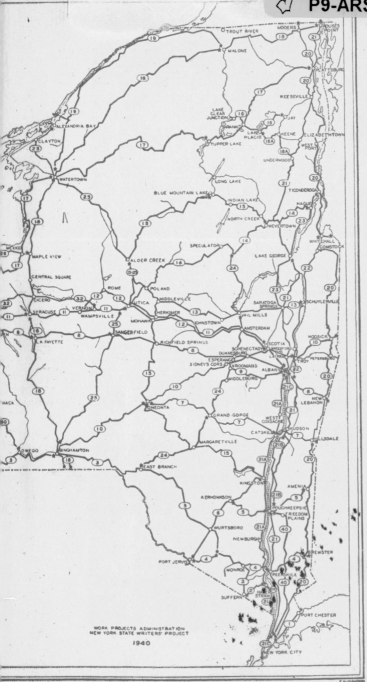

WORK PROJECTS ADMINISTRATION
NEW YORK STATE WRITERS' PROJECT

1940

NEW YORK

A Guide to the Empire State

NEW YORK

A GUIDE TO THE EMPIRE STATE

~~~~~~

Compiled by workers of the Writers' Program
of the Work Projects Administration
in the State of New York

AMERICAN GUIDE SERIES

ILLUSTRATED

SPONSORED BY NEW YORK STATE HISTORICAL ASSOCIATION

OXFORD UNIVERSITY PRESS · NEW YORK

BUREAU OF STATE PUBLICITY

NEW YORK STATE CONSERVATION DEPARTMENT

State-wide Sponsor of the New York State Writers' Project

LITHGOW OSBORNE, *Commissioner*

ALLAN REAGAN, *Director*

FEDERAL WORKS AGENCY

JOHN M. CARMODY, *Administrator*

WORK PROJECTS ADMINISTRATION

F.C.HARRINGTON, *Commissioner*

FLORENCE KERR, *Assistant Commissioner*

LESTER W. HERZOG, *State Administrator*

This Guide aims to present the colorful,
historic past and the many-sided contemporary life of New York State. Assembling
the data was a difficult job. On its
battlefields liberty was won and made
secure. From the days of the Indian fur
trade and the pioneer sawmill New York has
risen to preeminence among the States in
commerce and industry. Since the time
when its products fed the armies of the
Revolution, it has retained a high rank
in agriculture. In education, in public
welfare, in conservation it has shown the
way. Its people have achieved full self-
expression in religion, art and literature.

Here, in this book, are described side by
side, as they occur on city streets or
along State highways, great industrial
plants, broad farm lands, welfare institutions, parks and bathing beaches, colleges,
churches, battle sites, historic structures
of architectural interest, museums of art
and science, canals, bridges - all the
evidences of an active and enlightened
life. For the visitor it is an introduction to the Empire State; for the people
of New York it is in the nature of a
self-portrait.

Herbert H. Lehman
Governor.

Preface

THIS book could hardly have been compiled without the co-operation of the community which is its subject. The contribution of the New York State Historical Association and of the Bureau of State Publicity is indicated on the title page. Dr. David M. Schneider, Director, and Albert Deutsch, Research Associate, of the Bureau of Research and Statistics, State Department of Social Welfare, contributed the chapter on *Public Welfare*. Dean Samuel N. Spring of the New York State College of Forestry at Syracuse University contributed an article on forestry; Mr. A. E. Champlin, Director of the New York State School of Agriculture at Cobleskill, contributed an article on agriculture. Other unnumbered State and local officials, and private citizens with public spirit, lent their aid.

Office space and equipment have been provided for Project workers by the Grosvenor Library, Buffalo; Sibley, Lindsay & Curr, Rochester; the Cayuga Museum of History and Art, Auburn; and by a number of cities, villages, and counties.

The drawings illustrating the chapter on *Architecture* are by Mr. T. C. Bannister. For the head and tail pieces the Writers' Project is indebted to the skill of Mr. Harry Tedlie of the New York State Art Project.

My personal gratitude goes out to the several hundred men and women who had a hand in the preparation of this book. Many of them have found a place in private employment; several have established themselves as free-lance writers. They will all take pride in the achievement which this Guide represents. The human story behind the book they will keep in their memories.

With the exception of a few of the smaller towns and villages, the population figures used in the Guide were taken from the preliminary report of the 1940 Census.

BERTRAND M. WAINGER
Supervisor

August 1, 1940

Contents

Part I. The General Background

Part II. Cities and Special Points of Interest

Part III. Tours

Part IV. Appendices

Illustrations

THE COUNTRYSIDE—*Continued*

Maps

General Information

Railroads: New York Central System; Erie R.R.; Delaware, Lackawanna & Western R.R. (D.L.& W.); Pennsylvania R.R. (Pennsy.); Long Island R.R.; Delaware & Hudson R.R. (D.& H.); New York, New Haven & Hartford R.R. (New Haven); Baltimore & Ohio R.R. (B.& O.); Boston & Maine R.R.; Rutland R.R.; Lehigh Valley R.R. (Lehigh); Central Railroad of New Jersey (Jersey Central); Staten Island Rapid Transit Ry.; Hudson & Manhattan R.R. (Hudson Tunnels).

Highways: 85,000 miles of highways, 51,000 miles paved; 547 numbered State highways, including 13 designated as Federal. Rigid State police patrol. Federal gas tax, 1¢; State gas tax 4¢; tax on oil absorbed by vendor.

Bus Lines: Adirondack Transit Lines, Arrow Bus Line, Blue Bus Line, Champlain Frontier Coach Lines, Greyhound Lines, Hoosic Valley Coach Lines, Hudson Transportation Lines, Interstate Bus Corporation, Martz Lines, Peter Pan Bus Line, Short Line, Vermont Transit Lines, Blue Way Trailways, DeCamp Bus Lines, Edwards Lakes to Sea Stages, Flying Eagle Whiteway Lines, Gray Line, Old Colony Coach Lines, Lincoln Transit Co., Manhattan Transit Co., New England Transportation Co., Pan American Bus Lines, Public Service Interstate Transportation Co., Safeway Trailways, Yelloway Busses, Boston & Maine Transit Co.; numerous short lines.

Air Lines: American Airlines Inc., daily service at Syracuse, Rochester, Buffalo, Binghamton (Johnson City), and New York City; Pennsylvania-Central Airlines, daily service at Buffalo; Airline Feeder System, Eastern Air Lines, Transcontinental & Western Air Inc., and United Air Lines, daily service at New York City; Pan American Airways, service at New York City (Port Washington, L.I.).

Boat Lines: Day line between New York and Albany (*see Albany*), with stops at intermediate points; lake steamer service between Buffalo (*see*

Buffalo) and Lake Erie points, Detroit, and Chicago; coastwise and trans-oceanic service from New York City; lake steamer service on Lake George, Lake Placid, and Chautauqua Lake.

Ports of Entry: Buffalo, Dunkirk, Niagara Falls, Lewiston, New York, Albany, Rochester, Fair Haven, Oswego, Sodus Point, Syracuse, Chateaugay, Clayton, Fort Covington, Malone, Mooers, Morristown, Roosevelttown, Rouses Point, Waddington.

Citizens of the United States require no passports to enter Canada, but should be prepared to furnish evidence of identity. Foreign-born citizens and alien residents of the United States should carry credentials establishing legal residence.

Travelers permitted to import, duty-free and for personal use, merchandise to the value of $100 every 30 days. One gallon of alcoholic beverage may be brought in duty-free. Once every four months Canadians are allowed $100 in merchandise duty-free, provided they have been in the United States for a period of not less than 48 hours. Failure to report at the United States Customs entails a $100 fine for driver and car and $500 for each passenger.

Traffic Regulations: Reciprocity with other States is practiced with regard to operating licenses, except that a foreign license may not be used to drive for hire within the State.

No State speed limit, but speed in excess of 40 m.p.h. for $\frac{1}{4}$ m. is considered presumptive evidence of reckless driving. In special cases maximum speed is indicated on road signs. Incorporated villages and cities establish speed limits never less than 20 m.p.h.

Driving while intoxicated is punishable by revocation of operator's license as well as fine or imprisonment, or both. A plea of guilty to this charge in order to expedite trial entails loss of driving privilege.

Accommodations: Hotel and restaurant accommodations entirely adequate in cities and incorporated villages. Tourist camps, cabins, and houses available on most improved highways at varying rates (50¢–$1.50). Adirondack, Catskill, and Sullivan County resorts and the spas have many hotels and restaurants, some open year round; rates higher in summer season. Cities, the Sullivan County region, and the spas have *kosher* establishments.

Climate: The State is a region of moderate rainfall, but summer cloudbursts and winter blizzards are not uncommon; some roads occasionally flooded in the spring. Evening fogs in the fall common in Finger Lakes region. Temperatures range from −40° F. in winter to 110° F. in summer; Ontario-Erie region more temperate. January is usually the coldest month, July the warmest. Adirondack sections tend to have warm days and cool nights in summer. Winds are prevailingly westerly. Weather reporting stations in principal cities.

Protection of Plants: Do not pick or dig up trailing arbutus, flowering dogwood, mountain laurel, lotus, lady slipper, fern, or hart's tongue. Cutting, girdling, injuring, or destroying fruit, shade, or ornamental trees, plants, shrubs, or vines on State lands, highways, or public park land is a misdemeanor.

Liquor Regulations: Beer may be purchased for off-premises consumption in breweries, drugstores, grocery stores, restaurants, and hotels; for on-premises consumption in hotels, clubhouses, restaurants, grills, ships, and railroad cars.
Wine and liquor may be bought for off-premises consumption in licensed liquor stores and in drugstores which have permits; for on-premises consumption in bona-fide hotels, clubhouses, restaurants, ships, and railroad cars.
Sale of beer, wine, and liquor is prohibited for off-premises consumption on Sunday, weekdays between midnight and 8 a.m., and general or primary election days while the polls are open; for on-premises consumption on Sunday from 3 a.m. to 1 p.m., weekdays from 3 a.m. to 8 a.m., and on general or primary election days while the polls are open. Local county boards further curtail hours of sale in many localities. Many townships in the State, under local option, prohibit the sale of alcoholic beverages or permit it in bona-fide hotels only.

RECREATION

Camping: Free camping on designated State campsites and free temporary camping on other land in the Adirondack and Catskill forest preserves; free camping in several State parks outside the forest preserves. Some State parks charge 50¢ a night, $2 a week for camping privileges; and some provide cabins, rented by the day, week, month, or season at varying rates. Trailer camps in some State parks, and many, privately owned, along the main roads. The State Conservation Dept., Albany, furnishes free pamphlets on campsites in the State parks.

Swimming: June through August. Public and private parks and beaches throughout the State. Indoor pools in winter.

Hiking: State-maintained trails in Adirondack and Catskill forest preserves and in several of the larger State parks. Most private landowners do not object to trespass for hiking purposes only. The State Conservation Dept., Albany, furnishes free pamphlets on trails in the Adirondacks and Catskills.

Boating: April–November. A guide to the Adirondack canoe routes is issued free by the State Conservation Dept., Albany.

Skiing: December through February. Bear Mountain, Woodstock, Slide Mountain, Fleischmanns, Rotterdam, Berlin, Lebanon, Luzerne, Lake George, Ticonderoga, Gore Mountain, Lake Placid, Saranac Lake, Thacher Park, Cooperstown, Allegany State Park, and others. Novice, intermediate, and expert slopes. Week-end ski trains, January and February, from New York City, Albany, Schenectady, and Utica (schedules at D.& H.R.R. and N.Y.C.R.R. stations). A ski trail guide is issued free by Bureau of State Publicity, Conservation Dept., Albany.

Bobsledding: Mt.Van Hoevenberg at Lake Placid; expert run.

Skating: Late November through February. Many city parks, private ponds, and indoor rinks; indoor ice carnival at Lake Placid in July. Collegiate and preparatory school games on home rinks throughout skating season, weather permitting.

Baseball: April through September. Minor league games at Buffalo, Rochester, Syracuse, Albany, Binghamton, Elmira, and other cities. College and high-school games April to June. 'Twilight league' evening games throughout the State; also softball.

Football: Sept. 1 to Nov. 25. High school and college games throughout the State; professional games in New York City. Upstate major teams at U.S.Military Academy (West Point), and Syracuse, Colgate, and Cornell Universities.

Lacrosse: April to June. Principal teams at Union, Hobart, U.S.Military Academy, and St.Lawrence.

Track and Field: April to June: interscholastic, collegiate, and A.A.U. title meets throughout the State. September through October: interscholastic and collegiate cross-country races, often between halves at football games.

Tennis: April through October. Many municipal and private club courts throughout the State. Major competition at Rye; many county and sectional championship matches.

Golf: April through October. Municipal, State park, hotel, fee, and private club courses. Fees from 50¢ per day to $2 per round. Club, city, and sectional competitions at various times; P.G.A. sectional championships at club extending invitation.

Hunting and Fishing: Nonresident and alien license to trap, hunt, and fish, $10.50. Citizen resident license to trap, hunt, and fish, $5.25. Alien fishing license only, $5.50. Citizen nonresident license, 3 consecutive days, fishing ing only, $2.75. Resident citizen deer license, $1.25. Federal stamp for wild-fowl hunting, $1, at first- and second-class post offices. State licenses secured at Conservation Department, Albany, and branch offices, or from county, city, town, or village clerks or game protectors. For restrictions consult syllabus of State game laws obtainable at office issuing license or by mail from State Conservation Dept., Albany. A guide to the fishing waters of the State is issued free by the Bureau of State Publicity, Conservation Dept., Albany.

Licensed Guides: Licensed guides, displaying State badge, can be hired from Albany, Clinton, Columbia, Delaware, Essex, Franklin, Fulton, Greene, Hamilton, Herkimer, Jefferson, Lewis, Monroe, Oneida, Onondaga, Orange, Oswego, St.Lawrence, Saratoga, Schenectady, Sullivan, Ulster, Warren, and Washington Counties. Usual fees, $5 a day during deer season (Oct. 15–Nov. 15), $4–$8 in other seasons.

Fire Protection: Fire wardens have authority to call private citizens for fire duty; 25¢ an hour for actual service, mileage allowance for automobile if commandeered. Governor may close forest preserve lands to campers, hunters, fishermen, and hikers under conditions of fire hazard.

Public Information Service: Douglass M. Burckett, Chairman, Appalachian Mountain Club Ski Committee, 5 Joy St., Boston, Mass.; Rae

Galusha, Chairman Publicity Committee, Gore Mountain Ski Club, North Creek, N.Y.; Adirondack Mountain Club, Room 1935, 1220 Broadway, New York City; Publicity Dept., New York Central R.R., Grand Central Terminal, New York City; Publicity Dept., Delaware & Hudson R.R., Albany, N.Y.; New York Chamber of Commerce, 65 Liberty St., New York City; Martin J. Rennell, Secretary, Adirondack Resorts Assn., Port Kent-on-Lake Champlain, N.Y.; K.J.Lixtur, President, Schenectady Winter Sports Club, 2637 Augustine Ave., Schenectady, N.Y.; Charles H. Schenck, Executive Secretary, Mohawk Valley Towns Assn., Inc., Amsterdam, N.Y.; Bureau of State Publicity, State Conservation Dept., Albany, N.Y.; New York State Automobile Assn., 184 State St., Albany, N.Y.; Associated Industries of New York, Inc., 406 Root Bldg., Buffalo, N.Y.; Finger Lakes Assn., Watkins Glen, N.Y.; Travelers Aid Society, railroad stations in first- and second-class cities.

Calendar of Annual Events

JANUARY

First	at Newburgh	Middle Atlantic Speed Skating Championships
Ninth	at Bear Mountain	Interstate Ski Jumping Tournament
Twenty-second	at Utica	Ice Carnival (weather permitting)
Twenty-third	at Rosendale	Telemark Ski Jumping Tournament
Twenty-third	at Bear Mountain	Interstate Speed Skating Championships
Thirtieth	at Bear Mountain	Palisades Ski Jumping Tournament
Second week	at Saratoga Springs	Eastern States Skating Championships
Last week	at Schroon Lake	Winter Carnival
No fixed date	at Monticello	State and Middle Atlantic Ice Skating Championships

FEBRUARY

Twelfth	at Bear Mountain	Bear Mountain Ski Jumping Tournament
Twelfth	at Watertown	Northern New York Skating Championships
Twelfth	at Saranac Lake	North American Outdoor Speed Skating Championships
First week	at Alexandria Bay	Winter Carnival
First week	at Syracuse	Syracuse University Winter Sports Carnival
Second week	at Saranac Lake	Mid-winter Carnival, Dog Sled Derby, Carnival Ball

Third week	at Ithaca	Cornell Farm and Home Week
Third week	at Watertown	Winter Carnival
No fixed date	at Cooperstown	Winter Carnival

MARCH

First week	at Rosendale	Invitation Ski Jump Tournament
No fixed date	at Rochester	Hobby Show

APRIL

No fixed date	at Rochester	Festival of American Music

MAY

Tenth	at Ticonderoga	Fort Ticonderoga Day
Thirtieth	at Altamont	Automobile Racing
Thirtieth	at Rye	Hunt Race Meet
First week to first week in June	at U.S.Military Academy, West Point	Mon., Tues., Thurs., Fri., Battalion Parade at 4:30 p.m.; Sat., Regimental Review at 1:10 p.m.
Third week	at Batavia	Western N.Y. Apple Blossom Festival
Last week	at Rochester	Lilac Week
Early	at Kingston	Ulster County Apple Blossom Festival
Early	at Geneva	Three County Apple Blossom Festival
Late	at Larchmont	International Class Yacht Race
Late	at Rhinebeck	Vassar Horse Show
Late	at Tarrytown	Rockwood Hall Horse Show
No fixed date	at Elmira	Hobby Show
No fixed date	at White Plains	Music Festival
No fixed date	at Albany and New York	Albany-New York Outboard Motorboat Marathon

JUNE

First week	at Tuxedo Park	Horse Show
Second week	at U.S.Military Academy, West Point	'June Week' Ceremonies (all events except parades require invitation). Horse Show
Second week	at Port Chester	Horse Show
Second week	at Mt.Kisco	Dog Show
Third week	at Troy	Dog and Horse Show
Third week	at Mt.Kisco	Opening of Westchester Playhouse
Last week	at Rye to New London, Connecticut	American Yacht Club Race
Last week to mid-July	at Elmira	Annual National Soaring Contest
Last week	at Cooperstown	Intercollegiate and Inter-scholastic Outboard Regatta
Last week	at Poughkeepsie	Intercollegiate Rowing Regatta
Last week to last week in July	at Yonkers	Horse Racing, Empire City Track
No fixed date	at New Rochelle	Long Island Sound Championship Regatta
No fixed date	at Rochester	Rose Society Show

JULY

Third and Fourth	at Alexandria Bay	Water Carnival, Motorboat Races
First week	at Lake Placid	Men's Invitation Golf Tournament
Second week	at Rye	Horse Show
Third week	at Larchmont	Regatta, Larchmont Yacht Club
Fourth week	at Albany and Schenectady	Albany-Schenectady Amateur Marathon
Early	at Geneva	N.Y. State Outboard Motorboat Championship

Early	at Goshen	Trotting and Pacing (half-mile events)
Late	at Lake Placid	Water Carnival
Late	at Hill Cumorah near Palmyra	Mormon Religious Pageant
First half to last week in August	at Schenectady	Mohawk Drama Festival at Union College
Last week to last week in August	at Saratoga Springs	Horse Racing
Late, and August	at Chautauqua	Summer School
Late, and August	at Lily Dale	Lily Dale Assembly

AUGUST

First	at Rochester	Genesee Valley Open Golf Tournament
Second week	at Letchworth Park	N.Y. State Archery Tournament
Third week	at Goshen	Trotting and Pacing (one-mile events, including Hambletonian Stakes)
Early	at Lake Placid	Horse Show
Late	at Batavia	Genesee County Fair
Late	at Rochester	Rochester District Golf Association Tournament
Late	at Altamont	Albany-Schenectady County Fair
Late	at Avon	Horse Show
Late	at Rhinebeck	Dutchess County Horse Show
Late, and early September	at Syracuse	New York State Fair (Grand Circuit light harness races)
No fixed date	at Middletown	Automobile Racing
No fixed date	at Saratoga Springs	Yaddo Music Festival

SEPTEMBER

Second week	at Glens Falls	Glens Falls Open Golf Tournament
Early	at Tuxedo Park	Dog Show

Early	at Rye	Dog Show
Early	at Syracuse	Automobile Races (State Fair Grounds)
Middle	at Albany	Spaniel Field Trials
Late	at Scarsdale	Horse Show
Late	at Newburgh	Hudson River Senior Golf Tournament
No fixed date	at Lake Placid	Annual Indian Council
Last two weeks	at Yonkers	Horse Racing, Empire City Track

OCTOBER

Twelfth	at Buffalo	Columbus Day Celebration

NOVEMBER

Thanksgiving Day	at Troy	American Legion Marathon
Thirtieth	at Buffalo	St. Andrew's Day Banquet
No fixed date	at Rochester	Chrysanthemum Show

DECEMBER

Third week	at Rochester	Christmas Flower Show

Numerous other local events will be found listed in individual city descriptions; for events in New York City see *New York City*.

PART I
The General Background

The New York Countryside

By DIXON RYAN FOX

THE Empire State'—it would gratify the people of New York if they could discover who first dared that spacious adjective. It must have been a man of uncommon prescience, for in the early years of independence there was nothing imperial about the State. It was seventh in population. Its port-town at the mouth of the Hudson, about two thirds the size of Philadelphia, had been partially burnt during the Revolution and when its Whig inhabitants returned to claim it from the British army and the Tories, they found little to cheer their hope. The other inhabitants of the new State were clustered along the banks of the Hudson and on Long Island, with a few straggling settlements up the Mohawk and along the Susquehanna. Up to the time of the war, the Indians, chiefly Iroquois or tributary tribes, had held all north and west.

The Sullivan-Clinton campaign of 1779, which broke the Indian power, made it possible to penetrate the wilderness in peace, and in the last years of the eighteenth century settlers, chiefly from the thinner soil of New England, were wrestling with the primeval forest, planting corn and wheat between the stumps, setting up gristmills and log taverns, talking confidently of a great future. Washington, journeying through the new country with Governor George Clinton, hazarded a guess that New York might be the 'seat of empire'; but it was not until another generation had come to manhood and the first governor's nephew, De Witt Clinton, had induced the State to build the Grand Canal from the Hudson to Lake Erie, giving the farmers of the new western counties an outlet for their produce, that the city on Manhattan Island was secure against the competition of Philadelphia and the State was certain of a commanding destiny.

The fact that the water-level route from the ocean to the great interior spaces of the North American continent, a route used by turnpike, canal and railroad, ran straight across New York had much to do with the State's development; but the rushing streams near that great highway, or in the valleys that led toward it, soon did their ample share in turning the wheels of industry. Cities like Rochester, which milled the farmers' wheat into flour, and Utica, which was surrounded by small cotton manufactories, rose with miraculous speed, but on such a solid foundation of public need that they kept importance, and, when outdone in their original specialties by distant competition, adjusted themselves to other industrial production. From the hills by Lake Champlain the iron mines sent treasure to the city of Troy, until its foundries supplanted stagecoach making as the chief business of the place. Then when the rich deposits of the Minnesota ranges made New York iron unprofitable the citizens of Troy took up the clever idea of making detachable collars. Since detachable collars have sagged in popularity, industrial leadership has turned to other haberdashery. In every city of the State, and there are 60 of them, the presence or absence of geographical advantage and flexible, intelligent enterprise accounts for prosperity or the lack of it. Few, if any, New York State manufacturers have a competitive margin with respect to low labor costs. This circumstance accounts for neat and pleasant housing, generally speaking, but here and there it explains some smokeless factory chimneys as well.

New York holds its premier position in wealth and population by reason of its being an industrial and commercial State. But, the great metropolis aside, it is, especially for the tourist, primarily rural. It has been officially described for tourist interest as 'the State that has everything,' partly because of its striking contrasts. Ordinarily latitude and altitude are the chief factors in accounting for climatic differences. In these respects New York is scarcely to be compared, shall we say, with California. The 'long way' of New York is from east to west; as the traveler goes it is some 600 miles from Montauk Point to the Pennsylvania line at Lake Erie, an impressive distance in the eastern States. But nature has provided contrasts within even this narrow range of latitude. On Shelter Island, caught between the points of Long Island, the Gulf Stream influence permits the only stand of bamboo north of the Carolinas, while Owl's Head, in the Franklin County upland, each year reports winter temperatures about as low as any in the United States. The gardens of Westchester are blooming when ice still chokes the harbor in Buffalo. But the varying height of land tends to equalize the climate of the State as a whole. There are hills along US 20 and in Cattaraugus County, to say nothing of the Catskills, that are as high as Lake Placid in the Adirondacks. The rainfall grows heavier toward the south, except on Long Island, where Suffolk County has a maximum of sunshine.

The motorist entering New York is conscious first of the road on which he travels. Vaguely he apprehends that the cost of road construction must be high, because of the rolling country and the many streams. Until recently new construction was usually superimposed on old roadbeds, but during the past quarter-century, with the development of strong and reliable cars, the engineers have cut through many miles of 'virgin' territory up hill and down dale, to the shortening of distances. Yet, generally speaking, a long stretch of straight road is still rare in New York State; speed conditions are usually sustained by scientific banking of the frequent curves.

Of the 86,000 miles of road within the State 14,000 have been built directly by the State engineers, State roads having been begun in New York by the act of 1898, antedated only by the Massachusetts statute of two years before. But Massachusetts has never had a road problem comparable to that of New York, in mileage, burden, or unevenness of terrain, nor have many other States. New York has had to set standards of road-building for the country. Eighteen thousand miles of roads are on the county system, but with these, as with the 32,000 miles of market roads in whose responsibility the towns co-operate, the State pays a large share of the cost. Presumably the number of State roads will steadily increase, but reduced appropriations of the 1930's, enforced by necessary State economies, cut down the rate of building. The ten and a half billion vehicle miles estimated as the annual burden of New York State roads give them use and wear beyond those of any comparable area in the world.

The springy bituminous macadam will doubtless be preferred by many motorists, and the State is turning to it where a lighter traffic will allow, but the Portland cement construction is the more impressive. There are many three-lane cement roads, but there will be no more; the competitive center aisle has caused too many accidents. The four-lane roadway centered with a grassy mall is standard from now on for lines of heavy traffic, even though it costs $100,000 a mile under average conditions. The 110-foot cut through rocks a little north of Peekskill, though only a few rods in length, cost $1,000,000. Maps are drawn and calculations made for a 300-mile super-highway through a new right of way from Albany to Buffalo, carrying 12 lanes of traffic across streams and waterways and under or over every transverse road, at an estimated cost (probably too low) of $300,000 a mile.

In 1926 the State began building its own bridges, and its engineers take pride in the fact that no flood has washed out one of State construction. They are braced for 20-ton trucks, two at once, and the older spans that do not meet this high requirement are duly posted. But we live in a fast-changing time; the highway division has not yet contemplated its full military responsibilities in this new age of 70-ton tanks. Bridge tolls, which had been thought quite obsolete in the modern State, have come back again by reason of the enormous cost of the structures across the Hudson and East Rivers; the engineering marvel of the Triborough Bridge is certainly worth a quarter to experience at first hand, and the approaches to the Washington Bridge are now equally elaborate. At the other end of the scale we can still gain an antiquarian thrill from covered modern bridges in the Catskill and Adirondack regions. One at Blenheim is carefully preserved as a museum piece for posterity.

In the Mohawk Valley—in Schenectady and Montgomery Counties, to be precise—main roads have been lighted as brightly as city streets for an aggregate of over 50 miles, but the State is finding reasonable satisfaction for night driving in the reflecting guides at the side of the road, an idea borrowed from Michigan. The continuous installation from New York City to Albany is the longest in the world; its record in reducing accidents is out of all proportion to the moderate cost. In the daytime the number of accidents has undoubtedly been cut down by the system of road-marking introduced by New York in 1940, already copied in Canada and in all probability soon to be extended throughout the United States. The sign 'Unlawful to cross solid line on your side,' erected at intervals of five miles or more, might seem at first somewhat difficult to understand; but referred to the lines before you it is clear and simple. At any previous time comment on road markings would have been ephemeral, experiments followed so fast upon one another; but the present scheme seems likely to be permanent. Simple as it seems, the motorist may be interested to know that a twenty-six page pamphlet of directions is required to insure a proper application by road painters.

What gives New York most distinction in its travel routes, throughout the country and perhaps throughout the world, is its parkways, built and maintained by special commissions operating under special appropriations. The innovation came about thirty years ago, and under peculiar circumstances. The little Bronx River, flowing through Bronx Park in New York City, carried an odorous burden from the houses, shacks, small mills and refuse heaps along its banks far up into Westchester County. Something had to be done about it. A suggested tunnel was rejected not only because of expense and because it would deprive the park of a scenic asset, but also because it could not contain the swollen stream in springtime. Instead, a joint commission was set up by New York City and Westchester, the former bearing three fourths of the cost, to park the environs of the river to its source in Kensico Lake and to include a landscaped roadway. The three commissioners set a high example in acquiring thousands of properties and building the Bronx River Parkway, at $1,000,000 a mile for 15 miles, without a hint of waste or favoritism. But the effect was not so much of civic virtue as of landscape art. European visitors and others went home to tell of a masterpiece. In days of constantly increasing prosperity Westchester, with help from the State, constructed five other parkways, all models of beauty and convenience, and the State continued with the Eastern State Parkway, to have its terminus at Albany, and now completed to the neighborhood of Poughkeepsie. As western Long Island routes of traffic became increasingly crowded and confusing, Robert Moses was appointed to head a parkway commission for that region. Acquiring rights through closely settled districts and arguing down the opposition of the owners of country estates, this indomitable leader carried through the project of half a dozen parkways, built on Westchester lines without grade crossings. These principles have governed other recent parkways in the eastern States, notably the Merritt Parkway in Connecticut.

Despite the attractions of the open road, many thousands of passengers will see New York each week from the windows of railroad cars. The railroad in this State has a long and honorable history, beginning in 1831 with the 16-mile Mohawk and Hudson, which, cutting a chord across the wide arc of the Erie Canal, ran trains from Albany to Schenectady. With its line to Saratoga the following year Schenectady became the first railroad junction in America; it seems natural that one of the country's great locomotive manufactories should still flourish in that place. Success in this district led to ventures farther west, until by the early forties one could journey across the State from Albany to Buffalo by using eight different railroads. The trip, which theoretically could be made in 25 hours but scarcely ever was, became much easier in 1853 when the New York Central Railroad was organized from the constituent lines. Long before this New York City had begun the Harlem Railroad, ostensibly designed (to avoid the political opposition of steamboat men) only to tap the northern suburb on Manhattan Island, but actually in the course of time carried through to Albany by the State's most eastern valley—possibly the only American valley customarily called after a railroad. The better level was along the edge of the great river, but the building of the Hudson River Railroad on the east bank was delayed by the adequacy of water carriage during the eight months that ice did not impede. By the middle of the century, however, it reached Albany, a few months before the Harlem. About 20 years later the two roads were combined with the New York Central under the organizing genius of Commodore Vanderbilt. Under Vanderbilt's son it then absorbed the West Shore (built so that the Central would have to buy it), the Rome, Watertown and Ogdensburg, the Utica and Black River, and others.

From New York City to Lake Erie and the West the shortest line was obviously not along the water level; daring, or perhaps reckless, promoters projected a line straight across the southern hills. The charter of the Erie Railroad compelled it to build entirely within the State and its eastern terminus therefore was at Piermont, just above the Jersey border on the Hudson, where a long pier still exists to reach a proper depth for a steamboat landing; the other end at Dunkirk was almost as awkward, for Buffalo was and is the great New York harbor of the lakes. There is no time here to trace the means by which these errors of planning were corrected, or the greater errors of financing. Suffice it to say that starting May 14, 1851, a train moved through in four days, the most distinguished passenger being Daniel Webster, whose rocking-chair was strapped to a flat car so that he might better survey the scene between speeches. The Delaware and Hudson, chiefly a freight road handling coal, strikes across the State from Pennsylvania to the Canadian border at Lake Champlain; the Delaware, Lackawanna and Western and the Lehigh Valley, coming in from the south, spread their systems through the central and western counties. There are numerous tributary roads, some of them long independent. It was well on in the nineteen thirties that the eleven-mile Middleburg and Schoharie Valley Railroad, perhaps the shortest independent line in the country, gave up operation and with a favorable foreign market for scrap iron went far toward satisfying its bondholders. In earlier days it had been profitable for its officers to exchange passes with the other railroads of America.

To traverse the length or breadth of New York State one does not have to go by land. Many who read these pages will take the steamboat from New York City north to Albany through that spacious and magnificent fiord, the Hudson River. To say that any river route is incomparable in beauty may, of course, be extravagant, but there is nothing of its kind in the United States, at least, and Yorkers feel a thankful pride that this impressive scenery is included in their varied homeland. Not so long ago the steamer was the favorite means of traveling Lakes George, Champlain, Cayuga, Seneca, and many others, but, with the convenience of motor cars, this traffic has fallen off. Nevertheless, the steamer, the motor launch, the rowboat and the canoe are still the leisurely and wholly satisfying ways to see the shores of New York lakes—and there are thousands of them.

Perhaps there is a faint trace of nostalgia in the romantic interest that inland water travel holds for twentieth-century Americans. In days when horses and oxen, to say nothing of thigh muscles, afforded the only competition, water travel, where possible, was the swiftest, most convenient, and, as it still is, the cheapest, mode of transportation. It is a comfort now, in this new time, to brush aside the compulsions of the modern tempo and settle back into the nineteenth century. It was faith in the superiority of water transportation that led General Schuyler and his friends in 1792 to project canals from the Mohawk to Lake Ontario and from the Hudson to Lake Champlain. It was faith and persistent persuasion for many years by which De Witt Clinton got through the legislation that started the Erie Canal in 1817 and drove it straight across the State, an unprecedented distance. To invent the engineering methods needed and construct so long a waterway for $7,000,000 aroused the admiration of the country; its respect for the projectors' judgment was increased by the fact that the canal, charging moderate tolls, paid for itself in ten years.

The Erie Canal, whose old gray-stone lock walls can still be seen along State 5S, not only made New York City the port of the northern Middle West, but greatly increased population and land values for a wide district north and south of its own line. Its success stirred the State to build others, some of them feeders for this 'Grand Canal' and some of them independent links between natural waterways. The traveler now passes the ruins of the Chenango, the Chemung, the Black River and other canals, but he sees in full use and in greatly improved condition the canal from the Hudson to Lake Champlain (which is as old a project as the Erie), the Oswego Canal to Lake Ontario, and the Cayuga and Seneca Canal, which joins the two lakes to the main navigation-way across the State.

This principal waterway is now, of course, the Barge Canal, begun in 1903 (with no strong sympathy from the railroads) as a free way for Great Lakes barges to the Hudson, with its access to the sea. It follows in general the old Erie route, but in the eastern portion makes use of the Mohawk River. One hundred and seventy-seven million dollars have been expended in the twentieth century on this most extensive of American canal systems, to say nothing of annual maintenance appropriations which average above $3,000,000. With a 12-foot depth, it rises 565 feet to the level of Lake Erie. At its many locks, especially at Lockport, automobiles may oftentimes be seen clustered about, their occupants peering over the parapets to see a great petroleum power-barge being raised or

lowered. There is a vertical change of more than 200 feet along the Mohawk at Cohoes Falls. A few miles below, on the Hudson, is the Port of
Albany, to whose wharves there now comes ocean commerce from all
parts of the world.

No passenger boats now serve the public on the canal system, though
private motor boats and yachts ply its placid waters. Freight transportation is, of course, the major purpose, and it is not astonishing that the
State which has spent so much on these facilities does not unanimously
favor the mammoth project of the St.Lawrence waterway, however beneficial that would be to the northern counties.

We have lingered on the avenues of travel, as perhaps a guidebook must,
but whatever its other utility travel would lose much of its charm and instruction without a survey of the scene along the highway. Throughout
most of the State one realizes that he is traversing a prosperous farm
land. A stranger from the Mississippi Valley may be surprised to learn
that New York, which confines the largest population within an area but
twenty-ninth among the forty-eight States, yet ranks seventh in the
value of its agricultural product. Cattle grazing on innumerable hill-
pastures or knee deep in a thousand streams, lush meadows flecked with
sparkling flowers, ample barns with towering silos—all these are picturesque enough, but they are not maintained for scenic purpose. Half
the New York farmers' cash income is from the dairy industry, aggregat-
ing $300,000,000 annually. Other States surpass us in the production of
butter and cheese, but they look a little enviously upon New York with its
convenient and voracious market for whole milk, delivered without the
cost of processing. With its unique advantages of production and a great
consuming population—it supplies over 70 per cent of its own metropolitan market—New York is the only State that has engaged in a systematic
and extensive governmental campaign to advertise the values of milk as a
food and a beverage. Heavy milk trains are constantly *en route* through
the valleys of the State, and everywhere along the main roads one sees
the flashing aluminum tank-trucks of the great milk-distributing companies or of the co-operative Dairymen's League.

In the midst of modern scientific agriculture the mind goes back to the
Society Instituted in the State of New-York, for the Promotion of Agriculture, Arts and Manufactures, meeting year after year during the 1790's in
the city of Albany. It was not the first organization in the United States
devoted chiefly to agriculture, but the 150 names upon its roll, scarcely
one of which is without a State and national significance, indicates the talent here brought to bear upon the problem. One of the papers at an early

meeting was on the 'Advantages of Domesticating the Elk and the Moose.' It is cited not because it had the slightest practical consequence but because it represents the restless imagination of the early leaders in this State, as well as elsewhere, and the useful failures in the field that had to be made before practicable crops and breeds were hit upon. Some crops, like alfalfa, were rejected only to be profitably introduced a hundred years later; others, like mulberry trees for silk production, were enthusiastically promoted and hopeful investments made, only to go down in disappointment.

In the State census report of 1845 vegetables and chickens were 'not important enough to be listed.' Now there are nearly 200,000 acres devoted to vegetables within the State. In the southern valleys of the Finger Lakes the summer fields are alive with workers picking vegetables, especially beans, for the local canneries. New York is second among the States in potato production, a fact easily accepted by one who travels the length of Long Island surveying field after field covered with the full dark green of potato vines as far as the eye can see. On the Jericho Turnpike during midsummer nights there rolls a procession of trucks carrying their burdens of two-bushel bags to the great city markets, interspersed with like loads of cabbage, onions, lettuce, and other garden produce. Traveling the New York Central one can see the great muck fields south of Rome striped with thrifty vegetables, carefully tended by Italian-Americans, with their tradition of close gardening; the motorist in Orange County sees like tillage. On the slopes of the Catskills one looks upon the choicest of cauliflower, desired in every market.

Fruits, for a century past, have been an important interest in New York. Nearly a third of the currant production of the United States is centered in the Hudson Valley. There, too, are ample apple orchards, gay with blossoms in the spring and heavy with fruit in September. The Champlain slope is famous for the McIntosh; Monroe, Ontario and Wayne Counties produce an apple harvest each year surpassed in size only by a comparable area in the State of Washington. About a hundred years ago the volumes edited by Ebenezer Emmons for the New York Natural History Survey showed hand-colored plates portraying beautiful apples, but they represented rare approaches toward an ideal rather than the general fact in New York State. Today one sees the plowmen turning up the soil between the tree-rows, the sprayers forestalling the tent-caterpillars, the pruners lopping off dead branches, the planters putting in the grafted seedlings, other workers carefully applying fertilizer—and one realizes the sifting of methods, largely by the State experiment station at Geneva, which has brought the standard fact up to the ideal in pomology, as in every other branch of horticulture. Thousands of farmers, however, still grow 'cider apples,' taking what bounty they can from unassisted nature. Vineyards fill many a landscape in the Chautauqua, Niagara, and Finger Lakes regions; and the wineries at Hammondsport on Keuka Lake, served by skilled workers of French or German background, grow more famous each year. The Oswego County strawberry crop requires help from far and wide during the last two weeks of July. Twenty million chickens grow each year to the glory of New York State; the duck farms of Long Island give their region a strangely interesting aspect. The State ranks third in egg production.

A word may be admitted here on the production of maple sugar, a by-industry with small direct investment among New York farmers, but one in which, nevertheless, the State ranks second. In March one sees the roadside maples pierced with spouts and hung with buckets to catch the sap, but the sugar-house usually lies too deep in the woodlot to be visible to the traveler. It is affectionately known, however, to the young folk, who like to gather there in season to watch the sap boiled down in the great vat over a snapping fire and now and then to eat the flavorous wax formed by pouring the hot heavy syrup on pans of snow. The tract north of Utica, stretching along the Black River, was first opened on the bright hope of this industry when, in 1791, Gerrit Boon, for whom Boonville was named, representing investors in Holland, cleared 17,000 acres of all but maple trees and attempted mass production by catching dripping sap in an elaborate system of down-grade pipelines. The Amsterdam business-men were not alone in their dreams of an enormous maple-sugar market. When a New York landlord called on Jefferson in 1791, the Secretary of State assured him that 'in a few years we shall be able to Supply half the World.' Such ambitious ventures soon fell into decay, but individual farm-ers here and elsewhere in the State soon counted on their own maple trees for sweetening their food. In the early days of antislavery agitation it was hoped that, duly commercialized, this domestic product might supplant cane sugar entirely in the general market and thus make unprofitable the tropical slave-plantations. Another incipient reform was not promised comparable benefit, for certain projectors built high expectations on 'rum from the maple tree.'

If you talk with any official of the State's Department of Agriculture and Markets you will find an intense interest in the problem of grading produce for market. Following the example of California, the State gov-ernment has set up rigid standards, with but a small percentage of tolerance, and whether the product is eggs, apples, potatoes, or anything else the 'Empire State label' pasted on the box or bag gives the inspector's guaranty as first, second, or third grade. The farmer, therefore, markets his produce as he does his milk under the State's responsibility.

The temples of New York agriculture are found not only in the Grange halls that one sees in so many hamlets and which the official county agents visit to give instruction, as they likewise do the rural schools, but most impressively at the State College of Agriculture at Cornell University and at the State Fair grounds in Syracuse. When Elkanah Watson, the P.T. Barnum of our agriculture, established county fairs in New York during the second decade of the nineteenth century, he could scarcely foresee the splendid exposition buildings at Syracuse, where each year so many resort to see exhibits of the best achievement through all the 62 counties. It may seem surprising to include the city counties in this broad statement, yet even Manhattan Island makes its contribution to agriculture, from the laboratories of the department of agriculture in Columbia University.

Despite all that has been said of agriculture in its various forms, most Yorkers, as is well known, gain their daily bread in cities, and directly or indirectly from industry. In some towns the industrial roots run deep indeed: as in the gun manufactories in Ilion, which stem from the ideas of a farm-boy, Eliphalet Remington, at the beginning of the nineteenth century, and which family enterprise later extended to the making of typewriters; in the copper mills at Rome; and in the glass works at Corning. Some industries will attract the traveler's interest because of their unusual success in labor policy, with institutional expressions, as in the Endicott-Johnson shoe mills in the so-called Triple Cities—Binghamton, Endicott, and Johnson City. Others will draw attention not only because of mechanical efficiency but also because of the frontier explorations they are making in new fields of science, as the Eastman Kodak and the Bausch and Lomb Companies in Rochester, and the General Electric Company's parent establishment in Schenectady; and some because in themselves they represent new departures in our way of life, as the International Business Machines manufactories in Endicott and elsewhere. There are industries still located in New York because they once had a peculiar geographical propriety, like the packing houses in Buffalo; and some which are only a memory, like the farm-machine works that contributed so much to Auburn when western New York exported great quantities of grain and hay, or the giant tanneries of Prattsville, or certain ghost towns of the lumber trade. Abundant water power brought manufacturing to scores of towns in New York, like Rochester, Little Falls, Glens Falls, and Watertown;

cheap fuel in the form of natural gas did the same for others, as James-town, Olean, and Salamanca. And there are some industries that came about simply because the early inhabitants of the locality had a good idea and developed skill and enterprise irrespective of geographical advantage, like glovemaking in Gloversville, Johnstown, and Fonda.

But the city family wending its way through New York State may be concerned less with agricultural and industrial resources than with finding healthful and pleasant recreation. To mention this is to imagine the two tall and graceful ladies who flank the State seal, forgetting that they repre-sent Liberty and Justice and, swinging wide their arms, assuming each the character of Hospitality; for when New York advertises that it 'has everything,' it is thinking particularly of vacation opportunities. When the State was set up in 1777 few thought of summer, much less winter, vacations in the country; most people lived in the country anyway, and a vacation was simply a few days off for fishing or hunting, and even this had to be justified in terms of economic benefit. Next to this the American conscience accepted ill-health as a basis for compromise with leisure, and when nature withheld this excuse it had to be spuriously affected. The beaches at Rockaway were early recommended by medical men to pa-tients in the South; but New York's chief therapeutic attraction came in mineral springs, of which, as discovery, partly by reports from the In-dians, gradually revealed, the State had nearly a hundred. In the first years of the nineteenth century 'invalids of elegance and opulence' were advised to go to Ballston Spa and near-by Saratoga, and soon Lebanon, Sharon, Richfield, Clifton, and Massena had each its clientele. By the twenties leisure simply for rest and recreation had become respectable, and the Catskill Mountain House became a center of fashion. The Adiron-dacks, that great extension of the Canadian highland, were then all but unknown save to the most venturesome hunters. Not till Joel T. Headley, not long out of Union College, spent successive summers in the moun-tains to fortify his health and in 1849 issued his book, *The Adirondacks, or Life in the Woods*, was a broader curiosity aroused. In 1859 Paul Smith put up his hotel on St. Regis Lake, and others soon followed, catering not to hunters and fishermen alone but also to families who could pay for luxury in the wilderness. As the apostolate of William Henry Harrison Murray, better known as 'Adirondack' Murray, on hundreds of lyceum platforms shortly after the Civil War, popularized the idea of private camps and summer homes, the shores of Adirondack lakes and others throughout the State soon were strung with them.

The increasing urbanization of life in America, and particularly in New

York, brought more and more people to realize the charm and benefit of an annual month or fortnight in the country, and farmers found new income in the entertainment of summer boarders. Then enterprising city men themselves took over farms, enlarged the dwelling houses and set up as summer landlords, especially in Sullivan, Ulster, and Greene Counties. 'Fresh air' vacations for city children early attracted the support of philanthropic organizations and metropolitan newspapers; not only were the children scattered by carefully planned arrangement to farm and village homes throughout the State, but organized play camps, too, were soon set up. It occurred to some that the children of the well-to-do needed this latter type of recreation almost as much, and, in 1885, following a precedent in New Hampshire, Sumner F. Dudley, of Newburgh, inaugurated Camp Wawayanda at Warwick, with adequate fees from the patrons. It is scarcely necessary to say that camps of this kind have been set up in great numbers in the mountain and lake regions of the State. Doubtless. John Burroughs, of Ulster County, with his admirable nature essays, and Dan Beard, with his writings on camp techniques, did much to stir the interest of Boy and Girl Scouts and others in this movement.

It remains now to say something of what the State itself has done to provide facilities for outdoor recreation. State concern began in the Adirondacks, and two names stand out upon its early records. Franklin B. Hough, while supervising the State census of 1865, became alarmed at the denudation of the northern hills by lumbermen, and then, developing interest in scientific forestry under public control, not only influenced State legislation but ultimately organized the forest administration of the Federal government. Verplanck Colvin, a lawyer and topographical engineer, whose name is now appropriately borne by an Adirondack peak, spent his summers exploring the mountains and in 1872 ascended Mount Marcy and discovered Lake Tear-in-the-Clouds, the high source of the Hudson. On his application and under his superintendency there was instituted the Adirondack survey, which at last resulted in the great forest preserve of that region.

The Fish and Game Commission was interested chiefly in the preservation of wild life for the enjoyment of sportsmen, but since the inauguration of a separate Conservation Department in 1927 the State's interest has not been confined merely to serving and supervising the 2,000,000 hunters, fishermen, and trappers who use our wild land and waters, nor to the protection of the 2,400,000 acres of (wisely) abandoned farm land that the State has acquired, nor to flood prevention through water storage, as in the great Sacandaga Reservoir, which rivals Lake George in size and each spring prevents heavy losses by flood damage along the Mohawk and upper Hudson Rivers. More and more New York devotes itself to the accommodation of the tourist whether he travels on foot or in a motor car.

The State owns and administers 70 parks, ranging in size from the single acre of Squaw Island in the northern portion of Canandaigua Lake up to huge areas like the Allegany State Park, nearly 57,000 acres of highland within the bend of the Allegheny River in Cattaraugus County, with 70 miles of spring-fed mountain streams, 50 miles of woodland roads and 100 miles of hiking and saddle trail. In Taughannock Falls State Park near Ithaca is the highest single waterfall east of the Rockies; in Robert H. Treman State Park, off the Elmira road not far away, is the beautifully sculptured Enfield Glen with its 12 falls and its great fresh-water bathing-pool beneath the spray. Among the famous Thousand Islands in the St.Lawrence there are 10 State parks, and on Long Island 18. No one can realize the beauty of the State until he has explored the 15-mile scenic gorge of the Genesee in Letchworth Park, swept with his eye the almost endless view out from Thacher Park in the Helderbergs, climbed the paths of Bear Mountain and Harriman Section, skirted the royal mile of Storm King above the Hudson, and, in fact, sampled the resources of every State park. Doubtless the most impressive natural feature of the State is the great Niagara cataract itself.

Nothing need be said here of Niagara's majesty, but the reader may bear with a few words on how it was secured for public enjoyment through all time. Frederic Law Olmsted, the eminent landscape architect, seems to have been the first to propose public ownership, in 1869. Visitors then had to pay a fee to see the Falls, but were generally disappointed because of the ugly buildings cluttering the margin; Goat Island, it seemed likely, would be entirely surrendered to industry. In 1879, with Canadian co-operation, an active movement was begun for public purchase, eliciting the support of most of the leading members of the Federal government and university scholars, divines, littérateurs, poets, artists, statesmen, and philanthropists everywhere. The State was slow to respond, but under Governor Cleveland the bill was finally signed, and the Reservation dedicated on July 15, 1885. Dr.Charles M. Dow, its historian, has pointed out the significance of this action not only for the Falls but also for park policy throughout the country. The purchase by a State of property for purely esthetic purposes was a new departure.

The State does not own all the natural wonders within its borders—Ausable Chasm and the Howe Caverns and other caves in Schoharie and Albany Counties may stand as examples of private enterprise—but no commercial proprietor could be more solicitous in providing for the enjoyment of his visitors than is New York. Bath houses, boats, restaurants, picnic tables, *everything* is ready for comfort and satisfaction. In this respect perhaps the most impressive resort is the great development of Jones Beach, connected with Long Island parkways. Amid the beautiful masonry pavilions, faced everywhere by splendidly attired attendants, served expertly in every conceivable way, the guest can scarcely escape a pleasantly disturbing worry lest he has blundered into a first-class club and is mistaken for visiting royalty. At the Saratoga Spa the State has developed buildings and equipment that rival those of any bath resort in Europe.

But public hospitality is not confined to the State government. There is Westchester County, for example, with its astonishing Playland, its Glen Island Casino, its many other recreation parks and public golf courses. There are hundreds of golf courses in the State where with little expense the casual tourist can have opportunity to try his skill. And the State's hospitality to the vacationing public is not all for the day visitor. In the Adirondacks and the Catskills there are nearly 200 public campsites, large and small, many with resident supervision. There are rules to be observed, and in this sort of thing one needs the circulars of the Conservation Department, but the little societies of campers, constantly changing with going and coming, show a disposition to compliance. 'Hearthstone,' looking out on beautiful Lake George, apparently does not disturb the peace of costly private estates on each side.

Much has been said here of New York's facilities for a 'good time,' and for winter as well as summer, as there is skiing for long periods in a great part of the State, and tobogganing, bob-sledding, ski-joring and mushing. But a 'good time' is not always taken in terms of scenery or sport. Many a motorist will note particularly the monuments of culture and education. Some of them are humble, though neat and businesslike; there are 5,000 single-teacher school districts remaining in rural New York, so the 'little red schoolhouse'—generally white—is often seen. But in early morning or late afternoon one encounters school-busses and sees them gather in parking spaces of impressive buildings, oftentimes, though not always, within village limits. These are the centralized schools, which have grown in number from 48 to almost 250 within the past 20 years, representing a policy which, if the truth be told, has caused no little discussion along the countryside. These schools are for the younger grades. The high school, in New York certainly as much as anywhere else in America, usually occupies the outstanding building of the community, the characteristic temple of the

American spirit. In round numbers there are 1,000 of them in the State. At one time it seemed likely that they would sweep the field of secondary education; but for various reasons the good private academies have held their own and in recent years the number of church schools has increased. It is generally admitted—more than admitted by the Yorkers themselves —that in public education New York sets the standard for other States; no school system is more free of 'political' influences. In expenditure, either in total or per student, it stands ahead, with only California as a strong competitor. Stop at a taxpayers' meeting and you will find that this policy is not carried through without some controversy.

Church spires play their old parts in the skyline of every town and village, but the rural churches are less numerous now that the automobile has conquered distance on Sundays as on other days. The older Christian denominations are all represented, together with synagogues in the larger cities, but there are fewer variations than one meets in some States. Near New York City, as in other old regions of the Middle States, one sees the austere meetinghouses of the Friends, and the Dutch Reformed Church is conspicuous throughout the Hudson and Mohawk Valleys; but there is little to give a marked peculiarity to religion in New York. Knowing the predominance of Yankees among the early settlers of the nineteenth century, one may be surprised at the paucity of Congregational and Unitarian churches. But two facts may be remembered: the New York Yankees came from upland New England where neither orthodoxy nor later liberalism was conspicuously strong; and the many Congregationalists who did migrate found the expansive organization of the presbyteries better adapted to new settlements.

To Auriesville, beside the Mohawk, the most extensive Roman Catholic shrine in the United States, many thousands annually resort to beseech the intercession of the first American Saints. At Palmyra, in Wayne County, a stately shaft reminds us that on this hill of Cumorah the prehistoric conflicts of the Mormons on New York soil were revealed to Joseph Smith. Not far away the Fox sisters, listening to strange table-rappings, began American spiritualism, whose chief gathering place is now Lily Dale, in Chautauqua County. In Yates County one can visit the home-site of the extraordinary Jemima Wilkinson, the 'Universal Friend,' who explained her miracles by the circumstance that she herself had been raised from the dead. Near the Massachusetts border, as we see from ample architectural evidence, were the original co-operative establishments of the Shakers; in Oneida County remain the buildings and the intelligent enterprise of the Oneida Community, though their social tenets have been abandoned. Seneca Falls was the cradle of the women's rights movement whose symbol, though not whose guiding mind, was Mrs.Amelia Bloomer. To Saratoga County, near what is now South Glens Falls, we must go for the site of the first temperance organization, and to Warsaw, in Livingston County, for that of the first political convention of the antislavery men. New York is not without its shrines of religion and reform—of greater or less dignity.

Colleges and universities in New York State—and there are 62 of them —are historically connected with religion rather than with the slow-evolving public school system. Union (1795), first chartered of the upstate institutions, was an exception in its nonsectarian auspices; it was founded by petition of citizens of all affiliations in the region of Schenectady— hence its name. And Cornell, the largest and most famous of the upstate institutions, developed shortly after the Civil War from the secular philanthropy of Ezra Cornell, a New Yorker who had made a fortune in the telegraph, ably advised by a friend who became its first president, Andrew D. White, of Homer. But most of the early colleges, led by New England talent, were designed to qualify a ministry for their respective sects: Hamilton (1812), at Clinton, stemming from Samuel Kirkland's academy, a missionary means for Congregationalists; Colgate (1819), at Hamilton, and Rochester (1850), for the Baptists; Hobart (1822), at Geneva, for the Episcopalians; St.Lawrence (1859), at Canton, for the Universalists; Alfred (1857), for the Seventh-Day Baptists; Syracuse (removed from Lima in 1870) for the Methodists; and others. Most of them, however, whether or not organically related at the start, have long since divested themselves of sectarian supervision; and, generally speaking, the strictly church-controlled colleges are now those of the Roman Catholic and Lutheran faiths.

New York outrivals any State in the number of women's colleges— Vassar and Elmira (each claiming to be the first full-fledged chartered college of the type), Wells, Barnard, Hunter, Skidmore, William Smith, Russell Sage, Keuka, Sarah Lawrence, and Adelphi coming to mind, as well as New Rochelle, St.Rose, and others under the Roman Catholic Church; but coeducation, too, has its stronghold in New York. The junior college movement has made little penetration of the State. Separate schools of engineering began in America with the Rensselaer Polytechnic Institute in Troy, and besides university and college departments New York now has several other separate institutions granting the engineering degree: Brooklyn Polytechnic Institute, Pratt Institute, and, far to the north in Potsdam, Clarkson College of Technology.

The State relies chiefly upon the endowed colleges and the two State teachers' colleges at Albany and Buffalo for the preparation of its high school teachers, but takes most of its elementary school personnel from its nine normal schools, which now have certain degree privileges and doubtless soon will have more. Visitors from most States will be surprised at the absence of a State university and for a partial explanation of this circumstance must turn to the history of the University of the State of New York, which though doing no teaching itself has had, since its beginning in 1784, a sort of supervision of 'private' institutions, and in 1904 brought the entire school system within its control. Instead of maintaining higher academic instruction on the analogy of other States, it grants scholarships to the abler high school graduates each year, who may use them in any college within the State. At Cornell the instruction in agriculture, home economics and veterinary medicine, at Syracuse that in forestry, and at Alfred that in ceramics are financed by the State, and there are special agricultural schools at Farmingdale, Alfred, Canton, Cobleskill, Morrisville, and Delhi.

In the southwestern corner of the State is the unique Chautauqua Institution, begun in 1873 as a summer training conference for Sunday school teachers but gradually developed into a nationally influential center of adult education. The universities, from Buffalo to the Hudson, where Union has an organic connection with the Albany medical, law, and pharmacy colleges, provide opportunities for professional education sought by students from many States. The two-volume guide devoted to New York City describes in more detail the vast educational resources of the metropolis: with Columbia, of world fame and contact; New York University, serving every sort of instructional interest; Fordham, under the rigorous program of the Jesuits; and others—not to speak of the four huge municipal institutions for the city's own youth.

In the matter of reputation, the many-sidedness of New York actually puts the State at a disadvantage. One State has green hills and little else, another boasts the quaintness of its little harbors, here and there another its manufactures, its agriculture, or whatever its specialty may be. But New York is not a specialist State; and the State that 'has everything' is less likely to be identified in competitive comparisons. To some, therefore, it will be surprising that New York, all in all, can claim an easy primacy in educational opportunity. The thoroughgoing traveler, however, comes to realize it, and to remark its storied halls—at Union, with its gray old buildings in geometric order, wherein Joseph Jacques Ramée gave the American college its first systematic architectural plan a half-dozen years before Jefferson built his university at Charlottesville; in Philip Hooker's charming chapel, built a century and a quarter since at Hamilton; in the massive old Main Hall at Vassar; in the great quadrangle at Cornell, 'far above Cayuga's waters'; and more recently in the river campus at Rochester.

The tastes and interests of a people, as well as their fundamental needs, are well reflected in their architecture. Since buildings in most places are likely to outlast their builders, the traveler through a region has opportunity to gauge by architectural evidence not only the civilization of the present, but that of successive layers, as it were, in the structure of history itself. He is interested, particularly, in what distinguishes the local life from other life, now and formerly, by reason of peculiar personal and geographical circumstances. In architectural forms New York has its own distinction. The few memorials of the seventeenth century speak of utility and, in the gun-slits of the Van Cortlandt manor house at Croton, of defense against expected Indian attacks. The Dutch Colonial is a well-marked style along the Hudson and the Mohawk, with rounded gambrel roofs, or stepped-end gables, or the full-length overhang supported by a row of posts. In some of the old farmsteads, like the Mabie house by the Mohawk near Rotterdam, built in 1671, the slave quarters are a feature. But there are other notable characteristics of our ancient houses; President Franklin D. Roosevelt has contributed to books on Dutchess County frames and doorways. Two communities are whole museums of early eighteenth-century stone work: old Hurley, back of Kingston, and New Paltz, with its high-pitched roofs that sheltered—and still shelter—Huguenot families. One can follow the Dutch and German influence among churches, too, from the famous little edifice at Sleepy Hollow, dating from 1699, past the two in the Rhinebecks, up to the Palatine churches—that at Fort Herkimer with its beautiful high colonial pulpit, that at Stone Arabia, and that on the road from Nelliston to St.Johnsville, the last-named possibly the best-known landmark of the Mohawk Valley. Down in peaceful Schoharie is the old stone church which did duty as a fort in the Revolution and is now annually visited by thousands as a museum.

But the peculiar architectural record of New York is written not so much in humble farmhouses and in primitive churches as in the mansions of the landed families. The aristocratic land system was costly to New York in population and, perhaps, in basic prosperity, but it has left widely scattered monuments of gracious and expansive living that are not matched in other northern States. The Philipse manor homes at Yonkers and North Tarrytown, the Schuyler Mansion at Albany, the three Johnson houses at Amsterdam and Johnstown, homes of forest rulers, all breathe an air of feudal authority. These are convenient to the main roads and open to the public; but deep in private parks along the Hudson are the Livingston manor houses, far to the east are the manors of Gardiners and Shelter Islands, and there are many other lordly mansions lasting over from the eighteenth century, but visible to the stranger only in a distant view. The word manor is loosely used in most sections of the United States, but in New York it has a definite and legal meaning; in 20 spacious holdings, more or less, the 'lord of the manor' had the rights of his own courts, of nomination of the clergy, of exclusive property in treasure trove, mines, bridges, deodand—or the forfeiture of any instrument, vehicle, or boat that had been the means of death—etc.; but the practical peculiarity, not only in the manors but in certain other large estates as well, was in the perpetual leases by which the land was rented. Hence in Albany, Rensselaer, Columbia, Delaware, Dutchess, Putnam, and Westchester Counties there is still a vivid legend of antirent riots in the eighteenth and nineteenth centuries. The 20-mile-square domain of the old Patroon Van Rensselaer was not broken into independent farms until the 1840's.

The aristocratic idea, however vain and inappropriate it may seem to us today, set its pattern more deeply on upstate New York than is commonly realized. Many there were who sought to imitate the authentic manorial splendor by building mansions in the wilderness, centering in them an affection for conservative politics and the Episcopal church. Even the great land companies left memorials of frontier capitalism, like the Lincklaen house in Cazenovia and the Holland Company's office in Batavia. Some, like the Napoleonic *émigrés* in Jefferson and Lewis Counties, brought anomalous courtliness to astonish the backwoods farmers of the early nineteenth century. But when the Indian claims were settled, and the area of cheap available New York land thereby immensely increased, the colonial rent scheme became completely impracticable. The only profit in wild land was to clear and plant it with one's own hands or to sell it. Aristocratic pretensions on the frontier began to fade.

The excessively active land market, long held back by circumstances already adverted to, brought the lawyer into special prominence in New York State. The little law office out beside the road, just beyond the shadow of the substantial village home, that one sees in many counties, represents what came nearest to a ruling class in this commonwealth during the thirties and forties. Gradually the lawyer gave way to the industrialist, and found his living by advising in the problems of industrial wealth rather than in those of real estate.

Spiritually above and about the life that these represented was the classical tradition. It happened that the great growth of New York villages and cities came in the time when the Classical Revival was regnant in architecture, and scattered through the State are still found many of its best examples in domestic forms, on farms as well as in populous communities. The temple house with its heavily columned porch, so widely represented in our New York towns, was dark inside and not particularly comfortable, but in this day of self-indulgence it admonishes us that austere self-discipline and a reverence for standards played strong parts in producing the civilization we have inherited.

Andrew Jackson Downing, of Newburgh, did much to popularize the American Gothic, especially for smaller houses, and the Italianate style, with square towers rising from the ground and with wide overhanging eaves—the 'Hudson River Bracketed,' which supplied the title for one of Mrs. Wharton's novels. But Downing is more gratefully remembered for his landscape art, which spread its influence over the great estates along the river, where successful railroad men and manufacturers were taking on the style of English gentry. Here and there in New York, as in some other States, one passes a surviving witness of the mid-nineteenth-century vogue of octagon houses, extended from the monstrous example built north of Fishkill during the decade from 1848 to 1858 by Orson Squire Fowler, a Cohocton farm boy who had risen to fame as a phrenological lecturer and miscellaneous writer.

As America went on to greater and greater material prosperity businessmen ornamented our cities with gloomy brick or wooden mansions sprouting bay windows, towers, cupolas, narrow piazzas and anything else that came to the designers' minds, so long as it looked heavy and substantial. Most of those that time has left house lingering family remnants or stand unkempt and unwanted, shabby memorials of past power and glory. For vitality and prosperous hope, so far as domestic architecture is concerned, one now looks more to the suburbs, made easily accessible by the motor car. Here modern and historic styles mingle on surprisingly good terms and individuality has full play; yet the spacious front lawns with scarcely indicated boundaries give the aspect of parklike ensemble so characteristic of the New York and New England village, and envied by visiting Europeans accustomed to walled gardens.

Many of those who love this State hope that legislation may soon control the distribution of roadside billboards; but on a less inappropriate poster panel current at the moment of this writing a gasoline company may win some approval in advising the traveler to see 'Historic New

York.' The fact is, the State is drenched with history, as casual mention has already assured the reader. Some will be fascinated by the life of humble, ordinary people, as the scene suggests the changes that circumstances forced upon it in successive ages; some will seek out the folk-record of the New York mind, expressed in ballads, from that dashed off after the massacre at Schenectady in 1690, through those on the tragic Jane McCrea in Revolutionary days, to those of the Grand Canal and the early railroad engines—all set forth along with innumerable strange tales in Dr.Thompson's *Body, Boots and Britches*. Very properly the State Division of Archives and History has placed more than 6,000 tablet-markers along the road margins, for the American people come more and more to cherish the American tradition and to seek out its notable sites. Many of those marked in New York are, of course, of significance merely local, if the word 'merely' may be countenanced in a matter of such importance to the young folk of the respective regions; but many, also, call to mind events and personalities that have made America what it is.

Every New York child knows the debt his State owes to Dutch blood (seeing its record in the names spread through our town directories) and to Dutch custom, with its Santa Claus, Christmas stockings, cookies, crullers, cole slaw, winter sports, and other heritage. The day before these lines were penned the writer attended a Kermis, for which a complete Dutch village had been constructed on a spacious property beside a Dutch Reformed Church, where Dutch food prepared by Dutch chefs was dispensed, Dutch games and dances offered, Dutch silver and other art displayed, and a play of Dutch colonial life produced, while among the great throng present hundreds of ladies, Dutch descendants, proudly wore broad lace bonnets that, at one time or another, had been purchased in the old Fatherland.

In most counties the Yorker knows the local legend of the confederated Iroquois, noblest warriors of the forest, who rushed down upon their enemies along the streams that flow from New York in all directions. He knows of saints and soldiers who came, with holy cross and fleur-de-lis entwined, to brave Indian peril in the very heart of the woodland province where they hoped to plant the faith and culture of France. On Long Island he marks the old field boundaries of colonial towns and listens to the tales of Indian battles, pirate legends, and of off-shore whaling days and of voyages that sailed out from Sag Harbor across the seven seas. Not only from the magic pages of Francis Parkman but from the map itself he realizes that New York was the theater of the century-long conflict between the British and French empires, whose prize would be the control of a continent; hence those military ruins at Crown Point and Oswego and the fascinating fortresses that still stand at Niagara, where commandants and seigneurs received the diplomatic missions of tribes a thousand miles away; and Ticonderoga, toward which, in his mind's eye, he can see Abercrombie's barges as, crammed with redcoats, they came northward on Lake George in stately procession to death.

When the Revolution came it was natural that the largest number of engagements should be fought on New York land and water. Here were the gates to—and from—Canada. If the British could command New York they could divide the colonies and thereafter conquer them. Here the Tories and the Whigs were nearly matched, and bitter and bloody civil conflict stained many a neighborhood, often with the aid of Indian tomahawks. The bright uniforms of George III were an all too familiar sight from Southampton to the far Canadian borders; every mile of the lower Hudson and the Mohawk could tell its story of menace and suspicion, fire and death. One thinks of the intrepid Benedict Arnold brilliantly maneuvering his little fleet on Lake Champlain to hold back Carleton until it was too late for a deep invasion in '76; then at the great decisive battle of Saratoga; then in his shabby and disgraceful treason at West Point. But we reflect with gratitude upon the fortune that turned this highland fortress, happily saved, into a shrine of American patriotism, the seat of the great national military academy since 1802. In the War of 1812 the gates of Canada were again the centering points of American strategy, all too clumsy and ineffective. Nevertheless, the achievements of 1814— of Macdonough and Macomb in the neighborhood of Plattsburg and of Brown and Scott along the Niagara—brought glory again to our frontiers. Fancy needs but little aid to picture once again the military preparations of those fateful years at Sackets Harbor, where the old scene stands but little changed.

The State has done its due official part in keeping fresh the memories of this picturesque and consequential past. It cherishes and administers as museums the battlefields of Saratoga (now a national park), Newtown (near Elmira), and Bennington, which last-named engagement, it will surprise some schoolboys to learn, was fought on New York soil; likewise the Senate House at Kingston and Washington's Headquarters at Newburgh, whose acquisition by a company of public-spirited local citizens in 1850 for presentation to the State set a precedent for the establishment of historic-house museums in America. The State has taken scores of other historic properties under its care, but by far the greater part of them now open to the public are available by reason of the generous concern of county historical societies, the Daughters of the American Revolution, and the like. The New York State Historical Association, under whose sponsorship this book is published, maintains museums in newer buildings at two historic places, Ticonderoga and Cooperstown.

The best general view of the Adirondack highland is to be had from the Vermont side of Lake Champlain, just as for the best view of the Green Mountains one must stand in New York. Some detachment, some spiritual distance is essential to an understanding of a region and its people. Doubtless a visitor could better assess the meaning of New York than we who live within its borders. The poets, strangely enough, have passed it by, but it was fortunate for New York that it numbered among its citizens the first two American prose writers who attracted the attention of the world: Irving, who enveloped the Hudson Valley in deathless legend, and Cooper, who peopled the New York forest with immortal heroes. Scores of novelists since have been fascinated by the life lived in New York by sharply contrasting groups and classes through three hundred years. Many a visitor, therefore, will look upon the New York landscape as a scene that he has known well in his books, and its people as descendants or successors of old friends. To the native, scene and people are cherished with a rare emotional intensity.

'What has been said may justify a claim that there are certain traits and qualities, and certain prides and distinctions that we may rightly call our own—that there has been and is a person rightly to be identified as a Yorker. There is a present pride in being the greatest State in population and in wealth, but this the upstate citizen can scarcely claim, knowing that the larger part of both property and people is concentrated in a single city, not particularly his; he knows that outside of that the State must rank with Ohio or Texas. The pride of size but slightly pulls the heartstrings. There is more affection in the pride of beauty, in the satisfaction that comes from living in a land of wooded slopes and crag and pool, of sparkling lakes and noble rivers, of island strands, of gently rolling farms all finely cultivated, of busy towns not too much begrimed with soot. It is not a land of staggering wonders but one of varied loveliness. For all this it is loved, but for many its most persuasive charm is in its human associations so peculiar to itself. Certainly they play a rich part in the pride that qualifies a Yorker. The human story he recites with a twang of speech entirely his own.' [1]

1. D.R.Fox, *Yankees and Yorkers*, New York University Press, New York, 1940; pp.24–5.

Geology and Topography

IT IS no unfounded boast to say that North American geology had its beginning in New York State. Largely pioneered by Amos Eaton, Stephen Van Rensselaer, his patron, and Ebenezer Emmons, his student at Rensselaer Polytechnic Institute, the geology of the State became an impetus for scientific debate that still flourishes. Several of the formations of the State—Potsdam, Trenton, Normanskill, Helderberg—became reference rocks for those of similar age investigated later.

Since the North American continent rose out of primordial seas, the land area has undergone a rhythmic cycle of rise and fall, of elevation above and submergence beneath prehistoric waters, as land formations were eroded away in one place and deposited as sediments in another. The oldest rocks, nowhere surpassed in antiquity, occupy much of the northern lobe of New York State. A highly altered granite is probably the oldest formation, but the Grenville series of altered and considerably contorted gneiss, quartzite, and limestone, formed from sediments at the bottom of the first sea to flood the Adirondack region, is of about the same age. After their consolidation into rock, the Grenville strata were penetrated by several generations of igneous rocks that rose molten from the interior of the earth. The high peak area of the Adirondacks is made up of what appears to be the oldest intrusion, a soda-lime feldspar rock called anorthosite. Surrounding the anorthosite and responsible for a group of mixed rocks by virtue of their having dissolved some of the Grenville series, are, in probable order of genesis: syenite, granite, gabbro, and basalt.

The Highlands of the Hudson comprise a pre-Cambrian area of granite and granite-injected crystalline rocks, apparently faulted as a block upward through the younger sedimentary strata. Although some recent investigators do not concur, it is generally accepted that the crystalline rocks of Manhattan and Westchester, the Fordham gneiss, Inwood limestone, and Manhattan schist are similar in age to the Grenville of the Adirondacks. Tough and relatively resistant to erosion, they form a substantial rock foundation for the skyscrapers of New York City.

Following the creation of the pre-Cambrian rocks, a long period elapsed during which the land stood well above sea level. Erosion, tearing down the Adirondack highland, deposited sediments far to the east in an unrecorded sea. As the land wore down and the sea gradually encroached on the Adirondack region, the Cambrian sediments were laid down.

The lowermost Cambrian strata are now found east of the Hudson, a position they took during the close of the Ordovician period, when they were thrust westward. Beginning as sandstones, locally altered to quartzite, they are succeeded by limestones and shales. The limestones of the Massachusetts-Connecticut boundary and the Wappinger limestone of Dutchess and Orange Counties have a somewhat anomalous position, but their lower portion is of Lower Cambrian age.

A mountain-building movement in the Middle Cambrian re-elevated the land, so that only one formation, the Stissing dolomite of Dutchess County, represents that era within the State.

While the east remained elevated, the west was depressed, and Upper Cambrian sediments collected in a sea that surrounded the Adirondack region. The lowermost formation, the Potsdam sandstone, almost completely encircles the mountains; coarse sediments in its lower part indicate shallow-water conditions. As the sea deepened, with fluctuations indicated by the Theresa beds of alternating sandstone and dolomite, deposition of sand gave way to lime and formed the Hoyt and Little Falls formations, both built on foundations of lime-secreting algae known as *Cryptozoon*. Popularly called 'fossil cabbages,' the *Cryptozoon* were recently found by scientists of the Saratoga Reservation, near which they appear in classic exposure, to contain a high degree of radioactive potassium, which may contribute to the therapeutic value of the Saratoga mineral waters.

In the Upper Cambrian, fossils become profuse; beds contain relatively high forms of life represented by the lobsterlike trilobites and bivalve brachiopods. The creatures of earlier eons, from which these evolved, were probably too soft-bodied to be preserved, or mineral alteration in the pre-Cambrian wiped out the harder-shelled forms.

The first rocks of the following period, the Ordovician, occupy the area east and slightly west of the Hudson. A series of shale and sandstone with minor inclusions of limestone, they extend in age to the Middle Ordovician and appear to have been deposited in a sedimentary basin distinct from that of the rocks of similar age to the west. The Deepkill and Normanskill black shales are characterized by large numbers of many species of graptolites, extinct ancestors of modern bryozoa, which float on the surface of the sea. Other Ordovician strata, predominantly limestones, in the

Champlain Valley, contain a large fossil fauna of cephalopods, progenitors of the modern squid and pearly nautilus.

In the eastern part of the Mohawk Valley the Middle Ordovician rocks are mainly shales and sandstones; westward they become increasingly limy, until in the western Mohawk Valley and in the Black River Valley they are true limestones. The Trenton limestones are exceedingly fossiliferous; bryozoa, brachiopods, and trilobites are the outstanding forms.

Upper Ordovician rocks outcrop in the vicinity of Utica and through the Black River Valley northwest to the vicinity of Watertown. The great thickness of shale in the lower part is succeeded by shaly sandstones and, finally, by pure sandstones. Graptolites and brachiopods are the principal fossils.

The Ordovician period closed in the east with a mountain-building movement of great magnitude. The Lower Cambrian and Lower Ordovician strata of the east were crumpled and broken and thrust 100 miles or more westward to their position along the present Hudson Valley. West of the Hudson the folding rapidly died; and the central and western parts of the State were undisturbed. The present Taconic Mountains are but eroded stumps of the original Taconics, which must have been of Alpine proportions.

While the Taconics rose in the east, sedimentation continued in the sea which still covered central, western, and extreme southeastern New York. Thus the only formation of the Lower Silurian in the east is the Shawangunk conglomerate, which makes up the mountain range of the same name in Ulster and Orange Counties. Westward from the vicinity of Utica, Silurian strata are the principal surface rocks; and Lower Silurian beds cover most of the Lake Ontario Plain. Where the Silurian sea became deeper in the west, the basal Medina sandstone was succeeded by limestones. The Niagara limestone of the Middle Silurian forms the crest of Niagara Falls.

The Middle Silurian Clinton formation contains red iron ore, now mined only for paint pigment. The lower part of the Upper Silurian is dominated by the Salina formation, which contains beds of salt and gypsum of great commercial importance. These rocks indicate a period of transient, shallow seas and a warm climate. The remainder of the Upper Silurian is composed mainly of limestones, the various 'waterlimes' furnishing raw material for cement. The Rondout, Cobleskill, and Manlius limestones were deposited in the seas which once again flooded eastern New York in the Upper Silurian. No shallow-water formations preceded

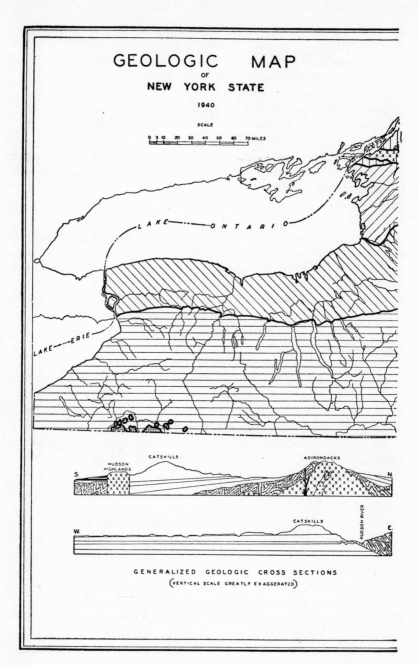

GEOLOGIC MAP
OF
NEW YORK STATE
1940

SCALE

0 5 10 20 30 40 50 60 70 MILES

LAKE ONTARIO

LAKE ERIE

GENERALIZED GEOLOGIC CROSS SECTIONS
(VERTICAL SCALE GREATLY EXAGGERATED)

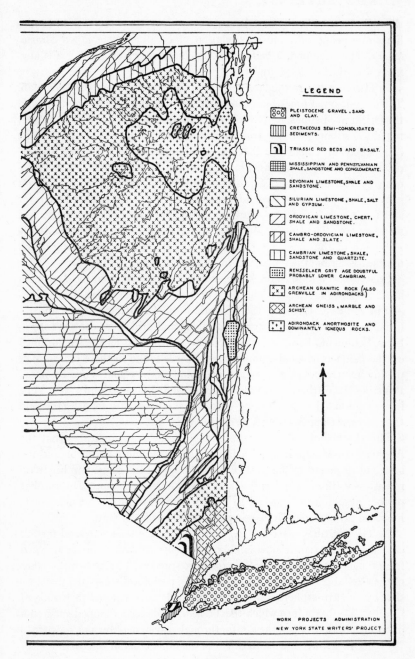

LEGEND

- PLEISTOCENE GRAVEL, SAND AND CLAY.
- CRETACEOUS SEMI-CONSOLIDATED SEDIMENTS.
- TRIASSIC RED BEDS AND BASALT.
- MISSISSIPPIAN AND PENNSYLVANIAN SHALE, SANDSTONE AND CONGLOMERATE.
- DEVONIAN LIMESTONE, SHALE AND SANDSTONE.
- SILURIAN LIMESTONE, SHALE, SALT AND GYPSUM.
- ORDOVICIAN LIMESTONE, CHERT, SHALE AND SANDSTONE.
- CAMBRO-ORDOVICIAN LIMESTONE, SHALE AND SLATE.
- CAMBRIAN LIMESTONE, SHALE, SANDSTONE AND QUARTZITE.
- RENSSELAER GRIT AGE DOUBTFUL PROBABLY LOWER CAMBRIAN.
- ARCHEAN GRANITIC ROCK (ALSO GRENVILLE IN ADIRONDACKS)
- ARCHEAN GNEISS, MARBLE AND SCHIST.
- ADIRONDACK ANORTHOSITE AND DOMINANTLY IGNEOUS ROCKS.

WORK PROJECTS ADMINISTRATION
NEW YORK STATE WRITERS' PROJECT

these limestones in the east because they were coral reefs, the Manlius limestone being built on a foundation of coraline algae called *Stromatopora*. The pteropod, *Tentaculites*, brachiopods, clams, and snails augment the fauna of corals and the algae.

Brief emergence of the land separated the Silurian from the Devonian. The deposition of limestones continued until shallower seas prevailed and the Oriskany, Esopus, and Schoharie grits were deposited. While the west remained submerged and true marine sediments accumulated, the east commenced an emergence that was the forerunner of the great Appalachian Mountain uplift. Thus, in the east, the Middle Devonian rocks became typical continental deposits, probably formed in a great delta off some westward-flowing river, and characterized by their oxidized red color and fossil remains of land plants, notably *Eospermatopteris*, the earliest seed fern tree. The Upper Devonian, all across the State, is like the Middle Devonian of the east—a series of red and green beds containing beach marine fossils and the remains of fresh-water fish and plants.

Continental and seashore sedimentation continued from the Devonian into the Carboniferous with hardly a break. The Appalachians rose gradually in the east, throwing the Cambrian and Ordovician shales and Silurian and Devonian limestones into folds and still more complex structures. Sediments became more typically continental as the seas drained off the flanks of the rising mountains. Fossils found in these rocks are of predominantly nonmarine types; and land plant remains are common. Probably the Carboniferous rocks once extended far north into New York but were eroded away, leaving only the small patches in Allegany and Cattaraugus Counties near the Pennsylvania line.

The absence of rocks of Permian age in the State indicates that the Appalachian Mountains had attained their maximum elevation and the seas had retreated to the west. Erosion attacked the range and began its relentless work of reducing the land to sea level once more. During that period, amphibians splashed in sylvan marshes and enormous insects hummed through giant ferns in what is now New York State.

In Triassic time, after the Permian period, the seas retreated farther east than the Atlantic now is. The sediments that were being stripped from the newly created Appalachians were spread out in fresh-water lakes of the coastal plain. These muds and sands, periodically exposed to oxidation by the atmosphere, formed the red beds now exposed in Rockland County. The basin into which the Triassic muds were dumped suffered a depression that dropped the strata, through a system of breaks, down into the older rocks. From time to time the unstable crust of the earth let basalt lava through to spread out on the surface of the red beds. A mass of this basalt forms the Palisades and Hook Mountain. The dominant creatures of the Triassic were reptiles, including dinosaurs. Their remains have not been found in New York, but that they roamed the region is indicated by the discovery of their footprints in similar Triassic red beds of the Connecticut River Valley.

During the succeeding or Jurassic period, the State stood well above sea level, and the sea was probably many miles east of the present New York harbor. In the next period, the Cretaceous, the ocean lapped farther up on the continent, and Long Island and Staten Island, as well as the entire coastal plain to the south, received deposits. By this time mammals had evolved from reptiles, but fossil remains of them are very rare within the State.

There are only small outcrops of Tertiary coastal plain sediments on Long Island, but they are known to underlie much of that island. The Tertiary was a period of erosion during which the State was evolving the basic features of the topography it now has. The Adirondacks stood higher than now; and streams carried mud to a sea which was inhabited by forms of life little different from those of today.

In the Pleistocene period, an ice sheet swept over the State. Two miles thick in places, it moved southward, scraping soil from the land surface, rounding off hilltops, and scouring out valleys. For 500,000 years or more the ice advanced or retreated as annual temperatures varied. Only the hardy plants and animals remained near the ice front; all others perished or fled south. Finally the ice sheet melted back to the north, while parts of it were left to rot. Large amounts of gravel, sand, and clay, frozen into the ice, were deposited as the ice melted. Such deposits form the Long Island terminal moraine, the Syracuse drumlins, and the Mendon kames, as well as the stony soil over much of the State. Banks of glacial debris provide clay for brick manufacture in the Hudson Valley and sand and gravel for concrete throughout the State.

Although man is supposed to have made his appearance during the glacial period, there is no trace of early man in New York. Many skeletons of mastodons and mammoths, kin of the modern elephant, have been found entombed in the muds of once-existing glacial lakes.

The great load of ice depressed the State area several hundred feet. Despite a partial return to the old elevation, the bedrock channel of the Hudson River is still well below sea level. During this lowering of the surface, the sea came up the St. Lawrence River and flooded Lake Champlain, around which shells of Pleistocene marine clams have been found. Since the termination of the Ice Age, about 10,000 years ago, erosion has been the dominant geologic process active in the State.

TOPOGRAPHY

Economically and socially significant is the fact that New York is the only State touching both the Great Lakes and the Atlantic Ocean. The State's boundaries, established by natural waterways, treaties, and inter-state arbitration, suggest in outline an early twentieth-century box-toed shoe, slightly dented as it boots Lake Erie, while Long Island trails like a loose spur from its worn heel into the Atlantic. About 550 miles of the State boundary is on land; somewhat more than that amount along or in water. The 47,654 square miles of land and water within these boundaries comprise a large variety of topographic forms.

The Adirondack Mountains, occupying the northern lobe, are made up of a great mass of rocks, which, by virtue of their superior resistance to erosion, tend to retain their altitude. They are mountains in the sense of their greater height rather than in the sense of being formed of folded structures. Drainage sought out geologic faults and formed valleys. At the close of the Ice Age, dams of glacial debris were left at the southern ex-tremities of the valleys, streams were backed up, and the many lakes of the Adirondacks were formed on north-northeast to south-southwest axes.

The loftiest mountains lie about 25 miles west of Lake Champlain. From them elevations decrease gradually in every direction. On the east they terminate abruptly at Lake Champlain; on the south and north they run out in fingerlike ridges; on the west they end in a peneplain with only minor hills. On the northwest the Adirondack rocks form a low ridge which cuts through northern Jefferson County and crosses the St.Law-rence River, in which it forms the Thousand Islands.

The Allegheny Plateau, largest single physiographic province of New York, covers almost the entire southern part of the State. Its fairly uni-form altitude of about 1,600 feet is cut by valleys some 500 feet deep. At its eastern margin it rises to the 4,000-foot altitude of the Catskill Mountains. At the northeastern corner of the plateau, massive limestone strata form a cliff known as the Helderberg Mountains. The sedimentary rocks of the plateau are inclined gently away from the northern oldlands. The drainage has a tendency to follow the dip-slope, so that the major streams of the area flow generally south.

The Catskill Mountains, like the Adirondacks, are not mountains in the sense of being composed of folded structures. Their separate peaks are lofty ground between the valleys of a deeply dissected plateau. As the streams that drain the area tend to form straight valleys through the plateau, the mountain peaks have a tendency to form more or less continuous ranges. Lakes are few and small; the only large bodies of water are Ashokan and Schoharie Reservoirs, both man-made.

The Finger Lakes lie in north-south valleys in central New York. Geologists believe that the lake valleys once contained southward-flowing rivers which were backed up by dams of glacial debris formed during the Ice Age, and that the new or post-glacial drainage was forced to seek the northward course it now takes. The sides of the valleys rise abruptly to the broad back of the Allegheny Plateau. Tributary streams, tumbling down the steep slopes, have cut glens and produced many waterfalls. Taughannock Falls near the head of Cayuga Lake plunges 215 feet, the highest waterfall east of the Rockies.

The Lake Ontario Plain extends 160 miles east and west along Lake Ontario, and reaches southward 30 to 40 miles. An extension of it forms a bench five miles wide along the shore of Lake Erie, southwest of Buffalo. The plain is a low-lying surface with an ill-defined drainage system giving rise to numerous swamps. Projecting 50 to 150 feet above the general level of the plain are glacial deposits, many of which stand like islands in swampy bottoms. These deposits are of two types: those dumped by the moving ice (drumlins), and those formed in temporary lakes during the Ice Age (kames). In the vicinity of Syracuse and Lyons, drumlins are numerous enough to give the plain a rolling and hilly appearance. In the vicinity of Rochester, kames predominate. Running east-west through the western part of the Lake Ontario Plain, the Ridge, an outcropping edge of the massive Niagara limestone, extends to the Niagara River and produces the waterfall. As the limestone ledge is undermined, its edge breaks off, the falls migrate upstream towards Lake Erie, and the deep Niagara gorge is lengthened approximately one foot a year.

The St. Lawrence Valley is a narrow inner-lowland north of the Adirondacks. About 18 miles wide and reaching northeast from the Thousand Islands to the Canadian boundary and then east to Lake Champlain, it has a mean altitude of about 300 feet. At its southern boundary, ground moraines of glacial sand have leveled off the terrain by filling the small valleys of the Adirondack foothills.

Between the Adirondacks and Lake Ontario is the Tug Hill Plateau, a cuesta separated from the Adirondack oldland by the narrow Black River inner-lowland, above which it rises 1,700 feet. Somewhat of a wilderness, the plateau is unfertile and is not traversed by State roads.

The Mohawk Valley is an inner-lowland between the Adirondack old-land and the Allegheny Plateau. Its head is near Rome, which stands on a narrow divide separating the drainages of the Ontario Plain, the Black River, and the Mohawk River. At Little Falls and at Sprakers, upthrust blocks of the ancient Adirondack rocks reach across the valley and form high spurs, or 'noses,' on both sides of the river. Between Sprakers and Schenectady the valley cuts into layers of limestone, forming rather high banks. East of Schenectady the valley widens out into a plain formed by a glacial lake.

The Hudson-Champlain Valley runs north and south across the State. Wood Creek, which flows into the long, narrow, southern end of Lake Champlain, is separated at its source from a tributary of the Hudson by a divide less than 20 feet high and half a mile wide.

From its source to Hudson Falls, the Hudson River is a typical Adirondack radial stream, making abrupt bends to conform to the system of faults. At Hudson Falls it enters the Hudson-Champlain Valley and flows south through a belt of shale. Below the confluence of the Mohawk it becomes an estuary, so that tides are felt 150 miles up from its mouth. Near New York City it enters the chasm it cut in its early development through the Highlands, south of which the Palisades form its precipitous west bank. West of the lower Hudson, the Shawangunks form a mountain range 2,000 feet above the Rondout-Neversink and Walkill Valleys.

South of Lake Champlain the region east of the Hudson River is occupied by the Taconic Range and its western foothills. The present summits are not the actual crests of the original upfolds, but rather the heights between valleys etched in the softer or more soluble rocks. The mountains, locally known as the Berkshires, extend across the New England line and are terminated on the south by the Highlands of the Hudson.

Long Island is an expanse of flat land underlaid by sand and gravel of the glacial period. This great glacial terminal moraine rests on a cuesta of relatively recent Coastal Plain sedimentary rocks, which faces the New England oldland across the sea-invaded inner-lowland called Long Island Sound.

In its early development the waterways of New York State formed perhaps its greatest natural advantage. Extending into the most fertile parts of the territory, and into the areas richest in forests and minerals, they opened up the land for settlement and provided water power and arteries of transportation. In time of war the shores and valleys became the objectives of strategy and the fields of battle.

Plant and Animal Life

THE ZONES of plant life closely correspond to the State's geographic divisions, though variations in wind exposure, moisture, and soil composition may destroy zonal uniformity. There are 149 species of trees, of which 116 are native, 33 naturalized, and 3 borrowed from neighboring States; virgin timber exists in relatively small patches in the remote parts of the Adirondacks. The list of flowering plants and ferns, briefly annotated in a report of the State botanist, occupies about 750 octavo pages.

The zone of lowest altitude and latitude borders Long Island Sound in southern Westchester County and Long Island, and has a native flora characterized by post and willow oak, short leaf pine, laurel magnolia, sweet gum, and hop trees.

The Hudson Valley, the lower Mohawk Valley, the Lake Ontario Plain, and the deeper, protected valleys of the Allegheny Plateau comprise a floral zone characterized by nut-bearing trees like oaks, hickories, and chestnut. Conifers are restricted to red cedar and the white pine and hemlock survivors of the lumbering spree. The chestnuts are second-growth immature trees or, more rarely, survivors of the blight which came as an undesirable alien into New York harbor. The American elm is a common and graceful component of valley woodlots and hedgerows. White, red, and post oak, maple, locust, gum, pepperidge, short-leaf pine, tulip, beech, and walnut are also at home in these valleys.

The Taconic foothills in the east, the broad surface of the Allegheny Plateau, and a wide circle around the Adirondacks are characterized by about 20 tree species. White pine and hemlock, once common, are now all but gone. Maples, beeches, birches, basswood, and white oak are widespread and commercially valuable.

The bulk of the Adirondacks, the Tug Hill Plateau, the Catskills, and the Taconic summits exhibit a tree flora in which red and black spruce, balsam fir, and mountain ash, rarely found in the lower zone, are most important. Maples, birches, and beech, as well as white pine and hemlock, persist.

The Catskill summits and the Adirondack slopes below the timber line are characterized by red, white, and black spruce, balsam fir, paper birch,

37

and mountain ash. Balsam and spruce, interspersed with contrasting white birch, beautify the Adirondacks.

Only hardy plants of the Alpine zone exist above the Adirondack timber line. Lichens, mosses, bearberry willow, glandular birch, black crowberry, Labrador tea, and Lapland rose bay form thickets where soil, slope, and sun permit. Virgin forests of the Adirondack region are mainly of red spruce, beech, yellow birch, striped maple, mountain maple, witch hobble, and shield fern. The spruce and birch often exceed 80 feet in height, towering over a carpet of rotting windfalls, leaves, and needles.

In forest areas many species of flowering plants pop up where light and rainfall permit. Wild sarsaparilla, Solomon's seal, bunchberry, star flower, trillium, enchanter's nightshade, sweet-scented bedstraw, Indian pipe, and goldthread are not uncommon. Over the greater part of the State, meadow flowers often form pied blankets acres in extent. Dandelions, cut as weeds from lawns, grow a foot tall on road shoulders, framing black macadam in borders of gold. Queen Anne's lace, devil's paint brush, white daisy, and black-eyed Susan bloom concurrently in bottom valleys, forming a tapestry of green, white, yellow, and orange. Buttercups are blended in grassy openings with violets, strawberry blooms, and clover. Goldenrod and wild rose (the State flower) hug the borders of woodlots. Cattails and blue flag thrive in tidal flats of the Hudson estuary; rushes, cut for chair bottoms, cover acres of the Finger Lakes shallows; and alders grow at the water's edge between the white and yellow water lilies and the dry shores of Adirondack lakes.

State and private planting have introduced a number of trees and plants. Foreign spruce, pine, and larch are replacing native trees on submarginal lands. Crack, white, and weeping willow, Lombardy and black poplar, European elm, mulberry, locust, Chinese ailanthus, Norway maple, horse chestnut, and catalpa thrive in New York soil and climate. The sequoia in Aurora and the cypress and cactus in Hudson, far from native climates, are surprisingly sturdy exotics. The black walnut stripped from rich valley bottoms of the lower zones for midnineteenth-century furniture factories is slowly being replaced by black walnut from other States.

While southern counties show upper austral (southern) species of animals and northern counties show boreal (northern) species, the largest part of the State is a transition zone where northern and southern species not only overlap but occasionally crossbreed. The higher Adirondack peaks are characterized by fauna of Arctic affinities: small, hardy species that prefer cold, barren isolation. Though several species of the native fauna have become extinct or all but exterminated since white occupancy, many more exotic forms have been introduced and are rapidly becoming abundant.

The peccary, horse, mammoth, mastodon, and giant beaver of the Ice Age are known only as fossil remains. The American bison, which roamed eastward to the salt licks at Syracuse, disappeared before white settlement. The wild turkey was exterminated by the white man's bullets. In 1871 the State legislature voted a $20 bounty on panthers and a $30 bounty on timber wolves, and the species disappeared. By 1900 the fur industry had all but exterminated the beaver; recent protective measures have fostered their increase to the point that their dams and reservoirs have become nuisances. The otter has been mercilessly slain. Mink, marten (sable), and fisher, sought for their rich brown fur, have dwindled in all but remote areas. Thoughtless gunners threatened many game bird species with extinction until conservation legislation was enforced. The Hudson River fishing industry of 50 years ago, abetted by stream pollution, reduced sturgeon, shad, and herring to noncommercial quantities. The wolverine was gone by 1811; elk have not been seen since 1840; and moose disappeared about 1860.

Introduced species that have gained firm foothold are Hungarian partridge, pheasant, English sparrow, European starling, a number of destructive insects and the praying mantis which feeds on them, numerous game fish, and the house rat, which came with European mercenaries during the Revolutionary War. Domestic cats, abandoned in mountain resorts and camps, have reverted to a wild state.

Rarely venturing out of the mountain, the Eastern black bear, weighing close to 500 pounds, is diminishing in number, though protected by law except for about one month in the late fall. The common deer is abundant in the State forests; only bucks may be shot during open season. While the Canada lynx is rare in the State, the wildcat still hides on the peaks of the Catskill Mountains, to which it gave its name, and in isolated Adirondack areas.

Classed as 'vermin,' the red fox ranges all over the State. Its southern cousin, the gray fox, joins it in the transition zone in a destructive hunt for rabbits, mice, and birds. Foxes may be taken at any time by any means, but traps are of little avail against this shrewdest of animals.

Whereas the varying hare or snowshoe rabbit is the common rabbit of the North Country, the cottontail, represented by several species, infests woods and fields of the lower zones. The larger hare is a recluse, but the cottontails invade kitchen gardens; both species are heavily preyed upon by foxes, cats, and hawks.

The porcupine is a not uncommon resident of the lower mountain zone. It will eat anything for a taste of salt, and even relishes glued paper cartons and varnish. Ranging through the State, the skunk is prized for its black and white lustrous fur, but is avoided because of its pungent scent.

Wherever burrowing is easy, but rarely in evergreen forest, the common and abundant woodchuck digs its hole with two exits. It greatly resembles an overfat prairie dog, but its appearance belies its speed and agility.

Rivaling the blue jay for excited chatter in Adirondack evergreen forests, the northern red squirrel ranges south to intermingle with its southern brothers and to fight with its southern cousin, the gray squirrel. Red squirrels seem to prefer wooded solitude, but the gray ones flourish in metropolitan cemeteries, parks, and backyards. Black squirrels are becoming numerous in the Southern Tier.

The southeastern chipmunk and the northeastern subspecies range throughout the State, building their nests in stone walls and rock ledges in or near thickets of dry, open woods. When they run they carry their tails vertically as signals of alarm; their striped backs afford protective coloration.

Widely distributed throughout the State, the muskrat prefers the watercourses of open country. Its fine, durable fur goes to market as 'Hudson seal'; and its abundance is responsible for New York's rank as second among the States in fur production.

The raccoon is rapidly multiplying as his more formidable enemy, the fisher, dwindles in number. A native of upland hardwood forests, the 'coon' often visits open lowlands to steal food, which it almost invariably washes. Its fur is of attractive shades of striped brown.

The fisher and its first cousin, the pine marten, are bearers of rich, brown fur (American sable). Uncontrolled slaughter has reduced their number to the extent that recent estimates allow five or fewer individuals per hundred square miles of Adirondack wilds. They are fierce little carnivores of the weasel family and prey on birds, mice, moles, and other small animals. The mink, represented by a northern and a southern species, is another tough, small carnivore of the weasel family. It snarls when opposed and its greed is often stronger than its caution.

From the point of view of numbers, the many species of mice hold the mammal record. The jumping or kangaroo mouse, about seven and one-half inches long, can jump more than a yard at a hop, and stores food in its squirrel-like cheek pouches. Several species of moles are prevalent; the star-nosed mole has the widest range. It infests soft, cool earth and often ruins golf greens with its tunnels, which it burrows just beneath the surface.

The birds of New York are divided into year-round residents, winter residents, summer residents, migratory species, and accidental visitors—in all, about 265 species. Among the year-round residents are the black-capped titmouse; that pestiferous import, the English sparrow; the common crow; the pileated, hairy, downy, and yellow-bellied woodpeckers; and the red-tailed and red-shouldered hawks. The most abundant summer residents are the robin, wood thrush, Wilson's thrush, catbird, bluebird, house wren, Maryland yellow-throat, red start, barn swallow, bank swallow, yellow bird, yellow-winged sparrow, song sparrow, red-winged blackbird, meadow lark, orchard and Baltimore orioles, kingbird, pewee, chimney swift, belted kingfisher, cuckoo, red-headed woodpecker, ruffed grouse, kildeer, Virginia rail, bufflehead duck, and common tern.

Among amphibians, the common toad of the genus *Bufo*, two species of the frog genus *Rana*, the spotted newt, and three genera of salamanders, including the giant hellbender of the Allegheny River, are widely distributed. Ponds and puddles abound with polliwogs in the spring.

Highly adaptable to varied environments, the garter snake has no venom and visits city gardens as well as Adirondack second-growth forest wilds. The sluggish copperhead, although dangerously venomous, keeps to itself in its Catskill and Hudson Highlands habitat. The Adirondacks were once infested with rattlesnakes, but their number has steadily declined as a result of a relentless war by summer residents. Large, black, harmless water snakes are common; and fields abound with finger-long, green grass snakes. Milk snakes are abundant.

An enormous number of fish species inhabit New York waters, but many of them are exceedingly rare. Natural distribution has been considerably upset by the stocking of waters with species harmful to the native fish, by canalization, and by pollution. Eleven kinds are abundant in all watersheds: yellow perch, darters, common suckers, common bullhead, common sunfish, smallmouthed bass, rock bass, shiners, dace, brook trout, and blunt-nosed minnow.

The upper Hudson watershed has a fair abundance of whitefish, imported German brown trout, northern pike, wall-eyed pike or pike-perch, and northern sculpin. Lake Champlain has gar pike, smelt, whitefish, and largemouthed bass; and brown trout and eel live in tributaries. The Raquette River watershed of the northern Adirondacks shows typical cool-water species; the Oswegatchie and Black River watersheds have the barred killifish in addition. Within the Oswego watershed, including the Finger Lakes, cisco and lake trout prefer the deep lakes; chain pickerel live in the south; the Cayuga minnow keeps to weedy shallows along with the northern pike; brook, rainbow, and brown trout inhabit the cooler streams; and catfish, pike-perch, and Oswego bass are found in the weedy rivers.

Lake Erie contains several types of commercial fish, outstanding among which are cisco, sucker, trout-perch, white bass, yellow pike, blue pike, sauger, sheepshead, and ling. German carp, spotted catfish, and northern pike inhabit the larger western New York rivers. The smaller streams abound with dace, trout, bass, shiners, sunfish, and suckers. While bass and whitefish are common Lake Ontario-St.Lawrence River fish, the rarer and larger muskellunge is principally sought by sportsmen.

As the only salt-water section of the Empire State, Long Island produces and markets seafood to the extent of $3,000,000 annually, while Long Islanders and visitors catch for sport food fish having another $1,500,000 in value. Pollack, flounders, sole, mackerel, blue fish, weak fish, striped and sea bass, black fish, butterfish, tuna, and swordfish are seasonally caught. Long Island is famous for its shellfish: lobsters, oysters, clams, and scallops.

While amateur naturalists and professional entomologists wave nets at colorful butterflies and moths, serious efforts are being made to exterminate these pestiferous insects. Swamp drainage operations aim to exterminate the mosquito, although it carries no malaria. The praying mantis, lady beetles, and dragon flies augment man's efforts by feeding on other insects. The gypsy moth of the southeastern counties, the Japanese beetle of the south, the widespread European cornborer, the widely distributed Dutch elm leaf beetle, the San Jose scale, and the Mexican bean beetle are all imported pests. The birch-leaf skeletonizer attacks particularly the white and gray birches.

Conservation and Recreation

IN THE Colonial period, exploitation of the natural resources of the New York area was limited only by the needs of the colonists and the means at their disposal. With trinkets, firearms, and firewater as means of exchange, the French, Dutch, and English encouraged the Indians in their wholesale destruction of beaver and mink. Wild animal life, an important food source, was considered fair game without sanctuary; and some species, like the wild turkey and the elk (eastern wapiti), were in time exterminated. Trees were cut for building, to clear land for cultivation, for fuel, and for naval stores. Soil 'conservation' was carried on in Indian fashion: when one piece of land was exhausted another was brought under the plow. Another form of 'conservation' resulted from the edict of the British Government reserving to the Crown all pine trees above a certain height as potential masts for the Royal Navy.

In the national period, destruction was intensified and expanded by a rapidly growing population, the reckless assignment of natural resources to private interests, improvements in transportation, and the development of industry. The Erie Canal and its feeders opened eastern markets to the farmers of the central and western parts of the State, encouraging soil exhaustion through specialization in the staple crops. Fish and game were taken without regard to breeding season and age. Stands of wood were burnt for potash; the magnificent forests of the Catskills and the Adirondacks, sold to individuals or private groups at a few cents an acre, were laid low—to provide hemlock bark for leather tanning and to feed the lumbering and papermaking industries.

The modern conservation movement can be traced to Verplanck Colvin and Franklin B. Hough in the fifties and sixties. In 1873 the State park commission, established the previous year, recommended a plan of State forest control to insure the preservation of water resources and to establish a recreational area. Nothing was done until 1883, when a bill was passed withdrawing Adirondack lands from sale and appropriating $10,000 for the acquisition of land of which the State was joint owner. In 1885, 25 years after it had lost its leadership in the lumber industry, the State

43

established a forest preserve in 15 Adirondack and Catskill Counties and set up a three-man commission for its control.

The commission, however, was ineffective, the State lost much of its land because of defective titles, and lumbering companies and individuals boldly invaded the preserve. In 1893 Governor Flower signed a bill legalizing timber cutting on forest preserve land. This action probably led to the incorporation of the heart of the law of 1885 in the State constitution by the convention of 1894 as Article VII, Section 7. This was changed in 1938 to Article XIV, Section 1, which specifies that 'The lands of the State, now owned or hereafter acquired, constituting the forest preserve as now fixed by law, shall be forever kept as wild forest lands. They shall not be leased, sold or exchanged, or be taken by any corporation, public or private, nor shall the timber thereon be sold, removed or destroyed.'

Because of its stringent language, this article has been 'the most loved and the most hated' of all State constitutional provisions. It has served to postpone the development of production forests by the State and even to delay the construction of new roads. Its chief supporters have been sportsmen, interested in the preservation of wild forest land as a sanctuary for game and as a playground for strenuous vacationers. Thus the New York State World War Memorial Highway was opposed on the grounds, first, that it would mar the beauty of Whiteface Mountain, and second, that it would open up the mountainous interior to mollycoddles who would climb a mountain only by automobile.

In 1892 the Adirondack Park was created; in 1904 the Catskill Park. These were outlined in blue on the maps of the conservation commission; and the 'blue line' became the line of battle. The fight was won by slow stages. Some land reverted to the State as a result of tax delinquencies; more was purchased. At first the legislature was niggardly with its appropriations, but later it became more liberal, so that by 1937 more than $16,000,000 had been spent on land purchases. By 1936 the State owned 2,159,795 acres in the Adirondack Park, about one half the entire area, and about 230,000 in Catskill Park.

Preservation of State forests involves an endless war on fire and disease. In 1899, 80,000 acres of trees went up in smoke and flame; in 1903 and 1908 a combined total of more than 865,000 acres was destroyed. As measures of prevention, fire wardens were appointed and fire towers erected; railroads were compelled to burn oil during dry summer months; and the governor was given power, which he frequently exercises, to close parks and forests in time of fire hazard. About 73 per cent of the fires in 1934 were traced to the carelessness of hunters, fishermen, campers, hikers, and children. State foresters, with the co-operation of the Federal Forest Service, the Civilian Conservation Corps, and private persons, have attacked the white-pine blister rust, birch-leaf skeletonizer, gypsy moth, Dutch elm leaf beetle, and other pests, by tearing up and burning intermediate hosts and infected parts of trees and by establishing barrier zones.

In 1898 the State established a school of forestry at Cornell University, but ceased its subsidies in 1903. In 1910 a department of forestry was created in the New York State College of Agriculture at Cornell. In 1911 the State College of Forestry was organized at Syracuse University.

Reforestation for production purposes was pioneered in New York on private plantations, the first in 1859. Reservoir watershed plantings were begun in 1902 on the banks of Hemlock Lake by the city of Rochester. The Delaware & Hudson Railroad in 1904 and the Santa Clara Lumber Company in 1905 established nurseries for reforestation purposes. The first State nursery was established near Lake Clear Junction in 1901. A nursery begun in 1902 near Brown's Station in the Catskills, under the direction of Clifford R. Pettis, evolved the methods now nationally used for raising conifers. In 1936 the four State nurseries distributed more than 72,000,000 trees to individuals and groups interested in the propagation and conservation of forest areas.

Under a law passed in 1929 and the Hewitt amendment ratified in 1931, the State is carrying out a 15-year plan to purchase and reforest upwards of 1,000,000 acres of idle and abandoned land outside the preserve at an estimated cost of $20,000,000. By the end of 1936, about 335,000 acres had been acquired and 250,000 acres reforested.

Conservation of fish and game has been promoted by hunting restrictions, natural propagation in game sanctuaries, and artificial propagation on game farms and fish hatcheries. The first State game and fish wardens were appointed in 1880. The large revenue from licenses, first acquired in 1908, encouraged artificial propagation. Early restocking of waters was not always successful; but after the Conservation Department had made its habitat and forage studies, the restocking activities were scientifically directed. In 1936 a total of 398,119,905 fish of all varieties were distributed from State hatcheries. Among the game birds, the imported Hungarian partridge and pheasant, propagated on a large scale, have readily adapted themselves to New York weather and food.

In 1927 the conservation activities of the State were placed under the control of the State Conservation Department. The department has had to step warily in order to mediate between varying views and interests within the ranks of conservationists. Organized sportsmen demand the stocking of their favorite lakes and streams, without regard to ecological principles. Hunters assert that reforestation with conifers is destroying the habitat of small game, deer, and bear; foresters reply that there will always be sufficient hardwood cover. Some conservationists charge that the department plants large numbers of Scotch pine and foreign larch, relatively useless woods, because they grow rapidly and make a favorable showing in a short time; State foresters reply that these trees are good soil binders and their fast growth therefore makes them the best agent to prevent soil erosion and too rapid runoff.

At first thought it might seem that conservation had little or no place in the economy of the metropolis. Yet there are 15,148 acres of park land within the City of New York, representing the conservation of land or water front and the beauty of woodland, lake, glen, and greensward. Nut trees attract chipmunks and red and gray squirrels. Within the parks are six bird sanctuaries, two of them in Central Park. Geese, pelicans, and herons are among the park's protected species. Wild bird species observed in Central Park number 168, those in Prospect Park, Brooklyn, 200. The bird sanctuary on Staten Island is 51 wooded acres in extent and includes a salt marsh for waterfowl and a strip of underbrush for quail, pheasants, and similar species. Outside the parks there are still more trees than buildings—more than a million of them—and nearly all are municipal property. In Bronx Park there is a virgin forest of hemlock—3,000 trees. Most New York trees, however, are imports, such as plane trees and Norway and Japanese maple. Poplars are forbidden because to reach water they sometimes pry into sewers and city mains. The ailanthus, a Chinese tree, flourishes in even the dankest tenement yard.

Other natural resources of the State have received little governmental attention. The activities of the three Federal soil conservation stations and other Federal services and of the State College of Agriculture and the State Planning Board have been largely limited to reconnaissance and recommendation. A survey completed in 1934 delimited 3,800,000 acres of submarginal land outside the Adirondack and Catskill park boundaries, and the State Planning Board recommended that four fifths of this extensive 'hardscrabble' area dotted with ramshackle farm buildings and abandoned fields be transformed into forest land paying dividends in forest products, watershed protection, fish and game preserves, and recreational opportunities. In other millions of acres, on which erosion has not yet progressed to a state of complete removal of top soil, preventive measures were urged.

The total available water-power resources of New York are estimated at 3,562,000 horsepower, of which about one third has been developed. Of the remaining potential power, one half is represented by the State's share of the St.Lawrence. This resource is awaiting development and a market.

For flood prevention and control, 18 reservoirs with a total capacity of 73 billion cubic feet have been built. Those in the Adirondack area are used primarily for river regulation. The Sacandaga Reservoir, completed in 1930, with a capacity of 30 billion cubic feet, is operated by the Hudson River Regulating District. In the Catskill area the reservoirs are used principally for water supply. The two largest, the Schoharie and Ashokan Reservoirs, provide water for New York City. Plans have been proposed for the construction of additional reservoirs with a total capacity of 379 billion cubic feet.

The State Conservation Department includes among its functions that of 'selling' the State to the touring millions and therefore continually expands the attractions available. In the depression years the department was faced with a possible curtailment of funds; but, with Federal services and aids, including the Civilian Conservation Corps and the Work Projects Administration, and the co-operation of private groups, it has been able to proceed with its long-time program. More than $50,000 is spent annually to restock lakes and streams with fish. Ducks are plentiful in the fall over the Hudson, Lake Champlain, and the Finger Lakes. Partridge, pheasants, quail, and woodcock are the principal land game birds and may be hunted with dogs; the principal wild animal game are deer, bear, and fox.

The three largest State parks—Adirondack, Catskill, and Allegany—provide picnic and camping grounds, cabins, foot trails with lean-tos for overnight shelter, and lakes for canoeing and swimming. The Conservation Department has mapped out a 150-mile canoe trip between Old Forge and Loon Lake and a 136-mile hiking trail between Northville and Lake Placid. Many of the smaller parks were established to preserve unusual physical features, like Taughannock Falls and Watkins Glen, which attract large numbers of tourists every season. In Jones Beach State Park on Long Island the State has reclaimed two miles of shore line and has provided attractive bathing facilities. In 1935 the State parks were visited by 23,500,000 persons.

With a wealth of waters, waterside yacht clubs, and boat liveries, boating is a State-wide activity; according to the Bureau of State Publicity, the State has 300,000 miles of waters navigable for craft larger than canoes. Outboards vie for national honors in the annual Albany-New York 150-mile marathon, and small power boats roar around courses on Seneca

Lake and Keuka Lake in annual regattas that attract top-flight competition. Long Island Sound turns white with sails as early in the spring as the weather permits; and sailing fervor reaches its peak late in May when the Larchmont socialite tars sponsor the International Class yacht races. On Great South, Shinnecock, and Peconic Bays, salt-water sailors vie in races and regattas for all classes of sailing craft. Fresh-water sailors of the Great Lakes challenge salt-water sailors to race off Rochester, smug in their knowledge that peculiarities of water and wind will baffle the ocean mariners. (*See also Sports.*)

Archeology and Indians

ARCHEOLOGISTS are eagerly searching for evidence of the first inhabitants of what is now New York State—presumably remote descendants of the Asiatic-Mongoloid wanderers who migrated to America across Bering Strait. These earliest inhabitants were possibly people of the widespread Algonquian linguistic stock, who appear to have come to the area by way of the Niagara Peninsula. They belong to what archeologists term the Lamoka Focus, and exhibit traces of a long established culture. Projectile points are long and narrow with a straight stem or faint side notches; no traces of pottery exist; and the absence of certain other implements suggests that these Archaic people were nomadic hunters rather than settled farmers.

Following them in the culture sequence thus far established by research came the Laurentian culture, the most widely disseminated in the State. It appears to have entered from the northeast through the St.Lawrence and Hudson Valleys and, like the Archaic, was produced by a hunting and fishing people. Chief among its distinctive artifacts are broad-bladed points of many forms, gouges, plummets, and ground slate knives.

The Vine Valley occupation, entering in two waves, probably from the west, brought a richer culture. Polished stone implements are more numerous; crude pottery and a greater variety of bone and antler tools suggest more stable settlement, leisure, and the progress of invention. This culture was also widespread.

The Hopewellian (Mound Builder) invasion, which preceded the Owasco Aspect, brought a people who often buried their dead in sizable mounds, made copper articles, ornaments, pottery, and pipes of superior quality, lived in villages, cultivated food plants and tobacco, and wove fabrics. Few traces of them have been found in eastern New York, but their handiwork unearthed in western counties exhibits an affinity with larger finds in Ohio.

The Owasco occupation was rooted to the soil and enjoyed a high degree of cultural attainment, as indicated by the superior temper, design, and ornamentation of pottery, clay smoking pipes, triangular arrowheads, and the domestication of corn and beans. The lack of intermixed European tools, utensils, or ornaments proves that this culture was definitely pre-Columbian, and it doubtless existed for several centuries before A.D. 1300.

The final wave of Algonquian penetration was probably that of the Lenni-Lenape. They were on the eastern seaboard of New Jersey and Pennsylvania to greet the white man, who found them banded in confederacies, tilling the soil, smoking tobacco, and inscribing rocks to denote tribal boundaries. To the white intruders these people were the Delaware, named after the river traversing the heart of their domain. The Lenni-Lenape dominated the southeastern part of what is now New York State. Not long before the coming of the white man, the irresistible infiltration of the Iroquois had begun on the southwest, south, and north.

The variety of geographical features, the abundance of nuts, fruits, edible roots, and wild game, the presence of flint, and, above all, the far-spreading system of interconnected waterways made the New York region a strategic stronghold that would endow with abundance and authority any Indian group able to win it and hold it.

Although the Algonquins equaled the Iroquois in bravery, intelligence, and physical prowess, they lacked the Iroquois genius for political organization and the Iroquois zeal for protracted warfare. The northern group of the Five Nations, who called themselves the 'Men of Men,' in the first half of the sixteenth century cut their affiliations with the Huron-Iroquois groups of Canada, slashed their way through the vigorous but futile resistance of the Algonquins, and settled along the Mohawk River; those who came from the south and west settled in the foothills south of Lake Ontario. The conflict lasted well into the early days of white settlement; the Battle of Kinguariones was fought in 1669, though a decade or two before that the mighty Iroquois had become the virtual masters of what is now New York State and had either absorbed the Algonquins or driven them out.

One source of Iroquois power was their confederation. Late in the sixteenth century, Dekanawidah, probably of Huron blood, recognized the urgent need for peaceful unity and devised a code of laws that would bring all men together as friends and brothers. Although his dream of eternal peace was soundly ridiculed by the warriors, Dekanawidah enlisted the aid of Hayonhwatha, a Mohawk by birth, and together they launched a campaign for Iroquois solidarity which they zealously promoted for five years. Hiawatha, who began his reforms among the Onondaga, combined political strategy with eloquent oratory and finally won over Adodarhoh, powerful Onondaga opponent of the plan, by offering this fiercest of warriors the position of moderator in the league council. Legend has it that this form of flattery 'combed the snakes from the head of Adodarhoh.'

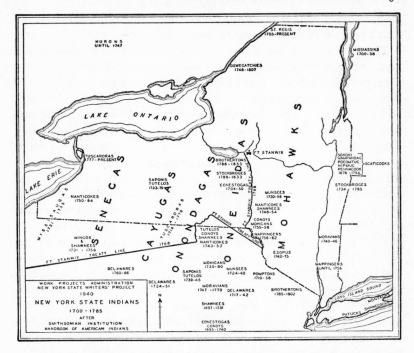

About the year 1570 the Mohawk, Oneida, Onondaga, Cayuga, and Seneca were welded into the Five Nations Confederacy; and the first great
council fire blazed high on what are now called the Pompey hills.

Although the founders of the league likened their new government to
'a long house where families dwell together in harmony,' the confederacy
was not established without considerable jealousy; fear of supersedence
and demands for special concessions were problems that had to be ironed
out with a high degree of diplomacy. But the desire to control the fur
supply of their neighbors to the north and west and thereby monopolize the
trade in European goods finally brought about a real union; the primacy
in matters of state went to the Mohawk, the Onondaga were granted
custody of the permanent council fire, and the Seneca were given two war
captains. These three nations together constituted the 'elder brothers';
across the fire sat the Oneida and Cayuga, 'younger brothers' of the larger
nations.

The league's constitution, as it developed, consolidated a civic and social system built on the old pattern of tribal society and embracing ideas
of universal peace and brotherhood, set up a policy of fraternal expansion,

and provided for the appointment of the peace chiefs by the women—in effect, gave the women the right to vote.

The 'Men of Men' did not call their women squaws; to them women were 'our mothers.' Although the Iroquois woman was practically the domestic slave of her arrogant spouse, she exercised a large influence in government, shared in religious rites and festivals, arranged marriages, and authorized divorce. All tribes recognized the descent of name and property through the female line.

The Great Law, which was transmitted orally from one generation to another, proved to be a governmental system well suited to the stage of culture for which it was designed. A federal council was established and each of the Five Nations was represented by delegates, or federal chiefs. Organization of the tribe began in the matrilineal family unit, called the *owachira*, of which the eldest woman was the nominal head; and two or more *owachiras*, believed to be related, made up a clan, which functioned within the tribe to ensure economic security and political representation for its members. Members of the clan shared certain property. The women of the clan elected its chiefs and subchiefs, who represented the clan in tribal councils. Privileges of membership included a common burial ground, the right to give childbearing women of the *owachiras* the power to elect and impeach chiefs, the right to clan personal names, help in securing a mate, and protection through 'blood revenge.'

Polygamy, practiced by the Algonquin and Huron, was not encouraged by the Iroquois, although it infrequently occurred. Marriage was arranged by the mothers. The girl signified her mother's choice of a husband by placing a basket of bread at the door of the youth's home. If the lad and his mother agreed on the advisability of the matrimonial venture, they sent back a basket of food as a token of acceptance; but if the match was not acceptable, the girl's gift was returned untouched. If both sets of parents gave their consent, the simple ceremony, consisting chiefly of a lecture on the duties of social life, was performed by the clan matrons, through the chiefs or some orator as their surrogate. A pair of impetuous lovers might ignore formal routine and stage an elopement, in which case one night away from home validated the marriage. Divorce was relatively simple, sufficient grounds being infidelity or failure to provide.

The birth of a child, male or female, was a welcome event, but female offspring were more highly valued. Most villages maintained small lodges to which women retired for childbirth; and the newborn babes were cared for in these crude maternity homes until they were ready to be shown to the family. Comparative lack of sanitary precautions, dietary deficiencies, and the rigorous climate resulted in an extremely high rate of infant mortality.

Although the Iroquois moved their habitations every 10 or 12 years, they built their villages strong for shelter and military protection. Trees were felled, peeled, and converted into pole frameworks. Elm bark was pressed flat into sheets, laid horizontally over the frames, and tied down with cords. They built homes ranging from individual bark cabins to log communal houses 200 feet long; erected stout stockades 16 to 30 feet high, with platforms on the inside wall for fighters, weapons, and water; and dug deep moats outside the barricades.

Agriculture was the chief basis of Iroquois stability. Each village had its fields and, in the 1700's, its orchards; the men cleared the land, the women planted and cultivated the fields. Corn (maize), which had been developed by deliberate breeding and was the Indian's particular grain, was planted in rows, so many kernels to the hill; and the intervals between the hills were measured by the 'long step.' These early New York farmers raised tobacco, beans, Jerusalem artichokes, and squash. Exhausting the soil and the supply of firewood in a dozen years, they moved the village to a new site.

Commerce in pre-Colonial days consisted principally of direct exchange of commodities among families and tribes. The measurements used included finger width, palm breadth, finger span, and the integral fathom, just as is the case, less directly, in England and the United States today, as indicated by the term 'foot.' Wampum, arrowheads, and beaver skins were the media of exchange.

The Indian was truly a craftsman. Combining his native patience with ingenuity, he made bone knives, serrated stone saws, and bow-operated drills; and with these tools he fashioned fighting and farming implements, made combs from antler, and built bark canoes, snowshoes, and toboggans. The women shaped clay into pottery and worked pelts into clothing.

Indian warfare, before the coming of the white man, was carried on with crude weapons: bow and arrow, tomahawk, and war club were the primary equipment for offense, and round shields and slat armor for defense. War expeditions rarely numbered 100 men and only on rare occasions did the Indians assemble a force that could be considered of army proportions. Their technique called for concealment, surprise—the swift swoop from ambush. Scalping, an aboriginal custom of the Iroquois which they probably introduced to the Northeast, was encouraged by both the French and English, who offered bounties for the dripping topknots of their enemies—white or Indian. With this stimulus the practice spread rapidly and became characteristic of Indian warfare. Cannibalism was a common practice among the Huron-Iroquois, and the New York Iroquois indulged in the practice at times, under the belief that a great warrior's heart if eaten would provide increased valor and strength.

Christianity was first brought to the Indian by the Franciscan Order of Recollects in 1615 and later by the courageous Jesuits. The missionaries suffered every hardship; blamed for epidemics, crop failures, and grass-hopper plagues, they were frequently subjected to extreme torture and killed. The Jesuit Relations abound with tales of such atrocities.

The white man's religion was all but incomprehensible to the red man. Intimate observations of nature formed the whole fabric of his philosophy; he knew hunger, the change of the seasons, the budding of flowers. To him life was practical and understandable. He envisaged a continuous conflict between good and evil spirits and was perfectly willing to bribe either group with generous offerings. He believed that all living creatures pos-sessed souls and that a supernatural force controlled all nature. Probably under the influence of the Jesuits, he came to believe in a land of souls, with separate villages for homicides and suicides, who were not admitted to the village of the blessed.

The Five Nations were continually at war with their neighbors, with the aim of controlling the fur trade. The Algonquin and the Huron, having suffered from these imperialistic tendencies, welcomed the arrival of the French, whose 'thunder poles' spoke death. In order to wreak vengeance upon the 'upstart' Iroquois secessionists, the Huron quickly formed an alliance with Samuel de Champlain and induced him to accompany a war party against the Mohawk. In the subsequent engagement near Ticonder-oga, Champlain and his two musketeers introduced the use of firearms in Indian warfare, and the dumbfounded Mohawk were easily defeated. This tragic experience was symbolic of the enmity which the Iroquois developed toward the French and which helped defeat French colonization in the New World. Again the contest for domination of the trade in beaver pelts was the motivating factor.

War then blazed in earnest. The Five Nations struck their foes at every vulnerable spot. Town after town was captured; French priests were tor-tured, thousands of Huron warriors were slain; women and children suf-fered extreme hardship. With the fall of the great village of Scanenrat in 1648, the Huron confederacy was completely broken and its people fled to their allies, the Erie, the Neutrals, and the Andaste.

Determined to wipe out the last vestige of resistance, the Five Nations proceeded to conquer and absorb these neighboring tribes, which had previously rejected league membership. The Neutrals, neighbors of the Seneca on the west, were the next to be crushed. The Erie, occupying the south-western corner of the present State, were battled into submission in 1654-5; and then the conquest of the Andaste in a bloody 10-year cam-paign completed the struggle for domination.

First tasting the bitter fruit of the white man's invasion at the hands of Champlain, the Iroquois established friendly relations with the Dutch and English; traded valuable beaver and mink pelts for flashy baubles, cotton cloth, guns, and rum; and were systematically cheated by the crafty Europeans. The Hollanders, chiefly interested in the profitable fur trade, paid little attention to the Indian's lack of Christianity, but the English recognized the great power of the Five Nations Confederacy and en-deavored to convert the Iroquois into loyal allies. The Episcopal Church sent out missionaries; John Stuart translated the New Testament into several Iroquoian languages; and Sir William Johnson, highly esteemed by the Indians, personally financed the publication of the Episcopal liturgy in Mohawk. Adding flattery to religion, the British formally denounced French interference with the Five Nations, and in 1687 James II issued a warrant to Governor Dongan authorizing protection of the Iroquois as subjects of Great Britain.

Proud of their new sovereignty, the Iroquois raided French settlements on the St.Lawrence with a bloodthirsty eagerness that threatened Mon-treal and caused bloody retaliation by Count Frontenac's vengeful hordes in the Schenectady massacre. The subsequent devastation of Iro-quois villages brought the Five Nations to their knees and resulted in a treaty with the French in 1701.

After the cessation of war with the French, the Iroquois enjoyed a long period of ascendancy. They diplomatically played off the British and French against each other, and made their own control of the fur trade more certain. The Delaware were subdued, several Pennsylvania tribes were annexed, and in 1722 the Tuscarora were admitted to the league, which thereafter became known as the Six Nations Confederacy.

Despite their smoldering hatred of the French, many Iroquois groups joined the sporadic raids made against the English by motley war parties of Algonquins and Hurons during the French and Indian War. This alien-ation of their allegiance was evidently caused by fear of the French, dis-trust of English land speculators, and the dismal failure of British military efforts. But even before the final British victory the Iroquois were won back into the British fold by Sir William Johnson, who staged a grand council at Fort Stanwix in 1768. This conclave, attended by more than

3,000 Indians, marked the end of the Cherokee Wars and created a line of territorial demarcation beginning at Fort Stanwix and extending south and west to a point north of Fort Pitt, then down the Ohio River to the mouth of the Tennessee. West of this line no white settlement was to be made. It was the subsequent violation of this boundary that caused much of the Iroquois bitterness toward the colonists.

The beginning of the Revolution found the Six Nations divided in allegiance between the English and the Continentals. The Mohawk, Onondaga, Cayuga, and Seneca remained steadfast British allies; the Oneida and Tuscarora, through the powerful influence of Samuel Kirkland, were friendly to the Colonials.

Joseph Brant, full-blooded Mohawk chief whose sister had married Sir William Johnson, joined the British forces in 1776, received a captain's commission, and played an important role throughout the Revolution. A force of Iroquois under Brant and Sayenqueraghta, supporting the British and Tories at Oriskany on August 6, 1777, was outbattled by Herkimer's makeshift militia. Smarting from this costly defeat, the Iroquois retaliated by desolating the New York and Pennsylvania frontiers. Chief Ojageght joined in Colonel Walter Butler's raids at Wyoming and Cherry Valley; Blacksnake, Little Beard, and Cornplanter left red trails of slaughter across the Unadilla hills; and Joseph Brant defeated the Continentals at the Battle of Minisink. But the Iroquois were forced into defensive fighting in 1779 by the Sullivan-Clinton expedition, which devastated their homes and their cornfields and drove them north to seek British protection. From this blow the Iroquois never fully recovered.

When the Revolution ended the Indians were entirely destitute. Joseph Brant went to England in 1785 to plead for the welfare of his people. He was cordially received in London, hobnobbed with high society, paid a formal visit to George III, and returned with a grant for a reservation on the Grand River in Ontario.

Many Mohawks, Onondagas, and Cayugas accompanied Brant to Canada, but many more remained, and their plight was entirely tragic. The Continental Congress and the State legislature passed resolutions; treaties were signed; Indian commissioners were appointed; and after 1784 reservations were established in New York State for the Oneida, Onondaga, and Cayuga. The Seneca obtained 10 tracts of land by the Big Tree Treaty in 1797, and later deeded a small section to the Tuscarora.

In this time of need and distress appeared Ganeodaio (Handsome Lake), who between 1799 and 1815 preached a doctrine of reform that became the most effective bar to the spreading of Christianity among the Indians.

He organized a characteristic messianic cult, like that of Tecumseh, the Shawnee prophet. Advocating strict adherence to Indian custom, he covered hundreds of miles on foot and preached a doctrine of chastity and temperance with an eloquence that gained many converts.

With the establishment of reservations, the Indian underwent a gradual metamorphosis. His warfare was obsolete. The small area of his habitations and the decimation of wild game made hunting unprofitable. Agriculture declined with the loss of land and the weakening of morale. Missionaries erected churches, Quakers established an Indian school, and the arrogant warrior became a disciple of the white man's progress. In the nineteenth century the Quakers achieved the only real success at making the Iroquois self-sufficient farmers.

Today practically the entire Indian population of the State, numbering approximately 5,000, is confined within the boundaries of reservations. Reservation Indians are a separate people, exempt from land and school taxes, and with power to regulate their internal and social relations. The only revenue the Indian receives from the Government is an annuity, under the early treaties, of from 68¢ to $1.35 and five yards of cloth, in addition to the rentals from his lands and their mineral resources. He ekes out a living by truck farming and by selling moccasins, splint baskets, and willowware. The State Department of Social Welfare provides the cost of home relief, medical care, and employment service, maintains an orphanage, and offers help in the improvement of agriculture; the Work Projects Administration has provided work relief and has sponsored a revival of the old handicrafts; and the State Education Department maintains Indian schools, though most pupils attend adjacent village schools.

The Indian's contributions to the civilization of the New World were of inestimable value. His cultivation of corn and tobacco, his vast knowledge of woodcraft and herbs, and his technique in trapping and hunting were all vital props in bolstering the self-reliance of the pioneering colonists. Even his methods of government were freely borrowed and used in the building of empire. Most definite, and lasting into our own day, has been the Indian contribution to place names, which has stamped upon the New York State map such names as Otego, Owasco, Canandaigua, Poughkeepsie, Schenectady, and Ticonderoga. Finally, the Indians left, hovering over brook and vale and mountain, legends of creation, of battles of gods and giants, of tragic elopements, of fools and wise men,—legends which, for the initiate, animate the landscape with a beauty and an interest beyond what the senses perceive.

History

IN 1609, Samuel de Champlain, a Frenchman, explored southward along the valley of the lake later named for him, and Henry Hudson, an Englishman in Dutch employ, sailed northward up the river later named for him. These two expeditions, occurring within two months of each other and penetrating to points only about 100 miles apart, prefigured a century and a half of struggle for control of a North American empire.

In 1614 Fort Nassau was built by the Dutch on Castle Island, south of the present city of Albany, to serve as a fur-trading post; after it was destroyed by a spring freshet in 1617, a new fort, Fort Orange, was erected on the west bank of the river near the present site of Albany. In 1621 the West India Company came into being. About 30 families, mostly Walloons, were transported in 1624 to New Netherland, as the area was called, and a majority of them formed the first permanent Dutch settlement at Fort Orange. The first substantial settlement on the island of Manhattan was made the following year; and after a fort was built there, the families at Fort Orange were moved down temporarily to enjoy its protection.

In order to encourage colonization, in 1629 the West India Company offered a large estate, or patroonship, in the new colony to each of its members who within four years would settle 50 colonists on the tract assigned to him. The only patroonship to survive Colonial times was Rensselaerswyck, a large area on both sides of the upper Hudson, of which the site of Albany was the approximate center; it was settled by its absentee owner, Kiliaen Van Rensselaer, with Dutchmen, Germans, Danes, Norwegians, Scots, and other nationals. The nonresident patroon, through his agents, enjoyed complete suzerainty over his domain and retained ownership of the land, letting it out principally on leases. He financed the settlers and was repaid slowly over a long period. The Fuyck, enjoying the protection of Fort Orange on the west bank of the Hudson, became the principal settlement. A quarrel over jurisdiction was ended in 1652 by the establishment of a new court at Beverwyck, which included Fort Orange and the Fuyck. This tribunal immediately overshadowed and finally absorbed the patroon's court in 1665. Other settlements in the upstate area were made during the Dutch period at Wiltwyck (Kingston) and several other points along the Hudson, and at Schenectady on the Mohawk. The settlement on Manhattan Island was designated as the city of New Amsterdam and given burgher government in 1653.

The Dutch West India Company, in common with other early trading and colonizing groups, looked upon its colony as a source of dividends. It bound the settlers by contracts that prohibited trade, change of residence, and the transfer of property; and it imposed heavy taxes, including taxes on imports, that discouraged enterprise, aroused antagonism, and insured minimum returns. It shirked all obligations of a social character, throwing on the Dutch Reformed Church the burden of education and care of the sick and the poor. This shortsighted policy, aggravated by the greed and ineptness of its officials in the Colony, brought the company to virtual bankruptcy. The Directors General of New Netherland—Minuit, Van Twiller, Kieft, Stuyvesant—had trouble, much of it of their own making, with the company's business agents, with the clergy of the Reformed Church, with Van Rensselaer's agents, with the New Englanders encroaching in Westchester and on Long Island, and especially with their own people, who demanded an effective voice in the government and wider freedom.

In 1664, when Colonel Richard Nicolls at the head of a British fleet demanded the surrender of New Amsterdam, Director General Stuyvesant found himself with little support and was obliged to capitulate. The Province and the principal settlement were renamed New York, Beverwyck became Albany, and Wiltwyck, Kingston. In 1673 the Dutch recaptured the Colony, but in 1674 it was restored by treaty to the English, who promptly resumed their sway.

The terms of surrender in 1664 were highly favorable to the Dutch. Land titles were confirmed, including that of Rensselaerswyck; toleration was granted to the Dutch Reformed and other Protestant churches. Transition to English political institutions was slow; in the Albany district and along the wharves of New York City the Dutch language persisted for generations. In 1683 the Province of New York was divided into 12 counties, two of which, Dukes and Cornwall, later passed to Massachusetts and Maine; the boundaries of Albany County extended north, west, and east without fixed limits. In 1686 charters were granted to the cities of New York and Albany.

The forced abdication of James II and the accession of William and Mary (1688–9) brought discontent to the surface. Following the lead of New England, Jacob Leisler, with strong support from the common people, seized power in New York City and governed, though in Albany his authority was at first not recognized. After the arrival of Governor Sloughter in 1691, Leisler and his chief lieutenant, Jacob Milborne, were hanged for treason; but their names were later cleared in England, and for a generation the memory of Leisler served as a symbol for the discontented.

The war between Britain and France that began in 1689, known in America as King William's War, was the first of a series of four conflicts that ended in 1760 with the British conquest of Canada. In these wars, because of geography and Indian relations, the Province of New York played a strategic role. In the days when natural waterways were the principal means of transportation, its lakes and rivers, connecting the Atlantic with the Great Lakes, the Mohawk and the St.Lawrence with the Susquehanna and the Delaware, and the Hudson with the Allegheny and the Ohio, made it the great crossroads of the East. The nations comprising the Iroquois Confederacy, which controlled the carries and the headwaters of this far-flung system of water routes, held the balance of power in the struggle. Albany was Montreal's successful rival in the fur trade, which, together with the routes to the interior, would be controlled by the side that won the friendship or the submission of the Iroquois.

On February 8, 1690, Schenectady was destroyed by one of three French and Indian war parties sent out by Frontenac, governor of Canada. Fearful lest Albany be taken and their western boundaries be opened to attack, in May of that year the English Colonies sent representatives to the first intercolonial congress in New York, at which a plan for military co-operation was made; but only Connecticut and Maryland joined New York in an abortive campaign against Montreal, the New England colonies busying themselves in an equally fruitless expedition by sea against Quebec. The New York legislature, absorbed in its controversy with Leisler, failed to provide adequate defense for the Albany-Schenectady frontier, and the population in that district fell off by a third. Credit for the preservation of the Iroquois friendship in these crucial days is due Peter Schuyler of Albany, who performed heroic service in defending the frontier, in pursuing French and Indian raiding parties, and in counteracting the solicitations of French agents in the Iroquois councils. But after the first French war the English Colonies never enjoyed the unanimous and wholehearted support of the Five, later Six, Nations of the Iroquois Confederacy.

After the Treaty of Ryswyck (1697) an important trade sprang up between Albany and Montreal; and the interested Albany and New York merchants were influential enough to stress the policy of neutrality in subsequent defensive wars. New England, which suffered the brunt of the attack during Queen Anne's War (1702–13)—the American phase of the War of the Spanish Succession—complained bitterly that the French Indians were shooting its people with guns bought in Albany. But Peter Schuyler learned from visiting Indians of contemplated attacks and forewarned New England authorities, and New York contributed its quota of men and money to the abortive expeditions of 1709 and 1711 against Canada.

During the 30 years of peace that followed the Treaty of Utrecht (1713), while the French strengthened their position by constructing a system of fortifications at strategic points, including Niagara (1726) and Crown Point (1731), the English Colonies went their individual ways. New York's advantage in the contest for supremacy lay in the preference of the Indians for Albany goods in the barter for furs, but that advantage was sacrificed by the direct sale of those goods to the French. In King George's War (1744–8), which grew out of the War of the Austrian Succession, New York again inclined toward a policy of neutrality, but it took part in the ineffective expedition against Canada in 1746.

During the six-year interval between the third and fourth French wars the trade of the British Colonies and their prestige with the Indians declined further. There was much to alienate the Iroquois: their business as middlemen in the fur trade was spoiled by the commerce of the western tribes directly with Montreal, made possible by the Albany trade with the French merchants; France seemed to have the upper hand in a military sense; the long sojourn of the Joncaires, father and sons, among the Seneca had won that strong nation's friendship for the French; and the English were neglecting to send the Indians the customary gifts. The Albany Congress of 1754 was called in an effort to secure united Colonial action and to conciliate the Iroquois, but failed to do either. Like Peter Schuyler in the earlier period, during the last two French wars Sir William Johnson possessed the confidence of the Iroquois and was able to keep them active in the British cause, or at least, in the darkest days, neutral.

The French and Indian War, the last British-American conflict with the French, begun in 1754 with the clash at Great Meadows, was marked in 1755 by Braddock's defeat and the failure of expeditions against Niagara and Crown Point. Though he did not take Crown Point, Sir William Johnson succeeded in holding the Lake George area by defeating Dieskau, for which achievement he was made a baronet and presented with £5,000 by Parliament. By taking Oswego and gaining control of the Great Carrying Place (the site of Rome) in 1756, the French dominated the important Mohawk River-Oneida Lake waterway. After these reverses all the Iroquois became neutral, with the exception of the Mohawk, who were kept loyal to the English by the efforts of Sir William Johnson. After Montcalm captured Fort William Henry and hostile Indians made successful raids on the English frontier in 1757, it required all of Johnson's influence to keep the Iroquois from going over to the enemy.

The year 1758, with William Pitt in power, proved the turning point in British affairs in North America. Encouraged by Pitt's promise of reimbursement, New York raised its quotas of men and money. The train of disasters was completed by Abercrombie's failure to take Ticonderoga (July 8), but in the same year Bradstreet with little effort captured Fort Frontenac (August 27), on the site of Kingston, Ontario. That victory enabled the English to establish themselves at Fort Stanwix (Rome) and revived the confidence of the Iroquois. As in a dramatic tragedy, once the climax was passed, the events of the dénouement piled up rapidly. In 1759, while Wolfe was taking Quebec, Amherst compelled the French to abandon Ticonderoga (July 26) and Crown Point fell to his hands (July 31), while Johnson captured Niagara (July 25) and reoccupied Oswego. In 1760 Amherst took La Galette, now Ogdensburg, and at Montreal accepted the surrender of all Canada to the British. In a council at Detroit in 1761, Johnson persuaded 13 Indian tribes formerly allied with the French to sign a treaty with Britain. Though peace was not signed in Europe until 1763, for New York the menace of the French and the Indians was over, and the Province was ready to begin its rapid progress to pre-eminence.

During the English period the Colony developed slowly. The Dutch occupied the Hudson and spread into the Mohawk Valley; English from New England settled along the east bank of the Hudson; Scots and Scotch-Irish settled on the west bank, in Cherry Valley, in northern New York, and in the vicinity of Johnstown, to which they were attracted by Sir William Johnson. In 1677 a small party of Huguenots settled New Paltz; in 1689 another group founded New Rochelle. The Palatines, comprising the largest mass immigration of the English period, came first to the Hudson Valley to produce naval stores, but with the failure of that enterprise many of them finally settled in the Schoharie and Mohawk Valleys. In 1760 the frontier settlements extended to about 40 miles north of Albany along the Hudson and about 80 miles west of Albany on the Mohawk. In that year New York ranked seventh in population among the thirteen Colonies.

Historians give three chief reasons for this retarded growth. The threat of French and Indian raids prevented expansion northward and westward; the Iroquois showed their displeasure at every effort to appropriate more

The Setting

Photograph by Roger L. Moore

WHITEFACE MOUNTAIN FROM COPPERAS POND

AMERICAN FALLS, NIAGARA

Photograph by Milton J. Washburn

NIAGARA RIVER, RAPIDS AND FALLS (American Falls, left; Horseshoe Falls, right)

HUDSON RIVER FROM BEAR MOUNTAIN

Photograph by courtesy of the New York Bureau of State Publicity

BIG FLATS VALLEY, NEAR ELMIRA

RAINBOW FALLS, WATKINS GLEN

THREE OF THE THOUSAND ISLANDS

LAKE CHAMPLAIN

ROLLING FARMLAND, MONROE COUNTY

Photograph by Josef Schiff

HEART LAKE AND MT. McINTYRE

Photograph by Roger L. Moore

of their land; and the prevalent system of large estates, with long-term leases preferred by the manorial lords to outright sales, discouraged settlement by immigrants to whom independence meant above all ownership of the soil they plowed.

Social and economic organization still reflected the medieval inheritance. The manor was an almost self-sufficient unit, its basic agriculture supplemented by handicraft and the importation of indispensable goods; the leaseholder paid his rent in kind, and was influenced by a personal loyalty to the lord of the manor that was transmuted by the latter into political power; and the manor house was the social center of the community, in which the humble leaseholder vicariously lived a fuller life. Labor was regularly hired by contract for a term of years, and the custom of apprenticeship was widely followed. In the cities, keeping shop and practicing trades were limited to freemen; 'freedom' could be purchased, the cost to merchants being about double that to tradesmen and handicraftsmen; apprentices to freemen were admitted by registration. Negro slaves made up more than 10 per cent of the population.

In the light of subsequent Revolutionary history, the most significant aspect of the political life of the Provincial period was the struggle for supremacy between the governor, representing the prerogative of the Crown and usually supported by the council, and the assembly, representing Provincial interests. It was not at the time a struggle for democracy but rather an effort by the Provincial aristocracy to achieve political power and by Provincial business and commerce to avoid taxation and throw off the restrictions of the mercantile system. The issue was settled by control of the public purse strings. At the end of the period the assembly had established a body of precedents that gave it control of finance and established it as the dominant element in the Provincial government.

It is not necessary to rehearse the conflicts between imperial policy and local self-interest and between British and Colonial theories of political rights, nor the series of specific clashes, that culminated in the American Revolution. In New York, as in other Colonies, the situation was complicated by the effort of the propertyless class—mechanics, laborers, and tenant farmers—to bend events toward the realization of a higher economic and social level for themselves, and, at the other extreme, by the presence of a large number of Loyalists who, while willing to plead with the Mother Country, refused to follow the Patriot party into armed rebellion. About 40,000 Loyalists left the State during and after the Revolution.

The steps involved in the actual accomplishment of revolution—the establishment of an effective insurgent government and the administration and financing of the war—were undertaken by a system of local committees. These appointed delegates to a Provincial convention, which in turn sent representatives to the Continental Congress. Until the establishment of State and local governments, the committees 'had to enact law and enforce it, perform judicial and police duties, suppress the Loyalists, raise funds, recruit soldiers, furnish military supplies and perform a thousand other duties.'

On July 9, 1776, the Provincial Congress of New York, meeting at White Plains, ratified the Declaration of Independence, and on the next day named itself 'the Convention of the Representatives of the State of New York.' The first State constitution was adopted and proclaimed in Kingston on April 20, 1777. That document represented a victory for the aristocratic group of the Patriot party in that it set up property qualifications for the franchise. George Clinton, chosen by the ballots of freeholders, took the oath of office as first governor of the State on July 30; and on September 10 in the Kingston courthouse the House of Assembly of the State of New York began its initial session. In the interval affairs were administered by an extralegal Council of Safety. Local governments were set up under the supervision of the Revolutionary committees.

In the military history of the Revolution, New York State bulks large: '. . . out of the 308 battles and engagements of the Revolution, 92, or nearly one third, took place on New York soil.' In the spring of 1775 Ethan Allen captured Ticonderoga, Seth Warner took Crown Point, and Arnold made a dash on St.Johns, Canada. The artillery captured at Ticonderoga was transported by General Knox to Boston and enabled Washington to drive the British from that city. Later in the same year Montgomery took Montreal. In the unsuccessful attack on Quebec on December 31, 1775, Montgomery was killed and Arnold was wounded.

In 1776, in the northern part of the State, Carleton defeated Arnold in the Battle of Valcour Island (October 11), one of the first engagements between a British and an American fleet, and thereby regained control of Lake Champlain, but failed to take Ticonderoga. In the southern part of the State, Howe drove Washington from Long Island and Manhattan and followed him northward. After the Battle of White Plains, Howe captured Fort Washington. Thereafter the scene of the campaign shifted to New Jersey. The British held New York City until the end of the war.

Under the British plan of campaign for 1777, Burgoyne was to move south along Lake Champlain and the upper Hudson; St.Leger was to land at Oswego, take Fort Stanwix, and march down the Mohawk Valley;

Howe was to ascend the Hudson from New York City; and the three forces were to meet at Albany, thus establishing control over New York and separating New England from the other Colonies. St.Leger was halted at Fort Stanwix (Rome) and settled down to a siege. On August 6, General Herkimer and his Tryon County militia, marching to relieve the fort, were ambushed at Oriskany, six miles east, but held the field against a Loyalist, British, Hessian, and Indian force in one of the bloodiest battles of the war. On the same day Colonel Marinus Willett made a bold sortie from Fort Stanwix into St.Leger's camp. This successful resistance, together with the arrival of reinforcements under Arnold, caused St.Leger to raise the siege on August 22 and retreat to Oswego. Arnold was left free to join in the campaign against Burgoyne.

Burgoyne moved south along Lake Champlain in June, took Ticonderoga (July 6), and advanced to Skenesborough (Whitehall) at the head of the lake. His continued advance was slowed by his heavy baggage trains and by Schuyler's strategy of obstructing the road by every possible means. During the delay the defending force was strengthened by thousands of volunteers, especially after the murder of Jane McCrea (*see Tour* 22). At Walloomsac, in the Battle of Bennington (August 16), Stark defeated two detachments of German dragoons on their way to take the supplies stored at Bennington. In the first Battle of Saratoga, at Freeman's Farm on September 19, the British held their ground; but in the second battle on October 7 they were defeated, largely by an assault, in defiance of orders, led by Benedict Arnold and powerfully supported by Daniel Morgan's sharpshooting riflemen. Burgoyne fell back to Schuylerville, where, finding his retreat cut off, he surrendered on October 17.

In the meantime Howe, not having received specific orders to move up the Hudson, went south to take Philadelphia. Sir Henry Clinton started up the Hudson on October 3 and advanced as far as Kingston, which he burned on October 16; but his messages to Burgoyne were intercepted, and, upon hearing of Burgoyne's surrender, he returned to New York.

Within 24 hours after receiving the news of Saratoga, the French Government decided to come to the aid of the Colonies and to declare war on Great Britain.

The years 1778 and 1779 saw a deadlock between Washington, defending West Point, and Clinton, holding New York City, neither strong enough to attack the other. The events of those years in New York took place on and beyond the frontier. In 1778 Loyalist and Indian bands under Sir John Johnson (Sir William's son), John Butler and his son Walter, and Joseph Brant—names that are to this day anathema to central New York State residents—raided a number of frontier settlements. In 1779 the carefully planned Sullivan-Clinton campaign, a punitive expedition into the central and western Iroquois country, struck a blow at the Confederacy from which it never fully recovered, though in 1780 retaliatory raids were made in the Schoharie and middle Mohawk Valleys. On October 25, 1781, six days after Cornwallis's surrender at Yorktown, Willett checked a combined force of British, Loyalists, and Indians in the Battle of Johnstown. In the pursuit after the battle, on October 30, Walter Butler was killed.

Following the surrender of Cornwallis, Washington made his headquarters at Newburgh until after the peace was signed. Here he rejected a crown offered him by a military faction, and here he prevented an uprising by the disgruntled Army. In the intervals he found time to make a tour of the battlefields in the upper Hudson and Mohawk Valleys and to invest in New York real estate. On May 6, 1783, he met with the British commander to plan the evacuation of New York; on November 25 he marched into the city.

The final act of the drama in which a unified Nation was molded was the adoption of the Federal Constitution. In New York the sharp conflict between the Clintonian faction, opposed to ratification, and the Hamiltonian faction, in favor of it, reflected the clash of interests between tenants and their manorial lords, between workers and their employers, and between the agricultural back country, which preferred State autonomy, and the city with its dominant commercial interest, which desired a strong central government to support commerce and provide a sound currency. The campaign for election of delegates to the ratifying convention was the occasion of the writing of the *Federalist* papers by Hamilton, Jay, and Madison. Two thirds of the delegates, elected by universal free male suffrage, were committed to vote against the Constitution; but the Federalists were aided by the march of events. The convention met in Poughkeepsie in June 1788. After New Hampshire ratified as the ninth State, and Virginia as the tenth, the fear of losing the lucrative trade with the other States, of the possible secession of the southern New York counties, and of having land claims in the present State of Vermont invalidated by the Federal Government, swung the convention over to ratification. The final vote, after more than a month of bitter debate, was 30 to 27. Four delegates, including Clinton, failed to vote.

After the Revolution, settlement extended northward and westward. The menace of the Indians was gone; the State purchased the titles to their lands and sold them to speculators: land speculation became the favorite form of financial gambling. In 1789–90 the Military Tract of more than 1,500,000 acres east of Seneca Lake, reaching from the southern tip of that lake to the shore of Lake Ontario, was set aside for Revolutionary veterans; but many of them sold their allotments to speculators. The classical names assigned to the townships of the Military Tract form a well-known characteristic of central New York.

Title to the western area of the State was disputed between New York and Massachusetts. By the Hartford Treaty of 1786, Massachusetts was awarded ownership and New York jurisdiction of the land west of the Pre-emption Line drawn through Seneca Lake. In 1788 Massachusetts gave two speculators, Oliver Phelps and Nathaniel Gorham, an option on the entire tract; but they obtained Indian title to only the land east of the Genesee River and about 200,000 acres on its western shore up from its mouth, and surrendered their option on the rest. They sold a large part of their holdings in 1790 to Robert Morris of Philadelphia, who resold it to the London Associates, headed by Sir William Pulteney. Morris bought the remaining land from Massachusetts in 1791 and sold all but a tract along the Genesee River to a Dutch group known as the Holland Land Company, which became the proprietor of about 3,300,000 acres in western New York. After Indian title was obtained in 1797, the company sent surveyors under Joseph Ellicott to mark out townships, and sales began at the land office in Batavia in 1801.

In the North Country the Macomb Purchase, 1791, including nearly 4,000,000 acres, was soon divided into smaller tracts. The Delaware, Susquehanna, and Champlain Valleys, and the territory north and south of the Mohawk River were taken up by innumerable small purchases.

A few pioneers had settled on some of these lands immediately after the Revolution, but once clear titles were available the migration took on the proportions of a stampede. A large majority of the settlers came from New England by way of the Mohawk and Cherry Valley routes, transporting their belongings—many now treasured in historical museums—by water and in large, boat-shaped covered wagons. Some came up the Delaware Valley from New Jersey, others up the Susquehanna from Pennsylvania. Eastern New Yorkers in large numbers sought their fortunes on the new western lands; and when the Holland Tract was opened up, some moved from central New York for a fresh start. New Englanders, French Canadians, and French émigrés settled the North Country.

The years just preceding and following the turn of the century were New York's frontier period. Many of the trail blazers, some of whom have become part of local folklore, moved farther west before the wave of permanent settlers. Clearings were made in the forests, log cabins were erected, and the land was brought under the plow. Gradually the clearings were enlarged and the homes improved. The New Englanders built villages in the image of Lexington and Concord. Churches were formed; schools were erected, then academies were organized, and finally colleges were founded. By 1820 the population of the new settlements totaled 500,000, and that of the State 1,372,812, representing an advance since 1790 from fifth to first place among the States.

In the first years the new settlers could produce no more than enough to meet their own needs. Then the demand for supplies during the War of 1812 brought a period of prosperity, for which trade with the enemy was responsible in a substantial degree.

Most of the land fighting of the War of 1812 occurred along the Canadian border within the State. Repeated invasions of Canada failed because of the inefficiency of troops and their commanders, aggravated by the difficulties of co-operation between the State militia and the National Army. In 1813 the Americans burned York (Toronto), and the British burned Lewiston, Black Rock, and Buffalo; but the end of the war found the opposing armies holding almost their original positions along the Niagara frontier. The British attack on Plattsburg (September 11, 1814) was turned back by Macdonough's naval victory on Lake Champlain.

Long before the War of 1812, the need for improved means of transportation was recognized, and by the time of the war the construction of turnpike roads was in full swing. But the war provided vivid proof that land haulage was too costly: it cost $400 to haul a gun weighing about three tons from the place of manufacture to Sackets Harbor. Prohibitive transportation rates made it impossible for farmers in the Finger Lakes and Genesee Valley regions to compete with those along the Hudson and the Mohawk. Without an available market for its products, western New York was retarded in its development. Surplus grain was turned into the more portable form of whisky, of which large quantities were consumed on the spot. Crop surpluses were also used to raise livestock, and for a period of years drovers clogged the turnpikes with herds bound for the slaughterhouses of Albany and New York. The commerce of the central and western parts of the State followed the natural waterways to market—down the Delaware to Philadelphia, down the Susquehanna to Baltimore, and down the St.Lawrence to Montreal. Farsighted leaders like De Witt Clinton saw that a canal connecting the Hudson with the Great Lakes would provide relief for the western farmer and, by deflecting the commerce of the area down the Hudson, would make the State an economic unit and raise New York City to commercial pre-eminence. But when the bill authorizing construction of the Erie Canal was up for passage in 1817, the representatives of the city in the legislature, uninterested in 'upstate' improvements, voted against it as one man. The bill, however, was passed, the canal was dug, and the stream of commerce thus stimulated became the decisive factor in determining the rapid growth of New York City. Before the canal was opened in 1825, the cost of hauling a ton of freight from Buffalo to New York City was $120; on the canal it was reduced to $14.

The canal and its feeders created a strong economic bond between the eastern and western sections of the State to the profit of both. The drastic reduction in transportation costs opened the eastern market to western grain, and a prosperous west bought the products of eastern factories, to which more capital was steadily drawn. Inland ports grew up along the canal, serving as transportation and shopping centers and providing local markets for agricultural products.

As the influence of the canal extended beyond the borders of the State and accelerated the development of the Great Lakes region, especially Ohio, midwestern grain entered the eastern market and New York farmers turned to dairying, truck gardening, and fruit-growing; and the cities, aided by inventions, available capital, an adequate labor supply, and access to power sources and markets, became industrial centers.

The railroads, extending their lines in the years following the completion of the canal, hastened the process of change; the Erie reached Lake Erie at Dunkirk in the fifties, supplying the Southern Tier with modern transportation for its products to New York City.

By 1850 the State had achieved a pre-eminent rank in industry and commerce and was still among the leaders in agriculture. In that year 'New York possessed one seventh of the true valuation of the property of the whole country.'

The twenties, thirties, and especially the forties (the period of the Great Irish Famine and abortive revolution on the continent) were marked by a large foreign immigration, principally Irish and German. The former dug the canals, then remained to build the railroads, and finally settled in large numbers in the urban centers. The Germans provided skilled workers and professional people and became a stimulus to an expanding cultural life.

Coincident with this economic development arose a struggle for political democracy. The Revolution and the ratification of the Federal Constitution left the landed aristocrats and commercial princes in power, and political leadership was largely identified with names like Van Cortlandt, Schuyler, Livingston, Hamilton, Jay, Morris, Van Rensselaer, and Clinton. The Hamiltonian principle of government by the propertied class for the protection of property prevailed, and the franchise was accordingly limited by property qualifications. But democratic doctrine had been rapidly gaining strength, especially in the newly settled western and northern counties and among the mill and factory workers of the cities. The constitution of 1821 represented substantial progress toward universal male suffrage, and the subsequent series of democratic reforms was completed by the constitution of 1846, which provided for direct election to high State executive and judicial offices. Other evidences of the growth of the democratic spirit were the gradual abolition of slavery; the organization of a Working Men's Party that demanded a mechanics' lien law, abolition of imprisonment for debt, and universal education; and the antirent wars, in which leaseholders on the large estates resorted to force in resisting the feudal inequities of the leasehold system of land tenure.

The same period was characterized by an epidemic of reform movements concentrated in central and western New York and probably attributable to the New England antecedents of the population. A strong anti-slavery sentiment expressed itself in political organization and in the activities of the Underground Railroad. The woman's-rights movement began in Seneca Falls. Temperance societies multiplied rapidly in the twenties and thirties, and total abstinence was endorsed by the State temperance society in 1835. The anti-Masonic movement was another western growth. And a number of novel religious sects, including the Mormons and the Millerites (Seventh Day Adventists), sprang up.

The detailed history of the political strife of the period is characterized by the multiplication of factional groups brought about by conflicts of personalities, interests, and issues. The robust nature of the politics is suggested in the names of the factions—Coodies, Bucktails, Hunkers or Hard Shells, and Barnburners or Soft Shells. The Native American Party gave expression to antiforeign, anti-Catholic sentiment in the State, caused mainly by the economic pressure arising from the new immigration. The anti-Masonic party developed in the western counties out of the disappearance of one Morgan, who had threatened to expose the secrets of the order. In the Albany Regency and in the political leadership of Thurlow Weed, New York State gave the country early examples of the thorough efficiency of the modern political machine based on patronage. The Tweed Ring, the Canal Ring, and the Railroad Lobby were active in Albany.

Its population and wealth made New York a pivotal State in national elections, enabling it to play a significant role in national politics. By 1850 it had given the Nation two Presidents, five Vice Presidents, and many cabinet officers and ambassadors. The slavery issue in the Civil War period crystallized political lines into the present Republican and Democratic Parties. To the Union cause in the Civil War New York State contributed its full share of men and money: the total number of New York troops engaged was nearly 500,000, of whom about one tenth were killed.

In the Civil War period industrial capitalism was introduced, with machine production, absentee ownership, corporate management, and the wage laborer. The railroads brought the raw materials to the industrial centers and carried away the finished products; the canals declined in importance, and many an inland port, once bustling and prosperous, became a sleepy milk station and a Saturday-afternoon shopping center for farmers. The factories attracted young people from the country, and the cities grew rapidly at the expense of the rural areas. Later, as the heavy industries moved closer to the sources of raw materials, New York State turned to the manufacture of intermediate products and consumers' goods. In the recent past the State gained new industries resulting from scientific advance, especially the production of radio equipment, electrical supplies, chemicals, and airplanes. New York City became the center of the Nation's banking, finance, and wholesale and retail merchandising; and Wall Street became the barometer, and to a growing extent the control center, of the Nation's business. In recent years the city has developed into the greatest seaport in the world. While agriculture in the State remained economically important, its character changed: cultivation of grain was superseded by dairying and the growing of fruits and vegetables for markets close at hand. Thus the wealth of the State today, unsurpassed in the Union, is securely founded on eminence in specialized agriculture, manufacturing, and commerce.

Urbanization and industrialization created problems that became the political issues of the post-Civil War period. In the late seventies bad harvests in Ireland drove thousands of Irish to New York. In the eighties began a stream of immigration, ending only with the World War, that brought new racial elements in large numbers to the State—Italians, Poles, Russians, and others, all from southern and eastern Europe—and that created new problems in economics and citizenship. The growing cities needed workers to lay streets, sidewalks, and sewers and to construct water, light, power, and rapid transit systems. Politicians in control of political machines were able, in granting contracts and franchises, to enrich themselves by betraying the public interest to the contractor or the public-utility promoter. Through the boss, Big Business controlled politics. The temptation of proffered graft was too strong to be universally resisted by elected representatives. Tilden achieved national renown, and all but won the Presidency, as a result of his exposure of the Tweed Ring and the Canal Ring. Conditions reached such a pass that a reputation for honesty and steadiness in local administration was sufficient, as in the case of Grover Cleveland, to place a public figure in the White House. Charles Evans Hughes first attracted wide public attention as a result of his investigations into gas and electricity rates and the financial practices of insurance companies.

In the World War, New York State contributed to the military and naval service more than 500,000 men, about 10 per cent of the entire national force. The number of casualties was about 55,000, including 14,000 deaths. Its financial and industrial contributions were commensurate with its wealth.

In the twentieth century the rapid development of machine industry and the recurring cycle of prosperity and depression gave emphasis to another set of social problems: women and children in industry, conditions of work in factories, workmen's compensation, the rights and duties of organized labor, unemployment insurance, and old-age security. In many of these fields New York State legislation has served as a model for other States. The same period saw a rapid extension of State activity and support in the fields of roadbuilding, education, conservation, and the care of its wards in penal institutions and asylums. Through its financial policy of offering grants-in-aid to local units for schools, highways, and public welfare, the State has been able to secure adoption of its standards by local governmental bodies. State expenditures increased from $59,000,000 in 1916 to $396,000,000 in 1938-9; but its credit has remained strong throughout the years of depression.

Early efforts to regulate public utilities by special legislative acts failed. The principal activities of the Public Service Commission in recent years have been regulation of gas and electric rates and of bus lines and elimination of railroad grade crossings. The problems of determining a just valuation of utility property as a basis for rate-making purposes and of exercising an effective control over holding companies are still largely unsolved. Public ownership as a substitute for regulation in New York State has largely been restricted to waterworks; some of the smaller cities, notably the city of Jamestown, Chautauqua County, own their electric generating and distributing systems.

In the determination of policy in regard to the State's water-power resources the issue was clear-cut between State development and operation, espoused by Governors Alfred E. Smith, Franklin D. Roosevelt, and Herbert H. Lehman, and private development under State supervision, supported by the Republican majorities in the legislature. In 1930, after a long struggle, possession of the State's water power was reserved to the people; but the issue was reopened by the constitutional convention of 1938. The campaign for the development of the potential power of the St.Lawrence River has not yet been brought to a decision.

As it extended the sphere of its activities, the State government expanded into an unco-ordinated mass of bureaus and departments without centralized responsibility; and reorganization became another issue. The political conflict was complicated by opposition between the metropolis and the upstate area and by the demand for city home rule. The present system of representation, adopted in 1894, prevents New York City, though containing more than half of the population of the State, from securing a majority in the legislature. In 1927, largely as the result of the efforts of Governor Alfred E. Smith, all administrative functions were consolidated in a small number of departments, with final responsibility in the hands of the governor; in 1929 the executive budget system was instituted, with responsibility again vested in the governor. Since 1938 the governor is elected for a term of four years. On November 8, 1938, Governor Herbert H. Lehman was re-elected to serve the first four-year term in the history of the State.

National interest in New York politics is always large; the governor of a State that has 47 votes in the Electoral College is always a potential candidate for the presidency. In recent years this national interest has been increased by the careers of Governors Alfred E. Smith and Franklin D. Roosevelt. Both men fought for popular programs—Governor Smith for reorganization of the State government, workmen's compensation, a six-day week for all workers, health insurance, improved hospitals and penal institutions, a better and larger State park system, and repeal of the prohibition amendment; Governor Roosevelt for old-age pensions, reform of local government and the courts, relief for agriculture, and public control of hydroelectric power: and the opposition of one or both of the houses of the legislature, Republican-controlled, served as a sounding-board to arouse Nation-wide interest in these programs and their sponsors. The administration of Governor Herbert H. Lehman has followed the same pattern, with, however, a more circumspect opposition from the Republican Party.

The history of the State of New York illustrates the history of the Na-

tion in all its stages; in some aspects the history of the State is well nigh
coextensive with that of the Nation. The mingling of the peoples of the
world; the development from wilderness to metropolis; the baptism of
war; the conflicts of politics; internal improvements and revolutions in
transportation and communication; the trend away from agriculture to
manufacturing and commerce, though with agriculture retained as a basic
activity; the growth of corporations and the multiplication of new industries; the domination of finance and the spread of foreign commerce; the
ever-widening responsibility of government in social welfare; and the
achievement of cultural self-consciousness and self-expression—in all these
aspects the history of New York comprises a large and important share of
the history of the Nation. One of 48 politically equal States, ranking
twenty-ninth in area, New York in 1929 contained 10 per cent of the
country's population and more than 12 per cent of its wage-earners, and
made 14 per cent by value of its manufactured products. It is the Nation's
greatest financial, mercantile, and cultural center. It lives up to every con-
notation of the name given it by common consent—the Empire State.

Transportation

A GLANCE at a relief map of eastern United States will show how the natural features of New York State, especially its system of waterways, determined its prime importance in the development of American transportation. The Hudson-Mohawk Valley, the only pass of low elevation through the northern Appalachians and the straightest one in the entire range, provided easy access to the Great Lakes and became the avenue of commerce between the West and the northeastern seaboard. River, turnpike, canal, railroad, motor highway, and air line traffic have all followed this route, and have made its bordering area the wealthiest, most populous, and most thoroughly industrialized section of the State. Besides this Hudson-Mohawk route, the State has the Hudson-Champlain route to Canada; the Black River route to the North Country; the Oneida route to Oswego; the Finger Lakes, approaching within portage distance of the Chemung-Susquehanna watershed and a downstream route to Chesapeake Bay; the Genesee River, cutting across from Pennsylvania to Lake Ontario; and the Allegheny route, including Chautauqua Lake, which reaches to the Mississippi.

For the Indian, whose light canoe was easily toted between watersheds, these rivers and lakes were open paths of war and trade. High up on the slopes, where the ground was dry, thinly wooded, and free from underbrush, ran the Indian trails. The Great Central Trail crossed from Albany to Lake Erie; the Susquehanna Trail led from Albany southwest to the Susquehanna River and into Pennsylvania; from Catskill on the Hudson a trail wound north along Catskill Creek to join one that followed Schoharie Creek to its junction with the Mohawk; another followed the course of the Genesee and crossed to the Allegheny; others led into the North Country from Lake Champlain and the upper Hudson and along the Black River.

White settlement brought relatively little improvement over routes or means of transportation for more than 150 years. Until the Revolution, settlement was largely restricted to the Hudson and Mohawk Valleys, and the rivers remained the chief arteries of travel and trade. Merchantmen loaded with goods from London and Paris sailed up the Hudson to Albany, sold their wares, and took on cargoes of pelts, ginseng, flax, and flour. Intra-valley shipments were carried by sloops; in 1749, 47 of them were plying the river. Passengers provided their own food and bedding; livestock was tethered to the mast. On the Mohawk, as the fur trade expanded and settlement crept westward beyond Schenectady, birchbark and log canoes were succeeded by clumsy, bargelike bateaux, usually poled by eight or ten men; these were in turn replaced by Durhams, broad, flat-bottomed boats with sails, decked fore and aft, with capacities ranging from 15 to 20 tons.

In this same period, a crude, narrow road was cleared along the bank of the Hudson and another was built across the 17-mile sand plain between Albany and Schenectady, which was later extended to Fonda, Little Falls, and beyond. Other roads were few and of small account except locally. Wheel tracks marked the trail of British expeditions over the Lake Champlain route during the French and Indian wars. The occasional overland traveler followed a rough and tedious way, waiting for rains to cease before fording rivers and following blazed notches on trees to find shelter in the scattered homes of settlers.

Soon after the Revolution, roads were somewhat improved and extended, mainly with the proceeds of a series of lotteries in 1797. Finding its financial resources inadequate to meet the growing needs, the State chartered turnpike companies to build roads with private capital and to collect tolls to obtain a return on their investment. The Albany-Schenectady Turnpike was completed in 1805 at a cost of $10,000 a mile. Other roads were built from Schenectady to Utica, from Utica to Canandaigua, and from Canandaigua to Lake Erie. Shortly after the War of 1812 this Mohawk route was completed across the State. Its outstanding competitor was the Great Western Turnpike, running west from Albany over the ridges south of the Mohawk Valley through Cherry Valley and Cazenovia. (Today State 5 and US 20, the two most heavily traveled east-west highways in the State, follow in the main the routes of those early roads.) Turnpikes leading west from Newburgh and Catskill later became short cuts to western New York. These were the most important pikes in a highway system that by 1821 included about 4,000 miles of improved roads.

The turnpikes presented a scene of varied activity: wagoners driving six- and eight-horse teams that hauled heavily laden wagons with broad-rimmed wheels; drovers herding cattle, sheep, or pigs to the eastern markets; tin peddlers in their slender wagons filled with notions; stagecoaches providing rapid transportation for travelers and mail; and emigrants moving west, their household goods packed in their covered wagons. Stage lines connected New York and Albany, and, with Albany and Troy as a hub, extended north, west, and east, joining far-flung communities. Travelers filled innumerable taverns from garret to bar; in 1815 there was on the average a tavern for every mile on the road between Albany and Cherry Valley. Since wagoners and drovers did not mix well, many taverns specialized in their clientele.

The turnpike era lasted about 30 years. The roads were never prosperous, paying small dividends at best, even in the days of heaviest travel, principally because of large maintenance costs. The competition of canals and railroads hastened the end of the private turnpike, and the roads were eventually turned over to the State.

Plans for the improvement of internal navigation were proposed by prominent men in the Colonial period, but no action was taken until after the Revolution. In the 1790's some improvements were made in the navigation of the Mohawk River. Boats with capacities of from 15 to 20 tons were built in Schenectady's shipyards. The demand for a trans-State canal came from the new settlers of the central and western parts of the State, who because of high freight rates could not profitably sell their surplus produce in the East, and from commercial men in the East who were eager to exploit the growing western market. A survey was made in 1808, and a commission explored the most likely routes in 1810, when De Witt Clinton gave his support to the proposal. The War of 1812 caused further delay, but a final survey was made in 1816 and construction of the Erie Canal was begun on July 4, 1817. The limitations of engineering skill made it necessary to build an artificial channel from the Lakes to the Hudson, rather than to attempt to canalize large bodies of water like the Mohawk. The original plan to run the canal to Lake Ontario was defeated by De Witt Clinton, who feared that trade might be diverted to the St.Lawrence and Montreal. The inland route to Lake Erie was adopted; and Buffalo was chosen as the western terminus.

In 1825 the 363-mile 'ditch' was completed at a total cost of more than $7,000,000. On October 26 a fleet of boats left Buffalo on the canal, and cannon relayed the announcement of the event across the State in 81 minutes. The first boat, the *Seneca Chief*, drawn by four gray horses, carried De Witt Clinton and his party. Another, called *Noah's Ark*, had on board 'a bear, two eagles, two fawns, with a variety of other animals, and birds, together with several fish—not forgetting two Indian boys, in the dress of their nation—*all products of the West*.' The fleet was welcomed at every stop by enthusiastic crowds, and an astonishing number of toasts were drunk. Green-eyed Philadelphia called the celebration a 'Roman Holiday.'

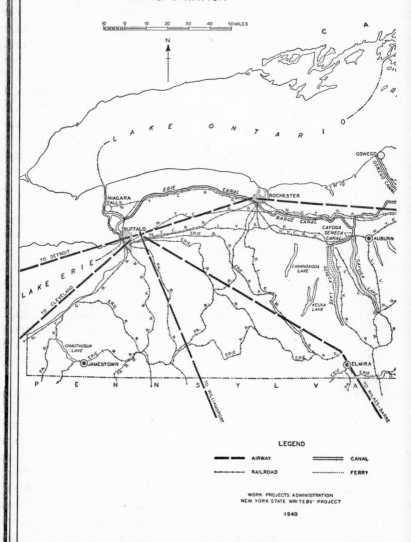

NEW YORK

TRANSPORTATION

10 0 10 20 30 40 50 MILES

N

C A

L A K E   O N T A R I O

OSWEGO

OSWEGO CANAL

NIAGARA FALLS

ERIE CANAL

ROCHESTER

BARGE CANAL

CAYUGA SENECA CANAL

AUBURN

BUFFALO

TO DETROIT

LAKE ERIE

TO CLEVELAND

CANANDAIGUA LAKE

SENECA LAKE

CAYUGA LAKE

KEUKA LAKE

CHAUTAUQUA LAKE

JAMESTOWN

ELMIRA

P E N N S Y L V

TO WILLIAMSPORT

TO WILKES-BARRE

LEGEND

——— AIRWAY   ═══ CANAL

+—+—+ RAILROAD   ········· FERRY

WORK PROJECTS ADMINISTRATION
NEW YORK STATE WRITERS' PROJECT

1940

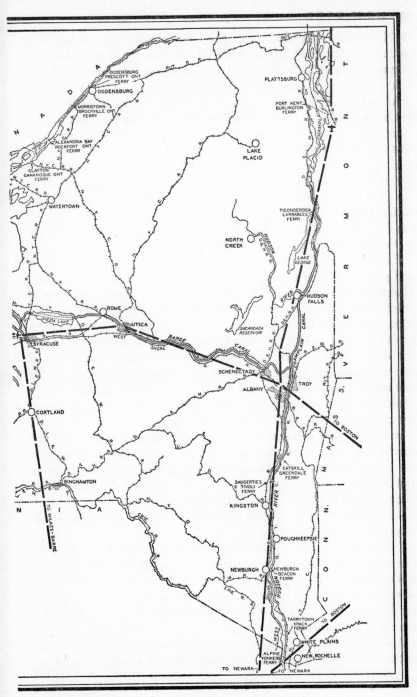

On November 4, in a solemn ceremony, Clinton poured a keg of Lake Erie water into New York Bay, and the 'Marriage of the Waters' was consummated. The Champlain Canal was completed two years before the Erie.

At first passenger traffic on the canal was greater than freight traffic, but by the end of the first decade of operation the freight tonnage passing West Troy had increased fivefold and the canal was definitely a success. The desire to provide the advantages of water transportation to every part of the State led to the construction of more than 10 branch canals, the most important of which were the Oswego, the Cayuga and Seneca, the Chemung, the Black River, and the Genesee Valley Canals. The first enlargement of the Erie was begun 10 years after its completion. Tolls on the Erie, abolished in 1882, more than covered the cost of its enlargements up to that date and the deficits of the other canals.

By building this canal system, the State interconnected its waterways and provided a tremendous stimulus to settlement and the development of agriculture, commerce, and industry through the drastic reduction in freight rates and the improved accessibility of markets and supplies. Like a great system of arteries, the canals carried a golden stream of commerce across the State and up and down the Hudson, bringing new wealth and life to every section of the State. At canal termini, and at strategic points where agricultural products were processed and freight had to be unloaded and reloaded, towns grew rapidly into business and financial centers and markets for local products. Branch canals brought Pennsylvania coal to the cities, supplying the fuel for the development of modern industry. New York City, export and import center for the entire system, became the Nation's commercial metropolis. Moreover, the canal, together with the short-line western railroads, gave growing States like Illinois, Indiana, and Minnesota access to the markets of the East, and thus linked their interests more firmly with those of the North in the Civil War crisis than would have been the case had the bulk of their products gone to market by way of the Mississippi.

In this same period, beginning in 1807 with the success of Fulton's *Clermont* on the Hudson, the steamboat became an important means of transportation on waters within the State and on its borders. The steam-powered lake ship strengthened Buffalo's position as the eastern terminal for the Lakes trade, and the ocean-going steamship made New York City the major world port of the Nation.

A year after the Erie Canal was opened for commerce, the first railroad in the State, the Mohawk & Hudson, was chartered. It began running between Albany and Schenectady in 1831. The rails were of wood, faced with strap iron and secured to granite blocks. The first locomotive, the *De Witt Clinton*, built in New York City, hauled a train of stagecoaches mounted on special trucks. Riding was accompanied by jerking and jolting, and the clothes of outside passengers sometimes caught fire from the pine embers blown from the smokestack. But improvements were rapidly introduced and the road was declared a success. In 1832 it established connections with the Schenectady & Saratoga Railroad, which opened that year as a horsecar line. In 1835 the Rensselaer & Saratoga Railroad was built between Troy and Ballston Spa, where it connected with the Schenectady & Saratoga. In 1836 the Long Island Railroad began operation..

In the early days of their development railroads were thought of as auxiliary to waterways, providing short cuts and feeders. As they grew in wealth and popularity and roads were planned to parallel the Erie Canal, the State imposed restrictions to protect its canal investments, especially in regard to the transportation of freight. Not until 1851 were all railroads allowed to carry freight at their own rates and retain the revenue. Thereafter began the competition which led to abandonment of some of the branch canals and greatly reduced the importance of the Erie.

In the thirties a number of short lines, varying in gauge, were built across the State: the Utica & Schenectady in 1836; the Syracuse & Utica in 1839; the Auburn & Syracuse in the same year; the Auburn & Rochester in 1841; the Tonawanda between Rochester and Batavia in 1837, extended in 1842 to Attica; and, in the latter year, the Attica & Buffalo. Thus eight short lines extended disjointedly between Albany and Buffalo. Trans-State travel had its difficulties, especially the several changes of cars and the uncertainty of schedules. In 1853 these roads, together with several branches, were consolidated to form the New York Central. North from New York City, the New York & Harlem, begun in 1832, crept gradually up through the easternmost counties, reaching Greenbush (Rensselaer), opposite Albany, in 1852. But it was beaten to this terminus by the Hudson River Railroad, constructed along the edge of the river. Cornelius Vanderbilt, prominent steamboat operator, acquired control of both roads between Albany and the metropolis, and then forced the New York Central to capitulate to him by refusing to furnish connections at Albany. The consolidated roads, headed by Vanderbilt, became the New York Central & Hudson River Railroad, and later, after reorganization, simply the New York Central. In 1871 the New York Central, which controlled—and still controls—the only right-of-way entering Manhattan from the north, built the first Grand Central Station at 42nd Street.

The railroads in general intensified and accelerated the economic processes stimulated by the canals. In sections of the State where the influence of the canals was limited, as in the Southern Tier and the North Country, the railroads supplied the primary impulse for development. The Erie Railroad provided the Southern Tier with an outlet to the eastern seaboard. Even before it was completed in 1851, between Piermont on the Hudson and Dunkirk on Lake Erie, the Erie began its checkered career. After many difficulties, caused in part by provisions in its charter, it was granted new termini—Buffalo in the west, which enabled it to compete with the New York Central for traffic, and Jersey City in the east, which brought it within the metropolitan district. Its track gauge was six feet, and 50 years passed before it adopted the standard gauge of four feet, eight-and-one-half inches. Overcapitalization and waste drove the road to Wall Street for aid, and it was turned into a financial football by Daniel Drew, James Fisk, and Jay Gould, at the expense of Vanderbilt, whom Gould outmatched in manipulation. The history of the Erie has been a succession of receiverships. Income from its immense freight traffic has failed repeatedly to overcome the effects of the financial maladministration that dogged it from the start.

The first line in the North Country, the Northern Railroad, completed in 1850 between Lake Champlain and Ogdensburg, was built by Boston interests to participate in the commerce with the Great Lakes area. The road is now a branch of the Rutland Railroad. Another important North Country road was the Rome, Watertown & Ogdensburgh (*sic*), formed in 1861 by a merger of two earlier roads. When it extended its lines and began to compete with the New York Central, it was absorbed by the latter. After a severe rate war the West Shore Railroad, built along the west shore of the Hudson and the south shore of the Mohawk and west to Buffalo— closely paralleling the Central throughout, suffered the same fate. The Albany & Susquehanna (now part of the Delaware & Hudson), together with its branches, and the Ulster & Delaware, joining Oneonta and Kingston, carried Pennsylvania anthracite to the industries of eastern New York and northern New England. In all, ten railway systems at present operate 8,260 miles of track in the State.

Men of New York have played a large part in the development of railroading since the time when scouts went out on horseback to locate late trains and brakemen stopped trains by the exertion of sheer physical strength. The first train order sent by telegraph is credited to Charles Minot, superintendent of the Erie. Henry Wells, of Albany and points west, and William Fargo, of Pompey, Buffalo, and points west, organized some of the earliest express companies. George Westinghouse, inventor of the air brake, was born in Central Bridge. The first sleeping cars were built in the late fifties almost simultaneously by Theodore Woodruff, of Watertown, and Webster Wagner, ticket agent at Palatine Bridge. In 1867 Wagner built the first drawing-room coach, or palace car, befrilled with plush seats, carved cupids, and crystal chandeliers; and in 1890 his company was merged with the Pullman Company to form the Pullman Palace Car Company. Within the last few years the Delaware & Hudson Railroad has developed in its Watervliet shops the 'velvet rail'—jointless, welded track a signal block in length, which reduces maintenance costs and eliminates the clickety-click of rail joints.

Another phase of railway transportation is represented by the streetcar, at first drawn by horses, later driven by electricity carried in wires strung overhead or laid in a channel between the rails. After the turn of the century this new public utility, widely applied, enabled the cities of the State to spread out in residential and industrial suburbs. A natural extension of the urban streetcar was the interurban trolley connecting upstate cities, in some cases paralleling the railroads, in other cases providing more direct connections than the railroads afforded. Some operators built picnic grounds and amusement parks at countryside terminals and encouraged week-end outings. Equally popular was the 'Twilight Trolley Tour,' for which cars decorated with colored lights were provided to rattle lovesick 'spooners' over 25-mile networks of trolley lines. But the introduction of the bus marked the beginning of the end for the trolley. The interurban lines have almost all been superseded, and within cities streetcar lines are being replaced by bus lines. Some of the old trolley cars have been saved from destruction by conversion into lunch wagons, and, thus transformed, stand stationary and disconsolate beside the roads they once traversed.

A bicycle craze that set in early in the trolley period led to the formation of cycling clubs, which built and maintained hundreds of miles of cinder paths out of the annual $1 fees paid by members. Their hard smoothness conducive to high speed, these paths produced the 'scorcher,' forerunner of the present-day automobile driver who has nowhere in particular to go but is in a terrible hurry to get there. Many of the old bicycle paths were widened to accommodate the first 'gas buggies,' 'steamers,' and 'electrics.'

In recent years, the large-scale use of the automobile—in 1939, 2,749,135 motor vehicles were registered in the State—brought to the fore the problems of a new age in transportation. The turnpike era was in a sense revived, in an extremely elaborated and accelerated—one is tempted to say a 'jazzed-up'—form. The highway became a motorway, subject to traffic that was dense and continuous, traveled by vehicles that were ponderous, vehicles that were swift, and vehicles that combined something of both qualities. The science of highway engineering had to be revised and re-learned, and the licensing and regulation of motor vehicles and, in large part, road construction and maintenance became functions of the State. From 1922 to the end of 1935 the State appropriated $568,000,000 for its highways, in addition to Federal and emergency grants of $128,000,000. But continued increase in traffic and speed demanded continued additions and improvements. A five-year plan, adopted in 1936, called for the recon-struction of 5,230 miles of State and Federal routes that did not meet the needs of modern traffic, to include 1,617 miles of three-lane and 929 miles of four-lane pavement.

Expansion of the highway system involved the construction of a num-ber of noteworthy bridges, including the George Washington Memorial, Bear Mountain, and Rip Van Winkle Bridges over the Hudson, the Thou-sand Islands Bridge over the St.Lawrence, the Champlain Bridge at Crown Point, and the Peace Bridge at Buffalo. Westchester County has developed a system of three- and four-lane boulevards through landscaped parkways leading into New York City, and the State has built extensions of these north toward Albany and east toward New England. Similar de-velopments have been carried out on Long Island. In the field of highway illumination the General Electric Company has introduced sodium vapor lights, which are now used along stretches of road in various parts of the State.

The private motorcar, the motor bus, and the motor truck have made serious inroads on railroad traffic. The railroads have in part solved the problem of the motor bus by gaining control of the largest company in the State; but the general problem of the railroad in a motor age is national in scope and waits to be dealt with as such.

Aside from the pre-eminence of New York City in transatlantic and coastal commerce, water transportation has remained a significant factor in the State's economic pattern. In 1918 the modernization and enlarge-ment of the old canal system was completed to form the Barge Canal, which accommodates boats of more than 2,000 tons' capacity. West to Rome the old Erie was abandoned and the Mohawk River canalized; be-yond, the new canal follows the route, though not always the bed, of the old, with short branches to Syracuse and Rochester. The Champlain Canal division of the new system utilizes the canalized Hudson north almost to Fort Edward and thence extends in a new channel to Whitehall. The remaining units of the Barge Canal, outside of feeders, are the Oswego and the Cayuga and Seneca Canals; other divisions of the original system have been abandoned. Great advances have been made in canal craft. Numerous barges are towed by a single tug, and Diesel-electric boats with shallow hulls and disappearing stacks now carry cargoes between the most remote Lake ports and New York without transshipment. In 1939 the total canal tonnage was 4,689,037, principally petroleum products. Since 1932 ocean-going steamers come up the Hudson to the Port of Albany, transporting petroleum, lumber, pulpwood, wheat, and molasses. In and out of the Great Lakes harbors—Buffalo, Rochester, Oswego—lake carriers transport coal, grain, pig iron, limestone, and automobiles.

It was a citizen of New York State, Glenn Curtis, who emerged as the foremost rival of the Wrights in the early days of the airplane. At Hammondsport, on Keuka Lake, Curtiss developed a plane that was a definite improvement on the Wright ship of the time. Though the Wrights, who were first to fly, sued Curtiss for infringement, they added wheels—a Curtiss innovation—to their landing gear; and the rivals finally settled down to work in peace. Curtiss made the first public airplane flight of more than a mile in the United States, was first to fly a plane from Albany to New York City, and among other feats, pioneered in developing hydroairplanes, flying boats, and military combat planes. Long Island became the cradle of aviation after 1908, and all early records for flights were made there on the Hempstead plains.

The effect of the airplane on transportation in the State is still largely undefined. American Airlines maintains regular schedules in the principal cities, and the Federal Bureau of Air Commerce has constructed five completely equipped emergency landing fields at strategic points along main routes. The routes from Albany to New York City and Buffalo are lighted by the Federal Government; the others in the State, except between Albany and Montreal, are commercially lighted. Radio beams on all the routes direct pilots flying blind. As part of the Government's emergency work programs, many millions of dollars have been expended on airport construction and improvement. In 1938, 97 airports and landing fields in the State were recognized by the Bureau of Air Commerce.

Agriculture

MENTION of the Empire State calls up a vision of large cities, urban populations, and the smokestacks of industry. Yet in 1936 New York ranked seventh among the States in the value of its farm products. It led in the cash values of its ducks, cabbage, fluid milk, and onions; was second in the value of its potatoes, apples, cauliflower, maple products, hay, buckwheat, grapes, cherries, and beets; third in the value of its eggs, carrots, and lettuce; and fourth in the value of its pears and celery. New York's production total of corn, wheat, barley, oats, rye, and buckwheat for 1936 was almost 50,000,000 bushels. Of buckwheat, a crop not widely grown elsewhere, the State raised some 2,000,000 bushels—about one third of the national production; and, incidentally, it enjoys a virtual monopoly of the production of dark, rich buckwheat honey. In canning, developed as an auxiliary industry to the growing of cash vegetable crops and fruits, the State ranked second in 1929, with 279 factories doing a gross business of $75,500,000.

Striking in the agricultural economy of the State is the fact that the 1935 figures for the number of farms and farm population approach those of 85 years ago. In round numbers, there were in 1850 some 170,000 farms totaling 19,100,000 acres; in 1935, there were 177,000 farms totaling 18,600,000 acres. But the value of farms in 1935 was almost double that of 1850; and the increase in invested capital is indicated by the rise in the value of livestock from $73,000,000 to $222,000,000 and of farm machinery and equipment from $22,000,000 to $173,000,000. The farm population in 1935 was 784,483.

In broad outline, the determining factors in the history of agriculture in the State were improvement in transportation, the rise of outside competition, and the growth of the metropolitan market. In the period during and after the Revolution, the Hudson, eastern Mohawk, and Schoharie Valleys were great wheat-growing districts, earning the title 'the granary of the Revolution.' When the Erie Canal and its feeders cut transportation costs, the wheat farmer of the Finger Lakes and the Genesee Valley was able to sell his grain in the eastern markets; and the eastern farmer turned to dairying and raising beef cattle. Accounts of the turnpike era in the development of transportation are enlivened with word pictures of drovers driving herds of beef cattle to slaughterhouses. It is said that Daniel Drew, financial buccaneer of Wall Street, laid the foundation of his one-time huge fortune by selling 'pre-salted' beef on the hoof in the city market. The story goes that Drew ordered that his cattle on the way to market be given no water but plenty of salt; then, just before they were put on sale, they were allowed to drink their fill, thereby improving their appearance and increasing their weight. Drew got top price for both beef and water. This business maneuver is said to have given rise to the term 'watered stock.'

In the latter half of the nineteenth century wheat from the western prairies drove New York State grains out of the market; and farmers of the central and western parts of the State turned to cattle raising and dairying, becoming especially well known for their cheese. The next step resulted from improvements in railroad transportation, especially the introduction of the refrigerated car. Western packed beef and Wisconsin cheese invaded the eastern market, causing the upstate farmer to devote himself largely to supplying fluid milk for the metropolitan market and growing fruits and vegetables. In 1935 about half of the State's farm land was devoted to crops and half to pasture; and dairying produced 50 per cent of the farm income.

The dairy industry grew rapidly with the expansion of the metropolitan milkshed. Its recent history is one of bitter controversy among producers, distributors, and consumers over the price spread between what the producer receives for milk and what the consumer pays for it. In August 1933, dairy farmers engaged in a general strike, blockading highways, dumping milk, and threatening to blow up milk plants and derail milk trains. In the 'Battle of Boonville,' 40 State troopers hurled tear-gas bombs and wielded riot sticks when 400 strikers attempted to block passage of milk trucks; eight strikers were beaten unconscious before a crowd of 800 spectators.

The State milk-control legislation of the next five years failed to settle the issue. On September 1, 1938, after approval by dairy farmers of the New York City milkshed, representing seven States, a new Federal-State milk-marketing program went into effect, aiming to help farmers get a fair and stable price for milk, prevent unfair competition among dealers, and assure consumers an adequate supply of milk at a reasonable cost. In midsummer of 1939 organized dairy farmers obtained higher milk prices by a brief, violent strike.

Poultry raising, second largest source of the State's agricultural income, is now largely concentrated on Long Island. In 1935 the 21,724,000 chickens raised in New York State, valued at an average of 68¢ each, together with the 1,323,000,000 eggs produced, placed New York fourth among the States in the value of its poultry industry. Ducks are raised extensively on Long Island, and 'Long Island duckling' has become a familiar item on the menus of quality restaurants.

Truck crops, forming the next important agricultural enterprise in the State, are grown intensively on Long Island, in Orange County, and on a wide strip of land just south of the ridge that runs parallel to and a few miles inland from the shore of Lake Ontario. Wayne County, at the eastern end of this area, ranks first among the counties of the Nation in the production of celery. North of this strip of truck land is the famous lakeshore fruit belt.

Until the middle of the nineteenth century, potatoes were not widely known in America, were grown in small beds as a garden crop, and were not considered proper food to serve at good tables. In the early 1840's an epidemic of potato blight swept the North American crop. Scientists were baffled. The Reverend Chauncey E. Goodrich of Utica believed that the potato could be rehabilitated by reverting to the seed. He sent to South America, habitat of the plant, for seed, from which he grew a new variety called 'Rough Purple Chile.' From this stock he produced Garnet Chile, the parent in 1861 of the Early Rose. From these two have been developed the 200 or more varieties that now constitute the potato flora of the United States. In 1936 New York produced 26,400,000 bushels of potatoes.

Onions are grown in Orange, Madison, Oswego, and Wayne Counties; in 1936 New York produced 3,248,000 bags (of 100 pounds each). In the same year the State grew 1,430,000 acres of commercial carrot crop, 5,940 acres of cauliflower, 3,960 acres of celery, and 8,900 acres of cabbage.

One of the most interesting farm enterprises in New York State is the maple-sugar industry, producing in an average season about 1,000,000 gallons of syrup and more than 500,000 pounds of sugar. St.Lawrence County in the north, Cattaraugus, Allegany, and Broome Counties in the Southern Tier, Cortland and Chenango Counties in the central part of the State, and Wyoming County in the west are the principal producers. A large portion of the New York product is exported to Vermont, where it is resold as 'Vermont' maple syrup.

Fruit growing is concentrated along Lakes Ontario and Erie, the Finger Lakes, and the Hudson-Champlain Valley. The New York apple crop is second in size to that of Washington. In 1935 orchards of the State contained more than 7,683,831 trees of bearing age and produced more than 16,875,000 bushels. Nearly 60 per cent of the crop is made up of three varieties: Baldwin, McIntosh, and Rhode Island Greening. Until recently the apple crop was marketed in barrels; now most of it is packed in bushel crates. Under depression prices, growers attempted to secure a larger proportion of the consumer's dollar by cutting freight costs through the use of trucks. The 43-per cent decline in the number of apple-bearing trees since 1890 represents a transition from a period when apples were generally grown to supplement the farm food supply, with the surplus for local sale, to the specialized commercial apple production of the present. Until recently orchards were not generally cultivated and were seldom pruned, and insecticides were unknown. Today, largely as the result of State-subsidized study and experiment, the scientific treatment of trees has become an important part of pomology.

Peaches have long been an important product of western New York orchards. In 1833 Lewis F. Allen purchased several thousand acres of land on Grand Island in the Niagara River, on which he planted peach trees and grew large crops. Eventually yellows destroyed these orchards; and the fruit industry moved from Grand Island to the mainland of Niagara County, which now produces more than twice as many peaches as any other New York county. The State production in 1936 was 700,000 bushels.

From 1825 to 1870 pears were a rarity and sold at as high as $1 apiece. Now they are grown generally throughout the State, with western New York producing the largest part of the crop. The 1928–32 average exceeded 1,000,000 bushels. The total production of cherries in 1935 was 22,500 tons.

Grapes, although small in the general total, are an important source of income in Chautauqua County and in the region bordering Keuka Lake. In 1936 the product amounted to 41,800 tons, which is about half the five-year average production. Chautauqua grapes, comprising about half the State crop, are marketed largely as table grapes and as unfermented juice. The growers in the Keuka district produce a large percentage of wine grapes, including the Concord, Catawba, Niagara, and Delaware. Ten wineries in this region produce still wines, which are highly flavored and command a premium in the market. The champagne industry, however, has made this region famous. Hammondsport produces 90 per cent of the 'fermented-in-the-bottle' champagne made in the United States.

In 1790 William Prince, nurseryman of Flushing, Long Island, planted the pits of 25 quarts of Green Gage plums, which later produced trees yielding fruit of every color. The Imperial Gage, Red Gage, Prince's Gage, and Washington plum are all descendants. In 1828 the Prince Nursery offered for sale 140 kinds of plums. To this nursery belongs the credit for giving plum growing in America its greatest impetus.

No American raspberries, strawberries, currants, or gooseberries were grown in New York before the middle of the nineteenth century. In 1850 H.H.Doolittle of Oaks Corners, Ontario County, found that the black raspberry could easily be propagated from tips. Growing this berry for the evaporator soon developed into a sizable industry concentrated in Wayne and a part of Yates Counties, and reached its height in the 1890's.

The marketing of farm products, which plays an important part in the State's agricultural economy, has become highly developed during the past 20 years. The Dairymen's League, fluid milk co-operative, is owned and managed entirely by dairymen, and grosses over $50,000,000 a year. The Sheffield Producers' Association, negotiating prices and conditions of sale, markets the milk of 15,000 members. The business of these and smaller co-operatives amounts to nearly $100,000,000 annually. New York State farmers lead the country in the co-operative purchase of farm supplies. The Co-operative Grange League Federation Exchange, Inc. (known familiarly as the GLF), an organization specializing in the purchase of feed, seed, and fertilizers for farmers, has its own mills for milling and mixing, 150 retail stores, and more than 400 dealers, who handle more than 1,000,000 tons of produce a year.

The State College of Agriculture at Cornell University, together with the experiment station at Geneva and six other State schools of agriculture, teaches the principles and practices of scientific farming to the oncoming generations of farmers, carries on scientific experimentation, makes local and State-wide surveys, gives winter short courses and provides extension work, conducts special radio programs for farmers, and prints and distributes pamphlets dealing with a wide variety of agricultural and farm home problems. Courses in agriculture are given in 200 of the high schools of the State. The aims of all these activities are to encourage soil conservation by crop rotation, the use of fertilizer, and the acquisition of submarginal land by the State; to instruct the farmer how to increase his income by more efficient farm management; to improve rural education and enrich farm life. The field representative of these activities is the county farm agent, employed by county farm bureaus with financial assistance from the State and Federal governments, who acts as clearing house for new developments and experiments, serves the farmer with his expert knowledge, and directs the organized activities of the younger generation, especially the 4-H Clubs.

Another and much older device by which the State distributes information to farmers and encourages agricultural progress is the system of State and county fairs. Although an agricultural society was formed in Albany in 1791, the fair did not come into existence in New York until 1816, when the Otsego County Fair was held at Cooperstown. Organized and promoted by Elkanah Watson, this first in the long procession of the State's agricultural fairs distributed the modest sum of $100 in premiums. In 1936, State subsidies totaling $250,000 were received by 34 county and 14 town fairs. The State fair, first held in Syracuse in 1841 with an appropriation of $700 and a handful of exhibits, has progressed steadily during its 99 renewals. In 1937, with an all-time record attendance of 271,152 and about 19,000 exhibits, $57,500 was awarded in prizes.

Equally humble were the beginnings of what is now the important State Department of Agriculture and Markets. Influenced by Watson's zealous missionary work for the advancement of agriculture and the approbation which the first county fairs received throughout the State, Governor Clinton in 1819 recommended the establishment of a State agricultural society, a board of agriculture, and a model farm. The farm, Watson's dream of what later developed into agricultural experiment stations, was blocked by legislative bickering, but an annual appropriation of $10,000 was made for agricultural societies and fairs under a board of agriculture. In 1884 a dairy commission was organized, which in 1893 became the Department of Agriculture. Today, with 15 bureaus in its headquarters in Albany, and branch offices in New York, Cortland, Buffalo, and Rochester, the State Department of Agriculture and Markets plays an important role in the economic life of the Empire State.

Industry

DUTCH New Netherland was primarily a fur-trading Colony. Frequently even the craftsmen sent over by the Dutch patroons deserted their trades for surreptitious but more lucrative barter with the Indians—exchanging cheap cloth and clothing, blankets, hatchets, kettles, and especially guns and liquor for the valuable beaver skin; and the service crafts were as a result maintained with difficulty. However, in the number and productivity of their sawmills the Dutch outdid their New England neighbors. Gristmills were plentiful, brick-making was common along the Hudson, and shipbuilding was carried on in New Amsterdam from the earliest years. Probably the first manufacturing plants in New Netherland were a distillery and a buckskin tannery, both established on Staten Island.

The transition from Dutch to British rule brought little change in the routine of life. English New York was primarily an agricultural province; by 1700 the fur trade had lost much of its economic significance, though as a weapon in the conflict with the French for control of the interior it was important politically. As the manorial system became established in the Hudson Valley, large landholdings were cut into farms and rented to farmers, who paid their rent in kind and were subject to the lord of the manor in many ways; and the agricultural interest became predominant in what is now upstate New York.

The application of Great Britain's mercantile policy restricted Colonial manufacture, except the production of naval stores. The Colonies were to be kept by the Crown as sources of raw materials and markets for finished products, with the balance of trade heavily favoring the Mother Country. But the proprietors of agricultural New York, by developing a triangular trade with Britain and the West Indies, managed to keep abreast of their indebtedness to English merchants. With the hard money derived from the favorable trade balance with the West Indies, the New York merchants canceled their debts in London; and the upstate land-owners, whose produce comprised the bulk of that trade, prospered.

The development of this lucrative commerce minimized opposition to the British policy of discouraging industry, so that manufacture was lim-

Science and Industry

Photograph by Daniel V. Nero

STATE GRAIN ELEVATOR, OSWEGO

Photograph by courtesy of the General Electric Company

EDISON AND STEINMETZ CONFER IN THE GENERAL ELECTRIC LABORATORY, SCHENECTADY

STUDENTS IN AN AERONAUTICS CLASS, RENSSELAER POLYTECHNIC INSTITUTE, TROY

Photograph by courtesy of Rensselaer Polytechnic Institute

ELECTRIC ARC WELDING, SCHENECTADY

POURING, IN AN IRON FOUNDRY

FINISHING RUGS, AMSTERDAM

EXAMINING FILM, BINGHAMTON

PRINTING WALLPAPER, HUDSON FALLS

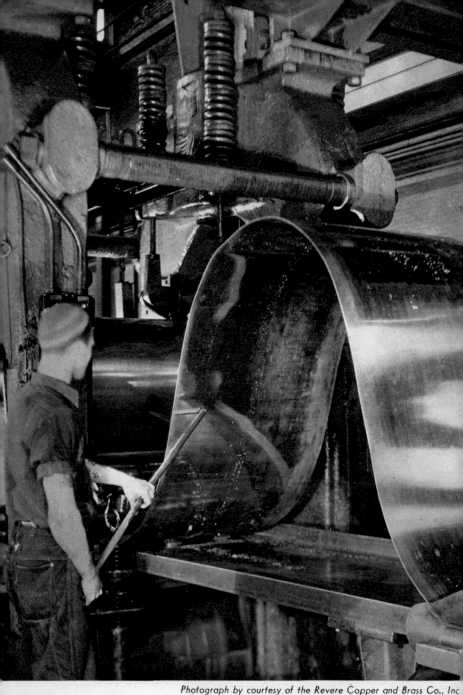

ROLLING COPPER, ROME

EXAMINING A 200" TELESCOPE DISC.
CORNING

Photographs by courtesy of the Corning Glass Works

BLOWING GLASS

Photograph by Paul Broad

BOTTLING MILK

CHAMPAGNE CELLAR, RHEIMS

Photograph by courtesy of the New York Bureau of State Publicit

ited mainly to the household production of some of the necessities of life. Craftsmen were employed by the lords of the manors, who frequently also served as middlemen in trade. In the country nearly every home had a spinning wheel and the womenfolk made the cloth for the family, principally linsey-woolsey, with warp of linen and woof of wool; the weaving was often done by itinerant weavers, and if the cloth was finished it was done at a local mill. In 1708 Caleb Heathcote reported that 75 per cent of the linen and woolen cloth used in the Colony was homemade; but homespun was never sold in stores. Shoes were similarly made to order from home-tanned leather, and other necessities were supplied by itinerant or local craftsmen. Clay for brick was puddled by the tread of horses and cast in rough wood molds.

Semi-agricultural industries like milling, cooperage, lumbering, and the preparation of potash expanded. Farmers derived an important part of their income from their wood ashes, which were refined into pearlash in local asheries and exported. Brewing and milling created a demand for barrels, popular because they required few nails and were sturdy and easily handled; and the farmers supplied the staves.

The principal iron mines were the Livingston works at Ancram and the Sterling Iron Works in Orange County, which produced pig and bar iron for domestic use and export. The colonists purchased iron in rods, and members of the family pounded out nails in the kitchen. In 1751 a charcoal blast furnace was built at the Sterling Iron Works for the manufacture of anchors and anvils; the metal was reputed to be as good for edged tools as Swedish iron. Peter Townshend, who took over the works in 1773, enlarged the plant, so that it was able to forge in six weeks the huge chain stretched across the Hudson between West Point and Constitution Island as a Revolutionary defense measure. The discovery in the 1760's of rich deposits of iron ore in Dutchess County stimulated iron production; and a furnace and foundry was erected at Amenia, which proved valuable to the Revolutionary government by supplying iron and steel for war purposes.

After the French and Indian War, British tax policy acted as a spur to Colonial industry. In 1764 the Society for the Promotion of Arts, Agriculture, and Economy was organized in New York City to encourage domestic manufacture; premiums were offered for excellence and quantity of products, and fairs were instituted for the display and sale of scythes, shovels, hoes, and the like. After the passage of the Stamp Act the movement was intensified, becoming so effective that from 1768 to 1769 the value of imports into New York fell from $490,674 to $75,931. At the same time, the increase in domestic industrial production was enormous; linsey-woolsey became the universal wear, and the manufacture of hats was well established.

For 50 years after the Revolution New York State remained dominantly agricultural, leading in the production of wheat. Capital was attracted to agriculture, trade, and internal improvements; labor was scarce and largely unskilled in the crafts. Britain forbade the export of machinery to the new Nation, discouraged the emigration of skilled labor, and dumped its own manufactured products upon the American market. But the Napoleonic wars, by shutting off imports from Europe, gave impetus to the increasing demand for domestic manufacture, and the incorporating act passed by the legislature in 1811, the first such State law in the country, served to facilitate industrial financing. When turnpike (toll) roads failed to pay attractive dividends, capital found its way into other fields, among them the industrial. Finally, after the War of 1812, Congress strengthened youthful American industry by erecting a protective tariff to prevent British dumping.

The spread of settlement through central, western, and northern New York provided a constantly growing market for factory products. Reduced freight rates on the Erie Canal enabled the farmers of the Genesee and the Great Lakes plain to sell in the State's chief urban markets, and eastern capital was drawn from agriculture to industry by the western demand for manufactured goods. The canal added its own demand for industrial products, especially boats and rope. Another important industry was the production of salt on the shores of Onondaga Lake.

Up to about 1830 manufactures increased in volume but did not change in kind. The thirties were years of marked change. Again the largest increase in production was in textiles, and the amount of cloth woven was remarkable. Although most of the work was still done in the homes, mills embodying new inventions and specializing in one or another process of cloth-making were established in Washington, Columbia, Dutchess, and Oneida Counties, attracted by superior water-power facilities. In 1823 there were 206 incorporated companies in the State, 62 of them manufacturing woolen and cotton goods, 36 cotton only, 16 woolen only, 10 glass, and 5 hardware. But domestic hardware met with sales resistance, the buying public preferring the imported product.

In 1826 Benjamin Marshall, a wealthy New York City merchant, established the Hudson River Print Works and the Ida Mills, both in Troy; for the first time in the State, these two plants brought under unit control the complete process of manufacturing cotton prints from raw cotton to the finished product. Ten years later the Marshall plants were reported to be turning out the finest shirtings and prints in the country. The rapid decline in the number of fulling mills after 1835 indicated that home industry was being displaced by the factory system of production. By 1840 the Harmony Mills in Cohoes were the largest producers of cotton goods in the State.

The Albany-Troy district was advantageously situated for trade and manufacture. It stood at the eastern portal to the Mohawk and Cherry Valley Turnpikes, on which the heavy stream of New England emigrants moved, and at the eastern terminus of the Erie Canal, which carried potash, Genesee flour, and Onondaga salt eastward and factory products westward. Albany was a flour-milling center, and the factories of the vicinity produced glass, potash, nails, starch, paper, tobacco, snuff, and chocolate. Excellent molding sand and plenty of limestone for flux turned the capital district to refining and manufacturing the iron ore discovered in the Adirondack and Lake Champlain areas. Castings of a relatively high grade were turned out, chiefly hollowware and agricultural equipment.

The first foundry in the capital district was established in 1804; the Townsend Furnace and Machine Shops, erected in Albany in 1807, produced mill gears, agricultural implements, and chilled rolls weighing from 100 to 6,000 pounds. In 1809 John Brinckerhoff of Albany started a slitting mill and nail factory on the Wynantskill in Troy and thereby became the pioneer in Troy's iron and steel industry.

Stoves were first assembled in the Albany district from New Jersey plate, but in the twenties and thirties Albany foundries began making their own stove castings. The first cupola in Albany expressly for stove castings was erected in 1838. At its peak, stove manufacture is said to have provided a living, directly or indirectly, for one of every six people in Troy and one of every eight in Albany. Henry Burden's improved process of iron manufacture and his invention of machines to turn out horseshoes and hook-headed railroad spikes fixed Troy's reputation as an iron center. Other Troy products of the period were bells and surveyors' instruments manufactured by Julius Hanks; coaches and carriages manufactured by Veazie & Barnard; and railroad passenger and freight cars made by Eaton & Gilbert.

The tanning industry, attracted by the extensive hemlock forests, first centered in the Catskill area, which in 1840–50 produced about a third of all the leather made in the country; the largest tannery was Zadock Pratt's at Prattsville. As early as 1808 Tallmadge Edwards began the manufacture of buckskin mittens, gloves, shirts, and trousers at Johnstown; and Fulton County became the leather goods center of the State.

The lumber industry was concentrated in Albany, though there were mills everywhere, and the towns fringing the Adirondack area were important producers. Troy led in the manufacture of rag paper, but as pulpwood came into increased use that industry moved close to the forests and to the excellent water-power sites at Watertown, Ticonderoga, Glens Falls, and other North Country towns. In the thirties and forties the State led in the manufacture of wood products and furniture.

In the same period, brick-making expanded in the Hudson Valley, especially after the introduction of machine production in the late twenties. Brewing and distilling spread across the State. In the milling industry Rochester and Oswego succeeded Albany as centers, and Buffalo began coming to the fore in the fifties. Buffalo also became an important center for the slaughtering of livestock for the market. The shipbuilding industry spread from New York City up the Hudson and was established along Lake Erie and Lake Champlain.

The forties were marked by the invention of the telegraph and the sewing machine and by the rapid expansion of railroads. The sewing machine made possible the growth of the clothing industry to its commanding position in the State, concentrating in New York City and Rochester; and its adaptation to shoe manufacture heralded the large-scale production of shoes in Rochester and in the Binghamton area. The demand of the railroads for rails and equipment stimulated an expansion of the Albany-Troy iron industry; and in Schenectady, an early railroad center, a locomotive works was established in 1848.

Characteristically, throughout this early industrial period, the manufacture of agricultural implements and household necessities expanded westward to keep up with the westward-moving market. In the late twenties, plow irons, small castings, and steam engines were produced in Buffalo, and scythes were manufactured in Amsterdam and Auburn. Utica had an engine-and-boiler works in the thirties, and in the forties was manufacturing stoves. By the middle of the century, Syracuse had foundries and machine shops and factories producing agricultural implements, boots and shoes, furniture, hardware, and silverware; Rochester had machine shops, cotton factories, breweries, boatyards, and coach and carriage, boot and shoe, and furniture factories; and Buffalo was producing stoves and hollowware, nails, furniture, bells, mirrors, millstones, soap, and candles.

By 1850 New York State had achieved its rank as the Empire State in industry. According to the census of that year, its manufactured products amounted in value to 23 per cent of the goods produced by the Nation. One third of the patents granted were issued to New Yorkers, most of them representing improvements on existing machines, which had not yet become standardized. In this mid-century period the factory system superseded handcraft and domestic production. Corporate organization invited investment capital, resulting in the separation of ownership and management and a sharper division between employer and employee. Workers organized for bargaining purposes and employers counterorganized to advance their interests. The industrialists became a powerful social and political group.

The Civil War stimulated improvement and expansion in every field of production. The exportation of foodstuffs increased sixfold; the textile industry expanded rapidly. Elmira turned out large quantities of cloth for uniforms; Rochester filled huge orders for military boots and shoes. The Remington plant in Ilion and the arsenal in Watervliet manufactured arms and ammunition; Troy iron mills produced the plates for the *Monitor*; the Union Cavalry rode to victory on Henry Burden's machine-made horseshoes. Out of the experience gained in the production of uniforms and equipment for soldiers came the adoption of a system of standard sizes, which made possible the large-scale production of ready-made clothes.

Since the Civil War, industry in New York State has shown a steady decline in the production of capital goods and a rapid rise in the manufacture of consumers' goods. The function of New York State industry has come to be 'the addition of high value to raw material, rather than the development of mass production or the turning out of crude products.'

The tanning and lumbering industries declined with the exhaustion of the natural resources on which they were based. In 1872, at the peak of the lumber industry, Albany alone shipped 660,000,000 board feet; today, instead of sending out cargoes of lumber to the ports of the seven seas, New York State imports for its own consumption 25 times as much as it produces. Lumbering survives in the Adirondack region, mainly to feed scrub timber to the paper and chemical industries.

Iron mining, yielding to the less costly production of the Great Lakes district, has all but ceased; today the only operating iron mines in the State are those in the Lyon Mountain and Port Henry areas. The low-cost Bessemer process of producing steel, together with the introduction of George Westinghouse's air brake, encouraged the rebuilding of railroads and the construction of larger cars and engines, in which the rail mills in Troy and the locomotive works in Schenectady and Dunkirk played a large part. But the center of iron and steel manufacture has since moved closer to the source of raw materials, leaving in the State only a few large plants, so that heavy products, especially agricultural implements, are now made elsewhere. In foundry and machine-shop products New York State dropped from first place in 1880 to fifth in 1933, and has turned to the manufacture of special equipment: valves, typewriters, bicycles, small forgings, cutlery, railroad signal apparatus, business machines, pumps, metal furniture, radiators, boilers, electrical fixtures, and the like.

The oil fields of New York, an extension of the Pennsylvania Bradford field, lie in the southwestern part of the State along the Pennsylvania border, with Wellsville and Olean as refining centers. The pools produce a relatively small share of the total national petroleum product, but the oil is so superior in lubricant quality that it always brings top prices, and a well yielding one third of a barrel a day can be profitably operated. Production reached a maximum of more than 5,000,000 barrels a year in the early eighties, and then declined rapidly to a low of 750,000 barrels in 1913. But introduction of the water-flooding method in 1920 (*see Tour* 3) resulted in increased production, which in 1936 reached 4,663,000 barrels valued at $11,380,000.

In 1933 New York State produced about 14 per cent of the Nation's manufactured products, by value, had about 18 per cent of the country's manufacturing establishments, and employed about 12 per cent of the country's industrial workers. The largest industry in the State is the manufacture of clothing and accessories, concentrated in New York City; bodily comfort and adornment call for products exceeding by half a billion dollars the total of the six next highest types of manufacture. In sum, New York State contributes annually about $1,700,000,000 in value toward enabling man and woman to appear as something better than a 'forked turnip.' Upstate, Rochester is important in the men's clothing and auxiliary industries; and Rochester and the Binghamton area manufacture shoes on a large scale. The production of women's clothes is centered in New York City, though small shops have been established in the Hudson and Mohawk Valleys, where rent is lower and labor is not so well organized. Clothing, chiefly men's, and hats and caps are made in Poughkeepsie, Beacon, Kingston, and Newburgh.

Printing and publishing, the second largest industry in the State, is also centered in New York City, though much of the printing of the city's vast output is done upstate and in neighboring States. The 1935 figures for the industry are 47,000 employed and $496,000,000 in value of products.

The food industries bulk large because of the volume of the State's agricultural products and the number of mouths it has to feed. Included are such items as $222,000,000 in bread and bakery products, $100,000,000 in flour and grain products, $33,000,000 worth of ice cream, and $37,000,000 worth of confectionery. Canning and preserving plants are scattered throughout the rural areas. In milling, New York State ranks second to Minnesota largely by virtue of the progress of the industry in Buffalo. Brewing, like baking, has developed into a large-scale, corporately owned industry concentrated in the large cities. Buffalo is the center of meat packing in the State.

The textile industry has remained one of the largest in the State because of transportation facilities, the size of the local market, and a skilled labor supply. In New York City there are more than 1,000 textile plants. In the upstate area the manufacture of underwear is concentrated in the western Mohawk Valley, with Utica as a center; Troy leads in men's collars and shirts; and knit goods, woolens, and worsteds are made in the cities of Rensselaer, Hudson, and Catskill, and Washington, Saratoga, Chautauqua, and Wyoming Counties. Important silk and rayon factories are in the Elmira and Buffalo areas. With Yonkers and Amsterdam as outstanding centers of manufacture, the State produces more than one third of the national output of carpets and rugs.

Rome leads the country in the manufacture of copper products, and the Hudson Valley is the largest producer of common brick in the world. Other clay products, ranging from common brick, through pottery, tile, and porcelain, to the finest table china, are manufactured in and around Syracuse; Buffalo leads in the heavier hotel tableware. Portland cement is produced in Columbia, Greene, Erie, Onondaga, Schoharie, Warren, and Tompkins Counties, with the largest plants in the city of Hudson.

The State has been fortunate in the extent to which new industries developing from the scientific and technological advances of the past 50 years have settled and grown within its boundaries. Schenectady ranks high in the field of electrical equipment by virtue of the main plant and research laboratories of the General Electric Company, in which heavy electrical generating machinery, radio transmitting apparatus, refrigerators, and induction motors are manufactured. Other large plants producing electrical machinery and appliances are in Syracuse and Rochester. Buffalo and Niagara Falls produce chemicals, dyes, abrasives, metal alloys; and Buffalo manufactures military airplanes and parachutes. Massena has the largest aluminum wire-and-cable manufacturing plant in the country. The automobile industry is represented by large assembly plants, which also make small parts.

Another interesting and important group of industries, many of them dominating the national and some even the world-wide market, owe their beginnings to local inventors and the availability of local capital or to the concentration of special local skill. Conspicuous examples are the glove and leather industry centering in Gloversville and Johnstown; the manufacture of special glass products in Corning; the production of billiard balls, checkers, and dominoes in Albany and of sandpaper in Troy, of photographic supplies in Binghamton, and of pneumatic tubes and conveyor systems in Syracuse; and in Rochester the manufacture of cameras and photographic supplies, optical goods, thermometers, safety check paper and automatic check writers, buttons, gears, and glass-lined steel tanks.

New York City is the Nation's major industrial center. In 1935, only five States, including New York State, surpassed it in wages paid, number of workers, and value of goods produced. Yet the city is far more important, in terms of dollars, as a market than as an industrial center. The value of its manufactured products in 1935 was $3,666,000,000; but in the same year its wholesale business totaled $9,618,000,000, and its retail trade $2,847,000,000—22 per cent and 8 per cent, respectively, of the Nation's business in these fields.

Labor

IN THE development of the labor movement in New York State, a cyclical pattern, begun about 1800, has repeated itself down to the present: organization and protest, collective action resulting in political pressure, then a period of disintegration and stagnation, and then again a resurgence of activity.

As a rule the initiative was taken in New York City, with reverberations soon shaking the upstate industrial towns. In 1822 the New York City hatmakers, who had organized in 1819, struck for higher wages and won; and as a result, hatmakers in Schenectady doing piecework received the almost unbelievable wage of $10 a week. In 1829 the Working Men's Party, known as 'Workies,' was organized in New York City, and the movement rapidly spread upstate. The mechanics and workingmen of Albany held a preliminary meeting in February 1830; Troy followed on March 24, and a little later an address was issued 'To the Journeymen Mechanics and Other Young Workingmen of the County of Rensselaer.' In Rochester, Utica, Syracuse, and other smaller places similar measures were taken and candidates were nominated for town and village offices.

The first State convention of the new party met in the courthouse at Salina (Syracuse) on August 25, 1830, with 78 delegates. The principal issues were the ten-hour day, a universal system of education, abolition of imprisonment for debt, and a mechanics' lien law. The convention nominated General Erastus Root for governor and General Nathaniel Pitcher for lieutenant governor, both old-line politicians, who betrayed the workers by withdrawing two weeks before election. The party was split by internal dissension on religious, racial, and intellectual questions; the depression of 1832–7 completed the disintegration, and labor activity returned to 'craft' action. A number of important gains, however, were made: better educational advantages for workers' children, abolition of imprisonment for debt, reform of the militia system, and in some industries better working conditions.

In 1840 President Martin Van Buren, with the aim, so often expressed since, of setting an example for private industry, proclaimed that ten hours a day should be the maximum on all public works. By that time canal and railroad construction had been responsible for increasing the average day's wages of common labor to 75¢ and $1.25.

After 1840 labor was diverted from its proper concern with wages, hours, and working conditions by many indirect issues: land reforms— with the slogan 'vote yourself a farm,' the gold rush, the Mexican War, the abolition of slavery, and such Utopian experiments as Fourierism and the Oneida Community. But after the middle of the century collective action started on the upgrade again. The New York Printers' Union was formed in 1850; in 1852 it became part of the National Typographical Union, which issued a charter to the Albany local on May 6, 1862, and became the International Typographical Union in 1869. The Typographical Union No.12, which at one time reached a maximum enrollment of 26,000 members, was organized in Rochester in 1859. In the same year the iron molders of Dutchess County were unionized. One of the oldest local unions in Schenectady County, also a molders' union, was established in 1860. Local clearing houses known as 'trades assemblies' were formed in industrial centers, principally as co-ordinating and advisory agencies with no power to declare strikes. The New York State Trades Assembly, later the Workingmen's Assembly of the State of New York, was organized on February 26, 1865. In the 1868 convention women appeared for the first time as delegates, and Kate Mullaney of the Laundry Workers' Union of Troy was appointed assistant secretary and national organizer.

The Knights of Labor, organized in Philadelphia in 1869, grew in New York State until in 1886 it numbered 700,000 members with local assemblies in all the major industrial centers. Paralleling this movement, and in many cases co-operating with it, were farmers' organizations, like the Patrons of Husbandry. The fact that one element in the Knights of Labor advocated violence aroused widespread opposition, and after it lost a number of major strikes the organization began to split and disintegrate. The confusion resulted in a return to craft unionism under the guidance of the 'pure and simple' philosophy of Samuel Gompers as expressed in the American Federation of Labor.

But the mass agitation of the Knights of Labor stirred up the State to the job of enforcing existing laws and adding new ones. The truancy law (1852) and the compulsory education law (1874) had little effect on child labor because no provision was made for enforcement; the same weakness existed in the eight-hour-day law (1867, 1870). But the 1870 amendment to the statute on conspiracy exempting trade union efforts to raise wages was a real gain for the labor movement. The State bureau of labor statistics was established in 1883. In 1886 the legislature passed an act prohibiting the employment of children under 13 in factories and limiting factory employment of minors to 60 hours a week, and creating the office of factory inspector to enforce these provisions. In the same year the legislature established a board of mediation and arbitration, the first such board in the United States. The fire in the Triangle shirtwaist factory in New York City in 1910, which cost the lives of 143 workers, mostly girls, aroused such public indignation that a State factory investigating commission was appointed, with Robert F. Wagner, Alfred E. Smith, and Samuel Gompers among its members; its 13-volume report, published in 1915, was responsible for the enactment of rigid standards of factory construction and inspection and the creation of the State Industrial Commission.

At a convention in Niagara Falls in 1910, the Workingmen's Federation of the State of New York became the New York State Federation of Labor. Activities upstate were slowed up during the World War, but the early twenties were marked by an epidemic of strikes for higher wages and union recognition. These were the issues of the shoe workers' strike in Rochester in 1922, supported by the Amalgamated Clothing Workers of America, which had established itself in that city as well as in New York on a collective bargaining basis. Other strikes occurred in the knitting industry and among streetcar workers. Most of these strikes were broken and the unions were beaten, and it required only the prosperity of the later twenties to stagnate the labor movement upstate almost completely.

The depression of 1930, however, brought a resurgence, stimulated by the National Labor Relations Act and the growth of the Congress of Industrial Organizations. As elsewhere, labor was on the march in Rochester, Syracuse, Schenectady, Amsterdam, Newburgh, and other upstate industrial centers. The conflict with the CIO was bitter and union success was gradual. The diversity of reaction to the Wagner Act is illustrated by two extreme cases: the General Electric Company plant in Schenectady, which after a Labor Board election recognized the United Electrical, Radio, and Machine Workers union as the exclusive bargaining agency of its employees; and the Remington Rand plants in Syracuse and Ilion, which fought a last-ditch fight against the decisions of the Board.

Again New York State has reached the phase in the labor movement when concentration upon organizational and strike activity passes to the political stage. In New York City the American Labor Party has become a determining factor in political campaigns, and upstate it has centers in Albany, Schenectady, Rochester, Buffalo, and Syracuse. The workers realize that great strides have been made in the position of labor during the 1930's, and that in order to fix and protect these gains they must become a power in the legislature and clinch their position with legislative support.

From its beginning as a statistical bureau in 1883, the State Department of Labor has grown into an organization of 14 major divisions and more than 1,500 employees. Its activities, reflecting recent advances in labor legislation, include the fields of workmen's compensation and insurance, industrial codes, industrial hygiene, the State Labor Relations Board, mediation, placement and unemployment insurance, women in industry and minimum wage, and the prevailing rate of wages on public works.

Ethnic Groups

THE polyglot character of the population of New York State is not a recent development. When the Empire State was still New Netherland, the Colony already had representatives of a dozen European nationalities. The first settlers of Fort Orange, now Albany, were French-speaking Walloons. Rensselaerswyck, the great patroonship on the Hudson, recruited its leaseholders from among the Norwegians, Danes, Germans, Scots, and Irish as well as Hollanders. English from Connecticut settled in the lower Hudson Valley in 1642, and others from the same colony and from Massachusetts Bay established themselves in the eastern half of Long Island. On Manhattan the pioneer Dutch element was soon swamped under a babel of tongues, races, and creeds, which included a group of 23 Jewish voyagers, come to New Amsterdam from Brazil. In 1644 Father Isaac Jogues was informed that 18 different languages were represented in the population of Manhattan and its environs.

After the British took over New Amsterdam in 1664, large numbers of English and Welsh arrived and settled on the southern tip of Manhattan and on Staten Island. Labor scarcity and high wages encouraged the importation of Negro slaves; by 1700 New York had 6,000 slaves in a total population of 40,000.

The largest mass migration of the Colonial period was that of the German Palatines, a small group of whom settled on the site of Newburgh in 1708-9. Two years later the British Government, adopting the plan of Governor Robert Hunter, subsidized the settlement of about 2,000 of them in the Hudson Valley to produce pitch, tar, and turpentine; but the entire undertaking was badly handled. After they were thrown on their own resources in September 1712, most of the settlers remained in the Hudson Valley, some of them on the Livingston estate; others scattered to New Jersey and Pennsylvania; and several hundred settled in the Schoharie and Mohawk Valleys, extending the New York frontier westward and northward.

Generally speaking, immigration into the Province of New York during the first half of the eighteenth century was discouraged by the threat of French and Indian raids, by the wider religious freedom offered by other colonies, and by the prevailing system of large land grants to political favorites, which narrowly restricted the opportunity of new settlers to acquire title to farms. Small numbers of Scotch-Irish, Germans, and New Englanders, however, formed precarious settlements along the upper waters of the Susquehanna and the Delaware, where they bore the brunt of the Indian attacks. After the close of the French and Indian War and the Treaty of Fort Stanwix, permanent communities were established in the central part of the State.

The Revolution brought immigration almost to a standstill. The Irish welcomed the war as an opportunity to strike back at their historic oppressor; the Germans, while they fought as valiantly—witness Oriskany—did their share not so much from revolutionary zeal as from the desire to protect their farms and homes.

As soon as the peace treaty was signed, American land agents launched a vigorous publicity campaign in Europe to attract settlers. Preference was shown for the 'bold and adventurous spirit of the Irish, Scotch and English and the patient, laborious and persevering genius of the Germans.' British subjects traveled in American ships to circumvent the obstructions placed in the way of emigration by the employing classes in England, who saw in this 'flagrant seduction' a threat to their own cheap labor market. A number of Portugese, Spanish, and French refugees from oppression in the West Indies added to the variety of nationalities.

While this new influx in the labor market eased its economic justification, the institution of Negro slavery was further weakened by the aggressive denunciaton of the Quakers. In 1799 the New York State legislature provided for emancipation in easy stages. But wage labor increased rapidly, and by 1817 the sentiment against Negro bondage was so strong that even slow emancipation was no longer acceptable and the legislature was forced to pass an act, effective in 1827, prohibiting slavery in the State.

When canal-building in the twenties and thirties increased the demand for labor, experienced Irish canal-diggers responded in droves, entering the State by way of Canada as well as through the port of New York. They swung picks and shovels, lived in leaky-roofed shanties, and worshiped God with missionary priests. Although wages as low as 50¢ a day fell short of what was promised, and although in numberless cases men were defrauded of their pay and discharged without cause, it has been said that 'the wild Irish behaved better than Revolutionary soldiers on the march.' By 1840 they had channeled the State with 13 canals totaling more than 900 miles; and from canal-building they turned to railroad construction. But they did more than dig ditches and lay rails; they 'were working on the foundations of three episcopal sees, were choosing sites for five hundred churches, were opening the interior of the State to the empire of religion, as well as of commerce.'

Beginning about 1840, additional hordes of Irish, fleeing the great potato famine at home, came to the American shore. Between 1847 and 1860 more than 1,000,000 Irish immigrants passed through the port of New York. Many thousands of them settled in New York City to work as teamsters, day laborers, streetcar conductors, and shipyard mechanics. Others pushed up the Hudson and Mohawk Valleys to the brick kilns at Haverstraw, the iron works and quarries at Saugerties, and the mills and factories in Albany, Troy, and Utica.

In the same period other nationals poured in from revolution-torn Europe. Italians fleeing from abortive revolts against Austria started coming as early as 1820; political refugees spilled out of Hungary and Germany by the ill-fated revolutions of 1848 came in shiploads during the fifties. In the three-year period of 1852–4, upward of 500,000 Germans landed in America.

The ebb and flow of immigration was, however, influenced by social, political, and economic conditions in this country as well as by those in Europe. During prosperous times in America the Europeans were invited, courted, and welcomed; but during periods of depression conflicts of interest and prejudice came to the surface, and the 'foreigner' was blamed for every misery and hardship. To the 'native' worker enduring a falling standard of living he was an economic threat; to the aristocracy of landlords and lawyers he was a political threat. As the Protestant newcomers were absorbed, the Roman Catholics were left in conspicuous isolation; and they therefore served as the target of the strong nativist movement in the State. In 1834 the New York Protestant Association was formed and two years later, in Brooklyn, stirred up an anti-Catholic agitation that was marked by the destruction of churches and other property of Roman Catholics. In 1843 the Native American party elected James Harper mayor of New York City, after a campaign in which crowds paraded on the streets with banners bearing the slogan 'No Popery.' Subsequently the party extended its activities to cover the entire State and broadened its aims to retain for the 'native' American his power and position threatened by immigrants schooled in European ideologies.

As successive waves of immigration broke over the State, nativism began to lose its effectiveness, despite the partial success of the Know-Nothing Party in 1852. By 1860 the two powerful nativist parties were swallowed by the Republicans and Democrats. From then on Catholics led more peaceful lives, and 'No Irish Need Apply' signs disappeared from employment offices. Another factor that helped to put the quietus on the nativist movement was the rise of the capitalist employer, to whom cheap labor meant more profits, and more immigrants meant more cheap labor.

Immigration during the 40 years before the World War was made up predominantly of Italians and Greeks and the peoples of the Slavic countries of eastern Europe: Poles, Lithuanians and Letts, Roumanians, Russians, and Russian Jews. These filled the steerages of westbound ships and were filtered through Ellis Island. Only the war and subsequent immigration restrictions checked what was one of the largest mass population movements in history. Many of these newcomers, especially the Italians, regarded coming to America as a temporary adventure from which they would return home with pockets full of money. Some did carry out that plan, but the vast majority became rooted in the new world.

In 1930 the foreign white stock in New York State included 3,191,549 foreign born, 3,351,491 native born of foreign parentage, and 1,133,307 native born of mixed parentage; the total comprised about 61 per cent of the population of 12,588,066. New York City has held in most cases a majority of each national group that has passed through its portals. In 1930, 73.3 per cent of its total population of almost 7,000,000 was of foreign white stock, including more than 1,000,000 Italians, almost 1,000,000 Russians, with Germans, Irish, and Poles ranging above and below the half-million mark. Cutting across national lines are 1,765,000 Jews. Besides a number of smaller white groups, there are 327,000 Negroes in the city, some 250,000 of whom live in Harlem.

Similarly in the upstate area, the national groups are heavily concentrated in the urban areas. The older Irish and German stocks are completely assimilated. The Irish have made the political field largely their own; the Germans are mechanics, brewers, and bakers; both are well represented in the professions and have played a conspicuous part in civil and commercial life.

The flood of Italian immigration reached its crest in 1907, when 300,000 passed through the port of New York. They settled mainly along the water-level route from New York City to Buffalo. In Rome they make up the bulk of mill hands employed in the large brass and copper plants. Another group, cultivating the black muckland at the city's southern border, produce tomatoes, celery, and onions in wholesale quantities. In Utica, where they occupy a distinct district, they are principally knitting mill workers. In Syracuse they dominate the city's north side and are employed in the steel mills, chemical plants, and clothing factories. Rochester's 55,000 Italians, less compact as a racial group than those in other cities, work in many industries, including clothing and shoe manufacture. Buffalo's 80,000 Italians, predominantly of Sicilian extraction, are represented in almost every type of commercial endeavor and share with the Poles the heavy labor in steel mills and iron foundries.

The Poles have always sought the centers of heavy industry like the steel mills and iron foundries in Syracuse and Buffalo. The latter city has 187,000 Poles, the largest Polish community in the State and the second largest in America. In recent years, the first full-fledged American generation of Italians and Poles has risen at a rapid pace to achievement in business, politics, and the professions.

The Russians began to come in large numbers after the Russo-Japanese War and the abortive revolution of 1905, and reached a peak in 1913. Lacking funds to go far afield, they found orientation to new conditions difficult and grasped desperately at any straw that would stave off starvation. They toiled for small pay and absorbed little of the language or customs of their adopted country. Russian Jews, on the other hand, adjusted themselves to the commercial tempo of America with amazing ease. Successive generations, educated in American schools, have attained high place in the State's commercial, industrial, political, and professional life.

The State's heterogeneous population is well exemplified in Binghamton, where the foreign born include 26 different ethnic types, with the Czechs and Slovaks, employed in the tanneries and the shoe factories, predominating. The local broadcasting station provides regular programs in the Slavic tongues every week. In Jamestown the residents of Swedish ancestry, who comprise 60 per cent of the population, predominate in the cabinet-making industry; they support a weekly Swedish newspaper and their restaurants specialize in Swedish cuisine. The French-Canadians have been filtering down across the line from the north for more than a century and number 83,057 in the State today, 28,955 of whom are foreign born. They are employed in paper and knitting mills, lumber camps, and factories. Sixty per cent of the population of Malone and half the population of Plattsburg and Cohoes belong to this group.

Each nationality, while attempting to keep alive its racial heritage, has contributed its share to our American culture. The Italians have been largely responsible for the addition of Columbus Day to our calendar of holidays and the delight of spaghetti to our tables. The Irish, with their genius for politics, have, since the succession of Irish governors—Dongan, Bellomont, Cornbury, Cosby—in Colonial days, played an active part in the evolution of our particular brand of democracy. The Germans, with their habit of relaxation after toil, lightened our celebration of Christmas, introduced the Christmas tree, and established the observance of gift-giving at Yuletide. Their love of music, reflected in the spread of choral groups, orchestras, and bands, has favorably affected the development of music, both vocal and instrumental. To our tables they have contributed sauerkraut, sauerbraten, frankfurters, and a general substantialness to cooking. The Syrians and Turks have given us the method of brewing thick Turkish coffee; the Greeks are famous for their 'candy kitchens,' an institution which no sizable town is without.

More clannish than the Italians and Germans and less influenced by American ways, the Poles have retained much of the folklore, language, and mores of their homeland. Business places in Polish communities display signs such as 'Apteka,' 'Adwokat,' and 'Gospoda,' indicating occupation or trade. In the larger cities 'little Polands' support daily newspapers printed in the native tongue. Italians bedeck city streets with flags and bunting to celebrate Saints' days. As always, the Jews cling to their ethnic traditions, and today our calendars are marked with their holidays.

The restriction of immigration during the past few years has given the potpourri of peoples in the State a chance to boil down to an even consistency. Racial differences have broken down considerably, and today men and women whose ancestry reach back into almost every European nation partake in a common economic and political life.

Folklore

NATURAL phenomena, special occupations like lumbering and mining, and stirring events, such as riots and wars, supply the stimulus for traditional stories, customs, ballads, and songs—for much that we call folklore. Particularly rich in such folklore are the mountain regions of New York State, the valleys of the Mohawk and the Hudson, and the St.Lawrence and Genesee regions.

Indian life and character have been popularized in sentimental-heroic style by James Fenimore Cooper and Henry Wadsworth Longfellow; the latter took the liberty of making the Onondaga chief Hiawatha an Ojibway and transplanting him from New York to the West. Historically, however, according to Arthur C. Parker, Hiawatha was an Iroquois chief who 'was spokesman for the greater mind of Dekanawidah whom the Mohawk nation recognizes as its great culture hero and the founder of its civic system.' In the Dekanawidah legend Hiawatha was born of a Huron virgin and was destined by his mother's dream to journey to the Many Hill Nation, the Iroquois, and raise up the Great Tree of Peace. After heroically overcoming many obstacles, he fulfilled his mother's dream, brought about peace and unity, and established the Confederacy.

Indian legends lurk in more than 500 Indian place names in New York State; and many others, often with the theme of young love ending in tragedy, are identified with conspicuous natural features like mountain ranges, waterfalls, and high cliffs overlooking rivers and lakes. Associated with the gorge of Kaaterskill Clove is a legend worthy of the fancy of a sculptor. Ontiora, an evil spirit, was transformed into the Catskills for his misdeeds. His bones became the rocks and crags, his flesh the rising ground, his blood the sap of trees. He lies prone with one knee raised, his face to the sky. His forehead is rough and vast, his nose long; his eyes are North and South Lakes, from which tears flow down in streams that seam and wrinkle his cheeks.

The story of early contacts between whites and Indians on the New York frontier is scattered through a mixture of fact and legend associated with the names of pioneers of the type idealized by James Fenimore Cooper in Natty Bumppo. Cooper once referred to one Shipman as 'the

Leather-Stocking of the [Cooperstown] region,' but controversy still rages as to whether this was David Shipman of Cooperstown or Nathaniel Shipman of Hoosick Falls. Ava, an Oneida County hamlet, believes its own Nathaniel Foster, Jr., was the original of Cooper's hero, while Syracuse supports Ephraim Webster for that honor. Like Onondaga's Webster, the Genesee's candidate, Ebenezer 'Indian' Allen, married Indian women but did not take his vows too seriously. In the Bumppo tradition also is Timothy Murphy, Schoharie's Revolutionary hero.

The themes of Dutch and English folklore, concentrated chiefly in the Hudson Valley, are ghosts and ghost ships and buried treasure. Out of the wealth of Dutch legend and the folk he knew so well Washington Irving gave the world Rip Van Winkle and the mountain dwarfs, Ichabod Crane and the headless horseman, Heyliger's adventures, and Diedrich Knickerbocker. Kinderhook folk know quite certainly that Katrina Van Tassel was the belle of the Van Alen family—you can see her picture in the old Dutch Van Alen house; and Ichabod Crane was the eccentric Merwin, who taught and flogged the Dutch boys in the little schoolhouse that stood where the white one does now. Wax manikins of both these persons have been placed in the local House of History.

There is a legend of the survivors of a Dutch crew who, unable to relocate a buried treasure because of a shift in the shore line and channel of Annsville Creek, swore to continue the search until they found the gold. At low tide, in the dark of the moon, folks say, their wraiths still pursue the unavailing quest under a weird light, while a white hound bays.

Tappan Zee, in the Hudson between Westchester and Rockland Counties, harbors many ghosts, goblins, and witches. In the old days Rambout Van Dam, who lived at Spuyten Duyvil, was in the habit of rowing to distant Kakait, a secluded hamlet at the north end of Tappan Zee. One fateful Saturday night he joined in a quilting frolic there, which was followed, as usual, by dancing and drinking. Van Dam lingered until past twelve. Then, heedless of warning, he set out to row home on the Sabbath, swearing that he would not land until he reached Spuyten Duyvil. A curse was put upon him, and he is doomed to ply his craft on the broad river until Judgment Day.

Thunder Mountain (Dunderberg), at the southern gate of the Hudson Highlands, was populated in Colonial days by a crew of goblins, whose Mein Heer was a Dutch-clad 'bulbous-bottomed goblin' in trunk hose and sugarloaf hat, with a speaking trumpet through which he bawled his orders for winds and lightnings. At his command the imps cavorted in the

air and played pranks with the rigging of passing ships, though they never
molested a mariner plying the river if he lowered his peak in homage to
Mein Heer, the keeper of the mountain.

The legends about Captain Kidd and his fabulous treasure are epic in
their completeness and circumstantial details. He is said to have buried
his loot near the eastern end of Long Island, on Gardiner's Island, in Gardiner's Bay, and at several points along the Hudson. The prospect of finding Kidd's treasure has stirred many people to dig at numerous places,
thus far vainly. Kidd's Plug, part of the craggy steep on the Hudson
called Cro' Nest, a knob projecting like a bung, is said to conceal a cavern
in which the pirate cached some of his gold. According to the most elaborate of the legends, Captain Kidd was anxious for the security of a Spanish maiden rescued in a fight in the South Seas from the pirate Ballridge.
Sailing secretly up the Hudson to Catskill, he entrusted his bride, Isabelle
del Puerto, to the care of an old Negro woman, Dora, who lived in a little
house at the foot of Kaaterskill Clove. During Kidd's absence Ballridge
spied Isabelle on the cliff above Fawn's Leap, pursued and caught her,
bound her to his horse, and rode off to his house near Leeds. Here he imprisoned her in a room, importuned her for her love, and persecuted her.
She escaped, was recaptured, and suffered a horrible death. After her
burial, her footsteps were heard nightly passing back and forth before the
door of the Leeds house, and a white horse was seen galloping home with
her ghost trailing from a rope. Captain Kidd was captured in the Red Sea,
taken to London, and hanged; and, says the legend, Ballridge wore a silk
cord around his neck until his death.

Often a ghost story was connected with a historical event. A Dutch family of Saratoga County filled up the well on their farm because it was
haunted nightly by the ghost of a woman without a head, believed to be
the spirit of one who had been massacred on the farm by Canadians and
Indians in 1748. Hans Anderson, who tilled a farm back of Peekskill, was
worried into his grave by the leaden-faced likeness of a British spy whom
he had hanged by General Putnam's orders. A ghost ship, which has been
sighted at intervals for 160 years off New Rochelle and along Long Island
Sound, is thought to be the phantom of a British warship seized by the
farmers of Long Island off Throgg's Neck in the bleak winter of 1777,
when the British crew were bent on felling their trees for firewood. The
battlefield of Bedford is haunted by apparitions of the Dutch and Indian
warriors of 1644; the whooping Indians who had been beheaded in the
fray battle again with their ghostly skulls teetering upside down on their
shoulders. Around Pelham, in Westchester County, treasure hunters were

once frightened away by a phantom troop of British Regulars, and a wedding breakfast was interrupted by a skirmish of Revolutionary ghosts. An old Huguenot tale tells of little girls on their way to fetch water being frightened by the ghost of a Hessian soldier. Even horses saw ghosts in Eastchester, where during a Thanksgiving turkey shoot three horses balked at passing a 'gallows tree' and their riders took down a stone fence in order to pass around it. On Long Island the spirit of Thomas Paine has been seen wandering, on dark nights, between his two graves. (He was buried in New Rochelle, Westchester.)

Numerous traditional stories, originating in events of the Revolution, the War of 1812, or the Civil War, have been colored in retelling until they have become part of local folklore. One story describes how by a ruse 20 spirited Colonials held up and captured the advance guard of the British at Bemis Heights. Popular in Rochester is the story that in May 1814, when 13 British ships threatened Charlotte, 33 Rochesterians marched in and out through a screen of trees and 'bluffed' the British Navy by creating the illusion of superior numbers. In the Robin Hood tradition is the story of Claudius Smith and his seven years of predatory warfare, and his hiding places in the Ramapo Mountains. There is the story of the 'scythe tree' in Waterloo, and in Tappan the account of the mysterious tar barrel in an elm tree that burned as a signal to the country of the signing of peace terms with Great Britain.

Belief in witches has been another rich source of folklore. Housewives feared the witch because she had power to bring bad luck to the family, sour the milk, and make churning abortive. Well-known charms were employed to break her spell: a silver coin was dropped into the churn; the horseshoe over the door was placed with open part up so that good luck would not run out. Since a witch could transform herself into a black cat, a strange cat was always a dreaded visitor and under no circumstances was allowed to cross one's path.

The traditional lore of Sullivan County includes Old Meg, the Hag, 'the seventh daughter of the seventh daughter,' hermit 'queen' of an intermarrying family of 400 who dwelt in cabins and caves in the wooded hills of Sullivan and Orange Counties. She was a withered old woman, over six feet tall and exceedingly thin; her skin was yellow, her hair was black and long, and her chin was covered with a three-inch beard. She had supernatural power in healing and in telling fortunes. One day Old Meg was missing. Sam Quick, hunting woodchuck, pushed through a half-hidden path and under a chestnut tree came upon Meg's body pierced by a large splinter of jagged stump thrust through her back and a foot beyond. On Saturday afternoon 200 men held a wake around her cabin, and at midnight set it afire and departed.

Writing in 1899 in the Port Jervis *Union*, J.V.Morrison told how as a boy he listened to witch stories in the slave cabins of the Delaware Valley. Tashee, a slave 'witch finder,' told Morrison that he could recognize the evil eye, the witch spots on the body, and the black cats that were imps of familiar spirits; and that he knew how to make compounds baleful to those he desired to injure, and talismans, amulets, and charms to protect him from witchery. He could put a spell on a tomb so that not even the Witch of Endor could raise the dead.

Old Tashee told about witches going to a farmer's pasture at midnight, clutching the manes of twin colts and riding them through the air to the witches' feasting place, and riding them back in the morning. They did this so often the colts became thin and weak and their manes all matted. Tashee greased, soaped, and unsnarled their manes and put them in separate pastures far apart. He then went to the farmer's house to find the witch. When an old maid came in he knew her to be the witch for 'she rolled up her evil eye' and turned up her nose at him. 'We took a shoe of the mare's right hind foot and put it in the fire among the coals and I told them next day noon, when she came there, to ask her to stay to dinner, and just as she was going to sit in the chair, one of them must take the tongs and slip the red-hot shoe in the seat for her to sit on. She was branded, the colts' manes came out all right, and I got a quart of whiskey and a dollar for the job.'

One of the chief delights of common folk in leisure time or as an adjunct to work has always been singing or chanting familiar songs and ballads. Usually these are handed down orally from generation to generation. Some of them—well-known ballads like 'Sir John Randall'—have been transported from the Old World; others, like 'Fair Charlotte' and the 'Jam at Gerry's Rock,' originated in other States: still others, like the 'Blue Mountain Song' and 'Low Bridge, Everybody Down,' are the creations of New York State folk groups or individuals. In any case, as the song has been absorbed by the community, the identity of the author or authors has been lost. The singing and the musical accompaniment are simple and artless—there are, for instance, farmers' families where an 'ear for music' has been inherited for several generations; and it is not uncommon to see the hard hand of the farmer 'pick a tune' on the old organ or fiddle.

During the winter evenings in the lumber camps of the Adirondacks the men were accustomed to sing, sometimes accompanied by dancing, around the fire. A few of their favorites, mostly of their own creation, were 'My Old Brown Coat and Me,' 'Jack Haggerty and His Flat River Girl,' 'Milking the Cows on the Farm,' and 'Gypsy Davy.' The 'Blue Mountain Song,' or the 'Belle of Long Lake,' is on the whole the most revealing of the shantyman's life in the woods. There are eight stanzas each followed by a chorus:

> Come all my gay gay fellows
> Wherever you may be
> Come sit down awhile
> And listen to me.
> The truth I will tell you
> Without a mistake
> About the rackets we have
> Around Blue Mountain Lake.
> Chorus: And its down, down, down,
>   Derry down.

Erie 'Canawl' songs are still cherished in the memory of the surviving 'canawlers' along the old route. 'Sing to our hosses? Never! We just said "Giddap"—or swore at 'em,' they say; but rollicking numbers were sung by the boatmen when loafing at the end of a run, though 'most of it ain't fit to print.'

The aged Mrs.Broadback lived on a canalboat when she was a girl and often sang the 'Boatswain's Boy.' The first stanza and chorus are:

> When I was young and about sixteen
> None was more bright and gay.
> I gamboled nimbly on the green
> Or sported in the bay.
> The bloom of youth was in my cheeks,
> My heart was full of joy.
> How happy were those days to me,
> The merry boatswain's boy.
> Chorus: For I was a boatswain's boy,
>   For I was a boatswain's boy—
>   Johnny, get your mule fed,
>   Johnny, get your mule fed—
>   For I was a boatswain's boy.

Elijah Leonard sold his pork in his grocery store at 'The Rock' about 1840, and for years it had a place in the song and story of the canal as 'Black Rock Pork.' Another short song gives the romantic history of the good old barge *Esther*. About 1877 'Corkleg' Johnny Bartley sang in Bonney's Theater, Buffalo:

> Whoa! Back! Giddap! Forget it I never shall,
> When I drove the team of spavined mules on the Erie Canal.

The 'Ballad of the Canal,' a longer song, is somewhat sardonic in tone with a characteristic chorus:

> So haul in your bowlines,
> Stand by the saddle mule,
> Low bridge, boys, dodge your head,
> Don't stand up like a fool.
> For the Erie is a-risin'
> An' the whiskey's gettin' low.
> I hardly think we'll get a drink
> Till we get to Buffalo.

Of the two most suggestive of life on the canal, one, 'Fifteen Years on the Erie Canal,' celebrates the virtues of a mule named Sal in verse that has been somewhat refined by Thomas S. Allen:

> I've got a mule, and her name is Sal—
> Fifteen years on the Erie Canal.
> She's a good old worker and a good old pal—
> Fifteen years on the Erie Canal.
> We've hauled some cargoes in our day,
> Filled with lumber, coal and hay,
> And every inch of the way I know
> From Albany to Buffalo.

The other, in more characteristic form, proclaims the virtues of a cook by the name of Sal:

> We were loaded down with barley,
> We were chuck up full with rye;
> And the captain he looked down at me,
> With his goddamn wicked eye.
> Oh the Erie was a-rising,
> The strap was getting low,
> And I scarcely think,
> We'll get a drink
>   'Till we get to Buffalo,
>   'Till we get to Buffalo.
>
> Drop a tear for big-foot Sal,
> The best damn cook on the Erie Canal;
> She aimed for Heaven but she went to Hell—
> Fifteen years on the Erie Canal.
> The missioner said she died in sin;
> Hennery said it was too much gin;
> There weren't no bar where she hadn't been,
>   From Albany to Buffalo.
>
> Low bridge! Everybody down!
> Low bridge! We're coming to a town!
> You'll always know your neighbor,
>   You'll always know your pal,
> If you've ever navigated on the Erie Canal.

Public Welfare

THOUGH privation and hardship were fairly general throughout the Dutch Colonial period, the number of actual dependents was small, and relief, when needed, was administered by the officers of the Dutch Reformed Church. Churches of other denominations were expected to care for their own poor, and in localities lacking a religious organization relief was a function of the civil authorities. Funds for the poor were raised through church collections, individual donations, and court fines for misdemeanors and violations of the excise laws.

Soon after the organization of the Colonial Government, several *sieckentroosters*, minor ecclesiastical functionaries, were sent to the Colony charged with the duty of visiting sick persons in their homes. These were the first social workers in what is now the Empire State.

For the dependent aged, almshouses were established by Dutch Reformed congregations at New Amsterdam, Rensselaerswyck, and other settlements, and a company hospital was erected in New Amsterdam in 1657 to care for sick soldiers and Negroes. Orphanmasters were appointed at New Amsterdam, Beverwyck (Albany), and Wildwyck (Kingston) to protect the interests of propertied widows and orphans, but when the latter became destitute they were turned over to the care of the deacons.

After the Colony came under English rule, poor relief in the southern counties was regulated by the Duke's Laws (1665), which made each parish responsible for its own poor and for raising funds by taxation. The few general poor laws enacted were directed against vagabonds, beggars, and others moving from their places of legal settlement. Until formally accepted as an inhabitant of a town, a newcomer might at any time be 'warned' to depart by the authorities. An undesirable was 'passed on' from constable to constable until he reached his place of legal settlement or the border of a neighboring colony.

The prevailing attitude toward dependency was stern, cold, and straitlaced; in many places the pauper was made to wear a brightly colored badge on his sleeve inscribed with a large letter 'P.' No attempt was made to segregate the types of dependents: the insane and the physically handicapped, the aged and the young, the inebriates and the sober were housed together. The first public institution for 'the employing of Poor and Indigent People' was established in New York City in 1734 and opened two years later under the name 'House of Correction, Workhouse and Poor House.' The only method of caring for destitute children was through apprenticeship and indenture, by which children were bound out singly or in groups with the specification that their masters have them taught to read, write, and cipher.

During the Revolutionary War the local poor relief system broke down in many communities. Refugees from areas controlled by the British or ravaged by raids, not being chargeable to either county or town units, became the first 'State poor,' cared for by State commissioners. In the wake of the Revolution a great wave of humanitarian reform surged over the new Nation. Private philanthropic organizations were set up, the most important being the Society for the Prevention of Pauperism established in New York City. A sweeping revision of the penal code in 1796 reduced the number of crimes punishable by death from thirteen to two and established the first State prison. Corporal punishment, such as confinement in the stocks, whipping, and branding, was gradually abolished. Reforms were made in the laws against debtors. Public poor relief was completely secularized: the office of overseer of the poor was made elective instead of appointive; and towns too small to maintain individual almshouses were permitted to join others in town unions for the purpose of providing institutional care. Poor funds continued to be raised by local taxation supplemented by income from fines.

Several severe yellow fever epidemics at the turn of the century resulted in such public health measures as systematized quarantine, general sanitation, isolation of patients, and appointment of public health officers. The Ladies' Society for the Relief of Poor Widows with Small Children was established in New York City in 1797 to help surviving dependents of fever victims. An offshoot of this Society founded the first orphan asylum in 1806. But child aid grew slowly, and for many years dependent children were herded indiscriminately with all other classes of dependents.

In the same period the insane were recognized as a separate social problem. In September 1792 the first mental patient was admitted into the newly opened New York Hospital, but treatment remained custodial rather than curative. The Bloomingdale Asylum, opened in 1821 as a separate unit of the New York Hospital, was the first institution for the insane in the State operated primarily on therapeutic principles. It received annual State grants for many years. The New York Institution for the Instruction of the Deaf and Dumb—second of its kind in the United States—was incorporated in 1817 and later received State grants.

In 1824 the secretary of state, J.V.N.Yates, published under legislative authority the first State-wide poor law survey, which revealed that be-sides almshouse and home relief, the indigent were being cared for under the 'contract system,' whereby the dependent poor were let out to house-holders at a fixed rate, and under the 'auction system,' whereby the poor were bid off to persons offering to maintain them for the lowest cost. After summing up the chaos, cruelty, and waste arising from prevailing poor law practices, Yates recommended a State-wide system of county poorhouses, where all paupers were to be maintained at county expense, the able-bodied to be set to suitable work and the children to be given ade-quate education.

As a result of the Yates report the legislature in 1824 passed 'An act to provide for the establishment of county almshouses'; but so many excep-tions were allowed that, although poorhouses were established in all but four counties during the ensuing decade, the attempt to put the county system into effect eventually collapsed and relief was returned to local re-sponsibility. However, the indiscriminate herding of dependents resulted in abuses so shocking as to lead to constant pressure for proper classifica-tion and segregation of different groups. The earliest effective changes took place in the field of child welfare. In 1824 the House of Refuge for Juvenile Delinquents, the first juvenile reformatory in the country, was established in New York City by the Society for the Reformation of Ju-venile Delinquents. It was supported mainly by State funds. In 1849 the Western House of Refuge (now the State Agricultural and Industrial School at Industry) was opened in Rochester as the first American juve-nile reformatory under complete State financial and administrative con-trol. The Asylum for Idiots (now the Syracuse State School) was estab-lished in 1851, the first of its kind to be opened under State ownership and control.

Several other important child welfare organizations were founded in the middle years of the nineteenth century, including the New York Juvenile Asylum (now the Children's Village at Dobbs Ferry) and the Children's Aid Society, which inaugurated the placing-out movement. The Thomas Asylum for Orphan and Destitute Indian Children was organized in 1855 under private auspices and taken over by the State in 1875. By 1866 the total number of privately managed orphanages exceeded 60.

A distinctive feature of this period was the development of State insti-tutional facilities for the mentally and physically handicapped. The State

Lunatic Asylum at Utica was established in 1836 and opened in 1843. The New York City Lunatic Asylum (now the Manhattan State Hospital), founded in 1834, was the first municipal mental hospital in this country. The blind had received separate care as early as 1831, with the founding of the New York Institution for the Blind. In 1865 the State Institution for the Blind (now the New York State School for the Blind) was established at Batavia to serve the western counties.

Mass immigration in the nineteenth century brought in its wake grave problems of public health and poor relief. Large numbers of immigrants needed medical care upon landing; many were poverty-stricken; others were mulcted of their meager savings by thieves and swindlers. Without friends or funds, they soon found themselves drawn into the slums or the poorhouse, or were obliged to engage in the meanest forms of work for low wages and under conditions that exposed them to vice, disease, and death. Alarmed by the growing hordes of indigent aliens, poor-law officials demanded State and Federal legislation to protect local communities. In 1847 a State board was created to help and advise newcomers and to reimburse local communities for immigrant relief. Funds for this purpose came out of head taxes and indemnity bonds imposed on immigrants. The agitation against 'alien pauperism' culminated in 1882 in an act of Congress regulating immigration and containing a provision intended to exclude persons likely to become public charges.

The effects of repeated economic depressions provoked increased dissatisfaction with the organization of public welfare. Following the crisis of 1837–42 the New York Association for Improving the Condition of the Poor was founded, with emphasis on individual and moral, rather than mass and material, relief. Horace Greeley and others raised the slogan 'Go West' as an alternative to the demands made for setting up public work projects for the New York unemployed. In the crisis of 1857–8 the jobless militantly demanded the 'right to work' and the 'right to relief'; and demonstrations, sometimes reaching threatening proportions, became almost daily occurrences.

After the Civil War, the increase in the number of institutions for dependents and the mismanagement of some institutions receiving State funds gave rise to the demand for adequate supervision, leading to the establishment in 1867 of a body later known as the State Board of Charities. The State Charities Act of 1896 defined the powers of the Board as including the right to visit, inspect, and supervise all welfare organizations except those under the supervision of the State Commission in Lunacy, established in 1889, and of the State Prison Commission. It was also empowered to correct improper treatment of inmates and to regulate the admission and retention of inmates maintained in private institutions at public expense. The Board's power to inspect private welfare agencies was later contested and restricted, but was partially restored in 1931 and written into the State constitution in 1938.

The last quarter of the nineteenth century was marked by successful campaigns to remove healthy children from public almshouses and to establish State institutions for the mentally ill, mental defectives, and epileptics in order to facilitate the removal of these groups from poorhouses. Another important development was the extension of the reformatory idea to the treatment of adult offenders between the ages of 16 and 30 convicted of a felony. The New York Training School for Girls was established at Hudson in 1881; the Albion State Training School was founded in 1890, and the Westfield State Farm in 1892. Another stimulus to progress was provided by private agencies. The State Charities Aid Association of New York, organized in 1872 by Louisa Lee Schuyler, did much to create public opinion favorable to needed developments in public welfare. The first charity organization society in America was founded in Buffalo in 1877, and was followed in 1882 by the establishment of the Charity Organization Society of New York City.

Recurring economic depressions again overtaxed welfare facilities. During 1873-9 more than 100,000 workers were jobless in New York City. Parades, demonstrations, and riots took place, and demands were made for work relief projects. The migration of thousands of jobless men created panicky alarm among public welfare officials over the 'tramp problem.' During the depression of 1893-7, many relief projects were set up under public and private auspices.

The turn of the century saw the rise of social reform movements with such goals as improved factory laws, better wage and living standards, workmen's compensation, child labor legislation, slum clearance, and improved housing; and attention was concentrated on the care, treatment, and possible prevention of mental and physical handicaps. Important institutions were established, such as the New York State Psychiatric Institute and Hospital in New York City, the New York State Hospital for the Treatment of Incipient Pulmonary Tuberculosis at Raybrook, the State Hospital for the Care of Crippled and Deformed Children (now the State Reconstruction Home) at West Haverstraw, and Letchworth Village for mental defectives at Thiells.

Although new institutions for the dependent and handicapped classes were being established, the twentieth-century trend was away from institutionalization and toward home care and treatment. The field of child welfare drew special attention because of the abuses of private orphanages in the care and placing-out of children. Juvenile courts were established in New York City, Buffalo, Albany, and Rochester in the first years of the century; and in 1922 a State-wide system of children's courts was established, with sweeping powers in dealing with delinquent and neglected children. The child welfare law of 1915 provided for a board of child welfare in each upstate county and in New York City to administer allowances to widows with one or more children under 16 years of age.

The panic of 1907 and the pre- and post-World War depressions were marked by the usual round of breadlines, soup kitchens, demonstrations of the unemployed, establishment of employment bureaus under private auspices, mushroom growth of citizens' emergency relief committees, and a sharp increase in the number of destitute migrants. An interesting outgrowth of this series of crises was the inauguration of many organized inquiries into the causes of periodical mass unemployment and methods of amelioration.

A new basic concept of welfare activity was written into the State public welfare law of 1929: 'As far as possible, families shall be kept together, and they shall not be separated for reasons of poverty alone.' Furthermore, the prevention of destitution, where possible, was expressly acknowledged to be a public duty. The new approach was evident in the creation in 1929 of a State commission on old age security, upon the recommendation of Governor Franklin D. Roosevelt, for the purpose of inquiring into the condition of the aged. The findings of the commission were embodied into the Old Age Security Act (Chapter 387, Laws of 1930), providing for allowances to needy persons 70 years old and over who were citizens of the United States, residents of New York State for at least ten years immediately preceding application for old age assistance, and proper subjects for noninstitutional relief.

The depression that began in 1929 overstrained the normal relief machinery. The number of those needing public relief in New York State rose 32 per cent in 1930, and 80 per cent more in 1931. The legislature, responding to a special message from Governor Roosevelt, unanimously passed the Wicks Act in September 1931, providing State aid to localities for unemployment relief. A Temporary Emergency Relief Administration was created to carry out the provisions of the law, and $20,000,000 was voted for a seven-month period. Not long after the establishment of the TERA it became apparent not only in New York but throughout the Nation that even State and local resources combined were not sufficient to cope with the human needs of the crisis. The Federal Government stepped in, first through advances made by the Reconstruction Finance Corporation, then through the establishment of the Federal Emergency Relief Administration, the Civil Works Administration, and the Works Progress (now the Work Projects) Administration, under which it assumed full administrative and financial responsibility for work relief. Under the Emergency Relief Appropriation Act of 1939 the State and its subdivisions must bear at least one fourth the total cost of projects. A revealing index to the tremendous needs arising out of the depression is afforded in the final report of the TERA, dated June 30, 1937, which shows that, during its five years and eight months of existence, expenditures for public relief in the State totaled $1,155,000,000.

The result of all these efforts was the realization that relief was not enough, and that a firmly grounded system of security must be established to absorb the shock to the individual, and to society as well. With this in mind, President Roosevelt, in June 1934, created a committee on economic security, whose recommendations served as the basis of the Social Security Act, which became law in August 1935. New York State proceeded to enact legislation conforming to the Federal act in order to derive from it the maximum benefit.

A far-reaching reorganization of the State's public welfare administration system took place during 1936. Chapter 873 of the Laws of 1936, amending the public welfare law, provided for the appointment of a new State Board of Social Welfare consisting of 15 members, with power to name the commissioner of social welfare. A permanent system of State participation in home relief was established, to the extent of 40 per cent of the costs. Chapter 358 of the Laws of 1937 provided State responsibility for all Indians and nonsettled persons and State reimbursement of 40 per cent for salaries of local public welfare personnel.

The extent of the public welfare program in New York State is indicated by the annual report of the State Board of Social Welfare for 1939, showing that in the last month of that year 434,530 cases involving 1,076,812 individuals received some form of public assistance at a total cost of $16,741,739. Of this expenditure it is estimated that localities paid $8,762,842, the State $6,243,816 and the Federal Government $1,735,081. In the same month the Federal Government spent approximately $10,109,000 in wages paid to about 154,300 persons employed on projects financed from WPA funds.

Constitutional amendments approved by the people of New York State in November 1938 broadened and deepened the definition and scope of social welfare for the State and widened the powers of visitation and inspection by the State Board of Social Welfare. Provision was authorized 'for the aid, care and support of the needy directly or through subdivisions of the State; or for the protection by insurance or otherwise, against the hazards of unemployment, sickness and old age; or the education and support of the blind, the deaf, the dumb, the physically handicapped and juvenile delinquents . . . ; or for health and welfare services for all children . . . ; or for the aid, care and support of neglected and dependent children and of the needy sick . . .' In this amendment the people gave recognition to the broader aspects of social welfare evolved under the pressure of events since 1929.

Religion

CHRISTIANITY entered the region of upstate New York from two directions, under two flags, and in two forms: ministers of the Dutch Reformed Church followed colonists from the Netherlands up the Hudson, and French Jesuit missionaries from the north early began to preach Roman Catholicism to the Iroquois. The Reformed Church made little effort to convert the Indians; the Jesuits, on the other hand, set the conversion of the natives as their sole aim. They endured torture and martyrdom and achieved some success, notably between 1668 and 1686. But their labors carried implications in the struggle between England and France for control of the fur trade. In some instances French punitive expeditions were sent against villages where Indian converts resided and, together with English intrigue, they largely undid the Jesuits' work. When the paths of the Dutch traders and French Jesuits crossed, their relations were friendly; and on several occasions the former rescued the latter from Indian captivity.

The English, like the Dutch, allowed religious freedom to all but Roman Catholics. New Dutch churches were established, in some of which the English language was not used until the close of the Colonial period. Other foreign-language churches were established by German Lutherans on Manhattan Island, by French Huguenots in Flushing, New Rochelle, Staten Island, and New Paltz, and by German Palatines in the Hudson, Mohawk, and Schoharie Valleys. Presbyterian churches, established by New Englanders and Scotch-Irish immigrants, dotted the valley of the Hudson; in the 1740's they divided into Old Sides and New Sides, but were reunited in 1758. A number of Quaker meetings were organized in Putnam and Dutchess Counties and on Long Island. The Church of England received support and encouragement from the Mother Country, and a number of churches were established along the Hudson. Beginning in 1693, the Episcopal clergy in the counties of Westchester, Richmond, New York, and Queens were for a time supported out of public funds. West of Albany there were a few Indian chapels, such as Queen Anne's Chapel at Fort Hunter and the Mohawk Mission at the upper Mohawk Castle, the present Indian Castle. During the Revolution the Episcopal

Church suffered because of its close connection with England and the Loyalists. In many cases the ministers were obliged to flee to Canada, and church edifices were desecrated.

The State constitution of 1777 separated church and State and provided for 'the free exercise and enjoyment of religious profession and worship, without discrimination or preference.' In the post-Revolutionary period the cause of organized religion suffered from the spread of deism, represented in New Rochelle by Tom Paine and in Newburgh by a society called the Druids. The frontier, notoriously irreligious, was chargeable with heavy drinking, Sabbath-breaking, and cursing. But the rapid settlement of the State and the spread of revivalism westward promoted the organization of churches. Immigrants brought their denominational preferences with them; Presbyterians, Methodists, Baptists, Universalists, and Quakers spread across the State. Another division on points of theological doctrine occurred among the Presbyterians in 1837, but the schism was healed in 1869.

The outstanding individual in the history of revivalism in New York was Charles Grandison Finney, who began his work in Western, Oneida County, in 1825 and achieved his greatest success in Rochester in 1830–1. Finney's emphasis on a life of practical piety stimulated church activity in missionary work, social reform, and education.

From the churches developed home and foreign missionary agencies, temperance organizations, antislavery societies, Sunday Schools, benevolent institutions, academies, and colleges. The absence of excessive sectarian competition is illustrated in the organization of Union College by a number of denominations, principally the Presbyterian and Dutch Reformed, and by the support of Hamilton College by Presbyterians and Congregationalists. But for the training of ministers the denominations set up separate theological seminaries, many of which evolved into the present-day nonsectarian colleges. Colgate and Rochester are Baptist in origin; Syracuse, Methodist; Hobart, Episcopalian; Hartwick, Lutheran; St.Lawrence, Universalist; and Alfred, Seventh Day Baptist.

In the decades before the Civil War, New York State churches were centers of antislavery sentiment, and their members manned the Underground Railroad, opposing the Fugitive Slave Act as a religious duty. Samuel R. Ward, born a slave in Maryland, was licensed by the New York Congregational (General) Association in 1839 and between 1841 and 1851 served as pastor in white Congregational churches in South Butler and Cortland. About 20,000 members of the Negro Cumberland Presbyterian Church met with white Presbyterian congregations, though a few Negro exhorters held separate meetings. Later they sought separate ecclesiastical organization and were set apart by the Presbyterian General Assembly in 1869.

After the Civil War the Protestant churches shared in the general prosperity, expanded home and foreign missions, and developed lay auxiliaries and women's societies, including the W.C.T.U., the Y.M.C.A., the Y.W.C.A., and Christian Endeavor. Intellectually they were for the most part stagnant, with no direct concern for the social changes, political and financial corruption, or philosophical upheavals. Scarcely before 1890 did modern Biblical criticism and evolutionary thought leave a mark; and then Protestantism was divided into 'conservative' and 'liberal' schools. During the 1920's this controversy assumed large proportions, the contending factions being known as 'fundamentalists' and 'modernists.' In the 1930's, however, attention shifted to social problems, and church groups were more concerned with unemployment, social security, and slum clearance than with the theory of evolution.

The movement of rural populations to the cities has left rural churches weakened in numbers and financial resources. In the cities the older church edifices have been surrounded by business blocks or recent immigrant settlements. City church federations point the way to a higher degree of interdenominationalism; and Protestant-Catholic-Jewish co-operation presents a united front against the enemies of faith and tolerance.

According to the United States Census of 1926 the Protestant churches of the State outside of New York City had a total membership of 1,200,000. The 14 principal Protestant denominations in New York City had more than 486,000 adherents.

Among Negro congregations the Baptist denomination—generally dominant in the Nation—leads in membership and number of church edifices in the State, with 111 buildings and 46,823 members. Total membership of Negro churches is 114,543, and number of edifices 352.

The first Roman Catholic church in upstate New York, excepting the early mission chapels, was St.Mary's, established in Albany in 1797. In the early years of the nineteenth century additional churches were established in Utica, Rochester, Auburn, and a few other centers. In 1806 Francis Cooper, a Roman Catholic elected to the State assembly, was unable to take his seat because his conscience prevented him from taking the required oath abjuring all foreign allegiance, ecclesiastical as well as civil. The objectionable clause was removed and Cooper took his seat. Throughout most of the nineteenth century the Catholic Church was obliged to contend for equal rights in ministering to inmates of public institutions and in sharing in public funds allotted for education, as well as to fight against the propaganda of 'No Popery' movements in politics. An article in the constitution of 1894 prohibited the use of public money to aid denominational schools, but an amendment adopted in 1938 permits the legislature to provide for the transportation of children to and from any school.

The Catholic Church grew rapidly as a result of Irish and German immigration, which began in the thirties and forties and reached a peak after the Civil War. St.Joseph's Seminary was established in Troy in 1864 to educate native priests. The diocese of Rochester was organized in 1866, the diocese of Ogdensburg in 1872, and the diocese of Syracuse in 1886. Bishop McCloskey, the first bishop of the Albany diocese, became the first American cardinal in 1875. In 1893 St.Bernard's Seminary was established in Rochester, and St.Joseph's in Yonkers in 1896. The large-scale immigration from eastern Europe beginning about 1890 added large numbers of foreign-born communicants to the Roman Catholic Church, especially Italians and Poles, who established and have retained separate parishes. Parallel with this growth has been the development of parochial schools, institutions of higher education, and religious and charitable institutions. In 1926, in the State outside of New York City, there were 1,381,470 members of the Roman Catholic Church, and in New York City there were 1,733,954.

Early Jewish settlers in New Amsterdam, and later New York City, traded up the Hudson River, but the first Jewish residents of upstate New York settled little, if any, earlier than the first years of the nineteenth century. A significant increase occurred after the middle of the century, due principally to the immigration of German and English Jews, who concentrated in the population centers—Albany, Syracuse, Rochester, and Buffalo. During the 30 years before the World War, immigration from Russia, Roumania, and Austria-Hungary swelled their number; but most of these settled in New York City, so that, while the Jews comprise about one sixth of the population of the Empire State, in 1926 outside the metropolis there were only about 135,000 Jews and 184 synagogues out of the 1,228 places of worship. In New York City, Jewish congregations had 1,765,000 members. Many of the congregations, principally those made up of German Jews, have modified the traditional orthodox doctrines and customs, and are known as reform congregations.

In the last years of the eighteenth and first half of the nineteenth century New York State was home to a number of new religious cults, some imported and some home-grown, the latter following the trail of New Eng-

land migration across the State and explainable, from a religious stand-
point, as the release under semifrontier conditions of the emotional tension
caused by the inwardness and repression of New England theology.
Mother Ann Lee and her original small following of Shakers came from
England in 1774. In 1776 they settled in Niskayuna, near Albany; and in
1792 the first Shaker community was established at New Lebanon. At its
peak before the Civil War the sect counted about 6,000 members; today it
is almost extinct. But it has made a permanent impress on the State by its
contributions to agriculture and by the products of its handicrafts.

Jemima Wilkinson, the 'Public Universal Friend,' who established her
short-lived 'Jerusalem' near Penn Yan in 1789, came from New England,
as did John Humphrey Noyes, the founder of the Oneida Community.
Joseph Smith, the prophet of the Mormons, was the son of a farmer who
migrated from Vermont.

In 1831 William Miller of Washington County, also from Vermont, began preaching the Second Advent; in 1843 and 1844 his followers throughout the central part of the State were driven to fanatical extremes in preparation for the Day of Judgment. Those of his followers who survived the
disillusionment met in Albany in 1845 and organized the parent body of
the various branches of the Adventist Church.

The Fox Sisters began their spiritualistic rappings in 1848 in Hydeville
and in the same year moved to Rochester, where the mother church of
modern Spiritualism was organized, though its theology was first formulated in the sixties by Andrew Jackson Davis, a Poughkeepsie tailor.
Lily Dale, in the western part of the State, is today a well-known spiritualist center.

Education

NEW YORK State has no State university in the usual sense of the term. In 1784 the legislature passed a bill 'for establishing a University within this State'; but by the term 'university' the legislators meant, not a school in the modern sense, but an entire system of education under State control. A Board of Regents was set up as a corporation to supervise this system. When a Columbia College group gained control of the Board of Regents, popular demand forced the establishment of a Department of Public Instruction to administer the 'common schools.' In 1904 the two agencies were combined in a State Education Department, and since 1910 the Board of Regents has been the head and the Commissioner of Education the chief executive officer of the Department. The Board, now numbering 12, is elected, one member each year for a 12-year term, by a joint session of the senate and assembly, and serves without pay. Thus, as a result of a historical development, the State educational system is governed in part by a group of public-spirited citizens devoted to its welfare.

The Education Department, acting through the Board of Regents and the Commissioner, performs a wide variety of duties. It charters colleges and universities, associations for the promotion of education, literature, science, art, and so on; it has a voice in budgeting the State-supported colleges of agriculture, veterinary medicine, and home economics at Cornell University, the College of Forestry at Syracuse University, and the College of Ceramics at Alfred University; it exercises complete jurisdiction over the six State agriculture schools, the merchant marine academy in New York City, the two State teachers' colleges and nine normal schools. It prescribes regulations for admission to professional study, and, with the exception of Law, issues licenses for the practice of the professions after examination; and for secondary schools it prescribes syllabi and examinations—formidable barriers known to high school students briefly as 'regents'—leading to a diploma generally accepted for admission to college. It administers the State library and the State museum and directs the preservation and publication of public records; and it reviews and licenses motion pictures to be exhibited in the State. Finally, at the annual convocation of the University of the State of New York it confers honorary degrees. The Commissioner of Education, as executive officer of the Department, with the approval of the Regents apportions State aid and exercises judicial power in all purely educational controversies.

While the general administration of the educational system has thus been centralized, a large measure of local independence remains. More than 150 cities and villages manage their own school affairs, subject only to review by the State Department. Outside of these the State is divided into districts under elected trustees and qualified district superintendents, who are responsible to the Commissioner of Education.

The first schoolmaster to teach in New Amsterdam had to take in washing to make enough to live on. A public school, free for 20 pupils, seems to have been opened in New York City in 1732, but for more than 150 years the clergyman dominated in the classroom. The most notable educational event of provincial times was the incorporation of King's College, now Columbia, under Royal charter in 1754. A free school for Negro children was opened by the Manumission Society of New York in 1787; and in 1805 the Free School Society, of which Mayor De Witt Clinton was president, was organized to provide educational opportunity for children not eligible for admission to the church schools. In 1826 the society became the Public School Society. A public board of education was established in 1842, which co-operated with the society until the bodies merged under legislative act in 1853. In the 48 years of its existence the society trained nearly 1,200 teachers, who instructed about 600,000 children; further, it started a free academy, which grew into the present City College.

When the rural districts were set up in the upstate area in 1812, they were made small because of the difficulties of transportation; and the result was the one-room, one-teacher school, the 'little red schoolhouse' over which the American public has waxed sentimental but which in the eyes of the professional educator is both expensive and inefficient. Under the Union Free School Act of 1853, a few hundred districts were consolidated into larger 'union free school' districts; and after 1925, under the stimulus of generous State grants, some 2,500 districts were consolidated into about 180 centralized districts, which erected the new central schools that enhance the appearance of many a roadside village. Yet in 1938 there were still 6,000 one-room, one-teacher schools, 2,000 of them with less than 10 children and 2,800 with from 10 to 20 children.

Secondary education in the State first took the form of private and semipublic academies, which were chartered in large numbers and which dominated the field until after the Civil War. Then, as the common school system was extended upward, most of these were absorbed within the expanding public high school system. The first teacher-training courses with State aid were given in several academies in 1835. The first State normal school was opened in Albany in 1844.

Union College, chartered in 1795, is the oldest upstate institution of higher learning. For many years before the Civil War, under the administration of Eliphalet Nott, it was the largest college in the country. The introduction of a civil engineering course in 1845 determined its permanent character, combining the pursuit of the liberal arts and pure sciences with the professional study of engineering within the limits of a small college. Hamilton College, chartered in 1812, has remained a purely liberal arts institution. Hobart was chartered in 1825. In 1826 Rensselaer Polytechnic Institute was incorporated 'for the purpose of instructing persons who may choose to apply themselves in the application of science to the common purposes of life'; today it is the oldest engineering school in the country. Madison—now Colgate—University was incorporated in 1846; Rochester in 1851; St.Lawrence in 1856; Alfred in 1857; Cornell in 1865; Syracuse, 1870; St.Bonaventure's, 1875; Canisius and Niagara, 1883.

While many female seminaries and 'colleges' existed earlier, Elmira, chartered in 1855, was the first institution of full collegiate rank in the country devoted to the education of women. Vassar College, incorporated in 1861, was opened in 1865; Wells College was chartered in 1868. Other institutions, like Cornell, Buffalo, St.Lawrence, Syracuse, and Rochester, are coeducational.

Best known of New York City's institutions of higher learning is Columbia University, with which are affiliated Barnard College, Bard College, and the New York Post-Graduate Medical School. New York University is another large institution, its Washington Square branch offering extensive cultural and professional curricula in evening classes. Fordham University is the largest Catholic institution of higher learning in the United States, and Manhattan College is another Catholic institution of considerable renown. Cooper Union, chartered in 1859 for the advancement of science and art, has given more than 200,000 students free instruction in science, engineering, and the fine arts. The city department of education exercises jurisdiction over the public libraries of the metropolis and controls the operation of City, Hunter, Brooklyn, and Queens Colleges, all financed by the city. From 400,000 to 500,000 adults annually take advantage of free educational facilities offered in New York City.

In 1936 New York State, including the city and Long Island, had 70 degree-granting colleges, universities, and professional schools; 1,200 high schools and academies; about 11,000 elementary schools, 100 vocational and continuation schools, 11 State teachers' institutions, 130 training schools for nurses, 16 schools for defectives and delinquents, and 22 Indian schools on the reservations. The student body included 1,750,000 in the elementary and 800,000 in the secondary schools, 100,000 in vocational and continuation schools, 150,000 in colleges and universities, 8,000 in teacher-training institutions, and 5,000 in special schools. About 400,000 pupils were enrolled in parochial and private schools. Members of the teaching profession in the State numbered close to 100,000. In 1936 expenditures for the public school system amounted to $350,000,000, one third contributed by the State, the rest raised locally.

When to these expenditures are added the sums spent for private schools and colleges and universities, it may safely be stated that the State of New York spends more than $1,000,000 a day on education. To complete the picture it is necessary to add the important contributions made by libraries and museums—historical, scientific, art—and their varied services, university extension, public forums, adult education, and education by radio.

Newspapers and Radio

WILLIAM Bradford's New York *Gazette*, issued on November 8, 1725, in New York City, was the first newspaper published in what is now New York State. Perhaps the most notable event in early New York journalism was the trial and acquittal of John Peter Zenger, editor of the rival *Weekly Journal*, who was prosecuted in 1734 in an attempt by the 'court party' to throttle the freedom of the press.

Although the Albany *Gazette* was founded in 1771, the power of the press was first felt in upstate New York in 1777, when John Holt, fleeing from the British, moved his New York *Journal and General Advertiser* from New York City to Kingston. When the British burned Kingston the next year, Holt moved to Poughkeepsie and published his paper there until the end of the war. Another refugee, Samuel Loudon, issued the first number of the New York *Packet and American Advertiser* in Fishkill in 1777. The Long Island *Herald* was first published in Sag Harbor in 1791.

The close of the Revolution ushered in an era of greatly stimulated journalistic endeavor. The young Republic was struggling to establish itself, and the people were avidly interested in news. Political issues were hot and discussion often took the form of scurrilous personal attacks. An attack on President Jefferson published by Harry Croswell in *The Wasp* at Hudson resulted in the second great battle establishing the principle of freedom of the press. In 1805 the State legislature enacted a law embodying the principle enunciated at Croswell's trial by Alexander Hamilton, who argued for the right to publish 'truth with good motives and for justifiable ends, even though it reflects on government.'

Newspapers were established in large numbers, multiplying in the older communities and spreading westward with the tide of settlement. By 1810 newspapers were being published at points as far west as Bath and Canandaigua; by 1820 they were appearing in Batavia and Buffalo, Watertown, Ogdensburg, and Plattsburg. Most of the papers were weekly or biweekly; the first daily west of Albany was the Rochester *Daily Advertiser*, founded in 1826. Among the important early papers were the Schenectady *Mohawk Mercury* (1796); the *Ulster County Gazette* (1798), which was a principal organ of the Federalist Party and died with that party in

1822; the Buffalo *Gazette* (1811); the Albany *Argus* (1813); the Rochester *Gazette* (1816); the Utica *Observer* (1817); and the Syracuse *Onondaga Gazette* (1823).

Making a direct appeal to the predominantly rural clientele, many papers carried the term 'farmer' or 'agriculturist' in their mastheads. The list included the *Farmer's Register* of Lansingburg and Troy (1803), the Republican *Agriculturist* of Norwich (1818), the Saratoga *Farmer* (1820), the *Seneca Farmer* of Waterloo (1823), and the Republican *Farmer's Free Press* of Herkimer (1830). None of these, however, could be considered agricultural journals. The *Plow Boy*, founded by Solomon Southwick in Albany, June 5, 1819, pioneered in the field of agricultural journalism in the State; but the *Genesee Farmer*, published in Rochester in 1831, was the first significant agricultural paper. Reflecting the practical experience of its editor and publisher, Luther Tucker, this paper became a powerful influence for agricultural progress. In 1853 it was merged with the *Country Gentleman*, another Tucker publication, printed in Albany. Other farm papers were the *Quarterly Journal of Agriculture*, Albany, 1845; the *Monthly Journal of Agriculture*, New York, 1845; the *Working Farmer*, New York, 1849; and the *Rural New-Yorker*, New York, 1850. The last named and the *Country Gentleman* survive as publications with national circulation.

The early upstate journalist was fundamentally a printer, his paper merely an appendage of his printing and stationery business and bookshop. Despite the fact that he was usually on the verge of bankruptcy, he wielded a wide influence in the affairs of his community. He was too busy with a thousand and one odd jobs to pen editorials, and often he was a typesetter at heart, with no ability or inclination to write; but he achieved full expression for his partisanship by clipping the writings of 'Camillus' and 'Aristides' from city papers and serving as a sounding board for the voices of party leaders. The rest of the paper was made up of republished public documents and advertising. The Albany *Register* of August 17, 1813, carried a full front page of advertisements, including 'A Proposal for Publishing a Periodical Work Entitled, Theological Magazine and Religious Repository'; a notice of 'Union College Lottery No.4. Second Part. Commence Drawing, October 1. Highest Prizes $25,000, $20,000, and $10,000'; announcements of steamboat sailings on Lake Champlain and the Hudson River; and offerings of Jamaica rum, lots on Patroon Street, Merino and common wool, and other goods for sale. Some papers featured a Poet's Corner, where the patriotic and sentimental effusions of local versifiers broke in upon the otherwise secondhand content.

For 50 years after the Revolution there was little improvement in the process of printing on crude, hand-driven presses. Legend has it that Elias Williams, who started the Genesee *Intelligencer* in 1807 with a secondhand press, spent an entire winter sorting out a box of old and considerably pied type. The publisher was further hampered by the difficulty of procuring paper. Since he could seldom afford to invest in a large stock, he depended upon the uncertain means of transportation from Albany and New York and often was obliged to scrimp while waiting for a fresh supply. In 1799 several issues of the Poughkeepsie *Journal* were reduced in size because a shipment of paper by boat from New York had been delayed. The printer often solicited materials for papermaking and urged his readers to save rags as a public duty.

In 1830 the Albany *Evening Journal* was founded by Thurlow Weed, who had previously enjoyed a varied newspaper experience in a number of upstate communities. He acted as reporter, editor, and proofreader; he penned terse Whig editorials, opposed the administration of Andrew Jackson, advocated the building of the Erie Canal, and co-operated with William H. Seward and Horace Greeley in the overthrow of the Democratic political organization known as the Albany Regency, led by Martin Van Buren and represented in the field of journalism by the Albany *Argus*. During the political campaign of 1838 Horace Greeley published the Albany *Jeffersonian*, a political journal that was discontinued the following year.

During the 1850's, with the problems of slavery, temperance reform, and free schools causing bitter factionalism along loosely drawn party lines, newspapers strongly reflected the tangled state of politics. Many sheets, formerly Democratic, transferred their support to the Republican party, and by 1865 the upstate press had become predominantly Republican. The Ithaca *Journal*, founded in 1827, is a case in point. A staunch Jacksonian organ, denouncing Harrison's policies and the Whigs in 1840, it wabbled editorially during the Mexican War, in 1848 swung its support to Van Buren and the Free Soilers, and finally supported Fremont and the new Republican party in 1856.

The Civil War produced a general change in journalism in which New York State newspapers shared. With readers clamoring for war news, weeklies became dailies and almost all papers increased their number of pages. Sunday editions appeared. Stereotyping, first tried in 1861, became a standard process. As a result of the increased use of the telegraph and the growth of the Associated Press and other agencies, papers improved tremendously in news value. But conservatism remained the keynote of journalism: the headlines announcing Lee's surrender were universally held to one column.

The development of the modern newspaper has been characterized by an ever-spreading standardization, facilitated by the growth of press associations, the establishment of feature syndicates furnishing low-cost articles and illustrations, and, above all, the extension of newspaper chains.

The process of standardization has extended to telegraph news, which is concentrated on the first page, and to features, so that a motorist, crossing the State in a day, will find in the city newspapers from Albany to Buffalo identical national and international news items, the same feature articles, and in some instances the same editorials. The independent small-town newspaper, while standardized and colorless in its wire news and dependent to some extent on pages of 'boilerplate,' still in many cases retains a degree of individuality as a personal rostrum for the editor-publisher, and frequently contains interesting feature articles on local history.

The upstate papers learned from the metropolitan press the value of lively reporting, a terse style, banner headlines built on positive statement and action, lurid features, and the other characteristics of the present-day newspapers. Until recently the Hearst chain included a number of papers in upstate urban centers, but in 1939 the Albany *Times-Union* was the sole survivor. Frank E. Gannett's chain of newspapers began with the merger of two papers in Elmira in 1907 to form the *Star-Gazette*; in Ithaca the *Journal* and the *News* became the *Journal-News*; in Rochester the *Union and Advertiser* and the *Evening Times* became the *Times Union*; in Utica the *Observer* and the *Herald-Despatch* became the *Observer-Despatch*. Within a period of 15 years Gannett purchased additional papers in Newburgh, Beacon, Olean, Albany, Ogdensburg, Brooklyn, Malone, Saratoga Springs, and Massena. Today the Gannett chain forms the largest group in the State and the third largest in the United States.

In the process of consolidation newspapers were dealt in like parcels of real estate with the advertising market as the determining factor. As a result many of them have lost much of their former prestige as community institutions and have become largely business enterprises and media for standardized propaganda and innocuous local news and gossip. In addition to its 211 daily and 1,057 weekly papers, upstate New York supports 52 college, 13 religious, and 15 foreign-language publications.

Today eight major dailies gather news for New York City, of which the *Times* is generally considered the best as a newspaper. Its nearest rival is the *Herald-Tribune*, descended from the famous papers of Horace Greeley and James Gordon Bennett. The *Post*, which had a national reputation under William Cullen Bryant, is interesting for its editorial outspokenness. The *Daily News*, a tabloid, has the largest circulation; the *Daily Worker* is the outstanding Communist paper in the country. The Brooklyn *Daily Eagle* is the best-known metropolitan newspaper published outside Manhattan. The foreign-language population is supplied by 35 dailies, of which 21 publish Sunday editions. New York Negroes support three weeklies. All the major press associations have their headquarters in the city.

RADIO

Technical progress in radio broadcasting during the past two decades has been tremendous. Scientists were carrying on laboratory experiments at the Schenectady plant of the General Electric Company before the World War, and Station WGY 'went on the air' February 20, 1922. Within a few weeks wire connections were made with churches, theaters, and hotels in Schenectady and Albany, and the first 'outside pick-ups' marked the beginning of an extensive wire network. The Schenectady station, distinctive in the field of radio broadcasting because of its pioneering activities, was the first to broadcast religious services direct from churches, world series baseball games, Presidential addresses, and ringside descriptions of prize fights—all before the organization of the National Broadcasting Company.

WHAZ, Rensselaer Polytechnic Institute station in Troy, followed WGY on the air in August 1922, and soon established a record for long-distance transmission when one of its regular broadcasts was picked up in New Zealand. Other early upstate stations were WCAD in Canton, WGR in Buffalo, WHAM in Rochester, and WSYR in Syracuse.

Sound effects, which have become one of the chief props of radio showmanship, were crudely introduced in 1922 when a small group of players began producing one-act plays over WGY. Actors reproduced the sound of running horses by pounding the pillows of the studio couch, the crackle of flames by rumpling a piece of paper in front of the microphone, and the drone of an airplane motor by holding cardboard against the blades of an electric fan. Full-length dramas presently replaced the one-act plays, mechanical gadgets and adroit trickery brought realistic sound effects, and a season of stage adaptations played by experienced actors proved the possibilities of radio drama and the existence of a large listening audience.

Commercial broadcasting has been guided by the principle of diversity. Program directors, failing to find an accurate measuring stick, aimed at the shifting target of popularity by mixing opera with jazz, comedy with drama. Stock market reports, political harangues, and lectures on literature, agriculture, and psychology were carried over the networks along with high-pressure blurbs about tooth paste, breakfast food, and cures for the common cold.

A New York City radio station, WEAF, established by the American Telephone and Telegraph Company, was the first to offer its facilities on a time-rental basis to commercial sponsors. This was in 1922. In the same year a New York station sent its program by wire to be broadcast simultaneously from Chicago, and WEAF became the originating point of a broadcasting chain. The four largest national broadcasting networks— NBC red, NBC blue, and the Columbia and Mutual Systems—have their home in the city, as do two regional networks and a tributary station of WLW, Cincinnati, one of the most powerful stations in the country.

Today New York State is served by 48 stations, nine of which are controlled by the National Broadcasting Company and eight by the Columbia Broadcasting System. A recent report of the Committee on Radio Research shows 2,993,100 radio-equipped homes in the State and places the State's radio audience at 11,670,000. Commercial revenues have grown each year; the income of the two major networks within the State rose from $4,000,000 in 1927 to well over $42,000,000 in 1936. In 15 years a toy became a large-scale industry.

Sports

EVERY reader of Washington Irving knows that the Dutch in the lower Hudson Valley played ninepins. They also enjoyed kolf, a game between teams not unlike modern field hockey, which was popular well into the eighteenth century, until a crimp was put in its popularity by a legislative enactment in 1760 prohibiting its being played on Sunday. The English introduced three sports—horse racing, cock-fighting, and animal baiting, the first now restored to favor, the last two prohibited, no doubt permanently.

In the first half of the nineteenth century sports were at an ebb. The horde of settlers from New England, revivalism, and new cults exercised a dampening influence; the feverish prosecution of expansion and internal improvement—canal digging and railroad building—seemed to leave no time or strength for play. But German and Irish immigrants, as they achieved a degree of economic well-being with accompanying leisure, gave vent to their love of sports and recreation. The Civil War was a decisive influence: men from different sections of the country were thrown together in camps and learned one another's games, with the result that the years after the Civil War were the period of organization and development of sports.

Abner Doubleday invented modern baseball at Cooperstown in 1839 and rules were formulated in 1845, but the present 'big leagues' date from the last quarter of the century. Out of a rough-and-tumble sort of rugby played by Americans of English descent, Gerrit Smith Miller of Cazenovia evolved in 1860-2 a scheme of co-ordinated team play that became the basis of modern American football. Horse racing was popular at the early county fairs, but the first jockey club was organized no earlier than 1868. In the light-harness field, while Hambletonian began in 1852 the siring of more than 1,200 foals, including Dexter, 'king of the turf,' and the dams and sires of many other champions, the organization of associations and the establishment of large purses waited until the seventies and later. Other sports—lawn tennis (first played on Staten Island), polo, track athletics, basketball—were introduced and organized in the same period.

Golf was introduced at Yonkers in 1888 and organized in 1894. The bicycle craze reached its peak in 1900.

Of New York City's three big-league baseball clubs, the Yankees draw the largest share of 3,000,000 customers each season. The Black Yankees represent the city in the National Negro Baseball League. Amateur and semipro baseball is hampered by lack of space for diamonds, but softball is played on all playgrounds and on many vacant lots. Most prevalent form of the game is stickball, played by boys with a broomstick and a rubber ball on almost any side street.

Professional baseball is represented in upstate New York by a number of minor leagues, the individual teams serving as 'farms' for big-league clubs. Semiprofessional twilight leagues, organized for the season, draw crowds through their appeal to local rivalries as well as to interest in the game. The teams are often sponsored by local business men, and the players, who share the proceeds of the hat collections, have regular occupations during the day. Softball is gaining in popularity, especially as part of intramural sports programs of colleges and large industrial and commercial organizations.

Boxing and wrestling are almost entirely limited to professional circles and are sponsored by local sporting clubs. Basketball, outside of school and college games, is also professionally played throughout the State under local auspices; it is said to attract more spectators than any other sport. First-class horse racing is carried on in Goshen, Saratoga, Yonkers, and Long Island; in the metropolitan area there are four tracks—Belmont, Jamaica, Aqueduct, and Empire City. The State Racing Commission supplements the work of the Jockey Club in guarding against irregularities and injustices; it introduced the use of the camera eye to decide closely contested races. Betting evils have been lessened by the action of the legislature and track stewards; pari-mutuel betting was authorized by vote of the people in 1939 and was introduced in 1940. The national center of light-harness racing is Goshen, but the sport is also featured at the State fair and at most county fairs. Competition is keen; many owners drive their own trotters and pacers; and purses and side bets are often large.

Professional football has not yet invaded upstate New York to any large extent, where the sport is still monopolized by college teams, the amateur standing of which is not always above suspicion. The 'big three' of the upstate area are Cornell, Colgate, and Syracuse; the Army team, representing the U.S.Military Academy, enjoys national support; the smaller colleges carry on intense rivalries. Receipts from admissions to football games finance a large share of the college sports programs, which include baseball, track, tennis, hockey, soccer, lacrosse, and rowing; basketball is usually self-sustaining. The culmination of the national college rowing season is the Poughkeepsie regatta in June.

In the metropolitan area five college football teams draw 1,000,000 spectators each season; the Army-Navy or Army-Notre Dame game pulls 90,000 more. Professional football, however, has proved one of the city's two wonder sports—the other is professional hockey. Boxing, hockey, and basketball—the big-time varieties—center at Madison Square Garden.

The two sports with the largest number of participants are tennis and golf. Every city and many a village and private organization have built tennis courts as part of their athletic facilities, and the number of municipal golf courses has been growing rapidly. More than 135 courses have reported to the Bureau of State Publicity as conditionally available to transients; the total number of courses in the State is much larger. Soccer is popular in New York City. Here, too, a number of exotic games are played by foreign groups: Italians lay out an alley for *bocci* wherever vacant ground is available; hurley is played fiercely by the local Irish at Innisfail Park; and in Van Cortlandt Park men from the West Indies play an adaptation of cricket.

Until recently winter sports have been limited to skating and coasting and to indoor games like bowling, volleyball, handball, and squash racquets played principally on local Y.M.C.A. courts. But in the past few years skiing has caught the popular fancy. Week-end snow trains and automobiles carry thousands to ski trails in the Taconics, the Hudson Highlands, the Catskills, the Adirondacks, and other sections of the State. Another newcomer is the Scottish game of curling, played on ice rinks; teams in Schenectady, Utica, and other upstate centers compete among themselves and with New England and Canadian teams.

The Arts

THE boundaries of a State are difficult limits to observe in any account of creative activity in the arts. That problem is especially acute in the State that includes New York City, which, by virtue of its great wealth, its concentration of population, its huge publishing industry, and the pre-eminence of its art critics and institutions, has long been the arbiter of the arts in the United States. The role played by the city has been adequately described in *New York Panorama* (1938) and *New York City Guide* (1939) of the American Guide Series. The short accounts that follow will therefore deal primarily with the upstate area.

In respect to the arts, upstate New York is but part of the hinterland that extends 3,000 miles west of the metropolis. Most of the writers, actors, artists, and musicians who were born within its boundaries were attracted to the center of activities in New York City and to the more mature and self-conscious environments of Europe; some of them lived long enough in the upstate area to carry its influence into their work; some returned to make its natural or its human scene the subject matter of their creative activity, in which they were joined by outsiders.

Because of its proximity to the metropolis, the upstate area was drained of its creative artists probably more rapidly and more thoroughly than other sections of the country. But in recent years it has been compensated by the widespread tendency of artists and writers to retreat from the crowded city and make their homes on its farms, among its mountains, and along its lake shores. Some of them settled in 'colonies'; others consulted their individual tastes and desires. A complete list of these would occupy too much space; it would include Max Eastman, Edna St.Vincent Millay, Floyd Dell, Stuart Chase, Waldo Frank, Maxwell Anderson, Herbert Asbury, Robert Benchley, Whit Burnett, Margaret Foley, Theodore Dreiser, Paul Corey, Ruth Lechlitner, Will Durant, John T. Flynn, Horace Gregory, Ben Hecht, Granville Hicks, John Howard Lawson, Sinclair Lewis, Lewis Mumford, Charles MacArthur, Burton Rascoe, William Seabrook, Vincent Sheean, Louis Untermeyer, Rockwell Kent, Margaret Widdemer, Brooks Atkinson.

LITERATURE

Early literature in New York consisted principally of sermons, historical writings, and letters and promotional pamphlets to attract settlers and investors; the verse, such as it is, is interesting only to specialists. An important source of information are the contemporary accounts of travelers and visitors. Cadwallader Colden wrote his *History of the Five Nations* to correct the false impressions of the Iroquois created by the French. William Smith was the first historian of New York, his *History of the Province of New York* appearing in London in 1757. In his *Letters from an American Farmer* St.John de Crèvecœur, who farmed for a number of years in Orange County, presents a sympathetic and eloquent picture of life on the frontier and its democratic processes. Mrs.Anne Grant, in her *Memoirs of an American Lady*, describes the tranquil, democratic society of Colonial Albany as she knew it in her childhood.

Between the passage of the Stamp Act and the adoption of the Constitution the quill was devoted primarily to protest, propaganda, and politics. Thomas Paine's *Common Sense* and *The Crisis* made him the most effective of the Revolutionary pamphleteers; after his English and French experiences, he spent his last years on his farm at New Rochelle. Philip Freneau, the poet of the Revolution, described with fervent patriotism, but in verse imitative of the English neoclassical poets, the 'atrocities' he suffered on British prison ships in New York harbor, and wrote delicate lyrics showing a keen, sensitive awareness of natural beauty. *The Federalist*, written by Hamilton, Madison, and Jay in defense of the Constitution and a strong central government, remains one of the outstanding works of American political thought.

Literary history proper may be said to begin in New York State with Washington Irving (1783–1859), its first outstanding man of letters. *Salmagundi* and *Dietrich Knickerbocker's History of New York* are satirical treatments of life in the city in his own day and during the Dutch period. But the determining factor in his literary career, taken as a whole, was his long absence abroad. *The Legend of Sleepy Hollow* and *Rip Van Winkle*, the two stories localized in the Hudson Valley upon which his continuing popular reputation rests, appeared in *The Sketch Book*, which was published in England and had English life and manners as its main theme. Thereafter Irving's chief interest was Spanish history, though he also wrote a life of Washington and an account of the fur trade for his patron, John Jacob Astor. At home near Tarrytown on the Hudson soon after his return from Europe in 1832, Irving brought the influence of a larger cultural world to the New York literary scene; but, like his famous character, old Rip, he was not altogether at ease in the bustling surge of a growing democracy.

James Kirke Paulding (1778–1860), Irving's *Salmagundi* collaborator, was the lesser artist but was more responsive to the native scene, pioneering in realistic fiction, welcoming the passing of the landed aristocracy, and satirizing the Whig party. Fitz-Greene Halleck (1790–1867) and Joseph Rodman Drake (1795–1820) co-operated in writing the humorous, satirical 'Croaker' verses; Halleck 'lamented the wane of romance'; Drake was one of the first to turn Hudson Valley scenery into accountable verse. John Howard Payne (1791–1852) collaborated with Irving in the writing of plays and achieved some reputation as a playwright, but is remembered only for his sentimental lyric, *Home, Sweet Home.* During his long editorship of the New York *Evening Post* William Cullen Bryant (1794–1878) supported every liberal cause, including the right of labor to organize, and risked the life of his paper by attacking the financial oligarchy of his day. Although considered essentially a New England poet, Bryant found inspiration for lyrics in the countryside about his Roslyn home, in the Catskills, and in the Hudson Valley.

The fame of James Fenimore Cooper (1789–1851) rests chiefly on the five Leatherstocking Tales, which comprise a biography of the scout, Natty Bumppo, one of the outstanding figures of American fiction. Vivid characters, sustained action, and a strong romantic atmosphere won for these novels a wide popular audience in both America and Europe. For his descriptions of the frontier wilderness Cooper drew upon his memories of New York State. If in these tales Cooper idealized the Indian as the 'unspoiled child of nature,' he can be forgiven in view of the prevailing characterization of the native as ignorant, bloodthirsty, and treacherous.

But the popularity of these romances and his sea stories has obscured the importance of Cooper's novels of manners and social purpose. Most significant are *Satanstoe* (1845), *The Chainbearer* (1846), and *The Redskins* (1846), in which he deals with the antirent wars and the decline of the aristocracy in New York State. Tied to the landed gentry by birth and marriage, Cooper fought against the equalitarian tendencies of the time. 'The notion,' he wrote in *The Redskins*, 'that every husbandman is to be a freeholder is as utopian in practice as it would be to expect that all men were to be on the same level in fortune, condition, education, and habits.' In his view, stability in democracy depends upon the recognition of a landed aristocracy as a reservoir of culture.

In the mid-nineteenth century, New York State, unlike New England,

had no 'schools,' no groups of writers clustered around and receiving coloration from a man or an idea. Writers here were rather isolated figures,
sharing, it is true, in the common romanticism, but achieving a sharply
personalized expression of that impulse. Herman Melville and Walt Whitman were both born in 1819, one in New York City, the other on Long Island; but their paths lay far apart and their readings of life are antithetical.

After a contented childhood in the city, Melville spent his teens in the
Albany-Troy district as a poor relation at the table of his mother's family,
the Gansevoorts. From 1841 to 1844 he sailed the seven seas on a whaler
and on an American man-of-war; and then he returned home to set down
his disillusions in *Typee*, *Mardi*, *Moby-Dick*, and *Pierre*. None of his books
after the first won immediate popular approval; and, though he lived
until 1891, his significantly creative life ended at the age of 33. Not until
the post-World War years was the significance of his bitter renunciation
of transcendental optimism adequately appreciated.

Whitman, on the contrary, was the last, most vociferous, and most un-
critical poet of transcendentalism, affirming in discursive physical imagery
his egotism and his utter faith in democracy based on an all-embracing
comradeship. Whitman lived his early years on Long Island, listening to
the surf, teaching school, carpentering, editing newspapers, crossing the
ferry to mingle with the crowds on the streets of Manhattan. The first edition of *Leaves of Grass* drew the scorn of the genteel men of letters of the
time; and his later verse, most of it reflecting his sobering Civil War experiences, was little better received. But appreciation of his significance in
literature has steadily grown. Aroused by Emerson's call to the youth of
America, he brought America's literary dependence on England to an end.
As an old man he settled in Camden, New Jersey, where he received homage as the 'good gray poet' and where he died in 1892.

For the rest, the pre-Civil War literary production of the State is more
notable for quantity than quality. Susan B. Warner (1819–85) and
Anna B. Warner (1827–1915), sister spinsters who lived on Constitution
Island near West Point, under the pseudonyms 'Elizabeth Wetherell' and
'Amy Lothrop' wrote novels heavy with moral teaching and sugared with
romance. The former's *The Wide, Wide World* was, after *Uncle Tom's
Cabin*, perhaps the most widely read book in nineteenth-century America.
Mary Jane Holmes (1825–1907), who lived in Brockport for many years,
won countrywide attention with *Tempest and Sunshine* and other novels.
The Reverend Joel Tyler Headley, born in 1813 in Walton, wrote more
than 30 volumes of biography, history, and travel, which by 1853 had
reached a total of 200,000 copies; the total up to his death in Newburgh in

1897 has not been computed. The letters of Nathaniel Parker Willis (1806–67), poet and journalist, and resident of Cornwall-on-Hudson, were widely popular in book form. As wife of a clergyman in Elmira, Mrs.Frances Miriam Whitcher, born in Whitesboro in 1814, wrote a number of mild satires for *Godey's Lady's Book* and other publications that almost caused her ostracism by her neighbors.

In the post-Civil War years one figure stands out, as much a product and part of upstate New York as Cooper and, though destined by his genre to a more restricted audience, of comparative stature. John Burroughs, poet-naturalist, was born near Roxbury in the Catskills in 1837, and as a boy ranged the mountains, observing birds, trees, and flowers while he steeped himself in the transcendental philosophy of Emerson. In his mid-twenties he worked in the Treasury Department in Washington, where he met Whitman. Thereafter, except for several long trips, his years were spent in his beloved Catskill Mountains, to which he belongs in much the same way as Wordsworth belongs to the Lake Country. On his farm on the west bank of the Hudson 80 miles above New York, and at his birthplace in the mountains, he wrote a book almost every two years. His development moved from a recording of the world about him, as in *Wake Robin* and *Birds and Poets*, through an interest in philosophical views of the world, to a wholehearted acceptance of the scientific approach that remained paramount until his death in 1921. Henry James said that Burroughs was 'a sort of reduced—more available, Thoreau.' Certain it is that he made the natural world of more interest to the American reading public than ever before. Raymond T. Fuller, in Sullivan County, and Alan Devoe, in Columbia County, carry on the Burroughs tradition today.

Upstate New York bulks large in two other fields of nineteenth-century American literature: in books for boys and girls—those read openly and those read surreptitiously; and in indigenous humor.

John T. Trowbridge (1827–1916), born in Ogden Township, Monroe County, published a number of adventure stories and Civil War novels. Frank G. Patchin (1861–1925), born in Wayland, produced more than 200 adventure books for boys and girls, including the Circus Boy series and the Grace Harlowe Overland Rider series. Charles Austin Fosdick, under the pen name 'Harry Castlemon,' rivaled the popularity of Horatio Alger,Jr., with his *Frank, the Young Naturalist* and his Gunboat, Rocky Mountain, and Boy Trapper series; Fosdick was born in Randolph in 1842, lived for many years in Westfield, and died almost forgotten in Hamburg in 1915. Edward Zane Carroll Judson (1823–86), under the name 'Ned Buntline,' popularized the American 'dime novel,' with William F.

Cody, to whom he gave the name 'Buffalo Bill,' as his hero. Judson's life was almost as melodramatic as one of his plots. Born in Stamford in 1823, he ran away to sea as a boy, beginning a career, notorious in his day, as infamous adventurer and political demagogue with the Know-Nothing Party, plus a very brief and ignoble period as a soldier in the Civil War. But the last 15 years of his life he spent as a respectable citizen in his native town.

In contrast to these were the books of Edward Payson Roe (1838–88) and Isabelle McDonald Alden (1841–1930); in a day when novels were considered instruments of Satan, the works of these two authors were not only permitted reading for the children of pious families on the Sabbath, but even had their place in Sunday School libraries. Roe, who lived in Cornwall-on-Hudson, was a country preacher turned author, and his elevating moral tales like *Barriers Burned Away* and *Near to Nature's Heart* sold hundreds of thousands of copies. Mrs.Alden, native of Rochester and wife of a Presbyterian minister, wrote more than 120 volumes, most of them books for girls—*Chautauqua Girls at Home, Six Little Girls*, etc. Dillon Wallace (1863–1939) wrote a number of popular boys' books based on his expeditions into Labrador. Finally, Lyman Frank Baum, one of the foremost writers for the young in the English-speaking world, who was born in Chittenango in 1856, achieved acclaim, long after he had left the State, for *Father Goose: His Book* and the *Wizard of Oz* series. Baum died in Hollywood, California, in 1919.

Best known of the humorists associated with New York State is Henry Wheeler Shaw (Josh Billings). Born in Lanesboro, Massachusetts, in 1818, Shaw attended Hamilton College, from which he was expelled in his second year. After 20 years in the West, he returned to New York, settling finally in Poughkeepsie as auctioneer, real estate agent, and politician. He began his career as a humorist in 1860 with his *Essa on the Muel bi Josh Billings*, and the success of his laconic essays, homely philosophy, and popular almanacs lasted beyond his death in 1885. In a similar vein was the humor of Melville De Lancey Landon (1839–1910), born in Eaton, Madison County; his 'Eli Perkins,' as Saratoga correspondent for the New York *Commercial Advertiser*, won him a Nation-wide reputation. Marietta Holley (1836–1926), living most of her life as a semi-recluse near her birthplace in Ellisburgh, New York, was popular both at home and abroad with her *Samantha* books—a simple, humorous portrayal of her own North Country people as observed by and reflected in 'Josiah Allen's wife.' Of more limited association with the State were: David Ross Locke (1833–88), born in Vestal near Binghamton, who left the State at the age of 17 and whose 'Petroleum V. Nasby' letters were an important contribution to Northern propaganda in the Civil War; Bret Harte (1836–1902), author of *The Luck of Roaring Camp*, who left Albany for California when he was a youth; and Mark Twain, once editor of the Buffalo *Express* and frequent summer visitor in Elmira, where he worked on several of his well-known books.

Of the upstate poets of the nineteenth century, few are worthy of note. The appeal of the sisters Davidson of Plattsburg—Lucretia Maria, born in 1808, and Margaret Miller, born in 1823—to the religious and sentimental readers of their time was enhanced by their untimely death from tuberculosis at the ages of 16 and 15. Two poems by Alfred Billings Street (1811–81) of Poughkeepsie, *The Gray Forest Eagle* and *Lost Hunter*, have given him a place among our minor poets.

Like native humor a transitional phase between romanticism and realism, the local color movement, stressing local scenes and local characters, first found expression, rather belatedly, in upstate New York in the last years of the century. *Seth's Brother's Wife* by Harold Frederic (1856–98), native of Utica, Albany editor, and foreign correspondent for the New York *Times*, depicts the drabness of upstate farm life. His *Damnation of Theron Ware* is a study of the lay and clerical leaders of the Methodist Church. *David Harum* by Edward Noyes Westcott, born in Syracuse in 1846, is an indulgent character study of a village banker; several publishers rejected the manuscript on the ground that it was 'unpleasant,' so the book was published only after Westcott's death in 1898, but it soon won a country-wide success. Irving Bacheller's novels, *Eben Holden* and *D'ri and I*, and his autobiography, *Coming up the Road*, portray the life of the North Country, where he was born in 1859. Grace Miller White's *Tess of the Storm Country* is a melodramatic account of the struggles of the despised squatters on the Ithaca lake shore with the respectable folk in the hill section of town. Samuel Hopkins Adams, born in Dunkirk in 1871, has written a number of successful books, often with a social theme as background; his *Siege* is a sympathetic study of an upstate strike, and *Revelry*, national in theme, is an exposé of the ruling clique during the Harding administration. Carl Carmer, native of Cortland, describes varied aspects of upstate life and folklore in *Listen for a Lonesome Drum*, and in *The Hudson* gives a vivid account of the State's most important river valley. Bellamy Partridge's *Country Lawyer* portrays life in the late Victorian period in Phelps, New York.

Partly overlapping this local color theme are the many historical novels that have mined the rich vein of history in upstate New York. Frederic's

In the Valley is a chronicle of the Mohawk Valley during the Revolution, climaxed by a graphic account of the stand at Oriskany. *Cardigan* by Robert W. Chambers (1865–1933), of Broadalbin, is a spirited romance with the same background. In *Jerusalem the Golden* Robert P. St.John tells the story of Jemima Wilkinson, the Universal Friend. In *Arundel* and *Rabble at Arms* Kenneth Roberts describes the Saratoga campaign. Roger Burlingame's *Three Bags Full* chronicles the development of central New York. Walter D. Edmonds, native of Boonville, has made the Erie Canal his subject in *Rome Haul*, *Erie Water*, and *Mostly Canallers*. His popular *Drums along the Mohawk* goes back to the Revolutionary struggle. Don Cameron Shafer, a resident of Schoharie, recasts the epic of the Schoharie Valley during the frontier period in *Smokefires in Schoharie*. The scene of *Artillery of Time*, Civil War novel by Chard Powers Smith, native of Watertown, is laid in the upstate area.

During the first quarter of the twentieth century New York State was the home of several successful writers of popular novels, including Grace S. Richmond of Fredonia, Mary Shipman Andrews of Onondaga, and Faith Baldwin of New Rochelle. Marjorie Rawlings, author of *The Yearling*, worked on newspapers in New York City and Rochester. Paul Horgan, born in Buffalo and associated with the Rochester Opera Company for several years, won the Harper prize in 1933 with his novel *Fault of Angels*, which satirized the pursuit of the arts in a provincial city.

Upstate New York's participation in the recent literary movements—realism, social revolt, muckraking, the new poetry, and the new criticism—has been the result of geographical location rather than of any indigenous stimulus. Hamlin Garland wrote much of his Middle Border series at his home in the mountains above Catskill. Theodore Dreiser came east and picked an upstate tragic figure for the principal character in *An American Tragedy*. Stephen Crane studied at Syracuse University but went to New York City to discover the slums and its 'creatures that were once men.' In poetry the renaissance championed in Boston by Amy Lowell and in Chicago by Harriet Monroe found a versatile promoter in Louis Untermeyer, who picked a mountain farm in the Adirondacks for a home. Edna St.Vincent Millay moved into Greenwich Village from Maine, but soon fled to the quiet of Columbia County hills. Max Eastman, who grew up in the Southern Tier, moved to New York to take part in the literature of revolt. Among the critics, Lewis Gannett grew up in Rochester, Lewis Mumford found a quiet spot in Dutchess County in which to write his books, and Granville Hicks selected the Grafton Mountains for his home.

THE THEATER

The early theater suffered the brunt of moral opposition to the arts. In 1750 a company in New York City was able to run continuously for four months. Lewis Hallam's troupe of London actors opened in a theater on Nassau Street in 1753, offering plays by Shakespeare, Congreve, and Addison. From 1758 to 1774 David Douglass operated with some security despite antagonism from the defenders of the public morals. The Dutch clergy denounced a performance of *The Beaux' Stratagem* by a group of British soldiers stationed in Albany in 1757, the first dramatic production north of New York City. In 1769 Douglass brought his company to Albany for a month. As late as 1785 the Albany *Gazette* mentioned a petition demanding that the Common Council refuse permission to play *The Taming of the Shrew* in that city, on the ground that the theater 'will drain us of our money, if not instill into the minds of the imprudent, principles incompatible with that virtue which is the true basis of republican liberty and happiness.'

During the Revolution the theater was kept alive only by the British officers stationed in New York, who, with the co-operation of women acquaintances, presented plays for six seasons. Political independence won, the call for cultural independence from England was answered by Royall Tyler (1757–1826) with his comedy, *The Contrast*, presented in New York on April 16, 1787. In it Jonathan, the first of the humorous Yankee characters, is a provincial boor with a Connecticut dialect; but his democratic principles, his patriotism, and his simple morality are extolled. William Dunlap (1766–1839), historian of the early stage, followed with *The Father; or, American Shandyism*, a comedy, and *André*, a tragedy.

The War of 1812 found the theater well established in New York and Albany. In 1813 John Bernard, actor-manager, opened the first theater built as such in the latter city. Moral opposition declined; a prologue promised

> No vile obscenity—in this blest age,
> Where mild Religion takes her heavenly reign . . .

and advised that

> . . . though 'mong players some there may be found
> Whose conduct is not altogether sound . . .
> Your remedy is good with such a teacher,
> Imbibe the precept, but condemn the preacher.

In Syracuse the top floor of a tavern was converted into a makeshift theater in 1823; the following year a theater was built in Rochester despite pleas that such wickedness be prohibited. In 1825 a modest playhouse was opened in Buffalo, its resident troupe traveling to near-by towns; the Troy Theater, in the Rensselaer House, opened with a resident company in 1828. Theaters were drab and meagerly equipped; Dunlap wrote of crude makeshift properties and of one set of costumes doing duty for the plays of an entire season.

By 1830 New York City had superseded Philadelphia as the country's theatrical center. But the stage in the upstate towns from Albany to Buffalo retained its independent vitality, presenting plays of the same quality as in New York and attracting the same stars. The repertory was principally Shakespeare and seventeenth- and eighteenth-century English drama, and many of the stars—Edmund Kean, Junius Brutus Booth, William Macready, Charles and Fanny Kemble, Ellen Tree—were imported from England. The showboat *Temple of the Muses* opened on the Hudson in 1845, playing *The Rent Day*, a popular London melodrama acidly portraying the grievous condition of English tenantry, which was warmly applauded by the Hudson Valley tenant farmers then in the midst of their antirent struggle. American plays, however, were well received, the two perennials being *Uncle Tom's Cabin* and *Rip Van Winkle*, in the latter of which Joseph Jefferson, third, starred from 1865 until 1904; and American stars like Edwin Forrest, Charlotte Cushman, and Edwin Booth shared the spotlight with their English colleagues. The first performance of George L. Aiken's adaptation of *Uncle Tom's Cabin* was given in Troy in 1852.

In the second half of the nineteenth century James W. Wallack and Augustin Daly subordinated the individual star to the well-rounded company. The eighties and nineties were the golden age of stock for both resident and road companies. Audiences were drawn by such melodramas as *The Black Crook* with its 'unprecedentedly generous display of the female figure,' *Under the Gas Light*, and *The Drunkard* interspersed with Shakespeare and other classical importations. It was in Albany's Green Street Theater in 1861 that Adah Isaacs Menken created a sensation when, clad in tights, she allowed herself to be bound to a horse for Mazeppa's wild ride; the incident has been called a forerunner of burlesque. The importance of Albany as a theatrical center is illustrated by the fact that the first performance in the United States of a play by George Bernard Shaw —*The Devil's Disciple*, starring Richard Mansfield—was presented in that city in 1897.

The modern commercialized theater began in the nineties and 1900's when Charles Frohman and the three Shubert brothers from Syracuse organized countrywide chains of theaters with headquarters in New York City. The new system overstressed the star at the expense of the supporting cast and produced plays with a sure-fire popular appeal. As a result a number of stage luminaries were developed—John Drew, Julia Marlowe, Otis Skinner, Ethel Barrymore; New York City was invested with monopolistic control of the American theater; the independent stock companies in Albany, Syracuse, Rochester, and Buffalo disappeared, and these cities became one-night stands for road companies repeating Broadway hits. This breakdown of the commercial theater upstate was made complete by the competition of the motion picture. A few resident stock companies and occasional traveling troupes, some of them acting in rural communities under tents, continued a fitful existence, performing three-year-old Broadway hits and old stand-bys like *Uncle Tom's Cabin, Ten Nights in a Barroom,* and other melodramatic thrillers. But in the thirties these disappeared, so that, except for an occasional visit of a New York City company, the stage in the upstate area lives today only in the widespread activities of amateur civic and college play groups and in the summer theaters, including the Mohawk Drama Festival directed by Charles Coburn at Union College, Schenectady.

From the earliest days the State has contributed its share of actors and playwrights. Frances Denny, born in Schenectady, became in 1820 'one of America's foremost actresses of tragic parts.' William James Florence, born in Albany, was one of the first great Irish comedians, and his wife, Melvina Pray, was the first American comic actress to play in London. Frances Starr, native of Oneonta, made her debut in Albany in 1901. Buffalo was the proving ground for several important figures of the stage—May Irwin, Chauncey Olcott, Katharine Cornell, and others. Clyde Fitch, one of the first playwrights to give drama a native vitality, was born in Elmira.

Ben Hecht lives at Nyack; his *Front Page, Crime without Passion,* and *The Scoundrel* achieved large success. Maxwell Anderson, author of *Winterset, High Tor,* and *Star Wagon,* the latter two dealing with the upstate scene, lives in New City. Rochester produced three successful contemporary playwrights: Philip Barry, who wrote the successful plays *You and I, Paris Bound,* and *Animal Kingdom*; George F. Abbott, who collaborated in the writing of *Broadway* and *The Fall Guy*; and George S. Brooks, whose *No Cause for Complaint* won first prize in a national social work play contest. Robert E. Sherwood, author of *The Petrified Forest, Idiot's Delight,* and other successful plays, was born in New Rochelle.

In New York City recent years have seen the rise of a number of experimental groups: the Provincetown Playhouse; the Theater Guild, out-standing in its success; the Workers' Laboratory Theater, the Theater Union, and the Group Theater—all of which have encouraged young American playwrights and brought the social-purpose play to the fore. The Federal Theater, part of the national relief program from 1935 to 1939, introduced the stage in a variety of popular and experimental forms to a new audience of thousands in the city and in the upstate area.

PAINTING AND SCULPTURE

Because settlers in Colonial New York thought of themselves as citizens of the Mother Country, early art was dominated by European influences. Even the folk art drew, though often remotely, from recollected European examples. In spring and summer itinerant portrait painters, or 'limners,' circulated from the cities among the rural settlements along the Hudson and Mohawk Rivers, carrying a stock of stiff, formal portraits, which they had painted during the winter months, with the faces left blank. For a small sum, often for food and lodging, a farmer could have his likeness introduced into a selected canvas.

The first stoneware kiln in America is said to have been that of Corselius on 'Potter's Hill,' New York City. The earliest recorded maker of the softer 'earthenware' was 'Dirick Benson, Pott Baker, 1698.' Johannes Smedes blew glass—probably crude bottles and 'bulls-eye' window panes —on Glass Maker's Street, now William Street, in 1654. Almost 100 years later Loedwyck Bamper started a more elaborate glassworks. The recent revival of interest in folk art has recovered many examples of early ships' figureheads, weather vanes, gravestones, and cast or hammered iron decorations.

New York craftsmanship reached its highest achievement in the rich yet classic skill of the dour Duncan Phyfe, whose furniture is almost unsurpassed for perfection of form and beauty of ornament. He came to Albany in 1783, where he was probably apprenticed to a coachmaker, and began his career in New York City in 1792 as Duncan Fife, joiner; but a year later he was Duncan Phyfe, cabinetmaker, and such he continued to be until he closed his workshop in 1848. The characteristic cosmopolitanism of New York is reflected in Phyfe's style, which was primarily English with French touches and American simplification.

Among the limners and painters of Dutch New York were Henri Couturier, a Frenchman, and four Duyckincks of three generations. Evert Duyckinck, who settled on Long Island in 1638, made the first stained glass in America and painted portraits of Stephanus Van Cortlandt and other notables. Jacobus Gerritsen Strycker, a prosperous farmer, trader, and official of New Amsterdam, painted a number of portraits, including one of Adrian Van der Donck, Patroon of Haarlem, which is said to be the second portrait painted in America. Pieter Vanderlyn (1687–1778) worked in the neighborhood of Kingston, painting inn signs and portraits of Dutch worthies. Among the native-born professional painters of the eighteenth century, who were associated with the English school but showed a leaning toward realism that reflected the rigorous, practical Colonial life, the outstanding New Yorker was Robert Feke, born on Long Island about 1705, who employed his unschooled talents on vigorous, statuesque, brilliantly colored paintings of Colonial families.

The painters of the young Republic were taught by Benjamin West (1728–1820), American expatriate in London, to depict historical scenes with an elevating patriotic appeal. John Trumbull (1756–1843) executed portraits of Revolutionary leaders and painted, among other historical canvases, the well-known *The Signing of the Declaration of Independence*. Other members of the school of West were Charles Willson Peale (1741–1827), historical painter; Robert Fulton—better known for perfecting steam navigation with the *Clermont*; Samuel F.B.Morse (1791–1872), inventor of the telegraph, whose portraits and landscapes are today arousing an increasing interest; and William Dunlap (1766–1839), whose *History of the Rise and Progress of the Arts of Design in the United States* records the lives and ideas of the artists of America to his own day.

Ezra Ames (1768–1836), who settled in Albany, achieved a considerable reputation for his portraits 'characterized by a homely soundness of approach.' John Vanderlyn (1775–1852), grandson of Pieter and born in Kingston, studied with Stuart in Philadelphia and then went abroad, where he came under the influence of David and French historical painting. His nude *Ariadne* was widely exhibited in America, and despite objections to its subject achieved wide popularity through the engravings of Asher B. Durand. John Wesley Jarvis (1781–1839) and Thomas Sully (1783–1872), both English born, worked in New York on portraiture and miniature painting. During this period John Ramage, Archibald and Alexander Robertson, Edward G. Malbone, and Benjamin Trott achieved remarkable success in exacting and delicate miniatures. Trott made copies of oil paintings; the Robertsons broadened their scope to include city views and landscapes for engravers; Malbone, the greatest of the group, achieved a highly refined technique.

Expansion and prosperity after the War of 1812, stimulated, especially in New York State, by the Erie Canal, produced a strong national self-consciousness. Although portraiture in the English style continued to be fashionable, the artists of the first half of the nineteenth century began to turn their attention to scenes from everyday life. Henry Inman (1801-46), who was born near Utica, important also for his portraiture, was one of the earliest to win popularity with his genre subjects, which include *Picnic in the Catskills*, *Rip Van Winkle's Awakening*, *An October Afternoon*, and *Mumble the Peg*. William S. Mount (1807-68), born in Setauket, Long Island, the son of a farmer, traveled through Long Island in a studio built on wheels, painting his neighbor farmers, field hands, tavern keepers, and Negro workers at their everyday tasks. His work reflects American provincial life, which was at the time perhaps in its most picturesque stage.

The American landscape was made the subject of art on a large scale by the Hudson River School. Under the same romantic impulse that stimulated Irving, Halleck, Drake, and Bryant in literature and Andrew Jackson Downing in landscape architecture, artists painted Hudson Valley scenes, especially the blue Catskills, with a detailed realism that was expected to arouse awe and humility. The technical deficiency of the members of the school in color and composition does not detract from their contribution in expanding and naturalizing the field of American art. Founder of the school was Thomas Doughty (1793-1856), a self-taught artist who was driven to extreme bitterness by public neglect of his work; its leading spirit was Thomas Cole (1801-48), who began with detailed landscapes but later introduced human figures to tell his story. Chief followers of Cole were Asher B. Durand (1796-1886), who had made a reputation as an engraver; John Kensett (1818-72), who achieved tremendous popularity with his meticulous landscapes of the Hudson Valley and the Adirondacks; and Frederick E. Church (1826-1900), who left the Hudson for the more grandiose and melodramatic aspects of nature that he found at Niagara Falls and in South America and Labrador. In the footsteps of these leaders a host of 'earnest, bearded young men' toured the Hudson Valley on foot and set up their easels to reproduce with the natural scene the romantic sentiments that it aroused in them. This same impulse toward a detailed recording of nature inspired John James Audubon's *Birds of America*.

Sculpture developed slowly in New York State. The first marble portrait carved by a native American—that of John Wells in old St.Paul's Church, New York City—is credited to John Frazee (1790-1852); the first equestrian statue to Clark Mills (1810-83), who introduced the industry of bronze-casting into this country. Thomas Crawford (1813-57), like

Mills, executed several important commissions in the National Capital. Henry Kirke Brown (1814–86), sculptor of the equestrian statue of Washington in Union Square, New York City, strove for a robust native realism, which was more adequately achieved by his gifted pupil, John Q.A. Ward (1830–1910), whose works include the *Indian Hunter* in Central Park, New York, *Henry Ward Beecher* in Brooklyn, and *Sheridan* in Capitol Park, Albany. The sculptured groups of John Rogers (1829–1904), tremendously popular in their day, are homely and pictorial illustrations of scenes from everyday life.

Improvements in lithography and increased newspaper and magazine publishing did much to popularize art. In 1850 Nathaniel Currier, operator of a lithograph print shop in New York City, and James Merritt Ives, artist, formed their famous partnership. Ives supervised a staff of artists, who produced prints on almost every subject of popular interest. Homes that no art had previously entered were decorated with these inexpensive prints characterized by detail, color, and action.

In the post-Civil War period a new spirit was infused into American art by the realists Winslow Homer (1836–1910) and Thomas Eakins (1844–1916), and the mystic Albert Pinkham Ryder (1847–1917). Homer was 'the trustworthy reporter' of the 'peoples, occupations and natural phenomena' of this country; Eakins, with a deeper insight into human character, unsparingly portrayed the money-grubbing society of the Gilded Age. Ryder, on the other hand, set aside the strident world and strove to convey the inner images that nature and legend aroused in him. A versatile figure concerned with the American scene as subject matter was Frederic Remington (1861–1909), native of Canton, well known as illustrator, painter, etcher, and sculptor of small bronzes. Most popular were his melodramatic western subjects—bucking bronchos, stagecoach hold-ups, fights with the Indians—celebrating the 'westward moving tide of empire.'

But these native forces were not to prevail until after American art had rounded out its education. In the second half of the nineteenth century, to a much greater extent than in the earlier period, American artists went to Munich, Dusseldorf, Paris, Rome, and other centers to submit themselves to training in the various European styles. The most prominent figure in this tradition was James A.M. Whistler (1834–1903), who went to Europe in 1856 and remained there throughout most of his life. John La Farge (1835–1910), a New Yorker of an old Jefferson County family, studied abroad and became an eclectic of remarkable range. As father of American mural painting he made it possible for the painter to co-operate with the sculptor and the architect to create harmonious interiors. La Farge was the pupil of William Morris Hunt (1824–79), who decorated the old Capitol in Albany and whose influence on American art was exerted largely through the painters who came under his guidance. Augustus St.Gaudens (1848–1907), who studied with La Farge before going abroad, brought the French influence into American sculpture in a personal style full of verve and feeling. His first important work was the Farragut monument in Madison Square, New York; his *Hiawatha* is in Saratoga Springs; his *Captain Randall* is in Sailors' Snug Harbor, Staten Island.

The predominant foreign influence came from French art. Taking their initial impulse from the Hudson River School, George Inness (1825–94), native of Newburgh, Alexander H. Wyant (1836–92), and Homer D. Martin (1836–97), born in Albany, moved on, under the influence of the French landscapists, to a more subjective treatment of views of the Catskills, the Mohawk Valley, and the Adirondacks. French Impressionism was introduced into American art by John Henry Twachtman, whose landscapes have a remarkable luminosity, often catching in a few delicate lines the whole substance of a subject. J.Alden Weir, with some of the poetic sensitivity of Ryder, was a vigorous painter of landscapes and figures.

In 1908 a group of artists under the leadership of Robert Henri (1865–1929) exhibited their work in New York City. Although their techniques were varied, in their work 'once again the influences of the past both native and foreign had been absorbed into an idiom of American experience.' Because of the subjects of their canvases—downtown streets, dock scenes, prizefights, beauty parlors, pool rooms—they were called the Ashcan School; now they are referred to as the New York Realists. The group included John Sloan, George Luks, Arthur B. Davies, Everett Shinn, Ernest Lawson, William Glackens, and Maurice B. Prendergast. To these may be added Edward Hopper, born and brought up in Nyack, and Charles E. Burchfield, who lived in Buffalo for a number of years. This new realism encouraged a revival of lithography and wood-engraving, represented, among others, by George Bellows, Rockwell Kent, and John Taylor Arms.

This re-emphasis of the American scene was partly the stimulus behind the founding of the Woodstock colony, the most important center of creative art in the upstate area. In 1906 L.Birge Harrison moved the summer school of the New York Art Students League to this Catskill village and brought to the place such artists as John Carlson, Walter Goetz, Henry Leith-Ross, and Frank Swift Chase. Henri came to Woodstock to teach and attracted George Bellows, Eugene Speicher, Henry Lee McFee, and John Carroll. Other early leaders were Ralph Radcliffe Whiteside and

Bolton Brown. The Woodstock colony has been credited with reflecting French modernism; but its product has been more varied than such a statement implies. From it has come the vivid and melodramatic work of Bellows; the solid figures of Speicher; the quiet dignity of Leon Kroll; the analytical realism of Kenneth Hayes Miller; the keen, humorous work of Peggy Bacon; the sensitive paintings of Alexander Brook.

The Tiffany colony in Oyster Bay and Yaddo in Saratoga Springs provide invited artists with the opportunity to work free from financial worries. The activities of the Art Program of the WPA have introduced indigenous art to a vast new public in the State. A group of artists in Buffalo have in recent years revealed a strong regional interest, painting local subjects such as canal and harbor scenes; their work, exhibited in New York City, has won much favorable comment.

MUSIC

Early music in New York was part of church services; secular music was frowned upon, though settlers in the central and western parts of the State had their fiddlers who managed to make their dancing tunes heard above the stomping of heavy-soled boots on barn floors. The Shakers at Colonie and New Lebanon made singing an integral part of religious rituals and harvest celebrations, accompanying song with simple dance movements.

In New York City musical societies were organized in the 1770's; in the upstate area they began much later, largely by the efforts of German immigrants, who brought a tradition of choral singing and a taste for instrumental music. Rochester had a brass band as early as 1817; the Maennerchor was organized in 1854, the Rochester Philharmonic Society in 1865. A local German choral group of 150 voices gave a concert of sacred music in Albany in 1830. In 1840 Professor Ferdinand Ilsely was engaged to teach music in Albany's public schools. Ilsely presented the oratorio *The Creation*, in 1839 and *David* in 1841; in 1850, the year before Jenny Lind sang in Albany, he organized the Harmonia Society and presented Haydn's *The Seasons*. Choral groups were organized in other upstate cities in the sixties and seventies, and local societies arranged for concerts by the great artists that visited New York.

With the establishment of the Philharmonic Society in 1842 and the opening of the Metropolitan Opera House in 1883, New York City laid the foundation for its pre-eminence in the musical world. But to a much larger extent than in the fine arts and the stage, music remained an activity in which large numbers of upstate people participated. The later Italian and Polish immigrant groups strengthened public interest and participation in music. Most large towns had choral groups, and even the villages sported local bands; the music teacher was an institution, instructing on the piano, the violin, and the wind instruments.

The silent motion picture increased professional opportunity for the musician, since even the smallest theater employed at least a pianist to accompany the movie and many had orchestras of several pieces. But the talking picture soon eliminated that field and the depression of the thirties added its blow by reducing the number of private pupils. The old marching bands were superseded by the modern jazz orchestras, but here a relatively few 'name' bands out of New York City, popularized by the radio, dominated the market. The Music Program of the WPA organized orchestras in the population centers of the State to give public concerts, thereby providing employment for musicians and creating a new impetus to musical activity and appreciation. The Buffalo Philharmonic Society, after sponsoring the WPA orchestra for several seasons, took over 54 of the project musicians and organized its own orchestra.

The musical pre-eminence of Rochester in the upstate area is supported by a long history of music activities. As a nucleus for the Eastman School of Music, opened in 1922, there was at hand, for George Eastman to purchase, the Institute of Musical Arts, established in 1913 by Herman Dossenbach, Alf Klingenberg, and Oscar Gareissen. The school's director, Howard Hanson, has composed, among other works, the opera *Merry Mount*; and the faculty includes a number of other outstanding composers and musicians. The Rochester Philharmonic Orchestra, Jose Iturbi, director, has created a national reputation through its radio broadcasts.

The other cities of the State also provide opportunities for the enjoyment of classical music. Each, with few exceptions, has a civic symphony orchestra supported by its citizens and a music association that sells subscriptions for an annual concert series featuring well-known vocalists, instrumentalists, and ensembles. Concerts given by local choral societies, usually with visiting artists, are events of community-wide interest. Chautauqua has for many years made music a major part of its summer activities, bringing to the western section of the State outstanding musicians from New York and other cities. In recent years musical education for the young has been taken over by the public schools, and music activities in colleges have expanded.

As in the other arts, New York has contributed a number of nationally known figures to the roster of American musicians. Antoinette Sterling,

born in Jefferson County, was famous in the nineteenth century as a ballad singer. Madam Albani, nineteenth-century opera star, although born
in Canada, lived in Albany until she went to Europe to study. Among the
Metropolitan Opera stars, Carmela Ponselle was born in Schenectady and
Richard Bonelli in Port Byron.

Architecture

FROM Indian lodge to skyscraper, the buildings of New York State have recorded and symbolized its dramatic history. Fire, the elements, and men have destroyed most of the early structures, but today those remaining are increasingly cherished and preserved, not in a spirit of romantic sentimentalizing, but rather with the realization that the essential character of New York culture is most clearly materialized in its architecture.

York State building begins with the forest-dwelling Iroquois, who, with stone knife and ax, framed their rude huts with pairs of light poles sunk in the ground, bent across and lashed in a series of light arches; horizontal pieces braced the structure longitudinally; overlapping bark slabs formed walls and roof. In size these dwellings ranged from single-family units to great 200-foot 'long houses' accommodating whole clans. After 1700, Indians often adopted the white man's system of log construction, witness the Seneca Council House in Letchworth State Park.

The first shelters of the Dutch consisted of large square pits dug in banks, roofed with timbers and green sod, floored with planks, and lined with bark. When other tasks permitted, these temporary dugouts were replaced by tiny one-story-and-garret cabins of logs or boards, with central hearths and smoke holes at the ridge of the thatched roofs. Mud and masonry chimneys were added later.

As soon as possible the Dutch erected permanent dwellings, several of which survive. Although bricks were sometimes imported from Holland, kilns were established in New Amsterdam by 1628 and in Beverwyck (Albany) soon after. Conforming to Dutch standards, these brick came to be called 'Holland' brick to distinguish them from the larger 'English' variety. The name has led to the usually erroneous belief that all so-called Holland brick were brought from the old country.

In form as in material, the early brick structures of Manhattan and Beverwyck preserved the medieval flavor of their Netherlandish prototypes. The typical two-story-and-loft town house faced its entrance stoop and stepped gable toward the street. The farmhouses of Rensselaerswyck, such as the Jan Breese House, built just south of Rensselaer in 1723, employ the one-and-a-half-story form common in all the Colonies, but borrow their steeply pitched gable roofs and wrought-iron beam anchors from urban cousins. Bricks of contrasting color were often introduced to record a date or create a decorative pattern.

Dutch dwellings in Ulster and Dutchess Counties were commonly of stone and had low-pitched gable roofs. John Brinckerhoff's house (1738), east of Fishkill, and William Stoutenburgh's home (1750), in East Park, are typical. Rockland County farmhouses, like those of northern New Jersey, reproduce the form and arrangement and the projecting 'flying-gutter' of the European peasant cottages of the Flemish farmers who settled this region. The rich rose-brown sandstone used in these buildings adds an attractive color note. Major John Smith's house (1735?), at Germonds, south of New City, is typical.

Under English rule, Dutch habits and traditions suffered little change, but increasing prosperity brought a demand for larger and more fashionable homes. Deeper plans produced single-pitched roofs of excessive height, as in the Hasbrouck House at New Paltz, but that difficulty was overcome after 1725 by the adoption of the New England two-pitched gambrel. The handsome brick house built in Beacon about 1750 by Abraham De Peyster, wealthy New York merchant, illustrates this aggrandizing and refining process. The main story with its central stair hall flanked by pairs of spacious, high-ceilinged parlors rests upon a high stone basement with service and servants' quarters. Beneath the broad gambrel an amazing number of large bedrooms are found. Cornice, doorway, staircase, and interior trim followed the new Renaissance fashion.

Several venerable Dutch barns are hidden in out-of-the-way corners of the Hudson and Mohawk Valleys. Their capacious square interiors are reached by a large wagon door in the center of the gable wall, while two small doors at the corners lead to cattle stalls under the low eaves. The Wemple Barn (1734), at Fort Hunter, and the Van Wyck Barn, south of Fishkill, exemplify the characteristic heavy timber construction.

The curious octagonal churches of the early Dutch period have all disappeared. Even the Sleepy Hollow Dutch Reformed Church, in North

Parsonage · Albany · 1657 ✤ Jan Breese Farmhouse · nr Rensselaer · 1723 ✤ Hasbrouck House · New Paltz · 1712

Tarrytown, whose rectangular stone walls date from 1699, has undergone such extensive alterations that its original form is almost unrecognizable. Later churches, such as that at Fishkill, built in 1784, adopt Georgian forms. Governmental buildings, known only from old prints, were but slight modifications of large town houses.

During the eighteenth century, English culture and architecture was largely confined to New York City and a few great manor houses along the Hudson and the Mohawk. In them was reflected the gracious, formal manner developed in England under the Restoration, Queen Anne, and the first three Georges. Fort Johnson (1749) not only followed the new fashion in its two-story rectangular stone mass, its symmetrically disposed windows, and its hipped roof with level eaves-line, but actually imported from London paneling, hardware, and other fittings. Albany's Schuyler Mansion, built of brick in 1762, with its square plan, its hipped gambrel roof with Chippendale railing, its spacious halls and rooms, and its richly carved stairrail, demands a prominent place on any list of great Colonial homes. Georgian additions or refittings, as at the Philipse Manor House, Yonkers, or the Glen-Sanders House, Scotia, often brought earlier dwellings stylistically up to date.

All in all, conservative half-Dutch New York spurned the elaborate academicisms so popular in New England and Virginia. An exception is the graceful Robert Morris (Jumel) House (1765), in New York City, which has the only pre-Revolutionary two-story 'colossal' portico in the Colonies.

In the smaller houses of farm and village, the English introduced the wood-frame-and-clapboard system of construction so prevalent in their New England colonies. From the simple salt-boxes of Long Island, related directly to Yankee prototypes, to the larger homesteads, such as Johnson Hall (1762), at Johnstown, carpenter and joiner everywhere adapted Georgian masonry details to wood with the light, gracious touch characteristic of Georgian Colonial.

The English, by direct subsidy, encouraged the establishment of Episcopal churches in the province, but architecturally the new congrega-

Maj. John Smith House · Germonds · 1735 ✤ Bushwyck Church · Brooklyn · 1710 ✤ Van Wyck Barn · Fishkill · XVIII Cent.

tions matured slowly. The first structure of Trinity Church, New York City, was built in 1696, but not until 1764 did Thomas McBean give the city its first authentic Georgian church, St.Paul's Chapel, directly inspired by Gibbs's St.Martin's-in-the-Fields, London. St.Paul's, Eastchester, 1761, and St.George's, Schenectady, partly 1766, are smaller and simpler, but still unmistakably Georgian Colonial. Several eighteenth-century Anglican chapels are extant. Christ Church, Duanesburg, though built in 1793, has a typical nonliturgical meetinghouse plan, and retains all the original furnishings. St.Peter's (1767), Van Cortlandtville, Trinity Church in Fishkill, begun about 1769, and the often altered Caroline Church (1729), Setauket, Long Island, are modest and charming examples.

Other ethnic groups made important architectural contributions to eighteenth-century New York. At Fort Niagara, the fortress built about 1725 by the military architect, Gaspard de Lery, simulates a French provincial manor house. The Huguenot-Dutch houses clustered together at New Paltz form an ensemble which in its humbler way is as informative and precious as Virginia's Williamsburg. The Palatine buildings along the Schoharie and Mohawk give no such cumulative effect, yet the same forthright character is apparent in 'Fort' Frey (1739), the Palatine Church (1770), and Schoharie's Old Stone Fort (1772).

The successful termination of the War for Independence not only created a new Nation but by the defeat of the Iroquois also gave New York a new frontier. For 40 years a stream of New Englanders poured westward and northward, intent on carving out of the wilderness a new Yankee domain. Symbolic of this struggle was that product of the woodsman's ax and jackknife, the ubiquitous log house, exemplified by Mary Jemison's cabin in Letchworth State Park. Some foresighted settlers took along prefabricated timber-framed houses, as did Neil McMullin, who in 1796 transported a house frame from Kingston to Oswego and erected it on the shore of Lake Ontario six years before the first sawmill was established in that region. Even earlier, Colden's report of 1723 mentions exportation of house frames ready to set up.

Although the Colonies had won political independence, England con-

Sir Wm. Johnson House · Ft. Johnson · 1749　✦　DePeyster House · Beacon · 1750　✦　Schuyler Mansion · Albany · 1762

tinued to be their architectural mentor for almost a century. During the Federal period, 1781–1830, marked by the boom of westward migration and the commercial expansion of New York City, the Georgian tradition remained strong, preserved by provincial craftsmen. Many of them were New Englanders, who, guided by Asher Benjamin's *Country Builder's Assistant* and other domestic or imported handbooks, followed the succeeding modes of delicate ornament popularized by Robert Adam, the bare stucco surfaces of Soane, and the idealized classicism of Palladio.

In such a dwelling as the massive Ludlow House, in Claverack, built about 1790, can be seen a fusion of Dutch solidity, Georgian symmetry, and Early Republican spaciousness, while at near-by Hudson the homes and warehouses of the Yankee proprietors preserve the flavor of pre-Revolutionary Nantucket. The village homes built by Ephraim Russ in Rensselaerville, from the Stevens House of 1809 to the Rider House of 1823, with its delicate blind arcade and gable window in the manner of Robert Adam, show the typical stylistic sequence and prove that by resourcefulness and taste a local builder could achieve remarkable civic unity.

Conservative post-Colonial architecture is best illustrated in the work of Philip Hooker (1766–1837), who singlehanded produced a worthy architectural setting for the capital city of the State. Arriving in Albany in 1790, he watched the Dutch village of 3,500 grow into a thriving town of more than 35,000. As architect, assessor, alderman, city superintendent, and surveyor, he built 16 public buildings—State Capitol, city hall, seven churches, two markets, two banks, two schools, and a theater—besides laying out new real estate subdivisions. His finest remaining works are the old Albany Academy (now the Joseph Henry Memorial), completed in 1817, and the Hamilton College Chapel (1828), both conceived in pure Georgian spirit. Even as late as 1827, Hooker's elegant marble façade for the house of Richard Hart, rich Quaker merchant of Troy, preserves the gracious warmth of the late eighteenth century.

Paralleling this conservatism, however, there is evidence that as early as 1792 the social and political aristocracy of New York State were cognizant

Christ Church·Duanesburg·1792 ♦ St. Paul's Chapel·New York·1756 ♦ Palatine Lutheran Church·1770

of more fundamental developments. In that year Staats Morris Dyckman erected handsome Boscobel House just south of Peekskill. Here the wide central hall with its superb divided stair leading to the large upper parlor, the projecting rooms, and the two superposed porches with slender columns and lambricated architrave indicate a new and freer solution of old elements. Even more remarkable is The Hill, south of Hudson, begun by Henry Walter Livingston in 1796, just after his marriage to Mary Penn Allen. Certainly Mrs.Livingston had visited Woodlands in her native Philadelphia, and, admiring the two elliptical salons there, ordered for her new home two similar rooms placed side by side, masked in front by a two-story portico. The stucco walls, massive columns, curved bays, and secondary projecting wings declare an architectural liberation from Colonial forms and indicate a growing interest in authentic Roman classical details.

If the post-Colonial manner symbolized the Anglophilia of the Federalists, the Roman Revival found its patrons in Jefferson and his Republicans, who, in romantically identifying the new Republic with the ancient prototype, decreed Republican architectural togas for the governmental buildings in Washington, D.C. In New York State, an unexpected and unique example of the Roman Revival appeared in the grand plan for Union College in Schenectady, drawn in 1813 by Joseph Jacques Ramée, trained architect and refugee from Revolutionary France, brought to America to build along the St.Lawrence the vast frontier estate of David Parish. Ramée's noble disposition of college buildings surrounding a wide mall, dominated by a classical rotunda, and flanked by fine formal gardens has been unjustly overshadowed by Jefferson's later University of Virginia. Romanized Palladianism is further apparent, first, in the Holland Land Office in Batavia, built in 1801 by Joseph Ellicott, then in Joseph's own house (now the Goodrich House) in Buffalo, built in 1823, and in several Geneva homes built in the 1820's by settlers from Virginia.

Between 1800 and 1830, knowledge of classical Greek architecture disseminated by such works as Stuart and Revett's *Antiquities of Athens* came to be increasingly applied to new buildings in Philadelphia and Washington. Completed in 1826, both Latrobe's Bank of the United

Ludlow House · Claverack · 1740 ✦ Stevens House · Rensselaerville · 1809 ✦ Rider House · Rensselaerville · 1823

States at Philadelphia and the Lee Mansion at Arlington by George Hadfield immediately captured popular imagination. Aroused by the Jacksonian revolution, fired by democratic dreams of another Periclean Golden Age, stimulated by sympathy for the contemporary Greek struggle for independence against the Turk, excited by the rapid commercial and industrial expansion following the opening of the Erie Canal, and fortified with Minard Lafever's *Modern Builder's Guide*, New York State went Grecian with a vengeance, literally lining the water level route with rustic Parthenons. Troy, appropriately enough, led off in 1827 with the Rensselaer County Courthouse, a Sing Sing marble Theseum now unfortunately demolished. Well-preserved, however, are the grave Doric First Presbyterian Church (1836), the graceful Ionic First Baptist Church (1846), numerous houses, large and small, and several business blocks. In the truly monumental four-story Doric portico of the Utica State Hospital (1839–42), New York possesses probably the grandest single work of the period, rivaled only by Robert Mills's Patent Office in Washington. An Ionic work of similar scale is Newburgh's American Reformed Church (1835). In the old State Office Building (now the Court of Appeals Building), built in 1839 in Albany by Henry Rector, a fashionable Sing Sing marble exterior encloses an interior noteworthy for its fire-resisting vaulted floors.

Typical large residences are General Aaron Ward's marble house (1835) in Ossining, and Rose Hill, southeast of Geneva, built of wood about the same time. Every hamlet had its temple-fronted cottage, but the General Spinner House (1840), in Mohawk, proves that the style could achieve flexibility both in plan and mass. Especially amusing are vernacular examples that sing the ancient modes off key, such as Child's Folly in Rochester (1837), with its extraordinary portico of five buxom Lysicratean columns. Possibly the finest residence of the period was Beverwyck, the manor house of William Paterson Van Rensselaer, built in 1839–43 in what is now Rensselaer. Its well-organized plan, refined detail, and dignified brown stucco exterior signalize the professional competence of its English trained architect, Frederic Diaper.

A third romantic revival was Gothic. Since the late eighteenth century,

Albany Academy · 1816 ◆ Dyckman House · Cruger Park · 1792 ◆ H·W·Livingston House · nr Hudson · 1796

pointed arches, wiry pinnacles, and crude tracery had been applied superficially to Anglican buildings which were fundamentally Georgian. An example of this 'Georgian Gothic' was the second Trinity Church, built in 1788 in New York City. St.Luke's (1824), Rochester, and St.Paul's (1827), Troy, represent more successful attempts to approximate medieval forms. In secular building, the 'castellated' style derived from English Tudor castles was preferred. Typical are Colonel James McKay's Castle (1837), Buffalo, the fine West Point Library (1841), and Lyndhurst, the Philip R. Paulding mansion, built in 1840 in Tarrytown by Alexander Jackson Davis, that prodigious peer of eclectic architects. Hyde Park's St.James Episcopal Church (1844), designed by the amateur, Augustus Thomas Cowman, shows further improvements.

It remained for the Englishman, Richard Upjohn, to introduce America to authentically designed and executed Gothic. In the third Trinity Church (1839–46) he achieved an effect of such dignity that Gothic soon replaced Greek as the popular style. New York State is particularly rich in Upjohn's work, outstanding examples being St.Paul's Cathedral (1850), Buffalo, and Albany's St.Peter's (1859). Especially worthy of note are Upjohn's charity jobs, the board-and-batten chapels sprinkled throughout the State; St.Paul's (1851), Kinderhook, is one of the most charming.

Since England was the fountainhead of New York State Gothic, it is not strange that John Ruskin's Victorian Gothic, based on the medieval buildings of northern Italy, quickly made its appearance here. Half Gothic, half Romanesque, the Nott Memorial Library of Union College, Schenectady, built in 1858–76 by Edward Tuckerman Potter, displays the salient features of the style in its polychrome masonry and polygonal, domed mass, inspired by the Baptistry at Pisa. Calvert Vaux and Frederick Withers, English architects who came to America to assist Andrew Jackson Downing, celebrated landscape architect of Newburgh, built in 1866–72 one of the most pretentious and costly Victorian Gothic monuments in New York, the Hudson River State Hospital, north of Poughkeepsie.

The pattern books of Downing and Vaux, which guided American house

Union College · Schenectady · 1813 ◆ First Court House · Troy · 1828 ◆ State Hospital · Utica · 1834-42

design in the forties and fifties, peddled every variant of the historic architectural styles. Taking their cue from George Harvey's romantification of Irving's Sunnyside in 1835, these volumes portrayed Tudor cottages, Italianate villas, Swiss chalets, and other homes in the 'American Bracketted Style.' Of all the buildings constructed under this influence, perhaps the most exotic examples are Renwick Castle, Syracuse, an unbelievable Norman hodgepodge built in 1851 by James Renwick, and the Persian villa which Frederick E. Church, leader of the Hudson River school of landscape painters, built overlooking the river opposite Catskill.

In the 1850's New York witnessed an interesting structural innovation in the development of commercial and industrial buildings whose walls, columns, and floor beams were entirely of cast iron. The new system aimed to secure greater fire resistance than the prevailing masonry-wall, timber-floor construction. The ease with which the prefabricated sections were cast encouraged an unusually profuse application of ornament.

In New York State as in the Nation, the close of the Civil War inaugurated an unprecedented expansion in population and industry; but despite a tremendous building boom, America remained an architectural province of Europe. The restless, picturesque Victorian Gothic continued in use for schools and churches. In commercial and governmental buildings, however, the English Renaissance gave way to the ostentatious bombast of Napoleon III's Second Empire style, the prestige of which was established by the reconstruction and expansion of the Louvre, 1852–68, and the building of the Opera, 1861–74, in Paris.

New York enthusiastically developed this new mode into an exuberant expression of its economic prosperity. One of the earliest Second Empire buildings in the State was James Renwick's Main Hall (1861–5), at Vassar College, Poughkeepsie, a somewhat ungainly and reduced brick version of the Louvre, complete with mansard roofs, superposed orders, and pavilion accents. A surer application of the same elements was begun in 1867 by Thomas Fuller and Augustus Laver in the incredibly expensive New York State Capitol in Albany, but the building was completed with unfortunate stylistic admixtures. In Rochester, the Powers Building (1870), by An-

Rose Hill · nr Geneva · 1835   Gen'l Spinner House · Mohawk · 1840   Beverwyck · Rensselaer · 1839-43

drew Jackson Warner, not only displays the latest in cast-iron construction but also the ultimate in mansarded commercial elegance. The old Buffalo City Hall (now the Erie County Building), built in 1872, also by Warner, is typical of numerous pretentious municipal buildings in this style. The summit of this superlatively parvenu period, however, was reached in the super-gorgeous Grand Union Hotel (1872) and United States Hotel (1875), which still preside over Saratoga Springs. Even factories aspired to modish grandeur: witness the 1200-foot long Building #3 (1866) of the Harmony Cotton Mills in Cohoes.

Upon this florid adolescent scene, four men appeared to establish that formal order that the architecture of any nation must possess to attain maturity. The first, Richard Morris Hunt, received a thorough theoretical and practical training in Paris as the first American student at the Ecole des Beaux Arts and as an assistant of his master, Lefeul, on the Louvre. Upon his return in 1855, his first independent commissions were rather tentative experiments: witness the Howland Library in Beacon. Although alert to the functional problems of his day—he built one of the first elevator office buildings in New York and the city's first apartment house—Hunt's greatest contribution came in the huge Fifth Avenue and Newport mansions in which he introduced the discipline of fine craftsmanship and accurately rendered historical details. To a select few of Ward McAllister's four hundred, his lavish architectural backgrounds provided a conspicuous and reassuring guarantee of social security. His masterpiece, the William K. Vanderbilt house, Fifth Avenue at 52nd St., begun in 1878 and unfortunately demolished in 1925, was a superb design in early French Renaissance. Levi P. Morton's half-timbered home, Ellerslie, built about 1886 on the Hudson near Rhinebeck, is a less elaborate example of his style.

The second great figure was Henry Hobson Richardson. While, like Hunt, he was trained in Paris, unlike Hunt he developed out of the French Romanesque a personal expression of masonry construction which attained great power, dignity, and beauty. The Buffalo State Hospital (1872–81) is a fine early example of his vigorous massing. Collaborating with Leopold Eidlitz on the State Capitol (1875–86), he designed that

St. Pauls Church · Troy · 1827   ✤   'Lyndhurst' · Paulding House · Tarrytown · 1840   ✤   Trinity Church · New York · 1839-46

brownstone fantasy of vegetative ornament, the famous 'million-dollar' staircase, Romanesque counterpart of Garnier's baroque stairhall in the Paris Opera. The Senate Chamber, his most sumptuous work, forms an interesting contrast to the restrained Victorian-Gothic Assembly Chamber by Eidlitz. The Capitol exterior suffers from composite authorship. Richardson's genius is most happily seen in the richly paneled Appellate Court Room (now removed to the Court of Appeals Building opposite the Capitol) and in the adjoining Albany City Hall (1882). This last great artist in masonry demonstrated that American architects could draw inspiration from the past without stooping to servile imitation.

Richardson never had to face the problems raised by the newly developed system of fire-resistant, steel-framed construction. The cast-iron structures of the fifties and sixties had failed to withstand the Chicago and Boston conflagrations of 1871–2, and in the reconstruction that followed the metal skeletons were for the first time consciously enclosed in protective sheaths of masonry. In subsequent Chicago and New York City building booms, the new system was extended to ever higher structures. In the early nineties, Adler and Sullivan of Chicago achieved the first rational expression of the new skyscraper form. Buffalo's Prudential Building (1894) is one of Louis Sullivan's finest designs. In its wide windows and slender piers, unashamed, unconventional verticality is frankly unveiled. If something of Richardson's round arches and rich foliage remains, Sullivan was able to transmute these into his own lyric style, and, at least symbolically, to reveal the slender steel supports beneath the superlatively ornamental terra-cotta sheath.

One step further remained to clear the way for a new American architectural synthesis. Sullivan's mantle passed to his pupil, Frank Lloyd Wright, who for almost 50 years has been producing building after building freshly approached in plan, imaginatively conceived in structure, and dynamically synthesized in a whole series of personal styles. The magnificent Administration Building (1904) of the Larkin Company in Buffalo is a mountain peak in modern architecture and a symbol of the growing importance of industrial structures. His Dana Martin House in the same

Hudson River State Hospital·Poughkeepsie·1866 ✦ Original Design· Capitol·Albany·1867 ✦ City Hall·Albany·1882

city displays the imaginative magic with which he invests the prosaic problem of a middle class house.

It was the tragedy of American architecture that the way pointed out by Richardson, Sullivan, and Wright was long obscured by the disciples of that other master, Richard Hunt. Hunt's success sent American student architects flocking to the Ecole des Beaux Arts. A few assimilated its basic teaching of sound structure and rational planning, but many returned with only a sketchbook of historical paraphernalia with which to mystify their unsuspecting clients. Even in a work of such manifest merit as the majestically planned Chicago Fair of 1893, dominated by Hunt's Administration Building and Atwood's Palace of Fine Arts, the public usually considered superficial stylistic detail to be the secret of success rather than the fundamental virtues of order, breadth, and competent finish.

It is only fair to acknowledge that the 'conservators of traditional values' have given us many fine if not progressive buildings. Stanford White's remodeling of Staatsburg (the Ogden Mills) House (1895) and his eloquent design for Hyde Park (1895), the Vanderbilt home, recapture much of the restrained elegance of eighteenth-century French chateaux. Cram and Goodhue's West Point, from 1903 on, forms one of the most romantic ensembles in all architecture. Claude F. Bragdon's New York Central Station (1914) in Rochester is a masterpiece of adaptation of classicism. Nor can the powerful magnificence of Palmer and Hornbostel's much maligned State Education Building (1912), in Albany, be denied. Marcus T. Reynold's Delaware & Hudson Building (1918), Albany, irrespective of its Flemish Gothic details, fulfills its splendid site with a charming vivacity. The Rundel Memorial Building (1936), in Rochester, by Gordon, Kaelber, and Waasdorp, is a successful free interpretation of the Italian Renaissance stripped of traditional ornamental details.

The appearance of most medium-sized New York towns records the progress of these nineteenth-century stylistic fashions. The central zone of brick business blocks with corbelled or bracketted cornices dates chiefly from post-Civil War expansion, but here and there a Greek Revival structure remains or a 'neon modernistic' creation replaces one destroyed by

Prudential Building · Buffalo · 1894 ◆ Larkin Building · Buffalo · 1903 ◆ New York Central Station · Rochester · 1914

fire. Surrounding this core, a band of mid-Victorian arks, once fashionable residences but now sheltering boarders and tourists, is interrupted along the chief arteries by blatant filling stations. Beyond, Eastlake jigsaw cottages of the seventies and eighties give way to 'Arts-and-Crafts' bungalows of 1900 and more recent homes of Colonial or English aspirations, with perhaps a few self-conscious moderns here and there. Outside the city limits, the radiating highways are lined with houses, shacks, and fruit stands that forego city services to escape city taxes. What architectural character such a typical community displays is usually the work of some local practitioner who year in and year out has supplied the necessary services and sooner or later adopts the current fad. Troy's Mark F. Cummings and Rochester's Andrew Jackson Warner are typical of almost forgotten personalities responsible for much of the civic scenery of their respective communities.

Although American architects sometimes seem preoccupied with stylistic matters, many of their most significant contributions have been made in the fields of construction and planning: for example, the steel-frame and reinforced concrete structural systems and the mechanical equipment that makes possible a remarkable degree of comfort and convenience. Developed and refined in the skyscraper, these technical improvements today enrich every type of building.

The skyscraper has revolutionized the process of construction. Where once a decade seemed too short a time to complete a large structure, today a 70-story office building materializes in less than 12 months. The steel framework of the Empire State Building grew four-and-a-half stories per week. Steel members were riveted in place within 80 hours after their departure from the fabricating plant in Pittsburgh. The methodical bolting into place of its 6,400 windows exemplifies the increasing trend toward standardization of parts. Surely such technical organization is a valuable addition to modern building. Furthermore, the experience gained in planning and operating industrial and commercial structures has established strict economic standards by which to judge the feasibility of building projects.

Williamsburg Houses · Brooklyn · 1937 ◆ Crum Elbow Quaker Meeting House · 1780 ◆ Grain Elevator · Albany · 1933
sketches · by · Bannister

Tremendous economic energy brought New York tremendous building activity, and this, in turn, has made the State a leader in all architectural fields, especially apparent in the many examples of new, highly specialized building types, such as Buffalo's New York Central Railroad Station, the Central Islip State Hospital, the great pavilions at Jones Beach, the Attica State Prison, and an ever-expanding array of educational institutions. Not only did new building types appear, but older forms underwent progressive change. Mangin's graceful City Hall in old New York and modern Buffalo's gigantic municipal skyscraper symbolize a whole history of urban development. Between the stinking, windowless, 'railroad' tenements of 1850 and the sunlit low-rental housing at Brooklyn's Williamsburg and Buffalo's Kenfield lies almost a century of crusading against speculator and jerry-builder. New York has always led in the development of the single-family, middle-class suburban house, that integration of city and country which is one of America's most important and most typical contributions to modern architecture. In Forest Hills, Long Island, and Sunnyside, Astoria, New York architects made notable advances toward the creation of a homogeneous, protected, traffic-free 'neighborhood unit,' a concept used increasingly in the design of modern residential communities.

New structural systems, new building types, and new planning methods led inevitably to a new aesthetic approach. In contrast to the conservators of traditional values, a school of architects has appeared that seeks to use these new resources and standards as the very bases of a new architectural synthesis. In the formation of a new manner, the first step has always been to renounce the prevailing mode and state the problem in starkly realistic terms. Such efforts have been seen in New York before. The asceticism of the Shaker buildings in Mount Lebanon and the Crum Elbow Friend's Meeting House near East Park, the forthright utilitarianism of the superb Schoharie Aqueduct at Fort Hunter, and the self-conscious craftsmanship which the Roycrofters of East Aurora inherited from William Morris, all have a close kinship to the majestic geometry of the great Port of Albany grain elevator, the 'International Style' exhibited in Howe and Lescaze's Hessian Hills School at Croton, and the lithe, soaring harmony of the Bronx-Whitestone bridge.

Whether the motive for negation of the past be religious, economic, or intellectual in origin, it often results in clean, bold forms of startling 'constructivistic' beauty. Despite their long pronouncements, the extreme abstractionists have not so much abandoned their inheritance of baroque grammar as they have substituted a 'constructivist' vocabulary of glass, steel beam, and concrete for traditional masonry forms. The World of Tomorrow, and the day after, will no doubt eschew extreme asceticism. Wright long ago demonstrated that a designer of soundly logical mind and vivid imagination can create new and stimulating buildings of genuine beauty that are neither reminiscent nor negative. Today a discerning eye can discover among the younger generation of architects many signs of better days ahead. Employing the new vocabulary of forms and materials, the better contemporary work, such as New York City's Museum of Modern Art (1939), by Philip Goodwin and Edward D. Stone, and the WGY Broadcasting Studio (1938), Schenectady, by Harrison and Fouilhoux, aims to achieve the qualities of all great architecture—order, breadth, and competent finish. No doubt the layman will be content to leave such aesthetic problems to practitioners and critics, and will find in the future his greatest satisfaction in the slow but steady growth of modern architecture, which promises him, in the words of Sir Henry Wotton, seventeenth-century architect-philosopher, buildings of greater 'commoditie, firmeness, and delight.'

PART II
Cities and Special Points of Interest

Albany

Railroad Station: Union Station, 547 Broadway, for New York Central System, Boston & Albany R.R., Delaware & Hudson R.R.
Bus Stations: 350 Broadway for Greyhound, Mountain View Coach, Champlain Coach and Hudson Transit Lines; 504 Broadway for Arrow Line, L.B.K.Line, Vermont Transit Co.; 426 Broadway for Interstate Busses Corp., Adirondack Trailways, Hudson Transit Lines; Plaza, Broadway & State St., for interurban busses.
Airport: 7.5 m. NW. on State 155. Local flights $1, $1.50; time 15 min.
Piers: S.Broadway, one block S. of Plaza, for Hudson River Day Line, May 25–Sept. 30; Port of Albany, S. city limits, freight service.
Streetcars and Busses: Fare 10¢; 13 tokens for $1.
Taxis: 25¢ up; zone rates.

Accommodations: 12 hotels; boarding houses, tourist homes.

Information Service: Tourist and Convention Bureau, Chamber of Commerce, 74 Chapel St.; Travel Bureau, Hotel Ten Eyck, 87 State St.; Albany Auto Club, Wellington Hotel, 136 State St.; De Witt Clinton Travel Bureau, De Witt Clinton Hotel, State and Eagle Sts.

Radio Stations: WOKO (1430 kc.); WABY (1370 kc.).
Theaters and Motion Picture Houses: Legitimate plays occasionally; 13 motion picture houses.
Swimming: Lincoln Park, Morton Ave. between Delaware Ave. and Eagle St.; locker 10¢.
Boating: Washington Park, Madison Ave. between Willett St. and Lake Ave., 25¢ per hr.
Golf: Municipal Golf Course, New Scotland Ave. and Whitehall Rd., 18 holes, 50¢.
Baseball: Hawkins Stadium, Broadway, Menands (State 32), Albany Senators of Eastern League, adm. 50¢–$1.10, night games.
Tennis: City parks, free.

Annual Event: Albany-New York outboard motorboat race, first week in June.

ALBANY (18 alt.,130,447 pop.), capital of New York State, inland seaport and port of entry on the west bank of the Hudson River, is built along the edge of a plateau that extends 18 miles northwest to the Mohawk Valley. Docks, railroad terminals, and factories occupy the narrow shelf at the water's edge. The Union Station, a massive rectangular building of late French Renaissance design, occupies an entire city block on Broadway between Steuben and Columbia Streets. The business section rises up the steep slope of the hill—a cluster of tall bank, hotel, office, and department store buildings: the main shopping area is in the Broadway, Pearl, and lower State Street section. The hill is crowned by the Capitol, the towering State Office Building, and the colonnaded State Education Building; other governmental structures border Academy Park. From this center spread the prim, tree-shaded streets of brownstone and brick

homes of Victorian Albany, interspersed with modern apartment buildings and occasional new residences. In the Pine Hills section, along Western and Madison Avenue, are pretentious homes built by wealthy residents in the 1890's and early 1900's. The Whitehall, New Scotland, and
West Albany sections were built up later. Beyond, the city spreads out in
boulevard developments and suburban bungalows. Twenty-five parks,
with an aggregate area of almost 300 acres, provide for playgrounds and
recreation.

Although Albany is an important manufacturing and wholesale distributing center, its personality is determined by its function as the capital of the State. For the 5,000 State employees, politics is the consuming
interest. During political campaigns, and in the early months of the year
when the legislature meets, the corridors of State buildings and hotel lobbies hum with politics. It is this large group of office workers that gives
Albany an essentially 'white-collar' appearance.

Albany's population is a composite of Dutch, English, Scots, Irish,
and Germans, with more recent immigrant elements including Italians,
Poles, and Russians. There is a small percentage of Negroes. The city's
churches are distributed among 16 denominations. Included in the public
school system are 24 grammar and four high schools. There are 18 parochial schools, five degree-granting colleges, and several private schools and
academies.

Aboriginal Indian trails running north and south along the Hudson
Valley and east and west between Massachusetts and Niagara crossed at
the site of Albany. Near by were one or two small Indian villages but the
plateau was used principally for campsites and the cultivation of maize.
On September 19, 1609, Henry Hudson anchored the *Half Moon* in the
shallows off the site of the present city—the farthest point north the ship
reached—and spent several days making friends with the Indians. In 1613
two vessels commanded by Captain Adrian Block and Hendrick Chris-
tiansen spent the winter near the head of navigation. In 1614, on Castle
Island (Van Rensselaer Island), now part of the Port of Albany, Christian-
sen built Fort Nassau, which was used as a trading post for four years; and
sporadic trade was thereafter continued by individual merchants. The
friendly relations maintained with the Indians during this early period
had a lasting influence on Albany's Colonial history.

The first permanent settlers, who came in 1624, were 18 families,
mostly Walloons from Holland. They built a second fort on the site of the
present river steamer landing and called it Fort Orange in honor of the
ruling house of Holland.

In 1630 Kiliaen Van Rensselaer, with two partners, purchased from the
the Indians land on both sides of the Hudson River with Fort Orange the
approximate center, and established the patroonship of Rensselaerswyck.
The patroon, who never came to the Colony, sent Dutch, Norwegians,
Danes, Germans, and Scots to settle on the land; he built sawmills, gristmills, homes, and barns for them; supplied foodstuffs and cattle; set up
laws regulating trade, hunting, and fishing; and collected rentals.

Father Isaac Jogues, the Jesuit martyr, described the settlement in

1643 as 'composed of about one hundred persons who reside in some twenty-five or thirty houses built along the river as each found most convenient . . . All their houses are of boards and thatched, with no mason work except the chimneys.'

Friction developed early between the patroonship and the Dutch West India Company, each claiming jurisdiction over the land on which Fort Orange was built. In 1652, Peter Stuyvesant, sent out by the West India Company as director general of New Netherland, set up a court and laid out space around Fort Orange for a new village called Beverwyck (Dutch, town of the beaver), and forbade the patroon to erect buildings near the fort. The Van Rensselaer agent tore down the proclamation and posted another maintaining the rights of the patroon. When the English threatened New Amsterdam (now New York City) in August–September 1664, Stuyvesant called on Rensselaerswyck for aid, but was refused. Under the new English rule the Van Rensselaers still claimed Beverwyck as part of their manor, but relinquished their claim to the village in 1685. Governor Dongan converted their patroonship into an English manor.

The British permitted the Dutch to retain their own language, customs, religion, local courts, and institutions, and admitted them to the governor's council. Their leaders, represented by such names as Van Rensselaer, Schuyler, Hendrick, and Winne, were joined by British tradesmen and officials, led by the Clintons, Yateses, Livingstons, and other families prominent in the Nation's history. In 1686 Albany, chief fur trading center of the English Colonies, was given a charter by Governor Dongan. For a quitrent of one beaver skin a year the king granted the city control of the fur trade to 'the eastward, northward, and westward as far as His Majesty's dominion may extend.'

The fur trade made Albany traders wealthy and intensified friction with the French. Control by the English of the interior and of the fur trade of the Great Lakes area depended on their alliance with the Iroquois and the defense of the Colonial frontier, of which Albany was the key. In 1690 the Massachusetts Council, concerned for the safety of Albany after the Schenectady massacre, wrote: 'Albany is the dam, which should it through neglect be broken down by the weight of the Enemy, we dread to think of the Inundation of Calamities that would quickly follow thereupon.'

The four Colonial wars kept the city in a state of anxiety from 1689 to 1763. During the early conflicts, when it bore the brunt of the defense, Albany protested the building of French forts to the west as a potential source of interference with the fur trade. In 1701, during a temporary cessation of hostilities, a substantial trade in Indian goods grew up between Albany and Montreal. To protect the trade, Albany agreed to remain neutral in case of another war, and the French agreed that Albany should not be attacked. Indians under French domination purchased arms in Albany to use against the New England colonies.

The Iroquois resented this trade with their commercial rivals, and their allegiance to the English cause was further weakened by French military successes. In 1754 the British Lords of Trade finally awoke to the danger and called a congress of all the colonies at Albany to make a treaty with the Indians and to consider colonial defense. The Indians were slow in arriving; their temper was expressed by King Hendrick, chief of the Mohawk, when he thundered, 'Look at the French; they are men, they are fortifying everywhere—but, we are ashamed to say it, you are all like women . . .' Benjamin Franklin's plan of union was adopted by the congress but was rejected by the colonies because it unduly limited their independence and by Britain because it impaired the royal prerogative.

During the French and Indian War, Albany served as point of departure for Colonial and British forces under William Johnson, Abercrombie, Bradstreet, and Lord Amherst on their way north and west against the French. After the Anglo-French treaty of 1763 the city was ready for peace, but farmers were disgruntled by taxes, merchants and lawyers were gauging anew the possibilities of Franklin's 1754 proposal, and young men back from the wars were restive under British rule. The break came with Stamp Act riots, the organization of the Sons of Liberty, and the burning of the city mail sleigh. Philip Schuyler proposed a censure of George III in the 1775 session of the Provincial Assembly, which carried 7 to 2 after the Loyalists had left the chamber.

Shortly before the Battle of Lexington a Committee of Safety was organized, which voted sums of money to Boston, patrolled the streets with its own militia, supervised defense operations, and erected gallows (near the present site of the State Capitol) to hang Tories who had tried to escape jail.

Capture of Albany was the objective of the British campaign of 1777. Mrs.Schuyler rode north in her carriage and burned the grain on the family estate at Old Saratoga (Schuylerville) to prevent its falling into the hands of the British. After the surrender of his army at Old Saratoga, Burgoyne became a prisoner-guest in her home in Albany. Lafayette spent part of 1778 in the city, preparing to lead an expedition against Canada. St.Peter's and the Dutch Reformed Church were turned into hospitals. Second to General Philip Schuyler as the city's hero was Colonel Peter Gansevoort, who commanded Fort Stanwix (now Rome), the western outpost, and with the aid of General Herkimer blocked St.Leger's advance down the Mohawk Valley. In 1779 local residents of the Second New York Continentals, under Colonel Goose Van Schaick, cut into the central wilderness to destroy the villages of the Onondaga. George Washington was made a freeman (i.e. voter) of the city during a visit in 1782; the following year, with Governor Clinton, he made a second visit.

The war at an end and the Indian treaties voided, Albany found itself at the crossroad of a free Nation in the making. Lands in the central and western parts of the State were opened to settlement; and the principal route from the New England States lay down the Hoosick Valley to the Hudson, south to Albany, and across the pine plains to Schenectady and the Mohawk Valley. The main stream of emigration poured westward through Albany; in 1795, five hundred vehicles a day pushed up State Street hill.

In 1785 Captain Stewart Dean, sailing from Albany to Canton, China,

was the second Yankee skipper to reach that port. A stagecoach line between Albany and New York was chartered in 1785. From 1783 to 1790
Duncan Phyfe, who later won fame as a furniture craftsman in New York
City, served his apprenticeship with a local coachmaker. Sailmakers and
chandlers opened shops along the city's three quays. Clothing, hat, and
glass factories were established. Within a few years glass manufacturers
developed an annual business of $380,000 in black bottles for the 'rum-to-
slaves-to-sugar-to-rum' trade of New England shippers. Lumberyards at
the northern end of the city absorbed the output of Adirondack forests.
After wandering from New York City to White Plains, Kingston, and
Poughkeepsie, the State legislature moved to Albany in 1797 and rented a
home for Governor John Jay.

In the closing years of the century, migration forced the first road improvements and the development of a number of turnpikes radiating from
the city. At the height of turnpike travel, 20 stagecoaches left Albany
daily over the Cherry Valley route (now US 20). The first steamboat to
make regular trips, the *Clermont*, built by Robert Fulton, steamed into
the Albany harbor on August 19, 1807.

The Champlain Canal was opened in 1822, the trans-State Erie was
completed in 1825. Albany built a pier 4,000 feet long, at which hundreds
of canal boats could be handled at one time. Wheat from the Genesee
Valley, salt and waterproof cement from Onondaga, butter, glass, and potash were unloaded on the Albany wharves. Packet lines carried pioneers to
Ohio, Indiana, Michigan, and Illinois. From 1820 to 1830 the population
of the city doubled. In 1831, 15,000 canal boats tied up at city wharves
and 500 sailing ships in the coastal and West India trade cleared from Albany.

Within a few years after the appearance of the first canal boat came the
first railroad. The diminutive *De Witt Clinton* made the first trip over the
Mohawk & Hudson Railroad to Schenectady on September 24, 1831. The
Hudson River Railroad, connecting New York City with Greenbush (now
Rensselaer) across the river, was completed in 1851. The first steam-
driven printing press in the country was operated here in 1828; the second
telegraph instrument in the United States was installed here in 1845; the
American Express Company was formed here in 1841. Cattleyards, developed at West Albany, at their peak handled 2,000,000 animals a year
from midwestern ranges.

In the twenties, thirties, and forties Albany was an important political
and journalistic center. The Albany *Argus*, founded in 1813, become famous as the mouthpiece of the political circle known as the Albany Regency, with Martin Van Buren its guiding spirit. The Albany *Evening
Journal*, founded in 1830 and edited for 35 years by Thurlow Weed, early
political boss, bolstered first the Whigs and then the Republican party.

The lumber industry reached its maximum development during the
Civil War years. Early in the nineteenth century log drives originating on
the upper Hudson made Albany a dominant lumber center. In 1872 the
lumber district extended for one-and-three-quarter miles along the canal
north of the city, with docks 1,000 feet long. The annual intake was

680,000,000 feet of timber. Destruction of the forests and the demand for conservation curtailed the lumber industry, and the 3,963 sawmills operating in the Albany district in 1865 dwindled to 150 in 1900.

The unleashing of energy and the spurt of industrialization that followed the Civil War, together with increased immigration, turned Albany into the path that led to its twentieth-century industrial and commercial importance. Groups of Irish settled in the city at various periods in the nineteenth century. Some Germans settled after the revolution of 1848, and many more came about 1870 to escape conscription in their homeland. In 1880 the population exceeded 90,000. During the last decades of the century Italians were attracted by labor opportunities.

Several of the city's largest manufacturing plants were established in the seventies and eighties. Early in the present century interest centered again on the canal system, and Albany profited from the construction of the Barge Canal. The seaboard returned to the city again, half a century after the disappearance of the clipper ship, when the Port of Albany was opened in 1932 and became a contributing factor to the city's growing commercial importance.

Together with its industrial neighbor, Rensselaer, Albany today has large factories making, among other products, checkers, dominoes, billiard balls, toilet paper and paper towels, papermakers' felts, drugs, textiles, woolens, carbonic acid gas, and electric car heaters. It is the third largest express transfer and sixth largest mail transfer station in the United States. It clears 148 passenger trains and 88 freight trains daily. Chain stores and mail-order houses maintain divisional warehouses in or near the city. In 1939 the Port handled the cargoes of 250 ocean-going vessels, consisting principally of petroleum, grain, and lumber.

The increasing importance of New York State in national politics after 1900 brought prominence to the State's capital city. The careers of Theodore Roosevelt, Charles Evans Hughes, Alfred E. Smith, and Franklin D. Roosevelt centered national interest on Albany.

POINTS OF INTEREST

1. The PARKER DUNN MEMORIAL BRIDGE, Broadway and Madison Ave., opened in 1933, the only toll-free bridge across the Hudson River between New York City and Troy, was named in honor of Parker F. Dunn (1890–1918), Albany war hero and recipient of the Congressional Medal of Honor. The elevating center span is the heaviest ever installed in this country.

2. The DELAWARE & HUDSON BUILDING, at the Plaza, Broadway at the foot of State St., a large granite structure designed in the Flemish Gothic style by Marcus T. Reynolds, has steep slate roofs and many ornamented dormer windows. Completed in 1918, it is four stories high with a 13-story central tower surmounted by a large bronze weather vane modeled after Hudson's *Half Moon*. A one-story vaulted arcade runs across the entire front of the building.

3. The FEDERAL BUILDING (POST OFFICE), SE. corner of Broad-

way and Maiden Lane, completed in 1936, is a five-story building of modern design with slight Greek influence, built of white Vermont marble on a white granite base. The simplicity of its design is relieved by the vertical setbacks around the doors and windows and a carved frieze depicting the story of the United States mail. A feature of the interior decoration is a series of nine indirectly illuminated ceiling maps which portray the nations of the world. The architects were Gander, Gander, and Gander.

4. The JOHN V.L. PRUYN LIBRARY (*open 9–9 weekdays; 2–6 Sun. for reading only*), SE. corner of N.Pearl St. and Clinton Ave., is of modified Dutch Renaissance architecture, with brick and stone walls, carvings, high stepped gables, steep roofs, tower, iron work, narrow mullioned windows, and richly decorated interior. Its imported fireplace tiles are Holland Dutch of 1580, and several pieces in the children's room are from churches and chateaux in France. The building was designed by Marcus T. Reynolds and constructed in 1901 on the site of the birthplace of John V.L. Pruyn (1811–77), lawyer, congressman, and Chancellor of the University of the State of New York.

5. The FIRST DUTCH REFORMED CHURCH (the North Dutch Church), SW. corner of N. Pearl and Orange Sts., begun in 1797, is the fourth building of the congregation, organized in 1642 and therefore the second oldest Protestant church body in America that has had a continuous existence. Philip Hooker not only furnished the design for the structure but also acted with Elisha Putnam as 'undertaker' (contractor). Hooker's original design, based on the Hollis Street Church in Boston by Charles Bulfinch, called for a fine pedimented portico with four brick Roman Doric columns, the whole flanked by twin baroque towers. The interior was severely plain. In 1858 the building underwent extensive alterations: the entrance portico was replaced by a projecting Romanesque block, and the steeples were covered with slate; within, the flat ceiling was masked by plaster groined vaults, windows received stained glass, and the walls were covered with medieval ornament.

The unusually wide central aisle is due to the retention of a seventeenth-century Communion service in which the whole congregation is seated at a

---

KEY FOR ALBANY MAP

1.Parker Dunn Memorial Bridge   2.Delaware & Hudson Building   3.Federal Building 4.John V.L. Pruyn Library   5.First Dutch Reformed Church   6.St.Joseph's Roman Catholic Church   7.Ten Broeck Mansion   8.St.Peter's Episcopal Church   9.City Hall 10.New York State Court of Appeals Building   11.Albany County Courthouse 12.Schuyler Monument   13.Lafayette Park and Academy Park   14.State Capitol 15.New York State Education Building   16.Cathedral of All Saints   17.New York State Office Building   18.Albany Institute of History and Art   19.Albany Academy for Girls   20.New York State College for Teachers   21.Bleecker Stadium   22.College of Saint Rose   23.Vincentian Institute Building   24.Bender Hygienic Laboratory 25.Dudley Observatory   26.Albany Academy   27.Albany College of Pharmacy 28.Albany Law School   29.Albany Hospital   30.Academy of the Holy Names   31. Washington Park   32.Roman Catholic Cathedral of the Immaculate Conception 33. State Executive Mansion   34.Lincoln Park   35.Schuyler Mansion   36.Port of Albany   37.New York State Bank Building

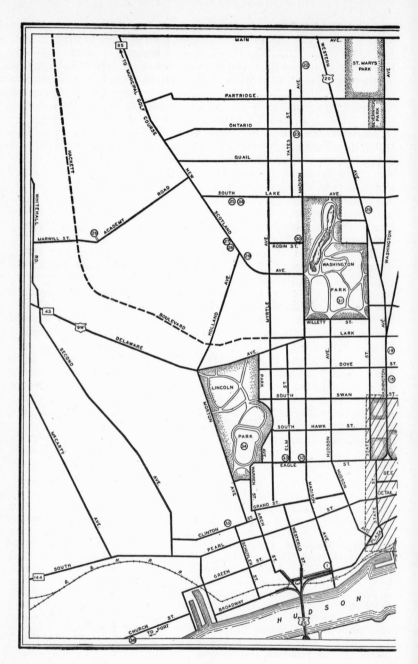

WORK PROJECTS ADMINISTRATION
NEW YORK STATE WRITERS' PROJECT

1940

ALBANY

SCALE

0   1/8   1/4   3/8   1/2 MILE

long table placed in the aisle. The oaken pulpit was carved in Holland in 1656. The box pew used by Theodore Roosevelt while governor of the State is marked with a bronze tablet.

6. ST.JOSEPH'S ROMAN CATHOLIC CHURCH, Ten Broeck St. between First and Second Sts., completed in 1860, except for the spire which was added about 1910, is in a parklike setting. It is constructed of blue stone in a modified Gothic Revival style; the trim was originally of French Caen stone, which, because it disintegrated in the severe climate, was replaced by Indiana buff limestone. The plan is cruciform, with high clerestory, nave, and transepts, and wide side aisles. The arched main entrance is through a square, buttressed, four-story tower surmounted by a high, dormered spire.

7. The TEN BROECK MANSION (*private*), 9 Ten Broeck Place, a solid, well-preserved brick building in the post-Colonial style, is two-and-one-half-stories high, with two prominent chimneys on each end. The ornamental hand-wrought iron beam anchors form the initials E and ATB and the date 1798. The house was built by Abraham Ten Broeck (1734–1810), Revolutionary patriot, member of the Albany Committee of Safety, 1775–7, member of the convention that framed the first State constitution, brigadier general in the Revolution, and mayor of Albany.

8. ST.PETER'S EPISCOPAL CHURCH, NW. corner of State and Lodge Sts., Gothic Revival in style, was designed in the French medieval tradition in 1859 by Richard Upjohn, the architect of Trinity Church in New York City. The square memorial tower, terminating in four pinnacles, the outside one higher than the rest and supporting an ornamented cross, was designed by Upjohn's son, Richard M. Upjohn, in 1876. The second rear east window was designed by Sir Edward Burne-Jones and made under his supervision by the William Morris Company, London, in 1880. The pulpit was designed by Robert W. Gibson in 1886; the figures in the reredos were sculptured by Louis Saint-Gaudens in the studio of his brother Augustus. The church body was organized in 1716. The grave of George Augustus, Lord Howe, killed in the attack on Ticonderoga in 1758, is believed to be beneath the vestibule floor.

9. The CITY HALL, Eagle St. between Maiden Lane and Pine St., erected in 1882, was designed by Henry H. Richardson in his characteristic modified French Romanesque style. The pyramidal-roofed tower houses the city carillon of 60 bells, the largest of which weighs 11,200 pounds. In the mayor's office is a portrait of the first mayor, Peter Schuyler, painted in London in 1710 by Sir Godfrey Kneller.

10. The NEW YORK STATE COURT OF APPEALS BUILDING, Eagle St. between Pine and Columbia Sts., constructed of white Sing Sing marble in 1835–42, Henry Rector architect, is Greek Revival in design, with a six-columned Ionic portico. Since it was originally built to house State offices, no expense was spared to make this building as fire-resistant as possible; therefore all the floors are composed of heavy masonry vaults. The thick rectangular mass has a central rotunda decorated with excellently executed superposed Greek orders and lighted from a skylighted dome. The two principal floors have 22-foot ceilings.

The stair to the left of the entrance is a notable example of self-supporting masonry. In a rear addition has been installed the Appellate Courtroom designed by H.H.Richardson in 1881. The room is paneled in light brown oak. Richardson's luxuriant Byzantinesque ornament is seen around the inglenook of the fireplace, which is faced with Siena marble and Mexican onyx, and in the old clockcase close by.

11. The ALBANY COUNTY COURTHOUSE, Eagle St. between Pine and Columbia Sts., erected in 1916, is a granite and limestone building in the neoclassic style, with engaged Ionic columns at the upper stories. The interior contains an open court from the roof to below the second floor ceiling, where it is covered by a large vaulted ceiling light. The lower court is striking with its columns and cream-colored Caen-stone walls.

12. The SCHUYLER MONUMENT, standing on a circular plot in front of the city hall, is the work of J.Massey Rhind. Philip Schuyler (1733–1804), born in Albany, supported the Revolutionary cause. He commanded the defenses of the northern frontier from 1775 until he was replaced by General Horatio Gates just before the Battle of Saratoga. Burgoyne and ranking British officers were his guests at the Schuyler Mansion for a week after the surrender. He played an important part in the earliest efforts to make the State's waterways navigable between the Hudson and the Great Lakes and in the chartering of Union College. Daniel Webster said Schuyler 'was second only to Washington in the services he performed for his country.'

13. LAFAYETTE PARK and ACADEMY PARK comprise a single stretch of greensward bounded by Washington Ave., and Hawk, Eagle, and Elk Sts. The western part is named in honor of the Marquis de Lafayette, who lived in Albany in 1778. The eastern part takes its name from the old Albany Academy building, erected in 1815, now called the JOSEPH HENRY MEMORIAL and occupied by the Albany Department of Education. The interior was remodeled in 1935 as a PWA project with Marcus T. Reynolds as architect. The two-story structure, designed by Philip Hooker and considered his masterpiece, is of formal post-Colonial architecture, constructed of brownstone, with Ionic pilasters, balustraded parapet, and a tall and graceful classical cupola. It was in this building that Joseph Henry (1797–1878), a quarter-century before Morse's telegraph, succeeded in ringing a bell over a circuit of wire strung around one of the rooms. A statue of Henry stands in front of the building.

14. The STATE CAPITOL (*open regularly 9–5 weekdays, 9–12 Sat.; June–Sept., 9–5 Sat., 10–5 Sun. for visitors*), in Capitol Park, bounded by Eagle, State, and Swan Sts. and Washington Ave., is an imposing, massive granite building crowning the hill. The exterior suggests a giant French chateau, with pyramidal red tile corner roofs and long, connecting gray slate roofs, high dormers, chimneys, and balustrades, and monumental eastern staircase extending 166 feet from the building.

The New York State legislature has met in Albany since 1797. Work was started on the present building in 1867. When it was formally occupied by the legislature in 1879, it was not yet complete; and even in 1898

Governor Black was able to say only that the building was 'practically completed.' It covers three acres and cost about $25,000,000.

Because of the many years of building, 1867–98, the influences of prevailing and passing styles of architecture, political personalities, and individual architects all found expression in the building, leaving it a mixture of styles and tastes. The exterior of the lower three floors is designed in the manner of the French Second Empire with Doric and Corinthian columns, arched windows, and rusticated stone work. The fourth floor is Romanesque: the columns are stubby in comparison with those of the second floor, the windows have a noticeably lower arch, the stone carvings are of natural objects—birds, trees, and flowers. On the fifth floor the towers, cornices, and dormers suggest the style of Francis I, the windows lacking the arches of the lower floors. The pedestals and balustrades of the monumental front staircase and the many chimneys are French Renaissance; the chimneys are adorned with clustered columns, bases, and capitals.

The plan, exterior decorations, and general massing of the building were the work of Thomas W. Fuller. The tower which he included in the original design and partly built was eliminated because the soil and the foundations would not safely carry it. The original plans were modified and added to by Leopold Eidlitz and H.H.Richardson in the prevailing styles of their day. To Isaac G. Perry as State Architect fell the duty of completing the designs of the other architects according to his own interpretation and subject to the needs of the State governmental departments. Eidlitz and Richardson were responsible for the Executive Chamber and the Court of Claims room; Eidlitz designed the Assembly Chamber and Richardson the Senate Chamber. The great western staircase and the main, eastern approach, with its corbels and arches, were designed by Richardson. Much of the exterior and interior stone carving and marble and wood paneling and carving was done by Perry.

The front staircase leads into the memorial rooms on the second floor, which contain Civil, Spanish-American, and World War mementos. The frescoes on the ceiling of the inner room depict military conflicts from the time of the Indian wars to the World War. The Executive Chambers are on this floor; the walls of the main room are wainscoted with mahogany and hung with portraits of Lafayette, Washington, and former governors of the State.

On the third floor are the Senate and Assembly chambers and the legislative library. The walls of the Senate Chamber are of Knoxville marble; the ceiling has massive carved oak beams. Two enormous fireplaces stand at one side of the room, with andirons more than four feet high. The walls of the Assembly Chamber are of sandstone, covered with sound-absorbing material; the ceiling is supported by four huge columns of Tennessee marble.

The building contains three notable staircases. The Senate staircase in the southeast corner is in the Gothic style; the Assembly staircase in the northeast corner is of simpler Gothic; the famous western staircase, the most ornate, is constructed of brownstone and lighted by an immense glazed dome and many clusters of lights.

The SHERIDAN STATUE, on the grounds E. of the Capitol, is a heroic equestrian statue of General Philip Sheridan (1831–88), native of Albany, cavalry commander under General U.S.Grant in the Civil War, and hero of Thomas B. Read's poem, *Sheridan's Ride*. The bronze monument on a base of polished granite was designed by J.Q.A.Ward and completed by his pupil, Daniel Chester French.

15. The NEW YORK STATE EDUCATION BUILDING, Washington Ave. between Hawk and Swan Sts., designed by Palmer, Hornbostel, and Jones, erected at a cost of $4,000,000, and dedicated in 1912, houses Chancellor's Hall, the State Library, the State Museum, and the offices of the State Education Department. The architecture is neoclassic, with modified Greek ornament. A colonnade of 36 Corinthian columns extends along the entire front.

Inside, to the right of the main entrance, is a broad staircase leading to the rotunda. Set in panels along the walls adjacent to the rotunda are 32 murals on the theme of education, designed and executed by Will H. Low.

On the second floor is the NEW YORK STATE LIBRARY (*open* 8:30 *a.m.–10 p.m. weekdays except holidays, Oct.–May;* 8:30–6, *June–Sept.*), founded in 1818. It possesses outstanding collections in New York State history and rare early American books. The manuscript collection includes the original drafts of Washington's *Farewell Address* and Lincoln's *Emancipation Proclamation*. The reading room is modeled on that of the Bibliothèque Nationale in Paris.

On the top floor is the NEW YORK STATE MUSEUM (*open* 9–5 *Mon.–Fri., 9–12 Sat. except holidays, Oct.–May;* 9–5 *weekdays,* 10–5 *Sun., June–Sept.*), which houses one of the largest collections of invertebrate fossils in the country. One group exhibit restores the tree fossils found at Gilboa, New York. In the Hall of Vertebrates is a specimen of the American mastodon, flanked by a restoration executed in plaster and coarse grass. On the west mezzanine are six dioramas of Iroquois Indians, grouped in realistic attitudes, depicting the daily activities of the Six Nations.

16. The CATHEDRAL OF ALL SAINTS, SE. corner of Elk and Swan Sts., seat of the Episcopal diocese of Albany, an unfinished edifice designed in the English Gothic style by Robert W. Gibson, is overshadowed by the higher, classical Education Building, which partly surrounds it. The exterior of the east portion, with its flying buttresses, and the aisles are constructed of rock-cut brownstone. The front, nave, and both transepts are of common brick without the stone facings; and the towers and lantern of the original plan are lacking, though there is a small flèche over the crossing.

The interior has been sufficiently completed to provide a cathedrallike atmosphere. Two rows of stone piers and arches, flanking the nave, accentuate the spaciousness of the building and draw the eye to the high altar, reredos, and large window of the east end. A delicate iron and brass rood screen separates the nave from the chancel. The stalls, imported from a church in Bruges, Belgium, are of carved oak, the carving dating back to 1655. The chancel and the south transept have elaborate stone carvings. The large stained-glass window in the west end is by John La Farge; the rose window in the north transept is by Maitland Armstrong; most of the others, including the east window above the altar, are by British designers.

The building was begun under the Right Reverend William Croswell Doane, first Bishop of Albany and author of the well-known hymn, *Ancient of Days*, whose tomb is directly under the high altar. The cornerstone was laid in 1884. The last major construction was done in 1902–4.

17. The NEW YORK STATE OFFICE BUILDING, Swan St. between Washington Ave. and State St., 33 stories in height, was completed in 1930 at a cost of $6,500,000. The massive exterior, of limestone and granite, is of modern design, built in a series of setbacks; the two lower floors are designed in the neoclassic manner. The Tower (*open weekdays all year; Sun. June–Sept.*) affords a bird's-eye view of Albany and the surrounding countryside.

18. The ALBANY INSTITUTE OF HISTORY AND ART (*open 10–5 weekdays, 2–5 Sun.*), 125 Washington Ave., a two-story gray brick building set back from the street, contains collections of American, English, and Dutch paintings, mostly of the nineteenth century, and period furniture. Special exhibits are held frequently.

19. The ALBANY ACADEMY FOR GIRLS, 155 Washington Ave., a private, nonsectarian institution, consists of three brick buildings, the main one in the Second Empire style with mansard roofs. The school gives elementary and college preparatory training to 250 girls. It was founded in 1814 and incorporated as the Albany Female Academy in 1821.

20. The NEW YORK STATE COLLEGE FOR TEACHERS, Western Ave. between Robin St. and S.Lake Ave., consists of a group of red brick buildings in Georgian Colonial and neoclassic style. Draper Hall, the administration building, built in 1908, is connected by colonnades with Hawley Hall on the left and Huested Hall on the right. The college, with a registration of 1,000 students, men and women, prepares teachers for secondary schools.

21. BLEECKER STADIUM, Clinton Ave. between Swinburne Park and Ontario St., with a field house of Georgian Colonial design, was built by the WPA. It seats 10,000 and has two baseball fields, a football field, a quarter-mile track, jumping and vaulting pits, and tennis courts.

22. The COLLEGE OF SAINT ROSE is on Madison Ave. between Main Ave. and Partridge St. Of particular note are Saint Joseph Hall on Madison Avenue, a red brick building with limestone trim, in modified Georgian style with a Corinthian colonnade on the upper story; and Science Hall, facing Western Avenue, a three-story brick and limestone structure. Chartered in 1924, the college, under the direction of the Sisters of Saint Joseph, has a student body of 300 girls, and grants baccalaureate degrees in liberal arts, science, music, and nursing.

23. In the VINCENTIAN INSTITUTE BUILDING (*open 7–6 daily*), N.E. corner of Ontario and Yates Sts., is the CHAPEL OF OUR LADY OF LOURDES, the sanctuary of which is designed in the manner of the Grotto of Lourdes, France. The stonework gives the appearance of a cave, an effect enhanced by a cascade, the murmur of which resounds through-

out the chapel. The altar is embellished with colored marble mosaics. The cave is illuminated by hidden lights.

24. The BENDER HYGIENIC LABORATORY (*private*), 136 S.Lake Ave., is a narrow, three-story-and-basement neoclassic building constructed of brick on a stone foundation. The laboratory was founded by a group of public-minded citizens in 1895, when the building was presented by Nathan W. Bender in memory of his wife. It carries on bacteriological examinations for the hospitals of Albany and vicinity, conducts scientific research, and holds classes in pathology.

25. The DUDLEY OBSERVATORY (*open 7-10 p.m. Tues.*), S.Lake Ave. N. of New Scotland Ave., founded in 1846, is part of Union University; the present building was erected in 1893. The refracting telescope is in the dome. A five-volume catalogue charting the movements of 33,000 stars, compiled by the observatory staff under the direction of Benjamin Boss, serves as a reference guide in all observatories. Visitors are allowed to look through the telescope when visibility is good.

26. The ALBANY ACADEMY, NW. corner of Academy Rd. and Hackett Blvd., a nonsectarian boys' preparatory school organized in 1813, is best known for the accomplishments of its distinguished professor, Joseph Henry. The present brick and marble building, completed in 1931, was designed in modified Georgian style by Marcus T. Reynolds.

27. The ALBANY COLLEGE OF PHARMACY (*open 9-5 Mon.-Fri., 9-12 Sat., except holidays*), 106 New Scotland Ave., a three-story building of modified Georgian design, is constructed of tapestry brick and limestone. Established in 1881, the college is part of Union University. The reconstructed O.B.Troop drugstore, which flourished in Schoharie in 1800, is on permanent exhibition in the building.

28. The ALBANY LAW SCHOOL, SW. corner of New Scotland and Holland Aves., erected in 1928, is a seam-faced granite structure designed in the Tudor Gothic style. The school was founded as a branch of the University of Albany in 1851 through the efforts of Ira Harris, Amasa J. Parker, and Amos Dean. In 1873 the University united with Union College, Schenectady, to form Union University. William McKinley, President of the United States, 1898–1901, graduated from the Albany Law School in the class of 1867.

29. The ALBANY HOSPITAL, New Scotland Ave. between Myrtle and S.Lake Aves., the oldest hospital in the city, was established in 1849. Its nurses' home is one of the largest in the State. The central building of brick with white stone trim was reconstructed in 1928.

Adjoining and connected with the hospital is the ALBANY MEDICAL COLLEGE, which occupies a four-story brick structure. The college, founded in 1838, is part of Union University.

30. The ACADEMY OF THE HOLY NAMES, 628 Madison Ave., a private Catholic preparatory school for girls, was founded by the Sisters of the Holy Names in 1884. The present stone and brick building, erected in 1914, is English Collegiate Gothic in style, with projecting wings, bay windows, and porches. The curriculum includes elementary and college preparatory courses.

31. WASHINGTON PARK, bounded by State and Willett Sts. and S. Lake and Madison Aves., occupying 90 acres, dates from 1865 and is Albany's largest park. It contains five miles of elm- and maple-shaded drives bordered by lawns landscaped with flower beds, flowering shrubs, and larch groves.

Near the Madison Avenue side of the park, facing the lake, is the KING FOUNTAIN, with figures in copper, by J.Massey Rhind, presented to the city in 1879 by Henry R. King in memory of his father. The figures represent Moses and his followers at the rock of Hebron.

East of the King Fountain stands the ROBERT BURNS STATUE, designed by Charles Calverly and erected in 1888. The seated figure is of bronze on a base of polished Scotch granite, set on a slightly elevated circular mound and overhung by maple and elm trees. At the northern end of the park, near the Northern Boulevard and State Street entrance, is the SOLDIERS AND SAILORS MEMORIAL, erected by the city in memory of its Civil War heroes.

32. The Roman Catholic CATHEDRAL OF THE IMMACULATE CONCEPTION, SW. corner of Madison Ave. and Eagle St., was dedicated in 1852. The large Gothic Revival building of warm brownstone stands on the crest of a hill. The two graceful front spires suggest those of Cologne Cathedral in Germany. The impressive Gothic exterior admirably complements the somber and spacious interior, with its altars and elaborately carved oak pulpit. Many of the former bishops of the diocese are buried in the crypt under the sanctuary.

33. The STATE EXECUTIVE MANSION (*private*), SW. corner of Eagle and Elm Sts., a large red brick building of the Civil War period, stands well back in a landscaped setting. On the first floor are the governor's office, the breakfast room, a large state dining room and kitchens, and the reception and check room. The second floor contains the living quarters of the governor and his family.

34. LINCOLN PARK, bounded by Eagle St. and Park, Morton, and Delaware Aves., is the second largest park in the city. In the southwest corner is the JAMES HALL BUILDING, erected by James Hall, State Geologist, 1836–98. This building served for 50 years as his residence, office, and laboratory, and was an active center of geological science. It was renovated in 1936 as a fresh-air school for undernourished children.

35. The SCHUYLER MANSION (*open weekdays 9–5, Sundays 1–5; admission free*), SW. corner of Clinton and Schuyler Streets, now a State-owned museum, was built by Philip Schuyler in 1762. The building, in its day called 'The Pastures,' is of Georgian Colonial architecture, with red brick walls, white trim, and a hipped gambrel roof set behind a delicate wood parapet railing and pierced by square chimneys and pedimented dormers. The octagonal vestibule is an early nineteenth-century addition. The interior is laid out in the typical Colonial plan with a wide center hall and central staircase and a fireplace in each room. In the room in the southeast corner of the first floor Elizabeth Schuyler was married to Alexander Hamilton. Much of the furniture now in the house belonged to the Schuyler family. Among the mementos in the second-floor collection are

General Burgoyne's shoe buckles, which the general gave to the Schuyler children on his visit after the defeat at Saratoga in 1777, and two pearl-encrusted lockets, one with a lock of George Washington's hair, the other with a braided strand of the hair of Alexander Hamilton and his wife.

36. The PORT OF ALBANY (*open*), Hudson River, S. end of Church St., one of the largest inland seaports and ports of entry in the United States, was completed in 1932, costing $13,000,000. The port occupies 217 acres, with a dock frontage of 4,400 feet, accommodating craft up to 27-foot draft. It has the largest single-unit grain elevator in the world.

37. The NEW YORK STATE BANK BUILDING, NE. corner of State and Pearl Sts., is a 17-story red brick office structure with stores on the first floor. When the present building was built in 1927, with H.I.Cobb as architect, the original structure, erected in 1803 and designed by Philip Hooker, was removed, except for the State Street façade, which now forms the main entrance. This portion is in the post-Colonial style, showing a strong Adam influence. The windows of the first story were originally doorways with small entrance stoops, and the present doorway was formerly a central window.

POINTS OF INTEREST IN ENVIRONS

John Boyd Thacher Park, 14 *m.* (*see Tour* 9). Fort Crailo and Beverwyck, 1 *m.*; Lindenwald, 22 *m.* (*see Tour* 21). Albany Rural Cemetery, 2 *m.* (*see Tour* 22).

Auburn

Railroad Stations: 150 State St. for New York Central System; corner of Clark and Monroe Sts. for Lehigh Valley R.R.
Bus Stations: 23 North St. for Greyhound and Giddings Bus Lines; Cayuga Omnibus Terminal, Osborne Hotel, 77 State St.
Street Busses: Fare 10¢; 6 tokens for 45¢.
Taxis: 25¢; 35¢ for 2 to 4 passengers.
Parking: Parking meters in business section; 1¢ for 12 mins., 5¢ for 1 hr.

Accommodations: 3 hotels; tourist homes, boarding houses.

Information Service: Cayuga County Automobile Association, Osborne Hotel, 77 State St.; Chamber of Commerce and Finger Lakes Association, 160 Genesee St.

Motion Picture Houses: 4.
Swimming: Owasco Lake, 2 m. S. on State 38; bathhouse 10¢, with locker 25¢.
Skating: Hoopes Park, E.Genesee St. Parkway.
Golf: Highland Golf Club, N.Hunter Ave., and Auburn Country Club, E.Lake Rd., greens fee $1.
Tennis: Pomeroy Park, 6 Bostwick Ave., 10¢.

Annual Events: Rose Show, June–July, Hoopes Park; Yacht Races, Owasco Lake, Memorial Day, July 4th, Labor Day.

AUBURN (650 alt.,35,705 pop.), once the junction point of the old Seneca and Genesee Turnpikes, has lost its robust stagecoach glamor. Cayuga County seat, important manufacturing and farm shopping center, it is an attractive city of Victorian homes on broad, quiet, tree-shaded streets. Through the Saturday afternoon shopping crowds on Genesee Street runs a farm atmosphere straight from the pages of *David Harum*. The factory sections of the town, principally in its western reaches, are the usual grimy huddle of brick blocks and smokestacks surrounded by nondescript homes of workers. The chief industrial products are rope, farm machinery, Diesel engines, shoes, carpets, and rugs. Foreign groups—Italians, Poles, and Russians, comprising about 20 per cent of the population—find employment in the factories, though some of the Italians do a little farming. A small Negro group, including descendants of runaway slaves, revere the memory of 'Aunt Harriet' Tubman, who helped slaves find freedom and who used the house and land given to her by Governor Seward as a home for indigent Negroes.

In 1793 Colonel John Hardenbergh, surveyor and Revolutionary veteran, built the first cabin on the present site of Auburn and a year later erected the first gristmill on the Owasco Outlet. At a meeting in 1805 the present name was taken from Goldsmith's *The Deserted Village*. In 1810 Governor De Witt Clinton reported that Auburn had 90 dwellings, 17 mills along the Outlet, and an incorporated library of 200 volumes. The opening of the State prison in 1817 and of the theological seminary four years later stimulated growth. In the 1840's Auburn was a rallying point for politicians. With William H. Seward and other national figures as adopted sons, it had hopes of becoming the State capital: Capitol Street is a reminder of that unrealized ambition.

Transportation facilities, abundant water power, and the practice, which was not abolished until 1882, of hiring out prison labor at ridiculously low rates, attracted industry. In 1818 Joseph Wadsworth transferred his scythe factory from Massachusetts to Auburn; in 1852 Carhart & Nye began the manufacture of carpets; in 1858 David Munson Osborne, a native son, founded the D.M.Osborne Company, which was absorbed in 1903 by the International Harvester Company. After 120 years existence, the Auburn Theological Seminary, chartered by the Presbyterian General Assembly in 1819, was merged with the Union Theological Seminary, New York City.

POINTS OF INTEREST

The AUBURN STATE PRISON (*not open to public*), 133 State St., bordering the Owasco Outlet on the south and Wall St. on the north, dominates the city skyline with tall smokestacks rearing from behind its concrete walls. The State Street gate is in the castellated Gothic style. The old main building was replaced in 1939 by a modern structure. 'Copper John,' the metal figure of a soldier which was perched atop the old building, has been transferred to the new one and remains the institution's mascot. The ambition of inmates is to look him in the face, which can be accomplished only from outside the prison walls.

The prison accommodates between 1,500 and 1,750 inmates; the products of its industries, with a value of about $600,000 a year, include cloth, school and office furniture, all the auto license plates and road signs for the State, baskets, brooms, and iron beds.

The original prison was constructed in 1816 on land donated by Auburn citizens, and the first building was patterned after the then typical congregate system. A small band of reformers, led by John Griscom of New York City, secured passage in 1819 and 1821 of laws requiring construction of solitary cells, the favorite prison reform panacea of the day. Since the laws did not specify the size of the cells, the contractor and the first warden, interested in economy, hit upon the smallest area in which a man could both lie down and stand up: $3\frac{1}{2}$ x 7 x 7 feet. These cages were erected in rows, back to back, and piled several tiers high, forming the first cell-block, which became the model of American prison architecture for the next hundred years and is still in use in Auburn in a modified form. It was soon discovered that, while the solitary convicts became anything but penitent and insanity increased among them, the prisoners in the old congregate rooms were earning profits for the prison by laboring for outside contractors. The 'silent system' was devised in 1823 by John Cray, Elam Lynds, and Gersham Powers, whereby the inmates were taken out of their cages during the day and marched in lockstep to the contractors' shops, where they worked under strict rules of silence, infractions being punished by the generous use of the 'cat-o-nine tails.'

Though public indignation was frequently aroused by the brutal excesses of punishment, the system gained official favor because of the economy of cell construction and the returns from contract labor. In 1825 Captain Elam Lynds took a crew of Auburn prisoners as his construction force to what is now Ossining and built Sing Sing on the Auburn cell-block pattern. After 1876 the more liberal discipline of the Elmira Reformatory gradually replaced the unnatural silent system. Long before that date, however, efforts had been made at Auburn to modify the harsh discipline. In 1847 whipping was replaced by the 'shower-bath': the convict was fastened in stocks and cold water was poured over him.

Thomas Mott Osborne (1859–1926), one-time head of D.M.Osborne & Company, was appointed State prison commissioner in 1913 and began his duties by serving a week's term in Auburn under the name of Tom Brown. To him a fellow-prisoner suggested the organization of the Mutual Welfare League as a means of fitting the prisoners for social life. Osborne introduced the plan, and although his league came to a bloody end at Auburn in the riots of July and December 1929, in which several convicts and a keeper lost their lives, the principle of enlisting the co-operation of inmates remains a feature of modern penology.

FORT HILL CEMETERY, 19 Fort St., includes a hill that once formed part of the ramparts of Fort Alleghan, believed to have been erected by the prehistoric mound builders. Artifacts taken from the site are in the State Museum, Albany, and in the Cayuga Museum of History and Art. Near the mound are the grave of William H. Seward and the 30-foot LOGAN MEMORIAL. Logan (1725–80), famous Indian orator and pacifist, was the white man's friend until in 1774 a group of white ruffians murdered his family in the Ohio Valley. In retaliation he gathered a party of warriors and began murdering whites up and down the countryside. Later in the same year, in a meeting at which he laid down his arms, he delivered an oration, a bitter indictment of white inhumanity, that is one of the most moving documents in Indian history. 'Logan never felt fear,' he concluded. 'He will not turn his heel to save his life. Who is there to mourn for Logan? Not one!'

The SEWARD MANSION (*private*), 33 South St., a brick, vine-covered post-Colonial home, stands in the center of a five-acre plot with Lombardy poplars, locust and cherry trees, and cast-iron griffins in the front yard. The house was built in 1816 by Elijah Miller, Seward's father-in-law. Here during the Civil War period Seward entertained many political leaders, American and foreign. In the small park adjoining the mansion is a statue of Seward.

William H. Seward (1801–72), born in Orange County and graduated from Union College, practiced law in Auburn and was elected to the State senate at the age of 29 by the anti-Masonic party. Later he followed Thurlow Weed into the Whig party and was elected governor in 1838. But his program of school expansion and internal improvements aroused antagonism, so that in 1843 he retired to his law practice in Auburn. After Horace Greeley and Weed had succeeded in absorbing most of the Free Soilers, Abolitionists, and Liberty Party into the Whigs, Seward was elected to the United States Senate, where he served from 1849 to 1861. By 1860 he was prominent enough to be a contender for the presidential nomination won by Lincoln. He was Lincoln's secretary of state, and an attempt on his life was made on the same day Lincoln was assassinated: a man named Payne stole into Seward's home and wounded him and his son. Seward was largely responsible for the purchase of Alaska in 1867; called 'Seward's Folly' and 'Seward's Frog Pond,' it has since paid for itself many times over.

The CAYUGA MUSEUM OF HISTORY AND ART (*open* 10–5 *Mon., Wed., Fri., Sat.; 2–5 Sun.*), 203 Genesee St., occupies the opulent Greek Revival house built in 1836 by John Seymour. The rectangular, four-story mass of unusually high proportions recalls numerous courthouse designs of the period. The four giant Ionic columns of the portico, the pediment above, and the cupola on the roof ridge are hallmarks of the style. The interior was slightly altered in the 1880's. The collections include Indian artifacts, Colonial implements, and books and records associated with William H. Seward and other famous sons of Auburn and Cayuga County. Changing art exhibitions are a main attraction.

The MEMORIAL CITY HALL, South St. near Genesee St., built in 1930, is a fine Georgian structure designed by Coolidge, Shepley, Bulfinch & Abbott, Boston architects. The building, of red brick with limestone trim and a wood portico of four Ionic columns, is a memorial to David Munson Osborne, manufacturer of agricultural machinery and mayor from 1879 to 1881.

POINTS OF INTEREST IN ENVIRONS

Enna Jettick Park, 2.6 *m*.; Cayuga Lake State Park, 16.4 *m*.; Fillmore Glen State Park, 19.5 *m*. (*see Tour* 8). Onondaga Reservation, 33.1 *m*. (*see Tour* 18).

Binghamton

Railroad Stations: 69 Lewis St. for Delaware, Lackawanna & Western R.R.; S.Depot St. W. of Chenango St. for Erie R.R. and Delaware & Hudson R.R.
Bus Stations: 81 Chenango St. for Greyhound, L.D.Dickinson, Hudson Transit, and Susquehanna Motor Coach Lines; 73½ Chenango St. for White Bus Lines; 56 Henry St. for Rapid Transfer, Blue Motor Coach, Hudson Transit Lines, and the Short Line.
Airport: Tri-City Airport, 10 m. W. on Campville Rd.

Accommodations: 10 hotels; tourist homes.

Information Service: Binghamton Auto Club, 124 Chenango St.; Binghamton Chamber of Commerce, 66 Chenango St.

Radio Station: WNBF (1,500 kc.).
Motion Picture Houses: 13.
Baseball: Johnson Field, N.Broad St. and Brocton Ave., Johnson City, home of the Binghamton Triplets of the Eastern League.
Golf: Ely Park, Ridge St. and City Line, 9 holes, greens fee 50¢.
Tennis: Ross Park, Park Ave. and Morgan Rd.; Recreation Park, Beethoven and Seminary Sts.; free.

BINGHAMTON (845 alt.,78,278 pop.), largest Southern Tier city, Broome County seat, and metropolis of the Triple Cities, which include Johnson City and Endicott, is at the confluence of the Chenango and Susquehanna Rivers. All main approaches to the city lead to the courthouse square, hub of the city's business district. Here, within a four-block radius, are the principal stores, hotels, and theaters, housed for the most part in plain, three-story brick blocks. On the west side of the Chenango River is the chief residential section. South of Main Street are stately old homes and modern stone and brick dwellings set in spacious, landscaped grounds. Northward, is a large foreign settlement of Polish, Russian, and Czechoslovakian factory workers; to the east is a large Italian colony.

Binghamton and its two sister cities have 107 industries, giving employment to 34,500 workers and distributing an annual pay roll of $48,-500,000. The significant co-operation between capital and labor, established in the early days of the shoe industry, has been reflected in all channels of the community's business, social, and educational life. Round-table conferences between workers and employers promoted employment stability, which in turn contributed to a high ratio of home ownership.

Little is known of the Binghamton area before the Revolution. The site was ceded to the whites by treaty at Fort Herkimer in 1785, and was sold in 1786 to William Bingham, a Philadelphia merchant. Joseph Leonard, first permanent settler, built his log cabin near by in 1787, and was soon joined by other pioneers, who called the new settlement Chenango. The following year Joshua Whitney learned that a bridge was to be built across the Chenango River near its confluence with the Susquehanna. At his suggestion a 'chopping bee' was organized, and land near the designated bridge site was cleared of timber. Several buildings were moved from the old village and the new settlement was called Chenango Point. In 1816 the first stagecoaches began weekly trips from Newburgh and Owego. Later the name was changed to Binghamton in honor of Bingham, who made liberal donations of land to the settlement. In 1834 Binghamton was incorporated as a village.

Completion of the Chenango Canal in 1837, establishing an important link between the coal regions of Pennsylvania and the Erie Canal at Utica, began an era of progress in transportation and industrial development. During this period the manufacture of photographic apparatus was begun by the E.& H.T.Anthony Company, progenitor of the Agfa-Ansco Corporation. In 1848 the Erie Railroad brought direct connection with New York and shortly thereafter with Buffalo and the Great Lakes. In 1851 the Delaware, Lackawanna & Western Railroad opened the way into Pennsylvania, and was followed by the Delaware & Hudson, which established a direct route to New England.

At the time of its incorporation as a city in 1867, Binghamton had a population of 11,000. Cigar making, its first important participation in manufacture for other than local consumption, was firmly established by 1870 and its rapid growth put the city in second place in the tobacco industry of the country. But the popular shift to cigarette smoking, combined with a cigarmakers' strike in 1890, caused a permanent slump. The manufacture of shoes, modestly begun in 1854 by Horace N. Lester and his brother George, developed into an industry that caused the founding of Johnson City and Endicott, brought a large-scale immigration of foreign factory workers, and resulted in the building of 22 factories, six tanneries, and two rubber mills located in Binghamton, Johnson City, Endicott, and Owego.

POINTS OF INTEREST

The BROOME COUNTY COURTHOUSE, on a plot bounded by Main, Collier, and Exchange Sts., erected in 1898, is constructed of Ohio sandstone trimmed with bluestone, the main entrance marked by a classic portico with tall Ionic columns. It is the last of a long line of courthouses, the first of which was erected in 1802, when Chenango Point was constituted a 'half-shire' of Tioga County. Broome County was separated from Tioga in 1806 and named for Lieutenant Governor John Broome, who, in appreciation of the compliment, presented the silver seal that is still used.

A plaque in the courthouse commemorates the founding in Binghamton in 1911 of the first farm bureau in the United States. The office of the bureau (*open 9-4 weekdays*) is in Room 302.

In front of the courthouse stands a statue by A.G.Newman of Daniel S. Dickinson, U.S.Senator, 1844-51. In the Democratic National Convention of 1852 Dickinson refused the nomination of Virginia, which might have made him the Democratic candidate for the Presidency, because of his loyalty to General Lewis Cass, to whom he was pledged.

The BINGHAMTON PUBLIC LIBRARY (*open 9–9 weekdays*), 78 Exchange St., a yellow brick building trimmed with limestone, neoclassic in style with pedimented, two-story front portico, is a Carnegie library and houses the MUSEUM OF FINE ARTS (*open 11–5 Mon.–Fri., 7–9 p.m. Sat.*), a small permanent collection of paintings, sculpture, and prints, and a collection of Indian artifacts.

CHRIST CHURCH (Episcopal), SW. corner of Washington and Henry Sts., built of stone, with steep slate roofs and a square, buttressed tower terminating in a dormered spire, was erected in 1855 from plans of Richard Upjohn,Sr. The tower was added in 1903. The congregation, incorporated in 1810 as St.Anne's and reorganized under its present name in 1816, is the oldest in the city.

ROSS PARK, Park Ave. and Morgan Rd., consists of more than 100 acres of wooded slopes, shady drives, paths, and picnic sites. It contains a deer park, a wading pool, tennis courts, and the Municipal Zoo, a large collection of American and foreign wild life.

MEMORIAL PARK, Washington and Water Sts., is an irregular oblong of about three acres bordering the Chenango and Susquehanna Rivers, which converge at this point. Here a detachment of General Clinton's army encamped during its expedition against the Indians in 1779.

RIVERSIDE DRIVE SOLDIERS AND SAILORS WORLD WAR MEMORIAL BRIDGE spans the Chenango River, connecting Riverside Drive with Water and Washington Streets. The eastern end of the bridge terminates in a circular plaza, in the center of which is the Spanish War Veterans Monument.

SUN BRIAR COURT (*open*), Riverside Drive near Helen St., model training stable owned by the estate of the late Willis Sharpe Kilmer, is named for the race horse that was credited with the largest cash winnings for 1917, and in the period 1917–20 sired several other famous horses. Within the large, circular wood building facing the entrance are an indoor track, a series of box stalls, and an equine hospital, including maternity clinic and nursery. In the clubhouse are displayed the trophies won by horses racing under the Kilmer colors.

The ENDICOTT–JOHNSON PLANT (*open during working hours upon application at office; guides*), 16 Susquehanna St., comprises three factories housed in red brick and wood buildings. The B.B.B. (Binghamton Busy Boys) factory is engaged mostly in the manufacture of children's shoes; the George F. Johnson factory fills orders for Army and CCC shoes; and the Binghamton Work Shoe factory makes everyday shoes. Other factories are in neighboring towns (*see Tour 3*).

The BINGHAMTON STATE HOSPITAL (*open 1–3 Mon., Wed., Fri.*), State Hospital Hill, east city line, housed in native stone and brick buildings, was founded in 1854. It is virtually a city in itself, with its own power plant, fire-prevention system, farms, shops, and nurses' homes. The institution provides treatment and care for the insane and the mentally deficient.

The ANSCO PLANT (*not open to public*), 40 Charles St., contains the laboratories and film production units of the Ansco division of the General Aniline and Film Corporation. It is the second largest and the oldest manufacturer of photographic supplies in the country.

POINTS OF INTEREST IN ENVIRONS

Johnson City, 2.1 *m.*; Endicott, 7.3 *m.* (*see Tour 3*). Chenango Valley State Park, 11.3 *m.* (*see Tour 10*).

Buffalo

Railroad Stations: New York Central Terminal, Lovejoy St. and Lindbergh Drive, for New York Central System, Michigan Central R.R., Pennsylvania R.R., and Toronto, Hamilton and Buffalo Ry.; Black Rock Station, Dearborn and Tonawanda Sts., for Michigan Central R.R. and Toronto, Hamilton & Buffalo Ry.; Lackawanna Station, Main St. at Buffalo River, for Delaware, Lackawanna & Western R.R., Baltimore & Ohio R.R., and New York, Chicago and St.Louis R.R.; Lehigh Valley Station, Main and Scott Sts., for Lehigh Valley R.R., Erie R.R., and Canadian National Ry.

Bus Stations: Greyhound Terminal, 640 Main St., for Central Greyhound Lines, West Ridge Transportation Co., Pennsylvania Niagara Lines, Dodaro Motor Coach Lines, Gray Coach Lines, Ltd., Genesee Coach Lines; Buffalo Bus Depot, Clinton and Ellicott Sts., for Hamburg Coach Lines, Blue Bus Lines, Martz Coach Lines, Canadian-American Coaches, Ltd.; Washington and Clinton Sts. for Lackawanna busses; Niagara and Church Sts. for Van Dyke busses.

Airport: Municipal Airport, Genesee St. and Cayuga Rd., 2 m. E. on Genesee Rd. (State 33), for American Airlines and Pennsylvania-Central Airlines; taxi 75¢ per person from Hotel Statler; busses 20¢, time 45 mins.

Piers: S. end of Main St. at Buffalo River for Chicago, Duluth & Georgian Bay Transit Co., Detroit & Cleveland Navigation Co., and Great Lakes Transit Corp. (Lackawanna depot) boats; E. end of Erie St. at Buffalo River for Cleveland & Buffalo Navigation Co. boats.

Toll Bridge: Peace Memorial Bridge, N. end of The Front; pedestrians 5¢, 10 passes for 25¢; cars, depending on length of wheelbase, 25¢–40¢; passengers 5¢ each; $1.50 coupon book for $1, $5 book for $3.25.

Taxis: 25¢ first mile; 5¢ each additional quarter-mile; no charge for additional passengers.

Streetcars and City Busses: 10¢, 3 tokens for 25¢; free city transfers.

Street Numbering: Streets beginning at lake or river are numbered north or east from there; north-south streets are numbered south to north; other streets intersecting Main St. are numbered east and west from that street. Each number represents 10 ft. frontage; No.528 is one mile from starting point.

Accommodations: 76 hotels; tourist houses.

Information Service: Automobile Club of Buffalo, Statler Hotel, Niagara Square; Chamber of Commerce, 283 Main St.; Buffalo Convention and Tourist Bureau, Genesee Bldg., Main and Genesee Sts.

Radio Stations: WGR (550 kc.); WKBW (1480 kc.); WBEN (900 kc.); WEBR (1310 kc.); WBNY (1370 kc.); WSVS (1370 kc.).

Theaters and Motion Picture Houses: Erlanger Theater, Delaware Ave., and W.Mohawk St., and The Playhouse, Lafayette Ave. and Hoyt Sts., legitimate stage plays; 67 motion picture houses; 4 art cinemas.

Golf: Grover Cleveland Park, Main St. at City Line, 18 holes, weekdays 50¢., Sat., Sun., and holidays 75¢; Delaware Park Meadow, Parkside Ave. entrance; Cazenovia Park, 410 Potters Corners Road; South Park, South Park Ave. and South Drive; all 18 holes, weekdays 25¢, Sat., Sun., and holidays 50¢.

Baseball: Offerman Stadium, 1515 Michigan Ave., home grounds of the Bisons of the International League.

Tennis: 66 municipal courts in city parks, 50¢ per season.

Swimming: Municipal Beach, Angola-on-the-Lake, 20 m. SW. of city on Lake Shore Road off State 5 (*see Tour* 11); basket locker, but no towel, free; season, Decoration Day to Labor Day. Public pools in Cazenovia, Riverside, and Houghton Parks, and at Massachusetts Ave. and Lawrence Pl.; open daily in season, free.

Annual Events: St.David's Day banquet, St.David's Welsh Society, Mar. 1; Italian 'Feste Carnelevare,' 10 weeks before Easter; St.Patrick's Day banquet, Friendly Sons of St.Patrick, Mar. 17; Polish Independence Day celebration, Dom Polski, May 3; Dominion Day, July 1; picnic of Friends of France, Bastille Day, July 14; Buffalo Yacht Club cup races and motorboat regattas, July 15; Erie Club (policemen's) Field Day, Crystal Beach, Canada, July 18; Shriners-Knights of Columbus Charity baseball game, July–Aug.; Deutscher Tag celebration, United German Singing Societies of Buffalo, second Sunday in Aug.; rowing regattas sponsored by National Association of Amateur Oarsmen, Labor Day; Air Races, Sept.; Columbus Day celebration, Federation of Italian Societies, Oct. 12; St.Andrew's Day banquet, St.Andrew's Scottish Society, Nov. 30.

BUFFALO (600 alt.,575,150 pop.), largest industrial and commercial center in upstate New York, is at the foot of Lake Erie, source of the Niagara River.

Broad avenues, branching in all directions from Niagara Square, form with intersecting streets the squares that are a distinctive feature of the downtown section. About one mile south are the harbor, the maw of Buffalo, and the milling district. Buffalo Creek meanders from the east through flat, low-lying lands, the city's industrial area. Buffalo ranks eighth among the Nation's industrial centers, with 1,400 major plants employing more than 200,000 workers and producing annually goods valued at about $500,000,000. Twenty-odd blast furnaces have an annual capacity of 3,000,000 tons of pig iron. Buffalo has the largest linseed-crushing plant and the largest dye plant in the country and makes three-quarters of the country's wallboard supply. Chemically suitable water has stimulated rubber manufacture, culminating in a $25,000,000 plant.

Delaware Avenue, the street of fashion and comfort, begins inauspiciously at the new county jail and is marred through the business district by parking lots and stores, but from beginning to end its broad asphalt is a motor speedway. Beyond North Street it is lined with impressive mansions, interspersed with older homes, modern apartment houses, and a succession of beautiful churches. North of Forest Lawn Cemetery, Delaware Avenue spreads out in a system of parks and parkways, with homes in a variety of styles—Elizabethan, Georgian, American Colonial. In 1924, when the street was widened at the sacrifice of hundreds of stately elms, a storm of protest arose; and Charles E. Burchfield, water-colorist, was stirred to the creation of his canvas, *Civic Improvement*, now hanging in the Metropolitan Museum of Art.

Main Street, running north and south, bisects the city, passing through the business district a few blocks east of Niagara Square. For many years Main Street was Buffalo. Slow in developing, it was largely responsible for Buffalo's reputation as an overgrown village. But with the coming of the automobile and suburban development at the turn of the century, it acquired more traffic space, more spacious buildings, and better lighting, until today it is a busy, seven-mile metropolitan thoroughfare.

The residential area is divided into sharply distinguished communities:

the German East Side, Little Poland, the West Side of the burghers, and an Italian and a Hungarian colony.

Little Poland, on the East Side, contains about one fifth of Buffalo's population. The foreign-born generally converse and do business in the Polish language and read Polish newspapers. Signs along the streets read *Apteka* (drugstore), *Adwokat* (lawyer), and *Gospoda* (tavern). Dom Polski (Polish hall), Broadway and Playter Street, erected in 1905, is the social center. Old country customs, mainly those of a religious nature, survive. Easter baskets are taken to church to be blessed, and miniature theaters portraying the Nativity are carried from house to house. Children believe in *Gwiazdor*, the Polish Santa Claus. On November 28 girls tell their fortunes by 'pouring the wax': they melt candles down, pour the mass into cold water, and read the hardened shapes like tea leaves. Christmas wishes are exchanged by 'breaking with you the wafer': the head of the family breaks a wafer and gives half to his wife; both break their wafers and hand half to others, and so on; each time the season's greetings are exchanged. Second and third American-born generations, however, are rapidly adopting American customs, and many of them are achieving recognition in the professions, in business, and in politics.

The Germans, formerly the dominating foreign group, rank a close second to the Poles. Because of long residence they are less closely knit as a national unit. The Italian colony of 80,000 spreads along the water front. The 15,000 Hungarians live in Black Rock. Like the Poles, each group is a cohesive unit with a newspaper and various organizations; a large majority are unskilled laborers. Most of the 13,500 Negroes occupy a well-defined section around Jesse Clipper Square (named for a local Negro hero of the World War) at Michigan Avenue and William Street. The 'first families' of the community go back to the days of the Underground Railroad, of which Buffalo was an important station. During the World War several thousand Negroes came to work in steel mills and packing houses and along the docks.

German, Polish, Hungarian, and Italian singing societies have long played an important part in the city's cultural life. Drama finds expression in amateur theatrical groups. The city's educational system is topped by four degree-granting colleges, two of them Roman Catholic. The WPA adult education program provides 300 courses to more than 30,000 students. The Grosvenor Library is the third largest reference library in the country. The Buffalo Historical Society, the Museum of Natural Science, and the Albright Art Gallery are active centers of popular education.

On August 7, 1679, LaSalle's ship, the *Griffon*, which had been anchored for three months off Squaw Island (within the present city of Buffalo), was towed through the short rapids and sailed on her maiden voyage. This was the first vessel built by white men to navigate the upper lakes. The first white settlement in this region, made by the French at the mouth of Buffalo Creek in 1758, was destroyed by the British the next year. A village of 1,500 Indians, established two-and-a-half miles above the mouth of Buffalo Creek in 1780, formed the nucleus of the Buffalo Creek Reserve, a tract of 84,000 acres retained by the Seneca when they gave up title to their lands after the Revolution. This was the home of Corn-planter, Red Jacket, and Mary Jemison. As white settlement spread, the Indians sold this tract and moved to the Cattaraugus and Allegany Reservations.

Although Joseph Ellicott chose and mapped the site of Buffalo for the Holland Land Company in 1799, it was not until 1803–4 that he divided the land into lots and offered them for sale. He modeled the city plan after that of Washington, D.C., which his brother, Major Andrew Ellicott, had helped draw up several years before. Ellicott called the place New Amsterdam, but settlers preferred the old creek name.

During the War of 1812 Buffalo was a mustering place for troops. In December 1813, when a British force pillaged and burned the settlement, the 500 inhabitants fled; but most of them returned in March to rebuild. From headquarters in Buffalo, General Jacob Brown directed the American troops that captured Fort Erie on the Canadian side, July 3, 1814. His army then marched toward Niagara Falls to the battles of Chippewa (July 5) and Lundy's Lane (July 25). In ensuing engagements the Americans, under Major General George Izard, suffered setbacks and had to retire to Buffalo on November 5.

Buffalo was incorporated as a village in April 1816. The first steamboat on the Great Lakes, *Walk-on-the-Water*, was built here in 1819. The early welfare of the settlement depended on its function as a trading center for emigrants who traveled difficult roads to the lake shore and then continued westward by boat. Chief rival for this trade was Black Rock, two miles north, its interests promoted by General Peter B. Porter. The rivalry reached its climax in the crucial struggle over the choice of a western terminus for the Erie Canal. Black Rock had the better harbor. The commission to choose the terminal met in Buffalo in 1822 under the chairmanship of De Witt Clinton; Porter appeared for Black Rock, Judge Samuel Wilkeson for Buffalo. After the meeting Buffalo improved its harbor, the new breakwater withstood the spring freshets, and Buffalo was awarded the prize.

The Erie Canal, opened in 1825, brought trade and prosperity on a new scale. Buffalo stood at the transportation break in the great east-west route, and its warehouses bulged with east-bound farm products and west-bound manufactured goods. Hundreds of emigrants arrived daily, and hotels were built to accommodate them while they waited for boat connections. Visitors to Buffalo a year or two after the opening of the canal were amazed at the rapidity of its growth. Mrs.Frances Trollope, who visited the city in 1828, wrote that 'all the buildings have the appearance of having been run up in a hurry, though everything has an air of great pretensions; there are porticos, columns, domes and colonnades, but all in wood.' In 1832, with a population of about 12,000, Buffalo was incorporated as a city.

Expanding commerce led Buffalo into manufacturing. In 1826 Edward Root built a foundry for the manufacture of plow irons and small castings. John Hibbard made the first steam engine here in 1829, devising tools for curving the iron sheets imported from England and for spacing and punching rivet holes. In 1836 Wilkeson & Goodrich advertised as iron founders and steam engine manufacturers. The Buffalo Steam Engine Works was incorporated in 1841; the Shepard Iron Works was built in 1847. In 1843 Joseph Dart invented a grain elevator propelled by steam, substituting mechanical power for human backs in the handling of cargoes. By 1845 Buffalo had an assortment of other pioneer industries: a stove and hollowware factory, a nail factory, a turner in metals, a cabinet factory, a silversmithy, a brass and bell foundry, plants making mirrors and picture frames, porcelain bathtubs, millstones, soap, and candles.

In the rapid development of railroads in the 1850's, Buffalo saw a threat to its commercial pre-eminence. It appeared that the railroads would supersede water and turnpike transportation and Buffalo would lose the advantage of its location at the break in the east-west trade route. The city sought a solution by diverting its capital and energy into the industrial field, and in 1860 the Association for the Encouragement of Manufactures in the City of Buffalo was organized. But these fears proved unfounded. The Civil War, by deranging the lines of communication and transportation in the middle States, threw a vast amount of commerce to the northern routes. Trade with the expanding West grew rapidly during and after the war, and Buffalo became one of the great grain and livestock markets of the world. The railroads, attracted by existing markets and established trade routes, converged upon Buffalo and made it a railroad center. With 11 main railroad lines served by five passenger terminals and 14 freight terminals, with 300 passenger trains coming and going and 3,000 freight cars clearing every 24 hours, it is today the second largest railroad center in the United States.

The stimulus to manufacture had its effect and Buffalo industry grew rapidly. In 1872 there were more than 800 small industries employing 18,000 workers out of a population of 150,000. Railroad connections completed with the anthracite coal fields of Pennsylvania in 1873. Pennsylvania coal and Lake Superior iron ore, transported by lake boats, provided the necessary elements for large-scale manufacture of metal products.

Buffalo began to take on the characteristics of a modern city. Streets were paved and lighted with gas; sewers and water and gas pipes were laid; street railways were built. Irish and German immigrants swelled the population. Churches and schools multiplied. The Young Men's Association opened a library, sponsored lectures, and in 1861 held the first public art show. The newly rich, aiming to outdo the established families, turned to the rococo architecture of the post-Civil War period, with its bell towers, serpentine wood carvings, cast-iron ornament, and colored windows. In the downtown section ostentatious hotels provided the expansive attractions of club life. Edwin P. Christy expressed the spirit of the time in his song hit, *Buffalo Gals, Can't You Come Out Tonight!*

By the turn of the century a new economic resource was created by the harnessing of Niagara Falls, with a potential 11,000,000 horsepower available at low rates, and Buffalo industry entered upon a new period of expansion. Blast furnaces were erected on the lowlands along Buffalo

Creek. Industrial concerns built long rows of cottages for laborers recruited from the new immigrant groups. The city spread rapidly to the north and east. Along the harbor huge modern grain elevators were built; lake shipping took on a new life with the introduction of iron ships. A golden stream of grain cleared through Buffalo. The World War brought new industries, especially the manufacture of dyes and airplanes.

Grover Cleveland was elected mayor in 1881 and by his aggressive opposition to municipal extravagance won State and national attention. In 1901 the city staged its Pan-American Exposition, marred by the assassination of President William McKinley by the anarchist Leon F. Czolgosz. On September 14, the day McKinley died, Theodore Roosevelt took the oath of office as President. In 1916 Buffalo established a commission form of government, with a five-man council elected at large on a nonpartisan ballot; but in 1928 the mayor-council form was restored.

POINTS OF INTEREST
(Downtown)

1. The McKINLEY MONUMENT, center of Niagara Square, was erected by the State of New York and unveiled by Governor Charles E. Hughes on September 5, 1907, in memory of President William McKinley, who was assassinated on September 6, 1901, while attending the Pan-American Exposition. The monument, of modified French Renaissance design, consists of an obelisk resting on a paneled classical pedestal; the shaft rises out of a series of pools decorated with crouching lions. A circular promenade approached by radial walks completes the design. The architects were Carrère and Hastings; the sculptor was A.Phimister Proctor.

2. The SITE OF THE MILLARD FILLMORE HOUSE, W.Genesee St. and Delaware Ave., is marked by a bronze tablet on the wall of the Hotel Statler, Niagara Square. Millard Fillmore (1800–74) was born in Cayuga County, studied law in Buffalo, and, after practicing for several years in East Aurora, returned to Buffalo, where he maintained his official residence for the rest of his life. He was elected Vice President in 1848 and became thirteenth President in 1850, upon the death of Zachary Taylor. After his retirement from public office, Fillmore played an active part in the community life of Buffalo. He lived in the house on this site from 1858 until his death in 1874. His grave is in Forest Lawn Cemetery.

3. The SPENCER KELLOGG ADMINISTRATION AND OFFICE BUILDING (open on application), NW. corner of Niagara Square and Delaware Ave., is a two-story-and-basement red brick office building designed in the post-Colonial style. It houses the main offices of Spencer Kellogg & Sons, one of the largest manufacturers of linseed products in the United States. A painting in the lobby by A.Forestier depicts early sixteenth-century uses of linseed oil.

The structure incorporates parts of the Sizer House, which was built in 1836 for Henry Huntington Sizer, wealthy Buffalo grain merchant. This house was the first Buffalo residence to use gas for illumination; and tradition has it that, when Sizer's daughter was married at high noon, she had all the shutters closed and curtains drawn, so that the 'elegant effect' of the new lighting might show to full advantage.

4. The BUFFALO CITY HALL, Niagara Square W., was completed in 1932. Designed by John J. Wade, the structure illustrates the adaptation of the commercial skyscraper to the housing of municipal offices. The monumental character demanded by Americans in their public buildings is achieved by the huge 32-story tower that dominates the building, by the 14-story wings flanking the tower, and by an incrustation of half-classic and half-modern decorative details.

The eight columns of the entrance loggia, three stories in height, are of modified Corinthian design and are surmounted by a one-story frieze carved with 21 figures symbolizing the economic and cultural life of Buffalo. On the massive bronze entrance doors appear the bear, beaver, snipe, and other emblems of the Iroquois clans.

Within, the lobbies and corridors have richly decorated vaulted ceilings, piers terminating in colossal sculptured figures, and wall paintings by William de Leftwich Dodge that deal with local history, especially the development of commerce, industry, and transportation. The council chamber has a modern decorative treatment.

In triangular plots to the left and right of the main entrance are large statues of Millard Fillmore and Grover Cleveland, the two Buffalo citizens who served as President of the United States. The sculptor was Bryant Baker.

5. TOWNSEND HALL, Millard Fillmore College, University of Buffalo (*open*), 25 Niagara Square, a four-story brick structure with Medina sandstone trim, houses the evening session and the treasurer's office of the University of Buffalo. Constructed in the middle years of the nineteenth century, the structure displays in its ornamental details the earliest phase of the Italian Renaissance Revival then under way.

6. The ERIE COUNTY HALL, Franklin St. between N.Eagle and Church Sts., the old Buffalo city hall, was erected in 1872. It is a three-story building with an eight-story tower. The style of the building is Italian Renaissance, with many Florentine Gothic details; the architect was A.J.Warner. The lobbies and vestibules are lavishly decorated in marble and bronze.

7. The PRUDENTIAL BUILDING, SW. corner of Church and Pearl Sts., a 12-story office building of structural steel and terra cotta erected in 1894, is a notable example of the work of Louis H. Sullivan, forerunner in the field of modern architecture. The use of skeleton steel construction enabled him to accent vertical lines by means of narrow piers and columns and to provide abundant light with more window area. All the exterior terra-cotta surfaces are reddish brown in color, with elaborate, interlacing ornament in designs peculiar to Sullivan. This ornamentation is also used on the ironwork of the elevators and stair grilles, the hardware, and the mosaic ceilings and upper wall surfaces of the main first floor corridors.

8. ST.PAUL'S EPISCOPAL CATHEDRAL, Shelton Square W., designed by Richard Upjohn in the Gothic Revival style, is of brown sand-

stone. It has a freestanding front central tower surmounted by a tall, graceful spire. Gothic arcades divide the nave from the side aisles. The ceiling over the nave is supported by heavy, open wood trusses. The site of the building was donated by the Holland Land Company to a congregation organized in 1817. The present edifice was named the cathedral church of the Episcopal diocese of western New York in 1866.

9. The U.S.COURTHOUSE, SW. corner of Franklin and Court Sts., harmonizes in design with the New York State Building, the two structures framing the fine vista from Niagara Square east to Lafayette Square. Designed in the neoclassic style, the courthouse has seven stories, but the two uppermost are set back to conform with the height of the earlier State Building. It was dedicated in 1936 by President Franklin D. Roosevelt.

10. The NEW YORK STATE BUILDING, Niagara Square at Genesee, Franklin, and Court Sts., is a rectangular five-story structure of neoclassic design, with a two-story rear wing. The exterior, faced with Indiana limestone, is a modern version of Italian Renaissance architecture. The high rusticated first story forms a massive base. The windows of the three upper floors are recessed in vertical strips; and the stone piers between them are fluted to suggest giant, three-story pilasters. The lobbies and corridors of the first floor are finished with richly colored marbles. Ceiling paintings by William Andrew Mackay and Louis J. Borgo depict in pastel tones scenes of Niagara Falls, the Niagara Frontier, Buffalo Harbor, and a canal lock of 1837.

The building was erected in 1928–31 during the administrations of

---

KEY FOR BUFFALO MAP

1.McKinley Monument 2.Site of the Millard Fillmore House 3.Spencer Kellogg Office Building 4.Buffalo City Hall 5.Townsend Hall 6.Erie County Hall 7.Prudential Building 8.St.Paul's Episcopal Cathedral 9.U.S.Courthouse 10.New York State Building 11.Soldiers' and Sailors' Monument 12.Buffalo Public Library 13.Michigan Avenue Baptist Church 14.St.Mary's Roman Catholic Church 15.Chippewa Market 16.Electric Building 17.Buffalo Savings Bank MIDTOWN 18. Trinity Episcopal Church 19.Buffalo Club 20.Grosvenor Library 21.Buffalo Courier-Express Building 22.Mark Twain House 23.New York State Institute for the Study of Malignant Diseases 24.Temple Beth Zion 25.Wilcox House 26.Saturn Club 27.St.Joseph's Cathedral 28.Milburn House 29.Buffalo Masonic Consistory NORTH 30.The Front 31.Old Breckenridge Presbyterian Church 32.Forest Lawn Cemetery 33.Delaware Park 34.Buffalo State Teachers' College 35.Buffalo State Hospital 36.Curtiss Aeroplane Plant 37.Site of the Assassination of President McKinley 38.Goodrich (Amherst) House 39.Martin House 40.Barton House 41.St. Mary's School for the Deaf 42.St.Vincent De Paul Roman Catholic Church 43.Canisius College 44.Irving Air Chute Plant 45.University of Buffalo EAST 46.St.Gerard's Roman Catholic Church 47.Chevrolet Motor Plant 48.St. Francis De Sales Roman Catholic Church 49.Humboldt Park 50.New York Central Terminal 51.East Buffalo Stockyards 52.SS.Peter and Paul Greek Orthodox Church 53.Niagara Frontier Food Terminal SOUTH 54.Buffalo Pottery 55.Larkin Administration Building 56.National Aniline and Chemical Plant 57.Republic Steel Plant 58.Buffalo Botanical Gardens 59.Ford Motor Plant 60.Buffalo Harbor

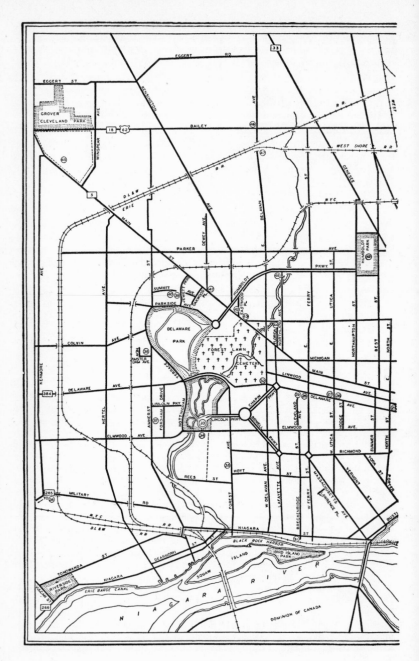

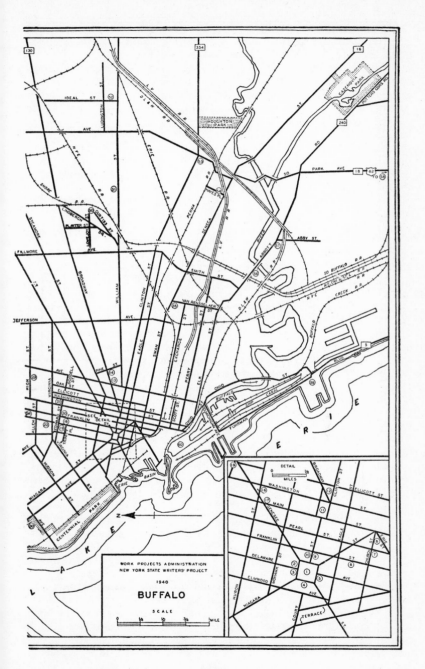

WORK PROJECTS ADMINISTRATION
NEW YORK STATE WRITERS' PROJECT

1940

BUFFALO

SCALE

0   1/4   1/2   3/4   MILE

Governors Alfred E. Smith and Franklin D. Roosevelt. The architects were William E. Haugaard, New York State Commissioner of Architecture, Edward B. Green & Sons, and A.Hart Hopkins.

11. The SOLDIERS' AND SAILORS' MONUMENT, center of Lafayette Square, erected in 1882–4, is a shaft of Vermont marble on an elaborately ornamented base surmounted by a statue of a female figure. The monument was designed in the Victorian Gothic style by George Keller and executed by Caspar Buberl.

12. The BUFFALO PUBLIC LIBRARY (*open* 9–9 *weekdays,* 2–9 *Sun.*), Broadway, Washington, Ellicott, and Clinton Sts., is the headquarters of the Buffalo Public Library system. The building, erected in 1885 and designed by C.L.W.Eidlitz, is of red pressed brick with a high brownstone and granite base; the style is Romanesque Revival.

The public library system provides traveling libraries for churches, classrooms, hospitals, industrial plants, and study clubs. To encourage home reading among children, it has more than 1,600 graded libraries in the classrooms of the city's elementary schools. Under J.N.Larned, its head from 1877 to 1897, the Buffalo library was one of the first in the State to undertake educational extension work.

13. The MICHIGAN AVENUE BAPTIST CHURCH (*open upon application to pastor*), 511 Michigan Ave., is a plain red brick structure with a high stone basement. Because they felt ill at ease in a church dominated by white folk, about 35 Negro members of the First Baptist Church withdrew in 1839 to organize the first Negro congregation in Buffalo. Services were first conducted in this building in 1845. The original pews have been replaced and are stored in the basement.

The building was an important station on the Underground Railroad. Many Negro families in Canadian towns near the border retain an affection for this church as the place from which their parents or grandparents made their last dash to freedom.

14. ST.MARY'S ROMAN CATHOLIC CHURCH, SW. corner of Broadway and Pine Sts., constructed of native limestone, is designed in the neoclassic style. The congregation, organized in 1844, comprised 600 German settlers. For a long time this was called the 'Woodchoppers' Church' because the members built the original structure in their spare time, hewing the timbers from the forest. The present building was consecrated in 1850.

15. CHIPPEWA MARKET (*open*), 50 E.Chippewa St., is a group of long one-story brick buildings and passageways with wood trussed roofs, containing 442 stands. The variety of produce sold is exceptionally large because the market caters to the many foreign groups in the city. Opened in 1856, the market is municipally owned.

16. The ELECTRIC BUILDING, Washington, Genesee, and Huron Sts., is a white terra-cotta office building constructed in 1912. The main feature is an octagonal tower on the corner rising sheer to 13 stories and then stepped back three times to a height of 327 feet, terminating in a large lantern. The rest of the building is seven stories high. The structure is modern in style, except for the neoclassic details on the three sections of

the tower. At night three searchlights, totaling 25,000 candlepower, play from the lantern, and the upper sections of the tower are illuminated in a variety of colors. The architects were Esenwein and Johnson. The building contains offices of the Niagara-Hudson and Buffalo General Electric Companies.

17. The BUFFALO SAVINGS BANK, NE. corner of Main and Genesee Sts., is a domed structure erected in 1899 and enlarged in 1933. Edward B. Green designed the building in the grandiose neoclassic style popularized by the Chicago World's Columbian Exposition in 1893. The murals on the interior are among the finest in Buffalo. The north wall mural shows Buffalo Harbor in the early forties, with the new Dart elevator—the world's first steam-operated grain elevator—canal boats and lake vessels in process of unloading, dock-wallopers, canalers, sailors, and passengers, and, in the offing, making its majestic entrance, a smoke-spouting side-wheeler. The painting on the east wall depicts the early purchase of land from the Indians headed by Red Jacket. Those in the four pendentives represent the foundations of Buffalo's civic greatness: commerce, industry, power, and the arts.

(Midtown)

18. TRINITY EPISCOPAL CHURCH, 371 Delaware Ave. opposite Trinity Pl., erected in 1884–6, is a brownstone edifice designed in the Victorian Gothic style. The exterior of the adjoining CHRIST CHAPEL is also Victorian Gothic; the interior, rebuilt and furnished in 1913, is in excellent modern English Gothic, with windows by John La Farge. The architect was W.H.Archer of Buffalo.

19. The BUFFALO CLUB (*private*), 388 Delaware Ave., a three-story mansion with mansard roof, was built as a residence by S.V.R.Watson in 1870. The organization, founded in 1866 with Millard Fillmore as president and William G. Fargo as one of the directors, purchased the place in 1887. While President William McKinley lay on his deathbed, September 6–14, 1901, the U.S.Cabinet met in the directors' room of the club.

20. The GROSVENOR LIBRARY (*open 9 a.m.–10 p.m. weekdays, 2–6 Sun.*), 383 Franklin St., a rambling red brick building covered with vines, has a circular tower at the corner. Here is housed one of the largest reference libraries in the country—about 300,000 volumes, including outstanding collections in medicine, chemistry, genealogy, local history, art, and music. The library was named for Seth Grosvenor, pioneer business man, who died in 1857, leaving $40,000 to found a reference library.

21. The BUFFALO COURIER–EXPRESS BUILDING (*open 7:30–10:30 p.m.; guides*), NE. corner of Main and Goodell Sts., erected in 1930, is a rectangular, five-story building of buff terra cotta with a polished brown granite base. Over the main entrance of this modern building are 16 black metal grilles depicting printer's marks. The architects were Monks and Johnson, Boston, Mass. In the first-floor lobby is a large mural by Charles Bigelow and Ernest Davenport, symbolizing the development of the newspaper in Buffalo. From the observation gallery off

the first-floor mezzanine overlooking the pressroom, visitors watch the first edition being run off.

22. When Samuel L. Clemens (Mark Twain) and his bride came to Buffalo in 1870, they found the MARK TWAIN HOUSE (*private*), 472 Delaware Ave., waiting for them as a wedding gift from the bride's father. They set up housekeeping in this place, a two-story brick structure with a mansard roof, and Twain began his work as co-editor of the Buffalo *Express* and as contributor of humorous articles to the *Galaxy*, a magazine. Their stay here was not a happy one. Twain's father-in-law died within the year; one of his wife's school friends died while a guest in this house. Shortly after, the first Clemens baby was born prematurely, resulting in a long illness for mother and child. Finding it impossible to continue his humorous writings in a house that had been the scene of so much sorrow, Mark Twain moved with his family to Elmira, after less than two years of residence in Buffalo.

23. The NEW YORK STATE INSTITUTE FOR THE STUDY OF MALIGNANT DISEASES (*open to visiting physicians*), 113 High St., is a three-story buff and red brick building. Founded in 1896, the institution cares for cancer sufferers and studies the cause, cure, and prevention of malignant diseases. The equipment includes four grams of radium for 'packs,' and nearly two grams, in the form of salts, for needles and other applicators.

24. TEMPLE BETH ZION (*open* 10–5 *daily*), Reform, 599 Delaware Ave., belonging to a congregation organized in 1847, was dedicated in 1890. Designed in the Byzantine-Romanesque style, the temple is square in plan, with towers at the front corners and a lunette treatment above the main entrance. A large, copper-covered dome over the auditorium rests on an octagonal drum and rises to a small lantern cupola. The temple was designed by Edward A. Kent of Buffalo, the school and residence at the rear and side by Dietel and Wade.

25. The WILCOX HOUSE (*open*), 641 Delaware Ave., is a gray-painted brick building with a pedimented portico and six Roman Doric columns, characteristic of the Classical Revival style. In this house, on September 14, 1901, upon the death of President McKinley, Theodore Roosevelt took the oath as President of the United States.

26. The SATURN CLUB (*private*), 977 Delaware Ave., of red brick and limestone trim, is in the style of an English Tudor manor house, with mullioned windows, leaded panes, full-story bay windows, and a fine Tudor doorway. The cornerstone was laid in 1921 and the building opened in 1922; the architect was Duane Lyman of Buffalo. Above the larger of the two fireplaces in the main lounge is inscribed the club's motto: 'Where the women cease from troubling and the wicked are at rest.'

27. ST.JOSEPH'S CATHEDRAL, NE. corner of Delaware Ave. and W.Utica St., dedicated in 1914, is the cathedral church of the Buffalo diocese of the Roman Catholic Church. Italian Gothic in style, it was built in 1912–14 after plans by Aristides Leonori of Rome, Italy. The exterior is faced with a veneer of Vermont and Italian marble. The two

Sports and Recreation

Photograph by Paul Broady

THE TRYLON AND PERISPHERE AND STATUE OF GEORGE WASHINGTON, NEW YORK WORLD'S FAIR

Photograph by courtesy of Fairchild Aerial Surveys, Inc., from Wide World Photos, Inc

JONES BEACH STATE PARK

BEACH, LAKE GEORGE

Photograph by courtesy of the New York Bureau of State Publicit

Photograph by Wide World Photos, Inc.

YACHT RACE, OFF OYSTER BAY

BAD WATER, ONONDAGA CREEK

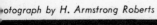

Photograph by H. Armstrong Roberts

SKI JUMP, LAKE PLACID

Photograph by John J. Vroom

Photograph by courtesy of the New York Bureau of State Publicity

GIRL ON SKI-TOW, LAKE GEORGE

HOCKEY, OLYMPIC ARENA, LAKE PLACID

Photograph by Roger L. Moore

OPENING DAY, SARATOGA

GRAND UNION HOTEL, SARATOGA

Photograph by Fred T. Loomis

GLIDERS, HARRIS FIELD

SARATOGA SPRINGS RESERVATION

Photograph by courtesy of the Saratoga Springs Commission

NEW YORK STATE EXPERIMENTAL GAME FARM, DELMAR

ADIRONDACK LEAN-TO

towers on the western façade originally had lanterns and lofty spires, which had to be taken down because of disintegration of the marble. Unusually broad proportions, necessitated by modern congregational seating, gives the interior a spaciousness not often found in medieval cathedrals.

28. In the MILBURN HOUSE (*private*), 1168 Delaware Ave., a brick structure of two-and-one-half stories, President William McKinley died on September 14, 1901, eight days after he was shot by Leon F. Czolgosz.

29. The BUFFALO MASONIC CONSISTORY (*open by permission*), 1180 Delaware Ave., dedicated in 1925, has four connecting units; Harold J. Cook was the architect. The three front units of graystone are designed in the Tudor Gothic style, with gables, steep green slate roofs, chimney pots, and mullioned windows. The main entrance is designed in the early English Renaissance style. The interior of the lobby, of marble in rich black and gold, is embellished with Greek Doric columns. A marble staircase leads to the ballroom, Renaissance in treatment, with wall panels depicting the history of the dance. The auditorium is designed in the neoclassic style; the ceiling is elaborately illuminated to produce stellar effects. A series of upper side wall treatments in the architectural orders, with paintings and ornaments, symbolize the principal Masonic steps to the thirty-third degree.

(North)

30. THE FRONT, entrance NW. corner of Porter and Busti Aves., is a 50-acre park extending along the water front. THE CASTLE, in the eastern section, is headquarters of the Buffalo Girl Scouts. This building, an excellent example in white limestone of the early castellated phase of the Gothic Revival, was designed and built in 1837 by Colonel James McKay, militarist and schoolmaster. The colonel's son, Steele MacKaye, noted actor-manager, was born here. The landscaped grounds contain several memorials to local regiments that fought in the Civil and Spanish-American Wars.

The STATUE OF OLIVER HAZARD PERRY, in the central plaza, was erected in 1915 in honor of the hero of the Battle of Lake Erie ('We have met the enemy and they are ours'), fought in September 1813. The sculptor of the heroic bronze figure was Charles H. Neihaus.

The PEACE BRIDGE, north end of The Front, the huge escarpment forming a striking feature of the scene, connects Buffalo and Fort Erie, Ontario. The completion of the bridge in 1927 marked the culmination of 100 years of uninterrupted peace between the United States and Canada.

31. The OLD BRECKENRIDGE PRESBYTERIAN CHURCH, 44 Breckenridge St., occupied by a plumber's supply shop, was constructed in 1835. It is the oldest building erected for church services now standing in Buffalo.

32. The FOREST LAWN CEMETERY, entrance at Delaware and Delavan Aves., has an area of 267 acres. A map of the plots is in the cemetery office.

The RED JACKET MONUMENT, inside Delaware Ave. entrance, is a bronze figure standing on a circular pedestal supported by octagonal stepped bases. An inscription reads: 'The Friend and Protector of his People.' It was erected in 1890 under the direction of the Buffalo Historical Society in memory of the Seneca chief (see Tour 8).

The FRANCIS TRACY MONUMENT, overlooking Crystal Lake, is a rectangular, stepped, altarlike monument of highly polished and carved brown granite in the Italian Renaissance style. On the west side is a bronze portrait in relief by Augustus Saint-Gaudens. Designed by Stanford White, the monument marks the graves of Francis W. Tracy (1839–86) and his wife Agnes (1845–1903), who as Agnes Ethel was a well-known light comedienne in America and Europe, and as Mrs.Tracy ruled over Buffalo society in the eighties.

The MILLARD FILLMORE MONUMENT is a reddish-brown polished granite obelisk on a dark gray granite pedestal and base. It stands in the Fillmore family plot, surrounded by a green-painted iron picket fence.

33. DELAWARE PARK, entrance from Lincoln Parkway, 350 acres, was designed and laid out by Frederick Law Olmsted in 1870.

The ALBRIGHT ART GALLERY (open 10–5 Tues.–Sat.; 1–5 Sun., Mon.), entrance on Elmwood Ave., is an impressive white marble building, given in 1905 to the people of Buffalo by John Joseph Albright. The building was designed by Green and Wicks of Buffalo. The central block with a pedimented portico is flanked by colonnaded galleries that lead to pedimented end gallery wings. The structure illustrates the monumental neoclassic manner, here rendered with strict adherence to the ornamental details of the Greek Ionic style. Each of the two side porches has four caryatids by Augustus Saint-Gaudens, directly inspired by those of the Erechtheum in Athens. The Elmwood Avenue façade includes a semicircular colonnade of 13 columns. In the interior, the large central Court of Sculpture is adorned with columns and pilasters; smaller rooms lead beyond to large galleries and, in the northwest corner, to the library, furnished in the modern manner.

The permanent collection of the gallery includes pairs of portraits by Gilbert Stuart and Ralph Earle, single paintings by Bellows, Inness, Burchfield, Speicher, and others, and a small collection of French masterpieces. The sculpture collection contains work by Brancusi, Maillol, Mestrovic, Epstein, Bourdelle, Noguchi, Haller, Despiau, Rodin, and Dobson. There are a number of outstanding individual pieces.

The gallery conducts more than a score of exhibitions yearly and carries on a number of cultural and educational services for school children and adults. It is managed by the Buffalo Fine Arts Academy.

The BUFFALO HISTORICAL MUSEUM (open 10–5 weekdays; 2–5 Sun.), Elmwood Ave. and Nottingham Terrace, in the northwest corner of Delaware Park, is a massive rectangular structure, neoclassic in style. The lake façade has an eight-column Greek Doric portico based on the Parthenon at Athens. Along the Elmwood Avenue façade is a series of three-quarter engaged Greek Doric columns. The building, erected as the New York State Building for the Pan-American Exposition, 1901, was deeded to the

Buffalo Historical Society by the State in 1902. The architect, George Cary, also planned the additions built by the City of Buffalo in 1927 and formally opened in 1929.

In the portico is Charles H. Neihaus's bronze statue of Lincoln. The bronze doors at the north entrance, with carved figures by R.Hinton Perry representing *History* and *Ethnology*, were presented to the society by Andrew Langdon.

The exhibits, presenting a visual history of the Niagara Frontier, include groups reproducing historic sites and events; Indian archeology and ethnology; collections of pioneer articles, military equipment, American glass, pottery, and pewter; and a series of costumes illustrating the changing fashions of the Niagara Frontier. The library has about 50,000 volumes, besides important collections of manuscripts and newspapers pertaining to the Niagara Frontier. Lectures are given during the fall and winter.

The new ZOOLOGICAL GARDENS (*open 1–5 Mon.–Fri.; 9–5 Sat., Sun., and holidays*), at Amherst St. and Parkside Ave., exhibit a wide variety of tropical and native mammals, birds, and reptiles. The new buildings were completed in 1938 by the WPA.

34. BUFFALO STATE TEACHERS' COLLEGE, 1300 Elmwood Ave., built in 1928–30, is a long two-story building of red brick with limestone trim in the post-Colonial style, with simple fenestration and detail. The State Normal School, organized in 1872, became a college by legislative enactment in 1927. It is coeducational and offers a four-year course leading to the degree of B.S. in Education. In addition to training teachers for the elementary grades, the college conducts courses in industrial art and home economics.

35. The BUFFALO STATE HOSPITAL (*visiting hours 2–4:30 Sun., Wed., Fri.*), 400 Forest Ave., maintained by the New York State Department of Mental Hygiene, accommodates more than 2,300 patients. Erected in 1871–81, the group of buildings is an important example of the work of the architect, H.H.Richardson. The central pavilion, four stories high, dominated by a pair of massive, steeply roofed towers, reflects Richardson's love of the Romanesque architecture of southern France. Stepping back, five on each side, and connected by quadrant passageways, are the lower wards, with three projecting pavilions, all in Victorian Gothic style. The 90-acre site was landscaped by Frederick Law Olmsted.

36. The CURTISS AEROPLANE PLANT (*not open to public*), NW. corner of Kenmore Ave. and Vulcan St., the largest military aeronautical plant in the country, manufactures and assembles service airplanes for the Army and Navy Air Corps. Planes are also manufactured for foreign powers with permission of the United States Government.

37. The SITE OF THE ASSASSINATION OF PRESIDENT McKINLEY, in the middle of Fordham Drive between Elmwood Ave. and Lincoln Parkway, is marked by a bronze tablet embedded in a low boulder set in a grass plot. On the afternoon of September 6, 1901, President William McKinley, while visiting the Pan-American Exposition, was receiving the public in the Temple of Music. As he was shaking hands with a

line of people, a young man approached with a handkerchief covering the revolver in his hand and fired two shots. The President died eight days later in the Milburn home. The assassin, Leon F. Czolgosz, was electrocuted in Auburn prison the following October.

38. The GOODRICH (AMHERST) HOUSE (*private*), 1150 Amherst St., a large white, post-Colonial building of frame construction, is the only existing structure definitely associated with Joseph Ellicott, head of the Holland Purchase survey. He began the house in 1823 on what is now the east side of Main Street just above High Street. Unfinished at his death in 1826, it was completed in 1831 by Colonel Guy H. Goodrich, who occupied it for many years. When the Medical School of the University of Buffalo bought the original site in 1891, the house was purchased by John C. Glenny, who moved it in sections to the present site and renamed it the Amherst House.

Although enlarged several times, the building presents an exterior that exemplifies the Roman Palladian phase of late Georgian Colonial architecture, which was introduced during the early Republic by Hoban's more sophisticated design for the White House in Washington. The two-story portico with its six widely-spaced Ionic columns, the crowning balustrade accented by graceful urns, the finely detailed cornice and entablature, and the formal panels beneath each window sill contrast curiously with the early provincial shutters. The entrance door has broad sidelights surmounted by a shell within a semicircular arch. The Palladian window above has been expanded to include two narrow sashes at each side in order to fill the entire space between the tapered pilasters.

39. The MARTIN HOUSE (*private*), 125 Jewett Parkway, built in 1904, is an important example of the work of Frank Lloyd Wright. Wright, a pupil of Louis Sullivan, evolved at the turn of the century a fresh and personal approach to residential design. The long, low horizontal line of the widely projecting eaves, the grouping of windows, the expansive porches, and the angular masses are all characteristic of Wright's early 'Prairie Architecture.' The house is of brick, with light parapet walls and large supporting piers, which make possible the thin screens of the banked windows. The interior, furnished completely according to Wright's designs, is notable for its facile plan arrangement.

There is an intimate affiliation of house and garden. Great stone vases are set on terrace walls; there are extensive flower boxes, and the planting is carefully distributed. A long pergola in the rear leads to the conservatory and stable, the roofs of which are accented with stone birdhouses.

40. The BARTON HOUSE (*private*), 118 Summit Ave., in the rear of the Martin House, is also by Wright. Forming an interesting contrast to its more opulent neighbor, this small house exhibits the same motif and manner of composition.

41. ST. MARY'S SCHOOL FOR THE DEAF (*open 9–3 daily*), 2253 Main St., occupying several three-story red brick buildings connected by covered passageways on a 23½-acre site, was formerly the LeCouteulx Deaf and Dumb Institute. Besides lip reading and voice building, the curriculum includes public and parochial school courses, a four-year high

school course, training in a number of trades, and courses for teachers of
the deaf. Receiving State aid since 1875, the school is open to afflicted
children of the State, regardless of race or creed.

42. ST.VINCENT DE PAUL ROMAN CATHOLIC CHURCH, NE.
corner of Main St. and Eastwood Place, is a well composed edifice in the
Byzantine style with some Italian Renaissance characteristics; it is built
of sandstone with limestone trim. The plan is cruciform, with a polygonal
dome and lantern over the crossing. The structure is richly ornamented
with Byzantine carvings and figures, rose windows, columns, and freestanding figures at the exterior base of the dome. The interior is rich in
conformity with the style. Over the high altar is a baldachin of marble
and mosaics. The mural in the apse, by Felix B. Lieftucher, represents the
Hand of God radiating gold rays. The church was opened in 1926; the
architects were Thomas, Parry, and McMullen, of Pittsburgh.

43. CANISIUS COLLEGE (*not open to public*), NE. corner of Main St.
and Jefferson Ave., is housed in a long three-story-and-basement building
of cream glazed brick with limestone trim erected in 1911. It is designed in
the neoclassic style. Over the arched main doorway, in the central pavilion, are four two-story engaged columns with entablature and pediment,
surmounted by a Roman dome.

This Jesuit college offers undergraduate instruction in the liberal arts
and graduate work leading to the Master's degree in chemistry, English,
French, and history. It has a fully equipped seismological observatory in a
vault under the approach to the main building. The college library has
several rare old Bibles.

44. The IRVING AIR CHUTE PLANT (*open 9–3 Mon.–Fri.*), 1671 Jefferson Ave., manufactures parachutes for a large part of the world market.

The Caterpillar Club was organized in 1920 by Leslie L. Irving and
George Waite of the Irving Air Chute Company. The condition of membership is to have had one's life saved by a parachute jump. The list of
members includes individuals from practically every country on the globe.
The gentle descent of the caterpillar on its silken thread suggested the
name and emblem of the club.

45. The UNIVERSITY OF BUFFALO, Main St., entrance opposite
Niagara Falls Blvd., occupies a campus of 174 acres. The buildings, set
far back from the street at the top of a landscaped slope, are impressive in
their gray quietness and neoclassic lines.

The University received its charter from the State legislature in 1846,
with the power to offer instruction and confer degrees in any branch of
professional or academic training; but for 40 years it consisted solely of the
Medical School (now at 24 High St.). Beginning in the eighties, the other
divisions were added. All coeducational, the various schools confer professional and advanced degrees. For juniors and seniors the College of Arts
and Sciences provides, within the usual structure of grouped departments,
individual tutorial work culminating in a comprehensive examination in
the student's specialized field.

The LOCKWOOD MEMORIAL LIBRARY (*not open to public*), facing the
center drive, almost square in plan, is built of limestone with a high rusti-

cated base. At the main entrance is a Roman Ionic portico two stories high. The architects were Green and James of Buffalo. Opened in 1933, the building was the gift of Thomas B. Lockwood, who also donated his private collection of about 2,500 rare books and manuscripts, including the first four folio editions of Shakespeare.

The older group of buildings is dominated by EDMUND HAYES HALL, a three-story stone structure, which was originally the Erie County Almshouse. The central four-story portion with pedimented front and stage tower is of late construction. The building houses administrative offices and classrooms. The BOOKSTORE, at the extreme western end of the campus, is a reproduction of the old Holland Land Office Museum in Batavia.

(East)

46. ST.GERARD'S ROMAN CATHOLIC CHURCH, NE. corner of E. Delavan and Bailey Aves., constructed of limestone, is a modified version of the Roman Baroque basilica. Originally built in 1902, the structure was remodeled in 1913; the architects were Carl Schmill and Son. The central section of the façade is articulated by two pilaster orders, Ionic below, Corinthian above. The central one of the three arched portals is framed by a classic motif of two engaged Ionic columns and a pediment. Above, the western window of the nave is topped with a curved pediment, while the adjoining bays contain framed niches with statues. The nave gable is treated as a pediment and contains a cartouche. The ends of the side aisles are plain; and to the south a three-stage tower, 110 feet high, completes the composition.

Within, the focal point of the interior is a life-size mural of *The Coronation*, by Harold Rambusch, in the semidome of the apse. Over the 12 massive granite columns symbolizing the Apostles is a richly paneled ceiling. The child in Christ's lap depicted in the baptistry window has the features of the first child baptized in the church.

47. The CHEVROLET MOTOR PLANT (*open* 10–2 *Mon.–Fri.; guides*), E.Delavan Ave. at the Erie R.R. tracks, an assembly unit, employs about 2,000 persons.

48. ST.FRANCIS DE SALES ROMAN CATHOLIC CHURCH, SW. corner of Humboldt Parkway and Northland Ave., built of Indiana limestone, is of early Christian architecture with both Byzantine and Romanesque features. The structure, cruciform in plan, is very high, with the graceful campanile rising to 140 feet. The roofs of the buttressed side aisles reach to the clerestory windows of the nave. The interior follows the same style. The sanctuary and the two side-chapels are semicircular in plan and covered with semidomes. The crossing of the nave and transepts is covered by a low, shell-like dome. The edifice was dedicated in 1928; the architects were Dietel and Wade.

49. HUMBOLDT PARK, entrance at Fillmore Ave. and Best St., 65 acres, is Buffalo's popular East Side resort. The grounds form an aboretum with 160 species of woody plants. In the NIAGARA FRONTIER ROSE GARDEN, under the supervision of the Rose Society of Buffalo, new and

established species of roses are cultivated. On the east side of the park is the CITY GREENHOUSE, where a chrysanthemum show is held each autumn, and where every year a 'pavilion' is erected, consisting of a 12-foot mound of densely growing flowers, with a century plant at the top. This novelty is on view from June 15 to September 1.

The BUFFALO MUSEUM OF SCIENCE (*open 10–5 weekdays; 1:30–5:30 Sun.; 7–10 evenings, 7–9 Sat., Oct.–Apr.; astronomical observatory periods 8–9 and 9–10 p.m. Fri.; guides*) is in the NW. corner of Humboldt Park, south of the intersection of Northampton St. and Humboldt Parkway. The two-story building has an exterior of Indiana limestone in modernized neoclassic style with an ornamented frieze replacing the heavy classical cornice. The central feature of the façade is a two-story loggia with four Corinthian columns. The building was opened in 1929; the architects were Esenwein and Johnson.

The exhibits, offering 'science in brief for busy people,' present a comprehensive and progressive account of the universe and of man, telling their story graphically and dramatically with the aid of specimens, individual and group models, and scientific devices. The museum program includes lectures, concerts, children's classes and clubs, courses for adults, loan services, and museum training courses.

50. The NEW YORK CENTRAL TERMINAL, Lindbergh Drive, Curtiss and Lovejoy Sts., rising above bare surroundings, is neoclassic in style. The exterior is of variegated tapestry brick with limestone trim and granite base. The dominating corner tower is 17 stories high, with a five-story office building adjoining. The architects were Felheimer and Wagner, New York City; the building was opened in 1929.

51. The EAST BUFFALO STOCKYARDS (*open 9–5 daily*), 1000–1200 William St., embrace the largest meat packing industry east of Chicago and the fifth largest in the world.

52. The SS.PETER AND PAUL RUSSIAN ORTHODOX CHURCH, 45 Ideal St., Buffalo's White Russian church, is constructed of cream-colored brick in greatly modified Byzantine style, with three onion-shaped domes surmounted by crosses. It was completed in 1933; the architect was Joseph Fronczak, Buffalo. Close by stands the small wood chapel in which the congregation began worshipping nearly half a century ago.

The interior is finished in a warm, buff, roughcast plaster, with decorative detail in the old Russian tradition. There are no pews, for the congregation stands through the two-hour mass. Icons hang on the pillars, and three-barred crosses are on the walls. From two standards hang the U.S. flag and the flag of old Russia surmounted by the imperial eagle. On the iconostasis (screen made of doors) are painted medallion-icons and brilliantly colored representations of saints and archangels. In the niche on the left beyond the iconostasis is a shrine to the Blessed Virgin. Before the icon, hooded with blue velvet, burns a wick floating in oil contained in a crimson glass globe which is suspended on brass chains.

During the high Easter season, which in the Russian and Greek Orthodox calendar falls about a fortnight later than in the Roman Catholic and Protestant churches, the church is crowded with worshipers and spectators. The choir in the gallery sings the responses to the Slavonic liturgies set to the music of Tschaikovsky and Rimsky-Korsakoff, and ecclesiastical dignitaries in the richly colored vestments of the Russian and Greek ritual offer prayers and burn incense before the iconostasis. After the day-long service, the social side of the Russian Eastern is observed, with music, tea from the samovar, and native cakes and fruit and cheese confections.

At the turn of the century the worshipers were but a handful, but since the Bolshevist revolution their number has swelled to about 5,000, including several members of the old aristocracy.

53. The NIAGARA FRONTIER FOOD TERMINAL (the Clinton-Bailey Market), NW. corner of Clinton St. and Bailey Ave., under private management, was opened in 1931. The site was provided by the Erie and Nickle Plate Railroads. It covers an area of 60 acres with a network of railway spurs for freight cars and groups of two-story buildings for produce, butter, egg, and poultry dealers.

Opposite the terminal, on the south side of Clinton St., is the FARMERS' MARKET, covering 10 acres, with a series of aisles separated by broad concrete avenues. Farmers from the near-by agricultural areas in Erie and Niagara Counties market their produce here.

(South)

54. The BUFFALO POTTERY (*open on application*), NE. corner of Seneca St. and Hayes Place, manufactures solid-color vitreous china, which it originated.

55. The LARKIN BUILDING (*open 9:30–5 weekdays July and Aug.*), 680 Seneca St., built in 1904–5, was designed by Frank Lloyd Wright. The location of this office structure suggested a plan in which the interior would be protected from the noise, grime, and odors of adjoining factories, refineries, and railroads. The five floors, occupied by the Larkin store and mail order divisions, look into a deep, narrow skylighted court, which contains the desks of the executives. The outer windows are doubly glazed and hermetically sealed. The building employed one of the first installations of air-conditioning, and interior noise reverberation was done away with by one of the first installations of acoustically absorbent material. All interior furnishings are of steel—one of the first such experiments—and were designed by Wright as an integral part of the building. Chairs are supported on swinging brackets to facilitate floor-cleaning. Adequate artificial lighting is assured by specially designed fixtures. The top story and the outdoor roof terraces provide for employee recreation.

Omitting any reflections of historical architectural styles, Wright achieved a clifflike red brick mass of great dignity and interest, entirely in terms dictated by the structural materials and the internal arrangements. The great corner blocks enclose skylighted stair towers; the simple side wing contains the entrance vestibule and employees' restrooms.

56. The NATIONAL ANILINE AND CHEMICAL PLANT (*open by application*), Abbott Road at Buffalo River, produces dyes and dyestuff of

the aniline type, medicines, tanning materials, synthetic resins, and perfumes.

57. The REPUBLIC STEEL PLANT (*open by special arrangement*), 475 Abbott Road, is the third largest producer of steel in the United States and the largest producer of alloy and special steels in the world. Its products range from carpet tacks to pig iron, and include steel for automobiles, lockers, and a variety of other articles.

58. The BUFFALO BOTANICAL GARDENS (*open 8-6 daily; guides*), South Park Ave. and McKinley Parkway, house the city's collection of rare plants. A fall chrysanthemum show and seasonal exhibits of native flora are held annually.

59. The FORD MOTOR PLANT (*open 9-12:30, 1:30-3 Mon.-Fri.; guides*), Fuhrman Blvd., foot of Ohio St., an assembly unit, has a capacity of 400 cars a day.

60. The BUFFALO HARBOR, Buffalo River, with a water front of 37 miles extending east and west from the south end of Michigan Ave., western terminus of the State Barge Canal and eastern terminus of Great Lakes shipping, presents a superb panorama of commercial and industrial Buffalo, with smokestacks of the Lackawanna plant of the Bethlehem Steel Company to the left, and the elephantine grain elevators, grain-dusted in mist or sun, to the right. Noisy switch-engines back produce-laden freight cars to the doors of grim warehouses that line the many slips. Fussy tugs churn the harbor waters and dash spray over the breakwall from rough Lake Erie beyond, where the Coast Guard station, white and neat, sits at the foot of the old lighthouse with its mooing foghorn. Passenger and freight boats constantly arrive and depart. Tugs with strings of barges in tow form an almost unbroken procession out of the Barge Canal. In winter, with shipping tied up and trade stilled for the season, the lethargic scene suggests mighty forces in hibernation. The panorama has been reproduced in etchings by Joseph Pennell.

The Port of Buffalo is first on the Great Lakes in value of gross tonnage, averaging $610,000,000 in the years 1932-6. More than 20,000,000 tons of freight are handled annually, principally grain, limestone, and iron ore. Forty grain elevators with a capacity of 50,000,000 bushels rear their cupolas along 10 miles of the water-front skyline. One fifth of the grain produced in the United States passes through these elevators, and the annual wheat tonnage of 480,000 has heaved the city into a leading position as a milling center; its flour mills have a daily capacity of 45,000 barrels. Eight railroads and the Barge Canal transport the cars and barges fed by the elevator 'legs.'

The outer harbor is more than a quarter mile wide and four-and-one-half miles long; it has a breakwater of 22,603 feet, the longest in the world. Within the breakwater an area of 715 acres is set aside for storing grain during the winter in icebound boats; in some seasons more than 33,500,000 bushels of grain have been stored here. The grain elevating, transferring, processing, and transporting industries give seasonal employment to 8,000 persons.

POINTS OF INTEREST IN VICINITY

Through FORT ERIE, Ontario, 3.5 *m.*, across the Peace Bridge, many American tourists enter Canada; a ferry supplements the bridge service. In recent years many American manufacturers have built subsidiary plants in the village. Annual horse races, July 3–15, on the one-mile track draw huge crowds from Buffalo. Many Buffalo residents maintain summer homes on the lake shore. Niagara Boulevard leads north along the west bank of the Niagara River to Niagara Falls, Ontario (*see Niagara Falls*).

FORT ERIE, at the south end of the village, was restored by the Niagara Parks Commission and opened to the public with elaborate ceremonies on July 1–4, 1939. The fort was the scene of some of the fiercest fighting in the War of 1812. In November 1814 the Americans blew it up; until 1938 the ruins were a popular picnic place.

CRYSTAL BEACH, Ontario, 13 *m.* (*boats from foot of Commercial St.*), is Buffalo's Coney Island, with sandy bathing beach, Ferris wheel, roller coaster, other midway attractions, and picnicking facilities.

Elmira

Railroad Stations: Union Station, Railroad Ave. between 3rd and Clinton Sts., for Erie and Pennsylvania R.Rs.; Lake St. S. of Washington Ave. for Delaware, Lackawanna & Western R.R.

Bus Stations: 269–71 State St. for Greyhound Lines, Dickinson Motor Coach Lines, and Edwards Lakes to Sea Stages; 506 Academy Pl. for White Star Coach Lines.

Taxis: 35¢ within city limits.

Busses: Fare 10¢; 3 tokens 25¢.

Accommodations: 4 hotels; tourist homes.

Information Service: Chamber of Commerce, E.Church and State Sts.; Elmira Auto Club, 230 Lake St.

Radio Station: WENY (1200 kc.).

Motion Picture Houses: Five.

Baseball: Dunn Stadium, foot of Phoenix Ave., home grounds of the Elmira Pioneers of the Eastern League.

Swimming: Municipal pool, Brand Park, Maple Ave. and Catherine St.; children free 9–2, after 2 p.m. 5¢; adults 25¢ including locker.

Golf: Chemung Golf Course, Mark Twain Park, Sullivan and Prechtel Sts., 9 holes, greens fee 50¢.

Tennis: Municipal courts, Horner and Falck Sts.; Westside courts, Hoffman and W. Church Sts.; free.

Annual Events: Hobby Show, Girls' Hobby Fair, May; Flower Show, June; National Glider Meet, two weeks ending about July 4, field determined by wind direction, headquarters at Harris Field.

ELMIRA (860 alt.,45,046 pop.), on both sides of the Chemung (Ind., big horn) River, occupies a broad, flat valley fringed by wooded hills. The north bank of the river is bordered by business structures; the principal business section extends along Water Street, which is too narrow for the congested pedestrian and automobile traffic of Saturday nights. Most of the buildings are three-story brick; a few select shops cater to the wealthy residents of Strathmont Park in western Elmira. In the older residential district, west of Main Street, stand the turreted mansions of the last century. The factories hug the railroad tracks and are surrounded by the humdrum dwellings of the workers.

About 10 per cent of the total population are foreign-born; about two per cent are Negroes. The relatively large Jewish group plays an important part in social, cultural, and educational activities.

The first white men to enter the region were the soldiers of the Sullivan-Clinton Expedition of 1779. At the mouth of Newtown Creek, beside the Chemung River, was the Seneca Indian village of Kanaweola, destroyed during the Battle of Newtown. Most of the early settlers were emigrants from Wyoming and Wilkes-Barre, Pennsylvania. In 1789 a famine struck the valley as a result of a frost that killed all the wheat. The only deaths that occurred resulted not from starvation but from overeating when food was finally obtained. By 1793 the community had developed sufficiently to support a Masonic lodge, one of the earliest in western New York. The Chemung Canal, connecting Seneca Lake with the Chemung River in 1832, stimulated the lumbering industry; and large amounts of timber moved through the village.

The present name was adopted in 1828. According to local tradition, Nathan Teall, one of the early settlers, had a daughter named Elmira, for whom her mother often called in a shrill, far-reaching voice. When it was decided to adopt a new name, several people suggested the one they had heard so often when Elmira was a child.

The Erie Railroad reached Elmira in 1849 and opened new fields for business activity. Woolen and lumber mills grew rapidly. In 1854 the Junction Canal was built to connect the Chemung Canal with the North Branch of the Susquehanna River in Pennsylvania. The metal industries had their inception in 1860 with the incorporation of the Elmira Rolling Mills. By the time a second and third mill were completed, 20 furnaces, eight engines, five trains of rolls, two roll lathes, and one Burden squeezer turned out 22,000 tons of iron annually.

During the Civil War, when the Union Army barracks in Elmira required large amounts of supplies, the Woolen Manufacturing Company turned out 16,000 yards of cloth for uniforms. In 1864, the year the town received a city charter, one of the barracks was turned into a prison camp. On July 6, 1864, the first detachment of prisoners arrived, and local merchants made profitable contracts for food.

During the nineteenth century the dairying industry in the vicinity grew in importance, and butter and cheese were shipped in large quantities from Elmira. In 1882 Abner Wright of Wellsburg, a neighboring village, first shipped raw milk to the New York City market in felt-jacketed milk cans surrounded by ice. In 1893 he and his associates organized the Chemung Valley Condensing Company and gave new impetus to the local dairy industry.

Superior transportation facilities have made Elmira a manufacturing center. The largest industry is the Precision Tool Company, a subsidiary of the Remington Rand Corporation, which was established in Elmira in 1935 and employs about 2,000 workers in the manufacture of office equipment and business machines. Other industrial products are fabricated structural steel, fire-fighting apparatus and chemicals, Bendix drives, glass bottles, silk goods, knit goods, and wood pipe and trim. In 1936 about 10,000 persons (10 per cent women) were employed in 79 manufacturing establishments.

POINTS OF INTEREST

The CHEMUNG COUNTY COURTHOUSE, Lake St. at E. Gray St., is composed of four units. The design of the older porticoed buildings reflect the Greek Revival style of the first half of the nineteenth century and are representative of Elmira's pre-Civil War boom. In the early days the courthouse, serving as community center, was also the scene of the first religious and Masonic meetings.

The ARNOT ART GALLERY (*open 2–5 Mon.–Fri.; 2–5, 7–9 Sat.; 2:30–5:30 Sun.*), 235 Lake St., occupies the Greek Revival mansion built by Mathias Arnot, one of the family of Arnots who were financial and political powers in Elmira during the last century. He bequeathed this red brick porticoed residence, as well as $10,000 for remodeling it, $200,000 for an endowment fund, and his art collection, to the community for a public art museum, which was opened in 1913. The permanent collection includes works of the Flemish, Dutch, German, and French schools. About 10 exhibits are held every year. Lectures on the exhibits are part of the curriculum of the city schools.

The STEELE MEMORIAL LIBRARY (*open 9–9 weekdays; 2–6 Sun. except July and Aug.*), corner of Lake and E.Church Sts., a Carnegie library, is a two-story red brick building trimmed with limestone. It also houses the Chemung County Historical Society. The name is in tribute to Joel Dorman Steele (1836–86), one of the most popular textbook authors of his time, and for many years principal of the Elmira Free Academy.

PARK CHURCH, SW. corner of W.Church and Main Sts., is built of greenish stone with red stone trim in a modified Romanesque style. It was erected during the pastorate of the Reverend Thomas Kennicut Beecher (1824–1900), brother of Harriet Beecher Stowe and Henry Ward Beecher, who is especially remembered for his pioneering efforts to make his church a center for social activities. A bronze statue of Beecher stands just east of the church.

In the second-floor lobby of the MARK TWAIN HOTEL, corner of N.Main and Gray Sts., are murals depicting Mississippi River steamboat scenes suggested by *The Adventures of Tom Sawyer* and a life-size portrait of Mark Twain. There are additional murals in the taproom.

GRACE EPISCOPAL CHURCH, SE. corner of W.Church and Davis Sts., is known for its beautiful interior. The pulpit was carved by Whipple in his studio at Exeter, England; the Calvary group of carvings was made in Oberammergau by leading actors in the Passion Play; and the sanctuary lamp is a reproduction of the lamp in St.Mark's Cathedral in Venice.

ELMIRA COLLEGE, College Ave. at Park Place, one of the earliest colleges for women, was founded in 1855, at a time when higher education for women was considered ridiculous. The college was financed by Simeon Benjamin, a wealthy resident of Elmira. At the first commencement in 1859 there were 17 graduates; today the alumnae body numbers more than 4,000, and the annual enrollment is about 375. The curriculum includes all liberal arts studies and courses in domestic science and nursing. COWLES HALL, College Ave. at Park Place, the original college building, named for Dr.Augustus Cowles, first president of the college, has a large central octagonal rotunda with several radiating extensions. It contains the administrative offices, the book store, the recreation room, several recitation rooms, and the chapel. According to local legend, a subcellar (*not open*) was a depot on the Underground Railroad.

WOODLAWN CEMETERY, north end of David St., contains the GRAVE OF SAMUEL LANGHORNE CLEMENS (Mark Twain) (1835-1910), American humorist and satirist. In 1870 he married Olivia Langdon, daughter of a wealthy Elmira businessman, and thereafter spent many summers in Elmira. He is buried in the Langdon plot. In the same plot is the GRAVE OF OSSIP GABRILOWITSCH (1878-1936), Mark Twain's son-in-law. He studied piano in St.Petersburg, Russia, his native city, and at the age of 16 won the coveted Rubinstein prize. In 1900 a concert tour brought him to New York. He achieved his greatest honors as conductor of the Detroit Symphony Orchestra. He met Clara Clemens while she was a pupil of Leschetizky, and they were married in 1909.

WOODLAWN NATIONAL CEMETERY, adjacent to Woodlawn Cemetery, contains the graves of 2,963 Confederate soldiers who died in the Elmira prison camp. The prison was hastily constructed, unsanitary, and crowded; most of the Southerners, brought here in 1864, died within the year. The Confederate graves, occupying the central portion of the six-acre plot, are surrounded by the graves of 322 Union soldiers. The cemetery office has a record of the burials.

The ELMIRA REFORMATORY (*open 3 p.m. Wed., 1 p.m. Sat., hours of military dress parade*), corner of Davis St. and Bancroft Road, is a massive brick structure painted gray, its grim buttressed side walls and towers typical of nineteenth-century prison architecture. In it are confined men between the ages of 16 and 30 convicted of a first-offense felony. Zebulon R. Brockway (1827-1920), superintendent from 1876 to 1901, evolved here the sytem of indeterminate sentence, under which the inmates, by accumulating credits, advanced through successive stages of increasing privileges until they received their parole. Brockway also developed industrial training, gymnastics, military drill, and a scholastic curriculum, all of which combined to make the Elmira system the pioneer pattern for modern penological methods.

The AMERICAN LAFRANCE–FOAMITE PLANT (*open by permission*), 100 E.LaFrance St., employing about 550 men, manufactures fire-fighting apparatus. The original firm was the Button Fire Engine Company, which began production in 1834 and rendered bucket brigades obsolete. Gasoline engines, power take-offs, and pumps, as well as trucks, are made in the Elmira plant. The firm also manufactures Foamite, a chemical for extinguishing fires.

The MARK TWAIN STUDY is on Quarry Farm, off East Hill Road, about half a mile beyond the city limits. Mark Twain himself described the structure as 'octagonal, with a peaked roof, each face filled with a spacious window, and it sits perched in complete isolation on the very top of an elevation that commands leagues of valley and city and retreating ranges of distant blue hills.' The place was built for him by Mrs.Theodore W. Crane, his sister-in-law, in 1874. That summer, and many of the succeeding summers until 1903, Mark Twain did much of his writing in this retreat, including portions of *The Adventures of Tom Sawyer, The Adventures of Huckleberry Finn, The Prince and the Pauper, A Tramp Abroad,*

Life on the Mississippi, and *A Connecticut Yankee at King Arthur's Court.*
In town he indulged his fondness for billiards.

POINTS OF INTEREST IN ENVIRONS

Newtown Battlefield Reservation, 4 *m.* (*see Tour* 3). Finger Lakes, 30 *m.* (*see Tours* 27, 28, 30).

Ithaca

Railroad Stations: Corner of W.Buffalo St. and Taughannock Blvd. for Lehigh Valley R.R. (ticket office also at 300 E.State St.); 710 W.State St. for Delaware, Lackawanna & Western R.R.
Bus Station: Green St. between Cayuga and Tioga Sts. for Greyhound, Giddings, and Geneva Bus Lines.
Airport: Municipal Airport, 1 m. NW. on Taughannock Blvd.; no scheduled service; flying instruction and local flights.
Taxis: 50¢ each for 1 or 2 passengers; 25¢ for each additional passenger.
Street Busses: 10¢; 12 tokens for $1.

Accommodations: 13 hotels; tourist homes.

Information Service: Chamber of Commerce and Ithaca Automobile Club, 211 E.Seneca St.

Radio Station: WHCU (850 kc.).
Theaters and Motion Picture Houses: Willard Straight Theater, Cornell University; 3 motion picture houses.
Golf: Newman Municipal Golf Course, foot of Willow Ave., 9 holes, 25¢.
Tennis: Stewart Park, foot of N.Cayuga St., free.
Swimming: Stewart Park, locker 10¢, suits rented; Beebe Lake, Cornell University campus, 10¢.

ITHACA (900 alt.,19,647 pop.), seat of Tompkins County, college town, and one of the principal gateways to the Finger Lakes region, fills the flat plain at the head of Cayuga Lake and climbs the steep slopes of the surrounding hills. From the business section, centered on State Street at the foot of East Hill, the city spreads out in modest residential streets.

Fall, Cascadilla, and Six Mile Creeks plunge down the deep, picturesque gorges that they have cut for themselves in the side of East Hill, and flow through the town. On the brow of East Hill, bordered by Fall and Cascadilla Creeks, is the elm-shaded campus of Cornell University. To the north is the incorporated village of Cayuga Heights, a residential district of new homes built on the hillside overlooking the far-winding lake.

While the city has several industries, essentially it is a college town, its chief economic activity consisting of supplying the needs of the more than 7,000 students and teachers of Cornell University and Ithaca College. The 'busy season' coincides with the academic year. The demands and activities of its college communities supply Ithaca with much better cultural, social, and recreational resources than are normally found in a city of its size.

Detachments of General John Sullivan's expedition crossed the site of Ithaca in September 1779, and burned Indian cornfields and orchards. The first settlers came in 1788 and 1789; but when the site was included within the Military Tract and title given to Revolutionary veterans, these pioneers were obliged to move on. The land was acquired by Simeon De Witt, surveyor-general of New York State, who gave the place its name. Solid growth began after the opening of Cornell University in 1868. In 1888 Ithaca became a city and turned to civic problems—streets, water, lighting, streetcars, traffic regulation, and social service. Members of the Cornell faculty have participated actively in city affairs.

For several years beginning in 1914 Ithaca was a center of the motion picture industry. *Dear Old Girl of Mine*, a picture of college life starring Francis X. Bushman and Beverly Bayne, and *Exploits of Elaine*, with Lionel Barrymore and Pearl White, were filmed with Ithaca and Cornell University backgrounds.

CORNELL UNIVERSITY

Cornell University, entrances on Stewart Ave., Eddy St., College Ave., and Thurston Ave., occupies a campus of 1,378 acres overlooking the city of Ithaca and Cayuga Lake. The campus has been called one of the most attractively situated in the country. The appropriateness of the Cornell Alma Mater, 'Far above Cayuga's Waters,' can be appreciated only after one has stood at one of the vantage points on the campus and looked down on the blue-green waters of the winding lake, with green and brown checkerboard fields rising up the slope of West Hill, or, better still, caught a sunset over the lake, its waters reflecting the roseate hues of the barred clouds. At night the depths of the gorges take on a mysterious blackness, the lights of Ithaca sparkle in rectangular rows in the dell below, and along West Hill the headlights of moving automobiles glitter through the trees.

The cosmopolitan community of about 7,000, including representatives from every section of the United States and many foreign countries, is in many respects self-contained, with its own theater, concerts, exhibitions, lectures, athletic games, periodicals, daily newspaper, store, and restaurants. Sixty fraternities and 14 sororities provide lodging for about 1,500 students, and the dormitories accommodate about 1,500 more; others live in private lodging houses near the campus. The outstanding social events of the year are Junior Week, during the second week of February, which is climaxed by the Junior Prom; and Spring Day, a traditional holiday usually celebrated on the third Saturday in May with a student carnival and intercollegiate boat races on Cayuga Lake.

The origin of Cornell University goes back to the meeting in Albany in 1864 of Ezra Cornell, State senator and chairman of the committee on agriculture, and Andrew Dickson White, State senator and chairman of the committee on education. The two men pushed through the legislature a bill awarding the entire land grant assigned to the State under the Morrill Act of 1862 to a new institution to be located in Ithaca and to be named for Ezra Cornell. Cornell gave the university 200 acres of land for a campus site and $500,000 in cash; and he bought from the State, in trust, the unsold land scrip, located lands with great care, and by his skillful management enormously increased the endowment derived from that source. The university was chartered in 1865 and opened in 1868.

The institution as organized expressed the interest of Ezra Cornell in the teaching of mechanics and the useful arts and of Andrew D. White in the teaching of modern history, languages, and literature by the side of the classics, and the preference of both men for coeducation and nonsectarian control. The College of Civil Engineering was established in 1868; the present College of Engineering comprises schools of civil, mechanical, electrical, and chemical engineering. The Law School was established in 1887; Veterinary Medicine, the first State-supported college, in 1896. The Medical College, the main unit of which is in New York City, was organized in 1898 and in 1927 combined with the New York Hospital to form the East Side Medical Center. In 1904 the State undertook the support of the College of Agriculture; the College of Home Economics was separately established in 1925. The three State colleges are financed by the State and administered by the university; tuition is free to residents of New York State.

The university with its nine colleges has come close to realizing the aim of Ezra Cornell to 'found an institution where any person can find instruction in any study.' It has something of the character of the midwestern State university, especially in its three State-supported colleges—all three leaders in their fields. By the side of these, the College of Arts and Sciences, the Graduate School, and the professional colleges have successfully attained the high standards of training and scholarship set by the older eastern universities. Free elective study has been a distinctive characteristic of Cornell from its inception.

CAMPUS TOUR

(The main entrance is on Eddy St. at Williams St. Unless otherwise stated, buildings are open 9-5 weekdays during the academic year.)

From Stewart Avenue on the west the campus rises in a series of terraces to the crest of Kite Hill, 900 feet high, with many of the buildings constructed to take advantage of the sharp slope. The heart of the lower campus is the main quadrangle, a level stretch of greensward crisscrossed by paths, shaded by spreading elms, and bordered by the older university buildings, with the conspicuous clock tower at its southwest corner. The main buildings of the upper campus are grouped around the 'Ag' quadrangle, with the athletic plant directly south.

1. MYRON TAYLOR HALL, designed by F. Ellis Jackson of Providence, R.I., and completed in 1932, was the gift of Myron C. Taylor, President Franklin D. Roosevelt's peace emissary to the Vatican and former chairman of the board of the United States Steel Corporation. It houses the Law School, which became a graduate school in 1925 and has published the *Cornell Law Quarterly* since 1915.

The building, of English Collegiate Gothic design, constructed of native bluestone with limestone trim, is L-shaped in plan, and has two main wings, a tower, and two connecting links, with walks and terraces completing the group. In the south wing is the library, a very large, arched room trimmed in light oak, with archaic sculptural ornament and Renaissance doorways with fine carvings. The mock courtrooms in the other large wing are equally impressive with fine plaster and wood detail.

2. SAGE COLLEGE (*private*), erected in 1873–4, is a women's dormitory. The building, together with an endowment of $100,000, was the gift of Henry W. Sage. It is a three-story Victorian Gothic structure with a tall, slender, pyramidal tower and lantern. The architect was the Reverend Charles Babcock, professor of architecture at Cornell, 1871–1913, and pupil and son-in-law of Richard Upjohn, architect.

3. SAGE CHAPEL (*open 9–5 weekdays; 11–12 Sun.*), the gift of Henry W. Sage, erected in 1874, was also designed by Babcock in the Victorian Gothic style. Sunday services during the academic year are conducted by visiting clergymen of various denominations. In the crypt under the Memorial Antechapel at the northwest corner are the graves of Ezra Cornell and his wife, Andrew D. White, Alonzo B. Cornell, eldest son of Ezra Cornell and governor of New York, 1880–3, and others. In the Sage Memorial Apse, at the east end of the nave, are the graves of Henry W. Sage and his wife.

4. WILLARD STRAIGHT HALL (*open 8 a.m. to midnight daily*), the student union, is the social center of the campus. Named for Willard D. Straight, class of 1901, the building was given by his widow to fulfill his desire that his estate be used to further human contacts among the students of his Alma Mater. Opened in 1925, it was designed by Delano and Aldrich, New York City, in the English Collegiate Gothic style.

The mural decorations in the lobby, by Ezra Winter, represent phases of the ideal human character. The Memorial Room, opening off the west end of the lobby, designed in the manner of an English college hall, is used for meetings, dances, and Sunday afternoon musicales. The other rooms are lounges for men and women. The upper floor contains barber shop, game room, and sleeping rooms. The lower floors contain dining rooms, cafeteria, and, in the northwest wing, a little theater (*adm.* 50¢–$1), in which plays are presented on Fridays and Saturdays almost every week of the academic year by the Cornell Dramatic Club.

5. The MEN'S DORMITORIES (*private*) comprise a group of dormitory units built of native bluestone and designed in the English Collegiate

---

KEY FOR ITHACA MAP

CORNELL UNIVERSITY CAMPUS TOUR

1.Myron Taylor Hall 2.Sage College 3.Sage Chapel 4.Willard Straight Hall 5.Men's Dormitories 6.Library Building 7.Morrill Hall 8.Statue of Ezra Cornell 9.McGraw Hall 10.White Hall 11.Sibley Hall 12.Goldwin Smith Hall 13.Statue of Andrew D. White 14.Bailey Hall 15.Martha Van Rensselaer Hall 16.Roberts Hall 17.James Law Hall 18.Balch Halls 19.Prudence Risley Hall 20.Suspension Bridge

POINTS OF INTEREST IN CITY

21.City Hall 22.Cornell (Ithaca Public) Library 23.Ithaca College 24.Tompkins County Courthouse 25.Stewart Park

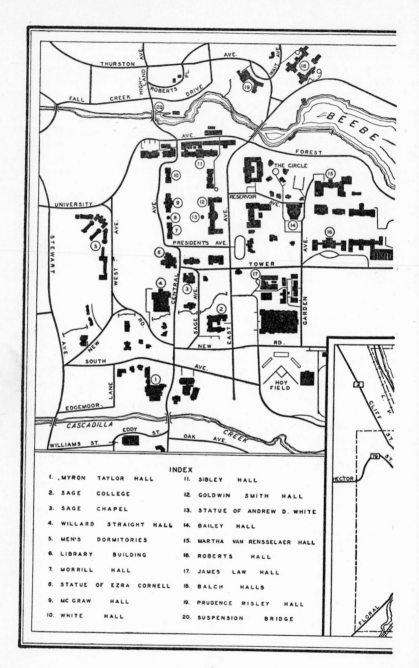

INDEX

1. MYRON TAYLOR HALL
2. SAGE COLLEGE
3. SAGE CHAPEL
4. WILLARD STRAIGHT HALL
5. MEN'S DORMITORIES
6. LIBRARY BUILDING
7. MORRILL HALL
8. STATUE OF EZRA CORNELL
9. MC GRAW HALL
10. WHITE HALL

11. SIBLEY HALL
12. GOLDWIN SMITH HALL
13. STATUE OF ANDREW D. WHITE
14. BAILEY HALL
15. MARTHA VAN RENSSELAER HALL
16. ROBERTS HALL
17. JAMES LAW HALL
18. BALCH HALLS
19. PRUDENCE RISLEY HALL
20. SUSPENSION BRIDGE

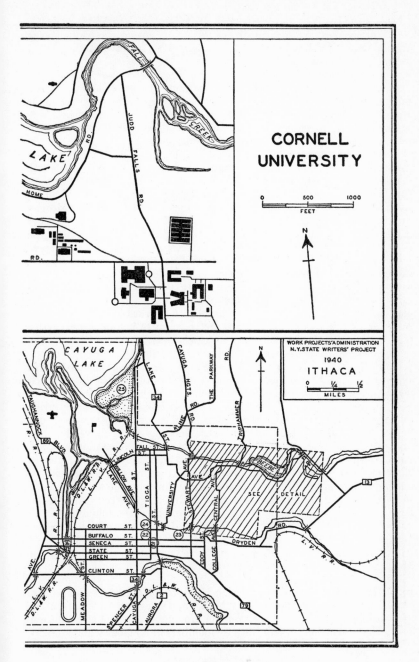

CORNELL
UNIVERSITY

0   500   1000
FEET

N

CAYUGA
LAKE

WORK PROJECTS'ADMINISTRATION
N.Y.STATE WRITERS' PROJECT
1940
ITHACA

0   ¼   ½
MILES

Gothic style by Day and Klauder of Philadelphia. The WAR MEMO-
RIAL along West Avenue consists of the Army Tower, the Navy Tower,
and a connecting arcade (*open at all times*) with traceried arches in the
manner of a Gothic cloister.

6. The LIBRARY BUILDING (*open, during academic year,* 8–5:30 *weekdays; summer,* 9–5 *weekdays*), at the southwest corner of the main quadrangle, erected in 1891, was designed by William H. Miller of Ithaca in the
Richardson Romanesque style, with massive stone arches and corbels.

The library, together with the various college and departmental libraries, has a wealth of special collections, including the Fiske Dante,
Petrarch, Rhaeto-Romanic, and Icelandic collections; the Charles Anthon
classical library; the Franz Bopp philological library; the Goldwin Smith
historical library; the White architectural library and Spinoza collection;
the Zarncke Germanic library; the Eugene Schuyler collection of Slavic
folklore; the Wordsworth collection made by Mrs.Cynthia Morgan
St.John; the Charles W. Wason Chinese collection; the James Verner
Scaife Civil War collection; the Emil Knichling library of engineering; the
Flower veterinary library.

The CLOCK TOWER (*not open to public*), south of the library and connected with it, is freestanding, square, campanile-like, constructed of the
same stone and in the Romanesque style. It is 173 feet in height and contains a chime of 14 bells, the original nine of which were donated by Miss
Jennie McGraw in 1868. When the university is in session the chimes are
rung for 15 minutes before 8 a.m., for 10 minutes before 1 p.m. and 6
p.m., and on Sundays before the 11 o'clock service in Sage Chapel. The
office of chimemaster has always been held by a student.

7. MORRILL HALL (*open, during academic year,* 8:30–4:30 *weekdays; in
summer,* 8–4 *weekdays*), built in 1866–8 of bluestone in the late French
Renaissance style, and named for the author of the Land Grant Act of
1862, is the oldest building on the campus. It houses the administrative
offices and, on the third floor, the laboratory of experimental psychology.

8. The STATUE OF EZRA CORNELL, founder of the university, is a
bronze of heroic size modeled by Hermon Atkins MacNeil and unveiled in
1919. As a young man Ezra Cornell (1807–74) managed mills and factories
along Fall Creek. After 1844 he devoted his attention to the extension of
telegraph lines and the organization of telegraph companies, among them
the Western Union. He retired in 1858 with a large fortune, and in the
next ten years achieved the great work of his life—the founding of the
university. He served as chairman of the board of trustees until his death.

9. McGRAW HALL, completed in 1872, the gift of John McGraw of
Ithaca, is designed in the late French Renaissance style, similar to that of
Morrill and White Halls. Its tower forms the dominant motif of this orig-
inal group of buildings.

10. WHITE HALL, similar in design to Morrill Hall, was completed in
1869. It is named for Andrew D. White. The College of Architecture, on
the third floor, middle entrance, conducts an almost continuous exhibition
of drawings, sketches, or paintings by members of its faculty and student
body.

11. SIBLEY HALL, the main building of the College of Engineering, is a composite structure, the two end sections dating from the seventies and the central section with the dome erected in 1902. It is named for Hiram Sibley of Rochester, who donated a large sum toward its endowment and equipment.

The large room under the dome (*open*) houses the college library and a study hall. On the west wall, in a glass case, is the original Morse telegraph instrument, presented to the college by Hiram Sibley, who, together with Ezra Cornell, was associated with Samuel F.B. Morse in the practical development of the electric telegraph.

A MEMORIAL SEAT AND TABLET, in front of Sibley Hall, commemorates the founding of Sigma Xi, honorary scholastic scientific society, at Cornell University in 1886.

A large hydraulic laboratory at the outlet of Beebe Lake provides facilities for numerous important hydraulic investigations carried on in cooperation with Government agencies. A 200-foot canal is used for the construction of model dams by means of which the problems of flood control are studied.

12. GOLDWIN SMITH HALL, with its heavy Doric portico, was erected in 1904–6 to house the College of Arts and Sciences. It was named in honor of Goldwin Smith (1823–1910), who was brought from England by Andrew D. White to serve as professor of English history. In his will he made a large bequest to the university. A marble portrait bust of him, executed by Sir Moses Ezekiel, stands in the lobby of the building.

13. The STATUE OF ANDREW D. WHITE, facing that of Ezra Cornell across the quadrangle, is a seated figure in bronze, of heroic size, wearing the gown of a doctor of civil law of the University of Oxford. It is one of the last works of Karl Bitter. At the unveiling in 1915 Mr.White made a brief address.

Andrew D. White (1832–1918) was born in Homer, New York. He was professor of history in the University of Michigan from 1857 to 1862. From 1863 to 1867, as member of the New York State Senate, he was instrumental in securing the State's share of the land grant of 1862 for Cornell University. He served as first president of the university (1867–85) and as U.S. Minister to Germany and to Russia and president of the American delegation to the first peace conference at The Hague. His best known published work is *A History of the Warfare of Science with Theology in Christendom*. He made many large gifts of books and money to the university.

14. BAILEY HALL (*private*), the auditorium of the College of Agriculture, used for major university functions, seats about 2,000. It is a semicircular structure adorned with Ionic colonnades. The building is named for Liberty Hyde Bailey (1858——), director and dean of the College of Agriculture, 1903–13, well known for his writings on botany, horticulture, and rural social and educational problems, and for his editorship of the standard cyclopedias of American horticulture and agriculture.

15. MARTHA VAN RENSSELAER HALL, erected in 1933 to house the College of Home Economics, is a large structure built of gray-buff brick,

with limestone trim, white painted sash, and spotted slate roof. In the northeast corner is the nursery, in which students are trained in the care of infants. Two-months-old babies, in perfect health and from good families, are kept here for the full college term; and girl students are assigned as 'mothers' for four-day periods of actual care of the infants.

The building was named for Martha Van Rensselaer (1864–1932), pioneer in the education of farm women, professor of home economics, and first director of the State College of Home Economics. She was also active on national committees on homemaking, housing, and child health. In 1923 she was named by the National League of Women Voters as one of the 12 most distinguished women of the United States.

16. ROBERTS HALL, the main building on the College of Agriculture quadrangle, is named for Isaac Phillips Roberts, director of the college, 1874–1903. It contains the college offices, including the publications office, which issues the many pamphlets published by the college to make available the results of the researches of its departments in scientific methods of agriculture. The State College of Agriculture performs a variety of services, including extension work, reading courses, a winter short course in agriculture, and an annual Farm and Home Week, at which the governor of the State is regularly a guest and speaker.

On the fourth floor of the building is the department of meteorology. The weather station on the roof, reached from the fourth floor, is maintained in co-operation with the U.S.Weather Bureau as the central station of New York State.

17. The three-story JAMES LAW HALL, the main building of the State Veterinary College, is in the late French Renaissance style. The building was named for the first director of the college, who was the first person to give instruction in veterinary medicine in an American university.

18. The BALCH HALLS (*private*), dormitories for women, were built in 1929. They are of an eclectic English-Italian Renaissance style; the entrance to the arcade is designed with a Palladian motif. The front balustraded terrace is a popular lounging place.

19. PRUDENCE RISLEY HALL (*private*), a dormitory for women erected in 1913, was given by Mrs.Russell Sage and named in memory of Russell Sage's mother. The pictures, statuary, and furniture in the main corridor and in the parlors on the ground floor were given by Andrew D. White.

20. The SUSPENSION BRIDGE, reached on the north by a path from Fall Creek Drive opposite Highland Ave., and on the south by a path off University Avenue just west of Sibley Hall, sways 100 feet above the rockbound waters of Fall Creek and affords a bird's-eye view of the rugged gorge. To the west are the Stewart Avenue bridge and Ithaca Falls; to the east, Triphammer Falls and bridge and the hydraulic laboratory at the foot of Beebe Lake.

POINTS OF INTEREST IN CITY

21. The CITY HALL (*open 9–5 Mon.–Fri., 9–12 Sat.*), NE. corner of Seneca and Tioga Sts., erected in 1842, is a rectangular building of red

brick and white wood trim, with elevated front portico and a stepped wood tower rising from the roof. On the upper floor are the city offices; the first floor is given over to the police department, city court, and fire station.

22. The CORNELL (Ithaca Public) LIBRARY (*open* 10–9 *weekdays*), 115 N.Tioga St., a red brick building of the Civil War period, was erected and endowed by Ezra Cornell in 1864. Besides the library, the building houses offices of the WPA and the city welfare department.

23. ITHACA COLLEGE, administrative offices at 120 E.Buffalo St., comprises a group of structures around De Witt Park and several additional buildings in the downtown section of the city. It includes departments of music, speech and dramatic art, and physical education. The student body, men and women, numbers 450, the faculty 44. Begun in 1892 as the Ithaca Conservatory of Music, the college was chartered by the Board of Regents in 1931.

24. The TOMPKINS COUNTY COURTHOUSE, corner of Court and N.Tioga Sts., is a modern classical building erected in 1931. In it are the headquarters and exhibit rooms (*open* 10–5 *Thurs.*) of the De Witt Historical Society of Tompkins County. The exhibits include Indian and Colonial relics and many items relating to local history.

25. STEWART PARK, at the head of Cayuga lake, the principal public park of the city, includes a bathing beach with bathhouses, picnic grounds, athletic fields, a small zoo, and the RENWICK BIRD SANCTUARY and FUERTES WILD FOWL SANCTUARY, which provide refuge for more than 300 species of birds. These sanctuaries were made possible by gifts from local citizens and were developed with the co-operation of the Department of Ornithology of Cornell University.

The memorial gateway at the waterfowl pond bears a bronze plaque in honor of Louis Agassiz Fuertes (1874–1927), native of Ithaca, ornithologist, and internationally known painter of bird pictures, many of the originals of which hang in the State Museum at Albany. He also supervised the designing and construction of several famous bird groups in the Museum of Natural History, New York City.

POINTS OF INTEREST IN ENVIRONS

Watkins Glen State Park, 29 *m.* (*see Tour* 27). Buttermilk Falls State Park, 2.3 *m.*, Robert H. Treman (Enfield Glen) State Park, 4.7 *m.*, Taughannock Falls State Park, 9.5 *m.* (*see Tour* 30).

New Rochelle

Railroad Station: Plaza between North and Union Aves. for New York, New Haven & Hartford R.R.
Bus Station: 244 Huguenot St. for Greyhound, New England, Blue Way, and Grey Bus Lines and local busses.
Streetcars: 5¢ within city; 10¢ to New York City subway in Mount Vernon.
Piers: Hudson Park, off Pelham Rd., for excursion and fishing boats; foot of Fort Slocum Rd. for Port Washington, L.I., ferry (cars $1.50 up) and Fort Slocum ferry (passes to visit Fort Slocum available at dock).
Taxis: 25¢–75¢.

Accommodations: 1 hotel; rooming and boarding houses.

Information Service: Chamber of Commerce, 272 North Ave.; American Automobile Association, 524 North Ave.; New Rochelle *Standard Star*, 253 North Ave.

Swimming: Glen Island, Weyman Ave. off Pelham Rd., general adm. 10¢; bathhouse: adults 35¢–40¢, children 15¢–25¢; parking 25¢–50¢. Hudson Park, Hudson Park Rd. off Pelham Rd.: residents of New Rochelle, with identification card (25¢), obtainable in park office, adm. free, bathhouse 10¢ (children under 14 yrs. free), season parking $1; visitors $1, parking 25¢.
Fishing: Hudson Park Dock for saltwater fishing (no license required, no restrictions on catch); boats leave 9 a.m. weekdays, 8 a.m. Sun.; equipment available; estimated day's cost $5; private boats also available.
Golf: Glen Rock Golf Course, Boston Post Rd. (US 1) between Stonelea Pl. and Palmer Ave., 9 holes; greens fee, 50¢ weekdays, $1 Sat., Sun., and holidays.
Tennis: Morgan St. courts, residents $1 a month, visitors 50¢ a game; tickets from Park Dept., City Hall.

Annual Events: Numerous regattas by yacht clubs on Long Island Sound each summer.

NEW ROCHELLE (72 alt.,57,415 pop.) is rich in historical landmarks and monuments scattered among its modern apartment houses, cottages, and estates. Main Street, the principal business thoroughfare, follows the route of the historic Boston Post Road, along which patriot messengers carried the news of Lexington and Bunker Hill to New York. From it branch tree-shaded avenues lined with two-story villa residences, each with its lawn and flower garden facing the road. Other residential sections, especially in the northern part of the city, are built up in a series of parks. New Rochelle was reputedly the scene of George M. Cohan's *Forty-five Minutes from Broadway*; the modern New Haven trains make the Grand Central Terminal in half an hour.

In the heart of the Westchester country club district (the Wykagyl Country Club and several others are in the city and the Winged Foot Golf Club and Travers Island are close by), and with nine miles of sheltered water front on Long Island Sound, the city prides itself on its sporting activities: golf, tennis, boating, yachting, and swimming throughout the summer months, and salt-water fishing in all weathers.

The fact that New Rochelle has one of the highest ratings of per capita wealth among the communities of the country is reflected in the rich architecture of its homes, its schools, and its churches. The city's diversified industrial products include powder puffs, surgical instruments, chemicals, and metal novelties.

In the poorer sections of the city live many Negroes, most of whom earn a living as servants in apartment houses and private homes, and 5,000 descendants of the Italian laborers imported in the eighties to lay railroad lines.

The city occupies the site of the villages of the Siwanoy, principal nation of the Wappinger Indian confederacy. In 1688 a small group of Huguenot refugees landed at what is now Bonnefoi Point. In 1689 they purchased from John Pell, second lord of the manor of Pelham, through the agency of Jacob Leisler, a tract of 6,000 acres and named the settlement for their old home in France, La Rochelle. In 1692 they built the first church in New Rochelle. With the passing of the years, they became communicants of the Anglican church. In 1698 a census showed a total population of 232, consisting of 188 whites and 44 Negro slaves.

Highlights of the Revolutionary period were the arrival of Paul Revere and other messengers from Boston to New York and the overnight stay of George Washington in 1775 on his way to Cambridge, Massachusetts, to take command of the Continental Army. General Philip Schuyler rode into town with him and left the next morning to take command of the defenses on the northern New York frontier. Schuyler was familiar with New Rochelle: as a boy of 15 he had attended the school of the Reverend Pierre Stouppe here, and his shore estate was near Pell's Point, five miles southeast.

New Rochelle became a village in 1857 and was incorporated as a city in 1899. As early as the 1890's it began to attract theatrical people, artists, and writers. Agnes Booth and Cora Tanner, famous in their day as stars of the melodrama *The Sporting Dutchess*, from time to time made the city their home, as did Eddie Foy, vaudeville actor and hero of the Iroquois Theater fire in Chicago. Francis Wilson, of *Erminie* fame, lived here; and Frederic Remington, sculptor and painter of western scenes, and Augustus Thomas, playwright, were commuters. Here, too, lived George Randolph Chester, who invented that delectable character of the old school, Get-Rich-Quick Wallingford. Faith Baldwin, novelist, was born in New Rochelle in 1893. A contemporary resident is Norman Rockwell, artist and illustrator.

The observance in the summer of 1938 of the 250th anniversary of the settlement of New Rochelle included a pilgrimage of children to New York City to commemorate the long trips to church taken by the first settlers. While the Huguenots, according to tradition, went barefoot all the way, the children put on their shoes and stockings after one block.

POINTS OF INTEREST

The JACOB LEISLER MONUMENT, North and Broadview Aves., erected in 1913 by the Huguenot Chapter D.A.R. and the Huguenot and Historical Association of New Rochelle, is the only American memorial to Jacob Leisler (1640–91). Following the abdication of James II and the overthrow of Edmund Andros in Boston, Leisler, a German immigrant, seized control and ruled the Province of New York from 1689 until the arrival of Governor Henry Sloughter, appointed by William and Mary. After laying down his power Leisler was tried for treason, found guilty, and executed, but his name was later cleared in England. Since no portrait of Leisler exists, the statue is largely imaginary, presenting a heroic figure dressed in a long cloak and a Dutch beaver hat and carrying a large staff. The sculptor was Solon H. Borglum.

The THOMAS PAINE MONUMENT, Paine and North Aves., enclosed by an iron fence, consists of a bronze bust on a square granite column, the cap of which has been chipped in several places. The monument was originally erected in 1839 and was restored in 1881; the bronze, dedicated on May 30, 1899, was modeled by Wilson MacDonald. The monument stands close to the site of the grave in which Paine was originally buried.

The PAINE COTTAGE (*open 2–5 Tues.–Sun.*), SE. corner of North and Paine Aves., a two-story post-Colonial frame house with shingle exterior, rough stone foundation, and solid blinds, has been moved from its original site (120 Paine Avenue) on a near-by hilltop, where it was occupied by Paine. It houses the Huguenot and Historical Association of New Rochelle; the collection includes a Franklin stove given Paine by Benjamin Franklin and the chair that Paine always used when writing.

Crossing the brook just south of the cottage is the HUGUENOT MEMORIAL BRIDGE, dedicated on June 27, 1917, and constructed of stones from the Huguenot Reformed Church that was built in 1710.

The PAINE MEMORIAL HOUSE (*open 2–5 Tues.–Sun.*), 989 North Ave., a two-story structure of natural stone, was erected in 1925 by the Thomas Paine National Historical Association. Ground for the building was broken by Thomas A. Edison, an ardent admirer of Paine's writings. The house contains a number of Paine's personal effects, including the trunk in which he carried the State papers of the Second Continental Congress, of which he was secretary, from Philadelphia after Howe's capture of the city in 1777. Across a wall of the main room is a painted replica of Paine's Rainbow Flag, which he proposed as an international symbol to be used by neutral ships in time of war. Photostatic copies of extant letters, first editions of Paine's works, his death mask, and a fragment of the mutilated gravestone complete the collection.

Thomas Paine (1737–1809), author of *Rights of Man* and *The Age of Reason*, was a participant in both the American and French Revolutions. His first great work, *Common Sense*, published anonymously in January 1776, crystallized Colonial opposition to the Mother Country into a demand for independence and strongly influenced the subsequent action of the Continental Congress. The installments of *The Crisis*, his other great American work of propaganda, which appeared during 1777, were read to the Continental Army.

After the war Pennsylvania presented him with £500 and New York with 300 acres of confiscated land in New Rochelle. After 15 stormy years in England and France he returned to the United States in 1802, and in 1804 made the New Rochelle farm his home. Denied the right to vote in 1806, he moved to New York City, where he died; the body was returned to the farm for burial. In 1819 William Cobbett, English political economist, removed the remains and shipped them to England, where they later disappeared, although some parts are said to have been returned and buried under the present monument.

The NEW ROCHELLE HIGH SCHOOL, Clove Rd. and Woodrow Wilson Drive, erected in 1926, is a notable example of Westchester County schools. It is a three-story building constructed of red brick with limestone trim and stone balustrades, designed in the late French Gothic and early French Renaissance styles. It is set well back beside Huguenot Lake amid large, well-equipped playgrounds. The composition of the whole is excellent. The architects were Guilbert and Betelle.

FANEUIL PARK, Huguenot and Main Sts., a triangular lawn plot set off by shrubs and walks and containing a war memorial, is named for Peter Faneuil, native of New Rochelle and successful Boston merchant, builder and donor of Faneuil Hall in Boston, the market building that came to be known as 'the cradle of liberty.'

SALESIAN COLLEGE (*open by permission*), 148 Main St., a school for training young men for the Catholic priesthood, was founded by the Salesian Fathers in 1919. The large modern gymnasium fronts the street. Driveways lead through the 30-acre campus.

HUDSON PARK, foot of Hudson Park Road, 13 acres along the city's harbor front, includes a public beach, the city boathouse and greenhouses, the shore station of the United States Coast Guard, and several yacht and rowing clubs. During the summer months excursion boats make frequent tours up the Sound as far as Playland and Rye Beach.

The present park is traditionally accepted as the landing place of the first Huguenot settlers. A granite boulder with bronze tablets commemorates the event. The monument overlooks the boat-studded inlets of the harbor and the still waters of the Sound, with the Oyster Bay section of Long Island a blue ridge on the horizon. This is a favorite shore vantage point for watching yacht races on the Sound during the summer.

The COLLEGE OF NEW ROCHELLE (*open by permission*), 29 Castle Place, occupies a heavily wooded 25-acre campus with 14 buildings, most of them designed in the Tudor Gothic style. Opened in 1891 by Ursuline nuns as a boarding school for girls, it received its charter as a Roman Catholic college for women in 1904, and today, with an enrollment of more than 700, ranks among the largest of its kind in the country.

FORT SLOCUM (*adm. by pass obtainable from officer in charge at dock*), on David's Island, reached by the Fort Slocum ferry, foot of Fort Slocum Road, is visible from the dock as a group of Army barracks. It is the overseas recruiting depot for foreign service enlistments of all casuals east of the Mississippi River. About 1,500 men a month are shipped, after a period of training, for service in China, the Philippines, Hawaii, and the Canal Zone. Visitors are permitted to inspect the old gun pits and military galleries of Civil War vintage.

GLEN ISLAND, foot of Weyman Ave., a 108-acre amusement park, privately owned until 1923, is now owned by the Westchester County Park Commission. The Island was visited by Aaron Burr, Daniel Webster, Washington Irving, Jenny Lind, General U.S.Grant, and James A. Garfield.

The GERMAN CASTLE, near the parking field, a garish structure built half a century ago as a beer garden and cafe, faithfully follows the pattern of medieval Rhine fortress-castles.

The CASINO, left of the entrance drive, is the park's luxurious dinner club.

The FIRST PRESBYTERIAN CHURCH, 50 Pintard Ave., designed by John Russell Pope in the manner of a New England Georgian Colonial church, was built in 1928 as the successor to the building erected by the French Reformed congregation of the Huguenot pioneers. The tower and spire, forming one transept, are graceful and lofty; the opposite transept wall has a Palladian window. The principal façade has a wood Ionic portico and pediment. The interior, lighted by narrow, arched, many-paned windows, is adorned with Roman Doric columns and pilasters. The vaulted ceilings of the nave and transept have a groined intersection.

The PINTARD MANSE, E. of the church, is a story-and-a-half early Georgian Colonial dwelling, used after 1774 as a country residence by Lewis Pintard, prominent merchant and patriot of New York City. The white-shingled walls and the delicately carved cornice act as a graceful, harmonious foil to the monumental stone church adjoining. The neoclassic porch and probably the dormers are later additions.

TRINITY CHURCH, NW. corner of Huguenot and Division Sts., is a Victorian Gothic church of the Civil War period, built of granite with brownstone trim. The roof is covered with slate of variegated colors, and the cast-iron cresting on the ridge is characteristic of the period. The spire is well-proportioned, light, and graceful.

At the rear of the church is the city's oldest cemetery, laid out by the Huguenots. Today the main line of the New York, New Haven & Hartford Railroad cuts through, its tracks at a level with the lichen-clad gravestones.

POINTS OF INTEREST IN ENVIRONS

Saxon Woods Park, 5 *m.*, Playland, 6.5 *m.* (*see Tour* 1). St.Paul's (Protestant Episcopal) Church, Mount Vernon, 4.5 *m.* (*see Tour* 20).

Commerce and Transportation

YANKEE CLIPPER TAKING OFF FROM LA GUARDIA FIELD, NEW YORK CITY

SKY CHIEF AND S.S. NORMANDIE LEAVING NEW YORK HARBOR

Photograph by courtesy of Wide World Photos, Inc

'DOWN HARBOR'—NEW YORK CITY (Statue of Liberty, right; Governors Island, left)

BUFFALO WATERFRONT

Photograph by Hare

TAKING ON CARGO, PORT OF ALBANY

AT LOCK 8 OF THE BARGE CANAL

C.C.BROTHERS

Photograph by Milton J. Washburn

PEACE BRIDGE, BUFFALO TO FORT ERIE, ONTARIO, CANADA

GEORGE WASHINGTON BRIDGE AND THE HUDSON RIVER, NEW YORK CITY

Photograph by courtesy of the New York Bureau of State Publicity

Photograph by courtesy of the Public Works Administration

BUILDING THE LINCOLN TUNNEL UNDER THE HUDSON RIVER

PARKWAY INTERSECTION, KEW GARDENS

VIADUCT IN HIGH BRIDGE PARK, NEW YORK CITY

Photograph by courtesy of Federal Works Agency

PARK AVENUE LOOKING TOWARDS GRAND CENTRAL STATION, NEW YORK CITY

BUFFALO AT NIGHT

Photograph by the Appleton Studio

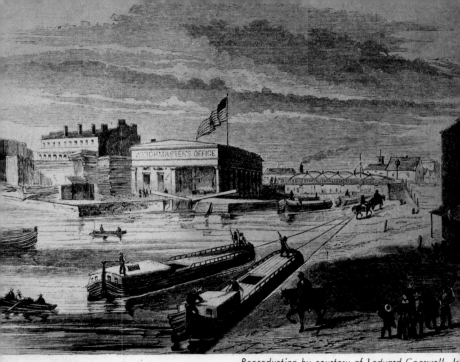

THE ALBANY BASIN OF THE ERIE AND CHAMPLAIN CANALS (1856)

THE *DE WITT CLINTON* (1831)

New York City

Altitude, 17.06 at Customhouse, Manhattan, and 409 at Todt Hill, Richmond; pop. 7,380,259; boroughs—Manhattan, Brooklyn, the Bronx, Queens, Richmond (Staten Island); area 322.83 sq. m.; settled 1625, incorporated 1653; government—mayor, city council, board of estimate, borough presidents, and numerous boards, commissions, and agencies.

Street Order and Numbering: While the other boroughs are a maze of streets, in Manhattan, except for the southern and, in part, the northern tips, the streets are laid out on a gridiron pattern, making it by far the easiest of the boroughs in which to get around. Avenues run north and south, streets east and west. Up to 138th St., where Fifth Ave. ends, the buildings on the cross streets are numbered east and west of Fifth Ave., and the street names are prefixed E. and W. accordingly. The section east of Fifth Ave. is popularly referred to as the 'east side,' that west of the same avenue as the 'west side.' In Manhattan, all north of 138th St. is west. The addresses of avenue buildings are numbered south to north.

'Uptown' and 'downtown,' popular directional expressions, are relative terms: traveling south from any point is to travel downtown, and north from any point uptown. By and large, however, the downtown district is below 14th St. Occasionally 'midtown' is used to designate the area embraced by Seventh and Lexington Aves. and 34th and 57th Sts. 'Cross-town' is from east to west and vice versa.

Railroad Stations: Grand Central Terminal, Park Ave. and 42d St., serving New York Central System and New York, New Haven & Hartford R.R.; Pennsylvania Station, Seventh Ave. between 31st and 33d Sts., serving Pennsylvania R.R. and Long Island R.R. Other terminals in Hoboken, Jersey City, and Weehawken, N.J., reached by ferry or motor coach. City ticket offices at 17 John St., 4 W.33d St., and 3 W.47th St.

Bus Stations: Capitol Greyhound Terminal, 245 W.50th St.; Dixie Bus Center, 241 W. 42d St.; Consolidated Bus Terminal, 203 W.41st St.; Gray Line Terminal, 59 W.36th St.; Hotel Astor Bus Terminal, 220 W.45th St.; Midtown Bus Terminal, 143 W.43d St.; All-American Bus Depot, 246 W.42d St.; Pennsylvania Motor Coach Terminal, 242 W.34th St. (All to be moved outside midtown section.)

Airports: La Guardia Field, Queens; Floyd Bennett Field, Brooklyn; Roosevelt Field, Mineola, Long Island.

Airlines Office: Union Airways Terminal, Park Ave. at 42d St., a central agency for tickets for all U.S. airlines.

Taxicabs: Basic meter rate 20¢ for the first quarter mile or any fraction thereof, 5¢ for each additional quarter mile. For articles left in taxicabs, call at Police Dept. Hack Bureau, 156 Greenwich St., Manhattan.

Public Transit Systems: The public transit systems, all owned by the city, converge on lower Manhattan. Both the IRT (Interborough Rapid Transit Corp.) and BMT (Brooklyn-Manhattan Transit Corp.) subway lines cross Times Square; the Eighth Ave. line (Independent City-Owned Rapid Transit R.R.) has an important station one block west at Eighth Avenue and 42nd Street. From Times Square the BMT runs uptown as far as 59th St., turns northeast to 60th St., then dips beneath the East River to Queens. The downtown segment of this line follows the course of Broadway and eventually emerges in Brooklyn to serve chiefly the lower part of that borough. At Union Square the 14th St., or Canarsie, spur of the BMT crosses, on its way from Eighth Ave. to Canarsie, Jamaica, and other points. The IRT has West side (Broadway-Seventh Ave.) and East side (Lexington Ave.) main lines, which serve commuters as far north as Van Cortlandt Park and the Bronx; both these lines also run downtown and into Brooklyn. A 'shuttle' links Times Square with Grand Central Terminal (42nd St. and Park Ave.).

From Times Square a spur breaks off east to serve Queens. The Eighth Ave. (Independent) Subway serves Eighth Ave., Central Park West to the northern tip of Manhattan, the Bronx, and part of Brooklyn. A branch line runs east on 53rd St. to Jamaica. Each subway car has an easily read road map showing the routes of its system, and all stations bear signs distinguishing local from express and uptown from downtown platforms.

The East side is served by the Third and Second Ave. elevated ('el') lines, the West side by the Ninth Ave. line. These north-south lines served Manhattan points east and west of the subways. Much of the cross-town traffic is handled by bus service. (The elevated lines are [1940] rapidly being demolished.)

As Manhattan is an island, a heavy traffic is carried by ferries, bridges, and tunnels. Fifteen bridges and 16 tunnels radiate from Manhattan. The Hudson Tubes system (Hudson & Manhattan R.R.) operates between Manhattan and Hoboken, Jersey City, and Newark, N.J.

Accommodations: Hotels and apartments to suit every purse; largest hotels concentrated in midtown area from 24th to 59th Sts., between Eighth and Lexington Aves. (Consult New York Hotel Assn., 221 W.57th St., for full information.) Thousands of restaurants; foreign restaurants listed separately in classified telephone directory.

Information Service: New York City Information Center, Pershing Square at 42nd St. (panorama map of Manhattan); police information booth, Times Sq., at 43rd St. and Broadway; American Automobile Assn., Pennsylvania Hotel, Seventh Ave. at 33rd St.; New York Convention and Visitors' Bureau, 233 Broadway; Esso and Socony-Vacuum Touring Services, RCA Building, Rockefeller Center; YMCA headquarters, 420 Lexington Ave.; YWCA Central Branch Information Desk, 610 Lexington Ave. (for addresses of 'Y' branches consult telephone directory); Hotel Assn. of New York City, 221 W. 57th St.; Daily News Information Bureau, 220 E.42nd St.; U.S.Travel Bureau, 45 Broadway.

Radio Stations: National Broadcasting Co.—WEAF (660 kc.), WJZ (760 kc.); Columbia Broadcasting System—WABC (860 kc.); WNYC (810 kc.); WQXR (1550 kc.); WEVD (1300 kc.); WMCA (570 kc.); WHN (1010 kc.); WBIL (1100 kc.); WBNX (1350 kc.); WOV (1130 kc.); WINS (1180 kc.); WNEW (1250 kc.); WFAB (1300 kc.); WBBR (1300 kc.).

Theaters: Mainly in the Times Square district, west of Broadway.

Night Clubs: Mainly from 42nd to 53rd Sts., between Eighth and Fifth Aves.; E.50's; Harlem.

Public Beaches: Brighton Beach, Brooklyn; Coney Island, Brooklyn; Jacob Riis Park, Queens; Manhattan Beach, Brooklyn; Midland Beach, Staten Island; Orchard Beach, Pelham Bay Park, Bronx; Rockaway Beach, Queens; South Beach, Staten Island.

Steamships: In normal times all the large transatlantic liners may be visited when in port. Consult shipping news columns in newspapers for dates of arrival and departure. Apply at piers for passes. Adm. 10¢–50¢.

Concerts: (Outdoor) New York Philharmonic Orchestra, Lewisohn Stadium, Amsterdam Ave. and 138th St., June–Aug. Goldman Band Concerts: June–Aug.; Sun., Mon., Wed., Fri. on the Mall, Central Park; Tues., Thurs., Sat., Prospect Park, Brooklyn. (Indoor) Brooklyn Academy of Music, 30 Lafayette Ave., Brooklyn, Oct.–Apr.; Brooklyn Museum, Eastern Parkway and Washington Ave., Brooklyn, all year; McMillin Academic Theater (Columbia University), Broadway and 116th St., Oct.–Apr.; Metropolitan Museum of Art, Fifth Ave. at 82nd St., symphony concerts, Sats. in Jan. and Mar.; Steinway Concert Hall, 113 W.57th St., Sept.–Apr. and scattered evenings throughout May and June; Washington Irving High School, Irving Place and 16th St., Oct.–Apr. WPA concerts throughout the city all year round.

Opera: (Indoor) Metropolitan Opera House, Broadway and 39th St., Nov.–Mar.; Hippodrome, 6th Ave. and 43rd St., Nov.–Mar. (Outdoor) Jones Beach Stadium, Jones Beach, Long Island, July–Sept.; Triborough Stadium, Randall's Island, July–Sept.

Annual Events: Jan., no fixed date, American Water Color Society exhibition, Motor Boat Show; Feb. 12, Lincoln's Birthday ceremonies; Feb. 22, Washington's Birthday exercises, including Sons of the Revolution church service; Feb., Six-Day Bike Race,

Sportsmen's Show; Mar. 17, St.Patrick's Day exercises, including Fifth Ave. parade; Mar., Golden Gloves Boxing Tournament, International Flower Show; Apr. 6, Army Day exercises, including Fifth Ave. parade; Apr. 26, Grant's Birthday exercises, including services at Tomb on Riverside Drive; Apr., Circus at Madison Square Garden, Rainbow Division Ball; May 1, May Day parade by labor organizations; May 30, Memorial Day exercises; June 14, Flag Day exercises, including Statute of Liberty celebration and Sons of the Revolution parade; July 4, Fourth of July exercises; July, Athletic Carnival at Randall's Island Stadium; Aug., swimming contests at Palisades Park; Sept., no fixed date, National Electrical and Radio Exposition, Outdoor Art Exhibition in Washington Sq., Camera Art Exhibition at Rockefeller Center, Mardi Gras at Coney Island; Oct. 12, Columbus Day exercises, including meeting at Columbus Circle; Oct., no fixed date, Drug Trade Exposition, National Hotel Exposition, National Business Show, Rodeo at Madison Square Garden; Nov. 10, American Legion Victory Ball; Nov. 11, Armistice Day exercises, including Mass at St.Patrick's Cathedral; Nov., Automobile Show, National Horse Show; Dec., International Ski Meet at Madison Square Garden, Chemical Industries Show at Grand Central Palace.

> No attempt can be made in this space to give more than an outline view of New York City. The subject is treated more comprehensively in *New York Panorama* and *New York City Guide* of the American Guide Series.

The average New Yorker, conditioned to crowds, speed, Wall Street, even violent death, takes his city for granted. The visitor approaching the city sees spread before him one of the most congested habitations of men on earth, the lofty towers of Manhattan marking the apex of a vast jungle of structures in which men work, sleep, eat, play. Little more than three centuries has sufficed for the building of this gigantic city. The miracle of its upsurge since the turn of the present century makes it a dynamic expression of American civilization. In that sense New York *is* America.

Two events were of decisive importance in this development: the opening of the Erie Canal in 1825, and the creation, under State charter, of Greater New York in 1898. The former established the commercial supremacy of New York—a position thenceforth never threatened—over the rival ports of Boston, Philadelphia, and Baltimore, and made the city the great gateway for European immigration. The creation of Greater New York brought into the city's jurisdiction not only areas as densely settled as lower Brooklyn, but also forests, farms, and marshes—a huge area for further expansion.

Most New Yorkers do not own their own homes; they rent apartments, and move about almost as freely as tent-dwellers. Population shifts in recent years have made Brooklyn the most populous borough, with the Bronx rapidly rising to challenge that primacy. Manhattan—the commercial, industrial, financial, and amusement center—is decreasing in population.

The city is a cluster of ethnic groups. Definite foreign colonies exist, but the lines are constantly shifting; and with the passing of the years, especially since drastic restrictions have been imposed on immigration, many Old World customs have been lost. On the other hand, much that has come to be considered peculiarly American is the direct contribution of these latter-day citizens. The Negroes are in some ways the most American of all.

If blood is to be used as the criterion for classification, there are more Italians in New York City than in Rome, more Irish than in Dublin, more Jews than in any other city in the world. Foreign white residents in the city in 1930 numbered 5,082,025, or 73.3 per cent of the total population. Of these the Italians led with 1,070,355, and were followed by the Russians (mostly Jews) with 945,072, the Germans with 600,084, the Irish with 535,034, the Poles with 458,381, and other groups trailing off into relatively small numbers. There are approximately 2,000,000 Jews in New York; a 1927 estimate gave 1,765,000.

Buying and selling goods remains New York's largest economic activity. In 1935 the city did a wholesale business of $9,618,000,000, or about 22 per cent of the national total. In the same year its retail sales amounted to $2,847,332,000, or about 8 per cent of the national total. Retail and wholesale establishments, owned by 114,882 individual proprietors and firm members, employed 522,908 persons in 1935, each person earning an annual average of $1,500. Nearly half the retail stores fall under the 'convenience goods' category—food, drugs, and so on—and are scattered over the Greater City. The 'shopping lines' and 'luxury goods,' on the other hand, are concentrated in well-marked districts, the most important of which is the midtown region fed by the city's two great railroad centers— the Grand Central Terminal and Pennsylvania Station.

Accessibility of capital, raw materials, and specialized machinery, geographical advantages, and concentration of population, including highly skilled workers, have combined to make New York the country's greatest industrial center. In 1935, the 485,144 workers employed in 26,061 factories were paid $582,298,673 for converting materials (including fuel and power) worth $1,756,473,582 into products valued at $3,666,218,239. The largest industry is the production of clothing and accessories, followed in importance by printing and publishing, and the manufacture of foods, beverages, fur goods, jewelry, metal products, textiles, wood products, chemicals, clay and glass products, paper goods, and tobacco products. Individual manufacturing establishments are relatively small.

Labor unions form an influential element in the city's industrial life. The strongest are the building trades unions, longshoremen's and maritime unions, the Amalgamated Clothing Workers Union, the International Ladies Garment Workers Union, the Hotel and Restaurant Workers Union, and the International Fur Workers Union. Since 1923 the Amalgamated has operated a bank which has built apartment houses for its members and frequently made loans to employers in the industry. The Congress of Industrial Organizations, since its inception in 1935, has increased labor consciousness by organizing new industrial unions. One of these is the Transport Workers Union, including subway, elevated, bus, and surface line workers and taxi drivers. White collar unions also have prospered. The passage of the National Labor Relations Act of 1935 was a boon to labor. The American Labor Party, organized in 1936, gave President Roosevelt 238,845 votes in New York City, and in 1938 furnished the deciding votes in the re-election of Governor Herbert H. Lehman.

Exclusive of part-time vocational schools and the education projects of the WPA, the public educational system of New York City conducts 849 day and evening schools serving 1,178,561 pupils and four colleges. Institutions of higher learning include Columbia, New York, and Fordham Universities. The New School for Social Research is primarily an institution of adult education. Cooper Union grants degrees in engineering and also has an art school. Brooklyn Polytechnic Institute is an engineering college. Pratt Institute grants degrees in such fields as engineering and library science and offers technical courses of noncollegiate grade. There are many other denominational colleges and institutions for the study of law, medicine, fine arts, and the social sciences.

New York is one of the greatest centers of museums in the world. Among the best known are the American Museum of Natural History, the Metropolitan Museum of Art, the Brooklyn Museum, the Washington Heights group, the Museum of Modern Art, and the New York Museum of Science and Industry.

Broadly, for every ill to which man is heir, one or more of the city's 1,167 social agencies offer aid. Every year 133 hospitals serve about 750,000 in-patients and about 2,000,000 out-patients. Clinics, 1,533 in number, specialize in a wide variety of ailments. In the fields of recreation, education, employment, and related activities, there are approximately 250 organizations.

New York City's contribution to the growth of the arts in America has been the provision of a market place and a critical audience for the artist's products. New York is the great center of the Nation's publishing industry. Relatively few of America's artists have been New Yorkers, but since the middle of the nineteenth century they have constantly sought out the book and music publishers, the periodicals, the newspapers, the stage, the art galleries, and the studios of Manhattan.

The city's tempo, its racy vernacular, its endless variety, its wilderness of brick and steel, and its tumultuous humanity have provided a rich reservoir for creative artists. Walt Whitman drew copiously from it. O. Henry chronicled the lives of the little people of Bagdad-on-the-Subway. Stephen Crane, sifting its cruel contrasts through his clear and honest vision, penned *Maggie, a Girl of the Streets*. Later writers, like John Dos Passos, have attempted to imprison its character within the covers of a book. The Armory Show, held in the city in 1913, still ranks as the most memorable event of the American art world. John Marin in his water colors has caught something of the city's squalor and grandeur. The multitude and magnitude of its skyscrapers constitute New York City's one great contribution to architecture. Tin Pan Alley has written down the city's folk music from minstrelsy through all the variations of jazz.

HARBOR AND RIVERS

The Port of New York, one of the largest in the world, and served by more than 300 motor truck lines and 10 trunkline railroads, embraces the area within a 25-mile radius of the Statue of Liberty with an approximate population of 12,000,000. In this region about 40,000 industrial establishments annually produce goods valued at $8,000,000,000.

The port is fringed by 771 miles of shore line. Along the more than 578 miles within the city limits are 1,800 piers, wharves, and bulkheads. The North (Hudson) River water front of Manhattan, the most intensively developed, is bordered with the piers of the great transatlantic and South American shipping companies.

On the Brooklyn water front are hundreds of large industrial plants, warehouses, and extensive drydocking and ship repair facilities; Bush Terminal is one of the largest docking, storage, and industrial developments in the world. On Staten Island is the only free port zone in the United States.

About 200 vessels nose into the harbor every day. In 1936 the total foreign and domestic water-borne commerce of the Port amounted to 110,697,688 tons valued at $7,864,339,142, of which more than four-fifths was domestic. The chief exports were wheat, flour, hay and feed, oil, kerosene, gasoline, motor vehicles, coal tar products, and copper manufactures, scrap iron, iron, and steel. Chief imports were petroleum, raw sugar, coffee, tea and cocoa, fruits and nuts, crude rubber, gypsum, iron ore, flaxseed, paper products, wood pulp, and bags and bagging.

In an apparent bedlam of intake and discharge, through a tangled skein of courses, the intra-port machinery functions with smoothness and precision. The loading and unloading operations are performed by 35,000 longshoremen; 15,000 men operate the 6,000 barges, scows, lighters, and carfloats of the port; 3,400 men run the railroad marine fleet of 1,600 craft. Private concerns own about 570 tugs. Fifteen thousand workers are employed in ship repairs and shipbuilding.

POINTS OF INTEREST

BEDLOE'S ISLAND: STATUE OF LIBERTY (1886) (*open daily, Oct.–May 9–5; during Sept. to 6; during June, July, and Aug. to 7; adm. 10¢; boat from Battery every hour on the hour; half-hour schedule every Sat. and Sun. during summer season; round trip, adults 35¢, children 20¢*), was executed by Frédéric Auguste Bartholdi, French sculptor, and presented by the French people to the people of the United States.

ELLIS ISLAND (*open 10–11 a.m. and 2–3 p.m., except Sat., Sun., and holidays; pass issued at South Ferry Barge Office for ferry leaving daily at 9:45 a.m. and 1:45 p.m.; phone Whitehall 4–8860 for reservation at least one day in advance*) lies about one mile SW. of the Battery in Upper New York Bay. Used by the Dutch as a picnic ground, in the early nineteenth century it was a Government arsenal. Since 1892 it has been an important immigration station.

GOVERNORS ISLAND (*from South Ferry Barge Office visitors transported free on Govt. ferryboat at 30-min. intervals, 5:45 a.m.–1 a.m. daily*), headquarters of the Second Corps Area, lies about 500 yds. off Battery Park in Upper New York Bay. Troops have left this island for the Seminole Wars, the Mexican War, the Civil War, the Spanish-American War, and the World War.

WELFARE ISLAND (*open only to visitors of patients; ferry leaves ft. of E.78th St., Manhattan, at 30-min. intervals, 5¢ each way, passes obtained at ferry; Queensboro Bridge, pedestrian passage to elevators on island*) lies in the middle of the East River from 52nd St. to 86th St., Manhattan. Up to 1921 known as Blackwells Island, it was the site of a city penitentiary and workhouse. Today, institutions of public service on the island are the Metropolitan Hospital, the New York City Home for Dependents, the Central Neurological Hospital, the Cancer Institute, the Welfare Hospital for Chronic Diseases, and the New York City Hospital.

BROOKLYN BRIDGE (1883), with Gothic pylons, is considered a masterpiece of design. Until 1903 this was the longest (6,016 feet) suspension bridge in the world. In this bridge John A. Roebling and his son, Washington A. Roebling, introduced several engineering methods that have since been widely employed, one being the use of semiflexible cable rests to allow for expansion and contraction during temperature changes.

TRIBOROUGH BRIDGE (1936), by the Triborough Bridge Authority, the second longest (17,710 feet) in the world, links Manhattan with the Bronx and Queens.

GEORGE WASHINGTON BRIDGE (1931), by O.H.Amman with Cass Gilbert in advisory capacity, links Manhattan with Fort Lee, N.J.; it is the only New York City bridge over the Hudson River.

HOLLAND TUNNEL (1927), twin tubes under the North (Hudson) River, is used by 12,500,000 cars every year.

LINCOLN TUNNEL (1938), is comprised of twin tubes under the North (Hudson) River.

QUEENS MIDTOWN TUNNEL is the only vehicular tube under the East River.

NEW TRANSATLANTIC PIERS, 44th to 57th St., North (Hudson) River: Pier 88 accommodates the *Normandie*, Pier 90 *Queen Mary*, Pier 92 giant ships of the Italian Line.

MANHATTAN

For most visitors to New York City, the center of interest is the Borough of Manhattan (pop. 1,871,474), the most explosive center of civilization in the New World. The borough is an island 12½ miles long, shaped like an index finger pointing to the south.

BROADWAY. *BMT subway, any station from 42d St. downtown; IRT Broadway-Seventh Ave. subway, any station from 42d St. uptown.*

BROADWAY, the longest and most fantastic street in the world, starts its 16-mile journey from the tip of Manhattan as a shipping lane, moves a few blocks north to the Wall Street financial center, passes by the civic buildings of the city, and takes a diagonal course from Union Square through the needle-trades area between 34th and 39th Streets. Between 42d and 53d Streets, Broadway is the Great White Way—renowned as an amusement and theatrical center. From 53rd Street to Columbus Circle it cuts through Automobile Row, center of the auto retail trade. It changes its diagonal course at 79th Street to parallel the island's high escarpment facing the Hudson River. Here it is lined with hotels, apartment houses, cafeterias, beauty salons, movie houses, and churches. At 114th Street it strikes a new note in the buildings of Columbia University, and another at 155th Street in a group of museums. From this point on it is a nondescript thoroughfare, ending as a semisuburban road as it approaches the city's limits.

POINTS OF INTEREST

(downtown to uptown)

NEW YORK AQUARIUM *(open daily, 9–5 Apr.–Sept., 9–4 Oct.– Mar.; adm. free)*, in Battery Park, contains the largest collection of marine life in the country.

FRAUNCES TAVERN *(open weekdays, adm. free)*, SE. corner of Pearl and Broad Sts., was built in 1719 as a residence by Etienne de Lancey, wealthy Huguenot. A merchant firm of de Lancey's grandson remodeled the building for use as a store and warehouse in 1757. It was sold in 1762 to Samuel Fraunces, a West Indian of French and Negro blood, who opened it as the Queen's Head Tavern. In 1783 George Washington bade farewell to his officers here. It now contains a restaurant frequented by bankers and brokers from the neighborhood.

TRINITY CHURCH (1846) *(open daily)*, facing Wall St. on Broadway, is a Gothic brownstone edifice by Richard Upjohn.

SUB–TREASURY BUILDING (1842), corner of Wall and Nassau Sts., by Ithiel Town and A.J.Davis, is an example of Greek Revival architecture.

THE CITY HALL (1811), in City Hall Park, by Joseph Mangin and John McComb, is reminiscent of a small palace of Louis XVI's reign.

The WOOLWORTH BUILDING (1913) *(tower open 9–6 daily; adm. adults 55¢, children 25¢)*, Broadway and Park Place, by Cass Gilbert, with Gothic details, is the first of the 'cathedrals of commerce.' It is 60 stories high.

BELLEVUE HOSPITAL (1816) *(open only to visitors of patients)*, First Ave., 26th to 30th Sts., is the oldest general hospital on the North American continent.

PENNSYLVANIA STATION (1910), between Seventh and Eighth Aves. from 31st to 33d Sts., by McKim, Mead and White, has a Roman Doric façade. At each end is a clock, with a dial seven feet in diameter, flanked by figures symbolizing Day and Night. The main hall is a copy of a Roman bath; the coffered vault is carried by eight Corinthian columns.

The METROPOLITAN OPERA HOUSE (1883), Broadway at 39th St., is New York's premier home of grand opera.

MADISON SQUARE GARDEN (1925), Eighth Ave. between 49th and 50th Sts., America's best known indoor arena, is the scene of the horse show ($315 a box), prize fights, political rallies, Ringling Bros.-

Barnum & Bailey circus, hockey, six-day bicycle races, rodeos, trade exhibitions, tennis, and even Paderewski—once.

AMERICAN MUSEUM OF NATURAL HISTORY (1877) (*open* 10–5 *weekdays, 1–5 Sun.; adm. free*), Central Park W. and 79th St., is one of the world's largest institutions devoted to natural science exhibits.

HAYDEN PLANETARIUM (1935) (*performances Mon.–Fri.* 2, 3:30, *and* 8:30; *Sat.* 11 *a.m.*, 1, 2, 3, 4, 5, *and* 8:30; *Sun. and holidays* 2, 3, 4, 5, *and* 8:30. *Adm.: adults, mat.* 25¢ *and* 50¢, *eve.* 35¢ *and* 60¢; *children* 15¢ *at all times*) is a separate unit in the group of National History Museum buildings, the gift of Charles Hayden. Main attractions are the Hall of the Sun and the Theater of the Sky.

CATHEDRAL OF ST. JOHN THE DIVINE (*open daily*), Cathedral Parkway (110th St.) to 113th St., Amsterdam Ave. to Morningside Drive, by Heins and La Farge, and Cram and Ferguson, is Romanesque and Gothic. Seven clustered chapels burst into the soaring splendor of the apse. When completed, it will be the largest Gothic cathedral in the world.

COLUMBIA UNIVERSITY (founded 1754 as King's College), Broadway and W. 116th St., its buildings grouped on Morningside Heights, has 30,000 students and 3,000 teachers.

AMERICAN ACADEMY OF ARTS AND LETTERS, the National Institute of Arts and Letters (*open* 10–5 *weekdays, 2–5 Sun. and holidays, Nov.–May; adm. free*), 633 W. 155th St., represents the country's nearest approach to the French Academy. It offers a permanent exhibit of sculpture, paintings, and manuscripts of Academy and Institute members.

The AMERICAN GEOGRAPHICAL SOCIETY (*open* 9–4:45 *weekdays; closed Sat. during summer; adm. free*), Broadway and 156th St., has largest collection of geographical publications and maps in the Western Hemisphere.

At the AMERICAN NUMISMATIC SOCIETY (*open* 2–5 *daily except holidays; adm. free*), Broadway and 156th St., is a collection of coins and currencies.

HISPANIC SOCIETY OF AMERICA (*museum open* 10–4:30 *weekdays, 1–5 Sun., except Thanksgiving and Christmas Days; library open* 1–4:30 *Tues.–Sat.; closed during Aug.; adm. free*), Broadway and 155th St., is devoted to the study of culture and history of the Spanish and Portuguese peoples; its library has more than 100,000 volumes, and canvases by Velasquez, El Greco, Goya, and others.

The MUSEUM OF THE AMERICAN INDIAN, Heye Foundation (*open* 2–5 *weekdays; closed July and Aug.; adm. free*), Broadway and 155th St., the only organization of its kind in the world, contains an extensive collection of items pertaining to primitive Indian culture.

COLUMBIA PRESBYTERIAN MEDICAL CENTER, Broadway to Riverside Drive, 165th–168th Sts., has four major units: Columbia University medical and dental group, Presbyterian Hospital group, Babies' Hospital of the City of New York, Neurological Institute of New York; the New York State Psychiatric Institute and Hospital is not affiliated, but adjoins the group.

JUMEL MANSION (about 1765) (*open* 11–5 *daily except Mon.; adm.*

free), in Roger Morris Park, on a cliff above Edgecombe Ave., between 160th and 162nd Sts., was the headquarters of George Washington until his defeat at Fort Washington and the Laurel Hill redoubt. The museum displays relics of Colonial and Revolutionary periods.

THE CLOISTERS (*open 10-5 weekdays, 1-6 Sun.; adm. Mon. and Fri. 25¢, other days free*), Fort Tryon Park, a branch of the Metropolitan Museum of Art, contains famous collection of medieval architecture, sculptures, and tapestries.

DYCKMAN HOUSE (1783) (*open 11-5 daily except Mon.; adm. free*), 204th St. and Broadway, is the only eighteenth-century farmhouse on Manhattan. Its museum contains a collection of Dutch and English Colonial furniture and curios.

WALL STREET. *IRT Lexington Ave. subway to Wall St. station; IRT Broadway-Seventh Ave. subway to Wall St. station.*

WALL STREET, focal point of the financial district, is a gloomy canyon along which multitudes of people scurry during business days; after sundown and on Sundays it is silent and deserted. The traffic of the banks, largest in the country, is staggering; through the New York Clearing House passes an enormous volume of exchange. Private banks bear the renowned names of Morgan, Kuhn, Loeb, Harriman, Belmont. Besides the security exchanges, cocoa from Venezuela and West Africa, hides from the Argentine, coffee from Brazil, sugar from the West Indies, cotton from Texas—all have exchanges here. The telegraph and stock-indicator ('ticker') record split-second banking transactions in London, Rome, Paris, Berlin.

CHINATOWN. *Second or Third Ave. el to Chatham Sq. station; IRT Lexington Ave. subway to Worth St. station.*

CHINATOWN lies west of Chatham Square and the Bowery and extends westward to Mulberry Street between Canal Street on the north and Worth Street on the south. Of the 18,000 Chinese in New York City, only 4,000 live in Chinatown. Despite its reputation, the district is as safe as any other in the city. So few women are seen, it appears to be inhabited by men only—and children. Men stand in little clusters before shop doors, discussing in the native tongue affairs of the moment with inscrutable expressions and in modulated tones, while in the narrow winding streets the children play American games and fling at each other American slang phrases. The shop windows are stacked with Chinese fruits, vegetables grown on Long Island, and strange unfamiliar foodstuffs. Curio shops display in piled-up disorder a variety of bric-a-brac. A movie front offers the prospect of Chinese pictures made in China or San Francisco. The Chinese restaurants are declared by the Board of Health to be among the cleanest in the city. Animosities that once divided the district have given way to unity in the face of the Japanese invasion of China.

LOWER EAST SIDE. *IRT Lexington Ave. subway to any station from 14th St. to Worth St.; Eighth Ave. Independent subway, Queens-Church Ave. line, to any station from Second Ave. to E.Broadway; Third or Second Ave. el to any station from 14th St. to Chatham Sq.*

The LOWER EAST SIDE stretches along the east of Chinatown, from Brooklyn Bridge to 14th Street. With the Bowery, a battered relic of its early days, the East Side is a notorious slum district. Here are tens of thousands of Jews and Italians, thousands of Poles, Greeks, Russians, Spaniards, Lithuanians, and a scattering of Turks, Persians, and Chinese: a concentrated melting pot of the Nation's immigrants. The one blatant characteristic common to them all is poverty. Ragged children play 'potsy' in the streets. Young mothers with old expressions search for pushcart bargains. Old men in threadbare clothes hobble along the sidewalks. Couples, flashy in cheap finery, dawdle here and there. Against the malodorous streets rise the façades of monotonous unbroken rows of brownstone structures with outside fire escapes and first-floor shops. Clotheslines straddle the huddled roofs. Grimy warehouses and sooty factories add their depressing touch. The average population to the acre for the city's residential area as a whole is 266; here are acres crammed with 600. The East Side is the birthplace of Alfred E. Smith, Irving Berlin, and others who have risen high in the world.

GREENWICH VILLAGE AND WASHINGTON SQUARE. *IRT Broadway-Seventh Ave. subway to Sheridan Sq. and Christopher St. station.*

GREENWICH VILLAGE streets, turning abruptly or crossing where they should be parallel, express the antic spirit of the community. For the Village has performed some amazing mental acrobatics. Not for nothing is it called the Latin Quarter, the Bohemia of New York City. Free love, Freudianism, Socialism, imagist poetry, and fads of all shades have waxed and waned here. Today the burden of its incessant talk is economics. The Village retires late, rises late. In eccentric night clubs visited by the curious, it listens to a crapulent poet melodramatically reciting his effusions. Its Main Street, 8th, is a bazaar of art objects and second-hand books, odd tearooms and studios cheek-by-jowl with drug and grocery stores, movie houses, tailor shops. The real-estate boom of the 1920's, with its intrusion of tall, ostentatious apartment buildings, has added a Midas touch.

WASHINGTON SQUARE, near the center of the Village, is dominated by an arch erected in 1892 in memory of Washington's inauguration. Washington Square College of New York University is on the east. The old red brick houses on the north were once the homes of the Nation's social leaders; and No.61, on the south side, has sheltered Theodore Dreiser, Frank Norris, Stephen Crane, John Reed, and Alan Seeger. Today along the tree-shaded walks of the Square stroll residents of the vicinity—the well-to-do of Fifth Avenue, members of the poor Italian section to the southwest, university students, and visitors from far and wide.

UNION SQUARE AND 14TH STREET. *BMT, Union Sq. station; IRT Lexington Ave. subway, 14th St. station.*

UNION SQUARE is America's open-air center of radical propaganda, the district of liberal and trade-union ferment. The Socialist Party, the Communist Party, the Rand School of Social Science, the American Civil

Liberties Union, and others share it with Tammany Hall. On a day in 1930, 80,000 workers and sympathizers met here to protest against unemployment. In the late night hours, the benches in the Square give rest to the wandering homeless.

Unmindful of the frothy political ripples in the Square itself, waves of bargain-hunters and amusement-seekers billow along FOURTEENTH STREET, the poor man's street of the city. Fourteenth Street has undergone change after change, each as violent as the other. Laid out in 1811, it soon attracted the prosperous; the theater made it the city's Rialto until the turn of the century; large retail stores made it the shopping aristocrat of New York. Then exclusive business moved northward and the needle trades took over the square. The old stately buildings disappeared or were broken down into offices and lofts, and even into rooms for rent. Flashy amusement spots, hole-in-the-wall eating places, cheap clothing shops, and cheaper dance halls now give the street its character.

THE GARMENT DISTRICT. *IRT Broadway-Seventh Ave. subway and BMT subway, both Times Square station; Eighth Ave. Independent subway, 42d St. station.*

The GARMENT DISTRICT, center of New York's famous garment industry, is set in the very heart of Manhattan, from 30th to 42d Streets between Sixth and Ninth Avenues. To see the district best is to see it at the lunch hour, when the sidewalks become surging masses of humanity spilling over into the streets; 'pushboys' maneuver their hand trucks loaded with garments through the crowds; 'pitchmen' hawk their gimcracks on the curb. Side streets are blocked by Gargantuan trucks loading and unloading.

The workshops are the lofts clustered about the three tall buildings—themselves garment factories—between 36th and 38th Streets on Seventh Avenue, and from them buyers carry the new styles to all parts of the country. Small production units and an antiquated system of manufacture make for expensive competition and a high percentage of bankruptcies.

TIMES SQUARE. *IRT Broadway-Seventh Ave. subway and BMT subway, both Times Square station; Eight Ave. Independent subway, 42d St. station.*

The glow in the sky when dusk has fallen is the reflection of TIMES SQUARE, amusement center of the country. At Times Square, Broadway becomes the Great White Way, its night turned into synthetic day by flashing, glittering, multicolored light-pictures advertising the Nation's products. The scene is cheap and tawdry, yet impressive and stimulating. The ebb and flow of the human tide never ceases here. The Times Square district, embraced by 39th and 57th Streets, from Fifth to Eighth Avenues, abounds in theaters, hotels, movie houses, small shops, lofts, spacious automobile showrooms, night clubs, restaurants, and 'taxi-dance halls.' Tin Pan Alley, workshop of the song-makers, jingles here. To the Metropolitan Opera House, Town Hall, and Carnegie Hall on the rim of the district come the great singers, the great solo performers, the great conductors, from everywhere. Its newest attraction is Rockefeller Center. The western section—Radio City—is devoted primarily to entertainment: the

RKO Building contains offices, and the adjoining Radio City Music Hall offers stage shows and first-run movies; the National Broadcasting Company's extension is the home of stations WJZ and WEAF; the Rainbow Room is a swanky night club requiring formal dress; the Rainbow Grill is less formal; the Center Theater has presented spectacular shows.

FIFTH AVENUE, MADISON AVENUE, PARK AVENUE. *Fifth Ave. bus; IRT Lexington Ave. subway, any station from 33d St. to 59th St.*

After four successive migrations northward, New York's principal shopping center reached its present location—between 34th and 59th Streets along Fifth and Madison Avenues—in the first decade of the twentieth century. The FIFTH AVENUE segment is called the 'Magnificent Mile.' But Fifth Avenue has lost something of its former exclusiveness; even the five-and-ten stores have arrived. Display windows have created a new art, fascinating to hordes of 'window shoppers.'

The section of MADISON AVENUE above 49th Street has become a smart shopping center, primarily because it lies between Fifth and Park Avenues. The shops here are smaller and more highly personalized in style than those on Fifth Avenue. Farther north are expensive food stores, antique dealers, and interior decorators, most of them in old brownstone buildings. Cafes and bars stud the area.

PARK AVENUE, east of these two shopping thoroughfares, is a street of large and expensive apartment buildings.

The long stretch of Fifth Avenue that faces Central Park from 59th to 110th Streets is called 'Millionaires' Row.' Here, in palaces of limestone, once lived Andrew Carnegie, Senator William A. Clark, Jay Gould, O.H. Havemeyer, John Jacob Astor, Mrs.Hamilton Fish, and others. Banker, broker, successful writer and artist live in the neighborhood; to it have come others seeking a pretentious address. The large apartment buildings extend almost three miles northward. In spite of changes, 'Millionaires' Row' has kept something of its old character and, because of its social traditions, remains New York's most impressive residential street.

POINTS OF INTEREST

The EMPIRE STATE BUILDING (1931) (*tower open* 8 *a.m.–*1 *a.m. daily; adm. adults* $1.10, *children* 25¢), Fifth Ave. at 33rd and 34th Sts., by Shreve, Lamb and Harmon, is the tallest building in the world: 1,250 feet. Fifty-mile panorama can be viewed from its tower.

The PIERPONT MORGAN LIBRARY (*main building open* 11–4 *Tues. and Thurs.*, 10–1 *Sat.; annex open* 10–5 *weekdays; adm. free*), 33 E. 36th St., the main building (1913) by McKim, Mead and White; the Annex (1928), at 29 E.36th St., by Benjamin W. Morris. Its exterior is severely formal, its interior sumptuously decorated and ornamented. It contains one of the most extensive private collections in the world: books, furniture, paintings, tapestries, sculptures, etc.

The NEW YORK PUBLIC LIBRARY (1911) (*open* 9 *a.m.–*10 *p.m. weekdays,* 1–10 *Sun.*), Fifth Ave. and 42nd St., by Carrère and Hastings, is an eclectic building based mainly on classical concepts. This is the central building of the New York Public Library, which includes branches in Manhattan, the Bronx, and Richmond.

GRAND CENTRAL TERMINAL (1913), Park Ave. and 42d St., is by Warren and Wetmore, and Reed and Stem. A feature of the 42nd St. façade is the sculptured group around the clock, by Jules Coutan, French baroque in conception; the three heroic figures represent Mercury, Hercules, and Minerva. The concourse leading from the waiting room is 385 ft. long, 125 ft. wide; the elliptically vaulted ceiling is carried by square piers 125 ft. high.

CHRYSLER BUILDING (1929) (*tower open 9–6 daily; adm. adults 55¢, children 25¢*), Lexington Ave. and 42d St., by William Van Alen, 1,048 ft. high, has a fantastic metal dome terminating in a spire. The building has a lobby finished in Rouge Flamme marble from Africa.

The NEWS BUILDING (1930) (*guided tours at 2, 3, 4, 5, 7:45, and 8:45 daily; reservations in advance; exhibits on main floor open 9 a.m.–10 p.m. daily*), 220 E.42d St., by John M. Howells and Raymond Hood, is considered a modern masterpiece. In its main lobby is a revolving terrestrial globe in a well under a faceted dome of black glass; walls carry weather maps and other meteorological items.

ROCKEFELLER CENTER (*guided tours: Rockefeller Center, 10–9 daily, adults $1, children 50¢; National Broadcasting Co. studios, exclusive of sponsored broadcasts, 9 a.m.–11 p.m. daily, 55¢; Sky Gardens, 10–5 daily, May–Nov., 50¢. Single adm.: Observation Roof, 10–midnight daily, adults 40¢, children 20¢*), between Fifth and Sixth Aves., 48th and 51st Sts., by Reinhard and Hofmeister, Corbett, Harrison and MacMurray, and Hood and Fouilhoux, comprises 14 buildings upsurging from a base of 12 land acres. The RCA Building is the tallest (850 ft., 70 stories) in the group. Four buildings are used as Fifth Ave. showcases for foreign nations: the British Empire Building, La Maison Française, Palazzo d'Italia, and the International Building East. Behind the last two rises the second International Building. The Time and Life Building, the Associated Press Building, and 30 Rockefeller Plaza (RCA Building Tower) surround the Plaza. The Fifth Avenue entrance is the most impressive. The Channel slopes from the avenue down to a flight of steps leading to the Sunken Plaza with series of fountains and other decorations.

NEW YORK MUSEUM OF SCIENCE AND INDUSTRY (*open 10–10 daily; adm. adults 25¢, children 10¢; lectures and motion pictures occasionally*), RCA Building, Rockefeller Center, presents a behind-the-scenes view of the industrial age—the most extensive, up-to-date exposition of its kind in America. The divisions of the exhibits—food industries, textiles, shelter, power, aviation, highway, railroad and marine transportation, communications, machine tools and electro-technology—contain about 2,500 items.

The MUSEUM OF MODERN ART (*open 10–6 weekdays, 12–6 Sun.; adm. 25¢, Sun. 10¢*), 11 W.53d St., houses exhibits of modern painting and sculpture.

The WALDORF–ASTORIA HOTEL (1931), Park Ave. at 49th and

50th Sts., by Schultze and Weaver, its chrome-capped twin towers rising 47 stories, is one of the largest and most costly hotels in the world.

ST.PATRICK'S CATHEDRAL (1879) (*open daily*), Fifth Ave. at 50th and 51st Sts., by James Renwick, is an example of Gothic Revival architecture. Geometric decorated tracery, twin spires, crockets, and dry coarse detail suggest the Cathedral of Cologne.

CENTRAL PARK is bounded by Central Park S., Fifth Ave., Cathedral Parkway (110th St.), and Central Park W. Its lakes, fields, and playgrounds are frequented in every season. South of the reservoir are Cleopatra's Needle, relic of the Pharaohs and gift of the Khedive of Egypt in 1877; the Menagerie (*open 11–5 daily; adm. free*), a favorite with children; and the Belvedere, a meteorological observatory of the U.S.Weather Bureau.

TEMPLE EMANU–EL (1929) (*open daily*), Fifth Ave. and 65th St., by Robert D. Kohn, Charles Butler, and Clarence S. Stein, is an example of early Romanesque architecture, its three separate units integrated into one design.

The FRICK COLLECTION (*open 10–5 weekdays; 1–5 Sun. and holidays; closed Mon., Decoration Day, July 4, Christmas, and month of Aug.; adm. free*), 1 E.70th St., is New York's only private home where art treasures are assembled and open to the public as a unit. It also includes the Bache Collection. Paintings, sculptures, enamels, Chinese porcelains, and other objects of art are on display. The mansion (1914), by Carrère and Hastings in the Louis XVI manner, is one of the showplaces of New York.

NEW YORK HOSPITAL AND CORNELL UNIVERSITY MEDICAL COLLEGE (buildings 1932) (*open 2–3:30 Mon., Wed., Fri.; 2–3:15 Tues., Thurs.; guides*), York Ave., E.68th to E.71st Sts., is popularly known as the East Side Medical Center. The buildings, by Coolidge, Shepley, Bulfinch and Abbott of Boston, are outstanding examples of modern architecture with a Gothic motif carried throughout the 15 units. The main building is 27 stories high. On the east side of the lot are three special hospitals: Psychiatric, Children's, and Women's Clinic; the buildings of the Medical College line York Ave.

METROPOLITAN MUSEUM OF ART (*open 10–5 weekdays, 1–6 Sun., 10–5 legal holidays, 1–5 Christmas Day; children under 7 must be accompanied by an adult; adm. Mon. and Fri. 25¢, other days and legal holidays free*), Fifth Ave. and 82d St., contains the most comprehensive collection of pictures and objects of art in America.

MUSEUM OF THE CITY OF NEW YORK (*open 10–5 weekdays except Tues., 1–5 Sun.; Sun. lectures Nov.–Mar. at 4 p.m.; adm. Mon. 25¢, other days free*), Fifth Ave. and 103d St., is devoted to the history of New York City. First floor: historical galleries trace growth of city from Indian village to present; Dutch furniture, portraits and miniatures of early settlers in corridor. Second floor: memorabilia of George Washington and Alexander Hamilton; changing fashions from Dutch period to end of nineteenth century. Third floor: display illustrating rise of communication.

The HARLEM RIVER HOUSES (1937), W.151st to W.153d St., Macomb's Place to Harlem River, comprise the first large-scale modern housing community provided for low-income residents of Manhattan. Built by the Federal Public Works Administration, they are operated by the New York City Housing Authority: 574 apartments, all modern facilities; average rent $5.20 a week per room.

RIVERSIDE DRIVE. *Bus. IRT Broadway-Seventh Ave. subway, Van Cortlandt Park extension, from 72d St. station uptown.*

Almost at the point where the great piers end, RIVERSIDE DRIVE begins its six-and-a-quarter-mile run along the high embankment of the Hudson River. During the last century this shore line was inhabited by squatters and their goats. Between the years 1872 and 1910 the Drive was developed in sections. The first to take advantage of its superb location, incomparable setting, and gifts of light and air were the newly rich; consequently it lacks tradition, and the older American families of wealth have kept away from it. The Drive, however, remains the most favorably located of Manhattan's streets. Its dips and rises and its winding course are a relief from the general run of city streets. And from its elevation the fluted cliffs of the Palisades are conspicuous across the wide river. Today its eastern flank is battlemented with apartment houses, a few mansions, and some well-known institutions. A narrow park borders it for most of its length. At the water's edge run the twin lanes of the new Henry Hudson Parkway, intended eventually to be part of a continuous express route encircling Manhattan on the rim.

POINTS OF INTEREST

RIVERSIDE CHURCH, Baptist (1929) (*observation tower open 10-5 daily; adm. 25¢*), Riverside Drive and 122d St., by Allen, Pelton and Collens, is a Gothic structure, whose tower contains the Laura Spelman Rockefeller Memorial Carillon of 72 bells.

GRANT'S TOMB (1897) (*open daily, 9-5, June 21 to Sept. 21; 9-4:30 Sept. 21 to June 21; adm. free*), Riverside Drive and 123d St., by J.H.Duncan, is the burial place of General Ulysses Simpson Grant and his wife. It has a ponderous square base and circular superstructure, motif of double colonnade of Doric design at entrance repeated on other three sides with recessed columns, and a cruciform interior.

HARLEM. *IRT Seventh Ave. subway, Lenox Ave. local, to any station between 110th and 145th Sts.*

HARLEM, shut in by the East and Harlem Rivers, by Morningside and Washington Heights, and by Central Park, was once a district of quiet farms where lived a few Hollanders, French Huguenots, Danes, Swedes, and Germans. Between 1830 and 1880 the railroad and rapid transit lines reached it and worked a miracle of transformation. For three decades the Germans were the dominant element, with the Irish ranking second. The immigration waves of the 1880's and 1890's brought in Jews and Italians. Then the Negroes began to come in—from downtown, from the South, from the West Indies, from Africa.

There are three Harlems: Negro, Spanish, and Italian—half a million people crowded into the largest slum area in New York. The Harlem River Houses, a large-scale modern housing development, accentuate the urgent needs of the community.

Of the 327,706 Negroes in New York City, 250,000 live here, paying 50 per cent higher rents than those charged for equivalent dwellings elsewhere in the city. One block in the district has 3,824 residents, or an average density of 1,100 an acre. The most noticeable feature of Negro Harlem is the color of the human faces—black to near white. The speech is often the sing-song drawl of the South. The Negroes practice their professions and enjoy comparative freedom from oppression and prejudice. Harlem's most recent messiah, Father Divine, has had phenomenal success. Clubs and societies flourish. The strident, ebullient life of the district is best seen at night, when the clubs are a riot of primitive abandon to the rhythm of Negro swing music.

Spanish Harlem clusters around the 110th Street station of the Lexington Avenue subway. It is a poor district; the restaurants, offering such Spanish dishes as *arroz con pollo* (rice with chicken) and *gazpacho* (Andalusian stew), draw much of their patronage from visitors. The population is about 120,000, of whom 85 per cent are Puerto Rican. During the World War they settled here because of low rents and freedom from racial discrimination. Sixty per cent of them have had no regular employment since their arrival. The market place that extends along Park Avenue from 111th to 116th Streets displays avocadoes, mangoes, guavas from Cuba, melonlike papayas, tamarinds used for making a drink called *tamarindo*, limes, tangerines, *garbanzos* (chick-peas), cassava, strings of red pepper, and so on. The air is redolent of spices. The purchasers show in their skins and features mixtures of Indian, Negro, and Spanish blood.

Italian Harlem, bordering the East River opposite Ward's and Randall's Islands, has a population of 150,000 living in an area of one square mile, the most densely populated section of Manhattan. It is the largest colony of Italian-Americans in the country. The market place presents the bright side of the district; the darker side is in the homes of the residents. Half the families had no income in 1937. During prohibition years it was the center of gang leaders. Social organizations, among them Harlem House, have exercised a reforming influence.

BROOKLYN

In Brooklyn 2,660,479 people are crammed into an area of 81 square miles. The borough is a vast residential cantonment with segregated shopping and service centers. The Flatbush, Shore Road, and Bay Ridge neighborhoods are occupied by the more prosperous elements of the community; Bay Ridge has a colony of Scandinavians; Brownsville is Jewish, Ridgewood German, the southern end Italian; Red Hook has a variety of national groups, largely Syrian and Arabian; the Irish and Poles are scattered.

About one fourth of the exports leaving New York is handled at Brooklyn's water front, which contains more than 6,000 industrial establishments with products ranging from foodstuffs to inks.

POINTS OF INTEREST

PLYMOUTH CHURCH OF THE PILGRIMS (1849) (*open daily*), Orange and Hicks Sts., was the pulpit of Henry Ward Beecher from 1847 to 1887. Its simple interior is suggestive of a New England meeting-house.

The LONG ISLAND HISTORICAL SOCIETY (*open 9-6 daily except Sun. and holidays; July and Aug., Mon. to Thurs. only; adm. free*), Pierrepont and Clinton Sts., houses a collection of books, pamphlets, and manuscripts especially devoted to life and history of Long Island. It has published six American historical works and a *Catalogue of American Genealogies*, all available for use.

BROOKLYN NAVY YARD (*open 9-5 Mon.-Fri.; 1-4 Sat., Sun., and holidays; adm. free*) has its main entrance on Flushing Ave. and Cumberland St.

The WILLIAMSBURG HOUSES (1937), Scholes St. to Maujer St., Leonard St. to Bushwick Ave., a slum-clearance and low-rent housing project, was completed under the Federal Housing program and is under the management of the New York City Housing Authority.

The BROOKLYN CHILDREN'S MUSEUM (1899) (*open 10-5 weekdays and holidays; 2-5 Sun.; adm. free*), Brooklyn Ave. and Park Place, was the first of its kind in the world and is rated the largest and best equipped. Exhibits: stuffed birds and animals, insects and minerals, handicraft and costume design, models of American historical events. Children may join the Museum League, Tree Club, Science Club, Mineral Club, Stamp Club.

KINGS COUNTY HOSPITAL, Clarkson and New York Aves., is a municipal institution with the largest bed capacity in the city, and cares for every ailment except contagious diseases and mental cases requiring prolonged treatment. The main building is a handsome brick structure, by Leroy P. Ward and Associates (1931).

BROOKLYN MUSEUM (*open 10-5 weekdays, 2-6 Sun. and holidays; adm. Mon. and Fri., adults 25¢, children 10¢; other days free*), Eastern Parkway and Washington Ave., is outstanding among American museums for the quality of its collections of the arts and crafts of American, primitive, and Asiatic peoples, and for its extensive educational program, consisting of concerts and dance recitals, demonstrations of various crafts, and lectures by writers, artists, and educators.

In the BROOKLYN BOTANICAL GARDEN (*open 8 a.m. to dusk weekdays, 10 a.m. to dusk Sun. and holidays; adm. free*), 1000 Washington Ave., are a brook, esplanade, trees, enclosed gardens, and glacial boulders. Special features are the Japanese Garden, the Rose Garden, the Rock Garden.

PROSPECT PARK, bounded by Prospect Park W., Prospect Park SW., Parkside, Ocean, and Flatbush Aves., covers 526 acres and is the borough's main public area. It contains a lake, pools, playgrounds, picnic grounds, parade ground, a Quaker cemetery, gardens, statues, menagerie, and the old LEFFERTS HOMESTEAD (*open 1–5 Mon., Wed., Fri.; adm. free*), which houses a collection of seventeenth- and eighteenth-century items. It is the site of the most important action of the Battle of Long Island, on August 27, 1776.

BROOKLYN COLLEGE (founded 1930), Ave. H and Bedford Ave., city-supported coeducational college of liberal arts and sciences, is a group of Georgian buildings, by Randolph Evans with Corbett, Harrison, and MacMurray as associates. Outside of summer school, graduate, and extension divisions, there is a student enrollment of 12,000 (divided between day and evening classes), with a teaching staff of 800.

FLOYD BENNETT AIRPORT (*IRT Flatbush Ave. subway to Flatbush Ave., then bus to field; BMT Brighton Beach subway to Ave. U, then bus to field; open free for inspection weekdays and Sat. mornings; sightseeing planes 9 a.m.–sundown daily; local flights $1.50 per person, over N.Y.C. $2.50 per person*), at the foot of Flatbush Ave. and Jamaica Bay, was the base of many famous flights.

CONEY ISLAND (*BMT Brighton Beach subway to Coney Island; BMT Sea Beach or West End subway to Stillwell Ave.; bus from Times Square, 50¢; boat from the Battery, leaving 11, 1, 2:30, 4, 5, 5:30, and 7 daily; season, May 30–second week after Labor Day; fireworks displays every Tues. 8:30 p.m.*), Surf Ave., Ocean Parkway to W.37th St., offers a bathing beach, two-mile boardwalk, two large amusement parks, bathhouses, dance halls, freak shows, carousels, roller coasters, penny arcades, assorted game booths, waxworks, ferris wheels, shooting galleries, souvenir shops, restaurants, tea rooms, chop suey parlors, and hot dog stands. It accommodates as many as 1,000,000 people in a single day.

THE BRONX

The Bronx, the only borough of the Greater City on the mainland, has 1,385,777 people on its 41.4 square miles. As late as 1850 its population, largely German, was but 8,000. Annexation of West Bronx to New York in 1874 and of East Bronx in 1895 encouraged development. Hordes of immigrants from the East Side of Manhattan, seeking more commodious quarters, moved in. In 1938 half the population was Jewish, the remainder a medley of other national groups.

The borough is primarily a residential area. West Bronx contains over three fourths of the population; East Bronx, less prosperous neighbor, is yielding some of its congestion to districts northward. Eastchester retains something of its early rural atmosphere. The Bronx boasts more park acreage (4,563) than any of the other boroughs.

POINTS OF INTEREST

THE BRONX COUNTY BUILDING (1934), 161st St. and Grand Concourse, by Joseph H. Freedlander and Max Hausle, is a modern courthouse.

POE COTTAGE (*open 10–1 and 2–5 Tues.–Sat., 1–5 Sun.; adm. free*),

Kingsbridge Rd. and Grand Concourse, a restored five-room frame house, was the home of Edgar Allan Poe during the last three years of his life (1846–9). It contains the bed in which Virginia Poe died, and a mirror, rocker, Bible, and spoon that belonged to the Poes.

HALL OF FAME (1901) (*accessible any time from either University or Sedgwick Aves.*), New York University, University Heights opposite W. 181st St., by Stanford White, is an arc-shaped colonnade integrating three beautiful buildings into a single handsome composition. Most illustrious of those represented by statuary in the Hall are Alexander Hamilton, Washington Irving, William Cullen Bryant, and Henry Ward Beecher.

FORDHAM UNIVERSITY (founded 1841), Fordham Rd. and Third Ave., is one of the largest Catholic educational institutions in the U.S., with a student body of 7,500.

BRONX PARK (IRT Bronx Park subway), Bronx Park E. and 180th St., covers 700 acres. Its most notable feature is the ZOOLOGICAL PARK (the Zoo) (*open daily 9 to half hour before sunset from April 15 to Oct. 15; 10–6:30 Oct. 16 to April 14. Adm., Mon. and Thurs. 25¢ adults, 15¢ children under 12; free other days and holidays*).

VAN CORTLANDT PARK (*IRT Broadway-Seventh Ave. subway to 242d St. station*), Broadway and 242d St., 1,132 acres, has two 18-hole golf courses, 21 baseball diamonds, tennis courts, horseshoe pitching courts, 2 cricket fields, 15 miles of bridle paths, archery and hockey fields, skiing hills, boating and ice skating, hiking trails, bird sanctuaries, children's day camps, wooded sections, meadows. The VAN CORTLANDT HOUSE MUSEUM (*open 10–5 Tues., Wed., Fri., Sat.; 12–5 Thurs., Sun.; adm. Thurs. 25¢, other days free*) is near the entrance at Broadway and 242d St., on a high bluff overlooking the lake. A gray stone structure, fine example of Georgian Colonial architecture (1748), it was occupied by Washington for a short time after the Revolution. The Museum contains a collection of Dutch and Colonial furniture and an exhibit of ancient arms and documents. North of the mansion is Vault Hill, site of the Van Cortlandt burial ground.

ORCHARD BEACH (*open daily 9–8 May 30 through weekend after Labor Day; lockers 15¢ and 25¢*), in Pelham Bay Park, Eastern Blvd. and Westchester Ave., was constructed with WPA aid. Opened to the public in 1936, the attendance for the 1938 season totalled 2,268,300. It contains a bathing pavilion, free playgrounds for children, game area, loggia, cafeteria; the Split Rock and Pelham Bay Golf Courses are about 1 m. from beach.

QUEENS

Queens, 121 square miles in area, is the largest of the boroughs; its population (1938) is 1,291,314. The growth of this borough, dependent in large part upon subway, road, and bridge extensions, was further stimulated by the establishment of the New York World's Fair at Flushing. Within recent years the 50 or so communities in Queens have steadily been crystallizing into one vast residential area.

POINTS OF INTEREST

LA GUARDIA FIELD (*Triborough Bridge, Grand Central Parkway to airport; Independent-Flushing subway to Junction Blvd., then bus to airport*), Grand Central Parkway and 94th St., North Beach, is the newest of the city's airports, and one of its two municipal fields. It is a combination landplane and seaplane terminal.

The NEW YORK WORLD'S FAIR (8 *m. from Times Square. Motor routes from Queensborough Bridge: Northern Blvd. [NY 25A], Queens Blvd. [NY 24], and Horace Harding Blvd. [NY 25], or Roosevelt Ave. From Triborough Bridge [toll 25¢]: Astoria Blvd. and Grand Central Parkway Extension. From New England: from Boston Post Rd. [US 1] follow Baychester Blvd., Eastern Blvd., and cross Bronx-Whitestone Bridge [toll 25¢]. Railway: L.I.R.R. [10 mins.]. Subways; from Times Square: IRT [23 mins.], BMT [26 mins.], and Independent [37 mins.]; 2nd Ave. el [30 mins.]*) extends from Flushing Bay front along Flushing Creek Valley for about 3.5 m. with an average width of 1 m. The Fair is divided into 7 zones: Government, Transportation, Communications, Production and Distribution, Food, Community Interests, and Amusement. The Fair theme for 1940 was 'For Peace and Freedom.' Its official colors: White, Dutch Orange, and New York City Blue. The Theme Center, dominated by the perisphere, symbolizing the infinite, and trylon, symbolizing the finite, faces eastward across a composition of pools, lagoons, pylons, waterfalls, and fountains, to the Federal Building. Extending from each side of this structure are buildings housing exhibits of States and foreign nations. A heroic figure of George Washington towers over Constitution Mall, gazing in direction of Statute of Liberty. Four tall figures in paved square east of Washington Statue represent freedom of press, religion, assembly, and speech. Two avenues, one running northeastward, another southeastward, both from Theme Center, cut fan-shaped section out of exhibition area. Immediately west of Theme Center stands New York City exhibit building. Another main avenue leads southward from Theme Center, over a bridge spanning World's Fair Blvd., to New York State Amphitheater on the north shore of Fountain Lake. The zone scheme, together with soaring trylon, makes for easy orientation. On the eastern side of Fountain Lake is the Amusement Section, embraced by a two-mile loop. In the Consolidated Edison Building, just southeast of Theme Center, is a diorama of New York City, largest ever made, depicting more than 4,000 of the city's buildings and occupying nearly a city block of space. Within the Perisphere is a model of the city of the future— 'Democracity'—viewed as from a height of two miles. The Transportation Section lies to the west of Theme Center.

The KING MANSION (before 1750) (*1–4:30 Mon., Wed., Sat.; free*), Jamaica Ave. near 153rd St., King Park, Georgian Colonial, was the country seat of Rufus King from 1806 to 1827. It contains a collection of Colonial furniture and relics, Colonial toys, books, documents, arms, army buttons, and Long Island money.

JACOB RIIS PARK, foot of Rockaway Beach Blvd. (or from foot of Flatbush Ave. across Marine Parkway Bridge, toll 15¢), partly a WPA project, was opened to public in 1937. It offers a bathhouse, boardwalk, play areas, two of which are free; music weekdays; fireworks every Wednesday evening.

RICHMOND
(Staten Island)

The borough of Richmond, a roughly triangular island, popularly known as Staten Island, has a population of 171,215. Although it is the third largest of the boroughs in area, Richmond is the least developed. A neat row of villages, some dating back to Colonial times, lines the north and west shores. Scattered along the north and northeast shores are shipbuilding yards, lumber mills, printing and publishing plants, and a large soap and oil plant. Storage tanks and the refinery units of New Jersey oil companies rise on the lowlands of the western district. The western section is given over to truck farms and unused meadowlands. Despite the fact that the island has the only free port in the country, its ocean-borne commerce is relatively negligible.

The older Dutch, English, and Huguenot families have preserved their ethnic purity to a large extent. Italians, Scandinavians, and Poles, comparatively recent arrivals, are grouped in the industrial areas.

POINTS OF INTEREST

STATEN ISLAND INSTITUTE OF ARTS AND SCIENCES PUBLIC MUSEUM (founded 1881) (*open 10–5 weekdays, 2–5 Sun.; adm. free*), Wall St. and Stuyvesant Pl., St.George, contains natural history, household, and insect collections, largely of Staten Island.

SAILORS' SNUG HARBOR (founded 1801; asylum opened in 1833) (*open 9–4 weekdays; adm. free*), Richmond Terrace and Tysen St., New Brighton, is a home for retired seamen.

STATEN ISLAND ZOO (*open 10–5 weekdays; 10–6 Sun. and holidays; adm. free*), Broadway, Clove Rd., and Glenwood Place, W.New Brighton, is noted mainly for its collection of reptiles.

The CONFERENCE, or BILLOPP, HOUSE (built before 1688) (*open Tues.–Sun., 10–6 May–Oct., 10–5 Nov.–Apr.*), foot of Hyland Blvd., Tottenville, was the scene of a conference between British and American authorities after the Battle of Long Island.

Niagara Falls

Railroad Station: New York Central Station, Falls and Second St., for New York Central System, Lehigh Valley R.R., Pere Marquette Ry., Michigan Central R.R., Wabash Ry., and Canadian National Rys.
Bus Stations: International Railway Terminal, Riverway opposite Prospect Park, for Canadian-American Trailways; Falls St. Terminal, foot of Falls St., for Greyhound, Great Eastern, Gray Coach, and Niagara Scenic Bus Lines, sight-seeing busses, and shuttle service to Canada.
Airport: 6 m. NE. on State 18D; no scheduled service.
Bridge: Whirlpool Rapids Bridge, Whirlpool St. and Mill Ave.; tolls: car and driver 25¢, each additional passenger 5¢. The border may be crossed quite casually. Naturalized U.S. citizens should carry proof of naturalization. Noncitizens require passport and visa. Automobiles may enter Canada for a 48-hour period upon deposit of registration card; 60-day tourist permits are free and renewable for 30 days. Corn on the ear and plants with roots may not be carried into Canada. U.S. residents returning from Canada are allowed to bring in, exempt from duty, goods up to $100 in value after a visit of not less than 48 hours.
Street Busses: Fare 8¢, 2 tokens for 15¢.
Taxis: 25¢ up; zone rates. Sight-seeing cabs slightly higher.

Accommodations: 16 hotels; wide range of tourist homes and tourist camps.

Information Service: Chamber of Commerce, 43 W.Falls St.

Motion Picture Houses: 8.
Golf: Municipal course, Hyde Park, Hyde Park Blvd. between Pine and Linwood Aves., 27 holes, greens fee 75¢.
Tennis: Hyde Park, free.
Swimming: Hyde Park, free.

NIAGARA FALLS, NEW YORK (575 alt.,77,374 pop.), stands in the corner formed by the river at the falls; and Niagara Falls, Ontario, stretches northward from the brink of the Horseshoe Falls. The world-wide reputation of the falls as a natural wonder attracts more than 1,500,000 visitors annually—particularly honeymooners—who promenade along Falls Street and through the parks, crowd the many tourist quarters, and purchase countless souvenirs and camera films. The State has carefully preserved the beauty of the area above the falls; and, in order to preserve the cataract as a spectacle, a British-American treaty limits diversion of water to 20,000 cubic feet a second on the American and 36,000 on the Canadian side.

The wide lawns of Prospect Park extend to the very edge of the roaring waters. Crowding the park and reaching northward along the gorge to Ontario Avenue is the business and shopping district, a collection of three- and four-story structures dwarfed by the 17-story United Office Building. The main industrial district borders the river above the falls, and from the smokestacks along Buffalo Avenue constantly rise the fumes of industry.

The large central part of the city is residential, the more exclusive district being the De Veaux area to the north, just east of Whirlpool State Park.

Control of this region was of strategic value in the Colonial period because of the seven-mile portage around Niagara Falls—the only break in the all-water journey between the St.Lawrence and the upper reaches of the Great Lakes. The first published view of Niagara Falls, reproduced in a volume in 1697, was a sketch made by Father Louis Hennepin, who visited the falls on December 6, 1678. In 1745 and 1750 the French built two forts near the falls to supplement Fort Niagara at the mouth of the river and to guard the upper end of the portage. Before the approach of the British in 1759, Chabert Joncaire, French master of the portage, burned the forts and retreated across the river.

Under British occupation, John Stedman received a grant of land along the river from the Indians and became master of the portage. Fort Schlosser, more substantial than its predecessors, was erected by Captain Joseph Schlosser, a German officer in the British army. An old stone chimney, the only part of the French forts not destroyed by Joncaire, was built into the mess hall of Fort Schlosser and now stands, reconstructed, on the grounds of the Carborundum Company.

Augustus Porter visited the place in 1795, returned in 1805 or 1806, purchased the land immediately surrounding the falls, moved his family there, built a gristmill, and succeeded Stedman as master of the portage. Visioning a manufacturing center that would rival the English city, Porter named the settlement Manchester. The fighting that took place on the Niagara Frontier throughout the War of 1812 culminated in the burning of Manchester and Fort Schlosser by the British in 1813. Only a few houses escaped the flames.

When Porter realized that the Erie Canal had destroyed business on the portage, he urged capitalists to develop Niagara power. As a result, a canal between the upper and lower rivers, begun in 1852, was completed in 1862 at a cost of about $1,000,000. In 1877 the entire property was bought at auction for $76,000 by Jacob F. Schoellkopf, whose descendants merged their holdings with the Niagara Falls Power Company during the World War. Niagara water power turned the first generator in 1881; power lines reached Buffalo in 1896 and Syracuse in 1905; today they extend into western and central New York, serving a population of more than 2,500,-000. The more than 450,000 horsepower of electric current generated, not only turns the wheels of local plants producing abrasives, paper, flour, foundry materials, and machinery, but also has made possible the remarkable technological development of the aluminum, calcium, carbide, ferro-alloy, silicon, and graphite industries. About one third of the city's population is of foreign stock, with Italians and Poles, who supply most of the labor in these factories, predominating.

POINTS OF INTEREST

The NEW YORK STATE NIAGARA RESERVATION, 412 acres in area, includes Prospect Park, Luna, Goat, and several smaller islands, and

Whirlpool and Devil's Hole State Parks. A decade of legislative setbacks preceded the actual transfer of the land in 1885. The bill was signed by Grover Cleveland as Governor. The largest unit in the reservation is Prospect Park, Riverway and Riverside Drive, which extends 1,000 feet along the river chasm and a mile along the rapids above the falls.

Points of Interest 1 to 7 are in the reservation and are listed in a sequence convenient for a tour.

1. PROSPECT POINT (*parking 10¢*), at the very brink of the ledge, offers a magnificent view of the AMERICAN FALLS, about 1,000 feet wide, the CANADIAN FALLS, with its curved crest of about 2,500 feet, and GOAT ISLAND, which separates the two cataracts. The 'Thunderer of Waters,' as the Indian name for the Falls is translated, pours 205,000 cubic feet of water a second over the ledge and plunges with an energy of about 4,000,-000 horsepower. Six per cent of the flow passes over the American Falls, the remaining 94 per cent over the Canadian Falls. The white, broken waters of the American Falls seem to hesitate momentarily, then roar over the brink and hit the rocks 157 feet below with a reverberating crash. The Canadian Falls, because of their distance, seem to descend in a smooth, noiseless sheet of water that gently bursts into an immense mass of surf and spray in the cauldron below. Both falls are tinted by rainbows and surmounted by mists that rise in pillars, then separate into lacy, floating clouds. In the evening, colored floodlights are trained on the falling waters. In the winter the freezing spray builds mountains of ice on both sides. Thrill-seekers walked from shore to shore over the ice bridge until tragedy befell a man and his wife in February 1912, when the ice bridge broke apart.

Daredevil stunts have been numerous. In 1829 Sam Patch leaped twice from a platform about 100 feet high into the gorge at the foot of the falls. In 1859 and 1860 Blondin, French tightrope walker, crossed and recrossed on a rope several times, once with his manager riding on his back. In the eighties several people navigated the rapids in barrels; in August 1886, William J. Kendall, a Boston policeman, passed through the rapids protected only by a cork life-preserver; in September 1889, Steve Brodie went over the falls in an India-rubber suit heavily padded and protected by steel bands. The first woman to go over in a barrel was Mrs.Annie Edson

---

KEY FOR NIAGARA FALLS MAP

1.Prospect Point 2.Hennepin Point 3.Goat Island 4.Luna Island 5.Cave of the Winds 6.Terrapin Point 7.Three Sister Islands 8.Niagara Falls Museum 9. Shredded Wheat Plant 10.Niagara Falls Power Plant 11.Whirlpool State Park 12.Whirlpool Rapids Bridge

NIAGARA FALLS, ONTARIO

13.Queen Victoria Park 14.Lundy's Lake Battlefield 15.Chippawa Battlefield 16.Niagara Gorge and Whirlpool Rapids 17.Spanish Aero Car 18.Niagara Glen 19.Queenston-Chippawa Generating Station 20.Queenston Heights Park

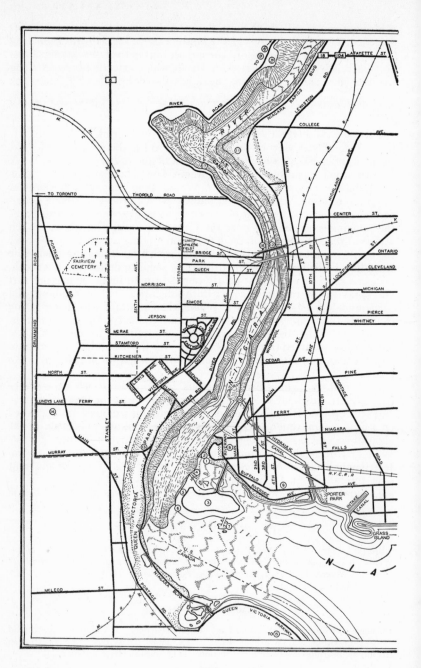

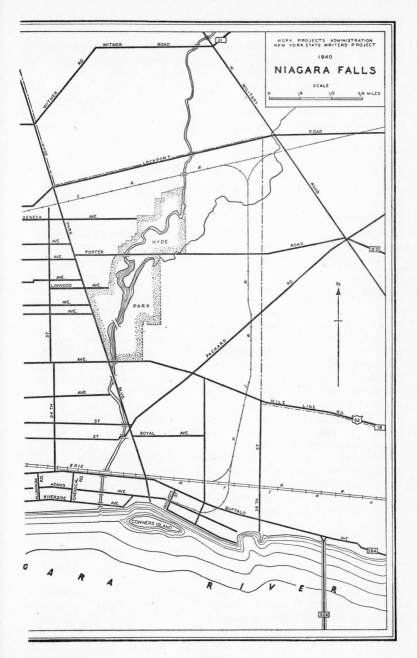

WORK PROJECTS ADMINISTRATION
NEW YORK STATE WRITERS' PROJECT

1940

NIAGARA FALLS

SCALE

Taylor, a schoolteacher, in October 1901. Bobby Leach, an Englishman, went over Horseshoe Falls in a steel barrel in July 1911, and then spent 23 weeks in the hospital recuperating. Jean Laussier shot over the Falls in July 1928, and came out smiling, thanks to a rubber ball of his own construction. Several publicity seekers have lost their lives.

At the close of the Ice Age, the Niagara River plunged over the truncated edge of a dolomite formation into Lake Ontario. At the foot of the fall, the swirling water in time eroded the soft shales from under this massive rock. Blocks of the dolomite, thus undermined, broke off and caused a recession of the crest of the waterfall. As the fall receded, it formed the gorge. This action is still going on; it is estimated that the fall has moved southward from the southern shore of Lake Ontario to its present position at the rate of about one foot a year. If the fall reaches Lake Erie it will disappear. Steps are being proposed to arrest the process and to hold the fall to its present location.

At the Prospect Point parking area, elevators (*open 9–6 daily, 8:30 a.m.–10:30 p.m. during July and Aug.; adm.* 10¢) lead to the foot of the falls, close enough to the plunging water for one to become soaked with spray and mist and deafened by the roar of Niagara. A small steamer (*75¢ a trip*) named *Maid of the Mist* bobs on the rushing currents and pierces the billowing spray beneath the cataract.

2. HENNEPIN POINT is said to be the spot on which Father Hennepin stood when he beheld the Falls and drew the first known picture of Niagara. There is a safe view down the precipice of 187 feet.

3. GOAT ISLAND (*picnicking free*), a 70-acre park banked by jagged perpendicular rock, splits the rapids into two cataracts and offers one of the best views of the Upper Rapids. The name is in reference to the bearded goat that was the only one of the herd to survive the winter of 1779, after having been left here by John Stedman. More than 200 rare plants grow here.

4. LUNA ISLAND affords a view of the brilliant rainbows that arch through the spray, even in the moonlight. In winter the island is transformed into a kingdom of ice.

5. The CAVE OF THE WINDS (*open 9–5 daily, May–Oct.; trip, including guides, flannel and rubber clothing, and special shoes*, $1), reached by two elevators leading to the foot of the American Falls, is alive with stinging spray and buffeting blasts of air. A series of paths and bridges offers a succession of unusual views. The climax is the walk to the Rock of Ages, where Luna Fall crashes.

6. TERRAPIN POINT is connected with TERRAPIN ROCKS by a handrailed walk. From the rocks is a view into the deep cleft that forms the apex of Horseshoe Falls, where the vast accumulation of water concentrates in a spectacular exhibition of power.

7. The THREE SISTER ISLANDS, named for the three daughters of General Parkhurst Whitney, builder of the Cataract House, provide splendid views of the Upper Rapids.

8. The NIAGARA FALLS MUSEUM (*open, summer,* 8 a.m.–12 p.m. *daily; winter,* 8–5 *daily; adm.* 25¢), Riverway opposite Prospect Park, is a

four-story stone building with a cupola. Founded in 1830 in Queen Victoria Park, Ontario, and moved here in 1864, the museum is one of the oldest in the country. The 700,000 exhibits include a tree 25 feet in diameter, the skeleton of a humpback whale, Indian relics, Eygptian mummies, the rubber ball of Laussier, the barrels in which Mrs.Annie Edson Taylor and Bobby Leach went over the falls, and the one in which Miss Martha Wagenfuhrer plunged through the whirlpool rapids.

9. The SHREDDED WHEAT PLANT (*open* 8–11, 1–4:30 *Mon.–Fri.; guides*), 424 Buffalo Ave., occupies two city blocks and employs 600 persons. Visitors are shown the processes in the manufacture of the company's products and are served luncheon.

10. The NIAGARA FALLS POWER PLANT (*open* 8–5 *weekdays; guides*), lower end of Canal Basin at the terminus of the hydraulic canal, contains three 70,000 horsepower units, among the largest hydroelectric generators ever constructed. Dating back to 1890, it marks the first and greatest development of hydroelectric power in the world. During the World War the company absorbed the earlier Niagara hydraulic developments.

11. WHIRLPOOL STATE PARK, Niagara Rapids Blvd. near College Ave., part of the New York State Niagara Reservation, provides splendid views of the swirling waters of the pothole whirlpool, 1,754 feet wide and 126 feet deep. Here the course of the river bends westward, and then, blocked by the jagged mouth of a filled glacial channel, curves back to follow the present gorge to Lake Ontario. Charles Dudley Warner wrote: 'When it [the Niagara River] reaches the whirlpool it is like a hungry animal returning and licking the shores for the prey it has missed.' The whirlpool has its gruesome side, for here Niagara usually gives up its dead; one old riverman has recovered 150 bodies.

12. WHIRLPOOL RAPIDS BRIDGE (*tolls: car and driver* 25¢, *passengers* 5¢ *each; pedestrian* 5¢), built in 1887, a double-deck steel arch structure crossing to Niagara Falls, Ontario, provides an impressive view of the gorge and upper rapids.

POINTS OF INTEREST IN ENVIRONS

Niagara University and Devil's Hole State Park, just N. of city line, 4 *m.* from Falls; Tuscarora Indian Reservation, 9 *m.*; Fort Niagara, 14 *m.* (*see Tour* 26).

Niagara Falls, Ontario

Railroad Stations: Canadian National Station, Bridge St. head of Erie Ave., for Canadian National Rys.; Michigan Central Station, SE. corner of Queen St. and Erie Ave., for Michigan Central R.R.
Bus Stations: 120 Bridge St. for Gray Coach Lines; Queen St. and Victoria Ave. for Canada Coach Lines.
Street Busses: Fare 10¢, 4 tokens 25¢.
Taxis: 25¢ in city, regardless of number of passengers; special rates for sight-seeing.

Accommodations: 9 hotels, numerous tourist homes.

Information Service: Chamber of Commerce, 1005 Victoria Ave.; Provincial Tourist Information Bureau, Bridge St. and River Rd.; Niagara Parks Commission Information Booth, Queen Victoria Park, Niagara River Blvd.

Motion Picture Houses: 2.
Tennis: Queen Victoria Park.
Swimming: Municipal Swimming Pool, Jepson St.; Niagara Parks Commission Pool, Dufferin Islands.

NIAGARA FALLS, ONTARIO (560 alt.,18,727 pop.), incorporated in 1903, is a modern city with an attractive business section. The river front is protected by law; River Road is kept free of unsightly structures, and the power houses are designed to blend with the sheer rock walls of the gorge. The city shares the large tourist trade with its neighbor across the border, and, like its neighbor, it has several factory districts close by avenues of homes and gardens and park areas. A number of nationally known United States concerns have built factories here to avoid paying duty on their products sold in the Canadian market.

POINTS OF INTEREST

The NIAGARA PARK SYSTEM, controlled by the Niagara Parks Commission, extends for 38 miles along the Niagara River between Lake Erie and Lake Ontario. Niagara Boulevard, a two-lane parkway bordering the river, provides convenient access to the points of interest on the Canadian side.

13. QUEEN VICTORIA PARK, at the falls, with its 196 acres of luxuriant lawns and gardens, offers the best views of both cataracts. At the north edge of the park is the OAKES GARDEN THEATRE, a reproduction of the Shakespeare theater at Stratford-on-Avon.

In the spray at the brink of the Canadian Falls is TABLE ROCK HOUSE (*open year round; 9–6 in winter, 9 a.m.–10 p.m. in summer; $1 a person including boots, waterproof coat, and guide through tunnel*). An elevator descends to a subterranean tunnel, which leads to lookout portals close to the falling water. Opposite the Upper Rapids is the TORONTO POWER GENERATING STATION of the Hydroelectric Power Commission of Ontario, a large cut-stone building with steel framework, designed in a modified Italian Renaissance style. The 11 great dynamos are visible through plate glass windows. The interior is finished in Italian marble. At the south end of the park are the DUFFERIN ISLANDS, with their numerous cascades and safe swimming places.

14. LUNDY'S LANE BATTLEFIELD, Lundy's Lane between Main Ave. and Drummond Rd., is marked by the Drummond Hill Cemetery. The bloody battle, fought in the evening of July 25, 1814, has been the subject of debate ever since. British and Canadian writers on the one side, and Americans on the other, claim the victory; others call it a draw. The cemetery contains a monument dedicated to American participants.

POINTS OF INTEREST IN ENVIRONS
(South of Bridge Street)

15. The CHIPPAWA BATTLEFIELD, 4.5 *m.*, is marked by a bronze plaque on a granite monument at the side of the parkway. The Battle of Chippawa was fought on July 5, 1814, 20 days before Lundy's Lane. The Americans under General Winfield Scott won a brilliant victory.

Niagara Boulevard becomes Queen Victoria Boulevard, which leads to the Peace Bridge, 20 *m.*, Fort Erie, 21 *m.*, and Buffalo, 21 *m.* (*see Buffalo*):

(North of Bridge Street)

16. A trip by elevator and through a rock tunnel reaches the bottom of the NIAGARA GORGE and WHIRLPOOL RAPIDS (*open 8 a.m. to dark daily, all seasons; 50¢ per person*). A 1,500-foot walk along the edge of the rapids offers a close-up view of the turbulent waters as they drop 50 feet in three quarters of a mile.

17. The SPANISH AERO CAR (*open 8 a.m. to dark daily, all seasons; 50¢ one way, 75¢ round trip*), 0.8 *m.*, offers a ten-minute thrill and an unusual view to passengers in a car suspended on six cables above the Whirlpool.

18. In NIAGARA GLEN, 2.8 *m.*, a dry gorge, huge potholes reveal to geologists the site of an ancient rapids and waterfall. Trails lead to the Lower Rapids.

19. The QUEENSTON–CHIPPAWA GENERATING STATION of the Hydroelectric Power Commission of Ontario (*open 9–4; guides*), 4.5 *m.*, cutting 300 feet into the side of the gorge, supplies 750,000 horsepower to Canada and the United States. Transmission lines reach 250 miles into New York State.

20. QUEENSTON HEIGHTS PARK, 5.7 *m.*, is on the site of the Battle of Queenston Heights, which took place on October 13, 1812. The BROCK MONUMENT, 185 feet high, is a statue of Brock standing on a Roman column supported by a high base and pedestal. It was dedicated in 1853 in memory of Sir Isaac Brock, British general who was killed in the battle. Refusal of New York militia to cross the river to reinforce their comrades was largely responsible for the defeat of the Americans.

The LAURA SECORD MONUMENT, near by, a granite marker, was unveiled in 1901 in memory of the American-born woman who on June 24, 1813, walked 25 miles on foot, all one day and into the night, to warn a Canadian force of an impending attack. Her warning enabled them to surprise and defeat a much larger American force in the Battle of Beaver Dams.

From Queenston a bridge (*toll 25¢ a car*) connects with LEWISTON, 7.5 *m.* (363 alt.,1,013 pop.) (*see Tour 26*).

Poughkeepsie

Railroad Station: Near foot of Main St. for New York Central R.R.
Bus Station: New Market St. for Mountain View, Flying Eagle White Way, Mohawk, Twilight, Harlem Valley, Pizzuto, and Greyhound Bus Lines.
Steamboat Docks: Foot of Main St. for Poughkeepsie-Highland ferry, 25¢ per car; and Hudson River Day Line, daily boats to New York City and Albany, May–Oct.
Busses: Fare 10¢, 3 tokens 25¢.
Taxis: At railroad station, 25¢; other, 20¢ within city limits.

Accommodations: 5 hotels; tourist homes.

Information Service: Chamber of Commerce, 57 Market St.; Nelson House, 28 Market St.

Motion Picture Houses: 6.
Golf: College Hill Park municipal course, N.Clinton St., 9 holes, 40¢–$1.
Tennis: Municipal courts in Butts Memorial Field, Church St. at Quaker Lane; College Hill Park; Eastman Park, South Ave. and Montgomery St.; King Street Park, Corlies Ave. and King St.; free.
Swimming: Wheaton Park, ft. of Mill St., children only; Greenvale Park, 3 m. SE. on State 376, adm. 5¢; Morello's Pleasure Park, 2½ m. NE. on Smith St., adm. 10¢.

Annual Event: Intercollegiate Regatta, late June.

POUGHKEEPSIE (175 alt.,40,237 pop.), on the east bank of the Hudson River midway between Albany and New York City, is the seat of Dutchess County and of Vassar College, and the scene of the annual Intercollegiate Regatta. The railroad bridge, of cantilever construction, and the Mid-Hudson Bridge, of the long suspension type, dominate the river front.

The city pattern is set by the long Main Street, which climbs the steep slope from the river and, lined with offices, shops, homes, and public buildings, extends eastward for about two miles. At the crest of the slope up from the river, where Main Street intersects with north-south Market Street, is the center of the downtown district. As in other cities feeding on industry and a large agricultural hinterland, the streets and stores are busiest on Saturday evening, with Main Street east of Market Street carrying the heaviest burden.

Downtown Poughkeepsie is composed of crowded brick and frame structures of varied heights. An occasional old residence has kept its foothold, the lower floor pressed into commercial service. The residential districts reflect the tastes and styles of their periods. The finest dwellings of the pre-Civil War era have almost all been destroyed or have fallen into ruin. Along the water front, where the largest industries have occupied what was once the most pretentious residential section, the scene is a mixture of activity and dilapidation.

The economic life of Poughkeepsie is about evenly divided between industry and commerce, with no one trade or product predominating. It is an important retail shopping and lumber distribution center, and manufactures cream separators and oil clarifiers, ball bearings, clothing, and cough drops. Clothes for men and women are made in small but numerous establishments employing women almost exclusively. In 1940, 38 per cent of the industrial workers in Poughkeepsie were women, almost all of them employed in these shops.

The Intercollegiate Regatta, most famous of American shell races, has familiarized the Nation with the name of Poughkeepsie. For two days in late June the city is host to a multitude of visitors from all corners of the continent, come to witness this pageant of rhythm and color. The three races—Freshman, Junior Varsity, and Varsity—are scheduled at one-hour intervals late in the afternoon, the exact time determined by the tide. The race course, on the imposing 'Long Reach' of the Hudson, is bordered by flag-flying yachts, launches, and rowboats, and the shores are crowded with thousands of people on foot and in cars. A bomb, fired from the Mid-Hudson Bridge, signals the start. Followed by the boats of referees and coaches and by an observation train that skirts the base of the west shore bluff, the shells glide smoothly down the channel to the finish line. Three times the spectacle is repeated, lasting, in all, about three hours. Then bets are paid, and the exodus begins; within a few hours the river scene is quiet, and by morning Poughkeepsie has resumed its normal routine.

The date given for the first modern intercollegiate regatta at Poughkeepsie is 1895. But the local history of rowing and allied sports goes back more than a century. The first recorded rowing regatta was held in 1839. Ice yachting began in Poughkeepsie in 1807; it came to an end about 1920, when icebreakers were introduced on the Hudson; in recent years the river has been kept open for ships plying to the Port of Albany.

Poughkeepsie is a modified Indian name, the original probably meaning 'reed-covered lodge by the little water place.' The first record of white settlement within the city limits is a deed of 1683 conveying land from an Indian, Massany, to two Hollanders. Growth in the eighteenth century was slow. Of the 170 inhabitants in 1714, all were Dutch save 15 slaves and a dozen French Huguenots and Englishmen. Public records, however, were written in a hybrid phonetic English.

Poughkeepsie was not involved in Revolutionary activities. In 1777 it was made the capital of the State and Governor George Clinton made his residence here. The chief event in the history of the town was the ratification of the Federal Constitution by the State on July 26, 1788.

Early in the nineteenth century the increased cultivation of the hinterland and the establishment of local factories brought Poughkeepsie into prominence as a river port. Eight large sloops sailed weekly to New York, transporting Dutchess County grain to the metropolis and bringing back supplies and settlers for the provinces. With the opening of the Erie Canal in 1825, however, western competition caused a decline in the value of Dutchess County produce, from which it has never recovered; and Poughkeepsie turned to industry and trade.

In the 1830's Poughkeepsie acquired a reputation as an educational center as a result of the establishment of more than a dozen private schools, but the most important educational advance came in 1861 with the founding of Vassar College.

In 1854, the year Poughkeepsie was granted a city charter, Henry Wheeler Shaw, the 'Josh Billings' of Yankee humor, took up his residence here and began his career as a writer under the pen name 'Efrem Billings,' which he soon changed to its classic form. Shaw contributed to local newspapers, took an active interest in civic affairs, and in 1858 was elected city alderman.

After the Civil War Poughkeepsie experienced a period of rapid industrial expansion, with a corresponding increase in population. Factories sprang up along the river front, displacing eighteenth-century wharves, warehouses, and residences. Families of wealth and social position, whose homes had occupied the picturesque slopes overlooking the Hudson, removed to the southeastern section of the city and developed residential areas on the eminences of Academy Street and along Hooker Avenue. With the passing of the years many of the new enterprises expired, but some of the wealth they created had gone into philanthropic institutions housed in various sections of the city. The most important economic development of recent years has been the establishment of numerous small garment factories.

POINTS OF INTEREST

The DUTCHESS COUNTY COURTHOUSE, SW. corner of Market and Main Sts., a three-story-and-attic structure of red brick with gray sandstone trim, built in 1902, stands on the site of four former courthouses. In the third of these, on July 26, 1788, the State convention, after warm and prolonged debate, ratified the Constitution of the United States by a vote of 30 to 27.

The new U.S.POST OFFICE, Mansion St. facing New Market St., was opened in 1939. The architect, Eric Kebbon of Washington, D.C., followed the design of the third Dutchess County courthouse, erected in 1785, in which New York ratified the U.S.Constitution. The style is therefore early Federal. The walls are of local stone, with white trim. The main block has a cupola, which holds the first bell to be installed in a post office. President Franklin D. Roosevelt took a personal interest in the plans for the building and laid the cornerstone.

The NELSON HOUSE, 28 Market St., a five-story red brick structure, stands on a site where, under various names and owners, an inn has been uninterruptedly maintained since 1777. Before the Revolution the Van den Bogaerdt farmhouse, which stood here, was used as an inn from 1725 to 1742. The central structure of the present hotel was built in 1875.

The VASSAR BROTHERS INSTITUTE (*open* 1–5 *daily*), 12 Vassar St., houses a museum of natural history, a natural science and historical library, and an auditorium. Fossils, Indian artifacts, and mounted specimens of fauna are exhibited. The red brick building, erected in 1881, is designed in the Victorian style characteristic of the several local institutional structures donated by the Vassar family, Poughkeepsie brewers.

The SOLDIERS' FOUNTAIN, South Ave. and Montgomery St., an ornately figured fountain unveiled in 1870 to the memory of the soldiers of the Civil War, is an example of 'folk art' in cast iron. The square in which it stands, at the entrance to Eastman Park, preserves more mid-Victorian civic atmosphere than probably any other civic square in the State.

CHRIST CHURCH (Episcopal), Montgomery and Academy Sts., is a striking red sandstone structure erected in 1888 and designed by William Appleton Potter in the English Gothic style. The tower was added in 1889. The Tudor rectory was built in 1903. The church body was organized in 1766.

ST.PETER'S CHURCH, foot of Mill St., a brick structure erected in 1853, with later additions, is an interesting example of 'folk Renaissance' architecture. This was the first Roman Catholic church in Dutchess County. From it is a fine view of the bridges across the Hudson.

The SMITH BROTHERS PLANT (*open 9–5 weekdays*), 134 N.Hamilton St., built in 1914, is a two-story brick building painted white, in which the nationally advertised Smith Brothers cough drops are made. The business was established before 1850 by William Wallace Smith and Andrew Smith, the famous bearded 'Trade' and 'Mark.' The two well-known faces were reproductions from actual photographs. The cough drops were first made in a basement by hand; now hand labor is eliminated and they are manufactured by the ton in this modern factory.

The CLEAR EVERITT HOUSE, known as the Governor Clinton House (*open weekdays 9–5, Sun. 1–5; adm. free*), NW. corner of White and Main Sts., is a historic State museum. Although dating from 1783, it is designed in the style of the early Dutch Colonial period. The attic section is built of wood; the foundations, two feet thick, are of rough field stone crudely laid; the walls are of the same material and workmanship. In the rooms are exhibited household implements and dishes of Colonial days, a number of original State documents, Revolutionary relics and weapons, and eighteenth- and nineteenth-century furniture.

The GLEBE HOUSE (*open 1–5 Mon., Wed., Fri.*), 635 Main St., built in 1767 as the rectory of the Episcopal Church, is a story-and-a-half structure of red brick laid in Flemish bond. The interior is planned with spacious rooms common to the houses of the period. The building was purchased for the city in 1929 by popular subscription, and the gathering of a historical collection is under way.

VASSAR COLLEGE (*open; closed to automobiles on Sun. and holidays; parking at gate*), Raymond Ave., Arlington, occupies a 950-acre campus landscaped with impressive trees and broad lawns crisscrossed by paths. The buildings are not arranged according to any regular plan, though the dormitory group, designed in the Tudor style with gables, bays, and battlemented turrets, form a quadrangle just north of the main entrance. The other buildings are of varied architectural styles. On the campus are an arboretum, a Shakespeare garden in which are grown the flowers mentioned in Shakespeare's plays, greenhouses, and an outdoor theater. Adjacent to the campus proper are faculty dwellings, two small lakes, an athletic field, and a nine-hole golf course. To the south lies the 700-acre Vassar farm, which supplies vegetables for the college dining halls.

Between classes the campus hums with bicycles operated under a system of licenses and traffic regulations administered by the students. There are no student-owned automobiles and no sororities.

The 31 academic departments are divided into four groups: art, foreign literature and languages, natural sciences, and social sciences. The curriculum is of sufficient scope to provide the student with a foundation for a professional career, for business, or for home life and citizenship. The student body is limited to 1,150; the faculty numbers about 180. During the summer months the Vassar Institute of Euthenics provides six weeks of study for parents, teachers, and social workers in the problems of child-rearing and the conduct of the family.

The college was founded by Matthew Vassar (1792–1868), Poughkeepsie brewer, in 1861, but the Civil War delayed the formal opening until 1865. From the time of Harriet Stanton Blatch, '78, through that of Inez Millholland Boissevain, '09, until suffrage was an accomplished fact, members of the college played an active part in the campaign for the enfranchisement of women. Other noted alumnae include Katherine Bement Davis, penologist; Edna St.Vincent Millay and Adelaide Crapsey, poets; Elizabeth Howe, well-known fashion designer and author of *Fashion Is Spinach*; Jean Webster, author of *Daddy Long Legs*; Constance Rourke, critic; Margaret Culkin Banning, novelist; and three college presidents: Katharine Blunt, Constance Warren, and Mildred McAfee.

TAYLOR HALL (*open 2–4 weekdays*), at the main entrance, constructed of seam-faced granite with limestone trim, is designed in the English Gothic style, with a heavy, square, battlemented tower over the entrance driveway, leaded-glass windows, buttresses, and oriel bays. The architects were Allen and Collens of Boston. The building houses the art department and the art collection, which includes several Rembrandt prints, watercolors by Turner from the collection of John Ruskin, a number of the paintings of the Hudson River School, and three bronzes by Jo Davidson.

The FREDERICK FERRIS THOMPSON MEMORIAL LIBRARY (*open 9–5 weekdays, 2–5 Sun.*), N. of Taylor Hall, like the latter, is designed in the English Gothic style with a large, square, buttressed and pinnacled tower. The roof is set behind a battlemented parapet. The main entrance, with small octagonal turrets, is typically medieval in design. The architects were Allen and Collens. The library contains 200,000 volumes, including the Justice collection of material relating to the periodic press and the Village Press collection printed by Frederic W. Goudy, of Marlboro, New York.

The CHAPEL, S. of the main entrance, dedicated in 1904, is constructed of yellow Weymouth granite trimmed with limestone. The exterior is designed like an English parish church in the Norman style, with massive round arches, square corner tower, and 'cart-wheel' window. The interior has hammer-beam trusses. The architects were Shepley, Rutan, and Coolidge of Boston. The stained glass windows are from the Tiffany studios, three of them designed by La Farge.

The MAIN BUILDING (*offices open* 8–5 *Mon.–Fri.;* 8–12 *Sat.*), facing the main entrance, was completed before the opening of the college in 1865. Designed by James Renwick, Jr., in the style of the French Second Empire, the five-story brick building is topped with a steep mansard roof. Until 1893 virtually all of the students and most of the faculty lived in this building. To it, especially in the eyes of the older alumnae, clings much of the tradition of Vassar. It houses the administrative offices, reception rooms, and accommodations for about 350 students and college officers.

The quadrangle enclosed by the dormitories north of the main entrance is said to have been the field in which the daisies were picked for the first daisy chain carried by sophomores on Class Day.

POINTS OF INTEREST IN ENVIRONS

Crum Elbow, 4.7 *m.*, Quaker Meetinghouse, 6 *m.*, Margaret Lewis Norrie State Park, 7.7 *m.*, Ogden Mills and Ruth Livingston Mills Memorial State Park, 8.7 *m.*, Fishkill Village, 12.2 *m.* (*see Tour* 21).

Rochester

Railroad Stations: Central Ave. between Clinton Ave.N. and Joseph Ave. for New York Central System; Main St.W. and Oak St. for the Buffalo, Rochester & Pittsburgh division of the Baltimore & Ohio R.R.; 35 Court St. for Erie R.R.; 357 Main St.W. for Pennsylvania R.R.; 99 Court St. for Lehigh Valley R.R.
Bus Stations: 83 South Ave. for Western New York Motor Lines (Blue Bus Line) and interurban lines; 72 Franklin St. for Central Greyhound Lines.
Airport: Municipal, 5.2 m. W. of city on State 35 for American Airlines; taxi, $1.25. Sight-seeing planes and aviation schools.
Piers: Foot of Boxart St. for Ontario Car Ferry; Municipal Pier, Beach Ave., for Canada Steamship Lines, season June 15–Sept. 12.
Taxis: 35¢ first 2 m., reduced charge for additional mileage.
Streetcars and Busses: Fare 10¢; weekly passes $1.
Subway: Rowlands to west city limits; fare same as surface lines, with 5¢ additional to Rowlands.

Accommodations: 17 hotels; tourist homes.

Information Service: Chamber of Commerce, 55 St.Paul St.; Rochester Convention and Publicity Bureau, Clinton Ave.S. at Monroe Ave.; Automobile Club of Rochester, 90 East Ave.

Radio Stations: WHEC (1430 kc.); WHAM (1150 kc.); WSAY (1210 kc.).
Theaters and Motion Picture Houses: Eastman Theater, Main St.E. and Gibbs St., operas, concerts, children's plays in winter; Masonic Temple Auditorium, Main St.E. and Prince St., legitimate plays during season; Community Playhouse, 820 Clinton Ave.S., amateur plays, Sept.–May; 31 motion picture houses.
Swimming: Municipal pool, 250 South Ave.; Genesee Valley Park, Elmwood Ave.; Seneca Park, St.Paul St. and St.Paul Blvd.; pools open weekdays 10–10, adm. free to 5 p.m., 25¢ thereafter. Beaches at Ontario Beach Park, Foot of Lake Ave., and Durand-Eastman Park, Lake Ontario.
Golf: Durand-Eastman Park, Genesee Valley Park; both 18-hole courses, greens fee: residents 50¢, nonresidents $1; season permit $5.
Baseball: Red Wing Stadium, Norton St. and Clinton Ave.N.; Rochester Red Wings, International League.
Tennis: City parks and playgrounds, 46 courts, season permit 50¢, players must furnish net.

Annual Events: Twelfth Night Celebration, Cobb's Hill Park, Highland and Monroe Aves., Jan. 6; Easter Flower Show, Lamberton Conservatory, Highland Park, Highland Ave. between Mt.Hope Ave. and S.Goodman St., Easter week; Music Festival, Eastman Theater, Apr.; Garden Club Exhibition, Convention Hall, Clinton Ave.S. and Monroe Ave., late May or early June; Lilac Festival, Highland Park, May or June; Rose Show, Chamber of Commerce Bldg., 55 St.Paul St., June; Yacht Races, Summerville, June–Sept.; Rochester Symphony Orchestra season, 12 concerts, Oct.–Apr.; Chrysanthemum Show, Lamberton Conservatory, Nov.; Christmas Flower Show, Lamberton Conservatory, Christmas week.

ROCHESTER (500 alt.,324,694 pop.), third largest city in the State, extends 12½ miles along both banks of the Genesee River to its outlet into

Lake Ontario. The river, called by the Senecas *Casconchiagon*, 'river of many falls,' bisects the city: to the south its grassy, tree-covered banks form the sloping margin of park and campus; in the center of the city it is lined by the dull brick walls and smokestacks of industry; north it flows through a scenic gorge. Ten bridges offer views of the river and of the city skyline dominated by Mercury a-tiptoe on the city hall annex, the modern aluminum wings on the Genesee Valley Trust Building, and the aluminum Eastman Kodak tower.

The Four Corners, the junction of Main with State and Exchange Streets just west of the Genesee River, was for 100 years the center of Rochester's life. Stately old structures, reminders of post-Civil War architecture with their horizontal belt courses, dormer windows, and mansard roofs, are jostled by modern bank and office buildings. The Four Corners has remained the financial center of the city; but in recent years, business, traffic, theaters, and hotels have moved eastward, following Main Street across the river to a new downtown district of irregular, heavily traveled streets.

From this main business area Rochester stretches out in every direction, merging into residential neighborhoods, each with its own shopping and amusement center. Several of these areas are characterized by individually owned homes with carefully tended lawns or backyards, a continuing expression of the period when the nursery industry prevailed in the city. East Avenue, shaded by overarching elms, is a street of pretentious homes behind spreading lawns.

Rochester is home to a number of outstanding specialized industries, some of which dominate in the national, others in the world market. These plants produce kodaks, optical goods, dental equipment, railway signal apparatus, gear-cutting machinery, thermometers, safety paper for checks and mechanical check-writers, and glass-lined steel receptacles. Other important products of the 1,000 local industries are shoes, clothing, food products, office equipment, unbreakable watch crystals, mail chutes, and carbon paper. The industrial plants are not congregated in any one section of the city; they dot its skyline with clean, modern structures, as a rule in park-like settings of wide, landscaped grounds.

As a result of the establishment of the Eastman School of Music and the activities of the Civic Music Association, Rochester has acquired renown as a music center (*see Music*).

Among the city's foreign groups, in point of numbers, the Italians lead with 55,000 people, the Germans come next with 40,000, then the Canadians with 20,000, the English 15,000, the Poles and Irish each 14,000, and the Russians 10,000. While the Italians and Poles for a time tended to congregate in separate sections of the city, there has never existed for any period a distinct foreign quarter.

Rochester schools originated or developed many modern educational practices. Sewing classes were organized in 1901 and cooking classes in 1908. Special classes for subnormal children were established in 1906, anticipating the State law by 12 years. The city was the first in New York State to establish the 6-3-3 plan (6 years in grade school, 3 in junior high school, and 3 in senior high school) and one of the first to develop the present 7-5 plan (7 years in grade school and 5 years in junior-senior high school).

The essential conservatism of Rochester is best exemplified in its architecture. The first large-scale period of construction coincided with the heyday of the Greek Revival, and that style has dominated local architectural taste ever since. Something in the severe, straight-line school of modern architecture strikes a responsive chord; but to the flight of fancy represented by the wings atop the Genesee Trust Building the city is not yet fully reconciled: it has an uneasy feeling in the presence of beauty that cannot be made to serve some utilitarian purpose.

The first settler on the site of Rochester was Ebenezer 'Indian' Allen, who was granted a 100-acre tract at the falls of the Genesee on the condition that he erect a mill for use by the Indians. Allen built his mill, near the site of the present Four Corners, in 1789. In 1792 he moved with his white and Indian wives to Mount Morris.

Allen's 100 acres, a dismal swamp infested with snakes and mosquitoes that threatened settlers with 'Genesee fever,' after changing hands several times was purchased in 1803 by Colonel William Fitzhugh, Major Charles Carroll, and Colonel Nathaniel Rochester, all from Maryland. In 1811 Colonel Rochester offered lots for sale; on May 5, 1812, Hamlet Scrantom moved with his family into a house on the site of the Powers Building and became the first permanent settler. Abelard Reynolds built a two-story home on the site of the Reynolds Arcade in 1813; in 1815 he opened a tavern; the first newspaper was published in 1816; the next year the village was incorporated as Rochesterville.

By that time the settlement was one of eight along the last 12 miles of the course of the Genesee. Most promising among these was Carthage, which in 1818–19 built a great bridge across the river to attract trade; but after 15 months the bridge buckled and fell. The ultimate supremacy was determined in 1823 by the construction of the Erie Canal through Rochester along what is now Broad Street; and eventually Rochester absorbed all her former rivals.

By drastically reducing transportation costs the canal opened eastern markets to the Genesee farmer. Flour mills multiplied along the river banks, and Rochester became the Flour City. It also became an important center of canal boat construction, and more than half the stock of the transportation companies operating on the canal was owned or controlled in Rochester. The cornerstone of the first Monroe County courthouse was laid in 1821; in 1822 the first sidewalks were voted and the name Rochester was legally adopted; in 1826 the population was 7,669; schools, churches, and bridges were built; and in 1833 Rochester applied for a city charter.

The social and cultural tone of early Rochester was set by the stern New England character. The first church organization was Presbyterian. Early 'charity schools,' which grew from the church, for a time offered educational advantages not supplied by the district schools. The first Sunday school, organized in 1818, was attended by Catholic and Protestant children alike. Early enterprises in the field of public amusement withered under the denunciations of the keepers of the public morals. Newspapers refused to accept theatrical advertisements. A change in sentiment did not come until the large German immigration of the late forties brought a taste for recreation and amusement that forced its influence upon the city.

With the development of the railroads and the expansion of the West, the flour milling industry on the Genesee declined slowly and was succeeded in economic importance by the nursery industry. Rochester then became known as the Flower City. In 1840 the Ellwanger & Barry establishment was organized and became one of the largest nurseries in the world, supplying trees for planting on every continent. Second in prominence was the firm founded by James Vick, which specialized in flowers and seeds. The nursery industry inspired the development of the city's parks; and real estate companies, affiliated with the nurseries, developed suburban districts and helped make Rochester a city of individually owned homes.

In the middle decade of the nineteenth century Rochester was a bustling city of more than 40,000 inhabitants. The early cultural frigidity was melting under the warmth of German *Gemuetlichkeit*. In 1847 the Turnverein built the Turnhalle; Corinthian Hall was erected in 1849 and became a center of musical and theatrical entertainment; and in 1854 the Maennerchor was organized. On the night of October 24, 1844, Millerites assembled on the Pinnacle Hills to witness the end of the world and be gathered up to heaven with a shout. In 1848 the Fox sisters moved with their family from near-by Hydeville to Rochester and began giving demonstrations of their spiritualist rappings. In 1847 Frederick Douglass, a runaway slave, began publishing the *North Star*, Rochester homes were used as stations on the Underground Railroad, and the movement for abolition was the first of the many reforms that kept the city in a ferment for the rest of the century. In 1850 the University of Rochester and the Theological Seminary were incorporated. In the early fifties, after Jesse W. Hatch adapted the Singer sewing machine to the stitching of shoes, Susan B. Anthony went about asserting the rights of women in industry on the ground that 'a man's clumsy fingers would never be nimble enough to master the machine that was invented for women.'

Although the shoe and clothing industries in Rochester can be traced to handicraft beginnings as far back as 1812, they did not achieve large-scale proportions until the Civil War. The invention in the fifties of machines for sewing and pegging enabled the shoe industry to respond to the stimulus of the abnormal wartime demand, so that by 1865 there were 25 shoe manufacturers. In 1898, 64 factories produced shoes for a world-wide market. In the clothing industry, the arrival of large numbers of immigrants, especially German Jews, skilled in the needle trades, the invention of the sewing machine, and improvements in transportation encouraged large-scale mass production. By 1881 between 5,000 and 6,000 persons were employed in that industry.

During the same period, 1850–80, Rochester's specialized industries took root. In 1851 George Taylor and David Kendall began manufacturing thermometers and selling them from house to house. John Jacob Bausch opened his optical store in Rochester in 1853 and a few years later began grinding his own lenses. His friend Henry Lomb bought a half interest in the business for $60. In 1876 William Gleason invented the first commercially successful machine for cutting bevel gear teeth, and his son James later added other inventions and improvements that made possible the development of the Gleason Works.

In 1880, after successful experiments in his mother's kitchen, George Eastman began the manufacture of photographic dry plates. His great work was the invention and manufacture of films for cameras. The invention by Edison of the moving picture machine resulted in a large demand for Eastman film. In 1888 the first Kodak was put on the market and brought photography within the reach of amateurs.

Casper Pfaudler began manufacturing glass-lined steel tanks in 1887. In 1889 Frank Ritter produced the first dental chair made in Rochester, and Libanus M. and George W. Todd invented the first of a series of mechanical devices to protect checks against alteration. In 1895 George B. Selden, a patent attorney in Rochester, was granted a patent on a compression gas engine, which gave him monopolistic control over the automobile industry until Henry Ford contested his claim in court and won.

Industrial growth made possible the physical and cultural development of the city. Horsecar lines ran in the streets in 1863; electrification began in 1889. In 1891 J. Harry Stedman invented the streetcar transfer in Rochester. In 1887 Ellwanger & Barry presented 20 acres of land to the city as the nucleus of Highland Park. This gift was the first unit in the park system established the following year under the supervision of Dr. Edward Mott Moore.

Rochester's shoe industry, already faced with competition from New England and the Midwest, suffered a severe blow in the strike of 1922, with union recognition as the chief issue. Most of the plants were forced to remain idle for months. Yet in 1931 there were 32 shoe factories employing 3,600 workers and producing shoes valued at $11,500,000, principally high-grade footwear for women and children. In 1933 the total product of the men's clothing industry in Rochester was valued at $32,000,000, with 7,500 workers earning a total of $11,845,500.

Conspicuous in the field of labor organization in Rochester is the Amalgamated Clothing Workers of America, an industrial union recognized in all the clothing factories. The history of the Amalgamated in Rochester illustrates the application of collective bargaining and arbitration to industrial relations. Strikes and lockouts have been eliminated and industrial peace and self-government established. By 1933 the capital-labor relations in the clothing industry were so well adjusted that for an 18-month period not a single grievance was brought before the arbitrator.

In 1916 the city line was extended north in a long arm to Lake Ontario. Rochester adopted the city manager form of government in 1925. In 1931 the Port of Rochester had its largest development; the harbor was deepened, and the municipal piers and accompanying terminal building were constructed.

POINTS OF INTEREST

(Central and East)

1. The POWERS BUILDING, NW. corner of Main St.W. and State St., eight stories high, built of Ohio sandstone and designed by Andrew Jackson Warner, is typical of post-Civil War architecture with its cast-iron decorations, many dormer windows, horizontal belt courses, and an unusual series of mansard roofs. When erected in 1870 it was hailed as the first fireproof structure in the city and the only building west of New York City equipped with elevators. Daniel W. Powers (1818–97), local banker and broker, built this office building and the adjacent hotel, both landmarks.

2. The MONROE COUNTY COURTHOUSE, SE. corner of Main St.W. and Fitzhugh St., is a four-story building of New Hampshire granite built in 1896 and designed in the Italian Renaissance style by J.Foster Warner. Four Roman Doric columns flank the main entrance, from which a wide marble stairway leads up to an enclosed courtyard. The millstones of Allen's gristmill are embedded in the west wall.

3. The BOARD OF EDUCATION BUILDING, 13 S.Fitzhugh St., a good example of Victorian Gothic architecture, was built in 1874 to house the Rochester Free Academy, the city's first public high school. On this site, donated to the city by Colonel Nathaniel Rochester, the first school in Rochester was built in 1814.

4. ST.LUKE'S EPISCOPAL CHURCH, 17 S.Fitzhugh St., a Gothic structure erected in 1824, is Rochester's oldest church edifice. The three

---

KEY FOR ROCHESTER MAP

CENTRAL AND EAST 1.Powers Building 2.Monroe County Courthouse 3.Board of Education Building 4.St.Luke's Episcopal Church 5.City Hall 6.Mechanics Institute 7.Jonathan Child House 8.Bevier Memorial Hall 9.Livingston Park Seminary 10.Fox Sisters' Home 11.Plymouth Avenue Spiritualist Church 12.Whittlesey House 13.Statue of Mercury 14.Broad Street Bridge 15.Rundel Memorial Building 16.Genesee Valley Trust Building 17.Reynolds Arcade 18.Chamber of Commerce Building 19.Frederick Douglass Monument 20.New York Central Railroad Station 21.Rochester Post Office 22.Masonic Temple 23.Gleason Works 24.Todd Plant 25.Cobbs Hill Reservoir 26.Stromberg-Carlson Telephone Manufacturing Plant 27.Early Mission Monument 28.Eastman Kodak Camera Works 29.Kodak Tower 30.Bausch & Lomb Optical Plant 31.Lomb Memorial 32.Platt Street Bridge 33.Bausch Memorial Bridge 34.Rochester Historical Society Museum 35.Edgerton Park 36.Maplewood Park 37.Kodak Park 38.Eastman Memorial 39.Veterans' Memorial Bridge 40.St.Bernard's (Roman Catholic) Theological Seminary 41.Old Charlotte Lighthouse 42.Ontario Beach Park 43.Port of Rochester 44.Durand-Eastman Park SOUTH 45.Clarissa Street Bridge 46.Colgate-Rochester Divinity School 47.Highland Park 48.Mount Hope Cemetery 49.Genesee Valley Park WEST 50.Taylor Instrument Plant 51.The Ritter Dental Plant 52.The General Railway Signal Plant 53.The Pfaudler Plant UNIVERSITY OF ROCHESTER 54.The Prince Street Campus 55.The River Campus 56.The Eastman Theater and School of Music 57.The Sibley Musical Library 58.The School of Medicine and Dentistry 59.The Rochester Dental Dispensary 60.The Eastman House

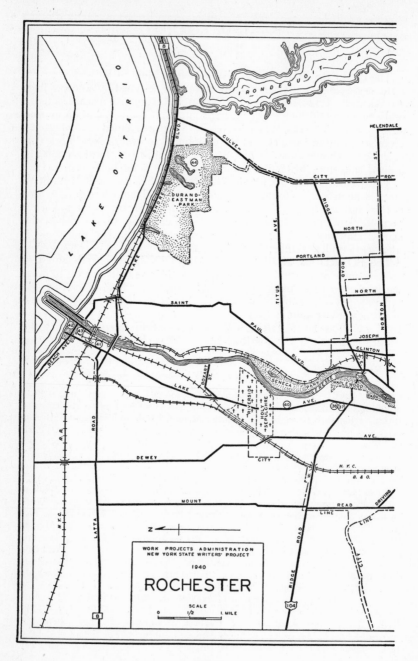

WORK PROJECTS ADMINISTRATION
NEW YORK STATE WRITERS' PROJECT

1940

ROCHESTER

SCALE
0   1/2   1. MILE

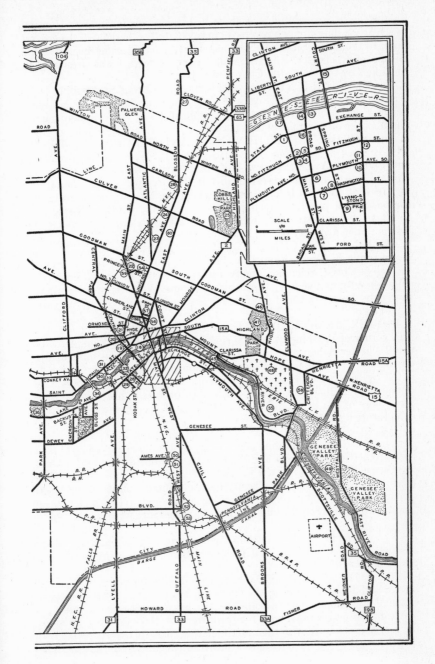

293

doorways are surmounted by high-arched stained-glass windows. Unusual at so early a date are two reversed-curve pointed arches above the central door. In the interior north wall is embedded a stone bearing the seal of the Bishop of Rochester, England, dated 1115–24, which was presented to St.Luke's by the Cathedral Church of that city.

5. The CITY HALL, NE. corner of Fitzhugh and Broad Sts., built in 1875, is a five-story structure of Lockport gray sandstone designed by A.J.Warner in a variation of the Victorian Gothic style. In the common council chamber are oil portraits of past mayors.

6. The ROCHESTER ATHENAEUM AND MECHANICS INSTITUTE (*open* 8:30–5 *Mon.–Fri.*, 8:30–12 *Sat.*), SW. corner of Broad St. and Plymouth Ave.S., is a two-story brick structure occupying an entire block. The Athenaeum was established in 1829 for non-occupational training. In 1885 Captain Henry Lomb founded the Mechanics Institute 'for the purpose of providing technical training for the youth of Rochester.' In 1891 the two institutions were merged. Nearly 4,000 students receive instruction in a variety of professional courses.

7. The JONATHAN CHILD HOUSE, 37 S.Washington St., an interesting example of Greek Revival architecture, is occupied by the Fourth Church of Christ, Scientist. The two-story-and-attic brick building is distinguished by its five lofty Corinthian columns. When it was constructed in 1837 by Jonathan Child, Rochester's first mayor, it was derisively called 'Child's Folly.'

8. BEVIER MEMORIAL HALL (*open* 8:30–5 *Mon.–Fri.*, 8:30–12 *Sat.*), NE. corner of Washington and Spring Sts., houses the School of Arts of the Rochester Athenaeum and Mechanics Institute. It was built in 1910 on the site of the home of Colonel Nathaniel Rochester with funds donated by Mrs.Susan Bevier of New York City. Claude F. Bragdon designed the building, and it can be described only as in his personal style. The colors of the brick and terra cotta suggest the Orient. Monthly art exhibits are held here.

9. LIVINGSTON PARK SEMINARY, 1 Livingston Park, a white two-story-and-attic wood building constructed as a residence in 1825, is occupied by the Gospel Mission and Welfare Association,Inc., and is known as the Gospel Tabernacle. In the Federal style, it is a reminder of the architectural splendor of early Rochester homes. Columns mark the front and side entrances. The interior trim is of carved mahogany, with columns of black walnut. In 1880 the building was converted into a private school for girls.

The terraced lawns of Livingston Park, guarded by iron grille gates and adorned with cast-iron animal figures, were the scene of many early Rochester social events.

10. The FOX SISTERS' HOME (*private*), NW. corner of Plymouth Ave.S. and Troup St., one of the cradles of Spiritualism, is a simple post-Colonial brick house. The two-story portico has Greek Doric columns.

After their first contact with the spirit world at Hydeville (*see Tour 32*), the Fox sisters moved with their family to this house in 1848. Meeting with skepticism, they conducted seances in their home; and from that small beginning the faith spread. The house later served as a station of the Underground Railroad.

11. The PLYMOUTH AVENUE SPIRITUALIST CHURCH, NE. corner of Plymouth Ave.S. and Troup St., is recognized as the mother church of modern Spiritualism. This Victorian Gothic brick building, designed in 1853, was originally a Congregational church. In the churchyard a marble monument, erected in 1927, commemorates the advent of Spiritualism in the home of the Fox sisters.

12. The WHITTLESEY HOUSE (*open 2–5 Fri.*), SW. corner of Troup and S.Fitzhugh Sts., is a two-story-and-attic brick building in the Greek Revival style erected in 1835. A high-columned portico extends across the Troup Street side, although the main entrance is on Fitzhugh Street. The interior of the house has mahogany trim, high-ceilinged rooms, and a wing stairway, all typical of the architecture that predominated in early Rochester homes. This house was purchased in 1937 by the Society for the Preservation of Landmarks in Western New York, Inc., for preservation as a historical shrine.

13. The STATUE OF MERCURY, by J.Guernsey Mitchell, a 28-foot copper figure atop the high chimney of the city hall annex, 34–54 Court St., towers 182 feet above the Genesee River. When it was placed in position in 1881, the building was the factory of the Kimball Tobacco Company, early manufacturer of machine-made cigarettes.

14. The BROAD STREET BRIDGE serves as a roof for what was once the Erie Canal aqueduct, built in 1842, which carried the canal across the Genesee River and was considered a marvel of engineering accomplishment.

15. The RUNDEL MEMORIAL BUILDING (*open 9–9 weekdays*), NW. corner of South Ave. and Court St., houses the Rochester Public Library, the Reynolds Reference Library, and the book and manuscript collections of the Rochester Historical Society. Completed in 1936, it is built of limestone in a modern 'stripped classic' style, designed by Gordon and Kaelber and Leonard A. Wassdorp. The building is constructed literally on stilts over a four-track subway and a river raceway. Through a series of 11 archways in the west base of the building the waters of the raceway spill into the Genesee River.

Funds for the building were bequeathed by Morton W. Rundel (1838–1911), art dealer and patron. The Reynolds Reference Library, of more than 90,000 volumes, was chartered in 1884 and enjoyed independent growth until 1936. It includes outstanding collections of official reports, State and national, and extensive back files of local newspapers. Art exhibits, mostly borrowed from America's leading art museums, are displayed each month in the gallery rooms.

16. The GENESEE VALLEY TRUST BUILDING, NW. corner of Exchange and Broad Sts., erected in 1929 of granite and limestone, is modern in style. The architects were Voorhees, Gmelin, and Walker of New York City. Severely straight lines characterize the first 12 stories, converging in a tower which supports four aluminum wings 42 feet high and weighing 12,000 pounds each. These wings add a distinctive touch to the Rochester skyline, especially under floodlights at night.

17. The REYNOLDS ARCADE, 10–20 Main St.E., a modern 10-story office building designed by Gordon and Kaelber and completed in 1932, occupies the site of the original Reynolds Arcade, which stood for a century and was the birthplace of the Western Union Telegraph Company and of the Bausch & Lomb Optical Company. George Eastman obtained his first job in an office in the Arcade, and George Selden had his office in the building.

18. The CHAMBER OF COMMERCE BUILDING, 55 St.Paul St., four stories high, of modified Italian Renaissance architecture, the exterior of Tennessee marble, was erected in 1916 with funds donated by George Eastman. A four-story addition was built in 1927 at the corner of Mortimer and Water Streets. The original structure was designed by Claude F. Bragdon, the addition by Gordon and Kaelber.

19. The FREDERICK DOUGLASS MONUMENT, Central Ave. and St.Paul St., a bronze statue on a granite pedestal, designed by Sidney W. Edwards, was dedicated in 1899 by Theodore Roosevelt, then governor of the State.

Frederick Douglass (1807–95) was born a slave in Easton, Maryland, and ran away from his master in 1838. His home on Alexander Street was a station on the Underground Railroad, and during the Civil War he helped organize Negro troops. Under President Benjamin Harrison he served as Minister to Haiti. His grave is in Mount Hope Cemetery.

20. The NEW YORK CENTRAL RAILROAD STATION, Central Ave. between Joseph Ave. and Clinton Ave.N., built in 1914 of smoke-brown tapestry brick and brownstone, represents one of the major architectural achievements of Claude F. Bragdon. The style is a free adaptation of the neoclassic. The four-story end pavilions are essentially traditional in design, but the connecting unit, with its three wide circular arches lighting the main waiting room of the station proper, is somewhat of a departure from the classic precedent. In the interior treatment of the waiting room, while some of the details are based on Roman prototypes, the beauty of the design is achieved by simplicity of line and proportion and by the able treatment of nonstylistic ornament.

21. The ROCHESTER POST OFFICE, Cumberland St. between Hyde Park and Ormond St., erected in 1934 at a cost of $1,700,000, is built of Ohio buff limestone in a modified Italian Renaissance style. The two curved entrances are adorned with columns of pink Tennessee marble having simplified Corinthian capitals. The walls and floor of the main lobby are of varicolored marble with woodwork of American walnut.

22. The MASONIC TEMPLE (*open 2–4 weekdays; guides*), SE. corner of Main St.E. and Prince St., dedicated in 1930, is built of pressed brick and limestone in a modern adaptation of the Gothic style. The architects were Osgood and Osgood, Grand Rapids, Michigan, with Carl Ade as associate. The lodge rooms on the upper floors are designed in the Georgian Colonial, Classic, and Gothic styles. The auditorium seats 2,600.

23. The GLEASON WORKS (*open by appointment*), 1000 University Ave., manufactures gears and gear-cutting machinery.

24. The TODD PLANT (*open by appointment*), 1154 University Ave., produces mechanical devices and chemically treated paper to protect checks against alteration, and mechanical check-writers and check-signers.

25. COBBS HILL RESERVOIR, entrance NW. corner of Monroe and Highland Aves., with a capacity of 144,000,000 gallons, is the largest within the city limits. A large central fountain aerates the water by sending a column 75 feet into the air.

The hill, with an elevation of 636 feet, affords an excellent view of the city. A LOOKOUT TOWER (*open* 10–10 *daily, June–Aug.*), near the reservoir, is equipped with a telescope. From it can be seen the downtown skyline with a residential section in the foreground, and, on a clear day, Lake Ontario to the north.

26. The STROMBERG–CARLSON TELEPHONE MANUFACTURING PLANT (*open* 9–4 *Mon.–Fri.*), 100 Carlson Rd., manufactures telephone apparatus and radios.

27. The EARLY MISSION MONUMENT, 1201 Blossom Rd., on the grounds of Our Lady of Mercy High School, a granite monument surmounted by a cross, was erected to commemorate the first building for Christian worship in the Rochester area. A small cabin for divine service was built of bark of trees near this site in 1679 by the Franciscan Recollect missionaries, Louis Hennepin, Gabriel de la Ribaud, and Zenobe Minord.

28. The EASTMAN KODAK CAMERA WORKS (*open by appointment*), NW. corner of State and Platt Sts., is a series of six- and seven-story brick buildings in which some 3,000 workers are employed in the manufacture of Kodaks, Brownies, Ciné-Kodaks, tripods, enlargers, and other photographic and developing equipment.

29. KODAK TOWER (*open* 8:30–5 *Mon.–Fri.*), NW. corner of State and Kodak Sts., 19 stories high, constructed of skeleton steel with exterior facing of terra cotta and completed in 1913, is designed in a modified French Renaissance style. The aluminum tower, built in 1931, rises 106 feet above the 19th floor. Known as the 'nerve center of photography,' this building houses the administrative offices of the far-flung Eastman Kodak organization.

30. The BAUSCH & LOMB OPTICAL PLANT (*open weekdays; three-hour conducted tours beginning at 9 and 2; planetarium open by special appointment, Tues. and Thurs. evenings, June–Sept.*), 635 St.Paul St., the largest of its kind in America, occupies 16 buildings, employs more than 3,500 workers, and manufactures upward of 17,000 products, including spectacle lenses and frames, instruments for testing and treating eyes, telescopes, microscopes, periscopes, binoculars, and scientific instruments. The company manufactures its own glass and maintains its own foundry, with one iron cupel and several brass and aluminum furnaces.

31. The LOMB MEMORIAL, on the plaza, facing Bausch St., is a black granite shaft, 48 feet high, on a base of pearl-pink marble, designed by Walter Cassebeer and Lewis Brew and erected in May 1930.

Captain Henry Lomb (1825–1908), born in Germany, emigrated to America in 1849 and worked as a carpenter. In 1853 he became Bausch's partner in his optical store. During the Civil War he sent a portion of his soldier's pay home to help support the business. In 1885 Lomb founded the Mechanics Institute; in 1903 he donated the initial funds for the Rochester Dental Clinic.

32. The PLATT STREET BRIDGE, St.Paul and Platt Sts., a steel arch bridge constructed in 1891, is 857 feet long, its roadway 114 feet above the river.

33. The BAUSCH MEMORIAL BRIDGE, St.Paul and Bausch Sts., is of steel cantilever construction with a span of 945 feet and a height of 105 feet above water level. The view embraces one of the centers of Rochester's industrial life.

Bronze tablets at the approaches to the bridge honor John Jacob Bausch (1830–1926), founder of the Bausch & Lomb Optical Company. Born in Germany and apprenticed there to the optical trade, Bausch came to America in 1848. After several difficult years, he opened an optical store in Rochester and began grinding his own lenses.

34. The ROCHESTER HISTORICAL SOCIETY MUSEUM (*open* 2–5 *daily*), 100 Lake Ave., was opened in 1937. Materials relating to the history of Rochester and the Genesee country, slowly collected by the Society since its organization in 1888, are displayed in rotating exhibits. Of special interest is an extensive collection of pioneer portraits. A program of special exhibits commemorating the anniversaries of historic events and personages was inaugurated on February 13, 1938, with the celebration of the 118th birthday of Susan B. Anthony.

35. EDGERTON PARK, Backus St. opposite Phelps Ave., 62 acres, is used for winter athletics. Near the main entrance a peristyle with stone columns adjoins a bandstand.

The ROCHESTER MUSEUM OF ARTS AND SCIENCES (*open, summer:* 9–5 *Mon.–Fri.*, 9–12 *Sat.; winter:* 9–5 *Tues.–Sat.*, 2–5 *Sun.*), south of the peristyle, housed in a four-story brick structure with the crenelated roof line of a feudal keep, was established by the city in 1911. The director is Dr.Arthur C. Parker, who has been cited as the most eminent man of Indian descent and an authority on Indian life. The Indian and archeological exhibit displays many artifacts discovered by Dr.Parker. There are also exhibits of local flora and fauna, geological specimens, and historical items.

36. MAPLEWOOD PARK, main entrance near intersection of Lake and Driving Park Aves., contains 145 acres bordering the west bank of the Genesee. There are two picnic areas with fireplaces, tables, and benches. A small artificial lake is used as a skating rink in winter.

37. KODAK PARK (*open weekdays; two-hour conducted tours*, 8 *a.m. and* 1 *p.m.*), NW. corner of Lake Ave. and Ridge Road W., with main entrance on Lake Ave., the largest Rochester plant of the Eastman Kodak Company, contains 83 major buildings over an area of 400 acres and employs 10,000 workers. The plant resembles a modern city in compact form, with a hospital, cafeterias, a small theater, a locomotive roundhouse, and an athletic field.

A six-story building near the main entrance houses the research laboratory, which has produced home 'movies,' natural color film, film that records images at a distance of hundreds of miles, and many other advances in photography.

Production at Kodak Park is confined to photographic films, plates, paper, and chemicals. In the departments where film and sensitized paper pass through the various stages of manufacture, white light is carefully excluded, and the work is carried on under an eerie glow of subdued orange, red, and green. In one building pure bar-silver is converted into silver nitrate, which, by its sensitivity to light, makes photography possible.

38. The EASTMAN MEMORIAL, at the Lake Ave. entrance to Kodak Park, is reached by three broad flights of steps leading down sloping banks to a large circular plaza paved with Georgia rose marble. A circular pedestal in the center of the plaza, containing a bronze urn with the ashes of Eastman, is surmounted by a cylindrical block of pink Georgia marble eight feet high, on which are carved two figures in bas-relief: a man heating a retort over a flame and woman holding aloft a torch.

George Eastman (1854–1932), born in Waterville, New York, came to Rochester with his family in 1860. While working as an office clerk for $4 a week, he spent much of his time and savings in experiments to simplify the making of photographs. In 1880 he began the manufacture of dry plates in a third floor loft on State Street, meanwhile keeping his job as a bank clerk. He opened a small factory in 1882, and in 1888 brought out the first Kodak. In 1889 he developed the flexible film that was used in Edison's moving picture machine. Eastman donated $72,000,000 to various institutions. His Rochester philanthropies include the Eastman School of Music and the Eastman Theater, the Eastman Building of the Mechanics Institute, the Rochester Dental Dispensary, and the Chamber of Commerce building. He also gave large sums to the University of Rochester. He died, leaving the message, 'My work is done; why wait?'

39. The VETERANS' MEMORIAL BRIDGE, carrying Ridge Road across the river, completed in 1931 at a cost of $2,500,000, is the longest of the city's bridges, with a span of 981 feet. It is a concrete arch type dressed with granite masonry, and has been widely praised for its classic architectural beauty. Gehron and Ross, New York City, were the architects and Frank P. McKibben was the consulting engineer.

40. ST.BERNARD'S (Roman Catholic) THEOLOGICAL SEMINARY (*private*), 2260 Lake Ave., is housed in a group of three-story buildings built of red sandstone in the Gothic style. The main building, with its chapel, classrooms, and living rooms, is flanked by the Building of Philosophy and the Theology Building, providing students' rooms, professors' living quarters, a library, and auditorium. The site was purchased in 1887 by the Right Reverend Bernard McQuaid (1823–1908), the first Bishop of the Rochester diocese.

41. The OLD CHARLOTTE LIGHTHOUSE, foot of Lighthouse St. off Lake Ave., was erected in 1822 of sandstone and brick. Octagonal, ivy-covered, it stands on a bluff about 2,000 feet from the mouth of the Genesee River.

42. ONTARIO BEACH PARK (*bathing—lockers* 10¢, *picnicking, playgrounds*), foot of Lake Ave., has 2,000 feet of sandy bathing beach on Lake Ontario.

43. The PORT OF ROCHESTER has a dock wall extending 1,200 feet along the west bank of the Genesee River and a large passenger and freight building adjoining the dock. The harbor accommodates regular lake traffic, freight steamers operating between the Atlantic coast and Great Lakes ports, and transatlantic steamers. Passenger boats ply regularly between Rochester and Toronto.

44. DURAND–EASTMAN PARK, main entrance in Sea Breeze L. from Culver Rd., has 506 acres of rolling wooded terrain. The mile-long sandy bathing beach along Lake Ontario is floodlighted for night bathing. Four small lakes within the park are stocked with fish. There are eight picnic areas equipped with tables, benches, shelters, and fireplaces, a zoo, and an 18-hole golf course. The park contains 395 varieties of native and foreign trees, shrubs, and plants.

(South)

45. The CLARISSA STREET BRIDGE, River Blvd. and Clarissa St., constructed in 1918, is a triple steel-arched bridge with four cast stone pylons, each consisting of four rusticated Roman Doric columns. The architects were Gordon and Kaelber.

46. The COLGATE–ROCHESTER DIVINITY SCHOOL, NE. corner of S.Goodman St. and Highland Ave., is on a hill. The administration building, the president's house, and the chapel comprise a group of English Gothic brick buildings designed by James Gamble Rogers. The square tower of the administration building, with its spires and pinnacles suggestive of English cathedral towers, is visible for miles. The main building, dedicated in 1931, marked the merger of the Colgate Theological Seminary, Hamilton, New York, founded in 1820, with the Rochester Theological Seminary, founded in 1850.

47. HIGHLAND PARK, entrance at Reservoir and South Aves., 108 acres, part of which was donated in 1887 by Ellwanger & Barry, early Rochester nurserymen, contains more than 400 species of trees, shrubs, and perennials, including a grove with 370 varieties of evergreens. Five greenhouses and a conservatory display flowers throughout the year, with special displays at Easter and Christmas. More than 400 varieties of lilac are displayed at the Lilac Festival in May.

48. MOUNT HOPE CEMETERY, 791 Mt.Hope Ave., extending over 250 acres, contains the graves of many prominent Rochester people: Susan B. Anthony (1820–1906), pioneer advocate of equal rights for women in politics, industry, and education; Colonel Nathaniel Rochester (1752–1831), founder and namesake of the city; Abelard Reynolds (1785–1878), the city's first innkeeper and postmaster; and Frederick Douglass, Negro leader.

49. GENESEE VALLEY PARK, main entrance at Elmwood Ave. and River Blvd., has an area of 640 acres, with the Barge Canal, Red Creek, and the Genesee River converging near its center. A public boathouse

rents boats and canoes and offers a sight-seeing trip in the river by motor launch (*fare* 10¢). The park contains picnic areas and facilities for a large variety of sports. Near the entrance to the park is a statue of Dr.Edward Mott Moore (1814–1902), 'father of Rochester's parks.'

(*West*)

50. The TAYLOR INSTRUMENT PLANT (*open* 10–4 *Mon.–Fri.*), 95 Ames St., manufactures instruments for recording, controlling, and indicating temperature, humidity, flow, and liquid level.
51. The RITTER DENTAL PLANT (*open* 8–5 *Mon.–Fri.*), 404 West Ave., manufactures dental furnishings and supplies.
52. The GENERAL RAILWAY SIGNAL PLANT (*open by appointment*), 801 West Ave., manufactures signaling apparatus.
53. The PFAUDLER PLANT (*open by special permission*), foot of West Ave., makes glass-lined steel containers.

THE UNIVERSITY OF ROCHESTER

The University of Rochester was founded in May 1850 by a convention of Baptists. The liberal purpose was indicated by the establishment of a four-year scientific course in addition to the traditional arts curriculum; the ancient languages were omitted. Housed in an abandoned hotel building, with 60 students and a faculty of five, the institution opened its doors on November 5, 1850.

The administration of Dr.Rush Rhees, 1900–35, covered the period of greatest expansion. In 1900, largely as the result of a movement headed by Susan B. Anthony, women were admitted on the same conditions as men; George Eastman made the first of a series of gifts in 1904; the Memorial Art Gallery was given to the university in 1912; in 1919 it received title to the Eastman School of Music and the Eastman Theater; in 1926 the School of Medicine and Dentistry was opened; the River Campus, which houses the College for Men, was dedicated in 1930, and the old campus became the College for Women.

The College of Arts and Sciences, with separate campuses for men and women, awards the degrees of Bachelor of Arts and Bachelor of Science. The Graduate School offers advanced study in several of the departments of the College of Arts and Sciences, the School of Music, and the Medical School. In 1939–40 the total number of students in the university, including summer session and extension department, was 5,247; the faculty, including part-time instructors, 573.

54. The PRINCE STREET CAMPUS, University Ave. between Prince and N.Goodman Sts., is the College for Women. The 27 acres, with the vine-covered buildings shaded by elms, form a park in the midst of a residential district. The College for Women is an integral part of the College of Arts and Sciences and classes are conducted by the professors who teach on the River Campus.

The MEMORIAL ART GALLERY (*open,* 10–5 *Tues.–Sat.,* 1:30–5 *Sun. and*

Mon.), L. of the University Ave. entrance, donated by Mrs.James S. Watson in memory of her son James G. Averell, was opened in October 1913. It is a limestone building designed in the Italian Renaissance style. The Palladian loggia forming the main entrance is similar to that of the Morgan Library in New York City. The architects were Foster, Gade, and Graham; an addition in 1926 was designed by McKim, Mead, and White.

The permanent collections of the gallery include paintings by old and modern masters, departments of Egyptian, Classical, Chinese, Medieval, and Renaissance art, including painting, sculpture, furniture, ceramics, stained glass, tapestry, and historical prints.

CUTLER UNION, R. of the University Ave. entrance, named for James G. Cutler, whose benefactions made it possible, was opened in 1933. This monumental building, designed in the English Collegiate Gothic style by Gordon and Kaelber, is constructed of shot-sawn limestone. The large assembly room on the main floor is used for major college functions. The lounge, of English 'great hall' type, is paneled in oak, with stained-glass Gothic windows reaching almost to the ceiling; the murals are by Ezra Winter.

Weathered ANDERSON HALL, occupying the central position on the campus, was built in 1861 and named for the first president of the university; for a long time it was the only building on the campus. Directly in front of it is a bronze statue of Dr.Anderson by J.Guernsey Mitchell.

55. The RIVER CAMPUS, River Blvd. and Elmwood Ave., 67 acres of rolling land on a high bluff overlooking the Genesee River, is occupied by the College for Men. The campus was dedicated in October 1930. The main buildings, in two groups, were designed by Gordon and Kaelber in the Georgian tradition.

The RUSH RHEES LIBRARY (*open during academic year,* 8 *a.m.*–9:30 *p.m. weekdays,* 2–6 *Sun.; in summer,* 2–6 *weekdays*) dominates the campus with its circular tower rising 186 feet. The foyer is of Indiana limestone with a floor of marble mosaic. Heavy stone columns mark the entrance to the grand stairway. The library contains about 188,000 books, and space is provided for expansion. It has the Adams collection of Johnsoniania, one of the most complete collections of original letters, manuscripts, and first editions of Dr.Samuel Johnson; also manuscripts and letters of Lewis A. Morgan and Thurlow Weed.

The BAUSCH-LOMB MEMORIAL LABORATORY, on the south side of the quadrangle, a gift of the Bausch and Lomb families, houses the physics department and the Institute of Applied Optics, which trains students in the industrial and scientific application of optical theory and techniques.

DEWEY HALL, next to the Bausch-Lomb Memorial, houses the departments of biology and geology. The rear and the south wing are occupied by the MUSEUM OF NATURAL HISTORY (*open* 8:30–5 *weekdays*). On the first floor are the study collections and the herbarium of the Rochester Academy of Sciences. On the second floor is the geological collection, the nucleus of which was gathered by Henry A. Ward, who established Ward's Natural Science Museum in Rochester and supplied the specimens for many of the large museums of America.

56. The EASTMAN THEATER AND SCHOOL OF MUSIC, SE. corner of Main St.E. and Gibbs St., completed in 1922, was designed by Gordon and Kaelber, with McKim, Mead and White as associate architects. The exterior of the structure is designed in a modified Italian Renaissance style. The two lower stories are of rusticated stonework, with an elaborate metal marquee extending the whole length of the building above the first floor. The third and fourth stories, of light gray Indiana limestone, are adorned with three-quarter engaged Ionic columns set on the curve of the building over the main entrance to the theater. The design is repeated in a series of pilasters alternating with pedimented and square-headed windows. An entablature, an attic story, and acroteria crown the building.

The Theater, with main entrance at Main St.E. and Gibbs St., is the largest unit in the building. Kilbourn Hall, with entrance on Gibbs St., is at the opposite end. Between the two, a central corridor, 187 feet long, forms the entrance to the School of Music. At the Kilbourn Hall end, the grand staircase leads to the second floor corridor. The School of Music also occupies a 10-story annex across Swan Street. While the faculty of the School of Music is separate from the faculty of the College of Arts and Sciences of the university, there is a close co-operation between the two schools, and tuition paid to one entitles the student to take approved courses in the other.

In the department of theory and composition, the school has a dozen eminent instructors headed by Dr.Howard Hanson, director. From 1932 to 1937 four of the six Prix de Rome awards of the American Academy in Rome were given to students of the composition department. In 1937 one of its students was awarded the New York Philharmonic prize for the best symphonic composition in a country-wide competition. The Eastman School Symphony Orchestra and the Eastman School Chorus, made up of students, give public performances in the Eastman Theater and broadcast regularly over the radio.

Kilbourn Hall, a memorial to Eastman's mother, Maria Kilbourn Eastman, is the assembly room of the school. The design is Italian Renaissance, embellished with colored ornamentation. The decorations were painted by Ezra Winter and the sculpture work was done by Paul Jannewein. The side walls are paneled in wood to a height of 21 feet, above which the smooth stone is hung with old tapestries. The ceiling is blue and gold in grille designs with heavy beams delicately ornamented and colored.

The Eastman Theater occupies the entire Main Street end of the building. An adjoining five-story building, directly connected with the stage, provides shops for the construction of scenery. The side wall spaces of the theater, unusually large because of the elimination of boxes, are finished in Caen stone and decorated in the Italian Renaissance style. High above the rusticated walls are murals by Ezra Winter and Barry Faulkner.

57. The SIBLEY MUSICAL LIBRARY (*open 9–6 Mon.–Fri., 9–5 Sat.*), 46 Swan St., a two-story brick structure with limestone trim, opened in 1938, is the only building in the United States used exclusively as a musical library. It contains about 42,000 volumes and a large number of musi-

cal scores and manuscripts presented to the University of Rochester by Hiram W. Sibley.

58. The SCHOOL OF MEDICINE AND DENTISTRY, 260 Crittenden Blvd., is combined with the Strong Memorial and Municipal Hospitals, which provide clinical treatment for more than 100,000 patients annually. The main building is constructed of red brick, with many wings and pavilions. The School of Medicine, opened in 1926, is active in medical research. Its dean, Dr.George H. Whipple, was awarded the 1934 Nobel Prize in medicine for his research in pernicious anemia. The School of Nursing offers a three-year course leading to a nurse's diploma and a five-year course leading to the degree of Bachelor of Science.

59. The ROCHESTER DENTAL DISPENSARY (*open* 9–4:30 *Mon.– Fri.*, 9–12:30 *Sat.*), 800 Main St.E., was established and endowed by George Eastman in 1916 to care for the teeth of the poor children of Rochester. The institution trains women for service in oral hygiene. The first dental clinic in the United States was opened in 1901 by the Rochester Dental Society with funds provided by Captain Henry Lomb. After Lomb's death in 1908, Eastman became interested in the clinic's activities and made his first donation. By the time of his death his subscriptions totaled $3,500,000.

60. The EASTMAN HOUSE (*private*), 900 East Ave., was built by George Eastman in 1906. He willed it to the University of Rochester to be used as the residence of the university president. The three-story mansion of 49 rooms is built of brick with stone trim in the Georgian Colonial style.

POINTS OF INTEREST IN ENVIRONS

Boyd-Parker Shrine, 30 *m.* (*see Tour 8A*). Caledonia State Fish Hatchery, 21 *m.* (*see Tour 11*). Hill Cumorah, 26 *m.* (*see Tour 29*).

Saratoga Springs

Railroad Station: Railroad Pl. and Division St. for Delaware & Hudson R.R.
Bus Stations: 351 Broadway for Hudson Transportation Line, L.B.K.Lines,Inc., Saratoga-Corinth Line, Champlain Coach Lines, and suburban busses; Adelphi Hotel, Broadway, for Adirondack Transit Co.
Airport: Municipal airport, 2.5 m. SW. on West Ave.; no scheduled service.
Streetcars: Interurban to Schenectady and intermediate points.
Busses: Fare 10¢.
Taxis: 25¢ in city; 50¢ a person maximum in Aug.

Accommodations: 27 hotels, 8 open all year; boarding houses, inns, and rooming houses during June, July, and Aug.

Information Service: Booth on Broadway in front of Congress Park, May to Oct.; Chamber of Commerce, Arcade, 374 Broadway.

Theaters and Motion Picture Houses: Spa Theatre in the Simon Baruch Research Institute, New York State Reservation, stock productions, July–Aug.; 2 motion picture houses.
Swimming: Saratoga Springs Reservation, outdoor pool; adults 75¢, children 35¢; Aug., $1 and 50¢.
Golf: Saratoga Springs Reservation, greens fee $1, including clubhouse privileges $1.50; McGregor Course, on US 9, 3 m. N. of city, greens fee $1.50, $2 in Aug.
Tennis: Saratoga Springs Reservation, hard court, per hour, 50¢ singles, 75¢ doubles; clay court, per hour, 75¢ singles, $1 doubles; locker, soap, and towel, 25¢.
Horse Racing: Saratoga Race Track, Union Ave.; grandstand and paddock, $1.50; field, $1.10; clubhouse, $4.

Annual Events: Winter Carnival with Carnival Ball and Eastern States Speed Skating Championship Races, mid-Jan.; Horse Racing, Saratoga Track, Union Ave., Aug.; Wildwood Kennel Dog Show, McGregor Golf Links, 3d wk. in Aug.; St.Michael's Day Italian Celebration, Sept. 29.

SARATOGA SPRINGS (330 alt.,13,169 pop.), resort city of the Adirondack foothills, famed for its mineral springs, its horse racing, and its old hotels, for eight months of the year is just another central New York State town. It stirs with anticipation in June, swings into preparatory activity in July, and rushes headlong into the full tumult of its summer season in August. In September the decline begins. In October the town resumes its character as a sectional trading center, settling into its winter normality, which is broken only by occasional social functions at Skidmore College and a winter sports carnival.

In August, the month of the races, Saratoga's population increases fourfold, beyond the resources of its numerous hotels and uncounted rooming houses. The main industry of the permanent inhabitants becomes the renting of homes, ranging in size and character from the unpretentious dwellings of Congress Street to the palatial mansions of Union Avenue, and of garages, automobiles, saddle horses, and what-not by the day, week, or month.

Horse racing, rich in turf tradition since the 1850's, draws thousands of summer visitors of every class. In the paddock, socialites rub elbows with stable boys, politicians prognosticate with rustics, and the famous mingle with the infamous. Night life during the racing season is gay and diversified. Entertainment ranges from black and tan revues in back-alley cafes to radio and stage headliners amid swank splendor. Until recent years gambling flourished: ivory balls clicked on the numbered slots of spinning roulette wheels; case cards flipped on faro layouts; no-limit dice games and table-stake poker were on tap in gambling halls, night clubs, and near-by roadhouses.

With the running of the final race on 'getaway day,' the exodus from Saratoga comes with startling abruptness. For a few hours the streets are congested, and then the town is deserted.

In September most of the large hotels close. A few of the smaller ones, clustered about the city's southern entrance, remain open, and their patrons make daily pilgrimages to the near-by Spa, where a monumental group of buildings houses the baths on a landscaped tract above the Vale of Springs. In this quieter atmosphere historic Saratoga comes into its own. Broadway, the wide main thoroughfare, is transformed from a 'Gay White Way' to a small town 'Main Street,' its ancient elm trees half revealing, half concealing the rambling old hotels of outmoded design flanked by more modern business buildings. An occasional horse-drawn hack hunts dejectedly for fares. The Grand Union and the United States hotels recall something of the spacious grandeur of the post-Civil War period; Canfield's Casino, citadel of chance during the halcyon days of the Gay Nineties, rests in quiet dignity on the green carpet of Congress Park; and Yaddo broods above the hushed beauty of its terraced, timber-guarded grounds.

The growth and development of Saratoga has been closely associated with its mineral springs, the waters of which have been in systematic use since 1774. Large numbers of wild animals, attracted by the saline properties of the water, made this section a favorite hunting ground for the Indians, who called it *Saraghoga* (place of swift water). The Mohawk and the Oneida built hunting lodges at the springs each summer, and the *Saraghoga* of that era was as well known to the Indians as the modern Saratoga is to the white man today. For many centuries High Rock Spring was called by the Indians the Medicine Spring of the Great Spirit.

Father Isaac Jogues, Jesuit missionary and explorer, is believed to have visited the springs in 1643. In 1767 Mohawk braves are said to have carried Sir William Johnson to the springs on a stretcher, that he might benefit from the waters. Johnson's strength was improved and he returned several times. In 1775 Dirck Schouten built a cabin near High Rock Spring, but he heeded Indian warnings and moved away from that beneficent abode of the Great Spirit. The Revolutionary War delayed settlement further, but the curative powers of the waters were recognized and the resultant value of the land was foreseen by many colonists. In 1783 George Washington attempted to buy High Rock and adjacent springs.

The development that has made Saratoga a place of international reputation began with arrival of the pioneer Gideon Putnam in 1789. In 1802 he bought the land around the present Congress Spring, cleared the heavy timber, and built the three-story frame Union Hall, 'the first commodious hotel erected at the springs for the accommodation of visitors.' People were attracted to the spot, and when they came to settle they found Putnam ready to sell them lots around his inn. Thus Saratoga Springs was built around a hotel. In 1811, during the construction of Congress Hall, his second venture, Putnam was fatally injured.

The first United States Hotel was built in 1824. The second railroad in New York State, the Schenectady & Saratoga, was opened in 1832. Saratoga soon surpassed the earlier popular Ballston Spa, which had the seeming advantage of a more solid foundation in industry and commerce, by devoting itself wholeheartedly to the service of its visitors. To its natural attractions for people who were health-bent, Saratoga added man-made attractions for those who were pleasure-bent, and the spa became the social and sporting center of the country. In 1841 a guidebook described the clientele of the hotels as a mingling of 'gentlemen of the turf, connoisseurs of the odd trick, and the amateurs of poker.'

In the Civil War period the Leland Opera House and the Grand Union Hotel were the centers of the North's social world. General U.S.Grant attended the grand ball that opened the opera house in July 1865. He held receptions at the Grand Union while President of the United States. Commodore Cornelius Vanderbilt brought his bride to the springs in 1869. Jay Gould and Mr. and Mrs. John Wanamaker were frequent visitors.

'Aunt Kate' Weeks, cook in a hotel on Saratoga Lake, one day attempted to make perfectly crisped French fried potatoes, but evolved instead the tidbit known for years as 'Saratoga Chips,' since grown widely popular under the name of 'potato chips.'

The Saratoga Association for the Improvement of the Breed of Horses was incorporated in 1865 by a group of sportsmen that included William R. Travers, Leonard W. Jerome, and Cornelius Vanderbilt, and the present track was built in the same year. On the older Horse Haven track, harness races had been held in the 1850's. The Association was subsequently taken over by John Morrissey, heavyweight bare-knuckle boxing champion of the United States, member of Congress, and State senator, who also erected in 1870 the first section of the present Casino, later made world-famous by the debonair patron of art, Richard Canfield.

For mid-Victorian America, Saratoga was the 'Queen of the Spas.' 'For gayety it was not to be surpassed on this continent, however gauche it may have appeared to visiting foreigners; the racing season, the gambling palaces, the "flirting and dancing" as advertised in one guide book, and the countless numbers of marriageable daughters, all displayed by their fond mothers like vegetables in a market stall, were but a part of Saratoga's charm . . . for the gossips there were the endless hotel verandas, for dancers bands playing Lanner and Strauss waltzes almost without stop.'

In 1890 discovery of a process for the extraction of carbonic gas from the waters of the springs brought a period of exploitation that for several years threatened the spa with eventual destruction. Wells were operated by pumps until the output reached 150,000,000 gallons a year and the levels of the springs were lowered to such a point that many ceased to spout. To prevent wholesale despoliation of its natural resources, the State in 1910 began a program of conservation and development which has resulted in the purchase of 163 springs and 1,000 acres of land surrounding them, and the construction of baths, a research institute, a Hall of Springs, and a hotel, the Gideon Putnam, at the center of the State reservation. The completion of the project was made possible by a loan of $3,200,000 from the Reconstruction Finance Corporation in 1933. A prime mover in the development of the Spa was George Foster Peabody (1852–1938).

POINTS OF INTEREST

1. HIGH ROCK SPRING, High Rock Ave. opposite Rock St., now inactive, was the first Saratoga mineral spring known to white men. According to tradition, in 1767, when Sir William Johnson was desperately ill, his friends, the Mohawk Indians, carried him to this 'Medicine Spring of the Great Spirit' to be cured. At that time the spring appeared a few feet down in the hollow core of a truncated cone-shaped rock, which still stands within a wired enclosure. Geologists have estimated that it took about 4,000 years for the cone to be formed by the precipitation of salts from the highly mineralized water. George Washington, Philip Schuyler, and Alexander Hamilton visited High Rock Spring in 1783 with the possibility of its exploitation in mind.

2. The UNITED STATES HOTEL (*open Aug. only*), Broadway and Division St., erected in 1875, is an imposing historic souvenir of the heyday of Saratoga. Occupying a site of several acres, the building, designed in the manner of the General Grant period, is a five-story brick structure laid out in the form of an irregular pentagon. The exterior is enriched by an elaborately bracketed three-story porch. The large interior court is ornamented with shade trees, fountains, and walks. The elegance of the period in which it was built is reflected in the marble fireplaces, the massive mirrors, the carved woodwork, and the highly polished wainscoting.

3. The GRAND UNION HOTEL (*open June–Sept.*), Broadway between Washington and Congress Sts., occupies almost an entire city block. Similar in style to the United States Hotel, it has pavilions, towers, and mansard roofs. A graceful piazza, three stories high, extends across the entire Broadway front. The interior courtyard has a promenade veranda running along three of its sides. The original structure, called Union Hall, a much smaller building but so pretentious for its day as to be labeled 'Putnam's Folly,' was erected by Gideon Putnam in 1802. In 1872 the property was purchased by A.T. Stewart of New York, who enlarged and renovated the building and gave it its present name. Once the center of Saratoga's social and political life, where Victor Herbert conducted daily

concerts, the hotel still preserves an imposing appearance, though, like the United States Hotel, it represents an outmoded era.

4. The STATE DRINK HALL (*adm.* 10¢), corner of Spring and Putnam Sts., a high, one-story frame building, contains a public drinking room with free water and table service.

5. CONGRESS PARK, Broadway between Circular and Spring Sts., is approximately 10 acres in area. The SPENCER TRASK MEMORIAL FOUNTAIN was erected by the citizens of Saratoga in tribute to Spencer Trask (1844–1909), broker and banker who after his retirement from business became chairman of the Saratoga Springs Reservation. The statue is by Daniel Chester French. Standing on a granite pedestal in an oblong pool against a background of evergreens, a winged bronze figure holding a cup of healing waters typifies the spirit of awakened life in the waters of the springs. The KATRINA TRASK PEABODY MEMORIAL, a granite stairway, is in memory of Katrina Trask, wife of Spencer Trask, who married George Foster Peabody after Trask's death. She died in 1922. The memorial was given by her family and the household of Yaddo.

The CASINO (*open 9-5 daily during Aug.*) is a conspicuous red brick building near the center of the park. Formerly owned by Richard Canfield and famed as a gambling house, it now provides quarters for the Saratoga County Historical Society. The middle section, originally a fashionable restaurant, has been converted into a convention hall; the adornments are elaborate, with columns, carvings, and fixtures.

The Casino dates to 1870, when John Morrissey (1831–78) erected it as an adjunct to the racing attractions and named it the Saratoga Club. Morrissey spent his boyhood in Troy. In his early twenties, he married and moved to New York, where he became a runner for a boarding house, his duty being to entice immigrants to his employer's establishment. Competition was keen, fist-fights were frequent, and Morrissey soon became adept as a rough-and-tumble fighter. He joined the ranks of professional boxers and in 1858 won the American bare-knuckle heavyweight championship by defeating J.C.Heenan in 11 rounds at Long Point, Canada. He retired undefeated. In 1866 Morrissey was elected to Congress from the sixth New York district and served two terms, 1867–71. During his last year as Congressman he opened his clubhouse in Saratoga. In 1875, despite the opposition of the antigambling group, he was elected State senator from the fourth New York district; in 1877 he was reelected from the seventh district.

In 1894 Richard Canfield (1865–1914) purchased the Saratoga Club for

KEY FOR SARATOGA SPRINGS MAP

1.High Rock Spring 2.United States Hotel 3.Grand Union Hotel 4.State Drink Hall 5.Congress Park 6.Skidmore College 7.Saratoga Race Track 8.Yaddo SARATOGA SPRINGS RESERVATION 9.Washington Baths 10.Lincoln Baths 11.Bottling Plant 12.Simon Baruch Research Institute 13.Hall of Springs 14.Roosevelt Baths 15.Recreation Unit 16.Gideon Putnam Hotel 17.Hayes Spring and Geyser 18.Orinda Spring 19.Karista Spring 20.Ferndale Glen 21.New York State Tree Nursery

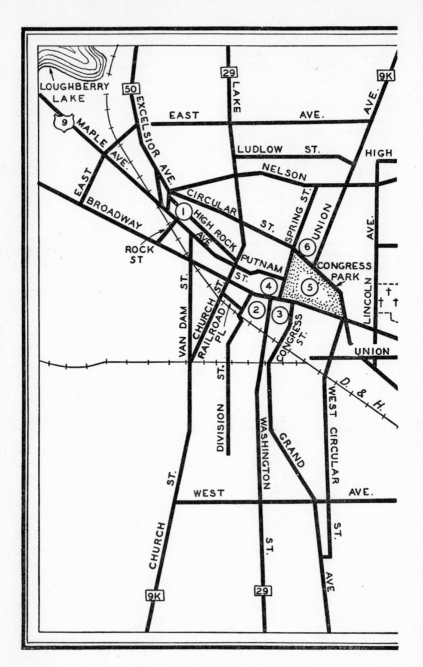

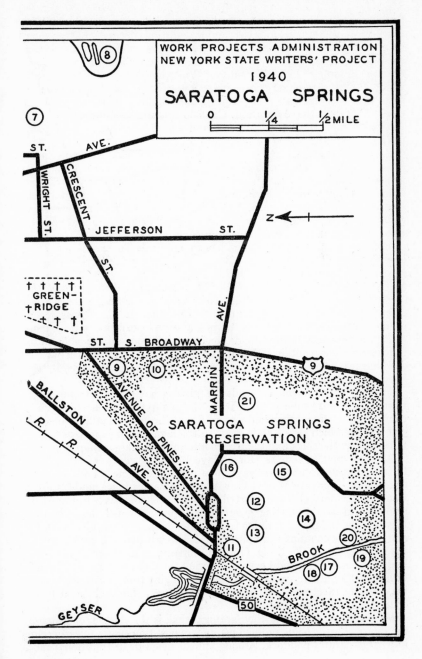

WORK PROJECTS ADMINISTRATION
NEW YORK STATE WRITERS' PROJECT
1940
SARATOGA SPRINGS

0   1/4   1/2 MILE

⑧

⑦

ST.
AVE.
WRIGHT ST.
CRESCENT
JEFFERSON   ST.
Z ←

GREEN-
RIDGE
ST.

ST. S. BROADWAY
MARRIN AVE.
⑨
⑨ ⑩
BALLSTON
R.
R.
AVE.
AVENUE OF PINES
㉑
SARATOGA SPRINGS
RESERVATION
⑯   ⑮
⑫
⑬   ⑭
⑪   ⑳
BROOK   ⑲
⑱ ⑰
GEYSER
50

311

$450,000 and changed its name to the Casino. In renovating the building Canfield outdid himself in lavish and ostentatious decoration. One room, its curved white ceiling flanked by stained glass windows and reflecting the light of a thousand carbon bulbs, is said to have been the world's first example of indirect lighting. Stanford White landscaped the grounds, for which Italian garden accessories were imported. In the Casino fabulous sums were won and lost in 'sky-limit' games, and many 'Monte Carlo suicides' are said to have occurred. Canfield solitaire was originated in the Casino's gaming rooms, and the club sandwich in its kitchen. Public disapproval and politics closed the place in 1907.

6. SKIDMORE COLLEGE, Circular St. between Union Ave. and Spring St., one of the younger colleges for women, was incorporated under its present name in 1922, but its origin can be traced back to 1903 when its founder, Lucy Skidmore Scribner, began her activities in the interest of creative education for women. The college combines liberal arts with specialized courses in the fields of fine and applied arts, health and physical education, home economics, music, nursing, and secretarial science. The campus covers about 10 acres and has 26 buildings. The enrollment averages 750 students. In the STUDIO BUILDING (*open 9–5 weekdays*) are exhibits of etchings, prints, pottery, and glass.

7. The SARATOGA RACE TRACK (*open free, 9–5 daily except during August races*), Union Ave. between Nelson and East Aves., is the scene of internationally famous horse races during August. The flower-decked grandstand, sprawling in the center of a 45-acre landscaped park, extends from the clubhouse to the 'Field' enclosure. The long arcade beneath the long rows of seats contains telegraph offices, refreshment stands, a bar, and a restaurant. A top-deck promenade extends along the upper level. Betting is by pari-mutuel machines.

Beyond the lawn, which extends the full length of the grandstand, is the racing strip, a 1⅛-mile oval. Within the main track is a steeplechase course that includes brush and water jumps. The infield contains an artificial lake on which swans glide beneath the high-arching spray of a fountain. Beyond the track and the trees bordering it is a large group of stables.

Across Union Avenue is Horse Haven, a small village of stables and training quarters. The roadways here carry the names of famous past champions. There are Man O'War Avenue, Roamer Place, and Campfire Court, in memory of the 'departed great whose hoofs have drummed the ancient turf of this testing ground for thoroughbreds.' Beyond Horse Haven is the Oklahoma training track, which is used for morning workouts and which also contains a jumping course. Directly across East Avenue are the sales stables of the Fasig Tipton Company, scene of the annual yearling auctions. Held several evenings during the race meeting, the auctions bring together a heterogeneous gathering ranging from socialites in evening dress to racetrack 'swipes,' come to witness the bidding on future champions and 'also-rans.'

Most colorful feature of the Saratoga track is the custom of watching the thoroughbreds being saddled just before post time under towering elms in a large natural paddock. Among annual renewals of traditional races run each August are the Travers, dating back to 1869 and known as the 'laurel wreath of the turf,' and the Hopeful, a $60,000 futurity test for two-year-olds. The colors of practically every prominent racing stable in the United States and Canada are represented in stake events.

8. YADDO (*grounds always open*), Union Ave., ¼ mile SE. of the race track, is a private estate dedicated to hospitality for creative artists. The land was first settled by Jacobus Barhyte in 1784. The increasing number of guests who came to partake of his notable trout dinners made necessary the erection of more commodious quarters in 1820. Edgar Allan Poe was a visitor at Barhyte's in 1843 and is said to have written the first draft of *The Raven* during his sojourn.

The estate, which includes 500 acres of land and four lakes, was later purchased and occupied by the Spencer Trasks; it was their young daughter Christina who gave it its name, which she said rhymed with shadow and 'made poetry.'

The landscaped grounds, hidden from the road by a dense wood, are ornamented with memorial statues, fountains, and a columned pergola. An Italian garden with more than 100 varieties of roses is at its best in June and early July. On a gentle slope in the background are sequestered studios and the Spencer Trask Mansion, a bulky, rock-cut stone building with tower and parapet suggestive of Norman architecture.

After the death of their children, Mr. and Mrs.Trask established the estate as a place where creative artists might 'find the Sacred Fire and light their torches at its flame.' The corporation of Yaddo was formed in 1922 and the first group of artists came in 1926. Among contemporary writers who have worked at Yaddo are Josephine Herbst, Lola Ridge, Evelyn Scott, Albert Halper, Newton Arvin, Raymond Holden, Louis Adamic, and Malcolm Cowley.

SARATOGA SPRINGS RESERVATION

The SARATOGA SPRINGS RESERVATION, a 1,300-acre tract between South Broadway and Ballston Ave., south of the Avenue of Pines, comprises the Washington and Lincoln Baths, a newer group of Georgian Colonial buildings completed in 1935–6, and Geyser Park.

9. The WASHINGTON BATHS (*open* 8–5 *weekdays; treatments*, $1.50–$3), S.Broadway at the Avenue of Pines, were among the first to provide facilities for mineral water treatments. The single-story structure of half-timber and stucco marks the northern boundary of the Reservation. The wings are equipped with electric bath cabinets, Turkish baths, and Baruch control tables. There are 108 rooms for natural mineral water baths.

10.The LINCOLN BATHS (*open* 8–5 *weekdays; treatments* $1.25–$1.50), S.Broadway directly S. of the Washington Baths, were erected in 1930. The two-story building is designed in a modified Renaissance style. The grounds are uniformly landscaped with evergreens, shrubs, and walks. There are 10 electric bath cabinets and four Baruch control tables, as well as extensive facilities for mineral water baths.

The AVENUE OF PINES, a one-mile stretch of macadamized road

flanked by a thick canopy of pine trees, leads from S.Broadway to the newer section of the spa. Bridle paths parallel the road.

11. The BOTTLING PLANT (*open 8–5 daily*), corner of Marrin and Ballston Aves., is of red brick in the Georgian Colonial style. Here are bottled the four most widely used waters, Hathorn, Coesa, Geyser, and State Seal. The first three are sparkling and highly mineralized: Hathorn is highly laxative, Coesa less so but valuable in mild cases of catarrh of the digestive tract; Geyser, a table water, is anti-acid and a digestive aid. State Seal is non-sparkling, non-mineral, and approximates distilled water. Visitors watch the bottling processes from a platform.

12. The SIMON BARUCH RESEARCH INSTITUTE (*not open to public*), S. of Marrin Ave. at traffic oval, was named for Dr.Simon Baruch, developer of the Saratoga system of cardiac therapy, and houses the laboratories, a library, a little theater, an auditorium, and the administration offices of the entire spa. It is here that experiments are conducted in an effort to discover new ways to utilize mineral waters in the treatment of disease, as well as to explain the origin and efficacy of the waters.

Built of Harvard brick with limestone trim and high, steep slate hipped roofs, the structure is Georgian in style. The dominant feature is a Roman Doric portico with pediment. Open arcades lead to end pavilions on both sides. The group of buildings facing the esplanade, of which the institute is one, was designed by Joseph H. Freedlander.

13. The HALL OF SPRINGS (*open 9–9 daily, adm. free, 10¢ for water*), directly across the esplanade, balances the Baruch Institute and harmonizes in exterior design. In the interior, the limestone walls are broken by 16 Casota limestone columns rising from the main floor to the mezzanine. From the ceiling of the main hall are suspended three great silver and crystal chandeliers. At the fountains, Geyser, Hathorn, and Coesa waters are served. Concerts are given during the summer season.

14. The ROOSEVELT BATHS (*open 8–5 weekdays; treatments by appointment*, $3), S. of the Institute and the Hall of Springs, complete the group along the esplanade. Georgian in style, with entrance loggias, the two one-story red brick buildings embody the most modern advances in curative work, and are so planned that wings can be added to increase their capacity to any desired extent.

The East House has 20 private mineral bathrooms. Some of the rooms have especially designed apparatus with which crippled patients are lifted in and out of tubs. Besides the usual hydrotherapy and electrotherapy sections, the East House has a mudpack section, in which mud of exceptional properties and heat-retaining quality found on the reservation is used for baths. The West House contains 40 mineral bathrooms; in the south wing are the inhalation and mechanotherapy sections.

15. The RECREATION UNIT (*open 9–9 daily; inner court 25¢*), S. of Marrin Ave., is a symmetrical group of four buildings in the Georgian Colonial style surrounding an interior court 150 feet by 220 feet. The swimming pool (*adults 75¢; children under 16, 35¢; Aug. $1 and 50¢; lessons $2 per hr.*) contains filtered and heated water. A water sports program is presented occasionally during the season. Directly across from the admin-

istration building is a gymnasium (*adm.* 25¢; *suit* 50¢), with complete units for men and women. On the north side is the bathhouse. There are also eight tennis courts, facilities for archery (75¢ *per hr.*), and a nine-hole therapeutic golf course designed to provide medically approved exercise.

16. The GIDEON PUTNAM HOTEL, Marrin Ave. N. of the Recreation Unit, named in honor of Saratoga's pioneer hotel builder, was erected by the Saratoga Springs Authority but is privately operated. It comprises fewer than 100 rooms. Designed in the Georgian Colonial style by Marcus T. Reynolds, the structure is of red brick with white wood trim. Its main feature is the front loggia with six Corinthian columns rising three stories and supporting a roof terrace. Murals depict early Saratoga events and scenes from the spa; the style of the furnishings and decorations is extremely modern.

The GEYSER PARK section of the spa lies south of the bottling plant. The park is skillfully landscaped without formality. Its beauty is enhanced by the tumbling waters of Geyser Creek, which winds through growths of conifers and birches. Miles of shaded walks and bridle paths lead through groves and vales and past spouting springs.

17. HAYES SPRING and ISLAND SPOUTER are west of the concrete bridge spanning Geyser Creek. On the knoll above the fountain is a summer house available for luncheon parties. A footpath leads to the Champion Geyser and the falls of Geyser Creek.

18. ORINDA SPRING, N. of Hayes Spring, with covered picnic site opposite, is a secluded spot in a rustic setting.

19. The water of KARISTA SPRING, S. of Hayes Spring, tastes somewhat of iron and is not highly gaseous.

20. FERNDALE GLEN, on the east bank of Geyser Brook, is a winding lane with small rustic bridges crossing the narrow brooklet which the path follows. It ends at a natural non-mineralized spring at the summit of a knoll. The path is shaded by a canopy of giant trees and bordered with ferns and flowers.

21. The NEW YORK STATE TREE NURSERY (*always open*), Marrin Ave. E. of the Gideon Putnam Hotel, is the largest nursery of its type in the United States. The project, started under the auspices of the New York State Conservation Department at Coesa Spring in 1910, now embraces a 230-acre plot with an average of 65,000,000 seedlings annually, which are marketed commercially and used to reforest idle lands in the State. Young trees can be obtained for the reforestation of private lands in the State at little or no cost.

POINTS OF INTEREST IN ENVIRONS

Saratoga Lake, 4 *m.*; Grant Cottage, 9.1 *m.*; Lake George, 28 *m.* (*see Tour* 21). Saratoga Monument, Schuylerville, 10.6 *m.*; Stark's Knob, 11.4 *m.*; Saratoga Battlefield, 20.1 *m.* (*see Tour* 22).

Schenectady

Railroad Station: Wall and Liberty Sts. for New York Central Systems.
Bus Stations: 26 Erie Blvd. for Greyhound Lines, Champlain Coach Lines, Interstate Busses Corp., and interurban lines; Hotel Mohawk, 134 Broadway, for Martz Lines; 512 State St. for Schenectady Railway Co. interurban cars and busses.
Streetcars and busses: Fare 10¢, 3 tokens for 25¢.
Taxis: 25¢ minimum, increasing by zones.
Airport: 3 m. N. of city on State 50, no scheduled service; local flights $1.25 up.

Accommodations: 5 hotels; boarding houses, tourist homes.

Information Service: Chamber of Commerce, 246 State St.; Schenectady Automobile Club, 8 State St.; Secretary, Union College, Union St. opposite Nott Terrace.

Radio Station: WGY (790 kc.), WGEA (9530 kc.), WGEO (9550 kc.).
Theaters and Motion Picture Houses: Occasional road shows in Erie Theater, 277 State St.; Civic Playhouse, 12 S.Church St., and Mountebanks Theater, Union College, amateur. 10 motion picture houses.
Golf: Municipal course, Oregon Ave. between Union St. and Consaul Rd., 18 holes; greens fee, 50¢ weekdays, 75¢ Sun. and holidays.
Tennis: Central Park, Central Pkwy. opposite Wright Ave., and Riverside Park, river front between Washington and Ingersoll Aves., free.
Swimming: Central Park, free.
Baseball: Central Park, semi-professional, State league.

Annual Event: Mohawk Drama Festival, Union College, July–Aug.

SCHENECTADY (220 alt.,95,692 pop.), on the Mohawk River, retains, with its modern industries and educational institutions, many evidences of its Dutch and English background.

The business section, clustered between State Street hill and the Mohawk River, is housed in severe brick and granite buildings three and four stories high, varied by the ornateness of theater and modern store fronts. Erie Boulevard, the filled and macadamized bed of the old Erie Canal, crosses State Street in the heart of the business district. Two blocks south looms the General Electric plant, a separate city, so to speak, of red brick and concrete buildings stretching away for more than a mile, with blue and gold and purple lights playing from a thousand windows; of long, high-ceilinged workshops, of aerials, steel masts, and giant stacks, with the GE sign, its 20-foot scrolled initials in a gold-lit circle, a bold crest against the night sky. North from the same intersection, extending to the northwest water front, lie the half dozen short, shaded streets of Colonial Schenectady, where old elms cast fretworks of shadow on yellow brick and white clapboarded houses with high gables and dormer windows. Along the cross streets of the upper State Street section two-family houses huddle in **regi-**

316

mented rows, monuments of the rapid industrial expansion between 1886 and 1920. East on Union Street, the sedate, parklike campus of Union College forms the boundary of a salaried middle-class residential section extending eastward beyond the city line.

Two of Schenectady's racial groups occupy separate districts. The Italians are concentrated around the locomotive works at the northern end of Erie Boulevard. The Poles are settled principally on Mont Pleasant in a tight community with its own social life, language, religion, and customs. Even the second and third generations cling to this transplanted culture while they rise in the city's business and professional life. The large German population, although held together by fraternal organizations and a Turnverein widely recognized for the excellence of its athletic units and its choral society, lacks the geographical homogeneity of the Italians and the Poles.

The economic life of the city is principally dependent upon the plants of the General Electric Company and the American Locomotive Company. Print shops, the manufacture of ice cream and of athletic equipment, insulator factories, and Union College play a lesser role. Emphasis on scientific research in the General Electric laboratories, among other factors, results in an exceptionally high percentage—about 6 per cent—of college graduates in the population, among them men of national and international repute.

The Mohawk Indians called the present city site *Schonowe* (big flats). The Indian original of the name Schenectady (at the end of the pine plains) referred to the sites of both Albany and Schenectady as the termini of the aboriginal portage between the Hudson and Mohawk Rivers. In 1662 Arent Van Curler, with a small group of Dutchmen, emigrated from Albany to the *Groote Vlachte* (Dutch, big flats) and made formal application to the governor for permission to purchase the land from the Indians. The application made its final appeal for the necessary permission in its postscript: 'P.S. If your Honor falls short three or four Muds [2.75 bushels] of oats as feed for your Honor's horses, please command me to supply your Honor with the same from my small store.'

In order to preserve for the residents of Beverwyck (Albany) their monopoly of the lucrative fur trade, Peter Stuyvesant granted the right to purchase land but coupled with it the restriction that none of the settlers should trade with the Indians. The prohibition failed to work: the villagers developed the art of 'bushrunning,' i.e., journeying upstream to bargain with the Indians for their best furs, thereby beating Albany traders to the market; and this illegal trade flourished for nearly 70 years.

The English seizure of the colony in 1664 had little effect on the village. The communal plan of living was followed, with garden lands along the river shore and on the islands held in common fief. In 1670 the magistrates purchased from the Indians the remainder of the valley flat lands, paying them 2,400 guilders' worth of white wampum, 6 coats, 30 bars of lead, and 9 bags of powder, with a rundlet of brandy thrown in. Later the Indians contended that though 'there are writings made of a sale of land,' yet 'it was never sold, but only the grasse . . . they have only bought the

Grasse and now are going to live upon it, but they ought to pay for the land as well as the Grasse.' The governor, however, upheld the villagers, informing the chiefs that 'it is the custom of the Government and amongst Christians when they sell the Grasse to sell the land allso.'

The Schenectady Patent covering this purchase, granted by Governor Thomas Dongan in 1684, was so framed that it became a source of trouble, discontent, and mismanagement for more than 100 years. Three of the five trustees were killed in the massacre of 1690; one left Schenectady; and the fifth, who controlled the lands for a quarter of a century, was an early dictator, acting as trustee for the town land but refusing to account for his actions.

Despite the insecurity of existence on the edge of a territory open to attack by the Indians and French and subject to the humors of Iroquois allies and English overlords, new settlers came and a few were bold enough to build their cabins farther west in the wilderness, beyond the protection of the stockade. A Dutch Reformed church society was organized in 1670; in 1682 Alexander Glen financed the building of the first church edifice, the sixth in the province, at the junction of State, Church, and Water Streets. The first resident minister, Domine Petrus Thessehenmaecker, arrived in 1683.

On the night of February 8, 1690, Schenectady suffered its worst disaster. A French and Indian force arrived at the settlement before midnight. According to local tradition, they found the stockade gate swung open with crude snowmen propped in the center of the passageway. Within an hour 60 of the inhabitants were slain, among them Domine Thessehenmaecker and three of the trustees. Seventy-eight of the 80 houses were burned. Twenty-seven villagers were dragged off to Canada. Forty horses were loaded and driven off. As Peter Schuyler, mayor of Albany, wrote a few days after the event, 'the cruelties committed at sd. Place no Penn can write nor Tongue expresse.' Symon Schermerhorn, wounded in one leg, hurried down the valley warning the other settlers, and reached Albany in six hours. The French escaped with only two men killed, though during the long hurried dash through the northern wilderness they abandoned much of the booty.

The massacre sent a shiver of fear through the English Colonies. Entire abandonment of the settlement at Schenectady was seriously considered. In accordance with the advice of the Mohawk, a new fort was built at the edge of the river (now the eastern end of the Western Gateway Bridge), but many of the survivors had lost heart and moved back to Albany or New York. In 1695 there were only 28 houses within the stockade and only 215 people in the district between Niskayuna and Hoffmans, a stretch of 15 miles. In 1705 Queen's Fort, named for Queen Anne, was erected at what is now the junction of Front, Ferry, and Green Streets, on the site of two earlier forts. In 1727 the settlers were granted free trade with the Indians; Albany's long monopoly of the fur market was ended, and the Schenectady bushrunners became honest fur-traders.

The first major migration of English into Schenectady began about 1700. In 1710 an Anglican congregation was formed, with infrequent sermons by the Reverend Thomas Barclay of Albany. In 1711 Fort Hunter was built 20 miles upstream. Settlement gradually spread west and north, and Schenectady ceased to be the western outpost of empire and became the eastern trading center of a new frontier. Local boatbuilders began constructing square, flat-bottomed bateaux, which were poled or towed upstream carrying one to five tons of cargo. With warehouses built along its bank, the Binne Kill, a branch of the Mohawk River (now used as the Barge Canal basin), became the center of activity.

In the middle years of the eighteenth century Schenectady had 300 houses in the area which includes the present State, Ferry, Church, Water, Jefferson, Center, and North Streets, and Washington Avenue. Most of the houses were built in the solid Dutch style. The Dutch Reformed Church tower held aloft the town clock. The Presbyterians rented a meeting house. The English began construction of St. George's Episcopal Church in 1759. Indian huts still stood within the stockade, but their domesticated inhabitants were reduced to a social level little better than that of slaves.

The shadow of French and Indian raids vanished with the Treaty of Paris in 1763. In 1765 the village was granted a borough charter and its dependence on Albany was ended. Expanding trade created a new aristocracy. When the Revolution came, most of the tenant farmers sided with the rebels; the majority of the landowners joined the Tory ranks, serving beside the loyal Iroquois in periodic raids on the Mohawk and Schoharie Valleys. Schenectady again became a center of warfare. A Committee of Safety was organized in 1775, and five local companies of Minute Men were formed to become units of the First New York Regiment of the Line, one of the best outfits in Washington's army.

Men—and boys—from Schenectady fought at Saratoga, at Newtown, at Stony Point, and at Yorktown. With the Mohawk and Schoharie Valleys forming the principal granary of the Colonial Army, Schenectady itself was of strategic importance in the war and became an important shipping center. The Durham boat, with a capacity of 15 to 20 tons, a strong, broad, flat-bottomed craft with straight sides, decks fore and aft, and sail rigging, was developed during the war period and was built exclusively in shipyards that sprang up along the town's water front. The first packet boats, similar to the Durhams but fitted out for 30 passengers and a little cargo, began trips up-river in the last year of the war: 'two days to Utica; 13 hours back.'

After the Revolutionary War, Schenectady remained a shipping center for the great western migration. The improved cart road between Schenectady and Albany was used for a daily stagecoach service after 1793, and other roads were extended westward. In the heyday of the turnpike era 300 people were engaged in carting goods to and from Albany.

In 1795, mainly as the result of the efforts of Philip Schuyler of Albany and the Reverend Dirck Romeyn of Schenectady, a charter was granted to Union College, the name symbolizing the joining of several religious denominations in a common effort for higher education. On March 26, 1798, Schenectady was granted a city charter. Joseph C. Yates, son of the chair-

man of the Committee of Safety, was appointed the first mayor. The alder-
men organized a fire department, passed laws controlling wood-cutting on
common lands and regulating the behavior of Negro slaves, and ordained
that pigs should wear rings in their noses to prevent them from tearing up
the streets.

After the completion of the Erie Canal in 1825, Schenectady lost much
of its importance as a river port; the day of the Binne Kill was over. In
1831 the city, with a population of 8,900, was an aggregation of streets
three and four blocks long, with square frame hotels along the towpath, a
half dozen saloons for 'canawlers,' the Dutch Colonial houses in their river
corner, and the gray stone buildings of Union College 'on the hill.' For
years Schenectady was affectionately called 'Old Dorp.' Its chief occupation was the growing of broom corn and the manufacture of brooms.

On September 24, 1831, the *De Witt Clinton* made its first trip from Albany to Schenectady on the Mohawk & Hudson Railroad. For several
years thereafter Schenectady was an important railroad center, with short
lines branching out to Saratoga, Utica, and Troy. But as soon as most of
these roads were combined with others westward to form the New York
Central, Schenectady became just another stop on the New York-Buffalo
run.

It was during this early period of railroad development, in 1848, that the
first locomotive factory, financed by local capital, was organized. Under
the influence of three generations of the Ellis family, the plant became one
of the largest locomotive works in the United States. For half a century it
was Schenectady's largest industry, familiarly known as 'The Big Shop.'
In 1901 the plant was taken over by the American Locomotive Company.

In 1886 Thomas A. Edison bought the two uncompleted and abandoned
factory buildings of the McQueen locomotive plant in Schenectady and
moved his small electric machine works from New York City. With this
event Schenectady entered upon its modern phase as an industrial city. In
1892 the Edison Company was consolidated with the Thompson-Huston
Company of Lynn, Massachusetts, to form the General Electric Company.
Schenectady was designated as the headquarters of the new corporation in
1894. In 1907, with a population of 65,000, it was granted a second-class
city charter. Schenectady became the city that 'lights and hauls the
world.' It has remained primarily a two-industry town.

Irish settled in the city after the construction of the Erie Canal. Italian
laborers were imported in the 1870's to build the West Shore Railroad.
The first Polish families to settle here were refugees from the Polish na-
tionalist revolution of 1879. The rapid increase in population after 1886
consisted in large part of further additions to these three immigrant
groups.

In 1911 Schenectady caught the attention of students of economics and
politics by electing George R. Lunn, pastor of the First Reformed Church,
mayor on a Socialist ticket. Under his administration Charles P. Steinmetz, the electrical wizard, served as member of the Board of Education
and president of the Common Council. In 1935 Schenectady adopted the
city manager form of government.

POINTS OF INTEREST

1. The GENERAL ELECTRIC PLANT (*open; tours* 10:30 *and* 3, *Mon.-Fri.*), 1 River Road, has 360 buildings on 670 acres housing factories, broadcasting studios, the general offices of the company, and its principal research laboratories. The red brick, gray concrete, and corrugated sheet metal structures are strung out along Works Avenue. Most of the local production is of heavy equipment for the generation, transmission, and control of electrical energy; but some consumer products are also manufactured, especially refrigerators, induction motors, and radio transmitter apparatus. Many nationally known scientists have worked in the laboratories: Willis R. Whitney, originator of the metalized filament lamp; Elihu Thomson, pioneer in arc lighting; William D. Coolidge, inventor of ductile tungsten, the Coolidge X-ray tube, and the first high-power cathode ray tubes; W.L.R.Emmet, whose work in the development of turbine generators made possible the electrical propulsion of ships; Irving Langmuir, winner of the Nobel Prize for chemistry in 1932, who developed the gas-filled incandescent lamp, atomic-hydrogen welding, and the high-powered vacuum tube; E.F.W.Alexanderson, radio pioneer; and Charles Proteus Steinmetz, dynamic mathematical genius, whose name is closely associated with that of the company.

The General Electric Company is noted for its excellent labor relations; to its employees it has been known as the 'generous electric company' and 'grandfather.' A mutual benefit association, a profit-sharing plan, and a company union were established in the plant; and the company has encouraged workers to own their homes. In 1937 the company recognized the United Electrical, Radio, and Machine Workers Union as the exclusive bargaining agency for its employees.

In its research laboratories the company maintains the 'House of Magic,' an exhibit of new and spectacular developments in the realm of electricity. Large groups may arrange for demonstrations.

The WGY STUDIOS (*open* 9–5 *daily, evenings by appointment*), outside the factory gates, are housed in a red brick and steel building, with the north wall of glass brick. The design of the structure, erected in 1938, Harrison and Fouilhoux, architects, is in the modern trend. WGY, a unit of the red network of the National Broadcasting Company, broadcast its first program on February 20, 1922. In the building also are the studios of WGEA and WGEO, the short-wave stations through which the polar expeditions of Byrd and Amundsen communicated with the world.

2. The WESTERN GATEWAY BRIDGE, State St. and Washington

KEY FOR SCHENECTADY MAP

1.General Electric Plant 2.Western Gateway Bridge 3.Robert Sanders Home 4.Schenectady County Historical Society Building 5.Mohawk Club 6.Dutch Reformed Church 7.Abraham Yates House 8.St.George's Episcopal Church 9.Indian Statue 10.Governor Yates House 11.Brouwer-Rosa House 12.Schenectady City Hall 13.Schonowee Village 14.Union College 15.Steinmetz House 16.American Locomotive Plant

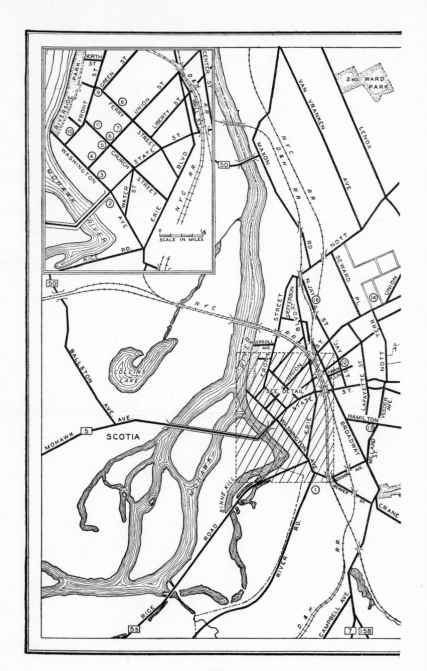

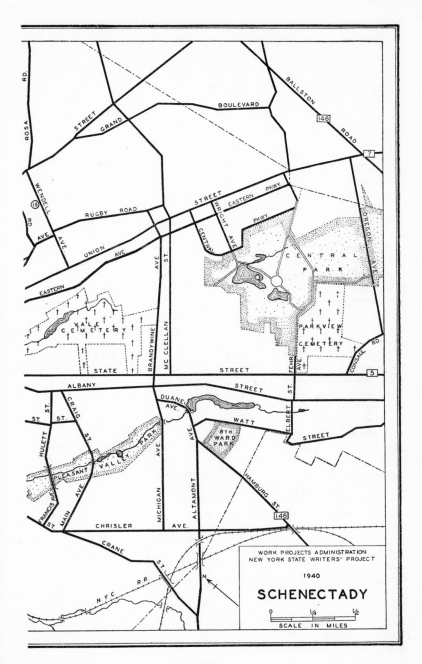

WORK PROJECTS ADMINISTRATION
NEW YORK STATE WRITERS' PROJECT

1940

SCHENECTADY

SCALE IN MILES

Ave., opened to traffic in 1926, spans the Mohawk River between Schenectady and Scotia (*see Tour* 11). Built entirely of reinforced concrete, supported by a series of piers and graceful arches, it clings low to the land and water.

3. The ROBERT SANDERS HOME (*private*), 43–45 Washington Ave., was built about 1750. Its brick walls are painted white with light gray trim at the windows and the cornice. Three high stories, with belt courses at the second and third floors, many 12-pane windows, and an arched, fanlighted doorway white against the faded brick, create a severe, dignified exterior. The heavy bracketed cornice is of later date. The house was once used as the quarters of the Schenectady Female Academy.

4. The SCHENECTADY COUNTY HISTORICAL SOCIETY BUILD–ING (*open* 10–12, 2–5 *weekdays*), 13 Union St., a two-story, yellow-painted brick structure, contains items identified with pre-Revolutionary, Revolutionary, and Civil War times, as well as articles illustrative of the growth and development of the city. A large mass of genealogical data on families of Schenectady and vicinity is on file.

5. The MOHAWK CLUB (*private*), NW. corner of Union and Church Sts., a three-story, vine-covered gray stone building, occupied by a leading social organization, stands on a site of historical interest. Purchased from the Indians in 1661 by Arent Van Curler, who is said to have erected a home here, the plot was within the original stockade built as a protection against Indian attacks. The present building was bought in 1817 to house the Mohawk National Bank; from 1872 to 1903 it was occupied by the Union Classical Institute, predecessor of the city's public high schools.

6. The DUTCH REFORMED CHURCH, NE. corner of Union and Church Sts., was built in 1862 from plans drawn by Edward Tuckerman Potter. The stone structure, Gothic Revival in design, is in the form of an L, with a square tower surmounted by a spire. The roof is of slate in variegated colors arranged in ornamental design. A 30-by-40-foot walnut-and-plate-glass screen separates the church and the consistory room. Four stained glass windows in the tower bear representations of the four earlier church buildings, the first of which was erected in 1682; and a rose window in the church proper displays the arms of the Dutch Reformed Church.

7. The ABRAHAM YATES HOUSE (*private*), 109 Union St., erected between 1720 and 1730 and still in the possession of descendants of the original owner, is one of the oldest homes in the city. It is of characteristic Dutch Colonial architecture, with a steep gable facing the street and stepped diagonal brick courses along its rake. The roof is carried over a lean-to in the rear; the side walls are finished with clapboards.

8. ST. GEORGE'S EPISCOPAL CHURCH, N. Ferry St. between Union and Front Sts., begun in 1759 and completed in 1766, is the oldest church in the Mohawk Valley. It is a stately, ivy-clad structure, built of gray limestone, with a gray slate hipped roof. A tall, finely proportioned wooden steeple surmounts the tower at the front entrance. The delicate Georgian Colonial detail of the exterior suggests the dignified and simple appointments within. Especially notable are the long 60-paned double hung windows with their arched heading.

During the first months of the Revolution, St.George's, closely associated with the English, was forced to close its doors. At the end of the war, inhabited by stray animals, the windows and doors broken, it was gradually restored to its earlier condition; but not until 1798 were regular services resumed. According to local tradition, unauthenticated by historical evidence, Walter Butler, leader of the Indians and Tories and hated enemy of the Schenectady Whigs, was secretly buried beneath St.George's Church in 1781.

9. The INDIAN STATUE, Front and N.Ferry Sts., enclosed in a circular iron fence, marks the site of Queen's Fort, erected in 1705 and used in connection with the barracks that extended along the east side of North Ferry Street almost to Union Street. During the Revolution the fort was torn down and the land sold, and Schenectady's career as a fortified town came to an end.

10. The GOVERNOR YATES HOUSE (*private*), 17 Front St., has two wings. The smaller dates from 1735; the other, of later but unknown date, was originally gambrel-roofed but has been so altered that it is now three full stories high. The house is built of brick painted gray, with white stone trim and green blinds. The present entrance replaces one that was demolished in 1902. The original doorway of the smaller wing is charming in its delicacy of detail. The larger unit was the home of Joseph C. Yates (1788–1837), first resident of the Mohawk Valley to become governor of New York.

11. The BROUWER–ROSA HOUSE (*private*), 14 N.Church St., is a two-story white frame house with wide, square-cut boards forming the front siding. The 12-pane windows have solid wood blinds painted an attractive shade of green. Electrified old wrought-iron lamps adorn the front entrance.

The original house was built by Hendrick Brouwer between 1690 and 1710 and remained in the family until 1795, by which time the structure was a fabrication of three Dutch cottages. About the latter year, James Rosa altered the two cottages fronting on Church Street to present the post-Colonial appearance of today; the third, or rear cottage, remains unaltered.

12. The SCHENECTADY CITY HALL, Jay St. between Liberty and Franklin Sts., is one of the outstanding modern buildings in the city. Designed by John M. Ryder in collaboration with McKim, Mead and White and built in 1931, the rectangular red brick structure with marble trim and slate roof is in the Georgian Colonial style. A white marble spiral stair graces the interior.

13. SCHONOWEE VILLAGE, Hamilton and Millard Sts., a group of five three- and four-story red brick apartment buildings of modern design, is a PWA slum clearance project developed with the co-operation of the Municipal Housing Authority. Accommodations for 219 familes are provided in 2-, 3-, 4-, and 5-room apartments renting for $6.50 a room. Facilities include a playground, a play room, and a game room. The tenants represent nearly every form of employment in the city, with clerks and business and factory workers composing the largest groups. The village was designed by R.L.Bowen with J.W.Montross associated.

14. UNION COLLEGE, Union St. opposite Nott Terrace, pioneer institution, second incorporated college in New York State, 'mother of college fraternities,' where 90 college presidents studied and worked, was chartered in 1795. The 100-acre campus, with broad lawns, giant elms, and shrub rows, is a sylvan retreat in the midst of a large industrial city. The U-shaped main quadrangle, with the old college dormitories at the two ends, represents part of the unique campus plan designed in 1813 by Joseph Jacques Ramée, French architect.

The first century of the history of the college was dominated by the figure of Eliphalet Nott, its president for 62 years. Nott attracted students from every section of the country and determined Union's permanent character by combining the liberal arts with science and engineering. Since 1934, under Dixon Ryan Fox, the social studies have been emphasized with the near-by State government in Albany as a 'laboratory.' The 800 students and 80 faculty members are grouped in four divisions: literature, social studies, science, and engineering. The lasting tradition of Union College is one of close companionship between faculty and students; a large number of both live on the campus.

Kappa Alpha, the oldest Greek letter college fraternity, was founded at Union in 1825; Sigma Phi, Delta Phi, Psi Upsilon, Chi Psi, and Theta Delta Chi followed in quick succession. The first chapter of Phi Beta Kappa in New York State was established at Union in 1817. William Henry Seward, Lincoln's Secretary of State, graduated from Union in 1820; Robert Toombs, Secretary of State for the Confederacy, graduated eight years later; Chester A. Arthur, 21st President of the United States, graduated in 1848.

Union College, though financially and administratively independent, is associated with the Albany Medical College, the Albany Law School, the Albany College of Pharmacy, and the Dudley Observatory in Union University.

SOUTH COLLEGE, built in 1814, with faculty homes in the two wings and student dormitories in the rest of the building, typifies Union post-Colonial architecture: dark, stucco-covered brick walls with white cement pilasters.

The NOTT MEMORIAL LIBRARY (*open*), in the center of the main quadrangle, is an unusual ten-sided building erected in 1858–76. The design, by Edward Tuckerman Potter, class of 1853, pupil of Richard Upjohn, is based on that of the Baptistry at Pisa. It is an excellent example of Victorian Gothic with some Lombard details. It occupies the site intended by Ramée for a classical rotunda.

The MEMORIAL CHAPEL is a modern adaption of the Classical Revival style treated with unusual simplicity and directness. The side elevations recall the design of the earlier college buildings; the front has a pedimented portico. The building was erected in 1924 with funds subscribed by the college community and the public to commemorate the Union boys who died in the World War.

JACKSON'S GARDEN, entrance through the Kappa Alpha Memorial Gateway between North Colonnade and the General Engineering Building, about 100 years old, is widely known for its beauty. One part is carefully landscaped in formal flower beds, and the rest is allowed to grow in a natural wildness, the quiet broken only by 'the brook that bounds through old Union's grounds.'

15. STEINMETZ PARK, 1297 Wendell Ave., is the site of the last home of Charles Proteus Steinmetz (1865–1923), prominent engineer who made invaluable contributions in the fields of alternating current, electromagnetism, and lightning phenomena. He was associated with the General Electric Company from 1892 until his death and was professor of electrical engineering in Union College, 1902–23. Within the house were the laboratories, libraries, and workshop where Dr.Steinmetz did much of his research. The house, which after his death was opened to the public, was torn down in 1944. A suitably inscribed tablet on a boulder commemorates this remarkable man.

16. The AMERICAN LOCOMOTIVE PLANT (*open to technical visitors; permits at N.Jay St. office*), junction of Erie Blvd., Nott and N.Jay Sts., is one of the largest manufacturers of steam and oil-electric locomotives in the United States. The factories, foundries, laboratories, and office buildings are long, low structures of brick or corrugated metal enveloped in bituminous dust and smoke.

The plant was established in 1848, re-organized in 1851, and in 1901 taken over by the American Locomotive Company. It is now the company's main unit.

POINTS OF INTEREST IN ENVIRONS

Glen-Sanders House and Alexander Glen House, 1 *m*. (*see Tour* 11). Mabie House, 6.3 *m*. (*see Tour* 12).

Syracuse

Railroad Stations: 807 Erie Blvd.E. for New York Central System; 225 W.Jefferson St. for Delaware, Lackawanna & Western R.R.
Bus Stations: W.Onondaga and S.Clinton Sts. for Greyhound Lines; Yates Hotel, Washington and Montgomery Sts., for Martz Coach Lines; 114 W.Genesee St. for Great Eastern System and Oswego Motor Lines.
Airport: 7 m. W. on State 173 for American Airlines; 4 planes daily.
Taxis: 35¢ minimum; zone system.

Accommodations: 11 hotels; boarding houses, tourist homes. Kirk Park, 1000 South Ave., trailer camp, 50¢ a day, $1.50 a week; running water, community stove, playgrounds.

Information Service: Chamber of Commerce, 351 S.Warren St.; Syracuse Auto Club, Onondaga Hotel, Jefferson and Warren Sts.

Radio Stations: WFBL (1360 kc.); WSYU (570 kc.); WOLF (1500 kc.).
Theaters and Motion Picture Houses: Civic Playhouse, 572 S.Salina St., productions by Syracuse University; 20 motion picture houses.
Baseball: Municipal stadium, 2d North St. and Hiawatha Blvd., home of the Syracuse Chiefs of the International League.
Hockey: Coliseum, State Fair Grounds, home of the Syracuse Stars of the International-American League.
Golf: Burnet Park, 321 S.Wilbur St., and Sunnycrest Park, 600 Teall Ave., 9 holes, 25¢, 35¢; Brooklawn, 1 m. N. on Thompson Rd., 9 holes, 40¢; Lyndon, 7 m. E. on State 5, and Tecumseh Hills, 2 m. SE., 18 holes, 50¢; Stonehedge, 6 m. W. on State 5, 18 holes, 50¢; Drumlins, 2 m. SE., 18 holes, $1, $1.50.
Tennis: City parks, free.
Swimming: City parks, free.

Annual Events: St.Patrick's Day celebration; Italian Day celebration, Aug; New York State Fair, Fair Grounds, Aug.–Sept.; Gemuetlichkeit Celebration, Thanksgiving Day.

SYRACUSE (400 alt.,205,637 pop.), an important commercial and manufacturing city at the approximate geographical center of New York State, occupies the flatlands at the head of Onondaga Lake, its newer residential sections pushing south and east into the valleys between the Onondaga hills.

Clinton Square, the heart of the city, is where nineteenth-century freight and passengers were transferred to canal boats at the Packet Dock. Traversing the square, wide Erie Boulevard, built on the fill of the old Erie Canal, carries the heavy traffic of State 5. The main business district, south of the Square, is dominated by wide Salina Street, with its clattering streetcars, its modern buildings conspicuous among the earlier structures of brick and stone.

From this downtown section the city spreads out into residential district with neighborhood shopping centers. James Street is the exclusive residential thoroughfare; the architectural styles of its homes vary from modified Spanish and Italian to Greek Revival and Queen Anne, from Victorian Gothic to Georgian Colonial. West Genesee Street, part of the original Genesee Turnpike, has undergone many changes since the old red mill was built on the banks of Onondaga Creek. For years a choice residential street, it became a business thoroughfare with the appearance of the automobile.

Some 87 large industries are scattered throughout the city. The principal ones, along Erie Boulevard and the city line and around the lake shore, manufacture typewriters, candles, pottery, gears, electrical and air-conditioning equipment, traffic signals, plated silverware, window fixtures for trains, cast stone building blocks, clothes-pressing machines, and doorknobs. The Solvay Process Company, just west of the city but an integral part of its economic life, produces ammonia, soda ash, oven coke, and their by-products.

Irish and German groups of the third, fourth, and fifth generations constitute more than half of the native population. Since they have merged with the earlier settlers to produce a typical American populace, their old-country traditions have all but disappeared. The Irish still celebrate St.Patrick's Day; the German retain their lodges and singing societies, and the festival of *Gemuetlichkeit* conducted by the Turnverein is still a highlight in the celebration of Thanksgiving.

The later immigrant groups, still bilingual, occupy well-defined districts. The Italians have all but supplanted the Germans on the 'north side' and have their own business section along North State and North Salina Streets. The Poles, attracted to Syracuse by the steel mills, live on the west side. Many of their homes huddle close to the grim plants of the Crucible Steel Company; others occupy a small district near Eastwood. Numerous lodge rooms and churches serve as social centers. The Russians, principally Ukranians, are settled along South State and Harrison Streets. Having but recently migrated, they still keep old country traditions alive. They still worship according to the Orthodox rite and still use the Julian calendar, celebrating Christmas on January 7. On that day the room in which the Christmas feast is held is sprinkled with straw, to simulate the manger in which Christ was born. Priests bless homes by sprinkling each room with holy water. In the Ukranian spring festivals, children and adults perform native dances in bright red, yellow, and green costumes handed down for generations. The Jewish people originally settled within the boundaries of State, E.Genesee, Irving, and Adams Streets, where they established businesses and built homes and synagogues; but as their businesses grew and they became prosperous, they moved their homes and synagogues to outlying districts. The Negroes, numbering about 3,500, live in the old east-central section of the city; very few are home-owners and rentals are low. There are three Negro churches—Baptist, Methodist, and Episcopalian, and Negro chapters of the fraternal orders of Elks, Masons, Knights of Pythias, and Odd Fellows.

In the field of fine arts, the College of Fine Arts of Syracuse University and the Syracuse Museum of Fine Arts exert definite influence; the Associated Artists of Syracuse is the largest and most active of a number of art groups. Morning Musicals, established in 1890, is the largest organization in the field of music. The Music School Settlement gives free instruction to talented children. The German Liederkranz is the best known of a number of music and social organizations among the older established foreign groups. Gone are the days of the old Weiting Opera House, where, during its prime in the late nineteenth century, world premieres and test runs of plays and light operas were held. Today the legitimate stage is kept alive by the efforts of the dramatic group of Syracuse University.

The beginnings and early growth of Syracuse are identified with salt, but a determining factor in the success of the city was the initiative of a succession of 'rugged individualists'—men like James Geddes, Joshua Forman, John Wilkinson, Thomas G. Alvord, and Vivus W. Smith.

What the French soldiers and Jesuits—the first white men to visit the site of Syracuse (1654)—saw, was a swamp. The salt springs were discovered by Father Simon LeMoyne, who reported that the Indians believed the water to be infested by a demon, rendering it fetid. The first white settler was Ephraim Webster, who came from Oriskany in 1786 and opened a trading station near the mouth of Onondaga Creek. Webster won the friendship of the Indians by his courage and his readiness to adopt their ways, even to marrying their daughters. Stories associated with his life are part of the folklore of the region; it is believed that James Fenimore Cooper's character Natty Bumppo owes much to the historical figure of Ephraim Webster. Webster's first Indian wife died shortly after their marriage in 1789. According to tradition, he promised his second Indian wife that he would live with her as long as she kept sober. After 20 years, Webster, reacting to the conventionalizing influences of the already large white settlement, began to desire a white wife and set out to make his Indian spouse drunk. For a long time she resisted every attempt but finally succumbed to the camouflage of milk punch. The next morning she left without uttering a word and soon thereafter died of grief. Webster married a white woman and raised a white family.

While on a hunting trip in Montgomery County, Webster slept in the barn of Major Asa Danforth in Johnstown. Webster's praise of the Onondaga country was so convincing that Major Danforth, his wife, his son Asa,Jr., and Comfort Tyler emigrated, and on May 22, 1788, erected the 'first Christian home' in the county. Asa's brother John followed him and began the manufacture of salt on the lake shore. In 1794 James Geddes settled on the west shore of the lake and in 1796 dug the first salt well in the present township of Geddes. The Indians claimed the springs west of the lake, but they adopted Geddes into their tribe and allowed him to continue to make salt. Other settlers came; little clusters of log houses were built around the scattered salt works along the lake shore, and for 70 years this industry formed the nucleus around which the activities of the communities revolved.

The most important of the salt settlements was Salina, also called Salt Point, now the north section of Syracuse. In 1797 the State took over the salt fields and established a reservation 11 miles long and 9 miles wide to obtain revenue from a tax on salt. Means of evading the duty were soon invented, and salt smuggling flourished.

The chief handicap of the infant industry was lack of adequate transportation facilities. Oxen wallowed through marshy land and hauled out salt on stone-boats. In 1804 James Geddes, then a member of the State legislature, interested Governor George Clinton in his plan to sell 250 acres of the State reservation and use the proceeds to build a road to the salt springs. The land, now the central portion of the city of Syracuse, was bought by Abraham Walton for $6,650. It was an unhealthy, almost impassable swamp, but gradually it was drained, cleared, and settled. A gristmill, the 'old red mill,' was built in 1805, a sawmill and tannery soon after; a tavern was opened by a man named Bogardus; and around these grew up the village of Syracuse. Across Walton's land Geddes laid out a 10-mile corduroy road, which later became part of the Genesee Turnpike.

Stimulated by this new utility, the salt industry developed rapidly. In the beginning the brine was dipped or pumped by hand from the springs for boiling. When the surface brine was exhausted, wells were dug and brine was pumped from them through pipes made of logs to 'salt blocks,' where it was boiled in huge kettles. The other method of manufacture was by solar evaporation: brine was exposed to the sun in huge vats and the salt precipitated by evaporation. If it started to rain a bell was rung, a signal for the workers to dash out and cover the vats.

The beginnings of manufacturing in Syracuse go back almost to the first settlements. Thomas Wiard began making wooden plows with iron staves in 1793. After the turn of the century Nicholas Mickles, who came from New England to lay the foundations of a fortune in what was then frontier country, erected the first furnace west of Oneida County. The enterprise, in which Joshua Forman soon had an interest, was known as the Onondaga Furnace; its site is contained within Elmwood Park. It manufactured kettles for the salt works and for the western country, and during the War of 1812 it cast shot for the army.

From the time of the commercial beginnings of the salt industry, the central New York waterways served as principal means of transportation. But these natural water routes were uncertain, difficult, and limited, and portages were slow and expensive. Syracuse salt manufacturers, especially Joshua Forman and James Geddes, were early propagandists on behalf of the Erie Canal project. With the lower freight rates on the canal, the production of salt increased rapidly, reaching a high point of 8,000,000 bushels annually during the Civil War period. Syracuse and Salina, situated on the canal halfway between Albany and Buffalo, and at the junction with the Oswego Canal opened in 1838, became important canal ports.

Salina was incorporated as a village in 1824, Syracuse in 1825. The latter had been known at various times as Bogardus Corners, Milan, Cossit's Corners, and Corinth. The name Syracuse was suggested by John Wilkinson, the first postmaster, who had read a poem describing the ancient Greek city in Sicily, which had also grown around a marsh and salt springs. At the time of incorporation the village had 15 merchants, one newspaper, a fire department, and several small industries.

John Wilkinson served as postmaster from 1820 to 1840 and as assemblyman in 1834 and 1835, and organized the Bank of Syracuse in 1838. His chief service was the construction of railroads radiating out of Syracuse, which gave the salt industry its final stimulus. The Auburn & Syracuse Railroad was opened for traffic in 1838; the Syracuse & Utica in 1839; the Oswego & Syracuse in 1848; the Rochester & Syracuse in 1853. The Syracuse & Binghamton Railroad, opened in 1854, brought coal from the Pennsylvania mines to be used as fuel in the salt fields. The salt industry had another able champion in Thomas G. Alvord, whose zealous efforts in its defense at Albany earned him the sobriquet of 'Old Salt.' He was elected to the assembly in 1845 and became lieutenant governor in 1864.

As early as 1840 leading citizens urged the consolidation of Syracuse and Salina and their incorporation as one city, but old antipathies blocked action. On New Year's Eve 1844, the rivalry culminated in a riot in Siegel's boarding house, which stood on the corner of Washington and Warren Streets. Tradition has it that salt-boilers from Salina descended upon the house to 'break up a party.' Mr.Siegel resented an insulting remark addressed to his wife and shattered the face of one of the intruders with a shotgun. A free-for-all followed, and the militia was called out. The event shocked both villages and negotiations for a city charter began. Terms were settled on January 3, 1848, and the two villages, together with Lodi, were incorporated as the city of Syracuse with a population of 22,000.

The new city was a center of the factional politics and the reform movements that swept across central New York State in the middle of the century. On October 1, 1851, occurred the Jerry Rescue, one of the most dramatic incidents in the antislavery movement. In June 1854, Horace Greeley, Thurlow Weed, and Vivus W. Smith met in Smith's home at the corner of West Onondaga Street and South Avenue in a historic conference, one of a series resulting in the birth of the Republican party. A meeting of the new party in Syracuse in 1859, at which a resolution 'to oppose treason" was adopted, foreshadowed the Civil War.

By 1860 Syracuse had several small foundries, machine shops, and factories producing agricultural implements, boots and shoes, furniture, saddlery, hardware, and silverware. The Irish, who came in large numbers to dig the canal and lay the railroads, remained to man the new factories. The Germans came between 1825 and 1850 and founded several of the industries that made Syracuse noteworthy in the nineteenth century. One group settled in the heart of the salt reservation, at the present village of Liverpool, and developed the willowware industry, which enjoyed wide fame for 50 years. In 1855, Anthony Will, a carpenter who had served his apprenticeship in Bavaria, melted wax over the family cook stove and started the candle industry in Syracuse.

In 1869 Charles Dickens came to the city to give a reading in the Weiting Opera House, stopped at the Syracuse House, and left in his letters a vivid picture of the 'Salt City':

I am here in a most wonderful out-of-the-world place, which looks as if it had begun to be built yesterday, and were going to be imperfectly knocked together with a nail or two the day after tomorrow. I am in the worst inn that ever was seen, and outside is a thaw that places the whole country under water . . .

I have tried all the wines in the house and there are only two wines, for which you pay six shillings a bottle or 15, according as you feel disposed to change the name of the thing you asked for. (The article never changes.) The bill of fare is in French and the principal article is Paeltie de shay! I asked the Irish waiter what this dish was and he said, 'it was the name the steward giv' to oyster patties—the French name.' . . .

We had an old buffalo for supper and an old pig for breakfast and we are going to have I don't know what for dinner at 6. In the public room downstairs, a number of men (speechless) with their feet against window frames, staring out at the window and spitting dolefully at intervals . . . And yet we have taken in considerably over 300 pounds for tomorrow night.

After the Civil War, salt manufacture declined under competition from Canada and Michigan. The central location of Syracuse, its railroads and canals, its access to raw materials, the presence of gypsum, brine, and limestone, ready money, and a large labor supply—all combined to attract varied industries; the acres devoted to salt works became more valuable as factory sites and the old industry was forced out.

John D. Gray moved his shoe factory from Little Falls to Syracuse in 1866. The pottery industry, which dug some of its clay near East Syracuse, was firmly organized in 1871. In the same year William Sweet started the first steel mill in the city. Harry Wiard, descendant of Thomas Wiard, invented the chilling process in plow manufacture, and in 1876 production of the improved plow was begun by the Syracuse Chilled Plow Company.

In 1887 the Smith-Premier, the first typewriter to bear the Smith name, was manufactured in Lyman C. Smith's gun factory on South Clinton Street. Alexander T. Brown, an employee, invented the machine, and Wilbert Smith, brother of Lyman, financed the construction of the model. Today the manufacture of typewriters ranks high among the industries of Syracuse.

H.H.Franklin opened a die-casting shop in 1894. In 1898 John Wilkinson, grandson of the first postmaster of Syracuse, was perfecting an automobile with an air-cooled motor. The facilities of the Franklin foundry were put at his disposal, and in 1902 the first Franklin stock car was turned out. As the automobile industry developed, Syracuse turned to the manufacture of gears and other parts requiring specialized labor skill.

In these years of industrial expansion Syracuse developed the facilities and felicities of modern city life. The first high school building was erected in 1868, the first public hospital was opened in 1870, the first park acquired in 1886. Syracuse University opened its doors in September 1871, and has grown with the city. In 1894 the modern water supply system was opened. Streets were extended and paved. Building went forward steadily and the area of the city was increased. Today Syracuse remains an industrial stronghold surrounded and supported by the rich agricultural area of central New York.

Syracuse established a special school for crippled children in 1930 and a children's court in 1932. Night schools for adults began in 1890; in 1936, under the WPA, 300 teachers provided instruction for 15,000 adults. The Milbank Memorial Fund, providing approximately $450,000 for public health projects during the nine-year period 1923–31, has helped give Syracuse a high rank in health standards.

In 1838 the Syracuse & Utica Railroad laid its tracks along Washington Street, and the New York Central retained the same right-of-way. For almost 100 years, trains, moving at a snail's pace along the street level, spread a pall of smoke and dust, and idle travelers caught intimate glimpes of soot-covered Syracuse, its people, its stores, and its houses. Syracuse was known far and wide as the city where the trains passed through the street. In 1936 the railroad tracks on Washington Street were removed; trains now run on concrete elevated lanes through a less central part of the city.

POINTS OF INTEREST

1. The JERRY RESCUE BUILDING (*not open to public*), NE. corner of Clinton Square, a dingy four-story brick structure, was erected in 1830 as a police station and is now used as a business office. It received its name from the Jerry Rescue incident of 1851.

Jerry, or William Henry, born in slavery in Buncombe County, North Carolina, about 1812, escaped from his owner and reached Syracuse, where he worked in a cooper's shop making salt barrels until discovered by his owner and arrested. An abolitionist group, headed by Dr.Samuel J. May and Gerrit Smith, attacked the police station, intimidated the guards, and rescued Jerry. He was smuggled from house to house for several days and was finally secretly taken to Canada.

2. VANDERBILT SQUARE, E.Washington St. between S.Salina and S.Warren Sts., was named for Commodore Cornelius Vanderbilt, who visited the city with his second bride in 1869. From 1837 on, Syracuse life for many years revolved around this square; the magnet was the railroad station, and the hostelries that grew up around it. In the old station Henry Clay was welcomed on his visit to the State Fair in 1849. Daniel Webster, General Winfield Scott, Louis Kossuth, John Brown, Stephen A. Douglas, and other notables were greeted here. On February 18, 1861, Lincoln, on the way to his inauguration, bowed from a coach platform; on April 26, 1865, his funeral train stopped for 30 minutes.

3. ST.PAUL'S EPISCOPAL CHURCH, SW. corner of Montgomery and E.Fayette Sts., a Victorian Gothic building of limestone erected in 1884, Henry Dudley, architect, is the church home of a congregation organized in 1824. Since that year the congregation has shifted its place of worship three times within an area of two blocks.

4. The ONONDAGA HISTORICAL ASSOCIATION BUILDING (*open* 10–12, 2–5 *Mon.–Fri.*, 10–12 *Sat.*), 311 Montgomery St., is a five-story red brick structure donated by William Kirkpatrick in 1906. It contains many early records, portraits, and printed volumes relating to Onondaga County history.

5. The SYRACUSE PUBLIC LIBRARY (*open 9–9 weekdays, 1–9 Sun.*), 335 Montgomery St., built in 1902, is a limestone, granite, and brick three-story building designed in the Baroque Revival style; the architect was

James A. Randall. The library contains important collections of old manuscripts and early examples of printing, a Whitman collection, and a collection of musical scores.

6. The STATUE OF COLUMBUS, Montgomery St., on the circular plot in the center of St.Mary's Circle, donated by Syracuse Italian societies in 1934, was designed and executed by Lorenzo Baldi, Italian sculptor.

7. The ONONDAGA COUNTY COURTHOUSE, 401 Montgomery St., completed in 1906, is a classical structure of stone and marble covering an entire block. The architect was Archimedes Russell. The murals by William de Leftwich Dodge represent episodes in Onondaga Indian history.

8. The CATHEDRAL OF THE IMMACULATE CONCEPTION, SW. corner of Montgomery and E.Jefferson Sts., was dedicated in 1886 as St.Mary's Church and in 1904 was named the Cathedral Church of the Central New York Roman Catholic Diocese. Of dark weathered Onondaga limestone, the church and the connecting offices are in the Victorian Gothic style.

9. The MIZPAH HOTEL and FIRST BAPTIST CHURCH, 215 E.Jefferson St., erected in 1912, Gordon Wright, architect, is a modern fireproof structure with elaborate tracery, mouldings, pinnacles, and tower, designed in the Perpendicular Gothic style. The church, with a high ceiling and a balcony, occupies the entire plot; the glass ceiling and roof over the platform and organ form the inner open court of the three-story hotel, which is U-shaped in plan. Steel columns supporting the upper structure extend through the church proper.

10. The STATE TOWER OFFICE BUILDING (*tower open*), 201 E.Genesee St., 22 stories high, is the tallest building in the city. Of concrete and steel construction with limestone and terra-cotta facing, it was erected in 1928 at a cost of $1,500,000. It occupies the site of the Bastable Theatre, where Mansfield, Irving, Drew, Terry, Goodwin, Bernhardt, and others gave performances.

11. The WEIGHLOCK BUILDING, 301 Erie Blvd., a two-story gray-painted brick structure with bracketed cornice, was constructed in 1850.

KEY FOR SYRACUSE MAP

1.Jerry Rescue Building 2.Vanderbilt Square 3.St.Paul's Episcopal Church 4. Onondaga Historical Association Building 5.Syracuse Public Library 6.Statue of Columbus 7.Onondaga County Courthouse 8.Cathedral of the Immaculate Conception 9.Mizpah Hotel and First Baptist Church 10.State Tower Office Building 11.Weighlock Building 12.Museum of Fine Arts 13.May Memorial Church 14. Leavenworth Mansion 15.Edward Noyes Westcott Home 16.Harold MacGrath Home 17.Lamson Factory 18.Continental Can Plant 19.L.C.Smith Typewriter Plant 20.E.C.Stearns Plant 21.Republican Tree 22.Remington Rand Typewriter Plant 23.Syracuse Chilled Plow Plant 24.Carrier Corporation Plant 25.Crucible Steel Plant 26.Onondaga Pottery Plant 27.Burnet Park 28.Woodlawn Reservoir and Standpipe 29.Elmwood Park 30.Old Arsenal Site 31.Experimental Station 32.Onondaga Valley Cemetery 33.Will & Baumer Candle Factory 34.Crouse Hinds Plant 35.Temple of the Society of Concord 36.Thornden Park 37.Oakwood Cemetery 38.Syracuse Medical Center 39.The Castle 40.Syracuse University

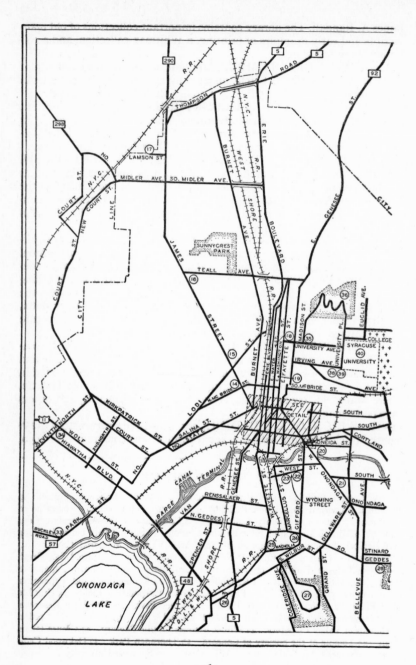

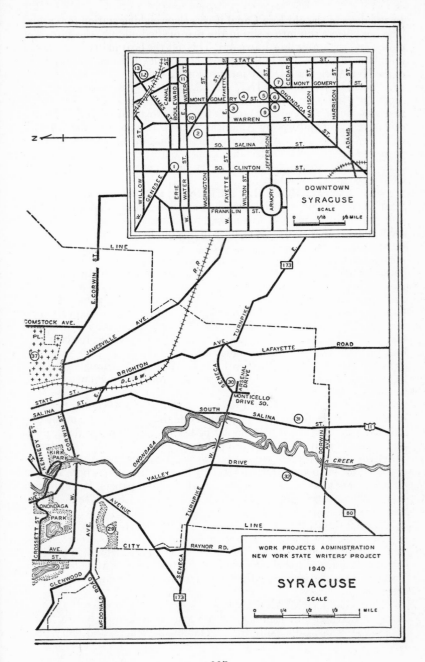

DOWNTOWN
SYRACUSE
SCALE
0   1/16   1/8 MILE

WORK PROJECTS ADMINISTRATION
NEW YORK STATE WRITERS' PROJECT
1940
SYRACUSE
SCALE
0   1/4   1/2   1/3   MILE

In the days of the old Erie Canal it was the weighing station for cargoes. The boats were run into a slip in the rear of the building; the gates were closed and the water was drawn out. This left the boat in dry dock, resting on immense scales. The building now houses the divisional headquarters of the New York State Department of Public Works.

12. The MUSEUM OF FINE ARTS (*open* 12–5:30 *weekdays*, 2–5:30 *Sun.*), 401 James St., organized in 1896 by Dr.George F. Comfort, was the first museum in the United States to form a permanent collection devoted exclusively to paintings by American artists. It also contains a notable collection of porcelains by Adelaide Alsop Robineau; etchings by Whistler; Japanese prints by Hiroshige and Yami; and other paintings and curios. The National Ceramic Exhibition is held here annually from mid-October to mid-November.

13. The MAY MEMORIAL CHURCH, 472 James St., known as the First Unitarian Congregational Society and also as the Church of the Messiah, was built in 1885. It was named in honor of its abolitionist pastor, Dr.Samuel J. May (1797–1871), born in Boston. Before coming to Syracuse he assisted William Ellery Channing in Boston. He was ardent in his support of the woman suffrage and antislavery movements, prominent in the Jerry Rescue, and used his home as a station for the Underground Railroad.

14. The LEAVENWORTH MANSION (*private*), 607 James St., is a Greek Revival structure built in 1842; the full-width front portico has large Ionic columns. General Elias W. Leavenworth (1803–87), born in Canaan, New York, practiced law in Syracuse and served as the city's second mayor before entering upon his military career.

15. In the EDWARD NOYES WESTCOTT HOME (*private*), 826 James St., an unpretentious dwelling, Westcott wrote the popular American novel, *David Harum*.

16. The HAROLD MacGRATH HOME (*private*), 1618 James St., built in 1912 in the English rural style, was at one time a show place of the city. The garden, surrounded by a poplar hedge, contains rock gardens, pools, and shrubbery. In the house are paintings and bric-a-brac collected by MacGrath in his travels around the world and a number of illustrations prepared for his books. Harold MacGrath (1871–1932) was born in Syracuse and served as reporter and columnist on local papers. His numerous books include *Arms and the Woman*, *The Man on the Box*, *The Goose Girl*, and *The Grey Cloak*.

17. The LAMSON FACTORY (*open* 9–4 *Mon.–Fri.*, 9–11 *Sat.*), 200 Lamson St., produces pneumatic tube and conveyor systems. In 1880 William Lamson, to make change for his clerks, cut a croquet ball in half, hollowed out the inside to hold money, and shuttled it across his notions store. From this Yankee idea grew the Lamson conveyor system, widely used in business.

18. The CONTINENTAL CAN PLANT (*open by appointment*), entrance at 1016 E.Water St., established in 1905, manufactures yearly about 200,000,000 cans, principally for vegetables, beverages, and dairy products.

19. The L.C.SMITH TYPEWRITER PLANT (*not open to public*), entrance at 701 E.Washington St., is an eight-story red brick factory. The first Smith-Premier typewriter was manufactured in 1887.

20. The E.C.STEARNS PLANT (*not open to public*), 224 Oneida St., makes power and hand mowers, shell hardware, and foundry material. Established in 1860, the plant first manufactured hollow iron tools and specialties, hollow augers, and saw vises. In the nineties it made the popular 'Yellow Fellow' bicycle.

21. The REPUBLICAN TREE, SW. corner of W.Onondaga St. and South Ave., is the historic elm that shaded the Syracuse editor, Vivus W. Smith, whose home stood near by, Horace Greeley, Thurlow Weed, and William H. Seward, when they met in pre-Civil War years to discuss the formation of the Republican party.

22. The REMINGTON RAND TYPEWRITER PLANT, 114 Gifford St., now abandoned, in 1936 was involved in a strike which lasted nearly a year. The company refused to recognize its employees' union for collective bargaining and forestalled a strike by shutting down the entire plant on the day of the intended walkout. One week later attempts were made to start production but strikebreakers were challenged by some 500 union men. Although the 329-day strike was officially ended in April 1937, the company appealed the findings of the National Labor Relations Board to the U.S.Circuit Court of Appeals. That court ruled in favor of the union, and its decision condemned the company's performance. The plant equipment was moved to Ilion in 1939.

23. The SYRACUSE CHILLED PLOW PLANT (*open by permission*), SE. corner of Marcellus and Wyoming Sts., covers almost two city blocks. Associated with the development of this industry were Thomas Wiard, who began to make plows in Syracuse in 1793, and Harry Wiard, who invented the chilling process in plow manufacture.

24. The CARRIER CORPORATION PLANT (*open 9–4 Mon.–Fri., 9–11 Sat.; guides*), 302 S.Geddes St., with 31 acres of floor space, employs about 1,500 in the manufacture of air-conditioning equipment.

25. The CRUCIBLE STEEL PLANT (*not open to public*), 104 Magnolia St., covers an area of 10 acres and employs about 1,200 men. High-grade tool steel for knives, cutters, and hammers is the principal product; bar steel and wire are made on order. Started about 1870 by William A. Sweet, the mill was purchased in 1876 by the Sanderson Brothers of Sheffield, England, who operated it until it was purchased in 1900 by the present owners.

26. The ONONDAGA POTTERY PLANT (*open by permission*), 1858 W.Fayette St., is owned by a company organized in 1871, one of the oldest in the industry in the United States. The four-story red brick building covers 14 acres.

27. BURNET PARK, main entrance at 321 S.Wilbur Ave., the largest park in the city, was donated in 1886 by Major John B. Burnet. Its 135 acres offer facilities for recreation and amusement, including gardens and a Zoo (*open daily, summer 7 a.m.–9 p.m.; winter 7–5*).

28. The WOODLAWN RESERVOIR AND STANDPIPE, 1900 S.Ged-

des St., draws its water from Skaneateles Lake, 17 miles southwest of the city. The round, bright red structure atop the hill is the storage tank for the reservoir. This point affords an excellent view of the city and environs.

29. ELMWOOD PARK, 204 Glenwood Ave., of 25 acres, is a natural beauty spot with a deep gorge through which Furnace Brook runs, so called because the furnace of Nicholas Mickles, in which he cast shot for use in the War of 1812, once stood on its bank.

30. The OLD ARSENAL SITE, Arsenal Drive and E.Seneca Turnpike, is indicated by a pile of gray stone blocks and a skeleton of walls. The arsenal was built in 1810 as a protection against the Indians; its ruins are Onondaga's only reminder of the War of 1812.

31. The EXPERIMENTAL STATION of the New York State College of Forestry (*open 9–5 Mon.–Fri.*), 5559 S.Salina St., occupies 93 acres. Since its beginning in 1912, this station has brought under control the strawberry weevil, which attacks the roots of pine and spruce trees, the Canadian saw-fly, which feeds on the leaves of spruce, white, and Norway pine, and the needle-miner, which infests lodgepole pine especially.

32. The ONONDAGA VALLEY CEMETERY, 1804 Valley Drive, has in it the graves of several old settlers, including those of Asa Danforth and his wife, the wife of Ephraim Webster, and Nicholas Mickles.

33. The WILL & BAUMER CANDLE FACTORY (*not open to public*), SE. corner of Park St. and Buckley Road, one of the largest candle factories in the United States, specializing in ornamental and church candles, dates back to 1855.

34. The CROUSE HINDS PLANT (*open by permission*), NW. corner of Wolf and 7th North Sts., is a three-story, red brick building, covering more than 25 acres. About 1,000 persons are employed in the manufacture of electric conduit fittings.

35. The TEMPLE OF THE SOCIETY OF CONCORD, 501 University Ave., a Jewish Reformed house of worship, is built of light gray stone with limestone trim; the style is neoclassic, with an impressive pedimented Doric portico. The society held its first meeting on November 21, 1841, at the residence of Jacob Garson in Mulberry Street (South State Street).

36. THORNDEN PARK, foot of University Place, 76 acres purchased in 1922, is considered the most beautiful in the city. The rose garden contains more than 7,000 plants in 150 varieties of hybrids and climbers. The old-fashioned perennial garden has more than 200 varieties of plants. The amphitheater, low in a rocky glen, surrounded by natural slopes for seats, is used for community events. The park also contains a swimming pool, a baseball diamond, a children's playground, and tennis courts.

37. OAKWOOD CEMETERY, College Place and Euclid Ave., containing 172 acres of sloping, tree-covered land, was dedicated in 1859 in what is known as Dedication Valley.

The cemetery contains the GRAVE OF COMFORT TYLER (1764–1827), pioneer settler of Onondaga Valley. Born in Ashford, Connecticut, he enlisted in the Revolutionary Army at the age of 14 and served until the close of the war. With Moses De Witt and others he surveyed the central and western portions of the State. In 1788 he and Major Danforth pushed into the wilderness and settled in Onondaga Hollow. Colonel Tyler felled the first tree in the Syracuse district, constructed the first piece of turnpike road in the State west of Fort Stanwix, and assisted in the first manufacture of salt. He represented Onondaga in the State legislature in 1798 and 1799.

38. The SYRACUSE MEDICAL CENTER, 736 Irving Ave., is in five units: the Syracuse Memorial Hospital, the University Hospital, the State Psychopathic Hospital, the University Medical School, and the City Communicable Diseases Hospital. The construction of the medical school building, completed in 1937, was made possible by a PWA grant of $825,-000; President Franklin D. Roosevelt laid the cornerstone in September 1936. The buildings form a harmonious group in the Georgian style.

The medical school, the oldest unit of Syracuse University, was established in 1834 as the Geneva Medical College, Geneva, New York. Later it was moved to Syracuse and took its present name in 1872. It includes a school of nursing.

39. The CASTLE, NW. corner of Irving Ave. and University Place, houses the Syracuse University School of Journalism, established in 1934. This rambling 'Norman' building was built in 1851 by James Renwick, architect of St.Patrick's Cathedral, New York City, for C.Tyler Long-street, who found it 'too large for comfort' and exchanged houses with A.C.Yates. The property was purchased by the university in 1905.

40. SYRACUSE UNIVERSITY, main entrance on University Place, stands on a hilltop that offers a panoramic view of the city. The campus of 84 acres is rectangular, with the buildings fringing its borders. The sunny court is a network of paths and drives outlined with tufa stones. Thirty buildings house the 17 separate schools.

The university has an enrollment of 9,293, approximately half men and half women. It offers a full roster of degrees. The John Crouse College of Fine Arts, organized in 1873, is notable as the first in the United States. Modern trends in higher education are exemplified in the College of Business Administration, the Maxwell School of Citizenship and Public Affairs, the School of Extension Teaching and Adult Education, the College of Home Economics, and the School of Speech and Dramatic Art. The New York State College of Forestry, established by the legislature in 1911, is State-supported. About 300 courses are offered during the university summer sessions.

In 1867 leading citizens of Syracuse called a public meeting and proposed that the city bond itself for $100,000 as a contribution to a college endowment with the provision that $400,000 be raised from other sources. The proposal was approved and the necessary legislation enacted in Albany. In 1870 Genesee College, then a small Methodist institution in Lima, New York, successfully raised the required endowment and in 1871 moved to Syracuse. As Syracuse University, coeducational and nonsectarian, it began its first semester in September of that year, the 41 students finding temporary quarters in the old Myers block at the corner of East Genesee and Montgomery Streets. The period of greatest growth occurred under Chancellor James Roscoe Day, who served the university from 1893 to

1922. During his administration the university expanded from three to 13 colleges, 22 buildings were erected, and the student body increased from 800 to more than 5,000.

HENDRICKS CHAPEL, at the border of the college green, is architecturally the outstanding building on the campus; the architect was Dwight James Baum. The plan is that of a Greek cross, constructed of brick with limestone trim and a high stone base. Neoclassic in design, it has a Doric pedimented portico at the entrance, side Palladian windows, large doors and foyer, and a dome. The interior details—pews, pulpit, lectern, organ, balconies, and furniture—are Georgian Colonial.

The NEW YORK STATE COLLEGE OF FORESTRY, S. of the chapel beyond the Archbold Stadium, is housed in three buildings designed in the Georgian style. The college is under a separate board of trustees and separate financial management; residents of the State receive free tuition. The extension division offers a variety of public services. The New York State Ranger School (*see Tour* 17), a department of the college in the western Adirondacks, trains men for work as forest rangers and tree-planting experts. The Charles Lathrop Pack Demonstration Forest, near Warrensburg (*see Tour* 21), serves as a field laboratory.

The CARNEGIE LIBRARY (*open* 8–6, 7–10 *p.m. daily*), facing the green on the south, donated in 1905 by Andrew Carnegie, is a three-story brick and terra-cotta building with elaborate French Renaissance details. Including separate college and departmental libraries, it has more than 250,000 books. The most valuable collection is the historical library of Leopold Von Ranke. The library also owns the Gerrit Smith-Miller collection of some 50,000 items, a valuable source of information on the antislavery, peace, temperance, and women's rights movements and on the economic development of central New York.

JOHN CROUSE COLLEGE, NE. corner of the campus, overlooking the city, houses the College of Fine Arts. A four-story Romanesque structure of red sandstone designed by Archimedes Russell, it was donated to the university in 1889 by John Crouse, Syracuse business man. A five-year course leads to the degree of Bachelor of Architecture; four-year courses lead to the degrees of Bachelor of Music and Bachelor of Fine Arts. The chimes in the tower, donated by Edgar Crouse, ring out the call to morning classes.

POINTS OF INTEREST IN ENVIRONS

Green Lakes State Park, 10 *m.* (*see Tour* 11). Onondaga Indian Reservation, 6.4 *m.* (*see Tour* 18). Forte Sainte Marie de Gennentaha, 4.2 *m.*; Salt Museum, 4.8 *m.* (*see Tour* 26).

In the Cities

STATE STREET, ALBANY (ABOUT 1830)
Watercolor by John Wilson

STATE STREET, ALBANY (1940)

UNION COLLEGE, SCHENECTADY

WORLD WAR MEMORIAL FROM WILLARD STRAIGHT TERRACE, CORNELL UNIVERSITY, ITHACA

Photograph by T. C. Bannister

UTICA STATE HOSPITAL

CLINTON SQUARE, SYRACUSE
*Photograph by courtesy of Syracuse
Chamber of Commerce*

DOWNTOWN BUFFALO
Photograph by Hare

MAIN STREET, ROCHESTER
Photograph by courtesy of Sibley, Lindsay & Curr

BINGHAMTON

Photograph by Joseph A. Buchta

SARA WEY TOMPKINS HALL, ELMIRA COLLEGE, ELMIRA

Photograph by John J. Vrooman

QUEENSBRIDGE HOUSES, NEW YORK CITY

Development, housing 3,149 families, built by the U. S. Housing Authority in the slum area of Long Island City. Queensborough Bridge over the East River, straddling Welfare Island. In the background midtown Manhattan; beyond, the Hudson River.

CENTRAL PARK, NEW YORK CITY

Troy

Railroad Station: Union Station, Union St. between Fulton St. and Broadway, for New York Central System, Boston & Maine R.R., Delaware & Hudson R.R., and Rutland R.R.
Bus Stations: 31 State St. for Greyhound Lines, Wagar Motor Coach, Hoosick Valley Coach, Taconic Valley, Miller Bus, Interstate Busses, and Boston & Maine Lines; Union Station for L.B.K. and Vermont Transit Lines.
Airport: S. city line; no scheduled service; local sight-seeing flights.
Busses: Fare 5¢ and 10¢.
Taxis: 25¢ minimum, zone system.

Accommodations: 9 hotels; tourist homes.

Information Service: Chamber of Commerce, 43 Fourth St.; Troy Automobile Club, Hendrick Hudson Hotel, Broadway and Second St.

Radio Stations: WHAZ (1300 kc.); WTRY (950 kc.).
Motion Picture Houses: 9.
Baseball: Semiprofessional at Laureate Grounds, River St. and Glen Ave.; New York State League, 115th St. and 7th Ave.
Golf: Frear Park, Oakwood and Frear Aves., 9 holes, greens fee 50¢; Sat., Sun., and holidays $1.
Tennis: City parks, free.
Swimming: Prospect Park, June–Sept., 10¢; children free mornings only.

TROY (34 alt.,70,117 pop.) stretches for seven miles along the eastern bank of the Hudson at the head of river navigation, opposite the junction with the Barge Canal. The mass of nondescript brick and wood buildings at the city's southern line gives way to a section of more stately homes of the Victorian era, Sage Park, public buildings, and the business district. Beyond are the high, confining walls of the shirt factories, and north of them is the residential section of old Lansingburgh.

In the downtown area the streets run directly north-south and east-west, with the east-west thoroughfares south of Liberty Street bearing consecutively the names of the Presidents from Washington to Polk, intercepted only by Ida Street, named for Mount Ida, the 360-foot buttress of Cambrian rock and glacial clay that is the center of the municipal Prospect Park, and Canal Avenue on the south bank of the Poestenkill. Eastward, modern residential sections stretch toward the Taconic hills in a maze of short streets. Almost hidden by the bulk of factory walls are the Poestenkill and Wynantskill, swift streams that were the first sources of power in the community.

Troy is an industrial, educational, and shopping center. There are 73 miles of paved streets, a $4,000,000 gravity water supply system, and a mile of new concrete docks bordering the 150-year-old harbor. Six public parks totaling 220 acres contain athletic fields, a golf course, and swimming pools. Besides its public school system, the city has Russell Sage College, Rensselaer Polytechnic Institute, and the Emma Willard School.

In 1609 a longboat from Henry Hudson's *Half Moon* explored north as far as the site of Troy. The crew found the flatland at the head of navigation planted in corn and beans, the cornstalks acting as poles for the bean vines. Pa-an-pa-ack, the Indian name of the site, has been translated as field of standing corn. The site was part of the patroonship granted to Kiliaen Van Rensselaer by the Dutch West India Company.

For 120 years Troy existed as the meadowland of stolid Dutch farmers, a green ribbon within sound of the Mohawk's falls and backed by the soft swellings of the Berkshires. In 1785 the greater part of the city site lay in three farms owned by the descendants of Derick Vanderheyden. The rent demanded by the Van Rensselaers was three bushels and three pecks of wheat and three fat hens or capons annually. The Lansings, northerly neighbors and relatives of the Vanderheydens, laid out their land in building lots shortly before the Revolution and established the village of Lansingburgh, first known as New City. A lively trade sprang up between Albany and the Lansings' settlers in the years following Burgoyne's defeat.

After the Revolution Benjamin Thurber purchased a lot at the intersection of the river road and the Hoosick road and opened a general store, which he called the Bunch of Grapes. Captain Stephen Ashley leased the Matthias Vanderheyden home which stood at what is now the corner of Division and River Streets, and turned it into a tavern. Jacob D. Vanderheyden, owner of the middle farm, for a while opposed settlement was but finally persuaded to lay out his holding in building lots. The land was surveyed for a town site in 1786. Philadelphia, a city of regular squares, was adopted as a model, and, except for the curving of the river road, now River Street, the plan was followed. Vanderheyden insisted that the village carry his name, but the half dozen houses were popularly known as Ashley's Ferry or Ferry Hook. The name Troy was adopted at a public meeting in Ashley's Tavern on January 5, 1789. Jacob Vanderheyden, reconciled to town building, rebelled anew against the name, and for years gave his address as 'Vanderheyden alias Troy.'

The townspeople were sober and intent, worshipping on Sundays even when there was but one man in the village who could make a prayer. In 1791, 64 Trojans took a step toward dominance of the area by subscribing 1,000 pounds toward construction of the Rensselaer County courthouse.

Bricks were first made in the locality in 1789; about the same year a dam and flume were built on the Poestenkill to operate the first paper mill in northern New York. Packet lines carried freight and passengers to New York City. In 1796 Troy was granted a post office, and in 1798 it was incorporated as a village. The Troy-Schenectady toll road, begun in 1802, provided a direct route from the West to the head of navigation on the Hudson and opened the Troy market to Palatine and Dutch farmers along the Mohawk. By 1806 Troy had a population of 3,200, including 80 free Negroes and 79 slaves.

The War of 1812 brought the settlement one of the largest arsenals of the United States, now the Watervliet Arsenal (*see Tour* 10), and immortalized Samuel Wilson, who supplied the soldiers quartered near by with what they called 'Uncle Sam's beef,' as the original 'Uncle Sam.' War trade, the beginning of iron manufacture, the unbroken stream of New England emigrants passing through on their way west, stimulated growth; and in 1816 a city charter was granted by the State legislature.

During the next decade, three people moved to the city who became leaders in three Nation-wide movements. The era of Amos Eaton, Emma Willard, and Henry Burden was Troy's golden age. Eaton, who spurred public interest in mechanical and scientific development, was appointed senior professor at the Rensselaer Polytechnic Institute in 1824. Emma Willard, pioneer in liberal education for women, brought her school to Troy in 1821. Henry Burden, who came to Troy in 1822, by his inventions stimulated the city's iron industry.

The first bell foundry in Troy began operations in 1825; the first stove-plates were manufactured in 1821. With the opening of the Erie and Champlain Canals began the smudged confusion of tugboats, barges, and cranes that still persists along the Troy water front. Charles Veasie and Orsamus Eaton opened coach shops that for years led the trade in these ornate vehicles. It was estimated in 1845 that 5,000 Eaton coaches were in use in North and South America. Troy's population jumped from 5,264 in 1820 to 11,556 in 1830.

In the first months of 1838, hard on a national panic, the city subscribed to all the stock of the proposed Schenectady & Troy Railroad in the hope of becoming a railroad center. Constructed with the first H-section iron rails laid in the United States, and well ballasted, the road was completed in 1842 and was pronounced the most comfortable then in use. But it proved a financial failure, was sold, and later was merged with the New New York Central. Coachmaker Eaton tried his hand at passenger cars for the new road. They were clumsy in comparison with modern coaches but so much superior to those in use on the Mohawk & Hudson Railroad that the firm received orders for much of the equipment used on the dozen lines built in the State during the next decade.

In 1825 Mrs. Hannah Lord Montague, a Troy housewife, developed a detachable collar for men's shirts; according to tradition she cut the dirty collars off her husband's shirts to save herself the trouble of washing the entire garment, and thereby created a new industry. Ebenezer Brown first began the manufacture of detachable collars in 1829, and in 1834 Lyman Bennett opened the first successful collar factory. Further stimulus was given to the trade by the introduction of cuffs in 1845 and the sewing machine in 1852.

During the 1850's Troy surged into national prominence as an industrial center, although it never passed its old rival, Albany, in size. Construction work on the canals and railroads drew the first contingents of Irish immigrants, and industries later attracted additional thousands of them. By 1860 the population was 39,235. The migrations that founded the city had pushed on 3,000 miles to the Pacific Ocean; iron products and 'fancy clothes' followed, and Troy supplied both. The boom period was intensified by the Civil War. Across the river in Watervliet the arsenal turned out ammunition and guns for the Union Armies, giving employment to hundreds of men. Henry Burden's horseshoe machine clanked out footwear for cavalry and artillery mounts at the rate of 60 a minute. The regiment of the Second New York Volunteers, which left the city in May 1861, was the first to land on Virginia soil during the war. Workmen in local mills turned out plates for the *Monitor*. Troy troops, entrenched at Fortress Monroe, watched the *Monitor* battle the *Merrimac* off the Virginia coast on March 9, 1862.

During the Civil War women drawn into the laundry and collar industries of the city developed their own union. In 1868 the powerful Collar Laundry Workers of Troy gave $1,000 to the Troy Iron Moulders Association and $800 to striking bricklayers in New York City. Coupled with this, they forced increases in their own wages from $2–$3 to $12–$14 a week. In 1869, however, a strike split the union members into factions and the movement disintegrated.

Visiting Europe in 1864, Horatio Winslow purchased the rights to manufacture and sell Bessemer steel in the United States and began production at his company's Troy works. Introduction of the metal brought a new order of mass haulage by rail, and Troy became the steel center of the country. Its supremacy was doomed, however, when in 1873 Andrew Carnegie set up a steel mill 12 miles from Pittsburgh.

Trade with the North Country and the establishment of knitting mills brought hundreds of French-Canadian families to Troy between 1860 and 1910. Italians settled in the city during the same period, supplying the labor for railroad construction and municipal improvements. After the expansion of 1901, when Lansingburgh was added to the city under a second-class charter, population swept to a peak of 76,000.

The city has lost its nineteenth-century pre-eminence in the manufacture of steel, wrought-iron, and foundry products; and changed conditions of transportation have diverted much of its jobbing trade. But Troy is still an important producer of valves, fire hydrants, and engineering and surveying instruments, as well as collars and shirts, and produces a substantial volume of women's wear.

POINTS OF INTEREST

1. The BETSY HART HOUSE (*private*), 59 Second St., was built in 1827 by Richard P. Hart, a railroad magnate and merchant of the mid-nineteenth century, whose wife, Betsy, was said at her death in 1886 to have been the richest woman in America. The two-story-and-attic house with its marble front is an excellent example of Georgian Colonial architecture. The arched entrance and window trim are enriched with fine details, and the wrought-iron balustrade, newels, and fence are elaborate.

2. The FIRST PRESBYTERIAN CHURCH, SE. corner of Congress and First Sts., a stuccoed brick building with a stone foundation, erected in 1836, resembles a Greek temple with its Doric pedimented portico, heavy pilasters, and cornice. The congregation, organized in 1791, is the oldest in Troy.

3. RUSSELL SAGE COLLEGE, NW. corner of Ferry and Second Sts.,
an institution of higher learning for women, was organized in 1916 through
the generosity of Mrs.Russell Sage. The three stone-and-brick college
buildings in Sage Park were formerly occupied by the Emma Willard
School; the remaining buildings are near by. The curriculum includes four-
year courses in the arts and sciences, nursing, business education, home
economics, and physical education, leading to the degrees of A.B. and B.S.
Enrollment is approximately 700. On the campus, facing Second Street,
a bronze statue of Emma Willard marks the site of the Troy Female
Seminary, predecessor of the Emma Willard School.

4. The HART MEMORIAL LIBRARY (*open, winter, 9–9 weekdays; summer, 9–6 Mon.–Thurs., 9–9 Fri., 9–12 Sat.*), NE. corner of Second and
Ferry Sts., headquarters of the Troy public library system, was erected in
1897 by Mary Lane Hart as a memorial to her husband, W.H.Hart. The
building, a two-story-and-basement marble structure, is suggestive of an
Italian palace, with two arched main entrances, pilastered and triple-
arched front windows, and five-arched loggia on the second floor of the
Ferry Street side. The ornamentation is Italian Renaissance.

5. The FIRST BAPTIST CHURCH, Third St. between Congress and
State Sts., erected in 1846, is a bulky red brick building with a massive
white wood portico of six Greek Ionic columns and a pediment. From the
roof rises a stepped tower and a tall, slender spire. The First Particular
Baptist Church of the village of Troy, as the society was called, was the
second church organization in the community. Founded in 1795, it erected
its first church building in 1805 on land donated by Jacob D. Vanderheyden in 1796. In 1824 there was installed in its tower the first town clock
which was guaranteed 'to be seen from more than 1,000 windows . . . to
strike a handsome blow, and to keep perfect time . . . and be an ornament
for the church and city.'

6. ST.PAUL'S EPISCOPAL CHURCH, NE. corner of State and Third
Sts., erected in 1827, the oldest church structure in the city, is built of
limestone with wood trim. The style is simple English Gothic. The severe
plainness of the pointed arch windows contrasts with the intricate cut
woodwork of the upper portion of the tower over the main entrance.

7. The CLUETT PEABODY PLANT (*open 9–2:30 Mon–Fri., guides*),
433–71 River St., is the largest shirt factory in the world. The main factory is a six- and nine-story modern building occupying an entire city
block. Bleaching operations are carried on across the river near Waterford.
The plant has 3,700 employees, 80 per cent of whom are women. The plant

KEY FOR TROY MAP

1.Betsy Hart House 2.First Presbyterian Church 3.Russell Sage College 4.Hart
Memorial Library 5.First Baptist Church 6.St.Paul's Episcopal Church 7.Cluett
Peabody Plant 8.Rensselaer Polytechnic Institute 9.St.Joseph's Seminary 10.
Emma Willard School 11.Belding House 12.Troy Orphan Asylum 13.Ludlow
Valve Plant 14.Poor & Co. (Rail Joint) Plant 15.Hudson Valley Fuel Coke Plant
16.Burden Iron Plant 17.Troy Furnace Plant 18.Oakwood Cemetery 19.Wendell-
Lansing House

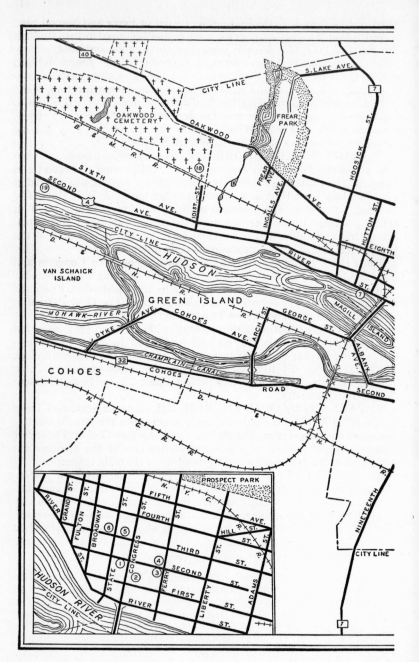

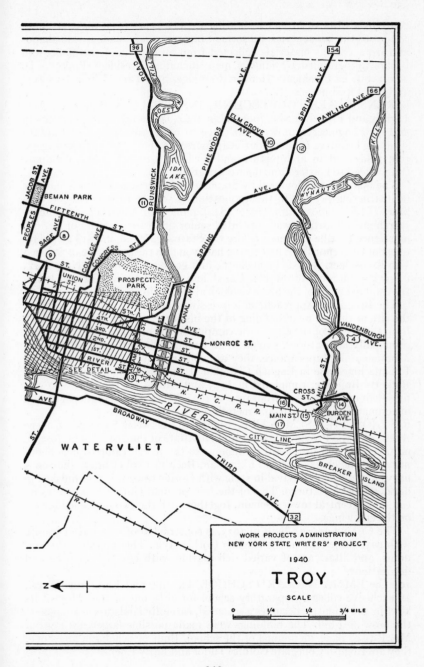

contains a COLLAR MUSEUM showing various types from the first 'Troy Made' to the latest styles; all sorts of bizarre collars made in odd shapes and from various materials collected from all corners of the globe; and collars autographed by famous men, including President Franklin D. Roosevelt, ex-Presidents Hoover, Coolidge, and Taft, Admiral Dewey, and Bob Fitzsimmons.

8. RENSSELAER POLYTECHNIC INSTITUTE, Sage Ave. between Eighth and Fifteenth Sts., founded in 1824, is the first college of science and civil engineering now in existence to be established in an English-speaking country. It offers four-year courses in the engineering and scientific fields and in architecture and business administration. Graduate courses lead to master's and doctor's degrees.

The institute was founded by Stephen Van Rensselaer 'for the purpose of instructing persons in the application of science to the common purposes of life.' Amos Eaton (1776–1842), pioneer in American scientific research and education, was appointed senior professor. A series of lectures on science that he delivered before the State legislature in 1818 at the request of Governor De Witt Clinton had won him the patronage of Stephen Van Rensselaer. In 1820 he made the first geological survey in New York, following the route of the Erie Canal, and created an interest that led to the establishment of the State Geological Survey in 1836.

The Broadway Approach, an impressive stone stairway constructed on the site of the old main building of the institute, offers a direct approach from the center of the city to the campus on the hill. The main buildings, principally laboratories, extend in an irregular line up the steep hillside. Monumental in appearance, they are constructed of Harvard brick and Indiana limestone in English Georgian style. The Palmer Chamberlaine Ricketts Building, completed in 1935 and named for the man who was president of the institute from 1901 to 1934, houses the newer departments of aeronautical, chemical, and metallurgical engineering.

9. ST.JOSEPH'S SEMINARY, Eighth St. between Sage and College Aves., now the Provincial House and Novitiate of the Sisters of St.Joseph, occupies the plot of ground contiguous to the R.P.I. campus. The Seminary and the chapel form a 'T' in plan. Built in 1856 of brick, the Seminary, Romanesque Revival in style with Gothic towers, is now finished in dark, rough-cast stucco. Two of the four original Gothic wood spires on the square central towers remain, together with the two pinnacled towers on the end wings.

The CHAPEL (*open*), built in 1933, is constructed of seam-faced granite with cast-stone trim in the English Gothic style. The interior walls, columns, and altars are of varied rich marble, with effective lighting and decorations.

10. The EMMA WILLARD SCHOOL, Pawling and Elm Grove Aves., an exclusive college preparatory school for girls, one of the oldest of its kind in the country, occupies a secluded, carefully landscaped campus on the brow of a hill. The buildings were made possible largely by a gift of Mrs.Russell Sage, an alumna of the school. Built of Schoharie limestone, they are English Collegiate Gothic (Tudor and Early English Renaissance)

in style. Open tracery and gargoyles distinguish the octagonal main tower. The gymnasium has an impressive clock tower.

11. The BELDING HOUSE (*private*), 9 Brunswick Road, is a fine example of the Greek Revival style. The pedimented portico with four fluted Ionic columns overlooks the mill pond across the road. The flush boarding of the main block is broken by floor-length parlor windows and on the left by an unusually squat side-lighted door surmounted by a wide transom. On each side are clapboarded wings with end chimneys. The interior retains its original doors, trim, and marble mantels. The house was erected in the late 1830's by Dennis Belding, Troy butcher, who owned the farm site from 1834 to 1854.

12. The TROY ORPHAN ASYLUM (*open by appointment*), SW. corner of Spring and Pawling Aves., is a private institution providing individual care for its inmates. The group of brick buildings in the Victorian Gothic style houses the dormitory, training quarters, recreational unit, chapel, hospital, power house, and barns. The institution is supported by voluntary contributions; admission is open to children of all sects from birth to 16 years of age.

13. The LUDLOW VALVE PLANT (*open 9–5 Mon.–Fri.; guides*), W. end of Adams St., makes giant gate valves.

14. The POOR & CO. (RAIL JOINT) PLANT (*not open to public*), Burden Ave. at entrance to the Troy-Menands bridge, manufactures insulated joints for block signals. The plant can turn a 900-pound steel billet into the finished product in one minute.

15. The HUDSON VALLEY FUEL COKE PLANT (*not open to public*), foot of Cross St., has an annual output of 375,000 tons of coke and 5,000,-000,000 cubic feet of gas. Other products include coal tar, ammonium sulphate, phenol, and benzol, which are shipped to all parts of the country and to foreign lands.

16. The BURDEN IRON PLANT (*abandoned*), Main St. W. of First St., which manufactured horseshoes, rivets, and merchant iron, had its origin in a rolling and slitting mill erected in 1809 on the south bank of the Wynantskill. Under the leadership of Henry Burden (1791–1871), the plant was enlarged in 1822 and its products were diversified. In 1825 Burden patented a machine for turning out wrought-iron railroad spikes; in 1834 the machine was revamped to produce hookheaded spikes. In 1835 he patented a machine for producing horseshoes and won a monopoly for his company in supplying the cavalry and field artillery of the U.S.Army during the Mexican and Civil Wars. His rotary concentric squeezer for removing slag from puddled iron was hailed in 1840 as one of the most important advances in the history of iron manufacture.

17. The TROY FURNACE DIVISION of the Republic Steel Corp. (*not open to public*), beyond foot of Main St., W. of the Burden Plant, operates a blast furnace leased from the Hudson Valley Fuel Corporation. The magnetic ore used is shipped from Port Henry by Barge Canal and rail. Three carloads of stone from Albany County are used daily for flux. The furnace has an annual capacity of 150,000 tons.

18. OAKWOOD CEMETERY, E. end of 101st St., extends over the

western slope of the hills on the northeastern border of Troy. The ROBERT ROSS MONUMENT, a heroic figure of Ross by J.Massey Rhind, was erected by the women of Troy, with the aid of Nation-wide contributions. Ross was martyred while defending the purity of the ballot at a city election on March 6, 1894. A State investigation and a trial focused the attention of the whole country on the political corruption of Troy at that time and on the lax election laws of the State of New York. Public opinion forced the passage of corrective measures culminating in the use of the Australian ballot.

The RUSSELL SAGE MONUMENT marks the grave of Russell Sage, (1816–1906), who was born in a covered wagon in Verona, New York, and came to Troy as a boy to serve as apprentice in his brother's store. In 1837 he purchased the store and thereafter extended his activities into several commercial fields. In 1852, while serving as the district's representative in Congress, he supported the movement to establish Mount Vernon as a national shrine.

The SAMUEL WILSON MONUMENT, a finely proportioned rough granite block, was dedicated by the Veterans of Foreign Wars in July 1936. Samuel Wilson (1766–1854) was a Troy brickmaker who early in the War of 1812 opened a slaughterhouse and sold meat to Elbert Anderson, Government contractor. Wilson's beef and pork were shipped down the Hudson to the Army cantonment at Greenbush, each piece stamped 'US—EA.' Soldiers invented the story that the US (United States) stood for 'Uncle Sam' Wilson. The phrase caught the public fancy and was applied to other Government property.

19. The WENDELL–LANSING HOUSE (*private*), 405 Second Ave., was built about 1750 in the early Georgian Colonial style. The white two-story superstructure is of Holland brick; the foundations are of cut stone, with a riverside wall more than three feet thick, probably to withstand ice floes brought down by freshets. The interior has been modernized.

POINTS OF INTEREST IN ENVIRONS

Watervliet Arsenal, 1 *m.*; Tomhannock Reservoir, 4 *m.* (*see Tour* 10). Van Alen Homestead and Lindenwald, 27.2 *m.* (*see Tour* 21). Saratoga Battlefield, 21.6 *m.* (*see Tour* 22).

Utica

Railroad Station: Union Station, Main St. near foot of Genesee St., for New York Central System, Delaware, Lackawanna & Western R.R., and New York Ontario & Western Ry.
Bus Station: 128 Genesee St. for Greyhound Lines, Central New York Coach Lines, and interurban busses.
Airport: Municipal airport, 6.9 m. W. on State 49; no scheduled service.
Streetcars and busses: Fare 10¢, 10 tokens 75¢.
Taxis: 35¢ anywhere in the city; extra passengers 15¢ each.

Accommodations: 8 hotels; boarding houses, tourist homes.

Information Service: Automobile Club of Utica, Hotel Martin, 225 Bleecker St.; information booths (summer only), north and south city entrances.

Radio Station: WIBX (1200 kc.).
Golf: Valley View municipal course, Roscoe Conkling Park, Pleasant St. and Seymour Ave., 18 holes, 50¢
Tennis: Roscoe Conkling Park; city playgrounds.

Annual Events: Welsh Eisteddfod, New Year's Day; Proctor Day, Sat. following July 4th.

UTICA (500 alt.,100,063 pop.), trading center and largest mill town of the Mohawk Valley, lies 20 miles east of the geographical center of the State. The almost level city area of about 22 square miles marks the western terminus of the Mohawk highlands; the foothills of the central Adirondacks rise to the north.

Baggs Square, the heart of old Utica, is approached from the north over the river and railroad bridges. Three blocks south is Utica's 'busy corner,' the junction of Genesee, Bleecker, and Lafayette Streets. The principal manufacturing plants are in the eastern part of the city; the knitting mills are in the eastern and western sections. A belt of parks, donated by Thomas R. Proctor and connected by the Parkway, a landscaped boulevard, extends in a rough semicircle across the southern section and is bordered by a residential area of prosperous modern homes.

Power from Trenton Falls, 15 miles north, whirls the wheels of the city's industries, producing about $50,000,000 in products yearly. Knit goods are the principal product; cotton cloth and cotton goods second, followed by beer, furnaces, metal furniture, firearms, machinery, and brass products. The surrounding rich farm and dairy section is the city's trading area.

Foreign groups—about one third of the population—include 13,000 Italians, 7,000 Poles, and 5,000 Irish. In the Italian section in northeast Utica, a distinct air of the homeland prevails. Weddings are gala affairs; at funerals files of marchers tramp to the dirge of a muffled band; and Saints' days are celebrated with parades and fireworks. In the Polish section, near the cotton mills in West Utica, the big social event is the wedding celebration, which lasts several days; every male guest dances with the bride and gives her a cash gift. The Welsh, of whom some 1,200 are foreign born, are occupied principally in the building trades. *Y Drych* (The Mirror), founded in New York City in 1851 and published in Utica since 1860, is the only Welsh language newspaper in the United States. The Cymreigyddion Society, the largest of a number of singing groups, sponsors the annual Utica Eisteddfod.

The Oneida Indian name for the vicinity of Utica was Yah-nun-da-da-sis (around the hill), in reference to the way their trails circled the near-by hills. At the city site was the only ford across the Mohawk River for many miles; and near by was the hub of trails leading northwest to the portage at Rome, west to Oneida Castle, and east to the settlements on the Mohawk and the Hudson. These trails became the routes of the white pioneers.

The site was included in Cosby's Manor, a grant of 22,000 acres made by George II to William Cosby, governor of the Province of New York, and others in 1734. In 1758 the British erected Fort Schuyler on what is now Main Street, just below Second Street, close to the river. It was never garrisoned, and was abandoned in the early 1760's.

In 1772 the Cosby tract, on which the quitrents were unpaid, was bought at public sale by Philip Schuyler, John Bradstreet, and others for about 1,300 pounds. In 1773 the Weaver, Reall, and Demuth families, descendants of the Palatines and staunch patriots, moved from German Flats to the north bank of the Mohawk River where it is crossed by the present North Genesee Street. In 1776 their settlement was destroyed during an Indian-Tory raid. After the Revolution new homes were erected; and in the floodtide of westward migration the settlement grew rapidly as a trading and transportation center. Among the early settlers was Peter Smith (1768-1837), who came in 1787 and who in later years was a partner of John Jacob Astor.

Quick to sense the possibilities of the place as an outpost for the Indian trade was John Post of Schenectady, who loaded family, employees, and merchandise on boats and made the trip west in nine days. Post erected a home and warehouses and sent his boats on regular trips to Schenectady, to bring back, not only goods to trade with the Indians and settlers, but also more Yankees and English to settle and become his customers. In 1792 a bridge was built across the river, and the next year stagecoaches ran from Albany; a church and a schoolhouse were erected in 1794. In 1796 Gerrit Boon, agent of the Holland Land Company for its northern tract, erected a three-story brick tavern; his purpose was to make the place a market and shipping point for the produce of his settlers. In 1798 the settlement, with a population of 200 in 50 houses clustered at the foot of the present Genesee Street, was incorporated as a village, and the present name was determined on by a chance selection from a hatful of paper slips.

After 1825 the Erie Canal brought new prosperity—new industries and Irish and German immigrants. The population, 2,972 in 1820, jumped to 8,323 in 1830. The city was chartered in 1832, and in the same year engine and boiler works joined the already existing plow factory, gristmill, iron foundry, and pottery. In 1836 the Chenango Canal and the Utica & Schenectady Railroad were completed and a clothing factory was opened. Stove and furnace manufacture was begun in 1842.

The textile industry, the backbone of Utica's economic structure, began with the opening of the woolen mills in 1847 and of the cotton mills in 1848. The manufacture of locomotive headlights was started in 1851, of steam gauges in 1861, of firearms in 1862, of knit goods in 1863. Frank W. Woolworth opened his first five and ten cent store on Bleecker Street in 1879; it was a failure. The manufacture of worsted and caps was started in 1886. A wave of Italian and Polish immigration, attracted by the varied industries, reached its crest in 1910. During the World War the Utica plant of the Savage Arms Company, which manufactured the Lewis machine gun for the British Government, had a total production equal to about two thirds of Great Britain's entire output of that weapon.

POINTS OF INTEREST

1. BAGGS SQUARE, junction of Main, Genesee, and Whitesboro Sts., the site of old Utica, was the center of the village until the Erie Canal stimulated growth. It is named for Moses Baggs, who built a log tavern on this site in 1798 and replaced it in 1813 with the Baggs Hotel, which was razed in 1932.

In the square is the PROCTOR MEMORIAL BUILDING (*open 9–5 daily*), a small one-story structure of early French Renaissance design, constructed of sandstone with a finial surmounting the sloping roof. The building, which contains the records of the Baggs Hotel, was erected in 1933 by Mrs.Thomas R. Proctor in memory of her husband, Thomas Redfield Proctor (1844–1920), who bought the Baggs Hotel in 1869 and made it one of the best known hotels in the East. In 1891 he married Maria, daughter of James Watson Williams, Utica capitalist. While on a European trip he conceived the plan of the magnificent park system that he donated to the city. Frederick Towne Proctor (1856–1929) came to Utica in 1887 and married Rachel, sister of his brother's wife.

2. The HORATIO SEYMOUR HOME (*private*), NW. corner of Whitesboro and Hotel Sts., a severe three-story structure in the post-Colonial

---

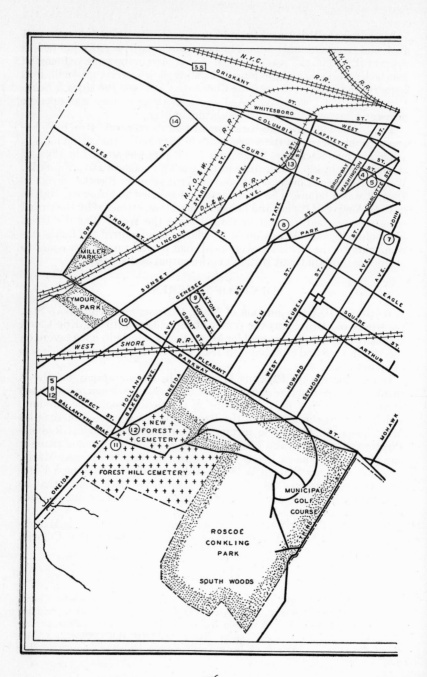

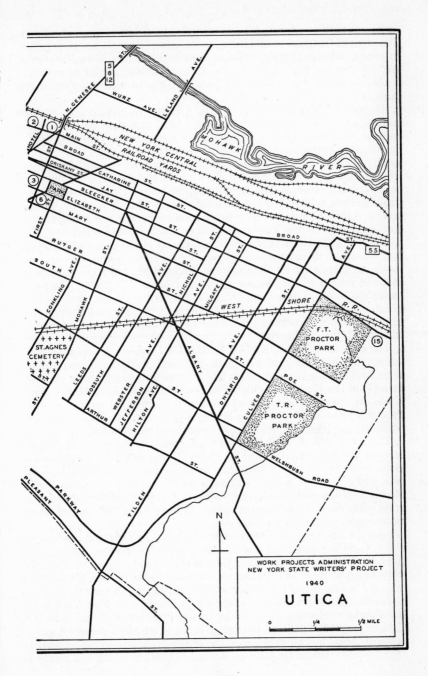

WORK PROJECTS ADMINISTRATION
NEW YORK STATE WRITERS' PROJECT

1940

UTICA

style, was built in 1810 and is now occupied by a manufacturing concern. The original Dutch oven and fireplace are intact. Horatio Seymour (1810-86), came to Utica at the age of nine from Pompey, New York. He studied law, represented the county in the State assembly, served as mayor of Utica and as governor (1853-5 and 1863-5), and in 1868 was Democratic candidate for President.

3. ST.JOHN'S ROMAN CATHOLIC CHURCH, SW. corner of John and Bleecker Sts., erected in 1869, a red brick structure in the Romanesque style with twin spires, dominates the downtown skyline. The leaded glass designs of the windows have been copied by other churches.

4. The UTICA CITY HALL, SW. corner of Genesee and Pearl Sts., erected in 1852-3, was designed by Richard Upjohn. The yellow brick building has a sober, Italian-Lombard Romanesque character which contrasts sharply with the English Gothic Grace Church near by, by the same architect. A heavy square tower subdivided by stone string courses dominates the exterior. The interior has been repeatedly altered.

5. GRACE CHURCH (Episcopal), SE. corner of Genesee and Elizabeth Sts., built in 1856-60, was also designed by Richard Upjohn. The entrance tower, added in 1870 by Upjohn's son, Richard M., has a tall stone spire that was rebuilt in 1933 by his grandson, Hobart B. Upjohn. The tower masks the broad reversed gambrel roof. The strong solemn dignity of the exterior contrasts with the richer character of the spacious interior. The nave is roofed with arched timber trusses. The chancel was designed by Richard M. Upjohn in 1890.

6. The ONEIDA HISTORICAL BUILDING (*open 2-5 weekdays, free*), intersection of John and Elizabeth Sts. and Park Ave., constructed of buff brick with steep tile roofs and stepped gable ends, is an excellent example of the Flemish Gothic style. Designed by Richard Morris Hunt, it was donated in 1896 by Mrs.J.Watson Williams, mother-in-law of the Proctor brothers. The building houses a collection of curios, paintings, portraits, and books and manuscripts associated with Oneida County.

7. The RUTGER B. MILLER HOUSE (*private*), Rutger Park, Rutger St. opposite John St., designed by Philip Hooker, is a two-story post-Colonial stone house with a three-bay main section topped by a hip-roof, twin end chimneys, and a 'captain's walk.' Begun in 1820 by Judge Morris S. Miller and completed by his son, Rutger B. Miller, about 1830, in its early days the house was called 'Miller's Folly' because of its remoteness from the village of that time.

Roscoe Conkling (1829-88) bought the house in 1863 and made it his home. Conkling practiced law in Utica, served as mayor, and married Julia, sister of Horatio Seymour. He was elected to Congress in 1858, and while still a member of the House was elected to the Senate. He resigned from the Senate in 1881, together with his colleague, Thomas C. Platt, as a protest against President Garfield's appointments in New York State and sought re-election as a rebuke to the President but was defeated. Conkling regarded political patronage in the State as his preserve, and as political 'boss' looked askance on the civil service reform movement. In 1877 he said, 'When Dr.Johnson defined patriotism as the last refuge of a scoundrel, he was unconscious of the then undeveloped capacities and uses of the word "reform".'

8. The MUNSON–WILLIAMS–PROCTOR INSTITUTE (*open* 9–5 *weekdays*), 312–18 Genesee St., occupies the former homes of Frederick T. and Thomas R. Proctor, yellow-painted brick Victorian mansions with bracketed eaves, set back on carefully landscaped grounds. The collection includes family heirlooms, paintings, and rugs. The institute was incorporated in 1920 but plans for its development were delayed until after the death of the members of the Proctor family, who bequeathed to it their homes and the bulk of their estates.

In 1936 the Arts Guild of New York City moved its school to a remodeled garage on the grounds of the institute and, under the name of the School of Related Arts and Sciences, began to offer courses in visual arts, the history and philosophy of art, and comparative symbolism.

9. The FIRST PRESBYTERIAN CHURCH, SE. corner of Genesee and Faxton Sts., erected in 1922, is a brick structure with limestone and wood trim in the late Georgian Colonial style, with pedimented portico and well-proportioned tower.

10. The BARON VON STEUBEN STATUE, at Parkway entrance facing Genesee St., donated to the city by its German citizens, was unveiled on German Day, August 3, 1914. The sculptor was J.Otto Schwizer. Cast in bronze and mounted on a high granite pedestal, it shows von Steuben in a cocked hat wrapped in his voluminous military cloak.

11. In FOREST HILL CEMETERY, Oneida St. at Ballantyne Brae, is the SACRED STONE OF THE ONEIDAS, a rounded oblong stone on a three-stepped granite base, which is said to have served as an altar for many Indian rites and for the councils of the entire Iroquois Confederacy. According to legend, the stone miraculously appeared in the Oneida village at the foot of Oneida Lake and magically followed the tribe from one settlement to another.

12. In NEW FOREST CEMETERY, Oneida St. at Baker Ave., is the FOUNDER RATHBONE MONUMENT, a white granite monument on the highest slope of the cemetery, erected in memory of Justus H. Rathbone (1839–88), native son of Utica and founder of the Order of the Knights of Pythias. Impressed by the story of Damon and Pythias, Rathbone set out to induce men to follow their example. In 1864, while working for the U.S.War Department, he organized the first lodge, composed entirely of Government clerks.

13. The UTICA & MOHAWK VALLEY COTTON MILLS (*open* 9–4 *weekdays; guides*), State St. between Court and Columbia Sts. extending to Fay St., represent the consolidation of several mills, the oldest of which was opened in 1848. The company is one of the world's largest manufacturers of sheets and pillow cases; the plant contains 138,000 spindles and 3,500 looms.

14. The UTICA STATE HOSPITAL (*open* 10–12, 2–4 *Wed. and Sun.*), Court St. between York and Whitesboro Sts., opened in 1843, was the first State institution for the insane. The main building was erected under the direction of three commissioners, General Francis E. Spinner, Captain

Elam Lynds, and Captain William Clarke. Clarke had built several Utica buildings and is credited with the design, though he may well have had the assistance of a professional architect. The structure, 550 feet long and constructed of gray Trenton limestone, includes a central four-story section of offices, staff quarters, and attic chapel and three-story side wings with self-contained groups of patients' rooms for classification by sex and ailment.

The exterior of the building comprises one of the noblest examples of Greek Revival architecture in the United States. The severely plain side wings, broken only by pedimented end pavilions, act as a foil to the august portico of the central block. The six Doric columns, built up of coursed limestone, have eight-foot diameters and are 48 feet high. The grand scale of this remarkable building recalls that other masterpiece of Greek Revival stonecutting, the Schoharie Aqueduct (*see Tour* 12). In 1857 a fire gutted the structure, leaving few traces of the original interior.

Dr.Amariah Brigham, the first superintendent of the Utica State Hospital, a pioneer believer in the therapeutic value of manual labor for patients, installed shops for carpentry, shoemaking, tailoring, blacksmithing, and whittling. For a number of years the patients wrote, edited, and printed their own magazine, *Opal*. Here Dr.Brigham began to publish the *American Journal of Insanity*, the first periodical in its field.

15. The MASONIC HOME, Bleecker St. near the east city limits, dates back to 1842, when Greenfield Poke contributed $1 toward its establishment. In 1889 the Grand Lodge purchased 160 acres and later acquired another 140 acres. The first building was erected in 1893; at present there are 19, arranged in a semicircle. The varied styles of the buildings reflect the changes in architectural taste since the nineties; most prominent are the Romanesque and neoclassic. The children attend the Utica public schools; those that show promise are given a college education.

POINTS OF INTEREST IN ENVIRONS

Oriskany Battlefield, 9 *m.* (*see Tour* 12). Adirondack State Park, 20 *m.* (*see Tour* 21).

West Point

U.S. MILITARY ACADEMY

Railroad Stations: West Point station for the West Shore division of the New York Central System; ferry at pier opposite railroad station (fare 25¢) to Garrison station on main line of New York Central System.
Busses: Storm King Stage Corp. busses between Highland Falls and Newburgh, on even hourly schedule 6 a.m.–12 p.m., fare 40¢, pass through Reservation on Thayer, Washington, and Lee Roads.
Pier: South Dock for Hudson River Day Line, daily boats in summer season to New York City and Albany; autumn schedule adapted to football games at West Point.

Accommodations: Thayer-West Point Inn, inside South Gate; 4 hotels and many restaurants in environs.

Information Service: Military police at North and South Gates and on grounds supply directory of all buildings and information on any changes in hours of ceremonies.

Directions and Restrictions: Visitors subject to military police regulations; speed limit 25 m.p.h.; visitors advised to visit grounds on foot. Guides available at Thayer-West Point Inn. Only public building is Thayer-West Point Inn; visiting hours posted for all buildings open to public. Rest rooms: railroad station; SE. corner of the lower floor of the Administration Bldg.; immediately N. of flagpoles; on main N.-S. road at south parking area opposite Cadet Hospital. Lunches may be eaten in an area N. of railroad station on Williams Rd. near power house. Cameras not requiring use of tripod permitted. Groups of 10 or more persons should communicate with Adjutant, West Point, New York, before visit.
Hours of Military Ceremonies (weather permitting and subject to minor change; daylight saving time, May to Sept.; no ceremonies on Sun. and legal holidays): Battalion parade, Mon., Tues., Thurs., Fri., 4:35 p.m., May and Sept. Inspection and regimental review followed by guard mount, Sat. about 1:10 p.m., Apr., May, Sept., Oct., Nov.

The United States Military Reservation, its site known as WEST POINT since Revolutionary times, lies just south of Storm King Mountain, between US 9W and the Hudson River. Including Constitution Island, donated by Mrs. Russell Sage and Miss Anna B. Warner in 1908, the reservation has an area of 3,500 acres. The buildings rise in terraces up the steep hillside, the rear of the Riding Hall, long, low, and massive, looking like the wall of a medieval castle, its base hidden by heavy foliage and fronted by a wide natural moat. Above it towers the Administration Building, a gray granite pile that dominates the lower, older buildings. On the higher plain, 200 feet above the river, is the main group, rising to the graceful Gothic lines of the chapel. Still higher on the hillside are Michie Stadium, the Howze polo field, blasted from the hillside, and the reconstructed Fort Putnam, 451 feet above river level. In the hills behind the Academy are seven redoubts, with connecting trails, remnants of Revolutionary fortifications.

The Academy's architecture falls into three major periods. The library is typical of a group of castellated Gothic structures, now for the most part replaced by modern buildings. Three structures, the Cullum Memorial Hall, the Officers' Mess, and the Bachelor Officers' Quarters, were designed by McKim, Mead and White in the neoclassic style popular in the late nineties. In 1903 Cram, Goodhue and Ferguson happily returned to the Gothic tradition. Succeeding architects have conformed to this decision, with the result that an impressive stylistic harmony binds together otherwise heterogeneous buildings. The grand picturesqueness of the dignified masses of the Gothic style achieves by some medieval magic a remarkably satisfying military character.

The living scene on the Reservation changes with the hour of the day. During academic hours the Plain is deserted; in the afternoon after classes it is a scene of intensive activity. On drill days squads and larger units engage in close-order maneuvers, map-making, and other military routine; on afternoons devoted to sport practically the entire regiment swarms over the field playing baseball, football, tennis, lacrosse, soccer, golf. During the summer months the cadets live in tents.

The cadet Corps, numbering 1,960 when all vacancies are filled, forms a regiment of 12 companies officered by members of the senior class. There are also stationed at West Point 275 regular Army officers and about 1,200 enlisted men. While all cadets receive considerable basic military instruction, particularly in the last two years, the West Point course is mainly academic, leading to a B. S. degree.

The cadets live a strict military life in an atmosphere of learning. They room in pairs, their twin cubicles separated by a partition and opening to a comfortably sized study, jointly used. After roll call, rooms are put in order; then comes breakfast, followed by morning classes, with one period of military training for Plebes (freshmen). In the afternoon classes continue until three o'clock; then comes supervised intramural competition in sports until Retreat and the lowering of the flag. Shortly after the evening meal, Call to Quarters is sounded; and from then until 10 p.m., when Taps sends them to bed, the cadets must be in their rooms studying.

Tradition permits recognition of the Plebe by upperclassmen only as duty or instruction requires. Plebes must double-time to positions whenever possible. They must remove their caps before entering the mess hall. They are detailed as 'gunners' to carve the meat or fowl, and as 'coffee corporals' to pour coffee. On graduation day the Fourth Classmen are 'recognized,' before Graduation Parade by the First Classmen, and after the parade by the other two classes; and the last painful memories of Fourth Class days of servitude are soon erased.

Many of the traditional ceremonies cherished by the older graduates have been discontinued. Hundredth Night and Two Hundredth Night, occasions when the Fourth Classmen were permitted to indulge in a free appraisal of upperclassmen without reprisal, are no longer celebrated. The old Ring Hop, at which the O.A.O. (one and only) of each First Classman placed the graduation ring on his finger and made a secret wish, is also a thing of the past. The Class Cup of the graduating class, presented to the 'class boy,' the first son born to a member of the class, is no longer cast out of the melted-down silver napkin rings of the cadets, but is purchased from class funds.

June Week brings the climax of the year's events. Graduation exercises are held in the Field House below the level of the Plain; the President or his designated representative presents the 2nd Lieutenant's commissions and the diplomas. The most colorful and dramatic scene is the graduation parade, when the Corps passes in review before the graduating class to the tune of *On to Victory* and *Alma Mater*. The battalions march off the Plain to the tune of *The Dashing White Sergeant*. As the band troops the line it plays *The Girl I Left Behind Me* and *Auld Lang Syne*, and finally *Home, Sweet Home*, tunes played at no other time.

The West Point region was one of four in the Hudson Highlands fortified during the Revolution. In early Army orders it was designated as 'the citadel and its dependencies,' the latter including river defenses north and south. Between 1778, after Sir Henry Clinton had retreated to New York, and 1780, Fort Putnam and Fort Arnold (later Fort Clinton) and a number of redoubts were built; and a great wrought-iron chain with protecting log boom was stretched across the Hudson to block British ships. After the failure of Arnold's plan to hand West Point over to the British in 1780, the area was never again threatened. The American flag has flown over West Point since 1778.

Although in October 1776 Congress appointed a committee to prepare plans for a military school and Washington twice recommended that such an institution be established at West Point, it was not until March 16, 1802, that Congress authorized the academy. On July 4 of that year the academy opened with 10 cadets. Under Major Sylvanus Thayer, who served as superintendent from 1817 to 1833, West Point became a military school of the first order; the basic system established by Thayer is continued today. During the Civil War, leaders on both sides—Lee, Grant, Jackson, Sheridan, Early, even Jefferson Davis—were West Point graduates.

Edgar Allan Poe was a cadet in 1830–31, but after eight months he was dismissed for insubordination. James A. McNeill Whistler entered the academy a month before his seventeenth birthday. He excelled in drawing, but his failure in chemistry eliminated him in his third year. 'Had silicon been a gas,' he later said, 'I would have been a major general.' Many of his sketches of cadet life are among the school's prized possessions. West Point gave General Grant his commission and an extra initial in his name. The Congressman who recommended him assumed that Ulysses was his first name and added Simpson, his mother's maiden name, to fill out. Thus he became U.S.Grant. He graduated in 1843, ranking twenty-first in a class of thirty-nine.

POINTS OF INTEREST

1. The THAYER–WEST POINT INN (*open all year*), just inside the South Gate, the only public building on the reservation, is a modern hotel

of modified Tudor architecture, having 225 rooms, grill, dance hall, and garage. Suites are reserved in the north wing for the President, the Vice President, and the Secretary of War.

2. The CAVALRY AND ARTILLERY DRILL FIELD, opposite the inn, provides the only available parking space for the cars of visitors attending football games. The barracks, stables, and gun sheds are plain but effective brick structures designed by Cram, Goodhue and Ferguson.

3. The ICE ARENA, off Mills Road, was dedicated in 1931. The walls enclose a 232-by-90-foot skating rink with a 10-foot promenade on the east and west sides. The game with the Royal Military College of Canada is the annual ice classic.

4. MICHIE STADIUM (*open only during games*), the football field, with a seating capacity of 26,000, was named in honor of Dennis Mahan Michie, class of 1892, captain of the first West Point football team, who was killed in action at San Juan, Cuba, in 1898.

5. FORT PUTNAM, approached by a steep foot trail from Mills Road, originally built in 1778 and partly restored in 1907–10, is on Mount Independence, 451 feet above tidewater.

6. The CHAPEL OF THE MOST HOLY TRINITY (*open 8–4 daily*), on a sharp rise of ground at the corner of Mills Road and Washington Road, is modeled on an English Carthusian abbey church. Consecrated in 1900, this Roman Catholic chapel was built and is maintained by private funds.

North from Washington Road, down the hillside toward the river, are the utilities building, service and auxiliary barracks, barracks of the band and the military police, and the ORDNANCE LABORATORY (*grounds open 9–4 daily*). Between these buildings and the lower edge of the plain above the West Shore Railroad tracks are the old Polo Field and the new Armory and Field House, in which an entire battalion can be maneuvered.

7. The OLD CADET CHAPEL (*open daylight hours*), at the entrance to the reservation cemetery, originally built in 1837 on the site now occupied by Jefferson Hall, was reconstructed here in 1911. The rectangular stone structure with its Roman Doric portico is a graceful example of the Renaissance Revival. Most prominent in the interior is an oil painting by Robert M. Weir entitled *Peace and War*. Black marble shields on the walls are inscribed in gold with the name, rank, and date of birth and death of every Revolutionary general. One, bearing only date of birth and rank, omits the name of Benedict Arnold.

In the WEST POINT CEMETERY, behind the chapel, the graves of enlisted men and civilians are side by side with those of Major Thayer and Generals Scott and Custer. It contains, among others, the graves of Margaret Corbin, Revolutionary heroine, and Susan and Anna Warner, popular authors who lived on Constitution Island and whose kindliness in the early days of the Academy eased the burden of homesick cadets.

Enlisted men's quarters line Washington Road on both sides, with more up the rise to the west. Along Lee Road, toward the North Gate, are the junior officers' quarters, the newest of which are modern homes of the duplex type.

8. The NORTH GATE, a brick and iron structure with Military Police sentry quarters, is the entrance for travelers from the north.

9. The CADET HOSPITAL, Thayer Road, built in 1924, Arnold W. Brunner, architect, is a massive stone structure with Gothic details. Study rooms adjoin the 20-bed wards.

The remaining points of interest must be visited on foot after car is parked opposite the Cadet Hospital.

10. The ADMINISTRATION BUILDING (*open* 10–12, 1–4 *weekdays except holidays*), Thayer Road, was built in 1904, Cram, Goodhue and Ferguson, architects. The powerful solid masonry of dark gray granite, trimmed with limestone, builds up into a picturesque mass dominated by the 160-foot tower-keep on the southeast corner. The battlements, buttresses, and cross-mullioned and traceried windows were inspired by the medieval castle. The entrance is ornamented with the rich heraldic seals of the Government and the Army and the Washington coat of arms, and is guarded by a raised portcullis. The large window at the rear lights the Academic Board Room, a vaulted hall with a carved stone chimney-piece, modeled by Lee Lawrie, which features the nine great warriors of ancient and medieval history. The ORDNANCE MUSEUM, upstairs L. of entrance, contains exhibits of multiple shot ordnance, including the French Mitrailleuse and the American Gatling gun, collections of flags and ammunition, artillery models, Indian relics, and Filipino and Chinese articles.

11. GRANT HALL (*open* 9–4, *evenings until Taps, daily*), the cadet reception hall, occupying a wing of the South Cadet Barracks across the driveway from the Administration Building, is finished in Tudor Gothic style, with State seals and insignia of Army divisions of the World War set into the ceiling. In the hall, informality prevails to a degree that astonishes visitors from abroad. But for their uniforms, the cadets are so many college boys.

12. The LIBRARY (*open* 9–6 *weekdays;* 2–5:30 *Sun.*), Jefferson and Cullum Roads, built in 1841, is the oldest surviving building now used by cadets. Major Robert Delafield, then superintendent, is usually credited with its Gothic Revival design, but its affinity with certain works of Alexander Jackson Davis, leading Gothicist of the period and very active in the Hudson Valley, suggests that Davis may have assisted in or at least inspired the design. The two-story stone structure has vine-clad, battlemented towers. The book collection contains more than 125,000 volumes; the military section is one of the most complete in the country. In the building are a portrait of Washington by Gilbert Stuart, a collection of portraits by Thomas Sully, including his portrait of Jonathan Williams, first superintendent of the Academy, and mementos of Whistler, Poe, and others.

Attached vertically to the north wall, near the library entrance, are two cannon: one, owned by the Confederates, several days before the attack on Fort Sumter fired the first shot in the Civil War at a steamer passing Vicksburg, Mississippi; the other fired the last shot before General Lee's surrender at Appomatox.

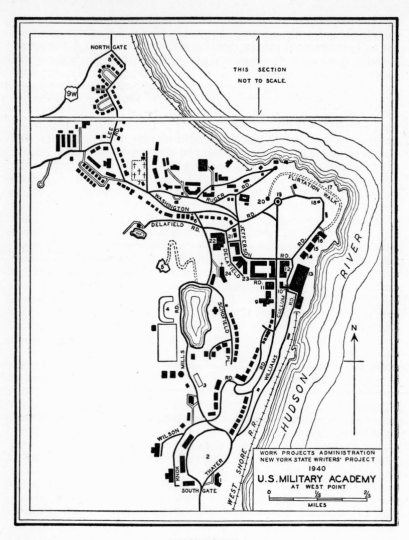

WEST POINT

(U.S. MILITARY ACADEMY)

1.Thayer-West Point Inn 2.Cavalry and Artillery Drill Field 3.Ice Arena 4.Michie Stadium 5.Fort Putnam 6.Chapel of the Most Holy Trinity 7.Old Cadet Chapel 8.North Gate 9.Cadet Hospital 10.Administration Building 11.Grant Hall 12.Library 13.Riding Hall 14.Officers' Club 15.Cullum Memorial Hall 16.Bach- elors' Building 17.Flirtation Walk 18.Kosciusko Monument 19.Washington Mon- ument 20.Battle Monument 21.Superintendent's Quarters 22.Gymnasium 23. Washington Hall 24.Cadet Chapel

13. The rugged granite walls of the RIDING HALL (*open 1–5 Mon.–Fri. except holidays*), built in 1911 by Cram, Goodhue and Ferguson, rise from the rocky river shore to the level of the east edge of the plain. In the arena, covering more than 16,000 square feet and lighted by skylights in the hinged steel arch roof, three riding classes meet simultaneously, field artillery units perform mounted drills, and polo teams enjoy the largest indoor field in the country. There are stalls for 100 horses, but most of the 250 mounts are kept in the south stables.

14. The OFFICERS' CLUB (*open to guests of members*), Cullum Road, houses the Bachelor Officers' Mess, one of the oldest in the service. The structure, one of the McKim, Mead and White buildings, is two stories high, designed in simple neoclassic style. It contains many battle paintings, engravings, and trophies. Silver candlesticks, formed by napkin rings joined vertically and engraved with the names of former members, adorn the table. A huge Chinese gong from the forbidden city of Peking, a trophy of the Boxer Rebellion, summons the members to 'chow.' There are dining rooms for married officers and their families, and the latest modern touch is the new rule admitting women to the cocktail lounge.

15. CULLUM MEMORIAL HALL (*open 10–12, 1–4 weekdays except holidays*), Cullum Road, dominates the neoclassic group of three buildings erected in 1898–1903 and designed by McKim, Mead and White. It is built of granite, two stories high, with hipped roof. The principal façade is adorned with a series of four three-quarter-engaged Ionic columns, with two antae, entablature, and acroteria. The building is the center of cadet social activities, especially the weekly hops. Flanking the main entrance are two guns cast in France in 1775 and taken at Santiago de Cuba in 1898.

16. The BACHELORS' BUILDING (*private*) is the third of the neoclassic structures. It contains the quarters of the bachelor officers assigned to duty at the Academy.

17. FLIRTATION WALK (*open only to officers, cadets, and their guests*), a gravel and rock foot trail, leaves Cullum Road just north of the Bachelors' Building and winds three quarters of a mile down the cliff to the river, past the lighthouse at Gee's Point, the beach where the western end of the great chain was anchored, the site of the chain battery, and the remains of the earthworks of Fort Clinton, and ends at Battle Monument.

Just before passing the lighthouse the path is overhung by KISSING ROCK, so called because, according to tradition, if a cadet passes underneath with his best girl and fails to kiss her, the rock will fall and crush them both.

Just beyond the point at which the walk turns south up the rise are (R) the boathouse, the north dock, and the airplane hangar.

18. The KOSCIUSKO MONUMENT, Cullum Road, designed by John H. Latrobe, class of 1822, was erected by the Corps of Cadets in 1828 to honor the Polish patriot who served with distinction under General Washington and helped plan the fortifications at West Point.

The Cadet Camp, of which the monument marks the northeast corner, was part of the site of Fort Clinton. It is occupied in summer only.

19. The WASHINGTON MONUMENT, in the circle at the corner of

Cullum Road and Thayer Road, is a replica of the one in Union Square, New York City.

20. BATTLE MONUMENT, a few steps west of the Washington Monument, is at the northern limit of the Plain, known as Trophy Point. The granite monument, designed by Stanford White and executed by Frederick MacMonnies, was erected to the memory of the 2,230 officers and privates of the regular Army killed in action in the Civil War. Standing on a circular pedestal, a Roman Doric column, five feet in diameter and 46 feet high, supports a winged statue of Fame. The five-step circular stairway around the base is broken by eight plain pedestals, each of which supports a sphere flanked by two cannon.

Near by, strung on stone posts, are a number of links from the 1700-foot, 180-ton chain which stretched across the Hudson from West Point to Constitution Island to block British ships during the Revolution. Each link was two feet nine inches long and about two and a quarter inches square. The display of cannon includes specimens captured in every major American war, together with several used by U.S. forces. There is also the telescopic periscope said to have been used in the World War by the German Crown Prince during the attack on Verdun and later captured by U.S. troops at Montfauçon.

21. The SUPERINTENDENT'S QUARTERS, Jefferson Road, was built about 1820 and was occupied by Robert E. Lee when he was superintendent of the Academy.

22. The GYMNASIUM (*open to visitors accompanied by officer or cadet*), originally built in 1908, has since been enlarged. It is the scene of intramural and intercollegiate athletic events, motion picture shows, stage productions, and dances.

On the south are the new Cadet Barracks.

23. WASHINGTON HALL (*open 10:30 a.m.–12 m. weekdays; 4–6 p.m. Sun. and holidays; cadet or officer must accompany visitor*), built in 1925–9, Gehron and Ross, architects, is the cadet mess hall. At meal time cadet companies march in in precise formation, take their places at the tables, and stand stiffly at attention until a signal is given from the main aisle by the Cadet Commander; then instantly the rigidness dissolves in a furious din and clatter.

Portraits of former superintendents and famous graduates hang on the walls. A large, multicolored window, picturing the outstanding events in George Washington's life, has 12 panels containing 12,000 pieces of imported glass in a surface of about 500 square feet. It is the product of two years of exacting work by artists and artisans of the Art Program of the WPA.

A statue of Brevet Major-General Sylvanus Thayer, as he was when he was superintendent of the Academy, stands on an inscribed pedestal on the lawn in front of the main entrance.

From the alley just east of Washington Hall, between it and the Central Cadet Barracks, several flights of stone steps lead up to the Cadet Chapel.

24. The CADET CHAPEL (*open 8–4 daily*), 300 feet above the river, is the dominant structure on the reservation. Completed in 1910, Cram,

Goodhue and Ferguson, architects, the high, gray granite building, neo-Gothic in style, is cruciform in plan, with a long nave and short transepts and a high buttressed tower at the crossing. The aisle walls of the nave are almost solid masonry; the high clerestory walls, by contrast, are all glass except for the stepped stone buttresses, which add to the impression of ruggedness.

The design of the Gothic interior is enhanced by the rows of battle flags hanging on both sides of the nave beneath the ceiling vaults, by the low aisle arches trimmed with stone, and by the slender piers supporting the vaulting.

The theme of war is carried out in the ornament: a series of figures representing the quest of the Holy Grail; King Arthur's Excalibur carved above the door; each of the 27 panels of the great chancel window representing a militant figure of Biblical history; angels dressed in suits of mail guarding holy places; even 'the Son of God goes forth to war.'

POINTS OF INTEREST IN ENVIRONS

Bear Mountain State Park, 6.5 *m.* (*see Tour* 4). Headquarters Park, Newburgh, 8.5 *m.*; Temple Hill and Monument, 12.3 *m.*; General Knox Headquarters, 12.4 *m.*; Stony Point Battlefield Reservation, 15.5 *m.* (*see Tour* 21A).

Yonkers

Railroad Stations: Foot of S.Main St. for New York Central System (main line); Broadway and Getty Sq. for New York Central System (Putnam Division); 12 suburban stations.
Bus Stations: Riverdale Ave. and Hudson St. (bus stop, not a terminal) for Greyhound, Flying Eagle, Gray, and Champlain Lines and interurban busses.
Ferry: Alexander St., foot of Ashburton and Wells Aves., to Alpine, N.J.; 6 a.m.–midnight; car and passengers, 40¢–50¢; pedestrians, 5¢.
Taxis: 30¢ first ¼ m., 10¢ each succeeding ¼ m.
Streetcars: 5¢ within city; connect with busses, interurban trains, and New York City subway.

Accommodations: 3 hotels; tourist homes.

Information Service: Chamber of Commerce, 20 S.Broadway; American Automobile Association, 284 S.Broadway; *Daily Herald-Statesman*, Larkin Plaza.

Motion Picture Houses: 5.
Swimming: Tibbets Brook Park, Midland Ave. between Yonkers and McLean Aves.; weekdays, children 15¢, adults 25¢; Sun. and holidays, children 25¢, adults 40¢; children under 12 free Mon., Wed., Fri. mornings.
Golf: Sprain Lake Golf Course, Grassy Sprain Rd. near north city line, 18 holes, greens fee: Mon.–Fri., 75¢; Sat. and holidays, $1.25; Sun. $1.50. Grassy Sprain Golf Course, Central Park Ave. at Tuckahoe Rd., 18 holes, greens fee $1; Sun. $1.50.
Tennis: City parks; season tickets $1, from Yonkers Recreation Commission, 283 Nepperhan Ave. Tibbets Brook Park (Westchester County Park Commission), 40¢ per hr. Mon.–Fri., $1 Sat., Sun., and holidays.

Annual Events: Polish Kosciusko festival at Kosciusko statue, Nepperhan Ave., Decoration Day; Italian Roseto festival, New Main St. and Park Hill Ave., July 16.

YONKERS (30 alt.,142,404 pop.) plays a double role as a residential suburb for New York City commuters and as an important manufacturing center. The 14 railroad stations within the city limits are supplemented by five additional ones—the latter the most heavily used—just beyond the eastern boundary.

The city occupies a huddle of hills and hollows on the east bank of the Hudson, its southern line forming the northern boundary of New York City. North Broadway runs between well-kept estates; South Broadway, its trolley line connecting with the northern terminus of the New York City subway system, is lined with apartment houses, secondhand automobile lots, and business establishments. The main business district centers in Getty Square, at a five-way intersection where Broadway crosses Main Street.

West of Broadway is the city's riverside industrial section; north and east along the Nepperhan River stretches a jumble of factories, mills, and warehouses surrounded by the drab homes of workers. East of Broadway, a maze of residential streets, broken by county parks and parkways, rises in a series of terraces from Locust Hill and Rose Hill along the Hudson to Nodine Hill and Valentine Hill, thence on to the Bronx River, which forms the eastern boundary. Valentine Hill was the scene of a skirmish after the Battle of White Plains, the only action of the Revolution within the present city limits.

The eastern part of Yonkers is composed of attractive residential districts. These communities—Crestwood, Mohegan Heights, Armour Villa Park, Sherwood Park, and others—have little to do with the commercial and industrial section to the west. Their inhabitants shop and receive their mail in Tuckahoe, Bronxville, and Mount Vernon, of which they consider themselves residents and to which their community spirit is tied.

The foreign groups of the industrial city, representing 28 nationalities and employed mostly in the mills and factories, comprise 25 per cent of the population; the public school rolls show 50 to 60 per cent of pupils of foreign parentage. The more recent Italian, Slav, and Polish arrivals outnumber the earlier Irish, Scotch, and German groups. These newcomers hold the balance of power in elections and take an absorbing interest in sports. The Empire City race track attracts turf followers in season. The city carries on an extensive program of recreational activities, and its sand lots frequently produce major league baseball stars. Golf was introduced in this country on the local St. Andrews course.

An Indian village—Nappeckamack—stood on the site of Yonkers, which was part of the Kekeskick Purchase (1639) made by the Dutch West India Company from the Indians. The city site was included in a grant of land made in 1646 by the company to Adriaen Cornelissen Van der Donck, the first lawyer and the first historian of New Netherland. By reason of his wealth and social position Van der Donck enjoyed the courtesy title of 'jonker,' the Dutch equivalent of 'his young lordship,' from which was derived the name of the city.

Van der Donck's colony, called Colendonck, was broken up into smaller holdings shortly after the British took possession in 1664. In the 20 years after 1672, Frederick Philipse, merchant trader and member of the Provincial Council, by a series of purchases acquired a tract of land extending along the east bank of the Hudson from Spuyten Duyvil Creek on the south to the Croton River on the north and eastward to the Bronx River. In 1693, by Royal charter, this domain became the Manor of Philipsburgh and its proprietor the lord of the manor. He erected the original Manor Hall, established mills, rented land to tenants, and soon had a flourishing colony, important in the eighteenth century for its iron mines. His great-grandson, the third and last lord of the manor, supported the Tory side in the Revolution, and the estate was confiscated in 1779.

In the early years of the nineteenth century, Yonkers was a village inhabited mainly by farmers; the land was well watered, the growing metropolis to the south provided a market, and transportation by boat was cheap. Development was accelerated by the opening of the Hudson River Railroad in 1849. In 1855 the village was incorporated with a population of 7,554. With the passing of the turnpike era, stagecoaches and taverns disappeared. Cheap transportation and the water power of the Nepperhan River attracted industries, such as Elisha G. Otis's elevator works in 1854, David Saunders's machine shop in 1857, and Alexander Smith's carpet mill in 1865.

In the second half of the nineteenth century, Yonkers enjoyed a national reputation for the products of its looms, spindles, and machine shops. New industries were added and attracted Irish, English, Scottish, and German immigrants, later to be followed by Poles, Hungarians, Italians, Armenians, and Russians. The city was chartered in 1872. In 1892 several dams, which at one time crossed the Nepperhan at seven levels, were torn out, industry turned to electricity for power, and the river, reduced to a trickle, disappeared beneath highways and buildings. Water transportation steadily decreased until it is no longer a factor; and the Hudson River docks, which once bustled with the traffic of sea-going craft, are practically deserted. The latest development in transportation has been the extension of the elaborate system of county parkways transecting the city.

Yonkers has more than 100 industries, employing about 15,000 workers and producing annually $100,000,000 in goods. Chief products are carpets and rugs, clothing—including women's dresses, men's hats and caps, and uniforms—elevators, books, patent medicines, and insulated wire and cable.

POINTS OF INTEREST

1. ST.JOHN'S EPISCOPAL CHURCH, SW. corner of S.Broadway and Getty Square, is designed in a modified Romanesque-Victorian Gothic style. The plan is cruciform, with a very high nave, high, broad aisles, and narrow, low transepts, much like side vestibules. The second lord of the manor gave a glebe for the church and cemetery and built the original edifice in 1752, which was partially destroyed by fire in 1791 and rebuilt in 1792. The old walls were incorporated in the present church, built in 1870.

2. The YONKERS CITY HALL, S.Broadway opposite Prospect St., occupying the crest of a sharp hill, is a three-story-and-basement structure built in 1908 of yellow pressed brick with buff stone trim. It is designed in the neoclassic style, its high, domed clock tower dominating the downtown section.

The WORLD WAR MEMORIAL, at the foot of the hill, is a semicircular monument of pink granite set into the rocky face of the hill and bordered by shrubs and flower beds. In the center stands a female figure in bronze executed by I.Konti.

3. PHILIPSE MANOR HALL (*open 9–5 weekdays, Sundays 1–5; admission free*), at the northwest corner of Warburton Avenue and Dock St., is an example of restored Georgian Colonial architecture, built of weathered brick with white wood trim. The building is L-shape in plan, with hipped slate roof, dormers, and roof balustrade. The symmetrical, five-bay façade with its fanlighted doorway and small Doric

portico is typical of the period. The older part of the house, the south wing facing Dock Street, was built about 1682; the northern portion was added about 1745. During the Revolution it was held alternately by Americans and British. In 1780, 16,000 British soldiers encamped on the estate for several weeks; in 1781 the grounds were occupied by Americans. A 300-acre parcel of the estate, including the manor house, was sold to Cornelius P. Low, New York merchant, in 1785. It was purchased by Yonkers in 1868 and became the village hall. When the new city hall was built, the preservation of Manor Hall as a shrine was made possible by a gift of $50,000 by Mrs. William F. Cochran. Title is vested in the State and the property is in the custody of the American Scenic and Historic Preservation Society.

The building contains Colonial furniture and objects of historical interest and a priceless collection of portraits of the Presidents from Washington to Coolidge and of a number of early American leaders, including the Tuckerman portrait of Franklin, portraits of George and Martha Washington by Gilbert Stuart, the portrait of Alexander Hamilton by James Sharples, and the portrait of John Quincy Adams by Thomas Sully. Of the five portraits of Washington in the collection, three are with brown eyes and two with blue eyes.

There is a local tradition that Washington courted Mary Philipse, sister of the third lord, in this house, and that in the midst of the feast following her marriage to Captain Roger Morris an Indian appeared and uttered the Sibylline prophecy, 'Your possessions shall pass from you when the Eagle shall despoil the Lion of his mane.' This came to pass when the manor was confiscated during the Revolution.

4. The OTIS ELEVATOR WORKS (*open by permission*), 44 Wells Ave., a number of old brick and new concrete buildings, manufactures electric elevators. Elisha G. Otis, the inventor, settled in Yonkers in 1852 and installed the first elevator to carry freight in his bedstead factory, in which for some years the Otis elevators were made. In 1853 he demonstrated his 'perpendicular stairway' at the Crystal Palace exhibition in New York, and the contrivance soon became popular.

5. The HUDSON RIVER MUSEUM AT YONKERS (*open 9-12, 1-5 weekdays, 2-5 Sun. and holidays*), 511 Warburton Ave., is housed in the Victorian Gothic Trevor Mansion. Built in 1876, it is of rock-cut stone, with square and round towers, many dormer windows, bracketed cornice, high, patterned slate roofs, bay windows, and balconies. The collections include manuscripts, books, newspapers, prints, maps; antique furnishings; American Indian, Philippine, Australian, and African native material. The museum serves the city schools and has special loan exhibitions.

6. The BOYCE–THOMPSON RESEARCH INSTITUTE (*open 9-5 Mon.-Fri.; 9-12 Sat.*), 1086 N. Broadway, is a center for the scientific study of plant growth. Alarmed by food shortages during the World War, the late Colonel William Boyce-Thompson founded the institution and equipped it with facilities for growing plants under controlled conditions.

7. GREYSTONE (*grounds open 10-5 Tues. May to Oct.*), 919 Broadway, built in 1873, is a solid graystone three-story structure designed in the

French Second Empire style with bulky square towers that rise an additional story above a mansard roof. The grounds are especially beautiful during the blooming of the rhododendrons in May and June. Once the home of Samuel J. Tilden, it was owned by Samuel Untermeyer until his death in 1940. The garden includes a cryptomeria walk, one-color gardens opening from the walk, Persian canals, Greek temples, and a 'living sundial' of flowers.

8. The ALEXANDER SMITH CARPET MILLS (*open to technicians by appointment*), with its general offices on Saw Mill River Road between Ashburton and Lake Aves. and its mills on near-by streets, is the largest industry in Yonkers, employing about 5,000 workers. During the last century, the carpet weaving industry was revolutionized by labor-saving looms invented in this plant by Alexander Smith and Halcyon Skinner.

9. ST.JOSEPH'S SEMINARY (*open by special permission*), 201 Seminary Ave., is an immense ashlar stone building, five stories high, with high attic, slate roofs, and cut stone trim. It is of modified French Renaissance design. The main entrance unit is marked by a pyramidal roof surmounted by a high open lantern and flanked by circular towers with conical roofs. The building is occupied by about 270 aspirants to the Catholic priesthood and their teachers.

10. The EMPIRE CITY RACE TRACK (*grandstand and paddock*, $1.50; *clubhouse*, $4; *July and Oct.*), Yonkers and Central Aves., is the smallest and least pretentious of the metropolitan tracks. It was built in 1898-9 by William H. Clark and in 1902 was purchased by James Butler, chain store magnate. After a long controversy with the Jockey Club, Butler was finally given a license for his track, and in 1907 he entered upon his colorful career as a racing promoter. Known as the 'poor man's race course,' Empire City attracts crowds ranging up to 35,000 daily.

Butler has become a legendary figure in Yonkers. 'The Squire of East View,' as he was known, was no flashy mixer of the 'Diamond Jim' type, but had a vast acquaintance among horsemen everywhere and was well liked by his Westchester neighbors. When one of his thoroughbreds stood in the winner's circle, Finnegan's Band invariably played *The Wearing of the Green*, and the crowd shouted its approval. Butler, however, never let sentiment interfere with business, and when the band became too great an expense it went the way of all unnecessary trimmings, Butler declaring that if the crowd must have its favorite tune of victory, 'Let 'em whistle it!' Butler would not look at golf or tennis. When his neighbor, John D. Rockefeller,Sr., invited him to play a few holes, Butler refused, declaring that golf was a rich man's game. He maintained the fiction of being poor by riding to his racetrack in a rickety automobile of outmoded design. For education, however, he loosened the purse-strings. Marymount College, on a high hill opposite Rockefeller's estate in Tarrytown, was founded by Butler.

11. SARAH LAWRENCE COLLEGE, a liberal arts college for girls, occupies an 18-acre campus just west of the Bronxville line. The main buildings, arranged in a rough semicircle, are built of Harvard brick and native stone and designed in the English Tudor style. The faculty numbers about

60; the student body about 275. The curriculum emphasizes music and dramatics.

The college was founded in 1926 by William Van Duzer Lawrence in memory of his wife, Sarah (Bates) Lawrence. The present campus was the Lawrence estate. WESTLANDS, erected in 1916, a large English Tudor mansion that was the Lawrence residence, is now the administration building of the college.

POINTS OF INTEREST IN ENVIRONS

Saxon Woods Park, 12 *m.*; Playland, 17.5 *m.* (*see Tour* 1). Wayside Inn, 7 *m.*; Kensico Dam, 17 *m.* (*see Tour* 20). Sunnyside, 11.2 *m.*; Sleepy Hollow Dutch Reformed Church and Sleepy Hollow Cemetery, 12 *m.* (*see Tour* 21).

PART III
Tours

Tour 1

(Greenwich, Conn.)—Port Chester—New Rochelle—New York City;
US 1.

Connecticut Line to New York City, 23.1 *m.*

New York, New Haven & Hartford and New York, Westchester & Boston R.R.s parallel route.
Four-lane concrete, macadam stretches in some towns.

This busy route, used by busses, trucks, commuters, and tourists between Boston and New York, follows the shore line of Long Island Sound across Westchester County. Since the eighties this has been an area of extensive and luxurious estates. Here are the homes of leaders of business and finance, of publishers, writers, artists, and stars of the stage and screen.

The Boston Post Road, like most other Colonial routes, followed old Indian trails. In 1704 Madam Sarah Knight wrote of her trip on horseback: 'The Rhodes all along this way were very bad. Incumbered with Rocks and mountainous passages, which were very dissagreeable to my tired carcass.'

Stagecoaches appeared on the Post Road early in the eighteenth century. Josiah Quincy, president of Harvard, describes a trip from Boston to New York: 'I set out from Boston in the line of stages of an enterprising Yankee, Pease by name; considered a method of transportation of wonderful expedition. The journey to New York took up a week. The carriages were old and shackling, and much of the harness of ropes. We reached our resting place for the night, if no accident intervened, at 10 o'clock, and, after a frugal supper, went to bed with a notice that we should be called at three which generally proved to be half-past two, and then, whether it snowed or rained, the traveller must rise and make ready, by the help of a horn lantern and a farthing candle, and proceed on his way over bad roads, sometimes getting out to help the coachman lift the coach out of a quagmire or rut, and arrive in New York after a week's hard travelling, wondering at the ease, as well as the expedition, with which our journey was effected.'

The recently completed boulevards (*see below*) provide an alternate route for those who wish to avoid trucks, cross traffic, and billboards.

US 1 crosses the BYRAM RIVER, 0 *m.*, here the boundary between Greenwich, Connecticut, and Port Chester, New York.

PORT CHESTER, 0.3 *m.* (34 alt., 23,074 pop.), first known as Saw Log Swamp and later as Saw Pit, was settled about 1650. Its factories produce candy, ammonia, nuts and bolts, furnaces, coal and gas ranges, soft drinks, and cartons.

The Bush Homestead (*open* 9–4:30 *Tues., Thurs., Sat.*), Lyon Park overlooking King St., is a well-preserved Georgian Colonial house built shortly before the Revolution by Abraham Bush, a sea captain; it was the headquarters of General Israel Putnam, 1777–8. The original furniture has been preserved, including the bed and desk used by 'Old Put.'

The Samuel Brown Home, Browndale Place, built in 1774 on the site of an earlier homestead, has been altered several times, notably by the addition of a wing. The interior walls, doors, and floors are unchanged.

The Brown Graveyard, at the rear of a vacant lot on Indian Road, a huddle of fallen tombstones among brambles, was the private burial ground of the Brown family from 1660 to 1900.

Right from Port Chester at the eastern end of town on Putnam Ave.; R. on King St. (State 120A) to the Hutchinson River Parkway, 2.4 *m.*, an alternate route between Port Chester and New York City. This is a four-lane road cutting through terraced, forested countryside (*speed limit,* 35 *m.p.h., strictly enforced*).

SAXON WOODS PARK, 9 *m.* (*riding, hiking, picnicking, golf*), is a 749-acre recreational development of Westchester County.

At a traffic circle, 13.8 *m.*, is the junction with the Cross County Parkway; R. here 2.4 *m.* to the intersection with the Bronx River Parkway (*see Tour* 40). The Cross County Parkway continues to YONKERS (*see Yonkers*) on US 9 (*see Tour* 21), which is 5.7 *m.* from the junction with the Hutchinson River Parkway.

On the Hutchinson River Parkway at 15.5 *m.* is (R) the Lincoln Ave. entrance to MOUNT VERNON (*see Tour* 20).

At 17.2 *m.* is the ramp leading to US1 (*see below*).

RYE, 2.9 *m.* (49 alt.,9,803 pop.), settled in 1660, is visible from US 1 as a series of apartment houses and mansions with landscaped grounds. The Haviland Inn (R), Purchase St. between Liberty Lane and Locust Ave., was built in 1730 and is now the Rye village hall. The old glass is intact; the beams are wooden-pegged; hand-split shingles cover three quarters of the structure. The inn was run by Dame Tamar Haviland, after her husband's death during the Revolution. In her time this was a notable stopping place on the old Post Road.

The Grave of John Jay (1749–1829), first Chief Justice of the U.S., is in a private cemetery on the Palmer Estate, Post Road and Barlow Lane, once the home of his brother, Peter Jay.

In Rye at 3.7 *m.* is an entrance ramp to the Cross County Parkway.

Left on ramp and R. on the parkway 1 *m.* to PLAYLAND (*open all year; bathing beach with accommodations for* 10,000, *boardwalk, swimming pool, dance hall, hockey rink, picnic grove, amusement devices. Parking* 25¢ *weekdays,* 50¢ *Sun. and holidays*).

Tied up at the Playland dock is the clipper ship, *Benjamin F. Packard* (*adm.* 10¢), built at Bath, Maine, by Cross, Sawyer & Packard in 1883. With a tonnage of 2,026 gross and a mainmast rising 147 feet from her deck, the *Packard* was one of the larger ships of her period. Her logs cover many voyages around Cape Horn.

MAMARONECK (Ind., he assembles the people), 6 *m.* (47 alt.,13,012 pop.), was settled by English farmers about 1650. Factories producing woolen cloth, perfume oils, and motor oils provide local employment for some of the residents, but the majority commute to work in New York City. Seven yacht clubs have private basins along the jagged shore line of the village.

The DE LANCEY MANOR HOUSE, 404 W.Post Road, known in its hey-day as Heathcote Hill, is now a gas station and restaurant; this was the ancestral home of the De Lanceys and in it James Fenimore Cooper married Susan A. De Lancey in 1811. The couple lived here for a time after the wedding. The building, which has been altered and enlarged, was bought at auction for $11 and moved to this place from its original position over-looking the Sound.

Colonel Caleb Heathcote, lord of the Manor of Scarsdale, wrote in 1704: 'Westchester—the most rude and heathenish country I ever saw in my life, which call themselves Christian; there being not so much as the least marks or footsteps of religion of any sort; Sundays being the only time set apart by them for all manner of vain sports and lewd diversion . . .'

Left on Orienta Ave. to beach and yacht clubs along the Sound, 1.3 *m.* On this street stood the early movie studios of D.W.Griffith, screen pioneer. *Way Down East, Or-phans of the Storm,* and *Valley Forge* were filmed with Mamaroneck backgrounds.

Southwest of Mamaroneck the Post Road passes large estates. Ethel Barrymore, James Montgomery Flagg, and Robert 'Believe It or Not' Ripley live near by. Approaching Long Island Sound (L) US 1 presents a view of dismal marshland, fishing huts, and small wharves. Chromium-trimmed taverns and elaborate filling stations follow in close succession.

LARCHMONT, 8.2 *m.* (100 alt.,5,955 pop.), is a residential commu-nity; more than half the total population commutes daily to New York City. Beach Ave. leads (L) to private shore and yacht clubs on the Sound. From the LARCHMONT YACHT CLUB the regattas on Labor Day are major events in eastern yachting circles.

NEW ROCHELLE, 10.5 *m.* (72 alt.,57,415 pop.) (*see New Rochelle*).

Left from New Rochelle on Echo Ave. to the junction with Pelham Road; R. on Pelham Road to State 1B (the Shore Road), which closely follows the shore of Long Island Sound to New York City. BOLTON PRIORY (R), 2.1 *m.*, was built in 1838 by the Reverend Robert Bolton, whose friend, Washington Irving, gave yellow bricks from the old Dutch church at Sleepy Hollow to outline the construction date on the wall above the door. A bloody battle between the Matinecocks and the Siwanoys took place on CEDAR KNOLL (L). The Siwanoys were routed and prisoners were de-capitated. Legend has it that when the moon is full, the spirits of the headless Indians perform a war dance, holding their heads in their hands.

The NEW YORK ATHLETIC CLUB (L), 2.4 *m.*, Italian Renaissance in style, stands on deep, landscaped lawns at Travers Island.

At the New York City line, 2.5 *m.*, State 1B becomes Pelham Parkway.

PELHAM MANOR, 12 *m.* (100 alt.,5,270 pop.), a residential commu-nity, is on land purchased by Thomas Pell in 1664 from the Siwanoy Indi-ans; the tract included what is now New Rochelle, Mount Vernon, the Pelhams, and Eastchester. In 1680 John Pell sold 6,000 acres for 'Sixteen hundred twenty and five *currant* silver money of the Province,' also 'to John Pell . . . every four and twentieth day of June yearly, and every year frowever if demanded, one fat calf.' Anne Hutchinson, rebel against Puritan conformity in Massachusetts, settled in this section in 1642 and was murdered in 1643 by Indians at Throgg's Neck, now Pelham Bay Shore.

Pelhamdale Ave., to the railroad station on Washington Ave., was the route of the tiny trolley said to have provided the inspiration for the *Toonerville Trolley* series of Fontaine Fox, the cartoonist.

At 12.5 *m.* is the junction with Split Rock Road.

Left on Split Rock Road to the New York City line, 0.5 *m.*, then through Pelham Bay Park to Pelham Parkway. Split Rock Road was once the private driveway from the manor house of Thomas Pell to the Boston Post Road. Washington's army retreated along this road after the Battle of Long Island. Some of the heaviest fighting in the Battle of Pell's Point, October 18, 1776, took place in the vicinity of the cleft 10-foot boulder, which is (R) near the New York City line.

At 12.6 *m.* is (R) the southern junction with the Hutchinson River Parkway, alternate route from the Connecticut State line (*see above*).

The New York City line, 12.8 *m.*, (*see New York City*), is crossed in a marshy area with rows of brick houses and many filling stations.

US 1 continues westward across the northern part of the city (*follow signs*), and crosses on the GEORGE WASHINGTON MEMORIAL BRIDGE, 21.2 *m.*, to New Jersey, 23.1 *m.*, at a point 12 miles north of Jersey City, New Jersey.

Tour 2

Junction US 202 and US 9W—Suffern—(Morristown, N.J.); US 202, 13 *m.*

Concrete roadbed.

US 202 is a short cut that avoids the larger cities between New England and the Philadelphia area. Between Haverstraw and the Bear Mountain Bridge it unites with US 9W (*see Tour 21A*) and east of the Bear Mountain Bridge with US 6 (*see Tour 4*). This section winds through sparsely settled country, part of the way along the edge of the Harriman-Bear Mountain section of the Palisades Interstate Park. The near-by hills are in places covered with forests that have received expert care in recent years and the area resembles a natural park.

The road follows an old Indian trail, as artifacts discovered during the road-building period indicate. During the Revolutionary War it was used by messengers between commanders of fortifications along the Hudson and detachments holding the Clove, the main Ramapo pass. New England troops and their French allies marched over it on their way from Stony Point and King's Ferry.

US 202 branches west from US 9W, 0 *m.*, at the northern end of Haverstraw, and at 0.5 *m.* passes (L) LITTLE TOR, the northernmost outcrop of the Palisades traprock. As the route reaches the valley of the Mahwah River, 6 *m.*, the Ramapo Mountains rise up in the west (*hikers in these mountains should be on guard against rattlesnakes and copperheads*).

The BAYARD LANE PROJECT (L), 9 *m.*, is a 40-acre tract devoted to the most recent of New York's long line of experiments in finding a happier way of living. Unlike the members of the communities of 100 years ago, the members of this one have no special religious or political programs; they are interested in providing themselves with attractive and comfortable homes in an efficient and economical manner. The ground is owned by the organization; the dwellings, conforming to plans approved by a governing board, are built for the individual householders by a cooperative. The members of the community have truck gardens for their own use but practically all male members of the village commute to jobs in New York City. This project, one of several being established, was inspired by Ralph Borsodi, economist and author.

SUFFERN, 11 *m.* (500 alt.,3,765 pop.), is a commuters' village and the local shopping center for many city people with summer homes near by. The main street of the village is treeless and sign-cluttered, giving little evidence of the spirit that has landscaped the riverbanks so attractively.

The SUFFERN SUMMER THEATER (*July and Aug.; seats* $1–$1.50) produces Broadway hits and is used for tryouts of plays that interest Broadway producers.

At 11 *m.* is the junction with a black-topped road.

Left on this road 0.4 *m.* to (L) the HOME OF DAN BEARD (1850——), teacher and author, best known as the founder of the Boy Scouts of America. The story-and-a-half white clapboard house with green shutters and roof is in a five-acre tract of woods and meadow.

On the southern outskirts of Suffern, at 13 *m.*, US 202 crosses the NEW JERSEY LINE at a point 35 miles northeast of Morristown, New Jersey.

Tour 3

(New York City, N.Y.)—Suffern—Binghamton—Elmira—Corning—Olean—Salamanca—Jamestown—Westfield, State 17.
New Jersey Line to Westfield, 406.4 *m.*

Erie R.R. roughly parallels route between the New Jersey Line and Jamestown. Two- and three-lane hard-surfaced roadbed.

State 17, the main east-west highway crossing southern New York, zigzags back and forth, connecting towns that achieved their growth after the construction of the Erie Railroad, which reached Lake Erie in 1851. This important road became as valuable an asset to the southern tier of counties as the Erie Canal was to the central part of the State. Construction was subsidized by nearly $5,000,000 from the State and handsome grants of land from counties, towns, and real estate owners eager to swing the route in their direction. In a speech in 1865 justifying this public aid, William H. Seward said that the people of New York could well afford it because 'we have not, and with the favor of God never will have, any aristocracy, pensioners and placemen in Church and State to consume the substance of the people.'

Section a. NEW JERSEY LINE to WESTERN JUNCTION WITH US 6; 33.2 m. State 17

This section of State 17 runs through the picturesque Ramapos, along the Ramapo River, and into a country of farms, some of them operated by wealthy summer residents as hobbies and others by families whose livelihood has for generations come from the land.

State 17, continuation of NJ 2, crosses the NEW JERSEY LINE, 0 *m.*, 25 miles north of New York City.

In the near-by hills live the Jackson Whites, whose ramshackle frame houses bespeak their poverty. During the Revolutionary War a trader named Jackson contracted to supply 3,500 British women for the entertainment of His Majesty's troops in America; after losing part of his cargo during the ocean voyage, he put into the West Indies to fill up his quota with Negro women. When the troops were withdrawn at the end of the war, the women were left behind in New York City, soon to be driven out by the authorities. They moved up into these hills, which already held other social outcasts—remnants of Claudius Smith's band (*see below*), runaway slaves, Hessian deserters, and a few Tuscaroras whose ancestors had left the main band during the journey north in 1714 to join the Iroquois Confederacy. The results of this racial interbreeding have been varied; many of the Jackson Whites are bronzed and show clear evidence of Indian blood; an unusually large number are albinos; others show Negro characteristics; and still others exhibit no evidence of Negro or Indian blood.

In SLOATSBURG, 2.6 *m.* (320 alt.,1,623 pop.), is the SLOT HOUSE (L). The main unit is a brick Greek Revival structure built by Isaac Slot in the early 1800's on the front of a much older one-story house erected by his father Isaac, for whom the village was named. At the southern end of the village line is SMITH'S TAVERN (L), built on the foundation of an old stagecoach tavern of the same name in which Washington stopped in June 1775. Facsimiles of military instructions from General Washington to General Anthony Wayne, dated 'Smith's tavern in ye Clove,' hang on the walls.

At Sloatsburg is the junction with Stony Brook Drive, leading into the Harriman Section of the Palisades Interstate Park (*see Tour* 4).

The village of TUXEDO, 5.5 *m.* (420 alt.,2,000 pop.), is chiefly the utility entrance to TUXEDO PARK (*open to public only on July* 4), which covers 13,000 acres around Little Wee, Big Little Wee, and Tuxedo Lakes. The beautiful tract was owned in the 1880's by Pierre Lorillard, the fourth. who decided to make it a refuge for America's early crop of millionaires. The land was broken up and sold in large tracts, on which were erected turreted mansions of the kind then fashionable. Proof that the

Tuxedoites had reached the eminence from which they could set the styles, rather than follow them, is found in the name of the dinner jacket that is now a formal uniform of the males of the Nation. For a long time Mrs.Emily Post, authority on etiquette, lived here.

Right from the railroad station in Tuxedo on a trail that leads to the CLAUDIUS SMITH CAVES, 1 m., shelter of a band of Tory highwaymen. The upper cave, about 9 feet high, 30 feet long, and 6 to 8 feet deep, housed the outlaws, while the lower one, of almost the same size, was the stable. Claudius Smith specialized in stealing horses and cattle from Whigs and selling them to the British; his disregard for human life made him particularly hated, and he was finally captured and executed.

At 8 m. is the junction with State 210, reached by an overpass.

Right on State 210, here part of the Seven Lakes Drive, into the HARRIMAN SECTION (see Tour 4) of the Palisades Interstate Park.

ARDEN, 12.3 m. (520 alt.,200 pop.), is primarily the railroad station of the Harriman Estate.

Right from Arden on a private road (open only to those with passes) into ARDEN, the 20,000-acre estate established by E.H.Harriman (1848–1909) and his wife at the beginning of the twentieth century. On the crest of the Ramapos is the 150-room chateau designed in the French Renaissance style and separated from the forest below by formal gardens of great beauty.

When E.H.Harriman died he left his $100,000,000 holdings intact to his wife, who continued their management until her death. She carried out his desire in transferring to the State the 10,000-acre section of the estate that is now the Harriman Section of the Palisades Interstate Park, and funds for its development as a public recreational area.

State 17 continues northward through HARRIMAN, 14.6 m. (560 alt., 657 pop.), a center of Harriman agricultural activities, to a junction with US 6 (see Tour 4), 17.5 m., on the western edge of Monroe. State 17 unites with US 6 between this point and a junction at 33.2 m. near Middletown (see Tour 4).

Section b. WESTERN JUNCTION OF US 6 to BINGHAMTON; 125.3 m. State 17.

This section of State 17 runs through the Shawangunk Mountains where in the early half of the nineteenth century considerable tanning was done. For many years the Shawangunk Mountains have been a summer resort for New Yorkers.

State 17 branches north from its western junction, 0 m., with US 6 (see Tour 4) on the southern edge of MIDDLETOWN, 2.3 m. (559 alt.,21,844 pop.), a trade center for farmers that has also become a manufacturing city. It produces printers' supplies, wrapping machines, shirts, machine tools, knives, women's underwear, and bags, and processes furs and leather. The city grew up along what had been the Minisink Trail, which ran from the Hudson to the headwaters of the Delaware and the Susquehanna.

The road crosses the route of the DELAWARE & HUDSON CANAL, 13.5 m., abandoned in 1899. After William and Maurice Wurts, Philadelphia merchants, had acquired anthracite coal fields in Pennsylvania, they determined to build this canal to carry the coal to the New York and New England markets. The State of New York was persuaded to help supply the funds for canal construction and John B. Jervis, a civil engineer, was placed in charge of the work. The public in general ridiculed the enterprise until December 3, 1828, when the first little fleet, bearing 120 tons of Pennsylvania coal, started down the Hudson. To bring the coal from the mines to the canal Jervis devised a railroad with seven inclined planes and nine miles of trestle. In 1830 he became chief construction engineer of the Mohawk & Hudson Railroad, for which he had a locomotive, the *Experiment*, built with such improvements as a forward four-wheel swivel truck to enable it to round curves.

WURTSBORO, 14.7 *m.* (560 alt.,423 pop.), and its environs have a large summer-vacation population. It is at the junction with US 209 (*see Tour* 6).

West of Wurtsboro is a picturesque region of lakes and woodland abounding in hotels, camps, and boarding houses in which thousands of New York stenographers, garment workers, clerks, embryo lawyers and doctors annually romp, take on sun tan, discuss world problems, and crowd into two weeks enough romance and adventure to carry them through another eleven and a half months. This is the locale of *Having Wonderful Time*, Broadway stage hit of 1937–8. All summer long the road is crowded with every make and age of automobile; the older the machine the greater its burden of sun-goggled, kerchiefed vacationists.

MONTICELLO, 27 *m.* (1,524 alt.,3,630 pop.), seat of Sullivan County, is the capital of this vacationland that spreads to the Neversink Valley on the east and the Mongaup Valley on the west. In and near the town are large rambling hotels—many of them advertising *kosher* meals; and half of the town's householders rent every room that can be spared from family needs.

Left near the western end of the town on State 42 to (L) MERRIWOLD PARK (*private*), 6.3 *m.*, a large resort club surrounding a small lake. The homes range from small log cabins to fairly elaborate mansions. One of the most picturesque is SHO FOO DEN (Jap., maple-pine palace), constructed in Japan and sent to the United States in 1904 to house the Japanese exhibit at the St.Louis Exposition. The structure was brought here by Dr.Jokichi Takamine, the Japanese chemist who first isolated adrenalin and who was the donor of the Japanese cherry trees in Washington.

State 17 turns northwestward to LIBERTY, 38.9 *m.* (1,581 alt.,3,789 pop.), a year-round resort with toboggan slides and ski trails and a program of winter carnivals and races. It also has a large private tuberculosis sanatorium.

At 50 *m.* is the junction with Johnson Hill Road (R) to BEAVERKILL STATE CAMPSITE (50 *fireplaces, swimming*), along a popular trout stream. This entire region is a favorite with trout fishermen.

At the western end of EAST BRANCH, 70.7 *m.* (1,007 alt.,300 pop.), is the junction with State 30 (*see Tour* 24). State 17 follows the East Branch of the Delaware River to HANCOCK, 82.5 *m.* (920 alt.,1,427 pop.), a summer resort at the junction of the East and West Branches of the Delaware. DEPOSIT, 96 *m.* (1,000 alt.,1,887 pop.), is another summer resort.

At 120.3 *m.* is a junction with US 11 (*see Tour* 18), which unites with State 17 to Binghamton.

BINGHAMTON, 125.3 *m.* (845 alt.,78,242 pop.) (*see Binghamton*), is at the junction with State 7 (*see Tour* 10) and US 11 (*see Tour* 18).

Section c. BINGHAMTON to ELMIRA; 57.7 m. State 17

This section of State 17 runs along the south bank of the Susquehanna and then the north bank of the Chemung River through rolling farm land. West of Binghamton the highway follows the trail used in 1779 by the Sullivan-Clinton expedition.

In BINGHAMTON, 0 *m.*, is the junction with State 17C, recommended as a better paved alternate between Binghamton and Owego.

Right from Courthouse Square in Binghamton on Main St. (State 17C), crossing the Chenango River. This 20-mile road runs through the communities that have grown up around the factories and offices of the Endicott-Johnson Corporation, manufacturer of shoes. The corporation has 29 factories, surrounded by the homes, gardens, and parks it has built for its 19,000 employees.

The corporation was built up and its policy determined by George F. Johnson, who was born in Massachusetts in 1857 and left school at the age of 13 to work in a small boot-making factory. In 1881 he secured a position in a shoe factory in Binghamton, and a few years later persuaded his employer to build a new factory outside the city at a place now called Johnson City on the theory that industry should be removed from congested centers. After the lean years of the 1890's Henry B. Endicott, the chief stockholder of the company, put Johnson in charge of reorganization. Johnson's program was, 'Cut out the frills and unnecessary costs and give the workers an incentive to produce—put them on piecework at a decent rate.'

As business expanded Johnson was able to put into practice his plan of providing homes that the workers could buy on time payments with a low carrying charge. When the company became a corporation he established a system whereby workers shared in the profits, and 2¼¢ were added to the cost of each pair of shoes to cover welfare activities for employees. In 1940 the employees voted against being represented by a CIO or an A.F.of L. union.

At the eastern entrance of JOHNSON CITY, 2.1 *m.* (847 alt.,17,952 pop.), is an archway, erected by Endicott-Johnson employees, with the inscription, 'Home of the Square Deal.' The Pioneer factory still stands. In the village are several recreational parks laid out by the company.

In ENDICOTT, 7.3 *m.* (840 alt.,17,657 pop.), are the headquarters and several factories of the Endicott-Johnson Corporation and of the International Business Machines Corporation.

State 17C continues through WEST ENDICOTT, 8.5 *m.*, newest and most delightful of the Endicott-Johnson villages.

UNION, 8.7 *m.*, was so named because it was at this place that the forces of Sullivan and Clinton met in August 1779. Sullivan had come up from Pennsylvania and Clinton down from the Mohawk. Endicott, Union, and West Endicott were consolidated in 1921.

At OWEGO, 21.2 *m.*, State 17C meets State 17 (*see below*).

State 17 crosses the Susquehanna to OWEGO, 22.3 *m.* (818 alt.,4,742 pop.), which came into existence on the site of Ah-wah-ga (where the valley widens), one of the Indian towns destroyed by the Sullivan-Clinton troops in 1779. Owego is an important railroad junction. The only factory of importance belongs to the Endicott-Johnson Corporation.

During the late 1800's Tom Platt's annual pancake breakfasts, the windup of Republican victory celebrations, were served in the main dining room of the AHWAGAH HOTEL, still in operation at 213 Front Street. At sunrise, after a night of hilarity, Platt and his cohorts, party workers from the Southern Tier, would gather at the hotel to eat pancakes and drink black coffee until midday. Thomas Collier Platt (1833–1910), born in Owego, was graduated from the Owego Academy. In 1870 he and Roscoe Conkling organized a powerful political machine that broke the hold Horace Greeley and Senator Reuben Fenton had on the State.

Owego is at the junction with State 17C (*see above*), State 2 (*see Tour* 30), and State 38 (*see Tour* 8).

When in 1915 Theodore Dreiser and a friend made a trip over this route, driving the whole way to Indiana in a 'handsome sixty-horsepower Pathfinder' with leather seats, the trip was enough of a novelty for Dreiser to write a book, *Hoosier Holiday*, about it. The adventurers had at first intended to take the 'State road'—up along the Hudson and across to Buffalo; but they daringly decided to cut across the lower part of the State. Before starting they equipped themselves with belted dustcoats and visored caps. They reported triumphantly that they had no difficulty in finding gasoline, though the price varied from $1.25 to $1.75 for seven gallons.

WAVERLY, 40.9 *m*. (839 alt.,5,662 pop.), on the Chemung River, is contiguous to Sayre and Athens, Pennsylvania; the three villages have a combined population of approximately 18,000. The Lehigh Valley Railroad shops in Sayre are the chief place of employment.

From DEVIL'S ELBOW, 44.3 *m*., so called from a sharp bend in the river, is an impressive view of the winding Chemung Valley.

At 54.8 *m*. is the junction with the Newton Battle Reservation Road.

Right on this road, up a steep grade, to the NEWTON BATTLEFIELD RESERVATION, 1.1 *m*., a 200-acre park, including the only real battlefield of the Sullivan-Clinton expedition. Here on August 29, 1779, the whites killed 12 Indians and the Indians slew three of the invaders.

ELMIRA, 57.7 *m*., (860 alt.,45,046 pop.) (*see Elmira*), is at the junction with State 14 (*see Tour* 27).

Section d. ELMIRA to OLEAN; 108.3 *m*. State 17

This section of State 17 runs through important manufacturing towns and through the State's oil fields.

Between ELMIRA, 0 *m*., and Big Flats, State 17E is the better and more direct route.

Left from Madison Ave. in Elmira on State 17E, which follows the northern bank of the Chemung River to the junction with the Harris Field Rd., 5.7 *m*.; R. here 1.5 *m*. to HARRIS FIELD, one of several glider fields in this vicinity used for the National Glider Meet, which is held annually in July; wind direction determines which field is used. New American altitude and distance glider records were established at the Elmira meet in 1938: Richard C. DuPont reached a height of 6,700 feet, and Peter Riedel glided from Harris Hill to Washington, D.C., a distance of 225 miles.

State 17E joins State 17 at BIG FLATS, 8.8 *m*. (*see below*).

West of Elmira, State 17 swings north, running in common with State 14 (*see Tour* 27) for 3.4 miles. BIG FLATS, 11.5 *m.* (900 alt.,600 pop.), is at the junction with State 17E (*see above*).

CORNING, 18.7 *m.* (937 alt.,16,140 pop.), is divided by the Chemung River; on all sides, steep slopes rise to the plateau, and the winter sun shines briefly here.

Corning is largely a one-industry town, depending on the manufacture of glass; and because glassmaking, as carried on here, requires the services of highly skilled workers and research staffs, the city has an air of stability and exhibits cultural interests unusual in a small manufacturing center, as evidenced by its Civic Orchestra, Choral Society, annual concerts by outstanding performers, and Little Theater Guild.

The village began to grow after the completion of the Chemung Canal in 1833. Erastus Corning of Albany had organized a company to speculate in local real estate and promoted the building of a railroad to carry Pennsylvania anthracite here for transshipment down the canal. In 1868, when the Flint Glass Company of Brooklyn determined to move its plant to a place where the cost of fuel and raw materials would be lower, it was induced to come here. The company was reorganized and Corning citizens subscribed to two fifths of the new stock issue.

The CORNING GLASS WORKS (*showrooms open to public, plant only by special permission*) is strung along the water front, a series of 40 brick buildings, some of which have been remodeled with the use of glass brick. In 1875 the glassmaking company, which then had only two furnaces and employed 100 workers, began to specialize in the production of special kinds of glass, including railway and marine signal lenses, lantern globes, thermometer tubing, gauge tubing, and laboratory ware. The bulb business was started in response to Thomas A. Edison's need for a practical electric light bulb. Today one factory unit produces more than half a million lamp and radio bulbs a day and manufactures much of the neon tubing used in the United States.

By 1910 the Corning Company had established its own research laboratory to study the physical and chemical nature of glass, and it now has the largest research staff in the glass industry. An important achievement of the laboratory was the invention of Pyrex, a tough borosilicate composition with heat, chemical, and electrical resistance far beyond that of ordinary glass. At first it was used only for chemical laboratory ware, but is now used for cooking utensils, railway lenses, and electrical insulators. The 200-inch Mount Palomar Observatory telescope mirror disc, the largest single piece of glass ever cast, was made here. Other products are special glasses that either filter or transmit X-rays, ultra-violet rays, and infrared rays.

In the Fibre Products Division, glass fibres, which have the appearance of silk and wool, are produced. The coarser grades of this material are used for building insulation, the finer grades in the manufacture of cloth, electrical insulation tape, chemical filters, battery separators, and filters for air-conditioning systems.

In 1938 new and highly ingenious automatic glassmaking machinery was installed; but in the Steuben Division, where very fine decorative glassware is made, each piece is individually created, and the delicate and precise manipulations of the skilled workmen are apparent in every piece.

The OBSERVATORY MUSEUM (*open* 8:30 *a.m.–*10 *p.m.*), center of the Public Square, was built in 1939 to house the first 200-inch lens cast in 1934 for the great telescope in the Mount Palomar Observatory in California. The museum is a small, round building of glass brick, constructed to resemble an observatory. The immense lens on display is about 17 feet in diameter, 27 inches thick, and weighs 40,000 pounds. It is made of the same kind of glass of which a casserole is made. To reduce the weight, cores were placed in the mold, and thus the back of the disc has a waffle-iron pattern.

When this disc was poured in March 1934, the heat of the molten glass was so intense (2,300 degrees Fahrenheit) that some of the cores broke loose and the disc was imperfectly molded. A second and perfect disc was cast a few months later and is now being polished in California. Small copies of the disc are sold as souvenirs at the museum.

PAINTED POST, 21.3 *m.* (950 alt.,2,332 pop.), at the point where the Tioga and Cohocton Rivers unite to form the Chemung, was so named because of a red-painted oaken post that was once here, probably erected as a memorial either to an Indian victory or to an Indian chief. The first white settler arrived in 1789, ten years after the Sullivan-Clinton expedition had wiped out the Indian village by the river. Most of the inhabitants of the town and vicinity are employed in Painted Post machine shops, foundry, and branch plant of the Ingersoll Rand Company.

Painted Post is at the junction with US 15 (*see Tour* 31), which unites with State 17 between this point and ERWINS, 25.2 *m.*, a hamlet. At the western end of JASPER, 49.3 *m.* (1,578 alt.,250 pop.), is the junction with State 21 (*see Tour* 29), which unites with State 17 for a short distance westward.

The divide (2,308 alt.) between the St.Lawrence and the Susquehanna watersheds, at 61 *m.*, marks the eastern rim of the New York oil field, part of the great field centering in Pennsylvania. This Allegany field differs from those of the Southwest in that no derricks dot the landscape and much of the production is carried on by independent landowners with small holdings.

The presence of oil in this region has been known by white men since 1627, when a French missionary priest reported that the Indians used a 'good kind of oil.' By 1789 the Indians were selling small quantities of petroleum to whites for use in lamps; a 1795 gazetteer of the United States referred to Allegany County 'Seneca oil' as 'a sovereign remedy for various complaints.' It was 1850, however, before a process for refining petroleum was invented.

Some prospecting was carried on in New York in the sixties but there were no spectacular strikes; the Triangle (*see below*) was producing in 1879 but attracted little interest. By May 1881, however, when the combined production of 13 wells near Wellsville was 219 barrels a day, the price of some Allegany County land had risen to $200 an acre. In the middle of the

decade production was 5,000,000 barrels a day. Then began a steady decline and only 750,000 barrels were marketed in 1913. But after the introduction of the 'flooding' technique—forcing the oil up out of the wells by
water pressure—production rose steadily; in 1937 Allegany County produced 5,478,000 barrels of petroleum.

WELLSVILLE, 76.3 m. (1,517 alt.,5,674 pop.), the hub of the Allegany County oil field, is a town of beautiful old homes and much wealth.
Settled in 1795 and named for Gardiner Wells, early settler and chief
landowner, it has continued to prosper since the completion of Triangle
No.1 in 1879, about four miles to the southwest. The well got its name
from the fact that it was the third of a series forming a triangle.

Wellsville is at the junction with State 19 (see Tour 35).

BOLIVAR, 90.3 m. (1,609 alt.,1,725 pop.), inhabited chiefly by workers
in the oil fields, was named for General Simon Bolivar when the South
American patriot was a popular hero. Some of the farmers near Bolivar,
with the help of donkey engines, collect oil in small quantities as a sideline
to agriculture; after milking their cows they go out to bring in the oil,
which is collected at the gate by truckers and hauled to refineries.

OLEAN, 108.3 m. (1,440 alt.,21,790 pop.), on the Allegheny River, an
important junction of the Erie and Pennsylvania Railroads, is a receiving
depot for the Socony-Vacuum refineries of the local oil field and manufactures glass, oil-well machinery, and steel cabinets. Like other towns in the
vicinity it came to life as a lumber camp. From their lumber settlers built
rafts to sell to emigrants who gathered here to await the spring flood which
would float them down the Allegheny and the Ohio to the West.

Olean is at junction with State 16 (see Tour 38).

Section e. OLEAN to WESTFIELD; 81.9 m. State 17

West of OLEAN, 0 m., the route runs through the Allegany Indian
Reservation, skirting Allegany State Park, and follows the shore of Chautauqua Lake.

At the eastern end of ALLEGANY, 3 m. (1,425 alt., 1,411 pop.), is (L)
St.Bonaventure College and Seminary, a Franciscan institution
chartered in 1875; it has about 450 students. The campus is beautifully
landscaped.

Opposite (R), on the brow of the hill, is St.Elizabeth's Academy, a
girls' school organized in 1859 and conducted by Franciscan nuns.

The eastern end of the 30,000-acre ALLEGANY INDIAN RESERVA-
TION is at 6.9 m.; the reservation extends for 40 miles in a long, thin arc
following the northern boundary of Allegany State Park. About 900 Senecas and a scattering of Cayugas live here on small farms. This reservation differs from others in the State in that a number of white settlements,
including the city of Salamanca, have been built within its confines. The
white men hold the land on long-term leases. The State appoints an attorney to guard the legal interests of the Indians.

At 10.9 m. is the eastern junction with US 219 (see Tour 39), which
unites with State 17 for several miles.

SALAMANCA, 18.9 *m.* (1,380 alt.,9,654 pop.), a market town, is be-coming a winter and summer resort. The first settlers came here from what is now West Salamanca in 1862, when a sawmill was established and the Atlantic & Great Western (now part of the Chicago & Erie Railroad) carried its single track line to this point. When the railroad company built shops and yards here, the grateful citizens named their village in honor of one of the important stockholders. Soon tanneries were opened and the population increased rapidly; everyone was sure that Salamanca was des-tined to become a metropolis when the Buffalo, Rochester & Pittsburgh and the Pennsylvania Railroads made the town one of their repair and division points. But the period of prosperity did not endure; the railroad shops were moved away and in time the growing furniture factories were moved to Jamestown.

In Salamanca is the western junction with US 219 (*see Tour* 39).

State 17 continues to RED HOUSE, 25.2 *m.*, the chief gateway to Alle-gany State Park.

Left from Red House on park roads into the 65,000-acre ALLEGANY STATE PARK, 0.8 *m.*, pleasant rolling woodland with numerous streams and high lookouts. The highest point is PARKER HILL (2,376 alt.). Wildlife is plentiful; the most in-teresting of the fauna is the giant hellbender, a large salamander of aquatic and noc-turnal habits; it is sometimes seen in the daytime moving slowly along the bottoms of streams.

Arrangements for use of park facilities are made in the ADMINISTRATION BUILDING, 2.8 *m.*, on Red House Lake, and at the camping headquarters in Quaker Run Valley. The park is well developed for use in summer and winter (354 *partly furnished cabins— bring your own linen*—$1.50 *a day,* $7 *a week,* $20 *a month,* $75 *a year; well-equipped trailer campsites,* 50¢ *a night,* $2 *a week*). In the administration building are a museum and a restaurant; several marked nature and hiking trails start here, and near by are picnic grounds, tennis courts, a lake (*bathing, fishing*), an athletic field (*free*), and rid-ing stables. Ski trails have recently been built.

The business and smoke-covered factory district of JAMESTOWN, 54.9 *m.* (1,400 alt.,45,502 pop.), clusters about the outlet of Chautauqua Lake; the prim residential districts with tree-lined streets cover the hill-sides. The city has an air of constant activity and bustle, accented by the clangor of many large red interurban electric cars.

Jamestown is one of the leading furniture-manufacturing centers of the United States; it also produces textiles, ball bearings, tools, milking ma-chinery, voting machines, and washers. The founder of the settlement was James Prendergast, who purchased 1,000 acres of land his brother had earlier bought from the Holland Land Company for $2 an acre. Among the early settlers were a number of skilled woodworkers, who began to make furniture to supply the needs of the pioneers in the region. In 1849 some Swedish immigrants appeared; after the close of the Civil War many others joined them. Most of the men were cabinet makers attracted by the furniture factories. In 1888, two years after Jamestown had become offi-cially a city, construction of metal furniture was begun.

The population is now predominantly of Swedish descent or birth. Swedish economic ideals are evident in the conduct of such enterprises as the locally owned and operated telephone services with annual rates as low as $20 and a toll-free service covering 250 square miles; and in the profitable municipally owned and operated electric light and power system. Swedish culture is also apparent in the restaurants of the city, which are notable for the quality and variety of their foods.

In six-acre FENTON MEMORIAL PARK, S.Main St. and Fenton Place, is a bronze STATUE OF REUBEN E. FENTON (1819–85), who was elected to the State Assembly in 1849 and to the House of Representatives in 1852 as a Democrat. He broke with his party on the slavery issue, helped organize the Republican party in the State, and as a Republican served in Congress (1856–64), as governor (1865–9), and as U.S. senator (1869–75). The 32-room FENTON HOUSE, a three-story red brick structure in the park, is used by veterans' organizations and their auxiliaries.

Left from Washington St. in Jamestown on State 17J (Third St.), an alternate to State 17 along the shore of Chautauqua Lake.

CHAUTAUQUA, 16.8 m. (1,340 alt.,300 pop.), with accommodations for 15,000 visitors (*hotels* $20 *to* $60 *a week; housekeeping apartments,* $50 *to* $150 *a season; cottages* $200 *up a season; facilities for boating, swimming, golfing, tennis*), offers a varied program during July and August, including a summer school conducted by New York University, a public lecture series, and outstanding musical concerts. The movement was the child of the revival-camp meeting and of the lyceum, offspring of the American passion for painless self-improvement, and the mother of the radio program and the university extension course. Despite variations and mutations, the basic characteristics of the family persist. The exhorters and lecturers of the revival and lyceum days were the backbone of the Chautauqua; many of its graduates, including Edgar Bergen, are radio stars.

In 1872 John Heyl Vincent (1832–1920), a clergyman, was corresponding secretary of the Methodist Sunday School Association and editor of its publications; distressed by the lack of interest and education among Sunday school teachers, he attempted to inaugurate a new kind of teaching at Camptown, New Jersey. His first innovation was to make a large outdoor map of Palestine and to have his adult pupils follow him over it, telling the stories of Biblical events at appropriate places. The experiment was so successful that, with the aid of Lewis Miller, a businessman, he planned to hold a short term of school for Sunday school teachers at the campmeeting grounds at Chautauqua. Those who attended the first session, in 1874, went home filled with enthusiasm. In a very few years the attendance had become Nation-wide and 'Chautauquas' had been organized in many other States. Before long the programs, always advertised as providing 'pure, wholesome entertainment,' were broadened, and by 1890 practically every type of entertainer now heard on the radio program was appearing before Chautauqua audiences—politicians, explorers, Swiss bellringers, banjoists, xylophonists, glee clubs, rabbis, priests. The exception was the 'actor.' The stage was still anathema to the church members of rural America and such actors as appeared—in carefully denatured versions of plays that were called 'readings'—were disguised as 'elocutionists' or 'readers.'

The all-time star of the Chautauquas was William Jennings Bryan, last of the line of American orators; audiences came year after year to hear him repeat the speech he made at the Democratic National Convention of 1896 in opposition to the gold standard, and swayed raptly as he concluded: 'You shall not press down upon the brow of labor this crown of thorns, you shall not crucify mankind upon a cross of gold.'

Chautauqua assemblies are still held, but in steadily decreasing numbers; the motion picture, the radio, and the motor car supply more entertainment than they can give and supply them the year round.

At MAYVILLE, 20.8 m., is the junction with State 17.

Northwest from Jamestown State 17 follows the northern shore of Chautauqua Lake through an almost continuous summer resort.

MAYVILLE, 75.9 *m.* (1,340 alt.,1,324 pop.), at the junction with State 17J (*see above*) and the head of Chautauqua Lake, is the seat of Chautauqua County.

State 17 continues westward through vineyards to WESTFIELD, 81.9 *m.* (748 alt.,3,466 pop.) (*see Tour* 8), at the junction with US 20 (*see Tour* 8).

Tour 4

(Danbury, Conn.)—Brewster—Carmel—Peekskill—Goshen—Port Jervis—(Milford, Pa.); US 6.
Connecticut Line to Port Jervis, 79.9 *m.*

Hard-surfaced throughout. Through traffic heavy and retarded by narrowness of streets and local traffic in many villages.

US 6, the Cape Cod-Los Angeles route, crosses the southeastern part of New York State through delightful rolling country. West of the Hudson it runs through the Bear Mountain Section of the Palisades Interstate Park.

Section a. CONNECTICUT LINE to PEEKSKILL; 26.7 *m. US* 6

East of the Hudson River US 6 runs through the Croton watershed, formerly the principal source of water for New York City and now part of the city's reserve system. From the first bright day in April till the end of Indian summer, every village, farmhouse, and group of cabins is filled with browned men, women, and children, half of whom seem to live in bathing suits. When the leaves become brilliant red and yellow, hikers are particularly in evidence. With the first snows many go skiing, or strap on snowshoes to mush their way through the woods. Later the ponds and lakes are bright with scarlet-, orange-, and brown-clad skaters.

US 6 crosses the CONNECTICUT LINE, 0 *m.*, 6.4 miles west of Danbury, Connecticut.

At 2 *m.* is the junction with State 121.

> Left on State 121 to PEACH LAKE, 2 *m.* (*bathing, boating, fishing, tennis, golf*), a popular resort.

At 3.8 *m.* is a junction with State 22 (*see Tour* 20).

BREWSTER, 3.9 *m.* (410 alt.,1,664 pop.), identified from a distance by the white spires that rise above its many trees, is essentially a farmers' trade center, although vacationists in shorts and slacks swarm in all summer long. HIGH MEADOW is the home of Rex Stout, creator of Nero Wolfe, the orchid-loving gourmet-detective.

At Brewster is another junction with State 22 (*see Tour* 20).

CARMEL, 9.2 *m.* (520 alt.,600 pop.), seat of Putnam County, is a leisurely village with solid old homes and streets shaded with elms and maples along the shore of Lake Glenida.

MAHOPAC, 14.4 *m.* (640 alt.,400 pop.), one of several straggling communities along Lake Mahopac, is the trading center for residents of the almost continuous line of summer cottages along the lake, named for a local Indian tribe.

At 20.4 *m.* is the junction with Eastern State Parkway (*see Tour* 40).

In SHRUB OAK, 20.5 *m.* (460 alt.,325 pop.), are several houses built in pre-Revolutionary times. Outstanding is (R) the HART HOUSE, at the western end of Main St., a frame structure built about 1770; it is the local library.

MOHEGAN, 22.8 *m.* (460 alt.,100 pop.), by Lake Mohegan, is another trading center for vacationists. Though the reflected lights of New York City can be seen from near-by hills, there are people who live near these resort villages who have never visited the metropolis. MOHEGAN LAKE ACADEMY, a preparatory school for boys, was established in 1867.

At 24.8 *m.* is the junction with the Bronx River Parkway Extension (*see Tour* 40).

PEEKSKILL, 26.7 *m.* (120 alt.,17,289 pop.), on hills that slope abruptly down to the Hudson, remains surprisingly rural in spite of the constant streams of tourist and commercial traffic. It is still the trade town for farmers it has been for nearly two centuries.

The city takes its name from Peek's Kill, the creek along its northern boundary named for Jan Peek, a Dutch trader who settled on its bank in 1665. During the early years of the Revolution, staff officers and troops moved back and forth through the settlement on their way between the river landing and their points of duty. There was little industrial development until the latter part of the nineteenth century. The Standard Brands plant, manufacturing yeast and alcohol, among other products, provides employment for about 2,500 people.

CHAUNCEY M. DEPEW PARK, in the center of the village, contains a statue of Depew, who was born in Peekskill in 1834 and was a lifelong resident. When Depew was 32 years old he was the attorney for Cornelius Vanderbilt's Hudson River & Harlem Railroad; in 1875 he became chief counsel, in 1882 a vice president, and in 1885 president of the Vanderbilt-owned New York Central. In 1899 Depew was elected to the United States Senate. Unlike most men occupying his position as counsel and confidential adviser, he was fond of appearing in public and gained a wide reputation for oratory. His *bon mots* are still quoted, though he died in 1928.

The PEEKSKILL MILITARY ACADEMY, on Oak Hill, a broad plateau overlooking the Hudson, was founded in 1833 and now has an enrollment of 400. The Gallows Oak Tree, from which the Revolutionary spy, Daniel Strange, was hanged, still stands on the campus.

The FIRST PRESBYTERIAN CHURCH, South St. east of Washington St., erected in 1846, is a handsome Greek Revival building. The front has flush boarding and the sides are clapboarded; heavy Doric pilasters frame the lower portion of the façade and tower.

Peekskill is at the junction with US 9 (*see Tour* 21).

Right from Peekskill on Oregon Road, concrete-paved, to VAN CORTLANDT-VILLE, 1.9 *m.*, which grew up around the UPPER VAN CORTLANDT MANOR HOUSE, still standing on a hill above Peek's Kill though much changed since it was built. This house, now St.Peter's School for boys, often sheltered Washington and other Revolutionary officers during the early years of the war when this area was a center of operations.

In the hamlet is ST.PETER'S CHURCH, an exceedingly simple structure built by the Van Cortlandts for the use of their tenants and opened in 1767. The straight-backed pew set aside for the family of the lord of the manor is unchanged; everyone else sat on rough-hewn benches.

Left from the hamlet 0.5 *m.* and across the creek to GALLOWS HILL, where Edward Palmer, a Tory spy, was hanged in 1777 by order of General Israel Putnam. Beyond Gallows Hill, at 1.5 *m.* is the SITE OF CONTINENTAL VILLAGE, a supply base that had barracks for 1,500 men. The barracks were burned by the British in 1777 and the site was not reoccupied until 1781.

Section b. PEEKSKILL to EASTERN JUNCTION WITH STATE 17; 20.7 m. US 6

This section of US 6 crosses the Hudson, offering magnificent views of the river valley, and cuts across the northern area of Bear Mountain Section.

West of PEEKSKILL, 0 *m.*, the road swings R. and L. on the Bear Mountain Bridge approach, a three-mile stretch carved through the rock directly above the Hudson River and affording splendid views of the Highlands; there are several parking spaces.

At 1.7 *m.* is the junction with Camp Smith Road.

Right on this road to CAMP SMITH, 0.3 *m.* (*visitors' day, Sat. during July and Aug.*), named for Alfred E. Smith, former governor of New York. Here the State National Guard holds its summer encampment. Troops were prepared here for the Spanish-American and the World Wars. Many Peekskill residents remember the arrival of Theodore Roosevelt's Rough Riders, 'the aristocracy of the wild men of the West, and the wild men of the aristocracy of the East.'

At 2.6 *m.* is the entrance to BEAR MOUNTAIN BRIDGE (*car with passengers,* 50¢; *trailer,* 35¢; *pedestrian* 10¢). The bridge, which was opened to traffic in November 1924, is 2,257 feet in length; the central span, with a clearance of 135 feet, is 1,632 feet long.

At 5.6 *m.*, just west of the western approach to Bear Mountain Bridge, is the junction with US 9W (*see Tour* 21*A*) and the eastern entrance to the BEAR MOUNTAIN SECTION of the Palisades Interstate Park. This 1,000-acre park, named for BEAR MOUNTAIN (1,314 alt.), which rises steeply above the Hudson, is one of the most popular recreational centers near New York City (*facilities for roller skating*—35¢ *including skates; bathing*—*lockers* 35¢ *weekdays,* 50¢ *Sun. and holidays; rowing*—*boats* 25¢ *an hour weekdays,* 50¢ *Sun. and holidays,* $1 *deposit; tennis*—*courts* 50¢ *an hour; baseball*—*diamond* $1 *an hour; tobogganing and skiing in winter*). The TRAILSIDE MUSEUM (*open, free*) informs visitors about plants and animals in their native setting; the ramparts of the Revolutionary Fort Clinton have been carefully restored.

US 6 continues westward through the park on Popolopen Drive. At 6.8 *m.* is the junction with Perkins Memorial Drive.

Left on this road, which climbs gradually, to the parking place near the SUMMIT OF BEAR MOUNTAIN, 2.3 *m.*, where a large parking space and an observation tower have been built for the convenience of those who wish to study the magnificent panorama of the Hudson Valley. The drive winds down the south side of the mountain to a junction, 4.7 *m.*, with Seven Lakes Drive.

On US 6 at 8.1 *m.* is the junction with Seven Lakes Drive.

Left on Seven Lakes Drive through the HARRIMAN SECTION of the Palisades Interstate Park. The main drive and side roads penetrate the heavily wooded area with 35 lakes, group camp area, bathing beaches, and boating and fishing facilities (*camping $3 a week; motor camp 75¢ for 24 hrs.; rowboats, per hour, 25¢ weekdays, 50¢ Sun. and holidays; bathhouse 10¢, 25¢; roller skating 25¢*). Roads lead out to State 17 (*see Tour 3*) and US 9W (*see Tour 21A*).

At the western end of MONROE, 20.7 *m.* (610 alt.,1,621 pop.), is the junction with State 17, with which US 6 unites for 15.7 miles.

Section c. EASTERN JUNCTION STATE 17 to WESTERN JUNCTION STATE 17; 15.7 m. US 6–State 17.

West of the EASTERN JUNCTION, 0 *m.*, the highway runs between high, rolling farms.

At 5.7 *m.* is a junction with State 45.

Right on State 45 to (L) YELVERTON INN, 0.4 *m.*, a two-story frame structure built by John Yelverton in 1765 and since then much remodeled. Here in September 1774 the Orange County delegates elected Henry Wisner as their delegate to the Continental Congress to 'protest against unjust taxation.'
In CHESTER, 0.6 *m.* (447 alt.,1,154 pop.), on Hambletonian Ave., is a slender red-granite obelisk marking the GRAVE OF HAMBLETONIAN, the trotter and progenitor of a strain of famous trotters, born on the farm of William M. Rysdyk in 1848. The Hambletonians are derived on both sides from Messenger through Rysdyk's Hambletonian, Abdallah, and Mambrins Messenger. Hambletonian's dam was the daughter of One Eye and granddaughter of Silvertail, the daughter of Messenger. Hambletonian's progeny includes Dexter (2:17½), Sunol (2:8¼), Goldsmith's Maid (2:14), Harus (2:13¾), Saint Julien (2:11¼), Jay Eye See (2:10), Nancy Hanks (2:4), Alix (2:3¾), and Directum (2:5¼). The second great trotting family, the Mambrins, is noted for racing quality and beauty.

At 6.2 *m.* is the western junction with State 45.

Left on State 45 to FLORIDA, (443 alt.,555 pop.), 4.5 *m.*, the financial capital of the Orange County onion-growing activities. Fifty years ago this region was a swampy and almost inaccessible jungle, owned by the State because the surrounding farmers considered it valueless. A few Polish farmhands began to acquire small patches at a few dollars an acre. They cleared them, planted onions, and in the five decades since 1890 the astonished natives have seen the land converted into one of the chief onion-growing centers in the East, with the land valued in places as high as $500 an acre. Quantities of celery are also produced. Today the population is predominantly Polish, with Polish church services, Polish stores, and Polish folkways. In summer, men, women, and children work across the flats under the hot sun, weeding and cultivating the rows of onion plants. On Main St. is the SEWARD MONUMENT; the BIRTHPLACE OF

WILLIAM H. SEWARD (*see Auburn*) is now a barn in the rear of a house near the monument.

State 45 continues southward to WARWICK, 9 *m.* (538 alt.,2,515 pop.), settled in 1746 by English immigrants from Warwickshire. The stone BAIRD TAVERN, at the corner of Colonial and Maple Aves., built in 1776, has been modernized. The BURT HOUSE (*open*), on Forester Ave. opposite the hospital, a much remodeled structure built in 1764, contains a small collection of Revolutionary relics.

On US 6 at 10 *m.* is the junction with State 207; close by (R) is the Good Time Track.

Right on State 207 (Main St.) to the center of GOSHEN, 0.7 *m.* (439 alt.,3,057 pop.), seat of Orange County and the Epsom Downs of light harness racing. In July and August the near-by roads are daily congested with horse lovers; it is hard to find rooms in the town and many people have to eat at the lunch counters that cluster near the tracks.

The settlers who came to this place in the early decades of the eighteenth century believed that the fertility of the rich soil would rival that of the Biblical land of Goshen. The solid prosperity of this tree-shaded town attests to the soundness of their choice. It exports dairy products and garden truck in large quantities. Claudius Smith, the bandit (*see Tour 3*), was hanged on the village green.

The kite-shaped, brown GOOD TIME TRACK, at the southern end of Main St. close to the junction with US 6, is owned by William H. Crane. Here during the second or third week in August are held the Grand Circuit meets, whose high spot is Hambletonian Day. Near the Good Time Track is the HARRIMAN TRACK, a half-mile oval sometimes called the Historic, which is crowded during the meet toward the end of July with men and women whose great-grandfathers raced their favorites over Orange County tracks and early roads. In 1940 the old auction pool was superseded by pari-mutuel betting windows.

Goshen's buildings represent almost every decade in its history, ranging from the Dutch-style BENJAMIN TUSTIN and ISAAC JOINTER HOUSES, on Main St. close to the junction with the Sarah Wells Trail, to the modern houses that might have been copied from current homemaking magazine pictures. The most solid and prosperous homes belong to the period when the favorite embellishments were jigsaw scrollwork, gables, turrets, and elaborate brackets. The mansarded barns are notable. Among the more modern buildings is a charming small Georgian-type LIBRARY.

The most interesting public building is the yellow-painted brick ORANGE COUNTY COURTHOUSE, on lower Main St., erected in 1845 and remodeled in 1895. Ivy-covered ST. JAMES EPISCOPAL CHURCH (1855), on Church St., was designed by Richard Upjohn in modified Gothic style. In the church there are windows made in the Tiffany studios and an altar designed by Cass Gilbert.

Well-paved State 207 continues northeast to NEWBURGH (*see Tour 21A*), 18.5 *m.*, passing several fine old mills.

At 14.5 *m.* US 6–State 17 skirts NEW HAMPTON (425 alt.,260 pop.). The NEW YORK CITY REFORMATORY (R), on a 620-acre tract of farm land at the eastern village limits, can accommodate 750 males from 16 to 30 years of age, first offenders convicted of minor charges, with sentences ranging from one day to three years.

At 15.7 *m.* is the western junction with State 17 (*see Tour 3*), which swings R.

Section d. WESTERN JUNCTION WITH STATE 17 to PORT JERVIS; 16.8 m. US 6.

This section of US 6 winds across steep hills.

West of the western junction with State 17, 0 *m.*, is SLATE HILL, 3.4 *m.* (505 alt.,130 pop.), visited by fishermen because of the numerous near-by streams and small lakes. The old BAPTIST CHURCH (R), erected in 1792, is of the rectangular frame New England meetinghouse type, with a steeple in four stages—one square, two octagonal, and a small spire. The interior is very simple; the pews have high backs and narrow seats. The seats for slaves were built in the far corner of the gallery.

The road now ascends to the summit (1,400 alt.), 13.9 m., of a ridge from which there is a wide view of the surrounding country.

PORT JERVIS, 16.8 m. (451 alt.,9,616 pop.), on the Delaware, calls itself the Tri-State City. The smoky haze that fills the lower part of town comes from the locomotives in the large railroad division yards, from the railroad machine shops, and from the factories producing glass. The Minsi band of the Lenni-Lenape did not give up the bottom lands here willingly, but Dutch and Huguenot farmers, who began arriving about 1698, were able to live in peace with them until Revolutionary times. For some years after 1779, when Brant led his Tory and Indian followers on a raid that wiped out the settlement, the place was deserted by the whites.

With the construction of the Delaware & Hudson Canal, 1826, the settlement began to assume importance and the grateful inhabitants renamed it to honor John B. Jervis, chief engineer of the canal company.

The MARTINUS DECKER FORT, 127 W.Main St., embodies part of the walls of the house in which the settlers huddled during the Indian raid of July 20, 1779. It was rebuilt in 1793 by Martinus Decker and his son, Martinus, whose initials, with the date of the reconstruction, are decipherable on one of the stones. When first built, the house had one-story walls of stone and upper half-story walls of logs; the saplings covering the roof were chinked with gravel and covered with a thick coating of clay.

Port Jervis is at the junction with US 209 (see Tour 6).

US 6 crosses the Delaware River on a free bridge, at a point 8 miles northeast of Milford, Pennsylvania.

Tour 5

Amenia—Millbrook—Poughkeepsie—Kerhonkson, US 44. 58 m.

Two-lane concrete or macadam.

US 44 is a direct route between the Berkshires and the West by way of the Mid-Hudson Bridge at Poughkeepsie.

Section a. AMENIA to POUGHKEEPSIE; 26.4 m. US 44.

This section closely follows the route of the Dutchess Turnpike laid down between Litchfield, Connecticut, and Poughkeepsie in 1805. It crosses the rich, rolling farm country of Dutchess County, which in the eighteenth century was the main source of supply of wheat and hides for New York City. Many old rambling mansions, usually set in a clump of weather-torn locusts, are relics of this period of prosperity. Quakers were among the first settlers; although but few of the sect are left here, several of their simple meetinghouses remain.

AMENIA, 0 m. (573 alt.,1,500 pop.), is at the junction with State 22 (see Tour 20).

At 0.9 m. is LAKE AMENIA (L), 0.5 m. long, with a bungalow colony (swimming, boating, fishing).

At 5.8 m. is the MILLBROOK THEATRE (L), where Broadway tryouts are held during July and August from Wednesday to Saturday (no matinees). The one-story frame building was originally a Quaker meetinghouse; the pews are still used and seat about 250 persons.

MILLBROOK, 10.4 m. (565 alt.,1,296 pop.), is a prosperous village surrounded by wealthy estates. The town also enjoys the patronage of an artist colony; the summer theater is enthusiastically supported; riding and hunting are popular diversions.

In Millbrook the Hicksite and Orthodox Quakers are still active. The Hicksites meet occasionally in the Brick Meeting House in Mechanic, on State 343, east of South Millbrook. The Orthodox joined with the Dutch Reformed and Methodist congregations in 1926 to build the Federated Church in Millbrook.

At 11.6 m. is the BENNETT SCHOOL AND JUNIOR COLLEGE (R), founded in 1891 at Irvington-on-the-Hudson by May Friend Bennett, and moved to its present site in 1907. Several of its graduates in drama have appeared on Broadway.

At 11.7 m. is the junction with State 343.

Left on this road to the entrance (R), 0.4 m., to the PHEASANT BREEDERS AND HUNTING ASSOCIATION (varying admission charge for privilege of hunting pheasants).

At 1 m. is the BRICK MEETING HOUSE (L), built in 1780 by the Nine Partners Meeting of the Society of Friends. The simple two-story brick building is in excellent condition. The interior was divided to separate men and women worshippers. Cast-iron wood-burning stoves remain in position on either side.

The SITE OF THE NINE PARTNERS SCHOOL lies 500 ft. east of the meetinghouse. Opened by the Society of Friends in 1796, the school offered a thorough academic course and at one time had an attendance of 100. It continued to prosper until the division of the Society of Friends in 1828 into Orthodox and Hicksite groups; the Hicksites withdrew from the school and established a separate and similar institution under the principalship of Jacob and Deborah Willetts. Jacob Willetts, author of popular arithmetic and geography textbooks, wrote the modern version of the useful lyric beginning 'Thirty days hath September.'

WASHINGTON HOLLOW, 17 m. (820 alt.,80 pop.), settled during the Revolution, was the campground for artillery trains bound for Sackets Harbor during the War of 1812.

At 17.1 m., about 200 ft. off the road and enclosed by a fieldstone wall, is the ZACHEUS NEWCOMB HOUSE (L), a very well preserved example of the early Dutch brick house, built in 1777 by Sarah Tobias Newcomb, while her husband, Zacheus, was away at war. The house, two stories high with a gambrel roof, has the usual eighteenth-century floor plan, with a bisecting central hall. The bricks are laid in Flemish bond. The south porch is an exact reproduction of the original, and the front door is the one built with the house, as are the mantels, window seats, corner cupboards, wood trim, and blue tile.

At 17.7 *m*. is a view (L) of the Hudson Highlands, strategic area in the Revolution.

At 19 *m*. is the junction with a dirt road.

Left on this road 0.7 *m*. to the JOHN NEWCOMB HOUSE (L), a two-story frame structure built in 1808 by John Newcomb, a son of Zacheus Newcomb. The house, an especially handsome one for its time and isolated location, is now occupied by a tenant-farmer. The front entrance is by way of a Dutch double door, around which are leaded lights. In the southwest bedroom is a carved mantel.

PLEASANT VALLEY, 19.2 *m*. (200 alt.,300 pop.), was settled in 1740 by Quakers and Presbyterians. A fine specimen of Quaker meetinghouse still stands here.

At 19.8 *m*., east of the power plant, is a curious old stone barn. Records of its origin are lost, but it is believed to have been erected in the 1750's as a defense post against possible French-Indian raids. In the walls are openings, narrow outside, flaring within, similar to the loopholes in early blockhouses.

At 23.4 *m*. is the junction with a macadam road.

Left on this road 0.4 *m*. to the ZEPHANIAH PLATT HOUSE (L). Constructed of native fieldstone, with a second story in brick and a gambrel roof, the house stands practically unaltered. The older portion, which consisted of but two rooms and a basement kitchen, was erected in 1735 by Gilbert Palen. Zephaniah Platt acquired the place in 1762 and built, before 1775, the addition at the right, which doubled the size of the house. The front door is of the Dutch double type and has a brass knocker of Revolutionary design.

Platt was a colonel of militia in the Revolution, a member of the New York Provincial Congress, State senator, and one of the members of the Ratification Convention at Poughkeepsie, whose courageous stand before the United States Constitution was ratified by New York State ultimately resulted in the adoption of the Bill of Rights. In the late 1700's Platt, his three brothers, and others from Poughkeepsie, moved to the northern part of the State, where they founded Plattsburg.

The road turns L. just beyond the Platt House; at 0.8 *m*. is the junction of three roads; left here 0.7 *m*., to the SLEIGHT HOUSE (L), of native fieldstone, two stories high, with a main hall bisecting it in the usual eighteenth-century style. Jacobus Sleight built it in 1798.

POUGHKEEPSIE, 26.4 *m*. (175 alt.,40,237 pop.) (*see Poughkeepsie*), is at the junction with US 9 (*see Tour* 21) and State 55 (*see Tour* 40).

Section b. POUGHKEEPSIE to KERHONKSON; 31.6 *m*. US 44

The route traverses one of the foremost fruit-growing regions of the State, and then climbs the ancient Shawangunk Mountains, offering again and again exciting vistas. The section was settled in the main by Huguenots, whose descendants still till its soil. Over the mountains roamed that relentless Indian-killer, Tom Quick, whose numerous exploits have inspired a fund of legend. He has been credited with having killed more than 100 Indians singlehanded in his lifetime; by his own account he slew many more, casually, while he was out hunting.

Of the many Tom Quick stories, there is one that the historian, Quinlan, averred to be true. It seems that one day Tom was deep in the woods splitting rails. As he was driving a wedge in a log, suddenly six dusky warriors stepped out of the underbrush and surrounded him; they asked to be directed to Tom Quick. It was their intention to take him alive and torture him. Tom asked if they would not first help him finish his work. To this the savages agreed, and Tom ranged them three on each side of the log to pull it apart while he drove the wedge deeper. As they held on, he knocked the wedge out, catching all six Indians by their fingers and then leisurely knocked them on the head one by one. Quinlan said he visited the precise spot where this incident occurred and saw the bleached bones of the Indians.

West of POUGHKEEPSIE, 0 *m.*, US 44 crosses the Hudson on the MID-HUDSON BRIDGE (*toll* 50¢), designed by Ralph Modjeski and Daniel E. Moran. It is a suspension bridge with a total length of 4,530 feet, including approaches. It crosses the river at the Long Reach near the official finish line of the annual intercollegiate rowing regatta.

At 1.4 *m.* in HIGHLAND (360 alt.,1,575 pop.) is the junction with US 9W (*see Tour 21A*).

Right from Highland on State 299 to NEW PALTZ, 6.9 *m.* (236 alt.,1,362 pop.), center for vacationists in the Shawangunk Mountains and home of the New Paltz State Normal School. HUGUENOT VILLAGE, Huguenot St., a group of fieldstone houses clustered along a ridge overlooking the Wallkill River, is a picturesque remnant of a settlement made by French Protestant refugees in 1677.

In the raid on Hurley and Kingston in June 1663, Esopus Indians kidnapped 45 white women and children to hold as hostages for the return of 20 braves shipped by Director General Stuyvesant to Curacao to become slaves. In early September a searching party took the Indians by surprise and set the hostages free. One member of the rescuing party, Louis DuBois of Hurley, in the midst of his joyful reunion with his wife and three sons, noted the fertile lowlands of the Wallkill. In 1677 he, together with 11 other refugees, purchased from the Indians and patented a large tract lying between the Shawangunk Mountains and the Hudson. Early in 1678 the 12 families loaded their possessions in three oxcarts and established their new home, which they called New Paltz after their first refuge, the Rheinish Pfalz. The little community prospered under the administration of the 'Dusine,' the 12 patentees, who allocated lands by lot and established whatever rules were needed. Until 1785, when the town was chartered by the State legislature, succeeding Dusines were chosen annually at town meetings from descendants of the patentees. No appeal from their judgment was ever recorded. Perhaps it was the influence of these Huguenots that explains the assertion that 'so fine and free from animosity and greed has been the life of the people of New Paltz that previous to 1873 no lawyer ever found a permanent residence here.'

About 1700 the community began replacing the original cabins by sturdy stone dwellings, six of which still stand, four practically unaltered, comprising a unique eighteenth-century ensemble.

The JEAN HASBROUCK HOUSE (Memorial House), opposite Front St., was built in 1712 by Jean Hasbrouck, one of the patentees. The design closely follows Ulster county types, and it has escaped to an unusual degree later 'improvements.' The rough stone walls are topped by a high, steep roof of medieval flavor. The simple entrance door is sheltered by a primitive shed-stoop. The interior has a typical central hall plan with two rooms on each side. In the hall, a glazed panel reveals the mud plaster, 'wattle-and-daub,' wall construction. In the attic there are two or three small garret rooms, but in the rest of the enormous space, broken only by light collar beams and struts, were stored great hogsheads of grain. The north right front room was used by Major Jacob,Jr., during Revolutionary times as a store; the bar is still in the attic.

Although rented after 1808, the house remained in the Hasbrouck family until 1899, when it was purchased by the Huguenot Patriotic, Historic, and Monumental Society, to be maintained as a memorial house.

Opposite, to the north, is the DEYO HOUSE, the walls of which were part of the house built by Pierre Deyo, the patentee. The dwelling suffered ruthless alterations in the nineteenth century. Again opposite and north, is the DANIEL DuBOIS HOUSE (the 'Old Fort'), the stone first story of which was built in 1705 by DuBois on the site of the Redoute, a stone fortress required by Governor Andros in the patent. Parts of the Redoute walls may have been incorporated in the new house. About 1835 the house, now a tea room, was enlarged and the interior refitted.

Next, opposite and north, is the BEVIER-ELTING HOUSE, the central part of which was built by Louis Bevier, the patentee, soon after 1699. This portion comprises a single room, attic, cellar, and wine subcellar. In 1735 Bevier's son Samuel extended the house to the east and possibly at the same time built the west addition fronting Huguenot Street. About 1765 the house was sold to Captain Josiah Elting.

North is the ABRAHAM HASBROUCK HOUSE. Abraham (d. 1717), patentee, brother of Jean and grandfather of Colonel Jonathan Hasbrouck, builder and owner of Washington's Headquarters in Newburgh, built the south portion with two rooms, garret, and cellar kitchen. Some time later, the central part was added, and finally, the north end with two rooms and a cellar with a great fireplace and primitive flagging. The house fortunately has escaped nineteenth-century alterations.

Just north is the HUGH FRERE HOUSE, erected in the early eighteenth century, but now defaced by a nineteenth-century porch.

The DUTCH REFORMED CHURCH, built in 1839, the fourth house of worship, is a trim example of Greek Revival with red brick walls and a wood portico of four Doric columns. Above the pediment is a fine steeple in two stages. The church body goes back to the Walloon Protestant congregation organized in 1683. The group assembled in a rude log building opposite the Jean Hasbrouck House until 1717, when a small stone structure with a tiny belfry replaced it. In town and church, French was the accepted language until in 1752 the church became affiliated with the Dutch Reformed faith. Not until after 1799 was English adopted. A third building, gambrel-roofed, was built just before the Revolution.

CLINTONDALE, 8.2 m. (552 alt.,603 pop.), is a fruit-raising center named in honor of the Clinton family. Orchards extend almost to the back doors of the homes. In 1830 William Cornell of Clintondale invented and patented a waterproof overshoe, the forerunner of the modern arctic.

From 13.8 m. the SHAWANGUNK (Ind., pile of white rock) MOUN-TAINS form the western skyline. They are the upturned edges of beds of resistant white and pink sandstone of Silurian age. The thick, jointed strata form cliffs several hundred feet high. Halfway up the mountainside is a view (R) of the Hudson River Valley—flat and velvety. The rock-strewn slopes of the mountain are covered with white pine, sugar maple, hemlock, and black cherry.

At 25.7 m. is the entrance (L) to LAKE MINNEWASKA (open May 30–Oct. 12; boating, bathing, tennis, riding, hiking). The name is from the Indian for floating waters—in reference to its position atop the mountain. Cliffs of white sandstone, 100 feet or more high, rise above the lake and are topped by two massive hotels. The lake was formed during the Ice Age when the ice sheet, several thousand feet thick, slid over the mountain top and plucked out blocks of the sandstone.

The road runs through a deep cut in the white rock. From the parking place (R), a view is unfolded of the Rondout Creek Valley, with the lofty peaks of the Catskill Mountains, rising as high as 4,000 feet above sea level, forming the distant horizon.

KERHONKSON, 31.6 *m.* (254 alt.,550 pop.), is at the junction with US 209 (*see Tour* 6).

Tour 6

Kingston—Ellenville—Wurtsboro—Port Jervis— (Milford, Pa.); US 209.
Kingston to Pennsylvania Line, 61.3 *m.*

New York, Ontario & Western R.R. parallels route.
Concrete with stretches of poor macadam.

US 209, connecting New England, upstate New York, and Pennsylvania by way of the Delaware Water Gap, follows a natural route that has been used successively as an Indian trail, a stagecoach road, and the path of the Delaware & Hudson Canal. Hurriedly built frame hotels and boardinghouses between Napanoch and Wurtsboro serve this playground for New York City during the summer; in the winter they are deserted.

US 209 branches west from US 9W (*see Tour* 21*A*) in KINGSTON, 0 *m.*

HURLEY, 3.8 *m.* (200 alt.,400 pop.), first called Nieuw Dorp (Dutch, new village), was renamed in 1669 for Francis Lovelace, Baron Hurley of Ireland. Maple-arched Main Street, with its high-steepled Dutch Reformed Church and almost uniform limestone houses, suggests an eighteenth-century village.

The VAN DEUSEN HOUSE (R), Main St., in the center of town, a one-and-one-half-story Dutch house, was built in 1723 with 24-light windows and a sharp gable pierced by four shed-roof dormers. The legislature, driven out when the British burned Kingston (*see Tour* 21*A*), moved first to Marbletown (*see below*), and later came here, making the Van Deusen House the capitol of New York from November 18 to December 17, 1777.

MARBLETOWN, 8 *m.* (213 alt.,90 pop.), is named for the eight-mile ledge of limestone from which much of the stone for the old houses of the township was quarried. In the ANDREW OLIVER HOUSE (L), another stone building, the State legislature met for a month after the burning of Kingston in 1777.

The CATSKILL AQUEDUCT, crossed at 12.2 *m.*, carries water from the Ashokan Reservoir (*see Tour* 15) to New York City.

ACCORD, 17.4 *m.* (250 alt.,359 pop.), was settled late in the seventeenth century. Shortly after the Revolution a cynical resident wrote to the Post Office Department in Washington suggesting the name Discord for this village because residents could not agree on a name. The post office was authorized, but the name was edited by an optimistic official.

The FARM OF TOM QUICK, 18.7 *m.*, was bought from the Indians in 1672 by the now almost legendary Indian-hating woodsman, who had followed the Shawangunk Range here from his native Pennsylvania (*see Tour* 5).

Historic Buildings

LOWER FORT, SCHOHARIE

TICONDEROGA

FRENCH ALTAR, FORT NIAGARA

Photographs by W. Lincoln Highton, courtesy of Federal Works Agency

KITCHEN, THE CASTLE, FORT NIAGARA

INTERIOR, FORT CRAILO, RENSSELAER

Photograph by T. C. Ban

INTERIOR, CHRIST EPISCOPAL CHURCH, DUANESBURG

Photograph by W. Lincoln Highton; courtesy of Federal Works Ag

INTERIOR, LINDENWALD

Photograph by Paul Broady

FIREPLACE, SCHUYLER MANSION, ALBANY

HASBROUCK HOUSE, NEWBURGH

Photograph by John J. Vrooma

HOLLAND LAND OFFICE MUSEUM, BATAVIA

Photograph by John J. Vrooma

hotograph by Paul Broady

FRANKLIN D. ROOSEVELT LIBRARY, HYDE PARK

PHILIPSE MANOR HALL, YONKERS

hotograph by John J. Vrooman

SENATE HOUSE, KINGSTON

Photograph by John J. Vrooman

OLD UNION HOTEL, SACKETS HARBOR

Photograph by John J. Vrooman

KERHONKSON (Ind., wild geese), 21.9 *m.*, (254 alt.,550 pop.), is at the junction with US 44 (*see Tour* 5).

At 26.5 *m.* is the entrance (R) to YAMA FARM (*references required*), a semiprivate inn of simple but extensive buildings in elaborately planted grounds. The high daily fee covers the use of all the country club facilities. In the early decades of the present century it was famous as a meeting place for literary figures, including John Burroughs and Hamlin Garland.

NAPANOCH, 27 *m.* (300 alt.,642 pop.), an attractive town with deep, shaded lawns, is a trading center for resorts and boys' camps.

The NAPANOCH STATE INSTITUTION FOR MALE DEFECTIVE DELINQUENTS (L), 27.1 *m.*, dwarfed by the sheer cliff backdrop, accommodates about 1,000 in its modern gray stone buildings. All able-bodied inmates are employed in the production of aluminum and sheet metal ware, gas billies, metal signs, wood handles, shoe materials, brooms, toweling, and baskets.

ELLENVILLE, 29 *m.* (360 alt.,3,977 pop.), between the Shawangunk Mountains and the Allegheny Plateau, is a center of the resort district of Sullivan and Orange Counties. Frame, brick, and cobblestone hotels and houses in and around the town feature *kosher* cuisines in serving the city visitors. The DUTCH REFORMED CHURCH and the COURTHOUSE are good examples of the Greek Revival period of American architecture. The OLD INDIAN FORT (R), now in disrepair, is a story-and-a-half stone building (1774) with a clapboard gable, its sweeping roof broken by two chimneys.

Abandoned DELAWARE & HUDSON CANAL LOCKS (*see Tour* 3) are (R) at 36.8 *m.*

WURTSBORO, 41.8 *m.* (560 alt.,423 pop.) (*see Tour* 3), is at the junction with State 17 (*see Tour* 3).

South of Wurtsboro the Shawangunks form the left slope of a 20-mile-long valley, as yet little exploited for summer tourists.

PORT JERVIS, 59.8 *m.* (451 alt.,9,616 pop.) (*see Tour* 4), is at the junction with US 6 (*see Tour* 4).

US 209 crosses the PENNSYLVANIA LINE, 61.3 *m.*, in the middle of the bridge over the Delaware River, 8 miles northeast of Milford, Pennsylvania.

Tour 7

(Great Barrington, Mass.)—Hillsdale—Hudson—Catskill—Grand Gorge—Oneonta; State 23.
Massachusetts Line to Oneonta, 100.5 *m.*

Two-lane macadam with stretches of concrete.
New York Central R.R. parallels route between Grand Gorge and Stamford and between Davenport Center and Oneonta.

East of the Hudson River State 23 crosses a hill country in which several contemporary writers have found refuge. West of the river it climbs over the northern stretches of the Catskills, summer playground for New Yorkers, with hotels and boarding houses sprawling up the slopes and the compact white homes of dairy farmers resting in the valleys. The landscape carries the romantic coloring of Dutch legend as elaborated by Washington Irving and of the more virile tales of James Fenimore Cooper.

Section a. *MASSACHUSETTS LINE to CATSKILL;* 23.8 m. *State 23*

Crossing over from Massachusetts at the crest of the Taconic range, the route hems the northern border of the Taconic State Park (*see Tour* 20) and climbs up and down the Columbia County hills. Artists and writers, forsaking Greenwich Village a decade or so ago, came to this region for the 'incredibly beautiful scenery,' but soon found the sturdy, earth-rooted farmers of Dutch and German stock as interesting and as timeless as the hills and valleys themselves.

State 23, a continuation of Mass. 17, crosses the MASSACHUSETTS LINE, 0 m., at a point 7.9 miles west of Great Barrington, Massachusetts.

Near HILLSDALE, 1.7 m. (686 alt.,500 pop.), at the junction with State 22 (*see Tour* 20), John Cowper Powys, British novelist, lived for several years in country 'more like England than any landscape I have yet seen in the whole of America.' Arthur Davison Ficke, author of *Sonnets of a Portrait Painter*, lives near by on his farm 'Hardhack,' named for the swamp brush that chokes the fields; here he wrote most of the poems in *The Secret*, published in 1936. In the shadows of Phudd Hill, Alan Devoe writes his nature essays in the tradition of Thoreau and Burroughs.

In the center of CRARYVILLE, 6 m. (640 alt.,128 pop.), is the junction with a macadam road.

Left on this road 2.9 m. to COPAKE (Ind., snake waters) LAKE, shaped like a horseshoe by a promontory which juts from the northern shore. Developed as a summer retreat, it was first used by Indians who had a village under sheltering hills at the outlet.

Taking much of its importance from the manor house of the lower manor of Rensselaerswyck, CLAVERACK (Dutch, clover field), 14.4 m. (209 alt., 400 pop.), was the Columbia County seat until it was superseded by Hudson (*see Tour* 21). Today principally a suburban residential district for Hudson businessmen and retired families, it steps out of the past with an array of old mansions.

The VAN RENSSALAER MANOR HOUSE (R), at the eastern village line, an L-shaped building with long shingled roof sloping unbroken to the first floor level to form a porch, is a conglomeration of additions to the original two-room dwelling, built probably about 1712. The lower manor was presented in 1704 by the fourth patroon to his brother, Hendrick Van Rensselaer.

The OLD HUDSON COUNTY COURTHOUSE (R), built in 1786 and used as a seat of justice until 1845, is a two-story-and-attic building of brick painted white with stone foundation. The style is Georgian Colonial; the portico has wood Corinthian columns and pilasters. Here in 1804 Alexander Hamilton argued for a retrial of Harry Croswell, publisher of *The Wasp* in Hudson, who had been found guilty of libeling President Thomas Jefferson. 'I contend,' said Hamilton, 'for the liberty of publishing truth with good motives and for justifiable ends, even though it reflects on government, magistrates or private persons.' The court divided on this case two and two; but in 1805 the State legislature enacted into law the principles which Hamilton had professed.

The LUDLOW HOUSE (R), said locally to be as 'old as the town of Claverak,' is a two-story weathered brick structure with varicolored slate gambrel roof, brown shutters, and wood trim and window jambs painted white. The MILLER HOUSE (L), built in 1767, a brick gambrel-roof dwelling, considerably altered in the interior, was used as a meeting place for courts-martial during the Revolution; prisoners were kept in the cellar. The VANDERBO HOUSE (R), a brick structure painted white, with green shutters, Greek Ionic columns on the entrance porch, shingled roof, and gabled ends, was built about 1800, during the village's prosperous era.

HUDSON, 18.1 *m.* (100 alt.,11,487 pop.) (*see Tour 21*), is at the junction with US 9 (*see Tour 21*) and State 9G (*see Tour 21B*).

State 23 runs in common with State 9G south of Hudson along the river, skirting swampland (R), haven for migratory ducks in season. Rising 543 feet beside the tidewater Hudson, MOUNT MERINO, 19.6 *m.* (R), was named for the sheep, among the first introduced in America, pastured on its rocky slopes by Chancellor Livingston (*see Tour 21B*).

At 22 *m.* State 23 branches right from State 9G to the RIP VAN WINKLE BRIDGE (*car and occupants* 50¢; *pedestrians*, 10¢), crossing the Hudson. Constructed in 1935 at a cost of $2,500,000, it is a deck cantilever-type steel structure 5,040 feet long and 142 feet above the river. In midstream the bridge rests on small Rogers Island, scene of one of the last battles between the Mahican and Mohawk Indians.

CATSKILL, 23.2 *m.* (75 alt.,5,414 pop.) (*see Tour 21A*), is at the junction with US 9W (*see Tour 21A*).

Section b. *CATSKILL to ONEONTA;* 76.7 *m. State* 23

The history of the region between Catskill and the Susquehanna Valley, supplemented by the present scene, shows to what uses man can put a mountain landscape: destroy its timber for tanbark and barrel hoops, tear jagged holes into it to quarry stone, clear its untillable acres for scratch farming, conceal stills in its secluded corners, tame it with manicured golf courses, and people it with figures of old romance. Through it all, the mountains have retained much of their beauty, thanks largely to the State, which has bought up the 232,000 acres of the Catskill Forest Preserve (*see Conservation*) to prevent further destruction and to rebuild. Fields have gone back to woodlot; the shorn hills have grown new timber.

At Catskill is the junction with State 23A (the Rip Van Winkle Trail), an alternate route between Catskill and Prattsville.

South on State 23A, which runs in common with US 9W (*see Tour 21A*) for a short distance. At 1.6 *m.* US 9W continues left (straight ahead) and State 23A branches right. Hidden among tall trees in the foothills is the ABEEL HOUSE (L), 5.1 *m.*, just visible from the road. In this one-and-a-half-story Dutch Colonial stone structure built in 1721, David Abeel was captured by marauding Indians during the Revolution and taken to Canada.

PALENVILLE, 10.1 *m.* (560 alt.,280 pop.), is the legendary home of Rip Van Winkle. Washington Irving wrote of the '. . . light smoke curling up from a village, whose shingle-roofs gleam among the trees.' During the Revolution there was a fortification on this site.

Right from Palenville on a macadam road 1.2 *m.* to the old OTIS ELEVATING RAILROAD STATION (R), now a private home, where nineteenth-century vacationists transferred from the narrow-gauge cars running between Catskill and the foot of the mountain to the cable car that hauled them up the steep wall to the Catskill Mountain House (*see below*). The straight gash of the tram's course up the mountain is now the path for an electric power line. At 2.9 *m.* (L) is the abandoned trail of the stagecoach road that hairpinned up the mountain in the days before the cable car. Here is a view of SLEEPY HOLLOW, the ravine halfway up the mountain designated by Irving as the place where the mythical Rip Van Winkle slept. Hikers who follow the abandoned coach road up the mountain stumble on the ruins, 1 *m.*, of the RIP VAN WINKLE BOARDING HOUSE, built in 1845 on the rim of Sleepy Hollow. The hotel had an enormous drinking bar to accommodate passengers during the rest and feeding period for the stagecoach horses. Before the visitors continued up the mountain they were shown the exact spot where Rip slept, with the indentations made by his shoulders in the rocks, and the tree under which he found the worm-eaten stock of his fowling-piece.

West of Palenville State 23A follows steep, narrow KAATERSKILL CLOVE and enters Catskill State Park (*see below*) at 11.2 *m.* Irving described the clove as 'wild, lonely, and shagged, the bottom filled with fragments from the impending cliffs, and scarcely lighted by the reflected rays of the setting sun'; William Cullen Bryant wrote a lyric about it, and Thomas Cole reproduced its beauty on canvas. Today swank homes and clubhouses cling to the steep slopes.

At HAINES FALLS, 15.2 *m.* (1,900 alt.,200 pop.), is the junction with an unmarked macadam road; right here 3 *m.* to the NORTH LAKE STATE CAMPSITE (*open May 25–Sept. 25, free*), from which trails lead to the upper rim of Sleepy Hollow and to NORTH POINT (3,280 alt.), commanding a wide view. At the campsite is the entrance to the grounds of the CATSKILL MOUNTAIN HOUSE (*adm. to grounds 25¢*), built in 1823. The huge, three-story white frame building, classical in design, with 13 wooden Corinthian columns supporting a long front portico, has been a show place for more than a century. From its veranda at the brink of a 1,400-foot cliff is an awe-inspiring view of the Hudson Valley floor.

At TANNERSVILLE, 17.3 *m.* (1,920 alt.,656 pop.), on Lake Rip Van Winkle, is the junction with a macadam crossroad.

1. Right 1.3 *m.* on this road to ONTEORA (Ind., mountain of the sky) PARK, an exclusive group of elaborate summer homes. Here Hamlin Garland wrote his Middle Border books and his memoirs. In 1927, after attending one of the colony's exclusive social functions, he wrote that 'luxury such as this may be debilitating.'

2. Left 2 *m.* on this road to ELKA PARK, another colony of private residences.

Twilight, Elka, Santa Cruz, and Sunset Parks are expensive resorts, separate in setting but under a single board of directors, admitting only those who can produce letters of introduction from persons known to the management. Here the top social strata of New York and Philadelphia come from expensive city apartments to the mountain wildness tamed by urban conveniences.

At 19.5 *m.* on State 23A is the junction with State 214; left here 7.8 *m.* to DEVIL'S TOMBSTONE STATE CAMPSITE (*free*), at the entrance to Stony Clove. Just north of the campsite, in the heart of the clove, is the junction for State-maintained foot trails to the tops of Hunter Mountain (4,025 alt.), Plateau Mountain (3,855 alt.), Sugarloaf Mountain (3,782 alt.), Twin Mountain (3,647 alt.), and Indian Head Mountain (3,585 alt.).

At 21.4 *m.* is the junction with a road across Schoharie Creek; left here 0.6 *m.* to COLONEL'S CHAIR (3,100 alt.), a mountain shaped like a chair, a gully forming the seat and ridges the arms. From here marked foot trails lead to the peak of Hunter Mountain, 4 *m.*, and a fire observation tower (*open when ranger is on duty*), Phoenecia (*see Tour* 15), Slide Mountain, Sugarloaf Mountain, and Indian Head Mountain.

Strung out for two miles in the narrow valley of Schoharie Creek, HUNTER 21.5 *m.*, (1,600 alt.,624 pop.), is an array of boardinghouses against the mountain wall. As early as 1880 the railroad through Stony Clove was depositing Jewish families in the valley town, and today it has a large year-round Jewish population and several *kosher* markets; fruit and vegetable stands cover the sidewalks, creating a decidedly urban atmosphere.

At 36.9 *m.* is the western limit of Catskill State Park; at 37 *m.* is the junction with State 23 (*see below*).

State 23 branches right from US 9W in CATSKILL, 0 *m.* Maples and elms, fencing the highway, shelter tourists' cabins, boardinghouses, and gas stations; life-size figures of Rip Van Winkle and other souvenir doo-dads are dangled as bait for the tourist trade.

Hereabouts legendary gnomes with bushy beards and eyes like pigs' worked in metals. Under the full moon they gathered on the mountain cliffs, dancing and capering until the night wore out. They brewed a liquor that shortened the body and swelled the head. When Hudson and his crew landed on the riverbank, the pygmies held a carouse in his honor; when the sailors departed they were distorted by the magic distillation, which, we moderns know, was Catskill applejack.

Today LEEDS, 3 *m.* (172 alt.,300 pop.), is a one-street town with hotels, souvenir shops, and stores advertising 'cure-all mineral waters' drawn 'through solid rock from a natural cave.' The REFORMED CHURCH (R), a two-story native stone structure with gable end facing the street, and the old STONE ARCH BRIDGE, built of local limestone, are about the only mon-uments left of the Dutch builders. The two eastern arches of the bridge, the oldest in the State, were laid in 1760 and the two western in 1792. The bridge was restored by the State in 1937.

West of Leeds once lived Ralph Sutherland, who caught his runaway white slave and tied her to the tail of his horse to drag her home; her skull was smashed against the rocks and she died. Sutherland was acquitted of her murder, but was required to wear a cord about his neck to remind his neighbors to shun him. The fertile imagination of the mountain people went to work: they heard a shrieking woman pass the house nightly, tied to the tail of a giant horse with burning eyes and smoking nostrils; they saw a woman on the garden wall with lights shining from her fingertips, ut-tering unearthly laughter. Sutherland died a lonely man.

Between Catskill and Cairo the road follows the bed of the old Catskill Turnpike, linking the Hudson and Susquehanna Valleys, over which huge, wide-wheeled freight wagons crawled behind straining teams of four oxen or six horses. As railroads were built, the turnpike shrunk, so that today, except where it runs in common with main-traveled roads, it is little more than a winding country lane, hub-deep in spring mud, hard and dust-choked in summer.

CAIRO, 9.8 *m.* (340 alt.,573 pop.), is another tourist town; villagers not

engaged in catering to summer visitors work in the surrounding apple
orchards.

Left from Cairo 1.4 *m.* on an improved road to PURLING (480 alt.,180 pop.),
known as Forge until 1895, when it was renamed for the purling of waters over the
stones in the Shinglekill. Here Enoch Hyde and Benjamin Hall built their forge. Iron
ore was brought up from the Hudson on mules. Later wooden-wheeled clocks, oaken
buckets, grain cradles, and furniture were manufactured with power supplied by the
creek.

ACRA, 13.3 *m.* (668 alt.,105 pop.), is surrounded by apple orchards. Local cider is distilled to potent Catskill applejack. In the last years of the
prohibition era, Jack ('Legs') Diamond moved his gang headquarters to
an innocent-appearing white farmhouse in a grove of trees just north of the
village. Hounded by rivals, the sallow-faced thug came to the isolation of
the Catskills to raise local stills to the status of an organized business.
Mountain bootleggers did not welcome the intrusion, and Diamond was
shot down in one of the mountain drinking joints. He survived, returned
to his Acra home, and had the trunks of the trees about his house painted
white to make an ambush attack impossible. Broken by legal battles, he
was eventually killed in a cheap rooming house in Albany.

Thurlow Weed (1797–1882) was born in a log cabin east of the village,
and spent several years among the rugged, superstitious backwoods people. Weed, last of the political journalists involved in the struggle between
Federalism and Jeffersonianism, rose from blacksmith, boathand, salt-
boiler, and printer to political dictator. He published an anti-Masonic
newspaper in Rochester in 1826 and cemented his political career in 1828
by swinging the anti-Masonic sentiment arising out of the Morgan incident (*see Tour* 11) to the support of John Quincy Adams for President. In
1829 the anti-Masons elected him to the Assembly so that he could be in
Albany to edit the Albany *Evening Journal*, which he made the undisputed
leader of the Whig press until the rise of Horace Greeley's *Tribune*. Weed's
political sagacity was as important to the birth of the Republican party as
was the antislavery issue.

West of Acra the characteristic Catskill red rocks appear; they formed a
part of the great Catskill delta, their red color resulting from oxidation
when the sea level was low. At 19 *m.* is (R) POINT LOOKOUT (2,400
alt.), with a 100-foot tower (*view from top* 10¢; *telescope* 10¢) at the edge of
the cliff, commanding a broad view northward to the Helderbergs and eastward across the Hudson to the Taconics, Berkshires, and Green and White
Mountains—'all creation,' as Leatherstocking said in Cooper's story. Windows in homes in EAST WINDHAM, 19.5 *m.* (1,920 alt.,100 pop.), a summer resort on the northeastern tip of the Catskill plateau, overlook an
1,800-foot drop into the valley of Catskill Creek.

At 22.4 *m.* is the eastern boundary of CATSKILL STATE PARK, covering 596,120 acres in Greene, Ulster, Delaware, and Sullivan Counties.
The State owns 232,000 acres outright and exercises water and forest control over the remainder. Within the protected area are many villages, summer resorts, farms, and hunting and fishing clubs; but mile after mile of
forest wilderness is guarded against spoliation, shielded from the ax, and

even from farming, pasturing, and habitation. Mountain and valley are for deer, fox, racoon, grouse, trout, and other wild life, and for the hiker who trails up the summits of high peaks and the hunter who crashes through the wilderness tangle in the fall.

In ASHLAND, 29.7 m. (1,422 alt.,196 pop.), Jairns Munson operated one of the first Catskill ropewalks—one of the 173 enumerated in the United States in 1810. Under the roof of a long, low building, spinners walked back and forth twisting the fibers so that by reciprocal friction they held together when strain was applied. In the summer the rope-making was often moved into the open to permit walks as long as 900 feet.

At 34.2 m. State 23 crosses the western boundary of the Catskill State Park, and at 36 m. is the junction with State 23A (see above), alternate route between Prattsville and Catskill.

PRATTSVILLE, 36.1 m. (1,150 alt.,384 pop.), a long, narrow town in the shadow of Prospect Hill (R), is supported by summer boarders, its creamery, and the trade of vicinity farmers.

Directly across the road is PRATTS ROCKS (picnicking), a public park donated to the village by Zadock Pratt, its namesake. Determined to perpetuate his name for posterity, Pratt left carved in the rocks a bust of himself, carvings of his favorite dogs and horses, and a bust of his son, Colonel George W. Pratt.

Born in Stephentown, Rensselaer County, Zadock Pratt (1790–1871) came to the Catskills and amassed a $14,000 fortune from a general store at Lexington. By 1825 he had built his own village, Prattsville, on Schoharie Creek, constructing more than 100 houses for settlers. At one time he operated the largest tannery in the mountains, a large gristmill, and a hat factory. Mountain neighbors regarded him as 'the most wonderful man the country ever produced.' He had a peculiar sense of humor. One hot Fourth of July, with the sun baking the Catskills, he hitched his white horses to his sleigh, strapped on the bells, bundled himself in his fur coat, and drove over the mountains to Catskill.

Soon after the War of 1812, the hush of Catskill forests was shattered by the ring of axes, the rumble of wagons, and the work songs of men. Shiploads of raw hides from South America hove up the Hudson and were trucked up over mountain peaks to tanneries blooming on the edge of every hemlock forest. Tanning required one cord of bark to every ten hides; since the largest wagon could carry only enough bark for five hides, tanners found it economical to bring the raw hides to the bark.

The hides were 'sweated' in liming vats for removal of hair, then passed to the first of a long row of tanning vats containing various solutions of tanbark, sumac acids, and water—the vats close together so that a husky man with a fork could lift a hide from vat to vat without waste of time. The hide finally emerged, tanned and ready for drying and shipping. The process, like a modern assembly line, was endless.

Tanbark peeling attracted many muscular migratory workers who worked for a few weeks in early summer while the sap was high and bark was loose. The work was hard, from sunup to sundown. A good bark peeler could pile two cords a day, for which he was paid as much as $2.75, bountiful wages for the times. Life was one continuous camping out, ever on the march for the retreating hemlock. The men lived in hemlock shanties slapped together in a few hours. The bark peeled off, millions of feet of potential lumber were left to rot and burn on the mountain sides. The dried, brittle logs were tinder for forest fires, and what man had failed to waste, fire did.

Following the bark-peelers, the hoop-making industry developed, prospered on a lesser scale, and died about 1890. In winter, sapling poles, eight feet long for barrels and five for kegs, were hauled to the hoop-makers' huts. The shaver split the sapling in the center, working on a bench similar to the old cobbler's stool. Leaning forward he placed his drawknife at the head of the pole and, with an oarsman's stroke of the body, pulled it toward him.

The hoop-shaving art was largely practiced by men of great solitude who lived in huts 'constructed almost as simply as those of the woodrats, made of sticks laid across each other without compass or square.' They had long and tangled hair; arms and backs bent by constant moving of the shaver's knife; 'dress that was a ludicrous mixture of two-years'-old store garments and the pelts of animals; tongues glued to taciturnity from endless weeks of silence . . .'

West of Prattsville State 23 passes, at 36.6 m., a small mountain (L) created by rock and dirt dumped from the SHANDAKEN TUNNEL, which carries water 18.1 miles under the mountain from Schoharie Reservoir (see Tour 24) to Esopus Creek and the Ashokan Reservoir (see Tour 15), and thence to New York. Named for the town of Shandaken, it aptly represents the Iroquois meaning of the name, rapid waters.

In GRAND GORGE, 41.2 m. (1,420 alt.,388 pop.), is the junction with State 30 (see Tour 24).

State 23 follows the Bear Kill and the Ulster & Delaware Railroad (R) through the Delaware County dairy, cheese, and cauliflower region. Hills are less densely wooded, and pasture and field climb well up the slopes. In June and July the hills smoulder with hawkweed, a pest to the farmers, but a gorgeous sight of yellow and tawny amid daisy white, buttercup yellow, and sorrel reddish-brown.

State 23 hugs the lower slopes (L) of MOUNT UTSAYANTHA (3,213 alt.), highest peak in the western Catskills. Here the beautiful Utsayantha, a Mohawk princess, fell in love with a Sioux brave, but Indian taboo barred the marriage. Utsayantha leaped into a lake and was drowned and her father buried her on the summit of the mountain. Her grave is preserved with a marker. Several years ago the grave was entered and nothing was found.

STAMFORD, 49.2 m. (1,827 alt.,1,103 pop.), with its 33 hotels, large and small, including the Hotel Habana, which caters exclusively to wealthy Cubans and South Americans who spend their summers here, is the largest and most pretentious resort in the Catskills. Excellent facilities for golf, tennis, swimming, riding, mountain-climbing, and fishing provide rural recreation without sacrifice of urbanlike hotel conveniences. Exclusive, a rich man's paradise in many ways, the village has reversed the economic rule: many of the so-called public recreation facilities, which are privately owned, have a sliding scale of prices; fees bound skyward for the 'undesirables' and decrease for those who are rich enough to be accounted desirable.

State 23 twists over rolling hills to the headwaters of the Susquehanna River, separated by less than two miles from the West Branch of the Delaware. HARPERSFIELD, 53.4 m. (1,752 alt.,50 pop.), was the scene of Indian-Tory raids during the Revolution, and later was one of the principal stops on the old Catskill Turnpike. Settled in 1771 by Colonel John Harper from Cherry Valley, the settlement, on the Indian trail between the Schoharie and the Susquehanna Valleys, was attacked in the spring of 1780 by Indians led by Joseph Brant (*see Tour* 8); three settlers were scalped and eight taken captive. Timothy Murphy avenged the loss in a single-handed attack on a camp of 27 Indians. When he left the camp, six Indians were dead and the rest scattered in the hills.

State 23 winds through hills along Center Brook, Middle Brook, and Charlotte Creek, all headwaters of the Susquehanna. At 74.5 m. the view of the broad Susquehanna Valley (R) throws fertile land, mountain, city, and river in bold contrast. At 76 m. State 23 joins with State 28 (*see Tour* 15) and runs in common with it for 0.6 mile.

In ONEONTA, 76.7 m. (1,120 alt.,11,649 pop.) (*see Tour* 10) is the junction with State 7 (*see Tour* 10).

Tour 8

(Pittsfield, Mass.)—Albany—Cherry Valley—Sangerfield—La Fayette—Auburn—Geneva—Canandaigua—Fredonia—Westfield—(Erie, Pa.); US 20.
Massachusetts Line to Pennsylvania Line, 387.6 m.

Two-, three-, and four- lane concrete, with stretches of two-lane macadam.
Rutland R.R. parallels route between New Lebanon and Brainard; Delaware and Hudson R.R. between Sharon Springs and Cherry Valley; Delaware, Lackawanna & Western R.R. between Richfield Springs and Bridgewater; New York Central R.R. and Lehigh Valley R.R. between Auburn and Geneva; and Pennsylvania R.R. between Geneva and Canandaigua.

In 150 years trails and woods-roads have been joined and improved to make US 20 a popular route spanning the Empire State but touching only two large cities—Albany and Auburn. From the crest of the Taconics the highway drops into the Hudson Valley; west of Albany it mounts the flank of the Helderbergs, dips into and out of the valley of Schoharie Creek, plunges into the upper valleys of the Susquehanna watershed, rides the serrated northern rim of the Allegheny Plateau, crosses the base of the Finger Lakes, then cuts across the rolling Ontario Plain to Lake Erie, and thence southwest to the Pennsylvania line. Steep grades through the eastern half of the route discourage commercial hauling and leave the highway open to light speed traffic. Following the trails made by moccasined feet, the route runs the length of the 'Long House' of the Iroquois Confederacy. Soldiers brought muskets to the red men; traders exchanged trinkets and rum for their furs; and the Jesuit missionaries, whose only weapon was the cross, offered salvation to their souls and suffered the worse for their pains. In the struggle for empire between Britain and France the allegiance of the Iroquois shifted with the fortunes of battle, until the British conquest of Canada made them staunch allies of the crown. In the early days of the Revolution they joined Walter Butler's Rangers and Sir John Johnson's Royal Greens to raid the outlying settlements. But this brought the Sullivan-Clinton expedition against them; the Patriot punitive force devastated the Long House, especially the land of the Seneca, and in the process cut the moccasin trails into roads.

The Revolution ended, Sullivan's soldiers went home to New England bearing tales of a fertile land to the west; and with the peace, the westward rush was on. The State set aside the Military Tract for veterans, and the western part of the State was sold to the land companies, which offered special inducements to new settlers. The great trek to the promised land crowded this Cherry Valley route. Obstructing trees were cut away and swampy sections were 'paved' with logs and gravel. Riding was rough: pioneer families, taking cows with them, put the milk into a churn and the jolting of the wagon churned the butter as they went along.

The migrating New Englanders, besides settling the region with stubborn, sturdy men and women, added their characteristic religious and political vagaries. Memorials of their sects and cults are scattered along the route from the Shakers at New Lebanon to the Brotherhood of the New Life at Brocton. The route exhibits houses, taverns, and meetinghouses built by them in the New England style. Side-stepped by bustling industry in the later nineteenth century, these buildings retain the pungent flavor of their salty builders.

Section a. *MASSACHUSETTS LINE to ALBANY;* 29.3 m. US 20

Shaggy Mount Lebanon rises north of the point where US 20 crosses the MASSACHUSETTS LINE, 0 m., 7.8 miles west of Pittsfield, Massachusetts. As the highway winds down the mountainside it passes several brown, barnlike houses (L), remnants of the MOUNT LEBANON SHAKER SETTLEMENT, established here in 1785. The Shakers were one of the earliest religious cults to sprout along the east-west axis of the Empire State. Its distinguishing tenets were celibacy, community of property, spirituality, and refusal to take oath or bear arms. The social unit was the large 'family' housed under one roof, but the men and women eating and lodging separately. The physical paroxysms accompanying their religious exercises gave rise to the name 'Shaking Quakers,' later abbreviated to Shakers.

The leader of the cult, Mother Ann Lee, represented the incarnation of the Divine Spirit, who, according to the hymn, *The Gospel Trumpet*,

> By her sufferings overcame
> And taught the way of self denying
> Put the nasty flesh to shame
> In which Old Adam's race were lying.

In response to a revelation, Mother Ann led six men and two women converts to America from England in 1774. This group settled originally at Watervliet, but Mount Lebanon was the first formal Shaker Society, organized by Joseph Meacham, a converted Baptist pastor.

A combination of communism, industry, and inventiveness built a prosperous society during the nineteenth century. Wide markets were found for Shaker herbs, garden seeds, blankets, brooms, and chairs, and many labor-saving inventions were provided for home and farm. But the sect's exclusive dependence upon converts and the adoption of orphans to recruit its numbers has led to a slow disintegration until today there is only a handful of aged Shakers left.

At 2.1 *m.* is the eastern junction with State 22 (*see Tour* 20), which unites briefly with US 20.

NEW LEBANON, 2.9 *m.* (720 alt.,400 pop.), was the birthplace of Samuel J. Tilden (1814–86), who as member of the State legislature and as governor pushed the investigations that smashed New York City's Tweed Ring and the upstate Canal Ring. Tilden was initiated into politics at an early age when conferences were held at his father's house by Martin Van Buren, Silas Wright, and other big-wigs of the Albany Regency. Influenced by the personal glamor of his mentor Van Buren, Tilden participated in the revolt of the Barnburner, or free soil, faction of the New York Democrats, and in 1855 was candidate of the softshell, or antislavery, faction for attorney general of the State. Many of the revolters joined the new Republican party but Tilden remained a Democrat. In 1876, as presidential candidate he won a majority of the popular vote. But the electoral vote was so close that a special commission was appointed, which, voting strictly on party lines, gave Rutherford B. Hayes the office by a majority of one. Dying a bachelor, Tilden willed a large part of his fortune to found the New York City Public Library; his grave is in the New Lebanon cemetery.

At New Lebanon is the western junction with State 22 (*see Tour* 20).

Just west of the village is (R) the SHRINE OF OUR LADY OF LOURDES (*open May* 1–*Nov.* 1), built around a spring. On the Sunday nearest the feast of St.Christopher (July 25), thousands of motorists drive to the shrine for the annual blessing of automobiles.

Crossing the narrow valley of Wyomanock Creek, the road passes between the LEBANON VALLEY SKI-JUMP COURSE (R) and TOBOGGAN SLIDE (L), 5.3 *m.*, thin crevices in the thick woods of the hillside.

BENJAMIN BUDD'S TAVERN, 11.2 m. (L), now a private residence, was built about 1800 on the site of the cabin of David Brainard (1718–47), Indian missionary.

At 11.8 m. is a junction with State 66.

Left on State 66 down the Kinderhook Creek valley to the BERKSHIRE THEATRE WORKSHOP, 3.5 m., a summer school for dramatic training, conducted by the Bishop-Lee School, Boston, Massachusetts. Students produce plays in the NELL GWYNN THEATRE (adm. 50¢), a huge old barn rebuilt to accommodate an audience of 250.

At NASSAU, 16.1 m. (403 alt.,670 pop.), when legal obstructions can be circumvented, greyhound races are run at the RENSSELAER COUNTY FAIR GROUNDS. Tickets for admission are distributed profusely without charge; the large profits are made from betting. The course is sometimes run with monkeys astride the dogs.

Skirting the Hudson Valley fruit belt, at 20.9 m. US 20 unites with US 9 (see Tour 21).

At 24.1 m. is the junction with US 4 (see Tour 22).

At 29 m. the route bears L. on the Parker Dunn Memorial Bridge.

In ALBANY, 29.3 m. (18 alt.,130,447 pop.) (see Albany) are the junctions with State 43 (see Tour 9), State 5 (see Tour 11), US 9 (see Tour 21), and US 9W (see Tour 21A).

Section b. ALBANY to SANGERFIELD; 93 m. US 20

West of Albany US 20 follows roughly the old woods-roads and Indian trails over which the Tory and Indian raiders struck eastward during the Revolution, wiping out settlements and isolated homes. Over this same route rode nineteenth century Paul Reveres, hunting horns blaring, to call the antirenters together to fight the sheriff and his deputies (see Tour 21).

Just west of ALBANY, 0 m., is McKOWNVILLE, 5.8 m. (209 alt.,62 pop.), a clambake and midget-auto racing paradise. Almost every weekend during the warm season, Albany clubs and organizations crowd McKown's Grove for a 'bake.' A cobblestone-lined pit is filled with cordwood, which is burned until the stones are almost white hot. Then the ashes are swept out and the pit spread with a layer of fresh seaweed. Wire baskets, each filled with two dozen or more washed and selected clams, two clambake sausages, one-half chicken, one white and one sweet potato, and one or two ears of corn (when in season), are set into the pit and the whole covered with a tarpaulin, edges sealed with wet clay. The steamed clams are supplemented by iced raw clams, bread, pickles, and olives.

On Sunday afternoons the Capital City Speedways sponsor midget auto races on the pear-shaped quarter-mile dirt track in McKown's Grove. The light, stubby cars, 500 to 950 pounds in weight, whirl 21 laps for the main event, their open exhausts clattering, adding din and dust to the general excitement.

In GUILDERLAND, 9.4 m. (210 alt.,225 pop.), is (R) the SCHOOL-CRAFT HOUSE (private), an excellent example of the mid-nineteenth-century fad, the Gothic Revival cottage. A yellow wooden structure, it is complete with carpenter-fashioned buttresses, drip moldings, and tracery.

The CASE TAVERN (L), a large, rectangular frame structure covered by white clapboards, was built by Russel Case in 1799. The building is typical of the 62 hostelries that at the peak of turnpike travel lined the 55 miles to Cherry Valley.

At 20.7 m. is the junction with a dirt road.

Left on this road 0.3 m. to the NORTH HOUSE (L), a square, two-story frame structure of Georgian Colonial design built in 1784–6 by William North (1755–1836). Born in Maine, North served during the Revolutionary War as aide to Baron Von Steuben, and was later adopted by Steuben as son, heir, and executor of his estate. Between 1798 and 1800 North was Adjutant General of the United States Army, and later served as speaker of the State assembly and as U.S.senator. His grave is in Christ Episcopal Church Cemetery, Duanesburg.

A short distance beyond the North House stands the 12-room Georgian Colonial structure known today as the DUANE-FEATHERSTONHAUGH HOUSE, built about 1816 by James Duane's youngest daughter Catherine. In form and plan the two-story frame dwelling marks a transition from boxlike structure by having unusually long proportions, front and side entrance porches, and a magnificent 70-foot-long, two-story porch on the garden side. In 1855 the estate was inherited by James Duane Featherstonhaugh.

US 20 continues to DUANESBURG, 21.9 m. (720 alt.,197 pop.), named for James Duane (1733–97), jurist, land speculator, and mayor of Manhattan 1784–9. Described as 'plump of body . . . the dignity of his appearance enhanced by such luxuries as gold shoe and knee buckles,' Duane had a 'jolly good humor which quickly won him friends . . .' Just prior to the Revolution Duane was zealously aligned with the conservatives; he was one of the prominent citizens who attempted to quell the Stamp Act mobs in 1765. In November 1766, he was 'busily employed in a new remonstrance to the Parliament respecting our trade.' He sat in the Continental Congress almost continuously until 1783, serving chiefly in connection with financial and Indian affairs and in assisting with the final draft of the Articles of Confederation. Duane's greatest nonprofessional interest was in land development. Besides inheriting a large tract of land here from his father, he acquired a number of other tracts.

In Duanesburg is a junction with State 7 (see Tour 10).

On his land here Duane built a lovely little church, around which he planned to promote a settlement that would eclipse Schenectady. Only the church, the CHRIST EPISCOPAL CHURCH (R), 22.9 m., surrounded by a few modest homes, remains, a plain, clapboarded square structure built in 1789–93. The oldest unaltered Episcopal church in the State, it still displays the interior arrangements typical of the eighteenth century when sermons from the high pulpit dominated the liturgy, which was recited at the miniscule altar to one side. The bright red desks and cushions contrast attractively with the white woodwork of box-pews, columns, and gallery, the latter built for slaves and servants. Only the circuitous stovepipes and the oil lamps show that time has passed since Duane and his family sat in the left front pew, which was curtained lest the villagers be distracted from their devotions by the presence of the lord of the manor.

At 28.7 m., in the Schoharie Valley, is the junction with State 30 (see Tour 24).

In 1806 General William North started to develop ESPERANCE, 29.2 *m.* (640 alt.,233 pop.), as a real estate venture on the newly opened Great Western Turnpike, renaming the original settlement of State Bridge. The PRESBYTERIAN CHURCH (R), a two-story gable-roofed stone structure, was erected in 1824 and remodeled in 1897.

On the northern edge of the village (R) an evergreen tree marks the grave of 'The Witch of Esperance.' According to the legend, during the Napoleonic Wars a French soldier brought his family to the village. Upon his death his widow, unable to speak English and mingle with the villagers, became an object of suspicion and mystery and was called the 'Grenadier Woman.' At a solemn conclave in the stone church her neighbors decided she was a witch and voted her death. Her executioners fired a silver bullet molded from a teaspoon through the window of the widow's cabin and killed her while she cooked at the open fire with her children playing beside her.

In 1838, in the same stone church which housed the witch-hunt posse, Sheldon Jackson (1834-1909), born in Minaville, was baptized. Fifty years later he was appointed superintendent of public instruction in Alaska, and during his incumbency he introduced reindeer into the territory as a food supply to end periodic famines among the Alaskan Eskimos.

West of Esperance US 20 follows Schoharie Creek (L) for several miles. At about 34 *m.*, in the old turnpike days, a branch road cut around a toll-gate and was known as the Shunpike Road. The Shunpike paralleled the main turnpike and joined it again a short distance east of Carlisle. This was one of the ways the early settlers had of beating the toll rates—12½¢ for a wagon, 25¢ for a coach, 20¢ for a score of horses, mules, or cattle, 6¢ for a score of sheep or pigs. This type of evasion also represented a protest against the poor condition of the turnpikes.

High up on the Mohawk-Schoharie divide is CARLISLE, 39 *m.* (1,250 alt.,200 pop.). In this region, on a summer evening the neighborhood folk occasionally gather on a churchyard green, beneath the yellow and orange glow of Chinese lanterns, to enjoy an 'ice cream sociable.' In the winter the women hold quilting bees; the hostess has the frames and groundwork of the quilts ready and some of the guests sew in the different designs and do the patchwork while others knot the quilting yarn.

In the CARLISLE CEMETERY (R) is the GRAVE OF CAPTAIN THOMAS MACHIN (1744-1816), an army engineer who aided in fortifying the American camp around Boston. His most distinguished achievement was the laying of chain and boom across the Hudson River at West Point in 1778 (*see West Point*).

From EIGEN'S POINT (R), 44.3 *m.*, is a superb view of the Adirondacks. On display here is an ancient stagecoach with an elegant but confining passengers' compartment, baggage racks on the top and behind, and a mail pouch recess under the driver's seat.

During the Revolutionary War, SHARON CENTER, 47 *m.* (1,442 alt., 68 pop.), became a hideout for Tories and Indian raiders; the Tories were offering an $8 bounty for each scalp taken and 50 acres of land to each person who joined their cause. On July 10, 1781, Colonel Marinus Willett,

test for accurately determining the percentage of butter fat in milk and cream. In 1830 Hiram Hunt and Albert Brockway, local farmers, invented the rotary rake, a machine for gathering hay.

In SANGERFIELD, 93 *m.* (1,246 alt.,225 pop.), is the junction with State 12 (*see Tour* 25).

Section c. SANGERFIELD to LA FAYETTE; 41.7 m. US 20

It is in this section of the route that the central New York State atmosphere is encountered in its full force and purity. Here the metropolitan aura of New York City definitely does not extend; the 'big city' is Utica or Syracuse. The villages are much alike, each with its Main Street, general store, candy kitchen, and, in the larger ones, a Bijou or Roseland cinema palace.

On the steep valley hillsides are herds of dairy cows and flocks of sheep. At sheep-shearing time, mounds of gray, dirty wool fluff against the gray walls of the shearing sheds. Prohibition almost killed the hop industry but repeal revived it, and today it has begun to flourish again.

Between SANGERFIELD 0 *m.* and BOUCKVILLE, 9.5 *m.* (1,149 alt., 250 pop.), is muckland striped with the lush green of pea and bean vines.

Left from Bouckville on State 12B, a macadam road, to HAMILTON, 5.1 *m.* (1,126 alt.,1,700 pop.), seat of Colgate University. Settled by New Englanders and incorporated in 1816, the village is built around a green reminiscent of New England. On the brow of a hill overlooking the village, COLGATE UNIVERSITY, main entrance at Broad St. and Kendrick Ave., spreads out over a landscaped campus of about 125 acres. The main quadrangle achieves a remarkable architectural unity by its use of the local golden buff sandstone. WEST HALL (1827) and EAST HALL (1834) are forthright post-Colonial dormitories, of fine simplicity in their rectangular mass, stepped gables, elliptical-arched entrances, and widely spaced windows. Similar in plan and use are STILLMAN HALL (1927), which finds its inspiration in early Georgian, and ANDREWS HALL (1922), which bows to Collegiate Gothic. The CHAPEL (1918), with sandstone walls and limestone trim, also adopts the English Georgian; it has a four-columned Roman Doric pedimented portico and a two-stage steeple reminiscent of Wren.

In the JONATHAN OLMSTEAD HOUSE, on lower Broad St., 'thirteen men of yore' met on September 24, 1817, and organized the Baptist Education Society of the State of New York, from which the university grew. In 1819 the State granted the society a charter, and seven years later Deacon Samuel Payne and his wife transferred to the organization their farm, the site of the present quadrangle. Until 1839 only men studying for the Baptist ministry were admitted to what was then called the Hamilton Literary and Theological Institution. In 1846 it was incorporated as Madison University; and not until 1890 was the name changed to Colgate in recognition of the benefactions and interest of William Colgate and his descendants. In 1928 the Theological Seminary became part of the Colgate-Rochester Divinity School (*see Rochester*). At present Colgate offers work leading only to the A.B. degree. The plan of education provides for preceptorial and tutorial work in the first two years and seminar instruction in the last two. The student body is limited to 1,000.

In the valley bottom west of Bouckville US 20 crosses the Chenango Canal and continues through muckland truck gardens. In the summer season makeshift tents and crude trailers cluster in hollows, and the smoke from the campfires of small groups of itinerant workers rises through the trees.

On the edge of the swamp MORRISVILLE, 14.7 *m.* (1,326 alt.,583 pop.), prospers around its STATE SCHOOL OF AGRICULTURE, which occupies a dozen buildings (L), including a former county courthouse, built about 1866, and jail. The school, opened in 1910, offers agricultural and auto mechanics courses to boys, home economics courses to girls. Experimental farming is conducted on the school's 200-acre farm south of the village.

Right from Morrisville on a macadam road, which follows the edge of Peterboro Swamp, to PETERBORO, 6 *m.* (1,321 alt.,330 pop.), a hotbed of antislavery radicalism when it was the home of Gerrit Smith (1797–1874). Smith labored in many reform causes, from vegetarianism to women's dress reform, but is best remembered as an abolitionist. Of the 800,000 acres left him by his father he converted a quarter into 50-acre homes for emancipated Negroes; he supported John Brown's activities, abetted the Underground Railroad, and organized posses to free fugitive slaves arrested in Syracuse. As one of the founders of the Liberty party, Smith was nominated for governor; he later declined the nomination for President, but was elected to Congress and served in 1853–4. The Gerrit Smith home burned in 1936, but many relics are in the village museum, and the library of Syracuse University has a collection of his letters and manuscripts. His grave is in the Smith family lot in the Peterboro Cemetery.

Near NICHOLS POND, 10 *m.*, stood the stockaded fort of the Oneida Indians, attacked on October 11, 1615, by Samuel de Champlain and an expeditionary force of French and Hurons. This was the second skirmish between the French and Iroquois warriors and the first penetration of central New York by white men. It contributed to the orientation of the Iroquois to the English cause in the Colonial wars.

West from Morrisville US 20 enters the first of the series of land purchases of post-Revolutionary times representing one of the largest real estate promotion booms in American history. The road drops down into the Chittenango Creek Valley to CAZENOVIA, 26.2 *m.* (1,200 alt.,1,788 pop.), an orderly village with shaded streets and classical and Colonial homes. It cups the heel of CAZENOVIA LAKE (R), called by the Indians Hoh-wah-ge-neh, the lake where the yellow perch swim, a four-mile strip of gem-blue water margined by fine modern residences and summer homes.

The village was settled in 1793 by John Lincklaen (1768–1820), local agent for the Holland Land Company (*see Tour* 11), which here owned a small tract. Lincklaen named it for Theophile Cazenove, general agent for the company, who was playing the 'grand seigneur' in Philadelphia. During the turnpike period the village was a stopover place; the Cazenovia House was a drover's tavern, accommodating York State cowboys and the livestock they drove to market; at such a hostelry stagecoach passengers were considered high society and were charged double.

The LINCKLAEN HOUSE (R), built in 1825, is a three-story hotel of yellow brick with green shutters; the front and side porches of stone are in the Greek Doric style.

On Seminary St. are the buildings of the CAZENOVIA SEMINARY AND JUNIOR COLLEGE (R), a college preparatory school founded in 1824 by the Methodist Church. The chapel, a two-story post-Colonial building of native stone and brick, was originally a wing of a building constructed in 1810 and used as a courthouse.

At the western edge of the village (L) is LORENZO (*private*), a two-story Georgian dwelling built in 1807 by Lincklaen after his first home had burned. It reflects the contemporary admiration for the work of Robert Adam in England by the delicate pilasters, elliptical arches, shallow projecting gable, and roof parapet.

Right from Cazenovia on State 13, down the Chittenango Creek Valley, 4.1 *m.* to the CHITTENANGO FALLS STATE PARK (*picnicking, parking* 25¢), where the creek cascades for 136 feet, the water roaring and rumbling over and under jutting rock ledges.

West of Cazenovia US 20 becomes a giant roller-coaster for 32 miles over the spurs of the Allegheny Plateau. At 29.5 *m.*, the route enters Limestone Creek Valley, which for centuries sheltered the villages and farms of the Onondaga Indians.

Near the western edge, 29.8 *m.*, of the valley stood the house in which Erastus Dow Palmer (1817–1904) was born. A graduate of Union College, he worked as a mechanic and carpenter until he was 29. Examination of a cameo portrait led him to cut a likeness of his wife on a shell; encouraged, he cut over 100 cameo portraits in two years. But failing eyesight forced him to attempt larger work, and in 1851 he exhibited at the Academy of Design in New York his first marble bust, *The Infant Cares*, for which one of his children served as model. Six years later he sculptured the group, *The Landing of the Pilgrims*, designed as a pediment ornament for the south wing of the Capitol at Washington, D.C., but never placed there. His *Angel at the Sepulchre* is in the Albany Rural Cemetery.

In POMPEY CENTER, 31.7 *m.* (1,260 alt.,211 pop.), is the junction with a macadam road.

Right here 3.4 *m.* to INDIAN HILL, today a green wave of corn, but until 1684 the capital of the Onondaga Indians, comprising 140 cabins. In the summer of 1654 the Reverend Father Simon LeMoyne, Jesuit missionary, was entertained here by the Indian chiefs; the following year in a chapel of bark and poles Fathers Joseph Chaumonot and Claude Dablon held Christmas service. So strongly was one chief impressed that he came to the door of the chapel the next morning and 'exhorted all the young people to listen well.'

High up on a ridge is POMPEY, 35.7 *m.* (1,700 alt.,100 pop.), one of the first settlements in the 1,500,000-acre Military Tract. For a decade Pompey was the western end of the Great Western Turnpike. Historical groups are making an effort to preserve the village as a historical model and to build a museum for the coffee mills, hand-forged rakes and hoes, and other cumbersome equipment brought to the vicinity by the first settlers and now rusting in Onondaga County attics.

Pompey was inhabited by hardy, alert, adventuresome, imaginative pioneers. The village, together with the surrounding farms, was the birthplace, between 1795 and 1830, of 13 members of the State legislature, one United States senator, two State governors, mayors of five cities as far west as the Pacific coast, three Supreme Court justices, one major general, several authors, and at least two business geniuses. Not counted among these was the farmer who in his winter leisure prepared the 'Pompey

Stone' hoax; the stone, bearing the date 1589, was for more than half a century accepted as the genuine record of the earliest advent of white men—Spanish, of course—in New York State.

Of the business men, William George Fargo (1818–81) stands out as a genial fellow who made friends easily. At the age of 13 he rode a mail route of 30 miles twice a week. Appointed in 1840 messenger for Pomeroy & Company, the express firm between Albany and Buffalo, he became their Buffalo agent the following year. Four years later he acted as messenger for Wells & Company, the first express concern west of Buffalo, which later became Wells, Fargo & Company.

Fronting on the tree-rimmed village green (R) stand frame post-Colonial houses and a general store built in 1836 of native limestone. Beside the store is a remodeled stone home built in 1797, which, as HANDY'S TAVERN, was the roistering place of the village when it was an important frontier crossroads.

On the right side of the green is the PRESBYTERIAN CHURCH, built in 1817–19 by the Congregationalists. It is a two-story frame building, the square tower topped by six pillars bearing the final octagonal spire and a wrought-iron weather vane, in the Christopher Wren style of church architecture.

Across from the village green stands (L) the rebuilt two-story BIRTH-PLACE OF HORATIO SEYMOUR (1810–86), State governor and presidential candidate against Grant in 1868. He learned the political ropes under Governor Marcy and joined the conservative Democratic faction known as 'Hunkers.' During his first term as governor his veto of a bill prohibiting the sale of intoxicating liquors brought down on his head a campaign of vilification that charged him with being a drunkard and called his attacks of dyspepsia a form of insanity, although he was in fact a 'teetotaling Episcopalian.' In the seventies Seymour helped Tilden tumble Tweed from the political heights and took an active part in early efforts to reform Tammany Hall.

Right from Pompey on State 91, down the slopes of the Allegheny Plateau, to the junction with State 173 in JAMESVILLE, 7 m. (580 alt.,495 pop.). Left on State 173 to the CLARK STATE RESERVATION (R), 1.2 m., containing limestone cliffs 200 feet high and a small, deep lake. The park contains one of the few American stations of the Hart's Tongue fern (*Scolopendrium vulgare*), which grows only on the slopes of limestone channels or plunge basins. The scientific name, from the Greek meaning centipede, is applied because of the resemblance of the rows of elongated sori along each side of the midrib to the legs of the centipede. The plant is common in the British Isles, in the Azores, and in Japan.

West of Pompey are apple orchards, pink in May, green in the height of summer, and startlingly red with fruit in the autumn.

LA FAYETTE, 41.7 m. (1,160 alt.,100 pop.), is at the junction with US 11 (*see Tour* 18).

Section d. LA FAYETTE to AUBURN; 25.4 m. US 20

Between LA FAYETTE, 0 m., and Auburn US 20 whips up and down over the ragged southern edge of the Lake Ontario Plain, the crests of the mile-long gradients providing brief glimpses of the blue Finger Lakes and farm-green valleys.

Set like a delicate cameo at the base of the little digit of the Finger Lakes, SKANEATELES, 18.6 m. (868 alt.,1,882 pop.), is today, in the minds of thousands of people, synonymous with KREBS (L), a story-and-a-half white frame house set off by deep lawns; and Krebs is synonymous with food. Here a one-time impoverished Alsatian caterer has provided a place to delight a gourmet. Krebs came to Skaneateles in 1900 for his health and started serving meals to make a living. By word-of-mouth the fame of his cuisine spread until now during the summer months more than 1,000 meals a day are served, continuing the original policy of giving customers more than they can possibly eat.

In 1750 Moravian missionaries from Bethlehem, Pennsylvania, visited the Indian village on this site. The Indian trails were widened through this area by a detachment from the Sullivan-Clinton expedition; even so, Abraham A. Cuddeback, believed to be the first white settler, who arrived here about 1792, required 43 days for his trip with family and effects from Orange County.

In 1841 a water-cure sanitarium was started here by Dr.W.C.Thomas, who conducted the cures for 40 years, and who could at least offer his long life, 107 years, as a recommendation of the curative value of the waters.

Before the Civil War the village was a headquarters for the abolitionist activities of Gerrit Smith and an important station on the Underground Railroad. In 1843–5 it had its touch of 'ism' in the form of a commune of 'infidels' led by John Anderson Collins (1810–79), who bought a 300-acre farm two miles north of the village and advertised in the papers for followers. The principles of the group were denunciation of individual property, negation of all force, easy divorce, universal education, and vegetarianism. The community attracted the usual seekers after free board and lodging and received the usual round of condemnation from outsiders. Disillusioned, Collins liquidated the venture. At the opposite pole from the antireligionists was the work of the Quakers. About 1818, Lydia P. Mott came to the region and started the Friends' Female Boarding School, known as the Hive.

At one time or another Skaneateles attempted to develop industries of its own. As a sideline to its effort in textiles, an industry flourished here which is almost unique: teasel raising. The fuller's teasel, a thistle-like biennial, native of the south of Europe, is used in tearing or raising a nap on cloth. While visiting his home in England in 1840, William Snook, a resident of Onondaga County, became interested in the plant and on his return brought with him teasel seed. Although the raising of teasel never spread far, it became an important means of livelihood for this area until foreign competition drove it from the market. Machines have been invented to supplant the teasel hook, but the plant, which is strong enough for the work and yet elastic enough to 'give' before breaking the cloth, is still the more practical.

AUBURN, 25.4 m. (650 alt.,35,705 pop.) (see Auburn), is at the junction with State 5 (see Tour 11).

1. Left from Auburn on State 38 along the western shore of Owasco Lake, past summer cottages, to (L) ENNA JETTICK PARK (*open Decoration Day to Labor Day; bathing, boating, fishing, picnicking, amusements*), 2.6 *m.*, a 38-acre, privately owned public park.

In MORAVIA, 18.5 *m.* (741 alt.,1,295 pop.), St.Matthew's Episcopal Church contains seven wood carvings by Hans Meyer of the Oberammergau Passion Players. A tablet commemorates the marriage in the church of Millard Fillmore to Abigail Powers.

FILLMORE GLEN STATE PARK (*parking 25¢; dancing, bowling, swimming, hiking*), 19.5 *m.*, contains 511 acres of forested slopes and ravines with picturesque waterfalls.

In LOCKE, 21.8 *m.* (800 alt.,315 pop.), is the junction with State 90; left on State 90 to Summer Hill, 5.2 *m.*, birthplace of Millard Fillmore (*see Buffalo*).

On State 38, in GROTON, 28 *m.* (1,020 alt.,2,086 pop.), a quiet industrial village, is the plant of the L.C.Smith and Corona Typewriters,Inc., employing between 800 and 900 workers and producing about 100,000 portable typewriters annually.

The GEORGE JUNIOR REPUBLIC, 35 *m.*, founded in 1894 by William Reuben ('Daddy') George, is a nonsectarian community in which boys and girls between the ages of 12 and 21 receive practical training in useful citizenship. Its constitution is modeled on that of the United States; the laws are those of New York State supplemented by special laws enacted by the young citizens in their town meeting. Discipline is also enforced by the young people. The motto of the Republic is 'Nothing without Labor.' Every citizen works for his token money; boys learn carpentry, printing, farming, plumbing, or aeronautics; girls learn office work or home economics. Buildings include a schoolhouse, governmental buildings, and a chapel.

At 46 *m.* is the junction with State 221; left on this road 0.6 *m.* to junction with a gravel road; right here 1.8 *m.* to junction with an unimproved road; left here 0.3 *m.* to the (L) reputed Birthplace of John D. Rockefeller (*see Tour 21*), not claimed as such by the Rockefeller family. The weatherbeaten two-story frame house is occupied by a caretaker.

State 38 continues south to OWEGO, 70.8 *m.* (818 alt.,4,742 pop.), at the junction with State 17 (*see Tour 3*).

2. Left from Auburn on State 34 to the Harriet Tubman Home (L), 1.7 *m.*, which was used as a station on the Underground Railroad. 'Aunt' Harriet Tubman (1821–1913), called the Moses of her people, was born a slave in Maryland. In the pre-Civil War period she led more than 300 Negro slaves to freedom, aided by the strong abolitionist sentiment in central New York. During the war, she nursed to health hundreds of white and Negro soldiers. In 1914 the citizens of Auburn erected a tablet to her memory in the Cayuga County Courthouse. Her small house and 25 acres of land were deeded to the A.M.E.Zion Church, which still owns it. In 1908 it was opened as a home for indigent Negroes. It is now unoccupied and deteriorating.

In FLEMING, 5.4 *m.* (910 alt.,68 pop.), is the junction with State 34B, which the side tour follows.

State 34 continues to the Waring Homestead (R), 1.4 *m.*, a two-story frame house built in 1806, which served the public as a tavern in turnpike days and was later used as a Masonic lodge, a schoolhouse, and finally as a farm homestead.

On State 34B, in SHERWOOD, 13.6 *m.* (1,060 alt.,100 pop.), is (L) the Home of Emily Howland (1827–1929), born here of pioneer Quaker stock, who worked long years to free and rehabilitate Negro slaves. In 1857 she went to Washington to teach in Miss Miner's School for Negro girls; during the Civil War she helped to organize the Freeman's Village for refugees at Camp Todd. After the war, her father bought land in Northumberland County, Virginia, to which she transported destitute families and opened a school for Negro children, maintaining it for 50 years, until the State took it over. In 1871 she founded in her native village the Sherwood Select School for white pupils and in 1882 assumed financial responsibility for it, erecting a new building and taking the teachers into her own household. In 1927 she relinquished the school to the State, and it was renamed the Emily Howland School, now a regular high school of the State public school system.

In POPLAR RIDGE, 15.3 *m.* (1,047 alt.,96 pop.), is (R) the Home of Jethro

WOOD (1774–1834), who invented the first cast-iron plow to contain no wrought iron, and patented it in 1819. Infringements on Wood's patent were frequent; though supported in his fight against them by outstanding legal talent, he died in 1834 before his rights were clearly defined; his family received only $550 from the patent.

In SOUTH LANSING, 32.2 *m.* (846 alt.,300 pop.), is the southern junction with State 34, which continues south along Cayuga Lake to ITHACA, 40.2 *m.* (400 alt., 19,647 pop.) (*see Ithaca*), at the junction with State 2 (*see Tour 30*).

Section e. AUBURN to WESTERN JUNCTION WITH STATE 5; 71.3 m. US 20

In the imagination of the Indians, the Great Spirit laid his hand upon their country in benediction, and left the crystal-blue Finger Lakes as his mark. Geologists explain these long, slender bodies of water as preglacial valleys whose south-flowing rivers were bottled up by glacial debris and their courses reversed. A roll is given to the landscape by rounded hillocks 60 to 100 feet high that fold away with smoothing monotony into the distance; early settlers thought these were Indian burial mounds, but the unimaginative geologist calls them drumlins, heaps of debris dumped by the glaciers.

West of AUBURN, 0 *m.*, US 20 runs in common with State 5.

At 10.6 *m.* is the junction with State 90.

Left on State 90, which skirts the eastern shore of Cayuga Lake, to MUD LOCK, 1.1 *m.*, junction of the Cayuga and Seneca branches of Barge Canal and a favorite spot for perch and bullhead fishing. Archeologists have discovered remains of a very ancient Indian culture here.

CAYUGA, 3.3 *m.* (420 alt.,466 pop.), settled in 1789, is one of the oldest Finger Lakes villages. To overcome the obstacle of the Montezuma Swamp and the lake to westward travel, the Cayuga Bridge, one of the engineering marvels of its day, was built in 1799. Across its one and one-eighth miles of wooden trestle, the Genesee Turnpike stages rumbled; during the War of 1812 the Army of General Wood and General Scott crossed it on its way to the Niagara Frontier. Today only the abutments remain.

CAYUGA LAKE (R), 40 miles long, 2 miles wide, and 435 feet deep, the longest of the Finger Lakes, is connected by canal with Seneca Lake on the west and with the Barge Canal on the north. In the nineteenth century it was an important transportation link between Ithaca, concentration point for the produce of southern New York, and the Erie Canal; a regular steamboat service was carried on until the 1920's, but now lake traffic is limited to pleasure craft and the slender shells of Cornell University crews. The moody blue waters of the lake and the life on its shores have been envisioned by two generations through Grace Miller White's novels.

UNION SPRINGS, 9.2 *m.* (419 alt.,894 pop.), takes its name from the numerous sulphur and salt springs in the vicinity. Rich archeological remains have been found near by and on FRONTENAC ISLAND, in Lake Cayuga. This is one of the very few islands in the Finger Lakes, a knot of land that was once an Algonquian burial ground but is now a bird and game refuge.

GREAT GULLY BROOK, 11.6 *m.*, is crossed by the highway at the site of an old Indian village, for many years the capital of the Cayuga, and near the site of the second Roman Catholic chapel in New York State, served by Father René Menard, 1656–8, and Father Etienne de Carheil, 1668–84. State and Knights of Columbus monuments stand on the sites. Father Etienne de Carheil, appointed to Father Menard's chapel, devised several original methods of showing the Cayuga the fallacy of worshipping animals. The Cayuga regarded the beaver as the master of their lives, and Father Carheil offered a prayer to the beaver: 'Thou, O, who canst not speak! Thou, who hast no soul, thou art master of my life who have a soul.'

At LEVANNA, 13.3 m. (424 alt.,100 pop.), is the site of a prehistoric Indian village; huge figures of a bird and animals outlined in stone and facing a primitive stone altar have been found here by archeologists. Reproductions of Algonquian villages of A.D. 900 have been built near this shrine.

AURORA, 15.6 m. (436 alt.,371 pop.), was named by General Benjamin Ledyard, who was impressed with the splendor of the site revealed in the first rays of the morning sun. The impressive campus of WELLS COLLEGE (L) rises from the lake shore. Henry Wells, co-founder of the Wells-Fargo Express Company, established this college for women in 1868. Most of the buildings are of brick in the Tudor Gothic style; some are adorned with sculptures by Erastus Dow Palmer. The curriculum includes courses in the liberal arts, dietetics, library science, and domestic science. The student body numbers about 270, the faculty 45.

'Frankie' Folsom (see below), as she was known to her schoolmates, went to school here while being courted by President Grover Cleveland.

At KING FERRY, 24.2 m. (950 alt.,320 pop.), is the junction with State 34B (see above). On the hills back from the lake shore are the ranks of Seckel pear trees, whose small russet, sugary fruit weigh down the candelabra-like branches. King Ferry boasts of the largest Seckel pear orchards in the United States.

The RENÉ MENARD MEMORIAL BRIDGE, 11.1 m., which carries US 20 across the Seneca River, was dedicated in 1933 in honor of Father René Menard. Beyond the bridge the road enters the Montezuma Swamp (see Tour 32), a dense growth of alder, willow, and maple, reeds and cattails, 1.5 miles wide where the road crosses it. This part of the swamp has been set aside as a bird sanctuary; migratory fowl stop here to feed and rest, and in the spring the trumpeting of the loons echoes and re-echoes over the dreary tangle with demonic fury. The Montezuma Swamp was one of the hide-outs of the famous Loomis gang (see Tour 25) and other swashbuckling highwaymen of the early nineteenth century.

At 12.9 m. is the junction with State 89.

Left on State 89 to CAYUGA LAKE STATE PARK (bathing, picnicking, games), 3.5 m.

At 6 m. is the SITE OF RED JACKET'S BIRTHPLACE (R). Grand sachem of the Iroquois and one of the wiliest diplomats in Indian history, Red Jacket (1750–1830) was used as a runner by British officers on the frontier and was given an embroidered red coat as a reward; he became so fond of it that he wore red coats on state occasions for the rest of his life. Thereupon the whites dubbed him Red Jacket. To the Indians he was Sa-ge-ye-wat-ha, he keeps them awake, a tribute to his oratorical powers. A fondness for rum brought him before the sachems several times on the charge that he was a disgrace to the tribes, but his quick tongue saved him from being read out of the clan. It was Red Jacket's influence that swung the Iroquois to the side of the Americans during the War of 1812 and kept the warriors from scalping enemy dead during that conflict.

SENECA FALLS, 16 m. (465 alt.,6,449 pop.), owes its early industrial development to the 50-foot waterfall which provided power, and its fame to great women who mothered the causes of woman suffrage, antislavery, and temperance. Seneca Falls gave the world the Holley inventions: a water system for municipalities and the rotary fire engine used throughout the Nation.

In Seneca Falls the 'New Woman' first asserted her equality with man and began throwing off her shackles. Mrs.Amelia Jenks Bloomer (1818–94), wife of the local postmaster, did not invent the 'bloomer'—that honor goes to Mrs.Elizabeth Smith Miller, daughter of Gerrit Smith—but she introduced it and advocated it as a uniform for the soldiers of the woman suffrage cause. The New York *Tribune* described the get-up as follows: 'Mrs.Bloomer was attired in a dark brown changeable tunic; a kilt descended just below the knees, the skirt of which was trimmed with rows of black velvet. The pantaloons were of the same texture and trimmed in the same style. She wore gaiters. Her headdress was cherry and black. Her dress had a large open corsage, with bands of velvet over the white chamesette in which was a diamond stud pin. She wore flowing sleeves, tight undersleeves, and black lace mitts. Her whole attire was rich and plain in appearance.' But the costume was abandoned when men stopped 'not to think of the cause for which it was worn but to grin and jeer,' and children trooped after the wearers chanting derisively

> Hi Ho,
> In sleet and snow,
> Mrs.Bloomer's all the go.
> Twenty tailors to take the stitches,
> Plenty of women to wear the britches.

Mrs.Bloomer worked persistently for woman suffrage and with Mrs.Elizabeth Cady Stanton (1815-1902) called the first convention of the movement at Seneca Falls in 1848. Mrs.Stanton, born in Johnstown, New York, moved to Seneca Falls with her husband in 1847. Her father disinherited her for her activities; she was arrested and suffered insult from judges and juries, was fined and imprisoned, but she persisted and was soon recognized as leader of the movement.

Woman suffrage was closely allied with other reform movements of the hectic forties and fifties, especially temperance and abolition. Mrs.Bloomer lectured ardently for temperance, and Mrs.Stanton shocked the delegates to a temperance convention in Rochester by advocating that drunkenness be accepted as grounds for divorce and by declaring that she believed in birth control for drunkards' wives.

Susan B. Anthony (1820-1906) was already interested in temperance and antislavery when in 1850 she met Mrs.Stanton in Seneca Falls. The two women worked together for 50 years. As a militant abolitionist Miss Anthony campaigned under the slogan, 'No union with slave-holders,' and advocated Negro suffrage. In 1872 she and 15 other women voted in Rochester in an attempt to test the legality of woman suffrage under the Fourteenth Amendment; she was arrested, but before the trial, held in Canandaigua, she voted again. The court, however, evaded the constitutional test and fined Miss Anthony $100; she refused either to pay or to go to jail, and the sentence was never carried out. Miss Anthony served as president of the American Women's Suffrage Association until 1900, when she resigned at the age of 80.

In the WESLEYAN METHODIST EPISCOPAL CHURCH BUILDING, corner of Fall and Mynderse Sts., now an automobile showroom, was held in July 1848 the first American woman suffrage convention, which, presided over by Henry B. Stanton, Mrs.Stanton's sympathetic husband, proclaimed that 'women have the right—or ought to have the right—to vote and hold office.'

At the entrance to the Fall St. bridge is (L) the SENECA FALLS HISTORI-
CAL SOCIETY, which has several pieces of Mrs.Stanton's furniture, including her rosewood piano.

The 78-acre GOULD PUMP WORKS (*open*), at the western edge of the village, is the largest of its kind in the country. Gould pumps are used not
only for moving water, but also for moving molten lead at more than 500
degrees Fahrenheit; moving bread dough from mixers to molding devices
in large bakeries; moving molasses in sugar refineries; and moving wood
pulp, road tar, and printing ink.

On the ashes of the Indian settlement of Skoiyase grew WATERLOO,
19.8 *m*. (450 alt.,3,992 pop.), which shares county seat honors with Ovid.
County buildings and a new high school border Lafayette Park in the center of the village. Near by stands the PATRIARCH ELM (R), a gigantic landmark nearly 20 feet in circumference and said to be 350 years old, which
was spared when the first road was laid out in 1795.

In the vicinity of Waterloo is Hi-Yan-ka Farms, operated by Clarence H. Van Wickle, who owned Sillon B, the largest horse in the world.
This proud stallion, foaled in 1930 and bought by Mr.Van Wickle for
$5,500, was a Percheron, weighing 3,000 pounds, standing 21 hands high
(7 feet) at the shoulder and 9 feet at the neck, and with a girth of 9 feet
4 inches. It took blue ribbons everywhere for size and beauty and was to
be exhibited at the Chicago World's Fair, but died in 1933.

West of Waterloo, US 20 follows the Genesee Road, early nineteenth-
century carrier for traffic from the headwaters of the Mohawk River west.

In 1861 James Wyburn Johnson, a farm boy, hearing of the firing on
Fort Sumter, made up his mind to carry on the tradition of John Brown.
Hanging his scythe on a six-inch sapling, now the SCYTHE TREE (R),
22.8 *m*., a large Balm of Gilead poplar, he said, 'Let it hang there till I get
back,' and enlisted. He was killed in battle in 1864. The tree has grown
around the scythe, so that today only six inches of the blade sticks from
the trunk; the handle has rotted away long ago. On Memorial Day ceremonies are held at the tree, and an American·flag flies over it at all times.

At 23.6 *m*. is the junction with State 2A.

Left on State 2A to ROSE HILL (R), 2.7 *m*., one of the finest Greek Revival houses
in the United States, on a splendid location overlooking Seneca Lake and the city of
Geneva. The great central block with its six-Ionic-columned portico is crowned by a
cupola and flanked by one-story wings with porches. The fine scale and restful majesty
of this mansion are marred only by the substitution of two-light sashes in the first-
story windows. The farm carries the name of Robert Selden Rose,Jr., who brought
his family here from Virginia in 1803. In the early thirties the property passed to a
Mr.Boody, who built this grand house about 1835.

GENEVA, 26.9 *m*. (460 alt.,15,543 pop.), at the foot of Seneca Lake,
is important for its nurseries and industries and as a center for Finger
Lakes tours. The untidy streets along the lake front contrast sharply with
the almost unbroken line of striking post-Colonial, Greek Revival, and
Victorian Gothic buildings, set off by landscaped grounds, on the ridge
above. In July crowds gather on the lake docks; the water is flecked with
sails and the put-put of outboard motors bounces against the hills, herald-
ing the Geneva Outboard Regatta.

The 2,400-acre tract covered by the city includes the site of the Indian settlement Kanadesaga (new settlement village), a name also applied to Seneca Lake, destroyed by the Sullivan-Clinton expedition in 1779. Soon after the Revolution settlers began to arrive. Captain Charles Williamson, agent for the Pultney Estate (*see Tour* 31), recognized the superb advantages of the site and lost no time laying out Main Street on the terrace overlooking the lake. Despite the incursion of motor traffic, the street retains an air of dignity and comfort seldom preserved even in somnolent 'ghost' villages. In its spacious Victorian days the place attracted an unusually large number of retired ministers and reconciled spinsters and was nicknamed 'The Saints' Retreat and Old Maids' Paradise.'

The outskirts of Geneva are fringed with the fields of 50 nurseries, growing fruit trees, berry bushes, and ornamental plants and shrubs. Foundries turn out ranges, furnaces, radiators, and high-grade cutlery; mills produce cereals, and canneries preserve the fruit of the countryside; factories make optical goods and enamelware.

The TRINITY EPISCOPAL CHURCH, 518–30 Main St., was begun in 1841 under the Reverend Pierre Paris Irving, nephew of Washington Irving. Although Calvin Otis was the nominal architect, his other work makes it clear that here he was supplanted as designer by an amateur architect, Dr.Benjamin Hall, then president of Hobart. Dr.Hall copied details from Trinity Church, New York, then being built by Richard Upjohn. Not the least of Trinity's distinctions was its famous quartet composed of Mr.Fox, Mr.Fowle, Mrs.Bear, and Mrs.Partridge.

HOBART COLLEGE, Main St., just beyond Hamilton St., a liberal arts college for men founded in 1822 by Bishop Henry Hobart by the union of the Fairfield Theological School and Geneva Academy, was called Geneva College until 1851. The oldest buildings, classical stone Geneva Hall and Trinity Hall, were financed in part by gifts from Trinity Church, New York. The Chapel, 1858–62, a stone Gothic Revival structure, was designed by Richard Upjohn. Later buildings include the Victorian Gothic library, 1901; Elizabeth Medbury and Coxe Halls in brick and stone, by Clinton and Russell, architects; and more recent neo-Georgian additions. Between 1834 and 1872 the Geneva Medical College was allied with Hobart. Here Elizabeth Blackwell fought her way through to graduation in 1849 to become the country's first woman physician. Four years later she established the New York City Infirmary for Women and Children. Dr.John Towler, Dean of the Medical College, long taught here an amazing array of subjects, which included modern languages, mathematics, philosophy, chemistry, anatomy, and medical jurisprudence.

The WILLIAM SMITH COLLEGE FOR WOMEN, adjoining Hobart College on the west, was founded in 1906 by Geneva's philanthropist, William Smith, who, ironically, was a bachelor with little use for women. Smith students attend Hobart classes. Blackwell House, a dormitory, was once the W.B.Douglas residence, built in 1861–3, from plans by Richard Upjohn. The polychrome brick bands and elaborately carpentered dormers give a rather jittery air altogether unwarranted by the straightforward rectangular plan.

The BURIAL MOUND (L), Castle St. west of the intersection with Old Preemption Road, was once the center of the Indian village of Kanadesaga. To win Indian assistance during the French and Indian War, Sir William Johnson sent Myndert Wemp and son here in 1756 to build a log fort amid the 50 long houses; the Indians, politely refusing a white garrison, manned it themselves. When Sayenqueraghta, local chief, became 'king' of the Seneca in 1763, the settlement took on a large importance. In 1765 Samuel Kirkland, missionary, hiked here on snowshoes from Johnstown in 23 days to teach Christianity to the Indians.

The NEW YORK STATE AGRICULTURAL EXPERIMENT STATION, Castle and North Sts., was founded in 1882, and has to its credit many important discoveries in entomology and agricultural bacteriology. It is associated with Cornell University (see Ithaca).

In the rear of the BROOKS HOME, 620 Castle St., is the observatory in which Dr.William R. Brooks discovered several comets, the most famous being the Pons-Brooks comet of 1883 and the Olbers-Brooks comet of 1887. The observatory now belongs to Hobart College.

At 41.7 m. is the junction with State 21A.

Left on State 21A to BARE HILL (R), 9 m., the sacred hill of the Seneca. Here, according to primitive Indian legend, the Creator caused the ground to open, allowing the ancestors of the Seneca nation to come into the world. A great serpent was coiled around the base of the hill, and one by one he ate the members of the newborn race. At last a young warrior, inspired by a dream in which the Creator commanded him not to fear, went down and slew the serpent with a magic arrow. In its death throes, as it writhed down the hill and into the lake, the serpent disgorged the heads of the Senecas he had eaten. For decades after white settlement began, delegations of warriors paddled across the lake, climbed the sacred slopes, and lit ceremonial fires at the summit. Lying in front yards and rock gardens of homes along State 21A today are large, rounded stones, divided into geometric patterns by veins and cracks, weirdly like weathered skulls. The Seneca believed the rocks to be the petrified skulls of their ancestors disgorged on Bare Hill; geologists explain that the patterns in the stones were formed by a slow deposit of lime in the post-glacial period.

US 20 curves around the base of CANANDAIGUA LAKE (L), 42.3 m., the thumb of the Finger Lakes. Its changing hues and varying moods have prophesied the weather to Indian and white alike: a streaky surface like mares' tails in the sky is a sign of storm.

In Canandaigua Lake is SQUAW ISLAND (L), which has been taken over as a State reservation because of its geologic interest. Pebbles on the shore of the island, locally called 'water biscuits,' are coated with algae, a soft, green plant that steals carbonic acid gas from the water and forms a lime deposit on the stones. According to legend, the island takes its name from its use by the Seneca as a sanctuary for their women and children during the Sullivan-Clinton expedition.

CANANDAIGUA, 44 m. (766 alt.,8,291 pop.), set in an agricultural region, has lined its upper streets with imposing post-Colonial and Greek Revival homes and public buildings surrounded by neat lawns and hedges. Industries of the town produce enameled ware, corsets, chemical solvents, and knitted goods.

After purchasing from Massachusetts all of New York State west of

Geneva and extinguishing the Indian title to a large part of the tract, Phelps and Gorham appointed William Walker as their agent and he opened here the first office for land sales in America. The first party of settlers, led by General Israel Chapin, arrived in May 1789, and within two years the town was overrun with emigrants from New England moving west over the Great Western Turnpike and up the Mohawk Valley. The first religious meeting was held in Judge Phelps's barn in 1790; the first academy on the Phelps and Gorham Purchase was established here in 1795; here the Ontario Female Seminary, organized in 1825, was a pioneer in the education of women.

The ONTARIO COUNTY COURTHOUSE, top of the Main St. hill, a two-story gray brick Greek Revival structure built in 1858, replaced the second courthouse, which is now the city hall. The bulbous dome with its octagonal drum and lantern is a motif reflecting in very diluted form the construction at that time of the great dome of the Capitol at Washington.

Here was held in 1873 the trial of Susan B. Anthony and her associates, who had voted in a national election in Rochester (*see above*). In 1937 women began jury service in this same courthouse where the pioneer suffragettes were found guilty of voting.

A boulder on the courthouse grounds commemorates the Pickering treaty signed here in 1794, whereby the Indians granted to the whites the right to settle the Great Lakes basin. Before the treaty was signed, however, Anthony Wayne had beaten the Indians in the Battle of Fallen Timbers and had won the Ohio country. It is said that the purpose of the treaty council was to distract the attention of the Iroquois from Wayne's campaign.

The CITY HALL, 2 N.Main St., erected in 1824, which served as the second courthouse until 1858, when it became the town hall, is a rectangular, two-story, gray-painted brick structure. The graceful pedimented portico has its slender Scamozzi Ionic columns paired at the corners, illustrating the Georgian Renaissance character of the late Federal period. If it is true that Francis, son of Gideon Granger, furnished the design for this building, he may well have been influenced by the Virginia State capitol, completed in 1798 by his father's friend, Thomas Jefferson. The felicitous belfry comes; however, not from Jefferson, but from ecclesiastical models.

The ONTARIO COUNTY HISTORICAL SOCIETY AND WOOD LIBRARY BUILDING (*open weekdays*), 55 North St., is a brick structure designed in the Georgian Colonial style by Claude F. Bragdon, architect, of Rochester. The Library was named for William Wood, brother of Mrs.Nathaniel Gorham,Jr., who established the Mercantile Library in New York and similar libraries in London and Liverpool, England. The Historical Society museum contains the original deeds and maps of the Phelps and Gorham Purchase, the Six Nations' copy of the Pickering treaty, and one of the two existing life masks of Abraham Lincoln.

The FIRST CONGREGATIONAL CHURCH, 58 N.Main St., erected in 1812, is a two-story brick structure. The unique façade adopts a pedimented gable above a wide, low-proportioned arch opening into a recessed porch flanked on each side by two fluted Ionic pilasters. The arrangement, ultimately derived from Roman triumphal arches, is somewhat startling when met in an American frontier village.

The CANANDAIGUA ACADEMY, corner of Main St. and Fort Hill Ave., built in 1905, is the modern successor to the original academy of 1795. Stephen A. Douglas, the 'Little Giant,' attended the old academy three years in the early 1830's.

The GENERAL PORTER HOUSE, 210 Main St., was built about 1800 by General Peter B. Porter (1773–1864), famous as the defender of Black Rock in the War of 1812. He lived in Canandaigua from 1795 to 1806, holding the offices of county clerk and member of the Assembly; then he moved to the Niagara Frontier, where he became a prominent figure; and he served as Secretary of War under President John Quincy Adams. In the same house John Canfield Spencer (1788–1855) spent 36 years in Canandaigua. Born in Hudson, he graduated from Union College in 1806. He held judicial offices in the State, and as special prosecutor in the famous anti-Masonic case resulting from the abduction of William Morgan he rose to national prominence. Under President John Tyler he served first as Secretary of War and then as Secretary of the Treasury. While he was Secretary of War his son Philip, a midshipman, was executed for attempted mutiny on board the brig *Somers*.

The GIDEON GRANGER HOUSE, 295 N.Main St., was built in 1814 by Gideon Granger (1767–1822) after his retirement as Postmaster General under Jefferson and Madison. Although the sides and rear of the house are clapboarded, the façade aspires to the Palladian order in its treatment of the first story as a high base for the second story, enriched by applied Scamozzi Ionic columns in the center and pilasters at the corner. Tradition attributes the design to Jefferson himself, and a certain facility with architectural paraphernalia might favor this view; but there is an English feeling and carpenter character present that would be difficult to reconcile with Jefferson's love of solid, heavy Roman forms. After Granger's death in 1822, his son Francis resided here.

Francis Granger (1792–1868) was, like his father, an important figure in State and national politics, and under President William Henry Harrison served, like his father, as Postmaster General. His long silver locks were responsible for the name of a faction of the Whig party, the 'Silver Grays,' bestowed when he was chairman of a Whig convention.

The DR.EDSON CARR HOUSE, 50 Gibson St., built in 1826, is an excellent example of a late Federal house. The broad five-bay façade is treated with flush boarding and is subdivided by two-story panelled Scamozzi Ionic pilasters. A light Doric cornice is surmounted by a light balustrade.

The U.S.VETERANS' HOSPITAL (*open to relatives of patients only*), Fort Hill Ave., south of Main St., cares for more than 500 veterans of the World War. The administration building is a four-story brick and stone structure of modified Tudor-Gothic design.

In the PIONEER CEMETERY, at the western city line, is the grave of Oliver Phelps (1749–1809), land speculator who laid the foundations for the settlement of western New York. Joining with Nathaniel Gorham, who never visited the region, he contracted for the 6,000,000-acre holding of Massachusetts in western New York. They bought the Indian title to the easternmost third of the tract—about 2,600,000 acres—and for several years did their utmost to meet the payments to Massachusetts, but they finally defaulted and the remaining two thirds were turned back to Massachusetts. Of the land they held, they sold about 1,200,000 acres to Robert Morris, who in turn sold the land to the London Associates, headed by Sir William Pulteney. The strain helped cause Gorham's death, but Phelps, though a heavy loser, kept his courage and turned to other fields, in five years acquiring title to nearly 1,000,000 acres along the lower Mississippi. When the land bubble burst in 1796 he was hopelessly involved; and fearing he would follow other land speculators to debtor's prison, he disappeared. In 1802 he turned up at Canandaigua, and until his death he managed what was left of his land and served as the first county judge of Ontario County and later as a member of Congress, 1803–5. Part of the inscription on his gravestone reads: 'Enterprise, Industry, and Temperance cannot always secure success but the fruits of those virtues will be felt by society.'

Canandaigua is at the junction with State 21 (*see Tour 29*).

At 49.7 *m.* is the junction with US 20A (*see Tour 8A*).

EAST BLOOMFIELD, 52.3 *m.* (1,060 alt.,365 pop.), is the original home in this country of the Northern Spy apple; Herman Chapin planted the first seed about 1800 and sprouts from the original tree were taken by Roswell Humphrey, who set them in his orchard. The original tree died but the cuttings flourished. The name Northern Spy grew out of the abolitionist movement rampant at the time: the apple was considered an interloper, hence a spy.

ROADSIDE CRAFTS (R), 52.7 *m.*, is a workshop rebuilt from a Baptist church erected in 1833. Handhewn beams in the ceiling are 43 feet long and pegged. The minute book, communion set, and antique collection box of the church are on display in niches on the stair-well. In the basement and on the first floor are rooms for weaving and woodworking; bedspreads made here are woven with the Cumberland mountaineer design.

In EAST AVON, 68 *m.* (821 alt.,250 pop.), is the junction with US 15 (*see Tour 31*).

AVON, 70 *m.* (583 alt.,2,337 pop.), is a farming and canning center with a considerable milk industry. The region is a horse-breeding area, and the annual Avon Horse Show, conducted by the Genesee Valley Breeders Association, draws a large gallery of spectators.

Up to about 1860 Avon was a noted health resort. The United States Hotel and a dozen others were filled with guests who came to drink of the sulphur springs. Old registers carry the names of princes, dukes, and counts, Presidents and Senators.

At 71.3 *m.* is the western junction with State 5 (*see Tour 11*).

Section f. WESTERN JUNCTION WITH STATE 5 to WESTERN JUNCTION WITH US 20A; 61.9 m. US 20

Making a beeline between Avon and Buffalo, US 20 crosses flat farm country, with fields of corn, grain, and hay sweeping away on each side;

it is as if the highway were suddenly crossing northern Illinois or Iowa. Large barns and freshly painted houses of inarticulate architecture indicate relative prosperity. Windmills tower above the trees in the farmyards; on the top of a barn or corncrib the propellerlike fan of a windmotor spins with sprightly enthusiasm as it charges the storage battery for the farmer's radio.

From the western junction with State 5, 0 *m.*, US 20 runs past the intersection with State 19 (*see Tour 35*), 15.7 *m.*, and through a dozen service hamlets for the farmers of the region.

At 25.5 *m.* in ALEXANDER (940 alt.,264 pop.) is the junction with State 98.

Left on State 98 to the ATTICA STATE PRISON (*open to relatives of inmates only*), 4.3 *m.*, completed in 1931 and accommodating 3,700 prisoners. Surrounded by high, massive walls, it looks like a fortress and is visible for miles. Modern methods of criminal rehabilitation are used.

ALDEN, 37.8 *m.* (862 alt.,954 pop.), had its black water baths as a starting impetus. Discovered in 1896, these black waters are said to be four times stronger than the Nauheim water of Germany and 40 times stronger than the waters of Aix-les-Bains, France. Patients still come from many lands for treatments in the four private sanatoriums.

Left from Alden on State 239 to COWLESVILLE, 4.8 *m.* (940 alt.,200 pop.). One mile beyond the village, on an intersecting dirt road (L), is the first of a series of five covered bridges crossing Cayuga Creek, no two alike. In the old days a toll tender served each bridge; charges included 'one man and his family in a surry, one span of horses 25¢.' Fines included $1 for traveling faster than a walk or within 30 feet of the vehicle ahead.

At 5.7 *m.* is the junction with an improved road; left here 6.6 *m.* to FOLSOMDALE (1,000 alt.,50 pop.) and the old FOLSOM MANSION, home of Frances ('Frankie') Folsom, who married President Grover Cleveland. The house is built in the Georgian Colonial style with heavy cornice supported by nine Doric columns. The Folsoms were early pioneers, 'lords of the manor.' They operated an inn about 1838, also a brewery in the glen beside Cayuga Creek. The brewery daybook, which has been preserved, shows that two quarts of the brew were retailed for 13¢.

In the Folsom house President Grover Cleveland courted Frankie, the daughter of his old Buffalo law partner. Frances Folsom, as Mrs.Cleveland, became one of the most popular women to be 'first lady.' It is told of her that her tact covered any situation; one incident is given of a great public reception where she had to shake hands with hundreds: after the handshaking ended, a little mouse of a country woman, among the guests, whispered to her, 'Dearie, be ye tired?' and 'Frankie' answered instantly, 'Yes, I be.' She is now (1940) Mrs.Thomas J. Preston,Jr.

TOWN LINE, 42.2 *m.* (750 alt.,350 pop.), is remembered for the fact that a majority of the townfolk seceded from the Union along with the Southern States, and the indignant minority called the town a 'nest of Copperheads'; at least five villagers joined the Southern army. Late in 1861 matters came to a head; 80 Town Line citizens voted for secession, 45 to support the Union. The latter threatened sedition charges, arrests, and even lynching; in August 1864 came the scare of an invasion by a wing of the Confederate force from Canada, and feeling ran so high against the Copperheads that most of them left town. The old desk on which the

CHITTENANGO, 37 *m.* (460 alt.,815 pop.), has an unusual series of churches. The PRESBYTERIAN CHURCH is another example of 'Georgian Gothic,' this time in stone; the building was erected in 1828, but the interior was remodeled after a fire in 1921. The EPISCOPAL CHURCH (1865) is an excellent example of 'Carpenter Gothic,' with vertical boarding, pinnacles, and buttresses. The BAPTIST CHURCH, erected about 1868, is a wood version of Second Empire.

Here is the junction with State 13 (*see Tour* 8).

At 40.5 *m.* is the junction with State 290.

Right on State 290 to (L) GREEN LAKES STATE PARK, 2.4 *m.*, a recreational area (*bathing, boating, golf, play and picnic grounds, and a maze of hiking trails*). The two lakes in the park have exceptionally high, densely wooded banks, and take their name from the reflected foliage. A difficult golf course (*greens fee* 50¢–$1.25), built to Bobby Jones's personal specifications, offers unusual hazards.

FAYETTEVILLE, 45.2 *m.* (500 alt.,2,008 pop.), takes one back a century to post-Colonial days, with its houses of colonnaded porches on sloping hillsides overlooking the business section. Small factories produce dies, furniture, and paper. Grover Cleveland spent his boyhood in the GROVER CLEVELAND HOUSE, 109 Academy St., a plain white frame building, occupied as a private residence.

Left from Fayetteville on State 92 to MANLIUS, 3.8 *m.* (540 alt.,1,538 pop.), home of the MANLIUS MILITARY ACADEMY, one of the highest ranking boys' schools in the United States. It was founded in 1869 by the Reverend Frederic C. Huntington, Episcopal bishop of central New York, and was originally known as St.John's Military School. It is under the direct patronage of the United States War Department and has been an honor school for the past 30 years. The English Gothic style buildings of stone and brick stand with inspection-ready trimness on the rolling, landscaped campus.

In 1794, at John A. Schaeffer's log tavern in the village of Manlius, Baron Von Steuben and General Van Rensselaer, while on inspection of frontier defenses, spent a bad night. Domestic noises, so the story goes, kept the Baron awake. From time to time he bellowed out of his bedroom door, 'Quiet!' The next morning he cursed the innkeeper roundly. Whereupon a woman left the room and returned with a lusty newborn boy, whom she placed in the Baron's arms, saying: 'This little fellow did not like the world he entered and objected strenuously to his admission.' The Baron calmed down and requested that the baby be named after him; later he gave his namesake some 250 acres in Oneida County.

SYRACUSE, 54 *m.* (400 alt.,205,637 pop.) (*see Syracuse*), is at the junction with US 11 (*see Tour* 18) and State 57 (*see Tour* 26).

1. Right from Syracuse on State Fair Boulevard to the NEW YORK STATE FAIR GROUNDS (L), 4.1 *m.*, covering 267 acres and valued, with the buildings, at $12,000,000. The New York State Fair was first held in 1841 at Syracuse under the auspices of the State Agricultural Society. After being staged in various other cities, in 1890 it returned to Syracuse, where it has remained ever since. Since 1900 it has been under the management of the State.

The Fair is held annually the latter part of August or early in September, usually for one week, occasionally two, and has the usual attractions, with livestock, agricultural, and industrial exhibits, and, among other contests, a Grand Circuit race meet on the half-mile track. About 250,000 visitors attend annually.

The COLISEUM, seating 6,500, is second in size in the State. The HARRIET MAY MILLS MEMORIAL BUILDING, named in honor of the ardent advocate of woman suf frage, is the center of social activities; it comprises two large structures with connecting wings, the main entrance marked by a two-story portico.

Close to the fair grounds entrance is the EMPIRE COURT, a magnificently landscaped, oblong-shaped lawn bordered by huge exhibition buildings. In the center is a concrete lagoon, built as a WPA project, swarming with fish in pools beneath its many cascades.

2. Right from Syracuse on Milton Avenue to the SOLVAY PLANT (R), 2.1 *m.*, a subsidiary of the Allied Chemical & Dye Corporation, which here manufactures the well-known Arm and Hammer brand of soda. The giant buildings occupy 81 acres. A large conveyor rises more than 150 feet overhead and extends from an immense pile of limestone to the crusher plant 800 feet distant. Across the street, facing the factories, are the employees' small frame houses, their exteriors crusted with the ever-present ash.

Section c. SYRACUSE to WESTERN JUNCTION WITH US 20; 97.8 m. State 5.

West from SYRACUSE, 0 *m.*, the route crosses a comparatively flat terrain relieved by numerous oval-shaped hills called drumlins, formed by the overladen ice sheet of prehistoric days.

CAMILLUS, 8.5 *m.* (420 alt.,1,036 pop.), which makes pocket knives, is one of the claimants to the title of 'birthplace of the Republican party' by virtue of a meeting called by 336 villagers and held in Rowe's Hotel on January 27, 1852, at which the principles of the Republican party were enunciated three years before the national organization came into being.

AUBURN, 26.5 *m.* (650 alt.,35,705 pop.) (*see Auburn*), is at the junction with US 20, State 38, and State 34 (*see Tour* 8).

West of Auburn State 5 runs in common with US 20 (*see Tour* 8) for 71.3 miles, branching off (R) at 97.8 *m.*

Section d. WESTERN JUNCTION WITH US 20 to BUFFALO; 64 m. State 5.

Branching right at the western junction with US 20, 0 *m.*, State 5 passes through CANAWAUGUS (Ind., malodorous waters), 1.2 *m.*, which occupies the site of the Seneca village of Ganowages, where two famous Indian leaders of the Revolutionary period were born.

Cornplanter (1732–1836) was the son of one O'Bail, or Abeel, an Irishman, who was an Indian trader, by a Seneca woman. Raised as an Indian, he rose to a position of commanding influence among the Six Nations. During the Revolution he served with Joseph Brant and took part in several of the British raids in the Mohawk and Wyoming Valleys. At Fort Stanwix in 1788, however, he counseled his people to sign the treaty with the 'Thirteen Fires' which opened up most of central and western New York to white settlement. Eventually he was recognized as liaison officer between the Government and the Indians, was officially honored by Washington, Adams, and Jefferson, and was inordinately proud of his breastful of medals, his sword, and his officer's uniform.

Handsome Lake (1735–1815), half-brother of Cornplanter through a common father, led a drunken, dissipated life until past middle age; then, when he was physically weakened almost to the point of death, he suddenly reformed and became a self-appointed apostle to the Iroquois. He walked from village to village exhorting his brethren to destroy the Demon Rum and live lives of temperance, hospitality, and humility. He died from exhaustion while on one of his pilgrimages and was buried on the Onondaga Reservation. Many of the Indians on New York State reservations still revere Handsome Lake as their prophet and accept his Code as their religious faith.

In CALEDONIA, 6.2 *m.* (669 alt.,1,222 pop.), is the junction with State 36.

Right on State 36 to the CALEDONIA STATE FISH HATCHERY, 1 *m.*, started as a private enterprise in 1864 by Seth Green and acquired in 1875 by New York State for its first experiments in the artificial propagation of fish for conservation purposes. On the 27.7 acres are six buildings where selective breeding of brook, brown, rainbow, and lake trout annually produce millions of fingerlings to be stocked in lakes and streams throughout the State. Some 40 ponds are used for this breeding; most of the hatching is done in indoor tanks, the water coming from Spring Brook at a temperature that varies less than ten degrees the year round. Mature specimens spawned here weigh as much as 20 pounds.

Birthplace of the stringless bean and home town of Jello, LE ROY, 13.4 *m.* (869 alt.,4,386 pop.), is a thriving village on Oatka (Ind., an opening) Creek, with more than its share of fine old post-Colonial houses, most of them grouped on Main Street adjacent to the one-block business section.

In the late 1870's Nicholas B. Keeney and his son, Calvin, of Le Roy, by cross-fertilizing some 40 or more bean plants over a series of years, weeded out all but the stringless pods, thus bringing to the market beans minus strings.

The LE ROY MANSION (*private*), 23 E.Main St., a massive, two-story post-Colonial stone house with stucco surface, was erected before 1812 as a land office by Egbert Benson. Jacob Le Roy, whose father had purchased a tract of 85,000 acres, came in 1821 as second land agent, enlarged the office, and opened a general store. Daniel Webster is said to have courted Caroline Le Roy, who became his second wife, on the broad back porch of the house.

The JELLO PLANT (*adm. by recommendation only*), North St., just beyond the railroad tracks, looks more like a group of private residences than a factory. The formulae of Jello flavors are carefully guarded secrets, and visitors see only the packing operations. Automatic machines select wax paper, cartons, and the proper flavors, and wrap the packages in two seconds each.

At 17.5 *m.* (R) are the EGG-LAYING TEST FARMS (*open*), where western New York egg-laying tests, sponsored by the State College of Agriculture, Cornell University, are held to determine and increase the fecundity of various poultry breeds. The tests have resulted in several world records. When they were started in 1931, the average was 189.9 eggs for 1,547 birds; by 1937 the average had increased to 227.8 eggs for 1,703 birds. In the latter year a new individual record was made for New Hampshires with 316 eggs, and a pen of 12 White Leghorn pullets averaged 305 eggs.

Midway between Rochester and Buffalo, BATAVIA, 23.4 *m.* (890 alt., 17,222 pop.), is a lively industrial city and a trading center for a wide agricultural area. Leading industrial products are plows, ladies' shoes, paper boxes, shoe dyes and polishes, and flavoring extracts. Italians and Poles make up about one-third of the population.

Historically, Batavia is noteworthy as the 'capital' of the Holland Land Purchase. In 1801 Joseph Ellicott, surveyor and subagent for the company, built a land office at the junction of the old Genesee Road and Tonawanda Creek, where two great Indian trails crossed, and where four State highways meet today. Ellicott proposed naming the place Bustia or Bustiville, for Paul Busti, the company's general agent; but the latter objected to the ferocious sound of the word and proposed Batavia, the name of the Dutch republic to which the proprietors belonged.

In 1802 James Brisbane, great-grandfather of the late Arthur Brisbane, was commissioned postmaster; the old Brisbane homestead is now the city hall. In those days mail was often sent collect; one Batavia woman, receiving a collect letter and lacking cash to pay for the postage, shouted, 'Hold that letter, Mr. Brisbane, while I skin a calf.' The first tavern was opened opposite the land office; the second, the 'Old Snake Den,' run by Stephen Russell at the present corner of Main and State Streets, advertised: 'We have clean sheets, only slept in a few times since new.'

Despite the rapid growth of neighboring Rochester and Buffalo, Batavia prospered, first as a farm trade center, later, with the development of railroads, as an industrial city and distribution point.

In OLD BATAVIA CEMETERY, Harvester Ave. between the Erie and New York Central Railroads, are the graves of Joseph Ellicott (*see below*) and a number of Batavia pioneers, and the MORGAN MONUMENT, erected in 1880 by the National Christian Association Opposed to All Secret Societies. When William Morgan (1775–1826) was denied membership in a Masonic lodge in Batavia, though he claimed previous membership in Rochester and Le Roy, he threatened to reveal the secrets of the order. After a series of arrests he was secretly carried off to Fort Niagara, where all traces of him were lost. A hue and cry was raised through the countryside, and a movement was set on foot to break the power of Free Masonry; tinged with patriotic and religious sentiment, it took form as a political party. For several years the vote of the 'infected district,' as this part of the State was called, determined the results of State elections. In the presidential campaign of 1828 the Anti-Masonic party polled 33,000 votes. Some time before the election a man's body was washed up on the shore of Lake Ontario and was identified as Morgan; when informed that the identification was doubtful, Thurlow Weed is reported to have said that it was 'good enough Morgan till after the election.' Morgan's fate has never been definitely determined.

The WIARD PLOW PLANT, Swan St. between the New York Central and Erie Railroads, manufactures plows, rakes, weeders, harrows, wheelbarrows, lawn mowers, and other farm machinery. The company was organized in 1804 by Thomas Wiard in East Avon; his first invention, the 'bull plow,' a wooden plow with wrought-iron points, was made by hand for pioneer farmers in western New York. The factory was moved to Batavia in 1876.

The RICHMOND MANSION (now the Children's Home), E.Main St., a large, gray-painted brick building with a pedimented portico of four Greek Ionic columns, was built by Dean Richmond (1804–66), bluff, forceful native of Vermont, grain elevator operator, banker, politician, and president of the New York Central Railroad. In his day the lavish interiors included a dining room famous for its yellow damasked walls and yellow velvet carpets; one of the baths had solid silver fittings. One of Richmond's emoluments as railroad president was to have all trains of the road, even the fastest expresses, stop at Batavia. According to tradition, Richmond's handwriting was so illegible that a dismissal notice written by him, with only the signature easily legible, was used by the dismissed employee as a free pass on the railroad.

The CARY MANSION, corner of Main and Bank Sts., is a gray-painted post-Colonial brick house built in 1817 by Trumbull Cary, a Batavia pioneer. The three-bay central block is flanked on each side by wings that are masked by the two-story Ionic-columned porches of the Greek Revival period. The graceful, elliptical-arched doorway exhibits the Scamozzi Ionic capitals favored in the earlier style.

The GENESEE COUNTY COURTHOUSE, Main St., erected in 1841, is a Greek Revival structure in Lockport limestone which eschews the temple form for a square cupolaed mass, probably reflecting the design of the first frame courthouse, which stood to the east of the present building until it burned in 1918.

The HOLLAND LAND OFFICE MUSEUM (*open summer afternoons, adm.* 10¢), W.Main St., erected by Joseph Ellicott in 1804, is a simple gray limestone building with a white wooden portico with four Roman Doric columns. Ellicott himself probably designed this graceful Roman Revival structure; its quiet dignity is closely akin in spirit to the Ellicott mansion (Goodrich House) built in Buffalo in 1823. Owned by the Holland Purchase Historical Society, the museum contains among its exhibits period rooms, early farming tools, uniforms, and local records.

The Holland Purchase included practically all of New York State west of the Genesee River, some 3,300,000 acres, sold in 1793 by Robert Morris to a group of Dutch capitalists who in turn financed the undertaking by selling shares. In 1797 Morris extinguished the Indian title by the Big Tree Treaty, and the sale was consummated. Joseph Ellicott was hired to survey the territory and lay out townships and in 1800 was appointed company agent. He was instrumental in the founding of scores of towns and villages, including Buffalo, but his especial pride was Batavia; 'I intend to do all I can for Batavia,' he said, 'because the Almighty will look out for Buffalo.'

The NEW YORK STATE SCHOOL FOR THE BLIND (*open* 10–12, 2:30–5 *daily*), corner of State St. and Richmond Ave., comprises a group of Victorian buildings set in landscaped grounds. Originating as an asylum under the State Department of Charities, it now is a school of regular academic standing under the State Education Department, with instruction extending through high school and including courses in music, home economics, and rug and basket weaving.

At 40.1 *m*. is the junction with State 93.

Right on State 93 to AKRON, 1.8 *m*. (720 alt.,2,254 pop.), which ships farm produce and manufactures gypsum products, plaster board, and dehydrated milk. In three
acres of low sheds, facing East Ave., mushrooms are grown, several crops a year; most
of the product is canned locally.

Right from Akron on Bloomingdale Ave. (State 267) 3.3 *m*. to the TONAWANDA
INDIAN RESERVATION, comprising 7,548 acres in Erie and Genesee Counties.
About 600 Senecas live here in small, modest homes, with here and there a garden;
the men find employment in the gypsum plants at Akron, on farms, and on roads.

At the edge of the reservation the WPA has built the TONAWANDA INDIAN COM-
MUNITY HOUSE, a structure of cypress planks and fieldstone foundation and chimneys,
resembling an Iroquois long house. Erected primarily to preserve and continue the
culture of the Indian, it contains a library, social rooms, a theater, a studio for Indian
arts and crafts, a health clinic, and a gymnasium. The building was turned over to the
State Department of Public Welfare on May 13, 1939.

The route enters the suburban area of Buffalo at WILLIAMSVILLE,
53.5 *m*. (665 alt.,3,607 pop.), where no industries mar the domestic scene.
The OLD MANSION HOUSE, 5495 Main St., a three-story graystone building, and the EAGLE HOTEL, 5578 Main St., a two-story frame structure,
have operated as taverns for more than a century. DREAM ISLAND (*picnicking, swimming, playgrounds*), the new village park built by WPA, extends along Ellicott Creek. GLENN PARK, Glenn Ave., is a small edition of
Coney Island, with a dance hall, side shows, and games of chance and
skill.

BUFFALO, 64 *m*. (600 alt.,575,150 pop.) (*see Buffalo*), is at the junction
with State 33 (*see Tour 33*), US 62 (*see Tour 37*), and State 16 (*see Tour
38*).

Section e. BUFFALO to PENNSYLVANIA LINE; 71 m. State 5

South of Buffalo the route, popular in summer, follows the shore of
Lake Erie, clinging to pine-clad cliffs, with sandy beaches below. The area
is part of the western State grape belt (*see Tour 8*).

In 1806, along this route, a man on foot carried mail between Buffalo
and Erie, the mail wrapped in a handkerchief; he arrived when he got
there, without a definite schedule. Stagecoaches began making the trip
daily in 1827; where a stream was too deep for fording, passengers were
paddled across one by one in a canoe, the horses swam, and the coach was
pulled across with a long rope. Today planes drop mail in Erie half an
hour after leaving Buffalo.

South of BUFFALO, 0 *m*., is LACKAWANNA, 4.8 *m*. (600 alt.,24,-
053 pop.), an industrial suburb, with treeless streets of row upon row of
drab brown and green houses and grimy steel mills. It was named for the
steel company that moved from Scranton, Pennsylvania, and erected its
plant here in 1899; ten years later the early hamlet of Limestone Hill,
Lighting District No.1, Town of West Seneca, was incorporated as a city.
About 30 per cent of the population is of recent European origin, mostly
Polish and Hungarian, and 10 per cent are Negroes.

The BASILICA OF OUR LADY OF VICTORY, SE. corner of Park Ave. and
Ridge Road, is one of two North American Catholic churches designated

by Papal decree as a basilica, the title conveying special privileges and indulgences. It is a large, rectangular structure of white limestone with a Byzantine dome 251 feet in circumference; the main entrance has two 165-foot towers with interlaced stone carvings; the interior is lavishly ornamented in 48 different kinds of marble.

The basilica is one of a large group of religious and charitable institutions known to western New Yorkers as Father Baker's Colony. The Right Reverend Monsignor Nelson D. Baker (1841–1936), native of Buffalo, was educated at Canisius College and Niagara University. Shortly after his ordination in 1876 he became director of a reform school in Lackawanna, which he converted into an industrial school; when his efforts to pay off the school's huge debt succeeded he enlarged the scope of his activities and continued to raise money and build institutions for the rest of his life. Today the basilica, orphanages, hospitals, schools, etc., representing an investment of about $25,000,000, stand as a memorial to the man.

The BETHLEHEM STEEL PLANT, Ridge Road and Turnpike (State 5), comprising more than 50 long, narrow two-story steel structures, produces about one-twentieth of the annual steel output of the United States. Its products include strip and sheet steel for automobile bodies, tin cans, office furniture, and countless articles of everyday use. The plant employs about 12,000 people. The Bethlehem Steel Company took over the Lackawanna plant in 1922, doubled its capacity by 1930, and in 1936 added a new $20,-000,000 strip mill.

Between 29.4 *m.* and 32.3 *m.* State 5 runs in common with US 20 (*see Tour* 8).

Despite its industries, DUNKIRK, 42.4 *m.* (600 alt.,17,606 pop.), is a city of homes set off by lawns and flower gardens on clean, well-lighted streets. Its water and electric systems were among the first in the country to be municipally owned and operated; rates are extremely low. Principal industrial products are oil-refining machinery, radiators, boilers, shovels, and silk.

In Dunkirk is the junction with State 39 (*see Tour* 34).

POINT GRATIOT PARK (R), 43.2 *m.*, 75 acres, has free picnic grounds and a sandy beach. On the point are a U.S.Government lighthouse and a New York State fish hatchery, which stocks Lake Erie with herring and whitefish.

LAKE ERIE STATE PARK (R), 50 *m.*, has a public bathing beach and bathhouse (*open May* 27–*Labor Day*), picnic areas, playgrounds, and camp sites.

BARCELONA, 60.3 *m.* (600 alt.,300 pop.), is a sea-food town, earning a living by fishing; fish frys are a featured dish on restaurant menus. The lighthouse on the lake shore, erected in 1821, was lighted for several years by natural gas piped in hollow logs from a gas spring near the village.

At 71 *m.* State 5 crosses the PENNSYLVANIA LINE, 17.5 miles northeast of Erie, Pennsylvania.

Tour 12

Schenectady—Canajoharie—Utica—Rome—Wampsville; State 5S.
107.5 m.

Two-lane concrete with short stretches of macadam.
New York Central R.R. parallels route between Schenectady and Rome.

Closely following the south bank of the Mohawk River, State 5S supplements State 5 (*see Tour* 11) across the river, the main highway through the Mohawk Valley. Twenty-one bridges connect the two riverbanks and join the opposite towns in a close community life. Frequently lifting above the valley floor, State 5S commands expansive views of river, flatlands, and wooded hills.

The south side of the river has its share of old Dutch houses, sites of Indian castles and Colonial forts, shrines to Jesuit missionaries, factories and railroads, Palatine settlements, Revolutionary battlefields, old taverns, and monuments to native sons who made good; but greater than these, though so unobtrusive as to be easily missed altogether, is a wide cattail-choked ditch paralleled by a bank wide enough for a set of automobile tracks—the old Erie Canal bed and towpath. Here and there the bed is filled in; stretches of it are marked by huge steel towers carrying high tension wires; the road runs along it for many miles, crossing and recrossing it from side to side, with the river stretching away to the right.

Today the canalized river is the main unit of the State's Barge Canal system, constructed in 1905–18; at intervals of from five to ten miles are huge modern concrete locks that can clear 2,000-ton barges; the 100-ton steel gates, electrically operated, can be opened or closed in 30 seconds. Such are the triumphs of modern engineering. But in the 1820's, when the first Erie Canal was being built, engineering skill was inadequate to the task of controlling river currents, so that it was necessary to dig an artificial ditch across the State paralleling the natural water courses. The ditch was dug with pickaxe and shovel; most of the laborers were Irish immigrants, three of whom could finish three rods of canal, four feet deep, in five-and-a-half days. Tanned, muscular, they worked bareback, harassed by mosquitoes that 'could drill through boots.' The canal offered 'the first great field of Catholic employment and avenue of Catholic emigration westward'; priests followed the faithful into the wilderness, building altars in the fields and then churches in the towns that sprang up on the sites.

The original Erie was 40 feet wide and 4 feet deep, accommodating boats of about 30 tons; between 1836 and 1862 it was enlarged to accommodate 240-ton boats—not very large, but large enough to be a decisive factor in the development of the Empire State and the Middle West by providing cheap transportation for goods and passengers. Westward-moving emigrants chanted:

> Then there's the State of New York, where some are very rich,
> Themselves and a few others have dug a mighty ditch,

To render it more easy for us to find a way
And sail up the water to Michigania . . .

Besides a few choice examples of Dutch, Palatine, and post-Colonial
buildings, this route and the one across the river display numerous and
varied Greek Revival structures that were the product of the first two
decades of canal prosperity. But the valley is noted for its post-Civil War
buildings: square, boxlike houses topped by functionless lanterns and ornamented with porches. One historian has called this the 'Mohawk Valley
style.' Perhaps the State's noblest and most significant architecture of the
mid-nineteenth century appears in the magnificently massive masonry of
the aqueducts and locks built during the first enlargement of the canal,
1836–62.

The western half of the route tells the story of the resistance offered by
British, Tory, and Indian forces during the Revolution by the farmer sons
of the Palatine emigrants. The events, which reach their climax at Oriskany and Fort Stanwix, have been narrated in Harold Frederic's *In the
Valley* and Walter D. Edmonds's *Drums along the Mohawk*.

West of SCHENECTADY, 0 *m*. (220 alt.,95,692 pop.) (*see Schenectady*),
State 5S skirts the GENERAL ELECTRIC PLANT (L), a compact group of red
and gray factory and office buildings stretching away for a mile under
radio towers and grimy smokestacks.

The MOHAWK RIVER (R) encircles several large islands, locale of the
legend of the passing of the last of the Mohawks. When he was called by
the Great Spirit, the old Indian gave his catch of fish to a white friend and
refused the usual firewater offered in return, saying, 'Great Spirit call,
Indian no need.' He sat down in the stern of his canoe, his arms folded,
and the craft moved swiftly upstream, pulled by some invisible power into
the setting sun. The next day his empty canoe was found floating in the
river.

At 1.6 *m*. the route crosses the ERIE CANAL BED AND TOWPATH;
at 2.3 *m*. are two well-preserved ERIE CANAL LOCKS (R), unusual in that
water still flows through them, the old ditch here carrying water to the
General Electric power plant. On hot summer days neighborhood boys
use the lock as a swimming hole; a hundred years ago 20,000 boats passed
through it in one season, an average of one for every 17 minutes night and
day. The canal was choked with barges pulled across the State by mules
and horses, carrying settlers' supplies to the West and farm products to
the markets of the East. Forty thousand emigrants rode the packets in
one year. Packets had priority over freighters; if a freighter neglected to
drop its tow rope to let a packet pass by, a sickle-like knife protruding
from the packet's bow cut the rope.

By 1845 the canal had become the State's biggest employer with 25,000
men, women, and boys working on 4,000 boats and barges and at the canal
basins; wages were about $20 a month for steermen, $12 for adult drivers,
$10 for boys, and $8 for deckhands. Child labor thrived: an estimated
5,000 boys, 'specimens of depravity' who gravitated to the canal from
city and country, drove the mules along the towpath; at the end of the
season they would 'haul up at either end and git what you can.'

The 'canawler,' half sailor and half landlubber, swore, drank, and fought hard. The boys fought for their turn through the locks and were often joined by captains and crews in knock-down, drag-out brawls. Whisky sold for 6½¢ a pint, applejack 25¢ a gallon. The story is told of a captain who sent a boy ashore for rum and bread; when the boy returned with two loaves of bread and one jug of rum he was thrashed for buying too much bread. At each lock and basin, the latter with coal, grain, and supply warehouses, there was a tavern where boat crews laying by overnight would gather, and 'the squawk fiddle and the wail of the accor-deen would mingle on the evening air with the rasp of rugged voices raised in song'; they created their own balladry, reflecting their hard, careless, per-egrinating life:

> 'Tis haul in your bowlines,
> Stand by that old sorr' mule;
> The cook she's on a racket,
> She acts just like a fool.
> For the Erie she's a-risin'
> An' our gin 'tis gett'n' low:
> An' I hardly think
> We'll strike a drink,
> Till we reach old Buffalo.

At 2.4 *m.* is the junction with Schermerhorn Rd.

Left on this road 0.3 *m.* to the BRADT HOUSE (*private*), a well-preserved example of the type of Dutch farmhouse found in the Capital District. Built in 1735 outside the Schenectady stockade near the river-flat farm of the Bradts, the story-and-a-half house reflects city models in its use of brick and in its steep gable with 'mouthteeth' courses. The end wings, dormer, and porch are nineteenth-century additions, but they cannot obscure either the fundamentally Dutch lines of the central mass or the Dutch details like the gable portholes and wrought-iron beam anchors.

At 4.2 *m.* (R) is a beautifully preserved three-arch aqueduct built about 1840. The road parallels the old Erie ditch and towpath (R).

The JAN MABIE HOUSE (R), 6.3 *m.*, is a characteristic one-and-a-half-story Dutch farmhouse built of local bluestone laid up at random without mortar, pointed and painted on the exterior and plastered on the interior. Only slight alterations mar the quaint Dutch flavor. The interior still retains the large cellar fireplace, the heavy beams—some 14 by 12 inches, and the wide pine floor boards. The first white owner of the land was Daniel Van Antwerpen; in 1705 he deeded half his land to Jan Mabie, who may have built this house.

AMSTERDAM, 16.5 *m.* (288 alt.,33,640 pop.) (*see Tour* 11), is at the junction with State 30 (*see Tour* 24).

At 20.1 *m.* is the junction with a macadam road.

Right on this road 0.5 *m.* to FORT HUNTER (300 alt.,700 pop.), a scattering of homes and churches, named for the fort built here by the British Governor Hunter in 1711. It was one of a chain of defenses to protect British gains in this territory against French and Indian aggression and depradations.

At the eastern end of the village is QUEEN ANNE'S PARSONAGE, erected in 1712 as a part of Queen Anne's Episcopal Chapel. Queen Anne ordered the chapel built at her own expense after the friendly Mohawk had asked for a place to worship the white man's God.

At the beginning of the Revolution, the remains of Fort Hunter were cleared away and a heavy stockade was erected around the chapel, with a blockhouse bristling with cannon at each corner. In the 1820's the chapel was razed to make a path for the Erie Canal, but the parsonage remains with but few changes—a new roof, new interior woodwork, and a new door in the south side.

One of the absorbing engineering problems in the construction of the Erie was how to get across transverse streams; the final solution was the aqueduct—a man-made river crossing a natural river over a bridge. On the western edge of the village is the SCHOHARIE CREEK AQUEDUCT, constructed, so runs the inscription on the parapet, by 'Otis Eddy, bldr., 1841.' This magnificent cut-limestone structure ranks with the Utica State Hospital as one of the finest pieces of monumental construction in the State preserved from the 1840's. Thirteen great piers carried the wooden trunk containing the 41½-by-7-foot water section of the canal, and 14 graceful 40-foot arches supported the towpath and braced the piers. It stands 624 feet long, a fitting monument to the confident grandeur of the imperial builders of the Empire State. European engineers came to view the remarkable feat of carrying a canal high above a river; artists sketched this and other Erie Canal aqueducts and carried the pictures back to England to be used for designs on English pottery.

The SHRINE OF OUR LADY OF MARTYRS (L) in AURIESVILLE, 22.5 m. (320 alt.,126 pop.), is a memorial to Father Isaac Jogues, brothers René Goupil and Jean de Lalande, and five mission priests, all of whom met martyrdom at the hands of the Indians and were canonized on June 21, 1925, the first North American Saints of the Roman Catholic Church. Father Jogues (1607–46), a French Jesuit, came to Canada in 1636 to work among the Indians. Captured by Mohawks in August 1642, he refused a chance to escape and saw Goupil chopped down at his feet. Tortured and dragged from village to village, he finally escaped with the help of Domine Megapolensis at Fort Orange (see Albany). After a brief visit to France he was back in America and in September 1646 returned to his charge among the Indians and to certain death. He was killed on October 18, 1646, in the Mohawk village of Osseruenon, on the site of which the shrine now stands.

In 1884 the Society of Jesus bought the land, erected a chapel, and developed the shrine, which now includes a coliseum, an inn, a cafeteria, and a replica of an Indian long house containing an exhibit of Mohawk artifacts. Each Sunday from April 15 to October 15 masses are celebrated, and on the Sunday nearest August 15 thousands of Catholics assemble at this quiet spot in the Mohawk Valley to honor the memory of the Saints who suffered martyrdom three centuries ago.

In KATERI'S GROTTO, adjoining the shrine, is the statue of Kateri Tekakwitha, 'Lily of the Mohawks.' Born in 1656 of a Mohawk father and a Christian Algonquian mother, she was left an orphan at the age of four during a smallpox epidemic, which also disfigured her. Withstanding the reproaches and tortures inflicted on her by pagan relatives, she persisted in Christian piety and escaped to a Christian Indian village in Canada, where she carried her religious fervor to such extremes of self-torture that she died in 1680 at the age of 24. Scores of accounts of extraordinary cures professedly achieved through the intercession of this Indian girl have been submitted to the Vatican for possible adjudication as miracles. If she is canonized, she will be the first American-born Saint.

The route continues to parallel the canal bed and towpath (L); an occasional well-hoed vegetable garden flourishes in the rich soil that carried the canal waters. Several major labor-saving devices were invented to meet the needs of the job of clearing the land and digging the ditch: a tree-puller—an endless screw with a cable attached to a tree; a grubbing machine propelled by horses, making possible the removal of 40 stumps a day; a plow with a second cutting blade, for work among roots and underbrush; and, most important, hydraulic cement. The common quicklime mortar first used would not slack; imported cement was too expensive; the canal project hung in the balance until Canvass White burned stone, pulverized it and mixed it with sand, placed the mixture in a bucket of water, and produced a cheap cement that set rigidly.

In October 1775, in a meeting on the river flats (R) at 23.6 *m.*, the Tryon County Committee of Safety, organized by a group of valley patriots to promote the cause of the Revolution, failed to persuade Mohawk chieftains to drop their loyalty to England and remain neutral during the struggle.

In 1666 Alexandre de Tracy, governor of Canada, led a French army against the Mohawk towns to convince the Iroquois of the strength of the French in the north. When he reached Andagoron, middle Mohawk castle of the Bear Clan (1642–66), the site of which is on Stone Ridge (L), 30.1 *m.*, he found the settlement abandoned, the Mohawk having fled to Iconderoga. Tracy left the castle in smoldering ruins and moved on to Iconderoga, where the Mohawk had massed for the attack. Overwhelmed by the number of invaders, the Indians fled without resistance, and de Tracy's men destroyed the last of the Mohawk towns.

CANAJOHARIE, 37.8 *m.* (320 alt.,2,573 pop.), a model village of the middle Mohawk Valley, depends for its prosperity chiefly on its food-packing industry, with other food products plants and a paper flour sack factory making their contribution. The name, from the Indian meaning the pot that washes itself, refers to a large pothole at the entrance to Canajoharie Gorge, south of the village, where the water boils endlessly; about a mile up the creek is a waterfall which drops 45 feet into the gorge. The village, settled by Dutch and Germans about 1730, was in 1779 the concentration point for General James Clinton's army.

The Beech-Nut Plant (*open; guide service*), main office on Church Street, packs bacon, peanut butter, strained baby foods, chewing gum, and candy. The 800 employees, most of them women in white uniforms, watch over complicated automatic machines that process and pack the products. The two-hour inspection tour covers curing, smoking, and packing bacon, making chewing gum, mixing peanut butter, etc.

The Canajoharie Library and Art Gallery (*open 9–12, 2–6 Mon.-Fri.; 9–12, 2–5 Sat.; 2–5 Sun.*), Church St. opposite the main office of the Beech-Nut Packing Company, occupies the Arkell Memorial Building. Erected in 1924 from plans by Tilton & Githens of New York City, it is reminiscent of the gambreled Van Alstyne House, but the scale is unfortunately disturbed by the Greek Revival entrance motive. The Gallery, the first established in the valley, displays more than 100 paintings, including a full-sized copy of Rembrandt's *Night Watch* and four originals by Winslow Homer: *Watching the Breakers, See-Saw, Boy on the Rocks,* and *On the Beach.*

The VAN ALSTYNE HOUSE (*open; apply to steward*), Moyer St., now the Fort Rensselaer Club, is a long, low, stone story-and-a-half house built in 1749 by Marte Janse Van Alstyne, an early settler. It contains a large collection of documents and relics relating to Mohawk Valley history. In 1774–5 it served as headquarters for the Tryon County Committee of Safety and was visited by General Washington in 1783.

At the eastern line of FORT PLAIN, 41.4 m. (320 alt.,2,761 pop.), at the confluence of Otsquago Creek and the Mohawk River, a gas station has been swung over the gray walls of an abandoned canal lock, the basin serving as a garage. To the right of the highway bridge are the five well-preserved arches of the Otsquago aqueduct.

On one of the main migratory bird routes, Fort Plain has a bird sanctuary in FISH AND GAME PARK, River Road, where native wild birds are fed in winter and protected during the nesting season. On ABEEL IS-LAND, in the Mohawk River at the north end of the village, there is a 50-acre game refuge for water and land birds and wild animals. The island was named for John Abeel, an Indian trader who married the daughter of a Seneca chief after the Indian fashion. Out of this marriage came the famous Indian warrior, Cornplanter.

The PARIS-BLEEKER HOUSE (*open*), on a private road between upper Main and upper Mohawk Sts., originally the old Paris Trading Post built in 1786 and now a D.A.R. chapter house and museum, contains many Indian and Colonial relics.

West of the village, at 42.5 m., is the SITE OF FORT PLAIN (L), built in 1776 to protect the valley settlements from raiders. It was considered one of the best fortifications in the valley.

On a wooded bluff (L) overlooking Nowadaga (Ind., place of mud turtles) Creek, the INDIAN CASTLE CHURCH, 51.4 m., marks the site of the upper castle inhabited by the Mohawk Bear Clan between 1700 and 1775. Here Sir William Johnson built Fort Hendrick in 1756 and named it for his friend and ally 'King' Hendrick, who had been killed the year before in the Lake George campaign; and here Johnson became enamored of Molly, the sister of Joseph Brant. After Johnson's death Molly returned to the castle and from here sent a warning of General Herkimer's plans to her brother, Joseph Brant, at Fort Stanwix, resulting in the ambush at Oriskany (*see below*). In 1779 the last of the Indians were removed from the castle and the land was turned over to white settlers.

The church, the sole surviving structure of all the Mohawk castles, was built in 1769 by Daniel Muller for Johnson, who presented it to his Indian friends. Brant, who had been educated at Eleazer Wheelock's school, now Dartmouth College, here translated St.Mark's Gospel into Mohawk. The simple clapboarded frame building originally had the entrance in the middle of the east side, like many other Colonial churches, and the Gothic Revival steeple was originally an open Georgian cupola.

The HERKIMER ESTATE (R), 53.8 m., is a 160-acre tract (*picnicking*) maintained by the State and containing the old Herkimer homestead, the

Herkimer family burial ground, and a 60-foot obelisk erected by the State to the memory of General Nicholas Herkimer (1728–77). The HOMESTEAD (*open weekdays* 9–5, *Sun.* 1–5; *adm. free*), built by Herkimer in 1764, is a substantial brick house, next to Johnson Hall (*see Tour 13*) the most pretentious dwelling in the valley. While the lower floor with its pine paneling remains the same as when Herkimer died in 1777, the exterior was radically disfigured in 1848 by Daniel Connor, the farmer owner, who 'modernized' it by replacing the small front stoop (now restored) with a long piazza, raising the roof and changing its form from a gambrel to a low gable, and adding a Greek Revival cornice and eaves windows. The house contains a collection of Colonial and Revolutionary relics and furniture.

This house stands in valley history as the counterpart to Johnson Hall; the latter was the home of the outstanding Loyalist of the valley, the former, the home of its outstanding Patriot. In 1775 the Tryon County Committee of Safety commissioned Nicholas Herkimer brigadier general. Herkimer had learned to fight during the French and Indian War; in those days Sir William Johnson was a close friend, and when Herkimer occupied this house he had as a near neighbor and friend Joseph Brant, who in 1777 led the ambush at Oriskany in which Herkimer was fatally wounded. After the battle the General was moved to the homestead, where his leg was amputated and he died on August 17, 1777. His grave is in the family burial ground close by.

The FORT HERKIMER REFORMED DUTCH CHURCH (R), 60.8 *m.*, was begun about 1730 by Palatine settlers to replace their humble log structure of 1723; but construction lagged, and during the French and Indian War, 1754–63, the walls and a temporary roof formed the center of Colonial Fort Herkimer. The inscription above the abandoned entrance on the north reads 'JHE (Johan Herkimer erbaut) 1767.' Johan Herkimer was the father of General Herkimer and 12 other children. He settled here in 1722 and established a trading post.

During the Revolution the church was part of a stockaded fort. On August 1, 1778, Tory-Indian raiders plundered the neighborhood but no lives were lost, thanks to the heroism of Adam Helmer, who ran ahead of the raiding force for 22 miles to Fort Herkimer, warning the settlers and enabling them to reach the safety of the fort before the Indians arrived.

In 1812 the church was altered and enlarged. The original structure came to the sill of the present gallery windows, the steep gable roof surmounted by a conical steeple; the entrance, on the north, led to a simple rectangular interior with the high pulpit and sounding board against the south wall.

MOHAWK, 64 *m.* (410 alt.,2,835 pop.), originally a Palatine settlement, was ravaged during the French and Indian and Revolutionary wars, but was rebuilt by Palatine descendants and Yankee newcomers. After the opening of the Erie Canal, the settlement boomed; near-by farmers turned to making cheese, an art introduced by the Yankees, and the village was second only to Little Falls (*see Tour 11*) as a cheese-shipping point. With the incorporation of the Mohawk Valley Knitting Mills in 1887 it became a factory town and today its workers make knit underwear here or across the river in Herkimer (*see Tour* 11), while others are employed in Ilion.

The GENERAL SPINNER HOUSE (*private*), corner of E.Main and Fulton Sts., is an example in brick of the Greek Revival style at its best. The central block, with a Greek Doric colonnaded porch and capped by a low pitched roof and square cupola, achieves the one-story effect so favored in this style, but it masks a banal two-story section in the rear.

Francis E. Spinner (1802–90) built the house in 1840. Later he rose to be Major General of the State militia and member of Congress, 1855–61. During the 1860 presidential campaign he was an ardent supporter of Lincoln. As United States Treasurer, 1861–75, appointed by Lincoln, he put his signature on Civil War greenbacks and was the first to employ women in Government service (*see Tour* 11); Miss Jane Douglass of Ilion, appointed by him, was the first woman to hold a Federal job.

The SHOEMAKER HOUSE (L), W.Main St., a two-story frame house with a hip roof, was once a Revolutionary tavern that catered to loyalists and rebels alike. A few days after the Battle of Oriskany, Walter Butler (*see Tour* 11) came here, well within the enemy's lines, with about 15 men, expecting to raise recruits for the Loyalist forces. But he was taken prisoner and kept captive in Albany, whence he escaped to wreak his vengeance at Cherry Valley (*see Tour* 8).

Mohawk is at the junction with State 28 (*see Tour* 15).

ILION, 65.8 *m.* (400 alt.,9,890 pop.), was saved from decay upon the ebb of the Erie Canal by the Remington industries, which still dominate the village. In 1800 Eliphalet Remington, farmer-mechanic, brought his family, including Eliphalet,Jr. (1793–1861), from Connecticut. Young Eliphalet inherited his father's mechanical bent; when he needed a gun for hunting he fashioned the barrel in his father's forge at Ilion Gulph and then trudged 15 miles to Utica to have it rifled. When neighbors asked for similar guns, father and son built a new forge and began the manufacture of firearms. Later they built a factory in Ilion, and the village spread over the flatlands along the Mohawk and up the hills to the south. Every war brought a spurt in production, but after the Civil War the industry collapsed because of overexpansion. Remington descendants carried on with new capital and tried to diversify their products by adding farm implements, typewriters, sewing machines, and electrical equipment; but in 1888 Remington control passed to new interests.

The REMINGTON ARMS PLANT, both sides of Main St., a group of brick buildings with third-story bridges crossing the street, is a Du Pont subsidiary, manufacturing guns and ammunition. The REMINGTON-RAND PLANT, Spruce St., making typewriters, office equipment, filing systems, and cash registers, stems from the Remingtons' first successful production of a commercial typewriter in 1873.

The Remington plants, employing more than 6,000 workers, are the industrial center of the Mohawk-Ilion-Frankfort community with a combined population of 28,000. An Ilion village ordinance prohibiting the sale or lease of property to foreigners, in effect for many years, succeeded in keeping out the recent immigrant groups. During the 1936 Remington-

Rand strike the company used a strikebreaking procedure widely publicized as the 'Mohawk Valley Formula'; after the strike the National Labor Relations Board ordered the reinstatement of the strikers.

Ilion has two large exhibits of guns; one in the Remington Arms plant and the other in RUSSELL PARK, foot of Park Ave., a 160-acre tract on a hill overlooking the village.

FRANKFORT, 68.1 *m.* (400 alt.,4,203 pop.), a stretch of plain dwellings on the flatlands along the river, with its large foreign population, is more typically industrial American than its neighbors. During the early years of the canal it outgrew Ilion, Mohawk, and Herkimer; the West Shore Railroad brought a railroad roundhouse, a boiler shop, a foundry, and many foreign laborers. Other industries sprang up, but all have disappeared except the manufacture of farm tools, road machinery, and milk products.

Frankfort's industrial past includes parentage of the American match industry. In 1843 William A. Gates began the manufacture of wooden matches in a tiny village shop and peddled them from house to house along the river. The match sticks were cut by hand from strips of wood three feet long and then dipped into a sulphur composition and allowed to dry. The process was slow and exacting; but later Gates invented a machine, made at the Remington plant in Ilion, that did away with much of the hand labor. After his death in 1877 the plant was merged with the Diamond Match Company and in 1893 was moved to Oswego.

In the 1890's, on what is called the Balloon farm, near Frankfort, Carl and Carlotta Myers, intrepid pioneer balloonists, equipped a building with laboratory and shop for the manufacture of balloons, including small hydrogen balloons used for Federal weather experiments. In their spare time Myers and his wife toured the country fairs with a balloon, taking awed spectators on flights.

The FOLTS HOMESTEAD (L), built in 1796 by Major Warner Folts, is a two-story structure with low gabled roof, end chimneys, and four-columned porch surmounted by an open balustrade. While extensively remodeled, the house retains the original hand-hewn beams and corner posts.

West of Frankfort State 5S cuts across fertile land to UTICA, 77.8 *m.* (500 alt.,100,063 pop.) (*see Utica*), at the junction with State 5 (*see Tour* 11), State 8 (*see Tour* 14), and State 12 (*see Tour* 25).

West of Utica State 5S follows the old Indian trail and military road connecting Fort Schuyler (*see Utica*) and Fort Stanwix (*see below*) through the broadening valley of the Mohawk. In YORKVILLE, 80.6 *m.* (420 alt., 3,406 pop.), a suburban residential community, is the INMAN HOME, corner of W.Oriskany and Whitesboro Sts., the birthplace of Henry Inman (1801–46), portrait and landscape painter. The house was built in 1792 by Inman's father, a distiller and real estate speculator; in 1812 the family moved to New York. Henry Inman was one of the founders of the National Academy of Design and painted portraits of Wordsworth, Audubon, Hawthorne, Fitz-Greene Halleck, Chief Justice John Marshall, President Martin Van Buren, De Witt Clinton, Clara Barton, and others. Once when he received $500—much less than he had expected—for a group painting ordered by a rich client, he asked that the picture be returned to him, then 'cut off all the legs and sent it back with $200.' He is also important for his landscapes and genre paintings, several of which depict scenes in the Catskills.

With its narrow, tree-shaded village green and stately nineteenth-century homes along Main Street, WHITESBORO, 81.7 m. (430 alt.,3,375 pop.), has preserved the flavor of the New England of its first settlers; its industries produce knit goods, furniture, and heaters. Judge Hugh White (1733–1812) left his Middletown, Connecticut, home in 1784, shipped by water to Albany, overland to Schenectady, and up the Mohawk by bateau to this western frontier; his son, driving a yoke of oxen, kept pace by land. The family's log house, thrown up in a hurry, was the first dwelling west of Utica on the Fort Stanwix military road.

ORISKANY, 85.1 m. (460 alt.,1,142 pop.), occupies the site of the Indian village of Oriska, on Oriskany Creek near its confluence with the Mohawk. In 1810 woolen fabrics were manufactured in the village from raw materials for the first time in the State; present industries produce iron castings and papermaker's felt. In 1819 the waters of Oriskany Creek were diverted into the newly dug bed of the Erie Canal for the passage of the *Chief Engineer*, the first boat to ply the canal between Rome and Utica.

Marked by a tall memorial shaft, the ORISKANY BATTLEFIELD (R), 86.8 m., on a hill commanding the Mohawk, was the stage for one of the bloodiest battles of the Revolution. On August 4, 1777, General Nicholas Herkimer led a force of 800 Tryon militiamen out of Fort Dayton (*see Tour* 11) to march to the relief of Fort Stanwix; on the night of August 5, he camped near the site of present Oriskany village and sent scouts ahead to inform Colonel Gansevoort of their approach and to arrange for the firing of a cannon as a signal that the garrison was ready to join in the attack. But on the morning of the 6th, Herkimer's officers became impatient with the delay, protesting to the point of mutiny: they called Herkimer a coward and a traitor, throwing up to him the defection of one of his brothers to the Tory side; against his better judgment Herkimer gave the order to march. They advanced about two miles; crossing a marshy ravine, they marched into a Tory-Indian ambuscade with a deadly fire from every side. Herkimer fell with a wound in a leg, but had himself braced in his saddle against a tree, lit his pipe, and directed the defense. For six hours the hand-to-hand fighting went on, neighbor against neighbor, with heavy losses on both sides. But the Americans—what was left of them—held their ground, and the Tories and Indians retired; the exhausted survivors of Herkimer's force returned to Fort Dayton. Oriskany was the first setback in the threefold campaign of 1777 (*see Tours* 21 *and* 22) and has therefore been called the turning point of the Revolution.

On August 6, 1933, the 'second battle of Oriskany' was fought. Farmers, revolting against low milk prices, strewed the road near the battlefield with planks bristling with sharp spikes to halt the passage of milk trucks. Twenty-four State troopers, reinforced by deputy sheriffs, ordered the 150 farmers to retreat but were answered with rocks and curses; three times they charged the rebels, and three times were forced to fall back. Again the embattled farmers won at Oriskany, though this time milk instead of blood was shed.

Covering the site of Fort Stanwix, ROME, 93.3 *m.* (440 alt.,34,217 pop.), extends over the flat, broad basin of the upper Mohawk River where in the 'horse-and-buggy days' school teachers 'used an ant hill as an illustration of what a hill looked like.' East and West Parks, facing James St., are flanked by several old public buildings, the new post office, the cathedral-like St.Peter's Catholic Church, the junior high school, the city hall, and a number of old homes. South of Dominick Street is Canal Village, where descendants of the city's first German inhabitants live; west of the village is a Polish settlement. The eastern section of the city is dominated by huge copper and brass mills. Within sound of the roar of industry are two communities of mill hands: the model town of Riverdale, with its attractive English-type residential cottages, community store, and athletic field, and the drab Factory Village, originally settled by Irish but now occupied by Italians.

Long before Rome was settled, its site, De-o-wain-sta (Ind., lifting or setting down the boat), the one-mile portage or 'carry' between the upper reaches of the Mohawk and Wood Creek, formed an important link in the water route connecting the Great Lakes region with the Atlantic seaboard. Beginning in 1725 the English kept the place fortified; in 1758 Fort Stanwix replaced two earlier forts.

The first settlement, a huddle of fur traders' huts outside the wall of Fort Stanwix, was destroyed by the American garrison before the siege of 1777. The first permanent settlers after the Revolution were New Englanders. In 1786 Dominick Lynch, whom George Washington called 'the handsome Irishman,' purchased 2,397 acres at Fort Stanwix, parceled out his land in village lots, and founded a settlement that he called Lynchville. Most of these lots were sold under a clause requiring the payment of a tax upon each transfer of title, which is still collected by Lynch's descendants. Dominick and Lynch Streets were named for the founder; James, Jane, Louisa, Jasper, and Depeyster Streets were named for his sons and daughters. Completion of a canal in 1797 connecting the Mohawk and Wood Creek started a new era of progress. In 1819 Lynchville was incorporated as the village of Rome, the name being in tribute to the 'heroic defense of the Republic made here.'

The Erie Canal was first run south of the village, but the route was later relocated and the Black River Canal was added. Rome bustled with the surge of transportation: canal boats carried farm implements west and grain and potatoes east; lusty 'canawlers' crowded the dock-lined basin with their craft, and taverns shook with their rough talk and loud laughter. Railroads followed the canals, the Rome Iron Works was established, and in 1870 the city was chartered. In 1891 the Rome Brass and Copper Company was incorporated and eventually evolved into the Revere Copper and Brass Company. Canals, railroads, and industries attracted Irish, Italians, and Polish immigrants. Today Rome processes one-tenth of all the copper ore mined in the United States; other industrial products include iron and steel, lumber, and sport and knit goods.

The SITE OF FORT STANWIX is bounded by Dominick, Willett, Liberty, and Spring Sts. The fort was built in 1758 by Brigadier General John Stanwix to guard the portage between the Mohawk and Wood Creek. In 1760, the French menace removed, the British abandoned the fort. A giant conclave staged by Sir William Johnson brought 2,000 Indians here and resulted in the Fort Stanwix Treaty of 1768 by which the English strengthened their Iroquois alliance and for $50,600 got possession of lands that now are part of New York, Pennsylvania, West Virginia, and Kentucky.

In 1776 the fort was garrisoned by Continental troops and named Fort Schuyler after General Philip Schuyler, but the old name stuck. In August 1777, Colonel Peter Gansevoort and a force of 550 successfully defended Stanwix against a three weeks' siege by Colonel Barry St.Leger's 1,400 British, Tories, Hessians, and Indians. General Herkimer's relieving force was stopped at Oriskany; but while that battle was waging, Colonel Marinus Willett made a successful sally from the fort, killing 50 British and taking much plunder.

After the battle John Butler (*see Tour* 11) and two officers entered the fort under the flag of truce and sat down with Colonel Gansevoort at a table spread with crackers, cheese, and wine to exchange neighborly greetings before turning to the business of demanding the surrender of the fort; to St.Leger's written message Gansevoort replied 'that it is my determined resolution, with the forces under my command, to defend this fort at every hazard, to the last extremity, in behalf of the United American States, who have placed me here to defend it against all their enemies.' That night Willett slipped out and made his way to Schuyler at Stillwater (*see Tour* 22) to request aid, and immediately Benedict Arnold was sent out with 800 men. On August 21 from Fort Dayton Arnold used a successful ruse, sending Tory and Indian 'fugitives' as messengers to Brant that he was approaching with 'an army as numerous as the leaves of the trees'; immediately the British Indians began to desert, and St.Leger raised the siege on the 22nd, abandoning supplies and, according to legend, dumping a large amount of gold bullion into Wood Creek, whence it is still to be fished up.

According to local tradition, the Stars and Stripes were for the first time flown in battle during the siege of Fort Stanwix; the flag was fashioned from a woman's red petticoat, a soldier's white shirt, and a captain's blue military cloak.

The REVERE COPPER AND BRASS PLANT (*open by appointment*), Seneca St., traces its origin to the Rome Iron Works, which was founded in 1866. Originally rolling iron rails, it began to roll brass in 1878 and added sheet copper in 1887. After several mergers, the present name, honoring the memory of Paul Revere, Revolutionary sentinel and first in the country to roll copper, was adopted in 1929. The local plant, one of six units, includes the largest copper rolling mill in the world, employs 4,000 skilled workmen, and produces brass and copper sheets, rods, tubing, cable, and screening.

The JERVIS LIBRARY (*open* 10–9 *weekdays*), corner of N.Washington and Elm Sts., was formerly the home of John B. Jervis, one of the chief engineers of the Erie Canal and builder of early railroads in the State. It contains a large painting by the Belgian-American artist, Edward P. Buyck, representing the siege of Fort Stanwix and the raising of the American flag for the first time.

Right from Rome on State 46 to the ROME STATE FISH HATCHERY, 4.1 *m.*, established in 1906 and taken over by the State in 1932, where brook, brown, and rainbow trout are raised by the State Conservation Department for restocking of streams. Trout propagation is unusually successful at this hatchery because of the relatively high temperature of the water, eggs hatching early and wintering fish attaining a good size before March.

ONEIDA, 105.3 *m.* (437 alt.,10,264 pop.), geographic center of the State, a city of broad, shaded streets and well-kept homes, produces caskets, period furniture, container caps, and canned goods. The establishment and early growth of Oneida resulted from a shrewd bargain made by Sands Higinbotham, owner of the city site, with the railroad whereby it received free right of way across his land, plus ample ground for a station, on the condition that it stop every passenger train at the depot ten minutes for refreshments. Higinbotham then built the Railroad House to serve meals to passengers. Settlers came in increasing numbers to this important stop, and Oneida became a thriving village. COTTAGE LAKE, Main St., the Higinbotham home, now houses the Madison County Historical Society.

WAMPSVILLE, 107.5 *m.* (480 alt.,280 pop.), is at the junction with State 5 (*see Tour* 11).

Tour 13

Schuylerville—Saratoga Springs—Johnstown—Dolgeville—Middleville; State 29. 79.7 *m.*

Mainly two-lane concrete, with stretches of macadam.
Boston & Maine R.R. parallels road between Schuylerville and Saratoga Springs.

Linking the towns in the southern foothills of the Adirondacks, the route offers glimpses of the mountains to the north and, from the hilltops, broad views of the Mohawk Valley to the south, falling away to the river and clambering up toward the Catskills beyond the horizon.

West of SCHUYLERVILLE, 0 *m.* (216 alt.,1,411 pop.) (*see Tour* 22), homemade signs invite tourists to stop at farmhouses; milk cans sit on roadside platforms; small patches of corn break the monotony of pasture land and hayfield.

SARATOGA SPRINGS, 11.1 *m.* (330 alt.,13,670 pop.) (*see Saratoga Springs*), is at the junction with US 9 (*see Tour* 21), State 50 (*see Tour* 21), and State 9K (*see Tour* 23).

At 14.3 *m*. is the junction with a dirt road.

Right on this road 0.6 *m*. to the PETRIFIED GARDENS (*open Apr.–Oct.; adm.* 35¢, *small children free, picnic facilities; geological museum*), a privately owned park exhibiting Cambrian Hoyt limestone and the fossils and solution cracks it contains. The fossils are the remains of lime-secreting plants known as Cryptozoon, which made up the base of a great reef surrounding the eastern and southern sides of the Adirondacks when the latter formed an isolated island in a broad inland sea.

In LESTER STATE PARK (R), 1.3 *m*., about an acre in size, solution cracks have been filled with concrete to preserve fossils by checking erosion (*do not remove specimens*).

Though the branding of cattle to identify ownership is associated with the western States, town clerks hereabouts kept the 'Book of Marks' before the West was settled. Peleg Taber's mark, registered in 1796, was 'a crop off the right ear tip, and knick under it'; Joseph Covert's mark, registered in 1800, was a 'swallow fork' in each ear.

The rock outcrop (R), 26.8 *m*., shows the line of contact between New York's oldest geologic strata (Archean) and beds of a period almost 500,-000,000 years younger (Potsdam), representing the enormously long period elapsing between rocks containing no traces of animal life and those with abundant marine fossils.

BROADALBIN, 33.7 *m*. (820 alt.,1,386 pop.), was named by its Scottish population when the post office was established in 1804. The first white settlers came in 1770, but the village developed slowly because of its comparative inaccessibility and the frequent Indian raids.

The HOME OF ROBERT W. CHAMBERS (1865–1933), N.Main and North Sts., is on a large estate. Here the novelist, who first won popularity with his historical romances of the Mohawk Valley, planned the books he wrote in a private New York City office. His grave, marked by a plain stone, is in a tree-surrounded clearing on the estate.

On the north side of Maple St. are the beautiful CHAMBERS ITALIAN GARDENS (*open by permission*).

VAIL MILLS, 35.2 *m*. (780 alt.,110 pop.), is at the junction with State 30 (*see Tour* 24) and at the southern extremity of the Sacandaga Reservoir (*see Tour* 23).

JOHNSTOWN, 44.2 *m*. (660 alt.,10,734 pop.), on the fertile Cayadutta Plateau, is a city with fine residences and a bustling business district, named for Sir William Johnson (*see Tour* 11), who settled here in 1762 at the height of his picturesque life as a frontier statesman and empire builder.

Johnstown and Gloversville (*see below*), centers of fine glove making, merge along Cayadutta Creek. Glove manufacture overshadows subsidiary industries like tanning and the making of glove lasts and cotton fleece.

On N.William St. just north of W.Main St. is the FULTON COUNTY COURTHOUSE, erected by Sir William Johnson in 1772, a low, red brick, gabled-roof structure with white painted doors and windows. In the octagonal cupola is the metal triangle used to announce the sessions of court since September 8, 1772.

The DRUMM HOUSE, on W.Green St., built by Sir William Johnson in

1763, was for some time occupied by Edward Wall, the schoolmaster who taught in the free school established by Johnson.

The GRAVE OF SIR WILLIAM JOHNSON, in the rear of St.John's Episcopal Church, N.Market St., is marked by a marble slab and four simple cornerstones.

The old FULTON COUNTY JAIL, corner of Montgomery and S.Perry Sts., a two-story stone building with a heavy cornice at the eave line, was built in 1772.

JIMMY BURKE'S INN, corner of S.William and Montgomery Sts., now the headquarters of the local chapter of the D.A.R., was a popular early nineteenth-century tavern. Built in 1793, the white clapboarded building has a one-story porch across its façade flush with the sidewalk.

The KNOX GELATINE PLANT (*open* 9–4; *guides*), W.Madison St., a white-painted concrete factory surrounded by greensward, packs consumer packages of plain gelatine and contains the home offices of the company, operated by the third generation of the Knox family.

Right from Johnstown on State 148 to GLOVERSVILLE, 4 *m*. (800 alt.,23,279 pop.), named for its outstanding industry. While the manufacture of heavy gloves and mittens has spread into every State, the making of fine kid gloves remains a Fulton County specialty. The larger factories are open to visitors during working hours.

Most of the steps in the process of manufacture require a high grade of skill; earnings are in most cases reckoned on a piecework basis. The sorter's practiced thumb separates the hides by grades and determines which will best take the various colors, the highest quality being reserved for the darkest color. In the shaving room the skins are thinned and cleaned; workers feed them under cylinders where emery paper takes off the rough surfaces. The cutters stand facing each other hunched over long tables, plotting out on the soft skins the rectangular 'tranks' from which the gloves are cut, and stretching and plying them to 'work out' the leather in order to assure a good fit; leather for cheaper gloves is not stretched so carefully. Pairs are matched for texture, weight, and color. 'Slitters' cut the entire glove, including the thumb and fourchettes (the small side-pieces for the fingers), out of the one trank with steel dies. In the silking room, men and women sit elbow to elbow over long rows of power-driven sewing machines running the designs on the back of the gloves; specially constructed machines make the more elaborate stitches. In the next step the thumb and fourchettes are sewed on and the glove is 'closed.' Then the sewn edges are trimmed, the glove is 'laid off'—steamed and ironed on hand forms, polished, and packed.

The beginnings of the industry in the county have been traced back to the 1760's when Sir William Johnson brought over as settlers a group of glovers from Perthshire, Scotland, who made gloves for local sale.

West from Gloversville, State 29A, a concrete road through a rough Adirondack lake district, crosses the Adirondack State Park boundary at 5.9 *m*. On the lake shores are private camps. PECK LAKE (R), 6.3 *m*., has good fishing. CAROGA LAKE STATE CAMPSITE (*bathing, fishing*), 9.3 *m*., is in the middle of a beautiful stand of hemlocks and hardwoods, one of the few remaining areas of virgin timber in the vicinity. CAROGA LAKE (*dancing, dining, boating, swimming*) is a favorite summer resort for Fulton County residents.

On the Nick Stoner Golf Course (R), 11.9 *m*., overlooking the road is the NICK STONER MONUMENT, a bronze statue of a man in a fringed leather coat, leggings, and fur cap, his left hand steadying a flintlock at rest. Major Nicholas Stoner (1762–1850) was a Revolutionary soldier and a pioneer trader and trapper in this southern Adirondack region. He became famous as a game hunter and Indian killer. He himself could not decide at any time whether he was married, and if he was whether to someone named Bessie; but the records credit him with several marriages, the last in 1840, when he was about 78 years old. To the end he was proud of the earrings he had worn since boyhood. His grave is in Prospect Cemetery, Gloversville.

The road continues past a chain of lakes: CANADA LAKE, 12.9 *m.*; GREEN LAKE, 13.5 *m.*; PINE LAKE (*dancing, dining, swimming, boating*), 15.3 *m.*; WEST LAKE, 16.9 *m.*; and PLEASANT LAKE, 19.7 *m.*

DOLGEVILLE, 33.4 *m.*, is at the junction with State 29 (*see below*).

West of Johnstown State 29 roughly parallels the blue line of the Adirondack State Park. The many streams of this hilly area, all tributaries of the Mohawk, furnished power for sawmills, gristmills, and tanneries during the nineteenth-century lumbering period.

Partly hidden by trees (R), JOHNSON HALL (*open 9–5 weekdays, and 1–5 Sundays; admission free*), 44.9 *m.*, Sir William Johnson's last home, was erected in 1761–2; it is owned by the State and managed by the Johnstown Historical Society. This two-story, white clapboard Georgian Colonial house has heavy dentiled corniced window headings and a Palladian window above the small entrance porch. The mahogany stair-rail of the fine Colonial stairway bears tomahawk marks said to have been made by Joseph Brant. After being inherited by Sir John Johnson, the estate was confiscated during the Revolution.

The heavy stone blockhouse close by is one of two built for the protection of the mansion, with which they were connected by tunnels.

The young evergreen forest, 61.7 *m.* (R), is State-owned and, like much of the land in the adjacent Adirondack Park classed as sub-marginal, has been planted by the State Conservation Department with quick-growing, soil-binding trees.

As the road tops the hill summits there are panoramic views of river, valley, and mountains on the left, and heavy evergreen forests on the right.

DOLGEVILLE, 67.5 *m.* (800 alt.,3,309 pop.), thriving on the manufacture of lumber and felt slippers, was named in 1881 for Alfred Dolge, a businessman who transformed the village of Brockett's Bridge into a factory town of several thousand workers. His factory, established here in 1875, was one of the first to manufacture felt in the United States and one of the pioneers in the earning-sharing scheme that provides employees with group insurance, pensions, disability benefits, and a mutual benefit society.

In Dolgeville is the junction with State 29A (*see above*).

MIDDLEVILLE, 79.7 *m.* (570 alt.,760 pop.), is at the junction with State 28 (*see Tour 15*).

Tour 14

Hague—Wevertown—Speculator—Utica; 127.4 m. State 8.

Two-lane macadam with stretches of concrete.
Good accommodations May to Oct.; in winter only in larger communities.

Rising up from the shore of Lake George and crossing the upper Hudson, State 8 enters a vast wasteland of stump—all that was left after the lumberjacks had passed over the once magnificent forests; now it is slowly being reclothed by second growth pine and hardwood, planted mainly by the State Conservation Department. In the 1880's came the summer boardinghouse as a source of livelihood. From lumber center to resort center: that is the short story of the mountain town. The area is one of the best hunting and fishing regions in the State.

West of HAGUE, 0 m. (330 alt.,550 pop.), on Lake George at the junction with State 9N (*see Tour 23*), the route crosses a second growth of hardwood and weaves through a deep, shady ravine noisy with cascading water.

At 5.7 m. is the beginning of a foot trail.

Left on this foot trail 0.6 m. to SWEDE MOUNTAIN OBSERVATION TOWER (1,930 alt.). The view extends to the broad-backed Green Mountains, hazy in the east; in the foreground, slopes rise from Lake George to the peak of Black Mountain; to the north, smoke from Ticonderoga's industries blurs the narrow thread of Lake Champlain.

Squeezed between mountain ranges, BRANT LAKE (R), 11 m., with its placid bays and sandy beaches, is surrounded by hotels, cottages, and private camps. In the fall, the hunters pre-empt the valley. In the winter the ice surface of the lake is dotted with small huts, heated with kerosene stoves, in which men wrapped in thick layers of clothes sit fishing through holes in the ice.

At CHESTERTOWN, 20 m. (854 alt.,700 pop.), is the junction with US 9 (*see Tour 21*), with which State 8 runs in common for 3.9 miles.

On the shallow, stony Hudson River, RIPARIUS (Riverside), 26 m. (883 alt.,150 pop.), is the Delaware & Hudson railroad station for this recreational area.

WEVERTOWN, 29.3 m. (1,040 alt.,225 pop.), is at the junction with State 28 (*see Tour 15*). The road cuts across a high ridge along rocky and wind-swept peaks, barren and jagged against the sky, to JOHNSBURG, 31 m. (1,295 alt.,275 pop.), a cluster of plain frame houses deposited and forsaken by the lumber industry. From this height is a sweeping view of Adirondack beauty: on the north, Oven Mountain (2,169 alt.) billows above an irregular mountain bulk; and the steep, broad range of Huckleberry Mountain (2,441 alt.) is the foreground for Crane Mountain (3,254 alt.) in the south.

The vanishing timber line left BAKER'S MILLS, 35.3 m. (1,580 alt., 75 pop.), once a prosperous lumbering town, a wasteland in the shadow of

Eleventh Mountain (3,303 alt.). Stumps rot in surrounding clearings; houses are run down; farm families barely subsist on the thin soil.

Into this cheerless wasteland came Samuel M. Coplon, self-appointed Santa Claus of the Adirondacks, who in 25 years distributed more than 20,000 gifts to poor mountain children. In 1904, Coplon, a toy salesman, went to North Creek to recover from illness resulting from service in the Spanish-American War. For a time he ran a country store in the backwoods settlement, coming to know at first hand the struggling, lonely life of the children to whom Santa was at best a story-book character. Back in Brooklyn, a well man again, Coplon collected sacks of toys and utility gifts and at Christmas took them to his mountain friends. Heartened by the joy they spread, Coplon related his adventure to manufacturers and jobbers with whom he did business, and they filled his packs; but he continued to buy gifts and paid the entire shipping cost. His task became so large as the years went on that he enlisted the help of churches, schools, and community organizations spread over seven mountain counties. In 1936 Coplon moved his Santa headquarters from North Creek to Baker's Mills, making his last personal appearance as Santa in 1937.

The route follows the East Branch of the Sacandaga River, a stony stream fed by numerous short tributaries reaching into the mountains. At 53.5 *m.* is the junction with State 30 (*see Tour 24*). SPECULATOR, 63.2 *m.*, (1,768 alt.,261 pop.), is a summer and winter resort on the northeastern tip of Lake Pleasant. Large, rambling white hotels, boardinghouses, and summer cottages string along the sandy shore line. On near-by OAK HILL (2,455 alt.) nine ski trails spring to life on winter week-ends. Heavyweight prizefighters, including Gene Tunney, Max Baer, and Max Schmeling, trained for heavyweight championship fights at Speculator. Isolated roads and trails through the hills offer ideal cross-country exercise, and vacationists swell the 'take' during the training period.

At 64.8 *m.* is the junction with a dirt road.

Right here 1.3 *m.* to MOFFITS BEACH STATE CAMPSITE (*open free, May 27–Oct.* 15), built by the CCC in 1936.

On a hill overlooking Sacandaga Lake is LAKE PLEASANT, 66.9 *m.* (1,791 alt.,200 pop.), a resort with large, lake-front homes radiating from the expansive hillside hotel. Spruce-covered Indian Head Mountain (2,443 alt.) towers above the settlement. Here 'Scout' Dunning, who served under Sir William Johnson, hunted and trapped, and here his son Alvah Dunning (*see Tour* 15) was born.

At 72.2 *m.* is the western junction with State 10.

Left on State 10 along the shore of Piseco Lake to SPY LAKE (L), 3 *m.*, and a popular hunting and fishing territory along the West Branch of the Sacandaga River.

In PISECO, 74.2 *m.* (1,680 alt.,20 pop.), a general store and gas station on the northern tip of Piseco Lake, is the start of a foot trail.

Left on this foot trail by easy stages up the shoulder of T Lake Mountain to T LAKE, 4.5 *m.*, with an open lean-to shelter, and T LAKE FALLS, 5.5 *m.*, a series of cascades on a tributary of West Canada Creek dropping 200 feet in a rocky gorge.

Poplar Point State Campsite (*fishing, bathing, boating*), 76.9 *m.* (*open free, May* 27–*Oct.* 15), occupies a narrow, sandy, wind-swept strip on the shore of Piseco Lake. Boats and supplies are available at Piseco.

At 77.8 *m.* is the start of a foot trail.

Left on this foot trail 1.2 *m.* to PANTHER MOUNTAIN (2,713 alt.), a half-hour climb to a panoramic view of Adirondack peaks in the distance and Piseco Lake spread out below.

In a hardwood grove, overlooking a long, sandy beach on Piseco Lake, is Point Comfort State Campsite, 79.8 *m.* (*open free, May* 30–*Oct.* 1; *tent sites*).

West of this lake region, State 8 twists through less rugged Adirondack ranges, passing an occasional sawmill, remnant of the once extensive lumbering operations, and penetrating a sparsely settled, thin-soiled farm area on the shoulder of West Canada Creek Valley.

At 94.9 *m.* is the junction with a dirt road.

Right on this road 12 *m.*, through a hunting and fishing country, to HONNEN-DAGA LAKE, which is part of a 275-square-mile tract reserved as a private hunting and fishing preserve for members of the Adirondack League Club.

The highway skirts HERKIMER NO.1 REFORESTATION AREA, 102.1 *m.*, a 10-acre State-owned tract of land blanketed with a healthy stand of red and jack pine.

At 125.6 *m.* is the junction with State 12 (*see Tour* 25).

UTICA, 127.4 *m.* (500 alt.,100,063 pop.) (*see Utica*), is at the junction with State 5 (*see Tour* 11) and State 5S (*see Tour* 12).

Tour 15

Wevertown—Blue Mountain Lake—Old Forge—Herkimer—Oneonta—Kingston; 277.7 *m.* State 28.

Two- and three-strip concrete or macadam open throughout the year.
New York Central R.R. parallels route between Thendara and Remsen, Oneonta and Kingston.
Hotel and tourist home accommodations May to October; in winter, larger communities only. Several public campsites in Adirondack region.

From the State land of the Adirondack Park to the State land of the Catskill Park, this recreation route starts in the foothills of the upper Hudson and ends in the valley of the lower Hudson. Picking its way across the central mountainous region of the Adirondacks, State 28 follows the Fulton Chain of Lakes, where early lumbermen left desolation behind them. Here woodsmen and trappers, an eccentric lot, catered to the first

Adirondack sportsmen, when the region's inaccessibility lent it a glamour that is missing in the comfortable sportsmen's lodge of the present time.

South of the Adirondack Park the route follows a straight course across the Mohawk Valley; past spas, not so gay as they were in the 90's; and along the Susquehanna Valley.

Between Oneonta and Kingston State 28 crosses the rich farmlands of the Delaware Valley. Through the Catskill Park it follows the route of early settlers of the Delaware and Susquehanna Valleys along Esopus Creek.

Section a. WEVERTOWN to BLUE MOUNTAIN LAKE; 35.1 *m.*

State 28

The route climbs toward the highlands of the central Adirondacks, which rise to the north above a forest of spruce, pine, and hemlock.

State 28 branches northwest from State 8 (*see Tour* 14) at WEVER-TOWN, 0 *m.* (1,040 alt.,225 pop.), settled in 1833 as a tannery site and still the center for small lumbering activities.

NORTH CREEK, 5.7 *m.* (1,060 alt., 600 pop.), is a winter and summer resort and the center of trade for the scattered residents within a large area. It is told that in a logging camp in the vicinity the mosquitoes were so bad that the lumbering people introduced bumblebees to fight the pests. But their plans went awry; the bumblebees mated with the mosquitoes and produced a swarm of hybrids with stingers at both ends.

At North Creek is the junction with State 28N.

Right on this road to MINERVA, 7.7 *m.* (1,400 alt.,210 pop.), which caters mostly to hunters and tourists. AIDEN LAIR LODGE (R), 14.3 *m.*, was one of the relay stations in Theodore Roosevelt's dash to North Creek to take the train to Buffalo to be sworn in as President of the United States.

The BOREAS BRIDGE STATE CAMPSITE (R), 15.6 *m.*, is a three-fireplace clearing along the stream, an ideal overnight stand for anglers.

On the ridge above the Boreas Valley a bronze plaque on a granite boulder (R), 19.7 *m.*, fixes the approximate spot where Theodore Roosevelt was when he automatically became 26th President of the United States upon the death of President McKinley.

At 21.4 *m.* is the junction with State 73, a dirt road, called the Roosevelt Marcy Highway; right here to TAHAWUS (Ind.), he splits the sky, applied to Mount Marcy), 1.9 *m.* (1,750 alt.,50 pop.). Left at the fork in the road to the junction, 6.8 *m.*, with the entrance to a foot trail; right on this trail (yellow markers) 4.2 *m.* to the summit of MOUNT MARCY (5,344 alt.), the highest mountain in the State. From State 73 are visible Mounts Marcy, Adams, McIntyre, Santanoni, Skylight, and Colden, which sit in a semicircle to the north.

On the bridge at 24.9 *m.* State 28N crosses the Hudson River near where it first assumes that name. From its source on Mount Marcy in Lake-Tear-of-the-Clouds, it plunges down the mountain sides and eventually, under the name of Opalescent River, merges with other tributaries to form the Hudson.

The road winds through several posted forest preserves set aside for wild life investigation and forest experimentation by the State College of Forestry at Syracuse University, Finch, Pruyn & Company of Glens Falls, and Cornell University.

At 30 *m.* is the entrance to the Mount Goodenow foot trail; left on this trail 2 *m.* to the forest fire observation tower on the summit of MOUNT GOODENOW (2,693 alt.).

LONG LAKE, 40.5 *m.* (1,660 alt.,225 pop.), is at the junction with State 10 (*see Tour 17*).

At 50.6 *m.* is the entrance to the Blue Mountain foot trail; left up this trail 1.8 *m.* to the forest fire observation tower at the summit of BLUE MOUNTAIN (3,759 alt.).

BLUE MOUNTAIN LAKE, 51.8 *m.* (1,800 alt.,300 pop.), is at the junction with State 28 (*see below*).

Along State 28 in isolated clearings are the homes of Adirondack natives, simple frame structures, the poorer ones with tar paper exteriors and sheet metal roofs. The men are guides, lumbermen, road workers, trappers, and hunters; the women add to the family income by managing gasoline stations and catering to tourists.

At 9.9 *m.* is the junction with a narrow dirt road (steep; chains essential after rain or snow).

Left on this road to the BARTON GARNET MINE (*open*), 5 *m.*, which produces a basic brownish red mineral suitable as an abrasive. From the mine a foot trail leads straight ahead (10 minutes) to the LEAN-TO OF THE GORE MOUNTAIN SKI CLUB, the start of nine trails. On winter week-ends the mountainside is alive with skiers in bright-colored costumes; a three-link ski-tow hums continuously upward, dragging the unwearied to the lower Skiland slopes. An annex of the North Creek American House offers warmth, the cheering cup, hot meals, and a place for technical ski-talk punctuated by the thumps of thick-soled ski boots.

In NORTH RIVER, 10.5 *m.* (1,071 alt.,170 pop.), is the junction with a dirt road.

Left on this road 5 *m.* to THIRTEENTH LAKE (*trout fishing*), with a scattering of camps on its mountain-bound shores. The HOOPER GARNET MINE, on the flank of Gore Mountain (L), is similar to the Barton Mine (*see above*).

West of INDIAN LAKE, 23.9 *m.* (1,650 alt.,400 pop.), is an undeveloped marshy country, a section of which has been posted as a sanctuary for migratory waterfowl.

Dr.Thomas C. Durant (1820–85) and William West Durant (1850–1934), father and son, were early promoters of this section of the Adirondacks. The father, financier and railroad builder, built a railroad from Saratoga to Blue Mountain Lake, and the son expanded his father's promotional activities. He built elaborate camps and sold them to J.P. Morgan, Alfred G. Vanderbilt, Collis P. Huntington, and others; he used to bring his friends up by railroad and across 40 miles of snow to enjoy Christmas dinner in the mountains.

BLUE MOUNTAIN LAKE (*speed boats available*, $1 *a person*), 35.1 *m.* (1,800 alt.,300 pop.), is a crossroads settlement of some half-dozen small houses of boxlike type and a few hotels, low, hip-roofed structures built to simulate log houses, scattered along the southern shore of the lake named for Blue Mountain.

At Blue Mountain Lake is the western junction with State 28N (*see above*).

Section b. BLUE MOUNTAIN LAKE to ALDER CREEK; 63.8 m.

State 28

West of BLUE MOUNTAIN LAKE, 0 *m.*, State 28 follows the Fulton Chain of lakes, part of a 150-mile canoe route between Old Forge and Loon Lake. This is one of the best hunting and fishing regions of the State; sportsmen rely on native guides, banded together in the Adirondack Guides Association, who plan and direct trips, lay out the schedule, and practically guarantee a full bag of game or string of fish.

The John Brown Tract, 210,000 acres in the Fulton Lake-Big Moose section of the Macomb Purchase, was bought in 1793 for $1 an acre. John Brown (1736–1803), businessman of Providence, Rhode Island, and member of the family instrumental in the establishment of Brown University, lived only long enough to have this waste land surveyed and subdivided into townships, which he named for the eight virtues he most admired— Industry, Enterprise, Perseverance, Unanimity, Sobriety, Frugality, Economy, and Regularity—and to assure himself, through several failures, that settlements could not be established here. After his death, Charles Herreshoff, his son-in-law, failed utterly in his attempt to restore his fortune in this 'region so barren that a crow would shed tears of sorrow while flying over it.' From 1819 to 1892, when the railroad opened the country as a resort area, Brown's Tract was deserted—free land for trappers and hunters, many of whom became the guides of early sportsmen.

EAGLE LAKE (R), 3.1 *m.*, and UTOWANA LAKE (R) are widened portions of the Marion River, which connects Blue Mountain and Raquette Lakes.

GOLDEN BEACH STATE CAMPSITE, 10 *m.* (*free; open May 30–Sept. 30; 65 campsites; picnic grounds*), occupies a shaded grove on a bluff overlooking a half-mile sandy beach on Raquette Lake.

At 13.6 *m.* is the junction with an unnumbered road.

Right on this road to RAQUETTE (Fr., snowshoe) LAKE (*boat trips July and Aug.*, $1 *a person*), 0.4 *m.* (1,800 alt.,50 pop.), a hotel resort community at the southwestern tip of the lake of the same name. On Raquette Lake the Durants built Camp Pine Knot, 1877–9, the first elaborate hunting lodge in the Adirondacks and for many years the showplace of the woods. In planning it the younger Durant combined the features of the Adirondack crude log cabin and the Swiss chalet, and so created the modern type of Adirondack lodge. He raised money for building an Episcopal church on an island in the lake, to which worshipers came on Sunday morning in boats.

Most famous of the early guides on Raquette Lake was Alvah Dunning (1816–1902). Alvah killed his first moose at the age of 11 and guided his first party at the age of 12; he claimed to have killed the last Adirondack moose in 1862. He had to leave Piseco Lake (*see Tour 14*) when he outraged public feeling by beating his wife, who had been unfaithful to him. The rest of his life was a long retreat from civilization. He rebelled against the city people, 'them city dudes with velvet suits and pop guns, that can't hit a deer when they see it, and don't want it if they do hit it'; he rebelled against property laws that would not recognize his squatter's rights; and he rebelled against the newfangled inventions. The crowning irony was the way he met his death: he was found asphyxiated in his bed in a hotel room in Utica: the gas jet had been leaking all night—he had blown out the light.

Close friend of Alvah Dunning was the Reverend William Henry Harrison ('Adirondack') Murray (1840–1904), Boston preacher who press-agented the Adirondacks as a health resort and vacation playground. His first book, *Adirondack Tales*, is said to have netted Murray $58,000 in royalties. But it was his *Adventures in the Wilderness* (1869) that started the stampede to the mountains that was called the 'Murray Rush'; Wendell Phillips said the book 'has kindled a thousand campfires and taught a thousand pens how to write of nature.' But there was another side to the picture: Murray had gone off the deep end in painting the attractions of the mountains, especially their health-giving powers; scores of tubercular people flocked to the Adirondacks, and Murray was charged with the murder of those who died there; editors of the day called the book a 'monstrous hoax' and referred to those who joined the rush as 'Murray's Fools.'

The moose almost completely disappeared from this once great moose-hunting district in the winter of 1854–5, but other game is still plentiful.

EIGHTH LAKE *(State-owned; excellent fishing)*, 17.2 *m.*, is (R) about half a mile from the road. This is the easternmost of the eight lakes known as the Fulton Chain, all of which flow into the middle branch of the Moose River.

At 18.6 *m.* is the junction with a dirt road.

Right on this road to the EIGHTH LAKE STATE CAMPSITE *(free, open May 27–Oct. 15; 25 sites)*, 0.5 *m.*, in a group of spruce and birch on the south shore of Eighth Lake.

SEVENTH LAKE is about 100 feet below the parking space at 20.2 *m.* White's Island in Seventh Lake was the retreat of sullen, hard-drinking Green White, the dread of Indians, whose longest speech was 'Indians never steal my furs but once.'

INLET, 24.1 *m.* (1,716 alt.,150 pop.), a resort community of several hotels, churches, and a cluster of frame houses, is at the western tip of Fourth Lake, the largest of the Fulton Chain. East of the village is one-mile-long Sixth Lake, surrounded by private camps. Adjacent and to the southwest is Fifth Lake, the smallest in the group.

At Inlet is the junction with the South Shore Road.

Left on South Shore Rd., an alternate between Inlet and Old Forge, following the south shore of the Fulton Chain, to THIRD LAKE STATE CAMPSITE *(free, open May 30–Sept. 30; transient stop-over, four campsites)*, 6 *m.*
The South Shore Road continues to Old Forge, 12 *m.* *(see below)*.

At EAGLE BAY, 25.9 *m.* (1,740 alt.,25 pop.), a resort colony on Fourth Lake, is the junction with a narrow, winding, hard-surfaced road.

Right on this road through a heavy forest of hemlock, spruce, and yellow birch, to the Big Moose country, a rectangular tract some 50 miles wide. In this locality, once nationally known for its deer-hunting, unsuccessful efforts have been made to propagate Wapiti, a type of elk, and to restock the forest with moose, imported from Canada. (Algonquian, *moos*, to eat off, is descriptive of the habit of the moose of eating foliage from standing trees.) More successful results came from the liberation of seven beavers in 1904 and 25 more in 1906. Their number had so increased by 1915 that their activities as dam builders made landowners their enemies, and the State Conservation Department was bombarded with demands for relief. A program of periodic legalizing of trapping in 1924 and 1925 made heavy inroads, since beaver pelts were selling for about $30 apiece. Today the beaver is a valuable economic resource.
DART LAKE (L), 4.1 *m.*, is named for William ('Bill') Dart, who built his first camp here in 1879 and bought the entire lake shore in 1892 when the railroad went through. The engaging personality of this guide won him a large following among sportsmen, who were transported to his simple camps by a two-seated spring wagon drawn by a 'gentle red bull.'

History

Reproduction from J.H. French's Historical and Statistical Gazetteer of New York State (1860)

BUFFALO HARBOR

GENESEE FALLS, ROCHESTER

Reproduction from J.H. French's Historical and Statistical Gazetteer of New York State (1860)

FORT GEORGE AND THE CITY OF NEW YORK (c.1760)
Reproduction from an old print published in London

MARKET PLACE, BROADWAY, ALBANY (c.1791)

SIR WILLIAM JOHNSON AT AN INDIAN COUNCIL
Mural by Henry Schnackenburg, Amsterdam Post Office

BURGOYNE SURRENDERS TO GATES, OCTOBER 17, 1777
From a painting by F. C. Yohn

ANTIRENT WAR
Detail of mural by Mary Earley, Delhi Post Office

RECRUITING IN CITY HALL PARK, NEW YORK CITY (1864)
Sketch by George Law

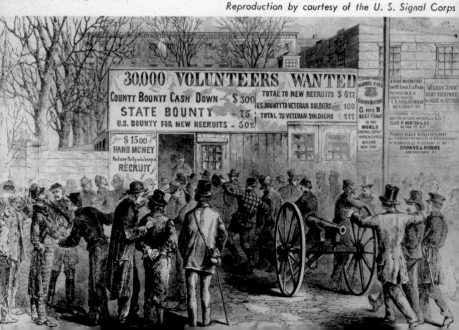

MILK STRIKE, MT. UPTON (AUGUST 1939)

PLAYING CROQUET, ONEIDA COMMUNITY

WILLIAM LYON PHELPS ADDRESSING CHAUTAUQUA

WOMAN SUFFRAGE PARADE, FIFTH AVENUE

Photograph by courtesy of Wide World Photos, Inc

FRANKLIN ROOSEVELT RECEIVES HIS NEIGHBORS' CONGRATULATIONS ON ELECTION NIGHT

THEODORE ROOSEVELT Addressing Visitors at Sagamore Hill, His Oyster Bay Home (1916)

Photograph by Paul Thompson; courtesy Roosevelt Memorial Associatio

The first permanent camp at BIG MOOSE LAKE (R), 5.6 *m.*, was built by Edwin L. ('Jack') Sheppard, 'so thin he has to step aside to throw a shadow.' In this region of rough trappers this student of geology, engineering, botany, and natural history was in great demand as a guide and of invaluable assistance to Verplanck Colvin in his survey of 1872.

At 6.2 *m.* is a crossroads; right here 0.2 *m.* to the GLENMORE HOTEL (*well-stocked general store; adequate boat landing*) on the lake shore.

At 31 *m.* is the junction with a foot trail.

Right on this trail 600 *feet* to RONDAXE (BALD) MOUNTAIN; the rocky ledges on the last quarter-mile are provided with stairs and railing. From the fire observation tower at the summit is an excellent view of the Big Moose and Fulton Chain country.

OLD FORGE, 35.3 *m.* (1,731 alt.,840 pop.), is an Adirondack metropolis of practical frame houses and a shopping district that serves the residents of a large surrounding area and the summer visitors and sportsmen who make this their headquarters. Old Forge is the starting point for short and extensive canoe trips through the Fulton and Raquette Lake regions.

THENDARA, 37.4 *m.* (1,705 alt.,200 pop.), was once the home of Nat Foster, a dead-shot trapper and guide, who carried spare bullets between his fingers. Otis Arnold, who ran an inn for hunters here, had 11 daughters, timid among human beings but at home on the horses they broke to saddle; his son was known for his terrifying snore.

The route follows the middle branch of the Moose River to its junction with the south branch. Passing several small lakes and resort towns, State 28 crosses the Adirondack State Park boundary in a sandy region of pine and spruce forest.

ALDER CREEK, 63.8 *m.* (1,200 alt.,150 pop.), is at the junction with State 12 (*see Tour* 25).

Section c. ALDER CREEK to ONEONTA; 85.9 m. State 28

This popular tourist route between the Adirondacks and the Catskills follows West Canada Creek to the Mohawk Valley, which it crosses at Herkimer, and continues along the Leatherstocking Trail to Lake Otsego, the headwaters of the Susquehanna. Between Lake Otsego and Oneonta the highway follows the widening Susquehanna Valley. The country south of the Mohawk was the wilderness setting for several of James Fenimore Cooper's Leatherstocking Tales.

South of ALDER CREEK, 0 *m.*, State 28 unites with State 12 (*see Tour* 25) to TRENTON, 11.6 *m.* (800 alt.,313 pop.).

At 7.7 *m.*, is the junction with State 46A.

Right here to the STEUBEN MEMORIAL PARK (*picnicking*), 3.5 *m.*, a wooded tract of about two acres which contains the marked GRAVE OF BARON VON STEUBEN (1730–94), the drillmaster of the Revolution, and a REPRODUCTION OF THE VON STEUBEN CABIN (*open to public, admission free*), which is being equipped with furniture of the Revolutionary period. The park is part of a 16,000-acre estate granted Baron Steuben by New York State in 1786.

At 13.8 *m.* is the junction with a macadam road.

Right on this road to TRENTON FALLS, 0.9 *m.*, a series of cascades in West Canada Creek, which, in cutting its way through a limestone gorge, has created ledges and uncovered formations of such geologic importance that the classification Trenton Epoch is applied to the limestone-making era evidenced by them.

At 19.3 *m.* is the junction with State 8 (*see Tour* 14), with which State 28 unites to POLAND, 20.9 *m.* (721 alt.,462 pop.).

At MIDDLEVILLE, 28.9 *m.* (570 alt.,760 pop.), is the junction with State 29 (*see Tour* 13).

HERKIMER, 37 *m.* (406 alt.,10,446 pop.) (*see Tour* 11), is at the junction with State 5 (*see Tour* 11).

At 38 *m.* the route crosses the Mohawk River, part of the State Barge Canal.

MOHAWK, 38.4 *m.* (410 alt.,2,835 pop.) (*see Tour* 12), is at the junction with State 5S (*see Tour* 12).

At 49.3 *m.* is the junction with US 20 (*see Tour* 8), with which State 28 unites to RICHFIELD SPRINGS, 49.9 *m.* (1,300 alt.,1,333 pop.) (*see Tour* 8).

South of Richfield Springs the route parallels CANADARAGO (Ind., on the lake) LAKE, 51.2 *m.*, which is swampy at its northern and southern ends.

COOPERSTOWN, 63.9 *m.* (1,240 alt.,2,909 pop.), a parklike residential and summer resort town, extends along the southern shore of Otsego Lake, the headwaters of the Susquehanna River.

The COOPER GROUNDS, Main St. opposite Fair St., is a landscaped two-acre memorial park dominated by a statue in heroic size of James Fenimore Cooper by Victor Salvatore. The monument stands on the SITE OF OTSEGO HALL, built in 1798 by Judge William Cooper, father of the author. In this house James Fenimore Cooper wrote *The Deerslayer* and several other romantic tales.

William Cooper came to Otsego Lake in 1785 to survey his landholdings and he soon founded the settlement that now bears his name. In 1790 he brought his family to their new home in the wilderness.

CHRIST CHURCH (Episcopal), S. of the Cooper Grounds, was erected in 1810 on land donated by Judge Cooper. Extensive alterations in 1840 were supervised by James Fenimore Cooper, a vestryman of the church, who endeavored to use the Gothic style of architecture he had admired in England.

The GRAVE OF JAMES FENIMORE COOPER (1789–1851) is in the Cooper family plot in the churchyard cemetery. In this wilderness outpost Cooper spent his childhood, developing the pioneer's independence and absorbing Indian lore that he later wrote into his novels. Following his expulsion from Yale for a college prank, and prior to his marriage in 1811 to Susan A. De Lancy (*see Tour* 1), Cooper spent a number of years as common seaman on a transatlantic merchant vessel and as midshipman in the U.S.Navy. An independence of spirit which later in life led him into controversial writing and wrangling in court was responsible for his starting to write. His first effort, a failure, was inspired by a dare from his wife when he said that he could write a better book than one they had just read. Further goaded by his own failure, he wrote *The Spy* and then *The Pioneers*, first of the Leatherstocking Tales, and was at once the center of attention from such contemporaries as Scott, Thackeray, Balzac, and Hugo. Cooper's fast-moving yarns, especially adaptable to translation, were sold the world over. N.P.Willis described him, in 1848, as 'a little increased in weight, weighing now two hundred and nine—but feels no other premonition of age. His peculiarly manly and rich voice certainly rings clear as ever, and his pale grey eye . . . sits as bright and steady in its full socket.' Democratic in principle but aristocratic in sentiment, Cooper won wide personal unpopularity: in England by his outspoken American patriotism; in the United States by his criticism of what he considered native vulgarities. He believed that democracy could not function unless led by a landed aristocracy to set up and maintain social standards.

The CENTRAL QUARTERS OF THE NEW YORK STATE HISTORICAL ASSO-CIATION (*open, summer 9–6 daily; winter 9–12, 1–5 Mon.–Fri., 9–12 Sat.; adm. adults 25¢, children 10¢, Association members free*), about a mile outside of Cooperstown on the shores of Otsego Lake, a Georgian stone building contains John H.I. Browere's remarkable series of 17 life-mask busts made about 1825 and including six of the first eight Presidents of the United States; a collection of New York State portraits, landscapes, and genre paintings; many items connected with the Cooper family; and printed and manuscript materials relating to Central New York.

The SITE OF THE CLINTON DAM is at the foot of River St. (R), at the outlet of the Susquehanna River. In July 1779, General James Clinton and his army, enroute to join forces with General John Sullivan, camped here. In order to raise the water level of the river to float the supply boats, Clinton had Otsego Lake dammed. On August 8 the dam was broken; the next day 208 heavily laden boats moved down the river, and the army marched along its banks.

COUNCIL ROCK, close by, is submerged except for its rounded top because the river has been dammed for water supply purposes. Here, according to Cooper's *The Deerslayer*, Indians came 'to make their treaties and bury their hatchets.'

Besides the Cooper family, Cooperstown has another claim to fame as the birthplace of baseball.

The NATIONAL BASEBALL MUSEUM (*open summer, adults 25¢, children 10¢*), Main St. between Fair and Pioneer Sts., an attractive two-story brick building, contains among other relics of the game a homemade baseball used by Abner Doubleday and a print illustrating Union soldiers engaged in a game at Salisbury, North Carolina, in 1863. The series of bronze plaques known as baseball's Hall of Fame honors retired players who have received votes from 75 per cent of the members of the Baseball Writers' Association in its annual poll. Among those elected are 'Ty' Cobb, 'Hans' Wagner, 'Babe' Ruth, 'Christy' Mathewson, Walter Johnson, 'Nap' Lajoie, 'Tris' Speaker, and 'Cy' Young.

LAKE FRONT PARK, Lake St. between Fair and Pioneer Sts., contains the INDIAN HUNTER, a statue of an Indian hunter and his dog, a replica by J.Q.A.Ward of the one in Central Park, New York City.

DOUBLEDAY FIELD, Main St. W. of Pioneer St., on the site used for the first baseball game, is a modern diamond and athletic field. Throughout

the summer of 1939 the centennial of the founding of the game was celebrated by a series of games between teams representing the various leagues.

Baseball grew quite informally from One Old Cat, a favorite boys' game
in Colonial days, played by a thrower, a catcher, and a batter. In 1839
Abner Doubleday, a student in a local military academy, later a major
general in the Civil War, limited the number of players to 11, outlined the
first diamond-shaped field, and drew up a memorandum of rules for the
game which he named baseball.

OTSEGO LAKE, called Glimmerglass in Cooper's novels, is described
in *The Deerslayer* as 'a broad sheet of water, so placid and limpid that it
resembled a bed of pure mountain atmosphere compressed into a setting
of hills and woods.'

North from Cooperstown on a macadam road to the Lakewood Cemetery, 0.8 *m.*;
the LEATHERSTOCKING MONUMENT, a shaft of white Italian marble surmounted by a
statue of Natty Bumppo, is a tribute to Cooper's most famous hero, the legendary
site of whose cabin is near by. Farther up the lake shore is NATTY BUMPPO'S CAVE,
2 *m.*, a narrow cleft in the rocks above the eastern lake shore.

South of Cooperstown State 28 parallels the east branch of the upper
Susquehanna as it winds past the long ridge of the Crumhorn Mountains
(1,900 alt.).

The HARTWICK SEMINARY BUILDINGS (R), 68.4 *m.*, housed the forerunner of the present Hartwick College in Oneonta (*see Tour* 10). This school
for Indians and theological students, the oldest Lutheran school in the
United States, was established in 1797 under the provisions of the will of
John Christopher Hartwick (1714–96), a Lutheran clergyman.

At COLLIERSVILLE, 80.3 *m.* (1,119 alt.,100 pop.) (*see Tour* 10), is the
junction with State 7 (*see Tour* 10), with which the route unites to ONE-
ONTA, 85.9 *m.* (1,120 alt.,11,649 pop.) (*see Tour* 10).

Section d. ONEONTA to KINGSTON; 92.9 m. State 28

From the Susquehanna Valley to the Allegheny Plateau and on to the
higher Catskills, State 28 follows the steep-walled water courses around
the mountain spurs, one of the routes of early nineteenth-century settlers
of the Susquehanna Valley.

South of ONEONTA, 0 *m.*, the road climbs to the crest of an S curve at
3.5 *m.*, high above the flood plain of the Susquehanna River.

DELHI, 20.3 *m.* (1,370 alt.,1,840 pop.), home of a State School of Agriculture, is a neat, modern town. Shortly after the Revolutionary War
Ebenezer Foote was so influential locally and as a member of the State legislature that he was nicknamed 'the Great Mogul.' At the suggestions of
facetious citizens the community was named for Delhi, India, the capital
city of the real Great Mogul. At Delhi is the junction with State 10, which
follows the valley of the West Branch of the Delaware, locally known as
Cat Hollow since 1843. At that time there was a lumber camp operating in
the valley that was dominated by an Amazon of a cook. Not only did she
knock out the bully who killed her cat but further punished the whole
crew by serving the pet in a surprise meat pie.

Near ANDES, 32.4 *m*. (1,600 alt.,395 pop.), occurred the climax of the 1845 antirent war (*see Tour* 21) in Delaware County. When under-sheriff Osman N. Steele attempted to evict a farmer for unpaid taxes, his neighbors, dressed as 'Indians,' with leather capes over their heads, cowhorns on their caps, and cowtails tied on behind, came to his aid, and in the struggle the sheriff was shot. Arrests were made and several convictions followed, but all sentences were commuted.

At 41.9 *m*. the route joins State 30 (*see Tour* 24), with which it runs in common for 3.2 miles.

MARGARETVILLE, 43.9 *m*. (1,325 alt.,771 pop.), catering to summer residents and tourists, is in a valley between 2,600-foot Pakatakan Mountain on the south and 2,211-foot Kettle Hill on the north, at the western boundary of Catskill State Park.

Right from Margaretville on a foot trail (blue markers) to a side trail, 10 *m*., which leads 0.2 *m*. to BALSAM LAKE. At 12.1 *m*. is the junction with a trail (yellow markers) leading (R) to HARDENBURG (2,200 alt.), 3.6 *m*. Camps consisting of lean-tos and fireplaces are at various points along the main trail and side trails.

An old wooden covered bridge, 45.8 *m*., built in 1845, carries the heavy Oneonta-Kingston traffic. It was erected without nails; all the heavy beams are held together by wooden pins.

In ARKVILLE, 45.9 *m*. (1,367 alt.,625 pop.), is the B.J.HARRISON PLANT (*open*), Roxbury Rd. A long two-story shingled building equipped with lathes, saws, and other wood-working machinery, it has operated continuously since 1840 as a furniture factory. The company operates its own sawmill, converting logs into lumber for folding chairs, bridge sets, and furniture specialties. The workers are skilled craftsmen, schooled by the early woodworkers in the mountains.

FLEISCHMANNS, 50.6 *m*. (1,515 alt.,495 pop.), is one of the major summer resort centers of the Catskill region. The town is built around its busy and colorful main street lined with stores and establishments for refreshment and amusement.

South of Fleischmanns State 28 runs through the central Catskills, where the wooded mountain sides are steep and each narrow hollow and valley has its stream, all excellent for trout fishing. Valley towns have become resorts much like Fleischmanns. Almost deserted in winter except for week-end skiers, they are alive in the early spring with sportsmen—flies in their hat bands, and trout as their principal topic of conversation; in summer they teem with gay New York City crowds that fill the porches of hotels and boarding houses, all of which advertise *kosher* food.

At PINE HILL, 55.1 *m*. (1,500 alt.,289 pop.), in the valley between Belle Ayr Mountain (3,380 alt.) and Rose Mountain (3,123 alt.), is the beginning of a foot trail.

Right on this foot trail (blue markers), which forms the backbone of a network of mountain trails in the Esopus Creek region to a system of ski trails on BELLE AYR MOUNTAIN, 1.2 *m*. The trail continues to the summit of EAGLE MOUNTAIN (3,700 alt.), 8.5 *m*.

At 57.9 *m*. is the junction with Big Indian-Claryville Road.

Right on this road, from which many hiking trails branch, to the junction, 8 *m.*, with the Slide Mountain Rd.; left here to the summit of SLIDE MOUNTAIN (4,204 alt.), 2.7 *m.*, and the SLIDE MOUNTAIN SKI TRAIL, suitable for novices or intermediates.

From the mouth of the SHANDAKEN TUNNEL (L), 63 *m.*, water from Schoharie Reservoir (*see Tour 24*) empties into Esopus Creek, which flows into Ashokan Reservoir (*see below*). This 18-mile tunnel through the mountains is one of the longest subterranean aqueducts in the world.

At 66.1 *m.* is the junction with a foot trail.

Right on this trail (yellow markers) through Woodland Valley, with a branch (red markers) over SLIDE MOUNTAIN (4,204 alt.), the highest Catskill peak.

In PHOENICIA, 67.4 *m.* (810 alt.,354 pop.), a crossroads summer resort, is the junction with State 214.

Left on State 214 to CHICHESTER, 1.6 *m.* (960 alt.,500 pop.), a village that in the summer of 1939 was on the auction block. For more than 100 years the woodworkers of the village earned a living making fine furniture in the community's one factory and living in the company's houses. But the firm failed in 1938, and, after a futile effort to revive the industry, the machinery was sold and the whole town was offered for sale.

At 78 *m.* is the junction with a macadam road.

Right here to the ASHOKAN RESERVOIR, 1.5 *m.*, completed in 1912, the largest of New York City's 24 reservoirs. For its construction more than 15,000 acres of land were acquired; seven villages were razed and their sites submerged; 32 cemeteries with 2,800 bodies were removed; 64 miles of highway were discontinued and 40 miles of new highway were laid out; 10 bridges were constructed for the new highways; a section of the Delaware & Ulster Railroad was transferred to another route; 2,000 inhabitants of the area were moved elsewhere.

Over 500,000,000 gallons of water flow daily to New York City from this 12-mile-long reservoir that has a water surface of 8,180 acres and an estimated capacity of 130,000,000,000 gallons. The aeration basin for the liberation of noxious gases is a vast fountain display of 1,599 sprays 50 feet high.

At 84.4 *m.* is the junction with State 375.

Left on State 375 to the junction with State 212, 3 *m.*; left on State 212 to WOOD–STOCK, 3.1 *m.* (560 alt.,350 pop.), widely known for the last 30 years as an artists' colony. The central part of the village bears a conventional appearance, with several fine old Colonial homes. The artists' studios are mainly clustered along the roads leading to the village and in outlying hamlets. Some of them are picturesque, and even eccentric, in their expression of the artists' personal tastes; many of them indicate the proverbial poverty of the artist. The colony numbers (1940) about 140 painters, sculptors, musicians, writers, and craftsmen. George Bellows was a member of the colony until his death in 1929; his family still lives in the home he built. Prominent residents are John F. Carlson, Eugene Speicher, Judson Smith, the Petershams, Norman Boggs, and John La Gatta. The Woodstock Art Association Art Gallery and the Gallery of the Sawkill Painters hold exhibitions during the summer.

Woodstock has almost all of the sport facilities associated with summer resorts. In recent years ski trails have been laid out on slopes close by the village.

The JOHN F. CARLSON SCHOOL OF LANDSCAPE PAINTING is the outgrowth of a school organized in 1902 by the Art Students League of New York City.

The WOODSTOCK SCHOOL OF MODERN ART, Judson Smith, director, specializes in mural painting.

BYRDCLIFFE, one mile north of the village on the slope of Outlook Mountain, was founded by Ralph Radcliffe Whitehead, who came here from England in 1902 and started Woodstock on its artistic career. The school has grown from a colony housed in one cottage to one of more than 30 buildings.

The truck farming country around WEST HURLEY, 85.2 *m.* (600 alt., 300 pop.), at the northeast corner of the Ashokan Reservoir, between the Hudson Valley and the Catskill Mountains, does not encourage laziness. Local farmers thought once to reform their Rip Van Winkle by the threat to bury him alive. Neither the threat nor the pine coffin, into which he permitted himself to be lifted, fazed him in the least. At last one soft-hearted neighbor offered two bushels of corn as the start of a new and industrious life. Lying back comfortably in his coffin, the lazy man said, 'Come on, boys. If it ain't shelled it ain't no use.'

State 28 crosses the highly cultivated Esopus Valley to KINGSTON, 92.9 *m.* (150 alt.,28,541 pop.) (*see Tour 21A*), at the junction with US 9W (*see Tour 21A*).

Tour 16

Jay—Wilmington—Lake Placid—Saranac Lake—Lake Clear Junction; 36.5 *m.* State 86.

Two-lane macadam, open throughout the year; icy in winter.
Hotels in villages; cabins between Wilmington and Lake Clear Junction; campsites between Wilmington and Saranac Lake.
Delaware & Hudson R.R. parallels route between Lake Placid and Saranac Lake; New York Central R.R. between Saranac Lake and Lake Clear Junction.

State 86 passes through farmland and conifer forests, past mountains and lakes, and crosses swamps where the dead trunks of trees rise skeletonlike, their gray-bleached knees deep in fern and moss-green stagnant water. The entire region is a grand vacation resort with every resource and device for summer and winter recreation, the principal centers being Lake Placid and Saranac Lake.

From the crest of a small hill west of JAY, 0 *m.*, (644 alt.,350 pop.), at the junction with US 9 (*see Tour 21*), is a glimpse of the grandeur of the high Adirondacks: Whiteface Mountain (4,872 alt.) towering in the foreground; Wilmington Mountain (3,458 alt.) rising to the northwest; and the peaks of Mount Marcy and Mount McIntyre cutting off the horizon to the south and west.

In WILMINGTON, 5.3 *m.* (1,020 alt.,574 pop.), is the junction with the NEW YORK STATE WORLD WAR MEMORIAL HIGHWAY (*open all year; tolls, adults $1, children 50¢*).

Right here up a serpentine mountain road to the parking area on WHITEFACE MOUNTAIN (4,872 alt.), 5 *m.* At the parking area, a few hundred feet below the summit, is the entrance to the elevator (*ascent 15¢, descent 10¢*) that rises through a giant shaft cut through the core of the mountain to a stone lookout tower at the summit, which can also be reached on foot over stairs and rock trails. The tower with a circle of windows is perched like a skull cap on the brow of the white mountain face.

Unlike Mount Marcy and the other high peaks, Whiteface is isolated, so that on clear days almost the entire northern part of the State is visible from its summit. To the south rises the humpy McIntyre Range; on the east stretches the irregular, gleaming spread of Lake Champlain, with the Green Mountains beyond; to the north is Mount Royal in Canada, marked by the pall of smoke over Montreal; and to the west is the St.Lawrence, and the rolling ridges that flatten out toward Lake Ontario. Weather instruments are anchored to knobs of rock on the eastern slope, and a radio station in the tower reports temperatures and atmospheric changes.

A State constitutional amendment was passed to permit construction of this $1,250,000 road over State-owned forest land.

South of Wilmington State 86 proceeds along a comparatively level stretch where both the valley and the stream become broader.

WILMINGTON NOTCH STATE CAMPSITE (R), 8.4 *m.* (*open, free, May 30–Sept. 15; 75 campsites; trout fishing*), is in a white birch grove overlooking the West Branch of the Ausable River.

HIGH FALLS GORGE (R), 9.5 *m.*, in Wilmington Notch, is a narrow defile between the precipitous slopes of Whiteface Mountain and the Sentinel Range which allows scant passage for river and highway. The gorge at the narrowest part of the pass has a falls with a 100-foot drop, access to which is controlled by a private concession (*adm.* 35¢).

NORTH AND SOUTH NOTCH TRAILS (L), 14 *m.*, for novices, are units in the Lake Placid ski trail system.

CONNERY POND STATE CAMPSITE (R), 14.4 *m.* (*open, free, May 30–Sept. 15; 8 campsites*), is a base for hikers climbing the trail to Whiteface Mountain.

From the campsite the Connery Pond Trail leads, by the shortest route, to the summit of Whiteface Mountain, 5.8 *m.*

At 17.2 *m.* is the junction with State 86A (*see Tour 16A*).

LAKE PLACID, 17.7 *m.* (1,880 alt.,2,930 pop.), built around Mirror Lake and surrounded by the highest Adirondack peaks, is a year-round sports community that has developed the surrounding natural resources for winter and summer activities: skiing, skating, bobsledding, ski-joring; golf, tennis, boating, swimming, fishing, and mountain climbing. Almost every sport has its annual competition, and the seasons merge in the midsummer indoor ice carnival. Exclusive clubs and large hotels provide city comforts for those who can afford them; tourist homes, cabins, cottages, and campsites accommodate vacationists who rough it on limited budgets.

The LAKE PLACID CLUB, on the east shore of Mirror Lake, was founded in 1895 by Melvil Dewey, inventor of the Dewey Decimal system for library classifications and advocate of phonetic spelling. A sports community in itself, this expensive club has its own post office, shops, and water supply, and complete recreational and sports facilities. Membership is by invitation; and it is said that even after they are in, members are classified according to degree of desirability. Forest Clubhouse, the main building, is the central unit for about 60 cottages, each containing as many as 10 rooms and renting for as much as $3,000 for the summer season.

The OLYMPIC ARENA, Main St., erected for the 1932 Olympic winter sports games, is 238 feet long and 143 feet wide. The ice rink, surrounded by seats for 3,360 spectators, is the scene of winter and summer ice carnivals and skiing contests. In summer the arena houses the Lake Placid horse show, flower shows, boxing matches, and special exhibits.

West from Lake Placid the route passes the PETTIS MEMORIAL FOREST (R), 19.8 m., a 3,000-acre area of white, red, Scotch, and yellow pine and Norway spruce, which was planted between 1906 and 1909 and named for Clifford Robert Pettis (1877–1927), a leader in New York State forestry.

The MEADOWBROOK STATE CAMPSITE (*open, free, Memorial Day to Labor Day*) is (L) at 23.1 m. on a seven-acre evergreen tract.

At 23.5 m. is the junction with a macadam road.

Right on this road to the RAY BROOK SANATORIUM, 0.8 m., a New York State institution for the treatment of incipient tuberculosis. The sanatorium accommodates 300 patients.

The WILL ROGERS MEMORIAL SANATORIUM (*open 9–10, 2–4*), 25.6 m. (R), on 48 acres of ground, is a three-story fireproof structure in the Norman style, with wings radiating from a central tower. Built in 1930 by the National Variety Artists Club for its tubercular members, the sanatorium is now open to radio and screen actors, who are rapidly supplanting the old vaudeville troupers in the show business. It was named for Will Rogers, the cowboy philosopher from Oklahoma.

SARANAC LAKE, 27.5 m. (1,540 alt.,7,132 pop.), on Flower Lake and about one mile northeast of the lake from which it gets its name, is a world-famed health resort for tubercular people. Sanatoria and houses have an air of being ready for the painter with their scaffoldlike sun porches.

Although classified as a village, Saranac is virtually an independent city of stores, banks, motion picture theaters, newspapers, hospitals, and churches run by the people who have settled here because their dormant tuberculosis becomes active in less beneficial climates. There is a carefree gaiety here typical of such resorts that makes the town a popular winter and summer recreational center for healthy people.

In its early days Saranac was a center for Adirondack guides and lumbering. Jacob Smith Moody, the first settler in the region, came here in 1819 and cleared 16 acres of land; while all of his sons became guides, Martin Moody, or Uncle Mart, guided the most distinguished list, including Governor Horatio Seymour, Presidents Chester A. Arthur and Grover Cleveland, and the members of the Philosophers' Camp (*see Tour 17*).

Captain Pliny Miller erected a sawmill here in 1827, and Saranac developed slowly as an isolated lumbering settlement. In 1876 Dr.Edward Livingston Trudeau (1848–1915), a New York physician who had contracted tuberculosis, came to Saranac to die, but was so benefited by the climate that he established here the first outdoor sanatorium (*see Tour 17*) for the treatment of tuberculosis, and also the first laboratory for the scientific study of the disease.

The SOCIETY FOR THE CONTROL OF TUBERCULOSIS, 64 Main St., was organized in 1907, with Dr.Trudeau as its first president, to educate the community in the proper sanitary care of tubercular patients, to inform the public on methods of controlling the disease, and to discourage the sending of indigent, hopeless consumptive cases to the Adirondacks.

The SARANAC LABORATORY FOR THE STUDY OF TUBERCULOSIS, 7 Church St., founded in 1894 by Trudeau in a small cottage where he first isolated the bacillus, is a modern stone, glazed brick, steel, and cement building with a white tile interior. The John Black Memorial wing contains the most comprehensive library on tuberculosis in the country. The staff of this privately financed laboratory, which makes approximately 5,000 examinations a year, has developed a bacteriological technique that has been widely adopted in the study and treatment of the disease. In the College for Physicians, under the management of the Trudeau Foundation, doctors are trained in methods of diagnosing and treating tuberculosis.

The STEVENSON MEMORIAL COTTAGE (*adm.* 25¢; *Wed. free*), Stevenson Lane, maintained by the Stevenson Society of America, is a simple two-story, white-painted, clapboard cottage with a large porch extending around three sides, the yard enclosed by a low white fence. During the six winter months of 1887–8, when Robert Louis Stevenson lived here under the care of Dr.Trudeau, he wrote a number of essays, including *Pulvis et Umbra*, *The Lantern Bearers*, and *Christmas Sermon*, finished the *Master of Ballantrae*, and revised the manuscript of *The Wrong Boy*.

The CLUBHOUSE OF THE SARANAC LAKE CURLING CLUB, 122 Beaver St., built in 1930 to replace its outgrown predecessor, is equipped with six ice sheets, a skating rink, and a heated spectators' balcony. Teams from eastern Canada and the United States compete here annually for the Patterson Memorial Trophy and the Mitchel Medal; the Gordon International Curling Match, the outstanding event in the sport, was played here in connection with the winter Olympics in 1932. With the growth of interest in winter sports, this national game of Scotland, which is much like bowling on ice, is spreading in the United States and Canada. The origin of the game is uncertain, but for more than three centuries it has been played in Scotland, where the Grand Caledonian Curling Club, established in 1838, formulated the rules that now govern the game.

Saranac Lake is at the junction with State 3 (*see Tour* 17).

In the STATE FOREST NURSERY, 35.3 *m.*, 28,000,000 trees are being grown for use in reforesting denuded areas and controlling erosion.

LAKE CLEAR JUNCTION, 36.5 *m.* (1,630 alt.,348 pop.), is at the junction with State 10 (*see Tour* 18).

Tour 16A

Lake Placid—Keene—Keene Valley—Junction US 9; 26.1 *m.* State 86A.

Two-strip macadam open throughout the year; icy in winter.

State 86A penetrates a section of the Adirondacks famous for winter sports, summer hiking, and year-round beauty. Trails lead from the highway to the summit of Mount Marcy, highest point in the State.

From LAKE PLACID, 0 *m.* (1,880 alt.,2,930 pop.) (*see Tour* 16), State 86A twists through rocky farmland toward a narrow pass between highwalled mountains.

At 2.9 *m.* is the junction with a hard-surfaced road.

Right on this road 0.6 *m.* to the State-maintained JOHN BROWN'S FARM (*open*), including his home, a weatherbeaten, clapboarded house now a museum for mementos of his life; his grave, fenced off and marked by a boulder; and a bronze statue of him dressed in the rough clothes and cowhide boots of an Adirondack farmer, with his arm protectingly around the shoulder of a Negro boy. The statue was erected by the John Brown Memorial Association, which conducts an annual pilgrimage to the place on May 9. At the age of 18 John Brown (1800–59), a Connecticut Yankee by birth, saw a slaveholder beat a Negro boy with a shovel and resolved to free the slaves. In 1849 he became associated with Gerrit Smith (*see Tour* 8), who was offering free farms on his land here to Negroes, and settled on this farm to help the Negroes till the soil. The venture failed because the land was unsuited for cultivation and the Negroes could not quickly adapt themselves to the rigors of Adirondack winters. But to John Brown this place remained home, and to it he returned between his excursions in liberation.

In 1855 he and five of his sons were fighting the free-soil battle in Kansas. In 1856 he was back East smuggling escaped slaves into Canada and meeting Thoreau and Emerson. On the night of October 16, 1859, with his sons Watson and Oliver at his side, he captured the rifle plant and the main arsenal at Harpers Ferry, Virginia, his purpose being to use this as a base for guerilla warfare in the South to free the slaves. The next day the militia stormed the arsenal; Brown was captured and his two sons were killed. In spite of appeals by Emerson, Thoreau, Whittier, and others, John Brown was hanged; he himself had observed prophetically: 'I am not incapable of error and I may be wrong but I think that perhaps my object will be nearer fulfillment if I should die.'

In 1920 the INTERVALES (Olympic) SKI JUMP (R), 3.2 *m.*, was constructed on Intervales Hill and in 1927 was redesigned by Dr.Godfrey Dewey. The total distance from the top of the tower to the foot of the lower hill is 660 feet; stands give spectators an unobstructed view. An annual tournament is held on Washington's Birthday and an intercollegiate meet between Christmas and New Year's.

At 4.6 *m.* is the junction with a macadam road.

Right on this road 5 *m.*, through wild, mountainous country, to HEART LAKE and ADIRONDACK LODGE (*accommodations for limited number of nonmembers*).

Henry Van Hoevenberg and Josephine Schofield, his intended bride, came here in 1880 and planned to build a home, but Josephine died within a year. Van Hoevenberg returned and built the original Adirondack Lodge as a memorial to her; it was destroyed by a forest fire in 1903. The present structure was erected a few years ago by the Lake Placid Club.

Van Hoevenberg blazed and improved many of the trails in the Mount Marcy region that start at Heart Lake. The longest is INDIAN PASS TRAIL, which cuts through one of the most rugged Adirondack gorges to Mount Marcy. Red markers denote the beginning of the trail at the junction of the road to Adirondack Lodge just north of Heart Lake. On this trail, INDIAN PASS, 5 *m.*, a great ravine about one mile long, whose vertical sides rise over 1,000 feet, is formed by WALLFACE MOUNTAIN (3,860 alt.) (R), an almost vertical wall, and MOUNT MacINTYRE (4,411 alt.) (L), its peak almost one mile overhead. From the trail branches lead to Lake Henderson and Mount MacIntyre. The summit of MOUNT MARCY (5,344 alt.), the highest point in the State, is at 18.3 *m.*

The MOUNT VAN HOEVENBERG BOBSLED RUN (*open about Dec. 20–Mar. 1; half-mile ride 50¢; mile $1*), 4.1 *m.* (R), was designed by Stanislaus Zentzytski of Berlin, engineer of the famous Schreiberhau run in Germany, and was constructed in 1930 at a cost of $250,000 by the New York State Olympic Winter Games Commission. After the 1932 Olympics, the run was taken over and is now operated by the State Conservation Department. The large steel bobs used for the ride weigh 485 pounds (four-man) and 352 pounds (two-man). In the 1932 Olympics, United States teams won both the four-man and the two-man events. Their time was 1 minute 54 seconds for the four-man sled, and 1 minute, 57 seconds for the two-man sled.

The run is about 1.5 miles long and has 26 curves; sleds on speed runs travel from 40 to 60 miles an hour. Some of the curves are 22 feet high, their banks almost vertical. The surface of the run is glare ice made by freezing a mixture of snow and water; the straightaway is covered with a thin frosting of snow to enable the sled runners to bite in and hold the track. Sleds are equipped with brakes, so that the speed is always under control. From seven telephones and control stations operators observe every foot of the slide; when one of the infrequent spills occurs, the starter is notified and the run is closed until obstructions have been cleared. The rustic Adirondack-style clubhouse at the bottom of the run has comfortable rooms, a special layout for viewing the last curve and finish, and a special circuit for operating the electrical timing device which records the speed of the bobs in hundredths of seconds.

At 7.4 *m.* is the beginning of a foot trail.

Right on this trail (*red markers, 2,000 ft. ascent, steady footing*) to the summit of CASCADE MOUNTAIN (4,092 alt.), 2 *m.* The right fork leads to the summit of PORTER MOUNTAIN (4,070 alt.) 2.5 *m.*

State 86A crowds through the narrow pass between Cascade and Pitchoff Mountains; a series of streams spider their way down the rocky wall of Cascade Mountain to the narrow bed of CASCADE LAKES (R), strung like a long, narrow ribbon along the road.

At 10 *m.* is the beginning of a foot trail marked by a small rustic bridge over a swift-running brook.

Left on this trail (*red markers, ascent 1,500 feet, steep footing*) to an open ledge at 0.8 *m.*, beyond which it veers to the northeast, reaching the summit of PITCHOFF MOUNTAIN (3,450 alt.), 1.8 *m.*, with sweeping views of mountain terrain: Owls

Head Mountain in the east, Cascade Mountain in the south, Sentinel Range and Lake Placid in the north and northwest.

KEENE, 14.1 *m.* (860 alt.,380 pop.), is at the junction with State 9N (*see Tour* 21), with which State 86A runs in common for 1.5 miles and then swings east across a flat plain with mountains rising to the south and east.

KEENE VALLEY, 17.5 *m.* (1,040 alt.,450 pop.), boasts of the oldest school district in the Adirondacks, its school records preserved from the year 1813. Some of the most famous of America's landscape painters have had studios here; among the earliest were John Fitch, Roswell Morse Shurtleff, A.F.Tait, and A.H.Wyant. The grandeur of the valley and the surrounding mountains was transferred to canvas and found its way into the leading art galleries of the country. Shurtleff, born in New Hampshire in 1839, was drawn to Keene Valley in 1868 by the paintings of John Fitch. He is credited with having designed the Confederate flag while a prisoner during the Civil War. Having bought a tract of primeval forest in the valley, in 1885 he built his studio from plans local carpenters called the 'damndest confusionedest things.' These practical builders of plain houses designed for comfort in winter could not understand the Japanese umbrella 16 feet in diameter that the artist designed for a ceiling.

Other nature lovers, scholars, and eminent professional men who made Keene Valley their summer home were Noah Porter of Yale, after whom Porter Mountain was named, Professors William James of Harvard and Willard Fiske of Cornell, Charles Dudley Warner, Felix Adler, the Reverend Joseph H. Twichell, and the Reverend Horace Bushnell.

One of the most colorful Keene Valley intellectuals was Thomas Davidson (1840–1900), who opened the Glenmore Summer School here for his Concord School of Philosophy. Although it started out in an old farmhouse, it gradually spread over a dozen or more detached buildings, but disintegrated after Davidson's death. As a leader of ethical socialism in England, he had previously founded the Fellowship of the New Life; the Fabian Society, formed by dissenting members, was an offshoot of this organization. The Bread Winners College in New York City's lower East Side was one of Davidson's more successful ventures.

At the Keene Valley Inn is the junction with the Johns Brook Trail, the oldest and best known eastern approach to Mount Marcy.

Right here, following the southern shore of Johns Brook, past junctions with other trails, to JOHNS BROOK LODGE, 4.2 *m.* (*open in summer; lodging, meals, supplies*), which is owned by the Adirondack Mountain Club and serves as a take-off point for the Mount Marcy trails. At 4.8 *m.* the Johns Brook Trail enters virgin timber, mostly conifer; Bushnell Falls (L), 5.5 *m.*, in a deep ravine, are named for Horace Bushnell, one of the group of climbing clerics who spent their summers in Keene Valley. At Bushnell Falls lean-to, 5.8 *m.*, is the junction with the Slant Rock Trail (red markers).

Left here to the summit of MOUNT MARCY (5,344 alt.), 9.3 *m.*, highest point in the State, from where there is an excellent view of the MacIntyre Range.

Orson Schofield ('Old Mountain') Phelps (1817–1905), who wandered into Keene Valley in 1845, is credited with having blazed the first trail to Marcy from the east in 1849. Charles Dudley Warner, whom Phelps knew as 'Charlie,' preserved his eccentricities in *The Primitive Man*, a portrait of the philosophic mind 'in the earthy exterior.' Shot into prominence by his friend Charlie, Phelps published *The Growth of a*

Tree, filled with his rugged, earth-tinged 'speckerlations.' 'Soap is a thing that I hain't no kinder use for,' he declared.

At 18.1 *m.* is the junction with a dirt road.

Right on this road 0.5 *m.* to ST.HUBERT'S INN, a large white frame building named for the patron saint of the hunted deer. It stands on the site of a hotel built by Smith Beede in 1876. The Ausable Lake and Mountain Club, owners of the present inn, has increased its holdings to 28,000 acres (*open with certain restrictions*), including Upper and Lower Ausable Lakes.

At 26.1 *m.* is the junction with US 9 (*see Tour* 21).

Tour 17

Plattsburg—Saranac Lake—Tupper Lake—Watertown—Hannibal; State 3. 247.9 *m.*

Two-lane concrete and macadam.
Delaware & Hudson R.R. parallels route between Plattsburg and Saranac Lake; Grass River R.R. between Tupper Lake and Cranberry Lake; New York Central R.R. between Benson Mines and Sackets Harbor.

Running north of the more popular Adirondack tourist routes, State 3 loops across the northern lobe of the State between Lakes Champlain and Ontario through regions where the ugly scars left by ruthless nineteenth-century lumbermen have not yet been covered over by second growths and where the tourist trade and thin-soil farming have been unable to take up the slack left by the declining lumber and iron-mining industries. The Black River Valley was part of the lands purchased by French *émigrés* in the early decades of the nineteenth century with the aim of establishing here a 'Little France.'

Section a. PLATTSBURG to TUPPER LAKE; 72.2 m. State 3

The Saranac Valley, which the highway follows for 40 miles, is a slice of backwoods America left stranded by the receding lumber and iron industries in the eighties. On the farms are weatherbeaten houses without barns but with rambling outhouses. Here and there a pioneer log cabin still serves as a home—logs hewn square around two or three rooms, the crevices chinked with plaster, the whole sometimes made gruesome with a ghostly coat of whitewash. But the Saranac Valley is no Tobacco Road. Besides farming, the men work on the roads, bolster the larder by hunting and fishing, and get a little hard money by selling surplus milk or lumber cut on the farm woodlot and sawed at one of the three or four sawmills operating in the valley.

Southwest of Saranac Lake, rugged, heavily timbered, mountain-bound State land is broken by innumerable ponds, lakes, and streams; in the Raquette River Valley are swamps ugly with the rotting stumps of once magnificent stands of timber.

West of PLATTSBURG, 0 *m.* (140 alt.,14,713 pop.) (*see Tour* 21), State 3 follows for several miles the route of a plank road built in 1850 to haul iron ore out of the mountains.

At 9.3 *m.* is the junction with State 374.

Right on State 374 through mountainous country to DANNEMORA, 5.2 *m.* (1,400 alt.,3,348 pop.), named for the city in Sweden because of the high quality of its iron deposits. A forbidding, 20-foot-high concrete wall (L), topped by round, glass-enclosed lookouts, encircles the CLINTON STATE PRISON (*not open to public*), with some 40 buildings and 2,000 inmates, on a tract of about 14,000 acres.

In 1845, 90 convicts from Sing Sing and Auburn were brought here to work privately owned iron deposits on Dannemora Mountain; the mines were taken over by the State in 1866, but, showing a steady loss, were abandoned in 1880. The combination of labor in the mines and the long, bitter winters earned the place the name 'Siberia of the North.' But mining has been replaced by the manufacture of toweling, ticking, and yarn, and by farming. Some 1,500 prisoners study courses ranging from reading and writing to engineering and the arts. In July 1929, a riot took place, said to have been led by 'lifers,' in which three prisoners lost their lives.

West of Dannemora, State 374 climbs the shoulder of Dannemora Mountain, descending to touch the foot of CHAZY LAKE (*fishing*), 11 *m.* At 14.2 *m.* is the beginning of a foot trail to the summit and fire observation tower of LYON MOUNTAIN (3,830 alt.), 3 *m.*

LYON MOUNTAIN, 17.6 *m.* (1,753 alt.,1,136 pop.), with its streets of uniform, frame company houses, is near the northwestern base of Lyon Mountain; dust from mine tailings covers the countryside and huge piles of slag identify the mines of the Chateaugay Ore and Iron Company, which has worked these beds since 1873. From a shaft sunk more than 1,600 feet into the mountainside, miners blast out the ore, which is crushed, separated, concentrated, and sintered in a tangle of buildings and conveyors on a hilltop, to emerge ore of such high quality that it is in demand in every part of the United States and Canada. The great cables of the Brooklyn and Golden Gate bridges get their strength from iron mined in the bowels of Lyon Mountain.

State 374 continues north through an almost primitive wilderness to LOWER CHATEAUGAY LAKE (*bathing, boating, fishing, hunting*), 27.8 *m.*

CHAUTEAUGAY, 35.8 *m.* (972 alt.,1,169 pop.), is at the junction with US 11 (*see Tour* 18).

State 3 follows the Saranac River past several decadent villages that were built around nineteenth-century lumbering activities and iron mines. The Saranac Valley iron industry reached its peak in the early forties and declined about 1880 because of competition from the western ore beds and the exhaustion of the local supply of wood for charcoal burning.

In REDFORD, 21 *m.* (1,100 alt.,500 pop.), Charles Corning and Gersham Cook of Troy established a glass factory in 1831 and permanently abandoned it 20 years later. The secret of manufacture died with the men who invented the process; white Potsdam sandstone was a principal ingredient and was melted in imported pots made of Stonebridge clay. Today the pale green Redford glass, in the form of goblets, vases, balls, canes, and crown window glass, is a collector's item.

In MERRILLVILLE, 35.1 *m.* (1,725 alt.,130 pop.), is the junction with State 99.

Right on State 99 to LOON LAKE POST OFFICE (*golf, riding, tennis, boating, bathing, fishing*), 3.3 *m.* (1,759 alt.), on the southeastern shore of Loon Lake. In 1879 Fred W. Chase built his crude 31-room hotel here; Chase's successors run a 3,000-acre resort colony with hotel rooms and sumptuous private cottages for 500 wealthy guests.

Loon Lake is one of the many lakes comprising a chain between here and Old Forge (*see Tour* 15), which affords a scenic canoe route.

State 3 crosses a rolling hill land of small farms with weatherbeaten houses, tangles of little outbuildings, fields of hay, corn, and potatoes, and thin pastures grazing a few cows and sheep.

Clinging to a hillside above the highway, TRUDEAU, 49.8 *m.* (1,650 alt.,225 pop.), is the home of the TRUDEAU SANATORIUM, the tuberculosis hospital established in 1885 as the Adirondack Cottage Sanatorium by Dr.Edward Livingston Trudeau (*see Tour* 16). Around the large central buildings the 22 large cottages housing 300 patients are grouped on the terraced hillside, each with its large screened or glass-enclosed cure porch where the 'curers' rest on their white cots. Near the entrance gate is the famous LITTLE RED (*open*), a small, two-room, red-painted wood cottage, one of the two structures in which Dr.Trudeau started his sanatorium, preserved as a memorial and containing mementos of the great pioneer in the cure of tuberculosis. In front of the Administration Building is the bronze TRUDEAU STATUE, a life-size figure by Gutzon Borglum representing the doctor in a reclining position, shawl over his shoulders, gazing thoughtfully over the panorama of river, valley, and mountain.

SARANAC LAKE, 51.2 *m.* (1,540 alt.,7,132 pop.), is at the junction with State 86 (*see Tour* 16).

Southwest of Saranac Lake State 3 cuts for nearly 16 miles through an almost unbroken wilderness and swampland along the eastern and southern shores of Lower, Middle, and Upper Saranac Lakes; the road, although graded, has not been completely surfaced (1940).

At 60.5 *m.* is the beginning of a foot trail.

Left on this trail, 2.7 *m.*, with a 1,700-foot ascent, to the crest of AMPERSAND MOUNTAIN (3,365 alt.). At its southern base is Ampersand Lake, along whose shore William J. Stillman bought 22,500 acres from the State in 1858 as a home for the Adirondack Club, which grew out of Camp Maples, as it was named by James Russell Lowell, or the Philosophers' Camp, as the guides called it. The Philosophers' Camp of August 1858 was an excursion of Boston's Saturday Club intelligentsia into the wilds of the Adirondacks on Follensbee Pond, near Tupper Lake; the company included, besides Stillman, Ralph Waldo Emerson, James Russell Lowell, Louis Agassiz, Ebenezer R. Hoar, and Jeffries Wyman. Longfellow was invited but, it is said, declined when he heard that Emerson was taking a gun along. Emerson, who wrote a dull poem describing the expedition, tried to smoke a pipe and be 'one of us' and got sick.

At 64.4 *m.* the highway crosses the INDIAN CARRY between Upper Saranac Lake and the Raquette River. Indian relics discovered here support the theory that a thoroughfare or chain of settlements extended between the Champlain Valley and that of the Upper St.Lawrence. The carry is one of the overland links in the 150-mile canoe route between Old Forge at the southern end of the Fulton Chain of lakes (*see Tour* 15) and Loon Lake (*see above*).

At 66.6 *m.* is the eastern junction with State 10 (*see Tour* 18), with which State 3 runs in common to Tupper Lake. The route skirts the lowlands and backwashes of the Raquette River and passes SUNMOUNT (R), 71 *m.*, the United States veterans' hospital for tubercular victims of the World War, a group of interconnected three-story brick buildings.

TUPPER LAKE, 72.2 *m.* (1,569 alt.,5,271 pop.), is two parts industrial and one part resort center. The village attracts fishermen in the spring, idlers in summer, hunters in the fall, and skiers in the winter. It was once the industrial and commercial metropolis of the Adirondacks, with large lumbering, papermaking, and woodworking plants. Only one plant remains, the Oval Wood Dish Company, making wooden butter dishes and employing about 200. In 1889 'Uncle John' Hurd extended his Northern and Adirondack Railroad to the shore of Tupper Lake and built a giant sawmill, around which the early village grew.

At Tupper Lake is the western junction with State 10.

Left on State 10, at 2.7 *m.*, is the beginning of a foot trail; left on this trail to the summit of MOUNT MORRIS (3,163 alt.), 4.5 *m.* The first fire observation tower in the Adirondacks was erected on Mount Morris in 1909.

Arising from the surface of BIG TUPPER LAKE (*fishing*), 6.4 *m.*, are many islands, gnarled and fistlike. Private camps line the lake shore; fishermen troll and cast for trout, whitefish, and landlocked salmon.

At 8.7 *m.* is the junction (R) with State 421; right here 1.6 *m.* to the AMERICAN LEGION MOUNTAIN CAMP for convalescent war veterans.

State 10 crosses LONG LAKE (*fishing*), 25 *m.*, a long, narrow body of crystal-clear water, which is actually the widened channel of the Raquette River. During spring floods the water level is sometimes raised as much as 14 feet; therefore boathouses stand on stilts.

LONG LAKE, 27 *m.* (1,660 alt.,225 pop.), is at the junction with State 28N (*see Tour* 15).

Section b. *TUPPER LAKE to WATERTOWN;* 103.1 *m. State* 3

For more than 50 miles west of TUPPER LAKE, 0 *m.*, State 3 twists past swampy backwashes and fields of rotting stumps, a wasteland despoiled by lumbering operations and slowly being reclaimed by second growths of birch, beech, and spruce. The few villages, bunched around lumber and paper mills, are ghosts of their former prosperous selves.

CRANBERRY LAKE (*fishing, hunting*), 26 *m.* (1,502 alt.,85 pop.), on the lake of the same name, is a summer resort of hotels and cottages.

At 34.2 *m.* is the junction with a macadam road.

Left on this road 1.7 *m.* to the NEW YORK STATE RANGER SCHOOL, associated with the State College of Forestry, Syracuse University; the school offers 45 or 50 young men between 18 and 35 years old a 44-week course in forestry, ranger service, management of forest estates and nurseries, and general conservation work.

West of the Adirondack State Park, whose western boundary is crossed at 54.5 *m.*, the countryside levels out and farms grow more numerous; but cultivation is a struggle, and farmers 'sow pebbles in the spring and reap boulders in the fall.'

At 66.8 *m.* is the junction with a macadam road.

Right on this road 1.5 *m.* to LAKE BONAPARTE, named for Joseph Bonaparte (*see Tour* 18), who bought several large North Country tracts as part of a plan to erect a 'Little France' in the northern wilds of New York.

NATURAL BRIDGE, 74.8 *m.* (820 alt.,400 pop.), is named for the arch eroded from the limestone by the Indian River; caverns (*boat trip* 25¢) extend 1,000 feet underground.

CARTHAGE, 84.2 *m.* (742 alt.,4,205 pop.), is an important papermaking town; the paper mills, on both sides of the Black River, produce tissues, bags, kraft, and board. One plant produces chemicals used in papermaking.

West of Carthage State 3 closely follows the Black River, which in the 26 miles to Lake Ontario drops 480 feet through a series of rapids and waterfalls, supplying water power for a number of paper mills, nuclei for communities of millworkers living in clusters of company houses. One of the largest of these is DEFERIET, 90.3 *m.* (641 alt.,739 pop.), which sprang up almost overnight after a paper mill was erected in 1900 by the St.Regis Paper Company. The place was named for Baroness Jenika de Ferriet, who about 1830 built a beautiful mansion, called the Hermitage, on the bank of the Black River. Here she lived with her servants, entertained other French *émigrés* including Joseph Bonaparte, cared for her flowers, and played on the first grand piano in the North Country. Shortly after her return to France in 1840 the house burned down.

In GREAT BEND, 92 *m.* (677 alt.,400 pop.), a papermaking village, is the junction with a country road.

Right 1 *m.* on this road to PINE CAMP, 13,000 acres of submarginal sand plain used by the U.S.Government as a summer military training camp and maneuver ground.

WATERTOWN, 103.1 *m.* (478 alt.,33,323 pop.) (*see Tour* 18), is at the junction with US 11 (*see Tour* 18), State 37 (*see Tour* 19), State 12 and State 12E (*see Tour* 25).

Section c. *WATERTOWN to HANNIBAL;* 72.6 *m.* State 3

State 3 pushes toward the blue expanse of Lake Ontario over the bed of the old Sackets Harbor-Watertown plank road and courses down the lake shore past War of 1812 battlefields, sandy bathing beaches, and summer cottage colonies.

West of *WATERTOWN*, 0 *m.*, are prosperous dairy farms, pastures close-cropped by blooded stock, and stretches of corn, oats, and hay broken by woodlots.

In 1823 Stephen Blanchard erected BLANCHARD'S LIBRARY (L), 3.9 *m.*, as an inn for the slowly developing North Country. Converted into a library in 1913, it houses a collection of rare manuscripts and books on the settlement of the area.

At 8.8 *m.* is the junction with the concrete Sackets Harbor Road.

Right on this road 0.5 *m.* to the GUTHRIE HOME, a two-story brick dwelling erected in 1801 and occupied from 1817 to 1848 by Dr.Samuel Guthrie (1782–1848), physician, chemist, and inventor, one of the three men credited with the discovery of chloroform, though he was unaware of its anesthetic value and used it to 'needle' his whisky. His invention in 1823 of a highly improved percussion pill and firing lock made the old flintlock obsolete.

SACKETS HARBOR, 1.5 m. (246 alt.,742 pop.), is a lakeside village of wide, shaded streets and spacious old dwellings settled in 1801. On July 19, 1812, five British battleships sailed into the harbor and were met by the American ship *Oneida* and a land force of farmers equipped with a single cannon, the 'Old Sow' (*see Tour* 25), which fired the first shot in the War of 1812. The men wrapped 24-pound balls, the only ammunition available, in old carpet to make them fit the 32-pound gun. The British fire 'broke nothing but the Sabbath,' most of their shots falling short of the bluff; a 32-pound ball from a British gun fell beyond the bluff and was rushed to the Old Sow, a sergeant crying, 'We've caught 'em out now, boys, send it back.' The shot tore the mast from the *Royal George*, British flagship; the *Oneida's* 16 guns had crippled the other ships; and the British withdrew.

MADISON BARRACKS (R), at the east village line, a U.S.Army post accommodating 45 officers and 1,040 enlisted men, consists of rows of brick and stone barracks and officers' homes around an oval-shaped parade ground. U.S.Grant was stationed here in 1843–9; contrary to popular legend about Grant's fondness for liquor, it is said that he organized the Sons of Temperance in Sackets Harbor.

In the OLD MILITARY CEMETERY (L), Broad St., surrounded by a fence that once enclosed the White House in Washington, are the graves of General Zebulon Pike, discoverer of Pike's Peak, and other soldiers of the War of 1812.

·SACKETS HARBOR BATTLEGROUND, north end of Main St., a public park overlooking the lake, contains a monument to the memory of the soldiers who fought in the Battle of Sackets Harbor.

The OLD UNION HOTEL (L), Main St., a stone building erected in 1817, is a museum maintained by the Sackets Harbor Civic League, containing Indian implements and documents and relics of the War of 1812.

The AUGUSTUS SACKET HOME (L), Main St., a spreading, white frame dwelling built in 1801 and still occupied, was used as a hospital during the War of 1812.

At 18.5 m. is the junction with a macadam road.

Right on this road 0.6 m. to HENDERSON HARBOR (*bass fishing*), a popular summer resort with hotels, cottages, and inns overlooking Horse Island in the Bay. During the War of 1812, sharpshooters were stationed here to harass the British in their attempt to reach the mainland from Horse Island.

The OTIS HOUSE (R), 28.5 m., a weatherbeaten frame structure with gable roof and end chimneys, was used as a hospital for British soldiers following the Battle of Big Sandy. A granite boulder, 28.8 m., marks the scene of that night skirmish.

The Americans at Sackets Harbor were building the *Superior*, a great ship of war, which was to carry 66 guns. A fleet of rowboats, loaded with guns and supplies for the ship, started up Lake Ontario from Oswego. Discovered and fired on by British men-of-war, the Americans put in at Sandy Creek, unloaded their stores and defeated a British landing party. All supplies, except a four-ton cable, were loaded into oxcarts and transported to Sackets Harbor. But no vehicle was sturdy enough to carry the cable. After a week's delay 100 soldiers from Colonel Stark's militia regiment shouldered the cable and trudged the 20 miles to Sackets Harbor in two days.

Southward several roads swing right from State 3 to lakeside resorts (*fishing, golf, bathing*). In PORT ONTARIO, 40.2 m. (280 alt.,75 pop.), is SELKIRK SHORES STATE PARK (*parking* 25¢), of 800 acres, opened in 1928. Improved by CCC workers, the park has 200 fireplaces and tables for picnics, a long pier jutting into the lake, and trails through dense woods. Fishing is good.

MEXICO, 48.2 *m*. (384 alt.,1,297 pop.), is at the junction with US 104 (*see Tour* 26). FULTON, 64.4 *m*. (400 alt.,13,337 pop.), is at the junction with State 57 (*see Tour* 26). HANNIBAL, 72.6 *m*. (330 alt.,410 pop.), is at the junction with US 104 (*see Tour* 26).

Tour 18

Rouses Point—Malone—Watertown—Syracuse—Binghamton—(Scranton, Pa.); US 11.
Rouses Point to Pennsylvania Line, 329.8 *m*.

Two-lane concrete.
Rutland R.R. parallels route between Rouses Point and Winthrop; New York Central R.R. between Potsdam and Syracuse; Delaware, Lackawanna & Western R.R. between Syracuse and the Pennsylvania line.

US 11 is the main artery of travel between Canada and New Orleans. Between Rouses Point and Watertown it parallels the Canadian border; then runs south through the heart of the State, a great dairying region, to the Pennsylvania line. Along the road are milk platforms on which the farmers leave their full milk cans to be picked up during the night by New York City milk trucks. There are several industrial cities. Around Watertown are landmarks recalling the romantic story of the French *émigrés* who settled in Jefferson and St.Lawrence Counties after the downfall of Napoleon. Other sites commemorate incidents in the War of 1812. Side routes lead to Canada and the Thousand Islands.

Section a.   *ROUSES POINT to MALONE;* 55 *m.   US* 11

Between Rouses Point and Malone US 11 goes through a region of pasture land and small fields of corn and potatoes. Originally an Iroquois war trail, this stretch became the Military Turnpike, a link in the overland route between Lakes Ontario and Champlain, which was completed in 1826.

In the middle 1800's hard-fisted, devil-may-care French-Canadian lumberjacks, packs strapped to their backs, came across the border to the camps of the North Country lumber industry, then beginning to boom. Upon depletion of the forests they settled on the land, eking a bare existence from the soil.

US 11 runs west from the border town of ROUSES POINT, 0 *m*. (120 alt.,1,920 pop.) (*see Tour* 21).

US 11 becomes the main street of CHAMPLAIN, 5 *m*. (120 alt.,1,197 pop.), which manufactures bookbinding machines and grows peonies. French Canadians who threw up cabins here in the late 1790's named their settlement for Samuel de Champlain, discoverer of the lake that bears his name.

At the 'Four Corners' in MOOERS, 13 m. (260 alt.,465 pop.), is the junction with State 22 (see Tour 20).

CHATEAUGAY, 42 m. (972 alt.,1,169 pop.), with its maple-lined streets and ample lawns, has a New England appearance. Named for the adjoining Canadian land grant owned by Charles Lemoyne, founder of an eminent Canadian family, the village was settled by French Canadians in 1796. A blockhouse was erected here at the outbreak of the War of 1812. General Wade Hampton's troops invaded Canada from here in 1813, retreating in rout after a brief engagement with the British.

MALONE, 55 m. (730 alt.,8,657 pop.), straddles the Salmon River, site of hydroelectric plants. Paper mills, woolen mills, railroad shops, tanneries, milk and cheese factories, and powder mills furnish work for about 1,500 persons. Slightly more than 60 per cent of the residents, Catholics of French-Canadian descent, speak both French and English. English is taught in the grade schools; parents teach their children French in their homes. The people listen to French programs from Montreal radio stations, attend ice hockey games at Montreal, and spend many winter hours snowshoeing across country.

The place was settled by Vermonters in 1802; the name was bestowed by William Constable, an early landowner, in honor of his friend, Edmund Malone, Shakespearian scholar. In 1866, 2,000 Irish-American members of the United States Fenian Society, formed in 1858 to supply arms and money to the movement in Ireland for an Irish Republic, came to Malone with the purpose of seizing Canada and then striking a bargain with England whereby the Dominion would be returned for the freedom of Ireland. Canada stationed troops along the international line and established a gun-boat patrol on the St.Lawrence. With no commissary, no discipline, and no lines of supplies, the poorly armed mob crossed into Canada on June 2, 1866, exchanged shots with a detachment of Canadians, and retreated in disorder to Malone, where they disbanded.

The WHEELER HOUSE, Elm St., now the clubhouse of the local Elks Lodge, was the home of William Almon Wheeler, Vice President of the United States under President Hayes, 1877–81. The present owners have preserved the front section of the building, erected in 1857, as it was when occupied by Wheeler.

Left from Malone on State 10 to MEACHAM WOODS, a thick stand of timber extending along the road for seven miles, 18.2 m. to 25.1 m. It was named after Thomas Meacham, hunter and trapper, who purchased the land in the early nineteenth century. MEACHAM LAKE STATE CAMPSITE (L), 22.7 m. (fishing, boats for rent), is one of the newer camping areas.

North from the campsite on a foot trail 2.5 m. to the summit of DEBAR MOUNTAIN (3,305 alt.).

State 10 continues southward, crossing the East Branch of the St.Regis River at 24.7 m. and passing through the largest State reforestation area in the Adirondack State Park, some 3,800 acres, burned over in 1903, and today containing a stand of

3,853,000 spruce and pine. The area is cared for by the CCC and protected by State rangers.

At 34.5 *m.* is the junction with State 192.

1. Right on State 192 to PAUL SMITHS, 0.3 *m.*, a hotel established in 1859 by Apollos A. Smith, a guide to wealthy sportsmen. It now has a private park of 33,000 acres, with a clubhouse, golf courses, and a bathing beach.

2. Left on State 192 to the EPISCOPAL CHAPEL OF ST.JOHN'S OF THE WILDERNESS, 0.3 *m.*, a beautiful little stone structure tucked away in the woods. Originally of oiled logs, it was established in 1877, burned in 1928, and was rebuilt in 1930. Dr.Edward Livingston Trudeau of Saranac Lake supervised the erection of the original chapel. The road continues to GABRIELS, 3.8 *m.* (1,704 alt.,200 pop.), and the GABRIELS SANATORIUM, conducted by the Sisters of Mercy, which has been caring for tubercular patients since 1897. State 192 continues to the junction with State 3 (*see Tour* 17), 9.1 *m.*

On State 10, UPPER ST.REGIS LAKE (R), 36.8 *m.*, is almost entirely surrounded by the luxurious camps of men of wealth. UPPER ST.REGIS LANDING (L), 37.6 *m.*, is a point of departure for short and long canoe trips through the Adirondack lakes.

LAKE CLEAR JUNCTION, 41.1 *m.* (1,630 alt.,348 pop.), is at the junction with State 86 (*see Tour* 16).

In the ADIRONDACK FISH HATCHERY, 43.9 *m.*, brook, lake, and rainbow trout and whitefish are hatched, and the fingerlings are used to restock the brooks and streams of the State.

At 45.8 *m.* is the junction with a macadam road; left here 0.5 *m.* to SARANAC INN (*open July* 15–*Oct.* 15). Begun in 1864 by James S. Hough on a small plot of land at the north end of Upper Saranac Lake, it is now a private park of 26,000 acres, with accommodations for 800 guests and a large variety of recreational facilities. Grover Cleveland was a frequent guest, and Charles E. Hughes, Chief Justice of the U.S. Supreme Court, has often vacationed here.

The FISH CREEK POND CAMPSITE (*fireplaces; canoes rented*), 49.9 *m.*, considered one of the most attractive Adirondack campsites, encircles the entire shore line of two small lakes. From the campsite there are several hiking trails; a popular canoe trip of about ten miles, with three carries, leads through several ponds.

UPPER SARANAC LAKE, 52 *m.*, has all types of Adirondack fish.

At 54.5 *m.* is the junction with State 3 (*see Tour* 17).

Section b. MALONE to WATERTOWN; 116.1 m. US 11

In this section are rich pasture lands, blooded cattle, and big barns. The road skirts the foothills of the Adirondacks, following the fall line between the Adirondack upland and the St.Lawrence plain, where the drop in the northward-flowing streams provides water power for paper mills and other factories. The people are almost all of hardy native stock, mainly Yankee.

West of MALONE, 0 *m.*, the route passes through a number of hamlets dependent principally upon small-scale lumbering and the farm trade. POTSDAM, 42 *m.* (433 alt.,4,136 pop.), is supported by dairy farmers, tourists, and the students and teachers of its two educational institutions.

In 1804 William Bullard and others came here from Massachusetts, pooled their resources, and purchased a tract of land, on which they established the 'Union.' Property was held in common, an accurate account of labor and materials contributed by each member was kept, and all proceeds were divided pro rata annually. The group prospered for a few years, but a demand by more indolent members for an equal division of income led to internal strife, resulting in dissolution in 1810, and the land was evenly divided among the members.

In the nineteenth century the sandstone quarries, now almost completely flooded by Hannawa Falls, employed hundreds of workers. The durable stone, of a deep, rich, lasting red color, was used in the construction of the House of Parliament, Ottawa, and All Saints Cathedral, Albany. But beginning with the late nineties, largely because of the cost of transportation, sandstone gradually lost its popularity.

The POTSDAM STATE NORMAL SCHOOL, Main St. above Park St., is a four-story red brick building erected in 1918. The school is an outgrowth of the old St.Lawrence Academy, founded in 1816, and turned over to the State in 1867. A three-year course provides training for prospective teachers. Besides regular practice teaching, students are trained in the education of subnormal children in a special practice school featuring manual arts, and in the care of children of pre-school age in the nursery school.

The THOMAS S. CLARKSON MEMORIAL COLLEGE OF TECHNOLOGY, Main St., known familiarly as Clarkson Tech., was founded in 1895 by Frederica, Elizabeth, and Lavina Clarkson as a memorial to their brother, Thomas S. Clarkson, Jr. The original red sandstone building provides facilities for woodworking, metal work, and chemistry. The student body numbers about 400, the faculty 35. Degrees are given in civil, chemical, industrial, electrical, and mechanical engineering.

Left from Potsdam on Pierrepont Ave., which becomes State 56, to HANNAWA FALLS, 4.8 m. (560 alt., 301 pop.), a hamlet spreading from the falls of the same name. Here the Raquette River, 300 feet wide, falls 85 feet. A masonry dam forms a pool almost three miles long that covers 200 acres.

Wide, tree-arched streets with bordering lawns lend a parklike atmosphere to CANTON, 53 m. (363 alt., 2,822 pop.), on the Grass River, settled by Vermonters in the early 1800's. It is the seat of St.Lawrence County and the home of St.Lawrence University and of a New York State School of Agriculture. The name, like that of Potsdam, was a chance selection from an atlas.

The story is told that in 1825, when the completion of the Erie Canal had made York Staters canal-minded, a local candidate for the assembly was elected as the result of a 'canal campaign'; his proposal was to join the St.Lawrence and Lake Champlain with a canal across the Adirondack Mountains.

On the crest of a hill on College Ave. are the buildings of ST.LAWRENCE UNIVERSITY, a coeducational institution chartered in 1856. The enrollment is approximately 700; the faculty numbers 86. The State School of Agriculture occupies land belonging to the university. Although the school is State-operated as a separate institution, the trustees of the university constitute the school's board of visitors. The Theological School (Universalist) has its own building and separate faculty, trustees, funds, and government. As provided by its founders, the College of Letters and Science is nonsectarian in its teaching and influence. The Law School, which became part of the university in 1903, is at 375 Pearl St., Brooklyn, New York.

Most conspicuous among the buildings is the GUNNISON MEMORIAL CHAPEL, an English Gothic structure with a corner tower and a steep slate roof, designed by Bertram Grosvenor Goodhue. The new dormitories are in part the gift of Owen D. Young, alumnus.

In 1878, at the age of 21, Irving Bacheller (1859——) moved here from his farm home in Pierrepont, six miles east, and entered St.Lawrence University. For 16 years after graduation, during which time he wrote for newspapers, Bacheller studied 'the hard-headed Yankee folk in the fertile valley of the St.Lawrence,' who were to serve as prototypes for the characters in his novel *Eben Holden* (1900). *The Master of Silence* (1892), *The Still House of O'Darrow* (1895), and *Darrel of the Blessed Isles* (1903) are among his other works.

Frederic Remington (1861–1909), artist, sculptor, and author, was born in the REMINGTON HOUSE (*private*), a large frame structure with portico, on Miner St. near Main St. He studied art with the Art Students League in New York City and at Yale, where he played on the football eleven captained by Walter Camp. After a year on a mule ranch in the West, he and Richard Harding Davis, novelist, were sent to Cuba by William Randolph Hearst to secure 'evidence' of Spanish brutality. Remington mailed his boss a few paintings, then, convinced that there would be no war, asked for his recall. Hearst is said to have cabled: 'You furnish the pictures; I'll furnish the war.'

Remington was fond of western subjects for his art; critics consider *Horses in Motion* his best canvas and *Bronco Buster* his foremost work of sculpture. His books include *Pony Tracks*, *Crooked Trails*, and *Stories of Peace and War*. A collection of his paintings hangs in the Remington Art Memorial, Ogdensburg.

GOUVERNEUR, 78 *m*. (428 alt.,4,015 pop.), on both banks of the Oswegatchie (Ind., black water flowing out) River, is the trading center for the 1,000 workers in the near-by talc mills and talc, lead, and zinc mines. Two small local industries—a marble quarry and a silk and hosiery mill—furnish about 100 jobs for men and women.

Gouverneur Morris purchased a large tract of land here in 1798, and seven years later the village was settled. In 1867 talc (magnesium silicate) was discovered in this region and it has since become an important product. In the mills, talc is ground to the fine finished form in which it is used as electrical and heating insulation, in the manufacture of rubber, and as a filler in paper, paint, roofing, rope, and plaster manufacture. Zinc mining began in 1915; the ore is sphalerite (sulphide of zinc). The lead ore (galena, sulphide of lead) is sent to St.Joseph, Missouri, to be refined.

At the eastern village limits is the unoccupied GOUVERNEUR MORRIS MANSION (R), a two-story stone house with hipped roof, erected in 1809. The rear of the building, facing the hillside, has no windows. Toward the end of a long political career, Gouverneur Morris (1752–1816) spent some time on his estate here. He had been Minister to France during the Reign of Terror and, so the story goes, had acquired costly jewels, plate, and other valuables from the fleeing French nobility, much of which he brought to this house. Since he had no children, relatives expected to inherit this wealth. To their disappointment, however, a son was born after Morris's death.

From these circumstances an elaborate ghost story has grown up. According to this story, his widow, Anne Morris, was sitting before the fire on New Year's eve, 1817, when she heard hoofbeats outside. There was a knock at the door and a man's voice demanded that she bring out her husband's will. At that moment the figure of Morris stepped down from a portrait on the wall, opened the door and frightened away the intruders, and then led the widow from room to room, showing her where the treasures were hidden.

At 90.7 m. is the junction with a macadam road.

Right on this road 6 m. to OXBOW (351 alt.,250 pop.), where the Oswegatchie River makes a complete loop, forming a bow-shaped lake. At the western end of the hamlet is the BENTON HOUSE, a large two-story brick structure built by Joseph Bonaparte in 1838. Joseph Bonaparte escaped to America after the Battle of Waterloo and, assuming the title of Count de Survilliers, settled in New Jersey and married Annette Savage, a beautiful Quakeress, despite the fact that he had a wife in Italy. In 1822 he moved his family to Natural Bridge, where he erected a house and a hunting lodge on the 80,000 acres he had purchased with the Spanish crown jewels. In 1838 the Bonapartes moved to the Benton House here.

The short, stout nobleman, invariably accompanied by four giant gendarmes who had fled France with him, became a familiar figure in this region. Here he was often host to French émigrés from Cape Vincent who rode on the lake in his gondolalike boat and ate from his plates of gold, while he, dressed in a green hunting suit, told jokes and recited poetry. Near the outlet of the lake, Bonaparte had a stump carved into a comfortable chair, from which he shot deer when they came down to drink. The chair was made very broad, since, in the words of one of his guides, Bonaparte 'had quite a beam amidships onto him, and he had to have room for himself.' In 1839, after settling a large sum on Annette and their daughter Caroline, Bonaparte rejoined his wife in Italy. He died in 1844.

During the Second Empire, Caroline accepted the invitation of Napoleon III and sailed for France with her daughter Josephine and her son Louis Joseph. She was legitimized by the Emperor, who said: 'You are a Bonaparte, my cousin. I see my uncle Joseph in your face.' Her daughter became maid-of-honor to the Empress. In 1871, after the retirement of the Royal family, Caroline returned to America with her daughter, leaving her son in a French military school. She died in Richfield Springs in 1890. Her grave is in the small Oxbow Cemetery.

The smokestacks of a large milk products plant pierce the skyline of EVANS MILLS, 105 m. (431 alt.,514 pop.), a farm center at the junction of West and Pleasant Creeks. Ethni Evans, New Hampshire millwright, who settled here in 1803, gave his name to the hamlet.

The PALMER HOUSE (R), Main and Factory Sts., a two-story brick hotel, was erected in 1821 and is still operating (1940). Here 'Prince' John Van Buren, son of President Martin Van Buren, lost his mistress by the flip of a coin. The girl was Maria Amerigo Vespucci, descendant of the man after whom America was named. The incident is described in Walter Guest Kellogg's novel, *Parish's Fancy*. Van Buren and George Parish of Ogdensburg had spent an evening at poker, with Maria watching the game. Van Buren lost $5,000 given him by a client for the purchase of land. 'You fancy the lady, Mr.Parish?' he asked. 'She is yours, if your luck holds good.' The girl was put up against the $5,000; a coin was flipped and Parish won. Van Buren complimented the winner, bid the lady adieu, and left.

In 1851 a group of farmers met in the OLD STONE HOTEL, Factory St. near Main St., now an apartment house, and organized the present internationally known Agricultural Insurance Company.

In the center of the village is the junction with a concrete road.

Left on this road 3 *m.* to LERAYSVILLE (532 alt.,60 pop.); right here on a dirt road 0.5 *m.*, to the stately French Renaissance LERAY MANSION (*open by appointment*), erected by LeRay in 1806–8. The main building is of two stories, with one-story wings; its principal feature is a wide, two-story Ionic portico surmounted by an open balustrade. Original ceilings, doors, and woodwork are well preserved.

James LeRay de Chaumont (1760–1840), French nobleman whose father had expended a large share of his fortune in the American cause, came to America in 1785 and presented his claims for reimbursement, which were settled by the Government in 1790. LeRay bought thousands of acres in the present Jefferson and Lewis Counties in 1802, erected a home, and brought his family to Leraysville six years later. He developed the new territory, building sawmills and gristmills, forges and blast furnaces, powder mills, wharves, and warehouses, and encouraging agriculture. His presence here attracted a number of French *émigrés* to this region.

Gateway to the Thousand Islands and the Adirondacks, WATERTOWN, 116.1 *m.* (478 alt.,33,323 pop.), a trading and industrial center, is bisected by the Black River, which falls 112 feet within the city, powering 55 industries. Manufactured products include paper, papermaking machines, air brakes, plumbing supplies, and surgical instruments. From the Public Square in the center of the city, bordered by business blocks and the huge bulk of the Woodruff Hotel, the principal streets radiate unsymmetrically, trailing off into residential sections.

In 1800 five New Englanders hacked their way up from the Mohawk Valley, stopped at the rocky Black River Falls, and named the site Watertown. They built sawmills and gristmills along the river, and burned piles of lumber for potash. Residents of near-by hamlets flocked to the settlement to work in carpenter and machine shops, barrel shops, and sash and blind factories.

The papermaking industry began with a rag mill in 1809 and reached its peak in the 1890's, when the Black River Valley was one of the Nation's leading papermaking districts. The industry started on the downgrade in the early 1900's when the supply of spruce dwindled.

The five and ten cent store originated here during county fair week in 1878. Frank W. Woolworth (1852–1910), a clerk in Moore & Smith's general store, piled leftover odds and ends on a table and put up a sign: 'Any Article 5¢.' The entire stock was sold out in a few hours. Inspired by this success, Woolworth opened his first store in Utica the following year.

The JEFFERSON COUNTY HISTORICAL SOCIETY BUILDING (*open Tues.–Sat.* 9–12:30, 2–5), 228 Washington St., contains collections of Indian curios, historical materials relating to the era of French settlement, and pioneer furniture.

The FLOWER MEMORIAL LIBRARY, Washington St., is a two-story-and-attic marble building in the neoclassic style of the Beaux Arts period of the early 1900's. The building was donated by Mrs. Emma Flower Taylor in memory of her father, Roswell P. Flower, governor of the State, 1892–5. The library exhibits relics of Indian life and French occupancy.

Watertown is at the junction with State 3 (*see Tour* 17), State 37 (*see Tour* 19), and State 12 and 12E (*see Tour* 25).

Section c.   *WATERTOWN to SYRACUSE;* 69.5 *m.*   *US* 11

South of WATERTOWN, 0 *m.*, the route crosses the flat Lake Ontario plain. The villages are much alike, with their tree-lined streets, truck gardens, one-family frame houses, and small industries. Most of the land is given over to pasture. Oxcarts of the pioneers followed an Iroquois war trail; during the middle years of the nineteenth century the road was turnpiked. The first automobile trip from Watertown to Syracuse, in 1900, took an entire day; gasoline was purchased in drug stores; repairs were made in blacksmith shops. In 1906 the same trip was made in two hours and 45 minutes, a record that stood for years.

In 1818 Charles Grandison Finney (1792–1875), a native of Connecticut, entered a law office in ADAMS, 13.8 *m.* (600 alt.,1,613 pop.), and was admitted to the bar two years later. At that time he 'manifested an antagonism to religion,' but Mosaic references in his law books led him to secure a Bible. Conversion came suddenly one day in 1823 when the Lord appeared before him and gave him 'a mighty baptism of the Holy Spirit.' Finney was ordained in 1824, and the same year converted the entire village of Evans Mills. A handsome, well-proportioned man, six feet, two inches tall, he made a profound impression upon his listeners. 'Violent physical manifestations resulted from his preaching; people burst into tears, shrieked, fainted, and fell into trances' as Finney portrayed 'the terrible guilt of sin and the consequences of the disobedience to God.' He continued his sensational work in Utica, Troy, Rome, and other towns. Some prominent members of his own sect, including Lyman Beecher, Moses Gillett, and Heman Humphrey, were displeased by his methods, and in 1827 a conference was held in New Lebanon to settle the matter; but the decision was in Finney's favor. In 1834, after a successful revival in a New York City theater, the Broadway Tabernacle was built for him. The following year he established the theological department at Oberlin College, then in its infancy. He was president of Oberlin from 1851 to 1856.

Mormons 'without scrip or purse,' led by Prophet Joseph Smith, arrived here in dusty, canvas-roofed wagons in 1841, put up in farmhouses, and started a drive for converts, which caused bitter dissension, often splitting families. Farmers sold their holdings and gave the proceeds to Smith, and some of them left with him for Ohio a year later.

The MORTON HOUSE (*private*), a small frame building on South Main St., was the birthplace of J.Sterling Morton (1832–1902), Secretary of Agriculture in the cabinet of President Grover Cleveland, who moved to Nebraska in his youth. Arbor Day is celebrated on his birthday, April 22.

Marietta Holley (1836–1926) lived most of her life in the HOLLEY HOUSE, 16.8 *m.*, a two-story frame house, now a tourists' home. Her birthplace near by has long since disappeared. A semirecluse, Miss Holley described North Country life and manners in her books with a sentimental humor; her *Around the World with Josiah Allen's Wife* was a best seller of the 1880's.

At the southern end of MANNSVILLE, 21.2 *m.* (630 alt.,313 pop.), is the KLAN HAVEN HOME (R), a roomy old frame house set on 300 acres of farmland. About 30 orphans of Klansmen are kept here; funds are supplied by Ku Klux Klan headquarters in Atlanta, Georgia. The boys are trained in farming, the girls in domestic science.

CENTRAL SQUARE, 52 *m.* (460 alt.,542 pop.), was the northern terminus of the Salina (Syracuse) and Central Square Plank Road, the first plank road in the country, 14 miles long and eight feet wide, built by George Geddes. The planking, laid crosswise on sills, was partially imbedded in packed earth to prevent decay. Millions of dollars were invested in plank roads before their popularity subsided in the seventies.

Right from Central Square on Phoenix Road to CAUGHDENOY, 3.4 *m.* (370 alt., 250 pop.), on the Oneida River (Barge Canal). Along the shore are the shacks of thirty-odd fishermen, each of whom pays the State $20 a year for the privilege of maintaining eel weirs, or traps, small wooden boxes with a wire entrance that opens inward but not outward. These traps are suspended from a wire stretched across the river at the proper depth. In early morning and late evening, the fishermen in rowboats empty the traps and transport the catch to the eel factory, an abandoned barn on the shore, where the eels are killed, skinned, and cooked. They are then pickled or smoked, cut into pieces from one to two inches long, and packed in glass jars. New York City delicatessen stores provide the main market. In the late nineteenth century, when eel appetizers were the fad, Caughdenoy factories packed 3,000 eels a day. Because of the diminished demand, the daily average has dropped to about 150.

CICERO, 59.9 *m.* (396 alt.,410 pop.), is famed for its frogs' leg dinners. In horse-and-buggy days, tally-ho parties came from Syracuse to enjoy the dish, said to have been introduced to this section by early French expatriates; today automobile parties make the same trip for the same purpose. Cicero Swamp, a 14-mile stretch that grows thick clumps of tamarack and balsam with underlying peat beds, supplies the frogs.

SYRACUSE, 69.5 *m.* (400 alt.,205,637 pop.) (*see Syracuse*), is at the junction with State 5 (*see Tour 11*) and State 57 (*see Tour 26*).

Section d. SYRACUSE to PENNSYLVANIA LINE;
89.2 m. US 11

This section is the most beautiful stretch of the entire route, especially north of Tully, where the road rides high above the farm-spotted Tully Valley and then drops abruptly into the Tioughnioga Valley. Fields of hay and corn stretch east and west from the road, backed by the hills that form the divide between the watersheds of the St.Lawrence and Susquehanna Rivers. Derricks standing over salt wells seem out of place in this pastoral panorama.

The road is built on one of the trails followed by the Sullivan-Clinton expedition. In the 1790's, New England pioneers, many of whom had served with Sullivan and Clinton, traveled westward in covered wagons over the Cherry Valley Turnpike, turned south at La Fayette, and erected cabins on the banks of the Tioughnioga. Fugitive slaves on their way to

Canada stole along the turnpike, remaining overnight or for days at a time in the homes of friendly farmers. A few of these Underground Railroad stations still stand. The population is about 75 per cent native born, and many trace their ancestry to the New England pioneers.

South from SYRACUSE, 0 *m.*, in NEDROW, 5.4 *m.* (520 alt.,250 pop.), is the junction with State 11A.

Right on State 11A to the hill-enclosed ONONDAGA RESERVATION, 1 *m.*, a 7,300-acre tract occupied by descendants of the Onondaga (Ind., people of the great hill) Nation, part of the Iroquois Confederacy. On the reservation are scores of unpainted two- and three-story houses, three churches, a two-story public school, two council houses, and a State health office. Less than 100 of the inhabitants are full-blooded Indians. Only a few work small farms on the reservation or hire out by the day on the near-by fruit orchards and truck gardens. Most of the Indians find work in Syracuse homes or factories, the more affluent driving to Syracuse daily in decrepit automobiles, the others hitch-hiking or walking the macadam road to Nedrow, at the end of the Syracuse trolley line.

The 200 descendants of the Oneida, the Cayuga, and Canadian Indians, who live among the Onondaga, do not receive the annual Government subsidy of a few yards of cheap cloth, a few pounds of salt, and $2 in currency, given to each Onondaga annually in accordance with the terms of the early treaties. Rentals received from white men's industries on the reservation—sand banks, a stone quarry, and pipe lines—are distributed by the sachems with the approval of the general body and of the Government Indian agent.

More than 70 per cent of the inhabitants have embraced Christianity; the others adhere to the doctrines of Handsome Lake (*see Tour* 11), nineteenth-century Indian prophet. The wary chiefs walk cautiously between the two religions. The green corn festival at the end of August, the week-long harvest feast in October, and the strawberry feast and thunder dances during the second week in June are advertised in newspapers. Tickets of admission are reasonably priced, and 'hot dogs' and soda pop are sold on the grounds. These festivals have been somewhat influenced by the circus; the ancient simple Onondaga headdress of a cap with three feathers has given way to the conventional feathered war bonnet of the prairie tribes.

The nation still retains the form of the ancient government of the Iroquois Confederacy, electing 14 sachems to the Iroquois Council; though the nominal rulers of the reservation, the sachems are subject to removal by mass ballot. Some 150 children are enrolled in the reservation public school. Many continue through high school in Syracuse, and several have been graduated from the State College of Forestry and other colleges of Syracuse University; only a few of the better educated Indians return to the reservation. Clinics held weekly by the State Department of Health have resulted in a marked improvement in health. In 1939, after a powwow that erased fear from the minds of the superstitious, the Indians allowed the installation of electric lights in their homes.

The ONONDAGA COUNCIL HOUSE (L), 2 *m.*, is a two-story structure, 68 feet long and 25 feet wide, built of white pine clapboards. The interior is a large meeting room with chairs and benches along the sides and a fireplace at each end. The GRAVE OF HANDSOME LAKE, in a small plot adjoining the Council House, is marked by a weathered granite stone.

At 16 *m.* is the junction with US 20 (*see Tour* 8). US 11A continues south to CARDIFF, 16.5 *m.* (676 alt.,100 pop.), which made newspaper headlines in October 1869, when the 'Cardiff Giant' was unearthed by workmen digging a well on the farm of William Newell. The giant figure, over 10 feet tall and proportionately broad, frightened Onondaga Indians, who immediately recalled their legend of the stone giant of the Cardiff hills who made forays into Indian villages each morning and chose a warrior for breakfast. As curious crowds gathered, Newell erected a tent over the hole and charged admission. Doctors and archeologists examined the figure and proclaimed it a petrified human being, even pointing out the stony pores. A group of businessmen from Syracuse and neighboring communities purchased the 'corpse' and placed it on exhibition. It was sold and re-sold, its value ever increasing until a one-eighth share was worth $25,000.

The hoax was revealed when physicians discovered that the giant was solid gypsum and had no petrified heart, lungs, or other internal organs. Investigation disclosed that George Hull of Binghamton, Newell's brother-in-law, had contracted to have the figure cut from a two-ton block of Iowa gypsum by stoneworkers in Chicago. A wet sponge filled with sand was used to erase chisel marks; the 'pores' were made with needles and a hammer. The figure was boxed, shipped by rail to Union, near Binghamton, then hauled overland at night in a large wagon and buried, late in 1868, at the future 'well' site. Despite the exposure, dozens of Cardiff Giants toured American medicine shows and fairs. P.T.Barnum, unable to purchase the original, had a duplicate made. In 1934 the giant was taken from a warehouse in Iowa, exhibited at the State Fair in Syracuse, then shipped back to Iowa to become a permanent exhibit in a private museum.

At 23.5 m. US 11A rejoins US 11.

LA FAYETTE, 12.1 m. (1,160 alt.,100 pop.), is at the junction with US 20 (see Tour 8).

HOMER, 31.7 m. (1,140 alt.,3,195 pop.), has a village green reminiscent of an old New England common, with churches and school in an orderly row. Brick structures of the Civil War period dominate the six-block business section. Industries manufacture flannel shirts and fishing tackle; beans canned here have a national distribution.

Homer was the locale of Edward Noyes Westcott's *David Harum* and the birthplace of David Hannum, around whom Westcott built his chief character. Hannum, a shrewd, quick-witted Yankee horse-trader, was faultless in attire, 'never appearing without his high silk hat and a kerchief in his breast pocket.' Innumerable legends have followed him down through the years. One tells of the time a man offered $15 for a white dog with black spots. Hannum completed the sale after paying an urchin 5¢ for a white dog on which he painted the required spots. Approached by the irate purchaser shortly after a storm, Hannum remarked: 'I guess I forgot to give you the umbrella that went with the dog.' 'Do others or they'll do you—and do 'em first!' was his business slogan. Late in life he lost his entire fortune in land speculation.

Francis Bicknell Carpenter (1830–1900), portrait painter, was born in the CARPENTER HOUSE, a two-and-one-half-story frame structure at the north village line. Carpenter made his first sketches with lampblack on scrap paper and on pieces of board. At the age of 16 he opened a studio in Homer. His original commission, for which he received $10, was to illustrate a book on sheep husbandry. His best known work, *Lincoln Reading the First Draft of the Emancipation Proclamation*, hangs in the Capitol at Washington. A group of his paintings are among the collection in the HOMER ART GALLERY (*free, 9–4 workdays*) in the Homer Academy, on the village green.

Andrew Dickson White (1832–1918), historian, State senator, first president of Cornell University (*see Ithaca*), and United States Minister to Germany and Russia, was born in the WHITE HOUSE, corner of Main and Albany Sts., a two-story Victorian brick home.

The STODDARD HOME, a two-story brick dwelling in the rear of the Braeside Inn, corner of Main and Albany Sts., was the birthplace of William

Osborn Stoddard (1835–1925), author of boys' books, inventor, and secretary to Abraham Lincoln. Besides his more than 70 books for boys, he wrote a *Life of Abraham Lincoln.*

At the north village limits is the junction with a macadam road.

Right on this road 0.7 *m.* to the SALISBURY-PRATT HOMESTEAD (*private*), a station on the Underground Railroad. This section of the railroad followed the Tioughnioga and Tully Valleys between Binghamton and Syracuse and the Oswego Valley between Syracuse and Oswego. In 1851, when Frederick Douglass, orator and journalist (*see Rochester*), was prevented from speaking in Homer by a barrage of missiles, Oren Carvath, abolitionist, who owned the house, resigned as deacon of the Congregational Church, sold his farm, and moved to Oberlin, Ohio. His son, Erastus M., who made the education of the Negro his life's work, collected funds for the founding of both Atlanta and Fisk Universities and was the first president of Fisk.

CORTLAND, 34.5 *m.* (1,122 alt.,16,113 pop.), is the home of 30 industries, manufacturing wire cloth, lingerie, corsets, truck parts, and other products. About 1,700 Italians live in the eastern section of the city close to the wire mills, where most of them work. Here customs of the homeland prevail: parades and fireworks feature the celebration of Saints' Days; wedding festivities continue long after the bride and groom have departed on their honeymoon.

As many as 250 Italian families, many from New York, are brought to Cortland County each summer in cannery-owned trucks and transported from farm to farm to pick beans—lima, string, and kidney. Some farms are company-owned, others company-subsidized. Workers live in company-owned homes, long wooden structures suggestive of the barracks found in Army camps during the World War. A company canteen sells food and other necessities. A family of four—two adults and two children —average about $200 during the working season, which lasts from late June to late August.

Elmer Ambrose Sperry (1860–1930), inventor, was born in Cortland. Sperry is credited with 400 patents, including the gyroscopic compasses and stabilizers used in ships and airplanes, high arc searchlights, and designs for improvements on electric street railway cars and electric automobiles.

Left from Cortland on State 13 to TRUXTON, 11.4 *m.* (1,150 alt.,609 pop.), birthplace of John J. McGraw (1873–1934), baseball's 'master mind.' Tiring of farm life at the age of seventeen, McGraw joined the Olean baseball team. A scrappy little lad with a passion for the game, he won the attention of baseball scouts, and was signed the following year by the Baltimore Orioles of the American Association, one of the most famous teams of all time. Among his teammates were Miller Huggins, later manager of the New York Yankees, and 'Connie' Mack, later manager of the Philadelphia Athletics. On July 19, 1902, McGraw became manager of the New York Giants, holding that position until June 3, 1932, when he voluntarily retired. Called the 'Little Napoleon,' he ruled the Giants with an iron hand, going to the extreme of calling every pitch from the dugout. Under his guidance the team won ten National League pennants and three world's championships.

At 70.5 *m.* US 11 joins State 12 (*see Tour 25*), with which it runs in common to BINGHAMTON, 76.4 *m.* (845 alt.,78,242 pop.) (*see Binghamton*), at the junction with State 17 (*see Tour 3*) and State 7 (*see Tour 10*).

South of Binghamton is a countryside of rolling hills and lush flatlands. Scattered homes house workers employed in the Triple Cities (*see Binghamton*). Irish section hands who helped lay the railroad through here objected loudly but unsuccessfully against the rule which compelled them to board with their section bosses. The food apparently left much to be desired, for the following song, later a vaudeville favorite, sprang into existence:

> The boss was a foine man, all aroun'
> Till he married a great big fat far down!
> She bakes good bread, and she bakes it well,
> But she bakes it hard as the hubs of—
> Eeee—yah!

At 89.2 *m*. US 11 crosses the PENNSYLVANIA LINE, 41 miles north of Scranton, Pennsylvania.

Tour 19

Malone—Massena—Ogdensburg—Watertown; 133.3 *m*. State 37.

Two-lane macadam or concrete.
The Grand Trunk R.R. parallels route between Fort Covington and Massena; New York Central R.R. between Ogdensburg and Theresa.

In a wide northern arc State 37 sweeps across the flat dairy country between Malone and Watertown, running for many miles close to the St.Lawrence River. The river rapids roll white between low, shelving shores; here two nations, proud of their century-old peace, build bridges rather than forts.

The North Country was opened up late. In 1776, when Sir John Johnson and 300 Tory sympathizers fled from Johnstown, traveling on foot for 19 days to reach the St.Lawrence near the mouth of the Raquette River, they pierced through an unknown region; as late as 1813 Spafford in his *Gazetteer* called Franklin County 'the least valuable county in the State.'

The vast St.Lawrence Valley ships millions of pounds of milk and milk products to the New York City market, produces aluminum products and electric power, transports Pennsylvania coal to Canada, and imports Canadian pulpwood. Inland lakes and the St.Lawrence and its tributaries provide extensive fishing.

Northwest from MALONE, 0 *m*. (730 alt.,8,657 pop.) (*see Tour* 18), State 37 follows the Salmon River through flat, sandy dairy country relieved by scattered patches of second-growth pine. Only ten years settled when the Embargo Act of 1808 was enacted, defiant pioneers refused to be denied their principal income, which came from the sale of potash in Canada. They used many subterfuges to evade the law; one was to throw up a flimsy hut on a border hilltop, fill it with barrels of potash, then remove a keystone from the foundation and let the hut and its contents topple down into Canada.

In the autumn of 1812 General Wade Hampton, guarding the border, built a blockhouse at what is now FORT COVINGTON, 15.8 m. (166 alt., 764 pop.). A year later General James Wilkinson left Sackets Harbor (see Tour 17) to join Hampton for an attack on Canada; but the British had stopped Hampton at Chateaugay, and Wilkinson was badly defeated in the Battle of Chryslers Field, across the border, on November 11, 1813. One of the Americans killed in the battle was Brigadier General Leonard Covington, for whom the village is named. Wilkinson returned to the fort here and dug in for the winter; some of his men died of cold and starvation. In 1814 the British captured the fort.

From 1818 to 1824, when the State matched bounties on wolves voted by counties, and a wolf's head brought $60, farmers in this region enjoyed lucrative hunting, using the same head several times and passing off dog and deer heads for those of wolves. During 1820–2 more than $55,500 was paid in bounties in Franklin County, amounting to an average of $12.50 for every man, woman, and child. A State investigation finally ended the fraud.

The ST.REGIS INDIAN RESERVATION, 19.9 m., nine miles long and three miles wide, half of it in Canada, is home for 2,800 United States and Canadian Indians, who live in straggling story-and-a-half cabins and unpainted frame houses. As a result of intermarriage, mostly with French Canadians, fewer than 100 full-blooded Indians remain. Governed by three elected chiefs, they are wards of the State, paying no taxes and receiving free medical care and schooling. Many of them earn a thin living making baskets and moccasins. Strands pounded from ash are dyed and woven together with sweet grass into baskets.

The St.Regis Indians take their name from John Francis Regis (1597–1640), French nobleman, philanthropist, and priest, canonized in 1793, who died in France before he was able to carry out his plan to cast his lot with the American Indians. The whole story covers a wide territory. Louis XV, impressed with the success of the French mission at Caughnawaga near Montreal, donated a bell to it; the vessel on which the bell was shipped was captured by the British, and the bell found its way to the tower of the Pilgrim Church, Groton, Massachusetts. During Queen Anne's War a party of Indians sacked the town and took away the bell and 100 prisoners, among whom were the Tarbell brothers, who in Caughnawaga married the daughters of tribal chiefs. Resentment over their growing power drove them from the mission, and they fled across the St.Lawrence to Akwis-as-ne (Ind., where the partridge drums), landing 'in the name of God and John Francis Regis'; and the name of the tribe was thus established.

In ST.JAMES CHURCH (R), 24.5 m., Eleazar Williams preached from 1850 until his death. His claim that he was the Lost Dauphin of France was widely believed. He was probably the grandson of Eunice Williams, daughter of a Massachusetts clergyman, who had been taken captive in an Indian raid. The rectory, a steep-roofed frame building, in which he lived, is called the Eleazar Williams House.

HOGANSBURG, 24.8 *m*. (178 alt.,112 pop.), is the trading center of the St.Regis Reservation. Indian-made baskets, moccasins, snowshoes, and novelties are displayed in the TRADING POST (L), a sprawling two-story frame structure.

Right from Hogansburg on a dirt road 2 *m*. to ST.REGIS (170 alt.,984 pop.), an Indian village of shabby story-and-a-half wooden houses around the ST.REGIS ROMAN CATHOLIC CHURCH, overlooking the St.Lawrence at the mouth of the St.Regis River. The historic Caughnawaga bell hangs in the belfry of this weatherbeaten frame structure.

State 37 crosses the St.Regis River and the western limit of the reservation near ROOSEVELTTOWN, 27.9 *m*. (208 alt.,48 pop.), formerly Nyando, but renamed for President Franklin D. Roosevelt in 1934 when he opened the ROOSEVELT INTERNATIONAL BRIDGE (*tolls: automobile $1, passengers 10¢ each; automobile with trailer $1.50; reduction on 24-hour trips; pedestrians 10¢*). The bridge has three links: the Raquette River Bridge, constructed without bolt or rivet, the longest all-electrically welded bridge in the world, crosses the Raquette River; the South Channel Bridge, across the international boundary line, connects the American shore with Cornwall Island, part of the Cornwall Indian Reservation; and the North Channel Bridge links the island with the Canadian mainland, offering a broad view of the St.Lawrence River with the Long Sault Rapids in the distance (L).

The road pushes through fertile farm country of close-cropped pastures and broad, level fields of corn and grain. President James Monroe followed this route on his horseback journey through the northern States in 1817. He was 'entertained at private houses and saw neither secret service man nor newspaper reporter during the whole trip.'

Industrial MASSENA, 37.9 *m*. (207 alt.,11,313 pop.), home of the Aluminum Company of America and hub of the State's second largest milk-producing area, lies along the Raquette and Grass Rivers. Its people, representing more than 30 nationalities, live in frame houses and modern bungalows on wide, shaded streets. The community also produces mica, silk, and milk powder. More than 50,000,000 pounds of milk and cream are shipped yearly, principally to New York City.

In 1792, Anable Fancher built a sawmill on the Grass River, naming his log cabin settlement for Marshall André Massena (1758–1817), veteran of the Napoleonic wars. In 1900, when the place had a population of less than 1,000, Henry H. Warren organized a company to dig a canal connecting the Grass River with the St.Lawrence; the water in the canal dropped 45 feet in three miles, generating 200,000 horsepower. This tremendous power source was responsible for Massena's growth.

The MASSENA WORKS OF THE ALUMINUM COMPANY OF AMERICA (*open by appointment*), at the north village limits, occupies 50 acres compactly built up with warehouses, mills, and shops. It is the only plant in the United States producing aluminum cable for transmission of electric energy and contains the world's largest mill for production of aluminum structural shapes.

Between 1822 and 1900 Massena was popular for its MINERAL SPRINGS, on the north bank of the Raquette River. St.Regis Indians first used the water 'that comes out of the ground, smells bad, but cures sick animals and sick Indians when they lick it.'

At 52.7 *m.* is the junction with a country road.

Right on this road 0.5 *m.* to the WADDINGTON-MORRISBURG FERRY (*open 6 a.m.– 12 midnight: car $1; passenger 25¢; free return trip same day*).

WADDINGTON, 54.9 *m.* (250 alt.,679 pop.), is a terminal for Canadian pulpwood and a milk shipping center. Here the St.Lawrence flows through the ruins of an eighteenth-century lock built to permit river traffic through the Rapide Plat.

For miles State 37 sweeps through broad acres of hay, alfalfa, wheat, oats, and corn and smaller patches of potatoes and soy beans.

There is a story that before surrendering ISLE ROYAL (R), 71.8 *m.*, to the British in 1760, the French commander secretly buried a large cache of gold. A century later a man named Pauchet, who called himself a grandson of the French commander, and Captain King, riverboat pilot, dug up 500 pounds of metal. As they were returning a storm broke over the river. Refusing to dump the gold into the river, Pauchet tied the bags to his waist, crying, 'If the gold goes, I go too!' The boat was swamped. King reached the shore, but the treasure still anchors Pauchet's bleached skeleton to the river bottom.

The ST.LAWRENCE STATE HOSPITAL (*open afternoons*), 72.9 *m.*, covering 1,219 acres of landscaped ground, is for the treatment of consumptives and mentally deranged. The institution houses 2,000 patients and 500 employees and offers a course in nursing.

At 73.5 *m.* is the junction with a gravel road.

Right on this road 0.5 *m.* to the 25-acre State-maintained ST.LAWRENCE FISH HATCHERY (*open Apr. 15–Oct. 1*), annually supplying 35,000,000 small mouth bass, perch, and muskellunge for streams and lakes in the State. The main hatchery is a small cement structure on the riverbank, backed by pump-fed raising basins.

OGDENSBURG, 75.3 *m.* (275 alt.,16,915 pop.), is a port of entry with five miles of irregular shoreline. A 21-foot channel, dug by the Federal Government and lined with docks, extends 300 yards up the Oswegatchie River, which here flows into the St.Lawrence; a 12-foot dam furnishes water power for mills, factories, and hydroelectric plants. Chief products are brass articles, silk and clothing, powdered milk, and casein.

About 60 per cent of the population is of French-Canadian descent, and relations with Canada are close and friendly. International friendship reaches a climax on Canadian Day, set aside annually by Ogdensburg to welcome Canadian friends, who come across in boatloads; streets are decorated with flags and bunting, stores offer special sales, and restaurants serve special dishes.

In 1749 Abbé François Picquet built Fort La Presentation at the mouth of the Oswegatchie River to serve as a rallying place for converted Indians, a fortification against the English, and a post for the French fur trade. In spite of the hard conditions that Father Picquet laid down—no more than one wife to a man and no drunkenness—the Iroquois settled here in large numbers; from Fort La Presentation came many of the Indians who helped defeat General Braddock in 1755. The British held the fort from 1760 to 1796. First called Oswegatchie, the town was renamed for Colonel Samuel Ogden, who purchased the site in 1792 and promoted its resettlement after the British evacuation.

In 1837 Ogdensburg was a base for American aid in the Patriots' War, an abortive effort by Canadian groups and American sympathizers to free Canada from 'the yoke of England.' Patriots under the command of Colonel N.G.S.Von Schoultz seized the steamer *United States* on the St.Lawrence and took in tow two arms-laden schooners; Von Schoultz landed below Prescott, Ontario, and mounted artillery for an attack on the village, but on the fifth day he was repulsed by a British attack from land and water.

The three-story brick REMINGTON ART MEMORIAL (*open*), corner of State and Washington Sts., which houses Indian relics, cowboy implements, paintings, statues, and books and sketches by Frederic Remington (*see Tour* 18), was originally the Parish mansion. It was built in 1809 by David Parish, English banker and large landholder in the North Country. In 1838 George Parish, David's nephew, who lived in the mansion, won, in a poker game at Evans Mills (*see Tour* 18), Maria Ameriga Vespucci, mistress of John Van Buren, son of the President. For many years Ameriga, called by the scandalized neighbors 'Parish's fancy woman,' lived in utter loneliness amid the splendor of this mansion with its palatial outbuildings —stables, coach houses, gardener's lodge, and conservatory, all enclosed by an eight-foot wall.

The MAPLE CITY MILL, E.River St., a two-story gray sandstone structure, was built in 1797 by Nathan Ford, agent for Samuel Ogden. It retains the original massive interior woodwork and still serves its original purpose as a mill, though the grinding stones have given way to mechanized grinders.

At the southern city limits are the ruins of the VAN RENSSELAER MANSION (L), built in 1832 by Henry Van Rensselaer, kin of the Hudson Valley patroon family. Opposite (R) is the ESTATE OF JUDGE JOHN FINE, early North Country pioneer; behind his large stone house is a stone barn with portholes, reminders of its service during the War of 1812. Adjoining the Fine estate is the stone VANDEN HEUVEL DWELLING, built by Jacob A. Vanden Heuvel, New York businessman who, in 1820, formed the settlement of Heuvelton southeast of Ogdensburg.

South of Ogdensburg colonies of summer cottages cluster in the pines along the mile-wide St.Lawrence. It was among these charming river scenes that Thomas Moore, Irish poet, wrote 'The Canadian Boat Song' while on a visit to America.

From MORRISTOWN, 86.1 *m.* (290 alt.,505 pop.), bass fishing center on a peninsula jutting into the St.Lawrence, the easternmost of the Thousand Islands are visible (*see Tour 25*).

State 37 swings through the Indian River lake region, extensively fished for pike and bass, to REDWOOD, 109 *m*. (365 alt.,524 pop.), trading post for vacationists and fishermen.

At 114.5 *m*. is a junction with State 26.

Left on State 26 to THERESA, 1.4 *m*. (376 alt.,873 pop.), birthplace of Roswell P. Flower (1835–99), governor of New York, 1892–5. Flower started as a poor workingman, employed in turn as farm boy, millhand, and teacher; and in his first campaign for Congress, against William Waldorf Astor, he used the slogan: 'My opponent counts his rents by the millions, while I have only the rents in my clothes.' But Flower grew wealthy rapidly: in the gubernatorial campaign of 1891 Tammany Hall introduced him as 'the flower that will never fade'; but anti-Tammany Democrats countered: 'By nominating a flamboyant millionaire, you propose to make the honor and power of the Republic a mere perquisite to the rich.'

At 115.4 *m*. is the junction with State 181.

Right on State 181 to LAFARGEVILLE, 7.5 *m*. (380 alt.,400 pop.), settled in 1816 by Reuben Andrus and named for John LaFarge, large landholder and father of John LaFarge, American artist, and grandfather of Oliver LaFarge, author of *Laughing Boy*.

WATERTOWN, 133.3 *m*. (478 alt.,33,323 pop.) (*see Tour 18*), is at the junction with State 3 (*see Tour 17*), US 11 (*see Tour 18*), and State 12 and 12E (*see Tour 25*).

Tour 20

(Montreal, P.Q.)—Plattsburg—Hoosick Falls—White Plains—New York City. State 22.
Canadian Line to New York City, 349.6 *m*.

Two-lane concrete or macadam.
Delaware & Hudson R.R. parallels route between Rouses Point and Whitehall; Rutland R.R. between Hoosick Falls and Lebanon Springs; New York Central R.R. between Hillsdale and New York City.

State 22, the easternmost road of the State, is essentially a rural route. Between Plattsburg and Whitehall it follows the long shore line of Lake Champlain; then it swings east to hug the New England boundary. In Westchester County it connects a series of restricted residential villages.

The section between Plattsburg and Whitehall began as a series of trails along the lake shore, followed by a part of Burgoyne's army. The southern stretch was opened to carry agricultural products to the markets of New York City. In the early decades of the nineteenth century, large herds of cattle were driven down this road, and the older taverns south of Hillsdale were built to accommodate the drovers, with large, enclosed yards for the livestock.

Section a.   CANADIAN LINE to WHITEHALL; 123.8 m.   State 22.

Traversing the Champlain Valley portal between Canada and the Hudson, this section of the route abounds in monuments of the Colonial and Revolutionary wars.

State 22, a continuation of Que.22, crosses the CANADIAN LINE, 0 *m.*, at a point 35 miles south of Montreal. At MOOERS, 3.9 *m.* (260 alt., 465 pop.), is the junction with US 11 (*see Tour* 18). Only scrubby second growth timber remains of a forest destroyed by a reckless lumber industry. The region is inhabited largely by descendants of French Canadians who came here as lumberjacks.

PLATTSBURG, 25.2 *m.* (120 alt.,14,713 pop.) (*see Tour* 21), is at the junction with State 3 (*see Tour* 17) and US 9 (*see Tour* 21).

Orchards in the foothills south of Plattsburg are famous for McIntosh apples. In the summer months the Little Ausable River, which runs through PERU, 35 *m.* (300 alt.,560 pop.), is filled with logs for a local mill. The village was named by some stretch of the imagination for the South American country because of its proximity to the mountains.

KEESEVILLE, 41.2 *m.* (400 alt.,1,794 pop.) (*see Tour* 21), is at the junction with US 9 (*see Tour* 21).

WILLSBORO, 53.7 *m.* (150 alt.,1,725 pop.), on the Bouquet River, has a large pulp mill, but thrives largely on its tourist trade. The district was first settled in 1765 by William Gilliland, a New York City merchant, who attempted to establish a feudal manor, but the Revolution put an end to the venture.

In June 1777, General Burgoyne, on his march toward Saratoga, encamped at Willsboro and here completed negotiations with the Indians, persuading them to take up arms against the Colonials.

At 57.9 *m.* are the grounds and buildings (R) of the DONTENWILL NOVITIATE OBLATE FATHERS. During the summer a choir and glee club of 70 voices present open-air musical programs on Sunday afternoons.

ESSEX, 58.6 *m.* (275 alt.,1,250 pop.), caters to a large summer tourist trade, and from here a ferry (*car and driver* $1; *passenger* 25¢) crosses the lake to Charlotte, Vermont.

At the north village line is the junction with Split Rock Road.

Left on this road to SPLIT ROCK, 4 *m.*, a slab 30 feet high with a surface of half an acre. The Indians believed that the spirit of a chief haunted the rock, and to placate him they threw gifts on the water whenever they passed in their canoes. According to legend, Arent Van Curler, founder of Schenectady, made an insulting gesture toward the dead chief as he passed by, and the outraged spirit raised a wind which upset the canoe and drowned the Dutchman. (Van Curler was drowned in Lake Champlain on his way to Canada.) Traditionally the boundary between the Mohawk and Algonquin, the rock was fixed as the northern limit of British possessions by the Treaty of Utrecht in 1713, became the boundary between New York and Canada in 1760, and was recognized as such until 1776, when Governors Moore and Carleton laid out the boundary, supposedly on the 45th parallel.

WESTPORT, 71.4 *m.* (271 alt.,790 pop.), lies on a natural terrace which encircles a deep bay extending in from Lake Champlain. Many of the stately homes have wide lawns, well-tended formal gardens, and iron fences with ornamental gateways. The Essex County Fair is held here annually in late August and the local yacht club puts on a summer regatta.

Summer residents double the population of PORT HENRY, 81.7 *m.* (600 alt.,1,937 pop.), which rises on a series of terraces above the lake. An iron smelter at the southern village limits employs 30 persons. Many of the citizens work in the near-by iron mines.

One of the winter pastimes of the villagers is to fish through the ice for smelt, perch, pike, and pickerel. In the winter, innumerable movable shanties, referred to in local idiom as the 'Stovepipe City,' dot the gleaming sweep of ice on Lake Champlain. Inside them, heavily clothed ice-fishermen sit huddled around kerosene stoves. The fish are hungry and rise to the bait eagerly.

In the center of the village is the junction with the Mineville Road.

Right on this road 0.3 *m.* to the PORT HENRY FREE CAMPING GROUND. MINE-VILLE, 4.6 *m.* (1,200 alt.,600 pop.), and WITHERBEE, 5.9 *m.* (1,300 alt.,1,567 pop.), are contiguous settlements in the heart of the Adirondack iron-mining area. The road is flanked by huge piles of black tailings and the smoke-stained huts of the miners. The present company is an outgrowth of one established in 1851.

In the mill the dynamited rock chunks are crushed and run over a large magnet to which the iron ore clings. The ore is scraped into a chute and the dirt and rock residue is conveyed to the tailing pile. A small part of the ore is locally sintered for use in fabricated steel; the rest is shipped to Troy, where it is smelted. With the exception of several Swedish deposits, the veins in this region produce the highest grade iron ore in the world, and remain the only iron mines in New York State commercially workable.

At 85.4 *m.* is the junction with State 8.

Left on State 8 to the CROWN POINT RESERVATION, 3.6 *m.* (*camping*), a 100-acre tract extending to Lake Champlain. At the entrance is the CROWN POINT TRADING POST, a log cabin said to be a replica of the one erected here by the French for trade with the Indians.

At 3.7 *m.* are the remains (R) of the LIGHT INFANTRY POST, one of the secondary defenses of Crown Point, which was erected by General Amherst in 1759 in conjunction with the construction of Fort Crown Point.

At 3.8 *m.* a road leads (R) to the CHAMPLAIN MEMORIAL LIGHTHOUSE, 0.1 *m.*, erected by the States of New York and Vermont in 1909 in honor of Samuel de Champlain, who in 1609 discovered the lake that bears his name. It occupies the SITE OF THE GRENADIER'S FORT, another of the secondary defenses of Crown Point constructed by General Amherst. The memorial is classical and French Renaissance in style, with heavy stone Roman Doric columns, entablature, ornamental frieze, and setbacks. The bas-relief of La France by Rodin was presented to the United States by the people of France and unveiled in May 1912.

At 3.9 *m.* (R) is the LAKE CHAMPLAIN BRIDGE (*car and occupants* $1; *trailers* 50¢), linking New York and Vermont. It is under the control of the Lake Champlain Bridge Commission, consisting of three members from each State.

At 4 *m.*, where the land shelves out into the lake to form a peninsula, are the ruins (R) of FORT ST.FREDERIC, erected on this commanding point by the French in 1731. A high, thick limestone wall enclosed a barracks, a chapel, and a lookout tower, all of stone. The armament comprised 63 cannons. It was the intention of the French, who collected a large force here, to make this the capital of their territory from the Connecticut River to Lake Ontario. They resisted English attacks in 1755–6; but in 1759 the garrison blew up the fort and retreated to Canada before the advance of Sir Jeffrey

Amherst. The parapet is partly traceable, and a granite monument marks the remains of the ammunition bins.

Opposite Fort St.Frederic is a small brick MUSEUM (*open summer months*), which contains a collection of cannon balls, arrowheads, and other Indian and Colonial relics.

At 4.1 *m.* is the entrance (L) to the ruins of FORT CROWN POINT, known for a time as Fort Amherst, which was begun by Sir Jeffrey Amherst in 1759 after his capture of Fort Ticonderoga and Fort St.Frederic. Amherst planned to make this a permanent British stronghold; but building was suspended before completion because the English realized the French had been driven out of this territory permanently.

A deep ditch, about one-half mile in circumference, which was dug out of limestone by the soldiers, still surrounds the fort. The ramparts, 25 feet thick, almost the same height, and faced with solid masonry, were formed from the stone and dirt thrown up from the ditches. The remains of two of the three barracks are preserved by the State. The barracks that face the entrance are in remarkably fine condition, their sides, walls, and fireplaces almost as good as when erected.

Together with Fort Ticonderoga, Fort Crown Point was captured by the Green Mountain Boys in May 1775. In 1777, upon the approach of General Burgoyne on his march to Saratoga, it was abandoned by the Americans, never again to assume military importance.

CROWN POINT, 89.5 *m.* (126 alt.,1,900 pop.), has capitalized on its historical environment to develop into a popular summer resort and tourist center.

Likewise TICONDEROGA, 97.4 *m.* (200 alt.,3,395 pop.), on the neck of land connecting Lake George and Lake Champlain, is a year-round tourist spot, with historic shrines and winter sports as attractions. The name is a variation of the Indian *Cheonderoga* (between two waters, or where the waters meet). The French built a military road along the path of the Indian carry between the two lakes and in 1755 they constructed Fort Carillon, later called Fort Ticonderoga.

The LIBERTY MONUMENT, Montcalm St. at Moses Circle, carved by Charles Keck, represents three centuries of local history. Around the stone base stand the bronze figures of a French soldier, an Indian, a Highlander of the Black Watch, and a Green Mountain Boy.

The HEADQUARTERS HOUSE OF THE NEW YORK STATE HISTORICAL ASSOCIATION, NW. corner of Montcalm St. and Moses Circle (*open, free; summer, 9–5 weekdays, 10–5 Sundays; winter, 9–5 weekdays*), is a reproduction of the John Hancock House, built in Boston, 1737–40. The reproduction, by M.H.Westoff, follows measured drawings of the original made by John Sturgis of Boston. Built of granite, the house has two stories with attic and basement, gambrel roof, and balustrade. The almost severe simplicity of the exterior is relieved by the balcony, which opens from the second floor through a doorway flanked by Corinthian columns and surmounted by a broken pediment. The wide entrance below this balcony leads into the spacious hall on the first floor. The Colonial staircase is a replica of the original in the Hancock House, with a Palladian window at the first landing. The furnishings on the lower floor are reproductions of fine early American furniture and originals on loan from the Metropolitan Museum of Art. The walls of the second floor hall are covered with a scenic wallpaper representing New York in 1716. Included in the collections are historical maps and paintings, mezzotints of famous characters, manuscripts, rare books, old newspaper files, and portraits of the governors of New York State.

The COMMUNITY BUILDING, 125 Montcalm St., is a three-story structure of New England granite trimmed with limestone, a charming adaptation of the Georgian Colonial style. This building, like the Headquarters House and the Liberty Monument, was a gift to the town from Horace A. Moses.

The BLACK WATCH MEMORIAL LIBRARY, 159 Montcalm St., the gift of Andrew Carnegie, honors the memory of the 42nd Regiment of Foot, better known as the Royal Highlanders, or the Black Watch, which lost more than 600 men killed and wounded in the Battle of Ticonderoga, July 8, 1758. The WORLD WAR MEMORIAL, on the grounds, was erected by the Ticonderoga chapter of the D.A.R.

Industrially Ticonderoga is known for its lead pencils, partially manufactured in the JOSEPH DIXON CRUCIBLE PLANT, Burgoyne Road (*open*), and the high-grade book and magazine paper produced in the TICONDEROGA PULP AND PAPER PLANT, on the same street. The pencil industry grew up around the graphite mine discovered here in 1815 and the invention 15 years later of a process of turning it into pencils. The first commercial production was begun in 1840. Today it is cheaper to import the graphite than to work the local mines.

In Ticonderoga is the junction with State 9N (*see Tour 23*).

At 98.7 *m.* is the junction with a macadam road.

Left on this road to the entrance, 0.7 *m.*, to the grounds of Fort Ticonderoga, marked by a stone arch and the caretaker's lodge (R).

At 1.2 *m.* a stone marker (R) commemorates the gallantry of the Royal American Regiment, composed of Colonial troops, which lost 279 men killed in Abercrombie's attack on the French fort here on July 8, 1758.

Another marker (R), at 1.3 *m.*, honors the Black Watch Regiment. Major Duncan Campbell, one of the officers mortally wounded in the engagement, is the subject of a famous ghost story. In Scotland Campbell once concealed a murderer and swore to keep his presence a secret; Campbell was true to his oath, though it transpired that the murderer's victim had been his cousin. The cousin's ghost appeared and warned Campbell, 'Farewell, Inverawe, till we meet at Ticonderoga.' Campbell discounted the warning; but before the battle his spirits fell and he resigned himself to death. He was wounded and died 10 days later. Stevenson made the story the subject of a ballad:

> And it fell on the morrow's morning,
> In the fiercest of the fight
> That the Cameron bit the dust,
> As he foretold at night;
> And far from the hills of heather
> Far from the isles of the sea,
> He sleeps in the place of the name,
> As it was doomed to be.

The position of the French lines are marked (R), at 1.4 *m.*, where Montcalm with 3,500 men withstood repeated attacks of Abercrombie's 15,000 British and Colonials on July 8, 1758. Parts of the trenches can be traced today.

At 1.5 *m.* is a memorial to General Montcalm.

FORT TICONDEROGA, 1.7 *m.* (*open May 1–Nov. 1; adm.* 50¢), is owned by Mr.S.H.P. Pell, who has been carrying on the work of reconstruction—not yet completed (1940)— for 25 years. Mr.Pell is a descendant of William Ferris Pell, who in 1820 bought the farms and fort at Ticonderoga from Columbia and Union Colleges; the land had been ceded to the schools by the State. The Pavilion, Mr.Pell's present home, was built by William Ferris Pell in 1826.

The PLACE D'ARMES, in the center of the fort, is surrounded by barracks and bomb shelters. The west barracks, fully restored, were the headquarters of Captain de la Place on the morning of May 9, 1775, when Ethan Allen and his Green Mountain Boys surprised the British garrison and demanded its surrender 'in the name of the Great Jehovah and the Continental Congress,' or, according to the folk version, with the command, 'Come out, you damned old rat.' This part of the fort now houses the MUSEUM, containing relics, prints, manuscripts, and paintings.

According to a legend, Ethan Allen, while attending church service shortly after the capture of Fort Ticonderoga, listened patiently for a time to the minister who again and again thanked the Lord for delivering the fort into the hands of the rebels, but finally he sprang to his feet and shouted: 'Parson Dewey! Please make mention of my being there!'

In 1777 Burgoyne set up a commanding battery on Mount Defiance, and General St.Clair, then in command at Ticonderoga, was obliged to retreat from the fort under cover of darkness. After Burgoyne's surrender the British abandoned the stronghold, but it was recaptured by General Haldimand in 1780. In that year Colonel John Brown failed to storm the bulwark for the Americans.

South of Ticonderoga, at 100.9 m., is the MONTCALM LANDING FERRY (car, $1) to Vermont.

WHITEHALL, 123.8 m. (123 alt.,5,191 pop.), mill town and railroad center at the northern terminus of the Barge Canal, is midway between New York and Montreal on the Hudson-Champlain trail. Silk mills and Delaware & Hudson Railroad shops furnish employment. One-third of the population is of Italian origin. In 1930 the owners of the local silk mill closed the factory and wrecked the machinery, forcing hundreds of people into unemployment. Almost immediately the people of Whitehall raised funds to purchase the mill property and new equipment and formed the Champlain Spinners,Inc., which has successfully carried on since.

In 1759 the place took the name of Skenesborough in honor of Major Philip Skene of the British Army, who settled here with about 30 families. Skene obtained patents to some 37,000 acres, but lost all as a result of his support of the British cause in the Revolution. He and his son acted as guides for Burgoyne's advance in 1777, but lavish entertainment at Skenesborough delayed the invading force and enabled the Rebels to multiply the obstructions. In the harbor of Skenesborough, Benedict Arnold constructed his motley fleet for the Battle of Valcour Island (see Tour 21). The settlement was razed in 1780 when General Haldimand, left in charge by Burgoyne, abandoned the place.

At Whitehall is the junction with US 4 (see Tour 22), which unites with State 22 southward for 7.2 miles.

Section b. WHITEHALL to HILLSDALE; 118.1 m. State 22

South of WHITEHALL, 0 m., State 22 turns abruptly toward the Vermont line and the Green Mountains and swings down the eastern border of the State. In the early Colonial days this route drew off the produce of the western New England valleys to Troy and Albany.

At 7.2 m., US 4 (see Tour 22) continues south (straight ahead) and State 22 turns abruptly left and crosses a bridge over the Champlain division of the Barge Canal. GREAT MEADOWS PRISON (*open* 9:30-11, 1-4 *daily*), 7.4 *m.*, built in 1810, is known as a semisecurity type of prison. It houses 200 guards and more than 1,000 prisoners, 'short-timers' transferred here from other institutions because of good behavior. Cells are cream colored and radio equipped; educational, recreational, and athletic facilities are provided, and every attempt is made to rehabilitate the offenders.

GRANVILLE, 17.8 *m.* (400 alt.,3,483 pop.), is a picturesque New England village, originally called Bishop's Corners when its first settlers, many of them Quakers, arrived from Vermont in 1781.

The site of the village was part of the hunting and fishing grounds of the St.Francis Indians of Canada, who made hatchets and arrowheads from slate and enjoyed friendly relations with the Mohawk. At many of the Indian campsites, relics have been unearthed, and the site of a fair-sized Indian village has been uncovered on East Main Street.

Industrially the village relies upon its slate quarries, which have been worked since 1850 and at present employ several hundred people, many of whom are of Welsh descent. In addition to the regular slate used for roofing and classroom blackboards, a valuable green slate produced here is used for marbleized finishing.

Slate is so plentiful in this region that the farmers have roofed their houses, barns, and outbuildings with it. South of Granville the ridge to the left is piled high with rubble—red, black, and pale green slabs and slivers —while the black towers and booms of derricks, strung with guy cables, spider against the sky.

Beneath the rampart of the Taconics to the east, State 22 runs west of the Vermont line. SALEM, 35.3 *m.* (500 alt.,1,081 pop.), with its well-kept houses and spreading maples and elms, is suggestive of Vermont communities. At the north village limits is GALLOWS HILL (R), where, until 1808, public executions were held. A hanging provided a holiday for hundreds of visitors, who arrived with lunches and dotted the surrounding meadow, picnic-fashion.

The LARMON HOME, E.Broadway, built in 1790 by John Williams, is an impressive residence in the Georgian Colonial style. A yellow clapboard building with handsome fanlighted doorway and green blinds, it has a double hip roof, the upper part almost flat. On W.Broadway, the UNITED PRESBYTERIAN CHURCH, known locally as the 'White Church,' is patterned after the white-painted frame, gable-roofed churches common in New England. The horse-and-buggy sheds are still intact. The congregation was organized at Dallibay, Ireland, in 1751 and in 1764 moved as a body to Salem. The present, or third, building on this site was erected in 1797 and is said to be the oldest Protestant church north of Albany.

CAMBRIDGE, 44.4 *m.* (500 alt.,1,762 pop.), its principal street lined with stately elms, is a farm shopping center, site of an annual agricultural fair and the Mary McClellan Hospital.

At 56.1 *m.* is the junction with State 67.

Left on State 67 to WALLOOMSAC, 1.1 *m.* (400 alt.,160 pop.). In the center of the village, indicated by a marker (R), is approximately where the second engagement in the Battle of Bennington took place, resulting in the defeat of reinforcements for Colonel Baum.

At 2.3 *m.* is the entrance (L) to the BENNINGTON BATTLEFIELD, a State park of 171 acres. The road climbs a hill which offers a sweeping view of the battle area, the surrounding hills, and the valley of the Walloomsac River.

On August 12, 1777, Burgoyne, then encamped at Old Saratoga (the present Schuylerville), dispatched an expedition of 500 men under Colonel Frederick Baum to take the stores collected by the Americans at Bennington. Burgoyne was under the impression that the supplies were guarded by a small party of militia and that the inhabitants of the area were largely of Tory sympathies. Meeting resistance, at about 3 p.m. on August 16, Baum drew up his force on the west side of the Walloomsac River. According to tradition, local citizens, equipped with sickles and pitchforks, came to him posing as Tories, and he ordered them given arms and ammunition. As the engagement grew hotter, the newly armed citizenry 'deserted' to the American forces under General John Stark on the east side of the river. Confused by the evaporation of his army, Baum surrendered after a few hours' fighting.

This victory was a major setback for Burgoyne in his invasion of 1777, and the failure of Baum to capture the much needed supplies led directly to 'Gentleman Johnny's' complete surrender at Saratoga (*see Tour* 22).

Upon a square granite rock at the high point of the battlefield, the State of New York has placed a bronze relief map of the engagement which indicates the various units in action and their respective positions. Other monuments memorialize General Stark and the Vermont and Massachusetts volunteers.

East of the battlefield is the STATE LINE HOUSE (L), built in 1784, lying partly in Vermont and partly in New York; the State line splits the dining room. In the days when men were imprisoned for debt, debtors in Vermont dined on the New York side and vice versa for New York fugitives.

HOOSICK FALLS, 58.3 *m.* (450 alt.,4,755 pop.), incorporated as a village in 1827, has utilized the falls in the Hoosick River to build a thriving industrial town, with a paper mill and an electrical appliance manufacturing concern.

At 62 *m.* is the junction with State 7 (*see Tour* 10), with which State 22 is united for 0.4 miles.

PETERSBURG, 70.3 *m.* (669 alt.,500 pop.), is at the junction with State 96.

1. Right on State 96 to the TROY TIMES FRESH AIR HOME (L), 4.2 *m.*, founded in 1887 by Charles Spencer Francis, publisher and U.S.Ambassador to Roumania. Two buildings accommodate 130 boys and girls at a time for a two-weeks' vacation.

GRAFTON, 5.6 *m.* (1,500 alt.,572 pop.), is a resort and trading center for dwellers in the summer homes and inns on privately owned lakes in the vicinity. Granville Hicks, critic and author, lives on a near-by farm; here he wrote *John Reed, Figures of Transition,* and *I Like America.*

TROY, 20.9 *m.* (34 alt.,70,117 pop.) (*see Troy*), is at the junction with State 7 (*see Tour* 10) and State 32 (*see Tour* 22).

2. Left on State 96 up the west slope of PETERSBURG MOUNTAIN to the 50-foot TOWER, 5 *m.* (10¢ *adm.*), which overlooks part of Massachusetts, New York, and Vermont—in clear weather a radius of 150 miles.

At the MASSACHUSETTS LINE, 5.2 *m.*, State 96 connects with Massachusetts State 2, 6 miles east of Williamstown, Massachusetts, linking the Hudson Valley with the Mohawk Trail.

BERLIN, 76.1 *m.* (810 alt.,750 pop.), turns out 100,000,000 lollypop sticks a month and grows 2,000,000 rosebuds a year.

LEBANON SPRINGS, 92 *m.* (800 alt.,400 pop.), owes its existence to the mineral springs, one mile north of the present village line. Indians who had long been acquainted with the medical value of the water brought Captain Thomas Hitchcock, a British officer, to the spring in 1766 after New England physicians had diagnosed his case as hopeless. The thermal waters effected a cure in a few weeks. Hitchcock returned in 1771 and built a bathhouse and roads. Columbia Hall, a large frame hotel on the old stage road between Boston and Albany, was erected soon after. From 1780 to 1830 the Spa was the American Baden.

At 93 *m.* is the junction with US 20 (*see Tour* 8), with which State 22 runs in common to NEW LEBANON, 93.8 *m.* (720 alt.,400 pop.) (*see Tour* 8).

Weaving through the foothills of the Taconics, State 22 passes the BERKSHIRE INDUSTRIAL FARM (L), 97.1 *m.*, a spread of stucco buildings and cottages on 1,100 acres, which cares for more than 100 New York City youths from the underprivileged class. The boys live in cottages under the care of house mothers. The grammar school and the trade school are under the supervision of the State Education Department; the latter trains boys in printing, the building trades, auto mechanics, and scientific farming.

AUSTERLITZ, 107.2 *m.* (1,210 alt.,150 pop.), was settled about 1750 by Judah Laurence and others from Connecticut and Massachusetts. Martin Van Buren, an ardent admirer of Napoleon, was incensed when a town in Seneca County was named Waterloo and moved to name this town Austerlitz. His point carried, he remarked triumphantly: 'There's an Austerlitz for your Waterloo!'

Three miles up in the mountains above Austerlitz are the red-roofed, white frame buildings of STEEPLETOP, the home of America's most popular woman poet, Edna St.Vincent Millay, and her husband, Eugene Jan Boissivain.

In the eastern edge of HILLSDALE, 118.1 *m.* (686 alt.,500 pop.), is the junction with State 23 (*see Tour* 7).

Section c. HILLSDALE to NEW YORK CITY; 107.7 *m. State* 22

South of Hillsdale, State 22 is flanked by broad fields of grain, hay, and pasture land, with here and there a fist of stone breaking the smooth sweep of the terrain. Distant hills gradually close in to become the Harlem Valley, rich in iron ore, limestone, and other minerals, which were once worked economically but have been supplanted by richer areas in the midwest.

This section of the highway was trodden out of the wilderness by immense herds of cattle being driven from northern pastures to the New York City market. Then came the period of iron manufacture when huge oxcarts loaded with iron ore, pig iron, and finished iron products rutted the roadway. Besides the drovers' taverns along the route, a string of Quaker meetinghouses were set up.

State 22 climbs and drops with the Taconic Highlands between HILLS-DALE, 0 *m.*, and COPAKE FALLS, 4.8 *m.*, (620 alt.,350 pop.). Once a flourishing iron town, Copake Falls now depends upon summer vacationists.

Left from Copake Falls on State 344 to the entrance to TACONIC STATE PARK (*parking 25¢; camping—tents and cottages for rent*), 1 *m.*, which extends into Massachusetts and Connecticut. At the park entrance a road leads (R) to the old Copake iron works, erected in 1846, where the smelter and some of the workshops still stand. The New York section of the park has 12 miles of roadways and 14 miles of trails. One trail leads to the head of the ski run. RUDD POND (*boating, fishing, swimming, camping*) is near the south end of the park.

The WEED IRON MINES, operated from 1776 to 1880 are just off State 22 (L) at 8.8 *m.* The old shaft of the mine is still visible.

At BOSTON CORNERS, 10.3 *m.* (727 alt.,98 pop.), in the decades of handlebar mustaches, derby hats, and gold-headed canes, bare-knuckle fighters would doff their shirts and stage gory battles. The most famous of those encounters was the one between Yankee Sullivan and John Morrissey. Sullivan, who won, was killed soon afterward.

At MILLERTON, 18.5 *m.* (700 alt.,919 pop.), State 22 joins US 44 (*see Tour 5*), and the two routes run in common to AMENIA, 26.9 *m.* (573 alt., 1,500 pop.), the home of Lewis Mumford, critic and author. His *Herman Melville* did much to revive interest in the neglected author of *Moby Dick*; later he published penetrating studies of cultural development, including *Technics and Civilization* and *The Culture of Cities*. J.E.Spingarn (1875–1939), one of the leaders in the 'new literary criticism' and author of several books on literature, spent his later years here.

South of Amenia the road winds through the narrow Wassaic Creek Valley. In WASSAIC, 30.3 *m.* (458 alt.,350 pop.), is the BORDEN MILK PLANT, now a milk station, where America's first condensed milk was produced under a patent granted to Gail Borden in 1856.

At 32.7 *m.* is the entrance (L) to WASSAIC STATE SCHOOL, a group of rugged brick buildings on a commanding elevation surrounded by the school farm. Administered by the State Department of Mental Hygiene, the school houses and trains 3,400 patients, mostly of adolescent age.

At 37.5 *m.* is the junction with a dirt road.

Right on this road to DOVER FURNACE, 2.1 *m.*, behind grass-covered heaps of slag, in which the smelting was done when Dover Plains played its part in the iron industry. In the rear of the furnace, a winding stream has cut a ravine through the hills, and an old dam spills a lichen-green water down the valley. Back in the hills are the iron mines.

At 2.7 *m.* is the entrance (R) to SHARPAROON POND, a large summer camp, operated by the New York Mission Society as a memorial to Russell Sage.

OLD DROVERS INN (R), 39.3 *m.*, a low-ceilinged, rambling structure, was erected about 1750 and opened in 1810 as an inn. The Georgian paneling and shell cupboards are well preserved, as is much of the handmade glass, the hardware, and the hand-hewn beams. The old tinder box, in which flint and steel were kept dry, and the pig-scalding boiler can still be seen.

Soon after its opening the inn became popular with the drovers on the road. Before a roaring fire, ballads were sung; one of them ended:

> So the Drover wed the tavern girl,
> The wedding soon was over;
> When morning dawned away she rode
> By the side of the jolly Drover.
> And gone forever is the bound-out girl,
> And gone is the jolly Drover,
> But still there are maids who'll love and trust
> In other towns than Dover.

'Love and trust' seems to have been a long suit in this neighborhood, for an old town record reports: 'Captain Thomas Baxter was married to Miss Ann Whitman after a long and tedious courtship of 28 years, which both endured with uncommon Christian fortitude.'

The JACKSON WING INN (R), 43.1 m., is a two-story red brick building. Numerous Wing families and their kinsmen, the Prestons, were prominent in the early settlement of the region. Jackson Wing is said to have built this house in 1806.

At 44.2 m. is the entrance (L) to the HARLEM VALLEY STATE HOSPITAL for the mentally defective. The buildings and grounds occupy 1,200 acres with accommodations for more than 4,000 patients and their attendants.

On a slight elevation at the northern end of the grounds stands the ALFRED WING HOMESTEAD (R), a white frame residence in a grove of trees. Greek Revival in style, it was considerably altered when converted into the home of the hospital steward.

The PAWLING SCHOOL FOR BOYS (L), 49 m., a college preparatory school, was founded in 1907 by Dr. Frederic L. Gamage. South of the school, in the cemetery (R) is a large granite memorial with an anchor in bas-relief, marking the GRAVE OF ADMIRAL JOHN LORIMER WORDEN, commander of the *Monitor* in its eventful battle with the *Merrimac* in 1862. In 1863 he commanded the *Montauk*, a newer *Monitor*, in the attack on Charleston, and succeeded in destroying the Confederate *Nashville*. From 1870 to 1874 he was superintendent of the U.S. Naval Academy at Annapolis, and from 1875 to 1877 he commanded the European squadron.

PAWLING, 49.9 m. (420 alt., 1,204 pop.), was settled about 1740 by English Quakers. Today it is the home of many wealthy New Yorkers.

At 50.8 m. is the junction with the Quaker Hill Road (State 341).

Right on this road to CLOVER BROOK FARM, 2 m., home of Lowell Thomas, well-known radio commentator and author. The house, remodeled on Colonial lines, was built by Quakers more than a century ago. A combination theater and gymnasium contains a radio studio with special broadcasting facilities.

At 3.3 m. on the same road are the grounds and buildings of the AKIN HALL ASSOCIATION (R), founded in 1882 by Albert J. Akin 'for the promotion of benevolence and mutual improvement in religion and knowledge and to provide a place of education, moral training and worship.' Upon his death in 1903 Akin left $100,000 for the maintenance of the association and an additional $50,000 for the completion and furnishing of a library. This AKIN FREE LIBRARY, down a dirt road (R) at 0.8 m., contains more than 4,000 volumes and a collection of Indian, Colonial, and Quaker relics.

At 5.3 m., just past the intersection, is (L) the OBLONG MEETING HOUSE, erected in

1764, one of the few survivors of the chain of Quaker churches which formerly extended from here into Westchester. During the Revolutionary War the structure served as a hospital, and across the road are the unmarked graves of many 'unknown soldiers' of the Revolution. Within its walls much Quaker history was made, including the famous 'Querie' against slavery, reputed to be the first antislavery protest in America.

The building is without architectural pretensions. It is unpainted; three sides are covered with weathered shingles; the north side still retains the old clapboards. Many of the 24-light windows are glazed with early wavy glass. On the interior are the straight-backed benches and the elevated seats of the elders, facing the congregation. The central sliding partitions could be raised or lowered by ropes to separate the sexes. The massive gallery is supported by crudely carved pillars.

After the Quaker schism in 1828 (*see Tour* 21), the meetinghouse was taken over by the Hicksites. For the next 75 years Orthodox and Hicksite each went his own way, a disunion that resulted finally in the disappearance of both groups from Quaker Hill.

At 53.6 *m.* is the junction with State 311.

Right on State 311 to PATTERSON, 1.7 *m.* (400 alt.,400 pop.), squatting in a broad valley formerly part of the Patterson Great Swamp, where cattle headed for the New York market were allowed to graze. The village, originally named Franklin, was settled about 1770 by Scotsmen discharged from the British army after service in the French and Indian War. The present name—after Matthew Patterson, an early settler—was adopted in 1808 when the legislature passed a law abolishing the numerous 'Franklins' in the State. At the time, local governmental offices included pathmasters, fence-viewers, and pound-masters, the duties of the latter including control of a large herd of hogs that roamed the neighborhood and wore rings in their noses to prevent them from burrowing the roads. A standing reward of one shilling was offered to the person who 'shall return a swine to his owner having a proper ring in his nose.'

A field to the east of the village, still known as the 'Militia Field,' was during the Revolution the scene of strenuous military exercises under the command of Colonel Henry Ludington, whose daughter Sybell is famous in local annals for her daring night ride to warn the sleeping countryside of the approach of the British just prior to the Battle of Danbury in 1778. The colonel and his daughter are both buried in the old cemetery jointly used by Presbyterian and Episcopal churches under an agreement of 1803.

The road skirts the eastern fringe of BREWSTER, 63.5 *m.* (410 alt., 1,664 pop.), at the junction with US 6 (*see Tour* 4).

CROTON FALLS, 68.5 *m.* (230 alt.,600 pop.), overlooks the Croton chain of reservoirs, part of the far-flung New York City water supply system. At the northern edge of PURDY, 70.3 *m.* (220 alt.,235 pop.), is the junction with State 116.

Right on State 116 to SOMERS, 1.7 *m.* (300 alt.,100 pop.), 'the birthplace of the American circus.' In the center of the hamlet is the wooden STATUE OF OLD BET, the first traveling elephant, standing on a granite shaft. In 1815 Hachaliah Bailey purchased the animal from a ship captain, who had brought her over from England. Bailey named her 'Old Bet' and began to exhibit her about the country. He added monkeys and a bear or two, traveling from place to place at night to minimize the 'free show' possibilities.

Then 'Uncle Nate' Howes, of South East, now Sodom, Putnam County, leased Old Bet from Bailey and introduced the first canvas-roofed 'round top' to the circus industry. But Old Bet was neither old nor docile, and since little or nothing was known about the handling of elephants, it was not surprising that her behavior often excited apprehension among the villagers. Finally a group of fanatics in Connecticut who detected in her a resemblance to the Behemoth of Scripture shot her down.

After the demise of Old Bet, a number of wagon shows were spawned in the vicinity of Brewster. Clowns were added to pep up the parade; Daniel Drew, from Carmel, later a famous financier, got his start as a clown, and 'Jim' Fisk, his partner, was once a menagerie man. George F. Bailey, nephew of Hachaliah, a tavern keeper, joined forces with Aaron Turner, a show promotor, and Phineas Taylor Barnum, a Connecticut storekeeper and lottery man. 'Uncle Nate' Howes had a young brother, Seth B. Howes, who became a partner in P.T.Barnum's American Museum and Menagerie. Seth Howes took the Great American Show to England and made a fortune out of it.

Opposite the elephant monument is the ELEPHANT HOTEL, a three-story brick structure, now the village hall of Somers. It was built by Bailey as a resort for the circus fraternity and for the entertainment of drovers, who were frequent guests.

At 76 *m.* is the junction with an unmarked road.

Right on this road to the JAY HOMESTEAD (*private*), 1 *m.*, at one time the home of John Jay, Federalist leader, governor of New York, and first Chief Justice of the U.S. Supreme Court. The house, partially destroyed by fire a few years ago, has been restored.

State 22 skirts the Kensico Reservoir (R) to the KENSICO DAM, 92.5 *m.*, which forces the inundation of 2,218 acres of land. Construction took 14 years and cost $158,000,000. Across the top of the dam is a broad highway that leads to the aeration plant with its 3,000 individual fountains that rise high in the air.

WHITE PLAINS, 95.7 *m.* (467 alt.,40,116 pop.), is well within the commuter's belt around New York City. On weekday mornings more than half the working population leave by train and auto for business in the metropolis. The city embraces almost 10 square miles of hilly terrain stretching between the landscaped banks of the Bronx River on the west and the Mamaroneck River on the east. Strictly a residential city, it has preserved seven square miles of its territory for one-family houses, of which there are almost 5,000. The industrial section occupies less than half a square mile. The rest of the city has been zoned for business and apartment houses.

The buying power represented by the large commuting population, supplemented by the trade of near-by villages, is responsible for the profusion of business places, including branches of New York department stores, that line Main Street and Mamaroneck Avenue and overflow into several cross and parallel streets. Narrow Main Street is cluttered with old two-story brick buildings and a few taller office structures. Mamaroneck Avenue, by contrast, comparatively recently converted to business, is marked by smart, spacious, one-story structures with modern fronts in glass and chromium. On Main Street and Martine Avenue, west of Mamaroneck Avenue, is a conspicuous group of civic and county buildings.

The early settlement, an established community by 1735, was the center of the county's iron mining activity, which remained important until the end of the eighteenth century, and the hub of stage routes to New York, Mamaroneck, Rye, Bedford, and Danbury. Troubled military conditions in New York City compelled the Provincial congress to move to White Plains. On July 9, 1776, it met in the courthouse, on the site of the present armory at the corner of South Broadway and Mitchell Place, and ratified the Declaration of Independence, which was read for the first time in upstate New York on the courthouse steps on July 11. The vote of the members on July 10 to call the assembly the Convention of the Representatives of the State of New York marked the break with Great Britain and the birth of the Empire State.

From October 21 to 26, 1776, Washington with his army of 25,000 ragged, hungry, and poorly equipped soldiers, most of them raw recruits, arrived in White Plains on his masterly retreat from Manhattan. On October 28 Lord Howe, with about the same number of seasoned troops, made his appearance. Howe sent his Hessians to take Chatterton Hill to the west of the Bronx River, which they did, but he made no attempt to press his advantage, so that the Continentals were able to retreat in good order and re-form their lines on the inaccessible heights of North Castle. After pondering the situation for two days, and realizing that he had been outgeneraled by Washington, Howe left for Kingsbridge by way of Dobbs Ferry. Four years later in Parliament, questioned why he had not pressed the attack after capturing Chatterton Hill, Howe said no more than that 'I have political reasons and no others for declining to explain why that assault was not made.'

After the Revolution, mining gave way to agriculture as the main source of livelihood. The railroad reached the settlement in 1844. In 1866, when the village was incorporated, the population numbered barely 1,000; by 1886 it had risen to 3,000. Then, almost overnight, New Yorkers discovered White Plains, and they moved here in large numbers and erected homes. By 1900 there were almost 8,000 inhabitants; in 1916, when the village became a city, the population was more than 19,000.

CHATTERTON HILL, the scene of the Battle of White Plains, October 28, 1776, is an elevation immediately west of the railroad station, lying between Chatterton Parkway, which skirts the Bronx River bluff that the British stormed, and Central Park Avenue. It is now a densely built residential section. There are markers along Battle Avenue, and a number of the streets are named for Presidents of the United States and Revolutionary War generals.

The WESTCHESTER COUNTY CENTER (*open* 10-10 *daily*), Bronx River Pkwy. at Central Ave., in a landscaped setting, is a large, majestic building planned and designed in the modern manner and devoid of all evidences of the historical styles. It was opened in 1930; the architects were Walker and Gillette. The main auditorium, with balcony, seats 4,600. The building is an active community center: it serves as an opera house, concert hall, and theater; dances and athletic events are held here; the little theater is used by 20 dramatic groups; the exhibition hall under the main auditorium is a large, unbroken area for banquets and exhibits.

The PURDY-FERRIS HOUSE (*private*), Spring St. between Mott and Water Sts., served as Lafayette's headquarters during the Battle of White Plains. The farmhouse is now in a sad state of disrepair.

The PRESBYTERIAN BURYING GROUND, N.Broadway at Rockledge Ave., contains the graves of early settlers and Revolutionary soldiers, among them the grave of Elijah Miller, whose house Washington occupied during the Battle of White Plains.

The MILLER HOUSE (*open* 10-12, 2-4 *Tues.-Sun.*), Virginia Road at the north city line, is a small story-and-a-half white frame farmhouse with a wide porch. Most of the furnishings and cooking utensils were used by Washington. The POWDER HOUSE, in the rear of the house, a deep hole roofed with stones, was used to store ammunition during the battle.

SCARSDALE, 99.9 m. (200 alt.,12,908 pop.), is a restricted residential village; many of its wealthy residents commute to the city. It takes its name from the Manor of Scarsdale, of which its site was a part, established by Caleb Heathcote, who came from Scarsdale, Derbyshire, England, in 1701. Today the town still patterns its life upon the horse-and-hound England from which its name comes.

The WAYSIDE INN, on the old Post Road, 0.5 mile east (R) of the railroad station, is a little frame building erected presumably by Caleb Heathcote about 1717. It was restored in 1919 under the auspices of the Women's Club of Scarsdale and now serves as the Scarsdale library. For 75 years it was conducted as a tavern by the Varian family. Sabre scars believed to have been made by De Heister's Hessians on their way to the Battle of White Plains mark the front door; the Hessians were only trying to arouse the landlord, who had hidden himself and his two most precious possessions, his Bible and his cow, in the cellar.

TUCKAHOE, 102.7 m. (120 alt.,6,575 pop.), is a suburb of Yonkers, where most of the working population are employed. The village originated around marble quarries, at one time a principal source of supply for New York City construction.

MOUNT VERNON, 105.1 m. (100 alt.,67,120 pop.), was developed as a refuge for industries and commuters escaping the high rents in New York City. The main business and shopping district is only a little less bustling than the main streets of Manhattan itself. The 115 industries of the city turn out clothing, chemicals, beverages, weather strips and screens, electrical equipment, dyes, machinery, and metal products. Many of the workers are of Italian origin.

The history of Mount Vernon goes back to the story of Eastchester, an attractive stretch of rolling countryside watered by small streams. Originally the region was known as Hutchinson's, after Anne Hutchinson, who found refuge here for a time after being exiled from Massachusetts. In 1664 a group of 10 families from Fairfield County, Connecticut, under the leadership of Thomas Pell, arrived and asserted the right of Connecticut to the territory 'as far south as the sea,' including Eastchester and Westchester. The settlers conciliated the Indians, but the boundary dispute between New York and Connecticut was not settled until many years later.

The modern city began as a planned community. In 1850 a group of New York City workmen, artisans, and others of moderate means formed the Home Industrial Association with the purpose of 'protection against the unjust power and influence of capital, and against land monopoly as the prime cause of poverty.' The immediate aim was to establish a home-making community outside the city. Members paid into the treasury not less than $25 and not more than $75. By 1852, 300 homes had been built and Mount Vernon became a regular stop on the New York, New Haven & Hartford Railroad.

The undertaking of the Home Industrial Association attracted the interest of many prominent men in the liberal circles of the day, conspicuous among whom was Horace Greeley. These men were accustomed to gather for discussion at Gould's Hotel, built in the new settlement by George J. Gould. The cuisine soon acquired a wide reputation, and the guest book displayed, among others, the signatures of Cyrus and Dudley Field, Frank Leslie, and John J. Huyler. Adelina Patti, as a very young girl, signed the guest book, and sang in the hotel parlor.

St. Paul's (Protestant Episcopal) Church (*open weekdays by appointment*), S. Columbus Ave. (old Boston Post Road) between S. 3d and Fulton Aves., a historic shrine on the marshy land beside the Hutchinson River, is today surrounded by giant gas and oil tanks and concrete factory buildings.

The church, built in 1761, its stone walls now weathered with age but still solid, is of a simple Georgian Colonial style, with a square tower at the front entrance. The bell, presented long before the Revolution and cast by Lester and Peck, who also cast the Liberty Bell, was buried in 1775 to prevent its being recast into cannon and is still rung at services.

After the Battle of Pell's Point, Hessian troops seized the church and used it as a barracks and hospital. Ninety Hessians, who died the first night in the church, were buried in a sandpit at the foot of the cemetery: the grave is now marked. The cemetery also contains a marker over an Indian grave dated 1687, and another stone dated 1704. George Washington Adams, son of President John Quincy Adams, drowned near by in 1829, is also buried here.

The list of names of the pewholders and vestrymen of St. Paul's at the end of the Revolution included Van Cortlandt, Rhinelander, Pinckney, Morgan, Drake, and Roosevelt. Aaron Burr pleaded cases in the church after the Revolution, when it was used as a court.

A part of the old Eastchester Village Green lies between the church and the sunken highway. Colonial troops drilled here for both the French and Indian and the Revolutionary wars. Coaches rolled by on an eight-day trip to Boston (today planes pass over the church on the 85-minute Boston run). In 1733 John Peter Zenger, New York newspaper editor, was arrested for his account of an election for assemblyman held here; his release several months later served to establish the American principle of the freedom of the press.

Fay's Tavern (*private*), S. Columbus Ave. opposite St. Paul's Church, was kept during the Revolution by one Billy Crawford and was a favorite rendezvous of British officers.

The Site of Guion's Tavern is at the corner of Kingsbridge Road and Columbus Ave. In the tavern Washington paid off his troops after the Battle of White Plains, October 28, 1776.

The Mount Vernon Library (*open 9-9, Mon.–Fri.*), 28 S. 1st Ave., is a large building designed in the French chateau style, with a sweeping stone staircase at the main entrance. Most of the windows are heavily leaded, seven of them decorated with glass inserts bearing the arms of medieval printers' guilds. Besides a collection of about 120,000 volumes, the library houses exhibits of pottery, enamelware, woodcuts, Audubon prints, old silver, drawings, and Mexican arts and crafts.

The STEVENS HOUSE (*private*), corner of E.4th St. and 6th Ave., a substantial late Georgian Colonial residence, was the home of John Stevens, leader of the Home Industrial Association and its agent in its first purchase of land.

At 107.7 *m.* State 22 crosses the NEW YORK CITY LINE, 12 miles northeast of Columbus Circle.

Tour 21

(Montreal, P.Q.)—Rouses Point—Plattsburg—Glens Falls—Saratoga Springs—Albany—Poughkeepsie—New York City; US 9.
Canadian Line to New York City, 327.1 *m.*

Hard-surfaced throughout, mostly concrete; narrow macadam between Schroon Lake and Warrensburg.
The Delaware & Hudson R.R. parallels route between Rouses Point and Albany; New York Central R.R. between Albany and New York City.

US 9, the main highway through the Lake Champlain-Hudson River Valley, swings westward from Lake Champlain through the eastern section of the Adirondack State Park, touches the lower end of Lake George, and crosses the low divide between the St.Lawrence and the Hudson River watersheds. At Albany, near the head of Hudson tidewater, it crosses the Hudson River to the east bank, which it roughly follows to New York City. Through the Hudson Valley, the Catskills rise on the west and the Berkshires and Taconics on the east.

For the French—and after 1776 for the British—the Champlain-Hudson Valley was an excellent route for the advance of troops from Canada to the heart of the Atlantic seaboard. It provided water transportation and was protected against flank attacks by high, heavily forested mountains, so that fortifications at a few strategic points could hold the entire valley. Conversely, the same route afforded an approach for a swift attack on Montreal and Quebec. When the Revolutionary War broke out, both sides based their strategy largely on the occupation of this natural thoroughfare. The Patriots got the jump on the British when Ethan Allen and Benedict Arnold captured Ticonderoga, and Seth Warner took Crown Point in May 1775. But the issue of the control of the valley was not settled until Burgoyne's surrender at Saratoga (*see Tour 22*) in October 1777. Similarly, the threat of British invasion from the north during the War of 1812 was halted by Macdonough's destruction of the British fleet on Lake Champlain in September 1814.

Section a. CANADIAN LINE to LAKE GEORGE; 130.8 *m. US* 9

Immediately south of the border US 9 runs along the low, level shore of Lake Champlain. South of Plattsburg the road turns inland and enters the Adirondacks, becoming a mountain road winding down creek valleys and over ridges.

US 9, a continuation of Que.9, crosses the NEW YORK STATE LINE, 0 *m.,* at a point 40 miles south of Montreal, P.Q. European visitors marvel at the absence of armed guards at the international boundary; the only uniformed officials are customs and immigration officers. At the U.S.CUS-TOMHOUSE (R) 0.1 *m.,* mirrors in the floor of the covered entrance reveal the undercarriages of vehicles (*for customs regulations see General Information.*)

More than 60 per cent of the population of ROUSES POINT, 1.4 *m.* (120 alt.,1,920 pop.), is of French-Canadian descent, and numbers of Canadians cross the border daily to enjoy the motion pictures and to buy American cigarettes.

Rose Ave. leads (L) to the ROUSES POINT BRIDGE (*tolls: car* $1, *trailer* 50¢; *pedestrian* 25¢), to Vermont, opened in 1937.

ISLAND POINT, an island in the lake, was the SITE OF FORT MONT-GOMERY, which replaced what had been called Fort Blunder, a fortification planned to guard the northern end of Lake Champlain but never completed. In 1819, when construction on the older fort was in progress, surveyors announced that the island belonged to Canada and the place was abandoned. Immediately after the boundary was established in 1842 by the Webster-Ashburton Treaty, a new fort was erected but it was never garrisoned.

Rouses Point is at the junction with US 11 (*see Tour* 18).

US 9 leaves the lake and turns inland to CHAZY, 10.8 *m.* (160 alt.,500 pop.), on the Little Chazy River. The first settler here was Jean From-boise, who arrived in 1763 but was driven off by Burgoyne's forces. He returned at the end of the Revolution and became the first apple grower in the North Country. The river and the village were named for Lieutenant de Chézy of the Carignan Salières regiment, who was killed near by in 1666 by a party of Iroquois. The regiment, brought to America in 1664, played a prominent part in the destruction of Iroquois villages by the French.

The COLONIAL HOUSE (L), 11.5 *m.* (*open May–Nov., adm.* 50¢), a two-and-a-half-story stone structure built in 1824, is now a private museum containing, among other relics, a chair that belonged to William McKinley, a sugar-loaf cutter once owned by Andrew Jackson, a wine cooler made for Abraham Lincoln, early American china, and Colonial furniture.

At 19.2 *m.* is the junction with a macadam road.

Left here 1 *m.* to the sandy beach of POINT AU ROCHE.

At 23.7 *m.* is a junction with a macadam road.

Left on this road 0.3 *m.* to CUMBERLAND BEACH, the municipal bathing beach of Plattsburg. Here in Cumberland Bay, on September 11, 1814, was fought the naval

Battle of Plattsburg, in which the British advance up the Champlain Valley was repulsed. The American commander, Thomas Macdonough, anchored his little wooden fleet across the mouth of the bay; auxiliary anchors were thrown out astern with cables running to the bows so that the ships could be readily swung around. The slightly larger British fleet was anchored in a parallel line. The first British broadside killed or disabled one fifth of the men on the *Saratoga*, Macdonough's flagship. When his starboard battery was disabled, Macdonough turned his ship around and brought his port battery to bear on Commodore Downie's flagship. Within two hours many of the British ships were disabled and the Union Jack was struck.

Tradition has it that when a cannon ball shot away the hencoop on the deck of the *Saratoga*, a rooster perched on the rigging, crowing and flapping his wings. The crew regarded him as a symbol of victory, and he is said to have been the inspiration for the innumerable weathercocks that adorned York State courthouses and barns in the nineteenth century.

PLATTSBURG, 25.3 *m.* (140 alt.,14,713 pop.), is at the mouth of the Saranac River, which has provided water power for manufacturing since 1785. The first mills ground corn and cut lumber for the settlers; the present ones make wood pulp and manufacture paper products, such as napkins and wallpaper. Nearly half the population is of French-Canadian descent.

The land engagements of the Battle of Plattsburg were fought in and north of the village. General Alexander Macomb, with a force of about 3,000 Americans, had advanced to oppose 11,000 British troops moving south under Sir George Prevost. On September 6, 1814, two skirmishes occurred north of Plattsburg. The Americans retreated south of the Saranac River and threw up fortifications. The British waited north of the river for Commodore Downie to clear the lake of the American fleet under Macdonough. On September 11, while the naval battle was in progress, the British attacked on land; but the news of the defeat on the lake caused Prevost to retreat during the night.

The MACDONOUGH MEMORIAL, S.River St. in front of the city hall, was designed by John Russell Pope. It is an obelisk of Indiana limestone, 135 feet high, and is decorated with reliefs and the names of the principal ships of Macdonough's fleet—*Saratoga*, *Ticonderoga*, *Preble*, and *Eagle*.

The KENT-DELORD HOUSE (*adm.* 50¢), 17 Cumberland Ave., is a long two-story structure with end chimneys and a one-story pedimented entrance portico. Chancellor James Kent is associated with the house only by virtue of having represented his wife in the sale of the property. It was purchased in 1810 by Henry DeLord, a French refugee from Martinique, who remodeled it. In the house are the DeLord family records and household treasures, including fine old furniture, an early Chickering piano, portraits, silver, and curios from Europe and China. An old chaise stands in the barn.

The CHAMPLAIN MONUMENT, Cumberland Ave., is a granite shaft surmounted by a statue of Champlain, who discovered the lake in 1609.

The PLATTSBURG STATE NORMAL SCHOOL, corner of Beekman and Brinkerhoff Sts., was established in 1889. The old buildings were destroyed by fire in 1929; the new structure is of modified Tudor Gothic design. The school prepares men and women for teaching in the elementary grades.

The UNITED STATES MILITARY RESERVATION, on the lake shore south of the river, covering 703 acres, was established six months after the Battle of Plattsburg. Many of the present buildings were erected in 1838. Troops of the Regular Army are stationed here and thousands of men attend the annual sessions of the Plattsburg Citizens Military Training Camp.

Plattsburg is at the junction with State 22 (see Tour 20) and State 3 (see Tour 17).

CLIFF HAVEN (L), 28.4 m., belongs to the Catholic Summer School of America. Extension courses of Fordham University and leadership courses of the Knights of Columbus Boy Life Bureau are given here.

Offshore at this point, in October 1776, the first Colonial Lake Champlain fleet had its initial engagement. The 16 little ships of the fleet, which were planned by Arnold and Schuyler after Montgomery's death before Quebec, were built by New England carpenters at Skenesborough (Whitehall) and were manned by New York and Massachusetts landlubbers. The British fleet of 29 vessels was intercepted here. On the first day the British guns did considerable damage to the American boats, but in the dense night fog Arnold crept through the enemy's line and reached Schuyler's Island, eight miles south, where he repaired his larger ships with lumber salvaged from the smaller craft. The next day he fought again and managed to bring off most of his boats to within ten miles of Crown Point. He burned the vessels to the water's edge in the shallows of Arnold's Bay on the Vermont shore and escaped overland with his men to Ticonderoga. The British fleet lingered near Ticonderoga until cold weather drove it back to St. Johns. As a result of the battle the British advance southward was delayed until the following year, thus giving the Colonials an opportunity to prepare defenses and arouse public support for the campaign of 1777, which ended at Saratoga.

In the summer of 1935, following a revival of public interest aroused by Kenneth Roberts's novel, *Rabble in Arms*, the hulk of the American vessel *Philadelphia* was raised and towed south to ports along the lake and was visited by large crowds. It is on display each summer at Crown Point (*adm.* 25¢).

The boundary of the ADIRONDACK STATE PARK is crossed at 37.3 m. The park—5,575,000 acres of private and public mountain, lake, and valley—embraces about two thirds of the great lobe of the State north of the Mohawk River between Lake Champlain and Lake Ontario, and includes the State-owned Adirondack Forest Preserve of 2,165,150 acres, which by law 'shall be forever kept as wild forest land' (*see Conservation*). Five separate mountain ranges—Luzerne, Kayaderosseras, Schroon, Bouquet, and the main Adirondack Range—parallel each other about eight miles apart through the eastern and southern regions of the park. The main range stretches 100 miles from Lake Champlain across Essex, Hamilton, and Herkimer Counties to the Mohawk River; rising from its back are the humps of Mount Marcy, the State's highest peak, Mount McIntyre, Mount Haystack, and Mount Skylight.

A network of picturesque lakes, rivers, and ponds interlace the valleys.

between the pine- and spruce-cloaked shoulders of the mountains. The principal lakes form an almost continuous chain, making possible a 150-mile canoe trip, with short carries, through an unspoiled mountain wilderness that in 1858 inspired Emerson's poem 'The Adirondacks' and, later, gentle fishing essays by Henry van Dyke. Here profitable lumbering was in some sections impossible, so that part of the Adirondack forest was saved from ruthless destruction. More than 500 miles of foot trails have been blazed over the principal mountain peaks. In 1938 more than 650,000 persons used the State campsites built along the lakes, rivers, highways, and foot trails.

In addition to conservation of forest lands, the Park insures improved water resources, increases fish and game, and provides recreation—hunting, fishing, hiking, skiing, and canoeing (*see also Tours* 14, 15, 16, 16A, 17, 18, 20).

Beneath the bridge spanning the gorge of the Ausable River, 38.9 *m.*, the water plunges 75 feet over a brown rock ledge to form Rainbow Falls at the southern end of the chasm.

Just north of the bridge is the entrance (L) to AUSABLE CHASM (*open May–Oct.; walking tour, 75¢; tour and boat ride, $1.50; boats do not operate on rainy days because of danger of high water*). Privately operated as a tourists' wonderland for 65 years, the chasm is crisscrossed by paths and steel bridges. Galleries cut in the face of the rock high above the river lead around rock formations named Pulpit Rock, Elephant's Head, Devil's Oven, Jacob's Well, Cathedral Rock, and the like. The boats run mild rapids at the northern end of the gorge.

The first settler of KEESEVILLE, 40.7 *m.* (400 alt.,1,794 pop.), was the Quaker John Keese, who arrived in 1806. Soon afterward he was joined by French Canadians attracted by the lumbering and iron-mining industries. A missionary priest was sent from Montreal and in 1835 he built the Church of the Immaculate Conception, establishing the second parish in the Ogdensburg diocese. Keeseville continued to be a roistering place for lumberjacks on the Ausable until 1919. At present its chief industrial activity is the manufacture of radio cabinets.

At Keeseville is the junction with State 9N.

Right on State 9N to AUSABLE FORKS, 11.3 *m.* (551 alt.,2,200 pop.), at the fork of the Ausable River. The largest single industry is a paper mill, whose wide yards along the river are pyramided with peeled, bleaching pulpwood chunks. On a farm just south of the village is the Cape Cod style cottage of Rockwell Kent, etcher and illustrator.

South of JAY, 17.9 *m.* (644 alt.,350 pop.), at the junction with State 86 (*see Tour* 16), State 9N follows the valley of the East Branch of the Ausable River through UPPER JAY, 21.6 *m.* (680 alt.,250 pop.), summer home of Donald Ogden Stewart, author-humorist, to KEENE, 28 *m.* (860 alt.,380 pop.), at the upper end of beautiful Keene Valley. With few arable acres in the mountain-shadowed valley, Keene's economic life depends upon tourists and vacationists. Immaculate white frame houses rise close to the tree-shaded sidewalks. Snug against a hotel is a gigantic elm with a spread of 91 feet and a base circumference of 21½ feet, reputedly the largest elm in the Adirondacks. Jagged mountains, the highest in the State, thrust their peaks above the village; Mount Marcy, blue in the cloudy distance, rises 5,344 feet in the southwest.

In Keene is the junction with State 86A (*see Tour 16A*), with which State 9N runs in common for 1.5 miles, then swings east through hilly country toward Lake Champlain.

At 37.6 *m.* is the junction with a dirt road; left here 2.4 *m.* along a swift mountain stream through a private forest plantation, to the end of the road and a foot trail to HURRICANE MOUNTAIN (3,687 alt.), 4.5 *m.* From the fire observation tower on the bare rock cone summit is a majestic view of the Adirondack terrain to the north, south, and west, and the blue waters of Lake Champlain to the east.

In ELIZABETHTOWN, 39.8 *m.* (550 alt.,636 pop.), is the junction with US 9 (*see below*).

Southward from Keeseville US 9 and State 22 (*see Tour* 20) are united for 4.1 miles. Continuing southwest, US 9 crosses low hills toward the black dome of Poke-O-Moonshine Mountain. According to authorities, the name is of Indian origin (the place where the rock is smoothly broken off), but local legend insists that the mountain was so named because of the moonshiners who set up stills near the summit in the days when stages ran to the lumber camps along the Saranac and Schroon Rivers. Here raw liquor, in delivery lots, became known as 'poke o' moonshine.' The dirt roads around the mountain were heavily traveled by bootleggers during the prohibition era.

In the shadow of the barren face of the mountain are entrances, (L) and (R) at 48.2 *m.*, to POKE-O-MOONSHINE STATE CAMPSITE (*free; open Memorial Day to Labor Day; two-week camping permits subject to renewal*), one of the 36 camping grounds operated by the State in the Adirondack area. A foot trail leads from No.1 fireplace to the wooded summit (2,162 alt.) of Poke-O-Moonshine, where a fire tower affords far-reaching views of the mountains and Lake Champlain.

ELIZABETHTOWN, 63.6 *m.* (550 alt.,636 pop.), hemmed in by the Adirondacks, lies at the head of a mile-wide flat land created by the Bouquet River. Lumbering reached its peak here about 1870, then rapidly declined. The rambling hotels were built when the invasion of summer visitors began in the seventies. In the ESSEX COUNTY COURTHOUSE is a painting representing the trial of John Brown, whose body lay in state in the building before its burial at North Elba.

In the village is the junction with State 9N (*see above*).

South of Elizabethtown the road follows the valley of the Bouquet River for eight miles, running along the eastern base of the main range of mountains. At 73.1 *m.* is the junction with State 86A (*see Tour* 16A), the most beautiful route in the park.

Within a five-mile radius of UNDERWOOD, 74.3 *m.* (1,120 alt.,235 pop.), are 14 ponds, all regularly stocked with game fish. SHARP BRIDGE STATE CAMPSITE (L), 78.4 *m.*, is on the bank of a branch of the Schroon River.

SCHROON LAKE VILLAGE, 94.2 *m.* (840 alt.,650 pop.), lies at the head of lovely nine-mile Schroon Lake. One tale is that the name was given by French scouts in the early eighteenth century, who compared the beauty of the long slim body of water with that of the young widow of Paul Scarron, the dramatist, best known as Madame de Maintenon, consort of Louis XIV. Hotels and tourist homes line the main street for two miles and spread along the side streets leading toward the lake. The vil-

lage is the trading center for the large number of summer visitors in outlying cottages, hotels, and camps. Within a five-mile radius are 70 lakes
and ponds.

The EAGLE POINT STATE CAMPSITE (L), 101.3 *m.*, borders the lake for a
mile.

At 108.4 *m.* is the western junction with State 8 (*see Tour* 14), which
unites with US 9 to the eastern junction in CHESTERTOWN, 112.3 *m.*
(854 alt.,700 pop.). The area was settled in 1780 by New Englanders, who
built gristmills and sawmills along the creeks.

A boundary of the CHARLES LATHROP PACK DEMONSTRA-
TION FOREST of 2,300 acres is crossed at 118.3 *m.*; it contains 240 acres
of virgin white pine. During the summer, students of the New York State
College of Forestry come here for practice work in planting, weeding,
thinning, and cutting. The tract was presented to the college in 1926.
Charles Lathrop Pack (1857–1937), the donor, was long active in the conservation movement and wrote *Trees as Good Citizens* and *Schoolbook of
Forestry.* His grave is in the forest about two miles from the administration
building.

WARRENSBURG, 124.4 *m.* (720 alt.,2,000 pop.), on the northern
shore of the Schroon River, was named for James Warren, who settled
here in 1804. Like Chestertown, it is a village with a year-round existence
largely dependent on the trade of farmers. During the middle years of the
nineteenth century, hemlock bark from the upper Schroon was shipped to
local tanneries. In the spring the settlement was overrun by loggers, as
drives from the upper Hudson and the Schroon met at the near-by junction of the two rivers for the final rush to the mills in Glens Falls.

Identified by its bandstand and a tall flagpole is FLOYD BENNETT ME-
MORIAL PARK, a small square of land given to the village in 1930 by the
local American Legion Post, No.446. Floyd Bennett (1890–1928), born at
North Caldwell, came with his parents to a small farm near Harrington
Hill, west of the village. After completing an automobile engineering
course in Schenectady, he returned to work as a mechanic in a garage at
Hague, and spent most of his waking hours tinkering with engines. In 1925
he was one of the naval mechanics assigned to service on the Donald Mc-
Millan expedition to Greenland; and he piloted Richard E. Byrd on the
first airplane flight over the North Pole, completing the round trip from
Kings Bay, Spitzbergen, to the Pole and return in $15\frac{1}{2}$ hours. In April 1928
Bennett developed pneumonia while on a rescue flight and died on
April 25 in a Quebec hospital.

LAKE GEORGE, 130.8 *m.* (350 alt.,848 pop.), seat of Warren County
and a year-round sports center, lies in the foothills of the Adirondacks at
the southern end of Lake George. All summer long, shoppers and strollers
throng the streets, parking space is at a premium, and the lake is alive
with boats and the seaplanes of wealthy New Yorkers who commute to
their offices by air four or five days a week. In recent years facilities for
winter sports have been developed on a large scale.

At the southern village limits (L), on the grounds of the Fort William
Henry Hotel, are the remnants of FORT WILLIAM HENRY, built in 1756 by

Sir William Johnson to protect the portage between Lake George and the Hudson. The fort, after having been successfully defended against 1,500 French soldiers and their Indian allies in March 1757, was captured by Montcalm in August of the same year. Montcalm had given promise of safe conduct for the garrison but he could not control the Indians, who massacred a large number of men, women, and children, and carried others into captivity. The French razed the fort, which was never rebuilt.

Montcalm St. leads west to a marked foot trail up PROSPECT MOUNTAIN (2,021 alt.). From the steel observation tower on the summit a vivid panorama of woods, mountains, and lakes unfolds, and on a clear day the spires of Albany are vaguely outlined. There are two Adirondack lean-to shelters for picnickers or overnight campers. South from the fire tower is the three-mile PROSPECT MOUNTAIN SKI TRAIL, approached in winter by a roundabout dirt road off US 9 just north of the village.

Lake George is at a junction with State 9N (*see Tour* 23).

Section b.   *LAKE GEORGE to ALBANY;* 60.2 *m.   US* 9

US 9, here a three- and four-lane highway, leaves the Adirondacks, crosses a monotonous plain, and descends gradually to Albany. During the French and Indian and Revolutionary Wars, this district was a bloody battleground; in the early years of the nineteenth century, it was the scene of much lumbering and paper making. Today the communities are supported by manufacturing and the tourist trade.

South of LAKE GEORGE, 0 *m.*, at 0.7 *m.* is the entrance (L) to State-maintained BATTLEGROUND PARK CAMPSITE, from which a graveled road winds into the LAKE GEORGE BATTLEGROUND PARK. At the main entrance is a large monument with two bronze figures representing King Hendrick, chief of the Mohawk, demonstrating to William Johnson the futility of dividing his forces.

On the morning of September 8, 1755, against the advice of King Hendrick, Johnson dispatched 1,000 Colonials and 200 Indians under Colonel Ephraim Williams to prevent Baron Dieskau from cutting his lines of communication with Fort Edward. About two miles south Williams encountered Dieskau in command of 1,000 or more Indians, Canadians, and French regulars; a sharp engagement—the 'bloody morning scout'—ensued, during which Colonel Williams was killed. Later in the same day Dieskau led his French troops in several futile charges against Johnson's barricade on this site. After several hours of fighting the Colonial forces poured over the barricade, charged the retreating French, and took many prisoners, including the wounded Dieskau. Johnson was given credit for the victory and was rewarded with a baronetcy.

In the park is the FATHER ISAAC JOGUES MONUMENT, a bronze statue by Charles Keck erected by the State of New York in 1939. The inscription describes the Jesuit martyr (*see Tour* 12) as an 'ambassador of peace from New France to the Five Nations of the Iroquois' and mentions his discovery of Lake George.

The RUINS OF FORT GEORGE consist of a mound 15 to 20 feet high and

100 feet long, covered with moss and grass, except where small sections of stone still stand. Construction of the fort was begun by Amherst in 1759 but was never entirely completed. Revolutionary troops sent to occupy the place retired before Burgoyne in 1777. After the Battle of Saratoga, the fort was again occupied by the Americans, who held it until surprised by Sir John Johnson in 1780.

At 1 *m.* is the entrance (R) to FORT GAGE PARK, a wooded area including the SITE OF FORT GAGE, on a rise of ground; this post is supposed to have been established early in the French and Indian War. Tradition has it that Lord Howe encamped here in 1758 with the advance guard of Abercrombie's troops and engaged in a game of 'jumping the stick' with other officers; Howe won when he cleared the bar at 6 feet 6 inches. The hill was later named for Brigadier General Thomas Gage, second in command under Amherst in 1759.

At 1.4 *m.* is the junction with State 9K (*see Tour 23*).

BLOODY POND (L), 2.4 *m.*, was so named because into it were thrown the bodies of French soldiers killed by a relief party during the Battle of Lake George.

The WILLIAMS MONUMENT (L), 3 *m.*, marks the spot where Colonel Ephraim Williams was killed during the opening moments of the 'bloody morning scout.' On his way to join Johnson, Colonel Williams had a presentiment of early death and at Albany made a will leaving most of his property to found a free school at Williamstown, Massachusetts. After 30 years this fund was used as the original endowment of Williams College.

Most of the business blocks of GLENS FALLS, 9.1 *m.* (343 alt.,18,715 pop.), show the trimmings of the mid-nineteenth century; the simplicity of the several new structures is in marked contrast. The residential districts, with large houses on broad lawns, reflect the high per capita wealth of the city. Paper, machinery, chemicals, dresses, and gloves are manufactured here.

The site of Glens Falls was part of the Queensbury Patent, 23,000 acres of land granted in 1759 to 23 men. The water power provided by the 60-foot falls in the Hudson, which the Indians called Chepontuo (a difficult place to get around), determined the location of the settlement. During the Revolution the village was in the direct path of invasion and in 1780 it was destroyed by the British. In 1788 Colonel John Glen of Schenectady acquired land and built mills here.

The history of Glens Falls is the story of a succession of industrial activities. First came lumbering, during which the huge log drives sent millions of feet of timber down the Hudson annually. The 'big boom,' built of timber and chains to catch and sort the logs, is still used near by. In addition to lumbering, the townspeople carried on the manufacture of lime from the limestone along the northern riverbank. When the demand for lime decreased, the limestone was used to make cement. The manufacture of paper began in the sixties, and by 1896 Glens Falls was producing 275 tons of paper a day; but after a bitter strike in the largest mill shortly after the turn of the century, most of the paper mills were closed. The mill that suffered from the strike now manufactures cellulose products on a relatively small scale. Shirt manufacturing began in 1879, expanded till it gave work to large numbers, and then succumbed to outside competition.

The FINCH PRUYN & COMPANY PLANT, 1–27 Glen St. (*open; guides at office*), with a huge pile of pulpwood always in the yard, produces paper, principally newsprint.

COOPER'S CAVE, beneath the bridge over the Hudson connecting Glens Falls and South Glens Falls, is reached by a spiral stairway. The low rock cavern at the foot of the falls is the scene of one of the most dramatic episodes of Cooper's *Last of the Mohicans*.

At 14.6 *m.* is the junction with a dirt road.

Left on this road 1.5 *m.* to a STATE FISH HATCHERY (*open April–Oct.*), containing open ponds and breeding pools for brown and lake trout. Approximately 500,000 fingerlings are grown here each summer, then transferred by tank car, truck, and airplane to Adirondack streams and lakes.

At WILTON, 20.4 *m.* (348 alt.,200 pop.), is the junction with a macadam road.

Right on this road, which runs up the slope of Mount McGregor, to the MOUNT McGREGOR SANITARIUM (R), 1.5 *m.*, a group of seven stuccoed buildings operated for employees of the Metropolitan Life Insurance Company. Near by is the GENERAL GRANT COTTAGE, State controlled (*admission free*), a two-story frame building. Suffering from cancer of the throat, General Grant came to this cottage on June 16, 1885, finished his memoirs, and died on July 23. The living room, dining room and office contain the furniture used by the Grants.

SARATOGA SPRINGS, 27.8 *m.* (330 alt.,13,670 pop.) (*see Saratoga Springs*), is at the junction with State 29 (*see Tour 13*) and State 9K (*see Tour 23*).

1. East from Saratoga Springs on State 9P to SARATOGA LAKE, 3.7 *m.*, popular summer resort. The Mohawk believed that the lake reflected their god's peaceful mind and that anyone crossing it would be drowned if he uttered a single sound. A white woman, to prove the superstition false, shouted while being taken across in a canoe, and nothing happened. The Indians brought her to shore and explained, 'The Great Spirit is merciful. He knows that a white woman cannot hold her tongue.'

Across the road from the WHITE SULPHUR SPRING HOTEL, 8.6 *m.*, where Jack Dempsey and Bob Pastor trained for world's heavyweight championship fights, is (L) WHITE SULPHUR SPRING (*open, free*).

At 12.1 *m.* State 9P rejoins US 9 (*see below*).

2. South from Saratoga Springs on State 50 to an entrance (L) to the SARATOGA SPRINGS RESERVATION, 1.6 *m.* (*see Saratoga Springs*). The COESA MINERAL SPRING (L), 2.9 *m.*, and the HATHORN No.3 MINERAL SPRING (L), 3 *m.*, are both known for their naturally carbonated, laxative waters.

BALLSTON SPA, 6.3 *m.* (340 alt.,4,433 pop.), has knitting mills and tanneries. Before the Civil War the place outranked Saratoga as a fashionable resort and watering place, but after the war the race track and the elaborate casinos attracted the crowds to Saratoga.

SCOTIA, 21.9 *m.* (240 alt.,7,944 pop.) (*see Tour 11*), is at the junction with State 5 (*see Tour 11*).

At 34.2 *m.* is a junction (L) with State 9P (*see above*).

The privately owned LUTHER FOREST PRESERVE (L), 37 *m.*, contains nearly 10,000,000 trees, chiefly varieties of pine. Red pine is best adapted to this region because of its immunity to the diseases that attack the other species.

In CLIFTON PARK, 43.9 *m.* (344 alt.,150 pop.), is (L) STEVENS' TAV-ERN, built about 1800. The 14 chimneys have been removed, but the heavy doors have the original wrought-iron hinges and iron bars. The second floor of the long wing was for a time used as a courtroom. Because the building was on the town line the court met at one end of the room for Clifton Park and at the other for Crescent.

CRESCENT, 47.6 *m.* (210 alt.,250 pop.), lies on the north bank of the Mohawk River at the top of the crescent made by the river in its bend toward the Hudson, four miles southeast. The village, with its neighbor Halfmoon, was one of the first Dutch settlements north of Albany.

The old Erie Canal formerly crossed the river on an arched concrete aqueduct just west of the bridge. Along the water front and on near-by farms live a number of the old 'canawlers' and their kin. In the village stand the decadent inns, once noisy with dances and 'shows'; the old red brick bank building; a two-story white house built around Granny An-drews's one-room select school where 'canawlers' paid 15¢ every Monday morning for their children's 'schoolin''; the community well; a country store with chairs around a big stove; the old mill and dam; and several squatters' homes.

At 53.5 *m.* a traffic circle marks the junction with State 7 (*see Tour* 10).
At 54 *m.* is a junction with State 155.

Right on State 155 to the ALBANY AIRPORT (R), 2.5 *m.*, owned and operated by the city of Albany.

The ANN LEE HOME (R), 2.6 *m.*, established in 1930 by Albany County as a farm colony for the care of the aged and homeless, comprises 787 acres of the richest farm-land in the county purchased from the United Society of Shakers in 1926. The home is named for Ann Lee, the Mother Ann of the Shakers (*see Tour* 8). The SHAKER CEM-ETERY (R), 2.7 *m.*, is a small plot with symmetrical rows of simple white slabs. Ann Lee's grave in the center is distinguished only by a slightly taller headstone. At 3.3 *m.* stand (R) the simple red brick buildings once occupied by the North Family of Shakers.

ALBANY, 60.2 *m.* (18 alt.,130,447 pop.) (*see Albany*), is at the junction with US 20 (*see Tour* 8), State 43 (*see Tour* 9), State 5 (*see Tour* 11), and US 9W (*see Tour* 21*A*).

Section c. ALBANY to POUGHKEEPSIE; 75.9 m. US 9

Between Albany and Poughkeepsie US 9 runs from two to five miles inland from the eastern bank of the Hudson River, following in stretches the route of the Albany Post Road of Colonial days.

This section of the State contains many reminders of Dutch settlement, especially family and place names—often puzzling in their Anglicized forms—and solid old houses with low first stories and steep gable or gam-brel roofs, small windowpanes, and thick doors. Below Hudson, stretching to New York City, is a magnificent succession of historic manor houses (*see also Tour* 21*B*) and great country homes.

The lovely countryside was one of the last strongholds of agricultural feudalism. The Dutch West India Company parceled out the land in enormous patroonships, and the British confirmed and extended the manorial system. Most important on the east bank of the Hudson were Rensselaerswyck, Livingston Manor, Van Cortlandt Manor, and Philipsburgh. The tenants who cultivated these estates were restless under the semifeudal system of long-term leases. In 1769 a real estate speculator on his way to his lands along the Mohawk kept a diary that reveals the unrest pervading the countryside. A tenant of Philipsburgh complained that his rent was seven pounds a year for 200 acres and that 'on his demise or Sale his Son or Vendee is obliged to pay to the Landlord one Third of the Value of the Farm for Renewal of the Lease.' A little farther north another said that he and his neighbors were planning to migrate because they had to pay seven pounds a year for 'about 100 acres including Rocks and Mountains.'

The hope of improving their economic lot made these tenants eager fighters in the rebellion against the Crown; but the political settlement after the Revolution did not break up the huge estates. After the Revolution, in a movement that reached its peak in the thirties and forties, tenant farmers took matters into their own hands and by the threat of force tried to prevent sheriffs from serving eviction notices for nonpayment of rent in arrears. In these 'antirent wars' the tenants often disguised themselves as Indians; and the old ballad relates that:

> The moon was shining silver bright;
> The sheriff came in dead of night;
> High on a hill an 'Indian' true
> And on his horn this blast he blew:
> Keep out of the way, old Bill Snyder;
> We'll tar your coat and feather your hide, sir.

These outbreaks were quelled by the militia; but wide popular disapproval and the opening of abundant cheap land in the West caused the breakup of the leasehold system. The tenants turned to political action and won their greatest victory in the adoption of the constitution of 1846, which abolished all feudal tenures in land and limited agricultural leases to a twelve-year period.

The industrial revolution caused another change in the cultural character of the valley. As new fortunes were made in finance, land and stock speculation, manufacturing, and trade, the Hudson Valley became a fashionable suburb of New York City. Everyone who made money wanted a country place where he could live in the style of the English gentry. The descendants of the old landed aristocracy set the tone of living in a tight little society of their own, to which newcomers were admitted only after they had shown in long years of residence that they understood and accepted the code. The city mansions of these gentry served as town houses, used during the winter social season and when business required that the head of the household be near his offices. Stages, carriages, boats, later the railroads, and finally the automobile provided transportation.

The Hudson reached its peak of fashionable importance in the decades following the Civil War; since 1900 that importance has dwindled steadily. The young people of today still dutifully go up the river for family reunions; but when the members of the older generation die, the heirs, preferring to live near the gay casinos and beaches of Long Island, sell the estates or give them to the State as public parks or to religious organizations or schools. So many of the places are being transferred to tax-free bodies as family memorials that the tax burden on the remaining property, especially in the case of farmers with small holdings, is becoming serious.

In ALBANY, 0 m., US 9 unites with US 20 (see Tour 8).

RENSSELAER, 1 m. (20 alt.,10,818 pop.), technically a separate municipality but actually a suburb of Albany, contains division shops of the New York Central and the Boston & Albany Railroads, and the water front is part of the Port of Albany, used particularly for lumber. Behind the wharves are factories producing dyes, chemicals, felts, and woolen goods. The city, formed in 1897 by the union of the villages of East Albany, Greenbush, and Bath-on-the-Hudson, stands on ground that was part of Rensselaerswyck, most successful of the patroonships.

FORT CRAILO (open weekdays 9–5, Sundays 1–5; adm. free), Riverside St. (L) south of Columbia, is a much restored brick dwelling now maintained as a public museum. The front or river block is believed to have been built by Hendrick Van Rensselaer in 1704, shortly after he received the Claverack tract and the Green Bush farm from his brother Kiliaen, the patroon. Within are huge hewn beams, large fireplaces, and broad floor boards. The interior of the rear wing, erected in 1762, illustrates, by contrast with the earlier structure, the progress of half a century: rooms are more spacious, paneling is more extensive, and double-hung sash supplant casements.

This building is also known as the 'Yankee Doodle House.' In 1758, while Abercrombie was preparing to attack Ticonderoga, Dr.Richard Shuckburgh, a British army surgeon, sat on the Fort Crailo well curb watching the provincial militia drill and wrote the derisive words of 'Yankee Doodle,' which later became the marching song of the Revolution.

BEVERWYCK, Washington Ave. opposite intersection with Eighth St., was built between 1840 and 1843 as the manor house of William Paterson Van Rensselaer, younger son of Stephen Van Rensselaer, upon the subdivision of the patroonship after the latter's death in 1839. The mansion was laid out on a truly aristocratic scale by Frederic Diaper, young English architect well known for his suave Italianate Fifth Avenue mansions and Wall Street banks. Stucco-covered brick to approximate cut stone, broad pilasters framing the triple windows, low attic, and one-story Greek Ionic porch produce a monumental effect. In the interior, a spacious hall with cantilevered stone stairs leads to the fine library with mahogany cases and Italianate ceiling painting in false-perspective. William resided here only a few years after completion of the house in 1843, since the estate was broken up as a result of the antirent wars. The Order of St.Francis bought the place in 1912 and established a monastery and training school here.

Right from Rensselaer on State 9J to the JAN BREESE (BRIES) HOUSE (L), 3.4 *m.*, built in 1723, the best remaining example of the brick farmhouses characteristic of the Albany region. Based on urban house forms, the trim story-and-a-half mass with its steep gable roof is in marked contrast to the low stone cottages of Ulster and Dutchess Counties. The walls of brick in English bond surround interior vertical timber members that support the floor beams, forming a structural system which, although it developed from medieval half-timbering, yet is surprisingly close in principle to modern skyscraper construction. The rear ell and dormer and the front porch are later additions. Inside, a central hall separates parlor and kitchen, which have beamed ceilings and large fireplaces. This important architectural monument is in a sad state of disrepair.

The VAN RENSSELAER-GENÊT HOUSE (L), 3.8 *m.*, built in 1742 by Kiliaen Van Rensselaer (1717–81), for his bride Ariaantje Schuyler, is a gambrel-roofed brick dwelling of the central-hall type. The porch and sash are nineteenth century. In 1802 George Clinton bought the house and farm for his daughter and son-in-law, Citizen Genêt, who resided here until they moved to the now destroyed Prospect Hill on the ridge.

Henry Hudson is supposed to have landed at the site of STUYVESANT, 18 *m.* (100 alt.,400 pop.), and named the place Kinder Hoek. The early Dutch settlers of the place moved up the hill to get away from malaria and mosquitoes and took the name with them.

At 22 *m.* is the junction with US 9 (*see below*).

On US 9–20, at 4.6 *m.* is the junction with US 4 (*see Tour 22*).

In the cemetery at the rear of the little Dutch Reformed Church (R), 5.5 *m.*, is the GRAVE OF EDMOND CHARLES GENÊT (1763–1834). Citizen Genêt, as first Minister of the French Republic to the United States, arrived in 1793, and caused much embarrassment to President Washington by outfitting French privateers at American ports and attempting to stir up American public opinion to force the Government into active support of France in its war with Great Britain. Washington succeeded in having Genêt recalled; but Genêt remained in this country as an American citizen and married the daughter of Governor George Clinton. On his farm along the river he carried on long and costly experiments that enabled him to obtain a patent in 1825 for 'an aerostatic vessel to be propelled by air.'

At 8.7 *m.* is the eastern junction with US 20 (*see Tour 8*).

At 17.8 *m.* is the junction with State 9H.

Right here 3.3 *m.* to the VAN ALEN HOMESTEAD (R), about 200 feet from the road behind three tall evergreens. The original brick house, built in 1737, contained two rooms, both with exterior doors, and a garret under the steeply pitched gable roof. In 1939 the house passed out of the Van Alen family for the first time. This was the home of Helen Van Alen, said to have been the original of Katrina Van Tassel in Washington Irving's *Legend of Sleepy Hollow.*

The ICHABOD CRANE SCHOOL (L), 3.4 *m.*, a one-room white-painted schoolhouse, stands on the site of the school taught by Jesse Merwin, the original of Irving's Ichabod Crane.

LINDENWALD (R), 4.2 *m.* (*small adm. fee*), was the home of Martin Van Buren from 1840, upon his retirement from the presidency, to his death in 1862. Built in 1797 by Judge William Peter Van Ness, with whom Van Buren studied law, the house was a typical post-Colonial, central-hall brick dwelling. Washington Irving, while visiting here in 1809 after the death of Mathilda Hoffman, his only love, tutored the Van Ness children and observed local characters, who later appeared in his humorous tales.

Van Buren, who named the property 'Lindenwald,' in 1849 had Richard Upjohn, architect of the just completed Trinity Church, New York City, renovate and enlarge the house. Upjohn obliterated the simplicity of the old mass by adding a steep front gable, consoled and gabled dormers, an eccentric cornice, a grotesque stoop, a supposedly Italianate tower, and wings on the south and west. Inside, Upjohn altered the stair and some of the post-Colonial woodwork. The architectural antiquarian will note with interest the hot air heating furnace dated 1834! Much of Van Buren's furnishings remain intact. Today the place is haunted by an eerie, romantic quality deepened by disrepair and unkempt planting.

At 15 m. is the junction with State 23 (see Tour 7).

At 18.7 m. is the junction with US 9 (see below).

KINDERHOOK (Dutch, children's corner), 20.6 m. (256 alt.,822 pop.), whose Dutch settlers brought the village name with them from their first settlement on the riverbank (see above), has well-cared-for old houses shaded by tall trees. It is said that Kinderhook had its own Boston Tea Party in the stormy days that led to the Revolution: a group of Dutch housewives raided a tea shop, bound the dealer, and sold his tea for him at a 'fair' price. A century-old copy of the Kinderhook Herald throws some light on the neighborhood spirit of the past: 'Slices of wedding cake have so often accompanied marriage notices that we shall for the future omit to acknowledge these dainties. Candidates for matrimony will please take notice that the following distinction will be made between those who remember the printer and those who do not—The names of the donner will be in "caps," while the others must be contented with small letters.'

The HOUSE OF HISTORY, near the center of Main St., built between 1810 and 1819 as a residence, is the headquarters of the Columbia County Historical Society and holds many old documents as well as a collection of historical relics. This large, two-story brick structure of the early post-Revolutionary period has a dignified stoop of modern workmanship. The entrance door is flanked by leaded sidelights and surmounted by a fanlight window under a graceful elliptical marble arch, complete with molded keystone and impost blocks.

Associated with the building are many stories and legends of the people of the Hudson Valley—the Van Burens, the Vanderpoels, the Van de Bogarts, and the Burts. Here Martin Van Buren talked plans with political henchmen and toasted political victories; here Aaron Vanderpoel earned the title of the 'Kinderhook Roarer' because of his stentorian voice. Thomas Burt, one of the founders of the Albany Argus and publisher of Rough Hewer, a Van Buren campaign paper, lived in the house for 45 years.

The one-story brick KINDERHOOK MEMORIAL LIBRARY (open 3–5 weekdays, 7–9 p.m. Sat.) is a rather heavy modern version of the Dutch Colonial house. Solid white shutters and a white picket fence add to the air of neatness.

The old brick walls of the BEEKMAN HOUSE (1736), Broad St., are now concealed by clapboarding. In the interior are an enormous fireplace and a Dutch closet-bed concealed by three doors with panels forming a Latin cross to protect inmates from witches.

ST.PAUL'S EPISCOPAL CHURCH, Sylvester Lane, is a fine example of 'board-and-batten' Gothic Revival. Richard Upjohn, who was remodeling Lindenwald for Martin Van Buren, furnished plans for the church; his original drawings are still in possession of the parish.

In the village cemetery (R) is the GRAVE OF MARTIN VAN BUREN

(1782–1862), who was born on Hudson Street, where his father, Captain Abraham Van Buren, kept an inn. Van Buren has been described as 'a bright blonde,' wearing 'a snuff-colored broadcloth coat with velvet collar; cravat orange with modest lace tips; vest of pearl hue; trousers of white duck; silk hose corresponding with vest; shoes morocco, gloves yellow kid and long furred Beaver hat with broad brim of Quaker color.' He became a power in the Albany Regency, which perfected the spoils system, and was successively County Surrogate, State Senator, State Attorney General, United States Senator, Governor, Secretary of State, Vice President under Andrew Jackson, and President of the United States succeeding Jackson.

At 26.5 *m.* is the southern junction with State 9J (*see above*).

Just south of this junction are (L) a HEXAGONAL HOUSE and an OCTAGONAL HOUSE, humble examples of the hundreds of 'spherical' homes built following the publication of Orson S. Fowler's treatise *A Home for All* (1849). After Fowler had collected a fortune by his lectures and writings on phrenology, a mid-century fad, he built a huge octagonal home near Fishkill and presented his architectural ideas to the world, asserting that the 'spherical' form was the most beautiful, enclosed the most space in the least compass, permitted entry of most sunlight, and made housework simpler. Dozens of the houses built during this period still stand in the Hudson and Mohawk Valleys. In the folk imagination the greatest advantage of the 'spherical' form is that the devil cannot corner the people who live in the house.

At 27.6 *m.* is the junction with a macadam road.

Right on this road, following the north bank of Stockport Creek, 1 *m.* to the MAJOR ABRAM STAATS HOUSE (R). Staats came to New Netherland in 1642, and after practicing for six years as surgeon of the West India Company, became a fur trader at Beverwyck (Albany). In 1654 he bought land at the mouth of Stockport Creek, built a house, and installed a tenant. In 1664 the house was burned by Indians, the tenant killed, and his wife carried off. The present stone dwelling, built soon afterward, may include foundations and walls of the original structure, but most of its original Dutch character was irretrievably lost by later nineteenth-century rebuilding of roof, porch, glass, and shutters.

The MACY HOUSE (L), 28.4 *m.*, built in 1816, is a spacious, yellow-painted brick structure with small rear corner wings. Altered from the original only by a Greek Revival stoop, it preserves the air of an elegant and comfortable summer home as planned by Captain Seth G. Macy, one of the sea captains who founded near-by Hudson.

The TURTLE HOUSE (R), 31.8 *m.*, on Penton Hook Farm, was built by Job Center, another sea captain, between 1800 and 1818. This unusual brick structure has a high first story and a very low second story under a low gabled roof. The central third of each façade projects forward in a semicircle that is sheltered by a semicircular two-story portico with a semicircular pediment supported by four Corinthian columns. The columns are solid timbers said to have served as the masts of old ships.

HUDSON, 33.3 *m.* (100 alt.,11,487 pop.), seat of Columbia County, is built on a slope that rises from the Hudson River. Its industrial plants produce machinery, woolen knit goods, ginger ale, matches, shirts and dresses, and flypaper. Two huge cement plants at the southeastern edge of the city gnaw at the limestone of Becraft Mountain.

Jan Frans Van Hoesen bought land here from the Indians in 1662, but there was no permanent settlement until 1783, when a number of New Englanders arrived, mostly Nantucket Quakers, whose fishing and whaling activities had suffered during the Revolution. The place has been called Claverack (Dutch, clover reach) Landing because of the fields of fragrant clover, but the new settlers, who had paid 5,000 pounds sterling for land and wharfage, changed the name to Hudson. On April 22, 1785, this New England community in a Dutch valley received the third city charter granted in the State. The proprietors soon built a mill, a shipyard, two tanneries, and a covered ropewalk. In 1790, 25 schooners in the whaling, seal, and West Indies trade registered Hudson as their home port.

Many of the old houses clearly show their derivation from New England precedent. No.7 Union Street is a typical five-bay brick Federal house with delicate Adamesque doorway, upper-hall triple window, and cornice. No.116 Union Street recalls wooden Nantucket cottages with their great central chimneys. No.126 Union Street illustrates the early New England gambrel roof.

PARADE HILL, foot of Warren St., is a promenade terrace commanding a magnificent vista up and down the Hudson. Granted to the Common Council in 1795 by the 'Proprietors,' this terrace is probably the only example of eighteenth-century civic planning to take advantage of the majestic Hudson scenery.

The COLLIER HOUSE (St.Nicholas Ukrainian Church), NW. corner of Partition and Second Sts., a large frame structure with a strongly proportioned Greek Ionic portico, is a fine example of Greek Revival. Another building in the same style is the FIRST REFORMED CHURCH, 451 Warren St., a brick edifice with wooden Greek Ionic pediment, entablature, and columns.

The WORTH HOUSE, 211 Union St., similar in style to No.7 Union St., unfortunately underwent, about 1850, renovation of door hood, window sash and heads, and cornice. In this house was born Major General William J. Worth (1794–1849), who served with distinction in the War of 1812 and the Mexican War and in the interval was superintendent of the U.S. Military Academy at West Point.

The ROBERT JENKINS HOUSE (D.A.R. Chapter House and Library), 113 Warren St., and the SETH JENKINS HOUSE, 115 Warren St., were the stately brick residences of the sons of Hudson's first mayor.

The GENERAL WORTH HOTEL, 215 Warren St., is a rare and unusually well-preserved example of Greek Revival architecture, rebuilt in 100 days after a fire in 1836.

The CHRIST PROTESTANT EPISCOPAL CHURCH, SE. corner of Court and Union Sts., was built 1854–7 by William G. Harrison, architect of the Episcopal Cathedral in Garden City, Long Island. The exterior is of Portland red sandstone and is chiefly remarkable for its thinly proportioned lancet windows and a 210-foot spire. The nave is covered with plaster tierne vaults. Ralph Adams Cram designed the polychromed oak reredos and the marble altar.

In Hudson is the junction with State 23 (*see Tour* 7) and State 9G (*see Tour* 21B).

At 38.5 *m.* is a view (L) of THE HILL (*private*), built just after 1796 by Henry Walter Livingston (1764–1810), grandson of Robert, third lord of the manor (*see Tour* 21B). Upon his marriage in 1796 to Mary Penn Allen of Pennsylvania, Henry Walter built this most splendid of all Livingston residences, an early example of Roman Revival style. The stuccoed brick house has a unique plan with two elliptical rooms, projecting as segmental bays on both sides but masked in front by the flat-roofed Scamozzi-Ionic colonnade. For 45 years following Henry Walter's death, the house, known as 'Widow Mary's Place,' continued to be famous for its hospitality, and today shows every sign of excellent care.

At 39 *m.* is the junction with State 82.

Left on State 82 to LAKE TAGHKANIC STATE PARK, 6 *m.* (*campsites, 50¢ a day; tents, 75¢ a day; two- to five-room cottages, $3–$8 a day; fishing facilities, hiking and ski trails*), which contains 750 acres with a 225-acre lake.

At 41.2 *m.* is the junction with a dirt road.

Right here 3 *m.* to the abandoned village of BURDEN, the center of iron mines worked from 1875 to 1898 by the Hudson River Ore and Iron Company. The mine shafts are now used as mushroom cellars. From Mount Tom ore, Troy mills turned out car wheels that puzzled ironmasters because of their superior tensile strength. Geologists have found that this ore contains some manganese.

At 44.9 *m.* is the junction with a macadam road.

1. Right here 1.6 *m.* to junction with a dirt road; left 0.5 *m.* to a mile-long, tree-lined lane leading (L) to THE HERMITAGE (*private*), a square brick building begun just before the Revolution by Colonel Peter R. Livingston. Colonel Peter, eldest surviving son of Robert, third lord of Livingston Manor (*see Tour* 21B), expected to be sole heir to his father's huge estate under the ancient law of entail and The Hermitage was intended to provide a suitably grand manor house with spacious apartments in the latest fashionable Georgian style; but war interrupted construction above the first story. At the conclusion of the Revolution, entail was abrogated, the estate was divided among numerous heirs, and Colonel Peter, his fortune greatly diminished, could only roof the unfinished mansion. In 1939, after long occupancy by tenant farmers, the main stair finally received a second story to lead to, porches were added, and The Hermitage approximated the original design. The divided Dutch door of the main entrance leads to a spacious hall, from which rooms open on each side. Many of the original mantels and much of the old trim remain.

Farther along on the dirt road is (L) TEVIOTDALE (*private*), 2.1 *m.*, the rectangular Georgian Colonial home built about 1773 by Walter Livingston (1740–97), son of Robert, third lord, brother of Colonel Peter of The Hermitage, and father of Henry Walter of The Hill. Constructed of rubble stone and covered with stucco, the house displays the typical five-bay, two-story-and-high-basement façade and hip roof of the period. The rear rooms have floor-length French doors, originally opening upon a porch that commanded a beautiful view south over the valley of Roeliff Jansen Kill. The house was inherited in 1797 by Harriet Livingston, who married Robert Fulton in 1808; they lived here until his death in 1815. After long occupation by farmers, the house and a small plot were acquired by General John Ross Delafield, who has repaired the major ravages of time and neglect.

2. Left from US 9 on the macadam road 0.7 *m.* to the BROCK LIVINGSTON HOUSE (R), the main block of which is a primitive one-and-a-half-story stone Dutch house. At 1.6 *m.* is the junction with a macadam road; right here to (R) the CALLANDER HOUSE (*private*), 0.4 *m.* Built about 1773 by General Samuel Ten Broeck, the brick dwelling is typical of Dutch domestic architecture of the late eighteenth century. Behind a rare original plaster-ceiled stoop, the heavy, divided Dutch door leads to a wide central hallway. The house was sold to General Henry Livingston, who bestowed the name Callander House after the Livingston ancestral home in Scotland.

CLERMONT, 46.6 *m.* (226 alt.,200 pop.), was once the chief village of the lower Livingston manor, inherited by the second Robert Livingston (*see Tour 21B*) from his father, first lord of the manor. In 1791, when the village happened to have a surplus of poor-relief funds, citizens petitioned the legislature for the right to use the money to erect and maintain a free public school. The enabling act, passed March 27, 1791, created the first public school chartered in the State of New York.

St.LUKE'S EPISCOPAL CHURCH (R), built in 1857, is one of the later examples of 'board-and-batten' Gothic by Richard Upjohn. Less simple and dignified than St.Paul's, Kinderhook, it illustrates Upjohn's later tendency to elaboration of ornamental effects.

One of the original POST ROAD MILESTONES is (R) at 49.1 *m.*, marked '109 miles to New York.'

At 50 *m.* is the junction with a macadam road.

Right on this road 0.8 *m.* to the REDDER HOMESTEAD, built about 1720, a one-and-a-half-story house of stone painted white, with green shutters and a very steep roof. The two-piece door has hinges, latches, and a knocker imported from Holland. The east wing, added in 1773, contains a living room with fireplace wall entirely covered with beautiful paneling.

The MARTIN HOMESTEAD (R), 53.5 *m.*, was built in 1732. The stone walls were recently covered with white cement, but the interior remains untouched, with large solid, hand-hewn beams and wide floor planks.

RED HOOK, 53.9 *m.* (200 alt.,996 pop.), was called Roode Hoeck by early Dutch navigators because of the profusion of red berries they saw growing on the hillsides. The village is a trade center for the apple growers of northern Dutchess County, and four cider-vinegar mills are operated here during the fall.

The road curves around the somber yellow EVANGELICAL LUTHERAN CHURCH OF St.PETER THE APOSTLE (R), 56.3 *m.*, known for more than a century as the Old Stone Church. It was built in 1730 on land donated by Gilbert Livingston and was remodeled in 1824, when a tower was added, and was again enlarged in 1842. In the cemetery behind the church are numerous Palatine graves.

At 56.9 *m.* is the junction with State 9G (*see Tour 21B*).

RHINEBECK, 59.3 *m.* (203 alt.,1,569 pop.), is a sedate old village that, like others along US 9, has benefited by the proximity of landed gentry. Several of the houses are noteworthy for their band-saw decorations. No.44 Montgomery Street, a Gothic Revival board-and-batten house, has an especially rich band-saw porch employing Gothic motives. Such examples of enthusiastic carpentering are as true a form of folk art as are samples, quilts, and cast-iron hitching posts.

The NORTHERN DUTCHESS COUNTY HEALTH CENTER (1931) is a model unit operated under the Thompson Trust; the clinic was established about 1900 by William Thompson. Opposite are the COONS GREENHOUSES, which began specialization in the production of English double violets when they were the most fashionable flower for corsages. The CHURCH OF THE MESSIAH (L), a low stone structure of the English parish type, was built in 1897 with Astor funds from designs by Stanford White; the Episcopal service is used.

The BEEKMAN ARMS, at the village center, has grown with each generation since the first two rooms and loft were erected about 1700 by William Traphagen; by 1769 it was two stories high. The third story was added in 1865, the wings and the portico yet later. This was a famous station in stagecoach days. Prior to the Revolution a sign in the office gave the rates:

> Lodging 3 pence
> With breakfast, 4 pence
> Only 5 lodgers to a bed
> No boots can be worn in bed.

The U.S.POST OFFICE, at the village center, was built in 1939. Designed by R.Stanley Brown, architect, the building reproduces the exterior of the oldest and main portion of the house of Hendrick Kip, which stood east of the Rhinecliff Road until it burned about 1912. Some of the old stone was utilized in the new building; the signature stone marked 'Ao 1700 HKAK' and a window sash from the Kip house are exhibited in the lobby.

South of the village center is (L) the REFORMED DUTCH CHURCH, built in 1808, the west and south walls of brick and the east and north walls of stone. According to tradition, the parishioners could not agree on the material that should be used for the building. Those who contributed money for the construction insisted that the walls be of brick and those who contributed in kind insisted on stone.

Northeast of the village are the DUTCHESS COUNTY FAIRGROUNDS, where the county fair is held during the first week of September. Every farmer, gentleman and otherwise, enters his best pigs, cucumbers, cows, pumpkins, and other products. In the races, an Astor is seen driving his own mules in competition with his neighbors.

Right from the center of Rhinebeck on State 308, which runs down to the river, 1.2 m. to the entrance to the VINCENT ASTOR ESTATE (R). The descendants of the first John Jacob Astor, who laid the foundation for his fortune by monopolizing the western fur trade and then investing in real estate, still keep a foothold here.

The ABRAHAM KIP HOUSE (R), 1.6 m., was built about the middle of the eighteenth century. The earlier western portion was a simple two-room structure; in the later eastern end, a hall and a pair of rooms were added. Abraham's father and brother operated the profitable canoe ferry to Kingston, while he utilized his house as an inn. The ruins of the HENDRICK KIP HOUSE (L) are at 1.8 m.

RHINECLIFF, 2.3 m. (50 alt.,300 pop.), is the eastern terminus of the Kingston ferry; left here on a macadam road to (L) ELLERSLIE (private), 3.6 m., home of Levi P. Morton (1824–1920), elected Vice President of the United States in 1888 and governor of New York State in 1894. When he acquired the estate in 1886, Morton erected the present half-timber building, which was designed by Richard Morris Hunt.

At 61 *m.* is the junction with the Old Mill Road.

Right on this dirt road 0.2 *m.* to GRASSMERE (L), a red brick mansion in wooded grounds, now the Fox Hollow School for Girls. Construction of Grassmere was begun by General Richard Montgomery, who was killed on December 31, 1775, while leading the attack on Quebec, and was completed by his young bride, Janet, sister of Chancellor Livingston (*see Tour 21B*). The house was burned in 1828; in rebuilding, some of the old walls may have been used.

The small DUTCH STONE COTTAGE (R), 61.3 *m.*, is typical of many that lined the eighteenth-century King's Highway. One room deep and two long, with steep winding stairs leading to a garret under the gable roof unbroken by dormers, this humble dwelling still houses tenant farmers. At 62 *m.* (R) is another, slightly smaller cottage. The rough, split stonework and the mellow tones of shingle and wood gables have acquired a patina envied by even the luxurious manor house.

At 63.9 *m.* is the junction with a paved road.

Right on this, the old Post Road, 0.9 *m.* to the ornate gateway (R) of the OGDEN MILLS AND RUTH LIVINGSTON MILLS MEMORIAL STATE PARK. This land was acquired in 1792 by Morgan Lewis (1734–1844), son of Francis Lewis, a signer of the Declaration of Independence. Morgan Lewis served in the Revolutionary War and the War of 1812 and held numerous public offices in a political career that began in 1783 after his marriage to Gertrude, sister of Chancellor Livingston; he was governor of New York 1804–7. The first Lewis home, called the Staatsburgh House, was ruined by fire in 1832, but a large portion of the masonry walls was incorporated in the new house, which was augmented by short wings and a four-column Greek colonnade. Lewis's great-granddaughter, Ruth, married Ogden Mills,Sr. In 1895 Mills had Stanford White remodel the house into the present mansion. The last private owner of the estate was Ogden L. Mills (1884–1937), Under Secretary of the U.S. Treasury during the Secretaryship of Andrew Mellon, whom he succeeded in 1932. As a public official Mr.Mills was notable for the scrupulous manner in which he observed the spirit of the law in paying taxes on his large holdings. The 200-acre estate was deeded to the public by his daughter as a memorial.

The MANSION, now a museum (*open 11–5 daily, except Mon.; adults 25¢, children 10¢*), standing on the crest of a hill, with a beautiful lawn sloping riverward, is a grand French Renaissance palace of 65 rooms. Stanford White achieved some of his finest interiors here; the Gold Parlor, the magnificently harmonious Green Marble Dining Room, and the oak-paneled Library attest his gift for opulent and luxurious color. All the interiors retain their priceless rugs, furniture, tapestries, and fittings.

STAATSBURG, 1.4 *m.* (50 alt.,500 pop.), was named for Dr.Samuel Staats and Dirck Van der Burgh, early landholders. Storage plants, built here in the 1850's to hold ice for New York City, and the Staatsburg Ice Tool Works, established in 1858, carry on a large business despite modern methods of refrigeration.

ST.MARGARET'S EPISCOPAL CHURCH (L), in the center of the village, is a stone building erected in the Civil War period and modeled on English parish church architecture. In the south walls are two three-panel windows of fine thirteenth-century stained glass from Chartres Cathedral installed here by Ogden Mills,Sr., as a memorial to his wife, Ruth Livingston Mills.

The Post Road rejoins US 9 at 2.1 *m.*

On US 9, opposite the southern junction with the old Post Road, 66.1 *m.*, is the entrance (R) to the MARGARET LEWIS NORRIE STATE PARK (*picnicking, swimming, hiking*), a 312-acre tract sloping down to the river.

The SITE OF PLACENTIA, last home of James Kirke Paulding (1778–1860), is at 68.3 m. Paulding, an author by desire but a public official from need, was born at Great Nine Partners, near Millbrook, where his family had taken refuge when Tories were rampant around Tarrytown, the family home. He collaborated with Washington Irving in the first Salmagundi Papers (1807), and their success confirmed them in their devotion to authorship. Paulding's Diverting History of John Bull and Brother Jonathan (1812) gave him a small reputation as a political satirist, and he was appointed to a minor political office. Martin Van Buren, his upriver neighbor, made him his Secretary of the Navy in 1837; Paulding, true to the romantic tradition, stubbornly opposed the replacement of sails by steam in the Navy. While Secretary of the Navy he published a book of fairy tales. 'Peter Piper picked a peck of pickled peppers' appeared in his Königsmarke.

Tree-shaded ST. JAMES EPISCOPAL CHURCH (L), 68.8 m., designed in the Gothic manner of the English parish church, has in the course of the century that has passed since its construction acquired a patina and a beauty well in keeping with this countryside of large, dignified estates. The church was founded in 1811 by Dr. Samuel Bard and General Morgan Lewis. The first church building was designed by the first minister, the Reverend John McVickar (1787–1868). In 1844, the old structure having been declared unsafe, the present edifice was built. Vestryman Augustus Thomas Cowman acted as amateur architect, making a trip to England to study ecclesiastical architecture. The stucco-covered exterior exhibits a long, low, gabled nave and a lower sanctuary, contrasting markedly with the slender western entrance tower. Within, the hammer-beam trusses, pews, and trim are of black walnut. The plastered walls carry many memorial tablets of the landed gentry. The two diamond-paned windows next to the door were preserved from the first church building; and two others utilized plain red, yellow, and purple glass from the Church of the Ascension, New York City. President Franklin D. Roosevelt has long been senior warden of this church, and here in 1939 King George VI and Queen Elizabeth attended services as his guests.

At 69.3 m. are the elaborate cut-stone gate and gatehouse (R) of HYDE PARK (adm. 25¢), the 700-acre estate of Frederick W. Vanderbilt (1857–1939). In 1705 Peter Fauconier, private secretary to Edward Hyde, Viscount Cornbury, Royal Governor of New York, obtained a patent for land, including this estate, which he named for his patron. In 1772 the property was laid out as a residential estate by Dr. John Bard, whose wife had inherited part of the patent. Dr. Bard was the first health officer of New York City, and was the first to apply quarantine regulations there. His son, Dr. Samuel Bard (1742–1821), the most distinguished physician of his day, retired to Hyde Park in 1797, built a square brick house, and began a serious study of horticulture and agriculture. His plantings included fruit trees imported from France and England, melons from Italy, and vines from Madeira. After his death, the place was bought in 1827 by Dr. David Hosack, Bard's former partner, professor of natural history at Columbia, and founder of the New York Botanical Garden. Hosack employed the

Belgian André Parmentier, the first professional landscape gardener in the United States, to lay out roads and plantings. Walter Langdon, the next owner, extended the original house, which, however, was demolished in 1895 by Mr.Vanderbilt to make way for the present great Renaissance mansion designed by Stanford White. Thus this estate has in 170 years become a gentleman's country seat combined with an arboretum containing specimens of species gathered from all over the world. In February 1940, President Roosevelt announced that 250 acres of the estate had been offered to the Government as an arboretum. Later in the same year it was taken over as a national park.

Since 1932, HYDE PARK, 69.5 m. (187 alt.,1,200 pop.), has ceased to be merely a quiet service center of the estate country. The name in the date line of a newspaper is as important as that of London, and the streets are clogged by the slow-moving cars of tourists eager to catch a glimpse of something connected with the President of the United States. The neat little village was once called Stoutenburgh, for Jacobus Stoutenburgh, the first settler, who arrived in 1741. There were enough houses here by 1777 to cause General Vaughn to cannonade the settlement as he retired down the river. In the early days the villagers did considerable sturgeon fishing; the meat was shipped to Albany and the roe was salted down and sent to New York City, where it was sometimes sold as 'Russian caviar.'

Below the crossroads is (R) the JAMES ROOSEVELT MEMORIAL LIBRARY (1927), built of fieldstone, the gift of Mrs.Sara Delano Roosevelt in memory of her husband. Near by is the white frame DUTCH REFORMED CHURCH, whose congregation was organized in 1789.

CRUMWOLD (R), 70.1 m., is a Herman Rogers estate. After the Rogerses had entertained Mrs.Wallis Simpson as their guest at Cannes before her marriage to the Duke of Windsor, businessmen in the vicinity hopefully fathered the idea that this might become the home of the Windsors.

The FRANKLIN D. ROOSEVELT LIBRARY (R), 71.1 m., is a fieldstone structure to be opened in July 1941. The cornerstone was laid by President Roosevelt on November 19, 1939. The building will house about 6,000,000 documents covering the President's career from the time he was elected State senator in 1910.

The entrance lane of CRUM ELBOW (R), 71.3 m., the estate of Mrs.Sara Delano Roosevelt, lies between rows of old trees and has frequently been guarded by sentries since 1932. This property was acquired in 1826 by Ephraim Holbrock, who built a two-story rectangular frame house, which forms the core of the present dwelling. In 1866 James Roosevelt, the President's father, bought the place, then called Spring Wood. The house, augmented by north and south wings, was a typical 'Hudson River-bracketed' villa; since 1900 the exterior has been transformed into a late Georgian dwelling. The stuccoed central block has two stories and an attic, with a hip roof crowned by a balustraded deck. On each side are low corner towers and projecting stone wings enclosing a balustraded terrace. The whole has a dignified solidity and generous scale in the best tradition of Dutchess County squiredom. The interior is less formal. Through the semicircular Roman Doric portico, the entrance hall and passage lead to the spacious library, the chief living room of the house, which contains a large collection of books on naval history and many prints of old ships and of naval engagements.

This house was the birthplace (1882) of Franklin Delano Roosevelt, elected President of the United States in 1932 and again in 1936. He was graduated from Harvard in 1904 and from the Columbia University Law School in 1907, entered the New York State senate in 1910, and served until he resigned in 1913 to become Assistant Secretary of the Navy. In 1920 he contracted infantile paralysis, but in 1928 he returned to public life when he entered a successful campaign for the governorship of New York. He left Albany to enter the White House.

The JAMES R. ROOSEVELT ESTATE, 71.5 m., is owned by the widow of the half-brother of Franklin D. Roosevelt. The two-story clapboarded house, painted dark red, was built between 1833 and 1835 by Joseph Giraud, but has undergone numerous changes.

ST. ANDREW'S NOVITIATE (R), 72.9 m., is a training school for novices of the Jesuit order; the school was moved here from Maryland in 1903. The wooded grounds surrounding the five-story red brick building are dotted with shrines.

The HUDSON RIVER STATE HOSPITAL (L), 74 m., opened in 1871 on a 208-acre site purchased from James Roosevelt, is an institution for the insane. The Victorian Gothic main brick building was designed by Vaux and Withers, New York architects. The 1,730-acre grounds have 83 buildings in a number of groups, making possible beneficial segregation of the various types of patients. Most of the recent buildings are built of red brick with light-colored stone or wood trim.

The inn of the WOODCLIFF RECREATION PARK (R), 74.2 m., was the Victorian home of John F. Winslow, partner of Erastus Corning in the Troy iron foundry that manufactured the first Bessemer steel produced in this country. Winslow was a staunch patron of John Ericsson, inventor of the *Monitor*; and the plans for that famous 'cheesebox on a raft' were drawn in this house.

POUGHKEEPSIE, 75.9 m. (175 alt.,40,237 pop.) (*see Poughkeepsie*), is at the junction with US 44 (*see Tour 5*), State 9G (*see Tour 21B*), and State 55 (*see Tour 40*).

Section d. POUGHKEEPSIE to NEW YORK; 71.8 m. US 9

Between Poughkeepsie and Peekskill US 9 bends slightly farther inland but continues to pass entrances to large estates. South of Peekskill it runs closer to the river and through a series of villages some of which are inhabited largely by people who commute to New York City. In Putnam and Westchester Counties are villages of the modern well-to-do residential type with strict regulations governing the kind of houses and stores that may be built.

South of POUGHKEEPSIE, 0 m., at 2.1 m., is the entrance (R) to LOCUST GROVE (*open by appointment*), the 100-acre estate that was the home of Samuel F.B. Morse (1791–1872) for the last 25 years of his life.

Morse was an artist of considerable talent; but like many artists of the early industrial era he diverted much of his energy to other fields. He is known chiefly in connection with the perfecting of the telegraph, the patent for which he took out.

The ABRAHAM FORT HOMESTEAD, (L), 4.6 *m.*, an attractive Colonial residence one-and-one-half stories high, was built by Johannes A. Fort about 1759. Through many alterations and additions, portions of the original woodwork and hardware have been preserved.

At 5 *m.*, at the foot of a steep hill, is the junction with paved New Hamburg Road.

Right on this road 1 *m.* to the entrance lane (R) of the 100-acre GALLAUDET HOME for aged and infirm deaf mutes. The institution was established in 1872 by Dr.Thomas Gallaudet, son of Thomas H. Gallaudet, who initiated systematic education of the deaf in America.

At 1.3 *m.* is the junction with a dirt road; right here 1 *m.* to the NEW YORK TRAP ROCK QUARRY, the largest dolomite producer in the world, with an average daily output of about 5,000 tons. Gray-white dust fills the air and covers the plant and the company-owned workers' dwellings. The stupendous bunkers are one of the most awesome sights in the valley. On the property is the site of De Witt Clinton's country home.

At 6.4 *m.* is the junction with State 9D.

Right on State 9D, a scenic route through the heart of the Hudson Highlands, to WAPPINGERS FALLS, 1.3 *m.* (116 alt.,3,336 pop.), named for the 75-foot cascade in Wappinger Creek that has provided water power since the place was settled. The chief industries are a bleachery and an overall factory. The MESIER HOUSE (L), Main St., now owned by the village, is a white frame structure with green roof and trim; the rear wing was built in 1741, the front in 1750. The house was acquired in 1777 by Matthew Mesier, tea merchant, who tried to profiteer when tea imports were curtailed, but local housewives combined to force a reduction in price.

Gateposts (R) at 8 *m.* indicate the entrance to MOUNT GULIAN, the Verplanck estate; the old house was destroyed by fire in 1931. This was the headquarters of Baron von Steuben toward the end of the Revolution; and here on May 13, 1783, a number of high-ranking officers organized the Society of the Cincinnati. There is nothing to indicate that these men had other than sentimental reasons for banding together, but the cry was instantly raised that the officers were attempting to establish a hereditary aristocracy by limiting membership in the future to descendants of the founders. In May 1789, the Tammany Society was founded, in part as the common soldier's opposition to the Society of the Cincinnati.

BEACON, 9.1 *m.* (150 alt.,12,181 pop.), was established in 1913 by the union of the seventeenth-century villagers of Fishkill Landing and Matteawan. The city is a helter-skelter grouping of factories along Fishkill Creek, brick and paper-carton plants along the Hudson, modest homes of the many Italian workers, and the larger residences of the well-to-do. Hats and brick have for many years vied for first place among some 40 factory products.

When, in 1663, the Indians agreed to sell Francis Rombout, acting for himself and his partner Gulian Verplanck, 'all the land that he could see,' they did not flinch from their bargain when he climbed South Beacon Mountain and encompassed 85,000 acres with his eyes. Rombout's share of 28,000 acres was inherited by Catharyna Brett, who came here in 1708 with her husband, Roger Brett. Brett was drowned in 1726, and Catharyna administered the estate with a masterly efficiency until her death in 1764.

Rombout tenants were active in the revolt against the Crown. After the War of 1812, John Jacob Astor, Peter Schenck, Philip Hone, and others, attracted by the waterfall in the Fishkill, built a cotton mill and a foundry here. For the rest of the century Matteawan set the pace in the manufacture of bricks, cotton goods, machinery, silk, wagons, and hats.

The BEACON-NEWBURGH FERRY (*car and driver* 50¢; *passengers* 10¢ *each*), foot of Beekman St., was established in 1743. Four modern boats constructed for ice-breaking maintain a year-round service. The crossing provides an excellent view of the north portal of the Hudson Highlands down to well below Bannerman's Island and Storm King (*see Tour* 21C). Historic LONG WHARF, below the ferry slip, was built between 1812 and 1816. Part of the yellow wooden building at the end of the wharf was an important inn when river traffic was heavy.

The entrance to the 900-acre grounds of the MATTEAWAN STATE HOSPITAL (*visiting hours* 1–4 *weekdays*) is at Verplanck Ave. and Cannon St.; the institution is for the treatment and confinement of the criminal insane. The reservation was formerly the estate of John J. Scanlon, whose trotters made records in the Hambletonian stakes. The Abbot ($2:03\frac{1}{4}$) and Kentucky Union ($2:07\frac{1}{4}$) were buried here.

The BRETT-TELLER HOUSE, Van Nydeck and Teller Aves., is the story-and-a-half structure Catharyna and Roger Brett built in 1709; the wing is of later date. The older house has long low lines and a gambrel roof that curves gently outward to form the roof of a porch. Scalloped cedar shakes cover the walls of the older unit. The kitchen end was probably built after the house came into the possession of Isaac de Peyster Teller, who married Alice Schenck in 1790. The present occupants (1940) are the seventh generation in direct line to own and occupy the homestead.

The HOWLAND LIBRARY, 477 Main St., a brick building of the Norwegian chalet type, was built in 1872. The architect was Richard M. Hunt.

ST.LUKE'S EPISCOPAL CHURCH, Wolcott Ave. between S.Liberty and Rector Sts., erected in 1868, Frederick C. Withers architect, is a stone structure in the English Gothic style. The cemetery north of the church contains the graves of Chancellor James Kent, author of *Kent's Commentaries*; Smith T. Van Buren, son of the President, and many early settlers.

CRAIG HOUSE SANITARIUM, Howland Ave., a private institution, occupies the home of General Joseph Howland, Civil War officer and philanthropist. The east wing was added in 1859 by the architect Richard M. Hunt.

The DE PEYSTER HOUSE, South Ave. across the railroad tracks, erected about 1743, was occupied by Abraham De Peyster, Madam Brett's nephew. It is a gambrel-roofed brick house on a foundation of Hudson River bluestone.

On Sargent Ave. south of Tompkins Place is (R) WODENETHE (*grounds open*), owned by the Craig House Sanitarium. This was formerly the estate of Henry Winthrop Sargent, to whom Andrew Jackson Downing (*see Tour* 21C) dedicated his *Architecture of Country Houses* (1850). The grounds here are still notable, the Roman garden attracting particular attention. The house, built about 1825 and remodeled by Calvert Vaux, Downing's partner, in 1853, is a large structure painted yellow with white trim; a three-story section is topped by a four-hipped, curved pyramidal roof. When Sargent and Andrew Downing's brother Charles brought out the revised fifth edition of Andrew Downing's *Cottage Residences* in 1873, Sargent appended a description of terraced Italian gardens and illustrated it with engravings of his grounds here.

Wolcott Ave. leads to the MOUNT BEACON INCLINED RAILWAY (30¢ *a round trip*), whose 2,200 feet of track carry its tilted cars 1,200 feet up the western spur of the mountain. From the casino near the head of the railway a trail leads 1 *m*. to the summit of MOUNT BEACON (1,500 alt.), one of the best observation points on the Hudson, used as a signal station during the Revolution. The trail continues to SOUTH BEACON PEAK (1,635 alt.), 2 *m*., from which the Empire State Building, New York City, is visible on clear days.

COLD SPRING, 16.9 *m*. (200 alt.,1,784 pop.), was named for a large spring at which, it is said, boats plying the Hudson filled their water butts. The Cold Spring Foundry, established here in 1814, turned out the famous Parrott rifled field pieces during the Civil War.

ST.MARGARET'S-IN-THE-HIGHLANDS, built in 1868, George E. Harney, architect, was modeled on an English parish church. It has bluestone walls, a simple gable roof, and a stone spire. The rectory was designed by Hobart B. Upjohn about 1930.

GARRISON, 20.7 *m*. (100 alt.,500 pop.), is a service center for the many estates covering the countryside between the old Albany Post Road and the river. The ferry here was important as a connection with West Point until the Bear Mountain Bridge was built.

ST.PHILIP'S-IN-THE-HIGHLANDS, just north of the junction with State 403, a small stone parish church, was built in 1861 by Richard Upjohn. Lacking the straightforward, simple mass of his earlier work, it illustrates his trend to the Victorian phase of the Gothic Revival. Upjohn was a vestryman here, 1852–78, and his grave is in the church cemetery.

From Garrison State 403 leads (R) to US 9, 2 m. South of Garrison State 9D joins US 6 (*see Tour 4*), 25.7 m., which is a Bear Mountain Bridge approach on which tolls are collected.

FISHKILL VILLAGE, 12.4 m. (200 alt.,553 pop.), is one of the most attractive towns along the Hudson. Though some Dutch settlers were living on the lowlands soon after 1700, at the time of the Revolution the village had only a dozen or so houses, two churches, a tavern, and a schoolhouse. Early in the Revolutionary War the Colonials fortified Wiccopee Pass, to the south, to block a land advance by the British. Barracks and storehouses were built here and the few houses were crowded with refugees from New York City. A few of the houses on the tree-lined streets were built shortly after 1800, but the majority belong to the post-Civil War period.

The FIRST REFORMED DUTCH CHURCH, Main St., was built about 1784. The exterior preserves much of its early character; the stuccoed stone walls are enlivened by brick quoins at the corners and around the openings. The weathercock has topped the steeple since 1795. The interior was entirely remodeled in 1854.

The congregation, organized in 1716, erected its first church in 1736. In this building the New York Provincial Convention met from September 5, 1776, to February 11, 1777, and then moved to Kingston. During the later war years the building was used as a jail for spies, deserters, and outspoken Tories. In Cooper's novel, *The Spy*, Harvey Birch was confined here with the Tories he had tricked into captivity, and was permitted to escape by secret arrangement

TRINITY CHURCH, Main St., a small clapboarded frame building, was erected about 1769. The exterior, with its curious cavetto cornice, remains unaltered but for the tower; the tall steeple became unsafe in 1803 and the upper stages were removed. The interior was entirely rearranged in 1860–70. During the Revolution the building was used as a hospital and in 1788 received 350 pounds as compensation, which the vestry used to repair and complete the structure. The parish was founded in 1756 by the Reverend Samuel Seabury, whose son became the first Episcopal bishop in the United States.

Trinity and the Dutch Reformed Church possess identical tankards which are inscribed in memory of Engelbert Huff, once attached to the Life Guards of the Prince of Orange; he died in Fishkill at the age of 128 years. It is told that when Huff was 121, he and a young man 100 years his junior courted the same lady.

On a steep bank beside the railroad crossing stands the OBADIAH BOWNE HOUSE, built in 1818. In an earlier house on this site the first State constitutional convention met. Here also Samuel Loudon printed the first number of the *New York Packet and American Advertiser*, the first copies of the Constitution of the State of New York, the first issues of the *Journal of the Legislature*, and some of Washington's military orders.

Left from Fishkill on State 52 to the WILLIAM DUDLEY HOUSE (L), 0.9 *m.*, an architectural curiosity of the first water. Dudley was a wrecker of buildings in New York City, and this house was fabricated in 1854 from pieces assembled from numerous Greek Revival structures: the porch columns once graced a lower Broadway church; the mantels, cornice, and solid mahogany doors are from various sources. The sill of the front door was once part of the cage of the giant bear Samson.

The DERICK BRINKERHOFF HOUSE (L), 2.4 *m.*, built about 1719, is now disfigured by an 1875 mansard roof. In the upper southeast room Colonel Derick Brinkerhoff sheltered the sick Lafayette during the Revolution. Across the road (R) is the site of Abraham Brinckerhoff's Mill, built in 1735, burned in 1777, and rebuilt at General Washington's command to grind grist for the American Army. Several cannon balls were found beneath the floor when it was demolished.

At 2.5 *m.* is the junction with State 82; left here 1.3 *m.* to the entrance (R) to a locust-bordered lane leading to the COLONEL JOHN BRINCKERHOFF HOUSE, an early one-and-a-half-story dwelling with stone walls; the southwest brick gable has the date '1738' set off in black brick. Washington was a guest here several times in the fall of 1788, occupying the rear west parlor-bedroom; his hostess is said to have tucked him in every night. Once when John Brinckerhoff was trying to pry some military information from his guest, Washington asked him whether he could keep a secret; when Brinkerhoff said yes, Washington assured him, 'So can I.' In 1926 the property was acquired by Teodar Wiitala, former champion marathon runner, and is now operated as a co-operative Finnish vacation resort featuring Finnish steam baths.

South of Fishkill on US 9 is the CORNELIUS C. VAN WYCK HOUSE (L), 13.5 *m.*, built in 1786 from lumber salvaged from Revolutionary barracks. The story-and-a-half dwelling has a central-hall plan. In the rear is a gray-painted DUTCH BARN, built in the mid-eighteenth century, one of the best examples remaining in the State. The square plan is covered with an unbroken gable roof, which descends to low eaves on each side. The large wagon doors in the end gable walls lead to a spacious interior framed with great timbers whose long tenons are held doubly tight by wedges and pegs.

At 13.6 *m.* (L) is the one-and-a-half-story clapboarded CAPTAIN CORNELIUS R. VAN WYCK HOUSE (*adm. on application*), built about 1785, although the architectural lines are pre-Revolutionary. The house was at one time the headquarters of General Putnam, and in it the Committee of Safety conducted the mock trial of Enoch Crosby. As a result of the allusions to the house in Cooper's *The Spy*, it is often called the Wharton Home.

An old red sandstone POST ROAD MILESTONE (R), 13.7 *m.*, reads: '66 Miles to N.York.' Directly opposite is the junction with a dirt road.

Left on this road, along the northern slope of the hills, to WILLOWLAKE (R), 6 *m.*, the home of Margaret Sanger (Mrs.J.Noah H. Slee), leader of the birth control movement.

In Indian legend this region was the home of a giant race, hunters of huge water rats that dwelt in a lake covering all the country north of the Highlands. To exterminate these enemies, the giants drained the valley; and then, their bathing place gone, the giants gradually solidified and became the high Fishkill Range.

The road passes through the southern defile of WICCOPEE PASS, the strategic point vigilantly guarded by three Colonial batteries from 1776 to 1783 to prevent the British from seizing the near-by military stores. The lines of the earthworks, several hundred feet apart in the form of a triangle, are still traceable on the hilltops. To the southwest is a lookout point used in relaying messages from Washington's headquarters in Newburgh. On the heights overlooking the pass Harvey Birch had his mysterious interview with Washington after his 'escape' from Fishkill, as narrated in Cooper's *The Spy*.

At 20. 2 *m.* is the junction with State 301.

Left on State 301 into the CLARENCE FAHNESTOCK MEMORIAL PARK (*camping, picnicking, hiking, boating, fishing*), 4 *m.*, a mountainous wooded area of 3,400 acres, with two small lakes stocked with game fish. It is bisected by the Eastern State Parkway (*see Tour* 40).

For 10 miles US 9 follows creek valleys between high hills. Here the ragged troops of Washington and Putnam dug in after their Long Island defeat. Almost every other mountain has a line of trenches, now overgrown with brush.

PEEKSKILL, 31.6 *m.* (120 alt.,17,289 pop.) (*see Tour* 4), is at the junction with US 6 (*see Tour* 4) and with an entrance to the Bronx River Parkway Extension (see *Tour* 40).

South of Peekskill US 9 skirts the western edge of BLUE MOUNTAIN RESERVATION, two miles wide, the head of the Peekskill-Briarcliff Parkway of the Westchester County park system, which contains a network of trails leading up Blue Mountain and Spitzenberg.

CRUGERS PARK (R), 35.1 *m.* (*camping, bathing: parking, weekdays* 25¢; *Sunday, Westchester cars* 25¢, *others* 50¢), a tract of 251 acres, was the estate of Staats Morris Dyckman; the present name stems from his granddaughter Elizabeth, who married John Peach Cruger. In the park is BOSCOBEL HOUSE, built by Dyckman in 1792, one of the finest Federal mansions still standing in New York State, now housing a tenant family and park equipment. The plan was clearly derived from the Georgian centralhall type, but the hall is here widened to accommodate a magnificent center stair and the flanking rooms are projected forward to break up the usual rectangular mass. Between these flush-boarded wings are two onestory porches, the lower with an elliptically arched doorway, the upper exhibiting a raised pediment with draperies and tassels carved in wood below the cornice. The trim and ornaments are extremely delicate in scale and crisp in detail. Inside, the stately mantels, trim, and doors, while in bad repair, reflect the taste and skill of the trained craftsman.

CROTON–ON–HUDSON, 38.7 *m.* (20 alt.,3,890 pop.), came into existence as the home of Irish and Italian laborers who were building the dam that created Croton Reservoir. About the time of the World War, Max Eastman and several others who had to live economically and wanted to escape from Greenwich Village tenements, acquired land on the wooded hills above Croton and built small houses; in time they were joined by Edna St.Vincent Millay, poet; Dudley Field Malone, lawyer; Doris Stevens, militant feminist; Mabel Dodge and her husband Maurice Stern, the artist; Floyd Dell, novelist; John Reed, radical journalist; Boardman Robinson, cartoonist and painter; Stuart Chase, economist; and others. The colony caused considerable excitement among the natives; it was reported that the women wore shorts, smoked cigarettes, and took sun baths, and that the men indulged in similarly shocking activities. After the war Harry Kelly, real estate promotor, conceived the idea of developing a suburban village here. He organized a company, bought up land, and advertised the place as a retreat for intellectuals and professional workers. One or two fairly large houses were built, but the majority were cottages. By 1926 enough children were on the scene whose parents wanted a more progressive school than could be developed in the village below, to make possible the establishment of Hessian Hills School, a co-operative enterprise. This school has become the center of community life and has, to a large extent, governed its development. The wilder fringe of the post-war years has disappeared, and most of the hill dwellers, some of them early settlers, are now sedate citizens with family interests.

Construction of HESSIAN HILLS SCHOOL, on a side road branching (L) from Mt. Airy Road, was begun a few months after the burning of an old farmhouse in which the classes were being held. A functional structure of concrete and glass designed by Howe and Lescaze, it has not yet been completed (1940) though some sections have been in use since 1932. The school was organized by Elizabeth Moos and Margaret Hatfield, and has approximately 90 pupils.

HARMON, 39.7 m. (20 alt.,1,500 pop.), is the northern terminal of the electrified section of the New York Central Railroad.

West of the village, by the river shore, is CROTON POINT PARK (*bathing, picnicking*), of 504 acres, a delightful peninsula with a sandy beach.

The VAN CORTLANDT MANOR HOUSE (L), 40.1 m., is one of the most historic dwellings in the Hudson Valley. Stephanus Van Cortlandt (1643–1700), son of the prosperous Dutch emigrant Oloff Stevense Van Cortlandt, was at 34 the first native-born mayor of New York City. In 1697 the 87,000-acre tract he had assembled along the Hudson, extending from the Croton River to Anthony's Nose and east to the Connecticut line, was erected into a manor, confirmed by a Royal charter that still hangs in one of the rooms of the house.

According to tradition, when Stephanus acquired from Governor Thomas Dongan the property on the north bank of Croton Bay, there was included the Governor's small hunting lodge, one story high and loop-holed, built half in a hillside, with thick stone walls and a low-pitched roof. This structure was soon enlarged by a second story and garret, and eventually both stories were extended by end rooms and long low porches. Today wooden steps at the eastern end mount to the main extrance on the second floor level.

Stephanus, the first lord of the manor, came to Croton Bay only in summer, but here he and his wife, Gertrude Schuyler, entertained all folk of quality that sailed up and down the Hudson. From 1700 to 1747 Philip Van Cortlandt and his wife Catherine De Peyster continued to use this as a summer residence. It was Pierre Van Cortlandt (1721–1814) who in 1749 established his permanent home in this house. Although offered rewards and honors by the English, Pierre Van Cortlandt cast his lot with the Revolutionists. From 1775 to 1795 he was lieutenant governor of New York State. In 1777, on the approach of British forces up the Hudson, his wife, Joanna Livingston, and the children fled the place. Barely escaping destruction by fire, the house was repaired upon the family's return in 1780. In subsequent years Washington, Rochambeau, Lafayette, and Von Steuben stopped here. The Reverend George Whitefield preached from the veranda and, so the records say, was heard distinctly across the bay.

OSSINING (Ind., stone upon stone), 42.4 m. (100 alt.,15,976 pop.), occupies part of what was Philipsburgh, the Philipse Manor, confiscated in 1779. The earliest settlement grew up before the Revolution around the natural dock at Sparta, just south of the present-day village. After the Revolution Hunter's Landing was settled and by 1813 was the incorporated village of Sing Sing, which outdistanced its older rival and became the shipping point for the hinterland as far as the Connecticut line. Farm wagons often jammed High Street to the top of the hill waiting to unload their produce. Early stores and residences clustered along Water Street, but long before they succumbed in the great fire of 1865 upper-class residences overlooked the gorgeous panorama of Tappan Zee from the eastern heights. Inhabitants grew tired of the jokes suggested by the association of their village name with the State prison and in 1901 had the name changed. Though porous plasters and maps are produced here, the town is primarily one of the chain of well-to-do commuters' centers that extends along the Hudson through Westchester County.

SING SING PRISON, along the river front, was established here in 1824 with the idea of working the Mount Pleasant marble quarries with convict labor. The following year Captain Elam Lynds, just dismissed from Auburn State Prison because of his excessively severe discipline, was put in charge and by May 1828 had completed by the labor of 100 prisoners a stone cell block of 800 cells. The new institution was operated from the first according to the Auburn system of silent group labor by day and solitary confinement by night. The lock step, rock pile, and lash were ordinary routine; mail and visitors were forbidden. Sing Sing marble was not only used in prison buildings but for a time enjoyed considerable vogue, especially for Greek Revival structures, witness the New York Court of Appeals Building in Albany. In contrast to the harsh and repressive practices of the past, the latest cell blocks at Sing Sing have beds, desks, running water, and radio earphones for most of the 2,500 inmates. Educational and recreational programs are carried on and 'varsity' teams compete with outside groups on Sunday afternoons (*open*, 50¢).

One of the first and finest residences to be constructed of Sing Sing marble is the GENERAL AARON WARD HOUSE, S.Highland Ave. near the high school, built in 1835. Of generous proportions and refined in detail, its handsome portico with four Greek Ionic columns is flanked by two-story wings. All the original interior decorations have been lost or mutilated by alteration.

The ROBERT HAVELL HOUSE, N. side of Havell St., is a square clapboarded dwelling with a porch and cupola. Robert Havell,Jr., born in 1793 in Reading, England, 'one of the greatest engravers in aquatint the world has ever seen,' was the engraver of all but 10 of the 435 plates of John James Audubon's *Birds of America*. Persuaded by Audubon's enthusiasm for American scenery, Havell came to America in 1839, bringing his family and his precious copper plates, and soon thereafter erected this house. In 1857 he moved to Tarrytown, where he died in 1878. Only 41 of Havell's plates are extant; the others were either damaged in a warehouse fire in New York City in 1845 or sold for scrap metal.

The famous DOUBLE ARCH, a bridge within a bridge, is on Broadway west from Main St. The upper bridge was erected in 1838–40 to carry the Croton Aqueduct across Kil Brook. In 1861 the timber bridge that carried Broadway through the aqueduct arch was rebuilt in masonry and the unique combination of arches was achieved.

South of here US 9 is crossed several times by the CROTON AQUEDUCT, constructed in 1837–42 at the cost of $12,000,000 to convey the impounded waters of the Croton River to New York City. The reservoir above Croton was enlarged between 1892 and 1906, but the original conduit is still functioning.

SCARBOROUGH, 44.6 *m*. (100 alt.,500 pop.), is a commuters' village in a region of large estates. Near the junction with Scarboro Road is the marble WORDEN MANSION (R), at one time occupied by John Lorimer Worden (1818–97), who commanded the ironclad *Monitor* in its battle with the *Merrimac* in Hampton Roads on March 9, 1862.

In the 1890's and later, the 15-mile stretch along the Hudson between Scarborough and Yonkers was called the Gold Coast because of the procession of elegant estates costing in the millions and representing in their owners a total wealth easily reaching into the billions. Among the owners were the Rockefellers, Vanderbilts, Wendels, and Morgans, Jay Gould, Amzi L. Barber (asphalt), Henry Villard (railroads), Charles L. Tiffany (jewelry), Louis and Isaac Stern (drygoods), William F. Cochran and John E. Andrus (carpets), J.Jennings McComb (cotton), and Daniel Reed (copper). In recent years several of these estates have been sold or rented to country clubs and others have been cut up into high class subdivisions and apartment house sites in an effort to retrieve some part of the huge investment.

ST.MARY'S PROTESTANT EPISCOPAL CHURCH (L), 45 *m*., a cruciform structure erected in 1851 of local granite, was designed by the Reverend Edward Nathaniel Mead, who took as his model the fourteenth-century Gothic parish church of St.Mary's, Scarborough, England. The western façade, with its window of five lancets recalling the Five Sisters of York Cathedral, is surmounted by a pert bell gable. The ivy on the church wall was brought from Sir Walter Scott's home, Abbotsford, by Washington Irving, frequent worshipper at St.Mary's. The interior is chiefly noteworthy for its pleasant proportions and the stained glass windows made by John Bolton of Bolton Priory, Pelham Manor, who, with his brother William, was among the first to make stained glass in the United States.

Within the church hangs the Perry Memorial Bell, 'captured at Tobasco, Mexico 1847' (really October 23, 1846) by Commodore Matthew C. Perry (1795–1858), negotiator in 1855 of the treaty which opened Japan to American trade.

ROCKWOOD HALL is visible (R) at 45.7 m. Now a country club, it was erected in the late forties by Edwin Bartlett, wealthy New York merchant. The mansion was described by a contemporary as having an 'extremely castellated appearance . . . in the latest style of English Gothic architecture.' The cold gray walls in two shades of local gneiss are dominated by an 80-foot corner tower and an ivy-covered carriage porch.

Rockwood Hall was long the home of William Rockefeller (1841–1922), brother of John D. of near-by Pocantico Hills, who played an active part in organizing the Standard Oil Trust. After the U.S. Supreme Court ordered the dissolution of the holding company in 1910, he, like his brother, retired from active business to the peaceful opulence of Tarrytown suburbia.

The WEBB-FRÉMONT HOUSE (R), 46.5 m., a black stone mansion built in the 1840's, was for several years the home of John Charles Frémont (1813–90), explorer, soldier of fortune, and first presidential candidate of the present Republican party.

The SLEEPY HOLLOW DUTCH REFORMED CHURCH (L), 47.6 m., is a small stone building 'erected and built by Frederick Philipse and Catherine Van Cortlandt, his wife, in 1699.' Little except the 30-inch-thick walls is original, for the structure has undergone many repairs, alterations, and restorations. In the early church only the Philipse family enjoyed pews; above was a gallery for slaves and indentured servants.

SLEEPY HOLLOW CEMETERY, in the rear, still suggests the picturesqueness called up by Irving in his famous legend. Here are the graves of Washington Irving, Carl Schurz, Robert G. Ingersoll, Andrew Carnegie, and Whitelaw Reid. Slaves were buried across the road.

NORTH TARRYTOWN, 48 m. (70 alt.,8,791 pop.), another commuters' village, has an assembly plant of the General Motors Corporation. At the foot of a hill US 9 crosses Gory Creek, or Pocantico River, on the WASHINGTON IRVING MEMORIAL BRIDGE. A short way upstream stood the narrow wooden bridge where Brom Bones threw the pumpkin head at Ichabod Crane.

Just south of the bridge, one-half block right on Bellewood Ave., is CASTLE PHILIPSE (L). Frederick Philipse, who came to New Amsterdam in 1653 as master-carpenter (architect) to the Dutch West India Company and rose to be the wealthiest citizen of the colony, began to assemble the Lower Plantation at Yonkers in 1672. He bought land on the Pocantico in 1680, and soon after built the Upper Mills. About 1683 he constructed this stone castle, now almost unrecognizable after many alterations. The main entrance now faces east on Bellewood Avenue and a shallow north wing creates the illusion of a Georgian Colonial façade, but inspection from the southwest shows that the original house was gambrelroofed and three bays deep and the entrance door was on the south. The Castle was only occasionally occupied by Frederick, but on his death in

1702 the Upper Mills passed to his second son, Adolphus (1665–1750), who established his permanent residence here. After he died the Upper Mills were reunited to the manor under the second and third lords of Philipsburgh, and the Castle fell into disuse. In February 1940, John D. Rockefeller, Jr., provided funds for the purchase and preservation of this property by the Tarrytown Historical Society.

Left from North Tarrytown on State 117 (Bedford Rd.), which passes the carefully guarded gate, 2.3 m., leading into POCANTICO HILLS, the 3,500-acre tract established as a family estate by John D. Rockefeller (1839–1937), known as the 'richest man in the world.'

During the first trust-busting era Rockefeller was the cartooned and execrated symbol of the 'malefactor of great wealth'; in his later years he was the shy but popular man who had poured half a billion dollars into educational, medical, and religious institutions and activities. But the later John D. Rockefeller differed little from the young man who entered the oil business in 1859 and revolutionized the industry. At one time, when he had been stung to self-defense, he wrote: 'I believe it is every man's religious duty to get all he honestly can, and to give all he can.'

John D. Rockefeller was a shining product of the system of *laissez faire*, but he would have been an outstanding figure under any economic system because of his organizing genius and his passion for order. When he entered the oil business it was in a state of chaotic and ruinous competition; by 1882 he had organized the Standard Oil Trust, which practically controlled the production and distribution of petroleum in the United States. Though this trust was legally dissolved in 1892, the Standard Oil units and affiliates continued to function in close harmony. The history of the organization, especially its efforts to maintain its monopoly, is punctuated with bloody and bitter episodes—strikes, rate wars, political manipulation, and dynamiting.

When Rockefeller determined to extend his holdings here he went about it with characteristic energy. He had railroad tracks moved and public roads rerouted. The village of Eastview is now occupied chiefly by people who work on the estate, which holds 75 buildings, including houses occupied by members of the family, their servants, and other employees.

The beautiful estate has 70 miles of roads, as well as bridle trails, which are carried across the highway by under- and over-passes. High, near the center of the grounds, is the large family mansion, formal Georgian in design. As each Rockefeller son married, a house was provided for his use, either a new one or a remodeled old one. The house built for John D. Rockefeller, Jr., is a rambling structure of more comfort than elegance. The homes of his sons, along the southern road, exemplify their tastes: Nelson's is a remodeled Dutch structure, Lawrence's a prefabricated steel house, and John's a modernized farmhouse. The children's playhouse is more elaborate than most clubhouses.

Washington Irving said that TARRYTOWN, 48.7 m. (70 alt.,6,785 pop.), was named by irate Dutch farm women who complained that their husbands lingered too long at the village tavern after depositing produce at the Philipse wharf; but more serious historians say that 'tarry' is a corruption of the Dutch word 'tarwe' (wheat). The first commuter to attract attention to the Tarrytown neighborhood was Washington Irving, who in 1835 decided to rebuild an old farmhouse as his home; he felt he could live here very cheaply, find seclusion for work, and yet be close to New York City. The village is now primarily a service center for large and small estates.

The TARRYTOWN HISTORICAL SOCIETY, 19 Grove St., has an exhibit of memorabilia of John D. Rockefeller, Sr., including the mahogany desk from his Cleveland home; Ledger A, his boyhood account book; copies of addresses before the Young Men's Bible Class of the old Fifth Avenue Baptist Church; and a collection of gift pennies and dimes.

At the northern end of the village is the ANDRÉ MONUMENT (R), a statue of a soldier on a granite pedestal. It is near the spot where John Paulding, David Williams, and Isaac Van Wart captured Major André on September 23, 1780. In the stockings of the British officer they found notes on the armament, gun emplacements, and defense posts of West Point. Arnold, who had connived with the spy, learned of the capture and made his escape; André was hanged a week and a half later at Tappan, across the river, in spite of British efforts to save him.

At the foot of W.Main St. is the NYACK FERRY (*boats every 30 min. during daylight hours*), which crosses the Tappan Zee (Ind. and Dutch, *cold spring sea*) to the western shore and affords beautiful views of the Palisades to the south and the Highlands, a hazy outline to the north.

Near the southern village line is (R) LYNDHURST (*private*), home of Jay Gould (1819–92) at the time he engineered the notorious financial deal that ruined his neighbor and former business associate, Cyrus W. Field. His name is also associated with watering the stock of the Erie Railroad and with the disastrous panic of Black Friday, September 24, 1869, resulting from his attempt to corner the gold market. The estate passed to his daughter, Mrs.Helen Gould Shepard, noted for her philanthropies; and in 1939, after her death, it became the residence of the Duchess de Talleyrand, another daughter, who after many years in France returned to this peaceful Hudson Valley home.

The mansion was built in 1840 for Philip R. Paulding by Alexander Jackson Davis (1803–92), one of the most fashionable and prolific architects of the mid-nineteenth century. The imposing mass of Sing Sing marble has an exceedingly picturesque silhouette dominated by the projecting carriage porch bay, now glazed in and augmented by another porte-cochere. The octagonal battlemented stair tower on the left balances the long range and lower tower to the north. Gables, chimneys, turrets, pinnacles, and tracery strive hard to justify a contemporary eulogy of the structure as 'one of the finest and purest specimens of the Pointed Tudor style in the United States.' Davis's medievalism, like his Grecian manner, was chiefly a fashionable veneer, inspired by current English vogues and aimed to give adolescent American society a backdrop of false but comforting tradition. Beneath the veneer, however, ingenious planning and creditable craftsmanship evidence Davis's architectural skill.

The WASHINGTON IRVING MEMORIAL (R), at the corner of Broadway and Sunnyside Lane, is a bronze and marble panel, with reliefs of Rip Van Winkle and Boabdil, the last King of Granada, facing a marble shaft topped with a bust of Irving. The memorial is the work of Daniel Chester French.

Down Sunnyside Lane, the Tarrytown-Irvington line, is SUNNYSIDE (*adm.* $1), a rambling conglomeration of buildings erected by Washington Irving around the ruins of the little Dutch house that had been built by Wolfert Ecker about 1690. The remodeled house was at first a modest structure, which Irving called the Roost, but in time he achieved a building in some ways resembling the home of his friend Sir Walter Scott.

Today ivy and wisteria half cover the walls and the porte-cochere. Irving (1783–1859) was the youngest of eleven children; when he exhibited much more interest in literature than in business or the law, which he had begun to study, his devoted older brothers encouraged him. In 1807 he and James Kirke Paulding, with some help from Irving's brother William, brought out the surprisingly successful *Salmagundi Papers*; in 1809 he published his Knickerbocker's *History of New York*, which was greeted so warmly that his brothers determined to subsidize his writing by making him a lay partner in their business. In 1815 Irving went to England to help his ailing brother Peter. There he continued to write and was soon a warm friend of Sir Walter Scott, his idol; in England he wrote, among others, *The Sketch Book*. By the time he returned home in 1832 he had achieved a wide literary reputation abroad as well as at home. In America, subsidized by John Jacob Astor, he wrote *Astoria* (1836), an account of his patron's fur-trading settlement at the mouth of the Columbia River. His other works, except for a life of Washington, dealt mainly with Spanish themes. After a term as Minister to Spain he returned home to be an object of admiration and imitation—America's first man of letters.

IRVINGTON, 50.8 *m.* (175 alt.,2,759 pop.), named for Washington Irving, is another metropolitan suburb ringed by wooded estates. Near the northern end of the village is (R) the ANNA E. POTH HOME for convalescent and aged members of the Companions of the Forest of America. The ornate brick mansion, hidden by a wall, was built in 1918 by Mrs.C.J. Walker (1867–1919), a pioneer Negro businesswoman. About 1905, when Mrs.Walker was a laundress in St.Louis, Missouri, she concocted a preparation to straighten tightly curled hair that revolutionized the appearance of members of her race. In 1910 she settled in Indianapolis, Indiana, where she established the Mme.C.J.Walker factory and laboratories for the manufacture of various cosmetics, and opened a training school for her agents and beauty culturists. Her interests were wide; in time her sales agents were acting as organizers of social welfare clubs and were carrying on educational propaganda of all kinds among Negroes. She eventually moved to New York and as 'Madame C.J.Walker of New York and Paris' became a leader in Harlem activities. A year after this house had been completed she died, leaving an estate worth more than $1,000,000, two-thirds of which went to educational institutions and charities. The house still contains her ivory-and-gold pipe organ, her tapestries, and some of her imported gold and ivory furniture.

From a point just south of the Anna E. Poth Home can be seen on the hilltop (L) THE CASTLE, another baronial estate designed by Alexander J. Davis in 1859 for John T. Herrick, wealthy flour merchant. The rough, rock-face stone, quarried on the site, is an interesting contrast to the smooth marble of Lyndhurst, built 19 years earlier. The 65–foot tower commands magnificent vistas up Tappan Zee.

ODELL INN (R), just south of the Main St. traffic booth, built about 1693, is now the superintendent's cottage of the Murray estate. When the Albany Post Road was opened in 1723, the one-and-a-half-story stone dwelling became a favorite stage stop. On August 31, 1776, the Committee of Safety of the State Convention met in the inn, then occupied by Jonathan Odell. Two months later the British took vengeance on Odell by destroying 1,000 bushels of his wheat, killing his hogs, cutting down his orchard, and carrying him off to a New York prison. In 1785 Odell bought the house and 463 acres from the Commissioners of Forfeiture, keeping the inn until his death in 1818.

ARDSLEY (L), 51.7 *m.*, was the home of Cyrus W. Field (1819–92) from 1868 to 1892. In 1866, after 12 years of work, Field brought to completion the first transatlantic telegraph cable. His later years were occupied chiefly with financial activities.

At the corner of Ardsley Ave., 52.1 *m.*, is the entrance (R) to NEVIS, erected in 1835 as the home of James Alexander Hamilton (1788–1878), third son of Alexander Hamilton, intimate of Van Buren and Jackson. The name is that of the island in the British West Indies on which Alexander Hamilton was born. The original house has been enlarged and the interior was altered in 1889 by Stanford White. One of the outstanding features of Nevis is a superb Early Republican garden, which led Mrs.T.Coleman du Pont to give the estate to Columbia University in 1934 for the establishment of a horticultural and landscape architecture center. The grounds contain 2,640 trees in 56 varieties and 1,928 ornamental shrubs, thus forming one of the largest arboretums in the United States.

Down Ardsley Ave. is the ARDSLEY CLUB, organized in 1895 by a group of millionaires and described by a society reporter of the 1890's as 'that pleasance of Midas.' This club had the third golf course laid out in America; the players at first used gutta-percha balls, which the caddies carried around in buckets of ice, to keep them in shape. The club members were also leaders in the introduction of bicycle parties; sometimes as many as 40 whirled over the roads of Westchester County on carefully polished, silver-trimmed wheels. And the members were of course among the first to own automobiles, exciting toys that they also tested in races for possible commercial value.

Before 1700 Jeremiah Dobbs was carrying people across the river at what was to become known as DOBBS FERRY, 53.1 *m.* (150 alt.,5,858 pop.). When Arnold was planning the betrayal of West Point he made an appointment to meet Major André at 'Dobbs Ferry,' which may have been either at the landing here or at the one on the other side of the river. After André had been captured, Sir Henry Clinton made an appointment at this place to meet General Greene in a vain attempt to save the popular young British officer from execution. The village is one of the line of towns along the river that provide fashionable addresses. The business and part of the cultural interests of the inhabitants are in New York City, but there is considerable local civic pride.

The CHILDREN'S VILLAGE, Walgrove Ave. (*open* 8:30–11 *a.m.*, 1:30–4:30 *p.m.*), a training school for problem children, occupies a 245–acre plot. The school, established in New York City in 1851 as the New York Juvenile Asylum, was moved here in 1901. The 40 buildings include schools, workshops, a printing shop, and residence cottages for 500 boys and girls.

ZION EPISCOPAL CHURCH, corner of Cedar and Main Sts., is a fine stone structure erected in 1834. Washington Irving served as vestryman from 1837 to 1843. In 1854 the tower was made higher, tracery mullions were introduced, and buttresses were added to the tower.

The PHILIP LIVINGSTON HOUSE (L), corner of Broadway and Livingston Ave., is an able restoration of the home of Philip Livingston. The oldest section to the rear is a three-story structure probably erected between 1690 and 1700 by Frederick Philipse, first lord of the manor of Philipsburgh. Since he was a trained master-builder, it is not improbable that this old dwelling was of his own design. Practically unaltered, the exterior has a long sweeping roof broken by five dormers. A two-story veranda faces south. Within, low ceilings, huge fireplaces, and wattle-and-daub partitions illustrate seventeenth-century techniques. When the confiscated Philipse lands were sold in 1785, Philip Livingston with two associates acquired the region that is now Dobbs Ferry. By 1796 Livingston had sole possession of the property. In 1806 he added on the west, towards the post road, a large, stately two-story block in the latest Federal style, making a striking contrast to the earlier Dutch building. High ceilings with plaster ornaments, spacious rooms, black and gold marble mantels, slender fluted columns, narrow clapboard, molded window frames, and hipped roof with balustraded deck are typical details of this fashionable era. In 1824 Livingston's son, 'rich, righteous, and rigid' Peter Van Brugh Livingston, acquired the house, but he soon began to break up the large estate, selling the house itself in 1830 to Stephen Archer. In 1916 the present owner saved the place from becoming a tavern, restoring and repairing the neglected building.

HASTINGS–ON–HUDSON, 54.7 m. (140 alt.,6,970 pop.), named for the English birthplace of William Saunders, a local manufacturer, has chemical, copper, and paving-block factories along the river front employing about one tenth of the population. Mustard gas for the American Expeditionary Forces in the World War was manufactured here.

Hastings, like Yonkers, began to grow after construction of the Hudson River Railroad in 1849. Horace Greeley was one of the commuters of the Civil War period; in 1862 a drunken mob, blaming him for having incited the draft riots in New York City, started down from Sing Sing village (Ossining) to blow up his house, but it was dispersed before it accomplished its purpose. When the first New Yorkers invaded the village to build country seats they found Johannus Stalton, an eccentric pearl button maker, living here; someone started the story that he had been the model for Rip Van Winkle and he enjoyed considerable prestige.

In GRACE EPISCOPAL CHURCH, Broadway and Main St., is a *Christ after the Temptation* by Carl Brandt, a portrait painter of some note in his time. One day when Brandt was very ill in Baltimore he woke from a stupor and demanded his brushes and a canvas; he had seen Christ, he said, and must paint him. His enthusiasm gave him such energy that he was able to return to his studio here to paint this picture; but his strength gave out before his work could be completed and his attendant, a giant Negro, had to hold him up before the canvas while he worked. He died soon afterward.

DRAPER MEMORIAL PARK, Broadway and Washington St., contains the DRAPER OBSERVATORY of Dr. John W. Draper (1811–82), president of the medical school of New York University. Draper came to the village in 1840, and a year later, with the aid of a glass tank filled with a solution of ammonia and copper sulphate, obtained the first photograph of the human face ever made in direct sunlight.

On the same grounds is the FARRAGUT HOME, occupied during the Civil War by the family of David Glasgow Farragut (1801–70), commander of the Union fleet in the Battle of Mobile Bay.

YONKERS, 59.1 *m.* (30 alt.,142,404 pop.) (*see Yonkers*).

US 9 follows Broadway through Yonkers. The apartment houses, shops, and garages form a solid line to Van Cortlandt Park.

NEW YORK CITY, 71.8 *m.* (17 alt.,7,380,259 pop.) (*see New York City*).

Tour 21A

Albany—Catskill—Kingston—Newburgh—(Jersey City, N.J.). US 9W. Albany to New Jersey Line, 130 *m.*

Two- and three-lane-concrete with short stretches of macadam.
New York Central (West Shore) R.R. parallels route between Albany and New Jersey Line; Erie R.R. between Nyack and Sparkill.

South from Albany US 9W follows the west bank of the Hudson, the western horizon formed first by the Helderbergs, a dim, distant crest; then by the Catskills, a jagged, rocky mass capped by oak, maple, and hemlock. Below Newburgh the road rides the crest of the Hudson Highlands—Storm King, Crow's Nest, Bear Mountain, Dunderberg—and looks dizzily down upon vistas of the river and its valley. From the majestic barrier of the Catskill fairyland to below Pyngyp, the region abounds with Indian legends, Dutch hobgoblins, and fables of lost mines and gold hoards cached somewhere—anywhere—by Captain Kidd.

The entire journey is marked by a steady procession of church spires. Church sociables, block dances, the rod-and-gun club, and the volunteer firemen comprise the main staples of social life. The large estates of an earlier era have been subdivided and resold to more recent arrivals in the well-to-do brackets. On the lower stretches of the road, where it skirts the placid expanse of Tappan Zee, well-kept villages combine touches of the Revolutionary era with modern commuter-style comfort and neatness.

South of Catskill, the highway is clogged during the summer season by caravans of vacationists in every breed of motor-driven conveyance packed to the mudguards with baggage and an occasional canoe or outboard motorboat lashed to the top, headed for the vacation lands of the Catskills.

During the Revolution this route was a vital line of communication which Burgoyne and Sir Henry Clinton tried to open between Montreal and New York City. As late as 1830 the road was still no pleasure-seeker's thoroughfare. One traveler wrote:

At the town of Goshen we changed the mail, thawed our garments, and ate our dinner. As we got north the sleighing got better, so we were accommodated with a covered box on runners . . . We traveled all night. The rain and snow descended through the roof, our hats were frozen to our capes, and our cloaks to one another. In the morning we looked like some mountains of ice moving down the Gulf Stream. And this is what the horse-flesh fraternity advertise as their safe, cheap, comfortable, and expeditious winter establishment for Albany.

Section a. ALBANY to KINGSTON; 56.7 m. US 9W

Between Albany and Kingston US 9W—running for the most part one to three miles west of the river—passes by fruit orchards and brickyards. Swinging buckets on spidery cable railways glide over the road on their way between the limestone quarry in the hillside and the cement plants at the river's edge. Here and there are abandoned factories and traces of once-vigorous lumber and boat-building trades. The villages still bear the indelible marks of their Dutch origin in their old stone houses and sturdy, stolid citizenry.

South of **ALBANY**, 0 m. (18 alt.,130,447 pop.), US 9W swings away from the river and at 3.6 m. crosses Normans Kill, named for an early Albany settler who erected a mill near the mouth of the stream around which the first cabins of Dutch traders were built. Called Tawasentha (waterfall) by the Indians, the Normans Kill Valley is said to have been the setting for Longfellow's 'Hiawatha.'

At 4 m. is the junction with the River Road.

Left on the River Road 1 m. to the junction with State 144. Right on State 144 to COEYMANS, 11.9 m. (100 alt.,1,506 pop.), where 40 years ago brick was made and ice was cut and both were shipped in large quantities to New York City. When New York began using stone for building and the electric refrigerator replaced the old leaking icebox, Coeymans came to a halt in its growth, though the brick industry is still important.

The angular overhead traveling cranes of the SUTTON & SUDERLEY BRICK PLANT, at the northern village limits (L), swing their 1,500-unit stacks of brick over the barges lining the docks, waiting to be loaded for the down-river market. Behind the cranes are the long roofs of the sheds, kilns, and molding plant. The clay is dumped into hoppers and a regulated amount of coke dust and silica sand added; powerful rotary knives knead the mixture as a bit of red iron ore is added: and the mix is ready for the molder. A thundering mechanism rams, presses, and extrudes the material into brick form and men arrange the wet brick on galvanized pallets to be cured on steam pipes. When properly dried, the brick are stacked by hand in loads of 1,500, so arranged that air can pass freely through the rick. Cranes lower the ricks into the kilns between rows of oil burners that can build up and maintain a temperature of from 1,800 to 2,600 degrees Fahrenheit. The firing ignites the coke dust, which distributes the heat within the brick, a function for centuries accomplished by straw, and the silica sand fuses to form a bond, toughening and strengthening the whole brick.

NEW BALTIMORE, 14.1 m. (100 alt.,734 pop.), settled in 1811 as a shipbuilding port, has the appearance of a Maine coast village. The ways, derricks, sheds, and barges of a prosperous shipbuilding past rot at the water's edge. Retired rivermen look out from the heights on ocean-going steamers in the broad channel and wistfully recall the pre-steel age when wooden ships built in New Baltimore slid down the ways.

At 16.2 m. State 144 rejoins US 9W.

At 9.7 m. is the junction with State 396.

Left on State 396 to SELKIRK, 1.5 m. (173 alt.,250 pop.), terminal yard for the New York Central Railroad. 'Manifest' freight which, before this yard was opened in 1924, had been forced to pass through Albany, suffered delay from grades and traffic congestion. The cutoff connecting Selkirk with Hoffmans west of Schenectady makes possible the routing of all freight bound between New York City or New England and the West without touching Albany. On the 256 miles of track stringing the yard, boxcars, flat cars, and gondolas roll and rumble. At the ice plant, with a storage capacity of 25,000 tons, refrigerator cars line up, ice-chest covers tilted back, while workmen lower the rainbow-hued cakes into the openings.

At 18.3 m. is the junction with State 144 (see above).
At 22.8 m. is the junction with State 385.

Left on State 385 to COXSACKIE (Ind., hoot of an owl), 1.6 m. (155 alt.,2,195 pop.), which, settled by the Dutch late in the seventeenth century, preserved its pure Dutch character until the 1790–1830 migrations from New England and Europe.

On January 27, 1775, 225 residents of the village—almost all with Dutch names—signed a 'declaration of independence' calling for opposition to 'the execution of several arbitrary and oppressive acts of the British Parliament.' The original document, antedating the Declaration of Independence of the Continental Congress by more than a year, is in the Albany Institute of History and Art.

As it did a generation ago, the town still makes bricks and cuts ice, though on a reduced scale. Farming in the vicinity has been static; as one old-timer put it, 'Those who have farms can keep going, but it is no place to start.' The AMERICAN VALVE PLANT, a sprawl of brick buildings (R), employs in its foundry and shop more than 100 villagers.

ATHENS, 7.9 m. (20 alt.,1,618 pop.), the third village in the State to incorporate (1805), also makes brick. Along the water front are buildings of the two shipyards run by the Federal Government during the World War. Old river steamers are tied up at the rotting docks; rebuilding of tugs and smaller craft continues on a small scale. The ice-harvesting industry once flourished here, as at other points along the river; ice cakes were cut and stored in huge icehouses along the water front and shipped to New York City during the summer. But mechanical refrigeration killed this chilly occupation and for a time the great icehouses stood empty. Then it was discovered that these windowless, well-insulated structures made ideal places for the mass production of mushrooms. Today they are filled with trays from floor to roof, from which sprout millions of buttonlike fungi. If the mushroom market is glutted, the production speed can be stepped down by a slight draft over the trays. Additional warmth and humidity increase the rapidity of growth.

The village was settled in 1686 by Jan Van Loon, a Hollander. Two of the Van Loon fieldstone houses built soon after settlement still stand: the ALBERTUS VAN LOON HOUSE (L), at the north village limits, a one-story structure built in 1724, and the JAN VAN LOON HOUSE, foot of Washington St., a solid one-story fieldstone building with gabled Dutch roof built in 1706.

New Englanders who settled the outskirts between 1790 and 1840 called the village Esperanza, after an unrealized dream of the Livingstons—Edward, Brockholst, and John—who lived across the river (see Tour 21B). Envious of the Nantucketers who were making Hudson a prosperous town, they planned a rival city on the west side of the river, envisioning it as a great market for western produce, and even speculating that it might become the terminus of a canal across the State to the Great Lakes. They had their draftsmen lay out the Esperanza Key, and named its streets Liberty, Equality, Happiness, Beer, Cider, Art, and so on. They sold a few lots, but while still in its early stages of development Esperanza was absorbed by Athens.

At the northern entrance to Catskill, 12.5 *m.*, is the junction with State 23 (*see Tour 7*) and the approach to the Rip Van Winkle Bridge.

In CATSKILL, 13 *m.* (75 alt.,5,414 pop.), is the junction with US 9W (*see below*).

South on US 9W at 24.2 *m.* is the entrance (R) to the BRONCK HOUSE (*open daily, June–Nov.*), headquarters of the Greene County Historical Society,Inc. The stone wing was built about 1663 by Pieter Bronck, only son of Jonas Bronck, after whom the New York City borough of the Bronx was named. In 1738 Pieter's grandson built the brick addition.

The stone house is a solid, plain building of the Dutch pioneer type, with high casement windows. The woodwork, including floors and huge, hand-hewn beams, has been restored. The Dutch doors retain their original hinges, knockers, and locks. In the upper room a steep ladder ascends to a platform, once a lookout and rifle station, with loopholes through the front wall. The later addition measures the advance of 70 years. Wooden-pinned beam supports of the interior suggest the influence of a ship's carpenter. The cellar houses a slave pen.

In the rear of the main house is the STEPMOTHER'S HOUSE, a one-room brick bungalow built in 1800 by Judge Leonard Bronck when his daughters by his first wife refused to live under the same roof with their stepmother. This miniature home has a fireplace furnished with crane, kettle, and Dutch oven, a tiny cellar, and an attic stair fitted with a pulley by which it can be drawn up to the ceiling.

The property remained in the possession of the Bronck family until in 1938 Leonard Bronck Lampman renovated the structure and presented it, with 16 acres of land, to the Greene County Historical Society.

On the hill west of the Bronck House, Indians operated a flint mine. They fractured the rock by first heating it with fire and then pouring cold water on it. From these chips they fashioned arrowheads, spear points, scrapers, and knives. Imperfect examples of these weapons are still found along the slopes.

Opposite the Bronck House is the entrance (L) to the STATE VOCATIONAL INSTITUTION FOR BOYS, which provides for 500 delinquents between the ages of 16 and 20. The architectural style of the enormous brick buildings harmonizes with the Colonial homes of the region. Although the windows appear to be ordinary mullioned ones, they are heavily barred. The aim of the school is to approach normal living conditions as closely as possible and yet make the inmates realize that they are confined for punishment and correction. The boys are taught trades in an effort to make them self-supporting after they are released.

At 32.5 *m.* is the junction with State 23 and the entrance to the Rip Van Winkle Bridge (*see Tour 7*).

CATSKILL, 33 *m.* (75 alt.,5,414 pop.), Greene County seat, crowds the narrow valley of Catskill Creek and stretches two arms up the sloping hillsides. In the spring the swollen creek waters rush through the town and frequently overflow their banks, leaving a deposit of mud in bordering cellars. In the summer, hordes of vacationists descend upon the town. Throughout the year, especially on Saturday afternoons, the hill natives come into the village to do their shopping. Small knitting mills, employing mainly Italian girls, and brickyards and distilleries in the vicinity, giving work to Negro residents, are the principal industries. A number of residents commute to work in Albany. On Saturday night the village seems to try to concentrate a week's life into a few hours; the narrow Main Street, with cars parked on both sides, is all but impassable.

Early tavern keepers in this community were known as 'retailers of liquid damnation.' Catskill mountain-brewed applejack was a staple during the prohibition era; the moonshiners outwitted the 'revenooers' by covering the jugs with burlap and burying them in the ground; when a customer came and identified himself with unimpeachable references the liquor was disinterred and sold. This trade and the inaccessibility of the hills to the west attracted the leaders of New York City gangsterdom, who established their hideouts in and near Catskill; as a result the village was associated with the careers of 'Legs' Diamond, Vincent Coll, and others of the gun fraternity; Diamond was tried in the Greene County courthouse in Catskill.

Originally known as Catskill Landing, the settlement on the river was subsidiary to the old Dutch hamlet of Kaatskill, still hibernating in the hills to the west, at the fall in Catskill Creek. Mountains, creeks, and village were named by the Dutch for the wildcats that occasionally came down from the hills, where they roamed in large numbers. In the heyday of turnpike and river transportation the place bustled with prosperity. Over the Susquehanna Turnpike across the mountains, the route in part of State 23 (see Tour 7), came a large part of the produce of the southern section of the State, and large mills were erected at Kaatskill to grind the wheat into flour, which was shipped to New York; shipyards at the Landing built boats for the river trade, and fishermen sent their shad and herring to Albany and New York City. The tanning industry in the mountains also shipped its leather from Catskill Landing. But the Erie Canal diverted the trade of the Southern Tier into its channel, the railroads superseded the river steamboat, and the tanneries followed the vanishing hemlock southward and northward.

In the late 1830's Charles L. Beach of Catskill got control of the stage and mail lines between New York and Albany on both sides of the Hudson and between Catskill and Ithaca. He improved vehicles, taverns, and speed of travel and made the trip between New York and Albany a pleasant 15-hour jaunt; in the winter the stages took to the smooth ice for speed and comfort. His most famous hotel was the Catskill Mountain House (see Tour 7). In 1843 he contracted with the New York Sun to get the governor's annual message to the legislature through ahead of the other newspapers. A copy left Albany a little after 2 p.m., with the famous driver Dimock at the reins; horses were changed every six or eight miles. From Goshen a special engine of the Erie Railroad carried it to Piermont, where a steamboat waited with a dozen printers ready to set type as the boat plowed toward the city. The next morning, to the Sun's proud headlines were added: 'by the Sun's exclusive express, from Albany through by horse and sleigh in 10 hours and ½.'

The THOMAS COLE HOUSE, Spring St. just north of Cedar St., was built about 1814 by the uncle of Cole's wife. Cole was one of the first of the Hudson River School of painters (*see Painting and Sculpture*) and a founder of the National Academy of Design. He spent much of his life in and around Catskill, painting scenes of the mountains. His *View of the Catskill Mountain House* is one of his most famous paintings. There are almost two score of his canvases still in the Cole House, several unfinished; outstanding among these are *Christ's Temptation in the Wilderness* and *Prometheus Bound*.

At 34.5 *m.* is the junction with State 23A (*see Tour 7*).

From the road south of the village are views (R) across the plateau to North and South Mountains and High Peak, jutting out from the northeast ridges of the Catskills, which rise an abrupt 3,000 feet above the plain and are cut by deep gorges known locally as 'cloves.'

MALDEN–ON–HUDSON, 43 *m.* (80 alt.,400 pop.), is a quiet village of frame homes, supporting itself by work in a local brickyard and neighboring cement plants, and by fishing. During the latter part of the nineteenth century the place throve on the mining of bluestone for sidewalks and street curbings. In its heyday the local Bigelow bluestone plant employed 125 men in its yards; but as the vogue for bluestone passed, the company went into receivership.

The two-story frame BIGELOW HOME, in the center of the village, is now (1940) the home of Poultney Bigelow, grandson of Malden's first postmaster and son of John Bigelow, Ambassador to France under Lincoln. Bigelow is a close personal friend of the ex-Kaiser of Germany, to whom he pays an annual visit. Mr.Bigelow gave the village its community hall and a school playground. Once a year the house and grounds are thrown open to the villagers for a field day with basket lunches and speeches by prominent guests.

Set in the hill slopes of the headland formed by the confluence of Esopus Creek and the Hudson River, SAUGERTIES (Dutch, sawyer's town), 45 *m.* (100 alt.,3,918 pop.), is an attractive village of Colonial, Greek Revival, and white frame homes with deep lawns, fences, and flagstone walks. Factories turning out paper, leather, and canvas do not mar the pleasing picture.

Saugerties was a live place in the days of the packet trade and the racing steamers; it was a terminus and port of call for the fleetest river boats, including the famed *Mary Powell*; people said in those days that 'Albany builds steamers, but Saugerties and Esopus (Kingston) build *racing* steamers.' At the mouth of Esopus Creek are the abandoned docks of the Saugerties Night Line, one of some dozen lines on the Hudson River that once maintained a daily passenger service to New York City.

The DUBOIS KIERSTEDS HOUSE, 119 Main St., a one-and-one-half-story stone structure, was built in 1727. The original doors, hardware, kitchen fireplace, and a bed recess in the west room have been carefully preserved.

At 54 *m.* the highway forks for two approaches to Kingston; the left fork is the through route, the right leads to the center of town.

KINGSTON, 56.7 *m.* (150 alt.,28,541 pop.), Ulster County seat, rises from the west bank of the Hudson River at the mouth of Rondout Creek.

The graceful lines of Overlook Mountain, with other Catskill peaks beyond, circle like a backdrop behind it. On a shelf between broad, muddy Rondout Creek and Chestnut Street is the lower town, a jumble of narrow byways with abrupt railroad crossings, sheds, docks, and oil tanks, its drabness unrelieved by a few stately old homes. Here center the maritime and industrial activities of Kingston. A score of factories manufacture refrigerators, hotel equipment, iron and bronze castings, road machinery, brushes, cigars, bricks, boats, cement, and hardware. In Rondout Creek are the rotting hulls of barges and canal boats, relics of the years when Kingston shipped millions of tons of cement annually. Tugs and barges still ply the creek under a graceful suspension bridge that connects with Port Ewen.

The upper town, on the plateau, is characterized mainly by neat one-family homes. An occasional Victorian dwelling holds itself aloof on a square of lawn, and a scattering of blue limestone houses built in the Revolutionary period impart an eighteenth-century air to the place. The business section, on Broadway, Wall, North Front, and John Streets, comprises groups of two- and three-story brick buildings with here and there a store front done in modern design.

In 1615 Dutch traders established a trading post at the mouth of Rondout Creek and named it Esopus. A group of Dutch colonists from Albany made the first permanent settlement in 1653. The Indians attacked the place on two occasions and took many lives. In 1658 Director General Peter Stuyvesant erected a stockade and blockhouse and in 1661 granted a charter to the village, which he called Wiltwyck (Dutch, wild retreat). In 1669 the English Governor Francis Lovelace gave it its present name in honor of Kingston L'Isle, his family seat in England. During the short Dutch reoccupation in 1673-4 the place was called Swanenburgh.

The memorable Revolutionary history of Kingston was crowded into the year 1777. Moving from place to place before the British advance, the temporary State Government met in the courthouse at Kingston beginning on February 19 of that year. In that building and in what is now known as the Senate House the first State constitution was adopted, the first governor was inaugurated, the first jury under the new constitution was impaneled, and the first session of the State legislature was held. On October 7 the legislature disbanded, again before the advance of the British, leaving the government in the hands of an extralegal Council of Safety. On October 16 the British burned the settlement.

The homes were soon rebuilt and the place was incorporated as a village in 1805. The foundation for the development of the city, which was incorporated in 1872, was laid by the Delaware & Hudson Canal, steamboat navigation on the river, and the manufacture of cement. The canal, opened in 1828 and enlarged in 1842 and 1851, stretched 107 miles, with a lock at every mile, from Honesdale, Pennsylvania, to Kingston, and made possible the introduction of Pennsylvania anthracite coal into profitable commercial use in the East. The canal began to die when the railroads reached the village in 1865 and 1866, and was doomed when the West Shore Railroad came in 1883.

Boat building and the cement industry came simultaneously about 1830. Cement reached its peak production about 1900, when Kingston and its environs produced 3,000,000 barrels annually. The industry waned with the appearance of Portland cement, which solidifies more quickly than the natural product.

The SENATE HOUSE and MUSEUM (*open weekdays 9–5, and Sundays 1–5; admission free*), are in a small park bounded by Clinton Ave. and N.Front and Fair Sts., the approximate site of the old Dutch stockade and blockhouse. The Senate House is a one-story structure with attic and basement, constructed of rock-cut limestone, with the exception of the rear wall of Holland brick. It was built by Colonel Wessel Ten Broeck in 1676. When the British burned Kingston in October 1777, the Senate House suffered little damage: only the roof was burned. The State purchased the building from a descendant of the original owner in 1887. The open porch on the northeast was added in 1888. In the interior, the furnishings, though not the originals, are of the Colonial period. There are four paintings by John Vanderlyn, native of Kingston.

In the most southerly room of this building the legislature of the State of New York held its first sessions, September 10–October 7, 1777. Here also John Jay convened the first State court on September 9 of that year.

The Museum, opened by the State in June 1930, is a solid fireproof structure of rough-cut bluestone, heavy chimneys, Dutch Colonial windows and blinds, and a simple entrance porch. The gable ends are irregular, a feature borrowed from the architecture of the old Dutch homes in the city. The first floor exhibit includes 28 paintings by John Vanderlyn— one a copy by the artist of his famous *Marius on the Ruins of Carthage*, the Alton B. Parker collection of governors' autographs, steel engravings of the Presidents, Indian artifacts, and relics of the Revolutionary and Civil Wars. The second-floor exhibits include the large steering wheel of the *Mary Powell*, queen of the Hudson River steamboats for decades (*see Tour 21C*); the bell of the *Norwich*, another river boat; and a collection of early glassware and china.

Another of the houses to survive the burning of the British with only superficial damage is the HOFFMAN HOUSE (D.A.R.Headquarters) (*open 9–3 weekdays*), corner of North Front and Green Sts., a substantially built two-story structure of stone painted cream color. The original small one-and-one-half-story house is believed to have been built about 1660; the place was owned by the Hoffman family from about 1707 until after 1900.

The VAN STEENBERGH HOUSE (*private*), Wall St. facing Franklin St., was the only house to escape altogether the burning of Kingston by the British. Originally it was a one-story-and-attic house built of limestone, with front center gable, end gables, and solid blinds. Tobias van Steenbergh,Jr., conducted a tavern in the building during the Revolution. Two local legends explain why the British spared the house: one is that admiration of the owner's beautiful daughter softened their hearts and stayed their hand; another that the redcoats tarried so long over a barrel of whisky in the cellar that when they were called to re-embark on their ships they lacked both the time and the poise to fire the house.

The CONRAD ELMENDORF TAVERN (*private*), 88 Maiden Lane, is a two-story-and-attic limestone building erected in 1725. The Council of Safety met here October 11–15, 1777.

A local newspaper is housed in the OLD KINGSTON ACADEMY BUILDING (*open by permission*), SW. corner of Crown and John Sts., a plain two-story limestone structure erected before 1770. This was the first academy in the State, chartered in 1773, opened in 1774, and incorporated in the city school system in 1864. Among its graduates were Governor De Witt Clinton and John Vanderlyn.

The DUTCH REFORMED CHURCH, at the junction of Wall, Main, and Fair Sts., erected in 1852, is a bluestone structure, rectangular in plan, of crude, heavy Roman classical architecture, with a square tower ending in a tall spire. The entire rear wall is taken up by a large colored leaded glass window and a pulpit. The pews are of the New England Colonial style. The congregation dates from 1659. In the burial ground adjoining the church is the GRAVE OF GEORGE CLINTON (1739–1812), first governor of New York State. Many of the surrounding headstones are pre-Revolutionary.

The ULSTER COUNTY COURTHOUSE, Wall St. between Main and John Sts., erected in 1818, is a two-story stone building suggestive of the post-Colonial style but not true in detail, especially in the main cornice brackets and the octagonal tower. The present structure occupies the site of the earlier courthouse in which the 'Convention of the Representatives of the State of New York' adopted the first State constitution on Sunday, April 20, 1777. Two days later the secretary of the Convention, standing on a barrel in front of the courthouse, read the constitution to the assembled crowd. On July 30, in the same building, George Clinton took his oath as first governor of the State; and his induction into office was proclaimed by the sheriff of Ulster County from the courthouse steps.

In Kingston are the junctions with US 209 (*see Tour* 6) and State 28 (*see Tour* 15).

Section b. KINGSTON to the NEW JERSEY LINE; 77.3 m. US 9W

South of Kingston the route is cradled in fruit orchard, vineyard, and berry patch; many of the farms are operated by Italians. South of Newburgh it winds over the gigantic buttresses of the Hudson Highlands past Revolutionary shrines. Campsites and resorts dot the valleys and the walls of Storm King and Bear Mountain, and the towers of West Point rear above a bulwark of trees.

South of KINGSTON, 0 *m.*, US 9W crosses RONDOUT CREEK. Site of a Dutch trading post built in 1614, the mouth of the creek was the busiest port along the mid-Hudson until the development of automobile transportation.

On October 16, 1777, when British men-of-war hove into sight, the American galley, *Lady Washington*, lay in the mouth of Rondout Creek. Cannonading began at 9; the British fire was answered by a battery of five guns on a hill above the creek. By noon the Americans had scuttled the

Lady Washington and the militia had spiked their guns and fled. Within three hours Kingston was in burning ruins.

US 9W follows close to the river on a plateau that stretches westward to the base of the Catskill wall. Across the river can be seen the Vanderbilt and Roosevelt estates.

In WEST PARK, 9.1 *m.* (170 alt.,700 pop.), is RIVERBY (L), the estate of John Burroughs. The two-story stone house, built in 1873, was designed by Burroughs. 'I built into my house,' he wrote, 'every one of those superb autumn days which I spent in the woods getting out stone.' In 1881 he built the one-room BARK STUDY, a few rods east. Its wide windows offer superb views of the Hudson; the huge cobblestone fireplace and built-in bookshelves filled with Burroughs's books are much as the naturalist-author left them. THE NEST, a rustic bungalow a few rods north, was built in 1902 by the naturalist's son, Julian Burroughs, who still lives here. On April 2, 1921, Henry Ford, Thomas A. Edison, and other distinguished persons gathered at The Nest for brief funeral services for the naturalist.

Right from West Park on a macadam road 0.9 *m.* to the entrance (L) to SLABSIDES, built in 1895 by Burroughs as a retreat when 'lion-hunters became too numerous,' and now owned by the John Burroughs Memorial Association. It is a rustic two-story structure with walls of slabs, fieldstone chimney and fireplace, and rustic furniture made by Burroughs. When President Theodore Roosevelt, a long-time friend, came to see Burroughs in a Government steam yacht, the tawny recluse was quite docile. Roosevelt arrived 'on the 10th of July, the hottest day of the whole year,' Burroughs reported; 'we walked from the river up to Slabsides, and Roosevelt sweat his white linen coat right through at the back.'

Just south of West Park, sloping down to the river, at a point directly opposite the Roosevelt estate, is (L) the 500-acre estate sold by Howland Spencer to Father Divine in July 1938 for a 'heaven,' one of the many pieces of property owned by Father Divine and his followers in Ulster County.

The origins of Father Divine (*alias* Joe Baker), who, his adherents say, is 'God himself,' are appropriately shrouded in mystery. His enthusiastic followers proclaim that he was never born but was 'combusted' one day in 1900 in Harlem at the corner of Seventh Avenue and 134th Street. He has, however, been traced back to the 1890's and to Savannah, Georgia, where he set up as a prophet. He arrived in New York in 1915 with 12 disciples and set up a communal organization in Brooklyn; but he found his green pastures in Harlem in the early thirties. To impoverished Harlemites, suffering from the depression and haunted by fear of the future, Father Divine brought his simple creed of peace and brotherhood and unlimited material abundance. He classifies his followers into 'Children'—people who go to his meetings but are not ready or willing to turn over everything to him, and 'Angels'—those who turn over to him all their worldly possessions, even their names, and are thereafter known by such names as Love Light, Rebecca Willing, Precious Love, Harmony, and so on. Father Divine's real estate holdings in Harlem include half a dozen apartment houses, in addition to 25 flats; he runs some 16 businesses, including a dress shop, a garage, a bakery, and several grocery stores. He also owns a number of residence and farm properties along the Hudson, most of them in Ulster County; some of his Ulster County followers are white.

At 14.9 *m.* is the northern junction with US 44 (*see Tour 5*); and at 15.4 *m.* is a traffic circle at the western end of the MID-HUDSON BRIDGE (L) and the southern junction with US 44 (*see Tour 5*).

The COLONEL LOUIS DUBOIS HOUSE (L), 22.6 *m.*, was built about 1757. The story-and-a-half clapboarded structure was given a jerkin head roof, dormers, and four false windows on the end wall about 1802. Colonel Du Bois was one of the few masters to free his slaves before the New York State law of 1825. But his act was a measure of economy rather than of principle; he felt that it was an extravagance to feed slaves all winter for doing his work when he could hire laborers during the farming season only.

In MARLBORO, 23.2 *m.* (180 alt.,1,000 pop.), the type designer Frederic William Goudy converted an old water mill into a workshop, in which he created his remarkable series of original type designs. Goudy is probably the only printer ever to carry the printing process from the original design to the printed book without outside help. This is the more noteworthy because he did not learn the technique and mechanics of type until he was 61 years old. In January 1939 the Goudy type shop caught fire, and the flames destroyed 75 or more original type designs, matrices of the 107 type faces originated by Goudy, the specially made precision instruments with which he created his masterpieces, and the press on which the English printer-poet William Morris got out the Kelmscott Chaucer. In 1940, on his 75th birthday, Goudy was appointed to the faculty of the Syracuse University School of Journalism.

CHRIST CHURCH (L), at the south end of town, is a modest brick structure designed in 1858 by Richard Upjohn, architect of Trinity Church, New York City.

At 24.6 *m.* is the junction with a lane.

Left here 0.1 *m.* to the MILL HOUSE (L). The stone first story was built in 1714 by Gomez the Jew, as a home and trading post for his fur trade with the Indians. Gomez developed so large a trade that he transported furs in his own boats to Spain and Portugal. In 1772, Wolfert Acker, grandson of the Wolfert Acker of Washington Irving's *Wolfert's Roost*, bought the Mill House, which became a meetingplace for Whigs during the Revolution. Acker added the second story, constructing it of brick made by his slaves.

NEWBURGH, 31.2 *m.* (160 alt.,31,797 pop.), is a city of tree-bordered streets rising in terraces above the broad expanse of Newburgh Bay. On the east the town drops down a maze of steep, winding streets to the river front, where cargoes are loaded on ocean-going freighters; the old residential section here is a series of faded brick blocks and sedate frame dwellings with broad piazzas and towers. The newer part of town spreads westward over a plateau reaching toward the horizon of the Shawangunk Mountains.

Water Street, narrow and congested, running parallel with the river, is the main shopping center. Broadway, 90 feet wide, climbs the westward slope, jammed at all hours with a stream of traffic between New England and New Jersey, Pennsylvania, and western New York. In sharp contrast, three blocks north is the courthouse square, an oasis of quiet.

In normal times the city's industries employ about 7,000 workers, producing lawn mowers, overalls, machinery, artificial leather, handbags and pocketbooks, carpets, and silk goods. Industrial buying power is augmented by a large summer tourist trade and an extensive commerce in fruit and farm produce.

Newburgh people are gregarious. The place is a stronghold of church activities, of playgrounds and parks, of sports, of secret and social clubs and organizations. The city cherishes its Revolutionary traditions, keeping them alive by emphasis in the school curricula, reading courses in the public library, and the activities of local patriotic societies.

The first settlement on the site of Newburgh was made in 1709 by a group of about 50 penniless German Palatines led by Joshua Kocherthal, a Lutheran preacher. They settled in the vicinity of Quassaick Creek, the present southern city line, under a patent covering 2,190 acres and known as 'The Palatine Parish of Quassaick.' As Scottish, Dutch, and English settlers moved in, the Palatines found it difficult to live in harmony with their new neighbors and sought out the larger groups of their own people up the Hudson, in the Mohawk Valley, and in Pennsylvania and Delaware. The present name was given to the settlement in 1762 in honor of the town in Scotland on the River Tay.

The significant Revolutionary history of the settlement is centered in the Hasbrouck House. After the Revolution, Major Isaac Belknap and others who before the war had sailed sloops of red cedar, staunch rather than speedy, re-entered the boating business, and by 1798 four lines of sloops were in active service from the growing town. Over the Newburgh-Cochecton Turnpike came from the hinterland the agricultural products that the sloops transported down the river. By the end of the century the trade of Newburgh had spread as far west as Canandaigua, whence wagon trails radiated in every direction. But this trade was rapidly diverted by the Erie Canal. For a short time the villagers found a substitute in whaling, and made futile plans for a Government shipyard. When the Erie Railroad was laid out, the plans excluded Newburgh, but repeated pleas were rewarded with a branch line from Chester, which was opened in 1850.

The city was incorporated in 1865 with a population of 13,000. A few years later, the completion of the Dutchess & Columbia Railroad to the east shore of the Hudson, and of the Newburgh & Wallkill Railroad west, with a free connecting barge service across the river, put Newburgh on the direct route between the Pennsylvania coal mines and the New England market. In 1881 the city became the western terminus of the New York & New England Railroad, and in 1883 the West Shore Railroad provided direct connection with New York City.

Attracted in large part by the multiplying rail facilities, between 1880 and 1891 factories came and began to manufacture flannels, overalls, paper boxes, iron products, hats, wire products and furniture, building supplies and paints, soap, electric motors, reed chairs, flour and feed, wallpaper, and lawn mowers.

DOWNING PARK, entrance corner of Carpenter Ave. and 3d St., was named for Andrew Jackson Downing (1815–52), native of Newburgh, who, with his brother Charles (1802–85), was largely responsible for the development of the Hudson Valley as a fruit-growing center and exerted a still visible influence on its architecture (*see Tour 21C*). From the peak elevation of the observation tower (*open*) on the grounds is a sweeping view of the Hudson.

The ORANGE COUNTY COURTHOUSE, Grand St. between 2d and 3d Sts., is a stuccoed brick building erected in 1841, Thornton M. Niver, architect.

ST.GEORGE EPISCOPAL CHURCH, SW. corner of Grand and 2d Sts., is a rectangular stone structure built in 1819. The Greek Revival steeple is one of the finest in the State.

The ASSOCIATE REFORMED CHURCH, NW. corner of Grand and 1st Sts., is a small clapboarded building erected in 1799 and rebuilt in 1821.

HEADQUARTERS PARK is a seven-acre enclosure with main entrance on Liberty St. between Washington and Lafayette Sts. The low, weathered graystone structure is the HASBROUCK HOUSE (*open 9–5 weekdays, 1–5 Sunday; admission free*), which served as Washington's headquarters from April 1, 1782, until August 18, 1783. The building incorporates in its southeast corner a house built about 1725 by Burger Mynders, second white owner of the land. In 1749 Burger Mynders,Jr., deeded the land to Elsie Hasbrouck, whose son Jonathan enlarged the house soon afterward and took title to the land in 1754. A second enlargement in 1770 gave the house the appearance as Washington knew it and as it now stands. After remaining in the hands of the Hasbrouck family for 100 years, it was taken over by the State of New York.

In this house Washington wrote his famous letter of advice to the governors of the States. Here on May 22, 1782, he received the formal letter in which Colonel Lewis Nicola, spokesman for a group of officers, proposed that Washington become king for the 'national advantage'; and here he wrote his reply that the proposal was received with 'surprise and astonishment,' 'viewed with abhorrence,' and 'reprimanded with severity.' Here, also, on April 10, 1783, Washington announced the cessation of hostilities.

The Headquarters were always overcrowded; and when a visitor remained overnight, he had to arise early so that his cot might be made up and the room turned over to the General as an office. Martha Washington spent a great deal of time here, and helped in receiving distinguished guests and in entertaining the Generals and their wives. Many pleasant evenings were spent at the Headquarters, Washington dipping from time to time into a great bowl of nuts that came on with the wine, and the company frequently convulsed with laughter at the tall tales of that great fisherman, Baron von Steuben, who proved to be something of a Munchausen.

That Martha Washington also mothered the Generals is brought out in the two letters following, sent from and received at the Headquarters:

Newburgh, March 6, 1783

Mrs.Washington presents her compliments to General Knox and begs his acceptance of two hair nets. They would have been sent long ago, but for want of tape to finish them and which was not obtained until yesterday.

West Point, March 8, 1783

General Knox has the honor to present his most respectful compliments to Mrs.Washington and to assure her he is deeply impressed with the sense of her goodness in favor of the hair nets for which he begs her to accept his sincere thanks.

Today the Hasbrouck House contains numerous objects of historical interest, including paintings and engravings of Washington and other Revolutionary personages and furniture of the Colonial and Revolutionary periods, a few pieces of which were used during Washington's residence. A large central room on the east side of the house—the famous 'room with seven doors and one window'—served the Washington family as a living room. Its unusual fireplace is without jambs; the fire was built against the wall with no protection, and the smoke rose to the chimney that begins at the level of the floor above.

The MUSEUM (*open* 9–5 *weekdays*, 1–5 *Sunday; adm. free*), in Headquarters Park, a two-story red brick structure in the Georgian Colonial style, was erected by New York State in 1910. It contains a large variety of historical mementos, principally of the Revolutionary period: firearms, battle flags, lace, beadwork, costumes, Indian artifacts, and objects associated with Washington and his wife, Lafayette, and Major André.

Among the smaller monuments and numerous cannon and war trophies in the park stands the TOWER OF VICTORY, a 53-foot monument erected in 1883, commemorating the disbanding of the Continental Army on October 18, 1783. In the open section of the tower is a life-size statue of Washington copied by William R. O'Donovan from Houdon's model.

Right from Newburgh on State 32 to the SITE OF THE LAST CANTONMENT (L), 2.5 *m.*, where the Continental regiments were encamped during the long armistice between the surrender of Cornwallis in 1781 and the signing of the peace treaty in 1783. These winter quarters along the Hudson are considered by many historians to have outdone in hardship the more storied quarters at Valley Forge; Washington wrote of 'the sufferings and privations of these heroic men, who ate at one time every kind of horse food but hay, and whose clothing was patched, nearly every substance of originality being lost.' The 8,000 troops quartered here included Continental regiments and brigades from Massachusetts, New York, New Hampshire, and New Jersey.

At 3.8 *m.* is the junction with Temple Hill Road; right on this road 1 *m.* to TEMPLE HILL (R), called the 'Birthplace of the Republic.' Memorial tablets on the 50-foot stone TEMPLE HILL MONUMENT, erected by the Masons, summarize the history of the site.

On this spot the soldiers erected in 1782–3 the Temple, a log structure that was the religious and executive core of the encampment. Here on March 15, 1783, before a convention of officers presided over by General Gates, George Washington made his 'Law and Order' speech in reply to the 'Newburgh Addresses' written anonymously by Major John Armstrong, later Secretary of War (*see Tour 21B*), inciting the soldiers to seize control of the government before peace was made and they were disbanded without their pay. 'Gentlemen,' Washington began, 'by an anonymous summons an attempt has been made to convene you together. How inconsistent with rules of propriety, how unmilitary, how subversive of all order and discipline; let the good sense of the Army decide.' Pausing a moment, he drew out his spectacles, carefully wiped and adjusted them, and then remarked, 'These eyes, my friends, have grown dim and these locks white in the service, yet I have never doubted the justice of my country.' And he concluded with an exhortation: 'I conjure you, in the name of our common country, as you value your own sacred honor, as you respect the rights of humanity, to express your utmost horror and detestation of the man who wishes, under any specious pretense, to overturn the liberties of your country, and who wickedly attempts to open the floodgates of civil discord, and deluge our rising empire in blood.'

At 3.9 *m.* on State 32 is the junction with State 45; left on State 45 to (R) the GEN-ERAL KNOX HEADQUARTERS (John Ellison House) 0.4 *m.* (*open 9–5 weekdays except Wed., 1–5 Sunday; adm. free*), a large white building of stone and frame construction. Part of the one-story wing was built in 1734 as the hunting lodge of John Ellison; the rest of the one-story section was added in 1754; the main two-story-and-attic stone house was added in 1782. It is today occupied by fourth-generation descendants of William Bull, builder of the stone portion; the State is represented by a curator.

As headquarters of General Knox, and for a time of General Gates, this house was a social center of the Last Cantonment, with less formality than was required in the presence of the Commander-in-Chief. The older section of the house contains a perfect specimen of a Dutch oven; there is a curious stairway to the attic, with staggered treads that are removable as the householder ascends, to pull a trap door up after him; and a door on strap hinges opens and closes by means of a rope with a weight at the end, running through a perforated wooden arm. The entire house is furnished with period furniture, fine old open fireplaces, mantels, and woodwork, which have been copied by visiting craftsmen of the present day.

In front of the house ran the Revolutionary highway, crossing Silver Stream by a small arched bridge of dry masonry, which still stands.

NEW WINDSOR, 33.1 *m.* (160 alt.,2,650 pop.), a Newburgh suburb, is the site of Washington's headquarters from June 24 to July 21, 1779, and December 6, 1780, to June 25, 1781. On July 4, 1779, in celebration of the third anniversary of American Independence, Washington granted a general pardon to all war prisoners under sentence of death, while 13 rounds boomed from the cannon at distant West Point. George Clinton, the first elected governor of New York State, lived here; and his nephew, De Witt Clinton, also governor in his turn, was born here.

The NEW YORK MILITARY ACADEMY (L), 35.6 *m.*, is one of the oldest military preparatory schools in the State. The military-type brick and concrete Gothic buildings occupy an estate of 350 acres. An accredited military school, it receives a regular allotment of guns, ammunition, and equipment from the U.S. War Department. It prepares students for West Point and college entrance.

In the 1840's, CORNWALL–ON–HUDSON, 36.3 *m.* (167 alt.,1,966 pop.), acquired renown as the home of Nathaniel Parker Willis (1806–69), poet, essayist, and historian, and later as the home of Edward Payson Roe, best-selling novelist of the 1880's. IDLEWILD (*private*), entrance on Spruce St., the Willis home, is a three-story-and-attic brick structure. On each side of the entrance door is the bronze figure of an American eagle with wings outspread, beak thrust forward.

US 9W swings into the STORM KING HIGHWAY at 36.8 *m.*, climbing the steep paunch of old Storm King itself. Known through the Colonial period as Butter Hill, the mountain, whose peak rises some 1,400 feet, and whose precipitous sides are heavily wooded, was given its present name by the poet, Willis. Curving high above the Hudson with only a low stone wall between it and a 500-foot drop, the highway offers spectacular views north to the Long Reach, south to West Point and the lower Highlands, and across the river to the gigantic bony knuckles of Breakneck and Bull Hill.

Construction is under way (1940) on a new road high up on the Highland ridge to the west, but work has been halted from time to time by injunctions obtained by villages which this new and almost equally scenic road is destined to ignore.

Once believed to be the haunt of hobgoblins and elves, the granite-walled Highland pass is today subdued and beaten by the gouging of rock quarries and the bestrewing of hidden clefts and valleys with bungalow villages, while the Hudson is fettered on each side by the gleaming steel of the New York Central main line and West Shore tracks.

At 40.9 m. is the junction with the road to West Point (see West Point).

Dipping left, US 9W curves through WASHINGTON VALLEY, 41.9 m., a wooded hollow where Washington had his headquarters during the winter of 1779. From the Moore House (demolished), the Commander-in-Chief issued an order forbidding profanity among Continental soldiers; and the next day, as if to compensate for this restriction, he ordered an extra ration of grog for everyone.

While teaching school in HIGHLAND FALLS, 45.3 m. (200 alt.,2,910 pop.), in 1862, John Burroughs discovered Audubon's *Birds*; the pictures so fired his imagination that he began his lifelong study of nature. Families of infantrymen, cavalrymen, and bandsmen stationed at the West Point Reservation have their homes here. For a century small boys of the village have been earning pocket money by selling 'smokes' to cadets during practice marches.

At 48.7 m. are (L) the grass-covered earth ramparts of FORT MONTGOMERY, built early in the Revolution. With Fort Clinton a mile south and Fort Independence across the river in the shadow of bulging Anthony's Nose, it guarded the Highland passes. General von Steuben expressed the opinion that upon the success or failure of the British effort to capture West Point and the Highland fortifications 'depends the fate of America.' Undermanned because of the demand for men to fight Burgoyne, both Fort Montgomery and Fort Clinton fell on October 3, 1777, before the force sent up the river from New York City by Sir Henry Clinton. The British continued on up the Hudson, burning villages and finally razing Kingston on October 16; but upon learning of Burgoyne's surrender, they retired to the safety of New York harbor.

Over two gracefully arched steel bridges US 9W sweeps to the junction at 49.3 m. with US 6 (see Tour 4); then past the entrance (R) at 49.5 m. to BEAR MOUNTAIN STATE PARK (see Tour 4).

The village of STONY POINT, 56.7 m. (120 alt.,1,000 pop.), derives its name from the rocky bluff that projects into the Hudson. Here the

Federal Government erected in 1826 a lighthouse 179 feet above sea level equipped with a mechanical fog signal and a 'fixed white light.' The village itself still has a few buildings that antedate the Revolution, but they are lost among glaring gasoline stations, diners, and tourist homes. Here James A. Farley won his first political victory—election as town clerk.

At 57.6 *m.* is the junction with a side road.

Left on this road 0.7 *m.* to the STONY POINT BATTLEFIELD RESERVATION, a site embracing the area held by the British forces and stormed and captured by 1,200 Continentals under General 'Mad' Anthony Wayne on July 6, 1779. In the daring charge, General Wayne was wounded and borne forward over the rampart to victory upon the shoulders of his men. An anecdote tells that during the discussion of Hudson River tactics, Washington asked Wayne if he thought he could storm Stony Point, to which Wayne replied: 'I'll storm hell, sir, if you'll make the plans!' Washington looked at him meditatively for a moment, then replied: 'Better try Stony Point first, General.'

The STONY POINT MUSEUM (*open* 9-5 *daily*), on one of the highest points of the promontory, is an L-shaped one-story structure with Dutch windows, containing murals, battle pieces, portraits, and maps bearing on the storming of the fort. The Museum was opened in 1936 under the supervision of the American Scenic and Historic Preservation Society.

Just south of the village is the NEW YORK STATE RECONSTRUCTION HOME (R), 58.8 *m.*, an orthopedic hospital for children established in 1900. It occupies the site of the homestead of Joshua Hett Smith, the TREASON HOUSE, in which Benedict Arnold and John André met to arrange for the betrayal of West Point to the British (*see below*).

At 61.3 *m.* is the junction (R) with US 202 (*see Tour 2*).

Swinging inland, US 9W crosses the Ramapo Valley; then begins the climb through HAVERSTRAW, 59.1 *m.* (20 alt.,5,906 pop.), which squats on the edge of the Hudson with its back propped against High Tor, Little Tor, and Pyngyp. Its main industry is the manufacture of brick and cement. Here James Wood discovered the modern system of burning brick and set up brickyards in the town, the beginnings of an industry which at the peak included 40 brickyards, producing 326,000,000 brick annually.

In 1825 the Franklin Community was established here by followers of Robert Owen; they wished to discard 'absurd and immaterial systems of religion' and the form of marriage based on them. But local antagonism soon put an end to this Utopia.

Left from Haverstraw on Riverside Ave. 0.3 *m.* to the RED STONE DOCK CAMPSITES of the Hook Mountain Section of the Palisades Interstate Park. When the local red stone, deposited in the Triassic Period, was being exploited in the 1820's, it was common to see from 10 to 12 vessels loaded with stone leave the docks each day.

At 62.9 *m.* is the junction with State 304.

Right on this road 3.9 *m.* to NEW CITY (200 alt.,1,000 pop.), seat of Rockland County. The ROCKLAND COUNTY COURTHOUSE (R), erected in 1928, was designed by Dennison and Hirons, architects. The interior is remarkable for the restrained use of color and for a historical mural map painted by James Monroe Hewlett.

Southwest of the Courthouse is the DUTCH MEMORIAL GARDEN, interesting not only for its landscape design but also for the use of brick in the pavilion, walks, and garden ornaments.

At 6 *m.* is the junction with a road; right here 0.4 *m.* to the MAJOR JOHN SMITH HOME (L), an unusually well preserved and unaltered example of primitive Rockland County farmstead built about 1735. The first-story walls of roughly cut red sandstone and the four-bay plan with an asymmetrically placed entrance door are typical early features. The gambrel roof still has the simple boarded cove treatment in the rear. The garret end walls are shingled; the cellar beams are of huge size; and there is an inside smokehouse.

Two hundred feet beyond is MAJOR JOHN SMITH'S BARN (R), the only such building in the State with stone walls. The plan is clearly derived from house forms rather than, as elsewhere, from the Saxonian peasant barns. Now a private garage, the structure is one of the mellowest, most picturesque relics of the early eighteenth century in New York State.

Although it has several small industries, NYACK, 70.1 *m.* (68 alt., 5,167 pop.), is essentially a bright and prosperous commuters' village. The water front offers swimming and boating; there is a public bathhouse just south of the village; and a favorite picnic and bathing place is a sandy beach in the shadow of Hook Mountain. Upper Nyack and South Nyack are separate incorporated villages.

The OLD STONE CHURCH, Broadway, Upper Nyack, is a simple rectangular structure with walls of the ubiquitous local red sandstone and a roof with boarded gables. In February 1813, William Palmer, Nicholas Williamson, and John Green met in Green's house in Upper Nyack and resolved 'that this be a meeting to organize and build a Methodist Episcopal Church; and that we begin to build the Church tomorrow morning. Carried.'

The MICHAEL CORNELISON HOUSE (Salisbury House), Piermont Ave., the southern village line of South Nyack, was built in 1770; it is a large two-story gambrel-roofed house commanding a magnificent prospect over Tappan Zee. The red sandstone came from near-by quarries, which extended along the road clear to Piermont. The second-story wall was erected after the Revolution; and the kitchen wing in the stepped gable 'Sunnyside' style, inaugurated by Washington Irving across the river, was added about 1840. The house was erected by Michael Cornelison, who had bought the land in 1765 from his father-in-law, Claes Jansen Kuyper, grandson and namesake of the original patentee.

PIERMONT, 74.6 *m.* (40 alt.,1,872 pop.), took its name from the mile-long pier (L) of the Erie Railroad. When the Erie was first completed in 1851, Piermont was made the eastern terminus because the railroad charter required the line to be constructed entirely within the boundary of New York State; connection with New York was by boat. The village was originally called Tappan Landing. Sir Guy Carleton came ashore here to discuss with Washington, then living at Tappan, peace terms and the orderly withdrawal of the British from New York City. Upon Washington's return visit to Carleton's flagship, the British for the first time saluted the flag of the United States of America.

Right from Piermont on a macadam road 1.5 *m.* to TAPPAN (80 alt.,1,200 pop.), a residential village associated with the beginning and the end of the Benedict Arnold-Major John André tragedy. In the DE WINT MANSION (*open, free*), Washington's headquarters in 1780 and again in 1783, the Commander-in-Chief entrusted to the embittered Arnold the command of West Point. Arnold immediately wrote to Sir

Henry Clinton in New York City, offering to betray the garrison to the British. Clinton sent Major André to arrange the details with Arnold at Joshua Hett Smith's house near Stony Point (*see above*). On his way back André was captured, and plans of West Point defenses were found in one of his boots, together with proof of Arnold's complicity. As soon as he heard of the capture, Arnold fled down the river to the British (*see Tour 21C*).

Near the De Wint House is the SEVENTY-SIX HOUSE (*open, free*), built in 1755, restored in 1897, and now used as an inn, which served as the prison of Major André. It contains a private collection of Colonial relics.

The REFORMED DUTCH CHURCH, on the village green, a fine brick edifice erected in 1835, the third on this site, retains, despite its Greek Revival details, the general arrangement and forms of the preceding Federal period. Typical of the early nineteenth century is the location of the pulpit against the façade wall. In the first church building on this site occurred the trial of Major André on September 27, 1780, before the Board of Enquiry appointed by General Washington.

To ANDRÉ HILL, André Hill Road, out Old Tappan Road, Major John André, adjutant-general of the British army in New York, and then just 29 years old, was brought just before noon on October 2, 1780, to be hanged. The large crowd of spectators was kept at a distance by a hollow square of 500 infantrymen. Washington and his staff were absent. Not until he turned up the Hill Road and saw the high gibbet did André realize that his plea to the Commander-in-Chief for a soldier's death before a firing squad was not to be granted. Restlessly awaiting the final preparations, he comforted his two weeping body-servants, who had been sent up from New York. Finally he leaped into the wagon stationed below the gallows crossarm, and, standing on the coffin, removed his stock, opened his shirt collar, took the rope from the clumsy hangman—the Tory prisoner Strickland—adjusted the noose about his own neck, and bound his handkerchief over his eyes. To the reading of the order of execution he responded, 'All I request of you, gentlemen, is that you bear witness to the world that I die like a brave man.' The signal given, the wagon rolled away, and it was done.

After the removal of General Richard Montgomery's body from Quebec to St. Paul's in New York, British authorities requested André's body in return. The owner of the hilltop field, who had refused many large offers for the land from speculators anticipating a large profit from this very situation, gave his assent; and in 1821 the remains were taken home and laid to rest in the south aisle of Westminster Abbey.

At about 77 *m.* the ramparts of the PALISADES begin their march.

US 9W crosses the NEW JERSEY LINE at 77.3 *m.*, 22.1 miles north of Jersey City, New Jersey.

Tour 21B

Hudson—Germantown—East Park—Poughkeepsie; State 9G. 44.4 *m.*

State 9G runs along the river to a point north of Rhinebeck, where it crosses US 9 (*see Tour 21*) and then parallels that road on the east to Poughkeepsie. The upper section, locally called the Apple Blossom Trail because of the many orchards that line it, offers the most convenient approach to several of the historic Livingston homes.

Livingston Manor was established by Robert Livingston (1654–1728). Born in Scotland, he migrated to Holland and thence in 1673 to America.

By 1686, when he was 32, he had accumulated by a series of purchases and grants a 160,000-acre tract along the east side of the Hudson, which was erected into a manor in 1686 by Governor Thomas Dongan. He bequeathed to his third son, Robert, who had saved the family from an Indian assassin, a 13,000-acre tract in the southwest corner of the manor, where Robert built a home and founded the Clermont branch of the family. The manor proper was inherited by Philip Livingston (1686–1749), second lord, a handsome, gay 'breaker of hearts.' His son, Robert (1708–90), third and last lord of the manor, had trouble with squatters from Massachusetts; militia was called out to protect his iron mines, which were a valuable source of supply during the Revolution. Upon his death in 1790, the prohibition of entailed estates forced the division of the manor among eight heirs.

The Livingston hold on the land was frequently, but unsuccessfully, challenged. The first challenges came from the democratic followers of the dictator Leisler. A century later, in 1795, several hundred inhabitants of the town of Livingston petitioned the legislature to investigate the Livingston title, stating that they leased the land upon conditions 'tending to degrade your petitioners from the rank the God of nature destined all mankind to move in to be slaves and vassals.' The manor had its share of antirent uprisings. In the end the estate was broken up only when the Livingstons chose to sell; members of the family still own much of it.

South from HUDSON, 0 m. State 9G runs in common with State 23 (*see Tour 7*) to the RIP VAN WINKLE BRIDGE, 3.9 m., and continues south past (L) CHURCH HILL (*private*), 4.8 m., reached by a winding lane through the woods. The house was the home of Frederick Edwin Church (1826–1900), famous member of the Hudson River School of landscape painters. As a young man, Church studied with Thomas Cole, founder of the school, at his studio in Catskill, across the river. Church imbibed Cole's love of wild, romantic nature, and, although he traveled far to paint erupting volcanoes and snowclad mountains, the genuine grandeur of the Hudson led him to build his home atop this 500-foot hill with its superb vista downstream. The plans, in Persianesque style, were by Church himself, although he consulted Calvert Vaux, the architect, on practical matters. The walls of rough local stone are trimmed in cut brownstone and bluestone. The entrance tower has surprisingly pleasing patterns in red, yellow, and black brick. The artist's touch is especially evident in the colorful decoration of doorway, cornice, and roof; the latter originally had even a few gilded slates. One of the most attractive features of the house is the picture window in the hall, which frames the dramatic river prospect to the south.

At 5.3 m. is a five-corner intersection.

Right on the dirt road 0.6 m. to the entrance (R) to OAK HILL (*private*), the home of John Livingston (1750–1822). Upon the death of the last lord of the manor, his son John received a large tract on the northern boundary of the manor. He climbed the tallest oak to survey his domain and selected this fine site with its splendid view of river and mountains on which to build Oak Hill, a stately early Federal brick mansion with the typical central-hall plan two rooms deep. The simple lines of the exterior are now obscured by a nineteenth-century veranda and mansard roof. In a day when fireplaces were the sole source of warmth, older members of the family warned John that he would surely freeze to death in these spacious rooms with lofty ceilings. Many family portraits, much silver and furniture, and one cast-iron fireback marked RML (Robert, third lord, and Mary Livingston) were brought to Oak Hill when the manor house (*see below*) was demolished about 1800. The mansion is now occupied (1940) by John's great-grandson, Herman Livingston.

At 7.3 *m.* is the junction with a macadam road.

1. Right here 0.4 *m.* to LINLITHGO STATION, at the mouth of the Roeliff Jansen Kill, once the busy river port and administrative center of Livingston Manor. The original manor house, erected by the first lord on a hillside above the settlement, was dismantled about 1800 by Robert Thong Livingston, grandson of the last lord of the manor.

2. Left from the junction 0.6 *m.* to LINLITHGO (145 alt.,200 pop.). In the center of the village stands the LIVINGSTON MEMORIAL CHAPEL, a plain brick structure built in 1870 by members of the Livingston family over the burial vault of the first lord of the manor and his wife Alida Schuyler. In recent years the bodies of eight generations of Livingstons, which once rested here, were removed to the family vaults in the churchyard of St.Paul's Protestant Episcopal Church at Tivoli (*see below*). The chapel stands on the site of the Livingston Reformed Church built in 1722 through the initiative of the first lord.

About 1,200 of the German Palatines brought over in 1710 by Governor Hunter to make tar and other naval stores were settled on Livingston land in and around GERMANTOWN, 11 *m.* (180 alt.,300 pop.), then called East Camp. Robert Livingston contracted to furnish bread and beer, to be delivered to the settlers at his manor house, at the rate of sixpence a day for adults and fourpence for children, and he also supplied flour and meat and made cash advances. The colonists were dissatisfied, asserting that they had been promised individual tracts of land in the Schoharie Valley, and a threat of revolt was put down by Governor Hunter with a show of force. The enterprise, however, failed because of mismanagement; in 1712 government subsistence ceased and the immigrants were told to shift for themselves. They scattered to Pennsylvania and New Jersey, to Rhinebeck on the Hudson and to the Schoharie and Mohawk Valleys; some of them accepted Livingston's terms and settled in the four villages of the manor.

At 14.9 *m.* is the junction with a macadam road.

Right here 1.7 *m.* to (R) CLERMONT (*occasionally open; watch for sign at gate*), the lower Livingston manor house. In 1729–30 Robert Livingston (1688–1775), who had been given a 13,000-acre estate here by his father, first lord of the manor, erected a substantial stone house. Judge Robert R. Livingston (1718–75), who inherited the estate, died in the same year as his father. The burden of administering the manor in the unsettled years of revolution fell on his widow, Margaret Beekman Livingston, and she proved heroically equal to the task. After the British burned Clermont in October 1777, she had it rebuilt the next year in its original form. The exterior has undergone numerous face liftings, but the interior escaped alteration. From the central hall with its fine staircase, mahogany doors in delicately carved frames lead to well-proportioned rooms with 12-foot ceilings.

Margaret Livingston's six daughters all married men who attained eminence in the affairs of State and Nation. Her eldest son, Robert R. Livingston (1746–1813), served as chairman of the committee instructed by the Continental Congress to draft the Declaration of Independence, first Chancellor of the State of New York, and chairman of the State convention that ratified the Federal Constitution. As Chancellor he administered the oath of office to President Washington on April 30, 1789. While Minister to France under President Jefferson, he negotiated the Louisiana Purchase. Having obtained from the legislature exclusive rights to steam navigation on the waters of the State—a monopoly that was not broken until 1824—he financed Robert Fulton's successful experiment with the *Clermont*, which was named for this estate. Chancellor Livingston was one of the founders of the American Academy of Fine Arts and its president in 1808. Interested in the improvement of agriculture, he imported fine cattle, introduced Merino sheep, and cultivated fruit trees. The mansion he built for himself just south of here burned down in 1909.

At 16.6 *m.* is the junction with a macadam road.

Right on this road 0.9 *m.* to TIVOLI (152 alt.,713 pop.), where in 1798-1802 Peter de Labigarre, who came to America after the French Revolution, built the Chateau de Tivoli, the first unit of a projected model community. Charles Balthazar Julien Fevret de Saint-Memin, an expatriate officer of the guard at the court of Louis XVI and an itinerant draftsman and portrait painter, drew the plan for the settlement. It was more visionary than practical. Two extant copies show a gridiron of 60-foot streets named Friendship, Chancellor (after Livingston), Liberty, Plenty, Peace, etc. The plan was so ill-adapted to the precipitious site that Zephyre Square, the central unit, would have been excavated in a hillside. Of the eighteenth-century dream only Flora Street, a road down to the riverside station, and Diana Street, a tiny private concrete driveway, remain. The scheme collapsed after De Labigarre's death in 1807, and Chancellor Livingston bought the property at a foreclosure sale.

CALLANDER HOUSE (*private*), entrance at head of Flora St., a large frame structure with thick, brick-filled walls, was built in 1794 by Henry Gilbert Livingston. Long known as Sunning Hill, it has always been occupied by members of the Livingston family.

ST.PAUL'S PROTESTANT EPISCOPAL CHURCH (L), Wood Road, was erected in 1868. The present stone structure was designed and supervised by Robert E. Livingston, grandson of the chancellor. A thick covering of ivy hides the Victorian Gothic details. In 1922 substantial modifications were carried out and the chancel and transept windows received memorial stained glass executed by Charles J. Connick of Boston. In a semicircle behind the church are eight burial vaults, several of which are owned by Livingston families.

At 18.9 *m.* is the junction with a macadam road.

Right here 0.3 *m.* to WARD MANOR (R), a 2,000-acre property donated by Robert B. Ward, prominent baker, to the New York Association for Improving the Condition of the Poor. Besides serving as a home for the aged, it also contains summer camps for boys and girls.

BARD COLLEGE (L), 0.7 *m.*, since 1928 a unit of Columbia University, was founded by Dr.John Bard in 1860 as St.Stephens College for sons of Episcopal clergymen. The CHAPEL OF THE HOLY INNOCENTS, begun by Bard in 1857 as a parish church and memorial to his son, burned in 1858 and was rebuilt by Charles Babcock, associate of Richard Upjohn. The interior has been redecorated by Ralph Adams Cram. Just to the north stands a quaint carpenter-Gothic Sunday School, now the music building.

The quaint hexagonal gatehouse (R), at 0.9 *m.*, marks the entrance to BLITHEWOOD (*private*), an estate established in 1795 by General John Armstrong (1758-1843), who married Chancellor Livingston's sister Alida. Armstrong was the author of the famous 'Newburgh Addresses' (*see Tour 21A*), U.S.senator 1801-4, Minister to France 1804-10, and Secretary of War 1813-14. In 1810 the place was purchased by John Cox Stevens (1785-1857), another brother-in-law of the Chancellor and one of the first influential amateur sportsmen in the United States. His yachts *Trouble* and *Black Maria* were built in a cove on the estate; in 1844, on his yacht *Gimcrack*, anchored off the Battery in New York harbor, the New York Yacht Club was organized. Stevens headed the syndicate that built the *America*, which in 1851 won the Hundred Guinea Cup at Cowes, England. Six years later this 'America's Cup' was presented as a perpetual challenge cup to encourage friendly competition with British yachtmen. Sixteen British and Canadian challenges between 1870 and 1935 failed of their purpose, and the cup has never left the United States.

Robert Donaldson, who acquired this property in 1835, employed the landscape architect Andrew Jackson Downing to lay out the grounds. Downing built the gate-house and planted the magnificent white pines along the driveway; the turf he planted is still in place. Dr.John Bard lived here after 1853; in 1899 Andrew C. Zabriskie erected the present late Georgian mansion.

At 1.6 m. is the entrance (R) to MONTGOMERY PLACE (*private*), built in 1805 by the widow of General Richard Montgomery, Janet Livingston, sister of the Chancellor. After Montgomery fell in the assault on Quebec in 1775, Mrs.Montgomery completed Grassmere (*see Tour* 21); but later, wishing a summer place near her family, she erected the Chateau de Montgomery. The house, with stuccoed walls, has the typical square plan of the Federal period. Mrs.Montgomery willed the estate to her brother Edward Livingston (1764–1836), author of the Louisiana Code, and Secretary of State and Minister to France under President Andrew Jackson. His widow had the architect Alexander J. Davis enlarge the house. Downing described the grounds as 'richly wooded, picturesque valley with dark, intricate, mazy walks, and musical with waterfalls.' The present owner and occupant (1940) is General John Ross Delafield, Livingston's great-grandson.

The QUINN HOUSE, 2.1 m., is a one-and-one-half-story gray stone structure of the early eighteenth century. The stone slave house still stands at the north end of the building.

On State 9G at 23.2 m. is the entrance (R) to ROKEBY (*private*), a two-story brick house erected during the War of 1812 by General John Armstrong, then Secretary of War, who had sold Blithewood. His only daughter married William B. Astor, the 'landlord of New York,' son of the first John Jacob, and wealthiest man in America in the sixties.

At 25.5 m. State 9G crosses US 9 (*see Tour* 21).

In EAST PARK, 38.2 m. (233 alt.,204 pop.), just beyond the intersection, is the WILLIAM STOUTENBURGH HOUSE (R), a one-and-a-half-story stone building erected in 1750–65. In the two-story barn adjacent, Otto Berge carries on the handicraft work in furniture begun by Mrs.Franklin D. Roosevelt in the Val Kill Center.

Left from East Park on a macadam road 2.6 m. to the junction with another mac-adam road; left here 1.6 m. to the CRUM ELBOW FRIENDS' MEETING HOUSE (R), a well-preserved, austere white clapboard building erected about 1780. The small east section was first constructed, but it soon became inadequate and was augmented by a larger western block, the line of separation appearing plainly in the roof. The modern concrete floor and turned porch columns add an incongruous worldly touch. In pros-perous days Quakers from the vicinity overflowed the hard benches on the main floor into the steeply stepped tiers in the gallery, now boarded up. Elias Hicks (1748–1830) frequently spoke here and engaged in those controversies that led in 1827 to the divi-sion into the Hicksite and Orthodox branches of the Friends. These names are some-what misleading, since it was Hicks who insisted that the personal 'inner light' was still the true guide and that those who sought to live by the letter of the law as laid down in the Bible and interpreted by the elders were following false principles.

South of East Park the FRANKLIN D. ROOSEVELT 'DREAM' COTTAGE can be seen (L), half-hidden among the trees on the highest hill east of State 9G. The one-story fieldstone structure was designed by President Roosevelt and built in 1938. He picked this high hill offering magnificent views of river and mountain for a retreat. Here in 1939 the President and Mrs.Roosevelt entertained the King and Queen of Great Britain at a frankfurter roast.

POUGHKEEPSIE, 44.4 *m.* (175 alt.,40,237 pop.) (*see Poughkeepsie*), is at the junction with US 44 (*see Tour* 5), US 9 (*see Tour* 21), and State 55 (*see Tour* 40).

Tour 21C

(HUDSON RIVER BOAT TOUR)

Albany—Hudson—Kingston—Poughkeepsie—Newburgh—New York City; 141.5 *m.* Hudson River.

Hudson River Day Line, daily boats (May to Oct.), from Albany and New York City.
The New York Central System parallels the river on both shores.
For more extensive treatment of points of interest on the east shore see Tours 21 and 21B; for those on the west shore see Tour 21A.

When it becomes a tidal estuary at Troy, the Hudson River has already traveled half its full length. It rises in the clear, cold lakes of the highest Adirondacks, among them Lake Tear-of-the-Clouds on Mt. Marcy. A shallow, bouldered stream fished for trout, it splashes and twists through the mountains, marking with its tributaries the trellis-like pattern of the Adirondack fault lines. It picks up the waters of the Jessup and Indian Rivers, the Boreas, the Schroon, the Sacandaga; between Warrensburg and Glens Falls it curves widely around Prospect Mountain and Lake George; at Hudson Falls it settles down to an ever deepening, south-running channel. The Batten Kill and Hoosic River bring it the waters of the western slopes of the Green Mountains and the Taconics. Between Waterford and Cohoes it receives the drainage of central New York and the higher Catskills through the Mohawk, here as large and deep as the Hudson itself. South of Troy it flows both ways, rising and falling as much as four and a half feet with the tide. Between Albany and New York dredging has provided a 27-foot channel for ocean-going steamers. In its southern reaches the river falls between the high folds of Storm King, High Tor, Dunderberg, Overlook, and Indian Head on the west, and the Taconics, older than the Catskills, on the east.

'We found a pleasant place between steep little hills. . . . And from those hills a mighty, deep-mouthed river ran into the sea,' wrote Giovanni da Verrazano, Florentine explorer, who nosed the first ocean-going ship into the mouth of the Hudson in 1524. On September 2, 1609, Henry Hudson started up the river in the *Half Moon*, feeling his way north with the flood tide, anchoring during low water, stopping to fish and exchange knives for Indian tobacco and corn. 'This is a very good land to fall with and a pleasant land to see,' wrote Robert Juet, officer on the *Half Moon*. The Dutch called the river the North River, the Great River of the

Mountains, and the River of Mauritius. It was 'for the most part a musket shot wide.'

From the earliest days of settlement the Hudson and its valley have been the main thoroughfare into the interior of the State. Navigation was as difficult as on Mark Twain's Mississippi: tides were erratic, wind currents temperamental, and the water was laden with hidden shoals. Dutch skippers measured the river by 'reaches'—14 of them between Albany and New York; and as they plied its waters they peopled the valley with hobgoblins. Manorial lords built large private docks and carried on a brisk trade. Sloops, 70 feet long with rounded bow and high aft, carried livestock tied to the mast, grain, flour, lumber, pork, hay, cider, potash, potatoes, brick, stone, and slate. In 1785 the square-rigged, 80-ton *Experiment*, Captain Stewart Dean, loaded with ginseng and furs, nosed into the channel at Albany, and in 1787 returned after a trip to Canton, China; the Albany river front was named Dean Street in the captain's honor.

The opening of the Erie Canal in 1825 enormously increased freight and passenger traffic. Fulton's *Clermont* introduced steam on the river, but the sloop was not eliminated until after the Civil War. Canal barges, cut loose from their towpath mule power, were towed down the river by steamers. Passenger boats, the pride of American inland waters, raced with one another for the blue ribbon of the Hudson until they burst their boilers. The river floated the products of a variety of industries. Hudson, supported by other river ports, challenged New Bedford as a whaling center. The river was fished for sturgeon and shad, and tons of 'Russian' caviar were prepared in Albany. Freighters carried raw hides to Catskill Landing to be carted up the mountains to the hemlock bark for tanning. Brick was shipped to New York City to erect its buildings and pave its roads. Boats for the thriving trade slid down the ways of river shipyards.

A century ago river towns were entertained by showboats that moved from one farm-banked shore to the other in one-night and two-night stands. Most popular play was *The Rent Day*, which depicted the deplorable conditions of English tenantry but in which Hudson River farmers read their own struggles against manorial rents. Where the Catskill Mountains rise above the river, American artists—Cole, Church, Bierstadt, and others—turned to painting the landscape, striving for naturalness, creating the illusion of looking upon the subject itself. Andrew Jackson Downing pioneered in landscaping river estates, and in architecture popularized the carpenter Gothic of the Hudson River-Bracketed.

Rapid transportation has robbed the river of much of its beauty and commercial importance. Ocean-going freighters loaded with lumber, pulp, and grain keep alive some of the tradition; in summer, day boats carry what little river passenger travel is left.

South of ALBANY, 0 *m*. (18 alt.,130,447 pop.), past the Albany Yacht Club pier, where the annual Albany-New York outboard motor race starts, and the Port of Albany (*see Albany*), the river divides farming and fruit-growing lowlands. The huge frame buildings that occasionally rise up out of the trees were storage houses for ice; many of them are now used as barns for growing mushrooms.

When shad fishing was an important river industry fishermen used SHAD ISLAND (R), 9 m., as a base. Nets were dropped as the tide began to rise, and were hauled in loaded with fish as the ebb set in. In recent years antipollution work by the State has revived fishing in the river.

COEYMANS (R), 12 m. (100 alt.,1,506 pop.), is marked by two widely separated brickyards almost flush with the shore, between which rows of dust-covered houses lean vertically up the slope.

On BARREN ISLAND (R), 13.5 m., Kiliaen Van Rensselaer's agents collected tribute from passing ships; skippers were given a choice—pay or be fired upon.

In 1939 Hollywood producers of *Little Old New York* came to NEW BALTIMORE (R), 15 m. (100 alt., 734 pop.), for scenes reflecting life on the Hudson in 1807: sailboats riding lazily in the harbor, old village homes, and retired rivermen swapping stories. In 1800 Paul Sherman was building schooners in the New Baltimore shipyard. When the Erie Canal brought a demand for barges, the yards rang with hammer and saw. Soon after Livingston's river steamboat monopoly was broken (*see below*), a steamer was launched out of a tangle of wood and iron. Later the local yard turned to building smaller craft and serving as a drydock for repairs and winter storage.

NOAH'S BRIG, a small rock-bound island in the ATHENS CHAN-NEL (R), 28.8 m., was named for Captain Noah, who one foggy twilight, approaching the channel with a fleet of rafts, sighted 'a dark object riding the waters'; it looked like a brig under sail. 'Brig ahoy!' he shouted. No answer. 'Brig ahoy! Answer, or I'll run you down!' No reply. Captain Noah kept to his course. Suddenly there was a crash and wood crunched on rock. Captain Noah had mistaken two trees on the island for masts with sails set.

On April 7, 1845, the *Swallow*, racing the *Express* and the *Rochester*, ran on the rocks of Noah's Brig and 15 lives were lost. Ira Buchman hauled the wreckage seven miles inland and built himself a two-story home known as the Swallow House.

The water front of HUDSON (L), 28.8 m. (100 alt.,11,487 pop.), consists of a time-eaten dock framed by a semicircle of decrepit brick buildings and several gas and oil tanks. In 1783 a fleet of Nantucket whalers, with frames for new houses aboard, dropped anchor here; and in a few years Hudson was a major port of entry with 25 sails on the high seas, many of them built in the local shipyard. Whalers slid down the river and returned with whale oil, sealskins, and other cargo. The War of 1812 tied the ships up; later the industry revived, only to die in the panic of 1837. Many sea stories survive in local tradition: one about Captain Judah Paddock, whose ship ran aground off the Barbary Coast. Captured by Arabs, Paddock served as a slave for six months, then, with two of his crew, was ransomed by the British for $1,700 and made his way home.

Below Hudson the river flows under the Rip Van Winkle Bridge, connecting Hudson and Catskill. On CHURCH HILL (L), towering above the eastern end of the bridge, is the CHURCH HOME, a gaily colored Persian castle designed and built by Frederick E. Church, landscape painter.

CATSKILL LANDING (R), 33 *m.*, is the river port for Catskill and its hinterland. Mountains loom in the background. Here in the early years of the nineteenth century ships brought raw hides to be transshipped to the mountain tanneries, and loaded for the return voyage with leather, brick, bluestone, and lumber. Here, too, New Yorkers disembarked for the stages to Catskill vacation centers. The CATSKILL MOUNTAIN HOUSE, one of the earliest and most popular of these, is visible as a white speck high on a mountain ledge (*see Tour* 7).

SAUGERTIES (R), 44.5 *m.* (100 alt.,3,918 pop.), once an important bluestone shipping center, is backed by an imposing cluster of Catskill peaks—Overlook Mountain, High Peak, and Sugarloaf Mountain. In James Fenimore Cooper's *The Pioneers* Natty Bumppo stood on the crest of Overlook and saw 'The river . . . in sight for seventy miles under my feet, looking like a curled shaving, though it was eight long miles to its bank.'

In the North Bay cove behind CRUGER'S ISLAND (L), 46.8 *m.*, on the Livingston estate, Robert Fulton's *Clermont* tied up on its initial trip to Albany. Chancellor Robert R. Livingston, who had financed Fulton's experiments, held a monopoly covering the making and operating of all boats propelled by 'force of fire or steam' on the waters of the State. That monopoly was broken in 1824 by Thomas Gibbons, who operated a steamboat between New York and New Jersey and whose case was successfully argued before the Supreme Court by Daniel Webster. After his victory, river commerce turned rapidly to steam.

KINGSTON POINT (*R*), 54.3 *m.*, with picnic grounds, has been a favorite outing place since the days of side-wheelers. Today it is also a landing place for Father Divine's peace-singing angels on their way to the many 'heavens' in Ulster County. The point marks the limit of the British advance up the river in 1777. From the dock the road winds up the slope to KINGSTON (*see Tour* 21A). Across the river is FERNCLIFF (L), the Vincent Astor estate.

Just south of the Point is RONDOUT (R), at the mouth of Rondout Creek, Kingston's river front. The rotting hulls of boats and barges along the banks of the creek suggest the one-time importance of the port.

In 1861 the *Mary Powell*, for half a century 'Queen of the Hudson,' entered the passenger service between Rondout and New York. Captain Absalom Anderson kept the ship free of all unessential 'tophamper,' in order 'to decrease the weight as much as possible and keep the hull near the surface of the water.' Her hull was coated with paint mixed with whale oil—so the story goes—to reduce resistance. In May 1881 she boiled up the river from New York to Rondout, 96 miles, including eight landings, in four hours and twelve minutes. Captain Anderson kept the ship a 'family boat,' on which mothers could trust their children: he would not tolerate drunkenness, he refused to run her on Sunday, and every morning at Irvington newspapers were taken aboard to complete the home atmosphere. On July 11, 1885, the *Mary Powell* lost the blue ribbon of the Hudson to the steam yacht *Stilleto*. In 1918 she was nosed into Rondout Creek, where she swung idly until junked in 1920. Her whistle still echoes over the Hudson waters from the *Robert Fulton*; her bell rings loud and clear on another boat; her blower engines and pistons are in the Ford Museum at Dearborn, Michigan; and the gilded globes that topped her masts ornament the gateposts at the entrance to the J.P.Morgan estate in Highland Falls. The *Mary Powell* never lost a life.

On the eastern shore, beginning at 55.3 *m.*, is a series of private estates: the estate of the late Ogden L. Mills, now a public park, with its marble palace, of which there is a momentary glimpse; Ellerslie, once the home of Levi P. Morton, Vice President of the United States and governor of New York; and the estates of the Huyler, Vanderbilt, and Rogers families.

RIVERBY (R), 64.2 *m.*, was the river home of John Burroughs. Near the rambling stone house is THE NEST, home of Julian Burroughs, his son. In the BARK STUDY, visible through the trees, Burroughs wrote many of his essays and was visited by Walt Whitman, John Muir, and Theodore Roosevelt.

The ROOSEVELT ESTATE (L), 64.5 *m.*, is the birthplace and home of President Franklin D. Roosevelt. Opposite, at a turn in the channel, is the former estate of Howland Spencer, sold in 1938 to Father Divine for a 'heaven.' South of here is the LONG REACH, an eleven-mile straight sailing course, named Lange Rak by Robert Juet in his log of the *Half Moon*. The straight channel of the Long Reach is the course of the annual June intercollegiate boat races. Boathouses along .the river are marked with college insignia and huge college letters have been blocked out on boulders by resting crewmen.

POUGHKEEPSIE (L), 70.6 *m.* (175 alt.,40,237 pop.) (*see Poughkeepsie*), is marked by two bridges, the up-thrusting gray towers and harplike cables of the Mid-Hudson Bridge contrasting sharply with the black, underslung, crisscrossing girders of the Railroad Bridge. When the April run is on, small fishing craft speckle the water, hauling up nets quivering with shad.

Opposite LOCUST GROVE (L), 71.2 *m.*, for 25 years the home of Samuel F.B. Morse, artist and inventor, is BLUE POINT (R), legendary anchorage of the phantom Storm Ship, which first appeared off Manhattan in the days of Wouter Van Twiller. During a violent thunderstorm burghers saw her come up the bay, her sails full-blown. Hans Van Pelt, harbormaster, fired a gun across her bow; the ship did not stop but sailed upriver dead against the wind. When a rowboat came within a few hundred yards, the ship disappeared. Thereafter she was reported hiding under bluffs, to appear only in unsettled weather, visible in flashes of lightning.

The DANSKAMMER LIGHTHOUSE (R), 80 *m.*, sentinels Danskammer Point. It is said that when Hudson's *Half Moon* rounded the promontory, the crew saw Indians dancing around a fire in a large cave and called it the *Duyvil's Dans Kammer* (devil's dance chamber). On the eastern shore, opposite the lighthouse, Baron von Steuben used to fish; arriving at Washington's headquarters in Newburgh one day, the baron held up an eel and exclaimed, 'A whale, nicht wahr?' Hudson fishermen long called eels 'Steuben's whales.'

NEWBURGH (R), 85.3 *m.* (160 alt.,31,797 pop.), rises high above the water in a series of terraces that almost blot out the Shawangunk Mountains in the background. Like Hudson and Poughkeepsie, Newburgh was an important whaling port, the *Portland* and the *Illinois* floating in with cargoes of spermaceti. After the collapse of the whaling industry, Captain George Austin headed his ship, the *Colonel Crockett*, for Africa for a cargo of ivory. A year later, off the African coast, the schooner ran aground on a hidden shoal, and the captain was roasted by cannibals.

At the southern end of the city there is a fleeting glimpse of the white, drop-roofed, frame HASBROUCK HOUSE, Washington's headquarters in the last years of the Revolution, and the TOWER OF VICTORY, a 53-foot shaft.

On the opposite shore, BEACON (150 alt.,12,181 pop.), sprawls at the foot of towering MOUNT BEACON, from whose summit signal fires blazed warning of British movements during the Revolution to the rebels on the Dutchess County plains below. The narrow line of the funicular climbing the mountainside to the white casino on the first summit looks like a silver wire. Beyond, the high rampart of the Fishkill Mountains is lost in a pastel-blue haze.

On BANNERMAN'S ISLAND, 88.4 *m.*, Francis Bannerman, starting as a dealer in munitions at the close of the Civil War, built himself a castle in 1900. Its towers, turrets, and battlements suggest the stronghold of a Rhenish robber baron. Since his death in 1918, his sons have carried on the business. Here they store their stocks of armor, guns, and munitions, which they buy at auction prices and resell as the demand arises. The island was once called Pollopel, for Mary (or Polly) Pell, who had two suitors, a farmer and a young minister. She preferred the former; her parents favored the latter. One day the minister took her sleighriding on the river; the ice broke and they fell in. The young farmer raced across the ice, jumped in, and brought them safely to this island. Polly embraced the young farmer so ardently that the minister saw the futility of his suit and married the couple then and there.

During the Revolution PLUM POINT (L), opposite, was fortified with a battery of 14 guns; now it is crowned by Alfred P. Sloan's handsome Georgian Colonial mansion.

CORNWALL (R), 89 *m.* (167 alt.,1,966 pop.), is a fashionable summer resort hidden among the trees. From Idlewild, his home in the village overlooking the river, Nathaniel Parker Willis, the 'dude poet of the Hudson,' watched huge loads of fruit and vegetables leave the east-shore docks; in the middle years of the nineteenth century he found the west bank of the river 'as much a wilderness . . . as any river-bank of equal length in the far west.'

Around a bend in the river the Hudson Highlands burst into view, gray rock cliffs, forest-crowned, on both sides of the river. STORM KING (R) rears its corrugated brow to a height of 1,340 feet, the Storm King Highway (*see Tour 21A*) making a deep crease across the ridge.

On the opposite shore are the twin bulks of BREAKNECK RIDGE and MOUNT TAURUS (Bull Hill). The story is that a wild bull once ranged this region, trampling farmers' crops. Armed with pitchforks, the farmers chased the beast over the first hill, which became Bull Hill, and on up the second, where the bull fell and broke his neck and thereby gave the ridge its name, Breakneck. To satisfy Victorian propriety, Bull Hill was for a time called Mount Taurus, but locally the Anglo-Saxon name persisted and has been officially restored.

Between the two hills is COLD SPRING (200 alt.,1,784 pop.). Parrot guns used in the Civil War were made in the village. When President Lincoln came to inspect the guns, Colonel Robert P. Parrott, the inventor, demonstrated his cannon by firing them across the river; but Lincoln was bored. 'I'm confident you can hit that mountain over there,' he said, 'so suppose we get something to eat. I'm hungry.'

Below Storm King is the bowl-shaped CROW'S NEST (L),

> Where the moon looked down on Ole Cro' Nest,
> And mellowed the shade of his shaggy breast.

High on its face is CAPTAIN KIDD'S CAVE, one of the many traditional hiding places of the notorious pirate's gold. William Kidd (1650–1701), one of the boldest sea captains sailing from New York, was recommended to the British as the man to send against the pirates. In 1697, carrying a Royal commission to exterminate pirates and prey on the French, he sailed his ship, the *Queda Merchant*, to Madagascar, and turned pirate himself, taking a number of rich prizes and amassing a treasure said to have amounted to £70,000 sterling. He made his way to America, was arrested and remanded to England, where he was convicted of the murder of a seaman and hanged. About £14,000 of his loot was recovered; the remainder has been a pot of gold at the end of the rainbow for treasure-hunters who have searched up and down the Hudson and elsewhere.

The remains of Fort Constitution on CONSTITUTION ISLAND (L) are visible only from the river among the jagged cliffs on the northwesterly side. Between the island and West Point an enormous iron chain, with links weighing more than 100 pounds each, was strung across the water along pointed timbers to prevent the British from ascending the river. This was the second chain, sturdier than the first, which the British had broken through on their advance to Kingston. At the north end of the island is FOUNDRY COVE, where cannon, shells, and shot were cast during the Civil War. The island is now a part of the West Point Reservation.

At WEST POINT (R), jutting into the river, the castellated buildings of the U.S.MILITARY ACADEMY (*see West Point*) rise in irregular tiers, the lower buildings appearing as if carved out of the rock on which they stand. Across the river are GARRISON (100 alt.,500 pop.), and the estate of Jacob Ruppert (1867–1939), brewer and owner of the New York Yankees. To the south is the tower of OSBORN'S CASTLE, home of William Church Osborn, foremost crusader against defacement of the Hudson Highlands.

South of Garrison rise FORT HILL and SUGAR LOAF HILL. In the Beverly Robinson House at the foot of Sugar Loaf, his headquarters as commander of West Point, on September 25, 1780, Benedict Arnold learned of the capture of Major John André. Washington and Lafayette were expected for breakfast, but Arnold mounted his horse and fled. Washington arrived to find the commander gone; from Alexander Hamilton he learned the details of Arnold's plan to betray West Point to the enemy.

ANTHONY'S NOSE (L), 99.6 *m.*, rising in the east, was named, according to tradition, for the nose of Anthony Corlaer, Peter Stuyvesant's trumpeter, which was 'of a vast lusty size, strutting boldly from his countenance like a mountain of Golconda.' On one occasion as they were passing by on a galley, a sunbeam fell on Anthony's gargantuan proboscis, 'the reflection of which did shoot straightway down hissing hot, and killed a mighty sturgeon that was sporting beside the vessel.'

Across the river BEAR MOUNTAIN dominates the western skyline. At its base is the landing dock for the BEAR MOUNTAIN SECTION (*summer and winter sports*) of the Palisades Interstate Park, favorite outing place for crowds from New York and New Jersey. In the park are the remains of Fort Clinton, a Revolutionary earthwork.

Early in the Revolution General George Clinton strung a huge chain across the river between the base of Anthony's Nose and Fort Montgomery, later called Fort Clinton, to block the river against the enemy. On October 7, 1777, a British fleet under Sir Henry Clinton attacked the fort; after hours of fierce fighting the Americans set fire to their ships, the *Constitution* and the *Montgomery*, and fled, General Clinton saving himself by sliding down a steep bank to the river and escaping in a waiting boat. By the light of the burning ships the enemy hacked away at the chain; the next day it gave way and the British continued up the river to Kingston.

Just south of Fort Montgomery is the GRAVE OF MARGARET CORBIN, Revolutionary heroine, who accompanied her husband as nurse; when he fell in battle at Fort Washington, she took his place until one of her arms was torn away by a cannon ball.

Rocky, wooded mountain heights crowding the ramps of the BEAR MOUNTAIN BRIDGE dwarf the two towers and the interlacing cables to make them look like slender spindles strung with black thread. On the left the toll road cuts like a sabre scar across Anthony's Nose. South of the bridge is IONA ISLAND (R), Government arsenal and supply depot. The circular shot-tower, marked with red and white squares, serves as a danger signal to aviators, who are forbidden to fly over the island.

Directly south, at the RACE, narrowest stretch of the navigable Hudson and most dangerous part of the river in the days of sail, is the DUNDERBERG (R), dwelling place of the Heer, bulbous goblin of the Dutch imagination, who touches off summer storms. Belches of fire split the heavens; barrages of thunder from unseen batteries ricochet off Dunderberg up the river, bounce off Taurus, and re-echo through the Highlands.

At the base of Dunderberg is KIDD'S POINT, where the pirate is said to have lived and hidden his treasure. Toward the middle of the last century a river boat got its anchor caught here in a submerged cannon, which was immediately proclaimed as a relic of Captain Kidd. A speculator organized the Kidd Salvage Company capitalized at $22,000, which built a coffer-dam and a pumping station to explore the river bottom for treasure; but in the end the sheriff wound up the business.

PEEKSKILL (L), 102.5 *m.* (120 alt.,17,289 pop.), climbs up a narrow valley at a sharp indentation in the shore line; its factory walls and smoke cut off the hills in the background. Freighters are warped against the docks, loading and unloading. Across the river a quarry has carved a deep bowl into the rock wall near the water's edge.

At INDIAN POINT (L), 103.5 m., long an Indian council place, the Hudson River Day Line has a large recreation park popular with New Yorkers.

STONY POINT LIGHTHOUSE (R), 106 m., guards a peninsula that juts like a crooked finger into the river from STONY POINT HEIGHTS, scene of a Revolutionary battle. During the Revolution the Point was connected with VERPLANCK'S POINT across the river by King's Ferry, the main water link in the east-west military line of communications between the New England and Middle Atlantic States. This ferry moved Washington's troops to Trenton and later to the decisive battle at Yorktown. While stationed at West Point, Baron von Steuben used the ferry frequently to reach the well-traveled Albany Post Road on the east shore, along which he preferred to ride his horse because there was less mud to stain his famous boots.

South of STONY POINT (120 alt.,1,000 pop.) is GRASSY POINT (R), another legendary cache of Captain Kidd's gold. 'Mad' Anthony Wayne and his troops scaled the sheer heights above Grassy Point on July 15, 1779, and recaptured the fort that had been lost to the British a month earlier.

On TREASON HILL (R), 107.2 m., Arnold concluded his negotiations with André. The sloop *Vulture*, which had brought André up the river, awaited him in Croton Bay downstream; but American land forces began cannonading the ship and forced it down river. André, learning of the attack, crossed King's Ferry and moved down the east bank. Near Tarrytown he was searched, and documents containing details of the plot to surrender West Point were found in his boots. When Arnold heard of the capture, he dashed from the Robinson house to the river, boarded a boat, and sped to the *Vulture*. Arnold wrote a plea to Washington that Mrs. Arnold, 'one year a mother and not two a bride,' be spared insult and injury because she had been ignorant of his plan. Alexander Hamilton wrote that when Arnold, about to flee, told her of his treason, she 'instantly fell into convulsions, and he left her in that state.' On the day André was captured, his poem *The Cow Chase* appeared in Rivington's *Royal Gazette* in New York, with its prophetic ending:

> And now I've closed my epic strain,
>   I tremble as I show it,
> Lest the same warrior drover, Wayne,
>   Should ever catch the poet!

Anthony Wayne was charged with the execution of André on October 2, nine days after the jingle appeared in the Loyalist paper.

Silhouetted in the rear of HAVERSTRAW (R), 110 m. (20 alt.,5,906 pop.), fronted by sprawling brickyards, are the three prongs of LITTLE TOR, PYNGYP (which owes its name to its resemblance to a Dutch loaf of bread), and HIGH TOR, a sharp-pointed craggy pinnacle shaped like a Dutchman's hat, which gave the title to Maxwell Anderson's play. Against a background of Dutch folklore humor, the playwright castigates those who would despoil the beauty of the Hudson Highlands to quarry profits out of them. On the side of High Tor is a line of grey concrete silos, like a giant pipe organ—the storage tanks for crushed rock dug out of the hills.

South of Haverstraw the west shore of the Hudson remains rugged, thrusting up sawtooth peaks; on the east the rolling plain melts into the distant horizon.

OSSINING (L), 114 m. (100 alt.,15,976 pop.), rises abruptly from the water's edge. Factories, coalyards, and docks hug the shore; church spires pierce the skyline. At the southern edge of the city is a flash of the hard walls of SING SING PRISON.

On the opposite shore (R) is the HOOK MOUNTAIN SECTION (*summer sports*) of the Palisades Interstate Park, a 1,000-acre craggy tract crowned on the north by Hook Mountain, goal of summer hikers, and on the south by Indian Head Mountain.

SLEEPY HOLLOW (L), 118 m., is the locale of Washington Irving's legend of the Headless Horseman who scared the daylights out of Ichabod Crane.

Upon entering the broad expanse of the TAPPAN ZEE, 118.5 m., legendary abode of ghosts and goblins, Dutch skippers shortened sail and implored the protection of the patron saint of sailors. Best known is the legend of Rambout Van Dam, who one Saturday rowed up from Spuyten Duyvil to attend a party in the Rockland hills. He danced and drank all Saturday night, and on Sunday morning started back home despite the warning of his companions that rowing on the Sabbath was an unpardonable sin. He never reached home, but was doomed to row perpetually up and down the waters of Tappan Zee.

Before the Revolution, the good ship *Pot Cheese*, so called for her broad lines and slow gait, made laborious trips between TARRYTOWN (L), 119 m. (70 alt.,6,785 pop.), and New York. Across the river is NYACK (68 alt.,5,167 pop.).

SUNNYSIDE (L), 119.5 m., was for many years the home of Washington Irving, who described the house as 'made up of gable ends and full of angles and corners as an old cocked hat.' In 1835 Irving wrote: 'The Hudson is in a manner my first and last love, and after all my wanderings and seeming infidelities, I return to it with a heartfelt preference over all the rivers of the world.'

DOBBS FERRY (L), 123.5 m. (150 alt.,5,858 pop.), was named for Jeremiah Dobbs, who in 1698 hollowed out a log and started the first river ferry. Across the river the PALISADES (R) begin their 14-mile march. This front of solid trap rock separates the valleys of the Hudson and Hackensack Rivers, which flow parallel for 30 miles. The Mahican Indians believed the Great Spirit raised this rampart to protect his favorite abode from man.

Opposite the crowded water front of YONKERS (L), 128.5 m. (30 alt.,142,404 pop.), is ALPINE GORGE (R), one of the few breaks in the Palisades.

On July 28, 1852, the *Henry Clay*, a 206-foot steamer, was plowing through these waters, putting on every ounce of steam to hold its lead over the *Armenia*. The race down from Albany had been packed with drama. The *Henry Clay* was well ahead when it docked at Hudson, but the *Armenia* passed it by omitting that stop. Near Kingston the *Henry Clay* came alongside the other boat; pilot Elmendorf gave the wheel a spin and cut across the bow of the *Armenia*; there was a crash of splintering wood— the *Armenia* was being shoved ashore. To avert being grounded, the *Armenia* cut steam and the *Henry Clay* moved triumphantly ahead. Women passengers begged the men to throw the captain overboard unless he stopped racing. At 3 p.m., a few miles out of Yonkers, a wisp of smoke curled from an awning amidship; suddenly the whole mid-section of the *Henry Clay* burst into flame. The pilot turned the ship and, full speed ahead, grounded it on the east shore, its bow rising out of the water. Andrew Jackson Downing, who had boarded the ship at Newburgh, stood calmly on deck giving orders and throwing buoyant objects to those struggling in the water; then he dove into the river, helped his wife and children ashore, and was drowned while helping others. Maria Hawthorne, sister of the novelist, went under. A Newfoundland dog seized a child struggling in water and bore it to shore. That night the coroner stood guard over 80 bodies, drawing his gun on pirates bent on plundering the dead. The next morning New York newspapers raged against this useless loss of life. The owners of the *Henry Clay* were acquitted of a murder charge; but public indignation resulted in legislation that ended steamboat racing.

Greatest loss to American cultural life was that of Andrew Jackson Downing. Only 37 years old, he had achieved a wide reputation with his *Treatise on Landscape Gardening* (1841), *Architecture of Country Houses* (1850), and *Cottage Residences* (1852), and his ideas had been applied in Hudson Valley buildings and estates. His principles were, first, fitness to use; second, truthfulness of expression; and third, beauty. Accordingly he ruled out the unpractical Greek Revival house, the use of the temple portico in place of the practical veranda, and the rustication of woodwork to make it resemble stone. He insisted that houses should be designed to harmonize with the country in which they stood, pointing out the fitness of high towers and peaked roofs for country mansions among the Highlands of the Hudson. He advocated the use of brackets, a novelty of the day produced by the application of steam power to millworking; but he used them with restraint.

Now a ship canal linking the Harlem River with the Hudson, SPUY-TEN DUYVIL CREEK (L), 132.2 *m.*, was so named, according to Washington Irving, because, when in 1664 Governor Stuyvesant, threatened by the British, sent Anthony Van Corlaer, his famed trumpeter, to arouse the colonists to the north, Anthony came to the creek and found it swollen by torrential rains but swore he would swim it 'en spuyt den Duyvil' (in spite of the devil). Halfway across, Satan seized Anthony's leg; Anthony blew a mighty blast from his trumpet and scared the devil into letting go.

But Old Nick recovered and pulled Anthony down. 'His ghost still haunts the neighborhood, and his trumpet has often been heard of a stormy night.'

The GEORGE WASHINGTON MEMORIAL BRIDGE, 135 *m.*, sweeps across the river between the sites of FORT WASHINGTON (L) and FORT LEE (R). After the Battle of Long Island Congress ordered General Nathaniel Greene to hold Fort Washington. In November 1776, General Washington looked on helplessly from Fort Lee as the American troops were decimated and Fort Washington was captured by Lord Howe.

South of the bridge there unfolds the New York City skyline. The river bustles with ferries, tugs, and freighters; transatlantic ocean liners rest at their docks. At 141.5 *m.* is the WEST 42D STREET PIER (L).

Tour 22

(Fair Haven, Vt.)—Whitehall—Hudson Falls—Schuylerville—Troy—Junction with US 20; US 4.
Vermont Line to Junction with US 20, 84.9 *m.*

Two-lane concrete.
Delaware & Hudson R.R. parallels route between the Vermont line and Fort Edward; Boston & Main R.R. between Schuylerville and Waterford.

US 4, paralleling the Champlain Canal and the upper Hudson, follows the trail of Burgoyne's invasion of 1777 through what is now a dairy region and past papermaking villages that grew up around Revolutionary forts at strategic points in the valley.

The route crosses the NEW YORK–VERMONT LINE, 0 *m.*, 3 miles west of Fair Haven, Vermont. From WHITEHALL, 8.2 *m.* (*see Tour 20*), US 4 runs in common with State 22 (*see Tour 20*) for 7.2 miles along the Champlain Canal.

After taking Ticonderoga (*see Tour 20*), Burgoyne's full force reached Whitehall on July 10, 1777; the much smaller American Army was only 20 miles south and might have been destroyed by a sudden attack. But Burgoyne, worried about provisions and slowed up by heavy artillery and cartloads of personal belongings, took three weeks to cover those 20 miles. In the meantime General Schuyler destroyed bridges, felled trees across the road, and ordered farmers to burn their grain before the advancing enemy.

FORT ANN, 19.5 *m.* (150 alt.,389 pop.), on the low divide between the Hudson River watershed and Lake Champlain, was the site of a series of Colonial and Revolutionary forts. A brief encounter between an advance British force and the Americans on July 8, 1777, is called the Battle of Fort Ann.

Right from the village on a country road 0.1 *m.* to the PIKE HOME (R), on the site of Fort Ann. A well on the grounds has been in use since 1690.

The COLONEL GEORGE WRAY HOUSE (L), 1 *m.*, erected soon after the Revolution by the paymaster of the British Army, is a well-preserved post-Colonial dwelling.

KANE'S FALLS (R), 2 *m.*, is the site of the blockhouse used during the Revolution; the falls furnished power for the first sawmill erected here in 1690.

HUDSON FALLS, 29.3 *m.* (280 alt.,6,449 pop.), a papermaking center, is at the sharp bend in the Hudson where the river changes its course from east to south. The village shares with Salem (*see Tour 20*) the county seat functions of Washington County.

The first white settlers came in the 1760's and built gristmills and saw-mills on the 70-foot falls; but at first the Burgoyne campaign delayed development, and then in 1780 Sir Guy Carleton burned the settlement. In the nineteenth century, pulpwood, floated down the Hudson River from Adirondack forests, established paper manufacturing as the dominant industry.

The UNION BAG AND PAPER PLANT (*open; apply at office*), its mills extending a mile along the river, employs 1,100 of the 1,700 village workers and produces the heavy paper used in making paper bags and wrapping paper, waterproofing material, and twisted and gummed paper products.

The IMPERIAL PAPER AND COLOR PLANT (*open; apply at office*), River St., originated and manufactures washable wallpaper and is one of the largest American producers of pigment colors. Color-splashed employees in grotesque protective masks work under colored lights.

FORT EDWARD, 31.3 *m.* (147 alt.,3,850 pop.), is another paper-making village, half the working population being employed in the mill of the International Paper Company, which stretches along the river.

As the Great Carrying Place, where Indians and whites toted their canoes between the Hudson and Lake Champlain, the site of Fort Edward was fortified throughout the French and Indian and Revolutionary wars. In July 1777, when Burgoyne was advancing a mile a day from the head of Lake Champlain, the American forces were stationed here, and, as the enemy approached, Schuyler retreated across the river. Burgoyne dallied here for another two weeks; on August 16 his Hessians were defeated on the way to Bennington; in the same week General Horatio Gates superseded Schuyler; on September 13 Burgoyne finally crossed the Hudson.

Just inside the gates of the UNION CEMETERY (L), on Broadway, is the GRAVE OF JANE MCCREA (L), enclosed by a high iron picket fence and marked by a six-foot white marble slab. Jane McCrea, on her way to the British lines to visit her fiancé, David Jones, a young Loyalist officer, was murdered and scalped by Indians in British employ who were over-eager to earn the bounty for American scalps. The atrocity was used by the Patriots as a weapon of anti-British propaganda. Feeling in this section had been lukewarm, but this event roused so many to join the Patriot army that some historians have asserted the Revolution was won by the murder of Jane McCrea.

At 35.3 *m.* a low white stone (R) surrounded by a shin-high rail marks

The Countryside

Photograph by courtesy of the Farm Security Administration

COUNTRY ROAD

GATHERING MAPLE SAP

Photograph by Daniel V. Nero

Photograph by John J. Vrooman

VINEYARD, CANANDAIGUA LAKE

DAIRY FARM

Photograph by courtesy of Farm Security Administration

Photograph by John J. Vrooman

DUCK FARM, LONG ISLAND

Photograph by W. Lincoln Highton

CHAPEL, HAMILTON COLLEGE, CLINTON

Photograph by courtesy of the U. S. Military Academy

PARADE, WEST POINT

CADET CHAPEL, WEST POINT

Photograph by John J. Vrooman

ST. JAMES CHURCH, HYDE PARK

Photograph by John J. Vrooma

'HOME, SWEET HOME', EAST HAMPTON, LONG ISLAND

INFIRMARY, SHAKER SETTLEMENT, MT. LEBANON

Photograph by courtesy of Chautauqua

CHAUTAUQUA

MARK TWAIN'S STUDY, ELMIRA

Photograph by John J. Vrooman

the original burial place of Jane McCrea and the site of an American camp at the time of her murder.

The route crosses the river at 41.7 *m*. On STARK'S KNOB (R), 42.6 *m.*, State owned (*adm. free*), Colonel John Stark set up his artillery after the second Battle of Saratoga, thereby gaining command of the river to prevent Burgoyne's retreat and compel his surrender.

The MARSHALL HOUSE (R), 43.3 *m.*, built before the Revolution, is sometimes called the Riedesel House after the German Baroness Riedesel, whose husband commanded the Hessians under Burgoyne and who here found shelter with her children during Burgoyne's retreat.

Revolutionary shrines in and around SCHUYLERVILLE, 43.9 *m.* (139 alt.,1,411 pop.), attract thousands of tourists. The original settlement, dating from 1689 and known as Saratoga, was destroyed by the Indians in 1745. The village was incorporated under the name of its illustrious patron, General Philip Schuyler, in 1831.

On Ferry St. (L), in the center of the village, is the FIELD OF GROUNDED ARMS, where the British forces stacked their arms and surrendered.

The SARATOGA MONUMENT (*open daily, May–Oct.; adm. free*), McCoyne Ave., standing 155 feet high on the hill where the British made their last stand, was dedicated on the centennial anniversary of the surrender. From the uppermost windows is a magnificent view of the Taconics and Green Mountains in the east and the Adirondacks in the west. In the base are four niches, three containing statues of Generals Schuyler and Gates and Colonel Daniel Morgan, and the fourth vacant, to symbolize Arnold's betrayal of the Colonial cause. A square room within the base contains Revolutionary relics, statues of Revolutionary heroes, and 16 tablets depicting memorable events in the Revolution. Legend has it that a mason, believing that nothing on this mortal sphere should be perfect, deliberately incorporated a palm leaf in place of a rosette in Schuyler's niche.

In Schuylerville is the junction with State 29 (*see Tour* 13).

At 44.9 *m.*, just outside the village limits, is the junction with a dirt road leading across a bridge.

Left on this road 0.1 *m.* to the SCHUYLER MANSION (L), a simple two-story-and-attic frame building set in a grove of trees. Built after 1777 by General Schuyler, it took the place of an earlier structure burned by Burgoyne. In its day the house sheltered Washington, Hamilton, and Lafayette. In the rear of the house are the fields where Catherine Schuyler, the wife of the General, burned the ripening wheat to prevent its falling into British hands.

VICTORY MILLS, 45.1 *m.* (200 alt.,473 pop.), is a ghost town. Cotton mills, 29 in number, established here in 1846, furnished employment for the village and countryside. In 1929 the owners closed the mills and shipped 328 carloads of machinery to Alabama. The huge mills and the company houses stand vacant by the side of the road.

The SARATOGA BATTLEFIELD STATE PARK, 51.9 *m.*, borders the road for about two miles. The parking space, on an elevation, offers a fine view across the Hudson River to the Green Mountains. In 1940 the battlefield was taken over by the Federal Government to be developed as a National Park.

The Battle of Saratoga was the turning point of the Revolution. Here the Americans checkmated the major movement in the British plan to occupy the Hudson-Champlain Valley and cut the rebellious Colonies in two. Burgoyne's slow advance gave the 'rabble in arms' time to organize themselves into an army. General Gates, reinforced by Morgan's famous Rifle Corps, entrenched at Bemis Heights upon the advice of Kosciusko. On September 19, 1777, the Americans, led by the fiery Benedict Arnold, attacked the enemy at Freeman's Farm. The British, particularly the Hessians, suffered heavy losses but held their ground. On October 7 Gates attacked a reconnoitering force led by General Simon Fraser, who was mortally wounded. Arnold, relieved of his command, and in violation of what little military discipline existed, galloped on the field amid the cheers of adoring troops and led the attack on the Hessian redoubt, which gave way and forced the British to retreat. But Burgoyne was as slow in retreat as in advance, and the Americans were able to surround his forces at Schuylerville. Despairing of help from Sir Henry Clinton, tardily on his way up the Hudson, Burgoyne surrendered on October 17. This victory decided France openly to support the American cause.

Adjoining the parking place is (L) a period BLOCK HOUSE (*open*), erected on the site of Fort Neilson, American headquarters. It contains collections of guns, flags, and other relics. Just beyond is (L) the building occupied by Morgan, Learned, and Poor. Beyond is the reproduced ARNOLD HEADQUARTERS (L), a small white, gable-roofed building. Down the slope of the hill (L) is the rebuilt powder magazine.

Across the highway are (R): a monument to Brigadier General Thaddeus Kosciusko (1740–1817), Polish military engineer, who, under the command of General Gates, selected and fortified the American position on the battlefield; the battlefield cemetery, containing the graves of soldiers who were killed in the two engagements; a memorial pavilion erected by the State; a memorial erected by the D.A.R. to mark the grave of an Unknown Soldier of the Revolution; and a monument, erected in 1938 by the Saratoga chapter of the D.A.R., honoring the 16 generals who took part in the battle, on which for the first time the name of Benedict Arnold appears.

A dirt road leads north from the parking space to a picnic ground; the Great Redoubt, where Arnold and Morgan routed the Hessians; Freeman's Farm, where the sharpest fighting of the first battle occurred; and the Arnold Monument on Breyman's Hill, where Arnold was wounded. The stone shows a left boot, symbolizing the wound Arnold received in his left leg, and the epaulets of a major-general, the rank to which he was promoted after the battle; the inscription records his achievements but pointedly omits his name.

In MECHANICVILLE, 61.1 *m.* (105 alt.,7,444 pop.), are yards, roundhouses, and repair shops of the Delaware & Hudson and Boston & Maine Railroads and the book-paper plant of the West Virginia Pulp & Paper Company, which employs about 800 persons. Other factories produce knit goods, dresses, and paper boxes. Italians comprise about one-third of the total population.

In the Hudson View Cemetery is the COLONEL E.E. ELLSWORTH MONU-
MENT, erected in memory of the first Northern officer killed in the Civil
War. Ellsworth was shot while removing a Confederate flag from the roof
of a hotel in Alexandria, Virginia. The body was taken to Washington and
the funeral services were conducted in the White House with Abraham
Lincoln as one of the mourners. Ellsworth had been active in the presidential campaign of 1860 and had accompanied the President-elect on his
journey to Washington.

WATERFORD, 69.7 m. (38 alt.,2,921 pop.), is at the junction of the
Champlain and Erie divisions of the Barge Canal; during the navigation
season the water front is a maze of barges and tugboats. Textile mills and
machine works provide local employment.

South from Waterford on State 32, following the west bank of the Hudson, to
COHOES, 1.8 m. (100 alt.,21,947 pop.), industrial city manufacturing rayon products, knitted goods, and, on a smaller scale, boats, fire hydrants, paper boxes, and
wallpaper. Fifty per cent of the population is of French-Canadian and 35 per cent of
Irish stock, with small Italian, Polish, Lithuanian, and Ukrainian groups.

Settled in 1665 by Gassen Gerritse Van Schaick, the city occupies part of Van
Schaick's Half Moon patent, a section of Rensselaerswyck, the northern boundary of
which is marked by Manor Avenue, and part of the grant belonging to Illetie Van
Slyck Van Olinde, a half-breed who received her land from the Mohawk in 1667.

At the intersection of Park and Van Schaick Aves. is the SITE OF CAMP VAN
SCHAICK, where the Continental Army was encamped when General Gates took over
command from General Schuyler before the Battle of Saratoga.

The VAN SCHAICK MANSION (open), Van Schaick Ave., was General Gates's headquarters when he planned the Saratoga campaign. A two-story Georgian Colonial
brick structure, it was built by Anthony Van Schaick, son of the first settler, in 1735.
The central one of the five cannons on the grounds was captured by the Americans in
the Battle of Saratoga. In the house is Colonel Daniel Morgan's rifle, which the sharpshooting patriot presented to his host as a token of appreciation.

Two hundred yards south of the house is the site of one of the first canals in this
country, constructed in 1795 by the Northern Inland Lock Navigation Company and
known in its day as 'Schuyler's Ditch.'

COHOES FALLS, best viewed from School St. near the electric power station, was
once a thundering 70-foot torrent about which Thomas Moore, the Irish poet, wrote a
poem in 1804. But diversion of the water of the Mohawk River for canal and power
purposes has reduced the flow to little more than a trickle.

At 3.4 m. is the junction with a macadam road; left on this road 0.8 m. to GREEN
ISLAND (40 alt.,3,983 pop.), industrial village, its principal industry being the FORD
MOTOR PLANT (open), head of George St., serving as an assembling and distributing
point and manufacturing radiators, batteries, and springs.

On State 32, WATERVLIET, 5.1 m. (27 alt.,16,097 pop.), is at the junction with
State 7 (see Tour 10).

The ALBANY RURAL CEMETERY (R), 8 m., contains the graves of Chester A. Arthur
(1830–86), 21st President of the United States; Colonel Peter Gansevoort (1749–1812),
defender of Fort Stanwix and participator in the Sullivan-Clinton campaign; Stephen
Van Rensselaer (1764–1839), last of the patroons, patron of science, and founder of
Rennsselaer Polytechnic Institute; William James (1771–1832), Albany merchant
and founder of the distinguished James family; Erastus Corning (1794–1872), iron
merchant, railroad pioneer, and politician; General Philip Schuyler (1733–1804); and
James Hall (1811–98) and John M. Clarke (1857–1925), scientists.

ALBANY, 12.3 m. (18 alt.,130,447 pop.) (see Albany).

US 4 crosses the Hudson to TROY, 74.5 m. (34 alt.,70,117 pop.) (see
Troy), at the junction with State 96 (see Tour 10) and State 7 (see
Tour 11).

South of Troy the route runs along a shelf of land overlooking the Hudson, from which there is an impressive view of the skyline of Albany (R).

At 84.9 *m.* is the junction with US 20-US 9 (*see Tours* 8 and 21).

Tour 23

Ticonderoga—Lake George—Saratoga Springs; State 9N and 9K. 70.8 *m.*

Two-lane concrete or macadam.
Delaware & Hudson R.R. parallels route between Lake George and Saratoga Springs.

State 9N makes its way between the mountains on the west shore of Lake George, squeezing through here and there to a view of the lake waters and the towering sentinel ridges opposite. Both shores of the lake provide semi-seclusion for private estates and large hotel colonies. State campsites on the west shore and at the head of the lake, among the most popular in the State, form a playground for shop and office workers and professional people. Some of the hotels stay open for the winter sports crowd.

Here ran one of the great Indian trails between the St.Lawrence and Mohawk Rivers. Father Isaac Jogues was the first white man to see the lake and named it Lac du Saint Sacrement, May 30, 1646. In 1755 it was given its present name by Sir William Johnson.

The region was inaccessible to settlers, but as part of the Hudson-Champlain gateway to Canada it was fortified and fought over by the British and the French. After Montcalm captured Fort William Henry in 1757, the English cause was kept alive by Robert Rogers and his rangers, as keen in woodcraft and scalping as the Indians, until 1759 when General Jeffrey Amherst captured Ticonderoga. The drumbeats of the Revolution again postponed settlement until after Sir Guy Carleton's raid of the region in 1780.

The summer resort trade began early; the first hotel appeared about 1800. Crude steamboats took passengers first from stagecoach stops and then from railroad docks to lake shore resorts and private homes. Since 1900 the State has kept much of the region open to the public.

South of TICONDEROGA, 0 *m.* (200 alt.,3,395 pop.), at the junction with State 22 (*see Tour* 20), State 9N is shadowed by wooded mountains that hide the lake.

At 1.8 *m.* (R) are the TICONDEROGA SKI TRAILS.

On the mountain slopes (L) opposite the ski trails took place the Battle of Snowshoes, March 13, 1758, the ambush of 180 English scouts under Robert Rogers by 600 French and Indians; only about 50 of the rangers, including Rogers, escaped. At 2.9 *m.* the road skirts ROGERS ROCK (L), where, according to tradition, Rogers, fleeing from the Indians after the battle, rolled his pack down to the lake below, retraced his steps, descended to the lake, and returned to his pack. When the Indians reached the precipice they saw Rogers skating up the lake, and, assuming he had performed the feat of sliding down the steep slope, gave up the chase.

At 5.2 *m.* the road touches the shore of LAKE GEORGE (L), hemmed in for the 32 miles of its length by forest-clad mountain ridges that dip down into the water, forming bays; dark, wooded islands look as tidy as though they had been painted on the water.

In the rock ledge (L), at 6.6 *m.*, are the INDIAN KETTLES, potholes 1 to 3 feet in diameter and 1 to 12 inches deep, which according to legend were used by Indians to prepare food.

In SILVER BAY, 15.1 *m.* (360 alt.,200 pop.), is the junction with a dirt road.

Left here 0.2 *m.* to the numerous buildings of the SILVER BAY ASSOCIATION. In July and August the association holds a series of religious and educational conferences sponsored by the Y.M.C.A. and Y.W.C.A. and attended by 300 to 400 girls and boys of college age.

At 19 *m.* begins (L) the Tongue Mountain foot and bridle trail system, which climbs the slopes of Fivemile Mountain and Tongue Mountain.

BOLTON LANDING, 29.7 *m.* (360 alt.,600 pop.), swells in summer to a population of about 2,000. Summer residences are opened; year-round dwellers share their homes with tourists.

South of Bolton Landing the route passes a series of large estates, including the summer homes of Madame Louise Homer, grand opera singer; the Right Reverend Ernest N. Stires, Bishop of the Episcopal Diocese of Long Island; and many leaders in industry and finance. The mansions find seclusion down private roads cut through dense stands of timber.

This 'Millionaires' Row' is invaded by the HEARTHSTONE POINT STATE CAMPSITE (*bathing, boating, fishing, playground*), 36.9 *m.*, which, with its 350 fireplaces and half a mile of choice lake front, is one of the most popular public campgrounds in the State.

LAKE GEORGE, 39.6 *m.* (350 alt.,848 pop.), is at the junction with US 9 (*see Tour* 21). The tour unites with US 9 to the junction with State 9K, 40.7 *m.*, which is now the route.

State 9K cuts through a heavily wooded region of lakes, forests, and dude ranches, which, providing active (but not too strenuous) outdoor life, with real horses and synthetic cowboys, have become popular in the southeastern Adirondacks. There is a 9,000-acre ranch on the north shore (R) of LAKE VANARE (*boating, swimming, fishing, horseback riding*), 48.3 *m.*, and another on LAKE FOREST (L), 50.3 *m.*

LUZERNE, 50.9 *m.* (635 alt.,800 pop.), is another summer and winter resort. North of the village are the STONE MOUNTAIN SKI TRAILS and the LUZERNE SKI TRAILS.

Right from Luzerne on a side road to the CONKLINGVILLE DAM, 6.5 *m.*, which impounds the waters of the Sacandaga River to form the 27-mile long SACANDAGA RESERVOIR (*boats, fishing, bathing*). The reservoir, completed in 1930, regulates the flow of the Hudson by controlling its tributary, the Sacandaga. The 42 square miles of water cover parts of the villages of Northampton and Mayfield and all of Osborn

Bridge. Homes were lifted from their cellars and moved to new foundations built above the high-water mark. In the short time since its completion, the reservoir has become a popular summer resort.

The U.S.EXPERIMENTAL FUR FARM (*open Wed. and Fri., July 1–Dec. 1*), 67.2 *m.*, conducted by the Department of Agriculture, carries on scientific breeding of fox, mink, and marten to improve fur production and publishes its findings for commercial fur farmers.

SARATOGA SPRINGS, 70.8 *m.* (330 alt.,13,670 pop.) (*see Saratoga Springs*), is at the junction with State 29 (*see Tour* 13) and US 9 (*see Tour* 21).

Tour 24

Junction with State 8—Amsterdam—Wright (Sidney's Corners)—Schoharie—East Branch; State 30. 156.9 *m.*

Two-lane macadam or concrete.
The New York Central R.R. parallels route between Grand Gorge and Margaretville; Delaware & Northern R.R. between Margaretville and East Branch.

State 30 follows the Sacandaga River out of the southern Adirondack area, rises with the Schoharie River up the western slopes of the Catskills, and descends with the East Branch of the Delaware into the Delaware River Valley.

Section a. JUNCTION STATE 8 to WRIGHT (SIDNEY'S CORNERS); 65.9 m. State 30

The junction of State 8 (*see Tour* 14), and State 30, 0 *m.*, is at the confluence of two branches of the Sacandaga (Ind., drowned lands) River, a rock-strewn mountain torrent.

At 7.2 *m.* the road cuts through the SACANDAGA STATE CAMPSITE (*open May 25–Sept. 25, free; register with warden*).

The small shed and the bridge-like structure slung across the river (R) at 8.7 *m.* is a STREAM GAUGING STATION of the U.S.Geological Survey. In co-operation with the Hudson River Regulating District, this station keeps a close check on the flow of the Sacandaga miles upstream from control reservoirs, electric generating stations, and mills.

NORTHVILLE, 20.4 *m.* (795 alt.,1,110 pop.), on one arm of the Sacandaga Reservoir, is a base for fishing in the reservoir (*pike, pickerel, bass, perch; boats rented*). Marking the southern end of the Northville-Lake Placid trail of the Adirondack Mountain Club, it is also an outfitting point for hikers and campers. Five small glove factories provide limited industrial employment.

VAIL MILLS, 34.5 *m*. (780 alt.,110 pop.), is at the junction with State 29 (*see Tour* 13). AMSTERDAM, 44.4 *m*. (300 alt.,33,640 pop.) (*see Tour* 11), is at the junctions with State 5 (*see Tour* 11) and State 5S (*see Tour* 12).

Between 61.4 *m*. and 61.8 *m*., State 30 runs in common with US 20 (*see Tour* 8) along Schoharie Creek.

Between 63.3 *m*. and WRIGHT (Sidney's Corners), 65.9 *m*. (610 alt., 24 pop.), State 30 runs in common with State 7 (*see Tour* 10).

Section *b*. *WRIGHT* (*SIDNEY'S CORNERS*) *to* *GRAND GORGE;* 32.1 *m*. *State 30*

Through the Schoharie (Ind., bridge of driftwood) Valley, the route follows a scenic and historic trail. Clustered along the road are the big red rambling barns and white houses of well-to-do farmers; the rich bottom lands grow heavy with meadow, wheat, and corn, potatoes, carrots, celery, onions, lettuce, cabbage, and tomatoes.

When the German Palatines found themselves trapped on Livingston Manor (*see Tour* 21B), they revived the legend that they had been promised the fertile fields of 'Skohare' and sent representatives to treat with the Indians. The latter, though they had already sold the title twice, were not averse to a third sale. In the fall of 1712 about 150 families moved to Albany and Schenectady; about one-third of them cut a way through the woods to Schoharie that same fall and lived through the winter somehow; the remainder followed in the spring. They settled in seven villages, named for the emigrant leaders and stretching from the present Central Bridge to Middleburg.

The Indians were friendly, and helped the white settlers; conflict threatened only when the more religious of the Palatines attempted to regulate the morals of the red men.

Not having been permitted to take with them the tools brought from England, the immigrants faced the frontier with only their hands and their axes to serve them. The cold of winter was hard to bear. As spring moved up the valley, it brought the settlers joy. Fields were prepared for planting, first with men dragging the crude wooden plow. Later community resources were pooled to buy a horse—a bony old nag that was hitched up with a cow to turn the soil. That horse adorns the seal of Schoharie County—not, however, the bag of bones of reality, but a dream horse with sleek body and flowing tail.

In planting, the whites followed the weather wisdom of the Indians: 'not until the leaves of the white oak are large as a squirrel's ear, is it time to plant corn'—a tradition that has been handed down through the years and is still heard on the farms of the valley. 'Remedies' have also been handed down: toe and fingernail trimmings, cut unbroken and wrapped in paper, put in a hole bored in a maple tree and secured by a pine plug, insure the owner against swollen joints.

No sooner were the Palatines settled than they were disturbed by other claimants to their land, but they discouraged these 'intruders' with no halfway measures: Nicholas Bayard was driven out of the settlement by an angry mob; when Adam Vrooman attempted to settle on land he had bought from a rival claimant, the Palatines tore his fences and beat his son; when a hapless deputy sheriff came from Albany with a warrant for the arrest of Conrad Weiser, a mob of women under the leadership of the Amazonian Magdalena Zeh took him in hand, dragged him through places 'where the sow delighted to wallow,' heaped unmentionable indignities upon him, rode him through the valley on a rail, and left him on the Albany road after Magdalena had laid a stick over him until 'two of his ribs made four and his organs of vision were diminished by one-half.'

The chief hindrance to expansion was the frontier fear of Indian raids, in the middle years of the century by Indians under French encouragement, during the Revolutionary War by Indians under Tory leadership. Because of its rich grain lands the valley was a particular target for enthusiasts in the British cause. After unsuccessful efforts to secure outside aid, the valley folk determined to defend themselves and constructed a three-fort defense—the Upper Fort above Middleburg, the Middle Fort below Middleburg, and the Lower Fort at Schoharie. The sporadic raids reached a bitter climax in the Johnson-Brant raid on October 17, 1780, which left the valley in burning ruin, though the forts withstood attack.

South of WRIGHT (Sidney's Corners), 0 *m.*, the route follows the left shoulder of the valley. The DIETZ TAVERN (R), 2 *m.*, a two-and-a-half-story frame post-Colonial house, with the colonnade rising to the top of the second floor, served as an inn at the junction of the Schoharie-Albany and Schoharie-Schenectady turnpikes in the early nineteenth century.

At 2.6 *m.* is the junction with State 43 (*see Tour 9*).

SCHOHARIE, 2.9 *m.* (611 alt.,827 pop.), is a village with many shade trees and expansive Colonial and post-Revolutionary houses. Its only industries are the cultivation of nursery stock and the quarrying of stone for crushing, the latter an enterprise that developed rapidly with the improvement of rural roads.

Community social life reaches its peak in the Thursday night street dances and open air motion pictures in summer. In a roped-off street square the villagers and their friends from neighboring communities unite for play and dance. In the twenty years that the street dance has been a Schoharie institution, the fiddling of the back-country amateurs has given way to blaring 'swing' orchestras.

Much of Schoharie's pride in its past is embodied in the LOWER FORT (*open daily*), known locally as the Old Stone Fort, a two-story structure with square tower constructed of native limestone, that stands (R) at the northern limit of the village on a small rise above the road and commands the valley. Erected in 1772 as a Dutch Reformed church, it was stockaded in 1777 to help defend the valley from raids; so secure was the stockade and so staunch its defenders that the sallies of Johnson and Brant on October 17, 1780, were repulsed.

Maintained by the county as a museum, the fort contains thousands of relics, including crude wooden implements that the pioneers fashioned to set up homes in their promised land: shovels fashioned from logs, tree trunks hollowed into mortars, mauls cut from huge wood-knots, grain forks whittled from forked tree branches. Shoes, except for moccasins, were crudely made of heavy leather and tied with leather thongs; a still cruder shoe was whittled from willow blocks. There is also the first automobile—a crude horseless carriage—owned in Schoharie.

The JOHANNES INGOLD HOUSE, on a knoll 200 feet from the highway at the southwestern limits of the village (L), is a two-story brick post-Colonial dwelling erected in 1795 on the site of an earlier house that was burned in the raid of October 1780. The rooms have paneled wainscoting and large fireplaces with carved mantels and ornaments. In the attic are exposed the huge hand-hewn timbers of the house frame, joined with sturdy oak pins. Near the head of the attic stairs stands the ancestral loom, and in a small basket are the weaver's patterns.

South of Schoharie the road sweeps up the valley toward the Catskills, past the SITE OF HARTMAN'S DORF (L), 6.9 m., largest of the seven Palatine villages, and at 7.2 m. crosses the grass-grown right-of-way of one of America's shortest railroads.

The story of the Middleburg & Schoharie Railroad is an epic of transportation change. Built at a cost of $90,000 in 1867-8 when iron rails were perfection in transportation, at the turn of the century the road grossed in a single year $97,000 carrying hops, timothy, and lumber 5.7 miles down the valley to the junction with the Schoharie Valley Railroad. But as the hard-surfaced road crept up the valley, the railroad was superseded. The single locomotive, built in 1895, snorted less frequently up and down the valley; during its last years it habitually jumped the tracks once a week and carried a huge jack on its stubby cow-catcher with which to restore its equilibrium. Toward the end, station stops meant nothing: the engineer stopped to pick up a fare wherever he received the hitchhiker's signal. This railroad and its wheezing engine once provided background for a motion picture of Edison's boyhood days as a telegrapher. The president of the road pointed out that although his road was not as long as some of the others, it was just as wide; he sent guest passes on his line to railroad presidents the country over, and they in return sent him passes over their roads, so that he saw America free. In its last days the road found difficulty in meeting a weekly pay roll of $46 and was closed in October 1936 by the State Public Service Commission. Sold at a public auction on March 15, 1937, the railroad brought $11,000 and the antique 40-ton locomotive, $1,265.

The SITE OF THE MIDDLE FORT, 8.7 m., across the field (L), will ever be sacred to true Schoharians because of its association with the insubordination of Tim Murphy, Schoharie Valley hero, which saved the fort, and possibly the valley, from capture by Sir John Johnson's Tories and Indians.

Timothy Murphy (1751–1818), a native of New Jersey, led the rough-and-tumble life of a frontier child, with the woods, a squirrel gun, and Indians as teachers. Owner of one of the first double-barreled rifles, he raised terror in the hearts of the Indians as the magic man whose gun would shoot without reloading; he killed Indians, it is said, skinned them, and used the hide for leggings. In 1776 he qualified for Morgan's Rifles, far-feared Virginia corps of sharpshooters. His dead-eye aim is credited with having turned the tide at Saratoga, when from his station in a tree he shot down General Frazer and demoralized the British defense.

On the October day in 1780 when the Tories and Indians swept down the valley plundering and killing, Murphy was stationed at the Middle Fort. In order to get information on the strength of the defenders, Sir John Johnson sent a flag of truce toward the fort; Major M.L.Woolsey, the commander, was ready to surrender and ordered the flag admitted; but Tim Murphy, in the face of a threat to kill him for insubordination, fired at the flag-bearers and drove them off. Thus Timothy Murphy saved the day and saved the valley and won himself a place in the heart of every true Schoharian.

Through MIDDLEBURG, 9.2 m. (650 alt.,948 pop.), the road winds down a shaded avenue with large post-Colonial and Greek Revival homes on spreading lawns and a rustic log and stone wall along the creek (R). From the post-Revolutionary period down to the coming of hard-surfaced roads, which brought a resort and tourist trade, the village has been the center of trade for the upper valley. Founded in 1712 by John Conrad Weiser and the first group of Palatine pioneers, Middleburg, first called Weiser's Dorf, is the oldest settlement in the valley. It was burned in the Johnson raid of 1780.

The DUTCH REFORMED CHURCH (L), a post-Colonial brick structure with its steeple immediately above the pulpit, was built in 1786 to replace the house of worship burned in the 1780 raid. In the MIDDLEBURG CEMETERY, on a hillside back of the village (L), are the graves of Timothy Murphy and Governor William C. Bouck (*see below*).

West of Middleburg State 30 crosses Schoharie Creek into the region of the valley's most prosperous farms. At the turn of the present century these were the richest hop fields in the world. Serried rows of uprights studding an occasional field are reminders of the time when Schoharie hops brought wealth to the valley farmers. Villagers today tell wistfully of hop-harvest dances that progressed up the valley night after night until dawn. There was little time for sleeping; with huge beefsteaks and apple pie for breakfast, the laborers returned to the fields to work, and then to the barns to dance again at night.

Decline of hop-growing began in the nineties when the blue mold, blamed on an excess of lime in the soil, blighted the fields. With no effective means to attack the scourge, farmers continued to grow hops for what they could get out of them, until prohibition forced them into dairying and the growing of wheat, oats, and buckwheat; some experimented with a blue potato or sought to solve the mystery of the sweet plum tree that, they contend, refuses to bear fruit if planted more than one mile from Tim Murphy's grave.

The route passes the SITE OF WILDER HOOK, 10.4 m. (L), principal Indian village at the time of the Palatine settlement, and MOUNT ONIS-TAGRAW (Ind., corn mountain), or Vrooman's Nose, 10.6 m. (R), cast like a bold profile of a man's nose and named in a spirit of caricature for the family that lived—and five of its members were massacred—in its shadow, at 10.8 *m.* (R).

On the morning of August 9, 1780, as Captain Tunis Vrooman was un-loading a rack of wheat, an Indian pounced from the shadows of the barn, tomahawked and scalped him. His wife was chopped down and scalped. Ephraim Vrooman ran to the house, picked up his small child, and hid in the cornfield. His wife, hiding near by, thoughtless of her own safety, stood up among the tasseled corn and called, 'Ephraim, Ephraim, where are you? Have you got the child?' She was dropped by an Indian bullet and was scalped. Another Indian spotted Ephraim and thrust a spear at him. Ephraim parried the blow and the child in his arms smiled. At the third thrust of the spear, the baby gurgled and laughed excitedly. The Indian's heart softened, and instead of scalping father and child he took them prisoner. The raiders left five Vroomans dead, houses plundered, buildings burned, and livestock shot, and took 30 prisoners. At the first night's en-campment, the scalps of the dead were stretched on hoops to dry before the eyes of relatives. The Vroomans later returned to the valley, and many descendants still farm Schoharie soil.

The SITE OF THE UPPER FORT is at 13.7 *m.* (L); here the first shot was fired on October 17, 1780, to warn the lower valley of the approaching Tory-Indian raiders.

Across the fields (L) at 14 *m.* is BOUCK'S ISLAND, on which stands the stately post-Colonial BOUCK HOME. William C. Bouck (1786–1859), zealous advocate of internal improvements, served the State in both houses of the legislature, as canal commissioner, and as governor, 1842–4. He was descended from a line of Schoharie farmers and his education was limited to a few winter terms in the local school.

BLENHEIM BRIDGE (L), 20.9 *m.*, built in 1855 by the famous Yankee bridge builder, Nicholas Powers, is 228 feet long, the longest single-span wood-covered bridge in the world. In 1931, when the bridge was threat-ened with destruction to make way for a new concrete structure, the county changed the course of the highway and preserved the old span as a monument to the ingenuity and skill of early American bridge builders.

The LANSING MANOR HOUSE (L), 24.5 *m.*, standing high on a plateau, is a study in the splendor of manorial days. The first-story bricks are cov-ered with lapped siding, and the walls of the second story are entirely of wood. Huge chimneys, rising above the low hip roof, vent the smoke of nine of the thirteen original fireplaces. John Lansing served as military secretary to General Philip Schuyler. Judge Jacob Sutherland, his son-in-law, was living in the mansion when called as a delegate to help alter the State Constitution in 1821. Later the mansion was owned by John A. King, governor of New York, 1857–9.

At 29.6 *m.* is the junction with State 342.

Left on State 342 to GILBOA DAM, 0.5 *m.*, impounding the waters of Schoharie Creek and creating the SCHOHARIE RESERVOIR, a unit in New York City's water supply. Waters impounded by the dam cover the oldest forests on earth—the fernlike trees of Middle Devonian time called *Eospermatopteris* (dawn seed fern). A group of FOSSIL TREE STUMPS, 1.1 *m.*, are preserved at the foot of the dam (R).

GRAND GORGE, 31.6 *m.* (1,420 alt.,388 pop.) (*see Tour* 7), is at the junction with State 23 (*see Tour* 7).

Section c.   *GRAND GORGE to JUNCTION WITH STATE* 17 (*EAST BRANCH*); 58.9 *m. State* 30

Following the natural trail of the East Branch of the Delaware River for 58 miles, State 30 rolls through scenes made famous in the essays of John Burroughs. In July and August the hills flame with the yellow and tawny of hawk-weed. In late summer the valley is a cauliflower field. In season, the East Branch and its feeder streams swarm with trout fishermen.

South of GRAND GORGE, 0 *m.*, State 30 squeezes through a narrow pass between high wooded hills. At 6 *m.* is the junction with a steep, winding, red-tinted country road, climbing Old Clump mountain.

Right on this road 0.8 *m.* to the junction with a country road; left here 0.1 *m.* to the OLD STONE SCHOOLHOUSE (L), in which John Burroughs, naturalist-writer, and Jay Gould, railroad tycoon and stock manipulator, were classmates. According to legend, in their schooldays their roles were reversed: Gould once wrote a poem for the future poet to save him from staying after school, and Burroughs bought Gould's grammar and geology textbooks for 80¢ when the latter was hard up. The school is now a private home.

The main side route continues up the hill to (R) WOODCHUCK LODGE (*open in summer*), 2.1 *m.*, in which Burroughs spent the last years of his life. It is a two-story frame house, preserved much as he left it; a few scabs of paint linger on the clapboards, and the vine-clad porch, where he used to sit and look out over the blue hills, has native trees for pillars and snaky saplings for lattice-work. Inside are many of the tools with which he worked. 'You'd think I'd escape visitors among these remote Catskill hills,' he wrote, 'but I have had as many as 40 or 50 come in a single day.' Here Dr.Clara Barrus, Burroughs's biographer, wrote most of the *Life and Letters*.

Born near by on April 3, 1837, the seventh of ten children, John Burroughs grew up from humble backwoods circumstances to become one of the world's foremost nature writers and essayists, wearing, in gentler fashion, the mantle of Thoreau. Through the 24 volumes of his published works, from *Wake Robin* to *The Last Harvest*, nature, much of it observed in this Catskill country, is the theme, though in his later years he turned to philosophical and critical writing. Older neighbors still remember him: 'Johnny Burris (the local pronunciation) was an odd one. He liked to come up here and watch us work and then write about it.' Today mementos of Burroughs, especially books and photographs, are on sale in Roxbury, and the village draws an income from the memory of the 'odd one' who sleeps on the hill.

Just beyond Woodchuck Lodge is the weatherbeaten HAY-BARN STUDY (L), where Burroughs wrote many of his essays, working on a desk improvised out of an old hencoop and looking out through the open barn door upon the fields and woods. Here Burroughs almost met death in one of the Model T's given him by his camping companion, Henry Ford. He learned to drive when he was past 75 and kept his car in the old hay barn. Once the car turned over on him, breaking his arm; doctors fixed his arm and Ford gave him another Model T.

Up the wild pasture (R), at 2.3 *m.* is BOYHOOD ROCK, a huge glacial boulder marking Burroughs's grave. He picked the site himself; here as a boy he sat and dreamed, viewing the panorama of valley and hills. Just before he died, on March 29, 1921, on a train speeding him back from the west coast, he rose from his pillow and asked, 'How far are we from home?' A simple bronze tablet on the face of the rock shows Burroughs shielding his eyes against the sun with his hand and looking off across the valley; underneath is inscribed, from his poem *Waiting*, the line 'I stand amid the eternal ways.'

In the BEECHWOODS (L), across the road, Burroughs and his camping companions,

Henry Ford, Thomas A. Edison, and Harvey Firestone, cooked thick steaks over an open fire.

Around the turn of the road at 2.6 *m.* is the ANCESTRAL HOME (R), a huge weather-beaten country house, backed up by large barns, where Burroughs lived as a boy and helped with the farming. Relatives of Burroughs still farm the fields. After the death of Burroughs, Henry Ford bought Woodchuck Lodge and the Ancestral Home to preserve them in memory of the naturalist. He deeded the burial field on Old Clump to the John Burroughs Memorial Association.

As Burroughs left his mark on Old Clump, so his schoolmate Jay Gould left his on ROXBURY, 6.8 *m.* (1,470 alt.,475 pop.). The houses are uniformly white, their blinds green, and their lawns trim and neat. The half-mile-long main street, immaculately clean, receives a daily sweeping in the fall when leaves are falling. This is a prosperous village with its large Gould holdings and its central position in the dairying country. Here live retired farmers, summer residents, men who run the village stores, and men who work on neighboring farms, especially the Gould estate.

Born May 27, 1836, on a poor uphill farm bordering Roxbury, Jay Gould began at the age of 16 to amass his $70,000,000 fortune. Between hours of work in the village store, young Gould learned the rudiments of business and surveying. He saved his money, and at 21 was ready for his first big venture. Investing in a small tannery and lumber business in Pennsylvania, he remained only long enough to make a handsome profit. With this capital he turned to railroad financing, buying a controlling interest in the Rutland & Washington Railroad. By 1880 Gould had gained control of more than 10,000 miles of rail—one-tenth of the mileage of the whole country. In 1881 he engineered the consolidation of competing telegraph systems into the Western Union Telegraph Company. The 'Black Friday' panic of September 24, 1869, credited to the spectacular attempt of Gould and 'Jim' Fisk to corner the gold market, brought a great wave of public anger and resentment. He died on December 2, 1892.

Near the north village line is the GOULD MEMORIAL CHURCH (R), built by the Gould family in memory of Jay Gould. Adjoining the church is KIRKSIDE, which was the spacious, immaculately kept summer home of Mrs.Helen Gould Shepard until her death in 1938. Back 300 feet from the highway is the GOULD LIBRARY (L), an old white structure, purchased and maintained by Mrs.Shepard as a village library. Jay Gould lived in this house while clerking in a local store and making his map of Delaware County. Here he wrote most of his *History of Delaware County*, a book that today brings as much as $25 at collector auctions.

At HALCOTTSVILLE, 14.3 *m.* (1,339 alt.,119 pop.), an old covered bridge (R), one of several similar structures that cross the East Branch, spans the river and connects two halves of the village. In MARGARET-VILLE, 19.8 *m.* (1,325 alt.,771 pop.), is the junction with State 28 (*see Tour* 15); the routes run in common for 3.2 miles. South of Margaretville State 30 and the East Branch form the western boundary of the CATS-KILL FOREST PRESERVE (*see Tour* 7).

The road runs past a succession of dairy farms, some crowded in narrow passes between steep hills, some spread out as hill slopes ease their climb. Gone are the old Delaware County apple holes: every fall 15 to 20 bushels of apples were dumped into a huge hole in the ground, packed with straw, and covered with soil; dug up in the spring, the apples had acquired a 'delightful earthy flavor' that made them a delicacy.

At 37 *m.* is another covered bridge (L), especially interesting for its lattice-like construction.

At SHINHOPPLE, 49.6 *m.* (1,060 alt.,100 pop.), 7,000 acres of unproductive soil are being converted into a forest and game preserve known as the BEAR MOUNTAIN GAME MANAGEMENT AREA. With the help of WPA labor, the Federal Soil Conservation Service is planting trees, building roads, and developing feeding stations and breeding grounds for wild game.

Early settlers found here an abundant growth of flowering vine, beautiful in the spring, but always tangling the shins and making walking almost impossible; and they expressively named the place Shinhopple.

EAST BRANCH, 58.9 *m.* (1,007 alt.,300 pop.), is at the junction with State 17 (*see Tour 3*).

Tour 25

Alexandria Bay—Clayton—Watertown—Boonville—Utica—Norwich—Binghamton; State 12.   209.9 *m.*

Two-lane macadam or concrete.
New York Central R.R. parallels route between Boonville and Remsen; Delaware, Lackawanna & Western R.R. between Waterville and Binghamton.

The sweeping arc of State 12 crosses the State between the Thousand Islands region of the St.Lawrence River and the Susquehanna River at Binghamton. Through both the Black River Valley of the North Country and the Chenango Valley of the Southern Tier it is an important milk truck route for two great dairy farming areas.

Section a. ALEXANDRIA BAY to UTICA; 119.9 *m. State* 12

South of the Thousand Islands summer resort area the route follows the Black River Valley between the Tug Hill Plateau on the west and the Adirondacks on the east. Village names and historical sites go back to the men who divided and settled the southern tracts of the huge Macomb Purchase. The Black River Canal, which carried grain and building materials south and clothing and machinery north, is traceable along a narrow ditch with fine masonry retaining walls and moldering wooden lock gates. Today the region is primarily interested in milk and butter and cheese.

ALEXANDRIA BAY, 0 *m.* (282 alt.,1,952 pop.), a village of white painted houses on clipped lawns, is a tourist and summer resort center for the THOUSAND ISLANDS REGION. Main Street, facing the St. Lawrence River and overlooking the northernmost of the Thousand Islands, is lined with large and small hotels. During the long winter months the river freezes over and the village slows down to the tempo of local farm trade.

A number of Thousand Islands motorboat tours leave Alexandria Bay daily: the trip to Boldt Castle ($1 *a person*); trips through the lower and upper sections of the islands (*each* $1.50 *a person*); and twilight tours (8 *p.m.*; $1 *a person*) past a group of islands not included in the daytime trips.

The Iroquois called the Thousand Islands region Manitonna (the garden of the great spirit), because it corresponded to the happy hunting grounds of their dreams. An early French explorer looked out upon the island-strewn upper reach of the St. Lawrence River and exclaimed, 'Les milles îles!' And the Thousand Islands they have remained, though there are more than 1,500 of them. Some of them are no more than projecting rocks with room but for a single dwarfish tree; others are rounded tufts of forest rising gently from the water; still others are miles long, supporting entire villages. Historical events and freak natural formations suggested such names as the Lost Channel, the Needle's Eye, Fiddler's Elbow, and Devil's Oven.

BOLDT CASTLE (*open*), on Heart Island, visible from the Alexandria Bay shore line, is a turreted, castellated structure erected for his wife by George C. Boldt (1851–1916), who rose from a hotel dishwasher to become president of the company owning the Waldorf-Astoria in New York.

MARY ISLAND STATE PARK (*camping* $2 *a week, rowboats* $1 *a day, bathing, picnicking, fishing*) is two miles by boat from Alexandria Bay.

CEDAR ISLAND STATE PARK (*camping* $2 *a week, rowboats* $1 *a day, bathing, picnicking, fishing*) is 10 miles by boat from Alexandria Bay.

South of Alexandria Bay, State 12 parallels the St.Lawrence River but without the elevation necessary for river views.

At 4.3 *m.* is the United States entrance (R) to the THOUSAND ISLANDS INTERNATIONAL BRIDGE (*tolls: autos with 1 to 8 passengers, $1.25; trucks and autos with trailers, $2; cyclists and pedestrians, 25¢*), dedicated by President Franklin D. Roosevelt on August 19, 1938.

The bridge, jumping across the St.Lawrence from island to island, consists of several parts: on the American side a suspension bridge connecting the mainland with Wells Island and a road across the island; on the Canadian side a long suspension bridge, a viaduct, and two short bridges connecting the mainland with Hill Island and a road across Hill Island; spanning the International Rift between Wells and Hill Islands is a 90-foot concrete structure, the world's shortest international bridge. From mainland to mainland the distance is about six miles.

On Wells Island, side roads from the bridge lead to THOUSAND ISLAND PARK and WESTMINSTER, both resort villages, and to WATTERSON POINT and DEWOLF POINT STATE PARKS (*camping* $2 *a week, rowboats* $1 *a day, bathing, picnicking, fishing*), also reached by boat from Alexandria Bay, Fishers Landing, and Clayton.

Off State 12 is (R) GRASS POINT STATE PARK (*camping* $2 *a week, rowboats* $1 *a day, bathing, picnicking, fishing*), 6.2 *m.*

Port of entry, railroad terminal, vacation and fishing center, CLAYTON, 11.8 *m.* (290 alt.,1,940 pop.), occupying a peninsula jutting into the river, is a square of right-angled streets surrounding the business district on Central Square. The village has several small industries, the largest making snowplows. In the summer, vacationists crowd the place; Saturday night band concerts and block dances bring in countryside residents. Pleasure yachts, fishing boats, and freighters tie up at the docks that line the water front.

The CLAYTON FERRY (*automobile*, $2.50, *passenger* 50¢) crosses to Gananoque, Ontario, except in severe winter weather.

From Clayton boats can be hired for GRINDSTONE ISLAND, one of the largest of the Thousand Islands, on which are CANOE POINT and PICNIC POINT STATE PARKS (*camping* $2 *a week, rowboats* $1 *a day, bathing, picnicking, fishing*).

At Clayton is the junction with State 12E, a longer alternate route to Watertown.

Right (straight ahead) on State 12E to (R) WILKINSON'S POINT, 0.6 *m.* Here General Jacob Brown repulsed a British attack in November 1813. In BART-LETTS'S POINT STATE CAMPSITE, 3 *m.*, an American battery was set up during the war.

CEDAR POINT STATE PARK (*camping, bathing, fishing, dancing*), 8.8 *m.*, covers 13 acres.

From RIVERVIEW, 9.2 *m.*, then known as Millen's Bay, in June 1812 a party of Americans led by Abner Hubbard crossed the channel and captured Fort Haldimand on CARLETON ISLAND, in the river opposite. The island has never since been fortified.

A few yards left from the stone bridge over Millen's Bay is SLAVE'S CAVE, the last stop on the Underground Railroad; from here the fugitives were spirited across the St.Lawrence to Canada and freedom. It is said that the cave was a hiding place for American spies during the Revolution and that in the Patriots' War of 1838 William Johnson used it as a refuge between sorties.

BURNHAM POINT STATE PARK (*camping, fishing, hunting*), 11.2 *m.*, comprises eight acres.

CAPE VINCENT, 15.2 *m.* (370 alt.,898 pop.), draws large numbers of tourists as a terminal point for Thousand Islands water tours; and near-by waters are noted for bass, muskellunge, and lake trout.

James LeRay de Chaumont (*see Tour* 18) induced a number of illustrious Frenchmen to settle here, including Count Pierre François Real, Napoleon's chief of police; General Roland, the Count's son-in-law; Camille Armand, painter; Professor Pigeon, private secretary to Count Real, who wore no hat, having sworn not to wear one so long as Napoleon was imprisoned; Louis Peugnet, a member of Napoleon's bodyguard; and Marshal Grouchy, whose failure to arrive in time at Waterloo is said to have caused Napoleon's defeat. A popular village legend is that these Frenchmen planned to rescue Napoleon from St.Helena and bring him here, and for that purpose built the Cup and Saucer House. Old pictures of the mansion, which burned in 1867, reveal a two-story octagonal structure with a rounded roof crowned with a cupola, looking like an inverted cup in a saucer. The cupola contained all the trophies of Napoleon snatched up by his followers when they fled from Paris, and on the round walls Armand painted scenes of Napoleon's battles.

At 21.4 *m.* is the junction with Long Point Road; right on this road 7.3 *m.* to the junction with an unmarked gravel road; left here 1.5 *m.* to LONG POINT STATE PARK, a 12-acre tract on Point Peninsula facing Chaumont Bay, frequented by fishermen and duck hunters.

CHAUMONT, 26.6 *m.* (295 alt.,553 pop.), is another fishing center and summer resort, named for James LeRay de Chaumont. From 1816 to 1855 thousands of barrels of ciscoes (whitefish) were shipped annually to every part of the country. For a time ciscoes became the legal tender and were commonly spoken of as 'Chaumont currency.' Ice-boating is here a popular winter sport.

BROWNVILLE, 35 *m.* (340 alt.,842 pop.), a paper manufacturing community on the Black River, was settled in 1800 by Jacob Brown. The BROWN MANSION, Main St. (*open*), a two-story house of native limestone built in 1811, was Brown's home until he moved to Washington as commander of the U.S.Army. Jacob Brown (1775–1828), a Quaker, commanded the frontier militia from Oswego to St.Regis during the War of 1812 and in 1813 defended Sackets Harbor.

State 12E continues to WATERTOWN, 40.8 *m.* (478 alt.,33,323 pop.) (*see Tour* 18).

DEPAUVILLE, 19.3 *m.* (297 alt.,300 pop.), was named for Francis Depau, early settler, who in 1834–5 built the stone DEPAUVILLE UNION CHURCH (R). The church is now owned by a union of Universalists, Baptists, Free Will Baptists, and Congregationalists.

WATERTOWN, 33.3 *m.* (478 alt.,33,323 pop.) (*see Tour* 18), is at the junction with State 3 (*see Tour* 17), US 11 (*see Tour* 18), State 37 (*see Tour* 19), and State 12E (*see above*).

South of Watertown the route climbs up and across a broad plateau, one of the greatest dairy farming areas in the State.

LOWVILLE, 63.4 *m.* (865 alt.,3,556 pop.), is a characteristic North Country village with tree-shaded streets, frame dwellings, and a neat brick business section. In one of the largest cold storage plants in the world, cheese and other farm products are gathered from the surrounding farms for shipment.

The HOUGH RESIDENCE, Collins St., a spacious brick house, was the home of Dr.Franklin B. Hough (1822–85), the 'father of American forestry.' Born in Martinsburg (*see below*), Dr.Hough was a Civil War Army surgeon, a mineralogist, a botanist, and a local historian. Pioneer in the conservation movement in New York State, he drew up the report of the State Park Commission in 1872 recommending a State forest preserve. In 1876 he was appointed Forestry Agent in the U.S.Department of Agriculture, and he was instrumental in the establishment of the Division of Forestry in 1881. He published 78 volumes, including several histories of northern New York counties.

In Lowville is the junction with State 26 (State 12D).

Right on State 12D-State 26 to MARTINSBURG, 4 *m.* (1,240 alt.,302 pop.), a quiet settlement of retired farmers. The GENERAL MARTIN TAVERN (R) was built in 1805 by Walter Martin, the first settler, who later served in the War of 1812. Admiring the architecture of Johnson Hall (*see Tour* 13), Martin set out to reproduce it in his residence. The central two-story stone building is flanked by one-and-a-half-story wings, which were added later.

HOUGH'S CAVE (R), 5.8 *m.*, which serpentines under the road and emerges some 500 feet away, was used by Horatio Hough, father of Dr.Franklin B. Hough, as a station on the Underground Railroad; in the daytime he hid the fugitives here and at night loaded them into his wagon and carried them to the next depot.

At 6.4 *m.* is the entrance (R) to WHETSTONE GULF CAMPSITE (*camping, picnicking, hiking*), a narrow, twisting gorge three miles long and 200 to 300 feet deep cut by Whetstone Creek in the soft shale.

In the narrow square of TURIN, 12.4 *m.* (1,264 alt.,260 pop.), stands (L) OLD SOW, a blunt brass cannon mounted on a square stone pedestal. It is said to have been sent to the Colonies by the British in 1689, captured by Ethan Allen at Ticonderoga, used by General Knox at Dorchester Heights, and finally, to have belched forth the first shot in the Battle of Sackets Harbor.

At 14.6 *m.* State 12D branches (L) to BOONVILLE, 9.4 *m.* (*see below*). State 26 continues (R) to CONSTABLEVILLE, 17.6 *m.* (1,260 alt.,348 pop.), named for William Constable, to whom part of the great 4,000,000-acre Macomb Purchase was transferred; in 1819 his son, William Constable,Jr., built CONSTABLE HALL (*grounds open*), near the western village limits, as his manor house. It is a high-columned, gray-stone Georgian Colonial mansion with one-story wings; between the two front bays is a recessed entrance with a pedimented portico, which rises the full height of the structure.

State 26 continues south to ROME, 43.7 *m.* (*see Tour* 12).

South of LYONS FALLS, 77 *m.* (865 alt.,882 pop.), the narrow ditch of the Black River Canal crosses and recrosses State 12; down the sharp hill slopes, the dilapidated locks, some of them still bearing their hand-operated wooden gates, appear like short stairways. The 35-mile canal was begun in 1838 and completed in 1855; it was not finally abandoned until 1926, when it was superseded in its final function as water feeder for the Barge Canal by the Hinckley and Delta reservoirs.

BOONVILLE, 87.7 *m.* (1,121 alt.,2,090 pop.), is built around a triangular park with a bandstand; the business section is composed of two- and three-story red brick buildings; along the residential streets are fine old homes occupied by the descendants of New England settlers, the business and professional men of the village.

As the forests gave way to dairy farming, the village became the distributing and shopping center for a large and important dairying region. Here the milk strike of 1933 reached its height of violence. Bands of from 400 to 800 farmers stopped milk trucks on the highways and dumped the milk into the ditches. State troopers armed with clubs and tear gas bombs attacked the farmers, who fought back with stones, clubs, monkey wrenches, and curses. In the second week simple weapons gave way to high-powered rifles, and rioting to guerilla warfare. Huge glass-lined trucks were fired upon; special deputy sheriffs were sworn in by the hundreds; Governor Lehman appealed to all sides in the struggle; finally, after 16 days of warfare a truce was arranged. The latest effort to settle the problem of milk prices is a Federal-State marketing agreement (*see Agriculture*).

In Boonville is the junction with State 12D (*see above*).

ALDER CREEK, 94.9 *m.* (1,200 alt.,150 pop.), is at the junction with State 28 (*see Tour* 15), with which State 12 runs in common to TRENTON, 106.5 *m.* (800 alt., 313 pop.) (*see Tour* 15).

UTICA, 119.9 *m.* (500 alt.,100,063 pop.) (*see Utica*), is at the junction with State 5 (*see Tour* 11), State 5S (*see Tour* 12), and State 8 (*see Tour* 14).

Section b. UTICA to BINGHAMTON; 90 m. State 12

Across the southern part of the State the route follows the beautiful Chenango Valley. Here and there can be traced the towpath of the Chenango Canal, opened in 1837 to connect the Susquehanna River at Binghamton with the Erie Canal; tolls failed to cover cost of upkeep, and the canal was abandoned in 1878.

Up to about 1900 this was a hop-producing area; as hop prices declined, dairying became the principal source of income; as marketing of milk developed price difficulties and transportation by truck improved, the region turned to growing vegetables, especially peas and beans, though dairying retains first rank.

South of UTICA, 0 *m.*, State 12 crosses a potato-growing region; the long, low barns built into the side hills are for potato storage. In PARIS, 9.7 *m.* (1,481 alt.,85 pop.), the cemetery (R) contains the grave of Isaac Paris,Jr. In 1789, when local crops failed, he sent settlers provisions from Fort Plain, taking his pay in ginseng, a medicinal root that abounded in this region. In 1792 the township was named for him, and in 1880 his remains were exhumed at Fort Plain and reinterred here with elaborate ceremonies.

WATERVILLE, 15.8 *m.* (1,231 alt.,1,298 pop.), settled before 1800 by emigrants from Waterville, Maine, was a hop-raising center until the close of the past century. With power available, industries were established and Waterville acquired a reputation for wealth and gentility. George Eastman (*see Rochester*) was born at 29 Stafford Avenue and went to school here; Charlemagne Tower, a prominent resident, served as United States Minister to Austria-Hungary and Ambassador to Russia and Germany.

Small hop yards have reappeared in recent years, and the natives take heart when they hear again the cheery voices of the hop-pickers in the late summer; the growers still search the vines for the bright-colored larvae called 'hop-merchants,' which they examine for the gold or silver spots by which they prognosticate the price they will get for the crop.

Summer mornings and evenings the road is alive with large stake-body trucks packed with Italian women and children being transported between Utica and the pea and bean fields in this region; they harvest the crops at so much a bushel, large families working co-operatively and building up a credit of several hundred dollars, which they receive in a lump sum at the end of the season. Some families prefer to accept the meager accommodations that the farmers provide in the low, one-story connected cells that straggle on the roadside and which the temporary inhabitants humorously christen 'Blue Heaven,' 'Never Rest,' and 'Bean Manor.'

South of SANGERFIELD, 17.8 *m.* (1,246 alt.,225 pop.), at the junction with US 20 (*see Tour* 8), the scraggly evergreens in the shallow valley (R) mark the northern tip of the one-time sinister NINE MILE SWAMP, headquarters of the notorious Loomis gang, which terrorized the countryside from 1848 to 1866. The father, George Washington Loomis, was a fugitive from Vermont; the mother was the daughter of a Frenchman who had fled France to escape embezzlement charges. They raised their brood of six sons and four daughters on a 385-acre farm in the swamp; the children grew up well educated, well mannered, and adept at stealing; the girls were the acknowledged beauties of the region. Accounts of their depredations have become colored by tradition: one time they attended a hop-pickers' dance and when young ladies' muffs began to disappear a daring young man lifted the voluminous drapery of a Loomis girl's hoop skirts, and there were the muffs encircling the Loomis limbs from ankle to knee.

In 1849, as horses and clothing disappeared from vicinity farms and all clues led to the Loomises, neighbors organized a search of the Loomis farm and found the stolen goods; one son, William, was arrested and suffered a short jail term—the only time a Loomis was convicted, although they were repeatedly indicted. Anyone who dared testify against them was likely to find his barn burned or his horses and cattle missing. By 1864, 38 indictments against them had accumulated. One September night the brothers broke into the firehouse at Morrisville, Madison County seat, cut the firehose, and burned the courthouse; learning that the records had been removed to the county clerk's office, they broke into his safe a few nights later and burned them. About a year later a posse shot and killed 'Wash,' the oldest son and leader after his father's death, and tried to kill Grove by rolling him in kerosene-soaked blankets and setting fire to them —but he was saved by his sister Cornelia. In 1866 a vigilance committee surrounded the farm, forced the family to surrender, but failed to extract a confession from Plumb Loomis, even by stringing him from a tree. But that marked the end of the gang: the girls married well; Plumb and Grove settled down; and the only evidences of the days of terror are the cellar ruins of the Loomis home and the crooked arm of an old tree, which Plumb used to point to in his later years and drawl, 'See that limb? Well, b'God, they hung me to that.'

Land in this region was purchased in 1788 by Governor George Clinton in a treaty signed with the Indians at Fort Schuyler (Utica). After the sale an Indian sat down on a log next to the Governor and crowded him. As the Governor politely moved away, the Indian continued to slide up and crowd him. When Clinton found himself at the edge of the log he demanded an explanation. The Indian explained: 'Just so white man crowd poor Indian. Keep crowding; keep crowding. By and by him clear off. Where poor Indian then?'

In SHERBURNE, 37.1 m. (1,071 alt.,1,077 pop.), textile and dairy center, is the junction with State 80.

Right on State 80 to the SHERBURNE STATE FARM, 1.2 m. a 275-acre game refuge for the propagation of pheasants, ducks, and geese.

Lewis Anath Muller, believed by many to have been Count Artois, erected a large dwelling on (R) MULLER HILL, 13 m., soon after 1808. When Bonaparte abdicated, he returned to France, leaving the place to fall in ruins.

NORWICH, 48.8 m. (1,015 alt.,8,378 pop.), is the seat of Chenango County. The NORWICH PHARMACAL PLANT (open, one-hour guide-conducted tours), Piano St., manufactures patent medicine products.

OXFORD, 56.9 m. (982 alt.,1,601 pop.), has two village greens: a round one in the center of town circled by country stores, and an oblong one in the old residential section, where some of the fine white clapboard houses with deep lawns and large elms are now the summer homes of New York City descendants of the early settlers.

The OXFORD ACADEMY, across the bridge, is a three-story Georgian Colonial brick building erected in 1924. The school goes back to 1794, when it was one of four chartered west of the Hudson River.

At 85 m. is the junction with US 11 (see Tour 18), with which State 12 runs in common to BINGHAMTON, 90 *m.* (845 alt.,78,242 pop.) (*see Binghamton*), which is at the junction with State 17 (*see Tour* 3) and State 7 (*see Tour* 10).

Tour 26

Maple View—Oswego—Rochester—Lewiston—Niagara Falls; US 104. 175.5 *m.*

Two-lane concrete or macadam.
The New York Central R.R. parallels route between Mexico and Webster and between Lewiston and Niagara Falls.

US 104, paralleling the Lake Ontario shore, bisects the great fruit belt of western New York, a region particularly beautiful in May when apple blossoms perfume the air and cover the landscape with their falling white petals.

The route was originally a line of communication among the Five Nations of the Iroquois. After the Revolutionary War it became a turnpike and towns grew rapidly. But by 1825 the Erie Canal had absorbed the traffic and nearly a century was to pass before the road regained its importance with the coming of the automobile.

Section a. MAPLE VIEW to ROCHESTER; 93.2 m. US 104

From the junction with US 11 in MAPLE VIEW, 0 *m.* (467 alt.,100 pop.) (*see Tour* 18), US 104 runs westward through a fruit- and vegetable-raising country. Most of the early settlers came from New England, and many of the houses and fences are built of fieldstone in New England fashion. More recently Italians have arrived to take up truck farming and berry raising. In the fall the villages become kitchens for the stewing, preserving, and canning of the crop.

In MEXICO, 4.3 *m.* (384 alt.,1,297 pop.), is the junction with State 3 (*see Tour* 17).

Right from Mexico on a macadam road to SPY ISLAND, 5.5 *m.*, a small State park in the Little Salmon River, named for Silas Towne, an American spy during the Revolution, whose grave on the island is marked by a marble shaft. In 1777 Towne secreted himself on the island to observe the arrival on the mainland of British troops under St.Leger. At night, he paddled down the river and then hurried overland by trail to Fort Stanwix, where his report enabled the garrison to prepare for and repulse the enemy.

OSWEGO, 19.4 *m.* (295 alt.,22,652 pop.), easternmost port on the Great Lakes, Barge Canal terminal, and seat of Oswego County, lies on Lake Ontario at the mouth of the Oswego River. The name, from the

Indian, means 'pouring out of waters.' Long before settlement, the strategic importance of the site as the western terminus of the Mohawk River-Oneida Lake-Oswego River water route was recognized; and the French and English contended for control. During the Colonial wars the region was an important base of supplies and Oswego was fortified after 1722. In 1756 the fort was captured by Montcalm but was reoccupied by Sir William Johnson in 1759; the British retained control until they surrendered it under the Jay Treaty in 1796.

Soon after military occupation ceased, the place was settled. Its commanding position at the terminus of the inland water route made the settlement a busy port. In 1810, 30,000 barrels of Salina (Syracuse) salt were shipped from the harbor. In 1817 the first steamboat on Lake Ontario, the *Ontario*, a paddle-wheeler, put into port. The *Vandalia*, the first steamer operated by Ericsson's invention, the screw propeller, was built in Oswego shipyards and launched in 1841.

The routing of the Erie Canal across the State to Buffalo destroyed Oswego's hope of becoming the largest port on the Great Lakes. Construction of the Oswego Canal, connecting with the Erie at Syracuse, and the opening of the Canadian Welland Canal between Lake Erie and Lake Ontario brought a boom period marked by the construction of mills, factories, and iron works. Completion of the outer harbor breakwaters begun in 1869 and the city's rail and hydroelectric advantages attracted other industries. Today Oswego factories produce matches, insulating board, boilers, pumps and machines, cotton, silk, and rayon goods, paper bags and boxes, confections, and other products. The city is an important depot for transferring coal, grain, cement, pulp, and pulpwood between trains, lake steamers, and barge canal craft.

Mary Edward Walker (1832–1919), physician and advocate of women's rights, was born in Oswego. During the war she served as a nurse with the Union Army. She was captured by the enemy, and was exchanged for a Confederate officer. After the war, she discarded woman's attire for long, full trousers and a long, flapping coat. She practiced medicine in Washington, where she participated in the agitation for popular election of United States senators and other reforms. In 1897 she founded a colony for women called 'Adamless Eden.'

The U.S.MILITARY RESERVATION (*open 6–6 daily; cameras permitted*), E. side of the Oswego River, with main entrance on 7th St., is garrisoned by the Third Battalion of the 28th U.S.Infantry and is the scene of the National Guard artillery maneuvers in the summer.

Within the reservation is old FORT ONTARIO, pentagonal in shape, with fronts facing the lake, the river, and the land. Its long history goes back to 1755. The present battalion post was laid out in 1903–5. During the World War the fort was used as a base hospital.

The U.S.COAST GUARD STATION (*open 1–5 weekdays, 8–5 Sun., holidays, and Navy Day*), on the lake shore at the foot of E.2d St., is a two-story white frame building housing a captain and a crew of 16. The Coast Guard cutter *Forward* is used for patrol duty.

The PONTIAC BOULDER, W.1st and Oneida Sts., marks the site of the council held between Sir William Johnson and Chief Pontiac in 1766, as a result of which Great Britain came into full possession of the Great Lakes basin. Addressing Sir William on the second day, Pontiac said: 'I speak in the name of all the nations to the westward, of whom I am the master. It is the will of the Great Spirit that we should meet here today; and before him I now take you by the hand. . . . Father, this belt is to cover and strengthen our chain of friendship, and to show you that, if any nation shall lift the hatchet against our English brethren, we shall be the first to feel it and resent it.'

OSWEGO HARBOR, foot of W.1st St., is the most easterly U.S. lake port with canal and rail connections to the Atlantic seaboard. An arrowhead of two Government-constructed breakwaters allows the largest lake vessels to dock without the aid of tugs. The port facilities include the New York State grain elevator with a storage capacity of 1,000,000 bushels and a freight warehouse with a floor space of 12,000 square feet. In the inner harbor is the northern terminus of the Barge Canal. The terminal lock is the only one on the siphon principle; it was modeled after the terminal lock of the Kiel Canal, Germany.

The COOPER HOUSE (*private*), 24 W.2d St., a small frame structure, was the home of James Fenimore Cooper in 1808–9 when he was a midshipman stationed in Oswego. The scene of his novel *The Pathfinder* is laid in the Oswego River Valley.

The OSWEGO STATE NORMAL SCHOOL, George Washington Blvd. near the city line, consists of two Georgian Colonial brick buildings. The student body numbers 500. At the entrance to the campus is a bronze STATUE OF EDWARD AUSTIN SHELDON (1823–97), whose efforts resulted in the opening of the first free school, called the 'ragged school,' in Oswego in 1848. In 1861 he founded the Oswego Primary Training School, which became the State Normal School in 1866, and headed it from 1869 until his death.

In Oswego is the junction with State 57.

Left on State 57, along the canalized Oswego River, to (R) BATTLE ISLAND, 6.7 *m.*, a State historical reservation, where on July 3, 1758, Colonel John Bradstreet repulsed an attempted ambuscade by French and Indians. According to legend, PATHFINDER ISLAND (R), 8.1 *m.*, is the locale of the fight between Natty Bumppo, hero of James Fenimore Cooper's *The Pathfinder*, and the Iroquois.

FULTON, 11.4 *m.* (400 alt.,13,337 pop.), ships milk and fruit and makes woolen goods, candy, paper containers, food products, ventilators, and linoleum felts. Settlement began because it was necessary to unload cargoes here and haul them in oxcarts around two falls in the river.

In the AMERICAN WOOLEN MILLS (*open*), W.Broadway and W.First St., giant machines tended by a few operators spin and weave yarn into cloth of intricate patterns.

The SEAL-RIGHT PLANT, 314 S.First Ave., grinds wood into pulp, rolls the pulp into cardboard, and shapes the cardboard into containers.

In Fulton is the junction with State 3 (*see Tour 17*).

In the 1920's, water from the natural spring on GREAT BEAR FARM (L), 16 *m.*, was bottled and shipped in large quantities all over the country; it is still bottled, though on a much smaller scale.

At THREE RIVER POINT, 22.6 *m.* (380 alt.,50 pop.), the Oneida and Seneca Rivers unite to form the Oswego River. The Jesuits; Champlain, Frontenac, and Montcalm; the British redcoats marching between the forts at Oswego and Stanwix; Walter Butler and Joseph Brant—all followed this natural water route, as well as many early settlers of western New York. Today the Barge Canal uses the dredged and locked river to Lake Ontario, to complete the shortest all-water route between the Atlantic and the Great Lakes.

At 24.4 *m.* is the junction with State 31 (*see Tour 32*).

LIVERPOOL, 31.6 *m.* (380 alt.,2,244 pop.), makes airplane and small delivery truck motors. Proximity of the famous Onondaga salt springs made it a nineteenth-century salt-producing center. About 1850 John Fischer, a German basket weaver, imported willow shoots and started the willow-weaving industry that was identified with Liverpool for 70 years. In its heyday 1,500,000 pieces of basketware and willow furniture were produced annually and tons of green willow were shipped to distant factories. As furniture styles changed and commercial laundries eliminated the clothes basket, the market waned. Much of the furniture made 25 years ago is still in use; 'I guess,' says an old German weaver, 'we made that willow furniture so good we worked ourselves out of a job.' Today about 20 old craftsmen eke out an existence at the trade.

The ONONDAGA PARKWAY DEVELOPMENT, 31.7 *m.*, follows the bed of the old Oswego Canal along the eastern shore of Onondaga Lake to Syracuse.

At 31.8 *m.* is the junction with Lakeshore Drive; right here through the Parkway 0.2 *m.* to the SALT MUSEUM (*open* 9–7 *daily*), built around the last remaining vat house and chimney of the State-owned salt reservation, and containing more than 100 items illustrating old salt-making machinery and several hundred photographs of the salt fields in their boom days. At 1.3 *m.* is (R) the reputed site of the founding of the Iroquois Confederacy under the leadership of Hiawatha and Dekanawidah.

On State 57 (L), FORT SAINTE MARIE DE GENNENTAH (*open* 9–7 *daily*), 32.3 *m.*, is a reproduction of the stockade erected to protect the 50 French colonists who attempted a settlement here in 1656. The exterior is of unfinished logs, the interior of rough-hewn boards; the furniture is reproduced. The exhibits include French, Indian, and Colonial relics.

The JESUIT WELL (L), 32.6 *m.*, is the traditional site of the salt spring visited in 1654 by Father Simon Le Moyne, Jesuit missionary to the Onondaga. He boiled some of the water down and took samples back to Quebec with him. Out of this beginning grew the salt industry that gave the city of Syracuse its start.

The DANFORTH SALT POOL (R), 33.3 *m.*, 700 feet long, is fed by natural springs. Stone for the adjoining bathhouse (*lockers* 10¢) was taken from the Geddes salt pumphouse, built more than 75 years ago at the height of the salt industry.

The southern entrance to the parkway development, 33.8 *m.*, at the northern Syracuse city line, is marked by two stone piers ornamented by illuminated panels depicting in silhouette scenes of the old Erie Canal and the salt manufacturing era of the Onondaga region.

SYRACUSE, 36.5 *m.* (400 alt.,205,637 pop.) (*see Syracuse*), is at the junction with State 5 (*see Tour 11*) and US 11 (*see Tour 18*).

HANNIBAL, 31.1 *m.* (330 alt.,410 pop.), a fruit-growing and dairy hamlet, is at the junction with State 3 (*see Tour 17*).

At 41.1 *m.*, is the junction with State 104A.

Right on State 104A to a junction with an unmarked road, 5.6 *m.*; left here to FAIRHAVEN BEACH STATE PARK, 1.8 *m.* (*picnicking, bathing*), 600 acres with large pine groves. Just west of the park property is a Federal lighthouse and pier.

West of WOLCOTT, 47.3 *m.* (378 alt.,1,324 pop.), US 104 enters the great Ontario fruit belt. Apples are the most important crop, but here and there is an orchard of pear, peach, or cherry trees. The sour cherries are picked early in July. Men, women, and children work in the orchards, living during the picking season in barns or any makeshift shelter they can find or erect. An adult worker averages between 300 and 400 pounds a day, for which he is paid about ¾¢ a pound. Cherries are picked stemless for the canneries, and workers must be careful not to break off the fruit spurs, from which next season's crop will grow.

Larger orchard fruits—pears, peaches, and apples—requiring the use of heavy ladders and greater skill in picking, are harvested exclusively by men. Peaches are picked in early August and apples in October. Expert pickers follow the harvest, earning from $3 to $4.50 a day. Usually a large part of the earnings is held up until the job is finished to prevent the workers from moving on.

Canneries, large and small, are in the villages along the route. Apples are peeled and cored by machine, cut by white-uniformed women into eighths or quarters, and steamed five to seven minutes. They are canned and the sealed can is left in boiling water 20 to 25 minutes. Pears, which used to be prepared in the canneries by hand, are now peeled, cored, and halved by machine. Peaches are left in a lye solution a few seconds to loosen the skin. They are split in half and the pit is removed with a special spoon.

RESORT, 53.4 *m.* (260 alt.,87 pop.), is a summer colony at the head of the east shore of Sodus Bay and the starting point for fishing expeditions on Lake Ontario. In August and September the bay is covered by large beds of American lotus, whose huge waxy white blossoms, almost six inches in diameter, rise two feet above the broad green pads on the surface of the water. The bed, one of the few of its kind in the country, is under the protection of the State Conservation Department. It is not known how the plants came here.

ALTON, 56.3 *m.* (380 alt.,350 pop.), is at the junction with State 14 (*see Tour 27*).

SODUS, 61.2 *m.* (475 alt.,1,513 pop.), is a pleasant village with comfortable old homes. Here as in several other places in western New York, the raising of silkworms was attempted in the 1830's. Large buildings were erected to house the worms and mulberry trees were planted to supply their food. In 1838 a newspaper declared that the manufacture of silk was 'as simple as feeding pigs and very easy to perform: one in which small children could be made useful, and also decayed widows and decrepit females. . . .' The attempt failed because the mulberry trees could not withstand the severe winters.

WILLIAMSON, 64.8 *m.* (452 alt.,1,000 pop.), is at the junction with State 21 (*see Tour 29*).

Reeds which flourish in the marshes of IRONDEQUOIT BAY, 88.2 *m.*, are harvested from early fall to early spring. Butt cutters ride in flat-bottomed boats and cut the reeds with sharp butt knives. The glue which forms within the stalks of the reeds is used to seal hogsheads against moisture leaks.

ROCHESTER, 93.2 *m.* (500 alt.,324,694 pop.) (*see Rochester*), is at the junction with State 2 (*see Tour 30*), US 15 (*see Tour 31*), and State 33 (*see Tour 33*).

Section b. ROCHESTER to NIAGARA FALLS; 82.3 m. US 104

West of ROCHESTER, 0 *m.*, US 104 continues through the fruit belt of western New York. This section of the road is called the Honeymoon Trail, because of the many honeymooners that travel it to Niagara Falls.

In CLARKSON, 15.8 *m.* (427 alt.,307 pop.), is the two-story brick SELDEN HOME (*private*), the birthplace of George B. Selden (1846–1922), called the 'father of the automobile.' In 1872, possessed with the idea of a 'horseless carriage,' Selden gave up the practice of law and constructed small engines to be propelled by steam, by ammonia gas, and by bisulphite of carbon. The following year he discarded the idea of steam for power, devoting his experiments to an internal combustion engine. In 1877 he made his first successful experiment with a 'lightweight, high-speed, three-cylinder gasoline compression engine.' Granted a patent in 1895, Selden received a royalty on all automobiles made until Henry Ford broke his monopoly in 1903.

In the center of CHILDS, 30.1 *m.* (425 alt.,75 pop.), is the COBBLE-STONE CHURCH, erected by the First Universalist Society in 1834. Three of the houses are also made of cobblestones. The principal cost in cobblestone construction was labor; the water-worn stone were found in glacial drift, remnants of the Ice Age. The stones were graded for size through holes bored in a plank. The builder laid one row of cobblestones, and while it dried went on to work on another house; sometimes the stones were laid in alternate rows of large and small, sometimes in herringbone pattern.

The apple-growing hamlet of GAINES, 31.3 *m.* (426 alt.,130 pop.), is named for General E.P.Gaines, who during the War of 1812 held Fort Erie for nine days against the siege of Drummond's British troops.

It is related that one of the pioneer settlers hired an old sailor, whose first assignment was to 'hitch up that span of oxen and the horse and go out and snake some logs.' Unaccustomed to land navigation, the elderly gob soon returned to the farmhouse, waving his arms and yelling: 'Pipe all hands! The larboard ox is on the starboard side, old Jan's in the riggin', an' the hull things goin' to hell starn foremost!'

At 56.7 *m.* is the junction with State 78 (*see Tour 36*).

At 74.2 *m.* the road skirts the northwestern edge of the TUSCARORA INDIAN RESERVATION, where about 400 members of the tribe till the the soil. The reservation contains 6,294 acres, acquired partly by treaty and partly by gift from the Holland Land Company and from the Seneca Nation. Two creeks and extensive woodland provide fishing and small game hunting.

None but Indians can buy or lease the land; among themselves, however, land sales are made. As a result, some of the more industrious and thrifty have acquired farms of from 200 to 300 acres, while the poorer ones have little or no land. The annual allotment by the Federal Government of a few yards of cotton cloth is the birthright of every Tuscaroran, secured by an early treaty. The Indians value highly their little red tickets which enable them to cross the United States-Canadian border as often as they wish without being molested by customs and immigration officials. This right also is based on an old treaty.

The reservation contains a community house, a church, and a school; the State furnishes hospital care and the services of a visiting supervisor. In all ordinary matters on the reservation the Indians are governed by their own councils, in accordance with old tribal laws.

LEWISTON, 75.6 m. (363 alt.,1,282 pop.), straggles along the Niagara River at the foot of a steep bluff. According to geologists, this was the site of Niagara Falls some 35,000 years ago. From a hill at the southern extremity is a view of the village, the lake plains, and the river to the point where it empties into Lake Ontario.

In 1626 a Franciscan missionary found here a settlement of the Attawandaronk or Neuter Indians. Twenty-five years later the village was destroyed by the Seneca. In 1678 René Robert Cavelier de La Salle and his men built a storehouse here and completed to the upper Niagara a portage trail which was used for a century and a half. Settlement did not begin until after the English troops surrendered Fort Niagara (*see below*) in 1796. The frontier village, named after Governor Morgan Lewis, was captured and burned by the British in 1813, but was rebuilt immediately.

The FIRST PRESBYTERIAN CHURCH, two blocks S. of Center St., a stuccoed stone structure with pointed arch windows and doors, was begun in 1817. The portico with its four Doric columns and the belfry are later Greek Revival additions.

The FRONTIER HOUSE, Center St., a large, gray stone three-story building, was erected in 1824; the porch was added in the late 1830's. Here, according to tradition, James Fenimore Cooper wrote *The Spy*. William Morgan (*see Tour 11*), who planned to publish secrets of the Masonic order, was seen by non-Masons for the last time at this inn on September 13, 1826.

In Lewiston is the junction with State 18.

Right on State 18 through YOUNGSTOWN, 6 m. (290 alt.,794 pop.), to FORT NIAGARA, 7 m. (*open 9–9 daily in summer, 9–5 other seasons; 25¢*). This 'patriotic shrine of four nations' overlooks Lake Ontario at the mouth of the Niagara River. Its situation at the mouth of the Niagara River, commanding the Great Lakes route, made the fort of strategic value during the entire Colonial period and on through the Revolution and the War of 1812. The first fort on the site was built by La Salle in 1678 and called by him Fort Conti. It was rebuilt as Fort Denonville by the French governor general of that name. Again rebuilt in 1725–6 by Chaussagras de Lery and named Fort Niagara, it was enlarged in 1756–7 by Captain François Pouchot; much of Pouchot's work still remains. In 1759 it was captured for the British by Sir William Johnson and held by them until it was taken over by the United States in 1796. During the War of 1812 the British recaptured the fort, but it was restored to the United States by the Treaty of Ghent in 1815.

Restoration was completed in 1934 at a cost of about $600,000, contributed by the Federal Government, the State of New York, Erie County, and the Old Fort Niagara Association. Plans in the Colonial archives of the French War Department were followed. A drawbridge, hoisted with the weight of large rocks, leads to the gatehouse with the French coat-of-arms. Immediately inside the entrance is a massive stone blockhouse with the English coat-of-arms. An underground passage of arched masonry, lighted with the original lanterns, leads to another blockhouse at the outer barrier of the fort.

In the center of the parade ground fly three flags: the American flag of 1796, with 15 stars and bars; the English Union Jack; and French fleur-de-lis of 1759. To the right stands a wooden cross, emblematic of the cross erected in 1688 by Father Jean Millet, Jesuit missionary. Here also is a Lombardy poplar planted by the French perhaps as early as 1669. Near by is a monument commemorating the Rush-Bagot Treaty of 1817, which defined the boundary between the United States and Canada and provided that the boundary remain forever unfortified.

The CASTLE, in the northwest corner of the fort, is an imposing two-story structure erected by the French in 1725-6 in the guise of a provincial manor house to deceive the Indians as to its real purpose. The walls were built four feet thick to absorb the material sway caused by the firing of cannon. The original building was enlarged by the British. The massive oak doors at the entrance, weighing 1,500 pounds, are so well balanced that a child can open them. The chapel, on the first floor, with altar, font, and statues, was restored in 1931. On the second floor are the gun ports with heavy shutters and the officers' quarters. The great hall was the council room in which Sir William Johnson signed the treaty of 1764 with the Indians. During the Revolution the building served as headquarters of Butler's Rangers and Britain's Indian allies; and the hall is said to have been piled with American scalps, for which the British offered a bounty of $8 apiece.

Thirty feet from the Castle is the Poisoned Well, 'whose water was poisoned by some demon in human form.' It was a story with the soldiers, believed by many, that at midnight the headless trunk of a French general was often seen sitting on the curb of the old well where he had been murdered and his body thrown into it. Credence was given the legend when the Americans, after taking possession of the fort, found the bones of a large-framed man and some military ornaments at the bottom of the well.

Adjoining the Castle is the Bake Shop, originally built by the French, and reconstructed by the British in 1759. The kitchen still contains the old wooden trough in which the dough was mixed.

NIAGARA UNIVERSITY (L), 79.8 m. comprises a group of tall, gray, rough stone buildings. It was founded in 1856 as Our Lady of Angels Seminary and was chartered as a liberal arts institution in 1883. One of the best known Roman Catholic colleges in the East, it has an average enrollment of more than 1,000; the faculty numbers 75. Women are admitted only for graduate work. The university maintains a center in Rochester where extramural courses are given, mainly in finance and accounting.

DEVIL'S HOLE STATE PARK (R), 80.2 m., encompasses the area adjoining the Niagara Gorge and the cavern gouged in the soft layers of rock at the water level of the river. The State has constructed picnic sites and lookout spots, which offer views of the lower rapids and of the gorge up the river toward the Whirlpool and down toward Queenston Heights.

One Indian legend has it that the cavern was the home of the Evil Spirit. According to another legend, the French explorer La Salle entered the cavern in 1679 and heard a mysterious Indian voice prophesy his death years later on the Mississippi. On September 14, 1763, John Stedman, the keeper of the portage, with 24 men and a wagon train was ambushed at Devil's Hole by a band of Seneca Indians. From the massacre which followed, only Stedman and one or two of his men escaped. Two companies of British soldiers stationed at Lewiston hastened to Stedman's relief only to fall into another ambush. Sixty-five soldiers were killed and eight or nine wounded.

NIAGARA FALLS, 82.3 m. (575 alt.,77,374 pop.) (see Niagara Falls), is at the junction with State 31 (see Tour 32) and US 62 (see Tour 37).

Tour 27

Sodus Point—Geneva—Watkins Glen—Elmira—(Troy, Pa.); State 14.
Sodus Point to Pennsylvania Line, 96.4 *m.*

Two-lane concrete with stretches of macadam.
The New York Central R.R. parallels route between Lyons and Watkins Glen; Pennsylvania R.R. between Starkey and Pennsylvania line.

A north-south route, State 14 crosses the Ontario fruit belt, runs up the west shore of 36-mile-long Seneca Lake, passes through Watkins Glen with its salt mines and scenic attractions and Montour Falls with its story of 'Queen' Catherine, and traverses a rolling countryside of dairy farms to Elmira and the Pennsylvania line.

Section a. *SODUS POINT to GENEVA;* 30.4 *m.* State 14

The Lake Ontario plain is an important fruit-growing area; rows of cherry and peach trees dip into the valleys and run over the rounded drumlins. Through this region the route cuts across the closely parallel main east-west routes across the State.

SODUS POINT (*bathing, boating, picnicking*) 0 *m.* (224 alt.,525 pop.), is a popular summer resort on Sodus Bay. On June 19, 1813, Sir James Yeo, War of 1812 commander of the British fleet on Lake Ontario, descended upon Sodus Point and landed a looting party, which overcame the defenders and burned every building but one.

The ALASA FARM (*open*), 3.7 *m.*, specializes in breeding shorthorn cattle. Its 1,600 acres were settled in 1823 by a colony of Shakers who erected large buildings and cultivated broad orchards and gardens; after 13 years they sold the land to a company interested in a proposed Sodus Canal to join Lake Ontario and the Erie Canal. The project fell through, and about 1844 the land was taken over by a group of Fourierists who pooled their property and joined together for pleasure and action in the harmony of a phalanx. But complaints against individual members and demands for the return of private property raised dissension and disrupted the phalanx within two years.

ALTON, 5.3 *m.* (380 alt.,350 pop.) (*see Tour* 26), is at the junction with US 104 (*see Tour* 26).

LYONS, 15.7 *m.* (420 alt.,3,838 pop.) (*see Tour* 32), is at the junction with State 31 (*see Tour* 32).

WEST JUNIUS (Five Points), 24.2 *m.* (490 alt.,170 pop.) (*see Tour* 30), is at the junction with State 2 (*see Tour* 30).

GENEVA, 30.4 *m.* (460 alt.,15,543 pop.) (*see Tour* 8), is at the junction with US 20 (*see Tour* 8).

Section b. *GENEVA to The PENNSYLVANIA LINE;* 66 *m.* State 14

For 36 miles the route runs along the western shore of Seneca Lake, touching the fringes of the few shore villages. The scenery is typical of the

Finger Lakes region: a long, gently curving body of water—normally placid but whipping up into whitecaps under rising winds—banked by low, sweeping hills, the unbroken slopes patched with vineyards, orchards, and hay fields rising to woodlots against the horizon. Toward the head of the lake rushing streams have cut narrow gorges in the rock that reach a climax of size and beauty in Watkins Glen.

South of GENEVA, 0 *m.*, State 14 follows the shore line of SENECA LAKE (L); its deep waters, fed by springs, have frozen over but four times in the memory of man. On summer nights the submarine rumbles of the mysterious 'lake guns' echo along the shores; to the Indians they were supernatural war drums calling them to the warpath; geologists believe them to be the poppings of natural gas released from rock rifts on the lake bottom. The largest outboard regatta in the East is held off Geneva every summer.

At 13.2 *m.* is the junction with State 54 (*see Tour* 28).

In LAKEMONT, 25.6 *m.* (840 alt.,200 pop.), is the LAKEMONT ACADEMY. Founded in 1842 as Starkey Seminary, it was reopened in 1939, after three years of inactivity, as a college preparatory school for boys, modeled after the English public schools.

At 33.2 *m.* is the junction with a macadam road.

Left on this road 0.5 *m.* to the INTERNATIONAL SALT PLANT (*open* 9–12, 1–4 *Mon.–Fri.*), an interconnected group of one- to four-story structures at the water's edge, with derricks rising up the hillsides marking the salt wells that average 1,800 feet in depth. Water is pumped into the wells, where it is saturated with salt; this brine is raised to the surface and the salt is extracted by evaporation.

This plant and the Watkins Salt Plant about 1.5 miles east of Watkins Glen, with a combined output of 170,000 tons a year, most of it table salt, make this area one of the State's leading salt producers.

Salt works, health springs, a lake front, a picturesque glen, and a rich agricultural back country make WATKINS GLEN, 36.1 *m.* (477 alt., 2,906 pop.), at the head of Seneca Lake, a combination farm shopping, industrial, and tourist center and spa.

WATKINS GLEN STATE PARK (*swimming, picnicking*), entrances on Franklin St. and county road at head of glen (*parking 25¢ for longer than* 10 *min., taxi between lower and upper entrances* 35¢), is the leading tourist attraction of the village. The Gorge Trail, with 700 steps and numerous bridges, enters the glen beyond the parking space through a tunnel, crosses and recrosses the twisted formations made by the stream in the rock, and reaches the head of the gorge 1.5 miles from the start and 600 feet higher.

The glen made the headlines in August 1934 when a newspaper correspondent discovered a deer marooned on an inaccessible ledge. During the Labor Day week-end 350,000 people came to see the stranded deer. A bridge was built across the gorge, but the deer refused to budge; a reservation Indian tried his deer lore on it for three days but with no avail; an elk head, borrowed from the local Elks, was set up near by, but again without result. One night the deer somehow scrambled down the sheer rock and escaped over the top of the gorge.

The nationally-known GLEN SPRINGS HEALTH RESORT HOTEL, Glen Ave., stands 300 feet above the lake with a view of a 30-mile sweep of water and hillsides. The water of the mineral springs, used on a wide scale in the treatment of disease, is similar in analysis to the waters of Bad Nauheim, Germany, but about five times as strong.

South of Seneca Lake State 14 follows Catherine Creek through narrow, winding Pine Valley. Markers trace the route of the Sullivan-Clinton expedition of 1779.

Within a short walk of MONTOUR FALLS, 39.5 *m.* (480 alt.,1,341 pop.), are seven glens, each with a distinctive claim to beauty in cascades, caverns, waterfalls, amphitheaters, and high and angular cliffs. The chief industry in the village is the Shepard-Niles Crane and Hoist Company, established in 1880, manufacturing electric hoists with lifting capacities ranging from a ton to 250 tons. David B. Hill (1843–1910), State governor, 1885–92, was born here.

The village occupies the site of Catherine's Town, a Seneca village of about 40 well-built houses, some of them with chimneys and glazed windows, which was destroyed by Sullivan's expedition. The white settlement on the site was named Havana in 1829; in the 1890's the name was changed to Montour Falls in honor of Queen Catherine Montour, said to have been the granddaughter of Count Frontenac, French governor of Canada, by an Indian woman. Catherine, 'a handsome woman of polite address who spoke French fluently,' married a Seneca chief, and after her husband's death ruled the village wisely.

Conspicuous in the village is SHEQUAGA (Ind., tumbling waters) FALLS, a 156-foot waterfall of exceptional beauty, which at first sight seems to drop right into the main street; the water plunges into a rip-rapped pool and flows off into Catherine Creek. On a visit to the place Louis Philippe, later Louis XVII of France, was so struck by the grandeur of the scene that he made a sketch of it which now hangs in the Louvre.

HORSEHEADS, 53.3 *m.* (903 alt.,2,430 pop.), within the metropolitan area of Elmira, manufactures bricks and optical goods. Known earlier as Fairport, in 1845 the place was named Horseheads, commemorating an incident in the Revolution that occurred here; General Sullivan's men slew their worn-out and starving horses for food and left the heads for carrion.

At 54.3 *m.* is the junction with State 17 (*see Tour 3*), with which State 14 runs in common to ELMIRA, 58.8 *m.* (860 alt.,45,046 pop.) (*see Elmira*).

At 66 *m.* State 14 crosses the PENNSYLVANIA LINE, 17 miles north of Troy, Pennsylvania.

Tour 28

Junction with State 14—Penn Yan—Hammondsport—Bath; 34.4 *m*. State 54.

Two-lane concrete or macadam.
New York Central R.R. parallels road between Dresden and Bath.

Swinging over the hills from Seneca Lake, State 54 joins the two long arms of Keuka Lake, curves down its west shore, and runs on through Pleasant Valley to Bath. All along the route, on the valley floors and over the hilltops, are patches of vineyards; the principal varieties of grapes grown are Catawbas, Isabellas, Ives, Delawares, Dianas, Elviras, and Ionas. The high natural sugar content of local grapes makes them among the best in the world for wine. In the villages and along the road are the wineries, their cellars pushing into the hillsides, though low temperatures are now in most cases maintained by air conditioning. On Labor Day their representatives meet with the growers to arrange the annual 'grape deal' —that is, to fix the prices for the year's crop. A few weeks later picking begins.

West of the junction with State 14, 0 *m*. (*see Tour 27*), State 54 passes through a region of tumbling hills checkered with vineyards.

PENN YAN, 5 *m*. (767 alt.,5,273 pop.), is guarded on three sides by hills and on the fourth faces the long eastern arm of Keuka Lake. The village wineries, canneries, and mills process and market the grapes, grain, fruits, and vegetables of the countryside, and small factories make grape baskets, boats, store fixtures, and bus bodies. A large tourist trade provides an additional source of income. Controversy between the settlers from Pennsylvania and New England over a name for the place was compromised by combining the first syllables of Pennsylvania and Yankee.

Southwest of Penn Yan the road hugs the eastern arm (L) of Y-shaped KEUKA LAKE (*bathing, boating, fishing*), the only one of the Finger Lakes with an irregular outline. Its waters flow from the main inlet at the base of the Y into one of its branches, and out again around a dividing bluff to its outlet at the tip of the other branch.

At 9.3 *m*. is the junction with the Keuka road and the Bluff Point road.

1. Sharp left on the Keuka road, 0.6 *m*. to KEUKA PARK, home of KEUKA COLLEGE (*swimming, fishing, tennis*). The campus has a half-mile lake front and the adjoining college farm rises up the vine-clad hillsides. First incorporated in 1888, Keuka has been a chartered college for women since 1924; the student body numbers about 200.

2. Left on the macadam Bluff Point road, along the ridge which separates the two arms of the lake, to the GARRETT MEMORIAL CHAPEL (L), 5 *m*., called 'the little chapel on the mount.' It is a memorial erected by his parents to Charles Garrett, who begged to be taken back to Bluff Point before his death from tuberculosis in 1930. The building is of seam-faced granite in the Gothic style; the sculptured ornaments and stained glass windows symbolize the interests and aspirations of childhood and youth. The view from BLUFF POINT, 7 *m*., embraces the main body of Keuka Lake stretching south from where it splits into its east and west arms.

In BRANCHPORT, 12.6 *m.* (740 alt.,300 pop.), is the junction with State 273.

Right on this road 4.1 *m.* to an uphill dirt road; left here to the FRIEND'S HOME (R) 0.3 *m.*, a large white clapboard frame house built about 1790. This was the home of Jemima Wilkinson, the Universal Friend. On an upper floor was her boudoir, elaborately furnished with her elegant mirror—the monogram 'U.F.' carved in the frame, her medicine case of wood inlay, her silver salver, her warming pan, and her perfume bottles. On the first floor she held religious meetings, appearing in a silk purple robe over a fine white muslin dress and a man's shirt and cravat bordered with lace, so that her costume was 'made to correspond neither with that of a man nor a woman'; her black eyes were brilliant, and her dark hair hung in curls over her shoulders. Her sermons were long and almost unintelligible, delivered in the illiterate speech of the New England back country. But her followers were devoted to her, performing menial tasks and parting with their possessions at her word that 'The Lord hath need of this.'

Jemima Wilkinson (1758–1819) was born the daughter of a respectable Rhode Island farmer. Aroused by the highly emotional revivals of the New Light Baptists, and probably in imitation of Mother Ann Lee of the Shakers, at the age of about 20, arising from a severe attack of fever she asserted that she had been dead, her carnal existence had ended, her body had been reanimated by the Divine Spirit, and she had returned as the 'Public Universal Friend' to warn sinners to flee from the wrath to come. For several years she preached in New England and gathered converts, among them well-to-do citizens, preaching celibacy and breaking up families by setting loyalty to sect above loyalty to spouse or parents. When opposition arose there, and later in Pennsylvania, she sent her followers to prepare a home for her in the wilderness. They settled in 1788 on the west shore of Seneca Lake.

As the tide of migration caught up with the settlement, the young people broke away to marry and live like their neighbors; her grasping after her followers' property alienated many; as she grew older her beauty faded and she lost her magnetic pull. After she 'left time' in 1819, the sect rapidly disintegrated. Descendants of the Jemimakins live in the country roundabout.

On KEUKA LAKE, opposite the highway at about 23.5 *m.*, on March 12, 1908, one of the world's first flying machines was carefully set up on the ice. Its official name was Drome No.1, but its familiar name was Red Wing, because its two long kitelike wings were covered with red silk. A 24-horsepower, eight-cylinder motorcycle motor, built by Glenn Curtiss in his Hammondsport shop, was installed between these flimsy wings. Casey Baldwin, John McCurdy, and Glenn Curtiss drew lots to see who would pilot the craft. Dr.Alexander Graham Bell, who had helped to design the 'aerodrome,' was not present, having been forced to leave Hammondsport because of his wife's illness. Casey Baldwin won the drawing and climbed into the pilot's seat. His assistants cranked the motor. Baldwin yelled 'Let go!' The Red Wing skimmed along on its runners for 250 feet, rose into the air six or eight feet, flew 318 feet and 11 inches, then crashed. Baldwin crawled out of the wreckage with a few bruises.

HAMMONDSPORT, 26.8 *m.* (718 alt.,1,102 pop.), at the head of Keuka Lake, is a center of the New York State champagne industry. In the early 1900's it was the aviation center of the Nation and it is proud of the title, 'Cradle of American Aviation.'

Glenn Hammond Curtiss was born here in 1878. As a builder of motors, he was sought out by Dr.Alexander Graham Bell to build a motor for a kite. Bell, Curtiss, Lieutenant Thomas Selfridge of the U.S.Army, and others began their work of building 'a practical aerodrome driven by its own motive power and carrying a man' (*see above*). On July 4, 1908, on Stony Brook Farm (*see below*), Curtiss flew the *June Bug* 2,000 yards. In 1910 he flew an airplane from Albany to New York, with two stops. In 1917 he joined with John N. Willis, automobile manufacturer, to supply airplanes for the World War. Later he designed and manufactured the *Wasp*, which established records for speed, climbing, and altitude.

At STONY BROOK FARM (L), 28.3 *m.*, in the spring of 1908, Dr.Bell, Glenn Curtiss, Lieutenant Selfridge, and their associates assembled their second 'aerodrome,' called *White Wings*, and lodged it in a circus tent attached to the side of the barn. Selfridge took off for the first time, hopped a fence, and landed with slight damage to the machine. Later Curtiss flew 1,000 feet and landed in a plowed field.

On July 4 all Hammondsport as well as citizens of near-by towns gathered at the race track on Stony Brook Farm to witness a great test. About 30 visitors came from New York City, including representatives of the Aero Club of America. The *Scientific American* had offered a silver trophy valued at $2,500 for the first flight of one kilometer (3,280 feet) by a heavier-than-air machine propelled by its own power. The new aerodrome, *June Bug*, which the group had built, was hauled out of its tent. Curtiss took the pilot's seat. On the first trial the machine stopped before it reached the line marked as the starting point. The wind was not right. At 7:30, just before sundown, a second attempt was made. This time the plane rose slowly to a height of 20 feet, crossed the finish line, banked to a half turn and landed safely. The crowd had followed, running and yelling. The official distance was 5,090 feet.

Clinging to the slope of the steep hill (L), the PLEASANT VALLEY WINERY (*open*), 29.6 *m.*, holder of U.S.winery license No.1, is one of the oldest champagne cellars in the United States. In 1860, C.B.Champlin, who had emigrated from France, organized the company and built the dank cellars running back under the hill; a head wine maker was brought from Rheims, France—his descendants still live in the valley—and the production of champagne from local grapes was begun. Today more than 3,000,000 bottles of champagne are being aged in these cellars.

After being sorted and cleaned, the grapes are dumped into giant evaporation casks; six months later the juice, called 'must,' is poured into 4,800-gallon aging casks in which fermentation goes on for two years, controlled by low temperature and the addition of yeast. Then a blend, or *cuvée*, is made of six or seven different grape wines according to a secret formula; rock candy for sweetening and a selected champagne yeast for fermentation are added; and the mixture is bottled in heavy champagne bottles, which are corked and placed neck downward in tiers of racks at a temperature of 50 degrees. During the second fermentation the carbonic acid is imprisoned in the bottles, giving champagne its sparkle; the pressure is so great that some of the bottles blow up. Twice a day, for six weeks or more, a worker lifts each bottle, shakes it slightly, and replaces it—this to force the sediment to settle on the cork. After fermentation is completed, the bottlenecks are inserted in brine to freeze about an inch of wine at the cork. Then the cork and the piece of ice, containing the sediment, are removed, a spoonful of syrup is injected slowly, a Spanish cork is mushroomed down the bottle mouth, and the champagne is ready for storage until used.

The COLD SPRINGS STATE FISH HATCHERY (*open*), 31.2 *m.*, raises fingerlings to stock the many trout streams of the State; the water is taken from an artesian well.

BATH, 34.4 *m.* (1,104 alt.,4,656 pop.), is at the junction with US 15 (*see Tour* 31).

Tour 29

Pultneyville—Naples—Hornell—(Knoxville, Pa.); State 21.
Pultneyville to Pennsylvania Line, 117.5 *m.*

Two-lane concrete or macadam.
The New York Central R.R. parallels route between Shortsville and Canandaigua; Delaware, Lackawanna & Western between North Cohocton and Wayland; the Erie between Hornell and Canisteo.

State 21 goes through fruit orchards, vineyards, and potato fields, and passes monuments of two nineteenth-century movements characteristic of central New York: Mormonism and the Underground Railroad.

Section a. PULTNEYVILLE to WAYLAND; 67.1 *m. State* 21

North of Canandaigua Lake is a fruit-growing region: west of the lake are the Bristol Hills, the most rugged part of central New York, with a sparse population of hill folk; and south of the lake is an important grape and wine district.

PULTNEYVILLE, 0 *m.* (274 alt.,257 pop.), an L-shaped, single-street village with a beach on Lake Ontario, was a hotbed of abolitionism and a terminus of the Underground Railroad; here the runaway slaves were smuggled under hatches across Lake Ontario to Canada and freedom. The local tradition is that while waiting for a boat the Negroes were concealed in large woodpiles on the docks from which the boats loaded their fuel; hence the expression 'a nigger in the woodpile.'

South of Pultneyville tall horse chestnut trees border the highway; of all trees native to New York State these have the most beautiful blossoms, white and upright like candles on a Christmas tree; but unfortunately the blossoms last only for about a week in the middle of May.

WILLIAMSON, 4.2 *m.* (452 alt.,1,000 pop.), is at the junction with US 104 (*see Tour* 26).

PALMYRA, 17.8 *m.* (470 alt.,2,706 pop.), is at the junction with State 31 (*see Tour* 32).

At 20.5 *m.* is the junction with a macadam road.

Right on this road 2 *m.* to the JOSEPH SMITH FARM (R and L), owned by the Mormon Church. The front portion of the frame clapboard farmhouse was occupied by the Smith family; the four rear rooms are a later addition. In the southeast bedroom Smith is said to have had the vision which led to the founding of Mormonism. In the house are a table and a chair made by Brigham Young and a number of antiques of the period of Smith's residence.

Joseph Smith (1805–44), born in Vermont, lived on this farm or in the vicinity from his tenth to his twenty-first year; he is described as a blue-eyed blonde with small hands and large feet, 'quiet, low-speaking, unlaughing.' The frontier climate was supercharged with religion: Methodists and Baptists held revivals, individuals enjoyed revelations and visitations, and new sects were organized around dominant personalities. In 1823 the Angel Moroni, son of Mormon, appeared to Joseph Smith in a vision and revealed to him where the gold plates of Mormon were buried, together with a key for translation. In 1830 the Book of Mormon was published; Smith had dictated the text to Oliver Cowdery, a Palmyra schoolteacher, in a style similar to that of the King James version of the Bible. The book, a translation of the plates, purported to be an account of the prehistoric inhabitants of America and of the establishment of primitive Christianity among them, which Smith was to re-establish in America. In the same year he organized the first Church of the Latter Day Saints at Fayette; and the first missionaries went out in the field soon thereafter. The existence of a sacred scripture and Smith's teaching that believers were endowed with the same powers of the Holy Ghost as the primitive Christians served as rallying points. By the end of 1831 the faith had representatives in 20 States and Canada. In that year the Mormons moved to Kirtland, Ohio.

HILL CUMORAH (L), 22.9 *m.*, a glacial drumlin, is the Mormon Mount Sinai, where Joseph Smith unearthed the gold plates that were the source of the Book of Mormon. 'Convenient to Manchester,' Joseph Smith wrote, 'stands a hill of considerable size, the most elevated of any in the neighborhood. On the west side of this hill, not far from the top, under a stone of considerable size, lay the plates, deposited in a stone box.' He saw them the first time in September 1823 and visited the place on each anniversary, until on September 22, 1827, he took them out of their hiding place. From 1827 to 1829 he translated them and then returned them to the angelic messenger.

On the summit, towering to a height of 40 feet, is the MORMON MONUMENT, dedicated in 1935 in the presence of thousands of members of the Church of Latter Day Saints. At night the shaft is illuminated by floodlights concentrated on the majestic figure of the Angel Moroni. Each of the four sides of the pedestal bears a bronze plaque representing, on the west, Joseph Smith receiving the tablets; on the south, the 'Three Witnesses,' who asserted they had seen Moroni and the gold plates and had heard the voice of God; on the east, the 'Eight Witnesses,' who asserted that they had seen and 'hefted' the gold plates; on the north, the exhortation of the Angel Moroni.

The MORONI HEADQUARTERS BUILDING, at the foot of the hill, dedicated in 1936, is built of split glacial stones gathered from near-by fields; the style is Mayan, the light stone trim bearing Mayan symbols, to represent the prehistoric American race believed by the Mormons to be described in the Book of Mormon. The building contains an information booth and living quarters for the attendants of the shrine.

MANCHESTER, 24.8 *m*. (590 alt.,1,329 pop.), is at the junction with State 2 (*See Tour* 30).

South of CANANDAIGUA, 32.3 *m*. (766 alt.,8,291 pop.) (*see Tour* 8), at the junction with US 20 (*see Tour* 8), State 21 passes a short distance west of Canandaigua Lake, hidden among the hills. To the west, and extending to Honeoye Lake, is the rough country of the Bristol Hills, a region of thick forest growths, narrow valleys, and small farms clinging to steep hillsides. The region and its inhabitants have been romanticized by Carl Carmer in *Listen for a Lonesome Drum*.

Jesuit missionaries wrote about burning springs with flames on the surface of the water, which they found in the Bristol Hills and which the Seneca Indians worshipped. The explanation is natural gas, which now lights the streets of many villages in the region.

The BALM OF GILEAD TREE (L), 53.5 *m*., a variety of poplar, was photographed in 1893, and the picture was exhibited at the World's Columbian Exposition of that year as the largest tree in New York State. When it was last measured it had a spread of more than 100 feet and the trunk was 29 feet in circumference and 125 feet high.

NAPLES, 55.2 *m*. (800 alt.,1,144 pop.), is the center of an important grape-growing and wine-making region. Grape culture was introduced in 1852 and the wine industry began about 1856, attracting Germans from the Rhine Valley, followed by Swiss and French; their descendants and more recent German and Swiss immigrants are employed in the wineries.

In 1882 the late D.Dana Luther of Naples discovered in Grimes Glen, in the village, the 'Naples tree' (*Archeosigillaria primerum*), which was evidence that trees grew on the earth during the Devonian period; theretofore scientists had believed that Devonian vegetation was limited to a species of fern. The restored fossil, 33 feet high, is in the State Museum, Albany.

WAYLAND, 67.1 *m*. (1,372 alt.,1,790 pop.), is at the northern junction with US 15 (*see Tour* 31).

Section b. WAYLAND to PENNSYLVANIA LINE; 50.4 m. State 21

South of WAYLAND, 0 *m*., at 1.4 *m*. State 21 branches right from US 15 (*see Tour* 31).

HORNELL, 21.6 *m*. (1,160 alt.,15,494 pop.), was 'made' by the Erie Railroad. In September 1850, a pigmy locomotive called the 'Orange No. 4' drew the first train into Hornellsville, a village of 100 scattered houses, two churches, and two schools; today the railroad shops employ 1,400 and city factories manufacture tile, brick, fence wire, silk goods, gloves, shoes, leather, carriages and wagons, electrical machinery, and farm tools. Potatoes and fruit from the surrounding territory are shipped by railroad and truck. In 1930, during a drought, the city fined persons convicted of wasting water; the flood of July 1935 caused property damage estimated at $4,000,000.

The first clearing on the site of Hornell was made by Benjamin Crosby in 1790. The city was named for George Hornell, an Indian trader who purchased the site in 1793, built the first gristmill and the first tavern, and became the leading citizen of the upper Canisteo Valley.

The ELIM BIBLE SCHOOL, W.Main St., occupying a 27-acre campus, has 60 to 70 tuition-paying students; it was organized in the 1920's by the Reverend Ivan G. Spencer to supplement the meager religious training provided in public schools. Outsiders come to watch the camp meetings held on the campus. The worshippers, sitting around a circle, listen to the music of a three-piece orchestra, maintaining an unbroken posture for hours at a stretch with no outward sign of physical discomfort; here and there one rises, raises his eyes heavenward, and chants hymn fragments; then, eyes partly closed, mumbling as in a trance, several throw their arms above their heads, cry out, and roll on the ground in the hysteria of emotion; all become convulsed with joy, and even the onlookers take the contagion and smile at one another with unaccustomed cordiality.

Right from Hornell on State 17F to ALFRED STATION, 7.1 *m.*; right from Alfred Station on State 244 to ALFRED, 1.4 *m.* (1,760 alt.,639 pop.), seat of ALFRED UNIVERSITY, the campus occupying an eastern hillside. The institution was founded as a 'select school' in 1836, became the Alfred Academy in 1843, and received a university charter in 1857. The two leading divisions of the university are the New York State School of Agriculture (1908) and State College of Ceramics, established in 1900 as the State School of Clay Modeling and Ceramics. The institution is coeducational, with a total student body of about 800. The STEINHEIM MUSEUM (*open Sun. and Thurs.* 2:30–5), built in the style of a German castle, is the second oldest college museum in the country. Exhibits include rare shells, mounted birds and animals, Indian artifacts and pioneer agricultural implements, early American pottery, Steigel and Sandwich glass, and samples of the finest workmanship in the ceramic arts.

State 17F continues south to ANDOVER, 16.1 *m.* (1,664 alt.,1,241 pop.), at the junction with State 17 (*see Tour 3*).

Wedged in the opening between 700-foot hills at the junction of the Canisteo River and Bennett Creek, CANISTEO, 27.2 *m.* (1,130 alt., 2,548 pop.), is a residential center for workers in Hornell and a shopping center for the farmers of the fertile valley bottoms.

In 1690 a French and Indian punitive expedition reached this spot and found Kanisteo Castle, a lawless refuge for Indians from various tribes, renegade Frenchmen, 'rascally Dutchmen,' Yankees that had fled the gallows in Connecticut, runaway slaves from Maryland, and footpads and highwaymen from the other coast colonies. The place was captured but continued its disorderly ways until finally in the 1760's Sir William Johnson sent an armed force against it and the inhabitants fled. In 1788 Solomon Bennett, Uriah Stephens, and other survivors of the Wyoming Massacre in Pennsylvania happened upon the valley and settled here.

JASPER, 39.6 *m.* (1,578 alt.,250 pop.), is at the junction with State 17 (*see Tour 3*), with which State 21 runs in common for 0.9 miles.

At 50.4 *m.* the route crosses the PENNSYLVANIA LINE, 4.5 miles north of Knoxville, Pennsylvania.

Tour 30

Rochester—Manchester—Waterloo—Ithaca—Owego; State 2. 121 *m*.

Two-lane concrete or macadam.
New York Central R.R. parallels route between Rochester and Victor, Manchester and Phelps; Lehigh Valley R.R. between Victor and Ithaca; Delaware, Lackawanna & Western R.R. between Ithaca and Owego.

Between Rochester and Waterloo State 2 follows the Indian trails that led to Lake Ontario. South of Waterloo it enters the central Finger Lakes area, traversing the high tableland between Seneca and Cayuga Lakes. Between Ithaca and Owego it goes through a dairying region. The farmers along the route trace their descent back to the pioneer settlers from New England.

Section a. ROCHESTER to WATERLOO; 46.7 m. State 2

From ROCHESTER, 0 *m*., State 2 follows the old Seneca trail to Indian Landing on Irondequoit Bay, trod by French Jesuits until Denonville came down in 1687 with his punitive expedition and destroyed the Indian villages to which the missionaries had carried a message of peace. This expedition was one of a series of warlike acts by the French that drove the Iroquois into the arms of the British.

PITTSFORD, 6.9 *m*. (500 alt.,1,573 pop.), is at the junction with State 31 (*see Tour 32*).

At 11.1 *m*. is the junction with Powder Mills Park Road.

Right on this road 0.5 *m*. to POWDER MILLS PARK (*picnicking, swimming, restricted camping*), 576 acres, maintained by Monroe County. The park contains breeding ponds operated in co-operation with the U.S.Bureau of Fisheries for the propagation and rearing of brook and rainbow trout. About 200 adult trout are kept for exhibition.

At 15.9 *m*. is the junction with State 251.

Right on State 251 to MENDON (560 alt.,350 pop.), 4.4 *m*., set in a hollow astride willow-lined Irondequoit Creek. Conspicuous in the village are a number of cobblestone houses, erected a century ago.

The BRIGHAM YOUNG HOUSE, corner of Cheese Factory Road and Ionia Road, a sturdy two-story white dwelling, was the home of the Mormon Joshua from 1830 to 1832. Brigham Young (1801–77), born in Vermont, was brought to Sherburne, Chenango County, in 1804, where he received a limited schooling and worked on his father's farm. At the age of 16 he set out to earn his own living as carpenter, painter, and glazier; at 22 he joined the Methodist Church and at 23 was married in Aurelius, Cayuga County. In the spring of 1829 he joined his father in Mendon. Here in 1830 he first saw the Book of Mormon, and on April 14, 1832, after two years of investigation and soul-searching, he was baptized into the church. Later in the same year he met Joseph Smith, and, called upon to pray, 'spoke in tongues,' in the language, said Smith, of Adam. 'It is of God,' the Prophet added, 'and the time will come when Brother Brigham will preside over the church.' After some missionary effort Young followed Smith to Ohio and Missouri, supporting the Prophet against opposition. In 1844, after Joseph Smith and his brother were killed in the Carthage, Missouri, jail,

Brigham Young became head of the church and led his flock west to Salt Lake City, where he established a co-operative religious society that built up the State of Utah. At his death he is said to have left an estate of $1,000,000, 19 wives, and 57 children.

The SITE OF BRIGHAM YOUNG'S CHAIR FACTORY is about 300 feet east of the house. Most of the chairs that he made have been bought up by Mormons to be cherished as relics; one, however, is in the Rochester Museum of Arts and Sciences, and another in the Holland Land Office Museum, Batavia.

VICTOR, 17.2 *m.* (580 alt.,1,107 pop.), occupies the site of a battle, the only one ever fought in Ontario County, between Denonville and a Seneca force in July 1687. On June 10, 1939, a monument was unveiled in the village in memory of Kryn, or Athasata, 'The Great Shadow,' the Mohawk chief who led the Christian Indian contingent of the French force against his own people.

Right from Victor on Holcomb Road 1.5 *m.* to BOUGHTON HILL, the site of Gandagaro, the largest Seneca village destroyed by Denonville's army in 1687. Father Joseph Chaumonot, Jesuit missionary, came to Boughton Hill in 1658 to preach and baptize among the Indians. Father Jean Pierron came here in November 1673 and a year or two later built St.Joseph's Chapel, the fourth in Seneca territory.

MANCHESTER, 26.6 *m.* (590 alt.,1,329 pop.), bustles with its Lehigh Valley freight transfer yard, in which some 500 Syrians, Ukrainians, and Italians load and unload 100 and more freight cars a day. Early residents named the settlement for Manchester, England.

In an old town cemetery is the grave of one Timothy Ryan, who was stung to death on May 14, 1814, by his own bees; the epitaph on his tombstone reads:

A thousand ways cut short our days—none are exempt from death.
A honey bee—by stinging me—did stop my mortal breath.
This grave contains the last remains of my frail house of clay;
My soul is gone, not to return, to our eternal day.

A neighborhood character until about 1860 was Ebenezer Horton, the Ontario Hermit, who lived and died alone in his hut near Cedar Swamp; he attended corn husking bees, and when the fiddles were brought out no one could 'cut it down' like Eb Horton: an original jitterbug, he put in somersaults and other improvisations, all in perfect time. Invited to join a sleigh ride party, when the sleigh arrived he climbed a tree; no amount of coaxing could bring him down, and since he was in danger of freezing to death, the tree was chopped down. He scrambled to a larger tree and perched himself on a branch. This time a fire was built under the tree and he suddenly jumped, breaking several bones; but he recovered under a doctor's care.

At 31.2 *m.* is the junction with a macadam road.

Right on this road 0.6 *m.* to CLIFTON SPRINGS (500 alt.,1,409 pop.), tree-shaded and landscaped like a park. The CLIFTON SPRINGS SANITARIUM, in the center of the village, occupies a 75-acre estate and gives treatment for all but mental and contagious diseases.

The trim industrial village of PHELPS, 35.6 *m.* (542 alt.,1,397 pop.), quarries stone and sand and produces grain drills, tinware, electric platform motor trucks, paint, fertilizers, and millwork; but principally it makes sauerkraut. Phelps is the scene of Bellamy Partridge's *Country Lawyer*.

The EMPIRE STATE PICKLING PLANT, Eagle St. off Main St., with its tile-roofed stucco office building and its gleaming tile block factory with row upon row of skylight windows, is the largest sauerkraut factory in the world; and the same company runs five additional plants within a radius of 15 miles.

As the cabbages move along on endless belt conveyors, batteries of machines extract the cores in split-second time without bruising the vegetable flesh, and uniformed women deftly pluck off the outer leaves; next huge circular slicers shred the white-green heads into long crisp fibers, which are carried in small trucks to 77 tanks, each 16 feet in diameter and 12 feet deep and with a capacity of three or four freight-car loads; the cabbage emerges in about three weeks as tangy, full-flavored sauerkraut.

The small QUAKER CEMETERY (L), 39.3 *m.*, is all that remains of what was once a Quaker village. A group of Quakers settled here in the early 1800's, and in 1860 purchased the cemetery land for $12.

FIVE POINTS (West Junius), 39.9 *m.* (490 alt.,30 pop.), is at the junction with State 14 (*see Tour 28*).

WATERLOO, 46.7 *m.* (450 alt.,3,992 pop.) (*see Tour 8*), is at the junction with US 20 (*see Tour 8*).

Section b. WATERLOO to OWEGO; 74.3 m. State 2

Between Waterloo and Ithaca the route follows the ridge between Seneca and Cayuga Lakes, the largest of the Finger Lakes group. The lakes are too far away to be seen, but side roads lead to their wooded shores broken by jutting points and deep ravines cut into the rock by short, turbulent streams.

Abundant game and fish made this a favorite Indian hunting ground. After the Revolution the State purchased the Indian titles to the land and set aside 1,500,000 acres, known as the Military Tract, to be distributed among the war veterans as a bounty. But when distribution began in 1791, confusion resulted: fraudulent claims were honored and rightful claims rejected; veterans who, tired of waiting, had sold their rights for a pittance nevertheless claimed their reward; legal owners found their titles challenged by squatters. For many years westward-moving pioneers passed by this land of uncertain titles, preferring to settle on the Phelps and Gorham Purchase west of Seneca Lake. The townships in the Military Tract, laid out in 1789 and 1790, were almost all given classical names— Lysander, Cato, Brutus, Cicero, Manlius, Sempronius, Fabius, Cincinnatus, and so on. It has never been determined who was responsible for this choice, but the action represented not merely an individual interest but the larger prejudices of the young Nation: English and Indian names were anathema because of the fresh memories of the Revolution, and the heroic spirit of the Roman republic had inspired many a patriot leader.

South of WATERLOO, 0 *m.*, is the junction, 2.8 *m.*, with a dirt road.

Right on this road 0.7 *m.* to the PETER WHITMER FARM, owned by the Mormon Church. Here in a log cabin, on Tuesday, April 6, 1830, Joseph Smith (*see Tour* 29) and his two brothers, David Whitmer and his brother Joseph Jr., and Oliver Cowdery, the Prophet's collaborator in writing the Book of Mormon, organized the Church of Jesus Christ of Latter Day Saints. From this farm Joseph Smith directed the missionary work of his followers for more than a year.

State 2 runs in common with State 414 between ROMULUS, 11.6 *m.* (330 alt.,79 pop.), and OVID, 17.6 *m.* (717 alt.,537 pop.). At Ovid, State 414 continues right (straight ahead) and State 2 branches left.

Right (straight ahead) on State 414 to HECTOR, 13.5 *m.* (860 alt.,60 pop.), a hamlet overlooking the lake. A temperance society was formed here in 1818; the founders aimed at total abstinence as the cure for the evils of drink, but they omitted wine and beer from the pledge lest they defeat their purpose. In the 1820's other New York State societies incorporated the ideal of total abstinence in their constitutions. In 1826 the Hector society voted to offer its members the choice of two pledges, one for abstinence from distilled spirits and the other for total abstinence; in recording the choices the secretary placed a 'T' before the names of those who had signed the total pledge, and they were called 'T-Totalers.' Teetotalism spelled the temporary decline of the local temperance organizations; many who would have subscribed to abstinence from hard liquor would not relinquish a glass of wine or a scuttle of suds. But Hector remained a desert for many years.

WATKINS GLEN, 22.7 *m.* (477 alt.,2,906 pop.) (*see Tour* 27), is at the junction with State 14 (*see Tour* 27).

From several high points on the road south of Ovid, Cayuga Lake is visible in a panorama of blue-green water sweeping to the eastern hills.

The name of TRUMANSBURG, 31.9 *m.* (1,000 alt.,1,128 pop.), was misspelled for that of its first settler, Abner Treman, a Revolutionary veteran who came here in 1792. At the southern village line (R) are the TRUMANSBURG FAIR GROUNDS, dull green exhibit buildings grouped around a dirt race track, annual scene of one of the fourteen blue ribbon fairs of the State.

At 33.5 *m.* is the official entrance to TAUGHANNOCK STATE PARK (*camping, picnicking, bathing, baseball, bowling*), comprising 400 acres with a long lake front. TAUGHANNOCK FALLS, more than a mile from the entrance, have a drop of 215 feet, 50 feet higher than Niagara. Except in the spring the volume of falling water is small, but the fall captivates by its quietness and by the dense spray which, rising from the bottom of the gorge, shrouds the lower half of the cliff in mist.

ITHACA, 43.5 *m.* (400 alt.,19,647 pop.) (*see Ithaca*).

Right from Ithaca on State 13 to BUTTERMILK FALLS STATE PARK (*parking* 25¢; *camping, hiking, swimming*), 2.3 *m.*, an area of 510 acres along Buttermilk Creek, which drops more than 500 feet in a series of rapids and cascades; a steep footpath follows the stream to the head of the rapids.

The ROBERT H. TREMAN (ENFIELD GLEN) STATE PARK (*picnicking, camping, hiking, fishing, bathing*), 4.7 *m.*, 823 acres, one of the most beautiful of the Finger Lakes parks, includes glacial potholes, rock formations, and a deep gorge boring 2.5 miles into a hillside. In the glen is a series of 12 waterfalls.

South of Ithaca, State 2 follows the route of the early Ithaca-Owego Turnpike, on which pioneer settlers hauled lumber and wheat to Owego. The road parallels stretches of the Ithaca & Owego Railroad, incorporated in 1828, which received the second railroad charter in the State; for the first six years the trains were horse-drawn.

At 72.5 *m.*, where Catatonk Creek joins Owego Creek, is the junction (L) with State 38 (*see Tour* 8). OWEGO, 74.3 *m.* (818 alt.,4,742 pop.) (*see Tour* 3), is at the junction with State 17 (*see Tour* 3).

Tour 31

Rochester—Bath—Painted Post—(Mansfield, Pa.); US 15. Rochester to Pennsylvania Line, 102.5 *m.*

Two-lane concrete, with stretches of macadam.
Delaware, Lackawanna & Western and Erie R.R.s parallel route between Cohocton and Painted Post; New York Central R.R. between Painted Post and Pennsylvania line.

US 15 crosses deep rural New York. In the northern part of the route the influence of Rochester is seen in the suburban cottages and truck gardens; but along most of the way are broad fields of potatoes, peas, beans, and forage crops.

South from ROCHESTER, 0 *m.*, US 15 runs in a straight line for some 20 miles. In WEST HENRIETTA, 8.6 *m.* (600 alt.,125 pop.), the village garage (R) with its cobblestone walls occupies an old carriage factory; the forges, workbenches, and bellows of a hundred years ago are intact.

EAST AVON, 18.2 *m.* (821 alt.,250 pop.), is at the junction with US 20 (*see Tour* 8).

LAKEVILLE, 23.6 *m.* (825 alt.,476 pop.), is at the junction with US 20A (*see Tour* 8A), which runs in common with US 15 to LIVONIA, 25.8 *m.* (1,044 alt.,747 pop.) (*see Tour* 8A).

SPRINGWATER, 40.3 *m.* (970 alt.,600 pop.), farm trading center, was the scene of a battle in 1866 between landowners and evicted squatters. The latter were defeated.

In the early days of settlement, when transportation costs were high, grain was too bulky to be shipped to market and was therefore turned into whisky, much of which was consumed on the spot. There is a local story about a farmer's wife who tried to cure her husband of excessive drinking by accosting him one night wrapped in a sheet; but he met the situation with a drunken calm, addressing the ghost thus: 'If you're a good spirit you'll do me no harm; if you're the devil, as I suspect, I've married into your family, and as you're much too much of a gentleman to injure a relative, I fear no danger from that quarter; so I pass.'

WAYLAND, 45.5 *m.* (1,372 alt.,1,790 pop.), was a stopping place for the stage between Elmira and Buffalo; the last 'coach,' a buckboard wagon, made its final trip on July 20, 1889. After the Erie Railroad was built in the fifties, German immigrants settled here and gave the place a reputation for hard work and thrift.

Wayland is in the northwest corner of Steuben County, one of the greatest potato-growing counties in the country; in recent years the canneries in the village have encouraged the growing of peas, beans, and corn. The village also has chair and silk factories.

Right from Wayland on State 39 to DANSVILLE, 6.4 m. (725 alt.,4,967 pop.), a nursery center and manufacturing village producing heating equipment, textbooks and magazines, tissue paper, and shoes. Here on August 22, 1881, Clara Barton, while recuperating from an illness at the Jackson Sanitarium, founded the first local chapter of the American Red Cross.

The MACFADDEN-DANSVILLE HEALTH RESORT, Health St., is a large Victorian hotel established as a sanitarium in 1858 by Dr.Caleb A. Jackson and reopened in 1929 by Bernarr Macfadden, publisher and physical culturist, as a health resort.

The hotel has won wide publicity as the terminus of the Bunion, or Cracked Wheat, Derby, as the newspapers call it, an annual hike by Bernarr Macfadden and enthusiastic disciples, who during the two-week trek live on cracked wheat, raisins, brown sugar, and honey.

In the first derby in May 1935, of the 100 crusaders who left New York City only 38 arrived in Dansville, 325 miles away, sunburnt, blistered, and weary. The fourth derby, in 1938, started from Cleveland, Ohio; of the 110 starters, 100 were in at the finish, the good showing probably due to the addition of grapefruit and raw vegetables to the diet. Through cities the hike becomes a triumphal procession with police escort, band serenaders, welcoming speeches, and appearances in local theatres; in Dansville the survivors are rewarded with a sumptuous banquet and a week-end at Macfadden's health resort, topped off by hikes into the countryside.

South from Dansville on State 36 to STONY BROOK STATE PARK, 9.4 m. (parking 25¢), which covers 560 acres of rough, rocky country. Stony Brook has here carved a deep gorge through the sheer rock, creating a number of waterfalls. Accommodations are being improved by a Federal work relief project.

In Wayland is the junction with State 21 (see Tour 29), which runs in common with US 15 for 1.4 miles.

At 48.7 m. the road crosses the site of a flood control project of the United States Soil Erosion Service; after the destructive flood of July 1935 in southern New York, Federal agencies co-operated to repair damage and prevent recurrence by building gradient dams in incipient gullies, straightening streams and deepening their beds to permit faster runoff, and building earthen dikes to keep streams within their courses.

At 61.6 m. the straightened highway skirts AVOCA (1,191 alt., 1,084 pop.), which manufactures brooms, hockey sticks, spools and reels, and potato graders. A local story tells of an early settler who, to teach a lesson to the Indians who stole his firewood, stuffed his wood with gunpowder; when the burning sticks exploded in the fire, the Indians thought the wood bewitched and never again stole wood from the white man.

BATH, 69.8 m. (1,104 alt.,4,656 pop.), is in a rich farming area and makes ladders, saddlery, and knit goods. Pulteney Square, lined with business blocks and the buff-colored brick Steuben County buildings, is the site of the first clearing in Steuben County made in 1793 by Colonel Charles Williamson (1757–1808), agent for the Pulteney Estate. Believing that the settlement and trade of central New York would follow the Susquehanna to Baltimore, Williamson chose the site of Bath on the Cohocton River as the location of the future metropolis that was to be the trading, industrial, and distribution center for the entire region. But he was too energetic to wait for the normal processes of settlement; his plan was to build the city first, which would then attract settlers. He set out to induce wealthy and socially prominent country gentlemen from Virginia and Maryland to buy land for either speculation or development; and to attract them he built roads, hotels, mills, and schoolhouses, started a newspaper, erected a theater which in 1799 advertised the performance of *The Mock Doctor or The Dumb Lady Cured* and *A Peep into the Seraglio*, and laid out a race track in the wilderness where he held annual racing meets and cattle fairs. Williamson's overhasty promotions cost his principals more than $1,000,000 and he was dismissed from his position in 1801.

In Bath is the junction with State 54 (*see Tour* 28).

PAINTED POST, 89.7 *m.* (950 alt.,2,332 pop.), is at the junction with State 17 (*see Tour* 3), with which US 15 runs in common for 4.4 miles.

At 102.5 *m.*, in LAWRENCEVILLE (1,000 alt.,300 pop.), US 15 crosses the Pennsylvania line 15 miles north of Mansfield, Pennsylvania.

Tour 32

Vernon—Weedsport—Newark—Rochester—Lockport—Niagara Falls; 209 *m.* State 234, 31.

Two-lane concrete or macadam.
New York Central R.R. parallels route between Weedsport and Niagara Falls.

State 234 branches northwest (R) from State 5 (*see Tour* 11), and runs into State 31. The latter bypasses Syracuse and west of Weedsport becomes the direct route between that city and Rochester. West of Rochester it runs parallel with US 104 ((*see Tour* 26) to Niagara Falls.

For almost 200 miles—between Montezuma and Lockport—State 31 runs beside the Barge Canal, which for the most part occupies the old Erie Canal bed, through a rolling drumlin countryside. The villages along the route were spawned by the Erie Canal in the days of mule-power to handle the local transshipment of produce, manufactured goods, and passengers. Today they earn a living by storing and canning fruits and vegetables and outfitting the farmers who raise them. These villages are reminiscent of the New England from which the early settlers came; each is built around a village green with shade trees, bandstand, a cannon or two, and a war monument or a memorial to a local person.

Section a. VERNON to ROCHESTER; 126 m. State 234, 31

The route follows the low southern shore of Oneida Lake, swings around Syracuse, and crosses the important muck-farming area of Montezuma

Swamp; west of the swamp the highway follows the Barge Canal into Rochester.

At VERNON, 0 *m*. (580 alt.,602 pop.) (*see Tour* 11), State 234 branches northwest from the junction with State 5 (*see Tour* 11) through hay, corn, and wheat fields. At 4 *m*. is the junction with State 5S (*see Tour* 12) and with State 31 (L), which the tour follows.

ONEIDA LAKE (*swimming, fishing, boating*) appears (R) at 12.8 *m*. In pioneer days it was an important link in the all-water route between the Hudson and the Great Lakes and today is part of the Barge Canal system.

At CICERO, 32.4 *m*. (396 alt.,410 pop.), is the junction with US 11 (*see Tour* 18).

At 39.9 *m*. is the junction with State 57 (*see Tour* 26).

BALDWINSVILLE, 44 *m*. (423 alt.,3,845 pop.), on the Seneca River-Barge Canal, has a large flour and feed mill, a cellulose factory, and a machine works. The first group of settlers, Revolutionary veterans occupying their bonus lands, died off rapidly because of the prevalent malaria, which was relieved when the lowlands along the river were filled in.

West of Baldwinsville is rolling drumlin country—swampy hollows, and uplands colored with the green of woodlot and cornfield and the brown and purplish sheen of timothy and clover.

WEEDSPORT, 62.4 *m*. (425 alt.,1,337 pop.), has lumber and feed mills, but many of the working population commute to Auburn and Syracuse. The village Whittlers' Club was formed in 1914 by local philosophers.

PORT BYRON, 65.8 *m*. (400 alt.,971 pop.), converging on a triangular village green, is a canal orphan, left high and dry when the Erie Canal was abandoned; a stagnant creek with ruins of masonry locks is all that is left of that artery of transportation. The principal industry is the manufacture of mincemeat.

Henry Wells (1805–78), co-founder of the Wells-Fargo Express Company and founder of Wells College in Aurora (*see Tour* 8), worked in the village as shoemaker from 1827 to 1830; Isaac Singer is said to have made his first model of a sewing machine in his workshop that stood near the present dam across Owasco Outlet; and Brigham Young (*see Tour* 30) lived for a short time in the small frame house behind the I.O.O.F. hall on Utica Street.

West of MONTEZUMA, 70.3 *m*. (400 alt.,300 pop.), for a mile and a half the route crosses an intensively cultivated part of the MONTEZUMA SWAMP, a flat marsh area stretching across much of north central New York. Digging the Erie Canal through these marshes, and building a bridge across them for the towpath, was a difficult task; workers, including Negroes, were felled by malaria, but the bog-trotting Irish dug through, malaria, mud, and all.

In the early spring tractors haul disk harrows over the soft black muck soil and workers direct potato planters and celery setters, making straight rows in the rectangular patches. Celery, the largest crop, is started in greenhouses and transplanted in the field; when the plants approach maturity the stalks are covered with banks of soil to exclude the light, a process called blanching. Harvest workers include native owners, Italian sharecroppers, local hired help, women and children, and migrants who have followed the truck farm harvest north from Florida and are housed in cabins and barns in near-by villages.

The route proceeds through a hilly region; on the highest hill (R) is the SITE OF ONONTARE, 74.7 *m*., a fortified village of the Cayuga, where Saint René Menard (*see Tour* 8) had a mission in 1657. The hill is locally known as Fort Hill because of traces of ancient earthworks probably erected on its summit long before the visit of the French Jesuit missionary.

The village park of CLYDE, 82.1 *m*. (420 alt.,2,354 pop.), contains a mineral spring around which settlers once hoped to build a spa. There are two factories making shoe counters, and a few other small industries. Almost half the population is composed of Italians who came to build the Barge Canal. In ST.JOHN'S EPISCOPAL CHURCH, 27 W.Genesee St., is the organ presented to Trinity Church, New York City, during the reign of Queen Anne; from the New York City church it was moved to a church in Geneva, and then here.

The road runs parallel with the Barge Canal, which here uses the bed of the old Erie.

LYONS, 89.4 *m*. (420 alt.,3,838 pop.), lies at the junction of Canandaigua Outlet and the Clyde River. The principal industries are a machine shop and a suspender factory.

The EXCHANGE BUILDINGS, NE. corner of Water and Broad Sts., a group of three Greek Revival commercial blocks built in 1835, are in an unusually fine state of preservation. The sturdy granite piers and entablature of the ground floor permit a considerable expanse of glass for store displays.

Lyons is at the junction with State 14 (*see Tour* 27).

NEWARK, 95.7 *m*. (456 alt.,9,642 pop.), produces paper containers, kitchenware, furniture, canned goods, extracts, and cosmetics, and has large flower nurseries.

The JACKSON PERKINS ROSE GARDENS (*open* 9–4 *Mon.–Fri.*), Madison St. opposite Jefferson St., display more than 40 new varieties of roses that were developed here and have been patented; perhaps the best known is the climbing rose, Dorothy Perkins, which was awarded the Nickerson Cup by the National Rose Society of Great Britain in 1908. Roses are grown here in 22 miles of outdoor hotbeds.

Right from Newark on State 88 to junction with a road, 1.5 *m*.; left on this road 0.6 *m*. to another junction; right here 0.1 *m*. to HYDEVILLE (420 alt.,40 pop.), called 'the birthplace of spiritualism.' A weed-covered lot by the side of the road is the SITE OF THE FOX HOME, in which lived the Fox sisters, 'through whose mediumship communication with the spirit world was established March 31, 1849.' The cottage was removed to Lily Dale (*see Tour* 8). The Fox family came here on December 11, 1847, and soon after their arrival they heard knockings at night, first in a bedroom, then in the cellar; other sounds were added, like a heavy body being dragged downstairs and someone shoveling in the cellar; the children told of a cold hand touching them in the dark. The youngest girl, Katy, began to converse with the spirit. 'Here, Mr.Split-foot, do as I do,' she said, snapping her fingers two or three times; and the spirit answered the correct number, counting as high as ten. Asked if he was a man, the spirit did not answer; asked if he was a spirit, he answered yes. Later he affirmed that he was the spirit of Charles B. Rosna, a peddler who had been murdered in the house four years previously; the cellar was dug up but water was struck before any evidence was found. In April the spirit began to rap in the daytime, and then he got 'tough,' slamming doors, moving the furniture about, seizing the girls with his cold hands, rocking the beds and dragging off the bedclothes. On almost every night was enacted the horrible death struggle between the peddler and his murderer, then the heavy thump of the dead body being dragged down the stairs, and the digging of the grave in the cellar. This, together with the rush of visitors, proving too much for the Fox family, they moved to Rochester, where the seances took a more regular form.

The name of PALMYRA, 104.3 m. (470 alt.,2,706 pop.), is associated with the beginnings of Mormonism; the Joseph Smith farm and Hill Cumorah are close by (see Tour 29). The principal industries make steam packing and paper boxes.

The WESTERN PRESBYTERIAN CHURCH, NE. corner of Main and Church Sts., erected in 1832, is a belated example of post-Georgian architecture. The body of the church, built of red brick, is almost square; the white pedimented portico has four Roman Ionic columns of stucco over rubble, of very slender proportions and devoid of any base except a tiny plinth. The three-stage steeple terminates in a short paneled spire.

The WILLIAM T. SAMPSON BIRTHPLACE, 112 Vienna St., is a clapboard house painted buff and brown, with a simple porch across the front. Admiral William T. Sampson (1840–1902) was the commander of the United States fleet in the Battle of Santiago during the Spanish-American War.

The GARLOCK PACKING PLANT (not open), at the northern village limits along the New York Central Railroad, makes packings used wherever steam is conveyed through pipes, pumps, or engines. In the late sixties one of the founders of the present company cut a ring from an old piece of rubber hose, pushed it in the stuffing box of a steam engine furnishing power for a sawmill, and started the steam packing industry.

PITTSFORD, 119.5 m. (500 alt.,1,573 pop.), is a residential suburb of Rochester.

BRIGHTON, 122.3 m. (470 alt.,900 pop.), another Rochester suburb, in point of time antedates the city by a number of years. The ORRINGH STONE TAVERN (private), East Ave. opposite Council Rock Ave., built in 1790, is the oldest private house in the Rochester area. In this post-Colonial frame structure, Aaron Burr and his daughter Theodosia, Joseph Brant, Lafayette, and Louis Philippe, 'citizen king' of France, were at various times entertained.

ROCHESTER, 126 m. (500 alt.,324,694 pop.) (see Rochester), is at the junction with US 104 (see Tour 26), State 2 (see Tour 30), US 15 (see Tour 31), and State 33 (see Tour 33).

Section b.   ROCHESTER to NIAGARA FALLS; 83 m.   State 31

West of ROCHESTER, 0 m. the route, still hugging the Barge Canal, passes apple, peach, and cherry orchards, hay and corn fields, fields of tomatoes, beans, and peas.

On Nicholas Road in SPENCERPORT, 10 m. (528 alt.,1,325 pop.), is the JOHN T. TROWBRIDGE HOME, a two-story frame farmhouse painted white, where John Townsend Trowbridge (1827–1916) lived the first 17 years of his life. Most of Trowbridge's 50 volumes are boys' books; his *Neighbor Jackwood* is said to have had a larger sale than any other American book before *Uncle Tom's Cabin*; his *Cudjo's Cave* depicts the hair-raising adventures of a runaway slave.

In BROCKPORT, 18.6 *m.* (539 alt.,3,584 pop.), the canal banks are landscaped with shrubs and rose bushes. Nurseries, cold storage warehouses, and canning factories supply work for those who do not commute to Rochester.

Brockport was the home of Mary Jane Holmes (1825–1907), popular post-Civil War novelist, whose books, many of them issued in paper covers, sold a total of more than 2,000,000 copies; most popular were *Tempest and Sunshine*, *English Orphans*, and *Lena Rivers*. Her sentimental plots, noble heroes, and swooning heroines are oversimplified for twentieth-century tastes; the heroine 'reclines on soft cushions,' from which she rises to proclaim that 'I would rather die than marry a man I did not love because of his gold.' Mrs.Holmes's grave is in the Brockport cemetery.

The BROCKPORT STATE NORMAL SCHOOL, end of College St., originally the Brockport Collegiate Institute, was opened in 1841. The old Medina sandstone buildings are to be replaced by new structures, the main unit of which, a large red brick, Georgian Colonial building, was completed in 1939 with PWA aid.

In Brockport is the junction with State 19 (*see Tour 35*).

In ALBION, 33.5 *m.* (519 alt.,4,651 pop.) the SNIDER PACKING PLANT (R), at the eastern village limits, consists, except for the brick main building, of long, low wood structures. This plant cans principally tomatoes and peas. The tomatoes are sorted and thoroughly washed, and the skin is loosened in scalding water. On the peeling tables girls peel off the skin and remove the cores with sharp knives, then place the tomatoes in cans, which are closed, cooked, and labeled—ready for the market. The plant also freezes peas and beans with the Birdseye system, invented by Clarence Birdseye.

The PULLMAN MEMORIAL UNIVERSALIST CHURCH, Main St. and E. Park Ave. is a low brownstone building designed in a modified Gothic style, with a vitrified tile roof. It stands on the site of the home of George M. Pullman (1831–97), born in Brocton, Chautauqua County, who was a cabinetmaker in the village from 1848 to 1855. It was probably here that, disgusted with the dirt, discomfort, and inconvenience of early passenger cars, he conceived the idea of a car with the luxuries of beds and upholstered seats. Pullman made his first cars in Chicago in 1858, using the olive-green paint and cherry wood trim that are still characteristic of Pullman cars. He sold to Webster Wagner (*see Tour 11*) the right to use his patented folding berths on Wagner's palace cars on the New York Central, but sued him for infringement when he sold his cars to the Michigan Central. Pullman donated land and money for the construction of this church.

In MEDINA, 43.6 *m.* (530 alt.,5,861 pop.), and vicinity, the local red Medina sandstone, used in Federal farmhouses, Greek Revival residences, Gothic Revival churches, and Second Empire business structures, gives a piquant flavor to all these styles. Two or three buildings in gray limestone, the normal building stone in the Rochester area, look ill at ease in the village. The Medina sandstone was quarried in the vicinity from the early days of settlement until late in the nineteenth century.

Besides the usual canning plant, Medina has several iron foundries. The population includes a large percentage of foreign groups, including about 1,000 Poles.

The H.J.HEINZ PLANT, Park Ave., a collection of rambling wooden frame structures and two-story brick buildings, makes a number of the 57 varieties—vinegar, pea soup, celery soup, and strained vegetables for infants and invalids, and cans prunes, carrots, and creamed diced potatoes.

The demand for labor in this fruit- and vegetable-growing and canning district fluctuates sharply with the season: in the spring and summer there is work to be done in the orchards and gardens; during the harvest, employment reaches a high peak both in the fields and in the canning plants, and workers are brought in from metropolitan centers; but as soon as the harvest is in the cans, employment drops rapidly and many of the workers are left stranded for the winter.

MIDDLEPORT, 48.8 *m.* (540 alt.,1,442 pop.), sprang up as a settlement upon completion of the Erie Canal in 1825, and took its name from its location midway between Lockport and Albion. The main industry is the manufacture of insecticides for spraying fruit trees, vines, bushes, and vegetable plants, and equipment for applying the spray.

LOCKPORT, 61.1 *m.* (550 alt.,24,308 pop.), grew around the series of locks built to carry the Erie Canal through the Lockport gorge. The surplus water from the lockings was diverted in a raceway that later became the source of power for the city's growing industries. The Barge Canal runs through the center of the city. The chief industrial products are electric alloy and other special steels, towels and linens, thermostats and automobile heaters, iron castings, wallboard and paperboard, milk bottles, paper boxes, and felt. Development of the farmlands and orchards of the Niagara frontier made Lockport an important marketing and milling center.

The businessman who put Lockport on the map in the 1870's was John Hodge, proprietor and manufacturer of Merchant's Gargling Oil, a remedy advertised to our grandparents as 'good for man or beast'; one of Hodge's stunts was to send a steamer bedecked with banners over the Niagara cataract. John J. Raskob (1879———), chairman of the General Motors Corporation and chairman of the Democratic National Committee, 1928–32, was born in Lockport.

The CANAL BRIDGE, over the Barge Canal at Cottage St., is 452 feet wide, and is frequently used for mass meetings, street fairs, and carnivals. The operation of the canal locks can best be watched from the Cottage Street end of the bridge. Two great Barge Canal locks raise and lower the barges a total distance of 60 feet. As originally built in 1825, ten locks, in two flights of five each, carried the canal between the two levels. The present locks have replaced the southerly set, but on the north the original design can still be seen, a tribute to the skill of Nathan S. Roberts (*see*

Tour 12), who declared that the greatest achievement of his career was the design and construction of the Lockport locks.

In Lockport is the junction with State 78 (*see Tour* 36).

The route runs past apple and peach orchards, vineyards, rolling pastures, and broad, flat weedy fields waiting for suburban development, to NIAGARA FALLS, 83 *m.* (575 alt.,77,374 pop.) (*see Niagara Falls*), at the junction with US 104 (*see Tour* 26) and US 62 (*see Tour* 37).

Tour 33

Rochester—Batavia—Buffalo; State 33. 71.2 *m.*

Two-strip concrete.

State 33, the most direct route between Rochester and Buffalo, goes through a flat countryside of grain fields, fruit orchards, and pastures.

This section of the State was part of the Holland Land Purchase. In the 1840's an old woman of 75 who had been one of the pioneer settlers north of Batavia, thus described her first home: it was a shanty 'about ten feet square, flat roofed, covered with split ash shingles; the floor was made of the halves of split basswood; no chimneys; a blanket answered the purpose of a door for a while, until my husband got time to make a door of split plank. We needed no window; the light came in where the smoke went out . . . For chairs, we had benches made by splitting logs, and setting the sections upon legs . . . We bought a cotton bag, and stuffing it with cattail, it was far better than no bed . . . We were soon on our way, house, or shanty keeping . . .

'Our first resource for bread, after exhausting the little stock we brought in, was to buy strings of corn of the Indians, burn out a hollow place in a stump, suspend a pounder by a spring pole, and thus make of the corn a coarse meal. One stump, pounder and spring pole, would answer for several families.'

But life was not all hard work and coarse bread: 'Some of our parties were got up by first designating the log house of some settler, and each one contributing to the entertainment; one would carry some flour, another some sugar, another some eggs, another some butter, and so on . . . Frolics in the evening would uniformly attend husking bees, raisings, quiltings and pumpkin pearings. All were social, friendly, obliging—there was little of aristocracy in those primitive days.' An indispensable part of every frolic was Russel Noble, the left-handed fiddler, of whom it was said—the remark casting an aspersion upon his music as well as his morals—that 'he used to have no more regard for time than he had for eternity.'

Southwest from ROCHESTER, 0 *m.* (500 alt.,324,694 pop.) (*see Roch-*

ester), State 33 cuts across pancake-flat farmlands. The DOLOMITE PROD-
UCTS QUARRY (L), 4.2 *m.*, is a huge hole in the ground out of which 350,-
000 tons of dolomite, a stone used in road building, are extracted annually.

NORTH CHILI, 10.8 *m.* (581 alt.,350 pop.), is the home of the CHES-
BROUGH SEMINARY (R), a free Methodist coeducational boarding school
founded in 1867. The campus covers 10 acres on the 200-acre dairy farm,
owned and operated by the institution.

In CHURCHVILLE, 15 *m.* (615 alt.,597 pop.), is the BIRTHPLACE OF
FRANCES E. WILLARD (1838–98), 24 S.Main St., a small frame house now
an addition to a store. Miss Willard lived most of her life in Illinois and
the statue of her in the Capitol at Washington was erected by the citizens
of that State. In 1894 she deserted her career as a college professor and
dean to devote the rest of her life to the cause of temperance, basing her
case on the moral need to protect the home and Christian life. During the
'Great Temperance Roundup' of 1883 she visited every State in the Union
seeking converts to the cause; when she arrived in a village a boy ran
around the streets ringing a dinner bell and shouting: 'Lecture at the depot!' Miss Willard set in motion the Home Protection Movement, was
secretary and then president of the Women's Christian Temperance
Union, served on the executive committee of the Prohibition Party, and
founded the World's Christian Temperance Union.

BATAVIA, 32.5 *m.* (890 alt.,17,222 pop.) (*see Tour* 11), is at the junction with State 5 (*see Tour* 11).

Since CORFU, 44.9 *m.* (860 alt.,460 pop.), was incorporated in 1868, its
principal industry has been the cultivation of flowers for the Rochester
and Buffalo markets, with as many as 26 greenhouses operating at one
time.

At 62.1 *m.* is the junction with State 78 (*see Tour* 36).

BUFFALO, 71.2 *m.* (600 alt.,575,150 pop.) (*see Buffalo*), is at the junction with State 5 (*see Tour* 11), US 62 (*see Tour* 37), and State 16 (*see
Tour* 38).

Tour 34

Junction with US 20A to Dunkirk; State 39. 85.9 *m.*

Two-strip concrete or macadam.
The Erie and Baltimore & Ohio R.R.s parallel route in stretches.

Milk is the most important product of the region traversed by State 39.
Herds of cattle graze on the hills; through the nights long milk trains and
huge milk trucks carry tomorrow's milk supply to Buffalo and New York;
local factories convert the surplus into butter, cheese, and powdered milk.

South from the junction with US 20A, 0 *m.*, is PERRY, 4.6 *m.* (1,320 alt.,4,505 pop.), which has large knitting mills and a septic and gasoline tank factory. In 1833 the Reverend William Arthur became pastor of the First Baptist Church in Perry; his son, Chester Alan, then four years old, was destined to become the 21st President of the United States. The parsonage in which the family lived, now considerably altered, stands in the rear of the W.T.Oline home on Elm Street.

CASTILE, 11 m. (1,360 alt.,898 pop.), is at one of the entrances to Letchworth State Park (see below).

At 12.3 m. is the junction with State 19A.

Left on State 19A to PORTAGEVILLE, 3.5 m. (1,245 alt.,300 pop.), at the entrance to LETCHWORTH STATE PARK (adm. free; campers must secure permits. Picnic areas, tent sites). The park is continually being developed as a recreational center; boundaries change as land is added by purchase, condemnation, or gift; park roads are being extended and improved and miles of additional foot trails marked. The deep gorge of the Genesee River, show place of the park, was etched by the erosive action of the river upon strata of horizontally bedded Devonian rocks. The park is named for William Pryor Letchworth, Buffalo manufacturer, scholar, and philanthropist, who donated much of the land.

One of the finest collections of Indian regalia and relics in existence is housed in the LETCHWORTH MUSEUM (L), 4.6 m. (open May 15–Oct. 15, 9–5). The modern fireproof building also contains a library and heirlooms of pioneer days in Wyoming County.

A short distance (L) off the main road, at 4.9 m., is the SENECA COUNCIL HOUSE, moved here from Caneadea in 1871. A typical Iroquois 'long house,' it is 50 by 20 feet, the walls of pine logs smoothly hewn and dovetailed at the corners, rising 12 or 13 feet; the only openings in the original building were two doors at the ends and two smoke vents near the center of the shingled roof. Here on October 1, 1872, was held the 'last Indian council,' attended by Colonel Simcoe Kerr, grandson of Joseph Brant, as representative of the Mohawk, and, for the Seneca, descendants of Red Jacket, Cornplanter, Mary Jemison, and other notables. These children of the Ho-di-no-saw-nee (Ind., people of the long house) sat on low benches around the council fire that burned on the clay floor; in a more comfortable chair sat the gray-haired Millard Fillmore, ex-President of the United States. During the ceremony Mr.Letchworth was adopted into the Seneca tribe under the name of Hai-wa-ye-is-tah (Ind., the man who always does the right thing).

Just beyond the Council House are the MARY JEMISON STATUE (L) and the LOG CABIN (L) that she built for her daughter Nancy. Mary Jemison, the 'white woman of the Genesee,' daughter of Irish immigrants, was taken prisoner by Indians at the age of 15 and lived the rest of her life among them. In the vicinity of present-day Pittsburgh she was adopted by two Seneca women, who named her Dehhewamis, 'beautiful girl,' and married her to a Delaware warrior; 'strange as it may seem,' she later said, 'I learned to love him and he made an agreeable husband and comfortable companion.' After her husband's death she accompanied her Seneca friends to their home on the Genesee, traveling on foot with a child a distance of nearly 600 miles through the wilderness, and settled at Little Beard's Town (Cuylerville); there she married another Indian, Hiokatoo, with whom she lived nearly 50 years and to whom she bore six children.

A short distance off the main road (L) at 5.1 m. are the PARK SUPERINTENDENT'S HOUSE and the GENESEE PARK COMMISSION ADMINISTRATION OFFICE.

Generally regarded as the best central vantage point in the park is INSPIRATION POINT OVERLOOK (R), 5.2 m., which offers an unexcelled view of the gorge of the Genesee, the Middle and Upper Falls, and a large part of the park itself.

From the crossroads at 17.1 m. the left fork road leads to Geneseo on US 20A (see Tour 8A).

At 17.2 m. is the junction with State 19 (see Tour 35), with which State 39 unites briefly.

ARCADE, 33.8 *m*. (1,479 alt.,1,675 pop.), has a milk plant and factories producing bowling pins, ladies' shoe lasts, barrels, and automobile tools.

In YORKSHIRE, 36.4 *m*. (1,438 alt.,306 pop.), is the junction with State 16 (*see Tour* 38).

In SPRINGVILLE, 47.8 *m*. (1,341 alt.,2,832 pop.), is the junction with US 219 (*see Tour* 39).

At 61.5 *m*. is the junction with US 62 (*see Tour* 37), with which State 39 runs in common to GOWANDA, 64 *m*. (760 alt.,3,042 pop.) (*see Tour* 37).

The route swings through western Chautauqua County, where archeologists have uncovered mastodon remains, stone implements, copper ornaments, and stone fireplaces, and earthworks believed to have been erected by mound builders.

FORESTVILLE, 76.9 *m*. (875 alt.,677 pop.), in an amphitheater of hills, was the birthplace of George Abbott, playwright and producer, author of *Boy Meets Girl* and other plays. Born here in 1889, he was educated in the Hamburg High School, the University of Rochester, and Harvard. After graduating he became an actor and later turned to writing and producing plays.

From the edge of the high plateau at 79 *m*. the hazy blue waters of Lake Erie are visible, smudged in summer by large black lines of smoke from lake steamers.

At 81.9 *m*. is the junction with US 20 (*see Tour* 8), with which State 39 runs in common for 0.8 miles. As the road approaches its western terminus the countryside takes on life and color from produce-laden trucks headed for metropolitan markets, train whistles in the near distance, roadstands, filling stations, billboards, and, approaching from the west, the grim smokestacks of the large industrial plants of DUNKIRK, 85.9 *m*. (600 alt.,17,606 pop.) (*see Tour* 11), at the junction with State 5(*see Tour* 11).

Tour 35

North Hamlin—Le Roy—Warsaw—Wellsville—(Galeton, Pa.); State 19. Lake Ontario to Pennsylvania Line, 110.9 *m*.

Two-strip concrete or macadam.
The Baltimore & Ohio R.R. parallels route between Le Roy and Silver Springs; Erie R.R. between Warsaw and Belfast and between Belvidere and the Pennsylvania line.

Transecting western New York between Lake Ontario and the Pennsylvania line without touching a single city, State 19 is a completely rural route through a general farming, dairying, and fruit-growing region.

The road runs in part through the easternmost districts of the Holland Purchase (*see Tour* 11) and in part through the Morris Reserve, a tract including the rich bottom lands of the Genesee to which Robert Morris retained title. First 'discovered' by General Sullivan's men during the campaign of 1779, the region was settled from New England, Pennsylvania, and eastern New York after the Revolution and after the Indian title had been vacated by the Big Tree Treaty (*see Tour 8A*).

Section a. NORTH HAMLIN to WARSAW; 46.7 m. State 19

South of NORTH HAMLIN, 0 *m.* (280 alt.,68 pop.), are orchards of gnarled apple, sour cherry, peach, and isolated plots of quince trees.

CLARKSON, 7.7 *m.* (427 alt.,300 pop.) (*see Tour 26*), is at the junction with US 104 (*see Tour 26*).

At BROCKPORT, 9.2 *m.* (539 alt.,3,584 pop.), junction with State 31 (*see Tour 32*), the road crosses the murky waters of the Barge Canal (*see Tour 32*).

Three corner gas stations, at 19.2 *m.*, mark the junction with State 33 (*see Tour 33*).

About three miles west of BERGEN, 18.4 *m.* (600 alt.,656 pop.), are the BERGEN SWAMPS, 15 miles long, an irregular marl bed surrounded by a dense cedar thicket inhabited by blacksnakes, deer, and rare birds; to the botanists it is interesting for its white orchids, small white lady's slipper, black chokeberry, fringed polygala, true and false miterwort, goldthread, bog violet, starflower, swamp valerian, twinflower, Labrador tea, dwarf cornel, bog cranberry, pitcherplant, and other rare plants.

On FORT HILL (L), 23.5 *m.*, a point of land at the junction of Fordham's Brook and Allen's Creek, was a fortified Indian stronghold; archeologists have found skeletons, pottery, beads, stone axes, and arrowheads; one of the pipes found here 'consists of a face having slitlike eyes and mouth, a long rectangular nose so modeled that it appears to look out from a hood with a triangular opening.'

LE ROY, 26.6 *m.* (869 alt.,4,386 pop.) (*see Tour 11*), is at the junction with State 5(*see Tour 11*).

Along the road, young, immature orchards rise beside the scarred stumps of older orchards that have been cut down. At 32.1 *m.* is the junction with US 20 (*see Tour 8*).

A single crude timber derrick near the road north of PAVILION, 34.6 *m.* (941 alt.,425 pop.), is all that remains of the development following the natural gas boom that started here in 1879.

The products of surrounding farms are processed in the canning and poultry feed plants of WYOMING, 40 *m.* (987 alt.,376 pop.), strung out beside the bit of green in the village square. Since they use inexpensive natural gas drawn from near-by shallow pockets, the street lamps of Wyoming are allowed to burn night and day in order to save the wages of a lamplighter.

The former MIDDLEBURY ACADEMY (*open by appointment*), Main St., a two-story brick building with a portico, erected in 1817, is now the studio of Bryant Fleming, architect, who has collected art objects from the far corners of the world. The academy, which functioned for 70 years before being replaced by a modern school, was noted as a preparatory school for Presbyterian divinity students.

WARSAW, 46.7 *m*. (1,000 alt.,3,541 pop.), is at the junction with US 20A (*see Tour 8A*).

Section b.   WARSAW to PENNSYLVANIA LINE; 64.2 m.   State 19

South of Fillmore the route threads along the flatlands of the Genesee Valley, bounded by low hills. Sullivan's men carried back to New England glowing accounts of luxuriant flats covered with grass 'tall enough to easily obscure and hide from observation not only the horse, but his rider'; where the land had been cultivated by the Indians 'the soil laughed with a bountiful harvest of corn, beans, squashes and gourds, when only slightly tickled with their primitive farming implements.' As soon as the peace was signed and title to the land cleared, the settlers' large covered wagons began rumbling in.

Valley towns reached the height of their prosperity during the construction of the Genesee Valley Canal, begun in 1836 and not completed until 1862; its four-foot ribbon of water was to join the Allegheny River at Olean with the Erie Canal at Rochester and thus channel the commerce of the entire Mississippi basin through New York State. But the canal never fulfilled its promises; in 1877, after the project had eaten up six and three-quarter millions of dollars, the legislature directed that the canal be abandoned.

South of WARSAW, 0 *m*., is a dairying and potato-growing region.

Farmers of the region about GAINESVILLE, 8 *m*. (1,616 alt.,283 pop.), during the 1938 season delivered 90,000 pecks of potatoes, all bagged and ready for sale, to a single grocery store chain. David Starr Jordan (1851–1931), biologist and president of Leland Stanford University, was born on a farm a quarter of a mile east of the village; Belva Ann Lockwood (1830–1917), lawyer, suffragist, and first woman candidate for President, was head of the Gainesville Female Academy in 1858; and Isabella McDonald Alden (1841–1930), author of moral tales for young people, wrote many of her stories in this vicinity.

At 12.9 *m*. is the junction with State 39 (*see Tour 34*), which unites briefly with State 19.

This is one of the largest maple sugar areas in the State; much of the product is marketed as 'Vermont' maple syrup. The season is in March and early April, when frosty nights alternate with warm, sunny days. Mornings the sap drips from the spouts into galvanized buckets hanging four feet up on the tree trunks; afternoons the run slackens and the farmers, wearing heavy sweaters and caps with earlaps lowered, gather the sap in larger pails on sleds or stone-boats and haul it to storage tanks beside the sugar house, where the sap is evaporated and sugared off. The carefully regulated heating in sheet-iron or copper pans over the blazing wood fires is a vast improvement over the Indian method of gathering the sap in bark containers and dropping hot stones in it to sugar it off. Like more modern and more technical chemical industries, this one has its by-products: maple sugar, maple cream, maple candy; from the skimmings and the scorched syrup good vinegar is made; and the second grade syrup is sold to tobacco companies for sweetening tobacco.

HUME, 20.3 *m.* (1,281 alt.,300 pop.), marks the northern limit of the former Caneadea Reservation of the Seneca Indians, one of the 11 set aside in the Big Tree Treaty of 1797; at the time it was as primitive a wilderness as western New York could offer. The Indians sold the land to a group of land speculators in 1826 and settled on the present State reservations.

Canal and railroad construction in the 1840's and 1850's attracted large numbers of Irish to this region, who remained as tillers of the soil.

HOUGHTON, 26.6 *m.* (1,200 alt.,300 pop.), dates from Genesee Valley Canal days, when, known as Jockey Street, it was a resort for gamblers and jockeys, with horse racing as the chief attraction.

HOUGHTON COLLEGE, its 15-acre campus with red brick Georgian Colonial buildings overlooking the village and the river, was established in 1883 by the Wesleyan Methodist Church largely through the efforts of the Reverend Willard J. Houghton, who aimed to found a school in which the development of Christian character would be emphasized; the college was chartered in 1923. Coeducational, it offers courses leading to A.B. and B.S. degrees; the School of Theology gives advanced courses in religious thought and history.

At CANEADEA (Ind., where the heavens rest on the earth), 29.5 *m.* (1,250 alt.,200 pop.), villagers hang their milk containers on the telegraph pole in front of the post office for the dairy farmer to fill and for them to pick up at their leisure. The place occupies the site of a Seneca village.

In the vicinity of WELLSVILLE, 54 *m.* (1,517 alt.,5,674 pop.), at the junction with State 17 (*see Tour 3*), are the oil wells of the New York section of the Bradford field (*see Tour 3*).

SHONGO, 62.4 *m.* (1,614 alt.,150 pop.), occupies the site of the summer village of the fierce Seneca Chief Shongo, who raided many American settlements during the Revolution.

At 64.2 *m.* the route crosses the PENNSYLVANIA LINE, 32.5 miles north of Galeton, Pennsylvania.

Tour 36

Olcott—Lockport—Depew; State 78. 30 *m.*

Two-strip macadam.
International Electric Ry. parallels route between Olcott and Lockport.

Clinging to Eighteenmile Creek, State 78 crosses the low-lying Niagara fruit belt, famed for its apples, peaches, and melons. South of Lockport it cuts across a flat, monotonous region of unkempt meadowland.

OLCOTT, 0 *m.* (280 alt.,300 pop.), enjoying beautiful vistas of Lake

Ontario, blue and white-capped on bright days, green or greyish in foul weather, is a summer resort, depending for a living on the June-to-August season. Bathing suits or bathrobes become the conventional garb of young women ambling along the sidewalks in company of young men clad in trunks. The air is heavy with charcoal smoke, the sounds of wailing concertinas and steam calliopes, and the shriek of merry crowds.

BURT, 1.5 m. (310 alt.,294 pop.), reaches the peak of its activity in the fall, when all roads leading to it are heavy with trucks loaded with apples, peaches, melons, cabbages, and potatoes, brought here to be freighted on the Rome, Watertown, & Ogdensburg Railroad.

Eighteenmile Creek has been harnessed at Burt, the water having been dammed up to form a lake two miles long. Beyond the dam are the ruins of old gristmills, burned by the British in the War of 1812.

NEWFANE, 3.2 m. (345 alt.,1,200 pop.), a fruit-farming community, specializes in tree nurseries, with a small felt and paper factory providing industrial employment. In 1939 a 140-year-old marker was discovered in a local backyard bearing the initials of William and John Willink, surveyors of the Holland Land Company. The stone had been placed by them to indicate the northern terminus of the Transit Road.

At 8.3 m. is the junction with US 104 (see Tour 26).

The FRIENDLESS CHILDREN'S HOME (R), 10.6 m., was founded by the wife of Washington Hunt, Governor of New York, 1851–3. The stone and frame building with tall chimneys, facing a winding entrance roadway, was Governor Hunt's summer home.

In LOCKPORT, 11.9 m. (550 alt.,24,308 pop.) (see Tour 32), is the junction with State 31 (see Tour 32).

South of Lockport State 78 becomes the Transit Road, a run of 25 miles without a bend, laid out by Holland Company surveyors in line with the North Star. TONAWANDA CREEK, crossed at 17.5 m., is a favorite fishing stream for black bass, perch, and muskellunge; it is restocked every season by the New York Conservation Association of Erie and Niagara Counties.

At 26.4 m. is the junction with State 5 (see Tour 11).

At 28.2 m. is the junction with State 33 (see Tour 33).

DEPEW, 30 m. (680 alt.,6,043 pop.), is a railroad center. Incorporated in 1894, it was named in honor of the late Senator Chauncey M. Depew, then president of the New York Central Lines. In contrast to its roundhouses, track mazes, smokestacks, and constant coming and going of trains, in the center of town is an attractive park with recreational facilities.

The village came into existence at the height of a frenzied land speculation following the establishment of the New York Central car shops in 1893. That year, nine miles of plank sidewalks and 6,000 feet of sewers were laid; the next year Depew had a population of 1,184. In 1930, when the car shops were removed to an eastern city, many citizens were absorbed in local industries, which produce storage batteries, food products, steel castings for railroads, bags, wrappings, mattresses, and cut and crushed stone.

In Depew State 78 merges with US 20 (see Tour 8).

Tour 37

Niagara Falls—Buffalo—Gowanda—(Warren, Pa.); US 62.
Niagara Falls to Pennsylvania Line, 102.1 m.

Two-lane concrete with stretches of three- and four-lane concrete and macadam.
Erie R.R. parallels route between Buffalo and Kennedy.

North of the village of Hamburg, US 62 runs through an industrialized section. Niagara Falls supplies the power and light to the manufacturing plants; the 'white coal' is carried by a network of overhead cables supported by tall steel towers. Huge freight trucks crowd the highway.

South of Hamburg is rural New York. Farmers send their milk to New York City; the small village industries produce glue, lollipop sticks, and other commodities.

South of NIAGARA FALLS, 0 m. (575 alt.,77,374 pop.) (*see Niagara Falls*), is the junction with old River Road, 1.9 m. In the Gay Nineties this road was traveled by the buggy-riding gentry on their way to clambakes at inns and taverns along the Niagara River.

At 12.7 m. is the junction with State 425.

Right on State 425 to NORTH TONAWANDA, 4 m. (575 alt.,20,224 pop.), on the northern bank of the Barge Canal, an industrial city manufacturing steel and iron products, musical instruments, amusement park furnishings, spark plugs, and filing cabinets. In the eastern part of town is an impressive residential district, with tree-lined avenues, parks, and gardens. The industrial section, with its large foreign population groups, faces the water front. In the Oliver and River Street section, the cheerless bungalows of Polish iron and steel workers are strung out in dense rows. Here Polish is commonly spoken and old-world customs observed. On the feast of St.Mary's, in the spring, blossoms are cut and brought to church to be blessed; an offering is made to secure bumper crops in the autumn. Corpus Christi Day begins with a solemn high mass; the Blessed Sacrament is exposed for three days for public adoration; 40-hour devotions are held; and the celebration closes on Sunday with bands, choirs, worshippers, and children in procession, waving banners and singing, stopping at street altars to pray and to receive the sacramental blessing from priests. The Italian section centers in Vanderwoort Street near Payne Avenue. The Columbus Day celebration calls for parades, with floats representing the discovery of America, banquets, and speeches. The RUDOLPH WURLITZER PLANT, 900-block Niagara Falls Blvd., makes theater and church organs, radio cabinets, mechanical pianos, and coin-operated phonographs. The firm was founded in 1856 at Cincinnati by Rudolph Wurlitzer, a young German, whose ancestors had been organ makers in Saxony for centuries. The North Tonawanda plant was opened in 1908.

TONAWANDA, 4.2 m. (575 alt.,12,973 pop.), a twin sister of North Tonawanda, is a transportation center with a web of railroads and a harbor accommodating large lake steamers; it produces shingles, office furniture, paper, motorboats, and beaverboard. Workers include large groups of Poles, Germans, Syrians, and Italians.

BUFFALO, 23.9 m. (600 alt.,575,150 pop.) (*see Buffalo*), is at the junction with State 5 (*see Tour 11*), State 33 (*see Tour 33*), and State 16 (*see Tour 38*).

South of Buffalo, at 34.5 m., is the junction with US 20 (*see Tour 8*).

At the HAMBURG FAIR GROUNDS (L), 37.9 m., the annual Erie County fair is held during the last week in August. Children's Day is marked by a pageant of as many as 30,000 children; Political Day brings oratory; Fireman's Day calls out 80 western New York organizations in a massed drill. The State police give riding exhibits; free dancing and vaudeville acts are offered; white and Indian boys vie in archery competition; old-time plowing contests survive in the form of horse-pulling matches.

The center of truck-farming activities is HAMBURG, 38.8 m. (826 alt., 5,428 pop.), settled by German immigrants about 1808. During the Canadian uprising of 1837–9 the villagers were sympathetic to the rebel cause and 400 recruits planned to cross Lake Erie one wintry night to invade Canada; but this heroic undertaking was stopped by New York State militia.

The undulating hills and hummocks south of Hamburg are the outposts of the Allegheny Mountains. This part of the State was settled by New Englanders; the soil has been cultivated by their descendants for generations, and the hardy New England influence is still in evidence: the zigzag rail fence, the solid stone or brick house, the neat flower garden.

NORTH COLLINS, 48.8 m. (830 alt.,1,178 pop.), has a chemical plant, canneries, a cheese factory, and brick kilns. The place was settled about 1809 by Quakers, who in 1813 built the first meetinghouse, still standing at the southern edge of town, a white clapboarded structure with slat-backed benches and white drop shutters. Natural gas, discovered on village farmlands in 1888, is still being piped to Buffalo and Springfield.

Between North Collins and Gowanda the route runs close to the eastern boundary of the Cattaraugus Indian Reservation. At 52.9 m. is the junction with a reservation road (see Tour 8).

At 55.9 m. is the northern junction with State 39 (see Tour 34); the two roads run in common to Gowanda.

The GOWANDA STATE HOMEOPATHIC HOSPITAL, 56.8 m., an institution for mental disorders, stands on a 500-acre tract. The community is listed in the postal directory as Helmuth, New York, named for Dr.William Tod Helmuth of New York City.

GOWANDA, 58.4 m. (760 alt.,3,042 pop.), tans leather, makes glue, carbonated beverages, cider, vinegar, wood barrels, and gelatine. Cattaraugus Creek attracted New England settlers in 1810, and they raised sawmills and gristmills. The intrepid Ahaz Allen (see below) built the first frame house in 1814. In 1830 Horace Greeley, who had hiked as a journeyman printer from Vermont to Erie County, came to Lodi, as the place was then known, in search of a job. In 1848 Lodi became Gowanda; three years later the Erie Railroad came through and brought industries.

Left from Gowanda on a paved road 7.2 m. into ZOAR VALLEY. Down Cattaraugus Creek in 1810 came Ahaz Allen and his family, all packed in a canoe. Stopping here, Ahaz looked out upon the pleasant valley and was reminded of Zoar, the city of plains, to which Lot once fled; and the valley got its name. In the eighties some of the largest gushers in the New York oil fields were struck in this region; in 1915 there were 23 wells, but these were all shut in, and the place is today a natural gas storage field.

The Erie Railroad bed in DAYTON, 63.2 m. (1,322 alt.,300 pop.), marks the watershed line, south of which all water flows into the Gulf of Mexico.

Left from Dayton on State 18 to CATTARAUGUS, 9.5 *m.* (1,383 alt.,1,236 pop.), which makes creamery supplies, wood veneer, meat skewers, and lollipop sticks. The Indian word means 'bad smelling banks,' referring to the natural gas that used to escape from rock crevices along Cattaraugus Creek. The place was settled comparatively late—in 1851—when the Erie Railroad came through; the gang workers who laid the tracks regularly blew their wages and turned the hamlet into a true western frontier town with their carousing, gambling, and fighting.

Joseph Plumb, who owned most of the land, was appalled by this lawlessness and decided to dedicate his property forever to temperance by inserting a clause in the conveyance of his lots which provided that title to any parcel of land should revert to him or his heirs if liquor were sold on the premises. When a man named Tubbs ignored this restriction and merrily went on selling hard liquor on a lot purchased from Plumb, a lawsuit resulted, which ended in a decision by the Court of Appeals upholding the validity of the prohibitory clause and reverting the lot to Plumb. The teetotaling but altruistic Plumb deeded the property back to the Tubbs family.

LITTLE VALLEY, 16.7 *m.* (1,594 alt.,1,196 pop.), Cattaraugus County seat, has a Borden milk plant and a cutlery factory. The vicinity is rich in archeological material predating Huron-Iroquois history.

Southward the road follows Little Valley Creek through the rising hills of the Alleghenies to WEST SALAMANCA, 25.5 *m.* (1,380 alt.,530 pop.). Originally called Buck Tooth, the place was once an important junction on the Erie Railroad, with turntables, shops, and engine houses; but when the farmers raised land prices, the railroad activities were moved to the present SALAMANCA, 27.8 *m.* (1,380 alt., 9,654 pop.) (*see Tour 3*), which is on State 17 (*see Tour 3*).

South of Dayton US 62 runs through a hilly area, following a series of creeks that finally join the Allegheny River in Pennsylvania. At 102.1 *m.* US 62 crosses the PENNSYLVANIA LINE, 12 miles north of Warren, Pennsylvania.

Tour 38

Buffalo—East Aurora—Yorkshire—Olean—(Bradford, Pa.); State 16, 16A.
Buffalo to Pennsylvania Line, 80 *m.*

Two-lane, macadam or concrete.
Pennsylvania R.R. parallels route.

Southeast of Buffalo is muck land worked by truck farmers; and beyond this black soil, as the land rises, are dairy and stock farms. Finally, near the Pennsylvania line, oil companies are still harvesting a crop which grew in a tropical jungle millions of years ago.

In the suburbs of BUFFALO, 0 *m.* (600 alt.,575,150 pop.) (*see Buffalo*), State 16 passes rows of peas-in-the-pod bungalows, viaducts, soot-stained rookeries at railroad sidings.

SPRINGBROOK, 11.6 *m.* (774 alt.,210 pop.), is a garden-farm community. Here and there are deep-retreating country estates, greenswards neatly edged, where gentlemen farmers raise blue-blooded horses.

In the 1860's a German nobleman, age 19, sought to emulate James Fenimore Cooper and came here to write a book about the frontier. For weeks he roamed the countryside with pencil and notebook. In 1868 appeared in Buffalo a book entitled *Hunt of the Buffaloes or A True Rapport of Perils with the Indians Whose Habitat is Near & Around Buffalo*, by Alexis Ferdinand von der Hoehe. There were few dull moments in the narrative: '. . . suddenly I hear a screech such as will by great necessity and suddenty curdle the blood of the veins in the human anatomy. I see a tall Indian rush out of the log cabin with a baby in arm and behind, crying with the most heart terrorizing sobs of the whole body the mother of the child, Mrs.Benson. "Thunder-lightning" I cry. "Stand still your pace in your tracks, you impudent fellow!" . . .'

In EAST AURORA, 15.5 *m.* (926 alt.,5,239 pop.), is the junction with US 20A (*see Tour 8A*).

South of East Aurora the monotony of the flatlands is broken by parallel lines of hills extending southward and covered with beech, basswood, and maple.

In YORKSHIRE, 37 *m.* (1,438 alt.,306 pop.), is the junction with State 39 (*see Tour 34*).

DELEVAN, 39.7 *m.* (1,442 alt.,558 pop.), is a favorite training place for pugilists and wrestlers. Many Buffalo fighters have trained here, among them the former heavyweight wrestling champion, George Nichols. The place was named in 1892 in honor of Jack Delevan, a trainer and hotel keeper.

LIME LAKE (*swimming, fishing, boating*), 43.5 *m.* (1,640 alt.,51 pop.), is a scattered summer resort along the irregular shore of Lime Lake.

At 45.9 *m.* is the junction with State 98.

Left on State 98 to FARMERSVILLE, 3.9 *m.* (1,837 alt.,50 pop.), at the watershed between the Allegheny River on the one hand and Cattaraugus Creek and a branch of the Genesee River on the other. Oldsters are fond of saying that there is a spot in the town where a man can, without moving, spit in the waters of the Gulf of St.Lawrence and the waters of the Gulf of Mexico.

The place was settled in 1816–17 by a group of men, all bachelors but one; in the true pioneer spirit the bachelors drew up and signed the following agreement: 'If any woman who is over fourteen years of age, shall come to reside in our village, and no one of this confederacy shall offer her his company, within a fortnight thereafter, then in such case, our board shall be called together, and someone shall be appointed to make her a visit; whose duty it shall be to perform the same, or forfeit the disapprobation of the company, and pay a fine sufficiently large to buy the lady thus neglected, a new dress.'

Factories in FRANKLINVILLE, 51.4 *m.* (1,594 alt.,2,021 pop.), produce kitchenware, cans, and cheese and other milk products. The place was settled shortly after 1800 by Joseph McClure, who surveyed for the Holland Land Company many of the early roads of Cattaraugus and Allegany Counties and was 'somewhat noted for his faculty of making them terminate at the settlement he had commenced.'

The new FRANKLINVILLE HIGH SCHOOL, N.Main St., which includes experimental agriculture in its curriculum, occupies the site of the old Ten Broeck Academy, once a dignified group of stone buildings on a four-acre campus, donated in the sixties by Peter Ten Broeck to provide free education, including astronomy.

ISCHUA, 59.1 *m.* (1,585 alt.,350 pop.), is in a pocket along Ischua Creek among quarried hills. In 1845 the settlers rose up against the Holland Land Company in the 'Dutch Hill War,' a bloodless affair. Farmers took to arms to defy ejection; one settler, an Irishman, accidentally discharged a gun as the militia, called by the company, approached. But that was all, and the agitated farmers returned home. The incident has been called the 'first agrarian strike in America.'

At 64.2 *m.* is the junction with State 63.

Left on State 63 to CUBA (1,500 alt.,1,422 pop.), 6.8 *m.*; left from Cuba on State 94 to the junction with a macadam road, 1.7 *m.*; left here 2.2 *m.* to CUBA LAKE (*bathing, picnicking, dancing, amusements*), an irregularly shaped body of water locally popular as a summer resort. On the same road, at the southwestern tip of the lake, is the CUBA RESERVATION, 4.7 *m.*, one square mile, which includes the first observed petroleum spring in America, discovered in 1627 by Joseph de la Roche D'Allion, a Franciscan friar. A stagnant, brush-grown pool, the spring is 18 feet in diameter and of unknown depth. An iron-bound cask, preserved by the oil, has occupied the center of the spring as long as anyone can remember. Indians used the oil for medicinal purposes. The spring and adjacent land was reserved in perpetuity to the Seneca Indians by the Big Tree Treaty of 1797; in 1937 but one lone Seneca lived in its confines.

At OLEAN, 71.3 *m.* (1,440 alt.,21,790 pop.) (*see Tour 3*), is the junction with State 17 (*see Tour 3*), and the junction with State 16A, which (straight ahead) becomes the main tour. South of Olean, State 16A passes through part of the New York State oil field (*see Tour 3*).

ROCK CITY (R), 76.3 *m.*, is a natural mass of conglomerate rock crisscrossed by fissures, producing the effect of a built-up city with regular street blocks. Near by are caves, some of which are large enough to shelter 30 people.

At 80 *m.* State 16A crosses the PENNSYLVANIA LINE, 10.3 miles northeast of Bradford, Pennsylvania.

Tour 39

Hamburg—Springville—Salamanca—(Bradford, Pa.); US 219.
Hamburg to Pennsylvania Line, 61.4 *m.*

Two-strip macadam and concrete road.
The Baltimore & Ohio R.R. parallels southern half of the route; Erie R.R. between Salamanca and Pennsylvania line.

US 219 traverses a pleasant, hilly farming region to Salamanca, east and south of which it cuts through the Allegany Indian Reservation along the eastern border of Allegany State Park, serpentining along the course of the Allegheny River and Tunungwant Creek.

Southeast from HAMBURG, 0 m. (826 alt.,5,428 pop.) (see Tour 37), the route follows Eighteenmile Creek. BOSTON, 8.3 m. (960 alt.,400 pop.), once manufactured cowbells. Ellen Beach Yaw, opera singer of the nineties who now lives in Covina, California, was born here in 1871. ST. PAUL'S EVANGELICAL CHURCH (R), was erected in 1834 by settlers from New England, who hauled the timbers from Gowanda.

SPRINGVILLE, 17.2 m. (1,341 alt.,2,832 pop.), was early known as Fiddlers' Green. David Leroy, 'famous and inveterate fiddler,' settled here in 1812, and he and other amateurs made it a habit to meet on the green and strike up popular tunes. Back from the road (R) is the BIOLOGICAL STATION OF THE GRATWICK LABORATORIES (New York State Institute for the Control of Malignant Diseases, Buffalo), in which cancer research is conducted on living tissue.

In Springville is the junction with State 39 (see Tour 34).

ELLICOTTVILLE, 36.6 m. (1,549 alt.,978 pop.), makes last blocks for the shoe trade, condensed milk, baskets, and prefabricated garages. The place was named for Joseph Ellicott, Holland Land Company surveyor. In 1859 three Franciscan Fathers, Pamfilio, Milian, and Sextus, established themselves here to administer to the spiritual needs of the Irish railroad workers. They remained for three years and then moved to Allegany, where they founded St.Bonaventure's College in 1859. In the belfry of ST.JOHN'S EPISCOPAL CHURCH, corner of Washington and Jefferson Sts., hangs a bell cast in 1708 in Malaga, Spain, and brought to the village in 1838.

In GREAT VALLEY 41.2 m. (1,460 alt.,214 pop.), is the junction with a dirt road.

Left on this road 2.4 m. to the BREATHING WELL HOMESTEAD (open). The 'Breathing Well' in the yard is a natural curiosity dating back to 1841. The phenomena of 'inhaling' and 'exhaling' are explained by the existence of a chain of subterranean caverns connecting with the well and ending at an as yet undiscovered outlet; variations in barometric pressure are said to cause the 'breathing.'

SALAMANCA, 47.8 m. (1,380 alt.,9,654 pop.) (see Tour 3), is at the junction with State 17 (see Tour 3).

At LIMESTONE, 59.6 m., in the valley of Tunungwant Creek, oil operations were started in the sixties when a well was sunk by Dr.James Nichols. A boom followed in the seventies, with 250 wells, some of them producing more than 170 barrels a day. It is said that the oil men planned to make Limestone their headquarters but exorbitant real estate prices drove settlers across the line to Bradford.

The road crosses the PENNSYLVANIA LINE, 61.4 m., 3.9 miles north of Bradford, Pennsylvania.

Tour 40

Poughkeepsie—New York City; State 55, Eastern State Parkway, Bronx
River Parkway Extension, Saw Mill River Parkway, 73.8 *m.*

Four-lane concrete; dangerous after snowfall until sanded.
40-mile speed limit strictly enforced.

The Eastern State Parkway, open (1940) as far north as Freedom
Plains, east of Poughkeepsie, connects with the Saw Mill River Parkway
and the Bronx River Parkway to provide a scenic boulevard route into
New York City, by-passing or over-passing all towns and crossroads
through the heavily traveled area north of the metropolis. The carefully
landscaped route rides the wooded hills of the eastern part of the State
through several State parks.

State 55 runs east from POUGHKEEPSIE, 0 *m.* (175 alt.,40,237 pop.)
(*see Poughkeepsie*), to FREEDOM PLAINS, 7.9 *m.* (340 alt.,84 pop.).
Right here on the Eastern State Parkway, which has two separate two-
lane highways, one northbound, the other southbound.

At 23.9 *m.* is the junction with State 301.

Right on State 301 to the CLARENCE FAHNESTOCK MEMORIAL STATE
PARK (*picnicking; parking 25¢*), 0.7 *m.*, 3,400 acres of forest land, much of which was
untrodden wilderness until the Parkway was opened.

At 37.3 *m.* the Eastern State Parkway runs into the Bronx River Parkway Extension.

Right here on the Bronx River Parkway Extension to PEEKSKILL, 1.9 *m.* (120 alt.,
17,289 pop.) (*see Tour 4*), junction with US 6 (*see Tour 4*) and US 9 (*see Tour 21*).

The NEW CROTON RESERVOIR, crossed on a bridge at 41.9 *m.*, is
the southernmost part of the Croton water system (*see Tour 21*).

At the HAWTHORNE TRAFFIC CIRCLE, 51.6 *m.*, is the junction with the
Saw Mill River Parkway, most convenient approach to the West Side,
Manhattan. The main route follows the Saw Mill River Parkway.

The Bronx River Parkway Extension, continuing south, runs into the Bronx River
Parkway, oldest unit in the Westchester County Parkway system, at the traffic circle,
3.5 *m.* At 6 *m.* is (R) the WESTCHESTER COUNTY COMMUNITY CENTER in WHITE
PLAINS (467 alt.,40,116 pop.) (*see Tour 20*). At 15 *m.* the Parkway under-passes the
CROSS COUNTY PARKWAY (*see Tour 1*). The BRONX RIVER PARKWAY ends at Ford-
ham Road, the Bronx, 21.5 *m.* Right on Fordham Road to the GEORGE WASHINGTON
MEMORIAL BRIDGE, 24.5 *m.*

On the Saw Mill River Parkway, a traffic circle, 65.7 *m.*, marks the
junction with the Cross County Parkway (*see Tour 1*). At 67.6 *m.* the
Parkway joins the Henry Hudson Parkway, which crosses the HENRY
HUDSON BRIDGE (*toll 10¢*) over the Spuyten Duyvil Creek at 70.7 *m.* At
73.8 *m.* is the entrance to the GEORGE WASHINGTON MEMORIAL BRIDGE
(R). The WEST SIDE ELEVATED HIGHWAY continues to the downtown area
and to the Lincoln and Holland Tunnels.

Long Island

Long Island, thrusting 125 miles eastward from New York Bay to a point abreast of New London, Connecticut, faces the New England coast across Long Island Sound on the north and fronts the open Atlantic on the south. The long, narrow outline of the island resembles that of a whale. Its eastern end is split by Peconic Bay; and the 50-mile peninsulas thereby formed are the north and south 'flukes.'

Topographically the island is almost a plain. On the north coast bluffs rise to a height of 200 feet. South of these, extending well into the island's midriff, run several chains of hills, with High Hill, the highest point on the island, attaining an altitude of 410 feet. From these elevations the surface declines gently southward toward the sea, forming the great plain, well suited for agriculture. On the south shore, between Rockaway and Southampton, the ocean waves break on a narrow ribbon of sand cut by several inlets and backed up by the waters of the Great South Bay. The west portion of this sandbar has been developed into a series of bathing resorts, chief among which are Rockaway, Long, and Jones Beaches.

Historians group the aboriginal inhabitants of Long Island, estimated never to have exceeded 1,000 in number, in two loose federations: the Montauk to the east, the Delaware to the west. No full-blooded aborigine remains. His memory survives in the names he supplied for villages, streets, and bays; and the reservations marked off at Shinnecock and Poosepatuck are the only estates left to his mixed Negroid and Indian heirs.

In 1609 Henry Hudson, seeking the fabled northwest passage, entered New York Bay and landed on Coney Island. Hollanders settled on the western end of the island, but were slow in extending their settlements eastward. In the next generation the restless English, descending from Connecticut and the Bay Colony, landed in Southampton, Southold, and other 'down east' points; by 1643 they were in Hempstead. The inevitable friction was followed by a division of control in 1650, the boundary line running from Oyster Bay south to the ocean. In 1664 the entire island became part of the Province of New York.

The island was little affected by events of the following two centuries. Slowly it gained in population, its economy built upon the soil and the bay waters. During the Revolution the east towns supported the patriots strongly, but by no means unanimously. In the western section there were many Tories who in the end paid heavily in confiscated estates for their preference for King George. After the Battle of Long Island in 1776, the English held the island in a firm grip until the final evacuation in 1784. During the War of 1812 the island was largely at the mercy of the British.

The off-shore whaling industry, a minor Colonial enterprise, boomed after the signing of peace. Sag Harbor and Greenport deep-sea vessels covered much of the world in the hunt for oil and bone. The opening up of the West turned Long Island farmers more and more to truck gardening. Meantime the fisheries expanded to meet a growing demand; Saddle Rock and Blue Point oysters were called for the world over. Fish for fertilizer is another Long Island product.

The coming of the railroad in the 1830's was the first step in modern transit. At first the inhabitants took to it unkindly: sparks from the engine burned their fields and destroyed their crops. In 1900 the Pennsylvania Railroad acquired control and provided for the Long Island Railroad a terminus in midtown Manhattan. Thenceforward the commutation passenger traffic on the Long Island Railroad increased rapidly.

The island comprises four counties: Kings (Brooklyn), Queens, Nassau, and Suffolk. The first two are constituent parts of New York City. The latter two present a marked contrast. Nassau, with a population of more than 300,000 and an area of 252 square miles, is made up of bustling villages containing the homes of the hordes of executives, clerks, and artisans who are disgorged every evening from the metropolis. The soil is secondary. Suffolk, with half the population on an area four times as large, depends primarily on agriculture and fishing. Its farmers, fishermen, clammers, and local shop people live in scattered villages, many with white wood churches casting peaceful shadows on village greens reminiscent of the New England coast and countryside. The tempo of life is slow, and traditional mores govern.

The backbone of the economy of Suffolk is truck farming. The light topsoil is easily worked, and the gravelly subsoil provides excellent drainage. The growing season is long, rainfall is generally ample, and, most important of all, close at hand is the largest market in the world. The two chief crops are potatoes and cauliflower. In 1930 Suffolk County produced 3,760,576 bushels of potatoes, more than twice as much as its nearest rival among the counties of the State; and Nassau grew 805,207 bushels. The average Suffolk cauliflower crop is 700,000 crates, comprising about seven-tenths of the State's total.

Livestock is largely limited to poultry; there are many egg and broiler farms, but no reliable figures are available on output. The Long Island duckling has been well advertised and no doubt impostors have crept to restaurant tables on his fame; but he does exist, 6,000,000 of him, whitening the shores of coves and canals from Speonk east, and adding from four to six million dollars to the yearly income of Long Island.

Oysters and clams furnish employment to a rather individualistic sector of the population—baymen of the south side and a smaller contingent out of the northern harbors. In 1930 the product of Nassau County waters was valued at $157,926; that of Suffolk, far in the lead, $880,795. Catering to the amateur fisherman is a thriving seasonal occupation calling for a rather heavy investment in small boats for landlocked waters and larger ones to face the sea off Montauk or to plow through the tides of the inlets.

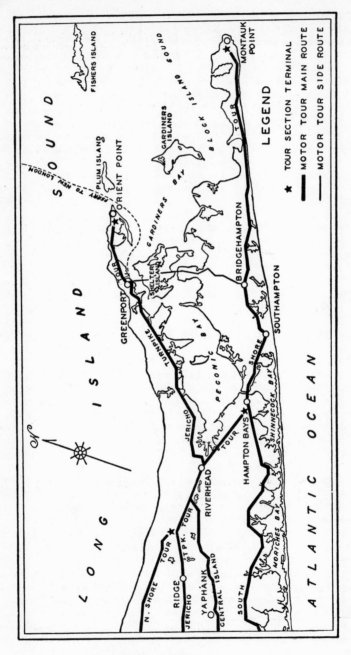

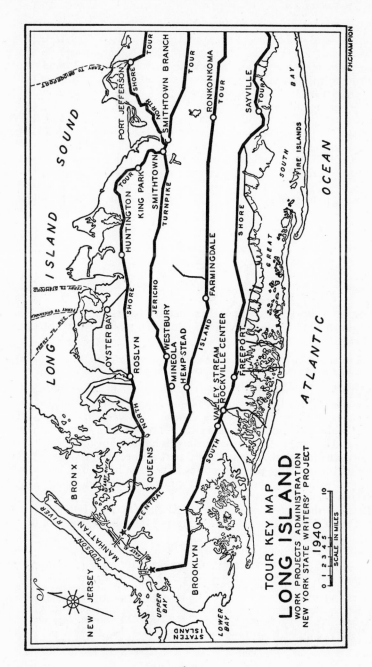

TOUR KEY MAP
LONG ISLAND
WORK PROJECTS ADMINISTRATION
NEW YORK STATE WRITERS' PROJECT
1940

SCALE IN MILES
0 1 2 3 4 5   10

F.H.CHAMPION

A large commuting population in its western quarter, farmers, fisher-men, and local shopkeepers—these are the foundations on which the island economy rests. During the winter months the communities go about their business quietly and methodically. With the coming of the summer month the island, with its bathing beaches, camp sites, yacht clubs, golf clubs, polo clubs, fishing grounds, and State parks, becomes a playground for the metropolitan millions.

Hard-surfaced roads gridiron the western quarter of the island, but far-ther east the pattern becomes more diffuse. The west-to-east road system is admirably balanced: two highways serve the 'north shore,' two the 'south shore,' one the middle island belt—all supplemented by two excel-lent State parkways built with an eye to scenic effect and offering speedy access to points well inland. Extensions, which will ultimately take these parkways to most of the principal State parks, are being built as planned.

NORTH SHORE TOUR

Queensboro Bridge—Roslyn—Huntington—Kings Park—Smithtown—Smithtown Branch—Port Jefferson—Junction with State 25; State 25A. 74.4 *m.*

Route paralleled in stretches by the Long Island Railroad. Hotel accommodations ample, but tourist camps and houses are few; restaurants are plentiful.

State 25A, reached from Manhattan Island via the Queensboro Bridge, serves the indented north shore of Long Island, and is paralleled one to five miles south by State 25 (*see Jericho Turnpike Tour*). Long Island Sound is always close and often in sight. Through some stretches the road, rising and dipping to the uneven surface, is bordered by oak forest.

Between New York City and Northport are necks on which several vil-lages and many large private estates have been built. The necks, while equipped with mayor, police, and civic machinery, are dominated by the rich landholders.

Between the eastern end of the QUEENSBORO BRIDGE, 0 *m.*, and the Nassau County Line, 11.7 *m.*, State 25A follows the streets of the bor-ough of Queens.

At 11.8 *m.* is the junction with Bayview Ave.

Left on Bayview Ave. to GREAT NECK ESTATES, 0.7 *m.* (2,004 pop.), SAD-DLE ROCK, 1.7 *m.* (74 pop.), and KINGS POINT, 2.8 *m.* (1,225 pop.).

East from Kings Point on Elm Road, past estates with residences screened by trees, to GREAT NECK, 4.4 *m.* (6,214 pop.), spread around a village green. Middle Neck Road, running south, connects KENSINGTON, 5.7 *m.* (926 pop.), GREAT NECK PLAZA, 5.9 *m.* (2,076 pop.), RUSSELL GARDENS, 6.1 *m.* (547 pop.), and THOMASTON, 6.3 *m.* (1,155 pop.). The contrast of these pastoral spots with the clamor of the adjacent metropolis is striking. Long winding roads run through the shade of trees and skirt landscaped plots. The region is exclusively residential, the large private estates barred to access. Saddle Rock, owned wholly by one family, has as its sole association with bygone days the ALLEN GRIST MILL (*private*), 2.2 *m*. (L), a two-and-a-half-story, weathered shingled bulk built in 1710 by Henry Allen and operated by tidal flow. Kings Point, which caps the peninsula, is made up of estates of the wealthy. Heavy woods restrict views of the water, to which only private roads lead. Great Neck, Kensington, and Great Neck Plaza are the business centers of the peninsula. Russell Gardens, a planned community, has bridle paths, a swimming pool, tennis courts, a golf course, and a clubhouse. Many of the wooded, hilly, barricaded estates on the neck have been popular with actors, song writers, playwrights, and authors. Will Durant, author of *The Story of Philosophy*, lives in Great Neck.

MANHASSET, 13.6 *m*. (2,827 pop.), is one of the oldest communities on the north shore. Facing State 25A, opposite Shelter Rock Road, is the old FRIENDS MEETING HOUSE, built in 1810; greenish weathered shingles and gray slate roof give the two-story structure the appearance of age. The ONDERDONK HOUSE, 2931 N.Hempstead Turnpike, built in 1836, is considered Long Island's finest example of Greek Revival architecture. The portico, two stories high, is composed of four Doric columns and triangular pediment, with the entrance doorway between the two left columns. One-story wings project from the main section.

In Manhasset is the junction with Plandome Road.

Left on Plandome Road to Manhasset Neck, which includes the villages of PLANDOME, 1 *m*. (893 pop.), PORT WASHINGTON, 3.3 *m*. (3,409 pop.), SANDS POINT, 5.2 *m*. (601 pop.), and FLOWER HILL, 13.9 *m*. (633 pop.). The old PLANDOME MILL (L) (*not open*), built in 1673, still stands by Leeds Pond. Port Washington is built on a hill overlooking Manhasset Bay, which in summer accommodates a swarm of water craft and the New York-Bermuda air liners. A ferry (*car and driver, $1.75; car, driver, and one passenger, $2; car, driver, and 2 or more passengers, $2.25*) connects Port Washington and New Rochelle.

Sands Point, a highly restricted residential community, is named for Captain John Sands (1649–1712), who mastered a packet plying between New York and Virginia ports and is said to have introduced the locust tree to Long Island.

ROSLYN, 16.9 *m*. (970 pop.), stretching along the curving shore of Hempstead Harbor, is backed by the wooded slopes of the Wheatley Hills. For many years the settlement was known as the Town at the Head of the Harbor.

William Cullen Bryant lived in Roslyn from 1843 to 1878; he came to New York in 1825 and a few years later became editor of the New York *Evening Post*, a position he held until his death. He divided his time between this house and his city home. A pair of Bryant's eyeglasses is exhibited in the ROSLYN GRIST MILL (L), Main St., a two-story building, half of which is below the road level. Originally the Onderdonk grist mill and the center of life for the village, it is now a combination museum and tea room. The water wheel still turns in the old raceway; inside, original millstones and mixers are exhibited along with Colonial heirlooms. John Robeson started to build the mill in 1698, but he failed to complete the job, and it was not until later that the mill began operations.

Bryant's house, CEDARMERE (L) (*private*), Bryant Ave., Roslyn Harbor, built in 1787, has been adorned with gray stucco; the two-and-a-half-story, gable-roofed dwelling bears little resemblance to the original. The poet's letters and writings abound in comments on the Roslyn countryside of nearly a century ago. The BRYANT LIBRARY (L) (*open 3–6 Mon.; 9:30–11:30, 3–6 Tues., Wed., Fri., Sat.; 9:30–11:30, 3–6, 7–9 Thur.*), 25 Bryant Ave., contains many of the poet's books. In the ROSLYN CEMETERY, E. end of village, are his and his wife's graves. Also buried in the Bryant plot is Parke Godwin, the poet's son-in-law, biographer, and successor as editor of the New York *Evening Post*.

As chairman of a committee appointed to seek a better name than Head of the Harbor, Bryant had much to do with the selection of Roslyn. The poetic and literary tradition of the village is carried on today by Christopher Morley, poet, essayist, and novelist, whose home, The Birches, is in Roslyn.

Bryant Ave., leading north from State 25A, enters the largest neck of the north shore.

North on Bryant Ave. to GLENWOOD LANDING, 2.1 *m.* (1,378 pop.), and the STEAM ELECTRIC GENERATING STATION (*open*) (L), which supplies Nassau and Suffolk Counties with much of their light and power. Over the masts of pleasure boats and beyond the blue water of Hempstead Harbor looms a sand and gravel pit.

SEA CLIFF, 3.3 *m.* (4,435 pop.), originally a church camp-meeting resort but now a residential village, clings to the side of a hill.

GLEN COVE, 5.6 *m.* (12,401 pop.), is one of Long Island's two incorporated cities and the business center of Cove Neck. Its narrow and hilly streets hum with activity in summer when vacationists at Lattingtown, Glen Cove Landing, and Bayville, near-by seaside colonies, do the week-end marketing. Charles A. Dana, who served with Greeley on the New York *Tribune* and organized the old New York *Sun*, came to Glen Cove in 1873 and died here in 1897. The weatherbeaten shingles of the FRIENDS MEETING HOUSE, NE. corner of Duck Pond and Birch Hill Roads, built in 1725 by Quakers averse to gambling, faces the ECLIPSE MONUMENT, erected to the 1823 winner of a three-heat race over a four-mile course near Hempstead.

East from Glen Cove on Forest Road to LOCUST VALLEY, 8 *m.* (2,304 pop.), a residential community, historically interesting as the spot where Captain John Underhill (1597–1672) acquired much land and lived his last years. Underhill came to Boston in 1630 to organize and command the Massachusetts militia. After a stormy career in New England he came here, where he fought Dutch discrimination against English settlers. He was led into wrangles with Peter Stuyvesant and narrowly escaped trial on the charge of sedition. The British occupation of 1664 elevated him to High Sheriff and made further belligerency unnecessary.

MATINECOCK, 8.9 *m.* (421 pop.), and MILL NECK, 10.5 *m.* (516 pop.), links in the cross-neck road, are residential. The entire village of Mill Neck and parts of the surrounding lands have been designated as a game sanctuary supported by private funds in co-operation with the State Conservation Department. There are approximately 3,800 acres of land and lakes; all wild life is protected and winter feeding is carried on.

Both Dutch and English were in OYSTER BAY, 12.5 *m.* (5,315 pop.), by the middle of the seventeenth century, and the varying and often conflicting interests of the two groups flavored the long history of the village. Because they could not agree, the village today has two main streets a block apart. RAYNHAM HALL (*adm. 25¢*), 25 W. Main St., the Townsend homestead built in 1740, a two-story residence with white shingled front and clapboarded sides and with a peculiar projection overhanging the front stoop, was the Revolutionary headquarters of the British Lieutenant Colonel John Graves Simcoe and his Queen's Rangers. He and his gay staff, Major André, and the three Townsend girls and their friends left an aroma of romance and of tragedy that endures, and a number of relics that the present custodians delight to show.

Oyster Bay is generally known as the home of Theodore Roosevelt (1858–1919), 26th President of the United States, but the neighboring incorporated village of COVE NECK, 14.7 *m.* (276 pop.), rightfully claims that honor. SAGAMORE HILL (*private*), Cove Neck Rd., the Roosevelt home on the east side of Oyster Bay, is open only to Boy Scouts one day each year. The ROOSEVELT GRAVE, Youngs Memorial Cemetery (R), 14.1 *m.*, surrounded by an iron picket fence, looks out over the harbor; the cemetery is bordered by the horseshoe-shaped ROOSEVELT BIRD SANCTUARY. ROOSEVELT MEMORIAL PARK is on the water front.

Theodore Roosevelt, in and out of office, kept the public eye as few, if any, Americans did before his day. Animated, aggressive, insatiably interested in everything around him, he held half a dozen offices from State assemblyman and New York City police commissioner to President of the United States, fought in the Spanish-American War as colonel of his Rough Riders, shook his 'big stick' at the 'malefactors of great wealth,' sponsored the causes of conservation and civil service, split the Republican party with the Bull Moose campaign of 1912, discovered the River of Doubt in South America, wrote a number of books on the West, and won the 1906 Nobel peace prize for his part in negotiating the peace that ended the Russo-Japanese War.

At 14.7 *m.* is the junction with State 25A.

At 26.5 *m.* is the eastern junction with the Glen Cove-Oyster Bay side route (*see above*).

In the DEPARTMENT OF GENETICS OF THE CARNEGIE INSTITUTE (*open*), 27.4 *m.* (L), experiments are carried on in organic evolution. At 28 *m.* (R) is a State fish hatchery (*open*), which breeds fresh-water fish for restocking lakes and streams.

COLD SPRING HARBOR, 28.7 *m.* (713 pop.), was a whaling port in the middle years of the last century. So many languages were heard on its main street, now State 25A, that the thoroughfare was called Bedlam Street. 'Bungtown,' a settlement but a stone's throw from the village, made barrels for whale oil. To the local taprooms strange and exotic objects were brought by sailors.

HUNTINGTON, 30.7 *m.* (6,693 pop.), at the foot of West and Dix Hills, spreads down to the bay front. The British soldiery during the Revolution converted the old cemetery, E.Main St. at the eastern end of the business section, into a fort, which, with grisly humor, they named Fort Golgotha.

The PRESBYTERIAN CHURCH, NE. corner of E.Main St. and Sabbathday Path, an impressive and graceful white-shingled structure, shows, by its quaint tower, spired lantern, and richly textured white-shingled walls, that forms derived from sophisticated metropolitan architecture can be translated into vernacular materials and still attain a dignified grace and charm. The contrast between the beautiful Georgian Colonial doorways and the naive double-carved projections immediately above is especially amusing. The present building, erected in 1784, is the third on the site; the first was built in 1665; the second, erected in 1715, was torn down by British soldiers in 1777 to furnish timbers for Fort Golgotha.

Left from Huntington on New York Ave. 1.2 *m.* to HALESITE, named for the American martyr, Nathan Hale. Right in Halesite on Young Ave. to HALE'S MONUMENT, 1.6 *m.*, a huge boulder set on a grassy plot facing Long Island Sound, marking the spot where it is thought the British captured Hale in September 1776, a few days after he had volunteered as a spy. He was executed in New York on September 22, 1776.

In CENTERPORT, 34.6 *m.* (434 pop.), is the junction with Little Neck Road.

Left on Little Neck Road to PLAISANCE, 1.1 *m.*, the marble-pillared Vanderbilt estate, and the VANDERBILT MARINE MUSEUM (*open by invitation*), in which is displayed the collection of marine life gathered by the owner from many parts of the world.

In the days of sail, ships out of NORTHPORT, 36 *m.* (3,079 pop.), circled the globe in search of markets for the expanding American trade. Between 1820 and 1884, 179 vessels were built in Northport yards, and allied industries thrived. Today the village is known as one of the most healthful in the State and famous for the fine views from its wooded slopes.

State 25A touches the SITE OF FORT SALONGA at 39.2 *m.*; the fort was a British post captured and destroyed by the Continentals in 1781. SUNKEN MEADOW STATE PARK (*parking 25¢ Sat., Sun., and holidays*), 42 *m.*, has a beach, picnic areas, and a playground for children. In KINGS PARK, 42.6 *m.* (232 pop.), is KINGS PARK STATE HOSPITAL, an institution for the insane. East of Kings Park are cabbage and cauliflower patches and potato fields.

At SMITHTOWN, 46.5 *m.* (71 pop.), is the western junction with State 25 (*see Jericho Turnpike Tour*), with which State 25A runs in common to SMITHTOWN BRANCH, 47.9 *m.* (951 pop.). At Smithtown Branch State 25A branches left.

STONY BROOK, 53.7 *m.* (790 pop.), is built on a hill sloping down to the water front. The houses are scattered along winding roads shaded with locusts and maples. In 1843, 24 vessels carried loads of cordwood to New York City. The harbor today can accommodate only craft of the lightest draft. The MOUNT HOUSE, NE. corner of State 25A and Gould Road, was occupied from time to time by William Sidney Mount (1807–68), genre painter and delineator of the common life. On Mill Road at the Stony Brook crossing is a gristmill, built in 1699, still doing its lively bit as the result of a discovery by a Manhattan physician that whole wheat flour, when ground slowly, is good for sufferers from stomach disorders.

At 55.3 *m.* is the junction with a macadam road.

Left on this road 0.9 *m.* to SETAUKET (384 pop.), an informal, rambling village with an unspoiled bucolic air, its shingled Cape Cod and 'salt-box' dwellings widely separated. It is at the head of the almost landlocked Setauket Harbor. The main street, running down to the water's edge, is cut by a long, narrow pond. Two churches, pinnacles of white shingle, face the tree-studded green, a triangular patch tilted on a slope. The PRESBYTERIAN CHURCH, rebuilt in 1811, with gable roof and gray trim, has a central front tower pierced by windows and terminated by a domed octagon. The CAROLINE EPISCOPAL CHURCH (1729), one of the oldest on Long Island, is notable for its odd little tower, now out of plumb and capped by a vestigial lantern and spire; the horse and wagon sheds still stand to one side. British officers during the Revolution were tongue-lashed by the rector for permitting the soldiers to steal while their superiors attended church. In a village house now gone, Benjamin F. Thompson (1784–1849), Long Island historian, was born.

Around the harbor of the same name lies PORT JEFFERSON, 58.1 *m.* (2,465 pop.). Once a thriving shipbuilding town, it has today two lace factories and several gravel pits; summer visitors supplement its economy. The shipyard still brings a small income from custom-built cruisers, sloops, and pleasure craft. A ferry (*car and driver* $4, *each passenger* 75¢) connects with Bridgeport, Connecticut.

East of Port Jefferson, State 25A links a number of hamlets and passes (R) the great Radio Corporation of America TRANSMITTING STATION (*open by permission from plant engineer of RCA Communications, 66 Broad St., N.Y.City*), 65.5 *m.* WILDWOOD STATE PARK (*parking, Sat., Sun., and holidays, 25¢; other days free; lockers, 25¢; camping 50¢ a day, $2 a week*), 71.2 *m.* (L), provides bathing, picnicking, and camping.

At 74.4 *m.* is the eastern junction with State 25 (*see Jericho Turnpike Tour*).

JERICHO TURNPIKE TOUR

Queensboro Bridge—Mineola—Westbury—Smithtown—Ridge—River-head—Orient Point; State 25. 105.2 *m.*

State 25, known in its western part as the Jericho Turnpike, misses most of the large communities of Long Island, providing the speediest route to Riverhead and the eastern arms of the island reaching into the Atlantic. Through the Westbury district the road passes walled-in estates and playgrounds of the rich. East of Smithtown is a rich agricultural region where straight rows of potatoes and cauliflower stretch across flat, sandy fields. East of Riverhead the route runs up the northern fluke to Orient Point.

Between the east end of the QUEENSBORO BRIDGE, 0 *m.*, and the New York City line, 13.5 *m.*, State 25 traverses a monotonous residential section of Queens and passes through the grounds of the New York World's Fair.

MINEOLA, 17.7 *m.* (10,107 pop.), at the junction of the main line and the Oyster Bay branch of the Long Island Railroad and traversed by east-west and north-south express highways, is the mercantile distributing center for the island. Large packing plants, vegetable depots, office buildings, and a glass factory differentiate the village from the surrounding residential communities.

At 19.1 *m.* is the ramp to the Northern State Parkway, leading to the south shore highway and beaches.

East of Mineola are the exclusive residential villages of OLD WEST-BURY, 20.3 *m.* (1,264 pop.), and WESTBURY, 21.7 *m.* (4,522 pop.). Trees and high walls bar all but flashing glimpses of the palatial estates which spread from both sides of the road. BOSTWICK POLO FIELD (L), 22.5 *m.*, playground for the social élite, was named for Pete Bostwick, gentleman jockey and polo player.

SANITA (L), 29.5 *m.*, was the country estate of millionaire-banker Otto H. Kahn. The 441 acres of rolling woodland and pasture, with the palatial mansion and other buildings, were purchased from the banker's widow in 1939 by the Welfare Association of the Department of Sanitation of New

York City for $100,000, to be used as a recreation and rest center for its 15,000 members, but local opposition, supported by the courts, forced the association to give up the plan. It was at Oheka, as the estate was formerly known, that Mr. Kahn entertained Georges Clemenceau, the French war premier, in 1922.

At 32.5 *m.* is the junction with State 110, connecting State 25 with State 25A on the north and State 24 on the south.

Right on State 110 to (L) the BIRTHPLACE OF WALT WHITMAN (*open 12–6 daily;* 25¢), 0.7 *m.*, a weathered two-story-and-attic, shingled cottage built as a farmhouse in 1810. Walt Whitman was born here on May 31, 1819. When he was four years old his father moved to Brooklyn to earn a living as a carpenter and housebuilder. Walt left school at the age of 13, and was therefore mainly self-educated. The next 15 years he spent at odd jobs—carpentering, school teaching, editing newspapers, and writing prose and verse. From a three-months' stay in New Orleans he returned with a deeper patriotism and the memory of a love affair. For a while he was his father's desultory assistant in building and selling small houses in Brooklyn. In the spring of 1855 he dropped his saw and hammer and began setting type for his book, *Leaves of Grass*, published in the same year. The book marks a milestone in the development of American poetry. In a free verse form he set out to celebrate the democratic personality that was Walt Whitman, and in and through himself to express the democratic spirit of his country.

The reception of the book was mixed, but Whitman persisted in his purpose and continued to add poems in the same style. The third edition (1860) contained one group of poems, *Children of Adam*, that dealt frankly with love between men and women, and another group, called *Calamus*, in which he celebrated somewhat obscurely the 'love of comrades,' or 'athletic love,' which was to be the basis of a Utopian human brotherhood.

Whitman set out to become a poet of democracy. But the public at large, shocked by his frank sensuality, puzzled by his natural mysticism, and antagonized by his stylistic novelty, ignored him for years. The paradox was complete when he was hailed as a poetic figure of the first magnitude by European critics.

In SMITHTOWN, 43.9 *m.*, is the junction with State 25A (*see North Shore Tour*), with which State 25 runs in common to SMITHTOWN BRANCH, 45.3 *m.* East of Smithtown Branch the route traverses a rich farming country of broad flat fields of potatoes and cauliflower.

At 54.3 *m.* is the junction with State 112, leading to Port Jefferson on the north and Patchogue on the south.

Thousands of quail are raised annually at the NEW YORK STATE QUAIL FARM (L) in RIDGE, 60.9 *m.* (40 pop.). The birds are shipped to various parts of the State by the Conservation Department for restocking woodlands.

At 62.1 *m.* is the junction with a road to Camp Upton.

Right on this road 1.2 *m.* to CAMP UPTON, one of the 14 great cantonments in which were billeted and trained division after division of the U.S. Army for service in France during the World War. Here Irving Berlin composed the soldier ditty, 'Oh, How I Hate to Get Up in the Morning.' In the fall of 1940 it was being rebuilt.

At 66.3 *m.* is the junction with State 25A (*see North Shore Tour*).

RIVERHEAD, 73.2 *m.* (5,396 pop.), is on the Peconic River about a mile from the mouth of the stream. The town depends for its prosperity largely upon the surrounding farms, the two main crops of which are potatoes and cauliflower. Within recent years the old predominant Yankee strain has dwindled and South and East Europeans, particularly Poles, have increased. Saturday evening shopping crowds also include many Negroes, who work on the farms.

The SUFFOLK COUNTY HISTORICAL SOCIETY (*open* 1–5 *daily*), corner of W.Main and Court Sts., a modern one-story-and-basement, red brick building with dormers and an iron-railed stoop, is designed in the Georgian Colonial style. An outstanding item in the exhibit is the Hulburt Flag, which is said to antedate the Betsy Ross flag by a year.

The SUFFOLK COUNTY BUILDINGS (*open* 9–5 *weekdays*), SE. corner of Griffin Ave. and Court Sts., are of neo-Georgian design. The central block, with three stories and basement, has a pedimented portico with six Corinthian columns and is flanked on each side by two-story porticoed buildings. Completed in 1929, the units house the Suffolk County executive, legislative, judicial, and clerical staffs.

East of Riverhead State 25 enters the long northeastern peninsula of Long Island known, by virtue of its resemblance to a whale's flipper, as the north fluke. Settlement by the British dates from the 1640's, the decade of Hempstead (*see Center Island Tour*) and Southampton (*see South Shore Tour*). For two centuries this was a bit of New England. Twice the war drums beat on the ears of the young men; always the sea lapped at their doorsteps. Eldorado called them in '49—but still the strain held staunch until into the last quarter of the nineteenth century. Thereafter the explosive effects of new technologies and wider opportunities stirred the inhabitants to adventurous change. Today, to much of the countryside the Puritan tradition is but a name.

The entire peninsula lures summer vacationists in large numbers.

LAUREL, 80 *m*. (39 pop.), named for laurel-bordered Laurel Lake in the vicinity, looks to seed time and harvest for the crests of its activity.

CUTCHOGUE, 86.1 *m*. (903 pop.), abounds in weathered, shingled, one-and-a-half-story Long Island farmhouses.

SOUTHOLD, 90.9 *m*. (1,651 pop.), settled in 1640, is one of the oldest communities on the island. Some building plots are still held by descendants of the original owners. The JOSEPH PRINCE HOUSE (1732), third on L. from foot of Youngs Ave., a much altered two-story shingled dwelling, houses a milliner's shop and shows no outward signs of its age. Several of the doors have cross paneling. FOUNDER'S LANDING, foot of Hobart Road, is a small public park occupying the spot where the 1640 colonists landed.

The fluke becomes so narrow beyond 93.6 *m*. that Long Island Sound (L) and Shelter Island Sound (R) are both visible.

GREENPORT, 95.7 *m*. (2,948 pop.), is the principal commercial center of the north fluke. The village is laid out in squares that slope down to the harbor; high bluffs face the Sound.

In the days of deep-sea whaling Greenport rivaled Sag Harbor, and the seafaring tradition lives in the multiplicity of relics in the old houses of the town. The village is now a center of the oyster trade. Since the local bivalve is held inferior in the market to that of Great South Bay, 400,000 bushels are sent yearly to Sayville (*see South Shore Tour*) for a finishing course that gives them the bulk and flavor of 'Blue Points.' Building of small boats is an auxiliary industry.

The CLARK HOUSE (1812), NW. corner of Main and Adam Sts., now the police station, was the inn in which, with their wives and sweethearts, the whalemen danced and made merry on the eve of three-year voyages. The simple beauty of the white-shingled inn has been spoiled by the addition of wings, a high stoop, and cornice brackets.

In EAST MARION, 98.1 m. (206 pop.), the WEBB HOUSE (*private*), fourth on L. of State 25, E. of Sunset Shores Road, built in 1730, is a good example of the weathered, shingled, one-and-a-half-story Long Island farmhouse with the deeply sloping rear roof.

ORIENT, 101.4 m. (616 pop.), as its name implies, is the most easterly of north fluke villages. Until a generation ago it was a favorite spot for honeymooners, and it remains a popular resort. The little weathered shingle houses, few more than one-and-a-half stories high, sit primly behind picket fences. In sun or storm the Atlantic winds roll in from Block Island Sound or whistle across Plum Gut; the 1938 hurricane rose to a roar and peeled tin and shingles from roofs like scales from fish.

ORIENT BEACH STATE PARK (*parking free, except Sun. and holidays* 25¢), 104.8 m., given to the State by the people of the village of Orient, comprises 342 acres of sand beach and bordering land. Comparatively new, it has only temporary facilities for bathing.

ORIENT POINT INN, 105 m., built in 1810 but several times remodeled, is a three- and four-story white shingled hotel at the point where State 25 bends sharply R. to terminate at the dock, 105.2 m., of the ferry (*May 27– Oct. 4; car* $5, *each passenger* $1) to New London, Connecticut.

CENTER ISLAND TOUR

Queensboro Bridge—Hempstead—Farmingdale—Ronkonkoma—Yaphank—Riverhead—Hampton Bays; 84.2 m. State 24, County Roads, State 25, State 24.

Long Island R.R. parallels route to Riverhead.
Accommodations poor on main route between Farmingdale and Riverhead; no service stations between Yaphank and Calverton.

Hurried drivers avoid this route because of its narrow, twisting macadam roads, while leisurely wayfarers with a taste for the sequestered are drawn to it. No population centers of any appreciable size are touched except Riverhead, Hempstead, and Farmingdale. Much of the route is through wooded country of stunted pine, scrub oak, and growths badly burned in 1936 and hurricane-torn in 1938. From the East River on the west to Flanders Bay, cradled in the gigantic arms which form Long Island's eastern reaches, the road bisects the island and affords access to

State parks, sport centers, aviation fields, and areas abounding in wild fowl, both land and water.

Between the east end of the QUEENSBORO BRIDGE, 0 *m.*, and the New York City Line, 13.2 *m.*, State 24 twists through a residential section of the borough of Queens.

BELMOMT PARK (*grandstand and paddock*, $1.50; *enclosure*, $4), 13.3 *m.* (L), named for August P. Belmont, financier and sportsman, is one of the great horse race tracks of America. The Withers, the Belmont, the Futurity, and the Metropolitan are its best-known stakes. The Turf and Field Club, associated with Belmont Park, numbers among its members the foremost sportsmen and sportswomen of the country.

HEMPSTEAD, 18.8 *m.* (20,859 pop.), is one of the largest population centers on Long Island. In the early days it was called the 'Town Spot'; local partisans now lean to 'hub of Nassau County.' In 1644 the first settlers found a well-watered grassy plain on which their cattle grew fat; the virgin soil was excellent for timothy, rye, wheat, and maize; the score or more families who made up the settlement prospered. Not before 1801, however, did the village begin to grow appreciably. At the end of the World War Hempstead was in aspect still a country town. After 1920 the automobile expanded the radius of the territory from which it drew its trade, and large concerns established branches in the village.

ST. GEORGE'S PROTESTANT EPISCOPAL CHURCH, Front St. opposite Liberty St., erected in 1822, is the third on the site. A simple gable-roofed, white shingled building, it has a square clock tower topped by an octagonal belfry. The weather vane, survivor of the preceding edifice, shows holes pierced by musket balls fired by British soldiers garrisoned in the town during the Revolution. In the RECTORY, 120 Prospect St., built in 1793, a white shingled building with five-bay front, Dutch gambrel roof, and balanced dormers, was born Edward Henry Harriman (1848–1909), who did much to revitalize several Western railroads and to save the beauties of the Hudson River from commercial encroachment.

The PRESBYTERIAN CHURCH, Fulton Ave. between Main and Washington Sts., was erected in 1846, but the society which it houses claims the distinction of being the oldest Presbyterian congregation in the country, its founding dating from the arrival of the Reverend Richard Denton and his followers in 1644. The building, of white-painted wood and shingles, has a hipped roof and a square four-story tower in the center of the façade. The porch with its low gable and flat Tudor arch, the hood moldings over the windows, the buttresses of shallow planks, and the wooden battlements, are details derived from English Gothic, here applied to a building essentially Georgian Colonial in mass and materials to produce an unusually interesting example of 'carpenter Gothic.'

HOFSTRA MEMORIAL COLLEGE, SW. corner of Fulton and California Aves., an affiliate of New York University, was founded in 1935 on William F. Hofstra's property donated for the purpose. It has 600 students. The buildings, designed by Aymar Embury II, neoclassic in style and with the severe plainness of the modern architectural trend, are constructed of white-painted brick and light limestone.

Left from Hempstead on Main St. to GARDEN CITY, 1.3 *m.* (11,225 pop.), a planned town, one of the wealthiest residential communities on Long Island, the realization of the dream of Alexander Turney Stewart, Manhattan merchant prince. Stewart bought 8,000 acres for $55 an acre and built the necessary railroad connection. Wide streets, shaded by trees of mature growth, are laid out in checkerboard pattern. Imposing residences stand on spacious plots; parks embellish the village. It is something of a social center and largely free from the turmoil of trade, although some fashionable city shops have branches here. The CATHEDRAL OF THE INCARNATION, Cathedral Ave. opposite 6th St., erected in 1885, is the See of the Episcopal Diocese of Long Island. Surrounded by a park of lawns, shrubs, and trees, the brownstone cathedral follows the English Decorated Gothic style. The plan is cruciform, with a square eastern bell tower terminated by steep gables and a crocketed spire. The sharply pointed windows are enriched with geometric stone tracery.

The COUNTRY LIFE PRESS (*open weekdays* 9–5, *Sat.* 9–12), Franklin Ave. opposite 5th St., built for one of the largest book and magazine publishing businesses in the country, has stood for three decades in large and beautifully landscaped grounds. The two-story-and-basement red brick buildings, with white stone trim and battlemented parapets, are designed in the Gothic style—a welcome departure from the conventional factory and a proof that industrial plants need not blight the property values of adjoining neighborhoods.

MITCHELL FIELD, Stewart Ave. at Clinton Road, is a U.S.Army flying field, largest Army aviation base on the Atlantic coast. In 1924 the first transcontinental airmail left this field for San Francisco. Much experimental work in air-land communication has been carried on here. Bordering the eastern end of the field is the INTERNATIONAL POLO FIELD, where crack teams from all over the world meet in championship competition for a cup representing supremacy in the most expensive of sports.

ROOSEVELT FIELD, Old Country Road at the east village line, named for Quentin, son of Theodore Roosevelt, who died as an aviator in the World War, is the airport from which Charles A. Lindbergh took off in 1927 on his historic flight to Paris. It is also associated with Post, Gatty, Pangborn, Byrd, Hawkes, and other aviators.

East of the flying field is the ROOSEVELT RACEWAY, an unusual auto race track. Abandoning the pattern of the conventional banked oval track, the engineers designed the speedway to test not only the driving skill of pilots but also the stamina and ruggedness of the cars.

MEADOWBROOK HOSPITAL (L), 23 *m.*, the Nassau County hospital, although of classic proportions and faithfully eclectic in pilasters, entablature, cornices, and attic stories, has rounded ends and long porches of distinctly modern treatment. The architect was John Russell Pope. A wide lawn separates the white concrete building from the highway.

At 27.3 *m.* is the ramp (R) to the Bethpage Parkway, which connects with the Southern State Parkway, Meadowbrook State Parkway, and Jones Beach (*see South Shore Tour*).

FARMINGDALE, 28.5 *m.* (354 pop.), the first village in American history to be 'blacked out' for a mimic night air raid, lies on the plain at the foot of Mannetto Hills. The village economy was founded on the surrounding farms. Silk dyeing and airplane manufacturing are recently added activities.

BETHPAGE STATE PARK, NE. corner of Main St. and Melville Road, has four 18-hole golf courses ($1 *weekdays;* $2 *Sat., Sun., and holidays*); bridle paths (*horses for hire*); a jumping course, a polo field, picnic grounds, and a playground for children.

The STATE INSTITUTE OF APPLIED AGRICULTURE ON LONG ISLAND, NW. corner of Melville and Broad Hollow Roads, founded in 1916, has a student body of 200 men and women, a faculty of 31, and offers courses in agriculture, estate management, ornamental horticulture, poultry husbandry, and allied subjects. The two-story-and-attic red brick buildings, spaced around a broad expanse of shrub-studded lawn, are designed in the Georgian Colonial style.

At 29.7 *m.* is the junction with State 110.

Left on State 110 to WALT WHITMAN'S BIRTHPLACE, 5.7 *m.* (*see Jericho Turnpike Tour*).

The large group of buildings (L) at 30.1 *m.*, houses the REPUBLIC AVIATION PLANT, backed by a vast expanse of level ground used as a testing field for planes.

East of Farmingdale, State 24 parallels the Long Island Railroad through a monotony of scrub pine and scrub oak, and touches several villages that are little more than railroad stopping places.

At 35.9 *m.* is the junction with Commack Road.

Left on Commack Road 2.5 *m.* to PILGRIM STATE HOSPITAL (R), second largest State asylum for the insane, with some 7,000 patients. The brown, pressed brick buildings cover a large area in the pine barrens, only electric power lines and the heating plant stacks breaking the skyline.

BRENTWOOD, 39.8 *m.* (741 pop.), was in 1851 the scene of an experiment in communism led by Joseph Warren and others. Labor certificates passed for currency, as the group believed that all wealth was created by labor. Like similar experiments elsewhere, it soon failed, leaving in its place a typical Long Island settlement.

East of CENTRAL ISLIP, 42.2 *m.* (1,615 pop.), is (R) CENTRAL ISLIP STATE HOSPITAL (*open*) 46.6 *m.*, with 8,000 patients, largest of the State institutions for the insane.

In RONKONKOMA, 47.4 *m.* (144 pop.), a mid-island hamlet, is the junction with Ronkonkoma Ave.

Left on Ronkonkoma Ave. to LAKE RONKONKOMA, 0.5 *m.* In recent years an increasing number of people have built summer cottages in the vicinity of the lake, and the dance halls and restaurants that they have attracted bring an ephemeral gaiety to the quiet waters and somber woodlands.

YAPHANK, 58.4 *m.* (350 pop.), furnished the title for Irving Berlin's war-time Broadway musical hit, *Yip, Yip, Yaphank.* The village was the railroad stop for Camp Upton, near-by military base during the World War (*see Jericho Turnpike Tour*).

The windings of the route eastward become more picturesque than comfortable as the roadbed grows poorer. At 63.3 *m.* the vegetation shows the ravage wrought by extensive forest fires in 1936. The suprisingly well-groomed bog at 68.2 *m.* is a commercial cranberry plantation.

The route joins State 25 at 73 *m.* (*see North Shore Tour*), with which it runs in common to RIVERHEAD, 76.1 *m.* (5,400 pop.). From Riverhead the route continues southeast on State 24 to HAMPTON BAYS, 84.2 *m.* (1,127 pop.), which is at the junction with State 27 (*see South Shore Tour*).

Manhattan Bridge—Valley Stream—Freeport—Sayville—Southampton —Montauk Point; 127.3 m. State 27.

Two- and three-lane macadam or concrete.

State 27, called the Sunrise Highway to Oakdale and the Montauk Highway east of there, links the mainland villages of the South Shore and parallels the Outer Barrier, the long beach that extends from Brooklyn to Southampton. The western communities of the South Shore are New York City suburbs; the central ones are farming and residential villages; the eastern ones are swanky summer resorts and deep-sea angling bases.

Between the east end of the MANHATTAN BRIDGE, 0 m., and the New York City line, 16.5 m., State 27 passes through Brooklyn and Jamaica.

VALLEY STREAM, 18.2 m. (16,978 pop.), developed after the World War. New streets shot out over the flat surface and through the woodland; new bungalows and cottages sprang up like mushrooms; new people came to Valley Stream. Where the morning trains once gathered a handful, they now take 1,700 commuters to Gotham.

On Merrick Road between Corona and Fletcher Aves. is VALLEY STREAM STATE PARK (*parking* 25¢, *swimming* 10¢, *picnicking, playgrounds*).

There were settlers in LYNBROOK, 19.8 m. (14,604 pop.), before the Revolutionary War. The SANDHOLE CEMETERY, corner of Merrick Road and Ocean Ave., still guards its relics of a century-old sea tragedy, the wrecks of the emigrant ships *Bristol* and *Mexico*, which foundered in 1836 and 1837 on the treacherous shoals off the Outer Bar.

In Lynbrook is the junction with Broadway.

Right on Broadway to the Rockaway peninsula, arbitrarily divided by corporation lines into several communities. The first settlers of Hempstead built a fence from the west end of Great South Bay to the shore of Jamaica Bay and turned their cattle into this pasture to fend for themselves. Much later the opulent of New York erected a social fence about it. The pull of Far Rockaway brought the exclusive to HEWLETT, 2 m. (550 pop.), CEDARHURST, 3.4 m. (5,501 pop.), and LAWRENCE, 4.2 m. (3,664 pop.). The Rockaway Hunt Club chased hounds about the meadows of the pioneers. Later came polo, tennis, and golf, and yachts on the bay waters. Today on the peninsula, abounding in tree-lined streets off the main road, the hum of activity seems as distant as the surf.

In Lawrence is ROCK HALL (*private*), Broadway opposite Lawrence Ave., erected about 1767. This white-shingled two-story-and-attic building, its gambrel roof truncated by a deck that is surrounded by a balustrade marked by Chippendale influence, is considered one of the finest examples of Georgian Colonial architecture on Long Island.

ROCKVILLE CENTRE, 20.8 m. (18,467 pop.), owes its name to the Long Island Smiths, of whom there were so many that qualifying names were needed to distinguish the various clans. Hence an odd list: 'Bull,' 'Tangier,' 'Wait,' and 'Rock' Smiths. To the last-named family belonged the Reverend Mordecai 'Rock' Smith, for whom the village was named. Among the island communities, Rockville Centre ranks third in population.

In Rockville Centre is the junction with Long Beach Road.

Right on Long Beach Road to OCEANSIDE, 1 *m.* (5,838 pop.). The first white settlers, a group of fishermen who arrived here nearly 200 years ago, called the settlement Christian Hook, but the name was changed to Oceanville in 1864 and Oceanside in 1889. Inhabitants are mostly city workers with a sprinkling of fishermen.

The wayside shrine, CHURCH OF ST.ANTHONY, built in a hillside at the corner of Windsor Parkway and Lincoln Ave., is sunk 30 feet below a beautifully landscaped rock garden. It was designed by the Reverend Robert Barrett, pastor, and built with funds bequeathed by his father. In the subterranean interior an ingenious system of lighting throws the main body of the cavern into reposeful shade and brings into relief in a blaze of light a golden tabernacle.

LONG BEACH, 6 *m.* (9,009 pop.), one of the two incorporated cities of Long Island, is an exciting mixture of Atlantic City and Coney Island. It sits on the shifting sands of the western end of the Outer Barrier, a mass of one-story bungalows, a hive of bathers and anglers in summer, a place of little movement in winter. A popular resort for city people of moderate incomes, its population varies with the season from 5,000 to 50,000. A superb boardwalk stretches two miles along the ocean front and all the accessories of a seaside resort are at hand.

Also in Rockville Centre is the junction with Merrick Road (State 27A), alternate route to Oakdale.

Right on Merrick Road (State 27A) to BALDWIN, 2.2 *m.* (11,205 pop.), a community of small homes spreading from the water front north to Hempstead, and historically an offshoot of the Hempstead colony of 1643. A watermill was built in 1686 on Milburn Creek and the surrounding area was gradually divided into farms. The U.S.Navy Plant, Milburn Ave., manufactures airplane flares.

State 27A runs through FREEPORT, 3.8 *m.* (20,369 pop.) (*see below*), crosses over the Meadowbrook State Parkway, 4.6 *m.*, and ducks under the Wantagh State Parkway, 7.8 *m.*

In MASSEPEQUA, 9.8 *m.* (1,260 pop.), is TRYON HALL (L), erected in 1770. It was the scene in 1779 of the abduction of Judge Thomas Jones, a Tory, in a successful effort on the part of the rebels to secure a prisoner to exchange for Major General Gold Selleck Silliman. The white shingled structure, Georgian Colonial in style, has a hipped-roofed central block, with unusual octagonally ended wings.

The CARMAN HOMESTEAD (*private*), 12.3 *m.* (L), the west wing of which was erected prior to 1776, has been continuously occupied by members of the Carman family. The west wing is a simple story-and-a-half dormered cottage, attractively set off by an arbor and window boxes. The main block is a Greek Revival addition, two-and-a-half stories high.

AMITYVILLE, 13.2 *m.* (5,040 pop.), a quiet village with a large commuting population, is on the dividing line of Nassau and Suffolk Counties. Several houses in this community are more than a century old. The IRELAND HOMESTEAD (*private*), SW. corner of Ocean Ave. and Montauk Highway, was erected about 1783.

Sailboat races on Great South Bay are sponsored by the Narrasketuck Yacht Club, which originated the 20-foot racing sloops known as Narrasketuck one-designs.

LINDENHURST, 16.1 *m.* (4,740 pop.), overgrown in pine and brushwood as late as 1870, was laid out by a German and still retains something of a mid-European flavor. One of the few industrial communities on Long Island, the village contains several small factories and a brewery.

Local tradition credits the founding of BABYLON, 18.5 *m.* (4,668 pop.), to Captain Jacob Conklin, who, shanghaied by Captain Kidd, the pirate, dove overboard, crossed the Outer Barrier, and landed on Sampawan's Neck, where the village stands. Great South Bay begins to widen here, and the village is a yachting center. Argyl Lake, its cascading outlet, and the park which surrounds it are an aesthetic asset. From the municipal dock, ferries cross to several of the beaches and cottage settlements on Fire Island at the eastern end of the Outer Barrier and to FIRE ISLAND STATE PARK (*bathing-lockers 25¢; camping 75¢ a day, $2.50 a week; picknicking, surf fishing*).

BRIGHTWATERS, 22.7 *m.* (1,550 pop.), is a city of gardens, and into its composition enter Inness-like views woven from green water and silver birches, oak, fir, and gleaming roadways.

BAY SHORE, 23.5 *m.* (6,467 pop.), was developed mainly after 1840. The narrow highway is flanked by unattractive buildings with no saving grace of masking trees. But the water front reveals a different picture. Great South Bay here is at its widest, over four miles. The residential section is well shaded, and many of the houses have achieved grace with the years.

ISLIP, 25.9 *m.* (4,000 pop.), and EAST ISLIP, 26.7 *m.* (1,817 pop.), grew gradually from little four-corner trading posts. There is still a spare commerce in furs gathered in the bogs and woodlands, but fish and farm products furnish the largest income.

At 27.8 *m.* is the entrance parkway (R) to HECKSCHER STATE PARK, with beaches on Great South Bay (*bathhouse 35¢; picnic grounds, playground, and camp sites*). Funds for the 1,518-acre park were provided by August Heckscher, New York philanthropist. For many years it was maintained as a private game preserve.

At 29.2 *m.* State 27A rejoins State 27 (*see below*).

At FREEPORT, 24.6 *m.* (20,369 pop.), largest of the south side villages, the five-story FIRST NATIONAL BANK BUILDING is conspicuous above the plain. Here the bay waters draw nearer and the town boosters have had the wit to exploit them. As a result of the advertising by real estate interests and fishermen, the village name has been made synonymous with tuna and other salt water fish.

The oldest house in the village is the DANIEL RAYNOR HOMESTEAD (*private*), South Main St., a boxlike structure erected in 1783 and now fast falling into ruin. Opposite the house, on the banks of Freeport Creek, stood the first saw and grist mills to be erected in Freeport, built and operated by Daniel Raynor and his three sons.

Lumber used in the JACOB BEDELL HOUSE (*private*), corner of Randall Ave. and North Main St., was prepared in the Raynor mill. The Bedell house was built in 1795 in what was then known as the Great South Woods. Painted white with green shutters, this large two-story Colonial house is in excellent condition.

At 25.4 *m.* is the junction (R) with the Meadowbrook State Parkway (*25¢ toll*), which connects Southern State Parkway with the Outer Barrier.

Right on Meadowbrook State Parkway to JONES BEACH STATE PARK, 5.2 *m.*, an engineering feat and a social benefit. In 1927 Jones Beach was an almost inaccessible sandbar on a wind-swept reef with a spare growth of sea grass and a few summer shacks. Purchased for and linked into the New York State park system, it was ready by 1929 for public use. Directly through the park run Bay Drive and Ocean Parkway, two-lane landscaped highways, the latter continuing to Gilgo State Park farther east. Underpasses for pedestrians, carefully planned construction of walks and drives, and parking spaces (*free Oct.–May, 25¢ May–Oct.*) for 15,000 cars at one time expedite traffic. Thickly planted shrubs and flowers form the basis of the landscaping. All architecture, neo-Gothic in design, is uniform down to the smallest service accessory. Briar Hill sandstone and pink Barbizon brick blend with touches of soft yellow or bright blue and green trim. The dominant structure is the WATERTOWER at the southern end of the Wantagh State Parkway and midway between the bathhouses. Its design suggesting an obelisk, it is 200 feet high and is capped by a copper roof weathered to a blue-green. Flower-bordered panel pools complete the trim. It holds 30,000 gallons of fresh well water to supply the park. Flood and beacon lights make it visible by night for more than 25 miles.

The EAST BATHHOUSE, with its two stubby towers with clocks facing the sea, accommodates 10,000 bathers (*lockers: children 15¢, adults 35¢; private dressing room 75¢*). It has a sundeck, first aid room, cafeteria, comfort stations, and beach accessory shops, and is connected by underpasses with the kindergarten and game areas and with the bathing area at Zachs Bay.

At the western end of Zachs Bay is a STADIUM (*1,500 free seats, reserved seats 25¢–$1.10*), seating 10,000, where, nightly except Sunday, operettas are performed on an Island stage—'Over the Water and under the Stars.' The program is changed each week, with the added attraction of fireworks on Monday night; Sunday night is reserved for grand opera.

The WEST BATHHOUSE contains a Marine Dining Room and Tea Terraces, one of which is reserved for patrons in bathing costume, where 500 diners can eat in full view of the Atlantic. Of the two heated salt-water pools, one, 150 feet by 100 feet, is reserved for adults; the other, 100 feet by 50 feet, is reserved for children. Tiled balconies surround the pools, which are illuminated by submarine lights for night swimming and the free nightly water shows and ballets.

The BOARDWALK, which joins the two bathhouses, is built like a ship's deck, even to the ship's rail at the outer edge and specially designed ship's lanterns. A lower deck is equipped for deck sports (*10¢ per person per half hour*), which include shuffleboard and paddle tennis.

In the park are various areas for children's play; archery ranges; an Indian Village presided over by Princess Rosebud Yellow Robe, a Sioux, who teaches children Indian lore—songs, basketry, and bead and pottery work; a pitch-putt golf course; softball and baseball fields; handball courts; and picnic areas. Mechanical thrillers like the rollercoaster, freak shows, and other ballyhoo are taboo.

On the northern or Great South Bay side of the park are a 3,000-foot sand beach, a fishing station, and yacht basins. Fronting the park on the south is the main beach—more than two and one-half miles of clean white sand lapped by the waves of the Atlantic and dotted in season by bright umbrellas and gaily dressed bathers.

A large orchestra in the MUSIC SHELL provides nightly melody for dancing at the central MALL, which has a cafeteria and comfort stations and remains open all winter for those who enjoy the cold sea air or the winter's stormy seas.

MERRICK, 26.4 *m.* (4,368 pop.), is the last of the suburban villages.

At 28.4 *m.* is the junction with the Wantagh State Parkway (*25¢ toll*), which connects Southern State Parkway with the Outer Barrier.

Right on Wantagh Parkway to JONES BEACH, 4.5 *m.*

East of WANTAGH, 28.6 *m.* (1,284 pop.), is FRANK BUCK'S ZOO (*open daily; evenings May 1–Nov. 1; adults 25¢, children 15¢*), 32.6 *m.*, housed in red-roofed, concrete block buildings, and exhibiting the zoological collections of Frank 'Bring-em-back-alive' Buck.

State 110, crossed at 33.6 *m.*, leads (R) to AMITYVILLE, 0.5 *m.* (5,040 pop.).

State 109, underpassed at 37 *m.*, leads (R) to BABYLON, 2.4 *m.* (4,668 pop.).

At 38.1 *m.* is the junction with Belmont Ave.

Left on Belmont Ave. to BELMONT LAKE STATE PARK (*parking 25¢, camping 50¢ a day, boats for hire*), 1.3 *m.*

Stretching from State 27 south to the water front are BRIGHT-WATERS, 39.9 *m.* (1,550 pop.); BAY SHORE, 40.4 *m.* (6,467 pop.); and ISLIP 43.4 *m.* (4,000 pop.).

In the traffic circle, 46.4 *m.*, is the junction with State 27A (*see above*).

The LA SALLE MILITARY ACADEMY (R), 48.6 *m.*, is operated by the

Christian Brothers and recognized by the U.S.Government as a training center for Reserve officers. Officers of the Regular Army serve as military instructors for the 200 students. Those completing the four-year course in military science are eligible for reserve commissions as second lieutenants in the U.S.Army. The War Department has designated the academy grounds as a military base in the event of war.

SAYVILLE, 51.2 *m.* (3,950 pop.), is an oyster center, packing the 'Blue Point' for shipment the world over. It is also a yachting center, with one of the best sailing courses on Great South Bay. Father Divine, the Negro cultist, maintained a 'heaven' in the village in 1929. A ferry, foot of River St., connects with Cherry Grove on Fire Island, as the Outer Barrier is here known.

PATCHOGUE, 56.2 *m.* (7,147 pop.), has been something of an industrial center for two centuries. Three small streams in the vicinity were dammed for lumber and gristmills probably before 1750. By 1800 the Union Twine Mill, third of its kind in the United States and the first to supply cotton carpet warp, was in operation. Later capital turned to the manufacture of lace, which now provides employment for about 800. The population includes a considerable number of Italians and Poles. LAKE-VIEW CEMETERY (L), State 27 near Waverly Ave., embraces the site of the former Hart's Tavern, visited by Washington in 1790, and contains the grave of Seba Smith, who wrote under the pen name of 'Major Jack Downey,' an early philosopher of the Sam Slick and Mr.Dooley fraternity. With him is interred his wife, Elizabeth Oakes Smith, writer of many books and short stories, and a pioneer in the agitation for equal suffrage for women.

East of Patchogue is a dwarf pine and oak country, through which the route hugs the Long Island Railroad.

At 61.1 *m.* is the junction with a concrete road.

Right on this road to BROOKHAVEN, 1 *m.* (510 pop.), the home of William Floyd (1743–1821), Revolutionary War soldier, statesman, and signer of the Declaration of Independence. He served as a member of the Continental Congress for several years.

At 65.6 *m.* is the junction with Mastic Road.

Right on Mastic Road, which bisects Mastic Neck, to the POOSEPATUCK IN-DIAN RESERVATION, 1.4 *m.*, a little colony of a dozen or so weatherbeaten and run-down clapboard cottages completely surrounded by woods. When the Poosepa-tuck, coming from the South, claimed affiliation and sought refuge on the Shinnecock Reservation, the Shinnecock disclaimed kinship, asserting that the Poosepatuck were Negroes, and thereby forced the establishment of a separate reservation. That the Poosepatuck have a strong strain of Negro blood is apparent. Mastic Neck is heavily wooded in oak, cedar, and spruce. Of it Dr.Thomas Hearne wrote:

None die except with age
Among the groves of Mastic.

East of Mastic Neck is a row of villages: MORICHES, 66.1 *m.* (250 pop.); CENTER MORICHES, 68.1 *m.* (1,000 pop.); and EAST MO-RICHES, 69.8 *m.* (847 pop.). The dunes begin to edge in here.

At EASTPORT, 72.8 *m.* (964 pop.), the Long Island duckling whitens the shores and waters of inlets. From an obscure beginning, the industry has grown in recent years to a $3,000,000 business, which gives employment to many during the summer months. Bordering the highway in this section are several large duck farms, each with an annual production of from 40,000 to 200,000 of the snow-white birds.

At WESTHAMPTON, 76.9 *m.* (700 pop.), is the junction with a side street.

Right here to WESTHAMPTON BEACH, 1.3 *m.* (963 pop.), a seaside community at the point where the Outer Barrier all but joins the mainland, leaving a small basin and Quantuck Bay. Two roads run out to the Outer Barrier, join, turn east, and continue to Southampton, passing Quogue and Shinnecock Bay and traversing Hampton and Tiana Beaches. The beaches and road suffered severe damage during the hurricane of September 21, 1938, in which about 40 persons lost their lives.

At 78.7 *m.* is (L) SANCTUARY NO.1 of the Southampton Township Wildfowl Association, where migratory ducks find safety near their domestic cousins. This section is noted for its duck-hunting and each fall attracts many hunters.

At 79.1 *m.* is the junction with a side road.

Right here to QUOGUE, 0.6 *m.* (623 pop.), summer resort village on Hampton Beach at the western end of Shinnecock Bay.

HAMPTON BAYS, 86.2 *m.* (1,127 pop.), at the junction with State 24 (*see Center Island Tour*), serves as supply base for the other small communities near by.

CANOE PLACE (L), 88 *m.*, made up of a two-and-one-half-story gambrel-roofed, weathered, shingled building with white trim and green blinds, and several rambling attached buildings, is a noted inn and summer 'hot spot' for the élite. At the east edge of the grounds is the SHINNECOCK CANAL, which the highway crosses at 88.1 *m.* and which connects Shinnecock Bay (R) with Great Peconic Bay (L). The Shinnecock Hills, gentle swellings at the western end of the south fluke, rise east of the canal. The general contour of the land in this section makes it an ideal place for golf. Here the National Golf Club of America has its clubhouse.

At 92.3 *m.* is (R) the SHINNECOCK INDIAN RESERVATION (160 pop.), which occupies the entire Shinnecock Neck. The unpainted dwellings of the Indians are scattered through the wilderness of scrub oak.

Neighbor to this Reservation is elegant SOUTHAMPTON, 94.4 *m.* (3,792 pop.), settled by emigrants from Lynn, Massachusetts, in 1640, and therefore one of the oldest villages on Long Island. Today it is a potato-growing center and a fashionable resort ranking with Bar Harbor, Newport, and Mt.Desert. Many mansions of the wealthy that overlooked the beach were all but destroyed during the 1938 hurricane. Branches of several New York City stores operate shops here in summer.

Job's Lane and Gin Lane are street titles of an earlier day. Job was the given name of the man who built the first house on the road; a 'gin' was an enclosure for cattle. The village has been well endowed by adopted sons—the wealthy summer residents.

The PARRISH MEMORIAL ART MUSEUM, 23 Job's Lane, founded in 1897 by Samuel L. Parrish, has a small but excellent collection of paintings and sculptures. The main building, one story high, of brick, has a simplified Renaissance character. The triple arched entrance loggia has a fine wrought-iron gate with low relief medallions at each side.

St. ANDREW'S-DUNES CHURCH, Dune Road at the foot of Agawam Lake, conducts services in summer only. Founded in 1879 and taking its present name in 1884, the church building is a composite: the central part of the nave was originally the life-saving station; in the west wall are three stones from York Minister, England (one of them formed a part of the molding of the tomb of Roger de L'Eveque, Archbishop of York from 1154 to 1181); the oak corbels supporting the corner posts under the belfry roof are from Blytheburg Church, Suffolk, England, which was built in 1442; the credence table stands on a shaft and base of Purbeck marble from one of the doorways of Netley Abbey, Southampton, England, erected in 1239 by Henry III; and the alms box is on a stone bracket from Tintern Abbey, subject of the poem by Wordsworth.

The OLD HOLLYHOCKS HOUSE, Main St., built in 1662, is the oldest of the remaining weathered shingled farmhouses.

In Southampton is the junction with North Sea Road.

Left on North Sea Road to CONSCIENCE POINT, 4.6 m., where the first white settlers landed in 1640 and founded what is now Southampton. A large glacial boulder bearing a bronze plaque marks the spot where the pioneers first set foot on this end of Long Island.

Silhouetted against a background of green grass and gay flowers, on several of the large private estates east of Southampton stand old wind-mills, which for many years ground grain into flour for Suffolk housewives.

BRIDGEHAMPTON, 100.5 m. (1,250 pop), settled in 1660, is in summer a lively shopping center for the countryside. WICK'S (BULL'S HEAD) TAVERN (*not open to public*), NW. corner of State 27 and Sag Harbor Road, a two-story, white shingled building, was built in 1686. During the Revolution it harbored British soldiers.

In Bridgehampton is the junction with Sag Harbor Road.

Left on Sag Harbor Road to SAG HARBOR, 4.5 m. (2,444 pop.), the most famous of the Long Island whaling towns. The townfolk fondly recall the days of 'Thar she blows!' James Fenimore Cooper found in Sag Harbor characters for his sea stories; and while here as agent for a whaling company he wrote part of his first novel, *Precaution*. Years later he drew, from Sag Harbor recollections, Long Tom Coffin, who belongs to the galaxy of John Silver and Equality Jack. David Frothingham began the publication of his newspaper, the Long Island *Herald*, the first on Long Island, in Sag Harbor on May 10, 1791. For many years the tower of the PRESBYTERIAN CHURCH (1844), Madison St. between Main and Union Sts., shaped like a sailor's spyglass, dominated the village and beaconed home-bound mariners out in Gardiners Bay; but the 1938 hurricane hurled it into the church yard. The MASONIC TEMPLE (*open*), Main St. opposite Union St., a lovely white Greek Revival home, was erected in 1845. The Masonic emblem is in the pediment and the name is on the entablature of the portico. The elegant Corinthian capitals, the elaborate entablature and pediment, the graceful metal cresting above the cornice, and the rich frames of the windows reflect the prosperity of whaling days. A whaleboat reposes in the area before the building, and inside are displayed relics of the whaler's trade.

In the center of OAKLAND CEMETERY, on the south line of the village, is the WHALERS' MONUMENT, erected in 1856. The 18-foot shaft is a broken mast with a hawser coiled around the base. One face of the die bears a dramatic whaling scene, another the names of six young men, all shipmasters of Sag Harbor and vicinity, who perished in the trade.

From Sag Harbor the side route continues on State 114. North of NORTH HAVEN, 6 m. (123 pop.) a ferry (*car and driver 75¢, each passenger 15¢*), 7.5 m., crosses to SHELTER ISLAND, 11 m. (1,250 town pop.), in 1652 a refuge for Quakers, now largely a summer resort. At 12.2 m. is (R) a monument to the Quakers who came to Shelter Island to escape persecution.

SHELTER ISLAND HEIGHTS, 13 m. (1,200 pop.), a resort community, is the southern landing for the ferry (*car and driver $1, each passenger 15¢*) to GREENPORT (2,348 pop.), on the north fluke (*see North Shore Tour*).

EAST HAMPTON, 106.8 m. (1,717 pop.), settled in 1648, is another of the early Long Island towns. Kentish yeomen who settled here named it Maidstone. Large mansions of varied architectural design, standing along the dunes south of the village, were struck by the full force of the 1938 hurricane; some were demolished, but all have now been restored. The trees which line the streets, survivors of the worst hurricane in more than 100 years, are of great age and remarkable beauty.

Lyman Beecher, progenitor of a remarkable family which included Henry Ward Beecher, noted orator and preacher, and Harriet Beecher Stowe, author of *Uncle Tom's Cabin*, was pastor of the Presbyterian Church here from 1799 to 1810. His salary was $300 a year and firewood, later increased to $400; but he resigned in 1810 to accept a call to a church in Litchfield, Connecticut.

A pond, a village green, and the OLD BURYING GROUND (R) cleave the main street. In the cemetery, still enclosed by the fence and turnstile of the days when cattle roamed the streets untended, is the grave of the first minister, Thomas James, who lies on the east side, head to east, in the hope that Gabriel's trumpet will bring him up erect and facing his flock. Here, too, is the grave of Lion Gardiner, first owner of Gardiners Island, and of another Gardiner, David, who became, posthumously, father-in-law to President Tyler; it was his accidental death on a Navy vessel that brought his daughter, Julia, and the President together.

HOME, SWEET HOME (*open; adults 25¢*), E. side of the green next to the church, is the birthplace of John Howard Payne (1791–1852), author of 'Home, Sweet Home.' The weathered shingle salt-box house, with gable end to the street, contains a collection of Americana and objects of art. The WINDMILL, in the rear of the house, built in 1774 and moved here from another site, also contains relics of historical interest.

Next to the Payne home and very much resembling it is the MULFORD HOUSE (R), once known as the Josiah Hobart House, built about the same time. Among the many Mulfords, Samuel, the champion of the Colonial whalers, stands out. When Governor Hunter in distant New York levied a tax upon the whale trade, for which, as he saw it, the whalemen got no benefit, Samuel packed his grip and sailed for London to see the king. But he found that too many polished officials stood between him and the royal presence. One day, as he waited a chance to pass the guards, his pocket was picked. He returned to his lodging, sewed some fishhooks into his pockets, and went back to his watch. Presently he heard a muttered curse;

he had caught his fish. The guard took charge of the thief, one of London's journals took note of the device, the story came to the king's ears, Mulford got his audience, the tax was lifted, and the south fluke chuckled at Sam Mulford and his tricks.

The GUILD HALL, SE. corner of Main St. and Dunemere Lane, is a community building with an octagonal auditorium dedicated to John Drew, actor and 'citizen of East Hampton.' The long, low, whitewashed brick building, built in 1931, is in an attractive version of Georgian Colonial architecture; the architect was Aymar Embury II.

The EAST HAMPTON FREE LIBRARY, directly across the street from the Guild Hall, has an annex housing the Pennypacker collection of Long Island historical material, the largest in its field.

CLINTON ACADEMY, Main St. east of the library, built in 1784, was the first academy chartered by the State of New York; William Payne, John Howard Payne's father, was the first teacher. The building has three stories, clapboard front, brick ends, shingled gambrel roof with five dormers in front, and a bell cupola composed of open framing and pointed roof. The school was named for Governor George Clinton, who donated the bell for the belfry.

AMAGANSETT, 109.5 m. (1,000 pop.), is still a fishing village, despite summer visitors and summer dwellers and houses of alien design, mostly of stucco with red or green roofs, among the dunes. It stands on a little elevation looking east over the Atlantic. It has no harbor, but the tradition of seafaring dates from its settlement in 1650 and from the inhabitants who, led by Indians, first attacked the basking whales beyond the surf. As late as 1907 the old cry 'whale off' rang in 'Gansett streets, and a crew of veterans went out with harpoon and lance to bring in a right whale, the bones of which now rest in the American Museum of Natural History, New York City. In the great days of the 'trade,' many 'Gansett boys sailed in bluff-bowed whalers out of Sag Harbor and Greenport. Age has come upon many of the houses, and sand and sea drift have silvered their sides.

East of Amagansett the Montauk Peninsula begins. The highway spans a sandy waste thinly grown to scrubby pine and oak and dwarfed herbage. The brown growths cover a rolling land, above which gulls poise and swoop. On the left is the bright blue of Gardiners Bay; on the right, the five miles of Napeague Beach, a favorite camping place.

HITHER HILLS STATE PARK (swimming, camping), 116.5 m., crossing the fluke from Napeague Bay to the Atlantic, is second in size among the Long Island State parks.

MONTAUK, 121.7 m. (608 pop.), terminus of the Long Island Railroad, is the most easterly of New York State villages. A thriving trade caters to fishermen who go out for tuna and swordfish off Montauk Point or angle for smaller fry inside Peconic Bay and Gardiners Bay. From the middle of March, when the flounders run, until the arrival of winter storms, the chase never slackens. During the summer a ferry (car $6, each passenger $1) operates to New London, Connecticut.

The Montauk Highway (State 27), here a parkway, rises and dips over the dunes within sight of water on the north and south; at 125.1 *m.* is a parking turnout (R) for a wide view of ocean and surf.

MONTAUK POINT STATE PARK, 127.3 *m.*, is at the end of the road. It is but a parking field with comfort stations and drinking fountains, encircled by ever-brown grass, scrubby oak, and shadbush. Of it Robert Moses, chairman of the State Council of Parks, said: 'Everyone who loves water, wind, sky and distance, and is not chilled by bleakness, must love Montauk.'

The park includes the entire tip of Montauk Point except that portion at the very extremity occupied by the U.S.Government LIGHTHOUSE (*open*), which was built in 1796. The documents connected with the purchase of the land for the lighthouse were approved by George Washington. The Atlantic breakers have snatched away more than half of the land that separated the black-and-white-striped tower from the ocean at the time of its construction. For many years the light was a steady beacon that burned whale oil, but now a more modern fuel feeds its intermittent gleam.

It was at Montauk Point that more than 25,000 men of the Cuban expeditionary force of 1898 landed on their return from the war. New York City had objected to the landing of the Army in its harbor because of the danger of infectious diseases.

PART IV
Appendices

Chronology

1609   Champlain, coming from the north, enters what is now New York from Canada and discovers Lake Champlain.
Henry Hudson discovers river now named for him and supplies the Netherlands with a claim to the region.

1614   The States General of the United Netherlands grant a Dutch commercial syndicate a three years' trading monopoly in 'New Netherland,' the charter being the first State document in which the name 'New Netherland' appears.
Hendrick Christiaensen constructs Fort Nassau, a trading-house, on Castle Island, vicinity of Albany.

1620   Puritans' petition to settle in colony denied.

1621   Dutch West India Company chartered, with jurisdiction over New Netherland for 24 years.

1623   New Netherland made a province managed by the Amsterdam Chamber of the West India Company.

1624   Dutch and Walloons, French Protestant refugees, make first settlement at Albany, and build Fort Orange.

1625   First colony settled on Manhattan Island.

1626   Peter Minuit purchases Manhattan Island from the Indians for trinkets worth about $24.
The settlement in the vicinity of Fort Amsterdam develops as New Amsterdam.

1629   Dutch West India Company establishes patroon system to encourage colonization.

1630   Kiliaen Van Rensselaer, nonresident patroon, establishes first settlers at Rensselaerswyck on upper Hudson.

1632   Great Britain presses claims to New Netherland.

1636   Jacob Van Curler purchases land on Long Island from Indians; first recorded grant in Kings County.

1640   Southampton and Southold, L.I., settled.

1641   Director General Kieft calls council of the people; board of 'Twelve Men,' first representative assembly, appointed.

1643   English from Stamford, Conn., settle Hempstead, L.I.

1646   Mohawks kill Father Isaac Jogues, Jesuit missionary.
Yonkers settled.

1647   Peter Stuyvesant becomes Director General of New Netherland.

1652   Esopus (Kingston) settled by Thomas Chambers.
Stuyvesant establishes court and village of Beverwyck (Albany).

1653   New Amsterdam is granted burgher government—the earliest city government in the United States.

1654   July 8. Jacob Barsimon, first Jewish colonist, arrives from Holland. In August, 23 Jewish refugees arrive from Brazil.

1659   Dutch Reformed Church at Esopus is established.

1661   Schenectady is settled by Arent Van Curler.

1664   New Netherland is included in territory granted by Charles II to the Duke of York.

New Netherland surrenders to the English and becomes the Province of New York.

1665   At Hempstead, L.I., Richard Nicolls, first English governor, publishes the 'Duke's Laws.'

1673   Dutch fleet recaptures New York.

1674   By Treaty of Westminster, the United Netherlands surrender New Netherland (New York), including New Jersey, to English.

1679   Fort Niagara, a stockade, is built by La Salle.

1683   Thomas Dongan becomes governor.

First 'elected representative' assembly meets in New York at Fort James and adopts Charter of Liberties.

Original 12 counties formed.

1684   At Albany the Five Nations submit to the king of England.

1686   July 22. Governor Dongan grants city charters to New York and Albany.

1688   New Rochelle settled by Huguenots.

1690   Schenectady massacre.

1691   Peter Schuyler with English and Dutch from Albany defeats the French at La Prairie, Canada.

1693   Episcopal Church organized in Colony.

1709–12   Palatines settle in the Hudson and Schoharie Valleys.

1713   By Treaty of Utrecht France recognizes British suzerainty over the Iroquois.

1731   New York–Connecticut boundary settled.

French build fort at Crown Point.

1746   William Johnson made head of Indian Department.

1748   Great Indian Council at Albany.

1754   Benjamin Franklin proposes a scheme of colonial union at Albany Congress.

King's College (Columbia) founded.

1755–63   French and Indian War.

1758   Abercrombie repulsed at Ticonderoga.

French rebuild Fort Niagara.

1760   Quebec captured by British.

1763   Peace treaty signed at Paris.

1764   New York Assembly urges united action against taxation without the consent of the taxed.

1765   Sons of Liberty organized.

Stamp Act passed.

1766   Stamp Act repealed.

1768   Assembly protests new taxes on glass, paper, lead, tea, and other commodities, and colonists boycott English goods.

1770   Duties repealed except on tea.

Battle of Golden Hill.

1771 Tryon named governor—last Royal executive of New York.

1772 Tryon (Montgomery) and Charlotte (Washington) Counties formed from Albany County.

1774 May 23. Committee of 51 sends letter to Boston by Paul Revere, proposing a Congress of Colonies.
First academy in State established at Kingston.

1775 May 10. Ethan Allen and Benedict Arnold capture Fort Ticonderoga.
May 12. Seth Warner takes Crown Point.
May 22. First Provincial Congress meets.
July 6. Necessity for war declared in a broadside.
Nov. 13. Montgomery captures Montreal.

1776 Jan. 20. General Peter Schuyler, commanding New York Department, forces Sir John Johnson to disarm and give his parole.
July 9. Provincial Congress at White Plains ratifies Declaration of Independence.
Sept. 15. New York City is occupied by the British.
Oct. 11. Battle of Valcour Island, Lake Champlain.
Oct. 28. Battle of White Plains.
Nov. 16. Forts Washington, Tryon, and George captured by British.

1777 Apr. 20. First State constitution adopted at Kingston.
July 27. Jane McCrea murdered.
July 30. George Clinton takes oath of office as first governor of State.
Aug. 3–22. St.Leger attacks Fort Stanwix.
Aug. 6. Battle of Oriskany.
Aug. 16. Battle of Bennington.
Aug. 19. General Schuyler superseded by General Gates.
Sept. 19. First Battle of Saratoga.
Oct. 7. Second Battle of Saratoga.
Oct. 16. Kingston burned.
Oct. 17. Burgoyne surrenders.

1778 Feb. 6. New York approves Articles of Confederation.
Nov. 11. Cherry Valley massacre.

1779 July 16. General Wayne captures Stony Point.
Aug. 29. Generals John Sullivan and James Clinton defeat Tories and Indians in Battle of Newtown.
Oct. 22. Loyalist estates forfeited.

1780 Indians and Tories ravage Mohawk and Schoharie Valleys.
Arnold's treason discovered; André captured at Tarrytown and executed at Tappan.

1781 Oct. 25. Last battle of Revolution in New York fought at Johnstown.

1782 Congress accepts New York's deed of cession of western lands and confirms State's western boundary.
American Army winters at Newburgh.

1783 Naturalization law enacted.
George Washington at Newburgh refuses a crown proffered by military faction.
Treaty of peace signed.
Washington's farewell to officers.

1784   May 1. University of State of New York established by legislature.

1786   Lynchville (Rome) settled by Dominick Lynch.

1787   Oct. 27. First issue of the *Federalist*.

1788   Phelps and Gorham purchase from Massachusetts 2,000,000 acres in western New York.

      July 26. New York ratifies Constitution of the United States in Poughkeepsie by a vote of 30 to 27.

1789   Washington is inaugurated in New York City.

      Two lots in each township in State granted by the legislature for educational purposes.

1790   New York relinquishes all claims to Vermont territory.

      Population 340,120.

1791   Holland Land Company purchase.

      Saratoga and Rensselaer Counties formed from Albany County.

1792   Western Inland Lock Navigation Company empowered to build canals and locks to Lake Ontario and Seneca Lake.

1795   First canal boat passes through Little Falls.

      Legislature appropriates $50,000 annually for five years to maintain schools.

      Union College receives charter.

      Jay becomes Governor.

1796   American flag raised at Fort Ontario, Oswego, Fort Niagara.

      Canal boats arrive at Oneida Lake.

1797   Legislature meets in Stadt Huis, Albany.

1798   July 31. State public records removed to Albany.

1799   Legislature provides for gradual emancipation of slaves.

      Cherry Valley Turnpike incorporated.

1800   Population 589,051.

1801   Public school system organized.

      State constitutional convention.

1802   West Point Military Academy formally opens.

1804   Aaron Burr kills Alexander Hamilton in a duel.

      Clinton chosen Vice President.

1806   Cornerstone of old New York State capitol laid.

1807   Robert Fulton's *Clermont* makes first trip, New York to Albany, in 32 hours.

1808   John Jacob Astor's American Fur Company chartered. Clinton re-elected Vice President.

      Importation of slaves prohibited.

1809   Schenectady County formed from Albany County.

1810   Population—959,049.

1811   Erie Canal authorized.

1812   War with Great Britain.

      Hamilton College, Clinton, receives charter.

1813   Ogdensburg is raided and looted.

      Gideon Hawley of Albany is appointed first State superintendent of schools.

1814   Americans abandon and blow up Fort Erie.

End of war on Niagara frontier.

Battle of Lake Champlain.

1815   Treaty of peace proclaimed.

1816   De Witt Clinton calls first State nominating convention in Albany.

First county fair in New York State is held in Cooperstown, Otsego County; organized by Elkanah Watson.

1817   Slavery in the State prohibited, effective 1827.

Ground broken at Rome for the Erie Canal.

Champlain Canal begun.

1818   A State library founded at the capitol.

Superintendent Hawley reports 5,000 schools organized and over 200,000 pupils.

1819   Erie Canal between Utica and Rome opened to navigation.

New York first called Empire State.

Charter granted to the Baptist Education Society, from which grew Colgate University.

1820   Population—1,372,812.

1821   State constitutional convention establishes general male suffrage.

Schools transferred to care of Secretary of State.

1823   Delaware & Hudson Canal Company incorporated in Pennsylvania and New York.

Joseph Smith, founder of Mormon church, has a vision revealing golden plates of Book of Mormon in Palmyra, N.Y.

Judicial system reorganized.

First State-wide survey of poor relief made.

1825   Geneva (Hobart) College chartered.

Erie Canal completed.

1826   Mohawk & Hudson River Railroad Company chartered.

New York House of Refuge, first juvenile reformatory in America, opened.

1827   Emancipation of all slaves in the State.

1828   Ithaca & Owego Railroad chartered.

Cayuga & Seneca Canal completed.

1829   Fanny Wright helps found the Working Men's Party.

Delaware & Hudson Canal completed between Rondout on the Hudson and Honesdale, Pa.

1830   Mormon Church organized at Fayette, Seneca County.

Book of Mormon first published.

Population—1,918,608.

1831   First Mohawk & Hudson Railroad train runs from Albany to Schenectady.

Joseph Henry of Albany develops electromagnet.

Imprisonment for debt abolished.

1832   Martin Van Buren of Kinderhook elected Vice President.

Buffalo and Utica granted city charters.

1833   The Chenango Canal between Utica and Binghamton started.

New York & Erie Railroad Company organized.

Chemung Canal between Watkins and Elmira completed.

Antislavery convention held in Utica.

Oneida Lake Canal Company incorporated.

Tower of Victory erected at Newburgh.

1834　Rochester granted city charter.

1836　Black River Canal between Rome and Boonville opened.

Martin Van Buren elected President.

1839　Antirent riots.

S.F.B.Morse patents his telegraph and makes first successful daguerreo-
type portraits.

1840　Governor Seward refuses to give up Negro fugitives.

Population—2,428,921.

1841　American Express Company formed in Albany.

1844　Long Island Railroad opened.

American Party organized.

1845　Consolidation of small schools.

Antirent war.

1846　Hudson River Railroad Company formed.

Third constitution adopted.

University of Buffalo founded.

1847　John Humphrey Noyes establishes the Oneida Community.

Syracuse granted city charter.

1848　Gerrit Smith, abolitionist, declines nomination of Liberty Party for President.

First women's rights convention held in Seneca Falls.

Millard Fillmore elected Vice President.

Slavery extension condemned.

Niagara Falls incorporated as village.

Auburn and Oswego granted city charters.

1849　Hudson River Railroad opened to Poughkeepsie.

1850　University of Rochester opened.

Millard Fillmore becomes President upon death of President Taylor.

Population—3,097,394.

1851　Erie Railroad opened.

Hudson River Railroad, New York to Albany, completed.

Delaware, Lackawanna & Western Railroad, Scranton to Ithaca, opened.

1853　New York Central Railroad Company incorporated.

1854　First Young Men's Christian Association in United States meets at Buffalo.

Separate State department of public instruction, with superintendent as
executive head, created.

1855　Elmira College founded.

Niagara Suspension Bridge completed.

1856　Genesee Valley Canal from Rochester to Olean completed.

1857　Financial panic.

Temperance law passed.

1860　Population—3,880,735.

1861　Vassar College chartered.

In Tweddle Hall, Albany, mass meeting held for 'conciliation, concession
and compromise' on slavery.

Legislature appropriates $3,000,000 to sustain Union.

Governor Morgan calls for 25,000 troops.

1862 Ericsson's *Monitor* launched at Rowland's Shipyard, Greenpoint, L.I.

120 regiments sent to war.

Martin Van Buren dies at Lindenwald, Kinderhook.

1863 Draft riots in Troy and New York City.

1864 Confederate prison established in Elmira.

1865 Cornell University chartered.

1866 Public schools made entirely free.

Constitutional convention.

Fenian raid into Canada.

1867 Mrs.Elizabeth Cady Stanton addresses the State assembly on woman suffrage.

1869 Susan B. Anthony and Elizabeth Cady Stanton present cause of woman suffrage before committee of U.S.Senate.

1870 Population—4,382,759.

1871 Cornerstone of New York State capitol laid.

Syracuse University opened.

Tweed Ring broken.

1872 Kingston incorporated a city.

1873 International bridge across Niagara River completed.

Financial panic.

1874 Women's whisky war.

First Chautauqua Assembly meets at Lake Chautauqua.

Compulsory education law passed.

S.J.Tilden elected as a reform governor.

1877 First State reformatory for adults established in Elmira.

1879 New capitol at Albany opened.

1880 State board of health established.

Population—5,082,871.

1881 Chester A. Arthur becomes President.

1883 A cantilever railroad bridge across the Niagara River at the Falls opened.

Civil service commission created.

1884 New York & West Shore Railroad opened.

Grover Cleveland of Buffalo elected President.

Public park at Niagara Falls opened.

1886 Strikes in various parts of State for eight-hour day.

Women admitted to practice of law.

1890 Population—6,003,174.

1891 First Empire State Express, New York Central, runs from New York to Buffalo in 8 hours and 42 minutes.

1892 Grover Cleveland elected President for a second term.

1893 New York Central engine No.999 establishes a world record for speed, running a mile in 32 seconds between Batavia and Buffalo.

1895 Empire State Express established long-distance record for speed, traveling from New York to Buffalo at an average of 64.34 miles an hour.

1899 State historical association organized, James A. Roberts president.

1900   Theodore Roosevelt elected Vice President.
        Population—7,268,894.
1901   Theodore Roosevelt, upon death of President McKinley, becomes President, the fifth from New York State.
        First dental clinic in United States opened in Rochester.
1903   People authorize use of $101,000,000 to convert Erie into Barge Canal.
1904   President Theodore Roosevelt re-elected.
        Ray Brook Sanatorium opened for patients with incipient tuberculosis.
1906   President Roosevelt awarded Nobel Peace Prize.
1907   Public service commission created.
        Albany granted second-class city charter.
1908   Curtiss airplane *Red Wing* makes successful trial trip.
        Glenn H. Curtiss at Hammondsport, N.Y., wins prize for flight in *June Bug*.
        Gambling at race tracks prohibited.
1910   Glenn H. Curtiss flies from Albany to New York City in 2 hours and 32 minutes, breaking former records.
        Population—9,113,614.
1911   Fire in State capitol.
        Direct primary election law.
1913   Governor William Sulzer impeached.
1915   Citizens Military Training Camp established at Plattsburg.
1916   Physical and military training in public schools made compulsory.
        Able-bodied male citizens between 18 and 45 become liable to draft by governor.
1917   Ashokan, now Catskill, Aqueduct, providing water for New York City, completed.
        State constabulary created.
1917–18 New York supplies 518,864 men to military and naval service during World War. Total number of casualties above 40,000, including 14,000 dead.
1918   New York State Barge Canal opened.
1919   Mrs. Ida B. Sammis of Suffolk and Mrs. Mary M. Lilly of Manhattan, first women members, are elected to New York Assembly.
        Theodore Roosevelt dies at Oyster Bay, L.I.
        Federal prohibition amendment ratified.
        Display of red flags in State prohibited.
        A commercial hydroairplane, carrying mail and small packages, flies from New York to Newburgh, Poughkeepsie, and Albany; on return trip stops at Hudson and Poughkeepsie.
1920   Five Socialists expelled from State assembly.
        Four Army Air Service planes fly from Mineola, L.I., to Nome, Alaska.
        Franklin D. Roosevelt Democratic candidate for Vice President.
        New York State dedicates granite shaft on Antietam Battlefield in memory of New York dead.
        Population—10,385,227.
1921   Membership or participation in Communist Party declared sufficient grounds for dismissal of public school teachers.
        State motion picture censorship commission established.

1922   Children's courts established.

$20,000,000 appropriated for highways.

1923   March 3. The Mullen-Gage prohibition enforcement law repealed.

1924   United Farmer-Labor Party of New York State organizes in convention at Schenectady.

Bear Mountain Bridge opened to traffic.

15,000 acres of land in the Adirondacks and Catskills swept by fire.

Alfred E. Smith re-elected governor for third term.

1925   Niagara Falls illuminated by 1,300,000,000 electric candlepower.

Bronx River Parkway, cost $16,000,000, officially opened.

College of home economics, Cornell, chartered.

1926   New York State Historical Association dedicates the John Hancock House, new headquarters at Ticonderoga.

State administrative reorganization adopted, effective January 1, 1927.

Governor Smith re-elected for fourth term.

1927   First radio broadcast of the roar of Niagara.

The Peace Bridge between Buffalo, N.Y., and Fort Erie, Ontario, opened to traffic.

Sept. 12. New York State celebrates its 150th anniversary at Kingston.

Oct. 8. Pageant of the Battle of Saratoga on 150th anniversary.

1928   Roosevelt Memorial Park, 38 acres of water front, dedicated at Oyster Bay.

Franklin D. Roosevelt elected governor.

1929 $450,000,000 power system formed, connecting every important city in New York State from Albany northward and westward.

Bridge between Crown Point, N.Y., and Chimney Point, Vt., opened.

1930   Charles Evans Hughes becomes Chief Justice of the United States.

First television feature act shown in Schenectady theater by Dr.Alexanderson of the General Electric Company.

Democratic and Republican State conventions declare for the repeal of the Volstead law.

Metropolitan Opera Company plays *La Boheme* in the new Westchester County civic center at White Plains; first grand opera in suburbs of New York.

Old Age Security Act passed.

Governor Roosevelt re-elected.

Population—12,588,066.

1931   'One million cubic feet of rock' at brink of Niagara Falls crashes.

Police teletype alarm system linking 46 municipalities established.

New York Temporary Emergency Relief Administration set up in Albany.

1932   Governor Roosevelt dedicates new Port of Albany and opens Winter Olympic Games at Lake Placid.

Buffalo celebrates centennial.

Model juvenile delinquency institution opened at Warwick.

Franklin D. Roosevelt elected President of the United States.

Herbert H. Lehman elected governor.

1933   March 13. New York State ratifies 21st amendment to Federal Constitution, repealing the 18th.

250th anniversary of the purchase of White Plains from the Indians celebrated.

Farmers of four counties dump their milk in protest against rates set by milk control board.

1934   State racing commission established.

Oath of allegiance to the Constitution required of all teachers.

Fort Niagara, recently rebuilt, dedicated by Secretary of War Dern.

250 feet of rock at lip of Horseshoe Falls plunge 160 feet into the Niagara gorge.

Nobel Prize in Medicine awarded to Dr. George H. Whipple, University of Rochester.

Herbert H. Lehman re-elected governor.

1935   Devastating floods in Finger Lakes region.

Unemployment insurance law passed by the legislature.

New York Spa at Saratoga formally opened to the public.

1936   Old Age Pension Bill enacted, making age 65 the initial year for pensions.

Governor Lehman appoints new State Board of Social Welfare.

President Roosevelt re-elected.

Governor Lehman re-elected.

1937   Cornerstone laid of the first community council house, Tonawanda Indian Reservation, erected by WPA.

Women permitted to serve on juries.

Unemployment Insurance organized.

1938   Eighth State constitutional convention.

July 14. Howard Hughes, having circled the globe in 91 hours, lands at Floyd Bennett Airport, L.I.

Eastern New York, especially Long Island, hit by hurricane.

Governor Lehman re-elected fourth time for first four-year term in history of State.

1939   New York World's Fair opens.

New York State Historical Association opens new central quarters in Cooperstown.

President Roosevelt entertains King and Queen of England at Hyde Park.

1940   Pari-mutuel betting introduced on race tracks.

Peekskill becomes a city.

Population—13,379,662.

Bibliography

This bibliography does not list many of the books, reports, and pamphlets issued by the various State agencies. Neither does it include county and local histories, regional and period novels, newspaper files, and State and local historical collections.

GAZETTEERS AND GUIDEBOOKS

Dutchess County. American Guide Series of the Federal Writers' Project, WPA. Philadelphia, William Penn Association,1937. 166p.,illus.

French,J.H. *Gazetteer of the State of New York.* Syracuse, R.Pearsall Smith,1860. 752p.,illus.

Hough,F.B. *Gazetteer of the State of New York,* Albany, A.Boyd,1872. 745p.

Lossing,B.J. *Pictorial Field Book of the Revolution.* New York, Harper & Bros., 1859. 2v.,illus.

—— *Pictorial Field Book of the War of 1812.* New York, Harper & Bros.,1869. 1084p.,illus.

New York City Guide. American Guide Series of the Federal Writers' Project, WPA. New York, Random House,1939. 708p.,illus.

Northeastern Tour Book. Washington, American Automobile Association,1939. 636p.,illus.

Rochester & Monroe County: A History and Guide. American Guide Series of the Federal Writers' Project, WPA. Rochester, Scrantom's,1937. 46op.,illus.

Spafford,H.G. *Gazetteer of the State of New York.* Troy, B.D.Packard,1824. 62op.

TRAVEL AND DESCRIPTION

Bacon, Edgar M. *The Hudson River from Ocean to Source.* New York, G.P.Putnam's Sons,1907. 59op.,illus.

Burroughs, John. *In the Catskills.* Boston, Houghton Mifflin Co.,1910. 25op., illus.

Carmer, Carl. *The Hudson.* New York, Farrar & Rinehart,Inc.,1939. 434p.,illus.

—— *Listen for a Lonesome Drum, A New York State Chronicle.* New York, Farrar & Rinehart,1936. 381p.,illus.

Carson, Russell M.L. *Peaks and People of the Adirondacks.* Garden City, Doubleday, Doran & Co.,1928. 269p.,illus.

Crèvecoeur, St.John de. *Letters from an American Farmer.* London, T.Davies, 1782. 318p.

Dickens, Charles. *American Notes.* New York, Harper & Bros.,1842. 92p.

Dwight, Timothy. *Travels in New England and New York.* New Haven, T. Dwight,1821-2. 4v.

Grant, Anne. *The Memoirs of an American Lady.* Albany, J.C.Wilson,1876. 397p.

Hall, Captain Basil. *Travels in North America in the Years* 1827–1828. London, Simpkin & Marshall,1829. 3v.

Haring,H.A. *Our Catskill Mountains*. New York, G.P.Putnam's Sons,1931. 350p.,illus.

Headley, The Rev.J.T. *Letters from the Backwoods and the Adirondac*. New York, John S. Taylor,1850. 105p.

Hungerford, Edward. *Pathway to Empire*. New York, Robert M. McBride & Co.,1935. 325p.

Hunt, Freeman. *Letters about the Hudson River and Its Vicinity. Written in* 1835–1837 *by a Citizen of New York*. New York, Freeman Hunt & Co.,1837. 252p.

Johnson, Clifton. *The Picturesque Hudson*. New York, Macmillan Co., 1909. 227p.,illus.

────── *The Picturesque St.Lawrence*. New York, Macmillan Co.,1910. 253p., illus.

Kalm, Peter. *Travels in North America*. London, John Reinhold, Forster,1770–71. 3v.,illus.

Nutting, Wallace. *New York Beautiful*. New York, Dodd, Mead & Co.,1927. 305p.,illus.

Reid, W.Max. *Story of Old Fort Johnson*. New York, G.P.Putnam's Sons,1906. 455p.,illus.

────── *The Mohawk Valley*. New York, G.P.Putnam's Sons,1901. 455p.,illus.

Rockwell, Charles. *The Catskill Mountains and the Region Around*. New York, Taintor Bros. & Co.,1871. 351p.,illus.

Smith, Richard. *A Tour of Four Great Rivers: Hudson, Mohawk, Susquehanna, and Delaware*, 1769. Ed. by Francis W. Halsey. New York, Charles Scribner's Sons,1906. 102p.

Towne, Charles Hanson. *Loafing Down Long Island*. New York, Century Co., 1921. 212p.,illus.

Trollope, Mrs.F.M. *Domestic Manners of the Americans*. New York, Dodd, Mead & Co.,1901. 2v.

NATURAL SETTING AND CONSERVATION

Annual Reports. Albany, Conservation Department, State of New York,1910–────. Illus.

Brigham,A.P. *Glacial Geology and Geographic Conditions of the Lower Mohawk Valley*. Albany, The University of the State of New York,1929. 133p.,illus.

Bureau of Biological Survey. *Biological Survey Reports: Genesee River System; Oswego River System; Erie-Niagara River; Champlain Watershed; St. Lawrence Watershed; Oswegatchie and Black River Watersheds; Upper Hudson Watershed; Raquette River Watershed; Mohawk-Hudson Watershed; Delaware and Susquehanna Watersheds; Lower Hudson Watershed; Allegheny and Chemung Watersheds*. Albany, Conservation Department, State of New York,1926–37. 12v.,illus.

Bureau of Game. *The Rearing of Game Birds in New York State*. Albany, Conservation Department, State of New York,n.d. 46p.,illus.

Burroughs, John. *The Writings of John Burroughs*. Riverby Edition. Boston, Houghton Mifflin Co.,1871–1923. 23v.,illus.

DeKay, James E. *New York Natural History Survey: Zoology of New York*. Albany, New York State Education Department,1842–4. 5v.,illus.

Eaton,E.H. *Birds of New York*. Albany, University of the State of New York, 1910–14. 2v.,illus.

Fairchild,H.L. *Geologic Story of the Genesee Valley and Western New York*. Rochester, the Author,1928. 215p.,illus.

Goldring, Winifred. *Handbook of Paleontology for Beginners and Amateurs*. Part I.*The Fossils*; Part II.*The Formations*. Albany, The University of the State of New York,1929–31. 2v.,illus.

—— *Guide to the Geology of Thacher Park and Vicinity*. Albany, The University of the State of New York,1933. 112p.,illus.

House, Homer D. *Wild Flowers of New York*. Albany, The University of the State of New York,1918. 2v.,illus.

—— *Ferns and Flowering Plants of New York State*. Albany, The University of the State of New York,1924. 759p.

Miller,W.J. *The Geological History of New York*. Albany, The University of the State of New York,1914. 130p.,illus.

Newland, David H. *The Mineral Resources of the State of New York*. Albany, The University of the State of New York,1921. 315p.,illus.

Seton, Ernest Thompson. *Lives of Game Animals*. Garden City, Doubleday, Doran & Co.,1928. 4v.,illus.

Tarr, Ralph S. *The Physical Geography of New York State*. New York, The Macmillan Co.,1902. 397p.,illus.

Whipple, Gurth. *Fifty Years of Conservation in New York State*. 1885–1935. Albany, J.B.Lyon Co.,1935. 199p.,illus.

ARCHEOLOGY AND INDIANS

Beauchamp,W.M. *History of the New York Iroquois*. Albany, New York State Education Department,1905. State Museum Bulletin 78. 340p.,illus.

—— *Aboriginal Place Names of New York*. Albany, New York State Education Department,1907. New York State Museum Bulletin 108. 336p.

—— *Aboriginal Occupation of New York*. Albany, New York State Education Department,1900. New York State Museum Bulletin 32. 190p.,illus.

Canfield, William W. *The Legends of the Iroquois*. New York, A.Wessells Co., 1902. 211p.

Colden, Cadwallader. *History of the Five Nations*. New York, A.S.Barnes & Co., 1904. 2v.

Hunt, George T. *Wars of the Iroquois*. Madison, University of Wisconsin Press, 1939. 209p.,maps.

Lydekker, John W. *The Faithful Mohawks*. New York, Macmillan Co., 1938. 312p.,illus.

Morgan, Lewis H. *League of the Iroquois*. New York, Dodd, Mead & Co., 1922. 2v.

Parker,A.C. *The Constitution of the Five Nations*. Albany, University of the State of New York,1916. New York State Museum Bulletin 184. 158p.

—— *Seneca Myths and Folktales*. Buffalo, Buffalo Historical Society,1923. 465p.,illus.

────── *The Archeological History of New York.* Albany, University of the State of New York,1922. 2v.,illus.

Sylvester,N.B. *Indian Legends of Saratoga.* Troy, the Author,1884. 47p.,illus.

HISTORY AND GOVERNMENT

Alexander,D.S. *A Political History of the State of New York.* New York, Henry Holt & Co.,1906–9. 3v.

Becker, Carl L. *The History of Political Parties in the Province of New York,* 1760–76. Bulletin of the University of Wisconsin. History Series II, No.I. Madison, Wis.,1909.

Beer, George L. *British Colonial Policy.* New York, The Macmillan Co.,1907. 327p.

Bobbé, Dorothie. *De Witt Clinton.* New York, Minton, Balch & Co.,1933. 308p., illus.

Campbell, William W. *Annals of Tryon County; or, The Border Warfare of New York During the Revolution.* New York, Dodd, Mead & Co., 1924. 257p.

Cheyney, Edward P. *Anti-Rent Agitation in the State of New York,* 1839–1846. Philadelphia, University of Pennsylvania,1887. 64p.

Day,R.E., and others, ed. *Papers of Sir William Johnson.* Albany, University of the State of New York,1921–39. 9v.,illus.

Donaldson, Alfred L. *A History of the Adirondacks.* New York, Century Co., 1921. 2v.,illus.

Earle, Alice M. *Colonial Days in Old New York.* New York, Charles Scribner's Sons,1896. 312p.

Flick, Alexander C.,ed. *History of the State of New York.* New York, Columbia University Press,1933–7. 10v.,illus.

────── *The Sullivan-Clinton Campaign in* 1779. Albany, University of the State of New York,1929. 216p.,illus.

────── *The American Revolution in New York, Its Political, Social and Economic Significance.* Albany, University of the State of New York,1926. 371p., illus.

Fox, Dixon Ryan. *Decline of the Aristocracy in the Politics of New York.* New York, Columbia University Press,1918. 460p.,illus.

────── *Caleb Heathcote: Gentleman Colonist* 1692–1721. New York, Charles Scribner's Sons,1926. 301p.,illus.

Frothingham,O.B. *Gerrit Smith, a Biography.* New York, G.P.Putnam's Sons, 1878. 381p.

Gabriel,R.H. *The Evolution of Long Island.* New Haven, Yale University Press, 1931. 194p.

Greene, Nelson. *History of the Mohawk Valley, Gateway to the West,* 1614–1925. Chicago, G.J.Clarke Co., 1925. 4v.,illus.

Halsey, Francis W. *The Old New York Frontier; Its War with Indians and Tories; Its Missionary Schools, Pioneers and Land Titles,* 1614–1800. New York, Charles Scribner's Sons,1901. 432p.,illus.

Hammond,J.D. *The History of Political Parties in the State of New York to* 1840. Syracuse, Hall, Mills & Co.,1852. 3v.

Harlow, Ralph Volney. *Gerrit Smith: Philanthropist and Reformer.* New York, Henry Holt,1939. 501p.

Harper, Ida H. *The Life and Work of Susan B. Anthony.* Indianapolis, The Bobbs-Merrill Co., 1898–1908. 3v.,illus.

Jameson,J.F.,ed. *Narratives of New Netherland, 1609–1664.* New York, Charles Scribner's Sons,1909. 478p.

Janvier, Thomas A. *Dutch Founding of New York.* New York, Harper & Bros., 1903. 217p.,illus.

Knittle, Walter Allen. *Early Eighteenth Century Palatine Emigration.* Philadelphia, Dorrance & Co., 1937. 320p.,illus.

Landon, Harry F. *History of the North Country.* Indianapolis, Historical Publishing Co.,1932. 3v.,illus.

Lincoln,C.Z. *Constitutional History of New York.* Rochester, The Lawyers' Cooperative Publishing Co.,1906. 5v.

Lodge, Henry Cabot. *Alexander Hamilton.* Boston, Houghton Mifflin Co.,1899. 317p.

Mahan, Alfred T. *Sea Power in the Relation to the War of 1812.* Boston, Little, Brown & Co.,1905. 2v.,illus.

Niles, Grace G. *The Hoosac Valley, Its Legend and Its History.* New York, G.P.Putnam's Sons,1912. 584p.,illus.

Nissenson,S.G. *The Patroon's Domain.* New York, Columbia University Press, 1937. 416p.

O'Reilly, Henry. *Settlement in the West. Sketches of Rochester; With Incidental Notices of Western New York.* Rochester, W.Alling,1838. 468p.,illus.

Parkman, Francis. *A Half-Century of Conflict.* Boston, Little, Brown & Co.1892. 2v.

Pound, Arthur. *Johnson of the Mohawks: a Biography of Sir William Johnson, Irish Immigrant, etc.* New York, The Macmillan Co.,1930. 568p., illus.

Redway, Jacques W. *Making of the Empire State.* Boston, Silver, Burdett & Co.,1904. 263p.,illus.

Roberts, Ellis H. *New York: the Planting and the Growth of the Empire State.* Boston, Houghton Mifflin Co.,1887. 2v.

Simms, Jeptha R. *Trappers of New York.* Albany, J.Munsell,1851. 287p.

Spaulding, Ernest W. *New York in the Critical Period, 1783–1789.* New York, Columbia University Press,1932. 334p.

Swiggett, Howard. *War out of Niagara: Walter Butler and the Tory Rangers.* New York, Columbia University Press,1933. 309p.,illus.

Thompson, Benjamin F. *History of Long Island.* New York, F.H.Dodd,1918. 3v.,illus.

Turner, Orsamus. *History of the Pioneer Settlement of Phelps and Gorham's Purchase, and Morris' Reserve.* Rochester, W.Alling, 1852. 588p.

—— *Pioneer History of the Holland Purchase of Western New York.* Buffalo, Jewett,Thomas & Co., 1849. 666p.,illus.

Weed, Thurlow. *Autobiography of Thurlow Weed.* Edited by Harriet A. Weed. Boston, Houghton Mifflin Co.,1883. 2v.,illus.

Wheeler, Mary A. *New York State, Yesterday and Today.* New York, Charles Scribner's Sons,1935. 432p.,illus.

Williams, Sherman. *New York's Part in History.* New York, D.Appleton and Co.,1915. 390p.,illus.

INDUSTRY AND TRANSPORTATION

Adams,C.F. *A Chapter of Erie.* Boston, Fields, Osgood & Co.,1869. 152p.

Andrews, Edward D. *The Community Industries of the Shakers.* Albany, The University of the State of New York,1933. 322p.,illus.

Bishop,J.L. *History of American Manufactures,* 1608–1860. Philadelphia, E. Young & Co.,1861. 2v.

Clark, Victor S. *History of Manufactures in the United States.* New York, McGraw-Hill Book Co.,Inc.,1929. 3v.

Cooper, William. *A Guide in the Wilderness; or the History of the First Settlement in the Western Counties of New York, with Useful Instructions to Future Settlers.* Dublin, Gilbert and Hodges,1810. 41p.

Harlow, Alvin F. *Old Towpaths.* New York, D.Appleton & Co.,1926. 403p.,illus.

Hungerford, Edward. *Men and Iron: History of the New York Central Railroad.* New York, Thomas Y. Crowell Co.,1938. 424p.,illus.

Ireland, Tom. *The Great Lakes-St. Lawrence Deep Waterway to the Sea.* New York, G.P.Putnam's Sons,1934. 223p.,illus.

Johnson,E.R.,et al. *History of Domestic and Foreign Commerce of the United States.* Washington, Carnegie Institute,1915. 2v.,illus.

Kimball, Francis P. *New York—The Canal State.* Albany, The Argus Press,1937. 105p.,illus.

Meyer,B.H.,et al. *History of Transportation in the United States before* 1860. Washington, Carnegie Institute,1917. 678p.

Munsell, Joel. *The Origin, Progress and Vicissitudes of the Mohawk and Hudson Railroad, and the First Excursion on It.* J.Munsell,1875. 20p.

Reports on the Growth of Industry in New York. Albany, New York State Department of Labor,1904. 2nd Report, Part 5. 670p.

Schlesinger, Arthur M. *The Colonial Merchants and the American Revolution.* New York, Columbia University Press,1918. 647p.

Sowers, Don C. *Financial History of New York State.* New York, Columbia University Press,1914. 346p.

Sutcliffe, Alice C. *Robert Fulton and the 'Clermont.'* New York, The Century Co.,1909. 397p.,illus.

Verplanck, William E., and Collyer, Moses W. *The Sloops of the Hudson.* New York, G.P.Putnam's Sons,1908. 171p.,illus.

Watson, Elkanah. *History of the Rise, Progress, and Existing Conditions of the Western Canals in the State of New York.* Albany, D.Steele,1820. 104p.,illus.

Whitford, Noble E. *History of Canal System of State of New York.* Albany, State of New York,1905. 2v.

——— *History of the New York Barge Canal of State of New York.* Albany, State of New York,1922. 610p.,illus.

Wilstach, Paul. *Hudson River Landings.* Indianapolis, Bobbs-Merrill Co.,1933. 311p.,illus.

AGRICULTURE

Beach,S.A. *Apples of New York.* Albany, State of New York,1905. 2v.,illus.

Downing, Andrew Jackson. *The Fruits and Fruit Trees of America.* New York, Wiley & Putnam,1847. 594p.,illus.

Fippin,E.O. *Rural New York*. New York, Macmillan Co.,1921. 381p.,illus.
Hedrick,U.P. *History of Agriculture in the State of New York*. Albany, J.B.Lyon Co.,1933. 462p.,illus.
────── *Cherries of New York*. Albany, State of New York,1915. 371p.,illus.
────── *Grapes of New York*. Albany, State of New York,1917. 564p.,illus.
────── *Peaches of New York*. Albany, State of New York,1917. 541p.,illus.
────── *Pears of New York*. Albany, State of New York,1917. 636p.,illus.
────── *Plums of New York*. Albany, State of New York,1911. 615p.,illus.
Van Wagenen, Jared, Jr. *The Cow*. New York, Macmillan Co.,1922. 153p.,illus.
────── *Golden Age of Homespun*. Albany, State Department of Agriculture and Markets,1927. 92p.,illus.
Van Wagner, Edith,ed. *Agricultural Manual of New York State*. Albany, State Department of Agriculture and Markets,n.d. 857p.,illus.

LABOR AND SOCIAL WELFARE

Abbott, Edith. *Women in Industry*. New York, D.Appleton & Co.,1910. 408p.
Annual Report of the Industrial Commissioner. Albany, New York State Department of Labor,1927–38.
Baker, Mrs.Elizabeth F. *Protective Labor Legislation*. New York, Columbia University Press,1925. 467p.
Bond, Elsie M. *Public Relief in New York State*. New York, State Charities Aid Association,1938. 64p.
Commons, John R. *History of Labor in the United States*. New York, Macmillan Co.,1918–35. 4v.
Cummings, John. *Poor Laws of Massachusetts and New York*. New York, Macmillan Co.,1895. 135p.
Economic Brief in Support of New York State Unemployment Insurance Law. Albany, New York State Department of Labor,1937. 356p.
Labor Law. Albany, New York State Department of Labor,1927–38.
Levinson, Edward. *Labor on the March*. New York, Harper & Bros.,1939. 329p.
McKee, Samuel. *Labor in Colonial New York, 1664–1776*. New York, Columbia University Press,1935. 193p.
Problems Relating to the Bill of Rights and General Welfare. Albany, Constitutional Convention Committee,1938. 684p.
Schneider, David M. *The History of Public Welfare in New York State, 1609–1866*. Chicago, University of Illinois,1938. 395p.,illus.
────── and Deutsch, Albert. *The Road Upward*. Albany, New York State Social Welfare Department, 1939. 64p.
Walsh, Raymond. *C.I.O., Industrial Unionism in Action*. New York, W.W.Norton,1937. 293p.

RECREATION

Bureau of State Publicity. 1001 *Fishing Waters of New York State*. Albany, New York State Conservation Department,n.d. 40p.,map.
────── *Ski Trails of New York State*. Albany, New York State Conservation Department,n.d. 55p.,maps.

Hopkins,A.S. *Lake George.* Recreation Circular 6. Albany, New York State Conservation Department,1939. 22p.,illus.

—— *The Trails to Marcy.* Recreation Circular 8. Albany, New York State Conservation Department,1939. 21p.,illus.

Howard, William G. *Adirondack Canoe Routes.* Recreation Circular 7. Albany, New York State Conservation Department,1939. 33p.,illus.

Mulholland,W.D. *Adirondack Campsites.* Recreation Circular 3. Albany, New York State Conservation Department,1939. 42p.,illus.

—— *Catskill Campsites.* Recreation Circular 4. Albany, New York State Conservation Department,1939. 14p.,illus.

—— *Catskill Trails.* Recreation Circular 9. Albany, New York State Conservation Department,1939. 34p.,illus.

—— *Lake Placid Trails.* Recreation Circular 10. Albany, New York State Conservation Department,1939. 22p.,illus.

Pettis,C.R. *Public Use of the Forest Preserve.* Recreation Circular 2. Albany, New York State Conservation Department,1939. 17p.,illus.

Skiing in the East: Ski Trails and How to Get There. Compiled and Written by Members of the Federal Writers' Project of the Works Progress Administration in New York City. American Guide Series. New York, M.Barrows & Company,1939. 334p.,maps.

State Council of Parks. *New York State Parks.* Albany, New York State Conservation Department,1939. 88p.,illus.

THE ARTS: LITERATURE, THEATER, PAINTING AND SCULPTURE, MUSIC

Adkins,N.F. *Fitz-Greene Halleck, An Early Knickerbocker Wit and Poet.* New Haven, Yale University Press,1930. 461p.,illus.

Austin, Mary S. *Philip Freneau, the Poet of the Revolution.* New York, A.Wessells Co.,1901. 285p.

Barrus, Clara. *Life and Letters of John Burroughs.* Boston, Houghton Mifflin Co.,1925. 2v.,illus.

Coad, Oral S., and Nims, Edwin J. *The American Stage.* Vol. 14 of the Pageant of America. New Haven, Yale University Press,1929. 362p.,illus.

Conway, Moncure D. *Life of Thomas Paine.* New York, G.P.Putnam's Sons, 1892. 2v.

Dunlap, William. *A History of the American Theatre.* New York, J. and J.Harper,1832. 420p.

—— *History of the Rise and Progress of the Arts of Design in the United States.* New York, G.P.Scott & Co.,1834. 2v.

Durand, John. *The Life and Times of A.B.Durand.* New York, Charles Scribner's Sons,1894. 232p.,illus.

Fielding, Mantle. *Dictionary of American Painters, Sculptors and Engravers.* Philadelphia, Lancaster Press,1926. 433p.,illus.

Godwin, Parke. *William Cullen Bryant.* New York, D.Appleton & Co.,1883. 2v.,illus.

Herold,A.L. *James Kirke Paulding, Versatile American.* New York, Columbia University Press,1926. 167p.

Hicks, Granville. *The Great Tradition*. New York, Macmillan Co.,1935. 341p.

Howard, John T. *Our American Music*. New York, Thomas Y. Crowell Co.,1931. 713p.,illus.

Isham, Samuel. *The History of American Painting*. New York, Macmillan Co., 1927. 316p.,illus.

Kolodin, Irving. *The Metropolitan Opera* (1883–1939). New York, Oxford University Press,1939. 646p.,illus.

La Follette, Suzanne. *Art in America*. New York, Harper & Bros.,1929. 361p., illus.

Mabie, Hamilton Wright. *The Writers of Knickerbocker New York*. New York, Grolier Club,1912. 121p.,illus.

Moses, Montrose J., and Brown, John Mason. *The American Theater As Seen by Its Critics*, 1752–1934. New York, W.W.Norton & Co.,Inc.,1934. 391p.

Mumford, Lewis. *Herman Melville*. New York, Harcourt, Brace & Co.,1929. 377p.,illus.

Noble, Louis L. *The Course of Empire, Voyage of Life, and Other Pictures of Thomas Cole*. New York, Cornish, Lamport & Co.,1853. 415p.

Odell,G.C.D. *Annals of New York Stage*. New York, Columbia University Press, 1927–39. 11v.,illus.

Parrington,V.L. *Main Currents in American Thought*. New York, Harcourt, Brace & Co.,1927–30. 3v.

Phelps, Henry P. *Players of a Century, A Record of the Albany Stage*. Albany, J.McDonough,1880. 424p.

Rees, James. *The Life of Edwin Forrest with Reminiscences and Personal Recollections*. Philadelphia, T.B.Peterson & Bros.,1874. 524p.,illus.

Spiller, Robert E. *Fenimore Cooper, Critic of His Times*. New York, Minton, Balch & Co.,1931. 337p.,illus.

Stone, Henry D. *Personal Recollections of the Drama*. Albany, C.Van Benthuysen & Sons,1873. 316p.,illus.

Taft, Lorado. *History of American Sculpture*. New York, The Macmillan Co., 1927. 622p.,illus.

Thompson, Harold W. *Body, Boots and Britches*. Philadelphia, Lippincott, 1940. 530p.,illus.

Tuckerman, Henry T. *Book of the Artists*. New York, G.P.Putnam & Sons,1867. 639p.,illus.

Williams, Stanley T. *The Life of Washington Irving*. New York, Oxford University Press,1935. 2v.,illus.

ARCHITECTURE

Bailey, Rosalie F. *Pre-Revolutionary Dutch Houses and Families in Northern New Jersey and Southern New York*. New York, W.Morrow & Co.,1936. 612p.,illus.

Downing, Andrew Jackson. *The Architecture of Country Houses*. New York, D.Appleton & Co.,1850. 484p.,illus.

—— *A Treatise on the Theory and Practise of Landscape Gardening Adapted to North America*. New York, A.O.Moore & Co.,1859. 576p.,illus. Supplement by Henry Winthrop Sargent.

Eberlein,H.D. *Manor Houses and Historic Homes of the Hudson Valley*. Philadelphia, J.B.Lippincott Co.,1924. 327p.,illus.

Edgell, George H. *American Architecture of Today*. New York, Charles Scribner's Sons,1928. 401p.,illus.

Hamlin, Talbot. *The America Spirit in Architecture*. Vol.13 of The Pageant of America. New Haven, Yale University Press,1926. 353p.,illus.

Lathrop, Elsie L. *Early American Inns and Taverns*. New York, Robert M. McBride & Co.,1926. 365p.,illus.

—— *Historic Houses of Early America*. New York, Robert M. McBride & Co.,1927. 464p.,illus.

Major, Howard. *The Domestic Architecture of the Early American Republic: The Greek Revival*. Philadelphia, J.B.Lippincott Co.,1926. 236p.,illus.

Monograph Series of the White Pine Bureau. New York, R.F.Whitehead, 1916–31. Covell,A.T. *Old Chatham and Neighboring Dwellings South of the Berkshires*. Vol.5,No.5. Embery II.,Aymar. *Farm Houses of New Netherland*. Vol.1,No.3. Keller,W.A. *Rensselaerville, An Old Village in the Helderbergs*. Vol.10,No.4. Moran,W.E. *Settlements on the Eastern End of Long Island*. Vol.5,No.2. Tallman,C.C. *Early Wood-built Houses of Central New York*. Vol.4,No.5. Trowbridge,A.B. *The Greek Revival in Owego and Nearby New York Towns*. Vol.7,No.3. Whiting,F.P. *Cooperstown in the Days of Our Forefathers*. Vol.9,No.3.

Mumford, Lewis. *Sticks and Stones*. New York, Boni & Liveright,1924. 247p.

—— *The Brown Decades*. New York, Harcourt, Brace & Co.,1931. 266p.

Reynolds,H.W. *Dutch Houses in the Hudson Valley before 1776*. New York, Payson & Clarke,Ltd.,1929. 467p.,illus.

—— *Dutchess County Doorways, 1730–1830*. New York, W.F.Payson,1931. 280p.,illus.

Rines, Edward P. *Old Historic Churches in America*. New York, Macmillan Co., 1936. 373p.,illus.

Root, Edward W. *Philip Hooker*. New York, Charles Scribner's Sons,1929. 242p.,illus.

RELIGION

Avery, Giles B. *Sketches of Shakers and Shakerism, A Synopsis of Theology of United Society of Believers in Christ's Second Appearing*. Albany, Weed-Parsons Printing Co.,1884. 50p.,illus.

Barnes, Gilbert H. *The Anti-Slavery Impulse, 1830–1844*. New York, D.Appleton-Century Co.,1933. 298p.

Evans, John Henry. *Joseph Smith, an American Prophet*. New York, Macmillan Co.,1933. 447p.,illus.

Hastings, Hugh. *Ecclesiastical Records of the State of New York*. Albany, J.B. Lyon Co.,1901–5. 6v.

Hewitt, William P.H. *History of the Diocese of Syracuse*. Syracuse, W.P.H. Hewitt,1909. 267p.,illus.

Linn,W.A. *Story of Mormonism*. New York, Macmillan Co.,1902. 637p.

Noyes, Pierrepont. *My Father's House*. New York, Farrar & Rinehart,1937. 312p.,illus.

Oppenheim, Samuel. *The Early History of the Jews in New York*. New York, American Jewish Historical Society,1909. 96p.

Parker, Robert Allerton. *A Yankee Saint: John Humphrey Noyes and the Oneida Community*. New York, G.P.Putnam's Sons,1935. 322p.,illus.

Seldes, Gilbert. *The Stammering Century*. New York, John Day Co.,1928. 414p., illus.

Thomas,A.C., and Thomas,R.N. *History of the Society of Friends*. New York, Christian Literature Co.,1894. Vol.XII of the American Church History Series.

Tiffany,C.C. *History of the Protestant Episcopal Church in the United States of America*. New York, Christian Literature Co.,1895. Vol.VII of the American Church History Series.

EDUCATION

Cole,G.W. *Early Library Development in New York State*. New York, Public Library,1927. 19p.

Horner,H.H. *Life and Works of Andrew Sloan Draper*. Urbana, University of Illinois Press,1934. 291p.,illus.

Fitch, Charles E. *The Public School: History of Common School Education in New York*. Albany, J.B.Lyon Co.,1904. 124p.

Sherwood, Sidney. *The University of the State of New York: History of Higher Education in the State of New York*. Washington, Government Printing Office,1900. 538p.,illus.

Index